The Cambridge Handbook of Communication Disorders

Many children and adults experience impairment of their communication skills. These communication disorders impact adversely on all aspects of these individuals' lives. In thirty dedicated chapters, *The Cambridge Handbook of Communication Disorders* examines the full range of developmental and acquired communication disorders and provides the most up-to-date and comprehensive guide to the epidemiology, aetiology and clinical features of these disorders. The volume also examines how these disorders are assessed and treated by speech and language therapists and addresses recent theoretical developments in the field. The handbook goes beyond well-known communication disorders to include populations such as children with emotional disturbance, adults with non-Alzheimer's dementias and people with personality disorders. Each chapter describes in accessible terms the most recent thinking and research in communication disorders. The volume is an ideal guide for academic researchers, graduate students and professionals in speech and language therapy.

LOUISE CUMMINGS is Professor of Linguistics at Nottingham Trent University. She is a member of the Royal College of Speech and Language Therapists and is registered with the Health and Care Professions Council in the UK.

CAMBRIDGE HANDBOOKS IN LANGUAGE AND LINGUISTICS

Genuinely broad in scope, each handbook in this series provides a complete state-of-the-field overview of a major sub-discipline within language study and research. Grouped into broad thematic areas, the chapters in each volume encompass the most important issues and topics within each subject, offering a coherent picture of the latest theories and findings. Together, the volumes will build into an integrated overview of the discipline in its entirety.

Published titles

The Cambridge Handbook of Phonology, edited by Paul de Lacy
The Cambridge Handbook of Linguistic Code-switching, edited by Barbara E. Bullock and Almeida Jacqueline Toribio
The Cambridge Handbook of Child Language, edited by Edith L. Bavin
The Cambridge Handbook of Endangered Languages, edited by Peter K. Austin and Julia Sallabank
The Cambridge Handbook of Sociolinguistics, edited by Rajend Mesthrie
The Cambridge Handbook of Pragmatics, edited by Keith Allan and Kasia M. Jaszczolt
The Cambridge Handbook of Language Policy, edited by Bernard Spolsky
The Cambridge Handbook of Second Language Acquisition, edited by Julia Herschensohn and Martha Young-Scholten
The Cambridge Handbook of Biolinguistics, edited by Cedric Boeckx and Kleanthes K. Grohmann
The Cambridge Handbook of Generative Syntax, edited by Marcel den Dikken
The Cambridge Handbook of Communication Disorders, edited by Louise Cummings

Further titles planned for the series

The Cambridge Handbook of Stylistics, edited by Stockwell and Whiteley
The Cambridge Handbook of Linguistic Anthropology, edited by Enfield, Kockelman and Sidnell
The Cambridge Handbook of Morphology, edited by Hippisley and Stump
The Cambridge Handbook of Historical Syntax, edited by Ledgeway and Roberts
The Cambridge Handbook of Formal Semantics, edited by Maria Aloni and Paul Dekker
The Cambridge Handbook of English Corpus Linguistics, edited by Douglas Biber and Randi Reppen
The Cambridge Handbook of English Historical Linguistics, edited by Merja Kytö and Päivi Pahta

The Cambridge Handbook
of Communication Disorders

Edited by

Louise Cummings

CAMBRIDGE
UNIVERSITY PRESS

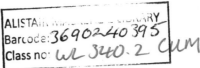

CAMBRIDGE
UNIVERSITY PRESS

University Printing House, Cambridge CB2 8BS, United Kingdom

Published in the United States of America by Cambridge University Press, New York

Cambridge University Press is part of the University of Cambridge.

It furthers the University's mission by disseminating knowledge in the pursuit of education, learning and research at the highest international levels of excellence.

www.cambridge.org
Information on this title: www.cambridge.org/9781107021235

© Cambridge University Press 2014

First published 2014

Printing in the United Kingdom by TJ International Ltd, Padstow, Cornwall

A catalogue record for this publication is available from the British Library

Library of Congress Cataloguing in Publication data
The Cambridge handbook of communication disorders / [edited by] Louise Cummings.
    pages   cm. – (Cambridge handbooks in language and linguistics)
Includes bibliographical references and index.
ISBN 978-1-107-02123-5 (hardback)
1. Communicative disorders–Handbooks, manuals, etc.   I. Cummings, Louise.
RC423.C24 2013
362.19685′5–dc23
2013018451

ISBN 978-1-107-02123-5 Hardback

In memory of
R. Steven Ackley
A committed author and audiologist

Contents

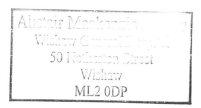

Figures

Tables

Contributors

R. Steven Ackley was Professor of Audiology and Director of the PhD Program in Hearing, Speech and Language Sciences at Gallaudet University, Washington, DC until his death in 2013. He was former Department Chair at Gallaudet and at the University of Northern Colorado. His research interests included auditory electrophysiology, balance disorders and deafness. His co-edited text *An Essential Guide to Hearing and Balance Disorders* (2007) gives an in-depth treatise of hearing and balance procedures and pathologies.

Kirrie J. Ballard is Associate Professor and Australian Research Council (ARC) Future Fellow at the University of Sydney in Australia. Her research interests are in the area of normal and disordered speech motor control and learning, with a strong emphasis on translational to clinical practice. She has authored over forty scientific articles and 100 conference presentations and is regularly invited to provide professional development workshops for speech-language pathologists. Her research has been funded by the National Institutes of Health (NIH) and the American Speech-Language-Hearing Association (ASHA) in the USA and by the National Health and Medical Research Council (NHMRC) and ARC in Australia.

Roelien Bastiaanse is Professor of Neurolinguistics at the University of Groningen, The Netherlands. She has over 150 publications on aphasia in English and Dutch. She has edited three books: with Evy Visch-Brink *Linguistic Levels in Aphasia* (1998); with Yosef Grodzinsky *Grammatical Disorders in Aphasia: A Neurolinguistic Perspective* (2000); and with Cynthia K. Thompson *Perspectives on Agrammatism* (2012). She has written two Dutch books and developed and published two Dutch treatment programmes, one of which has been adapted to German. She has co-authored with Susan Edwards and Judith Rispens the *Verb and Sentence Test* (2002), which has been adapted to English and Norwegian.

Gregory J. Benner is a professor and Executive Director of the Applied Research Center for Strong Communities and Schools at the University of Washington, Tacoma. Dr Benner specializes in preventive approaches for meeting the behavioural and academic needs of students, particularly those with emotional and behaviour disorders. He has expertise in building the capacity of educators to meet the social and emotional needs of youth who are least understood and struggling most. He is the co-author of the book *Instructional Practices for Students with Behavioral Disorders: Strategies for Reading, Writing, and Math* (2008). Dr Benner currently serves as Associate Editor for *Behavioral Disorders* and *Remedial and Special Education*.

Glenis Benson is a lecturer at the University of Wisconsin-Oshkosh in the USA. Her research focuses on pragmatic abilities in children with autism spectrum disorders and children with intellectual disabilities. Along with her colleagues at the University of Wisconsin-Madison, she is responsible for one of the early investigations of theory of mind in persons with intellectual disability. Glenis lectures but also supports persons with autism spectrum disorders and behavioural challenges through a private practice in Madison, Wisconsin.

Diane M. Bless is Professor Emeritus of Surgery and Communication Sciences and Disorders at the University of Wisconsin-Madison. She founded, developed and served as the Director of Voice Services at University of Wisconsin Hospital and Clinics for nearly three decades. She has authored chapters, books and scientific articles on voice issues, and given numerous lectures and workshops in the USA, Argentina, Australia, Brazil, Canada, Chile, China, Egypt, England, Ireland, Japan, Korea, France, Scotland, Malaysia and Sweden. The focus of her teaching, research and clinical practice has been on vocal fold functioning in health and disease, particularly as it pertains to assessment and treatment.

Tobias Bormann is a clinical neuropsychologist at the Department of Neurology of the University of Freiburg. He studied psychology at the University of Freiburg and held a position at Erfurt University. His research is concerned with acquired impairments of language, including studies of word-finding difficulties, impaired comprehension, dyslexia and dysgraphia. His research is mainly based on cognitive, single-case studies but also involves group studies with aphasic and unimpaired individuals. He is the co-author of several articles published in international journals including *Cortex*, *Brain and Language*, *Journal of Neurolinguistics* and *Aphasiology*.

Tim Bressmann is Associate Professor in the Department of Speech-Language Pathology at the University of Toronto. He also holds cross-appointments as an Associate Professor at the Faculty of Dentistry at the University of Toronto, an Adjunct Scientist at St John's Rehabilitation Program of the Sunnybrook Health Sciences Centre, and a lecturer in the Department of Special Education at the University of Munich. His research and teaching interests are in the field of structurally-related speech disorders, such as craniofacial syndromes, head and neck cancer, and voice disorders. A special focus of his research is the use of ultrasound imaging for the analysis of tongue movement. He has authored over 60 peer-reviewed papers, book chapters and contributions to conference proceedings.

Karen Bryan is Pro Vice-Chancellor and Dean of the Faculty of Health and Wellbeing at Sheffield Hallam University. She was, until 2013, a Consultant Speech and Language Therapist at the West London Mental Health Trust. She is the editor of *Communication in Healthcare* (2009) and co-editor with Jane Maxim of *Communication Disability in the Dementias* (2006). Karen Bryan was awarded a Fellowship of the Royal College of Speech and Language Therapists in 2011. She holds a Visiting Professorship in the Department of Neuropsychology, University of Warsaw.

Catherine Christo is Professor Emeritus in the School Psychology Program at California State University, Sacramento. Her interests are primarily in reading, dyslexia and learning disabilities. Dr Christo is a co-author of *Identifying, Assessing and Treating Dyslexia at School* (2009), and a chapter entitled 'Word Recognition' in the *Handbook of Reading Research, Volume IV* (2010). She is also the author of journal articles on reading, dyslexia, assessment, response to intervention and learning disabilities. Dr Christo provides training at a state and national level on these topics.

Nadine P. Connor is Associate Professor of Communication Sciences and Disorders and Research Director in Otolaryngology-Head and Neck Surgery at the University of Wisconsin-Madison. Her research interests are in the areas of voice and swallowing. She is particularly interested in the biological mechanisms of muscular adaptation to ageing and therapeutic interventions, specifically in the larynx and tongue. She also teaches courses at the University of Wisconsin-Madison in the areas of research methods and assessment and management of voice disorders. Among her students are otolaryngology-head and neck surgery residents.

Karen Croot is a lecturer in Applied Cognitive Psychology at the University of Sydney, Australia. Her research on speech production and speech impairments is carried out within the disciplines of cognitive psychology, cognitive neuropsychology and phonetics. She received her PhD from the University of Cambridge, and has held Visiting Fellowships at Royal Holloway, University of London, the Clinical Neuropsychology Research Group (EKN), Clinic Bogenhausen, City Hospital GmbH Munich and the Centre for Advanced Studies, Ludwig-Maximilians-University Munich. She is co-editor of *Progressive Language Impairments: Intervention and Management* (2009).

Louise Cummings is Professor of Linguistics at Nottingham Trent University in the UK. Her research interests are largely in pragmatics and clinical linguistics. She is the author of *Pragmatics: A Multidisciplinary Perspective* (2005); *Clinical Linguistics* (2008); *Clinical Pragmatics* (Cambridge University Press, 2009); *Communication Disorders* (2014); and *Pragmatic Disorders* (2014). Louise Cummings has edited *The Routledge Pragmatics Encyclopedia* (2010). She has held Visiting Fellowships in the Department of Philosophy at Harvard University and in the Centre for Research in the Arts, Social Sciences and Humanities (CRASSH) at Cambridge University.

Susan Ellis Weismer is Professor of Communication Sciences and Disorders and Associate Dean for Research, College of Letters & Science at the University of Wisconsin-Madison. She also holds affiliate faculty positions in the Departments of Psychology and Educational Psychology and is a principal investigator at the Waisman Center. Her research, which is funded by the National Institutes of Health, has focused on understanding the developmental course and mechanisms underlying language disorders in late talkers, children with specific language impairment, and children on the autism spectrum. She has published over 50 articles in peer-reviewed journals, 20 book chapters, and various reviews and abstracts.

Perrine Ferré is a speech-language pathologist and research professional in Montreal, Québec, Canada. Her clinical practice at the Hôpital de Réadaptation Villa Medica includes speech-pathology assessment, intervention and counselling for adults with neurological disorders and their proxies. As the coordinator of the clinical knowledge transfer branch of Yves Joanette's research team, she has contributed to various publications in the area of acquired communication disabilities, especially after right hemisphere damage. She is the co-author of journal articles in *Folia Phoniatrica et Logopaedica*, *NeuroImage* and *Rehabilitation Research and Practice*.

Sabina Flagmeier is conducting research alongside Dr Donald A. Robin in the neuroscience imaging programme at the University of Texas Health Science Center, San Antonio. Her current research focuses on understanding the neural contributions of voice motor control. Her work includes the use of non-invasive imaging modalities such as functional magnetic resonance imaging and electroencephalography as well as modelling techniques such as structural equation modelling and dynamic causal modelling.

Megan Hodge is Professor Emerita in Speech Pathology and Audiology at the University of Alberta in Canada where she heads the Children's Speech Intelligibility, Research and Education Laboratory. She has taught courses in anatomy and physiology of the speech mechanism, speech science and motor speech disorders. Her research publications address developmental aspects of normal and disordered speech production, perceptual-acoustic correlates of speech intelligibility, and linking theory with practice in evaluating and treating children with motor speech disorders. She has ongoing collaborations with community partners to translate and operationalize knowledge to improve services and outcomes for children with complex speech disorders.

Jinyi Hung is a senior researcher in the Cognition and Language Lab in the Department of Speech, Language, and Hearing Sciences at the University of Florida. Jinyi has previously studied speech-language pathology at the University of Tennessee Health Science Center. From 2009 to 2010, she was in the Neurocognitive Linguistics Lab at the University of Tennessee in Knoxville. Her previous research examined semantic processing difficulties in people with traumatic brain injuries during picture and word categorization tasks. She is affiliated with the Speech-Language-Hearing Association of Taiwan. Her research interests include semantic memory, dementia, cognitive-linguistic processing and cognitive rehabilitation.

Yves Joanette is Professor in Cognitive Neurosciences of Language at the Faculty of Medicine of the Université de Montréal. He is currently the Scientific Director of the Institute of Aging of the Canadian Institutes of Health Research, and Executive Director of its International Collaborative Research Study on Alzheimer's diseases. From 1997 to 2009, he was the Director of the Centre de Recherche de l'Institut Universitaire de Gériatrie de Montréal (CRIUGM), and then President and CEO of the Fonds de la Recherche en Santé du Québec as well as Chair of its Board. His research interests concern the ageing process and cognitive deficits in the elderly.

Laurence B. Leonard is Rachel E. Stark Distinguished Professor in the Department of Speech, Language, and Hearing Sciences at Purdue University. He conducts research on children with language disorders. Much of his work has been devoted to discovering the clinical profiles of children with specific language impairment across different languages, and understanding the source of these children's grammatical deficits. He is the author of the book *Children with Specific Language Impairment* as well as numerous research articles and chapters in edited volumes.

Anja Lowit is a reader in Speech and Language Pathology at Strathclyde University in Scotland. She teaches clinical linguistics and phonetics. Her research focuses primarily on prosodic disorders and motor speech disorders, with particular emphasis on the development and validation of novel assessment approaches. She has published in a number of international journals, and co-edited a book on *Assessment of Motor Speech Disorders* with Ray Kent (2011).

Patricia McCabe is Senior Lecturer and Course Director in the discipline of Speech Pathology at the University of Sydney, Australia. Her research, teaching and clinical practice are focused on developing and improving treatments for children with severe speech sound disorders, particularly childhood apraxia of speech. Tricia is interested in the application of the principles of motor learning to new treatments for childhood apraxia of speech in particular, and articulation and voice disorders more generally. She is also interested in the application of evidence-based practice in speech pathology, speech pathology service delivery innovations and professional voice user training.

Brigid McNeill is a senior lecturer in Literacy Education at the University of Canterbury, New Zealand. Her research primarily focuses on understanding the nature and educational consequences of developmental speech disorders, particularly developmental verbal dyspraxia. Brigid has published several articles evaluating the effectiveness of therapy designed to enhance speech and early literacy development for children with developmental verbal dyspraxia. She is a recipient of a New Zealand Marsden fast start research grant which is designed to support outstanding researchers early in their careers, and a Canterbury Teaching Fellowship to be undertaken at Trinity College, Dublin.

Julie Morris is a speech and language therapist and senior lecturer in Speech and Language Sciences at Newcastle University in the UK. She is Director of the Tavistock Aphasia Centre (North East). Her research interests focus on acquired aphasia, particularly spoken and written word comprehension and spoken word production. She is also interested in engagement with people with aphasia and is a trustee of the North East Trust for Aphasia. She is the author of several studies contributing to the evidence base about therapy for aphasia and is co-author of a series of theoretically motivated therapy resources (Newcastle Aphasia Therapy Resources, 2009).

Bruce E. Murdoch is the Director of the Centre for Neurogenic Communication Disorders Research at the University of Queensland. He is a recognized international authority on neurologically acquired speech and language disorders in children and adults. He has published 13 books in this field, over 395 peer-reviewed articles in high-quality, international journals, 70 invited book chapters and presented over 350 papers at major international conferences. Bruce Murdoch is a member of the editorial board of 10 international refereed journals and an editorial consultant to 25 other international journals.

J. Ron Nelson is a professor in the Department of Special Education and Communication Disorders at the University of Nebraska-Lincoln. He received the 2000 Distinguished Initial Career Research Award by the Council for Exceptional Children. He has developed a number of behaviour (e.g. Think Time Strategy) and literacy interventions (e.g. Stepping Stones to Literacy; Early Vocabulary Connections) that have been recognized by the US Department of Education. He is the co-author of several books: *Vocabulary Learning: Tools and Strategies for Teaching Students with Learning Difficulties*; *Instructional Practices for Students with Behavioral Disorders: Strategies for Reading, Writing, and Math* (2008); and *Comprehensive Behavior Management: Individualized, Classroom, and Schoolwide Approaches* (2012).

Courtenay Frazier Norbury is a reader in Developmental Neuropsychology at Royal Holloway, University of London. She worked as a speech-language therapist in East London before completing her DPhil in Experimental Psychology at Oxford University. Her research expertise centres on the nature of language impairment in developmental disorders, most notably specific language impairment and autism spectrum disorder. She co-edited *Understanding Developmental Language Disorders* with Dorothy Bishop and Bruce Tomblin, and co-authored the fourth edition of *Language Disorders from Infancy through Adolescence* with Rhea Paul. She was an editor of the *Journal of Speech, Language, and Hearing Research*, and is currently an editor of the *Journal of Child Psychology and Psychiatry*.

Ronald S. Prins was formerly Associate Professor of Patholinguistics at the University of Amsterdam, The Netherlands. In the 1970s, he developed a system for the analysis of aphasic spontaneous speech that is still widely used in The Netherlands, both for research and for clinical purposes. Furthermore, he is an expert in the early history of aphasiology, on which he has written several Dutch and international articles. He has published articles in a number of international journals including *Aphasiology*, *Applied Psycholinguistics* and *Brain and Language*. In 1999, he received an award from the Dutch Aphasia Association for his work on aphasiology.

Linda Rammage is Director of the British Columbia Provincial Voice Care Resource Program and a faculty member in the Department of Surgery and the School of Audiology and Speech Sciences at the University of British Columbia, Vancouver, Canada. She is a co-founder of the interdisciplinary Pacific Voice Clinic. Linda Rammage has published numerous papers and chapters and lectured internationally on assessment and management of voice disorders, psychopathology of voice disorders, voice care for professional and occupational voice users, muscle misuse voice disorders, the irritable larynx and various voice research topics. She is the author of several textbooks on management of voice disorders.

Jamie Reilly is an assistant professor in the Eleanor M. Saffran Center for Cognitive Neuroscience and the Department of Communication Sciences and Disorders at Temple University in the US. His research is focused on semantic memory and language learning in dementia. He is a co-editor of *Short-Term and Working Memory Impairments in Aphasia* (2012). He also serves on the editorial board of the *Journal of the International Neuropsychological Society*. Dr Reilly is a clinically licensed speech-language pathologist whose doctoral research training was in cognitive psychology and neuroscience.

John E. Riski is the Clinical Director of the Center for Craniofacial Disorders, and Director of the Speech Pathology Laboratory, Center for Craniofacial Disorders, Children's Healthcare of Atlanta at Scottish Rite. He is a former president of the American Cleft Palate-Craniofacial Association (2000–2001) and a Fellow of the American Speech-Language-Hearing Association (1992). His research interests lie in the study of surgical outcomes for speech problems related to cleft palate and craniofacial disorders. He has published over 70 professional articles and book chapters on the subjects of cleft palate and related craniofacial disorders, neurological and structural speech deficits and dysphagia.

Donald A. Robin is Professor of Neurology, Radiology and Biomedical Engineering and Chief of the Human Performance Division at the Research Imaging Institute, University of Texas Health Science Institute,

San Antonio and Professor and Assistant Director for Research at the Honors College of University of Texas, San Antonio. His current research programme focuses on the use of non-invasive brain imaging to understand neural network connectivity in speech and voice motor control, treatment effects and prediction of outcomes. He continues his work in apraxia of speech, examining neural substrates, modelling sensory motor control and developing and testing treatments for adult and child apraxia of speech.

Susan Rvachew is an associate professor at McGill University in Canada. Her research interests include the role of speech input in typical and atypical speech development and the evaluation of interventions for the remediation of speech, language and literacy deficits in children. She has co-authored, with Françoise Brosseau-Lapré, *Developmental Phonological Disorders: Foundations of Clinical Practice* (2012). She is also the author of over 50 scientific articles and book chapters.

Kathleen Scaler Scott is Assistant Professor of Speech-Language Pathology at Misericordia University in the USA. Her research interests are largely in cluttering and atypical disfluencies. She is the co-editor of *Cluttering: A Handbook of Research, Intervention, and Education* (2011) and co-author of *Managing Cluttering: A Comprehensive Guidebook of Activities* (2013), both with Dr David Ward. Dr Scaler Scott is the author of numerous publications and has spoken nationally and internationally on the topics of fluency and social pragmatic disorders. She was the first Coordinator of the International Cluttering Association.

Katherine Short-Meyerson is an educational psychologist and a senior lecturer in the College of Education and Human Services at the University of Wisconsin-Oshkosh in the USA. Her primary research interests include pragmatics and cognitive development. Dr Short-Meyerson completed a postdoctoral research fellowship at the Kennedy Center for Research on Education and Human Development at Vanderbilt University. Her work has been published in the *Journal of Intellectual Disability Research*; *Journal of Speech, Language, and Hearing Research*; *Journal of Child Language*; *First Language*; and *The International Handbook of Applied Research in Intellectual Disabilities* (2004).

Vesna Stojanovik is a senior lecturer (associate professor) in Clinical Linguistics at the University of Reading in the UK. Her research focuses on various aspects of language and communication in atypical populations with a special emphasis on populations with genetic syndromes such as Williams and Down's syndromes. Recently, her research has examined prosody development and impairment in children with Williams and Down's syndromes. She is one of the editors of *Speech Prosody in Atypical Populations: Assessment and Remediation* (2011) and is the author and co-author of several articles in international journals. Vesna Stojanovik is also the Chair of the British Association of Clinical Linguistics.

Leanne Togher is Professor of Communication Disorders following Traumatic Brain Injury at the University of Sydney in Australia. She is internationally recognized as an expert on communication disorders following traumatic brain injury, with the publication of over 80 journal articles, numerous treatment resources including the website and treatment manual *TBI Express*, and a co-edited book *Social and Communication Disorders following Traumatic Brain Injury* (2013). Leanne is a Senior Research Fellow of the Australian National Health and Medical Research Council and a principal research fellow of the University of Sydney.

Janet Webster is a lecturer at Newcastle University in the UK. She is a researcher and clinician who works in the Tavistock Aphasia Centre North East, based at the university. She has a particular interest in sentence processing and reading difficulties in people with aphasia, with a focus on developing assessments for differential diagnosis, evaluating the efficacy of therapy and promoting the availability of theoretically driven therapy materials for clinical use. She is co-author of *A Cognitive Neuropsychological Approach to Assessment and Intervention in Aphasia: A Clinician's Guide* (2013).

Anne Whitworth is an associate professor at Curtin University, Western Australia. She is a researcher, clinician and educator in the field of speech pathology, with particular interests in acquired neurological disorders. Her particular interests are in developing and evaluating theoretically sound assessments and interventions in aphasia, facilitating and measuring the real life impact of therapy for people with communication impairments, and supporting clinicians in carrying out research in the workplace. She is the co-author of the text *A Cognitive Neuropsychological Approach to Assessment and Intervention in Aphasia: A Clinician's Guide* (2013), which is now in its second edition, and is also the author of a series of research articles.

Maximiliano A. Wilson is Professor in the Département de Réadaptation in the Université Laval in Quebec City, Canada. He has held a postdoctoral fellowship in the Centre de Recherche de l'Institut Universitaire de Gériatrie de Montréal, Université de Montréal. Maximiliano is interested in the study of lexical and semantic processing in normal adults and in neuropsychological populations, such as mono- and bilingual aphasic patients and individuals with semantic dementia. He uses behavioural and brain imaging (fMRI) techniques to study normal and impaired language processing. He is the co-author of articles in *Behavioural Neurology*, *NeuroImage* and *Acta Psychologica*.

J. Scott Yaruss is an associate professor and Director of the Master's Degree programmes in Speech-Language Pathology at the University of Pittsburgh. He is an ASHA fellow and a board-recognized specialist in fluency disorders. His research examines methods for assessing and evaluating treatment outcomes in people who stutter. He has published more than 50 papers in peer-reviewed journals and nearly 100 other articles, papers and chapters on stuttering. He is author, co-author or editor of several booklets, books and brochures on stuttering, including the *Overall Assessment of the Speaker's Experience of Stuttering* (OASES) (Pearson Assessments, 2010) as well as *School-Age Stuttering Therapy: A Practical Guide and Minimizing Bullying for Children Who Stutter* (Stuttering Therapy Resources, 2013).

Preface

Communication disorders rarely achieve the prominence of a large range of other conditions that compromise human health and wellbeing. Yet, these disorders represent a significant burden on society in general, and compromise the quality of life and opportunities of the children and adults who experience them. In the UK, the Royal College of Speech and Language Therapists estimates that approximately 2.5 million people have a communication disorder. Some 800,000 of these people have a disorder that is so severe that it is hard for anyone outside their immediate families to understand them. In the USA, the National Institute on Deafness and Other Communication Disorders estimates that one in every six Americans has some form of communication disorder. If these figures do not make a compelling case for the assessment and treatment of communication disorders, then perhaps the reader will consider these comments made in 2006 by Lord Ramsbotham, the Chief Inspector of Prisons in the UK: 'When I went to the young offender establishment at Polmont I was walking with the governor, who told me that if, by some mischance, he had to get rid of all his staff, the last one out of the gate would be his speech and language therapist'. No statement more forcefully demonstrates how an individual's life chances are adversely affected by communication disorders, or the extent to which speech and language therapy can successfully intervene in these disorders.

Of course, speech and language therapy (speech-language pathology) is only possible to the extent that communication disorders are the focus of intensive academic study and clinical research. The chapters in this handbook are intended to bring to the reader the very latest knowledge of those disorders, from the epidemiology, aetiology and clinical features of communication disorders through to their assessment, treatment and theoretical significance. Each contributor has been chosen for his or her expertise in a particular communication disorder or group of disorders. This expertise is founded upon a substantial record of research in each case alongside direct clinical experience of the disorders in question. The result is a collection of chapters that represents the state of the art in communication disorders, both in terms of how these disorders are conceived and how they are clinically managed.

The expansion in clinical communication sciences has been such that each aspect of a communication disorder is now the focus of extensive research. The researcher who is concerned with investigating the epidemiology and aetiology of specific language impairment in children will certainly be aware of how this disorder is assessed and treated without directly contributing to the development of techniques in these areas. It is not possible to do justice to these different dimensions of communication disorders within single chapters. It is in an effort to capture the depth of research in each of these areas that the volume has been divided into five parts. Parts I, II and III examine the epidemiology, aetiology and clinical features of the full range of developmental and acquired communication disorders. These disorders include impairments in speech and language (Parts I and II) as well as voice, fluency and hearing (Part III). Part IV examines the clinical management of communication disorders. The chapters in this part reflect current thinking about how communication disorders can best be assessed and treated. In doing so, they address areas where the evidence base for clinical practice is poorly developed as well as areas where there is a much higher level of evidence in support of specific techniques and practices. Finally, a number of theoretical developments have enhanced our understanding of communication disorders. Similarly, communication disorders can make a significant contribution to theoretical debates in speech-language pathology and beyond. Part V in this volume contains chapters which explore theoretical developments at the levels of phonetics and phonology (speech production models), syntax (cognitive modularity), semantics (semantic models) and pragmatics (theory of mind).

Acknowledgements

There are a number of people whose contribution to this volume I would like to acknowledge. I want to thank Dr Andrew Winnard of Cambridge University Press. This handbook was proposed by Andrew. I am grateful to him for considering me as the editor of this work and for his ongoing support during the completion of this project. This handbook has been a huge undertaking and I received the assistance of others during its preparation. Rachel Eden, programme administrator at Nottingham Trent University, collated the final manuscript and bibliography. My sister, Judith Heaney, assisted me in preparing the index. Their combined efforts made my task a more manageable one and I thank them for their excellent contributions.

I owe an enormous debt of gratitude to the authors of the chapters that appear in this volume. The professionalism and commitment they have shown has been truly gratifying. I have gained intellectually from the experience of working with them. This volume simply would not have been possible without their expertise and dedication.

Part I

Developmental communication disorders

1

Cleft lip and palate and other craniofacial anomalies

John E. Riski

1.1 Introduction

Despite reports from the Centers for Disease Control and Prevention (2006) that cleft lip/palate is the most commonly reported birth defect, clefting remains a low incident disorder. Because it is low incident, there is often little impetus to include velopharyngeal function/dysfunction in educational programmes for speech-language pathologists. There are also limited numbers of patients and clinicians who can provide clinical expertise and training to students and practising clinicians. However, clefting can have a devastating impact on a newborn's ability to feed. Unrepaired or unsuccessfully repaired cleft palate can have a devastating effect on speech development and intelligibility, often preventing successful integration of the affected individual into society.

Velopharyngeal incompetence (VPI) can result from a number of congenital craniofacial anomalies and associated genetic disorders. VPI can also result from acquired neurological disorders such as stroke, head injury and neurological diseases. Also, it can result from ablative surgery from adenoidectomy and head and neck cancer. This chapter will focus on cleft lip and palate. However, understanding principles of evaluating velopharyngeal dysfunction and its treatments can serve clinicians faced with evaluating and treating patients with velopharyngeal dysfunction from other causes.

A cleft lip develops when the prolabium fails to fuse with the lateral lip segments (see Figure 1.1). A cleft palate develops when the palatal segments fail to fuse with the septum in the midline (see Figure 1.2). Clefts of the lip can be unilateral or bilateral. They can affect the lip, the palate or both.

A cleft palate can disrupt the palatal muscles that are responsible for elevation of the soft palate or velum. The levator muscle of the velum

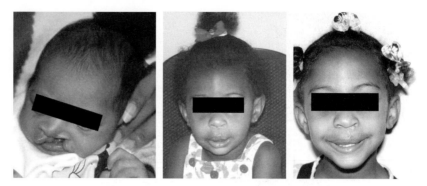

Figure 1.1 Children with cleft lip, unrepaired (left panel) and repaired (middle and right panel). (Permission granted for educational purposes.)

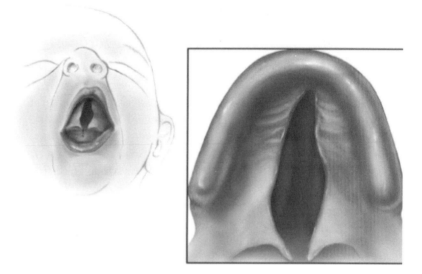

Figure 1.2 Drawing of midline cleft palate. (© 2012 Children's Healthcare of Atlanta, Inc. All rights reserved.)

functions to couple and separate the nasal cavities from the vocal tract during speech (see Figure 1.3). This function determines whether the voiced elements of speech have oral resonance or nasal resonance. It also helps to determine whether oral pressure can be impounded in the oral cavity for plosive, fricative and affricate sounds. Velopharyngeal incompetence or dysfunction of the soft palate often leaves speech unintelligible and hypernasal, lacking in aspiration of pressure consonant sounds.

A challenge to evaluation is that the aetiology of hypernasality and nasal airflow disorders is often occult or hidden. In reviews of patients receiving surgical correction for hypernasality, approximately 30 per cent did not have a cleft palate (Riski *et al.* 1992; Riski 1995). The aetiology in these children was an anatomically deep nasopharynx that can only be

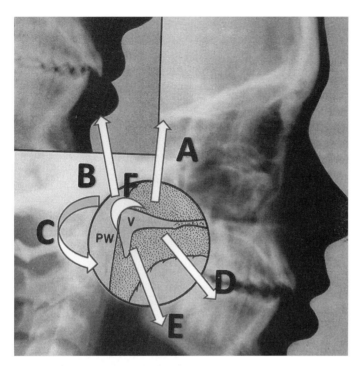

Figure 1.3 Muscles of the velum. The arrows show approximate direction of muscular attachment and direction of movement. A, tensor palatini; B, levator palatini; C, superior constrictor; D, palatoglossus; E, palatopharyngeus; F, musculus uvula; PW, posterior wall of the pharynx; V, velum.

diagnosed accurately by radiographic assessment. Normal velopharyngeal dimensions were described by Subtelny (1957) and highlighted by Zemlin (1997). Also, the anatomical defect of a disproportionately deep pharynx was described by Calnan (1971).

A mistaken concept in speech pathology is that non-cleft hypernasality is erroneously labelled as a 'voice disorder'. Labelling hypernasality a 'voice disorder' is ambiguous (it implies it is a disorder of the larynx), and often hampers successful management of the disorder. Because the physical defect is not recognized, speech therapies are often poorly designed and ineffective (Ruscello 2004). A cleft palate is identified prenatally or perinatally and palate closure is before one year of age (Riski 1995). In stark contrast, the average age of referral to our centre for children with non-cleft hypernasality resulting from 22q11.2 deletion (velocardiofacial syndrome or VCFS) was 9.2 years of age. Children with hypernasality resulting from cleft palate are generally referred to a craniofacial team. In contrast, children with hypernasality with no obvious form of clefting are referred to an ENT specialist, generally in a private office, who may or may not have experience of evaluating and managing velopharyngeal dysfunction. Delayed management of VPI leads to increased failure of surgical intervention and refractory speech deficits. The rate of complete success from surgery when VPI is managed before 6 years of age is 90.9%. The success rate falls to 73.9% between 6 and 12 years, 70.0% between 12 and 18 years, and 47.0% after 18 years (Riski *et al.*1992).

The evaluation of oral clefts and hypernasality is conducted by specialists in craniofacial clinics. However, in the United States, Public Laws 94-142 and 99-457, which culminated in the Individuals with Disability Education Act (IDEA, 1990, reauthorized in 1997 and 2004), mandated that special services, such as speech therapy, be provided through specialists in schools and developmental centres. The professionals in these settings usually have limited experience of cleft-related problems because these problems typically form a very small part of their caseload. This separation of evaluation and therapy can lead to poor communication between professionals and therapy plans that do not directly address the therapy needs of the patient. There is an unquestionable need for partnerships between evaluation centres and the settings in which therapy is conducted.

1.2 Epidemiology and aetiology of cleft lip and palate

In the United States, the Centers for Disease Control and Prevention (CDC) conducts a surveillance study of birth defects in 14 states. It is estimated that each year 2,651 infants are born with a cleft palate and 4,437 infants are born with a cleft lip with or without a cleft palate (Parker *et al.* 2010). The incidence and prevalence of clefting vary with epidemiological study. Bister *et al.* (2011) reported the incidence of facial clefts to be 0.127 per cent in a British population. Prevalence rates between 0.97 per 1,000 live births (Golalipour *et al.* 2007) and 1.47 per 1,000 live births (Gregg *et al.* 2008) have been reported. The condition is more prevalent in males than in females. Golalipour *et al.* (2007) reported the prevalence of oral clefting to be 1.08 per 1,000 male births and 0.86 per 1,000 female births. Prevalence rates also vary with the ethnicity of populations. Among Asian populations, Cooper *et al.* (2006) reported the prevalence rate of syndromic plus non-syndromic cleft lip with or without cleft palate to be 1.30 per 1,000 live births (Chinese), 1.34 per 1,000 (Japanese) and 1.47 per 1,000 (Other Asian). Compared to Caucasians, the prevalence of cleft lip with or without cleft palate is lower among Africans, higher among Native Americans and the same among Japanese and Chinese (Croen *et al.* 1998).

The distribution of different types of oral clefts has been examined in several studies. In an investigation of 835 cases, González *et al.* (2008) reported cleft lip and palate in 70% of cases, cleft palate in 21%, cleft lip in 8% and separate cleft lip and palate in 1%. Gregg *et al.* (2008) found a significant left-sided predilection for unilateral clefting of the lip. The aetiology of clefting is still uncertain. Studies from the CDC found that women who smoke are more likely to have a baby with an orofacial cleft than those who do not smoke (Little *et al.* 2004; Honein *et al.* 2007). Women who have diabetes are at increased risk of having a child with a cleft lip with or without a cleft palate (Correa *et al.* 2008).

Orofacial clefts can sometimes be diagnosed during pregnancy, usually by a routine ultrasound as early as 17 weeks. Riski (2006) found that 50% of families had a prenatal diagnosis of cleft by ultrasound, while Bister *et al.* (2011) reported that 65% of clefts were detected by antenatal ultrasound screening. Isolated clefts of the palate might not be identified until the perinatal period. Submucous cleft palate and bifid uvula might not be diagnosed until later in life. Bifid uvula has been identified in 2.26% of school-aged children and often occurs without any other palatal involvement (Wharton and Mower 1992). However, a bifid uvula highlights the need for a complete assessment of the velopharyngeal mechanism if there is any nasal regurgitation or hypernasality or if an adenoidectomy is planned. There are also children born with VPI without an observable cleft. These children have a deep nasopharynx identified only by lateral cephalometric radiographs (Calnan 1971; Riski *et al.* 1992; Riski 1995).

1.3   Effects of cleft palate

1.3.1   Feeding

An open cleft palate is a detriment to feeding in a newborn and can compromise nutrition. Furthermore, newborns with micrognathia, such as in Pierre Robin syndrome, will also have a compromised airway that complicates the normal suck–swallow–breathe coordination required for successful feeding. Craniofacial clinics should incorporate feeding specialists to evaluate and treat feeding problems found in newborns. The specialists should include speech-language pathologists who specialize in feeding of newborns, nutritionists, lactation consultants and nurses. They will first establish that the child has an adequate airway. There should be no sternal retractions or rapid respiratory rate. The effectiveness of feeding is established by measuring the volume of formula taken within a specific timeframe. Newborns with isolated cleft lip(s) might be able to breast-feed successfully if they have adequate tongue protrusion under the nipple to gain suction. Newborns with a cleft palate are difficult to breast-feed unless the mother hyperlactates and milk flow is rapid and requires little/no suction or compression. Failure to provide adequate nutrition to the newborn can lead to failure to thrive and more aggressive feeding options such as nasogastric tubes or gastrostomy tubes.

For all infants, feeding specialists will help ensure that the child is in a mostly upright position and will assess feeding effectiveness with various bottles and nipples. There are many specialty nursers and nipples available. Commonly used specialty bottles are the Mead Johnson Cleft

Palate Nurser, the Haberman Bottle and the Pigeon Bottle. The nutritionist is vital in documenting weight gain and recommending formulas that can increase the nutritional value of each feeding. The Cleft Palate Foundation (2012) has produced an instructional video for feeding newborns with cleft palate.

1.3.2   Articulation and resonance

Speech and resonance are affected by velopharyngeal incompetence, dental arch malformations and hearing loss. We will discuss some of the common articulation and resonance qualities associated with velopharyngeal function/dysfunction and discuss treatment of these anomalies in section 1.6.

Oral pressure is required for the production of stop-plosive, fricative and affricate sounds. Some languages have trills such as the trilled Spanish 'rr' that also requires oral pressure. Nasal pressure loss through an oral-nasal fistula or VPI can undermine that pressure. The lack of pressure for these sounds can render speech unintelligible. Typical compensations are the use of nasal substitution (e.g. [m] for /b/) or the development of maladaptive articulation errors such as use of the glottal stop or pharyngeal fricative.

Nasal air emission is the quality of non-acoustic sounds and is mostly easily perceived on unvoiced consonants. This quality results when the speaker is attempting oral pressure but it is leaking through a fistula or VPI. Nasal air emission may be inaudible in patients with patent nasal cavities when the air passes through the nasal cavity without creating any audible turbulence. The sound of posterior nasal frication (nasal air leak) in conjunction with oral airflow generally represents touch velopharyngeal contact. Velopharyngeal closing force is not maintained and the air leak through the port creates the posterior nasal frication. There is airflow simultaneously through the oral and nasal cavities.

Oral-nasal resonance is the balance of oral and nasal acoustic (voiced) energies. It is achieved by the appropriate coupling and isolation of the nasal cavities from the remainder of the vocal tract during speech by the movements of the velopharyngeal valve. Three English sounds require the nasal cavities to be coupled with the vocal tract (i.e. /m/, /n/, /ŋ/). All other sounds require the velopharyngeal valve to isolate the nasal cavities from the vocal tract. Hypernasality is the quality perceived by the listener when there is inappropriate nasal coupling with the vocal tract during speech. It is mostly easily perceived on vowel sounds. In contrast, hyponasality is perceived as inadequate coupling or obstruction of the nasal tract during production of those sounds normally associated with nasal energy. The obstruction may be posterior (e.g. hypertrophied adenoids) or anterior (e.g. hypertrophied turbinates, deviated septum). A speaker may also demonstrate mixed hyper-hyponasality when velopharyngeal closure is incomplete, but the nasal cavity is occluded anteriorly.

Compensatory articulations can develop in response to VPI or dental arch malformations. These articulations not only reduce the intelligibility of speech but have been found to be related to delays in language development in cleft patients (Pamplona *et al.* 2000). The classic compensatory misarticulations of glottal stops and pharyngeal fricatives have been expanded by Trost (1981) to include pharyngeal and midpalatal stops. In a pharyngeal stop, the point of stop is the tongue base to the posterior pharyngeal wall. This articulation is used as a substitution for /k/ and /g/. In a midpalatal stop, the point of stop is midpalate between the position of /t/ and /k/. This articulation is used as a substitution for /t, d, k, or g/. Other compensatory articulations include the use of clicks (Gibbon *et al.* 2008).

A unique, maladaptive articulation is the posterior nasal fricative. It is typically used as a substitution for sibilant and sometimes affricate and fricative sounds. During production of this fricative, the tongue is used to obstruct oral airflow. The airflow is forced through the constricted velopharyngeal valve which creates frication. There is no oral airflow. This is often seen in children without any cleft. Riski (1984) attributed this compensation to conductive hearing loss. Whereas the sibilant sound /s/ is one of the softest sounds that we produce at 20 dB, the posterior nasal fricative creates a relatively loud bone-conducted signal that bypasses fluid. We might also consider the anterior nasal fricative. This is similar to the posterior nasal fricative, but the point of frication is the anterior nostrils. Nasal grimacing may accompany this substitution.

The unique nature of compensatory or maladaptive articulation errors has led to speculation as to why these develop. The point of articulation is universally below the VPI and typically occurs at the larynx. Morr *et al.* (1988) speculated that these occur in response to certain respiratory receptors in the trachea, larynx and nasopharynx and operate to regulate vocal tract pressures and resistance during speech. In contrast, Netsell (1990) suggested that compensatory articulation is an attempt to generate acoustic distinctions that cannot be produced above the VPI. Additional study of speech compensations to VPI may provide greater insights into speech motor control.

1.3.3 Language

For some time, we have known that there are differences in language and reading abilities between children with isolated cleft palate (CPO) and children with cleft lip, with or without cleft palate (CLP). These differences were first brought to light by Richman and Eliason (1984). They reported significant differences on language measures, reading comprehension and type of reading errors between children with CLP and CPO. Their results suggested that children with CPO constitute a language disordered group with more severe reading disabilities. In contrast, they found that children with CLP were more likely to have verbal expressive deficits and milder reading problems.

In a follow-up investigation with a larger sample, Richman *et al.* (1988) reported that approximately 35% of students with cleft displayed a moderate degree of reading disability and 17% exhibited severe reading disabilities. Younger children were more likely to have reading disability than older children. However, when the two groups (CLP vs. CPO) were compared, older children with CLP had an incidence of reading disabilities similar to the general population or 9%. In contrast, the incidence of reading disabilities in children with CPO was 33%. They found that there were no differences in gender in the prevalence of reading disability.

Additional research by Broder *et al.* (1998) found that 46% of children with cleft had a learning disability, 47% had deficient educational progress and 27% had repeated a grade (excluding kindergarten). Males with CPO had a significantly higher rate of learning disability than other subject groups. Males with CPO and females with CLP were more likely to repeat a grade in school than were females with CPO and males with CLP.

1.4   Evaluation of velopharyngeal function and articulation

1.4.1   General considerations

The task of evaluating velopharyngeal function may be approached as a multi-level problem. The first level should include the perceptual assessment of resonance, nasal air escape and articulation. The trained ear is still the 'gold standard' of the evaluation. Resonance should be neither hypernasal nor hyponasal. The second level is the screening of velopharyngeal closure. This step uses inexpensive tools and is under-utilized. Patients who fail these two steps should undergo the third step of objective assessment with computerized instruments for voiced and unvoiced speech components. Finally, imaging should account for the three-dimensional nature of the velopharyngeal port and should include some combination of direct visualization using flexible fibreoptic nasendoscopy, radiography or fluoroscopy during speech.

Velopharyngeal function impacts speech proficiency. However, speech proficiency is not an adequate measure of velopharyngeal function (Riski 1979). It is possible to have severely defective speech and a competent velopharyngeal mechanism. However, normal speech usually cannot be produced without a competent velopharyngeal mechanism. Articulation should be evaluated separately with special attention to any compensatory misarticulations and the age-appropriateness of articulation. Also, longitudinal study of velopharyngeal port function has demonstrated its instability in children as their phonological system develops and craniofacial growth and adenoid involution occur (Van Demark and Morris 1983; Van Demark *et al.* 1988). Some children develop velopharyngeal incompetency as the adenoids involute (Mason and Warren 1980; Riski and Mason 1994). These studies demonstrate the need for longitudinal assessment of velopharyngeal function and the need to exercise some caution before performing a pharyngoplasty.

Each evaluation technique has its advantages and disadvantages. No one instrument provides all of the necessary information. An ad hoc committee of the American Cleft Palate-Craniofacial Association (ACPCA) suggested minimal standards for evaluation of velopharyngeal function. The standards included a perceptual evaluation of resonance and assessment using at least one instrument that provides evaluation during connected speech (i.e. fluoroscopy or pressure-flow) (Dalston *et al.* 1988). In 1993, an ACPCA consensus conference of 71 individuals experienced in the diagnosis and treatment of individuals with craniofacial anomalies developed the 'Parameters for Evaluation and Treatment of Patients with Cleft Lip/Palate or Other Craniofacial Anomalies'. These guidelines have been recently updated (American Cleft Palate-Craniofacial Association 2009).

1.4.2 Perceptual assessment

Perceptual assessment is still the mainstay of evaluation. It is even more important to observe a young child's speech if the child will not cooperate as an active participant in the evaluation. The observation of accurately produced pressure sounds (especially /p/ and /b/) are good prognostic indicators of future velopharyngeal competency (Van Demark 1979). Oral breath pressure behind the pressure consonants and nasal air emission should also be assessed. Oral breath pressure is that pressure which develops behind the oral articulators. For example, breath pressure develops behind the closed lips for the /b/ but not the /m/ sound. During conversation, the assessing clinician should listen to the force of the air stream behind the pressure consonants /p/, /b/, /t/, /d/, /k/, /g/, and the other pressure consonants. The presence of grimacing is typically a positive indicator of VPI. Grimacing is an attempt to occlude the nasal airway anteriorly.

1.4.3 Screening velopharyngeal closure

Numerous devices are available to screen velopharyngeal closure. Generally, anything that is sensitive to airflow can be used. The advantage of these devices is that they are inexpensive, portable, non-invasive and very accurate for determining the presence of nasal airflow. Examples of these devices include the See-Scape, nasal listening tube (Blakeley 1972; Riski and Millard 1979), nasal mirrors and paper paddles. Nasal airflow is monitored during words with oral pressure such as 'puppy, puppy'. The presence of any airflow indicates some degree of velopharyngeal opening and indicates that further objective testing is warranted.

1.4.4   Objective assessment

A range of instruments provide quantifiable information about hypernasality, hyponasality, oral pressure and nasal air escape. Pressure-flow study is an objective and reliable method for repeated, non-invasive measures of velopharyngeal port function for speech. Pressure-flow instrumentation measures the oral-nasal pressure differential and the volume-velocity of nasal airflow. The Perci-SARS (Palatal efficiency rating computed instantaneously-Speech Aeromechanical Research System) allows six channels of input including two pressure, two flow, a high speed voice channel and a DC (direct current) channel to input signals from other instruments. Software is included for velopharyngeal function, nasopharyngeal airway patency, laryngeal airway resistance and several other voice analysis measures.

The Nasometer has become a popular and useful instrument for evaluating the acoustic elements (i.e. hypernasality) of velopharyngeal function. The Nasometer provides an objective measure of nasality termed 'nasalance'. Nasalance is the ratio of nasal acoustic energy divided by nasal plus oral acoustic energy. Hardin *et al.* (1992) reported 91% agreement of nasalance scores with listener ratings of hypernasality. In addition, nasalance values greater than 26% were correlated with hypernasality, with values between 26% and 39% correlated with mild hypernasality and values greater than 40% correlated with moderate to severe hypernasality. Dalston *et al.* (1991a) reported a sensitivity of 89% and specificity of 99% for listener ratings of mild hypernasality. Dalston and Warren (1986) observed that nasalance scores and velopharyngeal area estimates change in concert with each other. Normative nasalance values were reported by Adams *et al.* (1989). A completely oral passage ('Zoo Passage') yielded an average nasalance of 15.53% (SD = 4.86). A mixed oral and nasal passage ('Rainbow Passage') yielded an average nasalance of 35.69% (SD = 5.20). Nasal laden sentences yielded an average nasalance of 61.06% (SD = 6.94).

Nasalance correlations with hyponasality have also been reported. Dalston *et al.* (1991b) reported a sensitivity of 0.48 and a specificity of 0.79. The measure may have been influenced by nasal air escape in some patients since the measures improved to 1.0 and 0.95, respectively, when patients with nasal air escape were eliminated. Hardin *et al.* (1992) reported that listeners' perception of hyponasality was related to nasalance scores less than 50 per cent. Researchers have defined nasalance norms for many languages. There is evidence that there may be differences between languages that will need to be clearly defined (Anderson 1996).

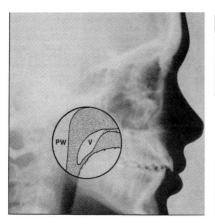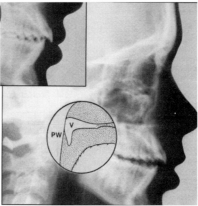

Figure 1.4 Lateral radiographs showing the velopharyngeal port in open position (left panel) and closed position (right panel). PW, pharyngeal wall; V, velum.

1.4.5 Imaging

A range of imaging techniques, including radiography, fluoroscopy and flexible fibreoptic nasendoscopy, may be used to evaluate velopharyngeal function. Lateral still cephalometric radiographs and videofluoroscopy have been used for some time to assess velopharyngeal function (see Figure 1.4). Sphincteric function during speech was demonstrated with the use of multiview videofluoroscopy by Skolnick (1970, 1975) who described and labelled three velopharyngeal closure patterns: coronal, circular and sagittal. A coronal pattern included active velar elevation with some simultaneous mesial movement of the lateral pharyngeal walls. Closure was in the coronal plane. A circular pattern was demonstrated by relatively greater lateral wall motion than velar movement. Finally, a sagittal pattern was characterized by lateral wall movement and contact with little velar elevation. These patterns are significant because pharyngoplasties have been designed and success reviewed with reference to the type and amount of movement. Videofluoroscopy allows the assessment of velar function in its dynamic state for connected speech. Still radiographs often misrepresent velar function because of the limited speech sample that can be employed (Williams and Eisenbach 1981). In addition, shadows and the two-dimensional nature of the still radiograph can distort the true nature of velopharyngeal function.

Flexible fibreoptic nasal endoscopes are a popular tool for evaluating velopharyngeal function because there is no irradiation and because they allow direct observation of the portal during connected speech. There are rigid endoscopes and flexible endoscopes. Rigid scopes provide better optics but flexible scopes are more comfortable to the patient. Each allows recording of the image using 35 mm, videotape or digital formats. Each suffers from the disadvantage that younger patients are often difficult to scope successfully. Endoscopy provides information similar to that obtained by base view videofluoroscopy. It provides information about the mesial movement of the lateral pharyngeal walls that cannot be provided by lateral radiography.

1.5   Methods of cleft palate management

Management of cleft palate for speech purposes consists of surgery, prosthetics and speech and language therapy. The details and timing of management techniques have been studied widely. However, no single technique has emerged as a unanimous choice for success.

1.5.1   Surgical intervention

Palatoplasty: A cleft of the lip is generally closed before a cleft of the palate is closed. The initial closure of a cleft palate (known as palatoplasty) usually occurs in the first year(s) of the child's life (see Figure 1.5). Children who have their palate closed early (before one year) often develop normal speech earlier and more easily than children who have the palate closed later (after one year) (Dorf and Curtin 1982). The best timing of palatoplasty has not been established possibly because studies have controlled only for chronological age and not for language age at the time of palatoplasty (O'Gara and Logemann 1988). The relationship of the timing of palatal closure to the onset of babbling is intuitive. It is at this point in speech and language development that a child must learn to coordinate velopharyngeal function with respiratory pressure, laryngeal abduction and adduction and oral articulation to produce consonants. In short, the child's first 'dada' is much more complicated than it appears.

Palatoplasty is successful in creating a competent velopharyngeal mechanism in approximately 80% of children and has not improved in recent decades (Riski 1979). However, some have found that the Furlow double reversing Z-plasty can improve the success rate to 90% (Gunther *et al.* 1998). This 80% success rate for palatoplasty may or may not be influenced by the initial type of cleft (Riski 1979; Riski and Delong 1984; Karnell and Van Demark 1986). One report demonstrated that the dimensions of the unoperated nasopharynx vary within each type of cleft and suggested that the type and extent of palatoplasty should be tailored to the preoperative dimensions of the nasopharynx (Komatsu *et al.* 1982). Furlow (1986) first described the double opposing Z-plasty for primary repair of cleft palate with good results.

Posterior pharyngeal flap pharyngoplasty: A pharyngeal flap surgery first elevates a flap from the midportion of the posterior pharyngeal wall (see Figure 1.6). This is usually left attached to the posterior wall at the top rather than at the bottom of the flap making it a superiorly based pharyngeal flap, which is pulled forward across the nasopharynx and sutured

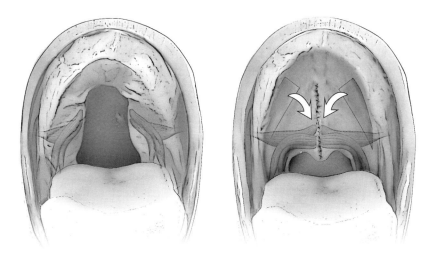

Figure 1.5 Closure of palatal cleft in a palatoplasty. White arrows show retrodisplacement of the levator muscle. (© 2012 Children's Healthcare of Atlanta, Inc. All rights reserved.)

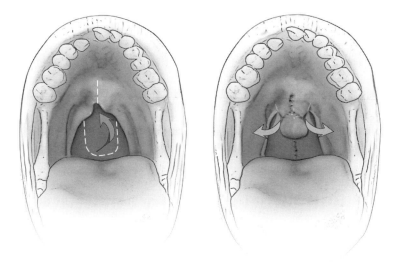

Figure 1.6 Pharyngeal flap. Arrow on left-sided figure shows elevation of the pharyngeal flap. Arrows on right-sided figure show lateral ports. (© 2012 Children's Healthcare of Atlanta, Inc. All rights reserved.)

into the soft palate. This obturates the midportion of the nasopharynx, leaving ports laterally for breathing and for nasal speech.

Postoperative studies of pharyngeal flap surgery have suggested several methods by which the nasopharynx is obturated. Studies have used electromyographic (EMG) analysis and endoscopic and videofluoroscopic imaging. The primary method of velopharyngeal closure is by active mesial movement of the lateral pharyngeal walls against the flap (Shprintzen *et al.* 1979, 1980). The pharyngeal flap is a static obturator of the midportion of the nasopharynx. Secondarily, circumferential scar contracture narrows the pharynx. Finally, contracture of the flap itself elevates the velum into the pharynx, diminishing the anterior-posterior dimension.

Crockett *et al.* (1988) suggested that three variables should be controlled for successful pharyngeal flap surgery: flap width, flap height or level, and lateral port size. Strategies have been developed to cope with these variables. The size of the lateral ports has been controlled (Hogan 1973), and the width of the pharyngeal flaps has been tailored to the amount of wall motion (Shprintzen *et al.* 1979). Some researchers have suggested that little strategy, if any, is needed for minimal VPI. Randall (1972) observed that if the VPI is minimal, any method should have a good result.

Posterior pharyngeal wall augmentation and muscle transposition: An attempt to augment the posterior pharyngeal wall was first reported by Wardill (1928, 1933). He created a permanent ridge of fibrous tissue on the posterior pharyngeal wall by making transverse incisions through the superior constrictor at the level of Passavant's ridge. The tissue was sutured vertically, creating a ridge with which the elevated velum could make contact. Hynes (1951, 1953), and later Orticochea (1968, 1970, 1983), advocated pharyngoplasties by muscle transposition that were similar in design but differed from each other in their intended function. Each procedure has undergone modification and refinement (Huskie and Jackson 1977; Jackson and Silverton 1977; Roberts and Brown 1983; Riski *et al.* 1984; Stratoudakis and Bambace 1984; Moss *et al.* 1987; Riski *et al.* 1992; Pigott 1993).

The Hynes or sphincter pharyngoplasty (see Figure 1.7) is designed as a passive, muscular prominence that is contacted by the elevated velum (Hynes 1953; Riski *et al.* 1984; Riski *et al.* 1992). Success of the procedure relies on insertion of the flaps at the height of active velar elevation (Riski *et al.* 1984). Pigott (1993) suggested that the procedure worked in any of three ways: by advancing the posterior wall, by reducing the lateral pharyngeal recess in a static manner, or as an active sphincter. Active sphinctering has been observed, although it may take 6 to 18 months to develop (Riski *et al.* 1984; Moss *et al.* 1987). The Orticochea pharyngoplasty was claimed to obturate the nasopharynx by active sphinctering of the palatopharyngeus flaps with the velum (Orticochea 1968). The only studies of this pharyngoplasty have evaluated the sphinctering by oral inspection during the sound 'ah' (Orticochea 1983). Even this observed sphinctering was found to diminish with age and was not observed in patients after 16 years.

Some investigators have studied postoperative pharyngeal movements by imaging and have concluded that the postoperative movement of the sphincter pharyngoplasty is active (Witt *et al.* 1998). The role of the palatopharyngeus in the observed sphinctering was studied more directly by Ysunza *et al.* (1999). Twenty-five patients who underwent sphincter

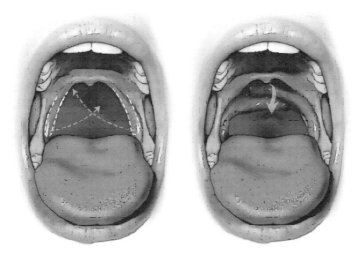

Figure 1.7 Hynes or sphincter pharyngoplasty. Arrows in left-sided figure show elevation of the lateral pharyngeal flaps from palatopharyngeus muscle. Arrow in right-sided figure shows flaps after insertion into the posterior pharyngeal wall. (© 2012 Children's Healthcare of Atlanta, Inc. All rights reserved.)

pharyngoplasty from 1985 to 1996 were evaluated using electromyography with simultaneous videonasopharyngoscopy. The following velopharyngeal muscles were examined: the superior constrictor, palatopharyngeus and levator veli palatini muscles. None of the patients showed electromyographic activity at the superiorly based flaps, indicating absence of activity of the palatopharyngeus muscles. However, all patients showed normal electromyographic activity at the superior constrictor and the levator veli palatini. They concluded that the observed sphinctering seems to be caused by the contraction of the superior constrictor.

Primary versus secondary pharyngoplasty: Several studies have reported the use of pharyngoplasty during primary repair of the palate. The pharyngeal flap is advocated to provide additional tissue when the palatal cleft is extremely wide (Tartan *et al.* 1991). Both the pharyngeal flap (Dalston and Stuteville 1975) and the sphincter pharyngoplasty (Riski *et al.* 1987) have been used at the time of primary palatal closure in an attempt to increase velopharyngeal competence. Both procedures have a higher rate of success than a palatoplasty alone. An inferiorly based flap combined with a palatoplasty has been shown to eliminate hypernasality in 94% of patients (Dalston and Stuteville 1975). A sphincter pharyngoplasty combined with a palatoplasty has been shown to have a 100% success rate (Riski *et al.* 1984). Controversy still exists about using any secondary procedure with primary palatoplasty because only 20–30% of patients will eventually require pharyngoplasty and because of the potential obstruction. The ability to predict which infants will eventually require a pharyngoplasty appears to be poor. One surgeon attempted to identify infants who would eventually need a pharyngoplasty by visual inspection of the nasopharynx at the time of palatoplasty. Sixteen of these children were later evaluated. The pharyngoplasty appeared necessary in only 50% (Riski *et al.* 1984). The remaining children achieved closure above the pharyngoplasty at the adenoids.

Timing of surgical intervention: The ideal age for both primary and secondary cleft palate management has been debated for some time. Most investigators have found better results in younger patients (Leanderson *et al.* 1974; Van Demark and Hammerquist 1978; Van Demark and Hardin 1985; Seyfer *et al.* 1988). A study by Moll *et al.* (1963) reported better results in patients younger than 15 years of age. Riski (1979) reported better articulation and resonance following pharyngeal flaps when performed earlier than 6 years of age than when performed after 6 years of age. Riski and colleagues reported better resolution of VPI with the Orticochea or sphincter pharyngoplasty when performed earlier than 6 years of age (Riski *et al.* 1984; Riski *et al.* 1992). Results of surgery after 18 years of age were poor.

Although VPI is usually diagnosed and treated in childhood, it is not uncommon for adults to present for management. Younger and Dickson (1985) treated eight adults with residual VPI following cleft palate repair as children. A superiorly based pharyngeal flap was used in each case. They reported 'significant subjective and objective improvement' although they reported no data. A more controlled study was reported by Hall *et al.* (1991). Twenty adult patients received a superiorly based pharyngeal flap. The authors reported normal resonance in 15 patients. However, speech intelligibility was not dramatically improved. Overall success of speech was dependent on preoperative articulation skills. A report on the success of pharyngeal flap surgery was recently provided by Fukushiro and Trindade (2011). Results were better in younger children than in older children and adults.

1.5.2   Prosthetic intervention

Prosthetic intervention is often desirable when surgical options are not available or if surgery is not possible for some time. Obturating hard palate fistula with a retainer-type device is fairly simple. Obturating a velopharyngeal incompetence with a pharyngeal speech bulb obturator and palatal lift is done by cooperative efforts. Prosthetic devices can be especially useful in individuals who have had ablative pharyngeal surgery for head and neck cancer or in cases of minimal soft palate movement associated with head injury or neurological disease. The use of computer evaluation and endoscopic imaging of velopharyngeal function can increase the efficiency and accuracy of obturator construction (Riski *et al.* 1989).

A hard palate fistula obturator may be fixed or removable. A fixed obturator is useful in young children who may be non-compliant for wearing the obturator. It should be removed by the dentist several times each

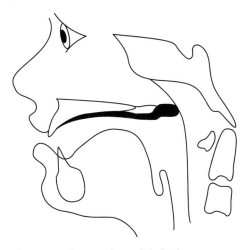

Figure 1.8 Pharyngeal speech bulb obturator.

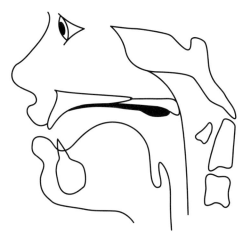

Figure 1.9 Palatal lift.

year for cleaning. A removable obturator can be used in older children who are compliant for wearing the appliance. A pharyngeal speech bulb obturator is used when there is a deficiency in the length of the soft palate to close the velopharyngeal port (see Figure 1.8). This is often the case in children with cleft palate or in cases of ablative surgery associated with head and neck cancer. A palatal lift is used when there is a deficiency of soft palate movement but adequate length of soft palate to close off the velopharyngeal port (see Figure 1.9). Both types of appliance require that the individual have healthy dentition which is in good repair and a minimal or a controlled gag response. When used to manage VPI associated with neurological problems, the individual should have good motion of the articulators and have sufficient manual dexterity or adequate supervision for inserting and removing the appliance.

1.5.3   Speech and language therapy

The goals of speech and language therapy in the child with a cleft palate or other resonance disorder are to establish correct articulatory placement, maximize oral pressure for pressure consonant sounds (plosives, fricatives and affricates) and maximize oral resonance (Kushner 2000). At the start of the process, parents are counselled regarding what to expect from their child's early speech attempts. Resonance will be hypernasal. The child will be able to articulate correctly words with nasal sounds, such as 'mama', but will not correctly articulate words with pressure sounds, such as 'dada'. Parents are instructed in play activities which focus on verbal interaction between parent and child and in appropriate modelling of speech and language. Parents can be asked to model babbling with pressure consonant sounds such as 'babababa' or 'dadadada' as well as to use gentle nasal occlusion to prevent nasal pressure loss.

Speech and language stimulation should continue with age-appropriate games, vocabulary and syntax. Parents are now asked to monitor the sounds that the child makes. If there are no confounding developmental problems, the child can be expected to begin making pressure consonants such as /p, b, t, d, k, and g/. Often, parents are asked to occlude the child's nose manually while playing 'sound games' such as repeating the syllable 'ba ba ba ba'. Occluding the nose prevents any nasal airflow and directs the air stream to the oral cavity. Parents are also asked to observe any signs of velopharyngeal dysfunction or oral-nasal fistulas. These include nasal reflux while eating or drinking, nasal airflow or facial grimacing, or the continued use of nasal sounds and the lack of pressure consonants while talking.

Exercises are generally unsuccessful in increasing velopharyngeal movements except in some very specific situations (Ruscello 2004). Increasing oral pressure for pressure consonants will maximize velopharyngeal elevation and may gain velopharyngeal closure for minimal VPI. A unique therapy technique using continuous positive airway pressure (CPAP) to the nasal surface of the soft palate has been developed by Kuehn (1991). Velar elevation for speech under the resistance of CPAP may improve velopharyngeal closure. Once VPI is diagnosed as adversely affecting speech or speech development, it should be evaluated and managed. Patients with VPI make little or no progress in speech therapy until it is managed (Riski and DeLong 1984; Van Demark and Hardin 1985). Articulation skills improve immediately following management of VPI (Riski 1979). When VPI is suspected or documented, speech therapy should be considered diagnostic and short term. Referral to a cleft palate-craniofacial team is appropriate after no more than several weeks of ineffective speech therapy.

Speech therapy for the child with a cleft palate is unique because the child may present with misarticulations that are not found in the non-cleft population (Trost 1981). There are a small number of children with normal soft palate function who use some form of nasal air emission as a sound substitution (Peterson 1975; Riski 1984). This is a sound substitution of a posterior nasal fricative for sibilant sounds and sometimes affricate or other fricative sounds. The characteristics include: normal resonance, sound-specific use of some form of nasal air escape, normal velopharyngeal function for correctly produced sounds, and the ability to correctly produce the sound in error without nasal air escape. This patient presents a special diagnostic challenge, and the differential diagnosis of an organic VPI from a 'functional' VPI is the key to appropriate management. Normal resonance and normal oral air pressure for plosive sounds and the ability to learn to make the problematic sound correctly without any nasal air escape are hallmarks.

Another common problem is the distortion of sibilant sounds. The cause of this distortion is often a collapsed dental arch. Airflow for sibilant sounds should be central. A simple drinking straw is very effective in determining the direction of airflow. The straw can be attached to a See-Scape to make the airflow 'visible'. This device is also an excellent therapy aid to teach sibilant sounds. Often, the stop sound /t/ is central. This can be released to create an acoustically acceptable /s/. A drinking straw placed at the central incisors will amplify this airflow and give positive feedback to both the patient and clinician. This technique is useful in teaching sibilant sounds no matter what the cause of the distortion.

1.6   Relationship of cleft palate and velopharyngeal dysfunction to craniofacial syndromes

Clefting is associated with more than 400 known syndromes including Apert's, Crouzon's, Treacher Collins, Pierre Robin, Stickler's, hemifacial microsomia and 22q11.2 deletion (Winter and Baraister 1998). Children born with Down's syndrome also have palatal anomalies (Lauridsen *et al.* 2001).

An inherited form of clefting is Van der Woude syndrome (VWS). The prevalence of this syndrome varies from one in 40,000 to one in 100,000 stillborn or live births (Rizos and Spyropoulos 2004). In addition to clefting, a hallmark of the syndrome is lip pits or mounds on the lower lip. VWS is caused by an alteration in a single gene (*IRF6*) on chromosome 1. Of individuals with this gene alteration, 95 per cent will have some features of VWS. Inheritance is autosomal dominant, meaning that individuals with this gene alteration have a 50 per cent chance of passing on the gene to each of their children (Rizos and Spyropoulos 2004).

Another inherited form of clefting is Stickler's syndrome. Although estimates vary, the incidence of Stickler's syndrome is approximately 1/10,000 in the white population of the United States (Francomano 2010). The (Pierre) Robin sequence is common in individuals with Stickler's syndrome. Characteristics of this sequence include cleft palate, macroglossia and micrognathia. These characteristics are present at birth and can lead to immediate breathing and feeding problems. Individuals with Stickler's syndrome commonly have eye problems and hearing problems. The degree of hearing loss is variable and can become more severe with age. Researchers currently believe that mutations in the *COL2A1*, *COL9A1*, *COL11A1* and *COL11A2* genes cause Stickler's syndrome. Since not all individuals with Stickler's syndrome have mutations in these genes, they also believe that other, unidentified genes may also play a role. There is an autosomal dominant inheritance pattern.

Velocardiofacial syndrome (VCFS) is due to a microdeletion at q11.2 on the long arm of chromosome 22. It is the most common microdeletion syndrome in humans with a reported population prevalence of 1:2,000 (Friedman *et al.* 2011). VCFS affects multiple organ systems. In addition to cleft palate and other palate deficits, it can include cardiac defects (most commonly ventricular septal defect), degrees of mental retardation, characteristic dysmorphic facial features and immune deficiency. Most 22q11.2 deletion cases are new occurrences or sporadic (occur by chance). The frequency of inherited 22q11.2 deletions varies with genetic study and can range between 10% and 28% (Kitsiou-Tzeli *et al.* 2004). The gene is autosomal dominant, therefore any person who has this deletion has a 50% chance of passing the deletion to a child.

Managing speech problems and velopharyngeal incompetence when there is a syndrome can be especially challenging on account of problems with cognition, hypotonicity (muscle weakness) or hypoplasticity (insufficient muscle formation). In addition to these problems, children with 22q11.2 deletion can also have Chiari malformation and cervical spine anomalies (Hultman *et al.* 2000). Success rate in managing velopharyngeal incompetence using sphincter pharyngoplasty falls from 87% (Losken *et al.* 2003) down to 78% when a child has 22q11.2 deletion (Losken *et al.* 2006). A recent investigation of children with hemifacial microsomia or Goldenhar syndrome found 18/26 (68%) had deficits in velar elevation (Riski 2011). Lack of movement was bilateral in two children and asymmetrical in 16 children (5 on the left side and 11 on the right side). An additional patient had a unilateral cleft lip and palate and two had submucous clefts. Eight (50%) of the patients with unilateral involvement had some degree of nasal air escape and demonstrated complete velopharyngeal closure. The nasal air escape was not significant enough to warrant management in any of the patients. Overall, one-third of the patients demonstrated posterior nasal fricative sound substitutions, probably related to conductive hearing loss.

1.7   Brain investigations in cleft palate

Since isolated cleft palate is a midline defect, evaluating how midline structures develop may shed some light on this anomaly. The neural groove and neural folds begin forming in the human embryo around 20 days gestation. At the superior aspect of the neural folds are the neural crest cells. The neural folds along with the neural crest cells migrate towards the midline, closing around 28 days gestation to form the neural tube which will become the spinal cord. The neural crest cells migrate to form many parts of the brain, cranial nerves and other midline structures, including the palate. Thus, there is an embryological connection between cleft palate and brain anomalies in cleft palate that is now being realized. In this section, the findings of several studies which support this connection will be examined.

Differences in the brain structure of individuals with clefts compared to individuals without clefts have been studied over the past decade. Nopoulos *et al.* (2007) examined height and head circumference of individuals with clefts. Brain structure was also analysed by means of magnetic resonance imaging (MRI). They found some significant differences in children with isolated cleft lip and palate compared to children without clefts. Individuals with clefts had a significantly smaller cerebrum and cerebellum. The frontal lobe was smaller and tissue distribution in the cortical grey matter and white matter within the cerebrum was abnormal. There was a larger cortical volume and smaller volume of white matter. Adult males with non-syndromic cleft lip and/or palate have been shown to have significantly lower temporal lobe grey matter volume than matched controls. This includes the superior temporal lobe, which is involved in the governance of auditory processing and aspects of language (Shriver *et al.* 2006).

Imaging studies by Weinberg *et al.* (2009) marked midline and surface landmarks from MRI brain scans in order to create a 3-D image for analysis of brain shape. The scans were of adults with non-syndromic cleft lip with or without cleft palate (CL/P), individuals with cleft palate only (CPO) and individuals without clefts. There were significant differences in brain shape among the three groups. Major brain shape changes associated with clefting included the selective enlargement of the anterior cerebrum coupled with a relative reduction in posterior and/or inferior cerebral portions, changes in the medio-lateral position of the cerebral poles, posterior displacement of the corpus callosum, and reorientation of the cerebellum. Thus, compared with controls, major brain shape differences were present in adult males with CL/P and CPO. Weinberg *et al.* interpreted the results to confirm and expand previous findings from traditional volumetric studies of the brain in clefting. These differences in brain size, it was argued, are a manifestation of the defect and not a secondarily acquired characteristic.

The ventral frontal cortex (VFC) is linked to social functioning including hyperactivity, impulsivity and inattentiveness. A recent investigation by Boes *et al.* (2007) found decreased volume and surface area of the straight gyrus portion of the VFC in individuals with isolated cleft lip and palate compared to individuals without clefts. They interpreted their findings to suggest that brain abnormalities may be responsible for social dysfunction rather than any psychosocial factors related to facial appearance. In a follow-up study from the same laboratory, Nopoulos *et al.* (2010) evaluated ventromedial prefrontal cortex (vmPFC). The vmPFC is a region of the brain that governs the behaviours of hyperactivity, impulsivity and inattention (HII). Compared to a non-cleft control group, individuals with isolated cleft palate demonstrated higher levels of HII and this was directly related to a significantly enlarged volume of the right vmPFC.

Other research has suggested that there might be a broader neurological impact from an isolated cleft lip or palate. Conrad *et al.* (2008) found that individuals with isolated cleft lip/palate showed significantly more evidence of neurological soft signs, especially at a younger age, than a healthy control group. Other brain differences have been identified by Yang *et al.* (2012). These researchers studied the central auditory pathway in infants with non-syndromic cleft lip and/or palate. They found no differences in general brain measurements including volumes of the brainstem and right hemisphere. However, they found statistically significant smaller volumes of the left thalamus and left auditory cortex and a significantly thinner left auditory cortex. They speculated that the development and maturation of the auditory cortex in infants with non-syndromic cleft lip/palate might be abnormal compared to infants without cleft.

The side of clefting has also been implicated in variations in brain development. Van der Plas *et al.* (2010) used MRI to evaluate brain structure in young boys with either a right-sided or a left-sided cleft lip and palate. They found that total white matter was significantly lower in boys with right-sided clefts compared to boys with left-sided clefts and healthy boys. White matter reduction was evident in both the cerebellum and the cerebrum in boys with right-sided clefts. In the cerebrum, white matter volumes were particularly low in the frontal lobes and occipital lobes.

Cerebellar structure has also been evaluated with regard to speech impairment in children with clefts. Conrad *et al.* (2010) measured cerebellar volume in boys and girls with non-syndromic cleft of the lip and/or palate and compared their findings to a control group of individuals without clefts. Imaging findings were also compared to speech measures. The group of boys with clefts had significantly smaller cerebellums than the control group. The girls with clefts demonstrated only regional size differences in the cerebellum. The size of the cerebellum also correlated with articulation skills for the boys. Conrad *et al.* interpreted the results to suggest that the cerebellum, along with other structural findings, may play a role in speech deficits, at least in boys with clefts.

Much of this research is still in its infancy. The differences in brain structure may explain some of the earlier language and behavioural differences seen in children with clefts compared to those without clefts.

However, further research is necessary in order to understand the full implications of these findings. Ultimately, information from brain studies of cleft children may lead to changes in protocols for evaluating language and cognitive development as well as enhancements in educational programmes for this client group.

1.8 Summary

The speech-language pathologist plays an integral role in the evaluation and treatment of speech and resonance disorders related to cleft lip and palate. Because cleft lip and palate is a relatively low incident disorder, there is limited training and experience for many clinicians. Further, understanding velopharyngeal function, evaluation techniques and treatment will help the clinician with other patients with velopharyngeal dysfunction. That would include patients with cerebral palsy, head injury, stroke, and head and neck cancer, among others.

The clinical assessment of velopharyngeal closure is quite simple and all speech pathologists should be skilled in the use of the relevant techniques. Understanding the basics of speech motor theory is important to understanding why individuals with velopharyngeal incompetence develop unique maladaptive speech habits. Recognizing these unique speech problems can be the first step to suspecting velopharyngeal incompetence and making necessary referrals to craniofacial centres. It is essential for clinicians in craniofacial centres to partner with speech-language pathologists in the community who provide much of the treatment to these patients.

Further research is necessary to help us understand velopharyngeal anatomy and physiology. In this respect, current studies using magnetic resonance imaging (MRI) are very promising (Bae *et al.* 2011). Enhancing educational programmes for speech pathologists to include a comprehensive understanding of velopharyngeal function, dysfunction and treatment is necessary.

2

Developmental dysarthria

Megan Hodge

2.1   Introduction

Developmental dysarthrias are a group of speech disorders caused by dysfunction of the immature nervous system that delays speech onset and impairs the strength, speed, accuracy, coordination and endurance of the muscle groups used to speak. Depending on the extent of impairment, one or more of the speech processes of respiration, phonation, resonance, articulation and prosody may be affected. Speech characteristics can include short breath groups (few words per breath), abnormal voice quality (e.g. harsh, breathy), poor control over pitch and loudness, difficulty using contrastive stress (i.e. all words are perceived as having primary stress), slow speaking rate, hypernasal resonance, nasal air emission, imprecise articulation and an overall perception of increased speaking effort. These children have particular difficulty producing sounds that require more precise spatiotemporal control of tongue postures and movements to make vowel and consonant manner and place distinctions (e.g. tense versus lax vowels; monophthongs versus diphthongs; glides versus liquids; stops versus fricatives versus affricates; alveolar versus palatal versus velar place). They also have difficulty producing the rapid, coordinated movements across muscle groups required for voicing distinctions and consonant clusters (Love 1999). In addition, their speech can be affected adversely by fatigue to a greater extent than for children without neuromotor impairment. Augmentative and alternative communication (AAC) systems are often provided to supplement their natural communication modes but children with dysarthria prefer to communicate using speech (Pennington *et al.* 2009a).

Typically, children with developmental dysarthria neither 'grow out of' nor are 'cured' of these neuromuscular abnormalities (Hodge and Wellman 1999). Outcomes can range from little or no functional speech known as 'anarthria' (i.e. a complete lack of speech due to severe motor impairment) to speech that has minimal distortions in articulation, resonance or voice or is produced at a slightly slower than expected rate. In some cases of congenital childhood dysarthria, the underlying condition progresses in severity (e.g. childhood muscular dystrophies). However, even when the underlying neurological damage or abnormality is non-progressive, the pathophysiological signs of the disorder, and how these are manifested in speech, change as the child grows and develops.

Given that the ability to communicate effectively is essential to creating and sustaining opportunities to stimulate social-emotional and cognitive-linguistic development, the speech-language clinician is concerned primarily with the effects of neuromuscular impairment on affected children's ability to learn to produce understandable, socially acceptable speech as part of their communication system. This chapter describes developmental dysarthria from biomedical and psychosocial perspectives, following the framework of the International Classification of Functioning, Disability and Health – Children and Youth Version (ICF-CY) (World Health Organization 2007a). Aetiologies of childhood dysarthrias are reviewed and the estimated prevalence, by neurological diagnosis, is reported for more commonly associated neurological conditions. The chapter concludes with a summary of the current state of our knowledge as it relates to diagnosis of developmental dysarthria, and highlights directions for future research.

2.2   Description of developmental dysarthria

The term 'dysarthria' was used first by neurologists to describe the condition of people who demonstrate difficulty speaking distinctly because of problems in executing movements that produce the sound patterns of speech. Dysarthria results when nervous system or muscle impairments cause abnormal signals to be sent along the pathways from the brain to the respiratory and bulbar (laryngeal, pharyngeal, soft palate, tongue, lip and mandibular) muscles that produce the rapid, precise and coordinated movements of speech. These impairments include abnormalities in muscle tone, strength, steadiness and endurance, which decrease movement speed, range, and coordination and, therefore, accuracy of speech. These movement disturbances distort the clarity and quality of the speech signal and frequently make it difficult to understand. Consequently, dysarthria may restrict the person's participation in situations that depend on intelligible, efficient spoken language.

Qualified speech-language clinicians commonly make the diagnosis of dysarthria based on (1) medical history, (2) neurological diagnosis and site of lesion information provided by a physician, (3) observed abnormal neuromuscular signs in the speech muscle groups during speech and non-speech activities, (4) perceived deviant speech characteristics, augmented by acoustic and physiological measures as indicated, and (5) measures of the impact of the speech disorder on intelligibility and speaking rate (Yorkston *et al.* 2010). Dysarthria subtype in adult-onset cases is commonly classified using the Mayo Clinic system that links brain pathology with speech behaviour (Duffy 2012; also see Chapter 11, this volume). This system recognizes spastic, hyperkinetic, hypokinetic, ataxic, flaccid and mixed forms of dysarthria.

When centres and pathways in the immature central or peripheral nervous system that control the execution of speech movements are impaired during the primary period of speech development, the speech disorder is referred to as developmental dysarthria. Developmental dysarthria differs from dysarthria which has its onset in later childhood and adulthood, when individuals have already acquired the phonological and phonetic system of their language with normal neuromuscular function. In developmental dysarthria, a child has to learn to control and coordinate the muscles used to speak with a faulty neuromotor substrate. Pennington *et al.* (2009a) used 3 years of age to distinguish developmental from later acquired childhood dysarthrias. These authors stated that, compared with children who acquire dysarthria after age 3 years, younger children with earlier acquired dysarthria 'may never have developed motor programmes for fluent speech or have memories of nondysarthric speech and may not see themselves as an intelligible speaker' (Pennington *et al.* 2009a: 11).

In addition, Pennington (2008) reported that children with severe speech and motor impairments due to congenital or early-onset pathologies have unusual patterns of communication development characterized by a predominantly responsive role and a limited range of conversational skills. Age of onset of neurological impairment relative to stage of speech development provides insights into what speech and communication interaction skills the child has learned with a normal speech motor control system (and might need to relearn or compensate for, depending on the nature of the impairment) and what speech and communication interaction skills the child still has to learn, using an impaired system.

Morgan and Liégeois (2010) questioned the validity of applying the Mayo classification system for adult-onset dysarthria to children, given that some conditions and syndromes associated with childhood dysarthria are developmental by nature, with no adult equivalent (e.g. cerebral palsy, neural migration disorders, seizure-related disorders and progressive disorders with childhood onset). In addition, relative to adults, children's brains are less mature and therefore may differ in patterns of recovery. Children may have higher potential for functional brain reorganization but may also have greater vulnerability to early brain damage.

Morgan and Liégeois (2010) identified the need for a neurobehavioural classification system that is specific to childhood dysarthria. They proposed that this be established and validated by pooling brain and speech outcome data across large numbers of children via international collaborations that follow standard protocols. These protocols would characterize speech outcomes and use neuroimaging data acquisition and analysis techniques that consider brain structure, function and connectivity for groups of children with similar aetiologies. Subgroups of dysarthria could then be defined by common clusters of speech behaviours. Neural correlates of these dysarthria subgroups could be examined to develop a brain-behavioural model for children. This model would underpin the classification system and consequently yield more sensitive diagnosis and management and enhanced speech outcomes. Morgan and Liégeois observed that in the absence of such a neurobehavioural classification system that is specific to children, clinicians rely on adult-based classification systems for dysarthria or child-based systems that are not specific to dysarthria or neuropathology. For example, the diagnostic classification system for developmental dysarthria proposed by Love (1999) and Webb and Adler (2008), and described later in this chapter, follows the conventions for adult-onset dysarthria.

The ICF-CY emphasizes the interaction between health conditions (function and disability) and contextual factors (personal and environmental) in influencing a child's success in learning and performing tasks and actions which permit community participation with greater or lesser independence. McLeod and Threats (2008) described how the ICF-CY might be applied to assessment and intervention practices of speech-language clinicians for children. Function and disability are described by associated impairments in body structure and function, the resulting limitations on the child's speech production abilities and communication activities, and how these may restrict the child's opportunities for, and independence in participating in life situations. A description of developmental dysarthria from the perspective of the ICF-CY components follows.

2.3   Function and disability in developmental dysarthria

2.3.1   Body structure and function

Impairments that result in developmental dysarthria can occur at one or more locations in the nervous system. Liégeois and Morgan (2012) reported the results of a systematic review of literature published between 1997 and 2010 that linked motor speech disorders (apraxia of speech and dysarthria) and brain abnormalities in children and adolescents with developmental (e.g. cerebral palsy), progressive or acquired (e.g. stroke, traumatic brain injury) conditions. The authors found no evidence that unilateral damage resulted in apraxia of speech or that left hemisphere lesions exhibited higher rates of apraxia of speech than right hemisphere lesions. They stated that 'the few studies reporting on childhood apraxia of speech converged toward morphological, structural, metabolic or epileptic anomalies affecting the basal ganglia, perisylvian and Rolandic cortices bilaterally. Persistent dysarthria similarly was commonly reported in individuals with syndromes and conditions affecting these same structures bilaterally' (Liégeois and Morgan 2012:39).

The results of this review agree with previous descriptions of neural correlates that have a major role in speech planning and execution. However, a key difference is the finding that, while in adulthood, damage to one hemisphere appears to be sufficient to result in chronic motor speech disorders, in childhood, bilateral disruption of these systems appears to be necessary to result in severe and long-lasting speech deficits. 'This suggests that either hemisphere has the potential to subserve speech functions in childhood' (Liégeois and Morgan 2012: 455).

Differences in motor speech characteristics of children and adults with similar site of lesion were also reported by van Mourik *et al.* (1997). By means of a systematic review, these authors documented features of childhood dysarthria (acquired before age 16 years) associated with lesions to areas that have been identified as neural correlates of speech production (i.e. cerebral cortices, cerebellum, basal ganglia, upper motor neuron pathways and brainstem). They found that highly similar speech features between children and adults were only observed for basal ganglia lesions. The results of these studies suggest that we can predict with some certainty that when known neural correlates of speech production are damaged in childhood, motor speech disturbances will result. However, with the exception of lower motor neuron lesions, we cannot predict with certainty what the clinical features of the motor speech disorder will be (childhood apraxia, dysarthria, or a combination of these disorders).

Even if there is not a primary lesion in the areas of the child's brain involved in learning and storing speech motor plans and programmes, function of these regions may be affected by primary lesions in other cortical regions and subcortical centres and circuits. This is because of the lack of experience that is needed to develop connections to these former areas with other areas of the speech motor system during speech learning (Guenther 2008). Early diagnosis of developmental dysarthria is complicated by delayed onset of speech and the increased complexity and decreased predictability associated with damage to the developing nervous system (Joffe and Reilly 2004). This delay in speech milestones and apparent difficulty in learning how to produce and control movements to generate speech sounds may initially resemble core features of childhood apraxia of speech (American Speech-Language-Hearing Association 2007). These features later diminish, while frank dysarthric signs appear as speech development progresses. A priority for future research is to develop and validate a standardized system for identifying and classifying developmental dysarthria that includes descriptions of how the dysarthria is manifested from the earliest stages of speech development through adolescence.

In the absence of an empirically driven, brain-behaviour model for classifying developmental dysarthria, speech-language clinicians who work with children should be familiar with the taxonomy of five developmental dysarthria types, described by Love (1999) and adapted by Webb and Adler (2008). This taxonomy recognizes spastic, dyskinetic, ataxic, flaccid and mixed forms of dysarthria. It is used in the following section to characterize early, childhood-onset dysarthria from the perspective of impairment in body function. With the exception of flaccid dysarthria, these subtypes are based predominantly on children with cerebral palsy after they have developed speech. As such, they reflect the classification of cerebral palsy subtypes. 'Cerebral palsy' is an umbrella term that covers a group of non-progressive but often changing motor impairment syndromes secondary to lesions or anomalies of the brain arising in the early stages of its development (Shevell 2009). The following descriptions are based on Webb and Adler (2008) and Workinger (2005).

Spastic dysarthria: This subtype of dysarthria is associated with bilateral damage to the upper motor neuron system that originates in the cerebral cortex. Axons from these neurons extend in both a direct pathway (cortico-bulbar and cortico-spinal tracts) and an indirect pathway to the lower motor neurons in the brainstem ('bulb') and spinal cord. Pathophysiological signs of damage affecting speech production include slow movements that are limited in range, muscle weakness, excessive muscle tone, muscle rigidity, persisting primitive oral-pharyngeal reflexes that normally disappear within the first year (e.g. rooting, suckling, bite) and hyperactivity of reflexes (e.g. jaw stretch, gag) that normally persist into adulthood. Associated speech characteristics include articulation errors (vowels and consonants), hypernasality, longer than expected word durations, lower than expected pitch for age, uncontrolled voice quality changes throughout an utterance, short breath groups and slow speaking rate. Chewing and swallowing problems and difficulties controlling oral secretions co-occur frequently because the underlying impairment also disrupts the skilled actions of the oral and pharyngeal muscles for these activities. Abnormal resting postures of the lips, jaw and tongue are common. Dental structure abnormalities, poor oral hygiene and sleep apnoea may occur as secondary health issues.

Dyskinetic dysarthria: This form of dysarthria is associated with damage to the basal ganglia control circuits that also act on the cortex to regulate upper motor neuron direct and indirect activation pathways. Pathophysiological signs of damage include athetosis (slow, writhing, involuntary movements) and other involuntary, uncontrolled movements. Associated speech characteristics include articulation errors (typically more frequent than in spastic dysarthria), hypernasality, pitch, loudness and vocal quality disturbances, inappropriate voice stoppage or release (e.g. pre-word vocalizations), disfluencies and slowed speaking rate. Athetoid cerebral palsy usually results in the involvement of all speech muscle groups. As in spastic dysarthria, chewing and swallowing problems, difficulties controlling oral secretions and abnormal resting postures of the lips, jaw and tongue frequently co-occur.

Ataxic dysarthria: Ataxic dysarthria is associated with damage to the cerebellum or cerebellar control circuits that also influence the direct and indirect activation pathways. Pathophysiological signs of damage include timing disruptions and poor coordination. When children with ataxic cerebral palsy are dysarthric, their speech is often affected mildly and characterized by slow rate, abnormal stress patterns and articulatory error patterns reflecting reduced coordination and accuracy of speech muscle groups (e.g. distortions, additions, timing errors).

Flaccid dysarthria: This form of dysarthria is associated with muscle weakness or paralysis resulting from damage to the cranial nerves (CN) (e.g. Möbius syndrome) or to the muscle tissue itself (e.g. muscular dystrophies). The cranial nerves are the final, common pathways to the bulbar muscles of the lips (CN VII), tongue (CN XII), mandible (CN V), soft palate (CN V, X, XI), pharynx (CN IX, X) and larynx (CN X, XI). Flaccid dysarthria can also result from damage to the spinal nerves that innervate the respiratory muscles (cervical 3–5; thoracic 1–12) (Hodge and Wellman 1999). Pathophysiological signs of damage include weakness, muscle wasting (atrophy), reduced or absent reflex responses, reduced muscle tone (hypotonia) and sometimes fasciculations, which are random contractions of a group of fibres within a muscle. Associated speech characteristics reflect the specific muscle groups that have been affected. Impairment of the lips, tongue and mandible will reduce articulation accuracy on sounds that are made with these structures. Impairment of the soft palate will result in hypernasal speech and distortion of high pressure consonant sounds (plosives, fricatives, affricates) and air escape. Impairment of the laryngeal muscles will result in a breathy voice quality while impairment of the respiratory muscles will result in reduced vocal loudness and short breath groups.

Mixed dysarthria: This form of dysarthria is associated with damage to two or more sites. It is most commonly a combination of spastic and dyskinetic types. The pathological signs and speech characteristics reflect a combination of those associated with the affected sites.

As noted, a major limitation of this classification system is that it does not address the evolution of speech characteristics as the child develops. For example, children with spastic and dyskinetic cerebral palsy and developmental dysarthria often show a persisting pattern of dependency of lip and tongue movements on jaw movement, and lack differentiated anterior and posterior tongue movements when producing speech sounds (Workinger 2005). This pattern is also seen in young children without speech disorders who gain independence of lip, jaw and tongue

Table 2.1 *Articulatory error patterns of children with cerebral palsy based on Bauman-Waengler (2008) and Hodge* et al. *(2011)*

Errors related to impaired motor control and phonetic placement	CONSONANTS	
	Developmental errors	Unusual errors
	• Fronting • Stopping • Gliding • Vowelization of [l], [r]	• Nasalization • Lateralization of apical and coronal fricatives • Backing • Dentalization of /s, z, l, n, t, d/
	VOWELS	
	Developmental errors	Unusual errors
	• Monophthongization	• Nasalization* • Centralization
Errors related to impaired temporal coordination	CONSONANTS	
	Developmental errors	Unusual errors
	• Consonant cluster reduction • Final consonant deletion • Stopping of fricatives • Weak syllable deletion • On and off glides	• Frication of stops • Prevocalic voicing • Variable realizations of voiced-voiceless cognates (e.g. voicing of unvoiced sounds; devoicing of initial consonants) • Inappropriate aspiration • Additions (sounds, syllables)

*May also result from impairment in temporal coordination.

movements in the preschool years as they develop and mature. However, without specific intervention, many children with developmental dysarthria do not elevate the tongue tip for lingual-alveolar place of articulation (use dental or interdental placement) and show a persisting pattern of undifferentiated tongue movements that are linked to jaw and lip movements (Love 1999). Associated with this are a persisting low resting posture of the tongue and immature swallowing pattern.

In some cases of developmental dysarthria, the aetiology and site(s) of lesion are unknown. Neural imaging studies are not done routinely in clinical practice, and when this information is available, site of lesion cannot be identified in all cases (Otapowicz *et al.* 2007). In addition, there are common perceptual speech characteristics across dysarthric subtypes. Most obviously, children show articulation errors that reflect a combination of delayed and disordered error types related to reduced spatial precision and temporal coordination that appear to vary in severity with severity of motor involvement of the speech muscle groups (Irwin 1968). Table 2.1 shows consonant error patterns that Bauman-Waengler (2008) classified by motor deficits. These patterns are further categorized by whether the error is considered to be developmental, and are revised to include vowel errors and additional error patterns which were identified in a phonetic transcription study of children with cerebral palsy and dysarthria (Hodge *et al.* 2012). Not surprisingly, in the majority of literature published in the past 10 years on childhood dysarthria, subtypes are not specified, and in many cases, perceptual characteristics of the dysarthria on a speech subsystem basis are not reported. Rather, the children are described by neurological diagnosis, severity ratings of dysarthria and/or intelligibility scores or ratings (e.g. Otapowicz *et al.* 2007; Pennington *et al.* 2010; Hustad *et al.* 2010; Sigurdardottir and Vik 2011).

The diagnosis of the presence of dysarthria in childhood is based typically on (1) neurological diagnosis and site of lesion information provided by a physician, (2) the child's medical, familial and developmental history, (3) observed abnormal neuromuscular signs in the speech muscle groups in speech and non-speech (e.g. feeding) activities during a comprehensive structural-functional examination and (4) perceived deviant speech characteristics. With respect to (3) and (4), the Verbal Motor Production Assessment for Children (Hayden and Square 1999) provides a standardized assessment protocol to identify dysarthric features in children between 3 and 12 years of age. It also serves to differentiate these children from those with characteristics of apraxia of speech or a speech disorder without a motor control component.

A speech-language clinician may be the first professional to suspect that a child has developmental dysarthria, especially when a child has no prior neurological diagnosis or other medical history suggestive of neurological abnormality. Key indicators include the following pathophysiological neuromuscular signs in the speech muscle groups: weakness, slowness, reduced range of movement, and muscle tone abnormalities (hypertonia, hypotonia) that reduce coordination and accuracy of muscle groups of the speech mechanism. These factors constrain development of differentiated, precise, dynamic actions of the oral articulators and their coordination with the respiratory-phonatory system to produce clear, efficient speech patterns. Other oral-pharyngeal and laryngeal-respiratory functions (e.g. chewing, swallowing, controlling saliva, resting lip, jaw and tongue posture, airway maintenance and clearance) can be affected. Early feeding difficulties and persisting primitive oropharyngeal reflexes are pre-speech risk factors for developmental dysarthria (Otapowicz *et al.* 2007). In contrast to childhood apraxia of speech, the motor control problem is neuromuscular in nature and is present regardless of task or context, involving speech and non-speech movements of the affected muscle groups.

At present, there is not an internationally accepted standardized protocol for identifying dysarthria in children. A priority for future research is to develop a standard set of reliable, valid and relatively simple procedures for this purpose which reflects the consensus of international researchers and professionals. This is a challenging task, especially for children with more subtle manifestations who do not have a prior neurological diagnosis. However, the availability of such a protocol would enable the creation of large, reliable databases, which would allow us to advance our knowledge of developmental dysarthria and significantly enhance early clinical decision-making.

2.3.2 Activity and participation

The ICF-CY defines activity as the execution of a task or an action by the child and participation as the child's involvement in a life situation. Activity and participation domains are divided into subdomains, three of which – oral communication (speaking, conversation, discussion), written communication (reading, spelling, writing) and interpersonal interactions and relationships – are of concern to us here. Restrictions on the activity of speaking that result from the neuromuscular impairments of children with dysarthria typically take the form of reduced intelligibility, abnormal sounding speech (reduced naturalness and acceptability), reduced speaking efficiency as a result of slow speaking rates and, in severe cases, lack of ability to produce functional speech (anarthria).

Intelligible speech is a key factor in successful communication. Intelligibility measures have been used to index the functional impact of dysarthria on speaking ability and reflect how well a listener can identify the words in speech produced by the child (Hodge and Whitehill 2010). In children with dysarthria, these measures may take the form of imitated words and sentences or conversational samples that are recorded from the child and judged by listeners at a later time using rating scales or word identification tasks (e.g. Hodge and Gotzke 2010; Hustad *et al.* 2010; Pennington *et al.* 2010). Figure 2.1 shows intelligibility scores (percentage of words identified correctly by listeners) for word and sentence imitation tasks on the Test of Children's Speech Plus or TOCS+ (Hodge and Gotzke 2010) for 36 children aged 4, 5 and 6 years with typical speech development (12 children at each age), 36 children aged 4, 5 and 6 years with speech sound disorder of unknown origin and age-appropriate receptive language (12 children at each age), and 18 children with cerebral palsy and developmental dysarthria who ranged in age from 4 to 12 years (mean = 6.3; SD = 2.5) and were able to perform the tasks.

Diagnosis by type of cerebral palsy was spastic (n = 13), Worster–Drought syndrome (n = 2), mixed spastic-dyskinetic (n = 2) and ataxic (n = 1). The children represented the full range of severity (levels I to V) on the Gross Motor Function Classification System Expanded and Revised (Palisano *et al.* 2007). All children with cerebral palsy had developmental receptive and expressive language ages of at least 3 years and hearing within normal limits at the time of testing. It is apparent that the children with dysarthria have a range of intelligibility deficits but, on average, present with poorer intelligibility than same-aged or younger children without

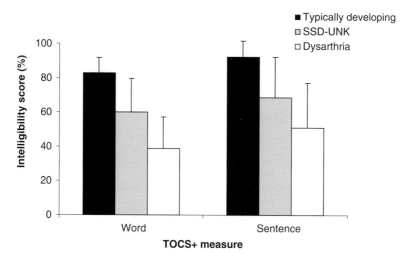

Figure 2.1 Word and sentence intelligibility scores on the TOCS+ for three groups of children: 4- to 6-year-olds with typically developing speech, 4- to 6-year-olds with speech sound disorder of unknown origin (SSD-UNK) and 4- to 12-year-olds with cerebral palsy and a diagnosed dysarthria.

dysarthria who have identified speech sound disorders. The word measure, which requires the child to make minimal pair phonetic contrasts for vowels, consonants and word shapes distinct to listeners (Hodge and Gotzke 2011), appears to discriminate among the groups slightly better than the sentence measure.

Communication partners require increased time and effort to decode speech that is difficult to understand (Coté-Reschny and Hodge 2010), and may limit the dysarthric child's opportunities to speak as a coping mechanism (Pennington 2008). This is compounded by the slower speaking rate of many children with dysarthria, which also increases the time required by communication partners to engage in conversation. Figure 2.2 shows speaking rates in words per minute (based on the number of words spoken in a sentence divided by the duration of the sentence) for the imitated sentence task performed by the same groups shown in Figure 2.1. It is apparent that the children with dysarthria varied in their speaking rates but, on average, used a slower rate than the other two groups of children. Figure 2.2 also shows intelligible words per minute (IWPM) scores for the three groups of children. IWPM is a measure of speech efficiency that combines accuracy (number of words identified correctly by listeners) with rate. It is determined by dividing the number of words identified correctly in the sentence set by the total duration of each of the sentences. When intelligibility and rate scores are combined, the difference between the children with dysarthria and the other two groups is even more apparent. However, it is not known if this measure differentiates children with suspected apraxia of speech from those with childhood

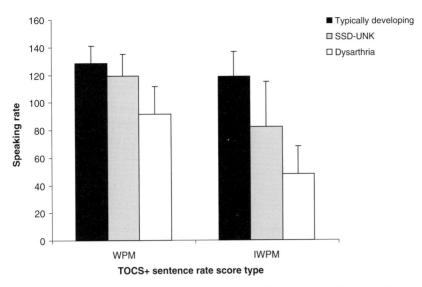

Figure 2.2 Words per minute (WPM) and intelligible words per minute (IWPM) speaking rate scores on the TOCS+ sentence measure for three groups of children: 4- to 6-year-olds with typically developing speech, 4- to 6-year-olds with speech sound disorder of unknown origin (SSD-UNK) and 4- to 12-year-olds with cerebral palsy and a diagnosed dysarthria.

dysarthria. More details regarding the calculation of these rates can be found in Hodge and Gotzke (2010).

Children with dysarthria and cerebral palsy are also at risk for difficulties in written communication activities (Hodge and Wellman 1999; Pennington 2008; Hodge 2010) even when receptive language skills are within the normal range. This may result from reduced opportunities to engage in learning how to read and write because of limited mobility and dysarthric speech, or from specific learning disabilities which affect written communication and may be part of the neurological impairment. Limitations in written communication activities will have major implications for children's academic success, vocational choices and access to information in general and may be functionally more limiting than reduced intelligibility in the longer term.

Ultimately, families, clinicians and teachers are concerned with how the child can perform the activity of talking as part of a larger communication system to converse with a range of communication partners in various contexts. Two classification systems have been published recently that provide direct measures of communication participation by classifying the everyday communication performance of persons with cerebral palsy into various levels. The five-level Communication Function Classification System (CFCS) (Cooley Hidecker *et al.* 2011) can be used by parents, caregivers or professionals familiar with the individual and has no age specifications. All methods of communication are considered including speech, gestures, eye gaze, facial expressions and augmentative and alternative communication. Three factors are used to distinguish among levels: performance in the role of communication sender and receiver, the pace of communication and the type of conversational partner (familiar/unfamiliar). The Functional Communication Classification System (Barty and Caynes 2009) also has five levels and was designed to classify communication in everyday situations for children between 4 and 6 years of age with cerebral palsy. Distinctions among the levels are based on independence in communication, type of communication partner (unfamiliar/familiar), range of messages/topics that are communicated and intentionality of communication.

These tools can be used in research and service delivery to describe functional communication effectiveness, select intervention goals that include both the child and his/her communication partners, consider how tasks, partners and environment affect the child's communication success and measure intervention outcomes. For example, the CFCS was developed by some of the same authors of the Gross Motor Function Classification System Expanded and Revised, a standardized measure that has wide acceptance internationally to describe the severity of gross motor function in children with cerebral palsy in research studies. Similarly, the CFCS could be used to describe the communication function of children with cerebral palsy in a universal manner across research reports. Pennington *et al.* (2009a) recommended that intervention studies for children with dysarthria include measures of activity and participation, even when they address speech specific interventions, to determine the impact of interventions on children's speech in everyday communication. A useful next step would be to validate these communication classification systems for other children with dysarthria.

2.3.3   Contextual factors

The ICF-CY recognizes that factors in the environment or that are part of the child's personality also influence the child's success in learning to communicate in everyday situations. One important implication is that 'disability can be reduced by changing the environment around the person, rather than changing the person' (Colver 2010: 2). Parents and caregivers are key factors in the environment. They influence the child's prelinguistic social-communication and later speech development via the type and frequency of social interactions they provide, and their motivation and ability to access speech and language services. Enhancing the skills of parents, other family members, teachers and peers through awareness, education and direct training that specifically address young children with motor impairment (e.g. Pennington *et al.* 2009b; Pennington and Noble 2010) may reduce the social disability experienced by children with dysarthria.

One of the findings of an international study of participation and quality of life of children with cerebral palsy living in Europe (Colver 2010) was that parents of children with cerebral palsy are more likely to experience significant stress than parents of children in the general population. Moreover, parental stress was far more likely if the child experienced pain, learning problems or communication difficulties. The study's authors recommended strategies to minimise parental stress such as ensuring that sufficient resources are in place to care for the child and that there is easy access to services and schools. This study also found that children with cerebral palsy who used self-report on a measure of quality of life had similar results compared with children in the general population of the same age and country. However, a measure of participation revealed that children with cerebral palsy took part in fewer activities than other children of their age. This finding supports the view that delays or limitations in the domain of communication may be due in part to limited opportunities to participate as a communication partner. Increasing mediated opportunities to practise communicating in a variety of contexts is another important goal for children with dysarthria, regardless of severity (Hodge and Wellman 1999).

Characteristics of the child that are not related directly to impairment in the speech muscles, such as attention and motivation, may also be impaired in the child with dysarthria. In addition to speech, other domains that are affected by the neurological impairment, including language understanding and use, learning style, cognitive ability and perception, influence how a child performs in various communicative situations. Hodge (2010) suggested that an important goal of intervention with children with dysarthria, regardless of level of speech proficiency, is to help them become as desirable conversational partners as possible, to increase the likelihood that others will engage them in communicative interactions.

In summary, diagnosis of developmental dysarthria is made at the ICF-CY level of body structure and function. Sophisticated neural imaging methods are becoming more widely available and can be used to understand the neural underpinnings of childhood dysarthria. These techniques can also provide information which is needed for the identification and classification of childhood dysarthrias and their differential diagnosis from other motor speech disorders such as childhood apraxia of speech. The influence of the ICF-CY is apparent in how children with motor impairments (particularly those with cerebral palsy) are being described in the literature, and in the availability of assessment procedures that specifically address activity and participation aspects of speaking and communication for children with dysarthria. Reports of measures of intelligibility (activity and participation levels) as outcome measures for interventions that address specific speech subsystem impairments, and more general clear speech strategies (e.g. Pennington *et al.* 2010; Fox and Boliek 2012) are starting to appear in the literature. The application of the ICF-CY to intervention studies to identify which combinations of treatment approaches that address body structure and function, activity and participation, and environmental factors are most effective for specific children with dysarthria, remains a challenge for the future.

2.4   Aetiological factors in developmental dysarthrias

Any factor that disrupts the development or impairs the function of the immature cortical and subcortical speech motor control centres and lower motor neuron pathways to the muscles involved in executing speech movements is a candidate cause of childhood dysarthria. There are a number of progressive and non-progressive conditions which cause damage to these structures and pathways, resulting in developmental dysarthria. This section examines these conditions in turn.

2.4.1   Non-progressive conditions

Developmental dysarthria occurs most commonly in children diagnosed with cerebral palsy. Cerebral palsy affects 2–2.5 children per 1,000 live births (Bax *et al.* 2006; Msall and Park 2009), and can result from many different causes. Bax *et al.* (2006) investigated clinical and neural imaging correlates of cerebral palsy in a population sample of 431 children from eight European countries who presented with the diagnosis in the 3-year period between 1996 and 1999. Magnetic resonance imaging (MRI) scans were performed on these children. Aetiological findings included a high rate (39.5%) of infections reported by mothers during pregnancy, 10.9% of children were very preterm and 12% of children were from a known multiple pregnancy. In 11.7% of children, MRI scans were normal. The children with normal MRI findings represented all clinical subtypes and severity levels of cerebral palsy.

For children with abnormal MRIs, 42.5% showed white matter immaturity (e.g. periventricular leukomalacia), 12.8% had basal ganglia lesions, 9.4% had cortical/subcortical lesions (e.g. watershed damage, multicystic encephalomalacia), 9.1% had brain malformations (e.g. polymicrogyria, cortical dysplasia, malformations resulting from in utero infections such as cytomegalovirus), 7.4% had focal infarcts and 7.1% had miscellaneous causes. The authors reported that children in this last group had high rates of other problems such as epilepsy and vision problems and suspected that some of these children may have had unidentified genetic abnormalities. The authors also reported that 58% of the children had speech and/or language problems. These problems were lowest in the diplegia and hemiplegia cerebral palsy groups and highest in the dyskinesia and quadriplegia groups.

Shevell *et al.* (2003) reported the results of a review of all consecutive cases diagnosed with cerebral palsy over a 10-year period in a single paediatric neurology practice in a major urban centre in Canada. An aetiology was identified for 82% of the 217 cases. Aetiologies identified by percentage of cases were periventricular leukomalacia (24.9%), intrapartum asphyxia (21.7%), cerebral dysgenesis (17.1%), intracranial haemorrhage (12.9%), vascular anomalies (9.7%), infection (5.1%), trauma (1.8%), atrophy (1.8%) and toxins such as alcohol and cocaine (1.1%). Multiple causes were identified in 15.6% of cases. Aetiology varied by type of cerebral palsy, gestational age and population (high risk neonatal or not). Cerebral palsy type by percentage of cases was spastic quadriplegia (35.5%), spastic hemiplegia (31.3%), spastic diplegia (18%), spastic monoplegia (2.7%), mixed (5.5%), ataxic-hypokinetic (5.5%), dyskinetic (0.9%) and Worster–Drought syndrome (0.9%).

Worster–Drought syndrome (WDS), also called congenital suprabulbar paresis, results from lesion sites above the lower motor neurons in the brainstem. WDS is a type of cerebral palsy that affects the bulbar muscles (i.e. lips, tongue, soft palate, pharynx, larynx). This causes persistent difficulties with swallowing, feeding, speech, saliva control and airway protection. Consequently, this condition has major significance for speech-language clinicians. The perisylvian cortex is thought to be the site of lesion (Clark *et al.* 2000), but other investigators have also reported subcortical basal ganglia lesions (Suresh and Deepa 2004). Like other types of cerebral palsy, WDS results from non-progressive disturbances in early brain development. Aetiologies include congenital bilateral perisylvian polymicrogyria (later neuronal migration/cortical organization disorders) in approximately 15 per cent of cases (Clark and Neville 2008). Genetic and vascular aetiologies have also been reported (Suresh and Deepa 2004; Clark and Neville 2008).

The core elements of WDS are spastic paresis of the bulbar muscles (weakness, exaggerated jaw jerk) and a mild spastic quadriplegia (bulbar muscles are more obviously affected than limb and trunk muscles). Clark *et al.* (2010) reported that in a prospective study of 42 children diagnosed with WDS, 36 had feeding difficulties and 23/38 had unintelligible speech. This was a significant barrier to learning and participating in peer groups. The majority of children who responded to testing had severe dysarthria (24/38) characterized by articulation difficulties (especially tongue movements), hypernasality and gross nasal air escape. Dyspraxia error types predominated in five children, while the remaining children exhibited mixed features. Use of a low-pitch and strained voice quality also reduced intelligibility in some children. Similar to previous reports, these authors found that some children had accompanying disturbances in cognition, behaviour (attention deficit hyperactivity disorder), social communication (autistic features) and epilepsy. According to Clark *et al.* (2000: 2160), 'WDS is startlingly absent from epidemiological studies of the cerebral palsies and rarely diagnosed, presumably because of lack of clinical awareness of the condition and lack of major gross motor impairments'.

There are other, non-progressive conditions in which congenital or early impairment of the neural substrates for speech production can result in dysarthria. At the level of the lower motor neurons, these conditions include Möbius syndrome. This is a congenital condition in which the CN VI and VII and in some cases IX, X, XI and XII do not develop normally (Bogart and Matsumoto 2010). Lip movements are absent or reduced, with the result that facial expression is lacking. This causes difficulties with social aspects of communication, in addition to labial sound production for speech. Soft palate and tongue movements may also be affected, which increases the severity of the dysarthria.

Non-progressive conditions that have reported the presence of dysarthria and specifically affect the cerebellum include Joubert's syndrome, congenital non-progressive cerebellar ataxia, opsoclonos–myoclonus syndrome (Liégeois and Morgan 2012), isolated cerebellar cortical dysplasia (Jissendi-Tchofo et al. 2012) and hypoplasia (Poretti et al. 2010) and those that affect more extensive areas of the brainstem such as Chiari's malformation (Albert et al. 2010). Children with chromosomal and gene abnormalities (e.g. Down's syndrome, fragile X syndrome, chromosome translocations) and other conditions where there appears to be global involvement of cortical and subcortical motor systems (e.g. global developmental delay of unknown origin) can also present with dysarthric characteristics. Inborn metabolic diseases resulting in dysarthria, with clinical signs apparent from speech onset or appearing in later childhood, include classic galactosaemia (Potter 2011), Niemann–Pick disease (Xiong et al. 2012), Sjogren–Larsson syndrome (Fuijkschot et al. 2009), sepiapterin reductase deficiency (Friedman et al. 2012) and those associated with childhood dystonia and chorea (Flamand-Rouvière et al. 2010).

Epilepsy disorders of childhood (e.g. rolandic epilepsy, acquired opercular epilepsy) typically appear after the age of 3 years and may be considered non-progressive if the seizures are well controlled. Rolandic epilepsy affects the primary motor cortices bilaterally. Liégeois and Morgan (2012) reported that rolandic epilepsy with normal MRI findings represented the majority of cases of dysarthria identified with epilepsy disorders. Oral-pharyngeal-laryngeal symptoms and speech arrest during seizures (duration of 1–3 minutes) have been reported in 40–50 per cent of cases (Bruni et al. 2012). Morgan et al. (2010) described the speech outcomes of 13 children (age range 4 months to 13 years) who underwent hemispherectomy to treat drug-resistant seizures. They found that all children were intelligible post-surgery and exhibited a mild dysarthria characterized by asymmetrical weakness and reduced quality and coordination of movements. Five of these children also showed signs of speech and non-speech oral apraxia.

The most common site for childhood brain tumours is the posterior fossa, which includes the cerebellum, basal ganglia, brainstem and cortico-cerebellar white matter pathways. Disorders of speech (mutism and dysarthria) are known complications of posterior fossa removal. In a consecutive sample of 27 cases, Mei and Morgan (2011) reported that mutism, dysarthria and/or dysphagia were apparent post-surgically in one-third of cases. These investigators provided a detailed description of the children's dysarthria, dysphagia and comorbid communication impairments. They reported deficits in articulation as the most common dysarthric feature but impairments in respiration, phonation and prosody were also observed. Eight children were identified as having dysarthria post-surgery and five were documented as having dysarthria at time of discharge. Cerebellar astrocytomas and medullablastomas account for about one-third of childhood brain tumours. Huber *et al.* (2007) found that in their study of 94 cases, survivors of these tumour types exhibited neuromotor speech disorders on long-term follow-up. They reported that tumour type and radiation treatment are factors that influence long-term outcomes.

De Smet *et al.* (2012) reported the result of auditory-perceptual analysis of speech in 24 children 1 to 12 years after cerebellar tumour removal. The most prominent speech features reported were distorted vowels, slow rate, voice tremor and monopitch that did not consistently fit the classic profile of adult-onset ataxic dysarthria. Presence of additional postoperative impairments, location of the surgical lesion and treatment with chemotherapy influenced long-term speech outcomes, with 63 per cent of cases showing persistent motor speech deficits at a minimum of 1 year post-surgery. Contrary to previous studies, de Smet *et al.* reported that motor speech deficits occurred following unilateral, bilateral and midline (vermian) lesions. These studies identify the need for speech-language clinicians to be involved in healthcare teams in routine assessment and follow-up of children with posterior fossa tumours.

2.4.2 Progressive conditions

After cerebral palsy, muscular dystrophy is the second most likely childhood neurological condition to present with a developmental dysarthria (Webb and Adler 2008). There are different types of muscular dystrophy including Duchenne's, myotonic and facioscapulohumeral dystrophy. Duchenne's dystrophy is a sex-linked, recessive condition that occurs predominantly in males, with clinical manifestations apparent by 3 years of age. The disease has a characteristic progression of muscular weakness initially affecting muscles of the pelvis and trunk and eventually affecting all skeletal muscles, including the bulbar musculature. As a result, flaccid dysarthria affecting articulatory, laryngeal and respiratory subsystems may appear in later stages of the disease. Cognitive impairment is present in approximately one-third of affected children and, regardless of level of cognitive impairment, boys with Duchenne's dystrophy have been found to perform more poorly on tests requiring attention to complex verbal information than on other verbal or memory measures (Hinton *et al.* 2000).

The infantile form of facioscapulohumeral dystrophy (FSHD) has also been associated with developmental dysarthria. This condition may occur in hereditary cases (autosomal dominant disorder) mapped to chromosome 4q35 or sporadically. Affected children may have generalized hypotonia and weakness of the shoulder girdle, facial and other bulbar muscles. Bilateral facial paresis or paralysis can be manifested before age 2 years, resulting in dysarthria, dysphagia, excessive drooling and poor suck. Some children with infantile onset also have sensorineural hearing loss. Hodge (1999) described the longitudinal speech intelligibility profile of a child with infantile-onset FSHD. The disorder manifested at 11 months of age as facial weakness and lip paresis. By age 3 years, the child had complete lip paralysis and at age 7 years, muscle wasting in the tongue and soft palate was marked and hypernasality was apparent.

Hereditary cerebellar ataxias are a family of neurodegenerative diseases that affect the cerebellum and may present clinical signs, including dysarthria, during childhood (Whaley et al. 2011). Spinal cord involvement, peripheral nerve disease, cognitive impairment, supranuclear ophthalmological signs, seizure disorders and psychiatric signs may co-occur. Charcot–Marie–Tooth disease is a complex group of inherited conditions that affect the peripheral nervous system (neuropathies) and may present with dysarthric features during early speech development (Patzko and Shy 2012). Other neurodegenerative diseases that present with dysarthria in adults can occur in children. For example, juvenile Huntington's disease and Parkinson's disease are rare in childhood but instances of these diseases with onset of dysarthric signs before ages 3 and 4 years have been reported (Liégeois and Morgan 2012). Myasthenia gravis is a disorder that affects the neuromuscular junction in the peripheral nervous system. Neonatal cases of myasthenia gravis with developmental dysarthria have been reported (Jeanner et al. 2008). Progressive vascular diseases in childhood (e.g. moyamoya) have also been reported to present with dysarthria as a clinical manifestation (Liégeois and Morgan 2012).

2.5   Prevalence and incidence

As observed by Pennington et al. (2009a), robust prevalence data are not available for developmental dysarthria or later-onset childhood dysarthrias. Moreover, incidence data have limited usefulness in studies of neurodevelopmental disabilities. This is because of the difficulty of identifying the onset of cases when these conditions develop in utero or shortly after birth (Yeargin-Allsopp and Drews-Botsch 2009). In the following section, available estimates of the prevalence of developmental dysarthria are reported for the more common conditions described in the previous section of the chapter.

The only population study of children with cerebral palsy located in the literature that specifically identified the presence of dysarthria included 152 Icelandic children ranging in age from 4 years to 6.5 years (Sigurdardottir and Vik 2011). These authors identified 16% of the children as being non-verbal (anarthric), 68% were classified as having normal speech or mild dysarthria (intelligible speech but with some deviations) and 16% were classified as having severe dysarthria (less intelligible or unintelligible speech). Children with severe dysarthria were less likely to be able to walk and were more likely to have spastic quadriplegic and dyskinetic subtypes of cerebral palsy. The majority of children (98%) with normal speech or mild dysarthria spoke in sentences compared with 32% of the children with severe dysarthria. Half of the children with severe dysarthria who spoke in sentences had normal or borderline cognition and the other half had mild intellectual impairment. The authors also reported that expressive language and speech status were highly associated with gross motor function, subtype of cerebral palsy and intellectual functioning. Most of the non-verbal children (88%) had multiple disabilities compared with 18% in the verbal group.

Pennington *et al.* (2009a) reported estimates of 40–50% for the prevalence of speech disorder in children with cerebral palsy in middle to late childhood. They did not specify if this prevalence estimate was specific to dysarthria or might also include children with features of apraxia of speech.

In a prospective study undertaken to identify speech and language profiles in a convenience sample of 34 children aged 4 years with cerebral palsy, Hustad *et al.* (2010) classified 23.5% of children as having no clinical motor speech impairment; 26.5% were classified as having motor speech involvement and typically developing language, 18% as having motor speech involvement and impaired language and 32% as unable to produce speech (anarthria). Because Hustad *et al.*'s study was not based on a population sample and did not classify severity of dysarthria or distinguish dysarthria from apraxic features, and Sigurdardottir and Vik's study combined children with no clinical evidence of motor speech impairment with those with mild speech impairment, these studies cannot be compared. However, in Hustad *et al.*'s study, the percentage of children with anarthria was twice as large and, overall, 77% of children had a motor speech disorder. Based on an estimated prevalence of cerebral palsy of 2–2.5 per 1,000, and using the range of prevalence data estimates (40–77%) of speech disorder in cerebral palsy from available studies cited in this chapter, approximately 1 to 1.9 per 1,000 children may have developmental dysarthria/anarthria associated with cerebral palsy other than WDS.

The prevalence of children with WDS who present with features of dysarthria is 100% by virtue of its being a core feature of the condition. Clark *et al.* (2010) suggested that the estimated prevalence figure of 2 to 3 per

100,000 live births for cases of WDS based on Shevell *et al.* (2003) was an underestimate, because late diagnosis (often after age 5 years) is common in WDS, and most cerebral palsy registers do not recognize WDS. A less conservative 'guesstimate' of 5 cases of WDS per 100,000 live births (0.05 per 1,000) by the author of this chapter would give a combined estimated prevalence range of 1.05 to 1.95 per 1,000 in the general population for developmental dysarthria associated with all types of cerebral palsy.

No prevalence data specific to the occurrence of motor speech disorders in children with stroke or traumatic brain injury acquired postnatally before 3 years of age are available. Morgan *et al.* (2010) reported an extrapolated incidence of 1.2% for dysarthria and 3.8% for dysphagia in all children admitted with traumatic brain injury sustained between 3 and17 years of age, identified over an 8-year period. When only children with severe traumatic brain injury were considered, the incidence was much higher (20% for dysarthria and 76% for dysphagia). In 2004, the National Cancer Institute in the USA reported annual incidence rates for childhood brain tumours of 3.2 per 100,000 (National Cancer Institute 2004). If one-third of childhood brain tumours occur in the posterior fossa and dysarthria is reported to occur following resection of these tumours in one-third to two-thirds of children (see section 2.4.1), a 'guesstimated' incidence of dysarthria occurring with childhood posterior fossa tumour resection by the chapter author is 1 per 300,000 population per year.

The highest estimate of Möbius syndrome in the general population is 0.02 per 1,000 (Bogart and Matsumoto 2010). Msall and Park (2009) reported a prevalence rate of 1 per 1,000 for Down's syndrome. Based on these data, combined with those for cerebral palsy, including WDS, the prevalence range of developmental dysarthria (onset before age 3 years) occurring in non-progressive conditions is 'guesstimated' by this author to be between approximately 2 and 3 per 1,000 in the general population. With respect to progressive conditions, Msall and Park (2009) reported a prevalence rate for muscular dystrophy of 0.5 per 5,000. However, at this time, there is not enough information available to estimate prevalence or incidence data for dysarthria in childhood progressive neurodegenerative diseases. These are relatively rare diseases and dysarthria is not present in all cases so the numbers are expected to be very low.

2.6   Current knowledge base and future directions

In the past 5 to 10 years, there has been a significant increase in the number of data-driven, international publications on childhood dysarthria, most notably by Pennington and colleagues in the United Kingdom and Morgan and colleagues in Australia. With the availability of more sophisticated MRI techniques and analyses, researchers are starting to investigate neural site of lesion correlates for childhood dysarthria. Based on current findings, persisting childhood dysarthria appears to occur most frequently in bilateral brain lesions, with the possible exception of some cases of post-surgical removal of posterior fossa tumours.

While similar sites of lesion appear to give rise to motor speech disorders in children and adults, clinical speech features correlated for site of lesion in adult-onset dysarthria do not follow the same pattern in children. Early-onset brain injury has quite different effects on speech behaviour in children even when the cause of injury and the site of lesion are the same as in adults. When a neurological insult occurs prior to speech development, dysarthria is often difficult to diagnose because of the lack of speech or speech-like behaviours which can be observed. However, early signs of feeding difficulties and speech delay are risk factors for dysarthria. As children become more verbal, new or changing diagnoses may be made. Developmental dysarthrias vary in their presentation within a child across development, and across children.

To date, there is no brain-based, empirical classification system for child-onset dysarthria and no standardized, internationally agreed protocol to ascertain dysarthria in children. These are high priorities for future research. Developmental dysarthria is currently diagnosed using clinical signs observed during a motor speech examination, including a comprehensive structural-functional examination, knowledge about neurological diagnosis and medical, developmental and family history. Milder dysarthrias and those where an underlying neurological condition may go undiagnosed, such as WDS, may not be recognized by speech-language clinicians. This often results in less than optimal treatment and poor speech outcomes. Educating developmental paediatricians and speech-language clinicians about these conditions should lead to higher identification rates, improved services and better speech and communication outcomes. No population-based studies of the prevalence of childhood dysarthrias are available. Based on the information presented in this chapter, the author estimates the prevalence rate of childhood dysarthria to be in the range of 2 to 3 per 1,000. However, with better methods of ascertainment, this number is expected to increase somewhat.

Children with developmental dysarthria often have co-occurring impairments in feeding and swallowing, and may have language and learning problems, behavioural problems and additional medical complications. They are also at risk for literacy problems. These factors limit their opportunities for engaging in activities and communicating with others. Their communication participation is also adversely affected by reduced speech intelligibility and slower speaking rates. Longitudinal studies are currently underway to describe the speech and language trajectories and outcomes in children with cerebral palsy and to predict the development of communication skills in children with motor impairment. The results of these studies will provide much needed data to inform clinical decisions regarding the timing and focus of speech, oral and written language, and communication interventions.

The persisting nature of developmental dysarthria, its evolution as the child develops, and the multiple areas of communication function that may be affected make it a candidate condition for management by means of integrated care pathways (Middleton *et al.* 2001; Great Ormond Street Hospital for Children NHS Foundation Trust 2007). Care paths outline the anticipated care, placed in an appropriate timeframe, to help clients (and their families) with a specific condition or set of symptoms move through clinical management to positive outcomes. Care paths elaborate the steps, decision points, investigations and interventions to be performed, criteria for referral to other professionals, milestones/outcome measures, guidelines or protocols and monitoring arrangements. Emphasis is on provision of appropriate care for each individual client in relation to the clinical evidence base and/or consensus of best practice. Care paths change as new evidence, guidelines and treatment patterns emerge. This will be a challenging undertaking for developmental dysarthria. However, establishing expected standards of care that (1) start at identification, (2) include early communication training, direct speech training, global strategies to optimize speech intelligibility and increase skill and confidence in conversing with others, and (3) support transitions between services and schools, would greatly improve professional practice and services for affected children and their families, reduce parental stress and improve communication outcomes for children with dysarthria.

Measures of activity and participation (intelligibility, communication) are available for children with cerebral palsy, but these have yet to be validated for children with dysarthria associated with other conditions. There is an expectation that measures at these ICF-CY levels be included as outcome measures in intervention studies. This will allow cross-study comparison of effect sizes. Quasi-experimental studies of the effectiveness of communication interventions and speech-specific treatments for children with cerebral palsy and motor speech impairment are beginning to appear in the literature (e.g. Pennington *et al.* 2010) and more are underway. It is expected that publications on the topic of childhood dysarthria will continue to increase exponentially over the next 5 to 10 years, given the increasing international interest in this population.

3

Developmental verbal dyspraxia

Brigid McNeill

3.1   Introduction

Developmental verbal dyspraxia is a controversial speech disorder with
continued debate over its existence, nature and diagnosis. Uncertainty
around these issues coupled with the typically severe and broadly affected
profiles of those affected present a challenge for clinicians. This chapter
presents an overview of current thought regarding the definition, characteristics, theoretical perspectives, assessment and intervention practices
for this population. A series of case studies are used to exemplify the heterogeneous nature of children with developmental verbal dyspraxia and
the changing face of this disorder over time.

3.2   What is developmental verbal dyspraxia?

Developmental verbal dyspraxia (DVD) is 'a childhood neurological
speech sound disorder in which the precision and consistency of movements underlying speech are impaired in the absence of neuromuscular deficits (e.g., abnormal reflexes, abnormal tone)' (American Speech-
Language-Hearing Association 2007: 3–4). A number of terms have been
used to label this disorder since its initial description by Morley and colleagues (Morley *et al.* 1954). Although DVD is the preferred label in the
UK (and will be the term used throughout this chapter), the disorder is
currently known as childhood apraxia of speech (CAS) in the USA. In fact,
the majority of research in the field has used 'CAS' as the label for the
difficulty since its adoption by the American Speech-Language-Hearing
Association in 2007. The terms are generally used interchangeably in the
research literature.

Although DVD more commonly occurs idiopathically (i.e. in the absence of obvious neurological injury and/or other neurobehavioural diagnoses), it may also present as a secondary feature within more complex difficulties such as rolandic epilepsy (Scheffer 2000; Kugler *et al.* 2008), galactosaemia (Shriberg *et al.* 2011), fragile X syndrome (Spinelli *et al.* 1995) and Down's syndrome (Kumin 2006). Possible concomitant presentation of DVD and autism has also been postulated. A recent evaluation, however, of the speech and prosody profile of 46 verbal children with autism showed no support for the co-occurrence of the two disorders (Shriberg *et al.* 2010a).

Epidemiological data for DVD is limited by the use of clinical rather than population samples in the calculation of figures, and by the use of varying diagnostic methods for identification of the disorder, which make it difficult to aggregate findings across studies. Despite such restrictions, all data indicate that DVD is a rare diagnosis. Delaney and Kent (2004) reported that about 4 per cent of 15,000 referrals of speech delay of unknown origin exhibited DVD. Broomfield and Dodd (2004) identified two potential cases of DVD out of 936 referrals to speech and language therapy services in the United Kingdom, equating to 0.2 per cent of referrals. Similarly, Shriberg *et al.* (1997a) estimated DVD to occur in 0.1–0.2 per cent of all children. Further research is needed to establish the prevalence of DVD within various neurobehavioural disorders.

Gender ratio analysis indicates idiopathic DVD is more prevalent in males than females. Lewis *et al.* (2004a) reported a 2:1 ratio of males to females in their sample of 22 children aged 3 to 10 years using a rigorous diagnostic method. Other studies have reported an even greater affection rate in males. For example, P.K. Hall *et al.* (1993) found that 74 per cent of 229 cases of DVD reported in the literature were male. Contrastively, the gender ratio of DVD occurring within neurobehavioural disorders is almost equal with a 0.9:1 ratio of males to females affected across studies (Shriberg 2010).

DVD appears to be a heritable condition with a large percentage of the family members of those affected experiencing speech, language and/or literacy disorders (Thoonen *et al.* 1997; Lewis *et al.* 2004a). Lewis *et al.* (2004a) found that 86 per cent of 22 participants with DVD had at least one nuclear family member with a speech and/or language disorder, while 59 per cent of participants had at least one parent affected with a speech and/or language disorder. There is, however, a low aggregation of DVD amongst family members of children with DVD. Lewis *et al.* (2004a) interpreted the familial aggregation of CAS with other speech-language disorders (rather than with CAS itself) as opposing a unique genetic cause of DVD. Rather, the authors posited that children with CAS hold extra risk genes for a general 'verbal trait disorder'.

Further demonstration of the heritability of DVD has been provided by the examination of the 'K.E. family', a family with approximately 50 per cent of its members exhibiting DVD (Hurst *et al.* 1990). Oral apraxia, speech errors, phonological processing problems, reduced non-verbal intelligence and syntactic deficits have been reported in those affected (Watkins *et al.* 2002). Genetic investigation of the family has identified a mutation at chromosome 7q31 (also called the *FOXP2* gene) (Lai *et al.* 2001). Although research on the 'K.E. family' has wide scientific benefit, the application of findings from this group to the general DVD population may be limited given failure to implicate *FOXP2* mutations in other children with DVD (American Speech-Language-Hearing Association 2007).

The aetiology of DVD is still broadly undetermined, but most definitions attribute a neurological origin to the difficulty (American Speech-Language-Hearing Association 2007; Royal College of Speech and Language Therapists 2009). Liégeois and Morgan (2012) reviewed the neurological functioning of 45 children with DVD who were reported across 12 studies. The majority (96 per cent) of descriptions of DVD with neurological findings were from children with concomitant neurobehavioural diagnoses. Most of the MRI brain scans reviewed did not show abnormalities. The authors concluded that neurological anomalies in DVD may thus lie at the sub-macroscopic, metabolic and/or neurotransmitter level in contrast to the broad lesions associated with acquired forms of apraxia. Further research is needed to identify the neurological functioning of those affected by idiopathic forms of the disorder.

3.3   What are the symptoms of DVD?

The following section describes the diverse motor, speech, prosodic, language and literacy symptoms reported in children with DVD. Historically, the broad nature of difficulties reported in DVD alongside the lack of specificity of the features (i.e. they also occur in other forms of developmental speech disorder) has led some researchers to question its existence as a unique clinical entity. Current developmental models of DVD highlight the complex interaction between motor speech and phonological development, making comorbidity of features across multiple levels of speech and language development an expected outcome of an underlying impairment in the planning and programming of speech production (Maassen *et al.* 2010; Burns 2011). Readers are referred to section 3.4 for further discussion of theoretical perspectives on the underlying difficulty in DVD.

3.3.1   Motor skills
Oral apraxia and limb apraxia have been reported in children with DVD. Features of oral apraxia reported in the population include impaired voluntary oro-motor control in isolated and sequenced oral movements (McCabe *et al.* 1998). For example, the child with DVD may have difficulty elevating his/her tongue in response to a verbal command, but

have no difficulty with spontaneous tongue movement. Oral apraxia is one feature of DVD that is not commonly reported in other developmental speech and language disorders. Earlier intervention approaches for DVD thus tended to focus on remediation of oro-motor control deficits (Pannbacker 1988). There is now general consensus in the literature, however, that non-verbal oral motor exercises are contraindicated in treatment approaches aiming to improve speech production in children with DVD (Forrest 2002; Lof 2003).

A history of feeding difficulties and low muscle tone is also reported in some children with CAS (Stackhouse 1992). Children with DVD are more likely than the general population to be diagnosed with comorbid limb apraxia and commonly exhibit fine and/or gross motor control difficulties (e.g. Dewey *et al.* 1998).

3.3.2   Speech production

Verbal dyspraxia is one of the most commonly cited features of DVD. Characteristics of verbal dyspraxia include slow and/or mis-sequenced performance in diadochokinetic tasks (i.e. repeating /p, t, k/) and articulatory groping (silent posturing for articulatory position) during speech (McCabe *et al.* 1998). There are a myriad of other speech production deficits that have been identified in children with DVD, all of which are also evidenced by children with other types of speech disorder. Speech symptoms include a limited phonemic repertoire, vowel errors, unusual or atypical speech errors, inconsistent speech errors on repeated words/syllables, sound sequencing errors, particular difficulty in the production of multisyllabic words or connected speech, and phonotactic deficits (see American Speech-Language-Hearing Association (2007) for a review). The speech production skills of children with DVD are reported to improve when producing automatic (or over-learned) phrases rather than spontaneous or imitated speech (Ozanne 2005). DVD is also generally associated with severe and persistent speech disorder that is resistant to speech and language therapy.

Table 3.1 presents the responses of a child with DVD called Sean to selected items of the Phonology subtest of the Diagnostic Evaluation of Articulation and Phonology (DEAP; Dodd *et al.* 2006). Sean is 5 years and 3 months old. He used gesture and sign to support his spoken attempts during the assessment and was noted to have trouble controlling his drool. Sean's responses demonstrate his limited consonant and vowel repertoire (e.g. his consonant production was limited to the /b/ and /d/ sounds), limited phonotactic skills (he only produced the CV syllable structure within the sample) and atypical speech errors (e.g. vowel errors). Deficits in a range of more complex speaking skills (e.g. connected speech, multisyllabic word production, inconsistent speech errors) could not be identified given Sean's limited verbal output. This case study data was taken from McNeill and Gillon (2011).

Table 3.1 *Sean's responses to selected items of the Diagnostic Evaluation of Articulation and Phonology (Dodd et al. 2006)*

Target word		Response
Boat	/boʊt/	/bu/
Rain	/reɪn/	/bə/
Zebra	/zebrə/	/bə/
Jump	/dʒʌmp/	/da/
Tongue	/tʌn/	/da/
Chips	/tʃɪps/	/dɪ/

Table 3.2 *Liam's responses to selected items of the Diagnostic Evaluation of Articulation and Phonology (Dodd et al. 2006)*

Target word		Trial 1	Response Trial 2	Trial 3
shark	/ʃak/	/gʌk/	/dʌ/	/gak/
elephant	/eləfənt/	/elfən/	/eləvən/	/eləbən/
tongue	/tʌn/	/kʌn/	/dʌn/	/kʌn/
kangaroo	/kæ gəru/	/dænuu/	/gænrɪn/	/kæru/
fish	/fɪʃ/	/bɪ/	/bɪ/	/bɪ/
helicopter	/helikɒptə/	/həkɪkɪ/	/həkɒhə/	/hɒlikɒhə/

Table 3.2 presents the responses of a child with DVD called Liam to selected items of the Inconsistency subtest of the DEAP. Liam is 7 years and 4 months old. The Inconsistency subtest is the only norm-referenced assessment measure of inconsistent speech production currently available. Children name the same 25 pictures across three trials (with another activity between each trial) in one assessment session. Liam's responses show a high level of inconsistent speech production, which includes atypical speech errors (i.e. he is not simply alternating between a correct form and developmental error such as kangaroo–kangawoo). A comparison between Sean's and Liam's responses shows that different features of DVD may be prominent within a child's profile at various points in development. For example, it is difficult to assess the consistency of Sean's speech given his restricted phonemic and phonotactic repertoires. This case study data was taken from McNeill and Gillon (2011).

3.3.3 Prosody

The prosodic symptom most commonly reported in children with DVD is difficulty with lexical and sentential stress production (Shriberg *et al.* 1997a, 1997b, 2003; Odell and Shriberg 2001). The stress production of children with DVD is routinely described as an 'excess and equal' stress pattern, which listeners may perceive as a monotonous or robotic sounding voice. Difficulties with volume, rate and resonance control have also been reported in children with DVD (McCabe *et al.* 1998).

Prosodic disturbances in DVD may be an important diagnostic indicator of the disorder. Shriberg *et al.* (1997a, 1997b) reported that around 50 per cent of children with DVD exhibited an excess and equal stress pattern. Further, excess and equal stress was the only characteristic that consistently differentiated children with DVD from children with other types of speech disorder. An excess and equal stress pattern has also differentiated children with DVD and adults with apraxia of speech (Odell and Shriberg 2001). Consistent with this research, atypical prosody (particularly stress errors) has been forwarded as a potential differentially diagnostic characteristic of DVD (see section 3.4).

3.3.4 Language

There is growing evidence for the presence of expressive and receptive language impairment in children with DVD. Lewis *et al.* (2004b) reported expressive and receptive language impairment in children with DVD that did not lessen as the children's speech production skills improved over time. At preschool age the language profile of children with DVD could not be distinguished from a group of children with combined speech-language impairment. However, the children with DVD exhibited more severe language deficits than the comparison group at school-age. Language impairment has also been incidentally reported in a number of DVD studies (Stackhouse and Snowling 1992; Thoonen *et al.* 1997; Moriarty and Gillon 2006).

One specific area of language development that has begun to be explored in DVD is expressive syntactic development. Ekelman and Aram (1983) examined the expressive syntactic performance within a conversational language sample of eight children with DVD aged 4; 4 to 11; 1 years. The authors reported a range of syntactic deficits including inflectional morpheme omission or substitution, pronoun errors and poor sentence structure due to copula or auxiliary errors. Many of the children's syntactic errors appeared unrelated to speech production skills.

Table 3.3 presents a personal narrative told by a girl called Anne in response to a photo prompt to tell a story about a school trip. Anne is 7 years and 6 months old. She participated in an intervention study for children with DVD and this sample was collected in her initial assessment battery (McNeill *et al.* 2009a). Anne's transcript shows that she is exhibiting difficulties in expressive morphosyntactic development that cannot be attributed to her speech disorder alone. For example, Anne is substituting the pronoun 'we' with 'us' and 'went' with 'go' despite being able to articulate both these words accurately. Anne's narrative also lacks structure and content, making it difficult to follow.

Table 3.3 *Anne's responses to a personal narrative speaking task*

We went to schooltrip.
It's called the the the …
I I forgot it now.
I know it now.
Um um it's like that (Anne points to the photo prompt).
Trains and cars like that.
It's like y* yours.
And and us went on the train.
Go to (the) the airport.
And and and us did go.
I was going to kindergarten.
And I go to schooltrip but um um tr* um b* about airplanes.
A and us go on a airport airplane.
And and that's all.

3.3.5 Phonological processing and literacy

Phonological awareness difficulties at the phoneme, rhyme and syllable levels are reported in children with DVD as compared to their typically developing peers (Stackhouse and Snowling 1992; Marquardt *et al.* 2002). Children with DVD may also be more likely than other groups of children with speech disorder to experience phonological awareness difficulties. McNeill *et al.* (2009b) compared the phonological awareness ability of 12 children with DVD to 12 children with inconsistent speech disorder (i.e. inconsistent speech production on repetitions of words without concomitant oro-motor planning impairment) and a typically developing comparison group. The two groups with speech disorder were matched for severity of speech impairment and level of inconsistent speech production. Children with DVD presented with weaker phonological awareness skills than both comparison groups. Deficits in broader phonological processing skills and working memory in DVD have also been reported (Zaretsky *et al.* 2010).

The close relationship between speech-language and literacy development means that children with DVD also experience heightened rates of reading and spelling difficulties. Lewis *et al.* (2004b) found that children with DVD performed more poorly than children with an isolated speech disorder on decoding, spelling and reading comprehension measures. Further, they presented with a more severe spelling deficit than children with combined speech-language impairment. Similarly, McNeill *et al.* (2009b) reported that children with DVD exhibited higher rates of impairment in decoding and spelling than children with inconsistent speech disorder.

The particular spelling difficulty experienced by some children with DVD is exemplified by Ryan's performance in an informal spelling task presented in Table 3.4. Ryan is 8 years and 8 months old. His responses show that his ability to plausibly represent the initial sound in a novel spelling item is emerging. He also exhibits minimal connection between

Table 3.4 *Spoken and written attempts by Ryan in an informal spelling task*

Item	Spelling attempt		Spoken attempt
rain		(welmn)	/weɪn/
kangaroo		(kaosne)	/dænəru/
girl		(lmal)	/dal/
shark		(amkl)	/zak/
teeth		(faim)	/tif/
fish		(faklo)	/frʃ/
chips		(sbrlo)	/zɪps/
dinosaur		(taoeegltl)	/daɪndɔ/
bridge		(wltmo)	/wedʒ/
cake		(kmko)	/deɪk/

his pronunciation of a word and its written representation. The predominance of non-phonetic spelling errors used by Ryan suggests difficulty in using phonological information in the spelling process.

3.4 Theoretical perspectives

Part of the controversy surrounding DVD is due to differing perspectives on the underlying impairment in the disorder. Traditional theoretical viewpoints have been polarized into motoric versus linguistic perspectives. Current theoretical perspectives on the disorder, however, are more adequately divided into those emphasizing speech motor planning processes in the disorder and those emphasizing representational and speech motor planning involvement (American Speech-Language-Hearing Association 2007). Despite the proposal of multiple theoretical accounts of DVD, there is limited evidence supporting or refuting these hypotheses (Maassen *et al.* 2010).

3.4.1 Motor speech planning/programming perspectives

The conventional perspective on the underlying cause of DVD is that its symptoms stem from a core deficit in speech motor planning and/or programming processes. Proponents of this perspective do not refute the wider linguistic deficits that have been described in DVD but view these difficulties as co-occurring with or being a consequence of speech motor control involvement.

A series of studies investigating possible prosodic markers of DVD concluded that stress and timing deficits in the speech production of children with DVD are due to pre-speech motor programming difficulties (e.g. Odell and Shriberg 2001; Shriberg *et al.* 2003). The authors dismissed the view that these prosodic difficulties were due to cognitive-linguistic deficits in the representation of stress assignment, as misplaced stress included excess stress on a usually stressed syllable rather than excess stress on the usually unstressed syllable. That is, children realized that a particular syllable needed to be stressed, but motor control difficulties meant that excess stress was placed on that usually stressed syllable. Finally, disrupted sensorimotor feedback systems in children with DVD have been attributed to speech motor control deficits. Odell and Shriberg (2001) posited that children with DVD may be unable to monitor motor performance during speech production and/or respond to sensorimotor feedback. The authors concluded that such deficits may render children with DVD incapable of adjusting inaccurate movement patterns during speech production.

3.4.2 Combined representational and motor speech planning/ programming perspectives

The representational and speech motor control perspective of DVD has been developed in an effort to account more parsimoniously for the speech, language and motor symptoms in the disorder. Unlike the motor speech planning perspective, these views conceptualize the more linguistic features in DVD as part of the core difficulty in the disorder.

Phonological awareness difficulties in DVD have prompted the development of the phonological representation deficit hypothesis of the disorder (e.g. Marquardt *et al.* 2002). This hypothesis states that indistinct phonological representations and/or impaired access to phonological representations underlie the broad range of difficulties associated with DVD. Specifically, children are thought to lack quality phonological representations from which to direct motor performance (Marquardt *et al.* 2004).

Similarly, Velleman and Strand (1994) highlighted the causative role of representational deficits in DVD. The authors postulated that children with DVD have difficulty with the hierarchical representation of linguistic components that impairs the organization of language sub-units (e.g. phonemes) into larger units (e.g. syllables). The hierarchical deficit is proposed to impact all levels of language organization (i.e. morphemes into words, word stress into phrasal stress, etc.). The deficit would thus have a widespread impact on the linguistic system and explain the diverse segmental and suprasegmental characteristics of DVD.

Combined representational and motor speech planning perspectives of DVD reflect recent neuroscientific findings that areas of the brain responsible for phonological-articulatory function develop interdependently, and are connected to those that contribute to expressive and receptive language function (Hickok and Poeppel 2007).

3.5   Assessment and differential diagnosis

The following section outlines some key issues in the assessment and differential diagnosis of DVD. Readers are directed to Chapter 21 of this volume for further discussion of the assessment of children with motor speech disorders (including children with DVD).

The diverse nature of symptoms associated with DVD and highlighted in section 3.3 indicates that a comprehensive assessment procedure that evaluates verbal motor planning, speech production, prosody-voice, language and literacy skills should be utilized for this disorder. Wider evaluation of children's functional performance is also recommended. Teverovsky et al. (2009) assessed the functional outcomes of 201 children with DVD via parental report. The children were likely to experience cognitive and learning problems (including literacy, calculation and memory deficits), social communication difficulties and behavioural dysregulation. The International Classification of Functioning, Disability and Health – Children and Youth Version (World Health Organization 2007a) provides a valuable framework for assessing the range of activities that may be affected by developmental speech disorders (McCormack et al. 2010).

The differential diagnosis of DVD from other speech and language disorders has been the centre of much controversy as no single characteristic has been identified to differentiate DVD from other developmental speech and language disorders. Currently, there is consensus in the literature that DVD does exist, and that the disorder presents a 'symptom complex' rather than a 'unitary disorder' (Shriberg et al. 1997a). A 'symptom complex' is a disorder that is diagnosed by a pattern of symptoms indicative of a common underlying cause. Such disorders cannot be diagnosed by one characteristic in isolation, meaning that different children may have different presentations of the same disorder.

The American Speech-Language-Hearing Association's (2007) technical report identified three potential differential diagnostic features of DVD: inconsistent speech errors on repeated productions of the same word/syllable; disrupted coarticulatory transitions between sounds and syllables; and inappropriate prosody. It is important that the usefulness of these features for diagnostic purposes undergo further examination, that operational definitions of deficit in these areas are identified, and that standard assessment procedures for evaluating these skills are established. Diagnosis of DVD is further complicated by the changing set of symptoms associated with the disorder over time. For example, a study by Lewis et al. (2004b) showed that speech production errors dominated the linguistic profile at preschool age, while language impairment, literacy deficits and prosodic difficulties dominated at school age.

3.6   Intervention practices

The following section outlines intervention procedures for DVD that focus on motoric, representational and prosodic features of the disorder. Augmentative and alternative communication (AAC) systems are a further intervention option for some children with DVD who have very limited verbal output to ensure that functional communication needs are met. Readers are directed to Chapter 21 of this volume for further discussion of intervention delivery for children with motor speech disorders (including those with DVD). Unfortunately, there is a dearth of intervention research to direct therapy practices for this population (Morgan and Vogel 2008).

3.6.1   Motor planning for speech

In line with the dominant view of DVD as a motor programming disorder, treatment approaches for DVD generally use principles of motor learning to improve speech planning and production. Case study and single-subject investigations show preliminary support for these approaches. One such approach is Dynamic Temporal and Tactile Cueing (DTTC) (Strand and Debertine 2000; Strand *et al.* 2006). The DTTC approach shapes movement for speech production, moving systematically from the most supported to most independent productions. In line with principles of motor learning, the intervention emphasizes multiple, repeated trials of intervention targets that are presented in frequent, short intervention sessions.

The usefulness of applying general principles of motor learning to speech motor planning interventions has begun to be explored. Edeal and Gildersleeve-Neumann (2011) reported that higher rates of production practice resulted in superior speech gains in response to a motor programming intervention for two children with DVD. Maas and Farinella (2012) compared the relative effects of random versus blocked practice schedules within the DTTC approach for four children with DVD. The assumed random practice advantage was found for two of the participants (with one participant showing greater gains in the blocked condition and another participant showing no speech gains). These results suggest that general non-speech principles of motor learning may not always be applicable to therapy approaches for children with DVD.

3.6.2   Phonological awareness and literacy

Preliminary studies suggest that integrated phonological awareness intervention (i.e. intervention that simultaneously targets speech production, letter knowledge and phonological awareness) may be a promising therapy for enhancing speech and literacy skills in DVD. McNeill *et al.* (2009a) reported that 9 out of 12 children with DVD exhibited significant growth in accuracy of treated speech sounds that was generalized to a connected speaking context for at least one targeted sound. Eight of the cohort also demonstrated significant growth in phoneme awareness skills. Follow-up of the programme's effectiveness showed that continued intensive support is likely to be necessary in order to ensure long-term accelerated growth in the speech and literacy skills of children with DVD (McNeill *et al.* 2010). Similarly, Zaretsky *et al.* (2010) demonstrated the benefits of providing ongoing specialist intervention to promote literacy development in a longitudinal case study of a child with DVD.

3.6.3 Prosody

Despite the attention that prosodic difficulties have received in the DVD literature, there has been little research focused on establishing effective methods for remediating this aspect of the disorder. Ballard *et al.* (2010) used a controlled, single-subject design to examine the effects of an intensive therapy targeting lexical stress contrast in three children with mild-moderate DVD. The intervention followed principles of motor learning. Results showed improved control of stress contrast, loudness and pitch in treated and untreated non-words. Generalization to real-word speaking contexts was not achieved.

3.7 Conclusion

DVD is a complex disorder that requires a multifaceted approach to clinical management. Current knowledge suggests that best practice for this population starts with a comprehensive assessment across speech, prosody-voice, language and literacy domains. A number of intervention approaches are emerging in the literature and it is likely that the appropriate therapeutic focus for a particular child will change as their communicative profile transforms over time. It is clear that further research, particularly in exploring the validity of potential diagnostic markers and establishing an evidence-base for various intervention approaches, is urgently needed to deepen our understanding and to direct clinical practice.

4

Developmental phonological disorder

Susan Rvachew

4.1 Introduction

Children with a developmental phonological disorder (DPD) misarticulate many more speech sounds than is expected for their age (Shriberg *et al.* 1997c) and suffer activity limitations and participation restrictions due to reduced intelligibility or social acceptability of their speech (McCormack *et al.* 2009). Given that the disorder is identified in relation to the speech abilities of age peers, a brief discussion of normal speech development is provided for context in this chapter. A review of the literature regarding the prevalence of DPD and long-term outcomes for children with this disorder follows. Current research on the aetiology and cognitive-linguistic underpinnings of DPD is considered and theoretical perspectives on subtypes of DPD are evaluated in view of this literature. Finally, approaches to intervention are discussed.

4.2 Normal phonological development

Phonological development begins in infancy and progresses throughout childhood via processes that involve aggregation and linkage of developing knowledge in the perceptual, articulatory and linguistic domains (Pierrehumbert 2003; Munson *et al.* 2005a). There is considerable evidence for an early word-based phonology with gradual emergence of phonological units as the lexicon expands (Ferguson and Farwell 1975; Metsala and Walley 1998; Beckman and Edwards 2000). Although most accounts of normal phonological development focus on the acquisition of individual phonemes (Sander 1972; Smit *et al.* 1990), knowledge of the prosodic structure of the language at supra- and intrasyllabic levels is also crucial (Bernhardt and Stemberger 1998). Initial milestones in phonological development are the shift from language-general to language-specific speech perception and the emergence of canonical babble (McCune and Vihman 2001; Kuhl *et al.* 2008). The pronunciation of first words may be highly variable and idiosyncratic while adapted to the form of the child's preferred word templates nonetheless (Vihman and Croft 2007). Subsequently, the child's speech is characterized by more predictable error patterns that gradually give way to improved accuracy as the repertoire of phones and syllable shapes expands and consistency in segment production increases (Preisser *et al.* 1988; Porter and Hodson 2001; Dodd *et al.* 2003). Most children achieve fully intelligible speech by age 4 years and adult-like levels of speech accuracy between 6 and 9 years (Smit *et al.* 1990). Ongoing improvements in precision are seen throughout childhood while the child adjusts to changing articulatory structure and increasing linguistic complexity (Smith and Zelaznik 2004; Goffman *et al.* 2007; Sadagopan and Smith 2008).

Efforts to identify universal principles that predict acquisition order for segments, features or markedness constraints have not been successful (Menn *et al.* 2009; Vihman 2010). However, acquisition is clearly impacted by input frequency, functional load and articulatory complexity (Stokes and Suredran 2005; Ingram 2012). Variability within and across children complicates the task of identifying children whose speech accuracy is sufficiently delayed relative to age peers to warrant a diagnosis of developmental phonological disorder. However, consistent with the International Classification of Functioning, Disability and Health – Children and Youth Version (ICF-CY; World Health Organization 2007a), a primary DPD can be diagnosed under the following conditions when the child presents with many speech errors in the absence of other concomitant or explanatory conditions: (1) the child scores below the tenth percentile on a standardized measure of speech accuracy, thus placing the child at risk for poor psychosocial, academic and vocational outcomes (for review and discussion, see Rvachew and Brosseau-Lapré 2012); (2) the child is older than 3 years and more than 75 per cent unintelligible to a stranger, placing the child at risk for activity limitations (Coplan and Gleason 1988); or (3) the child and/or significant others are concerned about participation restrictions that are associated with the child's speech accuracy at any age (McCormack *et al.* 2009).

4.3 Developmental phonological disorder: prevalence and outcomes

Reviews of the prevalence of DPD reveal no consensus as to the correct estimate of the proportion of cases with speech delay in the population at any one time (Shriberg *et al.* 1999; Law *et al.* 2000). Law *et al.* (2000) report a median estimate of approximately 6% for speech impairment, although it is not clear that this is a useful estimate given that estimates vary from 2.3% to 24.6% for isolated speech disorder. This broad range in estimates reflects differences in procedural quality, operational definitions and participant age across studies.

Probably the most reliable estimate is provided by Beitchman *et al.* (1986), who screened for language-only, speech-only and concomitant speech and language disorder in a stratified random sample of 5-year-old children in the Ottawa region of Canada using standardized procedures. The final estimate for the prevalence of speech disorders (including phonological, articulation, voice and fluency impairments with or without concomitant language impairment) was 11%, a group composed of 6.40% with speech-only impairment and 4.56% with concomitant speech and language impairment. More recently, McLeod and Harrison (2009) determined parent-reported prevalence for speech difficulties among Australian children to be 12% when measured in functional terms (e.g. parents reporting that their child's speech was 'not clear to others'). The prevalence of residual speech errors among older children was investigated by Roulstone *et al.* (2009), who observed that 18% of 8-year-old children had speech errors in a large-scale, population-based study conducted in the United Kingdom.

Comorbidity of DPD with specific language impairment is known to be high especially in clinic samples in which at least two-thirds of children with speech problems will have concomitant language impairment (e.g. Baker and Cantwell 1982). In samples drawn from the general population, overlap is less with Shriberg *et al.* (1999) reporting that only one-third of children with speech delay had concomitant language delay in a study involving kindergarten age children. Even when receptive language skills are within normal limits, children with DPD are very likely to have specific difficulties with productive use of finite verb morphology. Furthermore, their difficulties with expressive morphosyntax are significantly more severe than would be predicted from their articulation accuracy (Rvachew *et al.* 2005; Haskill and Tyler 2007) or their overall syntactic abilities (Paul and Shriberg 1982; Mortimer and Rvachew 2010).

Studies of short-term outcomes for children with a preschool history of DPD indicate an elevated risk of future difficulties with language and literacy skills during the school years. The risk of poor reading outcomes is enhanced when there is concomitant language impairment although there is a high likelihood of spelling difficulties even when the child's prior history involves isolated speech impairment (Bird *et al.* 1995; Larrivee and Catts 1999; Lewis *et al.* 2000). For example, Lewis *et al.* followed preschoolers with speech delay into third grade. For those with concomitant speech and language impairments as preschoolers, a large percentage in third grade presented with impairments in articulation (22%), language (60%), reading (46%) and spelling (58%) skills. The corresponding percentages for children with speech-only deficits as preschoolers were 4%, 14%,

4% and 30%, respectively. In this longitudinal study, however, children identified with 'speech-only' deficits had significantly less severe speech delays, higher IQs and higher socioeconomic status than children with concomitant speech and language impairments.

Short-term and longer-term follow-up studies reveal a higher risk of psychiatric problems for children who begin school with speech or language impairment with the elevation in risk of emotional problems for girls being especially striking (Beitchman *et al.* 1996). Again, concomitant language impairment plays a significant role and, in general, behavioural disorders are somewhat more likely in association with concomitant speech and language disorder whereas emotional disorders are somewhat more likely to be associated with isolated speech impairment (Baker and Cantwell 1987a; Beitchman *et al.* 2001; Brownlee *et al.* 2004).

Other studies have shown that the sequelae of preschool speech disorders persist through the school years and into adulthood. Felsenfeld *et al.* (1994) described educational and occupational outcomes for two groups of adults drawn from a large study of children who had been assessed repeatedly from prekindergarten through fourth grade and again in high school (the Templin Longitudinal Study). Two subgroups of adults were selected from the database to represent a group with moderately delayed development of articulation skills in the early school years (DPD group) and a comparison group with normal development of articulation skills (control group). Cognitive function was within normal limits for both groups but the DPD group had significantly lower verbal IQ than the control group. In comparison to the control group, adults with a history of childhood DPD performed significantly worse on tests of articulation accuracy, vocabulary knowledge and language skills. They required more remedial help at school, achieved poorer grades and completed fewer years of formal education. These adults were also more likely to hold unskilled or semiskilled occupations in comparison with the control group and their gender-matched siblings, who were more likely to hold professional positions. The authors pointed out that even when educational outcomes were similar, individuals with a history of DPD were likely to choose occupations that required lower levels of reading and writing competency.

4.4   Aetiology

On the basis of a large, population-based sample with blinded assessments, Campbell *et al.* (2003) found that speech delay was 7.71 times more likely in a child who had the three risk factors of male sex, mother not graduated from high school and family history of stuttering, articulation and/or language disorder. The heritability of speech disorders is now well established (Lewis *et al.* 2006; Bishop and Hayiou-Thomas 2008) and male

sex as a risk factor has been replicated in other large sample and population-based studies (Winitz and Darley 1980; Silva *et al.* 1984; Shriberg *et al.*
1999). Low maternal education is usually interpreted as an index of socioeconomic status, a variable that has been associated with speech delay in
other studies conducted in the United States (Winitz and Darley 1980).
Lower social class is more likely to be identified as a correlate if there is
concomitant language impairment than in the case of isolated speech disorders (Baker and Cantwell 1982). In contrast, socioeconomic status was
not associated with speech problems in studies conducted in Germany
(Fox *et al.* 2002) and in the United Kingdom (Roulstone *et al.* 2009).

Family aggregation and twin studies have confirmed that speech delay
is heritable. These studies invariably find that the participants' performance on measures of articulation (e.g. standardized measures of articulation accuracy in single words, percentage of consonants correct in
conversation), phonological processing (e.g. phonemic awareness) and
phonological memory (e.g. non-word repetition) are highly intercorre-
lated. These studies have found that speech delay and reading disability are jointly linked to regions on certain chromosomes, 6p22, 15p21
and 1p36 (Stein *et al.* 2004; Smith *et al.* 2005; Rice *et al.* 2009b). The candidate genes that have been proposed for these chromosome locations
are involved in neuronal or axonal migration during early maturation
of the central nervous system (for reviews, see Lewis *et al.* 2006; Bishop
2009). Bishop (2009) argues that the most likely explanatory model for
most communication disorders is the 'common disease/common variant'
model, in which many genetic variants combine with environmental factors to produce the full range of speech and language outcomes observed
in the population.

Brain imaging studies of children with DPD have just begun to emerge
in the research literature, and suggest deficits relating to phonological
processing in the perceptual and articulatory domains (Lewis *et al.* 2010;
Preston *et al.* 2010). Clearly, more research is required involving both
speaking and listening tasks and a broader age range of children.

4.5   Cognitive-linguistic and sensory-motor underpinnings

Findings from brain imaging studies are consistent with a large body of
literature which has revealed difficulties with various measures of phonological processing among children with DPD. In a recent review of 20
studies in which the speech perception skills of children with DPD were
compared to the speech perception skills of children with normally developing speech, only one study failed to find an association between speech
perception and speech production skills (Rvachew and Brosseau-Lapré
2012). Speech perception difficulties are directly associated with the children's articulation errors and typically reflect inappropriate cue-weighting

strategies rather than a complete lack of perceptual knowledge of a given phonemic contrast (Rvachew and Jamieson 1995). Usually children with DPD can perceive natural speech stimuli presented live-voice but have difficulty when stimuli are presented under conditions of reduced cue redundancy (e.g. Jan Edwards *et al.* 2002).

Studies that have compared the phonological awareness skills of children with and without DPD have also found significant differences with large effect sizes, both in cases of concomitant speech and language delay and in cases of isolated speech impairment (for reviews, see Preston 2010; Rvachew and Brosseau-Lapré 2012). The children's phonological awareness difficulties are associated with the quality of underlying phonological representations rather than the severity of the speech deficit itself (Rvachew and Grawburg 2006; Anthony *et al.* 2011). These difficulties with phonological awareness enhance the risk of later reading disability especially for children whose speech deficit persists past the age of school entry and for those children who have concomitant language delay or lower non-verbal intelligence (Bird *et al.* 1995; Larrivee and Catts 1999; Nathan *et al.* 2004; Rvachew 2007; Peterson *et al.* 2009). The risk may also be moderated by helpful environmental inputs such as access to high-quality language input, speech therapy and reading instruction. Further research to explain patterns of comorbidity among speech, language and reading disability within a multiple deficit model is required (Pennington 2006).

It is not clear that non-word repetition tests measure phonological working memory in children with speech problems because raw test scores are closely associated with articulation accuracy (for review and discussion, see Rvachew and Grawburg 2008). Non-word repetition skills have been assessed using an alternative strategy that taps underlying phonological knowledge in children with DPD and normally developing speech (Munson *et al.* 2005b). Non-word sequences were manipulated to ensure high- or low-frequency phonotactic probability but sequence length was held constant. Performance for the two types of sequences was compared. As would be expected, absolute accuracy of repetition varied between these groups and was significantly correlated with speech perception and speech production accuracy. However, the difference in repetition accuracy between low- and high-frequency phoneme sequences was not at all correlated with speech perception or articulation accuracy for any group. Furthermore, children with DPD did not show a greater disadvantage when repeating low-frequency sequences than did typically developing children, relative to repetition accuracy for high-frequency sequences. Munson and colleagues concluded that difficulties with abstract phonological knowledge are not the source of the articulation errors that are observed in children with DPD. Rather, these children have difficulties constructing word representations in the more primary phonetic domains. Shriberg *et al.* (2009) developed a repetition task that

makes fewer demands on articulatory skills by including only early developing stops and nasals. Preston (2010) assessed non-word repetition skills
in children with DPD using this test. But even under these circumstances,
articulation accuracy in general and the production of atypical error patterns in particular were significantly correlated with the children's syllable repetition performance.

Some children's speech errors can be traced to difficulties with speech
motor control. Electropalatography (EPG) has revealed that lateral bracing
of the tongue and independent control of the tongue blade is observed at
least by age 6 years in children with normally developing speech (Gibbon
1999). In contrast, EPG indicated the presence of 'undifferentiated lingual
gestures' in 12 of 17 school-aged children with DPD. Undifferentiated lingual gestures (ULGs) are characterized by simultaneous anterior and posterior contact of the tongue across the palate during production of the
lingual phonemes. ULGs can occur on misarticulated phonemes such as
target /k/ produced perceptually as [t] but also on phonemes that sound
perceptually correct such as target /d/ produced perceptually as [d] (Gibbon
and Wood 2002).

Gibbon (1999) argued that the articulatory patterns revealed by EPG
reflect motor constraints in children with DPD for three reasons: first, the
undifferentiated nature of the lingual gesture is a known characteristic
of immature oral motor control; second, the ULG can affect both perceptually inaccurate phonemes such as lateralized sibilants and perceptually accurate sounds such as alveolar obstruents in the same child; and
third, covert contrasts, wherein immature but topographically distinct
gestures are used to produce a phonemic contrast that is imperceptible
to the adult listener, indicate that the child has appropriate underlying
phonological knowledge. Thus far, however, ULGs have been observed in
a small number of children representing a particular subpopulation of
children with DPD (children with a trajectory of long-term normalization
often with atypical speech sound errors).

Another indicator of possible speech motor difficulties in older children
with distortion errors is reduced tongue strength, a finding that occurs
for a small minority of children (Fairbanks and Bebout 1950; Dworkin
1980; Dworkin and Culatta 1980; Robin *et al.* 1991; Murdoch *et al.* 1995;
Goozée *et al.* 2007). Low tongue strength is invariably associated with slow
diadochokinetic rates (DKRs), that is, poor ability to rapidly and repeatedly produce a single syllable. Studies of DKRs in children with DPD are
rare, possibly because DPD implies normal DKR performance by definition. Several researchers have examined alternate motion rates (AMRs)
in bi- or tri-syllable repetition tasks, however, and found that fewer than
5 per cent of children with DPD perform below normal limits on tasks
such as repeating the sequence [patakek] (Dodd and McIntosh 2008).

The contribution of difficulties with oral-sensory feedback has been
investigated in studies involving school-aged children and a variety of

research techniques. Ringel *et al.* (1970) reported the number of errors in oral form discrimination for 167 child and adult research participants with articulation deficits of varying severity. Children made many more errors than adults but errors increased with the severity of the speech deficit in both age groups. Poorer oral-form discrimination performance for children with articulation errors compared to children with normal speech was also reported by Sommers *et al.* (1972), McNutt (1977) and Speirs and Dean (1989), but contrary findings are reported by Lonegan (1974) and by Hetrick and Sommers (1988). Other tasks that have lower cognitive and linguistic load than oral-form discrimination include two-point discrimination on the tongue (McNutt 1977) and vibrotactile thresholds (Fucci 1972; Lonegan 1974), but insufficient research has been conducted and clear conclusions cannot be drawn.

4.6   Subtypes of developmental phonological disorder

Given that a number of cognitive-linguistic and sensorimotor causal-correlates of speech errors have been identified and that not all children with DPD share all of these symptoms, it is generally agreed that children with phonological disorders do not form a unitary population. However, there is no consensus on the criteria by which children might be classified into subtypes and no universally accepted diagnostic scheme.

Dodd (2005) recommends subtype classification on the basis of the consistency of the child's word productions over multiple repetitions and the types of error patterns that are observed in the child's speech. This subtyping scheme is expected to ensure exhaustive classification of children with DPD into four mutually exclusive categories that are developmentally stable and universally applicable regardless of the child's age or language background. An *articulation disorder* manifests itself as the inability to articulate a few specific phones, with distortion errors given as the most common example. *Delayed phonological development* is characterized by error patterns that would be typical of a normally developing but younger child. Examples of the error patterns are typical phonological processes such as velar fronting (*key* → [ti]) or cluster reduction (*blue* → [bu]). A child would be classified with *consistent deviant phonological disorder* if he or she consistently produced atypical phonological error patterns although these will likely co-occur with typical phonological processes. Examples of deviant or atypical error patterns might be consistent deletion of syllable onsets or gliding of fricatives (although we caution that this is specific to English – onset deletion is not deviant in French, for example, so it is essential to use language-specific norms for classification of error patterns). *Inconsistent deviant phonological disorder* is manifested by atypical phonological error patterns and inconsistent productions of words over repeated attempts to produce the same word, using a special word list and standardized test procedure as developed by Dodd.

Studies of English-, German-, Spanish-, and Cantonese-speaking children have found that similar proportions of children can be classified into these four categories in each language group (So and Dodd 1994; Fox and Dodd 2001; Fox *et al.* 2002; Broomfield and Dodd 2004; Dodd 2005), specifically: 10–12% articulation disorder; 50–60% delayed phonological development; 25–30% consistent deviant phonological disorder; and 10% inconsistent deviant phonological disorder. In terms of the validity of this approach to subtyping, it appears that the system can be used to reliably classify children into the four proposed subtypes at a given point in time. No studies have been conducted by Dodd and her colleagues to demonstrate that the categories are stable over time, however. In fact, all published data suggest that the four subtypes reflect the age of the child and the severity of the DPD rather than qualitatively distinct subtypes of phonological disorder (Broomfield and Dodd 2004; Dodd 2005). Furthermore, hypotheses regarding distinct psycholinguistic profiles underlying these subtypes have not been clearly supported (Broomfield and Dodd 2004). Williams and Chiat (1993) compared children with developmental versus deviant error patterns on four tasks tapping output processing and concluded that children with consistent deviant error patterns presented with a qualitatively similar profile to children with developmental phonological errors but with a more severe impairment.

Shriberg and colleagues outlined a three-parameter system for gathering and organizing information about a child (Shriberg 1994; Shriberg *et al.* 1997c). This system permits classification of the child's speech disorder according to a medical model that links observed characteristics of the child's speech to proposed underlying explanatory processes that are in turn linked to putative aetiological factors. The three parameters are: (1) the child's articulation competence, typically derived from a conversational speech sample; (2) the time course of the child's speech delay relative to age norms; and (3) all relevant developmental correlates of the child's speech problem. The *Speech Disorders Classification System* differentiated among the superordinate categories Normal (or normalized) Speech Acquisition, Developmental Phonological Disorders, Nondevelopmental Phonological Disorders, and Speech Differences. The category of Developmental Phonological Disorders encompassed multiple subcategories of residual errors and five subtypes of Speech Delay. Recently, the system has undergone considerable revision (Shriberg *et al.* 2012; personal communication). In addition to the renaming of DPD (now called Speech Sound Disorders), motor speech disorders have been removed from the Speech Delay category so that there are now three major types of developmental speech sound disorder: Speech Delay, Speech Errors and Motor Speech Disorders. Speech Delay is composed of three subtypes: Speech Delay-Genetic, Speech Delay-Otitis Media with Effusion, and Speech

Delay-Psychosocial Involvement. These subtypes in the Speech Delay category are presumed to arise from neurodevelopmental constraints in speech processes that impact upon phonological representations – either auditory-perceptual encoding (transforming speech input into acoustic-phonetic or lexical representations) or memorial processes (storing and retrieving representations). As these speech delay subtypes correspond most closely to developmental phonological disorder as defined in this chapter, they are discussed further. Motor speech disorders are covered in Chapters 2 and 3 of this volume.

The largest subcategory of Speech Delay is hypothesized to be heritable and of genetic origin (Shriberg *et al.* 2005). The authors proposed that the tendency towards omission errors in this subgroup – this occurs in at least 50 per cent of all children with DPD – may reflect an absence of phonological knowledge of the omitted phonemes. Their findings are consistent with the literature reviewed above which reveals heritability of DPD, frequent difficulties with speech perception and phonological processing in this population, and comorbidity of DPD and reading disability. Furthermore, children with DPD who have difficulties with phonological processing produce more omission errors (i.e. syllable structure errors) and atypical errors than children with DPD who do not have difficulties with phonological processing (Rvachew *et al.* 2007; Preston and Edwards 2010). Overall, support for this subtype is very strong at all levels of description in the scientific literature.

Shriberg (1994) observed that about a third of children with speech delay have histories of recurrent otitis media with effusion (OME) before the age of 3 years. This is a possible correlate of speech delay that may or may not overlap with family history. The findings on the impact of OME on speech and language outcomes are mixed (for review, see J.E. Roberts *et al.* 2004). This is most likely because the effects of OME interact with both environmental (Vernon-Feagans 1999; Yont *et al.* 2003) and genetic (McGrath *et al.* 2007) variables. Overall, the conclusion that OME interacts with auditory, cognitive, attentional and linguistic factors to produce mild delays in language skills as well as diffuse effects on speech intelligibility appears to be sound (Bennett and Haggard 1999; Shriberg *et al.* 2000).

The third aetiological subtype proposed in the Speech Delay category is associated with psychosocial issues. Hauner *et al.* (2005) proposed that genetic factors that determine temperament explain co-occurring negative affect and speech deficits in approximately 11 per cent of children with DPD. As reviewed above, speech and/or language deficits do place children at risk for concomitant or subsequent psychosocial illness, but direction of causality is difficult to determine. Zadeh *et al.* (2007), on the basis of linear structural equation modelling, and Beitchman *et al.* (1996), on the basis of longitudinal follow-up data, suggested that communication difficulties predispose the child to develop maladaptive coping strategies in social situations and thus psychosocial correlates may be an outcome of the speech deficit itself.

4.7   Intervention: approaches and efficacy

A recent meta-analysis of randomized trials of speech therapy for children with speech and language impairment concluded that there is evidence to support the efficacy of interventions for the treatment of expressive phonology deficits (Law *et al.* 2003). The review does not provide clear guidance about the clinical conditions under which a given approach to therapy is likely to be optimally effective. Behaviourist approaches that focus solely on the articulatory aspects of the child's speech deficit can be effective, but are likely to be inefficient and will require special effort to ensure transfer of training between word positions and from the clinic to the non-clinic environment (Mowrer 1971; Koegel *et al.* 1986; Forrest *et al.* 2000). Phonological approaches to intervention are designed to target patterns of error or underlying rules in the child's phonological system and use treatment procedures that highlight the contrast between phonological units that are present or absent in the child's system and/ or enhance the child's metaphonological knowledge (Hodson and Paden 1983; Dean and Howell 1986; Gierut 1998; Barlow and Gierut 2002; Hodson 2007). Phonological approaches have been shown to be effective and in some studies more efficient than approaches that focus on the articulatory aspects of sound production, with the *cycles approach* in particular being validated in a randomized control trial (Montgomery and Bonderman 1989; Klein 1996; Almost and Rosenbaum 1998; Pamplona *et al.* 1999; Bernhardt and Major 2005; Hesketh *et al.* 2007a).

Speech production outcomes are enhanced by the addition of computer-based speech perception training to ensure good quality acoustic-phonetic representations for the target phoneme (Wolfe *et al.* 2003; Rvachew *et al.* 2004). Live-voice 'ear training' procedures, when provided in isolation from speech production therapy, impact reading but not speech accuracy (Sommers *et al.* 1961, 1962; Shelton *et al.* 1978). Focused stimulation is another effective means for enhancing children's acoustic-phonetic representations for words, grammatical structures and phonological units (Fey *et al.* 2003). The procedures include providing the child with many exposures to a specific target form and recasting the child's production attempts if and when they occur. Tyler *et al.* (2003) demonstrated that this approach is effective when phonological and morphosyntactic goals are targeted separately in different sessions using an alternating goal attack strategy. Crosbie *et al.* (2005) suggested that treatment effectiveness is determined by the characteristics of the child and presented evidence to support implementing phonological approaches with children in the phonological delay subtype and the core vocabulary approach when children have inconsistent phonological disorder. Core vocabulary is a treatment procedure intended to improve phonological planning abilities by encouraging consistent production of specific words.

Very few studies have directly addressed optimum service delivery models in speech therapy, although it is clear that cumulative intervention intensity (Warren *et al.* 2007) is an important determinant of treatment outcomes. Non-experimental studies suggest that a minimum of 12 to 20 hours of service are required in order to achieve an observable functional improvement in speech production ability (Jacoby *et al.* 2002; Schooling 2003). Given the same number of sessions, it is possible that more frequent sessions over a shorter block may be more effective than less frequent sessions scheduled over a longer treatment interval, but research in the phonology domain is limited (Barratt *et al.* 1992; Allen 2009). Several studies have shown that parents are effective as adjuncts to or replacements for therapy provided by the speech-language pathologist. However, in these studies the parents received structured and closely monitored training in the application of the home programme and the time requirement for parent-administered intervention was not less than that required for the programme provided by the speech-language pathologist alone (Sommers 1962; Sommers *et al.* 1964; Eiserman *et al.* 1992, 1995). Therefore, the benefits of home programming are in the opportunity to increase treatment intensity and parent satisfaction. Similarly, group therapy can be as effective as individual therapy (Sommers *et al.* 1966), but only when session length is increased or other steps are taken to ensure that the effective dose of intervention per child is maintained in the group as compared to the individual therapy condition. The probable advantage of group therapy is in the social interaction between peers and the opportunity to enhance extra-clinic transfer of training.

Modern approaches to speech therapy properly incorporate scientific perspectives on the nature of DPD. New treatment approaches mentioned above target linguistic units beyond the segment, employ procedures to strengthen the child's knowledge at multiple levels of representation, and recognize comorbidity of DPD with language and literacy impairments. However, randomized controlled trials to date have been too small and too few to determine the essential procedures in any given treatment package, compare the relative efficiency of one approach with another, determine the optimum 'dose' of therapy, or identify the most effective match between therapy approach and child characteristics. More attention to these clinical questions in future research would provide a means for children with DPD and their families to benefit from the exciting developments in basic science that have occurred during the past two decades.

5

Specific language impairment

Susan Ellis Weismer

5.1 Terminology and classification

The term 'specific language impairment' (SLI) is used to refer to a type of developmental language disorder associated with no known sensory, neurological, intellectual or emotional deficits (Bishop 1997; Leonard 1998). Children with SLI form a heterogeneous group in terms of their linguistic profiles. Receptive and expressive language abilities can be affected in various domains of language, including phonology, morphology, syntax, semantics and pragmatics. Receptive language is relatively stronger than expressive language in most children with SLI, though this can vary across individual children.

Historically, a number of taxonomies have been proposed to delineate subgroups of children with SLI. Subgroup distinctions based on language modality (i.e. receptive versus expressive language) were identified in the Diagnostic and Statistical Manual of Mental Disorders (DSM-IV; American Psychiatric Association 1994). However, Leonard (2009a) has argued persuasively against the construct of purely expressive language impairment (other than in segmental phonology and prosody) on both theoretical and empirical grounds. The proposed DSM-5 classification of 'language disorders' does not include this distinction (American Psychiatric Association 2013).

Taxonomies focused on language domains that have been used most recently for research and clinical purposes include Grammatical-SLI (G-SLI) and Pragmatic Language Impairment (PLI). The G-SLI subgroup has been the focus of studies by van der Lely and colleagues (Gallon *et al.* 2007; van der Lely and Marshall 2011). This subgroup is defined on the basis of deficits in syntax, morphology and phonology. Children whose primary deficits involve pragmatic aspects of language and communication rather than structural language have been referred to as having PLI (Botting and

Conti-Ramsden 1999; Bishop and Norbury 2002). The proposed DSM-5 category of communication disorders includes a classification of 'social communication disorder' which is equivalent to PLI. Children classified as having PLI can be viewed as overlapping with typical SLI to some extent, but also as falling between SLI and autism classifications.

Conti-Ramsden and Botting (2004) noted that a shift has occurred over time in the boundary between SLI and pervasive developmental disorder in the UK. This issue of the overlap between language features observed in autism spectrum disorders (ASDs) and SLI will be considered briefly below (also see Chapter 9, this volume). In this chapter, children who have structural language deficits, with or without associated pragmatic impairments or phonological disorder, will be considered under the general category of SLI.

5.2   Epidemiology of SLI

SLI is a relatively common disorder that is typically identified during the preschool period. An epidemiological investigation conducted by Tomblin *et al.* (1997) in the USA established the estimated prevalence of SLI at 5 years of age to be approximately 7%. According to this study, the prevalence estimate for boys was 8% whereas the prevalence for girls was 6%. This resulted in a prevalence ratio of 1.33 boys to every 1 girl. These prevalence figures were derived from a definition of SLI in which children performed 1.25 standard deviations or more below the mean for their chronological age on at least two of five language composite scores (based on a model involving three language domains (i.e. vocabulary, grammar, narration) and two modalities (i.e. receptive and expressive language)). Clearly, the criteria and particular thresholds used to define the disorder affect the estimated prevalence rate (see Hannus *et al.* 2009; Bishop 2010a). An investigation of the prevalence of SLI in Finland was conducted through a retrospective analysis of all primary healthcare records of speech and language therapists from 1989 to 1999 (Hannus *et al.* 2009). Findings from this study indicated that the prevalence of SLI in Finland was less than 1%, with a 3.14:1 ratio of boys to girls. Clearly, these substantial differences in overall prevalence estimates and sex ratios across studies point to a need for more standardized diagnostic criteria and methods of ascertaining prevalence before international comparisons can be made.

In terms of developmental course, the vast majority of children with SLI have late onset of early language development. That is, most children who are subsequently diagnosed with SLI were previously late talkers who were delayed in vocabulary development and production of early word combinations. However, it is important to note that the relatively low percentage of late talkers who continue to display language delay by

5 years of age cannot account for the prevalence of SLI at that age (Ellis Weismer 2007; Leonard 2009a). Various investigations of continuity and discontinuity of early language delay, including large-scale population samples from several different countries, have indicated that there is a small percentage of children who do not display initial delay in language development (ranging from 18 to 24 months depending on the study), but who nevertheless have delayed language skills at a later point in development (30 to 48 months) (Dale *et al.* 2003; Westerlund *et al.* 2006; Henrichs *et al.* 2011; Bishop *et al.* 2012). It could be argued that this finding can be explained by the application of discrete categories to a continuous phenomenon (Dale *et al.* 2003) or that the extent of variation in language development before 2 years of age is so great that the validity of the initial identification of language delay at this point in development is suspect. Alternatively, it is certainly possible that some children who display typical early vocabulary development actually encounter difficulties in aspects of later language learning, as in the case of late emerging reading disability (see Catts *et al.* 2012).

5.3   Theories of causality

Although the cause of SLI is currently not known, theoretical perspectives regarding causality can be broadly divided into those that view SLI as a grammar-specific deficit and those that assume some kind of underlying cognitive processing deficit. With respect to the grammatical deficit views, the earlier proposals of 'feature blindness' (Gopnik 1990) or inability to learn implicit grammatical rules (Gopnik and Crago 1991) have largely been discounted. Two contemporary grammar-specific theories of SLI are those proposed by Rice and colleagues and van der Lely and colleagues. According to the extended optional infinitive (EOI) account (Rice and Wexler 1996a, 1996b; Rice *et al.* 1998), children with SLI go through an extended period of optional infinitive usage (which is also seen in typical development but is less protracted). During this time, children with SLI do not realize that tense marking is obligatory, so they express tense inconsistently or use a non-finite form instead.

An elaboration of the EOI account, referred to as the extended unique checking constraint, has been proposed by Wexler (2003) in an attempt to account for the fact that certain languages pose fewer morphological difficulties than English for children with SLI (see Kunnari *et al.* 2011). Children with SLI are assumed to display extended use of the unique checking constraint in which they can only check one feature (tense or agreement) at a time. This plays out differently across various languages depending on the relationship between tense and agreement marking.

Another grammatical deficit account of SLI espoused by van der Lely and colleagues is referred to as the computational grammatical complexity

(CGC) hypothesis (van der Lely 2005), which stems from the prior representational deficit for dependent relationships hypothesis (van der Lely 1998). The CGC account claims that there is a subgroup of SLI children, those with Grammatical-SLI, who have core impairments in syntax and morphology as well as often having deficits in phonology. According to the CGC hypothesis, it is only computation of hierarchically complex features of syntactic dependencies, morphological and phonological forms that are affected in SLI (van der Lely and Marshall 2011).

The processing deficit accounts of SLI include claims concerning difficulties with processing rapid auditory stimuli (e.g. Tallal and Gaab 2006), phonological short-term memory (e.g. Gathercole and Baddeley 1990), speed of processing (e.g. Kail and Salthouse 1994; Leonard *et al.* 2007), working memory and executive function (Ellis Weismer *et al.* 1999; Montgomery 2000; Im-Bolter *et al.* 2006; Marton 2008; Montgomery and Evans 2009), procedural memory (Ullman and Pierpont 2005; Lum *et al.* 2010) and implicit learning (Tomblin *et al.* 2007; Evans *et al.* 2009). These processing accounts vary with regard to the specificity of the mechanism assumed to underlie language impairment (e.g. phonological short-term memory versus generalized speed of processing), as well as the extent to which only language-specific deficits would be expected rather than broader deficits encompassing linguistic as well as certain aspects of non-linguistic abilities.

Reviews of processing accounts of SLI have been provided by Ellis Weismer and Elin Thordardottir (2002), Montgomery *et al.* (2010) and Snowling and Hayiou-Thomas (2010). Two processing accounts have been proposed by Leonard and colleagues to address specifically problems children with SLI have with grammatical morphology – the surface hypothesis (Leonard 1998) and the morphological richness account (Leonard 1998; Kunnari *et al.* 2011). The first account focuses on speed of processing limitations relative to spoken grammatical morphemes that are brief in duration. The second account emphasizes processing capacity limitations relative to the richness of the grammatical system inherent to the particular language that the child with SLI is learning. This account offers an explanation for different cross-linguistic patterns in SLI.

As noted by several investigators, none of the single-deficit accounts are entirely compelling or able to account for the heterogeneous nature of SLI. Accordingly, it is argued that multiple-deficit models of SLI are more likely to explain the disorder (Bishop 2006a; Ellis Weismer and Edwards 2006; Snowling and Hayiou-Thomas 2010). As a case in point, Hayiou-Thomas *et al.* (2004) induced SLI-like performance in typical talkers through manipulation of different processing demands (speed or memory). This study demonstrated that the particular linguistic profile of English-speaking children with SLI could be simulated in typically developing children by introducing cognitive stress factors into a grammaticality judgement task. Conditions simulating either reduced speed of processing or reduced memory capacity produced a pattern involving good performance on noun morphology and poor performance on verb morphology. Furthermore, Bishop *et al.* (2006) reported heritable components for both non-word repetition (phonological memory) and grammatical morphology, but these stemmed from distinct genetic effects (also see Falcaro *et al.* 2008). In sum, an interactive, multiple-deficit account of SLI appears most likely, such that there are various paths that can lead to language impairment.

5.4 Linguistic characteristics

5.4.1 Phonology

As noted above, children with SLI present differing clinical profiles with respect to their language deficits. One aspect of linguistic development that can be problematic for children with SLI is phonology. A distinction is usually made between SLI and phonological disorder. Children with phonological disorder, also referred to as speech sound disorder (SSD; Shriberg 2003), have developmental speech production errors that negatively affect intelligibility. There is some degree of overlap during the preschool and early school-age period between SLI and speech sound disorder. Findings from a large, population-based sample indicated that at 6 years of age approximately 5–8 per cent of children with SLI had SSD (Shriberg *et al.* 1999), with studies of younger, clinically referred children yielding much higher comorbidity estimates (e.g. Bishop and Edmundson 1987).

Independent of SSD, various investigations have reported that children with SLI demonstrate deficits in phonological representation and processing that impact on word learning (Gray *et al.* 2012) and grammatical morphology (Marshall and van der Lely 2007). Children with SLI also have difficulties with phonological awareness skills that are critical for literacy (Catts *et al.* 2002). Furthermore, studies have consistently found that, as a group, children with SLI exhibit deficits in non-word repetition abilities (Gathercole and Baddeley 1990; Dollaghan and Campbell 1998; Edwards and Lahey 1998; Ellis Weismer *et al.* 2000; Archibald and Gathercole 2007; Jones *et al.* 2010).

There is considerable debate about the mechanisms underlying difficulties with non-word repetition, with some researchers emphasizing phonological encoding/processing deficits and others focusing on maintenance and storage of phonological representations. The fact that several studies indicate a particular problem with multisyllabic non-words has been viewed by some as support for the role of phonological short-term memory limitations (e.g. Gathercole 2006). Alternatively, van der Lely and Marshall (2011) have argued that difficulties which children with SLI demonstrate are related to the arrangement of material in the prosodic hierarchy (i.e. the complexity of phonological structure) rather than the number of syllables per se (Gallon *et al.* 2007). Whatever the explanation(s) for non-word repetition deficits, the widespread difficulties observed for children with SLI as well as unaffected family members have led to the postulation that deficits in non-word repetition constitute a clinical marker of SLI (Bishop *et al.* 1996; Tager-Flusberg and Cooper 1999). As discussed below, non-word repetition phonological deficits have been used as a phenotype in genetic studies of SLI and examined with respect to possible links between SLI and other developmental language disorders such as dyslexia and autism.

5.4.2   Grammatical morphology

Deficits in verb morphology have been identified as a hallmark of English-speaking children with SLI (see review by Leonard 1998). Difficulties with grammatical morphology are evident in spontaneous language samples and elicited contexts. Findings have shown that children with SLI produce fewer grammatical morphemes in obligatory contexts compared to controls matched for age and mean length of utterance (MLU) (Rice and Wexler 1996b; Leonard *et al.* 2007). Bedore and Leonard (1998) analysed language samples from preschool children with SLI in terms of grammatical morphology. Using discriminant function analysis, they found that a finite verb morpheme composite (regular past tense–ed, regular third person singular –s, copula/auxiliary BE forms) could accurately classify children with and without language impairment with 84 per cent sensitivity and 100 per cent specificity. Conversely, spontaneous use of verb morphology was not found to adequately discriminate between *school-age* children with and without SLI (Moyle *et al.* 2011).

Under complex sentence processing conditions, adolescents with SLI have been shown to have persistent problems with past tense morphology (Leonard *et al.* 2009). Rice and colleagues have found that children with SLI between 6 and 15 years of age exhibit delays in finiteness marking based on grammatical judgements of BE copula/auxiliary and DO auxiliary in wh- and yes/no questions (Rice *et al.* 2009a). Numerous studies have focused on problems with finite verb morphology (tense and agreement) based on the predictions of the extended optional infinitive (EOI) hypothesis (Rice and Wexler 1996a, 1996b; Rice *et al.* 1998). Other investigators have explained morphological problems with tense in terms of the computational grammatical complexity (CGC) hypothesis (Marshall and van der Lely 2007).

5.4.3   Complex syntax

There is evidence that grammatical deficits in SLI extend beyond morphology to include difficulties with the comprehension and production of complex syntax. Various studies have found that school-age children with SLI display decreased proficiency in comprehending complex sentences such as verbal *be* passives (e.g. 'The man is eaten by the fish') and pronominal sentences (e.g. 'Bill said Joe hit him/himself') compared to age mates, despite having comparable comprehension of simple sentences (Bishop *et al.* 2000a; Norbury *et al.* 2002; van der Lely 1998, 2005; Montgomery and Evans 2009). Children with SLI also have difficulty comprehending sentences with centre-embedded relative clauses (e.g. 'The girl who is smiling is pushing the boy') (Montgomery 1995, 2000, 2004). SLI children's difficulties in sentence comprehension have been explained in terms of the CGC hypothesis by van der Lely and colleagues. These authors posit a specific grammatical deficit involved in computing syntactic dependencies between different sentence elements (van der Lely 2005; Marinis and van der Lely 2007; van der Lely and Marshall 2011). Other researchers have appealed to a processing limitation account, examining the role of memory and/or attention in complex sentence comprehension (Bishop *et al.* 2000a; Norbury *et al.* 2002; Montgomery and Evans 2009).

Various studies have investigated grammatical aspects of sentence production in SLI. In terms of argument structure, children with SLI have been shown to be more likely to omit obligatory subject arguments (e.g. '[The pig] is giving the cup to the mouse') than typically developing controls (Grela 2003) and to use less diverse argument structure (Elin Thordardottir and Ellis Weismer 2002). There is evidence from longitudinal spontaneous language samples in a case study of a child with SLI which indicates production errors in complex syntax during the school-age period involving omission of obligatory relative markers, complementizers, infinitival *to*, and wh- pronouns in wh- clausal complements (Schuele and Dykes 2005). Using elicitation tasks, Owen and Leonard (2006) found that 5- to 8-year-old children with SLI were significantly less proficient than age- and vocabulary-matched controls in producing both finite and non-finite complement clauses (e.g. 'Big Bird knew Elmo fed the dog' (finite) or 'Big Bird knew to feed the dog' (non-finite)). Using elicitation procedures with this same age range of children with SLI, Owen (2010) found that increased syntactic complexity (sentence type and clause order) resulted in decreased use of tense morphology for all groups. Compared to age-matched controls, children with SLI displayed less accuracy, but similar profiles, in their productions.

5.4.4   Lexical semantics

While grammatical deficits are a defining feature of SLI, other aspects of language can also be problematic for these children. Research has documented lexical-semantic deficits of various types. Evidence of deficits in this language domain comes from standardized assessment measures as well as experimental language processing tasks. Delays in early word acquisition are often observed in children who are later diagnosed with SLI (Rice *et al.* 2008). Children with SLI have been reported to have reduced receptive and expressive vocabularies relative to age-level expectations (Gray *et al.* 1999), and a subset of these children have word-finding deficits (Dockrell *et al.* 1998; German 2000). Word-finding difficulties can be characterized not only by a gap between receptive and expressive language abilities, but also by the use of empty words such as 'stuff' or 'thing', filled and unfilled pauses, sentence reformulations or other behaviours to compensate for the inability to retrieve the desired word (Messer and Dockrell 2006). Research suggests that word-finding difficulties cannot just be conceived as retrieval deficits but that children with SLI who display word-finding difficulties also have impoverished semantic representations and deficits in lexical-semantic organization (McGregor and Apel 2002; Dockrell *et al.* 2003; Sheng and McGregor 2010).

In addition to characterizing extant lexical-semantic abilities in children with SLI, numerous studies have examined word learning capabilities using both novel word (nonce) stimuli and unfamiliar real words. These investigations have focused on fast mapping or the initial phase of word learning (Dollaghan 1987; Rice *et al.* 1990, 1994; Ellis Weismer and Hesketh 1996; Alt and Plante 2006) as well as extended word learning within didactic contexts (Gray 2003, 2005, 2006; Nash and Donaldson 2005). The bulk of the evidence from the fast mapping/incidental word learning studies indicates that children with SLI are poorer than age-matched controls, and in some cases language-matched controls, in comprehending and/or producing newly acquired words. Rice *et al.* (1994) found that children with SLI comprehended significantly fewer unfamiliar words than normal language peers within an incidental learning paradigm after 3 exposures but were able to perform comparably after 10 exposures. This result was interpreted to suggest that additional exposures are necessary in order for children with SLI to establish a stable lexical representation. However, Nash and Donaldson (2005) reported that children with SLI were significantly worse than age-matched controls at learning new words even after 12 exposures as indexed by production responses as well as comprehension and recognition.

Incidental word learning appears more difficult in SLI than explicit instructional contexts. Studies by Gray (2003, 2005, 2006) have produced mixed results regarding explicit, extended word learning abilities of children with SLI. Nash and Donaldson (2005) directly compared both contexts and found that children with SLI exhibited deficits in incidental and explicit learning contexts. This finding implicated phonological deficits as well as semantic difficulties with inferring the meaning of novel words in the word learning problems of children with SLI.

5.4.5 Pragmatics

The extent to which children with SLI are deemed to have pragmatic deficits depends in large part on the criteria used to define SLI and on the theoretical approach to pragmatics that is adopted. A thought-provoking discussion of these issues has been provided by Fujiki and Brinton (2009), who make distinctions between the traditional formalist view of pragmatics, functionalist views of pragmatics, and the role of pragmatics within the broader construct of social communication. According to the traditional view, pragmatics is seen as one of several equal components of language (i.e. form, meaning and use). On this view, pragmatic impairment is conceptualized as difficulties that cannot be attributed to core structural language impairments in grammar, phonology or vocabulary.

Taxonomies have been proposed identifying a subset of children, referred to as having pragmatic language impairment (PLI), who primarily have problems with language use rather than form (see discussions by Bishop *et al.* 2000b; Fujiki and Brinton 2009). Characteristics of children with PLI include problems with discourse comprehension, difficulties with topic maintenance, overly literal interpretation of language, lack of semantic specificity and insensitivity to the needs of conversational partners (Conti-Ramsden and Botting 1999; Bishop 2000). There has been considerable discussion within the literature regarding the extent to which this classification overlaps with a diagnosis of autism spectrum disorder. It has been demonstrated that children with pragmatic difficulties, who do not meet criteria for autistic disorder per se, do exist (Bishop and Norbury 2002).

In addition to the proposed clinical taxonomy, there is experimental evidence that some children with language impairment have pragmatic difficulties in topic manipulation (Brinton *et al.* 1997) and conversational responsiveness (Bishop *et al.* 2000b) that extend beyond their structural language deficits. Employing a functionalist view of pragmatics in which the role of syntax and semantics is conceptualized more holistically in terms of the contribution to successful communication of messages, there is evidence that children with language impairment have pragmatic problems associated with structural deficits. Children with SLI/PLI perform more poorly than age-matched peers, but not language-matched controls, on mental state predicates/verbs (Johnston *et al.* 2001; Van Horne and Lin 2011), aspects of narration (Pearce *et al.* 2010), and inference construction in story comprehension contexts (Bishop and Adams 1992; Adams *et al.* 2009; Karasinski and Ellis Weismer 2010). When viewed even more broadly in terms of social communication deficits (Adams 2005), some children with SLI appear to have problems with social interactions (as discussed below) as well as with social cognition and social competence (Farmer 2000; Miller 2004).

5.5   Genetic influences in SLI

There has been considerable interest in examining genetic influences in SLI. Findings from this research indicate that that there is a strong genetic component in SLI (Bishop 2006a, 2008; Tomblin 2009; Snowling and Hayiou-Thomas 2010). Evidence from behavioural genetic studies includes investigations of familial aggregation and twin studies. As reviewed by Tomblin (2009), there is considerable evidence for familial aggregation in SLI based on use of the family history method as well as direct testing. In fact, having SLI in the family increases the risk for SLI in first-degree relatives by three to four fold (Tomblin 1996; Tallal *et al.* 2001).

Even more convincing evidence regarding genetic influences in SLI comes from twin studies, which allow investigators to estimate separately genetic effects versus environmental effects. Typically, twin studies have shown that the concordance rates for SLI in school-age children are higher in monozygotic (identical) twin pairs than in dizygotic (non-identical) twins (Lewis and Thompson 1992; Bishop *et al.* 1995; Tomblin and Buckwalter 1998). However, investigation of a large, population-based sample of 4-year-old twins in the Twins Early Development Study in the UK indicated that language impairment in the absence of speech problems primarily had an environmental aetiology (Hayiou-Thomas *et al.* 2005), whereas language impairment with additional speech difficulties that warranted clinical services was found to be highly heritable (Bishop and Hayiou-Thomas 2008). Higher heritability has also been reported when the SLI phenotype does not entail a discrepancy between language level and performance IQ than when such a discrepancy is used in defining SLI (Bishop *et al.* 1995; Hayiou-Thomas *et al.* 2005).

Molecular genetic studies directly measure the genotypes of large samples of individuals with language impairment and have attempted to identify the particular genes involved in SLI. Early molecular genetic research identified the *FOXP2* mutation in a three-generation family (known as 'KE') that was consistent with a single-gene autosomal pattern. This mutation resulted in non-specific speech and language impairment (Gopnik 1990; Gopnik and Crago 1991; Fisher *et al.* 1998). While this was an exciting breakthrough, subsequent studies have found no mutation of the *FOXP2* gene in large samples of children with SLI (Meaburn *et al.* 2002; O'Brien *et al.* 2003), indicating that *FOXP2* mutation is not a common cause of language impairment. There is, however, some research that suggests *FOXP2* regulates the expression of a different candidate gene, *CNTNAP2*, which may be implicated in prototypical SLI (Vernes *et al.* 2008).

Overall, current evidence has led to the conclusion that there is not likely to be a single language gene associated with SLI (Bishop 2006a, 2010b; Snowling and Hayiou-Thomas 2010). Linkage studies of SLI provide support for localization to candidate regions on chromosomes 16 and 19 as well as chromosomes 13 and 3, depending upon the phenotype to which they are linked (SLI Consortium 2002, 2004; Snowling and Hayiou-Thomas 2010). Thus, SLI appears to be a complex, multifactorial disorder that involves multiple genes operating in concert with various environmental factors (Bishop 2008, 2010b).

5.6   Relation of SLI to other developmental language disorders

Researchers have debated the extent to which SLI overlaps with other developmental disorders such as reading disorders and autism. They have questioned whether the apparent phenotypic similarities between these disorders reflect aetiological commonalities (Catts *et al.* 2005; Williams *et al.* 2008; Bishop 2008). Children with SLI are at increased risk of having reading difficulties relative to children without spoken language impairment. Early research focused on the overlap in phonological awareness problems observed in SLI and reading disabilities (Catts and Kamhi 1986), with subsequent studies exploring behavioural, neurological and genetic evidence of continuities across these developmental disorders (see Bishop and Snowling 2004). Based on their review of the literature, Bishop and Snowling (2004) proposed a two-dimensional model of the relationship between SLI and reading disorders, involving the presence or absence of deficits in phonological skills and non-phonological language skills (semantics and syntax). They argued that children with phonological processing deficits will have problems with reading decoding, whereas those with broader, non-phonological deficits will have oral language problems and reading comprehension difficulties.

Catts and colleagues examined the profiles of spoken language impairment and reading disabilities in a population-based, longitudinal sample of 2nd, 4th and 8th grade children (Catts *et al.* 2005, 2006). As predicted by the simple view of reading (Hoover and Gough 1990) and the phonological deficit hypothesis (Stanovich 2000), children with specific reading decoding deficits performed poorly on phonological processing measures but not on measures of spoken language comprehension, while 'poor comprehenders' showed the opposite profile (Catts *et al.* 2006). Findings from the Catts *et al.* (2005) investigation revealed a statistically significant, but modest, overlap between SLI and dyslexia in a representative sample of 527 children. Additional results indicated that phonological processing deficits were associated with dyslexia but not with SLI in the absence of dyslexia. Based on these findings, Catts *et al.* concluded that SLI and dyslexia are comorbid but distinct developmental language disorders. Recent genetic research has reported results consistent with the notion of a multiple gene model of comorbidity between language impairment and reading disability (Rice *et al.* 2009b).

SLI and autism have historically been viewed as distinct developmental language disorders. However, more recently research has begun to focus on similarities in particular aspects of these disorders. Investigations have reported certain overlapping language deficits (Kjelgaard and Tager-Flusberg 2001; Bishop and Norbury 2002; Geurts and Embrechts 2008), as well as similar patterns of cross-domain (i.e. lexical-syntactic) associations for children with SLI and ASD (McGregor et al. 2012). Imaging studies have identified neuroanatomical markers common to grade-school boys with SLI and grade-school boys with ASD who have language impairment with respect to symmetry reversal in the language association cortex (De Fossé et al. 2004) and enlargement of radiate white matter (corona radiata) (Herbert et al. 2004). Results from behavioural genetic studies have demonstrated an increased risk of ASD to siblings of children with SLI (Tomblin et al. 2003) and an increased risk of SLI to siblings of children with ASD (Folstein and Mankoski 2000). Further, quantitative genetics findings have suggested a locus of susceptibility common to ASD and SLI (Warburton et al. 2000; O'Brien et al. 2003).

At one point, Bishop (2003a) proposed the 'autism as SLI plus' hypothesis to explain the relationship between these disorders. However, as this debate has unfolded, Bishop and other researchers questioned whether the apparent language similarities between SLI and autism actually reflect a common aetiology (Bishop 2008; Williams et al. 2008). For instance, while children with SLI and autism both exhibit deficits in non-word repetition, there is evidence from genetic studies that these deficits are not familial in autism, unlike in SLI (Bishop et al. 2004; Whitehouse et al. 2007).

In a recent consideration of aetiological models of SLI and ASD, Bishop (2010b) rejected a 'phenomimicry' account which claims that similarities in these clinical phenotypes are superficial in nature and actually have different underlying causes. She argued instead that a simulated model that postulates overlapping aetiology for SLI and ASD through the incorporation of gene–gene interaction best accounts for the available evidence regarding data from family studies and molecular genetic research. This simulated model involves a modification of the 'correlated additive risks' (CAR) model which incorporates epistatic interactions (whereby the effects of one gene are modified by one or several other genes). Tomblin (2011) has provided a thought-provoking discussion of the potential relationship between SLI and ASD based on language data, brain imaging findings and genetic research. He contends that partial aetiological overlap seems likely. However, he points out the complexities inherent in this debate, including the heterogeneous nature of both SLI and ASD, the fact that features of SLI also occur in other neurodevelopmental disorders, and that our clinical classification schemes necessarily influence the features of the conditions under investigation.

5.7   Academic and social outcomes

While SLI is defined with respect to spoken language difficulties, it also has long-lasting effects on other areas of development such as academic performance (Botting *et al.* 2006; Catts *et al.* 2008, 2012; Conti-Ramsden *et al.* 2009; Durkin *et al.* 2009). There is considerable evidence that pre-schoolers with SLI are at increased risk for academic failure related to low literacy skills. This is not surprising given that spoken language abilities are foundational for reading (NICHD Early Child Care Research Network 2005) and that reading achievement is central to learning and academic success. Evidence for poor literacy and educational outcomes in children with a history of SLI comes from research conducted with clinically iden-tified samples as well as population-based samples from several different countries, using prospective longitudinal or follow-up designs.

Reading achievement at 8 years and at 15–16 years has been investi-gated for a cohort of speech-language impaired (S-LI) children originally studied by Bishop and Edmundson (1987) in the UK (Bishop and Adams 1990; Stothard *et al.* 1998; Snowling *et al.* 2000). Adolescent outcomes for this sample revealed that a subset of the S-LI children whose language delays had persisted beyond 5½ years performed significantly lower on literacy measures than the subgroup whose spoken language difficulties had resolved by that age. However, even the resolved S-LI group scored significantly worse on phonological processing and literacy tests than age-matched normal language controls (Stothard *et al.* 1998). At 15 years of age, the S-LI group as a whole performed more poorly than age-matched controls on tests of basic reading decoding, spelling and reading compre-hension, demonstrating worse reading accuracy during adolescence rela-tive to age expectations than at 8 years of age (Snowling *et al.* 2000).

Similar follow-up investigations of literacy skills were conducted for 11-year-old children with a history of SLI who had participated in the Manchester Language Study. Findings indicated that even when IQ, age and early reading accuracy were taken into account, spoken language abil-ities at 7 years were a significant predictor of reading abilities at 11 years (Botting *et al.* 2006). They also revealed that children with expressive-only language impairment outperformed those with combined receptive-expressive deficits on single word reading and reading comprehension (Simkin and Conti-Ramsden 2006).

Investigations based on a large-scale epidemiological investigation of SLI in the USA – Tomblin's Child Language Research Study – have under-scored the risks that early spoken language deficits pose for reading achievement. Approximately 50 per cent of 8-year-old (second grade) and 10-year-old (fourth grade) children in the language impairment group were classified as having a reading disability compared to 8 per cent in the normal-language control group. Furthermore, those children whose language abilities had improved at follow-up demonstrated significantly better reading abilities than children with persistent language impairment (Catts *et al.* 2002). Examination of reading achievement growth trajectories assessed at 8, 10, 14, and 16 years revealed that the children with language impairment had lower reading skills at 8 years of age and that they did not catch up with their peers (Catts *et al.* 2008). Unlike the findings reported by Snowling *et al.* (2000), there was no evidence that the children with language impairment were falling further behind over the course of development (i.e. the slopes of the growth trajectories for the two groups were similar). Using latent transition analysis to model changes in reading classification for this same sample, it was determined that 13 per cent of children could be identified as 'late-emerging' poor readers. These late-emerging poor readers (the majority of whom had problems in reading comprehension) often had a history of language impairment or low non-verbal cognitive abilities (Catts *et al.* 2012).

Educational attainment has consistently been shown to be poorer for adolescents with a history of early language impairment than for those with typical language development (Conti-Ramsden *et al.* 2009; Durkin *et al.* 2009). Young adult educational and occupational outcomes have similarly been reported to be relatively negative for individuals with a history of language impairment (Clegg *et al.* 2005; C.J. Johnson *et al.* 2010). Several studies have examined educational and occupational outcomes based on participants in the Ottawa Language Study, a 20-year longitudinal investigation consisting of a community sample of individuals in Canada with and without a history of speech and/or language impairment at age five years. At 25 years of age, those individuals who had a history of language impairment were found to have poorer outcomes in educational attainment and occupational status than controls without communication difficulties, as well as those individuals with speech-only impairments (C.J. Johnson *et al.* 2010). A significantly higher percentage of participants in the control and speech-only impairment groups had completed high school (92 per cent for both) than in the language impairment group (76 per cent). Additionally, the group with language impairment obtained significantly lower socioeconomic status ratings for their current occupations than the other two groups. Interestingly, however, there were no significant differences among the groups with respect to job satisfaction. Other research has shown that adults with a history of SLI are likely to have undertaken vocational training and to have occupations that do not depend on strong language and literacy competency (Whitehouse *et al.* 2009).

Social difficulties and emotional problems have also been associated with language impairment. However, the nature of this relationship appears to be quite complex (Redmond and Rice 1998; Fujiki *et al.* 2002; Hart *et al.* 2004; Conti-Ramsden and Botting 2004, 2008; Durkin and Conti-Ramsden 2007; Conti-Ramsden and Durkin 2008). School-age children with SLI demonstrate difficulties with peer interactions, such as gaining access to ongoing social exchanges and participating in cooperative learning activities (Craig and Washington 1993; Brinton *et al.* 1998). They have also been shown to exhibit elevated levels of reticence and withdrawal (Hart *et al.* 2004) and to be the target of bullying much more often than age-matched peers without language impairment (Conti-Ramsden and Botting 2004). Adolescent outcomes for children with a history of SLI have revealed reduced independence, poorer quality of close relationships, lower self-esteem and increased shyness despite typical levels of sociability, i.e. preference for being with others instead of being alone (Durkin and Conti-Ramsden 2007; Conti-Ramsden and Durkin 2008; Wadman *et al.* 2008).

Elevated levels of emotional problems, particularly depression and/or anxiety, have been found in adolescents and young adults with a history of SLI (Conti-Ramsden and Botting 2008; Whitehouse *et al.* 2009). However, evidence does not suggest that these emotional problems are a direct result of impaired communicative abilities. Adults who had severe receptive developmental language disorder as children were reported to have significantly poorer social adaptation (including fewer close friendships and romantic relationships) than controls, as well as increased risk for psychiatric disorders in adulthood (Howlin *et al.* 2000; Clegg *et al.* 2005). It is important to note that the criteria used to identify SLI need to be carefully considered in investigations of socio-emotional outcomes. Generally speaking, poor social outcomes have been associated with severe receptive language disorder and pragmatic deficits rather than with milder structural language impairments.

5.8   Conclusion

Children with SLI constitute a heterogeneous group with respect to their linguistic profiles, with most displaying particular problems with grammar. Current theories of SLI focus on either grammar-specific deficits or cognitive processing deficits. However, a multiple-deficit account appears most likely to explain this disorder. Genetic studies indicate that there is not a single gene responsible for SLI, but rather this complex disorder involves multiple genes interacting with various environmental factors. Given the prevalence of this developmental communication disorder and its adverse academic, social and emotional sequelae, there is a pressing need for continued research into the nature of SLI and its associated causal factors. An increased understanding of SLI is essential to the development of better prognostic indicators for individual children, and effective, targeted interventions that take into account the heterogeneous nature of the disorder.

6

Developmental dyslexia

Catherine Christo

6.1 Introduction

Print offers the magical transformation of our thoughts and voice into visual form and then back again into verbal form for others to experience. For children in love with stories and the magic of books, unlocking this cryptic mystery is probably the most important accomplishment of their early school years. And for those for whom print remains a stubborn unreadable cipher, despite their best efforts, it is likely to be the first of many failures school will provide for them.

Students may struggle in learning to read for a variety of reasons: poor instruction, lack of early exposure to print, poor vocabulary, low overall ability, emotional, behavioural or sensory disorders and specific deficits in cognitive processing. Those who struggle despite good instruction; adequate early experiences, vocabulary and general ability; and the absence of emotional, behavioural or sensory disorders, are likely to have dyslexia. The International Dyslexia Association has adopted the following definition (Lyon *et al.* 2003: 2):

> Dyslexia is a specific learning disability that is neurobiological in origin. It is characterized by difficulties with accurate and/or fluent word recognition and by poor spelling and decoding abilities. These difficulties typically result from a deficit in the phonological component of language that is often unexpected in relation to other cognitive abilities and the provision of effective classroom instruction. Secondary consequences may include problems in reading comprehension and reduced reading experience that can impede growth of vocabulary and background knowledge.

The National Institute of Neurological Disorders and Stroke (2011) provides this definition:

Dyslexia is a brain-based type of learning disability that specifically impairs a person's ability to read. These individuals typically read at levels significantly lower than expected despite having normal intelligence … common characteristics among people with dyslexia are difficulty with phonological processing (the manipulation of sounds), spelling, and/or rapid visual-verbal responding … Dyslexia can be inherited in some families, and recent studies have identified a number of genes that may predispose an individual to developing dyslexia.

The International Classification of Diseases (World Health Organization 1993: 192) provides the following definition of *specific reading disorder*, which is considered to be inclusive of dyslexia:

The main feature is a specific and significant impairment in the development of reading skills that is not solely accounted for by mental age, visual acuity problems or inadequate schooling. Reading comprehension skill, reading word recognition, oral reading skill … may all be affected. Spelling difficulties are frequently associated with specific reading disorder and often remain into adolescence even after some progress in reading has been made.

Commonalities among these definitions include the following:

- The difficulties in reading are not consistent with student performance in other areas or other cognitive abilities. In addition, they cannot be attributed to a lack of instruction or emotional disorders or other sensory disorders.
- The focus is on word-level processes. Students with dyslexia have problems with fluent word recognition and struggle with spelling and decoding, not with understanding (Vellutino *et al.* 2004). Secondary problems in reading comprehension and reduced reading experience can impede the development of both vocabulary and background knowledge (Cunningham and Stanovich 1997).
- Dyslexia is of neurobiological origin or is a brain-based condition. The reading difficulties of those with dyslexia result from a deficit in specific area(s) of cognitive processing.
- Difficulties in phonological processing are often the core cognitive processing deficit.

6.2   The prevalence and outcomes of dyslexia

Prevalence figures for dyslexia differ somewhat depending on the language of instruction. In the USA the prevalence of students identified as having a reading disorder and eligible for special education is around 4% (Christo and Davis 2008). The National Institute of Child Health & Human

Development (2010) suggests that up to 20% of people in the USA have some sort of language-based reading disorder. In studies providing intensive, early intervention for students struggling with learning to read, problems remained for 2–8% of the student population (Mathes *et al.* 2005; McMaster *et al.* 2005; Vellutino *et al.* 2006). Nicolson and Fawcett (2008: 13) state that there are '3 to 10 million dyslexic individuals in the U.K.'. Rates in other countries range from about 1% of the school-aged population in Greece (Anastasiou and Polychronopoulou 2009) to 10% in Russia and Finland (Spafford and Grosser 2005). It is possible that the prevalence rates may differ due to the differences in orthography and definition of dyslexia, which will be discussed later in this chapter.

In school-referred populations, the prevalence is much higher in boys than girls. However, some researchers attribute this to the school referral process (Shaywitz *et al.* 1992), noting that boys are more likely to be referred due to behavioural issues. From their review of studies on gender and prevalence, Liederman *et al.* (2005) concluded that the most likely ratio of boys to girls for reading disability was 1.74 to 2.0 in favour of boys.

For children with dyslexia and unresolved reading problems, the likely outcomes are bleak. Siegel (2010) reported that 82% of the street youth in Toronto and all the adolescent suicides in Ontario, tracked over a 3-year period, had undetected and unremediated learning disabilities. These children are at increased risk of dropping out of school (Frieden 2004) and face more difficulties in adult life (Mellard and Woods 2007). In addition, 75–95% of the Canadian prison population has learning disabilities. In the USA, estimates for the percentage of incarcerated youth with significant reading problems range from 34% to 43% (Finn *et al.* 1988; O'Brien *et al.* 2007).

6.3   Development of reading

"Mommy, I can't not read' – this young boy declared his mastery of possibly the most fundamental educational task: the development of automatic reading. Whether or not the process is truly automatic is open to some discussion (Stanovich 1991). But the seeming effortlessness of the process for successful readers is a given. Unfortunately for some learners, the development of the virtually effortless ability to decipher and decode is much more difficult to attain. And for some students it will remain a life-long struggle.

In order to understand developmental dyslexia, one must first have a general understanding of the process of learning to read. Becoming a reader involves both learning to decode the print and understanding how to construct meaning from that which is decoded. For dyslexic students the sticking point is the decoding or becoming efficient *word* readers. The simple view of reading (Gough and Tunmer 1986) posits that reading comprehension is a product of decoding and language comprehension. This view of reading has held up in numerous studies (Catts *et al.* 2005; Kendeou *et al.* 2009; Kirby and Savage 2008). In the simple view, decoding refers to word identification: to decode the symbols whether through automatic recognition or through using strategies such as phonetic decoding or analogy. Those with dyslexia, whether children or adults, may have strong language skills and be able to comprehend language that has been decoded for them. However, their comprehension may suffer when reading because of the conscious effort required in order to read individual words. The effort required to identify individual words both slows down their reading, thus impacting on comprehension, and uses up mental resources that should be in use for understanding the text. A word-based conceptualization of dyslexia is highlighted in the definitions provided previously. Dyslexia is exemplified by lack of skill in quickly and efficiently reading words.

As with any skill that one wants to develop to the level of virtual automaticity, it starts with being taught the basic rules and building accuracy. Then fluency develops. Following is a brief discussion of how children learn to read in a traditional, instructional approach (in an alphabetic writing system such as English) that focuses on teaching phonics and its use in word reading. Prior to the start of formal schooling, children are generally exposed to sound play such as nursery rhymes and songs and often create their own language play which may promote phonological awareness.

Ehri (2005) provides a four-stage model of how children learn to read words. In the first, pre-alphabetic stage, children often recognize common words through cues such as shape or print or trademarks. When formal schooling begins children are introduced to the graphemes that stand for the sounds of language and gradually learn the letter names and/or letter sounds. Along with learning to identify individual letters they learn how to blend the sounds together in order to read words. When children first start attending to the individual letters in words, they enter what Ehri terms the *partial alphabetic* stage. At this stage, children are starting to recognize words by linking some of the letters in words to the corresponding sounds. Their stored representations for words are not complete but only contain the most salient letter/sound combinations. Ehri notes that disabled readers often look like younger, partial alphabetic readers. Christo (1995) found that poor speller/good readers, who fit characteristics of compensated dyslexics, had poor implicit memory for common and recently seen words indicating that their stored memories for words are incomplete. The *full alphabetic* phase emerges as children 'learn sight words by forming complete connections between graphemes in spelling and phonemes in pronunciation' (Ehri 2005: 175). The *consolidated* phase emerges as children read more and more words and 'become familiar with letter patterns that recur in different words' (Ehri 2005:

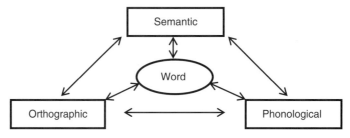

Figure 6.1 Information about words.

177). Through this process common letter-sound patterns become increasingly familiar and can be recognized more easily in different words. Thus, children become able to quickly read unfamiliar words through these already known connections. Ehri describes the process as moving words into 'sight word' status: through repeated exposure words are recognized on sight. The development of efficient word identification is foundational to reading comprehension (Adams 1990) and is a primary difficulty for students with dyslexia.

In addition to storing information about the letters and pronunciations of words, we also store information about the meaning of words. Various researchers have offered models representing how this information is stored and connected (Adams 1990; Berninger et al. 2008; Seidenberg and McClelland 1989). Figure 6.1 is derived from these models. In order to become efficient readers, the phonological, graphemic and semantic information about words must be well connected such that seeing the words (graphemes) leads to meaning and to pronunciation. Hearing the word (from hearing or from conscious decoding) leads to meaning. Thinking about the words we want to express leads to phonology (for speaking) and spelling (for writing). Context serves to speed up these connections by providing 'readiness' in likely candidates for correct pronunciation (e.g. desert, buffet), meaning or spelling (e.g. red vs. read). If these connections are not fast and accurate, we have incorrect or slow reading and poor spelling – common characteristics of dyslexia. Some children with particularly strong verbal skills are able to compensate for less automatic connections by using their verbal skills and background knowledge to 'guess' at words when reading. These students are often considered to be 'compensated dyslexics' and generally have poor spelling and fluency (Berninger 2007).

6.4   Characteristics and causes of dyslexia

As noted above, a lack of efficient word reading is the most prominent characteristic of dyslexia, but it is not the only characteristic. Berninger and O'Malley-May (2011) provide a list of characteristics that describe the 'hallmark phenotype' of dyslexia. The hallmark phenotype is exemplified by problems in pseudoword reading, spelling, phonological coding, orthographic coding, rapid naming, inhibition and rapid automatic switching. Hallmark phenotypes distinguish children with dyslexia from children with other developmental or neurological disorders that may affect the development of literacy. For example, children with dysgraphia only are distinguished by difficulties with legible letter writing, orthographic coding and rapid finger tapping tasks; children with oral and written language disorders will have problems in oral language as well as comprehension of text.

The core identified problem in dyslexia is a lack of efficiency in linking visual information (letters) to phonological information so that words can be read with relative automaticity. Thus, anything that interferes with this process is a candidate for the 'cause' of dyslexia. This includes: difficulties with phonological processing, an inability to process visual information efficiently, cognitive processes that lead to delays in processing this information, poor memory or global problems in automatizing skills. Following is a discussion of these candidate causes of dyslexia. The evidence for each of these processes in relation to (a) deficits in children with dyslexia, (b) ability to predict future reading skill and (c) the effectiveness of interventions that are based on improving functioning in the specific process (when available) will be provided.

6.4.1 Phonological processing

The work of researchers at Haskins Laboratory (Liberman 1999; Liberman and Shankweiler 1985) was instrumental in first identifying phonological processing as a core deficit in dyslexia. Phonological processing, as a term, encompasses phonological awareness and phonemic awareness. Phonological awareness is described by Torgesen (1995: 4) as 'sensitivity to or awareness of the phonological structure' of language (see also Wagner *et al.* 1999; Walsh 2009). Phonemic awareness is defined as the ability to manipulate the sounds of language. Phonological processing is both foundational to and fostered by learning to read. That is, the process of learning sound/symbol relationships appears to foster greater awareness of the individual sounds in words and greater ability to perform the above more complex tasks.

Phonological processing has been identified in numerous studies as deficient in students with dyslexia from very young children to college age students (Kitz and Tarver 1989; Liberman *et al.* 1989; Shaywitz 1996; Fawcett and Nicolson 2000; Vellutino *et al.* 2004; Fletcher *et al.* 2007; Christo *et al.* 2009). These deficits appear to be present in a variety of languages (Caravolas *et al.* 2005; Douklias *et al.* 2009) though to somewhat different degrees depending on the transparency of the alphabet. Phonological processing is highly predictive of success in early reading

(Shaywitz 1996, 2003; Torgesen *et al.* 1999). Intervention studies that have focused on improving phonological processing have been successful with struggling students (Foorman 2003; Torgesen 2002, 2004; Uhry and Clark 2004; O'Conner *et al.* 2009).

It is evident that tasks that assess phonological processing are strongly supported as indicators of dyslexia. In addition, instruction that focuses on directly teaching phonologically related skills (such as blending, decoding and segmenting) are effective (National Reading Panel 2000; Stuebing *et al.* 2008). What is somewhat less clear is what causes the phonological deficits that are such a hallmark of dyslexia. For example, is it lack of automatization (Nicolson and Fawcett 2008), problems with rapid processing (Tallal *et al.* 1996), visual processing deficits (Stein 2001), naming speed deficits (Wolf 2001) or verbal memory (Berninger *et al.* 2006)? Because reading is such a complex process, it may be that there is more than one 'cause' of dyslexia.

6.4.2   Naming speed

In studies of rapid automatic naming first undertaken by Denckla and Rudel (1976a, 1976b), children were asked to quickly name a row of numbers, letters, colours or pictures. At present, most assessments designed to evaluate the cognitive processing of students with reading problems include some measure of rapid naming (e.g. Comprehensive Test of Phonological Processing (Wagner *et al.* 1999), Process Assessment of the Learner II (Berninger 2007), Kaufman Test of Achievement II (Kaufman and Kaufman 2004)).

Poor readers show deficits in rapid naming of numbers, letters, colours and pictures (Ackerman *et al.* 1990; Bowers *et al.* 1999; Wolf and Bowers 1999; Fawcett and Nicolson 2000; Bowers 2001; Uhry and Clark 2004; Berninger 2006). In addition, naming speed differentiates children with specific reading disabilities from those with attention deficit disorders (Felton *et al.* 1987) and accounts for variance in reading skill beyond what is predicted by phonological processing (Spring and Davis 1988; Manis and Freedman 2001; Schatschneider *et al.* 2002; Christo and Davis 2008). Naming speed predicts current and later reading development (Spring and Davis 1988; Torgesen *et al.* 1997; Georgiou *et al.* 2006). However, the relationship between naming speed and reading varies across the age span and different levels of reading skill, being stronger for younger and poorer readers (Torgesen *et al.* 1997; Meyer *et al.* 1998; Manis *et al.* 1999).

There is debate as to whether naming speed is a distinct cognitive process or whether it should be considered as an aspect of phonological processing (Felton and Brown 1990; Wagner *et al.* 1999; Shaywitz 2003). Wolf and colleagues (Wolf *et al.* 2000a; Wolf 2001) see rapid naming as a distinct cognitive process and point to research showing differential response to intervention based on whether a student has phonological deficits, naming speed deficits or both (Bowers and Wolf 1993; Bowers 1996; Levy and Bourassa 1999). In addition, examination of phonological and naming speed deficits in reading impaired populations have identified subgroups with one or both of these deficits (Morris and Shaywitz 1998; Lovett *et al.* 2000). These findings lend support to the 'double deficit' hypothesis (Wolf and Bowers 1999). According to this position, readers with deficits in either phonological processing or rapid naming are less impaired and are more likely to respond to intervention than those with deficits in both areas. Other studies, however, fail to support the presence of naming speed as a distinct deficit separate from phonological processing (Cardoso-Martins and Pennington 2004; Waber *et al.* 2004; Vukovic and Siegel 2006). Supporters of a broad phonological deficit see problems in naming speed as an extension of global problems in phonology (Shaywitz 2003; Vellutino *et al.* 2004).

One can speculate on how speed of accessing name codes might impact on the ability to develop a mental storehouse of words that can be recognized effortlessly. Bowers (1996: 1) proposed that 'naming speed influences the ability to learn the orthographic pattern of words'. The classic Hebb rule states that 'cells that fire together wire together'. As readers are introduced to new words, many connections are made between letters that are commonly seen together and the words in which they are present. If readers are slower at pulling out the sound that attaches to individual graphemes, then the cells that were firing for beginning letters in words will no longer be firing by the time the reader has identified the letters and their corresponding phonemes at the end of words. Thus, it will take more trials for them to learn new words and their reading fluency will be affected, as is the case for dyslexics.

Interventions that follow from this theory focus on building fluency for identifying grapheme–phoneme connections, words and then text as well as on phonics instruction. RAVE-O (Retrieval, Automaticity, Vocabulary, Elaboration, Orthography) (Wolf *et al.* 2000b) is a reading intervention programme designed to accompany a phonologically based programme. Its focus is on addressing the multiple, possible causes of disfluency. Morris *et al.* (2012) indicate positive and lasting results from use of the programme.

6.4.3 Automatization deficit

Nicolson and colleagues (Nicolson and Fawcett 2008) have undertaken a variety of studies to explore dyslexic students' ability to learn tasks to automatization. Dyslexics were found to be deficient in relation to both chronological and reading level peers in automatization of a variety of simple tasks that were 'not likely to be taught but were subject to being learned to automatic level' (Nicolson and Fawcett 2008: 77). Nicolson posits that dyslexics need to consciously concentrate (use controlled processing) in order to reach the same level of performance as other children do automatically (without controlled processing). Students with dyslexia have also been found to take more time to learn skills to an automatized level, have more trouble initiating learning of new skills and difficulty unlearning strategies in response to changing stimuli (Nicolson and Fawcett 2008). Other researchers have found, however, that the lack of automatization is specific to reading (McBride-Chang *et al.* 2008; Deroost *et al.* 2010), that dyslexic readers do not show deficits with dual tasks (Wimmer *et al.* 1999) and that attention is the primary deficit.

Though the theory of a general automatization deficit as the primary cause of dyslexia is questionable, the educational implications and principles for intervention that follow from this theory appear to be the ones that are helpful for dyslexic students. For example, Nicolson notes that the automatization deficit theory would suggest that dyslexic students need direct, explicit teaching and that they will need more exposures and learning opportunities than normal readers in order to reach an automatic level. The Dyslexia, Dyspraxia Attention Treatment Programme (also known as DORE Program) is designed to address the cerebellar deficits purported to lead to problems in learning to automaticity. While some authors reported gains in targeted areas (but not reading), questions exist about methodology and findings (International Dyslexia Association 2009).

6.4.4 Visual processing

Because the first sensory system involved in reading is vision, it is intuitive to look for problems in that system. Early conceptualizations of dyslexia focused on visual processing (e.g. Hinshelwood 1917) and difficulties in the visual system or in interpreting visual input. Orton (1928) coined the term *strephosymbolia* to refer to children with symptoms of dyslexia. More recent theories of visual processing deficits have focused on two areas: difficulties in tracking and binocular vision, and deficits in the magnocellular pathways for visual processing (Lovegrove 1994; Stein 2001). Early tracking theories arose from the observation that poor readers displayed erratic eye movements when reading. Later research has demonstrated that the erratic eye movements of poor readers are a function of their inability to read the text rather than the cause of it. That is, they are looking for context clues to help in word identification.

Impaired magnocellular functioning has some support, at least for certain dyslexics. The visual magnocellular system detects motion sensitivity and functions during reading to help direct the eyes in moving across the page and in providing the quick stops and starts that are involved as readers focus and move on to the next target (Stein 2001; Thomson 2009). In dyslexics, this is demonstrated in the lab by poor motion sensitivity (Eden *et al.* 1996; Talcott *et al.* 1998) and difficulties with visual search

(Iles *et al.* 2000). Deficits in visual motion sensitivity appear to be linked more strongly with deficits in orthographic processing and spelling than with phonological processing. Questions regarding this theory include the inability to clearly relate the theory to deficits in reading (Skottun and Skoyles 2006), a lack of empirical support (Ramus *et al.* 2003; White *et al.* 2006) and problems with methods used to test various aspects of vision (Skottun and Skoyles 2008).

Visual attention deficits refer to problems in rapidly processing visual information so that the reader quickly processes all the letters present in his or her visual field (Valdois *et al.* 2004). This theory suggests that it is the visual processing per se and not the visual/phonological processing of reading that is the deficit. However, Ziegler *et al.* (2010) found that children with dyslexia were impaired in processing symbols that map to phonological codes but not in processing purely visual symbols.

There are few interventions linked to these visual processing deficits. Interventions based on optometric training to improve tracking or the use of coloured lenses to ameliorate symptoms of 'scotopic sensitivity' are not supported (American Academy of Pediatrics *et al.* 2009).

6.4.5 Temporal processing

Auditory temporal processing theories propose that the phonological problems of dyslexic readers arise from difficulties in perceiving rapid changes in the auditory signal. For example, children with dyslexia have difficulty distinguishing the rapidly changing acoustic signal that is found in transient consonant vowel sounds (Tallal *et al.* 1993, 1996; Tallal and Gaab 2006; King *et al.* 2008). Brain imaging has identified lack of activation for dyslexic children in areas of the brain typically active when making auditory pitch judgements (Gaab *et al.* 2007). Benasich and Tallal (2002) report that infant measures of rapid processing predict later language outcomes.

In contrast to these findings, other researchers have not reported a link between a deficit in rapid auditory processing and dyslexia (Mody and Studdert-Kennedy 1997; White *et al.* 2006). Johnson *et al.* (2009) tested the hypothesis that deficits in rapid auditory processing lead to phonological deficits using path analysis and hierarchical regression. They concluded that deficits in auditory processing did not lead to deficits in phonological awareness, but that performance on phonological tasks predicted performance on rapid auditory processing tasks.

FastForward is an intervention programme based on the theory of deficits in rapid auditory processing. The programme is computer based and trains participants to improve their ability to process these rapid changes in the speech signal by beginning with artificially slowed speech and progressing as the learner becomes better able to process the rapid speech sounds. Some studies have reported improvements in some reading skills (Scientific Learning Corporation 1999; What Works Clearinghouse 2007). However, Strong *et al.* (2011) note that previous meta-studies have not found positive effects for FastForward in relation to reading outcomes. They did not find any evidence that FastForward was an effective 'treatment for children's reading, or expressive or receptive vocabulary weaknesses' (Strong *et al.* 2011: 231) or that it improved the ability of participants to process rapidly changing acoustic information.

6.4.6 Memory

Berninger and colleagues (Berninger *et al.* 2006; Berninger 2007) have developed a model of dyslexia that utilizes working memory as a theoretical framework in which to understand the deficits in phonological and orthographic processing, rapid naming and executive function that are demonstrated by individuals with dyslexia. Deficits in working memory have been identified in adults and children with dyslexia (Swanson and Berninger 1996; Swanson and Siegel 2001; Berninger *et al.* 2006; Swanson *et al.* 2006). Functional magnetic resonance imaging (fMRI) studies have identified differences in brain regions that are associated with working memory in individuals with dyslexia compared to controls (Richards *et al.* 2006).

The working memory framework is composed of three components: '(a) codes for word-form storage and processing, (b) time-sensitive phonological and orthographic loops for maintaining information in working memory or outputting it, and (c) executive functions for language (e.g. rapid automatic naming, switching of attention)' (Berninger *et al.* 2008: 707). Three different kinds of information about words are stored: semantic, phonological and orthographic. While there are some shared storage areas, neuroimaging evidence also suggests that there are different storage areas for these different kinds of information about words (Berninger *et al.* 2008). The orthographic and phonological loops are important in helping to develop connections between these three word forms so that readers can both read and spell with ease. Executive function is important in allowing beginning readers to focus attention on the necessary components of words and orchestrate the linking of phonological, orthographic and semantic information about words.

The primary deficit noted for all struggling readers appears to be a deficit in the ability to link information across the different word forms (called *cross word form mapping*) (Berninger *et al.* 2008). Interventions that provide explicit information about the specific word forms have led to positive outcomes. Using the working memory architecture to more clearly identify whether a student has dyslexia, dysgraphia or oral and written learning disability can lead to more effective intervention (Berninger and O'Malley-May 2011).

6.4.7 Information from brain imaging

Imaging studies have provided clear evidence that the brains of dyslexics look different from the brains of typical readers when engaged in reading tasks. In the brains of typical readers there is a sequence of activation from the visual area of the brain to association areas where visual information is linked to phonological information and then to other association areas that provide semantic access (Pugh *et al.* 2001; Vellutino *et al.* 2004). Studies have generally found that dyslexic individuals have less activity in specific areas of the brain commonly activated by typical readers (Paulesu *et al.* 2001; Shaywitz *et al.* 2004; Cao *et al.* 2006; Hoeft *et al.* 2006). In typical readers, the left occipito-parietal region has been identified as an area that is activated during reading and becomes more active as children acquire new words that are 'automatically' recognized. This area has been dubbed the 'word form area' (Shaywitz 2003) or 'letterbox area' (Dehaene 2009). It is suggested that this area is important for the associations between letters, sounds and meaning to occur.

Imaging studies also indicate that dyslexic readers tend to compensate for under-activation in certain areas with over-activation in other areas. For example, there is greater activation in the right hemisphere and in Broca's area (for speech processing) (Thomson 2009). Perhaps the most promising finding of imaging studies is that interventions can lead to changes in the brain and that the brains of dyslexics come to more closely resemble the activation patterns in typical readers (Simos *et al.* 2002, 2006, 2007; Papanicolaou *et al.* 2003; Shaywitz *et al.* 2004; Gaab *et al.* 2007).

6.5 Cross-linguistic research on dyslexia

For several decades, research on dyslexia was conducted primarily with English speakers. English is considered to have a highly opaque orthography in comparison to other languages. In English the connection between graphemes and phonemes is not straightforward: the same sound can be written in different ways (ph, f) and the same letters or letter combinations can stand for different sounds (cough, though, through). In languages such as Greek and Spanish there is much more consistency between phonemes and graphemes. These languages are considered to be transparent because it is easy to learn the letter/sound connections for reading and spelling.

Grain size theory (Ziegler and Goswami 2005, 2006) hypothesizes that the size of the phonemic unit children must pay attention to in learning to read differs according to the transparency of the orthography. In very transparent orthographies the reader can rely on small phoneme units for word identification. In a language such as English, where there is a question about the letter/sound correspondences, readers pay attention to larger grain sizes and use other sources of information such as morphology or meaning to correctly read words. Concerns about this theory include a need to account for the use of morphological information (Durgunoglu 2006; Frost 2006) and the role of fluency in dyslexia in languages that are more consistent in their orthography than English (Wimmer 2006).

Dyslexia in more consistent orthographies is characterized by problems in fluency not in accuracy. In consistent orthographies, such as German, children become accurate readers of real and nonsense words during their first year of instruction (Wimmer and Mayringer 2002). Dyslexia in these languages is not characterized by inaccurate nonsense word reading but by slow reading of both real and nonsense words. While some researchers find rapid naming to be more associated with dyslexia than phonological processing in more consistent orthographies (Wimmer and Mayringer 2002), other authors argue that phonological processing deficits are present in dyslexia across languages (Paulesu *et al.* 2001; Pugh 2006; Ziegler and Goswami 2006).

As Pugh (2006: 448) points out, discovering the 'correspondences between print and speech' is the common task among readers across languages. Beyond discovering these correspondences is the need to develop the ability to rapidly access this information so that one is able to recognize multiple words with fluency. While phonological deficits may be more obvious in inconsistent and opaque orthographies such as English, the common behavioural manifestation is the lack of rapid word recognition.

6.6   Assessment of dyslexia

There are a variety of reasons for assessing students who are struggling to learn. Among them are helping children, teachers and parents to understand why a child is struggling; determining eligibility for any additional support services or legal protections; designing appropriate interventions; and providing information useful in future educational planning. These are all worthwhile goals and cannot be ignored in any assessment of a student suspected of having dyslexia. We also know that early intervention is particularly important for mitigating the learning problems that children with dyslexia are likely to encounter. Therefore, it is important to investigate early indicators of dyslexia.

6.6.1   Early risk factors

There is evidence that children at risk for dyslexia can be identified prior to school entry. Some of the factors that put children at risk for dyslexia include family history of dyslexia, global language deficits (Badian 1994; Catts *et al.* 2001; Catts and Hogan 2003), specific language deficits (Stackhouse 2006), oral language deficits (Scarborough 2005), vocabulary deficits, phonological processing delays and letter knowledge deficits (Christo and Davis 2008). Family history of dyslexia has been found to strengthen the predictive power of models designed to identify risk status (Puolakanaho *et al.* 2007; Snowling *et al.* 2003). Linkages have been found between dyslexia and identified genes in family studies (Grigorencko *et al.* 1997; Willcutt *et al.* 2002; Pennington and Olson 2005). Children's vocabulary prior to school entry is predictive of both early and later reading development (Dickinson and Tabors 2001; Snowling *et al.* 2003; Scarborough 2005). Having a bigger vocabulary may be an indicator of stronger underlying language skills that facilitate reading development. It has also been suggested that having a larger vocabulary enhances phonological development (Walley 1993; Goswami 2000, 2001).

As noted previously, phonological processing has been linked in numerous studies to early reading development. For young children this is usually measured through tasks such as rhyme detection and production, segmenting phonemes in words or in being able to categorize sounds. Differences in phonological processing, as measured by these tasks prior to school entry, are useful in predicting risk status (Wagner *et al.* 1997; Shatil and Share 2003; Castles and Coltheart 2004; Schatschneider and Torgesen 2004). However, it is important to point out that the evidence is strongest for the link between good phonological processing and low risk for reading problems than for the link between poor phonological processing and high risk for reading problems. That is, if a child is capable of performing a variety of phonological processing tasks, he or she is not likely to have reading problems. But problems in phonological processing don't necessarily mean the child is likely to have reading problems. Letter knowledge in preschoolers is a strong predictor of future reading skill (Muter 2000; Snowling *et al.* 2003). This is not surprising as letter knowledge is likely to be a marker for a variety of other factors such as memory, general ability, language skills and environmental factors. Finally, otitis media, or ear infections, has been investigated as a risk factor. While some researchers did not find a link between early ear infections and later reading difficulties (Roberts *et al.* 2002), others have found ear infections to be particularly common in students with reading problems (Winskel 2006).

Examples of preschool or early school years screening batteries are *Phonological Abilities Test* (Muter *et al.* 1997), *Ready to Learn* (Fawcett *et al.* 2004), *Test of Phonological Awareness – Second Edition: PLUS* (Torgesen and Bryant 2004), *Dynamic Indicators of Basic Early Literacy Skills* (Good *et al.* 2003) and *Test of Early Reading Ability – 3* (Reid *et al.* 2004).

To summarize, children who enter school with good language skills, some understanding of print and the alphabet and no family history of dyslexia are likely to be good readers. On the other hand, children who enter school with language delays (whether in vocabulary, speech or phonological processing), a lack of understanding and familiarity with print and the alphabet and/or a family history of dyslexia are at risk of having dyslexia.

6.6.2 School-aged assessment

Once children begin formal reading instruction, the first step in identifying those with dyslexia is to monitor progress on attaining early reading skills (National Reading Panel 2000; Gijsel *et al.* 2006). The ease with which children acquire these skills is predictive of later reading success or failure (Christensen 2000; Davis *et al.* 2007). Assessments such as *Dynamic Indicators of Basic Early Literacy Skills* (Coyne *et al.* 2001) and *AIMSweb* (Pearson Publishing 2010) provide information on progress of early literacy skills. These measures assess student progress in letter naming, identifying beginning sounds in words, segmenting phonemes in words, decoding nonsense words, reading lists of words and ultimately reading connected text (Coyne and Harn 2006). They are designed to assess mastery of each skill along with accuracy. Speed and accuracy are both measured. For example, the segmenting measure assesses how many phonemes in spoken words can be identified by the student in one minute. Benchmarks have been developed that provide markers regarding adequate progress in these skills (Good *et al.* 2001). These measures are designed to assess current level of performance and to be administered frequently enough to provide information about short-term progress. Graphing is a common way to provide a visual representation of student progress.

6.6.3 Evaluation of dyslexia

Lack of progress and performance below one's peers are not in themselves sufficient information for determining that a student has dyslexia. Once a student is identified as struggling with reading and failing to respond to appropriate instruction/intervention, a comprehensive evaluation is needed. Within the school system, this evaluation generally has three goals: (1) to determine whether the student is eligible for and in need of some type of special education support; (2) to determine if the diagnosis of dyslexia is appropriate for the child; and (3) to provide information useful in intervention planning. In this section, the focus will be on the second and third goals. A comprehensive evaluation will provide information useful to all of these goals.

The first requirement for determining the presence of dyslexia is significantly low performance on basic reading skills such as word reading, decoding or reading fluency. Older children will often show deficits in reading fluency and spelling only. Some authors suggest that in order for students to be considered as performing below their peers, they should receive a score in one of the basic areas of reading that is below the 16th percentile or a standard score of 85 (1 standard deviation below the mean) (Berninger 2007; Flanagan and Alfonso 2011).

Once the deficit has been identified, the next step is to determine that the student had appropriate instruction and intervention. The National Reading Panel (2000) has provided guidelines regarding best practices in reading instruction. These guidelines are based on an extensive review of previous research on effective reading instruction. Five areas were identified as essential instructional areas: phonological processing, phonics, fluency, vocabulary and text comprehension. The Panel concluded that direct, explicit instruction in each of these areas is important. When determining whether or not a student has had appropriate instruction/intervention, the guidelines of the National Reading Panel are useful in evaluating the programme and instruction provided.

The above steps occur within general education. Once these two conditions have been met, the next step is a comprehensive evaluation to provide information which is useful both in determining the presence of dyslexia and in informing further intervention. Berninger (2007) and Berninger and O'Malley-May (2011) suggest that the following developmental domains should be assessed: (a) cognitive development, (b) receptive and expressive language, (c) gross and fine motor skills, (d) attention and executive functioning and (e) social-emotional functioning. A comprehensive evaluation will probably have the following components:

- review of work samples and classroom progress in reading-related courses and other academic areas;
- review of developmental, medical and school history;
- health screening;
- observations;
- structured interviews with teachers and parents and student (as appropriate);
- rating scales for social-emotional status and behaviour, as needed;
- further assessment of component reading skills using norm-referenced tests;
- assessment of cognitive ability and specific cognitive processes related to reading; and
- assessment of language comprehension.

It is important to determine that the reading deficit is not primarily due to the presence of sensory deficits, environmental factors, second language issues, emotional disorders, low general cognitive ability or other handicapping conditions (e.g. attention deficit hyperactivity disorder and autism spectrum disorder), as these factors can affect the development of reading skills (see Figure 6.2). Co-occurring conditions are not uncommon in children with dyslexia. For older students, secondary emotional and behavioural issues may be present due to their struggles with reading. The essential question is to determine that these conditions are not the

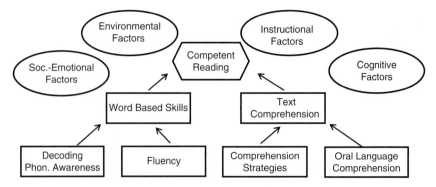

Figure 6.2 Development of competent reading.

primary cause of the reading problem. Once these conditions are ruled out, the next step is to determine the presence of a weakness in a cognitive process related to reading. This weakness should be present in an otherwise normal pattern of functioning. That is, the student should not show low overall cognitive ability but a weakness in specific area(s) that are known to be associated with reading disability and dyslexia. Those areas include the following: phonological processing, rapid naming, working memory, executive functioning and orthographic coding (Hale and Fiorello 2004; McGrew and Wendling 2010; Berninger 2011; Feifer 2011).

Phonological processing is generally assessed by tasks requiring the student to mentally manipulate the sounds of language. Phonological processing tasks range from simple (identifying rhyme or initial consonants) to complex (removing a phoneme from a consonant blend and recombining the sounds). Marshall *et al.* (2013) found that among reading-disabled students there was a significant difference in how well they performed on these tasks in comparison to their peers. The students in this study (many of whom had experienced a reading curriculum with an emphasis on blending phonemes) performed within the average range on a sound blending task but below average on an elision task requiring them to remove sounds and recombine the remaining sounds to form a new word. For school-aged children, rapid naming of digits and letters is most useful. In addition, tasks requiring rapid switching assess executive functioning as well as rapid access to name codes. Orthographic coding is assessed by tasks requiring quick storage and recall of letter combinations, knowledge of spelling and punctuation conventions and ability to differentiate homophones (e.g. PAL II (Berninger 2007), Test of Orthographic Competence (Mather *et al.* 2008)) and may be indicated in spelling.

Because dyslexia is considered a word-based reading disability, it is important to determine that the student has adequate oral language skills. Students with dyslexia may have difficulties with reading comprehension

Table 6.1 *Reading assessment flowchart*

If	Is	Then
Reading comprehension	Below expectations	Assess both oral language and reading fluency
Oral language	Appropriate	Focus on reading skills
	Below expectations	Provide language-based intervention
Fluency	Appropriate	Provide interventions in reading comprehension and vocabulary
	Below expectations	Assess word reading
Word reading	Appropriate	Provide text reading fluency interventions
	Below expectations	Perform detailed analysis of real and nonsense word reading in timed and untimed situations

as a 'secondary consequence' of dyslexia, but language comprehension is not the primary disability. Therefore, students should demonstrate average oral language skills in order to be considered to have dyslexia. If a student has poor oral language skills, then a more appropriate diagnosis may be oral and written language learning disorder (Berninger 2007, 2011). In addition, there should be a significant difference between the student's oral comprehension and the deficit in reading skill.

A detailed reading skills analysis will address the areas identified in Table 6.1. This table provides a 'drill down' approach for isolating a student's specific skill deficits. For a student who has reading comprehension problems, it is important to first determine that the student's oral language skills are within the average range. If not, then language deficits should be directly addressed. For a student who has adequate reading fluency but poor reading comprehension, instruction should focus on teaching comprehension strategies. For the student with poor text reading fluency but adequate word-based reading skills (identifying real and nonsense words), the focus for intervention should be on increasing reading fluency. For the student who has poor word reading skills, it is important to assess further to determine whether the issue is due to fluency, lack of phonics knowledge or failure to develop a mental storehouse of recognizable words.

A detailed analysis of word reading skill provides information relevant to areas of weakness and to designing interventions. This analysis requires assessment of reading of real and nonsense words in both timed and untimed situations. Table 6.2 provides information as to the specific components of word reading assessed. Untimed tests of nonsense words assess whether the student knows the requisite decoding information.

Table 6.2 *Word-level assessment*

	Timed	Untimed
Real words	Automaticity of word retrieval	Size of mental lexicon of stored words
Pseudowords	Automaticity of decoding skills	Knowledge of phonics

Untimed tests of real words provide information as to whether the student is developing a mental lexicon of known words. Testing decoding skill (reading of nonsense words) in timed situations provides information about the automaticity of decoding and the accessibility of that knowledge for the student. Timed measures of real word reading provide information as to whether the student has rapid, automatic access to an adequate number of stored words that are recognized on 'sight'. For a student who does poorly in both timed and untimed testing of nonsense word reading, an intervention that focuses on teaching decoding rules as well as fluency of decoding is appropriate. However, some students may be accurate, but slow decoders. These students need an intervention that focuses on speeding up the decoding process. Likewise, if a student is able to identify an adequate number of real words, but does so slowly, an intervention that focuses on developing automaticity of word recognition is needed. Spelling tests can also help with evaluating word level knowledge and skills. A student who spells incorrectly but in a phonetically correct way is demonstrating phonics/decoding knowledge. A student who puts unusual letter combinations together is demonstrating a lack of orthographic knowledge or familiarity with common conventions of print.

6.7   Dyslexia intervention

6.7.1   Instructional practices

Sound instructional practices are important for all students, but they are particularly important for students with dyslexia. While many students will learn to read by being immersed in a print rich environment and with minimal direct instruction, students with dyslexia need structured learning experiences (Torgesen *et al.* 2001; Torgesen *et al.* 2010). In designing interventions for students with dyslexia, it is important to keep in mind both the 'brain-based' and person-based aspects of instruction. That is, we must consider how to teach the brain to read – how to develop automatic word recognition skills that are problematic for children with dyslexia. Instructors must also recognize the importance of the student: the level of engagement and the emotional factors that can foster or hinder learning. The following are important instructional practices that address both these aspects of instruction:

- Use a systematic curriculum that teaches simple skills first and builds on previous knowledge to teach new skills.
- Provide direct, explicit instruction in the basics of reading such as how to decode words. This means clearly explaining the skill to be taught and explicitly bringing the learner's attention to key information.
- Demonstrate and model the skill to be taught.
- Provide practice with corrective feedback (Pany and McCoy 1988). Immediate corrective feedback will help prevent incorrect learning trials (e.g. misreading home for house) and will also help to prevent a student from learning incorrect or ineffective strategies.
- Scaffold instruction and practice to the student's level (Berninger and Wolf 2009).
- Engage previous knowledge and schemas.
- Provide multiple opportunities for practice.
- Provide positive reinforcement.
- Use engaging and motivating materials.

The National Reading Panel (2000) identified five aspects of literacy that should be targeted in instruction: phonological awareness, phonics, fluency, vocabulary and comprehension. Their recommendations regarding alphabetics stress the importance of explicit instruction in phonemic awareness and phonics. The panel found a lack of evidence supporting any particular instructional approach to increasing fluency but recommended that guided reading with practice was likely to be the most effective approach. In the area of vocabulary, the panel recommended that vocabulary be taught both explicitly and indirectly. In the area of comprehension, the panel did not find conclusive evidence about any one approach but recommended explicit teaching of comprehension strategies.

6.7.2   Programmes and curricula

Reading instruction and intervention programmes can be placed into three different categories: whole school programmes, reading curricula and supplemental programmes (Christo *et al.* 2009). Whole school programmes promote system change that involves an entire school. Examples of published programmes with clear guidelines for implementation include Success for All (Slavin *et al.* 1992) and Distar (Engelmann and Bruner 1983). The Response to Intervention (RTI) movement also encourages whole school change in how instruction/intervention in both reading and other academic areas is provided. While there are many different RTI models and methods of implementation, all RTI models have the same essential characteristics: (a) screening students to identify those at risk for academic failure, (b) monitoring the progress of students in response to instruction/intervention and (c) providing increasingly more intense, research-based interventions in response to student need (Christo 2005). RTI models hold promise for encouraging earlier identification and intervention for students with dyslexia.

The International Dyslexia Association (2007) provides information on programmes that they consider to be multisensory, structured language (MSL) programmes. These programmes include 'structured, explicit, systematic, cumulative instruction designed to promote understanding, memory, recall and use of spoken and written language' (International Dyslexia Association 2007: 1). This approach is built upon Orton–Gillingham programmes that had their origins in the 1960s (Gillingham and Stillman 1960). Both Orton–Gillingham and MSL programmes use instruction that is multisensory (visual, auditory, kinaesthetic and tactile) and teach all aspects of language (phonological awareness, alphabetics, syllable instruction, morphology, syntax and comprehension (Christo and Davis 2008)). These programmes are designed to provide explicit instruction and use a multisensory approach in order to enrich neural connections.

6.8   Summary

The most common characteristic displayed by individuals with dyslexia is difficulty with efficient word recognition. In languages that have an opaque or inconsistent orthography, issues in decoding are common, while in transparent or consistent orthographies, dyslexia is more often characterized by lack of fluency in word reading. At present, deficits in phonological processing appear to be a dominant factor in dyslexia. Naming speed has also been identified as deficient in many dyslexic individuals. Other purported causes of dyslexia include problems in automatizing skills, specific aspects of visual and auditory processing and memory. Research in languages other than English has increased and will continue to expand our understanding of dyslexia.

As a brain-based disorder, dyslexia is considered a life-long disability. Individuals will respond to early and appropriate intervention and also may learn to compensate for weak word identification skills. However, specific literacy-related deficits may remain (spelling, fluency). Early identification and intervention are crucial in order to reduce the secondary effects of poor reading.

7

Intellectual disability and communication

Katherine Short-Meyerson and Glenis Benson

7.1   Intellectual disability: terminology and diagnosis

According to the American Association on Intellectual and Developmental Disabilities (AAIDD), intellectual disability (ID) originates before the age of 18 and is characterized by significant limitations in intellectual functioning and adaptive behaviour (Schalock *et al.* 2010). These limitations are expressed in conceptual, social and practical adaptive skills, including communication. Historically, intellectual disability has also been referred to by other terms, such as 'mental retardation', 'mental disability' and 'cognitive disability' (Maulik and Harbour 2011; Wehmeyer and Obremski 2011). In the UK, the term 'learning disability' has also been used synonymously with intellectual disability (Fernald 1995). In this chapter, we will use the term 'intellectual disability' and focus on the communication of children and adolescents up to 18 years of age.

Individuals with ID are distinguished by their limited intellectual functioning or intelligence. Intellectual functioning is typically assessed with standardized intelligence tests such as the Stanford-Binet Intelligence Scale (Thorndike *et al.* 1986) and the Wechsler Intelligence Scale for Children – fourth edition (WISC-IV; Wechsler 2003) amongst others. For bilingual and limited-English-proficient students there are non-verbal tests of cognitive ability, including the Universal Nonverbal Intelligence Test (UNIT; Bracken and McCallum 1998) and the Naglieri Nonverbal Ability Test (NNAT; Naglieri 1996). Among other scores, these instruments yield an intelligence quotient (i.e. IQ score) based on a ratio of mental age to chronological age. In addition to other criteria, an IQ of approximately 70 or below, which is approximately two standard deviations below the mean, is needed for a diagnosis of ID to be made. Unfortunately, research on the validity of these measures has been minimal. Further research is necessary to ensure the valid interpretation and use of the results of these tests with all children and youth.

Traditionally, the degree of discrepancy of standardized intelligence test scores from the age-based norm has been described as mild, moderate, severe and profound. According to Maulik and Harbour (2011), the International Classification of Diseases (ICD-10; World Health Organization 2007b) is the most widely used classification system across all of its member countries. The ICD-10 describes IQ guidelines for levels of severity: mild (IQ = 50–69), moderate (IQ = 35–49), severe (IQ = 20–34) and profound (IQ <20). Most cases of intellectual disability (approximately 85 per cent) fall within the mild range.

A system describing the intensity of support needed by clients has also been proposed. The levels of support in the AAIDD classification manual (Luckasson *et al.* 2002) are: intermittent (occasional support), limited (e.g. a day programme in a sheltered workshop), extensive (daily, ongoing support) and pervasive (high level of support for all activities of daily living, possibly full-time nursing care). Level of support also varies by type, such as monitoring, prompting, partial physical assistance and full physical assistance. Educational needs are based on severity of ID, with educational plan teams developing appropriate instructional programmes.

In addition, limitations in adaptive behaviour, involving social skills, practical skills (e.g. eating, dressing, maintaining a safe environment) and conceptual skills (e.g. receptive and expressive language, reading, money concepts), distinguish individuals with ID. The limitations can be determined by using standardized tests such as the AAMR Adaptive Behavior Scale-School, second edition (Lambert *et al.* 1993) and the Supports Intensity Scale (Thompson *et al.* 2004), with performance that is at least two standard deviations below the mean being considered significant limitation. Assessment can also include other data, such as observations and interviews.

7.2   Epidemiology and aetiology

ID is the most common developmental disorder (Maulik and Harbour 2011). Reschly (2002) cites mild mental retardation, emotional disturbance, specific learning disabilities and speech-language disabilities as the four highest incidence disabilities. Estimates of the prevalence of ID among children and adolescents vary depending on diagnostic criteria used, study population and other factors. Internationally, the estimated prevalence is 'around 1% in high income countries and 2% in low and middle income countries' (Salvador-Carulla *et al.* 2011: 175). Especially for those in the mild range, prevalence tends to be greater for males than females (Maulik and Harbour 2011). The American Psychiatric Association (2000) reports a male-to-female ratio of 1.5 to 1.

The specific cause of ID is unknown for about two-thirds of individuals with mild ID and one-third of individuals with moderate to profound

ID. When the cause can be identified, it is often classified into one of several types. These types are preconceptual/genetic causes (e.g. Down's syndrome (DS) and fragile X syndrome (FXS)); prenatal causes (e.g. malformations of the central nervous system and teratogens); perinatal/birth process causes (e.g. intrauterine disorders and neonatal disorders); and postnatal causes (e.g. head injuries and infections) (Louhiala 2004; Maulik and Harbour 2011). In the past, not much attention was paid to aetiological differences, partly because aetiology was often unknown. Presently, however, aetiology is known in more cases because of advances in molecular biology. The American Academy of Child and Adolescent Psychiatry (1999) estimates that the classification that includes genetic disorder and monogenetic mutations, such as DS and FXS, makes up the highest percentage (32 per cent) of known causes of ID.

ID is often a multifaceted phenomenon, rather than a single, isolated disorder (Parmenter 2010). Individuals with ID often have at least one coexisting condition or disability. Comorbidities may include complex physical health problems, speech and language problems, autism spectrum disorder (ASD), mental health disorders and attention deficit hyperactivity disorder (ADHD).

7.3   Language development in intellectual disability

The acquisition of functional language in children with ID is less well understood than in normally developing children (Ogletree *et al.* 2011). This is especially true when ID is accompanied by severe speech and language deficits, as is often the case in DS, FXS or velocardiofacial syndrome (Sphrintzen 2000; Rondal 2001). The language of these children develops more slowly than that of children without disabilities. Yet, it is thought to have a similar developmental trajectory (Bates *et al.* 1995), albeit timing and outcomes are more varied and individual differences are more persistent in children with ID (Kaiser *et al.* 2001).

Individuals with ID often have delays in both expressive and receptive language. The major linguistic features that are delayed may include a combination of phonology, morphology, syntax, semantics and pragmatics. The specific area(s) that researchers identify as most affected depends on the characteristics of the individuals included in each particular research study. Characteristics such as severity of the ID (e.g. mild, moderate, severe, profound), whether the participants are speaking or non-speaking, and aetiology (e.g. DS, FXS, unknown) all play a role.

The cognition hypothesis (Cromer 1991) of delayed language acquisition in children with ID maintains that cognitive challenges in this group are responsible for the language delay. Mental age has been thought to dictate language ability in most children with ID (Chapman 1997; Rondal 2001). Indeed, in many studies the language level of children with ID has been commensurate with their mental age (Rondal 2001). However, unevenness in linguistic development in relation to mental age (some faster, some slower) has also been revealed. Mental age does not well predict weaknesses in speech production, syntax or intelligibility in children with DS (Roberts *et al.* 2007a). In children with non-specific ID (i.e. those without known syndromes), Van der Schuit *et al.* (2011) found that the vocabulary levels of children with ID were commensurate with their mental age, but that phonological working memory and syntax level were below their mental age. The vocabulary levels of other children with ID have been found to exceed their mental age (Facon *et al.* 2002).

One area of cognition that researchers of ID have been studying recently is working memory. Baddeley's (1996) model of working memory has three components: the central executive, the phonological loop and the visual-spatial sketchpad. The capacity of the phonological loop, which temporarily stores verbal information, is restricted in children (Russell *et al.* 1996; Jarrold and Baddeley 1997; Henry 2001; Henry and MacLean 2002) and adults with ID (Numminen *et al.* 2001, 2002). Furthermore, automatic rehearsal seems not to occur in children whose mental age is less than 7 years (Jarrold *et al.* 2000a). Schuchardt *et al.* (2010) compared the working memory of 15-year-olds with mild ID to four groups: 15-year-olds with borderline ID (IQ 70–84), 10-year-olds with borderline ID, children without disabilities matched for mental age, and children without disabilities matched for chronological age. Schuchardt and colleagues found that the children with ID had deficits in all three components of working memory compared to the children without disabilities, and those with mild ID had greater deficits than those with borderline ID. The deficit in the phonological loop was most severe.

Collectively, the communicative abilities of children with ID vary greatly (Van der Schuit *et al.* 2010). Additionally for children with ID, the predictive value of intelligence to later language skills remains equivocal (McCathren *et al.* 1999; Calandrella and Wilcox 2000). However, with the appropriate support, children with ID can acquire high levels of communication and literacy skills (Kaiser *et al.* 2001; Koppenhaver and Erickson 2003; Van der Schuit *et al.* 2010).

7.4   Non-speaking individuals with intellectual disability

The variations in language development of children with ID are sufficiently great (Gerber and Kraat 1992; Rondal 2001) that we have to make an arbitrary distinction between children with ID who are non-speaking and those children who become verbal communicators.

A subset of children with ID are unable to use natural speech to meet their communicative needs (Rosenberg and Abbeduto 1993; Romski and Sevcik 1997; Wilkinson and Hennig 2007). The additional cognitive,

Table 7.1 *Characteristics of types of communicators (from Ogletree et al. 2011)*

Expressive				Receptive
Communicator type	Intentional?	Symbol use?	Examples	
Perlocutionary	No	No	Grimace, cry, vocalize	Very limited May understand tone
Illocutionary	Yes	No	Gesture, tap on hand	General awareness of others' communication, but no flexible comprehension of language
Locutionary	Yes	Yes	Exchange communication card, verbally request	Comprehension is aided by augmented input (e.g. verbal message supported by tangible symbol)

motor and/or sensory deficits of these children can greatly interfere with the acquisition and use of spoken language (Van der Schuit *et al.* 2010). 'Complex communication needs' is the current term to describe these individuals with severe communication impairment (Bloomberg and Johnson 1990; Beukelman and Mirenda 2005). For these children, both expressive communication and receptive language are challenged. These insufficient language and communication skills result in the manifestation of problem behaviour for many of these children (Wacker *et al.* 2002; Sigafoos *et al.* 2003). It is not uncommon for them to use unconventional forms of communication (e.g. challenging behaviours, behavioural excesses, self-injurious behaviour) to express their needs (O'Neill *et al.* 1997; Sigafoos *et al.* 2002). The compromised communication skills of these children can adversely affect their quality of life as well as that of those who support them.

Complex communicators are highly diverse with regard to how they communicate. Some are pre-intentional while others have intentionality. McLean and Snyder-McLean (1988) used speech act theory (Austin 1962; Searle 1969) to characterize the communicative abilities of children with ID as perlocutionary, illocutionary and locutionary in nature (see Table 7.1). Ogletree *et al.* (2011) explained the various categories of communicator in the terms used by McLean and Snyder-McLean (1988). The distinctions between categories are fluid and there is overlap from one to another.

Most children with ID develop functional spoken communication skills during their childhood (Abbeduto 2003). Thus, children who do not eventually speak form a relatively low incidence population. Those who do not speak naturally are often able to use augmentative and alternative communication (AAC) (Van der Schuit *et al.* 2010). AAC is an intervention approach (Glennen 2000) that employs manual signs, communication boards and computerized voice-output devices. The relevance of AAC systems to perlocutionary, illocutionary and locutionary communicators with ID is undeniable. Beukelman and Mirenda (2005: 4) state that 'AAC should be thought of as a system with four primary components: symbols, aids, strategies, and techniques. An AAC system involves the use of multiple components or modes for communication.' AAC will be discussed further in section 7.6.

7.5   Speaking individuals with intellectual disability

This section is organized around three of the most commonly identified neurodevelopmental disorders associated with mild and moderate ID: Down's syndrome (DS), fragile X syndrome (FXS) and Williams syndrome (WS).

7.5.1   Down's syndrome

DS is the leading genetic cause of ID (Roberts *et al.* 2008). It is most commonly caused by an extra copy of chromosome 21 and is estimated to occur in 1 out of 920 births (Carothers *et al.* 1999). According to Abbeduto *et al.* (2007a), DS is associated with a pattern of strengths and weaknesses in communication which seems to distinguish it from other neurodevelopmental disorders such as FXS and WS. For example, 1- to 8-year-old children with DS have been found to have strong daily living and social skills relative to their communication skills (Dykens *et al.* 2006). Moreover, based on research by Chapman *et al.* (2002), the language phenotype of DS is described by Abbeduto *et al.* (2007a: 248) as 'likely to change with age, with both improvements and declines over the life course. Indeed there is evidence of continued progress in some language domains (e.g., productive syntax) alongside of declines, or regressions, in other domains (e.g., receptive syntax)'.

Substantial delays in the onset of first words and in expressive vocabulary relative to expectations for mental age have been widely reported for children with DS (Miller *et al.* 1995; Fidler *et al.* 2006; Abbeduto *et al.* 2007a). For example, Berglund *et al.* (2001) examined parental reports of word learning of 330 Swedish children with DS. They found that 3-year-old children with DS used productive words and sentences similar to 16-month-old children without disabilities. Likewise, 4-year-old children with DS used productive words and sentences similar to 20-month-old children without disabilities. Roberts *et al.* (2007a) examined older boys (4 to 15 years) with DS and found delays in their expressive vocabulary as well. By contrast, there are inconsistent results across studies on whether the receptive vocabulary of children with DS is equivalent to mental age expectations (e.g. see Chapman *et al.* 1991; Miller *et al.*1995; Price *et al.* 2007; and Roberts *et al.* 2007a).

Syntax is an area of special challenge for individuals with DS (Abbeduto *et al.* 2007a; Roberts *et al.* 2007a), with grammatical impairment present by 2 to 3 years of age (Chapman and Hesketh 2000). Expressive syntax is delayed relative to expectations for mental age (Roberts *et al.* 2008) and relative to syntax comprehension (Chapman *et al.* 1998; Eadie *et al.* 2002). However, there are inconsistent results across studies regarding whether children with DS show deficits in receptive syntax relative to non-verbal cognitive levels (e.g. see Thorndike *et al.* 1986; Chapman *et al.* 1991, 2002; and Price *et al.* 2007). Grammar is more affected than vocabulary in both expressive and receptive language (Laws and Bishop 2003).

In terms of pragmatics, or the social use of language, children with DS show an uneven profile with some strengths and some weaknesses (Coggins *et al.* 1983; Roberts *et al.* 2008). For example, Beeghly *et al.* (1990) found that children with DS did not differ from developmental age-matched children in topic maintenance or use of answers, comments or protests, but did use fewer requests. Roberts *et al.* (2007a) found that boys with DS, compared to boys without disabilities at similar mental levels, were less elaborative and produced a higher proportion of turns that were only adequate in quality during conversations with an adult. Children with DS also show an uneven profile in the narratives they produce (Boudreau and Chapman 2000; Miles and Chapman 2002; Kay-Raining Bird *et al.* 2004). Additional areas of difficulty for individuals with DS include speech production and intelligibility (Roberts *et al.* 2007a), grammatical morphology (Laws and Bishop 2003) and phonological memory (Abbeduto *et al.* 2007a).

For individuals with DS, Laws and Bishop (2003) note that language ability is not a simple function of non-verbal IQ. Moreover, expressive language seems to be especially challenging (Finestack and Abbeduto 2010) and it is often more affected than receptive language (Dykens *et al.* 1994; Laws and Bishop 2003; Roberts *et al.* 2007a). Roberts *et al.* (2008) report weaker expressive language skills for toddlers with DS than groups of children with mixed developmental disability and children without disabilities matched for mental age. During the school years the gap between expressive and receptive skills tends to widen (Miller *et al.* 1995; Chapman *et al.* 2002).

7.5.2 Fragile X syndrome

FXS is the most common inherited genetic cause of ID (Abbeduto and Hagerman 1997; Hagerman and Hagerman 2002). It is associated with a change in a gene called *FMR1* on the X chromosome. It affects twice as many males (1 in 4,000) as females (1 in 8,000) (Crawford *et al.* 2001). Males with FXS tend to be more severely affected than females with FXS (Abbeduto *et al.* 2007b). Most males with FXS have ID in the moderate to severe range, whereas only about one-third of females with FXS have ID and it tends to be in the mild range (Bennetto and Pennington 2002).

Most of the research on communication of individuals with FXS has included only males. Both expressive and receptive vocabulary are relative strengths for boys with FXS (Madison *et al.* 1986; Roberts *et al.* 2007b). In particular, Roberts *et al.* (2007b) investigated three groups of boys (2.9 to 14.4 years of age): boys with FXS and ASD, boys with FXS without ASD, and boys without disabilities. They found that boys with FXS (without ASD) were similar to boys without disabilities in terms of receptive and expressive vocabulary and speech skills. There were mixed results for boys with FXS and ASD. In addition, Roberts *et al.* (2007b) found that boys with FXS had higher receptive vocabulary than did boys with DS.

In contrast, both expressive and receptive syntax present challenges for boys with FXS. For example, Price *et al.* (2007) found that receptive syntax was delayed for boys with FXS relative to their non-verbal cognitive level. Price *et al.* (2008) and Roberts *et al.* (2007b) compared the conversational speech of boys with FXS to that of younger boys without disabilities. The utterances of the boys with FXS were characterized as shorter and less complex, with less complex noun phrases, verb phrases and sentence structure. Their questions and negations, however, were similar to those in the typically developing comparison group. The researchers propose that the observed syntactic differences were related to vocabulary limitations.

Unfortunately, because there is little existing research on girls with FXS, there is not enough research to determine how girls with FXS do in terms of their vocabulary or syntax (Roberts *et al.* 2008). Overall, the research that has included girls with FXS finds that they have less severe language delay than boys with FXS (Roberts *et al.* 2008). It is likely that the differences in the language of boys and girls with FXS reflect the degree of ID (Abbeduto *et al.* 2007b).

Girls and boys with FXS have difficulty with pragmatics (Abbeduto and Hagerman 1997; Abbeduto and Chapman 2005; Rice *et al.* 2005; Abbeduto *et al.* 2007b). Girls with FXS, for example, have difficulties in initiating and sustaining conversations (Freund *et al.* 1993; Mazzocco *et al.* 1997; Lesniak-Karpiak *et al.* 2003). In addition, girls with FXS tend to have a distinct style of talking, considered a run-on, disorganized and tangential style (Abbeduto and Hagerman 1997). Perseverative language, defined as 'excessive self-repetition of a word, phrase, sentence or topic', is characteristic of males with FXS (Abbeduto and Hagerman 1997: 317).

A number of researchers have compared the language and communication of individuals with FXS to those with DS and found distinct profiles.

For instance, findings suggest that the development of syntax is more delayed in individuals with DS than for those with FXS (Abbeduto *et al.* 2003; Price *et al.* 2008). Generally, the expressive and receptive language challenges of individuals with DS are more severe than those with FXS (Abbeduto *et al.* 2001; Price *et al.* 2007). In a study of high-functioning adolescents with FXS compared to those with DS, Finestack and Abbeduto (2010) found that adolescents with FXS had a better overall use of language than did those with DS.

7.5.3 Williams syndrome

WS is caused by the deletion of over 20 genes from the long arm of chromosome 7. It is rare, with an estimated prevalence of 1 in 7,500 to 1 in 20,000 live births (Martens *et al.* 2008). Individuals with WS have ID but their language and communication may be distinct from other groups, such as children and adolescents with DS. In particular, it has been argued that their language is an area of strength (Mervis *et al.* 2003) or that it is preserved or spared (Bellugi *et al.* 1997, 2000).

Bellugi *et al.* (1997) compared the language of individuals with WS to individuals with DS matched for age, full-scale intelligence quotient and educational background. They found that the vocabulary of those with WS was characteristic and unusual. Bellugi *et al.* (1997: 336) described it as a 'proclivity for unusual words'. For example, when asked to name animals, they included more typical/common types of animals and also more non-prototypical animals, such as yak, unicorn and sabre-tooth tiger. In terms of syntax, performance of the adolescents with WS on tests of comprehension of passive sentences, negations and conditionals was better than that of the individuals with DS matched to them on IQ and age. The spontaneous language of individuals with WS in narrative tasks, such as telling a story from a wordless picture book, tends to be phonologically and syntactically sophisticated compared to individuals with DS. Bellugi *et al.* (1997) describe their language as being rich in prosody and linguistic devices compared to those with DS or those without disabilities. This includes, for example, identifying the affective state of story characters and use of sound effects. Losh *et al.* (1997) have also found that adolescents with WS have advantages in spontaneous expressive language.

Stojanovik *et al.* (2006) found significant variability among four children with WS on standardized assessments of comprehension and production (focusing on syntax and semantics) and spontaneous speech. Some researchers describe the onset of language for children with WS as significantly delayed (e.g. Paterson *et al.* 1999) or as following an atypical pathway (Laing *et al.* 2002). For example, the order in which milestones (e.g. the vocabulary spurt, pointing and speech production) occur is different for young children with WS compared to young children with DS or those without disabilities (Mervis *et al.* 1999).

Furthermore, children with WS have difficulty in the area of pragmatics. Stojanovik (2006) found that a small sample of school-age children with WS, compared to children with specific language impairment (SLI) and children without disabilities, did not provide enough information for their discourse partner and relied too much on their partner's leads and contributions. In a study of the referential communication skills of school-age children with WS, John *et al.* (2009) investigated children's understanding of when a message was inadequate. They found that children with WS indicated a problem with an inadequate message less than half the time.

Laws and Bishop (2004) compared the pragmatic skills of children and adults with WS to three groups: children and adults with DS, children with SLI, and children without disabilities. All three groups with disabilities had lower pragmatic composite scores on the Children's Communication Checklist (CCC; Bishop 1998) than did the children without disabilities. The composite score of the group with WS was the lowest, although it was not significantly different from the groups with DS and with SLI. Moreover, the group with WS scored lower than the control group on all five pragmatic components of the CCC, which were inappropriate initiation of conversation, coherence, stereotyped conversation, use of conversational context, and conversational rapport. The scores of the subjects with WS on the stereotyped conversation and inappropriate initiation of conversation subscales were also lower than those of the groups with DS and with SLI. The overall pragmatic functioning of school-age children with WS, as assessed by the CCC-2 (Bishop 2003b), has been found to be higher though than that of children with ASD (Philofsky *et al.* 2007).

Generally, regardless of aetiology, pragmatics is often challenging for individuals with ID (Abbeduto and Hesketh 1997). This includes difficulties in identifying referents (Abbeduto *et al.* 1991; Brownell and Whitely 1992) as well as expressing and understanding speech acts, which seem to improve during adolescence and adulthood (Rosenberg and Abbeduto 1993). Additionally, delays in theory of mind have been reported for children and adolescents with ID (Abbeduto *et al.* 2004) and these have been linked to pragmatic deficits (John *et al.* 2009). However, school-age children with ID have been shown to be similar to school-age children without disabilities in terms of using common ground (knowledge that the speaker and listener are presumed to share) to understand and disambiguate referential expressions (Abbeduto *et al.* 1998). The challenges that individuals with ID face with pragmatics may have important consequences, such as hindering their successful inclusion in integrated programmes (Dolan 1997).

7.6   Intervention in intellectual disability

Language and communication skills are fundamental to quality of life. Hence, when they are compromised, as in children with ID, it is critical that remediation occur. In 1986, the National Joint Committee (NJC) for the Communicative Needs of Persons with Severe Disabilities was established in the USA with a view to recognizing the importance of communication in ID and improving communication through intervention. While determining the legitimacy of communication intervention with persons with severe disabilities may seem redundant, not all children with ID receive intervention to address their communicative deficits (Goldstein 2006). In the United States, and specifically in 31 states, if a child's language skills are commensurate with his or her cognitive level, services from a speech-language pathologist are denied, due to the mistaken belief that language skills cannot improve on account of cognitive constraints (Goldstein 2006). The NJC wanted to determine, first, if communicative abilities could be improved through intervention and, second, how some improvement could be made.

In 2005, the NJC reviewed the previous 20 years of communication intervention research in clients with severe intellectual and developmental disabilities, and assessed the results of this research against current evidence-based practice standards (Snell *et al.* 2010). The committee sought to identify the characteristics of the research evidence that supports intervention for communication in children with severe disabilities who had IQs of 44 or below. Snell and her colleagues concluded that systematic intervention can improve expressive and interactive communication skills of these children with complex communication needs. Furthermore, research demonstrates that language intervention benefits children with ID even when there is no language–cognition discrepancy (Cole *et al.* 1990, 1994). Intervention for communication skills is not dependent upon a language–cognition discrepancy, and improvements in communication skills of children with severe disabilities can be made when the intervention is systematic.

Most communication interventions with children with ID have a singular focus (Van der Schuit *et al.* 2010). Comprehension of linguistic concepts (Kim and Lombardino 1991), communication skills (Tannock *et al.* 1992; Sevcik and Romski 1997; Romski *et al.* 1999; Skotko *et al.* 2004) and mastery of an AAC system (Iacono and Duncum 1995; Romski and Sevcik 1996; Romski *et al.* 2003) have all been examined. Others have examined grammatical development (Warren *et al.* 1994; Harris *et al.* 1996), speech intelligibility (Dodd *et al.* 1994) and literacy (Erickson and Koppenhaver 1995).

Although singular in focus, the growth of communication intervention options for persons with severe disabilities has been increasing steadily since the 1980s. The early strict adherence to behavioural principles in narrow contexts has shifted to the current emphasis on functional, community-based efforts (Ogletree *et al.* 2011) in natural learning environments (Dunst *et al.* 2001a, 2001b). Utilizing the child's natural environment specifically for communication intervention has been emphasized over the past 15 years. The most recent emphasis on the natural environment for communication intervention is the direct result of the provision for 'natural environments' in the amendments to the American Public Law 105-17 (Walsh *et al.* 2000). In the Individuals with Disabilities Education Act (1997), the law states that interventions must be conducted in settings in which children without disabilities participate (Office of Special Education and Rehabilitative Services 2003). So in the USA, the utilization of natural environments is mandated.

There is an abundance of evidence both prior to and after the passage of this law that supports the claim that natural environments are best suited to promoting the acquisition of communicative competence (Halle and Holt 1991; McWilliam 1992, 2000; Barnett *et al.* 1993; Noonan and McCormick 1993; Kaiser and Hester 1996; Santos and Lignugaris/Kraft 1997; Prizant and Wetherby 1998; Odom *et al.* 2000; Dunst *et al.* 2001a, 2001b). Comparisons of the effect of special and general education placements on communicative development in children with ID have been conducted in The Netherlands (Peetsma *et al.* 2001), Australia (Foreman *et al.* 2004) and the USA (Fisher and Meyer 2002) and have found that the general education environment promoted the most progress in communication for these children.

These natural environments must also be contextually meaningful and complete with familiar, interesting tasks that are offered at the child's developmental level in order to tap into intrinsic motivation (Kolb 1984; Siegel-Causey and Bashinski 1997; Siegel and Wetherby 2000; Dunst *et al.* 2001a, 2001b; Siegel and Cress 2002; Roper and Dunst 2003; Beukelman and Mirenda 2005). For example, if a child loves animals (familiar and interesting) and has many pets, then learning the linguistic terms for animals while playing with the pets would be contextually meaningful, while seeing pictures of animals on flashcards, sitting at a table, would be non-contextual (Roper and Dunst 2003). Yet another example from Roper and Dunst (2003) demonstrates the contextually meaningful practice of reading books to a child who adores books, and how that activity can become decontextualized if contingencies were placed on the child to participate. For instance, if the adult would not turn the page until the child had identified a specific picture, or would not change books until the first book was finished, then the task loses its meaning for the child and would be considered non-contextual. By conducting communicative interventions in contextually relevant environments, the children with ID should have access to activities and routines that are motivating to them.

The broader communicative environment must also be taken into account during intervention. The people with whom children with ID interact in their environments (e.g. parents, caregivers, teachers, therapists, peers) are of major importance to both early language and literacy development (McCartney 1984; Whitehurst and Lonigan 1998; Dunst *et al.* 2001a, 2001b). There are vast differences between the communicative environments of children with ID in comparison to children without disabilities. While the former should be responsive to the child's lead and contingent, they are often adult-directed and directive (Light *et al.* 1985a, 1985b; Mahoney and Wheeden 1999; Dunst *et al.* 2001a, 2001b). Typically, children with ID spend more of their time in activities that are adult-directed and adult-centred than do children without disabilities (Marfo 1991). Children with complex communication needs spend much of their time in therapies, which are often adult-directed, thereby losing the intrinsic motivation that is so important to their learning.

Children with ID tend to eat and socialize with others who also experience communicative impairments, and their access to competent communicators is often limited to those who are paid to support them. Their access to students without disabilities is limited (Peetsma *et al.* 2001; Williamson *et al.* 2006; Cho 2008). When peers without disabilities are available, they can model desirable communication skills (Guralnick and Paul-Brown 1989; Goldstein and Kaczmarek 1992; Paul-Brown and Caperton 2001). In addition, peers without disabilities are effective when they are taught strategies to promote social communication with peers with ID (Goldstein and Cisar 1992; Goldstein *et al.* 1997; Guralnick and Neville 1997; Strain and Kohler 1998; Guralnick 2001). It is important to note that physical proximity to peers without disabilities, who are not taught instructional strategies, does not have beneficial effects on communication interactions for children with ID (Strain 1983; Guralnick and Paul-Brown 1989; Sigman and Rushkin 1999). Thus, to promote skills across a greater variety of communicative settings, communicative interventions should take place in the natural learning environment with engaged and skilled partners.

Milieu teaching (Warren and Kaiser 1988) is an approach to intervention that stresses contextually relevant natural environments that are child-centred and child-directed. Communicative partners are taught to follow the child's lead, prompt specific skills and target specific skills like communicative functions. The environment can be manipulated to increase the child's interest and subsequently communication (Goldstein 2006). Thiemann and Warren (2010) refer to this as the creation of communication opportunities. The child's interest can be piqued through sabotage (missing elements for an activity), providing interesting materials out of reach, setting up silly situations, providing inadequate portions and violating expectations for the purpose of motivating the child with ID to initiate an interaction. Combining environmental modifications (e.g. materials out of reach) with facilitative strategies employed by peers, throughout the day, has produced improvements in the communication abilities of children with ID (Goldstein 2006). Ogletree *et al.* (2011) elaborate on this concept by emphasizing that communicative activities should take place within routines; activities should have a discrete beginning and end (Snyder-McLean *et al.* 1988). These are scripted sequences that provide predictability regarding an activity while still being child-directed.

How interventions should take place is one issue, but the timing of interventions is most critical. Early intervention is necessary to stimulate language, communication and early literacy of children with ID, and to inform parents of the necessity of such intervention (Tannock *et al.* 1992; Erickson and Koppenhaver 1995). Evidence from brain research supports the use of intervention early in the child's development (Van der Schuit *et al.* 2011).

Determining what aspect of communication should be prioritized is an issue for all who are charged with conducting intervention. Since most problem behaviours of children with ID are the result of insufficient conventional communication skills (Wacker *et al.* 2002; Sigafoos *et al.* 2003), it is critical that communication interventions address the need for replacement communication skills. Ogletree *et al.* (2011) urge the recognition of the current idiosyncratic communication employed by the child with ID. A functional behaviour analysis must be conducted in order to determine the function of the current behaviour. The function, or the communicative intent, may be a request, a protest or the seeking of attention. Whatever the function is, the form of the communication needs to become more conventional. Teaching the replacement skill will be a necessary intervention strategy for children with behavioural challenges.

Augmentative and alternative communication (AAC) systems can also assist with the prelinguistic and cognitive skills necessary for language development in children with complex communication needs (Light *et al.* 1985a, 1985b; Romski and Sevcik 1996; Brady 2000). Ogletree *et al.* (2011) state that there are no prerequisites on the use of AAC. It may be justified at any age or cognitive level and AAC usage does not interfere with a child's acquisition of vocal/verbal communication (Cress and Marvin 2003). Although early access to AAC is essential for early communication development in children with complex communication needs, there are multiple reasons why many children do not receive this much needed intervention. According to Wetherby *et al.* (1998), many professionals lack the knowledge to facilitate such communication development. In addition, many of these young children have significant medical and physical challenges such that communication is not a high priority (Cress and Marvin 2003). While obstacles to the introduction and utilization of AAC systems abound, it is imperative that AAC systems be matched to the needs and skills of the child with complex communication needs (Wilkinson and Hennig 2007).

The advances in AAC during the past 20 years have been profound. The sophistication of the devices and the intelligibility of speech output have improved dramatically (Romski and Sevcik 2005). These advances alone had not translated programmatically into early interventions for young children. However, with the advent of AAC applications that run on the iPhone, iTouch and iPad, AAC interest and use has suddenly surged. Sennott and Bowker (2009) acknowledge the limitations of table-top digital devices. These are being replaced by more powerful, portable and affordable technologies that have only recently been made available. Lately, there has been a cascade of AAC applications, beginning with Proloquo2Go (Sennott and Niemeijr 2009) which reflects good practice in AAC (Farrell 2011).

The intervention elements discussed above are applicable to the wide variety of children with ID as they provide guidelines for the timing, environment, activities and partners that benefit the communicative development of the child with ID. Regardless of the level of their IQ, or their ability to speak, improvements can be made when intervening with the communicative abilities of children with ID. Critical to these inter-ventions is the provision of consistent, frequent, systematic and individu-alized instruction. Children with ID must be given ample opportunities in which to learn, practise and receive feedback on the effects of their communication across all environments with a host of social partners (Goldstein 2006).

The effects of communication and language interventions on chil-dren with developmental delays and disorders have been investigated for over 50 years (Warren *et al.* 2007). Indeed, hundreds of studies have been published, resulting in substantial evidence for a number of inter-vention approaches, and evidence that early intervention, in general, is beneficial (Guralnick and Neville 1997). However, there is much variabil-ity among children with ID and language interventions must be custom-ized to the child's specific profile (Gerber and Kraat 1992; Rondal 2001). Unfortunately, the transference of evidence-based practices from research to the frontline personnel, who develop and implement the program-ming for children with ID, has not been continuous (Olgetree *et al.* 2011). Survey findings suggest that many speech-language pathologists do not value, and therefore fail to provide, evidence-based intervention services to children with severe ID (Siegel *et al.* 2010).

7.7　Future directions

In many ways, the examination of communicative abilities of children and adolescents with ID is in its infancy. Although many studies have made attempts to examine and intervene, we know from literature reviews (Schlosser *et al.* 2005; Warren *et al.* 2007; Snell *et al.* 2010) that greater rigour must be applied to such investigations in the future. All aspects of these studies could be improved, from the definition of participants to the generalization and maintenance of treatment and everything in between (Snell *et al.* 2010). To allow for the implementation of research replica-tion, interventions must be described methodically, including setting, method of intervention, treatment duration and intensity (Warren *et al.* 2007; Snell *et al.* 2010; Thiemann and Warren 2010). We know this can be done. We also know that when provided with systematic interventions, communicative abilities of individuals with ID can improve.

It would assist future research greatly if consistent terminology and definitions were used worldwide. For example, the term 'intellectual disability', which has been used throughout this chapter and defined at its outset, is not used universally. In the UK the preferred term is 'learning disabilities' (Fernald 1995). However, in North America the term 'learning disability' has an entirely different meaning that excludes cognitive impairment. Additionally, there have not been investigations to date of ethnic differences with regard to communication and children with ID (Maulik and Harbour 2011). Yet, it would be reasonable to assume that this must be determined for culturally sensitive interventions to occur. We must also distinguish between girls and boys when it comes to profiling children with FXS. Although there has been work done with boys only, much of the research groups both genders together. Despite the cost of longitudinal studies, the wealth of information that could be gleaned over time regarding trajectories and intervention effectiveness for communication in children with ID would be well worth the cost.

Although we know the critical role of language comprehension in the production of language (Hollich *et al.* 2000), precious little has been done with regard to assessing or intervening on receptive language in children with ID. Similarly, we know that memory plays a critical role in language production and that children with mental ages less than 7 years of age do not rehearse (Jarrold *et al.* 2000a). However, we have yet to see this taken into account when it comes to communication intervention. Van der Molen *et al.* (2010) have shown that working memory can be improved. Perhaps improving working memory could lead to improved language production. Still looking at the need for improved production, few have examined the idiosyncratic communicative nature of behavioural excesses, and fewer still have chosen to measure communicative functions (Snell *et al.* 2010). We must prioritize what communicative skills are taught to children with ID.

The quality and quantity of research on communication of individuals with ID is rendered moot if frontline personnel cannot be motivated, or taught to implement the evidence-based practices with the individuals in their natural environments. We know that improvements can be made given systematic instruction. Now we must endeavour to motivate researchers to conduct more rigorous investigations and we must encourage those on the frontlines to employ the most promising interventions.

8

Emotional disturbance and communication

Gregory J. Benner and J. Ron Nelson

8.1   Introduction

US public schools provide special education and related services to nearly 500,000 students labelled with emotional disturbance (ED; Individuals with Disabilities Education Improvement Act 2004; US Department of Education 2002). However, while less than 1 per cent of school-age students receive special education services for ED as defined in the Individuals with Disabilities Education Improvement Act (IDEA; 2004), there are far more children and youth with ED who will go unserved during their educational years. Prevalence estimates suggest that 3–20 per cent of students have ED, with very conservative estimates suggesting 6 per cent (Kauffman 2013). Given that the majority of these students do not receive necessary individualized and specially designed supports for their behavioural challenges, these students have been referred to as the unclaimed children (Knitzer and Olson 1982).

The US Department of Education defines ED as at least one social or emotional characteristic exhibited over an extended period of time that adversely affects school performance, including (a) problems with learning or interpersonal relationships; (b) exhibiting inappropriate behaviour under normal circumstances; (c) disorders of affect, such as depression or pervasive unhappiness; or (d) exhibiting fears or physical symptoms in response to school or personal problems. The specific eligibility criteria for services under IDEA (2004: Sec. 300.8(c)(4)) include:

(i)   … a condition exhibiting one or more of the following characteristics over a long period of time and to a marked degree that adversely affects a child's educational performance:
    (A) An inability to learn that cannot be explained by intellectual, sensory, or health factors.

      (B) An inability to build or maintain satisfactory interpersonal relationships with peers and teachers.

      (C) Inappropriate types of behavior or feelings under normal circumstances.

      (D) A general pervasive mood of unhappiness or depression.

      (E) A tendency to develop physical symptoms or fears associated with personal or school problems.

   (ii) The term includes schizophrenia. The term does not apply to children who are socially maladjusted, unless it is determined they have an emotional disturbance.

As with all disability categories, states define ED and specify the eligibility criteria to be used by local school districts in the identification of students with ED. Although the eligibility criteria must be consistent with the federal definition, many states have adopted their own specific terminology and eligibility criteria (Swartz *et al.* 1987). For example, some states have dropped the socially maladjusted exclusion eligibility criterion. This criterion was dropped for two reasons: (1) there are no valid theoretical or empirical grounds for differentiating between social maladjustment and other ED, and (2) there are no reliable or socially validated instruments for making a distinction between social maladjustment and ED (Stein and Merrell 1992).

    Types of ED can be grouped under one of two broad bipolar dimensions: externalizing and internalizing (Achenbach 2001). Each of these broad bipolar dimensions includes specific syndromes (e.g. oppositional defiant disorder). Externalizing refers to all ED outwardly directed by the student toward the external social environment. Externalizing ED involves behavioural excesses considered inappropriate by parents, teachers, other professionals and peers. These behavioural manifestations often result in difficulties with social, academic and vocational functioning. Examples of externalizing behaviour problems include displaying aggression towards objects or persons, arguing, forcing the submission of others, defying the teacher, being out of the seat, not complying with teacher instructions or directives, having tantrums, being hyperactive, disturbing others, stealing and not following teacher- or school-imposed rules (Walker and Severson 1990). The most common externalizing syndromes include conduct disorder, oppositional defiant disorder, attention deficit hyperactivity disorder (ADHD) and adjustment disorder (American Psychiatric Association 2000). Additionally, high comorbidity rates are reported for externalizing syndromes (McConaughy and Skiba 1994).

    Internalizing ED involves behavioural deficits representing problems with self that are inwardly directed away from the external social environment. Internalizing ED is often self-imposed and frequently involves behavioural deficits and patterns of social avoidance. As with externalizing behaviour, these behavioural manifestations often result in difficulties with social, academic and vocational functioning. Examples of internalizing behaviour problems include having low or restricted activity levels, not talking with other children, being shy, being timid or unassertive, avoiding or withdrawing from social situations, preferring to play or spend time alone, acting in a fearful manner, not participating in games and activities, being unresponsive to social initiations by others and not standing up for oneself (Walker and Severson 1990). The most common internalizing syndromes include obsessive compulsive disorder, generalized anxiety disorder, social anxiety, separation anxiety disorder, post-traumatic stress disorder and child/adolescent depression (American Psychiatric Association 2000). Additionally, high comorbidity rates are reported for internalizing syndromes (McConaughy and Skiba 1994).

Youth with ED are likely to have language disorders that interfere with their ability to communicate (Nelson *et al.* 2005a). Indeed, the chief instrument of integration and order in human mental life is language (Vygotsky 1962). Language disorders are of two main types: receptive and expressive. Receptive (e.g. listening) language disorders include problems understanding language. Expressive (e.g. speaking) language disorders are problems using language (Owens 2008). Pragmatic language disorders, considered a component of language rather than a type of language disorder, are difficulties with the rules related to language use in social settings (e.g. speaker–listener relationship, turn-taking, eye contact, etc.).

Our knowledge about language dysfunction in students classified by the federal special education category of ED is growing. In contrast to a 4–7 per cent rate of language disorders in the school-aged general population (Paul 2007), language deficits appear to be much more common in youth with ED, and vice versa (Benner *et al.* 2002). A report of the Surgeon General on children's mental health indicated that successful use of language and communication is a cornerstone of childhood mental health (US Department of Health and Human Services 1999). Not only are strong language capabilities critical to the development of skills such as listening and speaking, but they are also fundamental to the acquisition of proficient reading and writing abilities. Parent and baby start to communicate with each other vocally as well as visually during the first months of life. Many, but not all, developmental psychologists believe that this early pattern of mother–infant reciprocity and interchange is the basis on which subsequent language and communication develop.

Language disorders appear to have a devastating effect on interpersonal relationships (e.g. those with family, companions and peers) throughout the lifespan. Children who are aggressive, for example, use less verbal communication and more direct physical actions to solve interpersonal problems due to limited language skills (Gallagher 1999). Children prone to non-compliance may have receptive language deficits that limit their ability to comprehend and comply to repeated warnings or verbal cues (Fujiki *et al.* 1999). As a result, such children may misinterpret communications, become frustrated, and consequently develop chains of miscommunication and antisocial behaviour patterns (Ruhl *et al.* 1992). The primary aim of this chapter is to illustrate that communication problems underlie the main presenting problem for students with ED, which is the inability to build or maintain satisfactory interpersonal relationships with parents, supervisors, peers and teachers.

The focus of this chapter is to summarize what we understand about the communication skills of students with ED and how to support these students in school. We also focus on the research and policies needed to meet the communication needs of this population. In this context, the chapter will describe the characteristics of students with ED (section 8.2) as well as the communication skills of these students (section 8.3). It will also examine how the communication needs of students with ED can be met (section 8.4). Finally, the chapter will discuss the research needs that need to be addressed with respect to this population (section 8.5) as well as certain policy needs (section 8.6). We begin with an overview of the characteristics of students with ED.

8.2   Characteristics of students with emotional disturbance

We begin by examining the behavioural, demographic and functional characteristics of students with ED. First, we present information on the behavioural characteristics of students with ED. Then, we describe the demographic characteristics of these students. Finally, we examine the functional characteristics of students with ED, including their cognitive and academic skills.

8.2.1   Behavioural characteristics

ED and the terminology used to classify associated disorders, such as emotional and behavioural disorders, resist easy and precise definition. ED is an umbrella term for a group of social and emotional function disorders that limit students' social, academic and vocational success. As noted above, students with such disorders are categorized as having an emotional disturbance under IDEA. The US Department of Education defines ED as at least one social or emotional characteristic exhibited over an extended period of time that adversely affects school performance, including (a) problems with learning or interpersonal relationships; (b) exhibiting inappropriate behaviour under normal circumstances; (c) disorders of affect, such as depression or pervasive unhappiness; or (d) exhibiting fears or physical symptoms in response to school or personal problems.

Other federal agencies that serve students with ED use different eligibility criteria than IDEA. The eligibility criteria adopted by the Center for Mental Health Services require the presence of a diagnosable mental, behavioural or emotional disorder of sufficient duration to meet diagnostic criteria specified in the Diagnostic and Statistical Manual of Mental Disorders (DSM; fourth edition, text revision; American Psychiatric Association 2000). Furthermore, the mental, behavioural or emotional disorder must result in a functional impairment that substantially interferes with or limits the child's role or functioning in family, school or community activities. The eligibility criteria employed by the Social Security Administration for the children's Supplemental Security Income programme require the presence of a mental condition that can be medically proven (Social Security Administration 2006). Moreover, the mental condition must result in marked, severe functional limitations of substantial duration. Given the differences in criteria, eligibility for services under the Center for Mental Health Services and Social Security Administration does not necessarily mean children are eligible for services under IDEA.

8.2.2   Demographic characteristics

Boys are more likely to have ED than girls. In a national study, more than three-quarters of students with ED receiving special education services were male (Wagner *et al.* 2005). This represented the highest proportion of males to females in any of the disability categories. Lower identification rates for females have been attributed to two factors. First, the assessment and identification process is largely subjective and influenced by schools' behavioural norms and standards (Wehby *et al.* 1997). Teachers may simply be less willing to refer girls for special education services for ED than they are boys. Second, girls are more likely than boys to exhibit internalizing ED that typically does not directly interfere with classroom management. Teachers are much more likely to identify students who exhibit externalizing ED than those with internalizing syndromes (Gresham *et al.* 1996).

While females are underrepresented among students receiving special education services for ED, African Americans are over-represented. Higher identification rates for African American students have been attributed to two factors. First, there may be a mismatch between the normative behaviour of African American students and teacher expectations regarding such behaviour (Horowitz *et al.* 1998). This mismatch in normative behaviour may result in higher referrals for special education services. Second, the over-identification of African American students may be due to the limited availability of culturally sensitive assessment instruments (Harry 1994). Current behavioural rating scales used to identify students with ED do not account for cultural differences in normative behaviour.

Additionally, students with ED are more likely than the general population to have demographic characteristics related to poor school outcomes. For example, people in the lowest income group are three times more likely to have a mental disorder than those in the highest income group (US Department of Health and Human Services 1999). As such, it is not surprising children and youth with ED receiving special education services are more likely to live in low socioeconomic homes than both students in the general population and those with other disabilities (Lewit *et al.* 1997; Wagner *et al.* 2005). More than 32 per cent of school-age students with ED live in poverty; among their general population peers, the figure is approximately 17 per cent.

8.2.3   Academic functioning

A plethora of research has demonstrated that students with ED are likely to have academic skill deficits (Nelson *et al.* 2004). Students with ED consistently show moderate to severe academic skills deficits relative to normally achieving students (Gajar 1979; Scruggs and Mastropieri 1986; Wilson *et al.* 1986; Meadows *et al.* 1994; Brier 1995; Wagner 1995; Greenbaum *et al.* 1996; Mattison *et al.* 1998) and students with learning disabilities (e.g. Gajar 1979; Scruggs and Mastropieri 1986). For example, Trout *et al.* (2003) reported that in 91 per cent (i.e. 31 of 35) of the studies reviewed over a 40-year timeframe (i.e. 1961 to 2000), students with ED showed substantial deficits in academic skills (i.e. below grade level or one or more years behind their peers).

8.3   Communication skills of students with emotional disturbance

In this section, we describe the nature of communication skills of students with ED. We begin with a discussion of the prevalence of language difficulties among students with ED, followed by the stability of these difficulties over time. We then discuss the interrelationships between the language, cognitive, demographic and behavioural functioning of students with ED and their contribution to the academic skills of this population.

8.3.1   Prevalence

Youth with ED are likely to have language disorders that interfere with their ability to communicate (Nelson *et al.* 2005a). Indeed, the concomitant prevalence of language disorders in children and youth with ED is 10 times that of the general population (e.g. Warr-Leeper *et al.* 1994). In the foremost study of language dysfunction in students classified with

ED (Nelson *et al.* 2005a), a prevalence rate of language disorders of 68% was found. This high occurrence in these 166 students with ED was consistent with an earlier major literature review of language deficits and psychiatric disorders (Benner *et al.* 2002). Benner *et al.* (2002) found an average of 71% for any language deficit in 18 studies in which a variety of language instruments and definitions for language deficit were used in children who met either a special education or a DSM definition of emotional or behavioural disorder. In contrast, a 4–7% rate of language disorders has been found in the school-aged general population (Paul 2007). In their review of the literature, Benner *et al.* (2002) found that, on average, approximately 90% of students with ED served in public school settings had expressive, receptive and/or pragmatic language deficits. The following percentages of all the grade-school participants scored ≤85 (at least one standard deviation below the mean (1 SD)) on each composite score of the Clinical Evaluation of Language Fundamentals-3 (CELF-3; Semel *et al.* 1995): 42% Receptive Language, 55% Expressive Language and 54% Total Language. Overall, 67% achieved at least one composite score in the clinical range, including 32% on all three scores.

Nelson and colleagues reported that the language deficits of students with ED were stable across age (Nelson *et al.* 2005a). Students with ED, on average, experienced large expressive and receptive deficits across the school years. This finding is supported by previous research conducted with children with ED who were served in clinical settings (e.g. Baker and Cantwell 1987b; Beitchman *et al.* 2001). For example, Beitchman *et al.* (2001) followed a sample (n = 301) of children with speech and language disorders over 14 years. The language skills of children with speech/language disorders remained relatively stable over the 14-year period. Just as antisocial behaviour patterns are stable and resistant to the current social development practices of schools (Kazdin 1993; Walker and Severson 2002), it appears that the language deficits of students with ED also may be stable and resistant to the current language development efforts of schools. This is not to imply that the language deficits of students are solely a function of their ED. Rather, they are likely to be a function of the complex interaction between the presenting problems associated with students' ED (e.g. non-compliance, inattention) and the social and language development practices provided to them.

Because successful language acquisition is a prerequisite for successful academic learning in all areas (Baker and Cantwell 1987b; Catts *et al.* 1999), the language deficits of students with ED are likely to have a negative influence on their academic achievement. Indeed, the Individuals with Disabilities Education Improvement Act (IDEA) of 2004 defined a specific learning disability as 'a disorder in one or more of the basic psychological processes involved in understanding or in using language, spoken or written, which may manifest itself in the imperfect ability to listen, think, speak, read, write, spell, or do mathematical calculations' (Sec.

602(30)(A)). In this context, Benner *et al.* (2009) examined the prevalence of four types of language disorders among public school students (n = 152) classified with ED. Nearly two out of three students with ED experienced a language disorder, with combined receptive-expressive disorders the most common (35.5 per cent). Students with a language disorder, particularly combined receptive-expressive disorder, showed significantly poorer achievement and more learning disabilities (LD) in all areas compared to students with no language disorder. Furthermore, nine out of ten students with any LD also had a language disorder.

8.3.2   Behavioural predictors

Researchers have studied the particular types of problem behaviour that are related to the academic skills of students with ED (Mattison *et al.* 1998; Barriga *et al.* 2002; Nelson *et al.* 2004). For example, Mattison *et al.* (1998) used the DSM-III to examine categories of problem behaviours that are related to the academic skills of students with ED. These researchers found that conduct/oppositional disorder was related to the academic skills of elementary and secondary aged students with ED. Externalizing behaviour appears to be related to language skills whereas internalizing behaviour is not (Nelson *et al.* 2005a). These results suggest that students with ED who exhibit externalizing ED are more likely to experience language disorders than students who evidence internalizing ED.

As well as behaviour predicting language disorder in ED, language disorder may also contribute to the behavioural difficulties of students with ED. Researchers have found, for example, that children prone to non-compliance may have receptive language deficits that limit their ability to comprehend and comply with repeated warnings or verbal cues (e.g. Fujiki *et al.* 1999). As a result, such children may misinterpret communications, become frustrated, and consequently develop chains of miscommunication and antisocial behaviour patterns (Ruhl *et al.* 1992).

8.3.3   Interrelationships among language skills, externalizing behaviour, academic fluency and academic skills

Nelson *et al.* (2006) used structural equation modelling to test the interrelationships among language skills, externalizing behaviour and academic fluency and their impact on the academic skills of students with ED. The construct of academic fluency, or academic processing speed, refers to the ability to work quickly and maintain focused attention when measured under pressure (Fry and Hale 1996). The Woodcock Johnson-III (WJ-III; Woodcock *et al.* 2001) Math Fluency, Reading Fluency and Writing Fluency subtests were used to measure the academic fluency of participants while performing rudimentary academic tasks. These subtests comprise the WJ-III Academic Fluency cluster.

As illustrated in Figure 8.1, results showed that language skills exerted a significant proximal effect and distal effect on academic skills. The effect of language skills was mediated through academic fluency (path coefficient = 0.389) but language skills also had a proximal effect on academic skills (path coefficient = 0.359). However, externalizing behaviour failed to have a statistically significant effect on language skills, academic fluency or academic skills. In consideration of the entire model, it can be seen that academic fluency mediated the influence of language ability on academic skills. Obviously, students' ability to efficiently process academic information and produce appropriate responses facilitated the students' academic abilities (Fry and Hale 1996; Berninger and Richards 2002). The interrelationships regarding language, externalizing behaviour, fluency and academic skills lead to a pragmatic postulate: up to 90 per cent of students with ED are likely to have concomitant language ability deficits (Nelson *et al.* 2005a).

Benner *et al.* (2008) investigated the mediating role of academic processing speed (i.e. academic fluency) on the relationship between (a) the externalizing behaviour and academic skills of K-12 (kindergarten to 12th grade) students with ED, and (b) language skills and academic skills of students with ED. Academic processing speed mediated the influence of both externalizing behaviour and language ability on academic skills. Externalizing behaviour was negatively related to academic processing speed, i.e. increased externalizing behaviour was associated with reduced processing speed (Al Otaiba and Fuchs 2002). Academic processing speed was positively related to academic skills and mediated the negative relationship between externalizing behaviour and academic skills. Language ability was negatively related to externalizing behaviour, suggesting students with better language ability were more likely to have lower levels of externalizing behaviours.

Replicating the Nelson *et al.* (2006) investigation, Goran and Gage (2011) used structural equation modelling to examine the interrelationship among language, cognitive ability, academic performance and history of suspension for students with ED and LD. With the exception of history of suspension, these researchers found no significant differences between students with LD and ED on any of the measures and concluded that the key distinction between the groups was behavioural performance in school. For both groups of students, Goran and Gage (2011) found that language was a significant predictor of cognitive ability and academic performance, but not behaviour. The most striking differences in the academic functioning of students with ED and LD may be the widening gap between them over time. For example, longitudinal research comparing the reading skills of students with ED and students with LD showed that the reading achievement scores of students with ED did not improve over time whereas those with LD showed significant improvement across the elementary school years (Anderson *et al.* 2001). Also, data from the Special

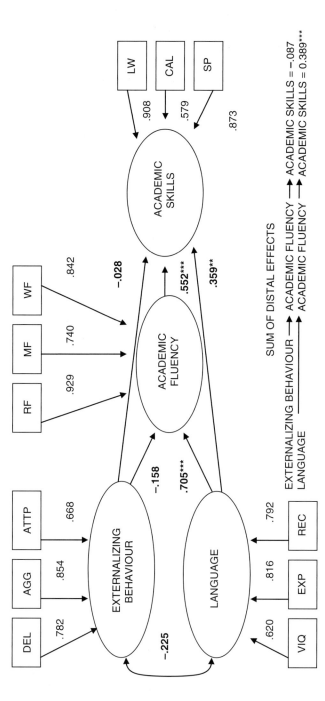

Figure 8.1 Structural model depicting the interrelationships among language skills, externalizing behaviour, academic fluency and their impact on academic skills (from Nelson et al. 2006).

Note: Observed coefficients represent the variance associated with the latent variables and the bold represents the path coefficients between latent variables. VIQ, verbal intelligence; REC, verbal reception; EXP, verbal expression; ATTP, attention problems; DEL, delinquent behaviour; AG, aggressive behaviour; WF, writing fluency; RF, reading fluency; MF, maths fluency; LW, letter-word identification; CAL, calculation; SP, spelling. *$p < 0.05$, **$p < 0.01$ and ***$p < 0.001$.

Education Elementary Longitudinal Study and the National Longitudinal Transition Study-2 show that compared with peers with and without other disabilities, students with ED experience the bleakest school and post-school outcomes (e.g. Wagner *et al.* 2006; Bradley *et al.* 2008).

8.4 Communication needs of students with emotional disturbance

Researchers have found that most ED students with a clinical language deficit do not receive language services. The recognition of language difficulties in public school children with ED is often eclipsed by the pressing challenge of managing the behaviour of these students in the classroom (Warr-Leeper *et al.* 1994). Researchers have indicated that the language disorders experienced by children with ED are largely overlooked and are consequently untreated (Walker *et al.* 1994). Approximately 33–40 per cent of children with ED served in non-public school settings (e.g. psychiatric settings) have undetected language deficits (Cohen *et al.* 1993, 1998; Cohen 2001). Those with undetected language deficits and ED appear to be the most delinquent, depressed and aggressive, and demonstrate more severe challenging behaviour than those with expressive language disorders (Cohen *et al.* 1993).

The overall increased percentage as well as the varying types of language disorders indicate that accompanying language disorders must be carefully ruled out in students at their initial evaluation for ED classification. The role of the testing psychologist is crucial, preceding any involvement of a speech-language pathologist. Practical red flags could include earlier speech/language services, underachievement in reading and/or written language skills, past or present parental and/or teacher concerns about language development, the presence of ADHD, neurological risk factors, student complaints of language difficulties and/or evidence of language dysfunction during the initial psychological testing and interview. Newer comprehensive tests of cognitive abilities (such as the Woodcock-Johnson III Tests of Cognitive Abilities; Woodcock *et al.* 2001) might better uncover language deficits, while abbreviated IQ tests are likely to prove inadequate (Benner *et al.* 2009). Sufficiently accurate screens for language dysfunction that can be administered by school psychologists still need to be developed for elementary and secondary students. Thus, at this point, it appears that school psychologists must primarily depend on heightened suspicion for language disorders in ED students, followed by key historical variables and discerning clinical interviews, which then lead to referral to speech-language pathologists for confirmatory assessment and specific planning.

There are several implications for the educational programming for students with ED. First, specific interventions for learning disabilities will often be necessary to sufficiently educate students with both ED and language disorders. Thus, academic intervention plans for many such students with comorbidity will become more complicated and difficult to coordinate. Special education agencies with large ED populations will have to ensure the continuing education of their ED teachers on the development and implementation of such complex treatment plans based on best-evidence interventions. Another approach would be to develop an ED staff person with special expertise in language and learning disorders who can then assist his or her colleagues with proper intervention planning. Second, a large majority of students with ED who have a learning disability also have a language disorder. Thus, teachers of students with ED must be highly suspicious of language disorders in their students who have learning disabilities, and closely observe whether such students show disrupted language skills or any of the practical red flags described above for assessment by school psychologists.

The addition of serious psychopathology further complicates the education of students with both ED and language disorders. Behavioural and emotional symptoms are usually treated with psychological interventions that depend on adequate language skills. Behavioural modification programmes require students with ED to understand verbal explanations, and participate in group counselling/discussion in order to learn better social interaction and problem-solving skills. Individual counselling depends on verbal exchanges with counsellors/therapists in school and/or in the community. What adaptations are required for these students to benefit from therapeutic interventions that depend so much on communication abilities, and specifically expressive language? The mix of serious language, achievement and psychological dysfunction in students with ED means that they have a guarded prognosis. We must better understand what early interventions (language and otherwise) can prevent or reduce the development of these precarious states in school. We also need to identify what interventions would most benefit them as they progress through their educational careers, from more intensive and complete services to alternative programming (such as vocational training and learning visual approaches to acquire knowledge). Lastly, how can we best help students with comorbid disorders as well as their families optimally understand and adapt to their language deficits?

Because successful language acquisition is a prerequisite for successful reading acquisition and academic learning in all areas (Baker and Cantwell 1987b; Catts *et al.* 1999), the language deficits of students with ED are likely to have a negative influence on their reading skills. Research has shown that when there are deficits in reading comprehension, there are always deficits in either decoding skills or language comprehension, or both (Catts *et al.* 2006). Reading comprehension is dependent upon the spoken language skills of morphosyntax (i.e. units of meaning in language and how they are put together in language), syntax (i.e. sentence structure), semantics (i.e. meanings of words, phrases and sentences) and discourse (i.e. world and conceptual knowledge). Thus, intermediate or secondary educators who serve students with ED should first assess reading comprehension. If the reading comprehension score of the student falls in either the 'at risk' or 'some risk' range, measures of decoding and language comprehension should be conducted. Educators serving students in the early grades (K-1) should begin with measures of decoding, such as the Nonsense Word Fluency subtest of the Dynamic Indicators of Basic Early Literacy Skills (Good and Kaminski 2002). The best reading intervention for a student with ED may actually be one that targets foundational language skills.

8.5   Where we go from here I: research needs

There are many unanswered research questions regarding the nature of language deficits among students with ED and how to treat them. We offer the following suggestions for future research. First, the range of different types of language disorders indicates the need for different language interventions, not only by school speech-language pathologists but also by ED teachers and associated staff. The evidence base for efficacious specific language interventions depending on the deficit profile is modest but growing, with long-term effectiveness more questionable especially in relation to more serious language disorders (Paul 2007; Peterson and McGrath 2009). The impact of language interventions on students who are also classified with ED is much less known. Studies have also not yet focused on the outcome of collaborative language intervention efforts by speech-language pathologists and ED teachers. It is likely that such targeted teamwork will have more positive impact than speech-language pathologists working alone with students with comorbidity during infrequent sessions over a school week.

Second, several researchers have highlighted the role of neuropsychological functioning as a mediating factor in the relationship between ED and language deficits (Hinshaw 1992; Hooper and Tramontana 1997; Hooper *et al.* 2003; Rogers-Adkinson 2003). Researchers have found that externalizing ED is related to deficits in three specific domains of functioning: (1) language-based verbal skills; (2) executive cognitive functioning (i.e. self-control functioning); and (3) processing speed (i.e. language and cognitive) (Giancola 2000; Lynam and Henry 2001; Hooper *et al.* 2003; Mattison *et al.* 2006). Researchers have demonstrated that evidence-based interventions increase neurological activity in areas of the brain that regulate information processing. Shaywitz *et al.* (2004) examined the effects of evidence-based phonological processing intervention on the reading fluency and brain organization of 77 right-handed 6- to 9-year-old children with reading disabilities. These researchers found that children in the experimental

condition (n = 37) made significant gains in reading fluency and demonstrated increased activity in the left hemisphere regions of the brain, particularly the occipitotemporal systems that are critical to processing speed.
These researchers also found that the occipitotemporal improvements in
the brain were maintained one year following the study and that as the
systems on the left side of the brain developed, the systems on the right no
longer needed to compensate for the lack of development on the left side.
Shaywitz *et al.* concluded that the use of evidence-based phonological processing interventions facilitate the development of the fast-paced neural
systems that underlie skilled reading and language development. Future
investigations into the relationships between ED, academic and language
deficits should build upon extant research on the underlying cognitive processes involved in language and social development.

Third, to date there have been no intervention studies focusing on
building the language skills of students with ED. However, in their best
evidence synthesis of the reading intervention literature, Benner *et al.*
(2010) concluded that supplementing classroom instruction with well-
targeted supplemental phonological awareness interventions is one
approach that is supported by relatively high-quality replicated research
(Lane 1999; Lane *et al.* 2001, 2007; Nelson *et al.* 2005a, 2005b). The structure and delivery of the phonological awareness interventions were consistent with previous research conducted with young children at risk of
reading problems (Leafstedt *et al.* 2004). The supplementary interventions
involved small groups, took place early in the children's schooling (i.e.
K-1), were relatively short and focused on identifying, manipulating and
producing sounds. The finding that supplemental phonological awareness
instruction improves the reading skills of students with ED has important
educational implications and suggests that it may be beneficial to provide
early intervention that stimulates phonological abilities in children with
or at risk of ED. It is also consistent with a plethora of research demonstrating the beneficial effects of supplementary phonological awareness
instruction (Wagner *et al.* 1993, 1994).

While the need for intervention studies is pressing, we believe that it is
important for language instructional interventions to be evaluated with
the service delivery context of schools in mind. To this end, there are
models of studies of reading interventions conducted with students with
ED where literacy instruction approaches and strategies fit contextually
in current school practices (e.g. Lane 1999; Strong *et al.* 2004; Nelson *et al.*
2005b). We believe that the usefulness of language research conducted
with students with or at risk of ED should be directed at the service delivery context of schools. More specifically, we believe that researchers
should contextualize their research in the following ways. Researchers
should conduct language research within the multi-level and Response to
Intervention (RTI) service delivery instructional (and behavioural) framework (National Center on Response to Intervention 2010). Placing the

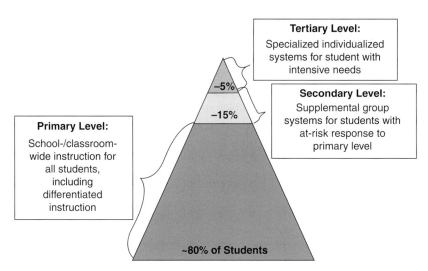

Figure 8.2 Multi-level prevention system in Response to Intervention (from Implementer Series Module 3: Multi-level Prevention System by the National Center on Response to Intervention, 2012).

language intervention programmes and approaches within such service delivery models would be useful to researchers and educators alike. The language difficulties of students with or at risk of ED, like all children, are best represented with a gradient or dimensional model (i.e. language skills fall on a continuum). Effectively improving their language skills requires a range of multi-tiered interventions and supports.

Researchers should conduct reading research on interventions at the secondary (Tier 2) and tertiary (Tier 3) prevention levels within the multi-level prevention framework (see Figure 8.2). We recommend focusing on these two levels because students with or at risk of ED, unlike typically developing students, tend not to benefit fully from primary (Tier 1) prevention language, arts and reading instruction provided in general education. Tier 2 and 3 programmes and practices should be based on three principles of effective instruction (Fuchs *et al.* 2003). First, Tier 2 and 3 require an explicit, didactic form of instruction in which the teacher directly guides students to ensure they learn. Explicit instruction involves instruction with a high level of teacher and student interactions. Second, the less visible and observable features of Tier 2 and 3 interventions are instructional design features that comprise the content and skills that are being taught. Well-designed programmes anticipate and eliminate potential misunderstandings by means of carefully sequenced and integrated instruction both within and across lessons. Third, given that problem behaviour interferes with academic outcomes (Al Otaiba and Fuchs 2002; Nelson *et al.* 2003), Tier 2 and 3 interventions should include embedded instructional management procedures and motivators to help students regulate their attention and behaviour as well as actively engage during instruction.

Finally, one of the greatest challenges facing schools seeking to implement evidence-based reading interventions for students with ED is the fact that a vast array of academic interventions claim to enhance the educational outcomes of students, and that they are evidence-based. The evidence for many of these interventions is based on poorly designed research. Schools must sort through these claims to decide which interventions merit consideration for their use. Thus, researchers should use research design features required for interventions to be designated as evidence-based. The US Department of Education created a review process to identify evidence-based interventions. These standards are used to review intervention studies for the What Works Clearinghouse. The What Works Clearinghouse review criteria provide a clear framework for intervention studies to determine whether the study provides strong evidence (Meets Evidence Standards), weak evidence (Meets Evidence Standards with Reservations), or insufficient evidence (Does not Meet Evidence Standards) (What Works Clearinghouse 2011). Although some would disagree, only well-designed and well-implemented randomized controlled trials are considered strong evidence whereas quasi-experimental designs with equating of experimental and comparison groups may only meet standards with reservations. Furthermore, although evidence standards for single-case designs and regression discontinuity designs have not been established, we believe that they will in the future, and that such high-quality designs can be used to demonstrate a functional relationship between a language intervention and improved communication outcomes for students with ED.

8.6   Where we go from here II: policy needs

It is our view that the main policy implication is federal funding for research interventions to build the communication skills of students with ED. Funding is pivotal in order for researchers to meet the high research standards that we have highlighted. A majority of the funding for special education research in the United States comes from the Institute of Education Sciences (IES). This is especially the case for academic focused intervention research. It is difficult to secure funding to conduct reading or language intervention research directed at students with ED. Indeed, we anticipate that we are likely to see lower-quality language intervention research because of the difficulty in securing funding to conduct high-quality intervention research. IES should support language intervention research with this population. No other population of students with disabilities experiences the same dismal outcomes as students with ED.

9

Autism spectrum disorders and communication

Courtenay Frazier Norbury

9.1   Introduction

Language is an arbitrary system of symbols that we use to encode our thoughts and feelings. The language code is multifaceted, consisting of phonology (the rules that govern how speech sounds may combine to create words), semantics (the meanings of those words and how meanings are connected) and syntax (the rules that govern how words combine to make sentences). In contrast, communication is a two-way exchange of information and ideas. We can communicate in a multitude of ways, for example, with a look or gesture, or by a shared language which enables us to communicate about abstract concepts removed from the immediate context. Animals can communicate, but only humans have language. The distinction is an important one when considering children with neurodevelopmental disorders, because they may be differentially impaired in language and/or communication abilities. For example, the prototypical child with specific language impairment (SLI) will have core deficits in structural aspects of language (i.e. phonology, semantics and syntax) but is often able to communicate effectively using limited language skills and non-verbal strategies (e.g. eye gaze, gesture).

Autism spectrum disorder (ASD) is characterized by persistent deficits in reciprocal social interaction as well as a restricted repertoire of interests and behaviours that are evident prior to the age of 3 years. In contrast to SLI, deficits in social communication are a defining characteristic of the disorder (Tager-Flusberg *et al.* 2005). Structural aspects of language in ASD are extremely variable and may range from minimal verbal expression to near-normal verbal fluency. Language ability plays a key role in understanding the developmental course of the disorder and remains an

This chapter was supported by an Economic and Social Research Council grant (RES-061-25-0409).

important predictor of long-term outcomes in social development, adaptive behaviour and educational attainment (Howlin *et al.* 2000; Szatmari *et al.* 2009).

Two key questions for researchers and practitioners are (a) what accounts for the heterogeneity in language development within ASD and (b) what is the impact of language impairment on other aspects of autistic cognition and behaviour? To address these questions, this chapter will review structural language, pragmatic language and social communication within ASD. It will then consider how individual differences in structural language, pragmatic language and social communication are associated with individual differences in aspects of autistic cognition, specifically impaired social cognition, weak central coherence and executive dysfunction. The chapter will also consider whether impairments in structural language are indicative of comorbid pathology using a framework in which ASD is seen as a multifactorial disorder in which vulnerability to language impairment overlaps with other neurodevelopmental disorders. Finally, it will argue that the need to take language ability seriously in understanding autistic communication in both research and clinical contexts is paramount.

Before proceeding, it is important to include a note on terminology. The term 'autism spectrum disorder' is used to refer to the broad spectrum of autistic persons and encompasses autism, Asperger's syndrome and pervasive developmental disorder-not otherwise specified. This reflects both common research practice in which these disorders are frequently included in the same group and the move to amalgamate all diagnostic labels into one ASD diagnosis (American Psychiatric Association 2013). There has been a recent move in the field to distinguish potentially distinct neurocognitive phenotypes that are identified on the basis of structural language ability (Tager-Flusberg and Joseph 2003). Where distinctions have been made, these are referred to as autism language impaired (ALI) and autism language normal (ALN). ALI is typically defined as a score of >1.5 SD below the normative mean on a standardized assessment of structural language competence such as the Clinical Evaluation of Language Fundamentals (CELF; Semel *et al.* 2003). The term 'autism language normal' implies that scores on this measure are within normal limits. However, the CELF does not assess aspects of pragmatic language or social communication, which may remain impaired in ALN.

The terms 'pragmatic language' and 'social communication' are used loosely and largely interchangeably in the research literature. In this chapter, these terms are distinguished from each other. The term 'pragmatic language' is used to refer to aspects of language in context that go beyond what is explicitly stated and includes inferencing, figurative language and scalar implicatures. The term 'social communication' is used to refer to dyadic social exchanges in which the ability to represent the mental states of others probably facilitates communication. Social communication includes skills such as discourse processing, narrative and referential communication.

9.2   Language in autism spectrum disorders

Language delay is often the first reason parents seek professional advice about their child's development (De Giacomo and Fombonne 1998). For the most part, language in ASD follows a protracted rate of acquisition, with first words acquired on average two years later than in typically developing peers (Howlin 2003). Nevertheless, a significant proportion of children with ASD go on to develop impressive vocabularies, often described as a 'peak of ability' (Mottron 2004). Even within the same study it is not unusual to find verbal scores (on language or IQ tests) spanning 50–70 points (e.g. Kamio and Toichi 2000).

Recent longitudinal research suggests that a significant percentage of children with minimal language skills in early life develop at least some spoken language skills by the age of 9, with only 9 per cent of children remaining non-verbal in later childhood (Hus *et al.* 2007). Other children apparently reach early language milestones as expected. Recent research has been directed at children with 'optimal outcome' (Kelley *et al.* 2006), who no longer meet criteria for ASD in the middle school years despite having received an ASD diagnosis in toddlerhood. These various language profiles prompt questions regarding how some children are able to acquire near-normal language abilities in the face of pronounced social and cognitive challenges, while others continue to have pronounced deficits in structural language. This chapter will examine these questions.

9.2.1   Speech and phonology

One consistent finding in the autism literature is that once some spoken language is acquired, articulation of speech sounds is relatively unimpaired across language phenotypes (Kjelgaard and Tager-Flusberg 2001). However, performance on more complex tests of phonological processing is less clear-cut. Numerous investigators have reported that a significant proportion of children with ASD perform poorly on measures of nonsense word repetition in which children repeat novel phonological sequences of increasing length and complexity (e.g. 'blonterstaping') (Kjelgaard and Tager-Flusberg 2001; Bishop *et al.* 2004; Whitehouse *et al.* 2008). In addition, atypical patterns in processing speech prosody are seen across the range of speakers with ASD from childhood to adulthood (Shriberg *et al.* 2001; Peppé *et al.* 2007), though these may be more prominent at sentence level than at the level of an individual word (Järvinen-Pasley *et al.* 2008). Although sound substitutions are rare, distortions of speech sounds and voicing patterns have been noted to affect intelligibility in adult speakers with ASD (Shriberg *et al.* 2001). In children, atypical spectral content and pitch variability discriminate between ASD and typically developing controls (Bonneh *et al.* 2011).

9.2.2 Lexical and semantic knowledge

Much research has been devoted to ASD children's word knowledge and the flexible deployment of this knowledge in different linguistic contexts. At the broadest level, vocabulary scores are consistently depressed in a large proportion of children with ASD relative to typically developing peers (Kjelgaard and Tager-Flusberg 2001; Loucas *et al.* 2008; Lindgren *et al.* 2009; McGregor *et al.* 2012). For a substantial minority of individuals with ASD, receptive vocabulary is considered to be a 'peak of ability' (Mottron 2004). However, what these children know about the words in their vocabularies may be qualitatively different from the knowledge of typical peers. For example, Norbury *et al.* (2010) found that children with ASD, matched to a comparison group on both raw scores and standard scores of the British Picture Vocabulary Scales-II (BPVS-II; Dunn *et al.* 1997), scored more than one standard deviation below the comparison group on a measure of verbal definitions.

Other investigators have suggested that, in general, the underlying organization of the semantic system in ASD is atypical and impoverished. For instance, individuals with ASD show attenuated priming effects for semantically related words (Kamio *et al.* 2007) and do not use semantic information to facilitate encoding and recall of semantic information (Tager-Flusberg 1991). However, the findings from many of these studies are somewhat hampered by large within-group variation and have failed to distinguish semantic profiles within ASD that might align with specific neurocognitive phenotypes. For example, McGregor *et al.* (2012) reported that semantic deficits were only seen in those children with ALI, yielding a profile similar to that seen in specific language impairment.

9.2.3 Morphosyntax and grammar

Relative to lexical-semantic skills, deficits in morphosyntax and grammar are more pronounced for children with ASD in general (Landa and Goldberg 2005) and for children with ALI in particular. As a group, children with ASD use fewer grammatical morphemes than non-ASD peers to mark verb tense and agreement (Howlin 1984; J.A. Roberts *et al.* 2004), although errors of commission (using the incorrect tense) are rare (J.A. Roberts *et al.* 2004; Eigsti *et al.* 2007). Analyses of spontaneous language samples have indicated that many children with ASD produce short and grammatically simple sentences relative to non-ASD peers, despite producing equivalent numbers of utterances (Scarborough *et al.* 1991; Eigsti *et al.* 2007). More structured tasks involving sentence repetition have also revealed poorer performance for individuals with ALI (Riches *et al.* 2010), highlighting the utility of this task as a marker for structural language impairment in ASD. Impaired sentence comprehension is a particularly striking feature of ALI (Loucas *et al.* 2008), although studies exploring comprehension of particular syntactic structures are lacking (but see Perovic *et al.* 2013).

9.2.4   Pragmatic language skills

Pragmatic language refers to the use of language in context. Competent language users are expected to infer meaning or resolve ambiguity generated by words and syntactic constructions by processing language in the context of their prior knowledge and experience. As a group, individuals with ASD are reported to have poor understanding of figurative and metaphorical language (Happé 1993; Norbury 2004), poor inferencing skills (Jolliffe and Baron-Cohen 2000; Norbury and Bishop 2002) and reduced ability to resolve ambiguities such as homographs or homonyms (Happé 1997; Norbury 2005a). Few studies have explored the extent to which pragmatic deficits align with neurocognitive phenotypes. Those studies that have explored this relationship report that children with ALI have more severe difficulties with pragmatic language tasks than peers with ALN (Snowling and Frith 1986; Norbury 2004, 2005a, 2005b).

9.2.5   Social communication skills

Despite variation in structural language and pragmatic language skills in ASD, deficits in social communication are universal in ASD (Tager-Flusberg *et al.* 2005) and are a defining feature of the disorder (American Psychiatric Association 2013). A broad definition of social communication would include an individual's understanding of speaker intentions and the verbal and non-verbal cues that signal those intentions. It would also include an individual's interpretation of environmental context, societal norms and expectations and how these coalesce with structural aspects of language to achieve successful communication.

Studies have shown that during conversation, speakers with ASD use too many or too few initiations, display poor topic maintenance, use fewer contingent conversational responses and produce non-contextual or socially inappropriate utterances (Tager-Flusberg and Anderson 1991; Adams *et al.* 2002; Hale and Tager-Flusberg 2005a; Nadig *et al.* 2010). These same deficits are also evident in narrative tasks. During narrative production, autistic individuals have been found to produce higher proportions of contextually irrelevant propositions (Norbury *et al.* 2013), to use poor referencing (Losh and Capps 2003; Norbury and Bishop 2003) and to provide little information about the motivations of characters in a narrative or the causal relationships between events (Diehl *et al.* 2006).

9.2.6 Unique language features in ASD

The deficits described so far are also seen in other neurodevelopmental disorders to varying degrees (Rice and Smolik 2007). However, language production in ASD also contains unusual features that are less common in typical development or in other neurodevelopmental disorders. Echolalia refers to the immediate or delayed imitation, or echoing, of overheard language (Tager-Flusberg and Calkins 1990). This may include language spoken to the child, or stereotyped utterances that the child has picked up from television or other media. Echoed language is less syntactically complex than non-echoed speech (Tager-Flusberg and Calkins 1990) but does appear to serve communicative functions such as turn-taking (Prizant and Duchan 1981). Pronoun reversals, in which the child uses 'you' for self-reference and 'I' for an addressee, have also been reported in ASD (Chiat 1982). In addition, neologisms or idiosyncratic word use is common in ASD (Volden and Lord 1991) and was noted in one of the first cases reported by Kanner (1943). The child reported by Kanner consistently referred to a saucepan as a 'Peter Eater'. Thus, both quantitative and qualitative differences in structural language, pragmatic language and social communication are evident in ASD.

9.3 Language impairment in ASD: consequence of autistic cognition, or comorbid disorders?

Until recently, language deficits in ASD have been viewed as a consequence of autistic experience. Investigators have argued that these deficits arise variously from reduced social experience (poor social cognition), from a reduced drive for coherence ('weak' central coherence) or from limitations in cognitive flexibility (executive dysfunction). This section will consider if any of these cognitive accounts is sufficient to explain the rich variation that occurs in structural language and pragmatic language in ASD. The evidence suggests that these accounts are not sufficient to explain this variation, and that structural language impairments may be best accounted for by comorbidity. In comorbidity, vulnerability to language impairment is shared with other developmental disorders, and is shaped by autistic cognition and experience. The intimate relationship between structural language and pragmatic language in ASD will be highlighted in this section.

9.3.1 Social cognition and language impairment

It has been argued that the core deficit in ASD is the 'failure of the social instinct' (Skuse 2012). This failure is manifest in reduced social interest and social engagement from early infancy, with cascading effects on both language and social cognitive development (Klin *et al.* 2003). In typical development, language develops within a social milieu, with adults providing contingent, salient and scaffolded input that aligns with the child's attentional focus (Baldwin 1991, 1993). Children, too, play an active role in establishing joint attention with their conversational partners, imitating verbal and non-verbal communicative gestures and responding in an emotionally engaged way to adult inputs (Baldwin 1991; Parladé and Iverson 2011).

In autistic development, this communicative dance is disrupted. Reduced social engagement results in the reduction of linguistic input, and input that may be qualitatively different with regard to content or timing (cf. Siller and Sigman 2008). Difficulties initiating and responding to bids for joint attention are well-documented in ASD and are predictive of later language competence (Charman *et al.* 2003). The ability to use joint attention cues such as pointing and eye gaze to discover new meaning crucially relies on attending to those cues and on being able to interpret their intended meaning. Individuals with ASD are reported to have difficulties with both (Norbury *et al.* 2010). The reduced ability to use speaker intention to map new word meanings is a particularly limiting factor in early language development (cf. Parish-Morris *et al.* 2007).

Problems with social cognition, or mentalizing, also have direct consequences for social communication abilities. For example, an inability to represent a listener's state of mind could account for the recognized limitations in providing the appropriate amount of information to minimize ambiguities in conversation in ASD (Tager-Flusberg and Anderson 1991) or in conveying sufficient information of interest to the listener in conversation and narrative tasks (Capps *et al.* 2000). Difficulties understanding speaker intentions have also been attributed to deficits in understanding figurative language such as metaphor and irony (Happé 1993) and in using referential communication (Nadig *et al.* 2009).

A strong prediction from any account that views language impairments in ASD as sequelae of a primary social deficit would be that language ability should be significantly correlated with degree of social competence. Indeed, there is evidence of a positive relationship between the two skill sets, at least in preschool children. Kuhl *et al.* (2005) tested preschoolers' preferences for infant-directed speech versus non-speech analogues, using the head-turn preference procedure. Here, the percentage of total time spent orienting to a particular sound was taken as a measure of social preference. Kuhl *et al.* found modest, inverse relationships between preferences for non-speech analogues and measures of initiation of joint attention and expressive language ability. Kuhl *et al.* also found a relationship between listening preferences and symptom severity, with increased listening time to non-speech analogues associated with higher symptom counts. However, a significant proportion of typically developing toddlers did not demonstrate a strong preference for infant-directed speech, and it is not clear whether a similar association

exists between social preference and language development in the typically developing group.

Paul *et al.* (2007) used the same procedure to gauge preferences for
infant-directed speech versus meaningful rotated speech in toddlers with
ASD. Time spent listening to meaningful, infant-directed speech was
positively correlated with receptive language scores. This relationship
remained significant 12 months later. However, the relationship between
language impairment and social deficit is less striking in older, cognitively able groups with ASD. Joseph *et al.* (2002) found that absolute level
of language ability was not associated with symptom severity, but that
discrepancies in which non-verbal abilities were more advanced than verbal skills were associated with more severe social communication deficits. In addition, ALI and ALN phenotypes have not differed significantly
on measures of social impairment and social adaptation (cf. Loucas *et al.*
2008; Norbury *et al.* 2009).

Another challenge for a strong version of the social account of structural language impairment in ASD is that while reduced social engagement and deficits in mentalizing are considered to be core deficits in ASD,
language impairments are not. Indeed, in a population sample, approximately 48 per cent scored within normal limits on standardized tests of
language, with vocabulary tests most likely to yield age-appropriate scores
(Loucas *et al.* 2008). This suggests that at least some individuals with ASD
have sufficient social skills to facilitate language learning (Luyster and
Lord 2009) or that they circumvent social weaknesses by relying on other
developmental skills. This implies in turn that those with ALI may have
multiple deficits that contribute to protracted language learning.

Aspects of structural language, pragmatic language and social communication are not mutually exclusive, but are likely to be highly
interactive. Individual differences on measures of pragmatic language
comprehension have been linked to both mentalizing, and structural
language abilities (see Gernsbacher and Pripas-Kapit (2012) for discussion
in relation to figurative language). For instance, Norbury (2005b) investigated metaphor comprehension in children with ALI and ALN. Children
with ALN did not differ from typically developing peers on a metaphor
task, whereas those with ALI had significantly lower scores. Moreover,
scores on measures of structural language predicted unique variance in
metaphor understanding, whereas scores on mentalizing tasks did not.
Studies of this type suggest that while structural language abilities may
not guarantee successful communication, they do strongly facilitate
pragmatic language comprehension. Also, deficits in social communication may be variable at the individual level, depending on the context.
For example, Nadig *et al.* (2010) reported that the topic of conversation
significantly influenced both verbal and non-verbal communication
behaviours of individuals with ASD. Thus, the core social deficit of ASD
does not necessarily yield impairments in structural language, nor is it

sufficient to explain variations in pragmatic language or social communication skill.

9.3.2 'Weak' central coherence and language impairment

Some aspects of communication do not rely so heavily on access to the mental states of others. For example, one can infer 'it was dark' by linking the two statements 'John walked into the room. He reached in the bag for his torch.' Inferencing requires the integration of linguistic knowledge with general knowledge and prior experience. This contextual processing is thought to be a challenge for many individuals with ASD. In his original descriptions of children with autism, Kanner noted that 'a story or a moving picture is experienced in unrelated portions rather than in its coherent totality' (1943: 250). Such observations formed the basis of the hypothesis that individuals with ASD lack the typical drive for global coherence, instead processing information in a piecemeal fashion (Frith 2003).

Weak central coherence theory has been enormously influential in attempting to explain some of the perceptual phenomena observed in ASD, and in recasting atypical abilities as a difference in cognitive style, rather than a deficit or dysfunction (Happé 1999; Happé and Frith 2006). For example, many individuals with ASD excel at tasks where detailed-focused processing is advantageous such as block design (e.g. Shah and Frith 1993). However, a cognitive style that is felicitous for detailed-focused processing of visuospatial stimuli could have deleterious consequences for language processing, especially pragmatic language, which by its nature requires integration of information in context in order to achieve meaning.

Early accounts of weak central coherence theory predicted that 'individuals with autism, of all ages and abilities, should be impaired at achieving context dependent meaning' (Happé 1997: 2). Ambiguous language, in which at least two interpretations of the same utterance are possible, has provided fertile testing ground for the weak central coherence hypothesis. It has been consistently reported that individuals with ASD make less use of sentential context when reading homographs such as 'tear'. In this case, they adopt the same pronunciation whether the linguistic context biases an interpretation of crying or ripping (Snowling and Frith 1986; Happe 1997). Deficits in understanding jokes and figurative expressions such as metaphor or idiom (Norbury 2004) and in making inferences, all of which require integration of information across a number of sentences (Jolliffe and Baron-Cohen 2000; Norbury and Bishop 2002), have also been attributed to weak central coherence.

The role of weak central coherence in explaining pragmatic language deficits in ASD has been challenged, because difficulties integrating information within a linguistic context are not specific to ASD, nor are they universal to the disorder (cf. Norbury 2005a). For example, problems with inferencing and understanding non-literal and ambiguous utterances have been reported in individuals with specific language impairment (Norbury and Bishop 2002; Norbury 2004), poor reading comprehension (Cain *et al.* 2005), hydrocephalus (Barnes and Dennis 1998), traumatic brain injury (Dennis and Barnes 2001) and schizophrenia (Solomon *et al.* 2011). Notably, none of these populations are renowned for exceptional visual processing, indicating that the source of difficulty with contextual processing need not be a domain-general difference in central coherence.

Furthermore, recent evidence suggests that the ability to integrate information in linguistic context is strongly associated with structural language abilities (Pijnacker *et al.* 2009). When consideration is limited to cohorts carefully matched to comparison groups on multiple measures of language ability, differences between ASD and typically developing peers is negligible (Saldaña and Frith 2007; Brock *et al.* 2008). Similarly, when language phenotypes are explicitly compared, the ALI group is generally less efficient at processing contextual information relative to ALN peers (Snowling and Frith 1986; Norbury 2004, 2005a, 2005b). In addition, across these studies, ALI groups have rarely differed from non-ASD comparison groups matched for language ability. These findings have led to the conclusion that deficits on verbal measures of central coherence are related to poor verbal ability, rather than to weak central coherence (cf. Norbury 2005a).

9.3.3 Executive dysfunction and language impairment

In addition to social cognitive deficits and weak central coherence, individuals with ASD are frequently reported to have deficits with executive functions, the set of cognitive abilities that underpin goal-directed behaviours. These abilities include working memory, planning, inhibition of prepotent (but irrelevant) responses, generativity, mental flexibility (set-shifting) and self-monitoring (see Hill (2004) for a review). There are at least two ways to conceptualize the potential relationship between executive function and language. First, deficits in executive function may impair language learning from the earliest stages. For instance, the ability to shift attention from interlocutors to objects in the environment may facilitate joint attention, the ability to hold novel phonological sequences in mind while mapping this code to novel objects, and the ability to monitor comprehension in order to trigger a search for new unfamiliar referents are all executive function skills that are likely to be important for early word learning. On this view, individual differences in executive function should predict variation in language outcome.

Second, acquisition of structural aspects of language may be unaffected by executive function, but flexible use of language for online social communication may be disrupted by executive function impairment. Studies of skilled adult language users have underlined this relationship, demonstrating that interlocutors are required to inhibit contextually irrelevant interpretations of discourse and flexibly adapt to their conversation partner's perspective (Brown-Schmidt 2009). With regard to ASD, difficulties with narrative production and the comprehension of ambiguous language, jokes, metaphors and idioms may be construed as sequelae of executive function deficits in planning discourse, shifting between literal and figurative meanings, and inhibiting interpretations that are irrelevant to the communication context. Either relationship predicts significant concurrent and longitudinal relationships between executive function and language measures.

Unfortunately, there is a paucity of longitudinal evidence with which to evaluate these hypotheses. Pellicano (2010) explored the development of executive function over a 3-year period in early childhood. While the ASD group demonstrated marked improvements in executive function (planning and set-shifting) over this period, changes in executive function were unrelated to language. However, participants were cognitively able and only one aspect of language, vocabulary, was measured. It is possible that relationships between executive function and more complex aspects of language, such as grammar, narrative or non-literal language comprehension, exist.

In a cross-sectional study, Landa and Goldberg (2005) explored the relationship between more complex language constructs and measures of executive function in school-aged children with ASD. They predicted that performance on tasks of sentence formulation and figurative language comprehension would correlate with measures of executive function that tapped planning, working memory and set-shifting. The ASD group were worse on both the language and most of the executive function measures relative to typically developing peers, but the expected correlations were not evident, nor did executive function skill relate to symptom severity. These findings led Landa and Goldberg (2005) to conclude that executive function impairment need not give rise to the structural language impairments or social challenges that characterize ASD. However, the youngest children in the study were 7 years old and, therefore, it remains possible that executive function deficits exert an early and lasting effect on language and/or social development.

A rather different conceptualization of the relationship between executive function and language is that language itself is a necessary prerequisite for executive function. The role of language, particularly self-directed or inner speech, in the development of executive function has been considered for several decades, with an emphasis on the importance of language as a self-regulatory function important for thinking, planning and self-regulation. More recently, Zelazo and colleagues have argued that development of executive function, specifically conscious control and cognitive flexibility, are dependent on structural language, particularly the ability to label relevant stimuli (Zelazo 2004; Jacques and Zelazo 2005). Labelling one's subjective experiences drives the capacity for self-reflection of those experiences at higher levels of consciousness. That very young children profit from verbalization of task-relevant rules provides additional support for the importance of structural language for executive function development (cf. Müller *et al.* 2004).

Thus, once again, variation in structural language ability may influence the developing cognitive phenotype of autism, rather than being the result of cognitive differences or deficits. Furthermore, the fact that a significant minority of children with ASD develop age-appropriate structural language abilities despite equivalent degrees of social deficit and symptom severity strongly suggests the possibility that structural language impairment is a comorbid disorder (Tager-Flusberg and Joseph 2003; Tomblin 2011).

9.4   Language impairment in ASD and differential diagnosis

In clinical practice, differential diagnosis of ASD versus other forms of developmental language impairment has long been a challenge. Also, recent research has been focused on delineating the similarities and differences between ALI and more 'specific' language impairment (SLI) (Tomblin 2011). Some investigators have argued that when structural language is impaired in ASD, ASD and SLI are comorbid disorders, sharing common behavioural and aetiological risk factors (cf. Tager-Flusberg 2006). Other researchers have disputed this claim because of qualitative differences in behaviour (Whitehouse *et al.* 2008; Williams *et al.* 2008) and an apparent absence of shared familial risk (Whitehouse *et al.* 2008; Lindgren *et al.* 2009). This debate will be briefly revisited in this section from the perspective of a multi-deficit model of neurodevelopmental disorders (cf. Pennington 2006).

According to the comorbidity view, some aspects of structural language are impaired in both ASD and SLI because of shared genetic and environmental risk factors in these disorders. However, by definition, children with ALI experience additional deficits that are not seen in SLI. We must, therefore, view the nature of structural language impairment in ALI through a lens of pronounced deficits in social interaction and a pattern of repetitive and compulsive behaviours and interests that is rarely seen in individuals with SLI (Bishop and Norbury 2002; Leyfer *et al.* 2008; Lindgren *et al.* 2009). As a result, there will be qualitative differences in performance on measures of structural language between the two groups, but this does not invalidate the possibility of aetiological overlap between the disorders.

Kjelgaard and Tager-Flusberg (2001) first noted that when a heterogeneous group of children with ASD was parsed according to performance on an omnibus test of language function, those who scored more than 2 SD below the normative mean (ALI) had a pattern of language impairment that closely resembled the profile associated with SLI. In other words, these children had age-appropriate articulation skills and low-average vocabulary scores, but pronounced weaknesses in grammar (especially the ability to mark grammatical tense on verbs) and nonsense word repetition, a measure of phonological short-term memory (Kjelgaard and Tager-Flusberg 2001; Tager-Flusberg and Joseph 2003). Both tense-marking and nonsense word repetition have been identified as potential clinical and heritable markers of structural language impairment (Falcaro *et al.* 2008).

Numerous studies have now replicated the finding that individuals with ALI identified on global measures of language competence have nonsense word repetition deficits (Whitehouse *et al.* 2008; Lindgren *et al.* 2009; Loucas *et al.* 2010). However, there is continuing debate about whether these deficits stem from different underlying mechanisms, as both quantitative and qualitative differences between ALI and SLI have been reported. For instance, Botting and Conti-Ramsden (2003) reported that children with SLI were more severely impaired on nonsense word repetition than a heterogeneous group of peers with ASD. Importantly, the authors did not divide the group into ALI and ALN phenotypes and the claim for comorbid nonsense word repetition deficits is most likely to be applicable to the ALI subtype. Length effects in nonsense word repetition are consistently reported for individuals with SLI, while increasing syllable length does not necessarily affect performance in ALI (Whitehouse *et al.* 2008; Riches *et al.* 2010).

In addition, while Whitehouse *et al.* (2008) did not find significant differences between SLI and ALI groups on nonsense word repetition, division into subgroups based on repetition performance suggested that the source of impairment may differ between the clinical groups. Specifically, children with SLI and poor repetition had greater difficulty with oro-motor control. In contrast, children with ALI who also had poor nonsense word repetition had higher symptom severity scores on the Social Communication Questionnaire (Rutter *et al.* 2003). The authors interpreted this result as the nonsense word repetition deficit in ASD stemming from a severe autistic presentation, characterized by multiple cognitive deficits including lack of social interest and poor imitation. In contrast, the repetition deficit in SLI is seen as indicative of phonological short-term memory deficits and/or limitations in oro-motor control. However, given the small participant numbers, variable age groups and eclectic diagnostic criteria used in this study, it is difficult to reach firm conclusions about the possible origins of the nonsense word repetition deficit in either group.

Another 'clinical marker' of SLI is relatively severe and persistent deficits in grammar relative to other aspects of language. In English-speaking environments, this is most commonly realized as an inconsistency in marking grammatical tense and agreement (e.g. past tense –ed and third person singular –s) in obligatory contexts (Rice *et al.* 1998). Children with ALI also have significant difficulties with these aspects of morphosyntax (Tager-Flusberg and Joseph 2003; J.A. Roberts *et al.* 2004). However, qualitative differences in the error responses of children with SLI and ALI have led some to question whether quantitatively similar impairments share common aetiologies (Williams *et al.* 2008).

Specifically, Williams *et al.* (2008) noted that children with SLI make errors of omission in which the verb stem is left bare (e.g. 'he walk to school yesterday'). In contrast, the ALI group studied by J.A. Roberts *et al.* (2004) had a large proportion of alternate verb errors or no responses. In fact, the ALI group made a range of errors, including errors of omission, but they also failed to respond or made errors that suggested difficulties with understanding the demands of the task. Thus, the social and pragmatic impairments prominent in ASD are likely to result in qualitative differences in error responses that reflect the interaction of structural and pragmatic language difficulties. Indeed, Loucas *et al.* (2008) reported that in addition to expressive grammar deficits, children with ALI had significantly poorer receptive language skills than either ALN or SLI comparison groups, suggestive of additive effects. Therefore, the pattern of more severely impaired grammatical abilities and pronounced deficits in marking tense are highly suggestive of overlapping language vulnerabilities in ALI and SLI.

Finally, the structural and pragmatic language deficits seen in ASD are characteristic of other neurodevelopmental disorders in varying degrees and combinations (Rice and Smolik 2007). For example, structural language development is vulnerable across a wide range of disorders of both known genetic origin (e.g. Down's syndrome, Williams syndrome, fragile X syndrome) and disorders of complex and multiple genetic influence (SLI, ASD, reading disorders). The behavioural manifestation of genetic risk to language impairment is influenced by the interactions amongst risk genes (Bishop 2010b), interactions between genetic influences and environmental circumstances (Bishop 2009) and interactions between cognitive abilities and behaviour. There is also increasing evidence that at least some genetic influences on language impairment may be shared across a number of clinical boundaries (Newbury *et al.* 2010).

Comorbidity in neurodevelopmental disorders is the rule rather than the exception, and is perhaps best understood as a complex interplay between biological, cognitive, environmental and behavioural features. Applying such a multifactorial model of language impairment and communication disorder to ASD may help us to understand the rich phenotypic variation that exists. Such a model has also been applied to comorbidity in other neurodevelopmental disorders. An elegant example of this approach is provided by Pennington and Bishop (2009) in their exploration of the overlap amongst three disorders: speech sound disorder, SLI and reading disorder. Like ASD, there has been intense research and clinical debate about the relationship between SLI and reading disorder. Resolving this debate has been similarly hampered by a complex phenotype that changes with development and a reliance on categorical diagnoses that impose arbitrary thresholds for disorder on what are essentially continua. The solution to these obstacles is first and foremost to recognize that SLI and reading disorder, and indeed ASD, result from the complex interplay of multiple interacting genes and environmental influences, which shape language outcomes in probabilistic ways. This recognition encourages a focus on structural language, pragmatic language and social communication as continuous traits rather than diagnostic categories (Bishop 2006b).

Adopting this approach, Pennington and Bishop (2009) identified shared vulnerabilities for particular traits across SLI, reading disorder and speech sound disorder at the genetic, biological and cognitive levels. At the same, there exist unique features that give each disorder its distinctive flavour. The combination of risk and protective factors that any one individual experiences may go some way to explaining individual differences within a diagnostic group. Importantly, Pennington and Bishop highlight the power of genetically informed designs (such as twin studies) in elucidating the biological relationships across disorders. At the present time, few such studies exist. Nevertheless, we can begin to consider aspects of language and communication that may be vulnerable across all disorders, including ASD, and how factors unique to ASD may further shape language phenotypes.

For example, a child with both SLI and ASD risk factors may be particularly poor at nonsense word repetition and experience disrupted social engagement. Such a combination would be especially deleterious for new word learning, with downstream consequences for grammatical development and discourse competence. Alternatively, a child with the social impairments characteristic of ASD, but without the shared SLI vulnerability, may be particularly tuned to the sound structure of language with reduced attention to semantic or social meaning (Norbury *et al.* 2010). This in turn may facilitate novel word mappings and give rise to exceptional receptive vocabulary scores, although qualitative differences in vocabulary knowledge may still exist (Norbury *et al.* 2010). The number and combination of risk factors a child experiences may affect both the severity of the deficit (cf. Loucas *et al.* 2008) and the quality of the language errors, producing both similarities and important differences between language phenotypes.

9.5   The role of language in understanding ASD

This final section addresses why it is important to distinguish different language phenotypes within ASD. From a research perspective, investigations into the genetic and neurobiological factors associated with ASD are frequently hampered by the heterogeneous phenotype. Where studies have distinguished language phenotypes, genetic signals may be enhanced (Spence *et al.* 2006) and differences in neural architecture, particularly in the cortical networks supporting language, may be evident (De Fossé *et al.* 2004; Hodge *et al.* 2010). Similarly, parsing heterogeneity associated with language has yielded differences in social viewing (Norbury *et al.* 2009), differences in the relationships between social viewing and social-behavioural outcomes (Rice *et al.* 2012) and differences in the degree to which children with ASD can process language in context (Snowling and Frith 1986; Norbury 2005a).

For instance, Norbury *et al.* (2009) examined the eye movements of adolescents with ALI or ALN and those of typically developing peers as they viewed dynamic scenes of social interaction. In line with previous investigations, those with ALN demonstrated reduced fixations to eyes (cf. Klin *et al.* 2002). Individuals with ALI, however, did not differ from the typically developing peers though there was considerable variation in all three groups. More importantly, fixations on the mouth were associated with greater communicative competence, suggesting that such a viewing pattern is not necessarily maladaptive.

Differences between language phenotypes have prompted a re-evaluation of cognitive theories of ASD and the causal pathways to structural language impairment and social communication disorder. But do they also have implications for clinical outcomes and interventions? It is well known that the acquisition of verbal language in early childhood is an important prognostic indicator of later outcome (Rutter 1970), but beyond a minimal level of competence, variation in language level is less predictive of social success (Howlin *et al.* 2004). Thus, even for individuals with ALN, their superb verbal skills may not be sufficient to compensate for the social deficits or behavioural rigidity that may present barriers to education, employment and social acceptance. For these individuals, interventions directed at increasing cognitive and behavioural flexibility and developing social awareness and understanding may be prioritized.

For individuals with ALI, developing social competence may not necessarily yield improvements in structural language or pragmatic language ability. For these children, targeted interventions that support development of phonological processing, vocabulary knowledge and grammar are necessary. Improving these skills should have positive consequences for literacy development and reading comprehension (Norbury and Nation 2011) and aspects of narrative and discourse comprehension that involve using linguistic context to make inferences or recover ambiguous meanings (cf. Norbury 2005a). Consideration of language phenotypes may also be an important factor in explaining differences in treatment response (cf. Fidler *et al.* 2007).

9.6   Conclusions

Within ASD, variations in structural language, pragmatic language and social communication skill are more variable than perhaps in any other developmental disorder. In addition, language and communication develop in the context of variation in non-verbal cognitive reasoning, pronounced difficulties with social interaction and social understanding and restricted repertoires of behaviour and interests. It is likely that individual differences in each of these domains contribute to the rich variation in language and communication ability observed within the autism spectrum. Despite the seemingly unique profile of autistic language and communication, a multifactorial view of neurodevelopmental disorder (Pennington and Bishop 2009) suggests points of commonality with other clinical conditions. Recognizing that structural language impairment might be a co-occurring disorder, rather than a consequence of autistic cognition, invites researchers to consider the impact of structural language on other aspects of cognitive and communicative development. It also points to essential targets for remediation and careful consideration of how improving early structural language capacities may alter the pragmatic and social communication trajectories of children with ASD during development.

Part II

Acquired communication disorders

10

Head and neck cancer and communication

Tim Bressmann

10.1   Cancer of the head and neck

Our face, our voice and our speech are our most important means for making social contact with fellow human beings. Head and neck cancer can have a devastating impact on the patient's facial appearance, voice and speech. The tumour and its treatment can critically affect vital biological functions such as breathing, swallowing, eating, smelling and tasting. The treatment and the treatment sequelae can be psychologically and socially devastating for the patient and the road to recovery is often protracted and difficult.

After heart disease, malignant tumours are the second most common cause of death worldwide (Lopez *et al.* 2006). Head and neck cancers are the eighth most common form of cancer in males internationally (American Cancer Society 2007). In Canada, epidemiological estimates of these cancers are published by the Canadian Cancer Society (2011). For a population of approximately 34.7 million Canadians, there were an estimated 3,600 new cases of oral cancer in 2011 (67% male), accounting for around 2% of new cancer cases. Oral cancer had an estimated mortality figure of 1,150 (66% male; 1.5% of all cancers). There were 1,150 new cases of laryngeal cancer (81% male), accounting for 0.6% of all new cancer cases, with an estimated 490 deaths (80% male; 0.6% of all cancer-related deaths). The estimated 5-year survival ratios for the period 2004 to 2006 were 63% for oral cancers and 64% for laryngeal cancers (Canadian Cancer Society 2011).

In developed countries, patients with head and neck cancer are normally assessed, treated and rehabilitated by a multidisciplinary team. The patient's avenue of treatment is decided upon in a team conference,

The author would like to thank Ms Christina Khaouli Tannous, HBSc, Communication Disorders Assistant, for providing the drawings in Figures 10.3, 10.4 and 10.5. Mr Brett Ayliffe, DDS, contributed the photo in Figure 10.2.

which allows the team members to share information and achieve the best possible outcome (Machin and Shaw 1998). The core members of the team include surgeons (depending on the country and the institution, these can be otolaryngologists, plastic surgeons, or oral and maxillofacial surgeons), radiation oncologists, medical oncologists and radiologists. The larger team comprises allied health professions such as oncological nurses, physical therapists, dieticians, dentists, prosthodontists, psychologists and speech-language pathologists. In head and neck cancer patients, the speech-language pathologist is an integral part of the rehabilitation team. He or she has an important role regarding the rehabilitation of the patient's voice, speech and swallowing.

Head and neck cancer and its treatment can result in surgical resections, organ loss or motility restrictions. These can significantly alter the patient's ability to breathe, swallow and speak. Indeed, the work of a clinical speech-language pathologist in head and neck cancer will often focus on the rehabilitation of swallowing because aspiration-related pathologies can become life-threatening for the patient (Logemann 1994). Since the focus of this handbook is on communication disorders, the discussions in this chapter will be limited to the structurally related speech disorders associated with head and neck cancer. However, occasional reference will be made to related topics such as swallowing and respiration.

10.1.1   Pathomechanisms and causative factors

The cells in our bodies have a limited lifespan. In order to allow us to survive into old age, a cell that reaches the end of its lifespan reduplicates and divides into two new cells through the process of mitosis. In order to reduplicate, the cell copies its deoxyribonucleic acid (DNA), which contains its genetic code. The myriad of daily DNA reduplications in the body will occasionally result in a copy which contains an error. Cells with aberrant DNA will normally be discovered and destroyed by the immune system. However, some DNA mutations will result in cells that will withstand the immune system. Such neoplastic cells can then reduplicate and reach critical mass until a tumour has formed (Kleinsmith 2006).

Tumour cells are characterized by uncontrolled cell division, growth and movement. Benign tumours show uncontrolled growth but, otherwise, they have no destructive intent. However, benign tumours are not as friendly as the name suggests. The tumour can take up space and compress, constrain or damage adjacent structures. Treatment, such as a surgical resection, may often be necessary. Malignant tumours have a more sinister agenda. These tumours are aggressive and may become life-threatening for the patient. Malignant tumours invade and infiltrate the healthy tissue of an organ. The cells of the tumour may spread in the body through the lymphatic system or the bloodstream, allowing them to cause distant metastases (Kleinsmith 2006).

The aetiology of head and neck cancer is multifactorial, meaning that the cancer is probably the result of the confluence of a number of different genetic, environmental and lifestyle variables. Major exogenic factors that are cited in the genesis of head and neck cancer are the triad of smoking, alcohol use and poor oral hygiene (Johnson 2001; Brouha *et al.* 2005). Occupational exposure to carcinogenic materials such as chemicals, textile fibres and wood dust may also contribute to the genesis of head and neck cancer, particularly when combined with smoking. In recent years, the human papillomavirus type 16 has been identified as an aetiological factor, especially for cases of oropharyngeal cancer in younger patients, with the highest proportion of human papillomavirus-positive squamous cell carcinomas found in tonsillar tumours (Kreimer *et al.* 2005).

A diagnosis of head and neck cancer cannot be made based on visual inspection or medical imaging alone. It is always necessary to carry out a tissue biopsy to evaluate the tumour cell histology. Most head and neck cancers are malignant squamous cell carcinomas. Exceptions are the tumours of the salivary gland, which are frequently pleomorphic adenomas or, less frequently, adenoid cystic carcinomas (Eveson 2011). Squamous cell carcinomas grow aggressively, and they invade and infiltrate surrounding structures. Squamous cell tumours metastasize via the lymphatic system. Therefore, it is important to evaluate and treat the adjacent lymphatic structures together with a primary head and neck tumour.

To assess how large and involved a tumour is, its severity is classified according to the international tumour-node-metastasis (TNM) system (Wittekind and Sobin 2002). On the T-scale, the tumour is labelled as T0 (absent) to T4 (severe). This rating depends on the organ affected by the tumour. For example, the tongue is larger than the vocal fold. As a result, a T3 tumour of the tongue could be considerably larger than a T3 tumour of the vocal fold. Lymph node metastasis is rated as N0 (absent) to N3 (involvement of lymph nodes distant to the site of the primary tumour). Distant metastasis is scored as M0 (absent) or M1 (present). The TNM scores are then used to determine an overall tumour stage, with Stage I as the relatively mildest and Stage IV as the most advanced and severe cancer stage. The TNM classification and tumour staging allows the treatment team to gauge the patient's prognosis for survival and to determine an appropriate treatment response to the cancer. It is important to note that the TNM system cannot be used to make predictions about post-treatment function and the resulting quality of life.

10.1.2 Principles of cancer treatment

Recent decades have seen significant changes in the philosophy and the treatment principles underlying cancer treatment. Historically, cancer surgery and other treatments were often radical. Since the patient's survival was the sole priority, the treatment team would accept severely disabling and disfiguring procedures and treatment side effects. However, the advent of more refined surgical techniques and a better understanding of cancer biology prompted changes in the way that cancer therapy was delivered. In the past two decades, the concept of quality of life has changed the paradigms of cancer care. While the main goal of cancer treatment is still successful cure, the treatment team also tries to ensure that the patient survives with reasonable function, quality of life and dignity. This also means that treatment alternatives are presented to, and carefully discussed with, the patient so that survival and functional limitations may be carefully weighted (Myers 2005; Chandu *et al.* 2006).

Cancer treatment can have curative or supportive goals. Curative treatment is aimed at removing or neutralizing the tumour and restoring the patient to health. Supportive treatment aims to ease pain and discomfort that the patient may experience as a consequence of the treatment. Curative and supportive care approaches will often be combined to make the patient as comfortable as possible during and after the treatment. Palliative care is used to decrease the suffering of a patient who is not expected to survive the cancer.

There are two general approaches to the treatment of a tumour. One approach is to remove the tumour with a surgical resection. The second approach is to destroy the cancer cells and render the tumour harmless with radiation therapy, chemotherapy or combined radiochemotherapy. Both general approaches can be used in the treatment of head and neck cancer. The choice of treatment will depend on the tumour size, tumour location and the expected functional impairments following from treatment. Treatment preferences may differ between treatment centres and healthcare systems. The two general approaches to treatment will be described below.

A surgical approach is appropriate for a tumour that is confined and surgically accessible. In the case of a benign tumour, the surgeon can remove the neoplastic growth and reconstruct the resulting defect, if necessary. However, in the case of a malignant tumour, the surgeon must also resect an appropriate safety margin around the tumour because malignant cells may already have invaded and infiltrated the surrounding tissue. The resection of a safety margin reduces the risk of a relapse. Together with the tumour resection, the surgeon also ensures that lymph node metastasis in the neck is addressed. Since the lymphatic ducts provide a route for squamous cell carcinoma metastasis, a neck dissection procedure removes affected or suspicious lymph nodes from the neck, together with associated veins and adjacent neck muscles (Cummings *et al.* 2004; Wang *et al.* 2012). A neck dissection may affect the normal lymph drainage, which can leave the patient with postoperative lymphoedema (Deng *et al.* 2011).

The surgical removal of a neoplasm may leave a defect that is functionally or aesthetically unacceptable. If the resulting defect is suitably small, the surgeon may decide to just let the tissue heal over (primary wound healing). However, if a tissue defect is larger, a surgical reconstruction may be necessary. Depending on the defect, the surgeon may have different options for how such a surgical reconstruction can be completed. The simplest approach is to close the defect locally by bringing the wound margins together and suturing them together (local closure). The suturing of the wound margins may change the orientation of muscle fibres and affect the execution and direction of movements, for example by tethering an organ such as the tongue to the floor of mouth. A surgeon may also decide to close the defect with a tissue flap. If the flap tissue is harvested locally, the procedure is called a local flap. In a local flap, the blood supply continues to come from the donor site. As an example, if an extensive neck defect arises after a total removal of the larynx (laryngectomy), the surgeon could pull up breast muscle (musculus pectoralis major) to the neck defect. The blood supply for the pectoralis flap would continue to come from the patient's chest area. Local flaps provide a safe and effective way to close surgical defects. However, the flap tissue may add weight to an organ or tether the patient's movements. A local closure of a neck defect with a pectoralis flap may affect the patient's ability to turn or extend the neck.

Since the 1990s, surgeons have started using free flaps on a more frequent basis for the closure of resection defects related to head and neck cancer. In a free flap procedure, tissue is harvested from another part of the body. For head and neck cancers, popular donor sites are the radial forearm or the inside of the thigh (see Figure 10.1). In order to successfully connect the transplant tissue to the recipient site, the surgeon connects the blood vessels in the flap to blood vessels in the resection site (anastomosis). With the blood supply from the resection site, the flap tissue can heal in and cover the defect. The advantage of a free flap is that the surgeon can make the flap relatively large and try to reconstruct the defect in a manner that is as physiological as possible. For example, the shape and bulk of the tongue can be recreated after a partial tongue resection (partial glossectomy). As with a local flap, the free flap tissue does not move actively and may add dead weight to the movement of an organ (Matthews and Lampe 2005).

The other general approach to cancer treatment aims to spare the affected organ from surgery and to use radiation therapy or chemotherapy to kill mostly the cancer cells and preserve the healthy cells. This treatment approach capitalizes on the fact that cancer cells reduplicate constantly. As a result, they are often in a near-constant state of mitosis, which means that their DNA is being copied in preparation for cell division. During the active mitotic stage of the cell cycle, the DNA is more vulnerable to exogenic influences such as toxic substances or radiation. If

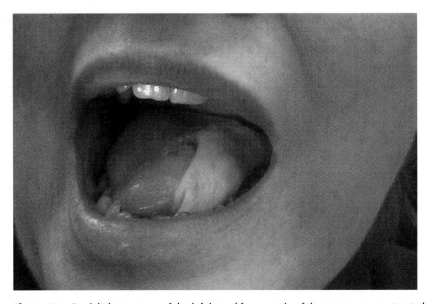

Figure 10.1 Partial glossectomy of the left lateral free margin of the tongue, reconstructed with radial forearm free flap.

a cancerous cell's DNA is sufficiently damaged, the cell cannot redupli-cate any more and spread the cancer (A. Abitbol *et al.* 1999).

Such an approach to treatment affects all cells in the treated area. In radiation therapy, all cells in the exposed area are irradiated. In chemo-therapy, the chemotherapeutic agent spreads throughout the body. The challenge for the oncological treatment team is to achieve optimum treat-ment efficacy while keeping the treatment side effects to an acceptable level. The decay rate of both tumour and healthy cells does not follow a lin-ear trajectory. In the example of radiation therapy, the radiation-induced tissue necrosis progresses exponentially once the treatment effects take hold. The tumour cells are inherently unstable, and they will be affected by the treatment before the healthy tissue. However, the healthy tissue is also stressed by the treatment, and non-cancerous cells start perishing soon after the tumour cells. The radiation oncologist therefore needs to calculate an exact radiation dose to maximize the treatment results while minimizing the necrosis of the surrounding tissue.

To facilitate exact and efficient delivery of radiation to the tumour cells, radiation oncologists now follow an approach called intensity-modulated radiation therapy (IMRT) in head and neck cancer. In IMRT, computer-controlled linear accelerators deliver carefully controlled radiation doses to the affected tissue while minimizing the exposure of surrounding healthy structures according to a previously established dose intensity pattern. The approach allows radiation oncologists to increase the radi-ation dose to the tumour. The IMRT relies on exact imaging of the tumour site using medical imaging methods such as computer tomography or magnetic resonance imaging (Wang *et al.* 2011). To increase the efficacy of radiation treatment in head and neck cancer, radiation oncologists currently advocate for small adjuvant doses of cisplatin, a chemotherapeutic agent which helps to improve the treatment efficacy. High-dose radiochemotherapy can reduce or eliminate the need for surgery, thus preserving organs (Kelly 2007; Wang *et al.* 2011). However, the long-term side effects of radiation therapy can be significant.

The damage that radiation therapy causes to cells is immediate and irreversible. However, the appearance of radiation necrosis can be delayed by the mitotic cycle of the cell. Tissues that have relatively short mitotic cycles such as skin and mucosa cells will often show a pronounced irritation during and immediately after the radiation therapy, seen as radiation dermatitis and radiation mucositis. Patients also report distortion of taste (dysgeusia), which often results in an abnormal perception of sweetness and can affect appetite and interest in food. These early effects of radiation therapy will usually reverse within a few weeks or months after the end of therapy.

An early occurring side effect of radiation therapy that can often be irreversible is dry mouth (xerostomia). Xerostomia is characterized by a sharp decrease in the serous component of saliva, so that the mouth becomes dry and only sticky mucus is produced (Brosky 2007; Eveson 2008; Scrimger 2011). The pH value in the mouth drops, meaning that the oral cavity gets more acidic. The increased acidity can promote dental caries. The dry oral mucosa can become irritated and fungal infections such as *Candida albicans* are difficult to stave off. Saliva is important for the lubrication of food during chewing and swallowing. The xerostomia makes dry or sticky foods difficult to eat for the patient. There is no curative treatment for xerostomia, so most patients constantly carry a water bottle in order to keep rinsing and lubricating the oral cavity. Adding a pinch of baking powder to the water helps to reduce the acidity of the oral cavity. Alternatively, there is oral spray available which contains artificial saliva that is based on elm bark extract. *Acmella oleracea* (also called spilanthes or toothache plant) can also be used to reduce the irritation caused by the xerostomia. In patients receiving radiation therapy to the pharynx or the retromolar trigone, Seikaly *et al.* (2004) advocate surgical relocation of one submandibular salivary gland into the anterior floor of the mouth. This protects the relocated gland from radiation damage and ensures that the patient will not have xerostomia.

Muscle, bone and nerve tissue have much slower mitotic cycles, so any radiation damage to these structures will only be visible with a considerable delay. In the case of bone, the osteoradionecrosis may take years to develop fully. In particular, the jaw is vulnerable to the development of osteoradionecrosis. The affected mandible becomes brittle and fragile, and the inflamed bone may break or extrude through the skin (O'Dell and Sinha 2011). The situation becomes even more serious if there are still teeth in the affected bone because radiation can damage dental enamel and cause extensive caries. It is possible to protect the teeth in the radiation field with shielding and an intensive fluoridation regimen, but in many cases the treatment team will opt to extract all teeth before radiation therapy (Miller and Quinn 2006; Hong *et al.* 2010).

Radiation-induced muscle fibrosis also has a lengthy and insidious onset. Fibrotic muscles become stiff and indurated. One muscle that is often in the radiation field is the masseter muscle. Of all the muscles in the body, the masseter has the highest density of muscle fibres. If it becomes fibrotic, the patient experiences a permanently clenched jaw (trismus), which is painful and interferes with eating, oral hygiene and speech (Stubblefield 2011). Stretching exercises for the jaw can improve the condition for some patients (Barañano *et al.* 2011). For other patients, it becomes necessary to surgically release the muscle. Radiation fibrosis can also cause a stiff and immobile tongue, which affects the patient's swallowing, eating and speech. Similarly, radiation fibrosis can affect the ability of the soft palate to close off the velopharyngeal sphincter sufficiently.

Irradiated tissue shows slower wound healing. That means that any kind of surgery or reconstruction of previously irradiated tissue is complicated and the outcome less certain than in a non-irradiated patient. Because the side effects of radiation treatment can be so pronounced, intensity caps are imposed and the absorbed radiation dose is limited to 60–70 Gy for the patient's life (some radiation treatment protocols go as high as 80 Gy). This means that the patient will not be allowed to receive any more radiation in this part of the body and that radiation is no longer a treatment option, should the cancer recur (A. Abitbol *et al.* 1999; Kelly 2007).

10.2   Cancer of the tongue

10.2.1   Glossectomy

The tongue is an important sensory organ for taste and touch. Its movement is important for eating, swallowing, speech and other oral manoeuvres. The tongue is largely composed of interdigitating muscles. It is considered to be a hydrostat organ (Kier and Smith 1985), i.e. an organ without a skeleton that stabilizes its movement by compressing water in its cells. Lingual cancer manifests itself in lesions on the lateral free margin of the tongue, on the floor of the mouth or in the retromolar trigone. The cancer is usually removed surgically with an appropriate safety margin. Depending on the defect location and size as well as the surgeon's assessment and skill level, the defect can be reconstructed with a local closure, a local flap or a free flap (see section 10.1.2). The resection and reconstruction are tailored to the location and the extent of the tumour, so every glossectomy surgery is individual. Historically, large tongue cancers were often treated with total glossectomy surgery, i.e. complete removal of the tongue, sometimes even combined with a laryngectomy. Total glossectomy surgery is performed very rarely today but may sometimes still be necessary. Modern glossectomy surgery is as circumscribed as possible in order to minimize detrimental effects on swallowing and speech for the patient (Smeele 2007).

Because the tongue is anatomically complex and composed of many different muscles, it is often difficult to predict the outcomes of partial glossectomy surgery for swallowing and speech. For swallowing, resections of the tip and blade of the tongue will mainly affect the patient's ability to manipulate food in the oral cavity. However, anterior resections do not affect the safety and efficiency of the patient's swallow as much as posterior resections. Resections of the base of the tongue can lead to difficulties with bolus clearance. In terms of speech, while larger defects will lead to more severe articulatory distortions, the reconstruction of the defect is also important for overall speech outcome.

Both the extent and the location of the defect have an impact on the patient's ability to speak after glossectomy surgery (Nicoletti *et al.* 2004). Bressmann *et al.* (2009) estimated that a resection of approximately 20 per cent of the tissue of the tongue constitutes the cut-off point after which speech acceptability deteriorates markedly. While some surgeons argue that post-glossectomy reconstruction should ensure maximum motility of the tongue (Imai and Michi 1992), other authors have argued that lingual reconstruction should recreate the bulk and the overall shape of the patient's tongue (Kimata *et al.* 2003). A number of studies have indicated that speech outcomes of glossectomy patients tend to be a little better in patients reconstructed with local closure procedures than in those with free flaps (Konstantinovic and Dimic 1998; Pauloski *et al.* 1998; Nicoletti *et al.* 2004). However, if the defect is relatively large, a local closure is often not feasible and the defect must be closed with a local or a free flap.

Glossectomy surgery can change the movement of the tongue in an unpredictable way. In a local reconstruction, the orientation of the muscle fibres can change so that when a patient activates the tongue muscles for the production of a word or a phrase, the learned nerve activation patterns for sound production lead to asymmetrical lingual movements. If a lateral lingual defect is closed by suturing the side of the tongue into the floor of mouth, this can have a tethering effect. Local reconstructions can be done with tissues such as the platysma muscle from the neck. While the platysma provides a supple and pliable flap, it often does not have very much mass and cannot be used to close a large defect. The pectoralis flap is an example of a local flap that was historically very popular and is still used today (Avery *et al.* 2010). In this procedure, chest muscle is mobilized and brought up along the neck into the oral cavity. This flap works well to reconstruct the floor of the mouth in a patient with an extensive lingual resection. However, the flap attachment to the chest can limit the patient's head movement. A free flap that is often used for the reconstruction of lingual resections is the radial forearm flap. This tissue is soft and supple which makes it appropriate for lingual reconstruction. Another advantage of the inside of the forearm is that there are few hair follicles so that the patient will not experience hair growth on the tongue after the reconstruction. If the defect is very large and the surgeon wants to create a bulky flap that mimics the shape of the tongue, the gracilis flap from the inside of the thigh can be used. While free flaps lead to a more normal looking tongue on oral inspection, the flap tissue of a bulky flap can add weight and hamper the movement of the tongue (Konstantinovic and Dimic 1998).

Jacobson *et al.* (1995) and Beck *et al.* (1998) underline the importance of meticulously documenting the extent and the shape of the resection and the reconstruction. Both teams of researchers advocate the use of graphical templates that the surgeon should ideally fill in directly after the surgery. The exact knowledge of the defect is necessary to gauge what kind of tongue movement can be expected following partial lingual ablation. Nevertheless, speech and swallowing outcomes remain difficult to predict (Beck *et al.* 1998). Since muscle tissue is resected and the reconstruction may be tethering, the standard expectation is that the tongue will lose strength and movement range, resulting in an inability to reach articulatory targets (Korpijaakko-Huuhka *et al.* 1999). While this is certainly the case for near-total glossectomies, this view neglects the fact that the speaker with a glossectomy will not just passively endure the altered lingual configuration but will actively try to compensate to the best of his or her abilities. Rastadmehr *et al.* (2008) demonstrated with ultrasound imaging that small- to medium-sized lateral lingual resections lead to increased postoperative raising of the tongue in the oral cavity and higher tongue velocity during a reading task. Bressmann *et al.* (2005a, 2005b, 2007) used three-dimensional ultrasound imaging to investigate the tongue shapes of partial glossectomy patients during sustained speech sounds. It was found that partial glossectomy leads to a decrease in midsagittal grooving along the length of the tongue. There was also a higher degree of postoperative height asymmetry between the affected and the unaffected side of the tongue. The decreased midsagittal grooving correlated moderately with the speakers' corresponding change in speech acceptability (Bressmann *et al.* 2007).

10.2.2   Rehabilitation of glossectomy patients

In the nineteenth century, the English theologian Edward Twistleton wrote a treatise debating whether glossectomee speech was evidence for a divine miracle or simply the result of physiological adaptation to a lingual resection (Twistleton 1873). Despite the fascination with the subject, the functional rehabilitation of glossectomy patients has not been the focus of a lot of research in speech-language pathology. As a result, the treatment recommendations in the literature are vague and unspecific. In part, this can be attributed to the complexity of the anatomical change after a glossectomy. Since the patient's articulatory gestures are difficult to predict, speech-language pathologists cannot assume that traditional articulation therapy techniques will be helpful or applicable to the patient. Unfortunately, there is not a lot of literature to guide the clinician. In fact, there have only been two books about glossectomy speech rehabilitation written to date.

Skelly's (1973) *Glossectomee Speech Rehabilitation* provides a careful description of the spontaneous compensatory manoeuvres that the author observed in patients with total glossectomies. After a complete resection of the tongue, patients will only be able to convey minimal phonetic contrasts with labial and lingual articulatory gestures. Obviously, the patient's available vowel space will be greatly reduced and only a few consonant sounds can be produced. Nevertheless, many patients with even a total glossectomy are able to converse relatively successfully with family members and other individuals who are familiar with their speech. Skelly (1973) described different successful compensatory manoeuvres for the information of speech-language pathologists and their patients (see also Skelly *et al.* 1971). However, because the physiological differences between patients can be quite stark, none of the described manoeuvres would be equally appropriate for all patients. Today, total removal of the tongue is a rather rare procedure and speech-language pathologists in head and neck cancer centres or in private practice will not encounter such cases very often. Skelly (1973) also discussed speech therapy exercises for patients with partial glossectomies, focusing particularly on secondary compensatory strategies such as vowel lengthening, reduction of rate of speech, and the use of exaggerated inflections, all of which were meant to maximize the patient's speech intelligibility.

Appleton and Marchin (1995) focus their treatment recommendations on the use of range of motion exercises for the tongue and the facial muscles. These range of motion exercises aim to reduce the effects of radiation-induced muscle fibrosis. The recommendation for oral motor exercises is echoed by Leonard (1994) and Lazarus *et al.* (2007). Leonard (1994) suggests that the speech-language pathologist should try to establish new articulatory targets and movements that take the changed lingual anatomy into account. However, such new articulatory gestures would have to be individually tailored to the patient. Therefore, it is difficult to make generic recommendations. Furia *et al.* (2001) studied the effects of a therapy programme on glossectomy speech focusing on articulation therapy and oral motor exercises. They found that the therapy improved speech intelligibility significantly for patients with total and subtotal glossectomies. However, patients with more confined partial glossectomy resections were not able to improve their speech much beyond the initial, pre-therapy outcome. In the end, not every patient with a partial glossectomy will even get a full course of speech therapy. The available resources in different healthcare systems are often limited, and many patients with glossectomy will only receive non-speech oral motor exercises, to be done at home.

An alternative approach for the speech and swallowing rehabilitation of patients with a partial glossectomy is the use of prosthodontic devices. Specialized maxillofacial prosthodontists can fit their patients with palatal drop/augmentation prostheses. The aim of a palatal drop prosthesis is to lower the palatal surface towards a hypomotile tongue. Therefore, the device facilitates the contact between the tongue and the palate (Shimodaira *et al.* 1998; Leeper *et al.* 2005). Marunick and Tselios (2004) found that there has not been much scientific investigation of palatal drop prostheses and that descriptions are limited to small patient numbers. While some authors have argued that a palatal drop may improve the oral phase of swallowing for the patient with a partially resected tongue, it is difficult to shape the palate in such a way that it will be helpful for speech production.

A palatal drop prosthesis is made by asking the patient to perform different lingual manoeuvres such as swallow or elevate the tongue against dental impression material (Leeper *et al.* 2005). If the patient's lingual movement is very restricted, this can make the palatal prosthesis bulky, which can further impact the production of lingual consonants. However, Leonard and Gillis (1990) were able to demonstrate that a palatal drop prosthesis improved various aspects of the speech of five partial glossectomees. De Carvalho-Teles *et al.* (2008) documented treatment outcomes in a comparatively large group of 36 patients and argued that the patients' perceived speech intelligibility and vowel differentiation improved as a result of the prostheses. Although the evidence for palatal drop prostheses is currently not conclusive, the idea of counteracting the effects of a lingual resection with a modification of the palatal height and shape remains fascinating and will hopefully be explored by more research in the future.

10.3   Nasopharyngeal and maxillofacial cancer

The pharynx is divided into the anatomical regions of nasopharynx, oropharynx and hypopharynx. Oropharyngeal and nasopharyngeal tumours can affect the function of the velopharyngeal sphincter. It was mentioned in section 10.1.1 that especially tumours related to the human papillomavirus tend to affect the tonsils and the retromolar trigone (Kreimer *et al.* 2005). Resections and reconstructions in this region may impact the function of the velopharyngeal sphincter. The velopharyngeal mechanism is responsible for the regulation of oral-nasal balance in speech. Velopharyngeal closure is achieved both by elevation of the velum and contraction of the lateral pharyngeal walls (Smith and Kuehn 2007). Tumour resections that involve the velum or the faucial arches will affect velopharyngeal valving and the patient will exhibit hypernasality, i.e. he or she will have air and sound coming through the nose when speaking. Hypernasality affects the intelligibility and the acceptability of speech. It is difficult to achieve functional surgical reconstruction of the velopharyngeal sphincter that will restore normal oral-nasal balance for the patient.

The standard surgical techniques used to facilitate velopharyngeal closure were developed for patients with cleft palate and other craniofacial syndromes. Pharyngeal flap surgery involves the mobilization of a muscle and mucosa flap from the posterior pharyngeal wall. This flap is then used to elevate the velum permanently and connect it to the posterior pharyngeal wall. Alternatively, pharyngoplasties support velopharyngeal closure by surgically narrowing the pharynx, therefore making it easier for the velum to close off the nasopharynx (Peterson-Falzone *et al.* 2010). However, head and neck cancer patients are usually not very good candidates for these types of surgeries because their resections are quite extensive. If the patient has undergone adjuvant radiation treatment, the wound healing properties of the tissue are diminished.

In head and neck cancer patients with palatal and velopharyngeal defects, prosthodontic treatment is often the preferred intervention. Defects of the hard palate will result in hypernasality because air will escape through the nasal cavity. When the patient has food in his or her mouth, nasal regurgitation may occur. Since the hard palate does not move, it is relatively easy to make a palatal obturator prosthesis. The device closes and covers the defect of the hard palate. The obturation of a palatal fistula will restore the patient's oral-nasal balance for speech (Rieger *et al.* 2003).

Defects of the velopharyngeal sphincter are more difficult to treat with a prosthodontic appliance. The velopharyngeal sphincter comprises dynamic, muscular structures that move actively. The speech prosthesis has to help the patient achieve good velopharyngeal closure, but it also has to be comfortable to wear and must not affect swallowing and nasal breathing. If the velum is still in place but its ability to elevate for velopharyngeal closure has been compromised, a palatal lift prosthesis can be used. These appliances consist of a palatal retainer and a shoehorn-shaped pharyngeal extension that serves to elevate the velum. If the velum has been partially or totally resected, the palatal prosthesis must fill a larger gap. In this case, the prosthodontist makes a device called a speech bulb (see Figure 10.2). Both the palatal lift and the speech bulb prostheses are based on pharyngeal impressions of the patient. After the basic shape has been established, the prosthodontist incrementally

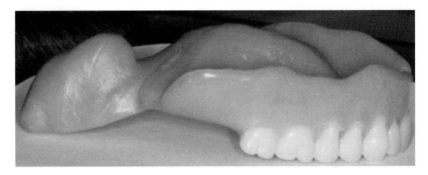

Figure 10.2 Speech bulb appliance, integrated into a full denture.

builds up the pharyngeal extension until it reaches a size that makes it beneficial for the patient's speech but is still comfortable during breathing and swallowing. The speech-language pathologist may have a consultative role during this process. Following the successful adaptation of the appliance, the speech-language pathologist may also be of help while the patient learns to make the best use of the appliance (Leeper *et al.* 2005; Lazarus *et al.* 2007).

Maxillofacial tumours may sometimes require a facial resection which may include the removal of one of the patient's eyes. The resulting defects are treated with facial prostheses (epitheses) that try to match the patient's facial features and skin tone as closely as possible (Van Doorne 1994). The epithesis can be retained with glasses, or the prosthodontist can attach it to implants. While the silicone rubber prosthesis will not look completely natural, the epithesis will allow the patient to interact with other people and to insert themselves into different social situations. For speech production, it may often be helpful to fill the facial defect behind the prosthesis with gauze to dampen the extra resonances.

10.4   Cancer of the larynx

10.4.1   Partial laryngectomy

Partial laryngectomy surgery aims to remove a tumour and restore the patient's health while maintaining his or her ability to breathe, swallow and speak as normally as possible. Since the larynx is important for both airway protection and voice production, this is a delicate balancing act. In a partial laryngectomy, the surgeon aims to resect the tumour specifically to its location and its size. The surgery attempts to preserve as much structure and function as possible. As a result, the procedures and outcomes of partial laryngectomy surgeries can be variable between surgeons. The description in this chapter will be limited to a general introduction to the most common types of partial laryngectomies.

There are differences in the treatment approach to laryngeal cancer in different healthcare systems and even within different sociodemographic groups (Chen *et al.* 2011). If radiation therapy is favoured over surgical interventions, patients with small- to medium-sized tumours will usually receive radiation therapy first. However, after the patient has received a full life-time dose of radiation, a partial laryngectomy is no longer a good second treatment option if the patient then has a cancer recurrence. In such a case, a total laryngectomy would be considered a safer surgical option. Healthcare systems that prefer surgical interventions over primary radiation treatment will offer a larger range of partial laryngectomy options. The treatment success of both options is comparable (Spielmann *et al.* 2010), but the treatment sequelae of radiation and surgery are different.

Small tumours that are confined to one vocal fold can be resected with a unilateral cordectomy. In this surgery, the surgeon excises the affected part of the vocal fold and a safety margin. The defect can either be reconstructed or left to heal over by itself. The surgery usually leaves the patient with an acceptable and functional speaking voice. While most normal voice users will be content with the postoperative voice, the change may make a big difference for speakers with high vocal demands, such as singers, actors and professional speakers. Since glottic tumours that qualify for a circumscribed cordectomy are by definition relatively small, partial cordectomies are also sometimes done with laser surgery. The laser sublimates the tissue from a solid state to vapour. This allows the surgeon to leave a smooth resection that will show good wound healing. Zeitels (2005) argues that local conservative primary laser ablation allows reliable control of small laryngeal tumours. The disadvantage of the approach is that the surgeon cannot gauge if the invisible pseudopodia around the visible tumour have been adequately controlled. Because the tumour is vaporized, it is not possible to analyse samples of the wound margins. After the laser surgery, the patient's larynx therefore has to be examined on a regular basis to rule out recurrence.

A tumour that has become larger in size or that is beginning to invade surrounding structures such as the ventricular fold must be resected with a more comprehensive approach. In a hemilaryngectomy, the surgeon vertically splits the larynx in half, roughly along the midsagittal plane. The muscles and cartilages are preserved on the non-affected side. When the patient's throat is reconstructed, a layer of scar tissue remains on the affected side. This will serve as a counterpart for the preserved vocal fold. As a result, the patient will be able to adduct the remaining vocal fold and produce voice. A more conservative variety of the hemilaryngectomy is called a vertical partial laryngectomy. The aim of this procedure is to preserve the arytenoid cartilage on the affected side. If some arytenoid movement can be preserved, the patient will find it easier to protect the airway and to produce voice (Balm 2007).

If a tumour is confined to the supraglottic aspects of the larynx, it is possible to limit the surgery to the laryngeal structures above the level of the vocal folds. In a subtotal supraglottal laryngectomy, all laryngeal structures above the vocal folds (including the epiglottis and the hyoid) are removed so that only the cricoid cartilage, the arytenoids and the vocal folds are preserved. This leaves a comprehensive defect. The rationale for the surgery is that the remaining vocal folds should allow the patient to protect the airway against aspiration and to produce voice. Unfortunately, because of the extent of the defect, patients will often suffer from aspiration of saliva and food into the lungs. Many patients will also require a tracheostoma to ensure safe breathing. Because of the extent of the surgery, the voice quality is poor and the voice does not project well (Doyle 1994). A more conservative version of this surgery is the supracricoid partial laryngectomy with cricohyoidoepiglottopexy (Laccourreye *et al.* 1990). In this surgery, the hyoid and the epiglottis are spared. To achieve better airway protection and swallowing safety, the cricoid cartilage is pulled up and attached to the hyoid and epiglottis. This modified procedure reduces the risk of aspiration. The voice quality has also been reported to be better than in the standard subtotal supraglottic laryngectomy (Crevier-Buchman *et al.* 1995). Nevertheless, this is an extensive surgical resection that will have complex functional sequelae for the patient.

10.4.2   Voice therapy for partial laryngectomees

The postoperative voice problems of patients after partial laryngectomy surgery may run the gamut from mild hoarseness to complete aphonia. Patients may also have undergone multi-pronged cancer treatment, involving surgery as well as radiation or radiochemotherapy. As a result, the resulting functional consequences are often complex. Voice rehabilitation following partial laryngectomy is inherently interdisciplinary in nature (Sparano *et al.* 2004). The involvement of the speech-language pathologist in the head and neck cancer team may go beyond the patient's voice and speech rehabilitation and encompass related medical problems such as swallowing and airway management. While these latter problems may initially be more acute and urgent than voice production, the patient with a partial laryngectomy will usually require the help of the speech-language pathologist to make optimum use of the resected and reconstructed structures.

Doyle (1994) observes that a partial resection of the larynx can cause rather different symptoms and trigger very different functional adaptations between patients. The resection may cause a deficiency of vocal fold closure, resulting in a weak, breathy and insufficient voice. Alternatively, patients may actively increase or modify their vocal fold closure. Paradoxically, the resection can then result in a hyperfunctional voice disorder. If one vocal fold has been stripped or resected, patients may also compensate by either producing ventricular phonation or mixed glottal-ventricular phonation.

There is no fixed voice therapy programme that can be uniformly applied to all partial laryngectomees. For this population, speech-language pathologists will tend to choose voice therapy techniques that meet the needs of the individual patient rather than strictly follow a specific school of thought. Boone *et al.* (2010) developed a set of voice therapy exercises that Stemple (2010) classifies as *symptomatic*, i.e. as a collection of independent intervention techniques. Within the symptomatic exercises proposed by Boone *et al.* (2010), a number of techniques can be classified as promoting increased vocal fold closure and adding tension to a hypofunctional voice. Using the hands to push against an object or against each other increases the muscle tone in the upper body, and this in turn can increase the strength of vocal fold closure. Similarly, the use of hard vocal attacks ensures that the patient will achieve maximum vocal fold closure. The half-swallow boom technique combines a swallowing manoeuvre with voice production.

If a patient is demonstrating a hyperfunctional compensation pattern, the speech-language pathologist should choose therapy exercises to relax the voice and promote easy, effortless phonation. An appropriate technique from the symptomatic exercises proposed by Boone *et al.* (2010) is the chanting voice, which employs an elevated pitch and a slightly breathy voice quality in a psalm-style chant. The voiced lip trill makes use of the fact that the lips are heavier than the vocal folds – when the patient is blowing a voiced raspberry, the vocal folds have to be slightly parted to allow for sufficient airflow. The chewing technique uses exaggerated mandibular and lingual motion to relax the patient's voice.

These different techniques can be supplemented by posture adjustments or slight finger pressure on the neck as some patients find that a slight turn or tilt of their head crowds and compresses the tissue on the affected side of the neck, resulting in better vocal fold closure. Stemple *et al.* (2010) propose a generic set of vocal function exercises that can be used as isometric strengthening and stretching exercises for the vocal folds. Partial laryngectomies with smaller resections could probably benefit from this approach. Colton and Casper (1996) describe the use of a 'confidential voice' speaking style for the immediate post-surgical phase. The authors describe this speaking style as 'much like the voice that one would use to exchange a confidence with a friend when one does not wish others nearby to hear' (Colton and Caspar 1996: 286). While this technique was not developed specifically for head and neck cancer patients, the slight glottal gap and the breathy voice quality could be helpful for patients who show hyperfunctional compensation or who show a crossed glottal-ventricular phonation pattern.

Doyle (1994) emphasizes the importance of finding strategies to maximize the intelligibility of the patient's speech through careful over-articulation and over-inflection. Depending on the extent of the resection, therapy goals for the patient have to be adjusted. For many patients, hoarse voice quality can be an acceptable therapy result if the voice is functional and relatively effortless to produce. The speech-language pathologist may even work with a patient on optimally employing their ventricular or mixed glottal-ventricular phonation. If the patient produces mixed or ventricular fold phonation with ease, and if the resulting voice quality and quantity is better than the glottal voice, this phonation style may fulfil a communicative purpose.

10.4.3   Total laryngectomy

Historically, total laryngectomy was a common and frequent procedure for patients with larynx cancer. While the surgery is comprehensive, there are a number of clear management approaches that may be used for postoperative vocal rehabilitation of the total laryngectomy. Today, the procedure is becoming increasingly less common as a primary treatment approach. Before resorting to a total laryngectomy, the treatment team will first attempt an organ preservation approach, using radiotherapy, possibly supplemented with chemotherapy. If a surgical approach is chosen, the surgeon will tend to employ a partial laryngectomy approach to preserve as much of the larynx as possible. A total laryngectomy is used as a last resort when a more conservative approach has failed.

In a total laryngectomy, all laryngeal muscles and cartilages are removed together with the hyoid bone, the epiglottis and several tracheal rings. The trachea is bent forward to form a permanent tracheostoma in the neck that will allow the patient to breathe. Since all laryngeal structures are removed, the patient's airway and food passage are completely separated. Together with the laryngectomy, a radical neck dissection is often performed to reduce the risk of lymph node metastasis (Balm 2007).

Total laryngectomy ensures that the airway remains patent and that the patient breathes directly from the neck. This requires a number of adjustments on the patient's part. The patient has to protect the tracheostoma from dust, fumes and irritants. Even insects can pose a risk for aspiration into the lungs. Also, strong perfumes or air fresheners may irritate the laryngectomee's lungs. Normal breathing is predominantly nasal. The nasal passages serve to warm and moisten the inhaled air. In contrast, the total laryngectomee will experience the full temperature and humidity differential directly at the lungs. On cold and dry days, heat and moisture will quickly evaporate from the lungs. However, hot muggy days may be equally unpleasant for the laryngectomee. Laryngectomees tend to cover the tracheostoma opening with special fabric or foam covers that are either tied around the neck or attached with an adhesive. To reduce the loss of heat and moisture from the tracheostoma, there are also heat and moisture exchangers (also called artificial noses), which use foam pads to insulate the trachea against the ambient air (Hilgers *et al.* 1991; Ward *et al.* 2007a).

After surgery, the patient loses the ability for thoracic fixation because the larynx cannot seal the air pressure in the lungs any more. The patient has to learn to manage the airway differently during manoeuvres such as coughing or sneezing. The inability to build up pressure in the lungs also means that the laryngectomee will not be able to build up muscle force based on thoracic fixation during activities such as lifting, climbing stairs or shovelling snow. Thoracic fixation is equally important when bearing down to evacuate the bowel. Laryngectomees have to relearn many every-day tasks such as washing their hair or taking a shower. Activities such as bathing or swimming carry an extreme risk for laryngectomees (Ward *et al.* 2007a). Another initial change is an almost complete loss of the sense of smell and taste after surgery. Lingual taste buds only relay basic flavours to the brain but more complex aromas are acquired using nasal receptors. Total laryngectomees have to learn to manipulate residual air in their oral and nasal cavities to regain smell and taste (Van As-Brooks *et al.* 2007).

Swallowing after a total laryngectomy can be affected by reduced opening of the upper oesophageal sphincter. The cricopharyngeal muscle is opened by the upward and forward movement of the larynx and hyoid. After these structures have been removed, the patient has to rely on positive pressure from the base of the tongue to move the bolus past the upper oesophageal sphincter. This can make the swallow more inefficient and laborious. Because the cricopharyngeus loses its opponents, a stricture may develop, which can aggravate the problem (Ward *et al.* 2007b).

10.4.4 Voice rehabilitation of laryngectomy patients

Total laryngectomy requires the patient to learn a completely alternative method of phonation and speech. There are three general approaches, and each of them is suitable for different patients. These approaches are the use of artificial larynges, oesophageal speech and tracheo-oesophageal speech.

In most industrialized countries, patients will automatically receive or buy an artificial larynx after surgery. Even if the patient is able to use a different method of voice production, the artificial larynx is an important back-up device. Most laryngectomees will always carry the device and many will use it as their primary method of communication. The most common type of artificial larynx is the transcervical electrolarynx (see Figure 10.3). This device consists of a battery-powered oscillator that produces a low-frequency sound under a plastic cover. The patient holds this plastic diaphragm against his or her neck so that sound waves from the

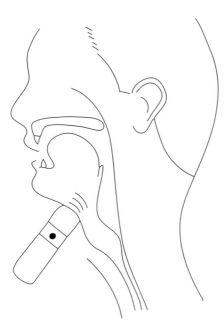

Figure 10.3 Transcervical electrolarynx.

electrolarynx are transmitted through the neck into the pharynx. The patient can then use this sound to speak. There is usually a sweet spot that allows particularly good sound transmission. The speech-language pathologist is often instrumental in helping the patient identify his or her individual sweet spot. Some patients find that alternative placements on the cheeks or the lips allow for the best sound transmission. To speak with the electrolarynx, the patient uses residual air in the oral cavity to produce consonant sounds such as plosives and fricatives. These need to be strongly articulated to ensure that the speaker will be intelligible to the listener (Doyle 1994).

The sound of electrolarynx speech has been described as robotic and monotonous by listeners (Meltzner and Hillman 2005). Unfortunately, a relatively low fundamental frequency is necessary because the longer wavelength ensures better transmission of sound through the tissue. Therefore, the core features of electrolarynges have stayed relatively constant over the last decades (Keith *et al.* 2005). It is important that the speaker carefully coordinates the electrolarynx sound with his or her speech. It is also a good idea for the speaker to make clear pauses between phrases in order to avoid tiring the listener with the sound of the electrolarynx (Doyle 1994; Graham 1997). Some electrolarynges have pitch control features that allow the patient to maintain some prosody in their speech. The presence of two frequencies allows the patient to use the higher frequency for emphasis. In more elaborate devices, the pitch is controlled with a touch-sensitive switch so the patient needs good

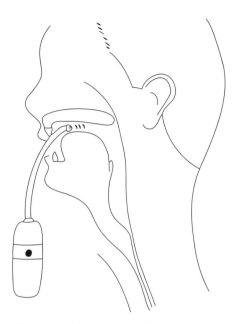

Figure 10.4 Electrolarynx with oral adapter.

dexterity as well as a keen ear. In the end, many patients will be content to use just one single frequency. Recent research has investigated how to use electromyographic signals from the laryngectomee's neck to develop a hands-free switching mechanism and pitch control mechanism for the electrolarynx (Kubert *et al.* 2009).

Laryngectomy surgery and neck dissection create scar tissue that may make the neck stiff and attenuate the sound from the transcervical electrolarynx. Tissue fibrosis secondary to radiation therapy or flap reconstructions may add to this effect. Patients who experience these difficulties may use an oral adapter that transmits the sound into the oral cavity via a plastic tube (see Figure 10.4). The end of the tube is placed on or near the dorsum of the tongue, and the patient uses the sound to produce speech. As with the transcervical electrolarynx, the patient will have to search for a sweet spot for the tube to ensure that the movement of the tongue does not muffle and block the sound. Because the tube is placed in the mouth, the patient has to be aware of potential hygiene issues associated with handling the device. Starting in the 1970s (Knorr and Zwitman 1977), there have also been repeated attempts to place the complete device in an intraoral dental prosthesis, but these devices are not very common.

Historically, the first successful artificial larynges were pneumatic (Keith *et al.* 2005). These continue to be available from a number of small manufacturers. This design is sometimes referred to as a Tokyo larynx (Nelson *et al.* 1975). The proponents of this artificial larynx argue that their design is superior to that of electrolarynges. Pneumatic artificial larynges use an adapter that is placed over the tracheostoma. When the patient exhales, the air pressure is used to excite a rattle or a reed that generates a sound. As in the oral electrolarynx, a cannula is used to transmit the sound into the oral cavity. The patient can use the air pressure to change the fundamental frequency of the sound, which makes the device interesting for speakers of tonal languages (Chalstrey *et al.* 1994).

Oesophageal voice is another method of voice production after total laryngectomy. The upper oesophageal sphincter can be used to produce audible eructations (burps). In a ructus, air passes from the oesophagus back into the pharynx. Along the way, it excites the tissue of the cricopharyngeus, which produces the ructus sound. It is possible to deliberately charge the oesophagus with air for this kind of sound production. Oesophageal voice has a low fundamental frequency and a rough quality. As in electrolarynx speech, the patient uses the residual air in the oral cavity to produce pressure consonants (Stemple *et al.* 2000). It could be argued that oesophageal speech is the ideal form of post-laryngectomy voice rehabilitation. No equipment is required and the voice is always available for the patient. However, oesophageal speech is laborious and requires the speaker to practise on a regular basis in order to stay proficient. The insufflated air in the oesophagus is a precious commodity for the speaker, and many oesophageal speakers are forced to keep their phrases brief and to the point.

More than any other method of laryngectomy speech rehabilitation, oesophageal speech depends on individual aptitude and disposition. Some patients find that they have a particular talent for this type of speech production whereas others are not able to consistently produce oesophageal voice. Proficient oesophageal speakers are able to produce complete sentences on a single insufflation. Unfortunately, oesophageal speech is difficult to teach (Graham 2005). Many patients have trepidations because they have been raised not to burp in company. These concerns can often be alleviated by pointing out to the patient that eructations are the result of digestive gases forming in the stomach whereas an oesophageal insufflation only builds up air in the clean upper third of the oesophagus. Another problem is that speech-language pathologists are often not very good at teaching oesophageal speech. Historically, some laryngectomees have taken training to become oesophageal voice instructors and to instruct their fellow laryngectomees. In North America, training for oesophageal voice teachers is provided by the International Association of Laryngectomees. As total laryngectomy is becoming an increasingly rare procedure, it is becoming more difficult to find laryngectomee volunteers to fill this role.

For instruction purposes, two methods of charging the oesophagus are distinguished. Injection manoeuvres build up positive pressure in the oral cavity and transfer some of this pressure into the upper oesophagus. There are different techniques such as air swallows, glossopharyngeal

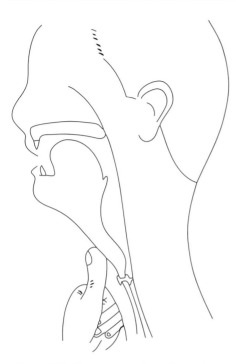

Figure 10.5 Tracheo-oesophageal speech.

pumping or articulation of an unreleased plosive sound. Inhalation manoeuvres make use of the fact that inhalation widens the lumen of the trachea, which in turns also widens the oesophagus and increases its negative pressure. The increase in negative pressure facilitates oesophageal insufflation. Fluent oesophageal speakers will use both methods in parallel (Doyle 1994; Graham 1997, 2005).

The third method of post-laryngectomy speech rehabilitation is tracheo-oesophageal speech (see Figure 10.5). Tracheo-oesophageal speech is oesophageal speech powered by pulmonary air. The trachea and the oesophagus, which are completely disconnected after laryngectomy, are reconnected through a surgically created fistula in the tracheo-oesophageal wall just below the level of the upper oesophageal sphincter. This fistula can either be made at the time of the laryngectomy, or it can be created in a secondary procedure, after wound healing has been completed. A tracheo-oesophageal voice prosthesis with a one-way valve is inserted into the fistula. The one-way valve allows air to flow from the trachea into the oesophagus. However, secretions and food from the oesophagus cannot enter into the trachea and lungs, so the patient is safe from aspiration. When the patient wants to speak, he or she occludes the tracheostoma, either with a finger or by attaching a special self-closing speaking valve to the tracheostoma. The pressure in the trachea then opens the tracheo-oesophageal puncture prosthesis and exhaled air flows into the oesophagus and vibrates the upper oesophageal sphincter (Hamaker *et al.* 1985; Blom 2000; Van As-Brooks and Fuller 2007). The resulting voice quality is rough and low, similar to oesophageal speech. However, because the patient is using pulmonary air to produce the voice, the utterance length is comparable to normal speech, and the speaker can maintain a fairly natural speaking rate. Listeners prefer the voice quality to both electrolarynx and oesophageal speech (Williams and Watson 1987; Clements *et al.* 1997).

Depending on the healthcare system, care for the tracheo-oesophageal prosthesis is the responsibility of either the head and neck surgeon or the speech-language pathologist. The first step is the selection of an appropriate prosthesis, based on the size of the puncture prosthesis, the thickness of the tracheo-oesophageal wall, and the characteristics of the prosthesis. Prostheses differ in terms of the pressure required to open the one-way valve, their shape, the insertion mechanism and the length of time that they may stay inserted (Van As-Brooks and Fuller 2007). While the patient will usually require no help learning to use the prosthesis for speech, the wearing of the tracheo-oesophageal puncture prosthesis requires careful monitoring and regular maintenance. In particular, the patient must be able to flush the prosthesis on a regular basis to keep the one-way valve clean and patent. Patients must have a good understanding of the functioning of the tracheo-oesophageal puncture prosthesis and the risks associated with wearing it. Patients must also have sufficient vision to check the tracheostoma and adequate manual dexterity to remove a leaky prosthesis and replace it with a plug. This means that not all laryngectomy patients will be eligible to receive a tracheo-oesophageal puncture prosthesis.

Despite the advantages of the procedure and the superior voice results, not all patients who use the tracheo-oesophageal puncture prosthesis will be able to permanently use the prosthesis. The silicon prosthesis gets colonized and clogged by bacteria in some patients. Other patients experience irritation, inflammation or the formation of fistulas around the device (Izdebski *et al.* 1994). The constant build-up of air pressure in the trachea can distend the neck of the patient. In the end, some patients decide for themselves that the effort of maintaining the tracheo-oesophageal puncture prosthesis outweighs the benefit of this kind of post-laryngectomy voice rehabilitation, and they resort to the electrolarynx or to oesophageal speech for their communication.

11

Acquired dysarthria

Bruce E. Murdoch

11.1   Definition and classification of acquired dysarthria

'Acquired dysarthria' is a collective term for a group of neurologically based speech disorders. These disorders result from abnormalities in the strength, speed, range, steadiness, tone or accuracy of movements required for control of the respiratory, phonatory, resonatory, articulatory and prosodic aspects of speech production. Damage to the nervous system, which causes disruption to any level of the motor system involved in the regulation of the speech production mechanism, can lead to dysarthria. Depending on which component(s) of the neuromuscular system is affected, a number of different types of dysarthria may be recognized. Each is characterized by its own set of auditory perceptual features. Parts of the neuromuscular system that can be affected include the lower motor neurons, upper motor neurons, extrapyramidal system, cerebellum, neuromuscular junction as well as the muscles of the speech production mechanism.

Historically, a number of different systems have been used to classify the various types of dysarthria including age at onset (congenital and acquired dysarthria), neurological diagnosis (vascular dysarthria, neoplastic dysarthria, etc.) and site of lesion (cerebellar dysarthria, lower motor neuron dysarthria, etc.). The most universally utilized system of classification, however, is that devised by Darley *et al.* (1975) and known as the Mayo Clinic classification system. The six clinically recognized types of dysarthria identified by the Mayo Clinic classification system together with their lesion sites are listed in Table 11.1.

These different types of dysarthria are described below in terms of their neuropathophysiological basis and clinical features, including perceptual, acoustic and physiological characteristics. The various speech disorders identified by the Mayo Clinic classification system presumably

Table 11.1 *Clinically recognized types of dysarthria together with their lesion site*

Dysarthria type	Lesion site
Flaccid dysarthria	Lower motor neurons
Spastic dysarthria	Upper motor neurons
Hypokinetic dysarthria	Basal ganglia and associated brainstem nuclei
Hyperkinetic dysarthria	Basal ganglia and associated brainstem nuclei
Ataxic dysarthria	Cerebellum and/or its connections
Mixed dysarthria, e.g.	
mixed flaccid–spastic dysarthria	Both lower and upper motor neurons (e.g. amyotrophic lateral sclerosis)
Mixed ataxic–spastic–flaccid dysarthria	Cerebellum/cerebellar connections, upper motor neurons and lower motor neurons (e.g. Wilson's disease)

reflect underlying pathophysiology (i.e. spasticity, weakness, etc.) and correlate with the site of lesion in the nervous system.

Unfortunately, no such neurobehavioural classification system exists in acquired childhood dysarthria. This is possibly due in part to the relative lack of systematic studies of acquired childhood dysarthria relative to the adult literature. Furthermore, the relatively few paediatric studies that have been reported have focused either on characterizing the speech behaviour with a noticeable lack of attention given to the precise neural basis of the dysarthria, or on the neural basis with little description of the speech characteristics of the disorder. In the absence of a paediatric based system, use of the Mayo Clinic system with childhood dysarthrias was advocated by Murdoch *et al.* (1990). However, in that this system was devised primarily for adult dysarthrias, some limitations to this approach have been identified in the literature. For instance, the Mayo Clinic system identifies a category of dysarthria for disorders either rarely seen or not seen in children (e.g. Parkinson's disease). Furthermore, it has been suggested that terms such as 'spastic' and 'flaccid', which are derived from descriptions of limb and trunk motor disturbances, may not be appropriate for disturbances of oral muscles due to differences in physiological and neurological control of the subsystems governing speech movements versus limb movements.

Van Mourik *et al.* (1997) appear to have been the first to challenge whether an adult classification system could be validly applied to children. More recently, Morgan and Liégeois (2010) further questioned the validity of applying an adult diagnostic model to acquired dysarthria in childhood, suggesting that a child-specific diagnostic model would yield more sensitive diagnosis and management. Until such time as empirical speech data are available to enable derivation of a classification system specific to acquired childhood dysarthrias, it would seem appropriate that the Mayo Clinic system of classification be used to define dysarthria in children in the same way as it is used to define the equivalent speech disorders in adults.

11.2   Acquired adult and paediatric dysarthria

11.2.1   Flaccid dysarthia
'Flaccid dysarthria' is a collective name for the group of speech disorders arising from damage to the lower motor neurons supplying the muscles of the speech mechanism and/or the muscles of the speech mechanism themselves. Lesions of the motor cranial nerves and spinal nerves represent lower motor neuron lesions and interrupt the conduction of nerve impulses from the central nervous system to the muscles. Consequently, voluntary control of the affected muscles is lost. In that the nerve impulses necessary for the maintenance of muscle tone are lost, the muscles also become flaccid (hypotonic). The term 'flaccid dysarthria' is derived from this major symptom of lower motor neuron damage, namely flaccid paralysis. Muscle weakness, a loss or reduction of muscle reflexes, atrophy of the muscles involved and fasciculation (spontaneous twitches of individual muscle bundles) are further characteristics of lower motor neuron lesions. All or some of these characteristics may be manifest in the muscles of the speech mechanism of persons with flaccid dysarthria, with hypertonia, weakness and reduced reflex activity representing the primary characteristics of flaccid paralysis. The actual lower motor neurons which, if damaged, may be associated with flaccid dysarthria are listed in Table 11.2.

The muscles of the speech mechanism, with the exception of the muscles of respiration, are innervated by the motor cranial nerves which arise from the bulbar region (pons and medulla oblongata) of the brainstem (i.e. cranial nerves V, VII, IX, X, XI and XII). Bulbar palsy, the name commonly given to flaccid paralysis of the muscles supplied by the cranial nerves arising from the bulbar region of the brainstem, can be caused by a variety of conditions which may either affect the cell body of the lower motor neurons or the axons of the lower motor neurons as they course through the peripheral nerves. The major disorders of lower motor neurons which can cause flaccid dysarthria are listed in Table 11.3.

In addition to lesions in lower motor neurons, flaccid dysarthria can also be associated with impaired nerve impulse transmission across the neuromuscular junction (e.g. myasthenia gravis) or disorders which involve the muscles of the speech mechanism (e.g. muscular dystrophy and polymyositis).

As in the case of adults, the lower motor neurons that innervate the muscles involved in speech production can be damaged by a variety of neurological conditions in childhood, including viral infections

Table 11.2 *Lower motor neurons associated with flaccid dysarthria*

Speech process	Muscle	Site of cell body	Nerves through which axons pass
Respiration	Diaphragm	Third to fifth cervical segments of spinal cord	Phrenic nerves
	Intercostal and abdominal	First to twelfth thoracic and first lumbar segments of the spinal cord	Intercostal nerves, sixth thoracic to first lumbar spinal nerves
Phonation	Laryngeal muscles	Nucleus ambiguus in medulla oblongata	Vagus nerves (X)
Articulation	Pterygoid, masseter, temporalis, etc.	Motor nucleus of trigeminal in pons	Trigeminal nerves (V)
	Facial expression, e.g. orbicularis oris	Facial nucleus in pons	Facial nerves (VII)
	Tongue muscles	Hypoglossal nucleus in medulla oblongata	Hypoglossal nerves (XII)
Resonation	Levator veli palatini	Nucleus ambiguus in medulla oblongata	Vagus nerves (X)
	Tensor veli palatini	Motor nucleus of trigeminal in pons	Trigeminal nerves (V)

(e.g. poliomyelitis), brain tumours, cerebrovascular accidents (e.g. embolization resulting from congenital heart disease), degenerative disorders and traumatic brain injury. In particular, damage to cranial nerves V (trigeminal), VII (facial), X (vagus) and XII (hypoglossal), located in either the cranial nerve nuclei in the brainstem or in their peripheral course, can lead to flaccid dysarthria.

Unilateral trigeminal lesions in children may result from traumatic brain injury and brainstem tumours involving the pons. Only minor alterations in speech occur, however, as a result of unilateral trigeminal lesions, in that movements of the mandible are impaired only to a small extent. A much more devastating effect on speech occurs following bilateral trigeminal lesions, the muscles responsible for the elevation of the mandible being too weak in many cases to approximate the mandible and maxilla. Bilateral flaccid paralysis of the masticatory muscles in children may be seen in bulbar poliomyelitis.

A number of different acquired disorders can cause malfunctioning of the facial nerves in children. In some cases the facial palsy may have an idiopathic origin, such as in Bell's palsy. Bell's palsy usually causes unilateral facial paralysis. Prognostically, in the region of 80 per cent of Bell's palsy cases recover in a few days or weeks. Unilateral facial paralysis can also result from traumatic brain injuries, damage to one or other facial nerves during the course of a forceps delivery, compression of the

Table 11.3 *Neurological disorders of lower motor neurons causing flaccid dysarthria*

Site of lesion	Disorder	Aetiology	Signs and symptoms
Peripheral nerves (especially cranial nerves V, VII, IX, X, XI and XII)	Polyneuritis	Inflammation of a number of nerves. Acute type – may follow viral infections, e.g. glandular fever. Chronic type – may be associated with diabetes mellitus and alcohol abuse	Sensory and lower motor neuron changes usually begin in the distal portion of the limbs and spread to involve other regions including the face, tongue, soft palate, pharynx and larynx. The muscles of respiration may also be involved. Bilateral facial paralysis may occur in idiopathic polyneuritis (Guillain–Barré syndrome)
	Compression of and damage to cranial nerves	Neoplasm, e.g. acoustic neuroma causing compression of the VIIth nerve. Aneurysm, e.g. compression of the left recurrent laryngeal nerve by an aortic arch aneurysm. Trauma, e.g. damage to the recurrent laryngeal nerve during thyroidectomy	Localized lower motor neuron signs dependent on the particular nerves involved
	Idiopathic facial paralysis (Bell's palsy)	Pathogenesis unknown in most cases but may be related to inflammatory lesions in the stylomastoid foramen. Approximately 80% of cases recover	Abrupt onset of unilateral facial paralysis
Cranial nerve nuclei and/or anterior horns of spinal cord	Brainstem cerebrovascular accidents	Lateral medullary syndrome (Wallenberg's syndrome) – caused by occlusion of the posterior-inferior cerebellar artery, vertebral artery or lateral medullary artery	Damage of the nucleus ambiguus (origin of the IXth, Xth and cranial portion of the XIth nerve) leads to dysphagia, hoarseness and paralysis of the soft palate on the side of the lesion. Impaired sensation over the face, vertigo and nausea are also present
		Medial medullary syndrome – caused by occlusion of the anterior spinal or vertebral arteries	Damage to the hypoglossal nucleus leads to unilateral paralysis and atrophy of the tongue. A crossed hemiparesis (sparing the face) and sensory changes are also present

Table 11.3 *(cont.)*

Site of lesion	Disorder	Aetiology	Signs and symptoms
		Lateral pontine syndrome (Foville's syndrome) – caused by occlusion of the anterior-inferior cerebellar artery or circumferential artery	Damage to the facial nucleus causes flaccid paralysis of the facial muscles on the side of the lesion. Other symptoms may include deafness, ataxic gait, vertigo, nausea and sensory changes
		Medial pontine syndrome (Millard–Gubler syndrome) – caused by occlusion of the paramedian branch of the basilar artery	Symptoms include facial paralysis on the side of lesion, diplopia, crossed hemiparesis and impaired touch and position sense
	Progressive bulbar palsy	A type of motor neuron disease in which there is progressive degeneration of the motor cells in some cranial nerve nuclei	Progressive weakness and atrophy of the muscles of the speech mechanism
	Poliomyelitis	Viral infection which affects the motor nuclei of the cranial nerves and the anterior horn cells of the spinal cord	Paralysis and wasting of affected muscles with lower motor neuron signs. Paralysis may be widespread or localized and can affect the speech muscles, limb muscles and muscles of respiration
	Neoplasm	Brainstem tumours – these are more common in children than adults	Tumour may progressively involve the cranial nerve nuclei causing gradual weakness and flaccid paralysis of the muscles of the speech mechanism
	Syringobulbia	Slowly progressive cystic degeneration in the lower brainstem in the region of the fourth ventricle. Congenital disorder with onset of symptoms usually in early adult life	As the cystic cavity develops there may be progressive involvement of the cranial nerve nuclei leading to lower motor neuron signs in the muscles of the speech mechanism
	Möbius syndrome (congenital facial diplegia)	Congenital hyperplasia of the VIth and VIIth cranial nerve nuclei	Bilateral facial palsy (VII) and bilateral abducens palsy (VI)

facial nerve by tumour (e.g. acoustic neuroma) and damage to the facial nucleus by brainstem tumours (e.g. glioma). Bilateral facial paralysis may occur in idiopathic polyneuritis (Guillain–Barré syndrome). In addition, sarcoidosis, bulbar poliomyelitis and some forms of basal meningitis may also cause facial diplegia, as can some congenital disorders such as congenital hypoplasia of the VIth and VIIth cranial nerves (Möbius syndrome).

Lesions of the vagus nerves can affect either phonatory or resonatory aspects of speech production or both, depending upon the location of the lesion along the nerve pathway (see section 11.3). Lesions involving the nucleus ambiguus in the medulla may be associated with occlusion of the posterior inferior cerebellar artery (lateral medullary syndrome) or brainstem tumours. In most cases, damage to the vagus nerve affecting speech involves the recurrent laryngeal nerve unilaterally. Such damage may accompany surgery to the neck or occasionally chest surgery, especially on the left side where the nerve loops around the aortic arch. Bilateral damage to the recurrent laryngeal nerves is rare. Hypoglossal nerve lesions are rare in children and more commonly result from damage to the hypoglossal nucleus in the brainstem than from damage to the peripheral nerve itself. Some isolated cases of damage to the hypoglossal nerve are seen as the result of the child falling with something (usually a pencil) in their mouth.

11.2.2 Spastic dysarthria

The term 'spastic dysarthria' was used by Darley *et al.* (1975) to describe the speech disturbance seen in association with damage to the upper motor neurons (i.e. the neurons that convey nerve impulses from the motor areas of the cerebral cortex to the lower motor neurons). The reference to 'spastic' in the term 'spastic dysarthria' is a reflection of the clinical signs of upper motor neuron damage present in the bulbar musculature of these patients, which include spastic paralysis or paresis of the involved muscles, hyperreflexia (e.g. hyperactive jaw-jerk), little or no muscle atrophy and the presence of pathological reflexes (e.g. sucking reflex).

Lesions that disrupt the upper motor neurons causing spastic dysarthria can be located in the cerebral cortex, the internal capsule, the cerebral peduncles or the brainstem. The upper motor neuron system can be divided into two major components, one a direct component and the other an indirect component. In the direct component the axons of the upper motor neurons descend from their cell bodies in the motor cortex to the level of the lower motor neurons without interruption (i.e. without synapsing). The direct component is also known as the pyramidal system. The indirect component, previously called the extrapyramidal system, descends to the level of the lower motor neuron by way of a multi-synaptic pathway involving structures such as the basal ganglia, thalamus and reticular formation. The indirect motor system appears to be primarily responsible for postural arrangements and the orientation of movement in space, whereas the pyramidal system is chiefly responsible for controlling the far more discrete and skilled voluntary aspects of a movement.

Because in most locations (e.g. the internal capsule) the two systems lie in close anatomical proximity, lesions that affect one component will usually also involve the other component. The term 'upper motor neuron lesion' is usually not applied to disorders affecting only the extrapyramidal system (e.g. in basal ganglia lesions). Such disorders are termed 'extrapyramidal syndromes' and include conditions like Parkinson's disease, chorea and athetosis, which are discussed under hypokinetic and hyperkinetic dysarthria.

The pyramidal system can be subdivided into those fibres that project to the spinal cord and those that project to the brainstem. In all, three major fibre groups comprise the pyramidal system: the cortico-spinal tracts (pyramidal system proper), the cortico-mesencephalic tracts and the cortico-bulbar tracts. The fibres of the cortico-bulbar tracts originate from the motor areas of the cerebral cortex and terminate by synapsing with lower motor neurons in the nuclei of cranial nerves V, VII, IX, X, XI and XII. For this reason, they form the most important component of the pyramidal system in relation to the occurrence of spastic dysarthria. Although the majority of cortico-bulbar fibres cross to the contralateral side, uncrossed (ipsilateral) connections also exist. In fact, most of the motor nuclei of the cranial nerves in the brainstem receive bilateral upper motor neuron connections. Consequently, although to a varying degree the upper motor neuron innervation to the cranial nerve nuclei comes predominantly from the contralateral hemisphere, in most instances there is also considerable ipsilateral upper motor neuron innervation. One important exception is the part of the facial nucleus which gives rise to the lower motor neurons that supply the lower half of the face. It seems to receive only a contralateral upper motor neuron connection.

Clinically, the presence of bilateral innervation to most cranial nerve nuclei has important implications for the type of speech disorder that follows unilateral upper motor neuron lesions. Although a mild and usually transient impairment in articulation may occur subsequent to unilateral cortico-bulbar lesions, in general bilateral cortico-bulbar lesions are required to produce a permanent dysarthria.

Unilateral upper motor neuron lesions located in either the motor cortex or internal capsule cause a spastic paralysis or weakness in the contralateral lower half of the face, which may be associated with a mild, transient dysarthria due to weakness of the orbicularis oris. There is no weakness of the forehead, muscles of mastication, soft palate (i.e. no hypernasality), pharynx (i.e. no swallowing problems) or larynx (i.e. no dysphonia). A unilateral upper motor neuron lesion may, however, produce a mild unilateral weakness of the tongue on the side opposite the lesion. In the case of such a unilateral lesion it seems, therefore, that the ipsilateral upper motor neuron is adequate to maintain near-normal function of most bulbar muscles, except those in the tongue. Although most authors agree that the hypoglossal nucleus receives bilateral upper motor neuron innervation, for some reason the ipsilateral connection seems to be less effective than in the case of other cranial nerve nuclei.

Damage to the upper motor neurons is associated with two major syndromes: pseudobulbar palsy (also called supranuclear bulbar palsy) and spastic hemiplegia. Both of these conditions are characterized by spasticity and impairment or loss of voluntary movements. Pseudobulbar palsy takes its name from its clinical resemblance to bulbar palsy (pseudo = 'false') and is associated with a variety of neurological disorders which bilaterally disrupt the upper motor neuron connections to the bulbar cranial nerves (e.g. bilateral cerebrovascular accidents, traumatic brain injury, extensive brain tumours, degenerative neurological conditions such as motor neuron disease). In pseudobulbar palsy, the bulbar muscles, including the muscles of articulation, the velopharynx and larynx, are hypertonic and exhibit hyperreflexia. In addition, there is a reduction in the range and force of movement of the bulbar muscles as well as slowness of individual and repetitive movements. The rhythm of repetitive movements, however, is regular and the direction of movement normal. Symptoms of pseudobulbar palsy include bilateral facial paralysis, dysarthria, dysphonia, bilateral hemiparesis, incontinence and bradykinesia. Drooling from the corners of the mouth is common and many of these patients exhibit lability. A hyperactive jaw reflex and positive sucking reflex are also evident and swallowing problems are a common feature.

By contrast, unilateral upper motor neuron lesions produce spastic hemiplegia, a condition in which the muscles of the lower face and extremities on the opposite side of the body are primarily affected. The bulbar muscles are not generally affected, with weakness being confined to the contralateral lips, lower half of the face and tongue. In addition, the forehead, palate, pharynx and larynx are largely unaffected. Consequently, unlike pseudobulbar palsy, spastic hemiplegia is not associated with problems in mastication, swallowing, velopharyngeal function or laryngeal activity. The tongue appears normal in the mouth but deviates to the weaker side on protrusion. Only a transitory dysarthria, comprising a mild articulatory imprecision, is present rather than a persistent spastic dysarthria.

Hypoxic ischaemic encephalopathy is the most common cause of spastic dysarthria in childhood. In most cases this is associated with intrapartum asphyxia, although severe anoxic brain damage at any stage can cause the same disorder. Brainstem ischaemia with infarction resulting from embolization in association with congenital heart disease can also cause pseudobulbar palsy in children (as it can bulbar palsy). Spastic dysarthria may also be seen in children who have suffered head injuries with elevated intracranial pressure and a midbrain or upper brainstem shearing injury (as a result of a deceleration/acceleration type of injury). Although a common cause of pseudobulbar palsy in adolescents and young adults, disseminated sclerosis is not a common cause of spastic dysarthria in prepubertal children. Degenerative disorders, such as metachromatic leukodystrophy, can also cause childhood pseudobulbar palsy.

11.2.3 Ataxic dysarthria

Damage to the cerebellum or its connections leads to a condition called 'ataxia', in which movements become uncoordinated. If the ataxia affects the muscles of the speech mechanism, the production of speech may become abnormal leading to a cluster of deviant speech dimensions collectively referred to as 'ataxic dysarthria'.

Although even simple movements are affected by cerebellar damage, the movements most disrupted by cerebellar disorders are complex, multi-component, sequential movements. Following damage to the cerebellum, complex movements tend to be broken down or decomposed into their individual sequential components, each of which may be executed with errors of force, amplitude and timing, leading to uncoordinated movements. As speech production requires the coordinated and simultaneous contraction of a large number of muscle groups, it is easy to understand how cerebellar disorders could disrupt speech production and cause ataxic dysarthria.

Located in the posterior cranial fossa, the cerebellum is composed of two large cerebellar hemispheres connected by a midportion called the vermis. As in the case of the cerebral hemispheres, the cerebellar hemispheres are covered by a layer of grey matter or cortex. Unlike the cerebral cortex, however, the cerebellar cortex is uniform in structure throughout its extent. The cerebellar cortex is highly folded into thin transverse folds or folia. A series of deep and definite fissures divide the cerebellum into a number of lobes. Most authors recognize the presence of three lobes: the anterior lobe, the posterior lobe and the flocculonodular lobe. The posterior lobe, also referred to as the neocerebellum, is the largest of the three lobes and is most concerned with regulation of voluntary muscle activities.

The central core of the cerebellum, like that of the cerebral hemispheres, is made up of white matter. Located within the white matter, on either side of the midline, are four grey masses, called the cerebellar or deep nuclei. These are composed of the dentate nucleus, the globose and emboliform nuclei (collectively referred to as the interpositus) and the fastigial nucleus.

Although the cerebellum does not initiate any muscle contractions, it monitors those areas of the brain that do. Its function is to coordinate the actions of muscle groups and time their contractions so that movements involving the skeletal muscles are performed smoothly and accurately. It is thought that the cerebellum achieves this coordination by translating the motor intent of the individual into response parameters that then control the action of the peripheral muscles. In order to be able to perform its primary function of synergistic coordination of muscular activity, the cerebellum requires extensive connections with other parts of the nervous system. Damage to the pathways comprising these connections can cause cerebellar dysfunction and possible ataxic dysarthria, the same as damage to the cerebellum itself. Briefly, the cerebellum functions in part by comparing input from the motor cortex with information concerning the momentary status of muscle contraction, degree of tension of the muscle tendons, position of parts of the body and forces acting on the surfaces of the body originating from muscle spindles, Golgi tendon organs and so on. It then sends appropriate messages back to the motor cortex to ensure smooth, coordinated muscle function. Consequently, the cerebellum requires input from the motor cortex, from muscle and joint receptors, receptors in the internal ear detecting changes in the position and rate of rotation of the head, skin receptors and so on. Conversely, pathways carrying signals from the cerebellum back to the cortex are also required.

The major afferent pathway connecting the cerebral cortex and the cerebellum is the cortico-pontine-cerebellar pathway. This pathway originates primarily from the motor cortex and projects to the ipsilateral pontine nuclei from where secondary fibres project mainly to the cortex of the neocerebellum. Other afferent pathways project to the cerebellum from structures in the brainstem such as the olive (olivo-cerebellar tract), the red nucleus (rubro-cerebellar tract), the reticular formation (reticulo-cerebellar tract), the midbrain (tecto-cerebellar tract) and the cuneate nucleus (cuneo-cerebellar tract) as well as from the spinal cord (spino-cerebellar tracts). Efferent pathways from the cerebellum originate almost entirely from the deep nuclei and project to many parts of the central nervous system, including the motor cortex (via the thalamus), the basal ganglia, red nucleus, brainstem, reticular formation and the vestibular nuclei. The feedback loop provided by the extensive afferent and efferent connections of the cerebellum give it the means to monitor and modify motor activities taking place in various parts of the body to produce a smooth, coordinated motor action.

The major diseases of the cerebellum are listed in Table 11.4. The signs and symptoms of cerebellar dysfunction are generally the same, regardless of aetiology. However, in those disorders where the lesion is slowly progressive (e.g. cerebellar tumour), symptoms of cerebellar disease tend to be much less severe than in conditions where the lesion develops acutely (e.g. traumatic head injury, cerebrovascular accident). In addition, considerable recovery from the effects of an acute lesion can usually be expected.

Major causes of acquired ataxia in childhood include posterior fossa tumours (e.g. medulloblastomas, cerebellar astrocytomas), traumatic brain injury, infections (e.g. cerebellar abscess), hereditary ataxias (e.g. Friedreich's ataxia), degenerative disorders (e.g. metachromatic leukodystrophy), metabolic and endocrine disorders, and toxic exposures (e.g. heavy metal poisoning).

Table 11.4 *Diseases of the cerebellum associated with ataxic dysarthria*

Diseases	Example	General features
Congenital anomalies	Cerebellar agenesis	Partial to almost total non-development of the cerebellum. May in some cases not be associated with any clinical evidence of cerebellar dysfunction. In other cases, however, a gait disturbance may be evident in addition to limb ataxia (especially involving the lower limbs) and dysarthria
Chromosomal disorders	Trisomy	Diffuse hypotrophy (under-development) of the cerebellum may be present which may be associated with symptoms ranging from no clinical symptoms of cerebellar dysfunction through to marked limb ataxia
Trauma	Penetrating head wounds (e.g. bullet wounds)	May be associated with either mild, slowly developing cerebellar dysfunction or rapid, severe cerebellar dysfunction
Vascular disease	Occlusion of anterior-inferior cerebellar artery	Hypotonia and ipsilateral limb ataxia
	Occlusion of posterior-inferior cerebellar artery	Dysarthria, nystagmus, ipsilateral limb ataxia and disordered gait and station
	Occlusion of superior cerebellar artery	Disordered gait and station. Ipsilateral hypotonia, ipsilateral limb ataxia and intention tremor. Occasionally dysarthria
Infections	Cerebellar abscess	Most frequently caused by purulent bacteria but can also occur with fungi. Cerebellar abscesses most frequently arise by direct extension from adjacent infected areas such as the mastoid process or from otological disease
Tumours	Medulloblastomas, astrocytomas and ependymomas	Primary tumours of the cerebellum occur more frequently in children than adults. Medulloblastomas occur most commonly in the midline of the cerebellum in children and usually have a rapid course with a poor prognosis. Astrocytomas are more benign than medulloblastomas and generally occur in children of an older age group than medulloblastomas. Ependymomas are relatively slow growing and again are more common in children than adults
Toxic metabolic and endocrine disorders	Exogenous toxins, e.g. industrial solvents, carbon tetrachloride, heavy metals, etc.	Signs of cerebellar involvement usually associated with symptoms of diffuse involvement of the central nervous system following these intoxications rather than appearing in isolation to other neurological deficits
	Enzyme deficiencies, e.g. pyruvate dehydrogenase deficiency	Ataxia most marked in the lower limbs

Diseases	Example	General features
	Hypothyroidism	Cretins show poor development of the cerebellum. Ataxia present in 20–30% of myxoedema cases
Hereditary ataxias	Friedreich's ataxia	The most commonly encountered spinal form of hereditary ataxia. Pathological degeneration primarily involves the spinal cord with degeneration of neurons occurring in the spino-cerebellar tracts. Some degeneration of neurons in the dentate nucleus and brachium conjunctivum may also occur. The first clinical sign of the disease is usually clumsiness of gait. Later limb ataxia (especially involving the lower extremities) also occurs. A large percentage of cases also exhibit dysarthria and nystagmus and cognitive deficits may also be present
Demyelinating disorders	Multiple sclerosis	Usually associated with demyelination in a number of regions of the central nervous system including the cerebellum. Consequently the dysarthria, if present, usually takes the form of a mixed dysarthria rather than a purely ataxic dysarthria. Paroxysmal ataxic dysarthria may occur as an early sign of multiple sclerosis

11.2.4 Hypokinetic dysarthria

As pointed out in section 11.2.2, the descending motor pathways can be divided into two subsystems, one a direct system and the other an indirect system. The indirect or 'extrapyramidal' system consists of a complex series of multi-synaptic pathways which connect the motor areas of the cerebral cortex to the lower motor neurons. Components of the extrapyramidal system include the basal ganglia plus the various brainstem nuclei that contribute to motor functioning. Diseases which selectively affect the extrapyramidal system without involving the pyramidal pathways are referred to as 'extrapyramidal syndromes'. They include a number of clinically defined disease states of diverse aetiology and often obscure pathogenesis (e.g. Parkinson's disease, chorea, athetosis). Movement disorders are the primary features of extrapyramidal syndromes and, where the muscles of the speech mechanism are involved, disorders of speech may occur in the form of either hypokinetic or hyperkinetic dysarthria.

Darley *et al.* (1969a, 1969b) first used the term 'hypokinetic dysarthria' to describe the speech disorder associated with Parkinson's disease. An acoustically similar form of dysarthria, however, has been observed in persons with progressive supranuclear palsy (Steele–Richardson–Olszewski syndrome) (Metter and Hanson 1986).

Parkinson's disease is a progressive, degenerative neurological disease associated with selective loss of dopaminergic neurons in the pars compacta of the substantia nigra. The condition arises from nigrostriatal dopaminergic cell degeneration which produces an activity imbalance within dopamine-regulated pathways of the basal ganglia. A clinical presentation of bradykinesia plus (one of) rigidity, tremor or postural instability confirms the diagnosis of Parkinson's disease (Valls-Sole 2007). A speech disorder may in some cases be the first symptom to emerge. It has been estimated that 60–80 per cent of clients with Parkinson's disease exhibit hypokinetic dysarthria, with the prevalence increasing as the disease advances. The medical management of Parkinson's disease has conventionally involved the administration of dopamine replacement (e.g. levodopa) and dopamine enhancement (e.g. dopamine receptor agonists) drug therapies. Recognized limitations in dopaminergic pharmacotherapy, such as the development of dyskinesias and on/off states, have prompted a re-evaluation and more general application of neurosurgical techniques such as pallidotomy, thalamotomy and deep brain stimulation to treat the Parkinsonian symptom complex.

Progressive supranuclear palsy is conventionally taken to refer to the subcortical degenerative syndrome first described by Steele *et al.* (1964). This is a progressive neurological disorder with associated akinetic-rigid syndrome, pseudobulbar palsy and dementia of frontal type. At autopsy, neuronal loss with neurofibrillary tangle inclusions in a proportion of the remaining neurons, and gliosis are characteristically found in the basal ganglia, brainstem and cerebellar nuclei but not in the cerebral or cerebellar cortex. The initial symptoms of progressive supranuclear palsy have been described as feelings of unsteadiness, vague visual difficulties, speech problems and minor changes in personality. As the disease progresses, symptoms include supranuclear ophthalmoplegia affecting chiefly vertical gaze, pseudobulbar palsy, dysarthria, dystonic rigidity of the neck and upper trunk and mild dementia as well as other cerebellar and pyramidal symptoms. The disease is rapidly progressive, resulting in marked incapacity of the patient in two to three years.

Patients with progressive supranuclear palsy tend to have mask-like facies and akinesia as seen in Parkinson's disease. They do not, however, exhibit tremor and have relatively good associated movements (e.g. arm swinging when walking). Affected individuals have a peculiar erect posture with backward retraction of the neck. Although reported by Steele *et al.* (1964) to have only minimal rigidity in the extremities, these patients do have severe rigidity of the axial musculature, especially in the latter stages of the disorder. The aetiology of progressive supranuclear palsy is unknown.

Parkinson's disease occurs most commonly in persons in their 50s and 60s. However, a syndrome, which like idiopathic Parkinson's disease in adults is associated with either a reduced level of dopamine in the substantia nigra or blockage of the dopamine receptors in the basal ganglia, also occurs in childhood. This syndrome is referred to as hypokinetic dyskinesia. In addition, a number of other conditions also predispose an individual to the occurrence of Parkinson's disease in childhood. Drug-induced Parkinsonism, for instance, can occur at all ages and subacute meningitis, such as that associated with measles, may also present with a Parkinsonian-like picture. Furthermore, postencephalitic Parkinsonism secondary to epidemic encephalitis was common in children in past years.

11.2.5 Hyperkinetic dysarthria
Hyperkinetic dysarthria occurs in association with a variety of extrapyramidal syndromes in which deviant speech characteristics are the product of abnormal involuntary movements which disturb the rhythm and rate of motor activities. Although known to be associated with dysfunction of the basal ganglia, the underlying neural mechanisms by which these abnormal involuntary movements are produced are poorly understood. Anatomically, the basal ganglia consist of the caudate nucleus, the putamen, the globus pallidus and the amygdaloid nucleus. Some neurologists also include another nucleus, the claustrum, as part of the basal ganglia. Although a number of brainstem nuclei, including the subthalamic nuclei, the substantia nigra and the red nucleus, are functionally related to the basal ganglia, they are not anatomically part of it. Collectively, the globus pallidus and the putamen are referred to as the lenticular nucleus (lentiform nucleus).

Any process that damages the basal ganglia or related brain structures has the potential to cause hyperkinetic dysarthria including degenerative, vascular, traumatic, inflammatory, toxic and metabolic disorders. In some cases the cause of hyperkinetic dysarthria is idiopathic. The major types of hyperkinetic disorders together with their effects on speech are outlined in Table 11.5.

11.2.6 Mixed dysarthria
A number of disorders of the nervous system affect more than one level of the motor system. Consequently, although pure forms of dysarthria do occur, mixed dysarthria, involving a combination of two or more types of dysarthria, is often exhibited by neurological cases referred to speech pathology clinics. A variety of neurological disorders can cause mixed dysarthria, including central nervous system degenerative diseases

Table 11.5 *Major types of hyperkinetic disorder*

Disorder	Symptoms	Effect on speech
Myoclonic jerks	Characterized by abrupt, sudden, unsustained muscle contractions which occur irregularly. Involuntary contractions may occur as single jerks of the body or may be repetitive. Two forms may affect speech – palatal myoclonus and action myoclonus	Speech disorder in palatal myoclonus usually characterized by phonatory, resonatory and prosodic abnormalities, e.g. vocal tremor, rhythmic phonatory arrests, intermittent hypernasality, prolonged intervals and inappropriate silences Action myoclonus – speech disrupted as a result of fine, arrhythmic, erratic muscle jerks, triggered by activity of the speech musculature
Tics	Brief, unsustained, recurrent, compulsive movements. Usually involve a small part of the body, e.g. facial grimace	Gilles de la Tourette's syndrome characterized by development of motor and vocal tics plus behavioural disorders. Vocal tics include simple vocal tics (e.g. grunting, coughing, barking, hissing, etc.) and complex vocal tics (e.g. stuttering-like repetitions, palilalia, echolalia and copralalia)
Chorea	A choreic movement consists of a single, involuntary, unsustained, isolated muscle action producing a short, rapid, uncoordinated jerk of the trunk, limb, face, tongue, diaphragm, etc. Contractions are random in distribution and timing is irregular. Two major forms – Sydenham's chorea and Huntington's disease	A perceptual study of 30 patients with chorea demonstrated deficits in all aspects of speech production (Darley *et al.* 1969a)
Ballism	Rare hyperkinetic disorder characterized by involuntary, wide-amplitude, vigorous, flailing movements of the limbs. Facial muscles may also be affected	Least important hyperkinetic disorder with regard to occurrence of hyperkinetic dysarthria
Athetosis	Hyperkinetic disorder characterized by continuous, arrhythmic, purposeless, slow, writhing-type movements that tend to flow one into another. Muscles of the face, neck and tongue are involved, leading to facial grimacing, protrusion and writhing of the tongue and problems with speaking and swallowing	Descriptions of the speech disturbance in athetosis largely relate to athetoid cerebral palsy rather than hyperkinetic dysarthria in adults

Disorder	Symptoms	Effect on speech
Dyskinesia	Two dyskinetic disorders are included under this heading: tardive dyskinesia and levodopa-induced dyskinesia. Basic pattern of abnormal involuntary movement in both of these conditions is one of slow, repetitive, writhing, twisting, flexing and extending movements often with a mixture of tremor. Muscles of the tongue, face and oral cavity most often affected	Tardive dyskinesia – abnormal involuntary movements typically choreoathetoid type. Articulatory deviations most prominent speech symptoms. Accurate placement of the articulators of speech may be severely hampered by presence of choreoathetoid movements of tongue, lip pursing and smacking, tongue protrusion and sucking and chewing behaviours Levodopa-induced dyskinesia – abnormal involuntary movements usually choreic involving muscles of tongue, face and mouth. Tongue may demonstrate fly-catcher movement, lips may pucker and retract and jaw may open or close and move side-to-side spontaneously
Dystonia	Characterized by abnormal involuntary movements that are slow and sustained for prolonged periods of time. Involuntary movements tend to have an undulant, sinuous character that may produce grotesque posturing and bizarre writhing, twisting movements	Dystonias affecting the speech mechanism may result in respiratory irregularities and/or abnormal movement and bizarre posturing of the jaw, lips, tongue, face and neck. In particular, focal cranial/orolingual-mandibular dystonia and spasmodic torticollis have the most direct effect on speech function

(e.g. amyotrophic lateral sclerosis, Wilson's disease), cerebrovascular accidents, traumatic brain injury, demyelinating disorders, brain tumours and toxic-metabolic and inflammatory diseases. As examples, three neurological diseases that typically display symptoms of mixed dysarthria are described in this section: amyotrophic lateral sclerosis, multiple sclerosis and Wilson's disease.

Amyotrophic lateral sclerosis (ALS) is a form of motor neuron disease characterized by a selective and progressive degeneration in the cortico-spinal and cortico-bulbar pathways and in the motor neurons associated with the cranial nerves and anterior horn cells of the spinal cord. The aetiology of ALS has not been determined to date, although there is evidence to suggest that immunological and metabolic disturbances contribute to the manifestation of the disease. The clinical features of ALS include muscle weakness and atrophy which are often asymmetric and sporadic, fasciculations, cramps, dysarthria, dysphagia, fatigue, spasticity, emotional lability, hyperreflexia and progressive respiratory impairment. Less typical features include oculomotor dysfunction, sensory abnormalities and autonomic nervous system involvement.

The presence of a severe speech disorder is a common finding in ALS, usually in the form of a mixed flaccid-spastic dysarthria. However, the speech disturbance may not always present as mixed throughout the course of the disease. It is possible that initially the dysarthria will present as either flaccid or spastic with a predominance of either type as the disease progresses (Duffy 1995). For those patients where upper motor neuron involvement predominates, the dysarthric speech disturbance is associated with spasticity of the tongue, the presence of primitive reflexes and emotional lability, consistent with pseudobulbar palsy. Bulbar dysfunction resulting in dysarthria and/or dysphagia has been found to occur in most individuals with ALS. The clinical signs of the dysarthria resulting from predominantly lower motor neuron involvement (bulbar palsy) consist of fasciculations, weakness, atrophy, reduced mobility of the tongue, and lip and jaw muscle dysfunction. Swallowing and chewing difficulties are closely associated with the presentation of dysarthria, particularly in those patients with bulbar palsy, and reflect the neurological involvement of the tongue (force and coordination), pharynx and jaw musculature.

Multiple sclerosis (MS) is the most common primary demyelinating disease and is a major cause of neurological disability in young adults in most western countries. The disease tends to vary in incidence and prevalence across different regions of the world, being most common in the temperate areas of the world and rare in the tropics. In about two-thirds of cases the condition is characterized by periods of exacerbation and remission so that the course of the disease is variable. In the remaining one-third, the course of the disorder is progressive without remissions. In terms of neuropathology, MS manifests in the form of irregular grey islands known as 'plaques' scattered throughout the white matter of the central nervous system, including the cerebrum, brainstem, cerebellum and spinal cord. The plaques represent areas of demyelination of nerve fibres, although the axons and neuron cell bodies remain relatively well preserved. As yet, the aetiology of multiple sclerosis is undetermined, although a number of possible explanations have been proposed.

Due to the disseminated neuropathology that may occur in MS, the clinical signs and symptoms of the disease are highly variable. A multitude of abnormal motor, sensory, cranial nerve/brainstem, cognitive and autonomic nervous system features have been described. Dysarthria is the most common communication disorder, occurring in about 47% of the MS population. Despite Charcot's (1877) inclusion of dysarthria in the triad of symptoms considered to be pathognomonic of the disease, this speech disturbance is now not regarded as a consistent feature of MS. In a study of 168 patients with MS, Darley et al. (1972) found that only 41% of individuals exhibited some form of deviant speech behaviour, with the majority of these demonstrating a mild speech impairment. A similar incidence of dysarthria was noted by Hartelius *et al.* (1993) in a group of 30 subjects, 47% of whom were dysarthric. Surveys of MS populations, conducted by Beukelman *et al.* (1985) and Hartelius and Svensson (1994), have reported incidences of speech disturbances in 23% and 44% of respondents, respectively. The severity of dysarthria would seem to be mild initially, with an increase in speech impairment corresponding to an increase in the overall severity of the disease, the number of neurological systems involved and the general deterioration in functioning of the individual. Indeed, the dysarthria associated with MS can be severe enough to warrant augmentative communication (Beukelman *et al.* 1985).

Given central nervous system involvement in MS, it is generally accepted that the dysarthria is predominantly mixed, although specific types of dysarthria may present in some individuals at various stages of the disease. The type of dysarthria exhibited by the individual will be dependent, therefore, on the sites of demyelination. Based on perceptual evidence and knowledge of neurological involvement, Duffy (1995) concluded that ataxic and spastic dysarthria and a mixed ataxic-spastic dysarthria were the most frequently observed forms of dysarthria, although other types or combinations of dysarthria may present in association with the disease.

Wilson's disease, or hepato-lenticular degeneration, is a rare, inborn metabolic disorder involving an inability to process dietary copper. As a result, copper builds up in the tissues of the liver, brain (especially the basal ganglia) and cornea of the eyes. The first symptoms of the disease typically occur in late adolescence or early adulthood, at about 15 to 17 years of age. The clinical presentation of Wilson's disease includes neurological, hepatic, haematological and, in some cases, psychiatric symptoms. The most common clinical signs and symptoms of the disease are Parkinsonian and hyperkinetic neurological behaviours. Reported symptoms include dysarthria, tremor, writing difficulties, ataxic gait, hepatomegaly, splenomegaly and thrombocytopenia, while other investigators have reported the presence of dysdiadochokinesis, dystonia, rigidity, facial masking, wing-beating tremor, bradykinesia, dysphagia, drooling, and gait and postural abnormalities. Dysarthria is considered to be a characteristic feature of Wilson's disease and has been reported to occur in 51–81 per cent of patients. The disordered speech takes the form of a mixed dysarthria consisting of mainly spastic, ataxic and hypokinetic components (Duffy 1995).

11.3   Clinical features of acquired dysarthria

The clinical features to be described below of the various types of dysarthria recognized under the Mayo Clinic classification system are largely derived from descriptions of adult cases. In general, the clinical features of each type of dysarthria observed in children are similar to those described for adults. However, it must be remembered that children, depending on age, are either beginning to develop or are still developing speech concurrent with damage to the nervous system. Consequently, unlike adults, motor speech disorders in children are complicated by the interaction between the acquired and developmental components of the disorder (Murdoch and Hudson-Tennent 1994). The impact of an acquired nervous system lesion on the developmental continuum of speech is unclear, as is the contribution of developmental speech patterns to the perceived acquired dysarthria and to its resolution or progression (Murdoch and Hudson-Tennent 1994).

11.3.1   Flaccid dysarthria

The principal deviant speech characteristics manifest in patients with flaccid dysarthria vary from case to case, depending on which particular nerves are affected and the relative degree of weakness resulting from the damage. Consequently, a number of subtypes of flaccid dysarthria are recognized, each with its own speech characteristics determined by the specific nerve or combination of nerves involved. Despite the variation in deviant speech features, the occurrence of these features has been attributed primarily to muscular weakness and reduced muscle tone and the effects of these neuromuscular problems on speed, range and accuracy of the movements of the speech musculature.

Collectively, the trigeminal (V), facial (VII) and hypoglossal (XII) nerves regulate the functioning of the articulators of speech (i.e. tongue, lips, jaw, etc.). The motor fibres of the trigeminal nerve run in the mandibular branch and innervate the muscles of mastication, including the temporalis, masseter, medial and lateral pterygoid muscles, mylohyoid, anterior belly of the digastric, the tensor veli palatini and the tensor tympani of the middle ear. Unilateral trigeminal lesions cause only a minor impairment in the client's ability to elevate the mandible and consequently are associated with only a minor effect on speech intelligibility. By contrast, bilateral trigeminal lesions have a devastating effect on speech production in that the elevators of the mandible (e.g. masseter and temporalis) may be too weak to approximate the mandible and maxilla. As a consequence, the tongue and lips may be prevented from making the necessary contacts with oral structures for the production of labial and lingual consonants and vowels.

The facial nerves supply the muscles of facial expression, including the occipito-frontalis, orbicularis oris and buccinator. Other muscles supplied by the facial nerves include the stylohyoid, the posterior belly of the digastric and the stapedius in the middle ear. Unilateral facial nerve lesions as occur in Bell's palsy lead to unilateral flaccid paralysis on the ipsilateral side of the face, causing distortion of bilabial and labio-dental consonants. In that these clients are unable to completely seal their lips to prevent air escaping from the mouth, the production of plosives, in particular, is defective. In clients with bilateral facial paralysis or paresis (as occurs in Möbius syndrome, for example), the above symptoms are more extreme. Speech impairments range from distortion to complete obliteration of bilabial and labio-dental consonants, with vowel distortion also occurring in severe cases due to problems with either lip rounding or lip spreading.

All of the intrinsic and most of the extrinsic muscles of the tongue (with the exception of palatoglossus) are regulated by the hypoglossal nerves. Unilateral hypoglossal nerve lesions cause ipsilateral paralysis of the tongue. Although this may be associated with mild, temporary articulatory imprecision, especially during production of labio-dental and linguopalatal consonants, in most cases the client learns to compensate for the unilateral tongue weakness or paralysis. More severe articulatory disturbances do occur in association with bilateral hypoglossal nerve lesions. In particular, speech sounds such as high front vowels and consonants that require elevation of the tip of the tongue to the upper alveolar ridge or hard palate may be severely distorted.

The motor fibres of the vagus nerves innervate the muscles of the pharynx, larynx and the levator muscles of the soft palate. Lesions of the vagus can therefore affect either the phonatory or resonatory aspects of speech, or both, depending on the location of the lesion along the nerve pathway. Brainstem lesions that involve the nucleus ambiguus (intramedullary lesions) or (extramedullary) lesions that involve the vagus near to the brainstem (e.g. in the region of the jugular foramen) cause paralysis of all the muscles that are supplied by the vagus. In such cases, the vocal cord on the affected side is paralysed in a slightly abducted position. This leads to flaccid dysphonia which is characterized by moderate breathiness, harshness and reduced volume. Additional voice characteristics that may also be present include diplophonia, short phrases and inhalatory stridor. The soft palate on the same side is also paralysed, causing hypernasality in the patient's speech.

If the lesion is bilateral, the vocal cords on both sides are paralysed and can be neither abducted nor adducted. Along with impaired bilateral elevation of the soft palate, this causes severe breathiness and hypernasality. The major clinical signs of bilateral flaccid vocal cord paralysis include breathy voice (reflecting incomplete adduction of the vocal cords that results in excessive air escape), audible inhalation (inspiratory stridor, reflecting inadequate abduction of the vocal cords during inspiration) and abnormally short phrases during contextual speech (possibly as a consequence of excessive air loss during speech as a result of inefficient laryngeal valving). Other signs seen in some patients include monotony of pitch and monotony of loudness. Bilateral weakness of the soft palate is associated with hypernasality, audible nasal emission, reduced sharpness of consonant production (as a consequence of reduced intraoral pressure due to nasal escape) and short phrases (reflecting premature exhaustion of expiratory air supply as a result of nasal escape).

Lesions to the vagus nerve distal to the branch that supplies the soft palate (the pharyngeal branch) but proximal to the exit of the superior laryngeal nerve have the same effect on phonation as brainstem lesions. However, such lesions do not produce hypernasality since functioning of the levator veli palatini is not compromised. Lesions limited to the recurrent laryngeal nerves (as may occur as a consequence of damage during thyroidectomy or as a result of compression of the vagus by intra-thoracic masses or aortic arch aneurysms) are also associated with dysphonia. In this latter case, however, the crico-thyroid muscles (the principal tensor muscles of the vocal cords) are not affected and the vocal cords are paralysed closer to the midline (the paramedian position). Consequently, the voice is likely to be harsh and reduced in loudness, but with a lesser degree of breathiness than occurs in cases with brainstem lesions involving the nucleus ambiguus.

Respiratory hypofunction in the form of a reduced tidal volume and vital capacity and impaired control of expiration can result from lesions involving either the phrenic or intercostal nerves. In general, diffuse impairment of the intercostal nerves is required to have any major effect on respiration. Spinal injuries that damage the third to fifth segments of the cervical spinal cord (i.e. the origin of the phrenic nerves) can paralyse the diaphragm bilaterally, thereby leading to significant impairment of respiration. Respiratory hypofunction may affect the patient's speech, resulting in abnormalities such as short phrases owing to more rapid exhaustion of breath during speech and possibly a reduction in pitch and loudness as a result of limited expiratory flow volume.

Multiple cranial nerve lesions are most commonly caused by intracranial conditions affecting the brainstem. In that the functioning of several cranial nerves is compromised simultaneously, the resulting flaccid dysarthria is usually severe. For example, in bulbar palsy the muscles supplied by cranial nerves V, VII, IX, X, XI and XII may dysfunction simultaneously. As a result, functioning of the muscles of the lips, tongue, jaw, palate and larynx are affected in varying combinations and with varying degrees of weakness. Disorders evident in the affected person's speech may include hypernasality with nasal emission owing to disruption of the palatopharyngeal valve; breathiness, harsh voice, audible inspiration, monopitch and monoloudness associated with laryngeal dysfunction; and distortion of consonant production owing to impairment of the articulators.

11.3.2 Spastic dysarthria

All aspects of speech production including articulation, resonance, phonation and respiration are affected to varying degrees in spastic dysarthria. The condition is characterized by slow and laboured speech which is produced only with considerable effort. Based on a perceptual analysis, Darley *et al.* (1969a, 1969b) identified the most prominent perceptible speech deviations associated with spastic dysarthria as: imprecise consonants, monopitch, reduced stress, harsh voice quality, monoloudness, low pitch, slow rate, hypernasality, strained/strangled voice quality, short phrases, distorted vowels, pitch breaks, continuous breathy voice and excess and equal stress. The deviant speech characteristics clustered primarily in the areas of articulatory/resonatory incompetence, phonatory stenosis and prosodic insufficiency. Chenery *et al.* (1988) identified a similar set of deviant perceptual features in their group of subjects with pseudobulbar palsy.

Oro-motor examinations of individuals with spastic dysarthria also reveal a characteristic pattern of deficits. In particular, these examinations usually show the presence of weakness in the muscles of the lips and tongue with movements of the tongue in and out of the mouth usually performed slowly. The extent of tongue movement is often very limited, such that the client may be unable to protrude the tongue beyond the lower teeth. Lateral movements of the tongue are also restricted, although the tongue is of normal size. Voluntary lip movements are also usually slow and restricted in range. Based on an assessment using the Frenchay Dysarthria Assessment, Enderby (1986) identified the major characteristics of spastic dysarthria to be (in decreasing order of frequency of occurrence): poor movement of the tongue in speech, slow rate of speech, poor phonation and intonation, poor intelligibility in conversation, reduced alternating movements of the tongue, poor lip movements in speech, reduced maintenance of palatal elevation, poor intelligibility of description, hypernasality and lack of control of volume.

To date, very few instrumental investigations have been conducted to examine the physiological impairments underlying the deviant perceptual speech dimensions observed in patients with spastic dysarthria. Consequently, there is still a need for further research into the nature and type of physiological deficits occurring in the speech mechanism of persons in this group. In general, the findings of those physiological and acoustic studies that have been reported tend to support the results of perceptual investigations, indicating the presence of deficits in the function of all aspects of the speech production mechanism in persons with spastic dysarthria (Murdoch *et al.* 2008).

11.3.3 Ataxic dysarthria

Ataxic dysarthria is associated with decomposition of complex movements arising from a breakdown in the coordinated action of the muscles

of the speech production mechanism. In particular, inaccuracy of movement, irregular rhythm of repetitive movement, incoordination, slowness
of both individual and repetitive movements and hypotonia of affected
muscles seem to be the principal neuromuscular deficits associated with
the cerebellar damage that underlies ataxic dysarthria.

The disrupted speech output exhibited by individuals with cerebellar
lesions has often been termed 'scanning speech', a term probably first
used by Charcot (1877). According to Charcot (1877: 192), 'the words
are as if measured or scanned: there is a pause after every syllable, and
the syllables themselves are pronounced slowly'. The most predominant features of ataxic dysarthria include a breakdown in the articulatory
and prosodic aspects of speech. According to Brown *et al.* (1970), the 10
deviant speech dimensions most characteristic of ataxic dysarthria can
be divided into three clusters: articulatory inaccuracy, characterized by
imprecision of consonant production, irregular articulatory breakdowns
and distorted vowels; prosodic excess, characterized by excess and equal
stress, prolonged phonemes, prolonged intervals and slow rate; and phonatory-prosodic insufficiency, characterized by harshness, monopitch
and monoloudness. Brown *et al.* (1970) believed that the articulatory problems were the product of ataxia of the respiratory and oral-buccal-lingual
musculature, and prosodic excess was thought to result from slow movements. The occurrence of phonatory-prosodic insufficiencies was attributed to the presence of hypotonia.

Based on the performance of ataxic speakers on the Frenchay Dysarthria
Assessment, Enderby (1986) also observed perceptual correlates of articulatory and prosodic inadequacy to be prominent among the 10 features she
believed to be the most characteristic of ataxic dysarthria. These features
included poor intonation, poor tongue movement in speech, poor alternating movement of the tongue in speech, reduced rate of speech, reduced
lateral movement of the tongue, reduced elevation of the tongue, poor
alternating movement of the lips and poor lip movements in speech.

11.3.4 Hypokinetic dysarthia

Overall, the speech characteristics associated with hypokinetic dysarthria follow largely from the generalized pattern of hypokinetic motor
disorders, which includes marked reductions in the amplitude of voluntary movement (akinesia), initiation difficulties, slowness of movement (bradykinesia), muscular rigidity, tremor at rest and postural reflex
impairments. According to Darley *et al.* (1975), marked limitation of the
range of movement of the muscles of the speech mechanism is the outstanding characteristic of hypokinesia as it affects speech. These authors
stated that reduced mobility, restricted range of movement and supranor-
mal rate of the repetitive movements of the muscles involved in speech
production lead to the various manifestations of hypokinetic dysarthria.

Although impairments in all aspects of speech production (i.e. respiration, phonation, resonance, articulation and prosody) have been identified in individuals with Parkinson's disease, these individuals are most likely to exhibit disturbances of prosody, phonation and articulation. According to Darley *et al.* (1975), prosodic disturbances constitute the most prominent features of hypokinetic dysarthria. The reported features of the speech disturbance in Parkinson's disease commonly include monopitch and monoloudness, decreased use of vocal parameters for effecting stress and emphasis, breathy and harsh voice quality, reduced vocal intensity, variable rate including short rushes of speech or accelerated speech, consonant imprecision, impaired breath support for speech, reduction in phonation time, difficulty in the initiation of speech activities and inappropriate silences.

11.3.5 Hyperkinetic dysarthria

As indicated in Table 11.5, a variety of extrapyramidal disorders may cause hyperkinetic dysarthria. Each of these disorders is characterized by the presence of abnormal involuntary muscle contractions of the limbs, trunk, neck, face, and so forth which disturb the rhythm and rate of normal motor activities, including those involved in speech production. The major extrapyramidal disorders that cause hyperkinetic dysarthria include myoclonic jerks, tics, chorea, athetosis, dyskinesia and dystonia. The abnormal involuntary movements involved vary considerably in their form and locus across the different diseases of the basal ganglia. Consequently, there is considerable heterogeneity in the deviant speech dimensions that manifest as the speech disorders collectively termed 'hyperkinetic dysarthria'. Any or all of the major subcomponents of the speech production apparatus may be involved, with disturbances in prosody also being present. In that different types of hyperkinetic dysarthria are associated with the different hyperkinetic movement disorders, the hyperkinetic dysarthrias are usually clinically described in the context of the underlying movement disorders causing the speech disturbance.

11.4 Concluding remarks

Clinically, six major types of dysarthria are recognized: flaccid dysarthria, spastic dysarthria, ataxic dysarthria, hypokinetic dysarthria, hyperkinetic dysarthria and mixed dysarthria. The type of dysarthria resulting from damage to the nervous system is dependent upon the site of damage to the neuromuscular system. Parts of the neuromuscular system that can be affected are the lower motor neurons, upper motor neurons, extrapyramidal (indirect) system, cerebellum and neuromuscular junction as well as the muscles of the speech production mechanism themselves.

Although acquired dysarthria in children is currently classified according to a classification system developed for adults, the need for a neurobehavioural classification system specifically for acquired childhood dysarthria is increasingly being recognized. It must be remembered that children, depending on age, are either beginning to develop or are still developing speech concurrent with damage to the nervous system and hence will exhibit both acquired and developmental aspects to their speech disorder.

12

Apraxia of speech

Donald A. Robin and Sabina Flagmeier

12.1 Apraxia of speech: definition and features

Apraxia of speech (AOS), which is one of a family of motor speech disorders
(Duffy 2005), affects the programming of speech movements. Pioneering
work in AOS emerged from an extensive study of motor speech disorders
by Darley, Aronson and Brown in 1975, which resulted in the publication
of their now classic textbook (Darley *et al.* 1975). However, the nature of
AOS, its diagnosis and treatment have been topics of great controversy,
and it is only recently that consensus has been reached on some of these
issues. For example, because AOS and Broca's aphasia are often comorbid
symptoms, AOS has been associated with other co-occurring pathologies
such as aphasia.

The term 'apraxia' was first coined by Steinthal (1871) and was subsequently elaborated upon by Liepmann as a 'disorder of voluntary movements not attributable to the loss of strength, coordination, or mental
faculty and restricted to certain body parts and functional activities'
(Liepmann 1913: section XI, part II; Ballard *et al.* 2000: 970). In 1969, Darley
presented the concept of apraxia as it applies to speech (Darley 1968,
1969). Darley suggested that the term would only be applicable when
assurance could be given that the patient had the intent, the underlying
linguistic representation and the fundamental motor abilities to produce
speech, but could not do so volitionally (Darley *et al.* 1975). However, the
precise characterization of AOS has been debated for a number of years.
The controversy that surrounds apraxia of speech focuses in part on the
unique features that are used to define AOS. For example, Martin (1974)
challenged the use of the term 'apraxia of speech' as it was applied to
select subject populations for study. He argued that the specific features
used to differentiate AOS from other speech disorders were in fact not
able to do so. Investigators are also divided on whether the pathogenesis
of AOS is phonological or phonemic in nature.

In 1997, an extensive summary of AOS was published by McNeil and colleagues (McNeil *et al.* 1997). In this work, they proposed a new definition of AOS and presented what they believed were the key differential characteristics of the disorder. The definition and characteristics of AOS proposed by McNeill and colleagues have been used in many studies since that time, and in particular were invoked by a committee that evaluated evidence-based practice standards in AOS (Wambaugh *et al.* 2006a). Specifically, McNeil *et al.* (1997: 44) proposed the following definition of AOS (see also McNeil *et al.* 2009):

> Apraxia of speech is a phonetic-motoric disorder of speech production. It is caused by inefficiencies in the translation of well-formed and -filled phonological frames into previously learned kinematic information used for carrying out intended movements. These inefficiencies result in intra- and interarticulator temporal and spatial segmental and prosodic distortions. It is characterized by distortions of segment and intersegment transitionalization and coarticulation resulting in extended durations of consonants, vowels, and time between sounds, syllables, and words. These distortions are often perceived as sound substitutions and as the misassignment of stress and other phrasal and sentence-level prosodic abnormalities. Errors are relatively consistent in location within the utterance and invariable in type. It is not attributable to deficits of muscle tone or reflexes, nor to primary deficits in the processing of sensory (auditory, tactile, kinesthetic, proprioceptive), or language information. In its extremely infrequently occurring isolated form, it is not accompanied by the above-listed deficits of basic motor physiology, perception, or language.

12.2   Neurological basis of AOS

Currently, three distinct aetiological classifications have been proposed for apraxia of speech: neurological, complex neurodevelopmental and idiopathic neurogenic forms of AOS (Shriberg 2006; Shriberg *et al.* 2006). The neurological form is typically caused by a stroke or cerebrovascular accident (CVA) to the left hemisphere of the brain. The complex neurodevelopmental form is commonly thought to stem from genetic and metabolic aetiologies (Shriberg 2006; Shriberg *et al.* 2006). The idiopathic form of AOS, which is also known as childhood apraxia of speech or developmental apraxia of speech, is most common in children and has an unknown origin. It should be noted that while there are considered to be three distinct aetiological classifications for apraxia of speech, the behavioural phenotype is similar across all three subtypes. Therefore, it is suspected that the underlying neural mechanisms behind the disorder are also similar across these subtypes (with differences related to developmental levels, genetic expression and acquired lesion). Although the main hypothesized areas for the lesion associated with AOS are still being debated, potential regions include Broca's area, the lateral premotor cortex, subcortical structures and the anterior insula (all in the left hemisphere). Each of these lesion sites will be examined in turn below.

12.2.1   Broca's area and AOS

One of the first recorded accounts of a lesion related to AOS was described by Paul Broca in the famous case of 'Tan' (Broca [1861]1977). Broca's patient, after suffering a lesion in the left frontal lobe, was only able to utter the word 'tan' repetitively. The problem with this observation is that several inferences were made about the relationship between the presented symptoms and the damaged neural tissue. Since the time of Paul Broca, many researchers have continued to study the effect of lesions to the left inferior frontal gyrus, known as BA 44. Many writers have described left cortical lesions as the cause of clinical symptoms consistent with the diagnosis of AOS (Jackson [1893]1915; Wilson 1908; Nathan 1947; Wertz *et al.* 1970). Unfortunately, in the absence of in vivo imaging, confirmation of the site of these lesions could not be made, leaving most of this work based on inference and postmortem evaluation. It is with the advent of modern brain imaging techniques such as computerized tomography (CT), magnetic resonance imaging (MRI) and positron emission tomography (PET) that light has been shed on the underlying neural mechanisms involved in apraxia of speech and the involvement of Broca's area in speech production.

12.2.2   Lateral prefrontal cortex and AOS

The left premotor cortex may play an important role in speech motor programming. Evidence for this emerged from lesion studies. Subjects who suffered a single left hemisphere CVA and who meet current guidelines for AOS diagnosis (e.g. Hageman *et al.* 1994; Seddoh *et al.* 1996; Robin *et al.* 2008) with no concomitant aphasia or dysarthria, underwent structural MRI scans taken as a part of a project designed to explore human lesion-behavioural relations. All participant lesion data were acquired using a standardized lesion plotting method (Damasio and Damasio 1989) with scan analyses performed by Dr Hanna Damasio. Results from this study indicate that a lesion in the inferior segments of the left prefrontal gyrus (BA 6) is associated with AOS.

Josephs *et al.* (2012) conducted a study to determine if AOS can present as an isolated sign of neurodegenerative disease. Thirty-seven subjects underwent speech and language, neurological, neuropsychological and neuroimaging testing. Twelve of these subjects did not have any signs of aphasia. Neuroimaging consisted of both volumetric resonance imaging and positron emission tomography (PET) using 18F-fluorodeoxyglucose. Voxel-based morphometry results showed both grey matter and white matter atrophy in the lateral premotor cortex as well as in the supplementary motor area. White matter loss extended from the lateral premotor cortex into the inferior premotor cortex and into the corpus callosum. Using diffusion tensor imaging analysis, reduced fractional anisotropy and increased mean diffusivity of the superior longitudinal fasciculus, particularly in the premotor components, were observed. PET scans uncovered hypometabolism associated with the lateral premotor cortex and supplementary motor area. This suggests that the premotor cortex plays an important role in speech motor programming.

12.2.3   Subcortical lesions and AOS

While many attribute apraxia of speech to cortical lesions, leaving subcortical lesions to account for dysarthrias (e.g. Darley *et al.* 1975; Van der Merwe 1997), some have determined that damage to subcortical regions, specifically the basal ganglia and other lower structures, can result in AOS. Kertesz (1984) reported data on 10 patients with subcortical lesions. All of these patients demonstrated some type of aphasia, as all had a slow rate of speech and frequent 'phonetic substitutions'. Nine out of 10 of these subjects had internal capsular involvement, while seven of the 10 had lesions to the putamen or caudate nucleus (or both). In another study Marquardt and Sussman (1984) found comorbid aphasia and AOS as a result of subcortical lesions. However, it is important to note that the level of behavioural description and the presence of aphasia make results difficult to interpret.

12.2.4   Anterior insula and AOS

Dronkers and colleagues have argued strongly that the anterior insula is critical to motor programming and, when it is lesioned, results in apraxia of speech (Dronkers 1996). This group has employed both CT and MRI techniques to examine this phenomenon. Specifically, Dronkers used these two methodologies to assess the location of the lesion in AOS and to examine its relationship to speech behaviours. Results showed that 100 per cent of the subjects identified as having AOS had lesions involving the superior precentral gyrus of the insula, while those that did not have AOS had no damage to this area. While this would have been a remarkable finding, the selection criteria were for linguistic rather than motoric speech disorders. Therefore, there is no evidence for the underlying neural substrates of AOS.

12.2.5   Brain imaging and AOS

Lesion studies have been considered to be the 'gold standard' in speech and language research. As such, most research stems from lesion/behavioural studies. In the past 20 years, however, functional imaging has provided insight into functional lesions of brain-injured patients as well as insight into task-related brain activity. Among the most commonly used techniques are PET and functional magnetic resonance imaging (fMRI).

In 2004, Hillis and colleagues examined the involvement of the insula in apraxia of speech using diffusion and perfusion-weighted MRI (Hillis *et al.* 2004a). Approximately half of the patients with AOS showed insular lesions while two-thirds of those without AOS also had insular damage. As a result, the authors concluded that there is no association between AOS and lesions of the insula.

In a report from the Mayo Clinic, structural and functional imaging in patients with progressive aphasia and AOS was studied (Josephs *et al.* 2006). Of the 17 patients studied, seven had AOS only, seven had primary progressive aphasia with AOS and three had progressive non-fluent aphasia with AOS. A retrospective analysis was made of single photon emission computed tomography (SPECT) scans and a region of interest analysis technique was also used. From analysis of the structural images, it was determined that AOS involves grey matter atrophy bilaterally in the superior premotor cortex with extension to the anterior bank of the precentral gyrus. Involvement from the supplemental motor area was also observed. SPECT results from five patients, two of whom had a diagnosis of AOS with primary progressive aphasia, two with progressive supranuclear palsy, and one with progressive non-fluent aphasia-AOS with corticobasal degeneration pathology, showed decreased activity for the posterior frontal and anterior parietal lobes and basal ganglia in all patients. Josephs *et al.* concluded that AOS is associated with structural damage to the premotor and supplemental motor cortices.

Josephs *et al.* (2010) examined 24 subjects using fluorodeoxyglucose F18 positron emission tomography. Of the 24 patients, nine were classified as having non-fluent speech output, 14 were classified as having fluent speech output and one was unclassified. Three subjects had apraxia of speech as determined by agreement between three clinicians. Researchers found distinct patterns of hypometabolism for specific non-fluent and specific fluent syndromes. Specifically, those with AOS were associated with superior frontal and supplementary motor cortex hypometabolism. Furthermore, contrary to previous stroke studies (e.g. Dronkers 1996), the authors failed to identify the insula as associated with AOS. Josephs *et al.* (2010: 603) concluded that AOS may be 'originating from the superior frontal lobe and supplementary motor cortex in progressive aphasia, while agrammatism and telegraphic speech is originating from the posterior inferior frontal cortex ... Given the patterns of hypometabolism ... observed in ... nonfluent patients, ... a downward progression from the posterior superior frontal and supplementary motor cortex to the posterior inferior frontal lobe [is hypothesized] in patients presenting with dominant AOS who later develop nonfluent aphasia'.

12.3   Differential diagnosis of apraxia of speech

The diagnosis of AOS is rooted in the definition of the disorder by McNeil *et al.* (1997, 2009) and is perceptual in nature. Differential diagnosis of AOS requires the use of speech errors that uniquely distinguish AOS from phonological disruptions (and ideally from other motor speech disorders). The primary clinical characteristics that are considered necessary for a diagnosis of AOS include: (1) slow rate of speech, typified by lengthened sound segments and intersegment durations; (2) sound distortions; (3) errors that are consistent in terms of type and location in a word; (4) prosodic abnormalities particularly de-stressing of stressed syllables; and (5) segmentation of speech which results in each syllable being produced without concatenation to the ensuing syllable and with equal stress on each.

Errors can occur in AOS which are not differential. They include articulatory groping for the correct articulator placement, increasing errors as length of utterance increases, more errors initially than in other parts of a word or syllable, awareness of errors, speech initiation problems, increased errors as rate increases, increased errors as phonemic complexity increases, islands of error-free speech, expressive-receptive speech or language gap, presence of fewer errors with increased speech automaticity and presence of limb or oral apraxia. Finally, errors that exclude the diagnosis of AOS are fast or normal speech rate, normal prosody and sound substitutions. Additionally, anticipatory errors and transposition errors are symptomatic of disorders that disrupt linguistic processes and are not part of AOS symptomatology.

12.3.1   AOS versus dysarthrias

Dysarthrias are a family of disorders described by Darley *et al.* (1975: 2) as 'disturbances in muscular control of the speech mechanism resulting from impairment of any of the basic motor processes involved in the execution of speech'. Given this very general description, dysarthrias have been used to cover a range of motor disorders. However, they do not include disorders of speech that have an anatomical, psychological, dental or malocclusal basis or are related to learning problems, aprosodia or stuttering. Unfortunately, the term 'execution' in the definition is poorly defined. Therefore, any one or a number of the physiological parameters of tone and reflexes along with the kinematic parameters of strength, speed, range, accuracy and steadiness are necessarily aberrant in dysarthria (McNeil *et al.* 1997: 314). However, the presence or absence of any of these characteristics must occur during speech and cannot be diagnosed by acoustic/kinematic parameters alone. Indeed, Darley *et al.*'s definition of dysarthria is not able to differentiate dysarthria from AOS, but they did suggest that AOS should be separable from the dysarthrias. This is done using perceptual measures of speech and is similar to the way that a clinician might tease apart two different forms of dysarthria.

12.3.2 Phonetic/motoric characteristics of AOS

It has been proposed that phonetic patterns have the ability to differentiate AOS from other speech and language disorders. Blumstein (1981) was the first to investigate this and found that those with AOS (called anterior aphasia in Blumstein's article) did in fact show deficits in voice onset time and nasal sounds. Indeed, durations of vowel and consonant patterns have been shown to distinguish apraxic from aphasic patients (Collins *et al.* 1983; Ryalls 1984, 1986; McNeil and Kent 1990; Seddoh *et al.* 1996). However, Odell *et al.* (1991) showed that the presence of vowel errors alone failed to differentiate AOS from aphasias and dysarthrias. Also, the number of syllables in a word did not affect the vowel error rate across groups in this study.

Clinical assessments routinely assess movement control and strength of the speech articulators during speech and non-speech activities. If movement control or strength of the articulators is judged to be abnormal in any of these activities, the diagnosis is typically that of dysarthria. For a diagnosis of AOS to be made, it is required that movement control and strength be judged to be within the normal limits. However, studies have found that forces and postures of the articulators are significantly poorer in those with AOS than in healthy controls and are not differential from those with dysarthria (McNeil and Adams 1991). Furthermore, Hageman *et al.* (1994) used visual motor tracking at 0.3, 0.6 and 0.9 Hz and found that participants with AOS have impaired ability to track a predictable target when compared to healthy individuals. Apraxic individuals' ability to track unpredictable targets was similar to that of healthy controls. Interpretation of these findings is that movement control is impaired in those with AOS in non-speech tasks. Also, because participants with AOS did not differ significantly from those without apraxia in the unpredictable task but were poor predictors of target movement, the authors suggested that the apraxic participants had difficulty retrieving or developing motor programmes to complete the intended action.

Slower rate of speech as compared to healthy individuals without motor speech impairment is a key feature of AOS. This slower rate of speech has been captured using perceptual, acoustic and kinematic methods of analysis. X-ray microbeam systems have been used to track inter-articulator timing abnormalities between the lip, velum and tongue dorsum in a subject with AOS (Sasanuma 1971; Itoh *et al.* 1980). Strain gauge transducers have also been used to compare labiomandibular durations, displacements, velocities and dysmetrias showing that movement durations across transitions from vowel to vowel are significantly longer for AOS participants (McNeil *et al.* 1989). In addition, strain gauge transducers have been used to determine normal peak velocity and time to reach normal peak velocity (Robin *et al.* 1989; McNeil and Adams 1991). In fact, McNeil and Adams (1991) found that individuals with apraxia take abnormally long times to reach peak velocity compared to normal, conduction aphasic and ataxic dysarthric participants. These investigators also showed significantly longer total utterance durations for apraxic, conduction aphasic and ataxic dysarthric participants compared to normal participants.

Electropalatographs have been used to describe general discoordination of the tongue tip, blade and body in an apraxic speaker (Hardcastle 1987). Katz *et al.* (1990) used electromagnetic articulography to investigate the labial and velar kinematic aspects of speech for those with apraxia. These investigators found that subjects with 'anterior' lesions produce more variable on-target movements than controls. Starting with Shankweiler *et al.* (1968), electromyography (EMG) has been used to investigate muscle activity. Using EMG, antagonistic muscle co-contraction was monitored. Shankweiler *et al.* found that the characteristics of AOS could not be captured using this method (Fromm 1981; Fromm *et al.* 1982; Forrest *et al.* 1991).

12.3.3 Speech prosody

Prosody, intensity, fundamental frequency and duration have been investigated when evaluating speech in AOS (e.g. Sasanuma 1971; Deal and Darley 1972; Rosenbek *et al.* 1973). Both Kent and Rosenbek (1983) and Lebrun *et al.* (1973) reported amplitude uniformity which leads to the neutralization of stress pattern dysrhythmia – part of the characteristic dysprosody often described in AOS. Furthermore, Odell *et al.* (1990) found that AOS and dysarthric individuals had substantially more errors on stressed syllables than did individuals with phonemic paraphasia. Furthermore, frequent errors involving sound transitions, as reflected by open juncture, separated the small sample of persons with AOS from those with conduction aphasia who demonstrated virtually no such errors.

12.3.4 Effort

'Sense of effort' has been found to be aberrant in patients with speech and voice disorders (e.g. Parkinson's disease, dysarthria, apraxia of speech). In these patient populations it is frequently found that excessive effort is exerted in order to produce speech when compared to healthy controls. Fatigue in the oral motor system over time accompanies the perception of an increased sense of effort. Pierce (1991) suggested that the notion of effort may be tied, to some degree, to the concepts of consistency, variability and successive approximation (trial and error behaviour) towards a correct target and cannot unambiguously be assigned to the person with AOS (Joanette *et al.* 1980; Kohn 1984; Hough and Klich 1987).

Following the development of reliable measures of sense of effort using the Iowa Oral Performance Instrument, Robin and colleagues investigated the relationship among motor abilities and sense of effort in normal and brain-damaged individuals (Solomon *et al.* 1994, 1996; Somodi *et al.* 1995). Results show that subjects produce consistent reliable pressures related to effort level. Somodi *et al.* (1995) hypothesized that the perception of effort derives from a central source that operates across various motor systems. Furthermore, Clark and Robin (1998) speculated that brain-damaged individuals may not be sensitive to task demands and may require external feedback to allocate resources effectively to motor or other tasks.

12.4   Treatment of apraxia of speech

Lack of uniformity amongst clinicians concerning the diagnosis of AOS has negatively affected research into the treatment of this motor speech disorder. In recent years, new research findings relating to treatment have emerged. Here, we provide a brief introduction to therapy approaches, practice schedules and feedback in AOS treatment. A more detailed discussion of AOS treatment can be found in Chapter 22.

Past studies employed treatment therapies that fell into one or more of the following four categories: articulatory kinematic, rate and/or rhythm, alternative/augmentative communication (AAC) and intersystemic facilitation/reorganization. Articulatory kinematic approaches refer to those therapies that focus on the positioning of the articulators. Rate and rhythm treatments are those that are designed to control prosody of speech. AAC therapies aim to substitute or provide a supplement to verbal communication. Lastly, intersystemic facilitation/reorganization approaches utilize intact systems to facilitate speech production (Rosenbek *et al.* 1976; Wambaugh *et al.* 2006a).

It is suggested that AOS treatments should be structured around the principles of motor learning (e.g. Robin *et al.* 2007). As defined by Robin *et al.* (2007: 78), learning is 'the maintenance or retention of a skill after treatment has stopped, and the generalization or transfer of learned behaviors to related but untreated target sounds or to new environments'. This is in direct contrast to 'acquisition', which is the change in a skill during treatment. To promote long-term retention, the two most important factors are the structure of practice (random/blocked) and the nature of the feedback provided (Schmidt and Lee 2005).

Sessions typically begin with pre-practice. The first goal of pre-practice should be to motivate the patient to participate in the therapy. This is especially true for children. The structure of the actual practice is critical to motor learning. There are two types of practice that are commonly used: blocked and random practice. During blocked practice the patient practises a specific behaviour for a number of repetitions before moving on to the next behaviour (e.g. 'pa'). Random practice involves the patient practising several different behaviours in a random order for the duration of the practice session (e.g. 'pa', 'ba', 'pa', 'ta'). Numerous studies support the idea that random practice promotes retention and transfer of skill, while blocked practice results in greater short-term improvements (e.g. Lee and Magill 1983; Li and Wright 2000; Wright et al. 2004).

Feedback is also critical to the treatment of apraxia of speech. There are two broad categories of feedback. The first is knowledge of results (KR) feedback. The second is knowledge of performance (KP) feedback. KR feedback provides information to the patient concerning the outcome of a given action. Examples of KR feedback are 'Yes, that was correct' or 'Oops, you got it wrong this time'. KP feedback provides the patient with feedback concerning the specific aspects of the behaviour. Examples of KP feedback are 'Yes, that was great. You got your lips together'.

Robin et al. (2007) argue that while KP feedback may be beneficial for learning, KR feedback is critical. Three key components of feedback are specificity of the feedback, temporal locus of feedback and frequency of feedback. Regarding the temporal locus of feedback, it has been found that delaying KR feedback is advantageous because it allows the patient to not rely on external feedback, but rather to reference internal feedback in order to determine if the targeted behaviour was performed in the correct manner (Swinnen et al. 1990; Park et al. 2000; Wright et al. 2004).

12.5   Theoretical models and AOS

The execution of speech requires conversion of an abstract idea into a linguistic code. This code is then transformed into a set of motor commands for the spatial and temporal coordination of muscle contractions that produce speech. Motor control for speech production is highly complex given the need for coordination across multiple muscle groups, the speed with which the speech articulators need to move and the unique differences in muscle structure (e.g. the tongue operates as a muscular hydrostat). Central planning and programming of speech movements is crucial to the execution of speech and is vital to the understanding of AOS.

Given the understanding of AOS as a motor programming deficit, it is reasonable to assume that patients with AOS suffer from a breakdown in developing and/or executing motor programmes. However, it is necessary to operationally define 'motor programme'. The most influential motor programming model is devised by Schmidt, who proposed a 'schema theory' of motor control and learning (Schmidt 1975, 1976, 2003; Schmidt and Lee 1999, 2005). This theory assumes that rapid movements require the retrieval of a motor programme from memory that is tweaked for the particular situation. Due to variation between particular situations, he proposes the concept of a generalized motor programme. Generalized motor programmes are operationally defined as relative timing and/or forces of an action, which can be examined by measuring the time or amplitude relations among kinematic landmarks of a movement pattern (e.g. Schmidt and Young 1991; Clark and Robin 1998). Schmidt (2003) recognizes generalization of a motor programme as the ability of a programme to be executed in several different ways to provide multiple variations in the performance of the same action. By contrast, individual parameters of a given movement represent absolute temporal and spatial constraints.

Data to test this operational model of motor programming in AOS were garnered by Clark and Robin (1998). These investigators examined differences between patients with AOS and those with conduction aphasia by analysing the temporal and spatial coherence of kinematic landmarks during articulatory movement. Subjects viewed a visual target wave and were instructed to replicate the wave in its absence using labiomandibular opening and closing movements. Results showed that only patients with AOS were impaired on the task and that the deficit involved either a breakdown in the generalized motor programme or the parameterization of the movement (that is, the factors that define the articulators' proper operation).

Healthy individuals are thought to have intact ability to create motor programmes and to execute existing ones with little reference to an external cue. Ballard and Robin (2007) used a visual motor tracking paradigm to determine if AOS interferes with the development of motor programmes or alters existing motor programmes. This paradigm required subjects to track either a predictable sinusoidal or unpredictable target both with and without visual feedback. Results show that subjects with AOS are unable to track a predictable target. This ability further deteriorates with increasing target frequency. Furthermore, healthy subjects maintained a 'phase lead' for predictable targets and a 'phase lag' for unpredictable targets. In other words, healthy subjects, relying on an internally generated model, were producing the sinusoidal pattern before external feedback was given. These same subjects were behind in producing the pattern for unpredictable targets due to the necessity of external feedback. While also producing a 'phase lead' for predictable targets, apraxic subjects were less accurate in timing and amplitude parameters than healthy controls. When comparing feedback versus no feedback, results further confirm that those with AOS have impaired temporal control and coordination when compared to healthy individuals. These findings demonstrate that motor programme development and feedback integration are impaired in patients with AOS.

Klapp (1995) developed a model of motor programming that he tested with speech sound production (syllables) and that has been expanded to finger and limb movements. The Klapp model conceptualizes motor programming as having two processing stages. One stage involves the buffering of individual motor units (programmes) in working memory. This stage is what Klapp refers to as the internal representation of the programmes for a given skilled movement and is termed INT. The next stage of pro-gramming – Klapp refers to it as SEQ – involves putting the individual units of action into the correct sequence. Klapp presented data to show that INT is the pre-programming stage and is sensitive to unit complexity, while SEQ is a phase of programming that involves assembling units in the correct order for execution and transitions between movements.

In order to fully test the Klapp model, Wright developed a new experi-mental paradigm called the self-select paradigm (Maas *et al.* 2008a; Wright *et al.* 2009). In this model, a self-regulated study time follows the pres-entation of a stimulus. Participants then indicate when they are ready to produce the movement. This is called study time and represents the INT processing demand. After a variable time delay (buffering) subjects see an imperative GO cue and they produce the requested movement(s) as quickly as possible. The reaction time for starting the action from the GO signal is an index of SEQ processing demand. Increases in study time indicate greater load on INT associated with increased programme com-plexity. Data for speech (Wright *et al.* 2009) and limbs (e.g. Magnuson *et al.* 2008) have shown that increases in INT occur when the complexity of a single unit is increased with no increases in SEQ processing. However, an increase in the number of units (to be ordered) resulted in increased SEQ (reaction time) processing but not in INT (study time). Utilizing this para-digm and assuming that a syllable is the smallest unit of speech, Maas *et al.* (2006) found that when increasing the number of syllables there is an increase in INT but not in SEQ. This suggests that syllables were already concatenated into a single unit. As a result of limb and speech data, it is concluded that AOS is a disruption of the pre-programming (INT) stage of the model.

Supporting this finding, work by Deger and Ziegler (2002) demonstrates that speakers with AOS show increased reaction times and intersyllable intervals for alternating syllable types, whereas those without apraxia do not show this sensitivity for syllable type. The inability to switch from one syllable type to another lends support to the idea that those with AOS have a disruption in the pre-programming stage of the model.

12.6 Summary

Apraxia of speech is a motor speech disorder that prevents the transla-tion of phonological representation into kinematic parameters despite intact functionality and strength of the speech articulators. Considerable controversy surrounds this speech disorder and the criteria that should be used in a differential diagnosis of AOS. Although the exact basis of AOS is still unclear, aetiological classifications have converged around neurological, complex neurodevelopmental and idiopathic forms of the disorder. Research studies of treatment in AOS reveal that interventions which emphasize motor learning are most effective. Clinicians must also consider the use of pre-practice, the structure of practice (blocked versus random practice) and the nature and temporal locus of feedback during treatment. Theoretical models have been advanced in order to explain AOS. They include Schmidt's schema theory and Klapp's two-stage model of motor programming.

13

Aphasia

Roelien Bastiaanse and Ronald S. Prins

13.1   Introduction

Aphasia is an acquired language disorder that is caused by a focal brain lesion after the period of language development. The most obvious symptoms occur in speech production. Frequent phenomena are: word-finding problems, speech errors and sentence construction problems. Apart from these difficulties, almost all individuals with aphasia encounter problems with language comprehension. However, language comprehension problems are usually less obvious and sometimes only detectable through language testing. Most aphasic people have reading and writing difficulties alongside disorders in speech production and comprehension of spoken language. In this chapter, the types of brain damage that may result in aphasia are examined. The symptoms and syndromes of aphasia, the relation between brain and language, and some current topics in aphasiology will also be addressed.

   Although aphasia is usually manifest in the four language modalities of speech, comprehension of spoken language, writing and reading, the differences between individual speakers with aphasia can be large, both in nature and in severity. In many aphasic individuals, some linguistic abilities, such as spontaneous speech production, naming and reading (aloud), can be significantly impaired, whereas other language functions, such as comprehension of spoken language and (silent) reading, are relatively intact. There is a clear relation between the impairments of aphasia and the location of brain damage. Accordingly, aphasia can provide useful information about the neural basis of language and about the way different modes of language use (e.g. naming of objects, comprehension of written sentences) are organized in the brain.

13.2   Aphasia: some background

13.2.1   Definition of aphasia

Aphasia is a disorder in the production and comprehension of spoken and written language. It is caused by a unilateral localized brain lesion in individuals who had normal language development.

Several features of this definition of aphasia are noteworthy. The first is that aphasia is a *language* disorder. In this chapter, the expression 'language disorder' is used to show that aphasia is a central deficit affecting both comprehension and production and both spoken and written language. Defining aphasia as a language disorder distinguishes it from articulation disorders, such as dysarthria (a motor speech disorder; see Chapter 11, this volume) and apraxia of speech (a disorder in programming and monitoring articulation, see Chapter 12, this volume). Such disorders often accompany aphasia, but can also occur without aphasia. Brain damage may affect articulatory abilities, for example, because the motor area is affected. In such cases, the person will display speech problems (a dysarthria). However, he or she will still be able to write and to understand both spoken and written language, because the language system itself is intact. Also, disorders in auditory and visual perception due to brain damage are excluded by this definition. Such disorders may result in auditory comprehension or reading problems, but these are not the consequence of a language disorder.

Communication disorders as a result of dementia are also excluded by this definition of aphasia. This is because there is no unilateral brain lesion and the language problems in dementia are progressive (see Chapter 15, this volume). Communication disorders due to psychiatric conditions (such as schizophrenia and depression) are also outside the scope of the definition, because in these cases there is no acquired brain lesion (Chapter 17, this volume). Aphasia should also be distinguished from developmental language problems in children. In order to make this distinction, aphasia is defined as an *acquired* language disorder. Developmental language disorders may have several origins: neurological damage that arises perinatally, specific genetic syndromes (as in Down's syndrome; see Chapter 7, this volume), but often there is no known cause (as in specific language impairment; see Chapter 5, this volume). The nature and the development of all these disorders may be very different from those in aphasia and, therefore, they are excluded from the definition of aphasia. If children acquire brain damage during the critical period of language development (e.g. due to a traumatic injury or a stroke), language problems may arise. This is called '(acquired) childhood aphasia'.

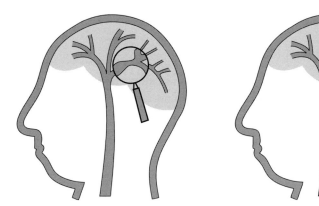

Figure 13.1 Illustration of how blood flow diminishes due to thrombosis (left) and how an embolus blocks the artery (right). (Reprinted from Bastiaanse (2010) with permission of the publisher.)

13.2.2   Causes and prevalence

By far the most frequent cause of aphasia is a cerebrovascular accident (CVA), commonly known as a stroke. A CVA causes around 85 per cent of aphasia cases (Bastiaanse 2010). It can occur in two ways. The first kind of stroke is an infarction. There are two possible causes of an infarct. First there is thrombosis. A thrombosis is a blood clot ('thrombus') in the artery. In damaged arteries blood clotting may occur because the inner tissue of the artery is affected. When these blood clots grow, they partially or entirely block the artery. As a consequence, the area behind the clot is insufficiently supplied with oxygen and necessary nutritional substances and, as a result, ceases to function (see Figure 13.1, left diagram).

A thrombosis may not be situated in the brain itself but be found in the heart or the carotid artery in the neck. Regardless of its location, parts of a thrombosis may tear off and flow into smaller arteries in the brain, which then may be (partially or totally) blocked. Again, the area behind the blockage will cease to function. A blood clot that tears off is called an embolus (see Figure 13.1, right diagram).

The second kind of stroke is a haemorrhage. This occurs when there is a rupture in one of the arteries supplying the brain. Blood flows out of the artery (see Figure 13.2) with the result that the area supplied by the damaged artery receives insufficient oxygen and other vital nutrients and ceases to function. Additionally, the blood that leaks out of the artery into the confined space within the skull increases the intracranial pressure. This blood puts pressure on the tissue surrounding the artery and prevents that area from functioning. Thus, the surrounding tissue is damaged as well.

The second most frequent cause of aphasia, after stroke, is traumatic brain injury (TBI). The term 'traumatic' refers to the fact that damage arises from some form of trauma, which in peacetime is most commonly

Figure 13.2 Illustration of a weak spot in the artery (left) resulting in a haemorrhage (right). (Reprinted from Bastiaanse (2010) with permission of the publisher.)

a road traffic accident. TBI may also be caused by violence, gunshots and falls. This explains why aphasia due to TBI is more often seen in younger people, whereas aphasia due to stroke is usually found in older people.

Within TBI, a distinction is made between open and closed head injury. This distinction refers to whether or not the skull is damaged. Open head injuries bring a risk of complications due to infection that add to the severity of the condition. In TBI, the lesion may be large and diffuse rather than focal or there may be multiple lesions. As a consequence, aphasia due to TBI is usually accompanied by other severe and often more prominent cognitive disorders, such as memory and behavioural problems. An exception to the large lesions in TBI is the small and well-defined lesion caused by a gunshot or shrapnel. These small lesions have contributed significantly to our knowledge of aphasia and the representation of language in the brain. Many soldiers who acquired head wounds due to gunshots or shrapnel in the first and second world wars have been extensively studied by aphasiologists in the Soviet Union, the UK and the USA.

The third type of brain damage that may cause aphasia is a tumour. Whether a tumour is malignant or benign is immaterial as far as the aphasia is concerned. A tumour is usually growing and occupies space. Since an inflexible skull protects the brain, the tumour will press on healthy tissue as it grows. If this tissue is involved in language, then aphasia is the result. The final and least common cause of aphasia is an infection in the brain, such as meningitis or encephalitis. This rarely occurs and the descriptions of aphasia after an infection are restricted to a relatively small number of case studies (e.g. Stewart *et al.* 1992).

Usually, aphasia is not a separate diagnostic category in medical registration systems and, therefore, there are no exact data on the frequency of occurrence of aphasia. For the USA and the UK, the estimate of the incidence (the number of new aphasia cases per year) is 170,000 for the USA and over 35,000 for the UK (Code 2010). The number of individuals suffering from aphasia (the prevalence) is around 0.37 per cent for both countries, that is, around 1 million for the USA and around 220,000 for the UK (Code 2010).

13.2.3   Recovery and prognosis

Brain cells only function properly if sufficient oxygen and essential nutrients are transported to the brain by the blood. In case of a lack of these nutrients, the brain cells become hypo-ischaemic and 'die'. This is known as necrosis. Until recently, it was thought that brain cells do not regenerate and that, therefore, brain damage is irreversible. It was thought that once a person becomes aphasic, the condition is permanent. However, it is now known that this is not the case. During the first few months after the occurrence of brain damage, significant improvement and even complete recovery in functioning are possible. Some cells that fail to function because of a lack of oxygen may regenerate. This phenomenon provides an explanation for the changes that are often seen in people with aphasia.

There are other explanations for improvement of aphasia after brain damage and these are more widely accepted. When the brain is wounded, swelling known as oedema often occurs. Because the brain is within the confined and non-expandable space of the skull, this swelling causes pressure in the brain to increase. As a result, some cells die while others may receive insufficient oxygen and nutrients to function (but enough to survive). After the immediate acute stage (around 2–3 months), the swelling diminishes as does the pressure on the brain. This allows non-functioning brain cells to regain their function. There is also some evidence that certain connections between the cells may regenerate during the first few weeks or months (e.g. Carmichael 2006). This explains why in most individuals spontaneous recovery of cognitive and physical functions takes place in the weeks and months immediately after brain damage. After this period of spontaneous recovery, aphasia in most cases will be permanent, although improvement of language and communication is still possible.

There are four major factors that further influence the recovery and prognosis of aphasia:

(1) Severity: Individuals with a severe aphasia, usually due to a large lesion, have a poorer prognosis than individuals with mild aphasia, especially beyond the period of spontaneous recovery.
(2) Age: In general, recovery is better for younger people. This age effect is shown in both stroke and trauma victims, although the degree of recovery is usually larger in the first group.
(3) Cause: Aphasia due to trauma has, in general, a better prognosis than aphasia due to a stroke. This may be related to the fact that people with TBI are usually younger than stroke victims.

(4) Left-handedness: Left-handed individuals and people who are ambi-
dextrous have, in general, a better chance of (spontaneous) recovery
than people who are right-handed. This is probably related to bilateral
language organization in left-handed individuals.

It cannot be excluded that some factors such as the (premorbid) intelligence, general health condition and motivation have some positive influence on the recovery process in aphasia. However, the effect of these factors has not been clearly demonstrated. Furthermore, aphasia therapy
aims to influence the recovery process, but as yet, there is no consensus
about the most effective method (see Chapter 24, this volume).

13.3   Aphasia symptoms

Aphasia is virtually always manifested in both productive (speech and
writing) and receptive (comprehension of spoken language and reading)
language modalities. Although linguistic symptoms may vary, it is usually
impairments in speech production, specifically everyday language use,
that are most prominent and disturbing for the aphasic individual and
people in his or her environment.

13.3.1   Spontaneous speech

Linguistic impairments in spontaneous speech may occur at the phonological, lexical-semantic and grammatical level. Phonological problems
are evident in the production of phonemic paraphasias, in which one or
more sounds ('phonemes') of the target word are substituted (e.g. 'diger'
instead of 'tiger'), omitted (e.g. 'tain' instead of 'train'), transposed (e.g.
'sarmaphy' instead of 'pharmacy') or added (e.g. 'ancknowledge' instead
of 'acknowledge'). If an aphasic speaker corrupts the word in a way that it
is no longer recognizable for the listener, the result is called a 'neologism'
(e.g. 'lackle'; 'fatalogle').

Most aphasic speakers have problems finding the right words at the
right moment. These lexical-semantic difficulties or word-finding problems are most prominent during a naming task, in which pictures of
objects and animals are shown to the aphasic individual who must name
them. However, word-finding problems may also occur in spontaneous
speech in one of the following ways:

(1) The aphasic individual has no articulation problems and speaks fluently, but his speech is characterized by a lack of explicit information
('empty speech'), because a relatively large number of content words
(nouns, verbs and adjectives) are omitted and substituted by common
words such as 'thing', 'there', 'do' and/or personal pronouns without a
clear referent.

(2) The aphasic individual hesitates and blocks before key words, for example: 'and then I go wa- … eh with water … no with … yes with water yes … to make and then eh …' (searching for the word 'wash'). Often the aphasic speaker indicates that he or she cannot find the word, for example, 'I cannot say it, but …', or 'what's the name again?'

(3) The aphasic speaker produces verbal paraphasias (word substitutions) that are often related in meaning to the target word, for example, 'boy' instead of 'girl'. This is called a semantic paraphasia. If there is no relation with the target word, then such a word substitution is called an irrelevant or unrelated paraphasia. An aphasic speaker may produce so many paraphasias that he or she is hardly comprehensible. This is called semantic jargon. A typical example is the following fragment in which the aphasic speaker tries to explain how she usually spends her day (… = pause).

Yes and I do like drying and riding my bike and … when the weather is nice here on the deck … and how I … well I know the most beautiful from I eh play me strike with gauze and I play with it me strike with my toe … I can do what I want on it and I give presents to everything with so called presents … what we do eh and I goes in the evening before we will, as they say … when we had dinner then I help the room help I all dipping.

Most aphasic speakers have additional problems with formulating sentences. These grammatical problems appear in two different forms: (1) impoverished sentence structure and simplification of the grammatical structure (agrammatism or telegraphic speech) and (2) erratic application of the grammatical rules (paragrammatism). Agrammatic speech is usually slow and effortful and is characterized by short sentences. It consists mainly of content words – function words (articles, prepositions and conjunctions) are largely lacking. A typical example of agrammatic speech is shown below. Here, the aphasic speaker is talking about her home town (the words of the interviewer are between square brackets):

Amsterdam … and eh … beautiful … eh … I … nice … walk [Okay. Where?] Where? Eh … Amsterdam [Are you walking around the city?] No bike or no eh … eh … car eh … shopping … and eh … eh call and eh … first eh … eh … cup of coffee … eh … Mary and eh … talking a bit.

Paragrammatic speech is fluent with normal speech rate and intonation. Although sentences are long and syntactically complex, they are often incorrectly structured. Many function words and inflections ('affixes') are substituted and sentence structures are often entangled or left incomplete. Paragrammatic speakers often use many phonemic and verbal paraphasias, making them hard to comprehend, as shown by the following extract:

[If I enter your house, what does it look like?] If you enter, you get immediately space that is for the space that is around the front door that is left rather small, but then furthermore for the rest everything in the house remained space. Downstairs, I should say a space that camou camouflage, downstairs a room that is left rather spacious. Herewith a space for the garage and above garage where you so big big/grit/ [neologism] your /grit/ with not in the middle in the house, out interior design rather bi rather big.

13.3.2   More expressive symptoms

Apart from these expressive characteristics, individuals with aphasia can demonstrate several other symptoms, such as stereotypes, speech automatisms, recurring utterances, echolalia and perseverations. In stereotypes, the aphasic speaker produces a word, phrase or sentence that is communicatively more or less appropriate, more frequently than normal, for example 'and so on', 'damned' (and other curses), 'I don't know', 'what's the name?', 'I can't say it'. The speaker cannot convey more specific information even when asked to do so. A speech automatism is a word or phrase that is repeated over and over again, but which is not communicatively appropriate. Most often, this is the only speech that the individual with (severe) aphasia is producing. It can be accompanied by (often unreliable) production of 'yes' and 'no'. Usually the speaker is able to apply a variety of intonation contours, resulting in (limited) transfer of information. Some aphasic speakers use the same speech automatism for years, for example 'Sunday morning special' and 'from the government'.

Recurring utterances are similar to speech automatisms, but are non-words that are continuously repeated. They usually have a very simple structure consisting of a vowel and a consonant or a consonant and a vowel. Consonant clusters are hardly ever observed. Examples are 'popopo' or 'tatatata'. As in speech automatism, prosody and intonation seem to be preserved which means that sometimes some information can be transferred. In echolalia, the aphasic speaker repeats the words or sentences of the conversational partner. This can be a literal repetition, with even the same intonation pattern (although this phenomenon is mainly observed in individuals with dementia), but usually parts of a sentence are repeated as an answer to a question:

Conversation partner: Did you sleep well last night?
Aphasic speaker: Slept well last night.

The term 'perseveration' refers to the repetition of a preceding activity at a moment when it is no longer appropriate. In relation to speech production, perseveration can occur at the sound level (e.g. 'ki-ki-king') and at the word level (e.g. the aphasic individual first names his nose correctly, but then refers to his eye and ear with 'nose' as well). Perseveration can also occur in spontaneous speech:

> [Have you been living in London?] No, in London, in London, no in London, oh, in Lond, no in London, it is London, it is *not* in London. [In Oxford?] Yes!!

The difference between a speech automatism and perseveration is that perseveration changes all the time, whereas a speech automatism is constant for a long time.

13.3.3   Auditory comprehension

Apart from the quite striking speech impairments described above, individuals with aphasia usually have language comprehension deficits as well. These can have different manifestations. Some aphasic individuals have problems distinguishing speech sounds. In extreme cases, this can result in 'word deafness', when the person cannot understand anything that is said to him, although hearing is unimpaired. However, most aphasic individuals have problems understanding the meaning of certain types of spoken words, specifically low-frequency words (e.g. 'snail', 'hour glass', 'sea horse') and abstract words (e.g. 'negotiation', 'redistribution'). Also, understanding of a word series (e.g. 'point to your nose, your eye and your ear') and grammatically complex structures such as passives (e.g. 'the lion is bitten by the tiger'), comparatives (e.g. 'the girl is taller than the boy') and genitive constructions (e.g. 'how would you call the brother of my wife?') is usually impaired.

13.3.4   Reading and writing

All aphasic individuals have problems with reading and writing. Reading disorders ('alexia') and writing disorders ('agraphia') are usually more severe than comprehension and production of spoken language, respectively. Most aphasic people cannot read the newspaper and hardly any aphasic person is able to write a letter without error. The fact that aphasic individuals usually experience more problems with written than spoken language cannot only be explained by the fact that they (like healthy people) have 'less experience' with written language. Reading and writing are derived from spoken language. They also demand additional skills such as visual recognition of letters while reading and application of spelling conventions and differential hand movements while writing. These skills can each be affected after brain damage. Moreover, many aphasic people are forced to write with their left hand because of a right-sided paralysis, delaying the writing process and distorting the handwriting. However, this poor motor control of the preferred hand is usually not the full explanation for the poor writing skills of aphasic individuals, because often the same writing errors (omissions, substitutions, etc.) are observed in typing.

13.4   Aphasia syndromes

Aphasia can manifest itself in different ways. The grouping of aphasia symptoms that is largely determined by the organization of language in the brain is far from arbitrary. That is, some symptoms often occur simultaneously, whereas other symptom combinations hardly ever occur. Although many different aphasia classification systems have been proposed over the last century, the most important aphasia types that are distinguished nowadays are still the same as the ones that were described at the end of the nineteenth century by German and French neurologists. The major so-called 'classical' aphasia types are Broca's aphasia, Wernicke's aphasia, anomia and global aphasia. For a detailed description of the classical aphasia types, see Goodglass *et al.* (2001).

13.4.1   Broca's aphasia

The most important characteristics of Broca's aphasia are effortful articulation, reduced vocabulary and grammatical limitation resulting in very simple sentences and stereotypical constructions. In severe cases, speech is limited to one-word utterances (often mainly consisting of 'yes' and 'no'). In less severe cases, speech is characterized by short, grammatically simplified sentences which consist mainly of content words (i.e. nouns, verbs and adjectives). This output is called 'telegraphic speech'. An example of telegraphic speech is shown below:

> [Where did you buy a new house?] In Cambridge, centre of Cambridge, middle of Cambridge. ah, beautiful place. [What does it look like?] new housing estate … premium estate … beautiful house … oh dear, yes, beautiful house … eh … magnificent from the outside … windows, very very lovely house [How big is it?] room … ninety metres … no! nine metres… all thresholds gone … beautiful garden … lovely.

Naming of objects, auditory comprehension (of single words and simple sentences) and silent reading are usually hardly affected. However, action naming, comprehension of grammatically complex sentences (such as reversible passives, e.g. 'the cat is chased by the dog'), reading aloud, repetition and writing are impaired. Nowadays, the term 'Broca's aphasia' is mainly used when grammatical comprehension disorders are studied. For production studies, the terms 'agrammatic aphasia' or 'agrammatism' are more common.

13.4.2 Wernicke's aphasia

The main characteristics are impaired auditory comprehension and fluent, well-articulated speech with paraphasias. In severe cases, an individual with Wernicke's aphasia will not understand spoken language and produce so many neologistic, phonological and/or verbal paraphasias that he or she is no longer understandable ('jargon aphasia'). Individuals with Wernicke's aphasia are usually not aware of their speech errors. In milder cases, they only have problems understanding low-frequency and abstract words and complex sentences and they only occasionally use paraphasias.

Although individuals with Wernicke's aphasia can produce long and complex sentences, these are often ungrammatical, because they are incomplete and grammatical constructions are mixed up. This is called 'paragrammatism'. In the following extract, the sentence endings have been marked with full stops, which are mainly based on intonation:

> [How are you these days?] I've got the idea that I've been taken better. You can hear that with the talking of course. On one side but I think it's nice, my idea too. But if it does not work then it does not work. I think quite easy about that. We never say it is not possible or it does not work. And that's what I did. That's the way I am, right?

Object and action naming, repetition of words and sentences, silent reading and writing are usually severely affected, while reading aloud can be more or less normal.

13.4.3 Anomic aphasia

The most important characteristics of anomic aphasia, or anomia, are the relatively severe word-finding problems that occur in the context of fluent, grammatically well-formed speech production and relatively intact auditory comprehension. In severe cases, the speech of these individuals is typically lacking explicit information. This is called 'empty speech'. Naming of objects and actions is relatively severely impaired, but repetition of words and sentences is usually good. Reading and writing can vary from normal to entirely impossible. An example of the word-finding problems that occur in anomia is given below (the speaker is attempting to name a picture of a tree):

> Ah … yes, how should I call this? You would like to know how you would how I would call it. People, but look, there are fat ones and fat ones (points to the branches) under a … how should I call it? A branch, I think that's enough.

13.4.4 Global aphasia

This form of aphasia is usually associated with large brain lesions. It is not mentioned in all aphasia classifications, since for a long time it has been considered to be a mixture of Broca's and Wernicke's aphasia. Since global aphasia is often observed in clinical practice and can also be caused by smaller lesions in which Broca's and Wernicke's areas are spared, there is no reason not to consider global aphasia as a specific aphasia type.

The most obvious features of global aphasia are very limited speech production with poor articulation and prosody, many speech automatisms and severely affected language comprehension. Only rarely is the individual with global aphasia able to produce a meaningful utterance, usually as an answer to a question and often in the form of echolalia. Many global aphasic speakers have a tendency to perseverate and sometimes speech production is even more hampered by dysarthria or apraxia of speech.

A specific form of global aphasia is characterized by speech restricted to speech automatisms or recurring utterances, for example, 'kitkit' or 'dododo'. These consonant–vowel combinations are produced fluently and with intonation that expresses affective information (e.g. agitation, question, doubt). Despite limited speech production, individuals with global aphasia may be able to repeat some words, albeit often with neologisms or perseverations. Naming of objects and actions is severely affected. There is either no reaction to the stimulus, or a neologism or speech automatism is produced. Perseveration on naming tests often occurs. Auditory comprehension, reading and writing are severely impaired.

13.4.5   Other aphasia syndromes

The four aphasia types examined above are the most common kinds found in clinical practice and research studies. However, there are other types of aphasia. Goodglass and Kaplan (1972, 1983; Goodglass *et al.* 2001), following the classical aphasia typology of Lichtheim (1885), mention three other aphasia syndromes. These syndromes can be distinguished from the ones above by a remarkable impairment or preservation of repetition of words and sentences.

Individuals suffering from conduction aphasia are severely impaired in repetition. Speech is fluent and grammatically well-formed and contains many phonemic paraphasias. Language comprehension is relatively intact. The person with conduction aphasia is aware of his or her errors and often tries to correct them. This can result in a sequence of approximations to the target word, for example 'scrapple, strapple, strample' for the game 'scrabble'.

Transcortical motor aphasia is a rather rare type of aphasia. Repetition is relatively well preserved compared to severely limited speech output. Individuals with transcortical motor aphasia hardly speak spontaneously, but they are able to give short, well-articulated answers to structured questions. Auditory comprehension, naming and reading are relatively intact, but writing is impaired to the same extent as speaking.

Transcortical sensory aphasia is a rare aphasia syndrome that has the same characteristics as Wernicke's aphasia. However, it differs with respect to the relatively intact ability to repeat words and sentences. Usually the aphasic individual does not speak spontaneously, but when addressed, may respond with fluent, well-articulated sentences that are littered with paraphasias and neologisms.

Finally, Goodglass *et al.* (2001) describe some aphasias that can arise from lesions in subcortical structures, such as the thalamus and the basal ganglia. These subcortical aphasias can occur in a fluent and non-fluent form depending on the lesion site. Anterior subcortical aphasia, in which the frontal branch of the internal capsule and the putamen are damaged, is characterized by sparse output with severe articulation problems and hypophonia (a weak voice resulting in soft speech). More extended lesions may result in global aphasia. In the case of more posterior lesions of the thalamus and adjacent white matter, fluent aphasia has been observed that, in some cases, may resemble Wernicke's aphasia.

13.4.6 Classification issues

Although a large part of aphasia research in recent decades consists of group studies with the classical aphasia syndromes, it is highly debatable whether individuals classified with the same type of aphasia form a homogeneous group. Evidence for this claim can be found in the fact that the frequency of occurrence of the classical aphasia types varies significantly by research centres. According to some researchers (e.g. Prins *et al.* 1978), only 20–30 per cent of aphasic individuals belong to a classical aphasia type, whereas other researchers (e.g. Kertesz and Sheppard 1981) claim that all individuals with aphasia (i.e. 100 per cent) can be classified as having one of the classical aphasia types. Such differences can only exist because researchers are not using the same classification criteria. For example, according to some researchers, 'telegraphic speech' is the defining feature of Broca's aphasia (Obler *et al.* 1978), whereas others (e.g. Lhermitte and Gauthier 1969) claim that less than 10 per cent of individuals with Broca's aphasia speak telegraphically. Opinions also differ regarding auditory comprehension in Broca's aphasia. According to some authors (e.g. Graetz *et al.* 1992), this is intact or at most minimally disturbed, while other authors (e.g. Kertesz 1981) claim that auditory comprehension in Broca's aphasia can vary considerably and may even be worse than in Wernicke's aphasia.

The above comments suggest that the results of many group studies on Broca's aphasia (and other aphasia types as well) may not be compared, because similar definitions of aphasia syndromes have not been used. Therefore, reliable generalizations about the psycholinguistic and neurolinguistic mechanisms underlying the classification of aphasia cannot be drawn. As a result, several researchers (e.g. Badecker and Caramazza 1985; Miceli *et al.* 1989) no longer accept group studies on the basis of classical aphasia typology and argue that research in aphasiology should only be conducted on the basis of case studies of carefully selected aphasic individuals. The debate between advocates and opponents of group studies has been quite heated, as is illustrated by the following quotations:

> ... the classification of patients into categories such as Wernicke's aphasia, conduction aphasia, expressive aphasia ... is not only useless but positively harmful for research into the nature of cognitive disorders and the structure of normal cognitive processing (Caramazza and McClosky 1988: 519).
>
> ... to prohibit group studies is to prohibit any generalization over data from more than one patient. Thus, an appeal to case-studies as the only one 'defensible methodology' guarantees a dead end ... Experience has shown that maintaining the traditional classificatory system, or refined variations thereof, has borne results, and ... case-studies have led nowhere (Grodzinsky 1990: 76–7).

13.5　Localization of aphasia: language and the brain

Until the present century, almost all our knowledge of the anatomical structures underlying the language faculty was based on studies of the localization of brain lesions in aphasic individuals. The most important sources of information were postmortem studies of the brains of individuals with lesions due to vascular disease and trauma, the latter caused by gunshots and shrapnel wounds in young soldiers. These studies were undertaken in Russia by Luria (e.g. Luria 1970) and in the USA by a group of aphasiologists (Harold Goodglass, Edith Kaplan, Frank Benson, Norman Geschwind and others) who worked in the Aphasia Research Center of the Boston Veterans Administration Hospital (now called the Harold Goodglass Aphasia Research Center).

In the 1970s, brains could be observed in vivo for the first time by using computed axial tomography (CAT scans). It was then possible to see which areas in the brain did not take up oxygen and were, hence, affected by a brain lesion. In the 1980s, activity in the brain could be observed in healthy persons for the first time by using positron emission tomography (PET scans). In the 1990s, PET was followed by functional magnetic resonance imaging (fMRI). By using magnetic radiation rather than radioactivity, fMRI was supposed to be a safer brain-imaging technique. These latter two methods are adequate to localize cognitive functions, including language, in healthy brains. Hundreds of studies have now been conducted using these techniques. The results of these studies show a large degree of overlap with what we knew already from classical localization doctrine as formulated by Paul Broca (1861, 1865), Carl Wernicke (1874) and Lichtheim (1885) and updated by Geschwind (1974). This theory can be sketched as follows.

In 95 per cent of cases, aphasia is caused by a lesion in the left hemisphere of the brain. In less than 20 per cent of left-handed individuals, language functions are localized in the right hemisphere (Rasmussen and Millner 1977). This unilateral control of language functions is called 'cerebral dominance'. Recent neuroimaging studies have shown that the ('non-dominant') right hemisphere also plays a role in some specific language functions in right-handed individuals (for an overview, see Stowe et al. 2005), but damage to these areas does not result in aphasia. Three cortical areas in the dominant hemisphere are critical for language (see Figure 13.3): (1) Broca's area and its vicinity in the frontal lobe of the brain; (2) Wernicke's area and its surrounding areas, including the angular gyrus in the temporal and parietal lobes, respectively; and (3) the (in-between) area in the inferior part of the pre- and post-central gyri, including the (subcortical) arcuate fasciculus. A lesion in one or more of these interconnected language areas will most probably result in permanent aphasia. A lesion in the surrounding areas will seldom lead to aphasia and if it does, the aphasia is usually transient (Luria 1970).

The classical localization doctrine can explain a large number of aphasia symptoms and syndromes, such as poor speech production in combination with relatively good auditory comprehension in Broca's aphasia, the fluent speech production and poor comprehension in Wernicke's aphasia, and the poor repetition abilities in conduction aphasia. As an illustration of the explanatory power of the classical localization doctrine, a concise analysis of the anatomical model of the naming of objects is presented (based on Geschwind 1974). The choice of naming of objects is not accidental. Learning to name objects in the world around us can be considered to be the basis of our language faculty. One could argue that humans, in contrast to other mammals including apes, have a specific brain structure available for object naming.

In naming an object such as an apple, at least six anatomical sites and psycholinguistic stages can be distinguished (see Figure 13.4). First, the target stimulus (the visual image of an apple) is projected onto the primary visual cortex, where sensory-specific processing takes place. Second, the visual pattern is transferred to the visual association cortex for perceptual analysis and synthesis (i.e. object recognition). Third, the association between the visual image of the apple and the sound image for apple stored in Wernicke's area is made in the angular gyrus. This is where the 'rules' for recoding visual perception into auditory perception, and vice versa, are stored.

From both an anatomical and a functional point of view, the angular gyrus is a transition area between the temporal, occipital and parietal lobes, where auditory, visual and tactile-kinaesthetic information is processed, respectively. The angular gyrus performs a synthesis of these three kinds of sensory information by its typical location. It is especially important for generating auditory-visual associations that play a fundamental

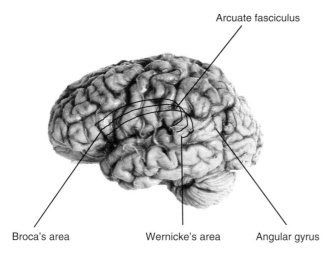

Arcuate fasciculus

Broca's area   Wernicke's area   Angular gyrus

Figure 13.3 Localization of the 'language areas' of Broca and Wernicke, their connecting track, the arcuate fasciculus and the angular gyrus on a lateral view of the left hemisphere. (The photo of the brain is taken from The Digital Anatomist Project at the University of Washington, with permission.)

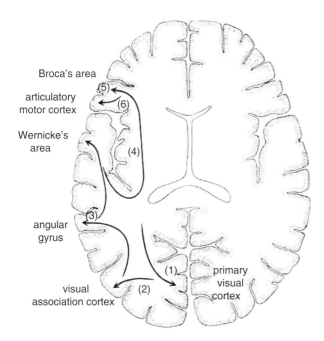

Broca's area

articulatory motor cortex

Wernicke's area

angular gyrus

visual association cortex

primary visual cortex

Figure 13.4 Six stages of naming a visually perceived object, shown on a horizontal slice of the brain. (Reprinted from Geschwind (1972) with permission of the artist, Bunji Tagawa.)

role in naming and, hence, in language acquisition. Fourth, the auditory form of the word 'apple' is (in abstract form, of course) transmitted to Broca's area through the arcuate fasciculus that connects Wernicke's area to Broca's area. Fifth, in Broca's area the articulation programme of the word 'apple' is triggered. Sixth, on the basis of the articulation programme the muscles of the articulatory organs (e.g. lips, tongue) are innervated via the primary motor cortex. The phoneme structure of the word 'apple' can then be pronounced.

Although this associationists' model of the naming process is, of course, very simplistic and leaves many questions unanswered (for example, how does a child learn abstract words like 'love', 'beautiful', 'but' and 'if'?), it can explain a variety of aphasic symptoms. For example, a lesion in Wernicke's area disrupts not only the naming of objects, but also the comprehension of object names. This is because the underlying (phonological) word form is no longer present (or accessible) and can, therefore, not be matched with the corresponding meaning. When the lesion is in Broca's area, comprehension of single words is unaffected, because the underlying word forms in Wernicke's area are still intact. However, words cannot be pronounced properly, because the correct 'articulation patterns' are no longer available. In other words, the problems are not in selecting the correct word, but in the motor realization and/or linear organization of the speech sounds that, together, constitute the phoneme structure of the word.

Even though the classical localization doctrine of Wernicke, Lichtheim and Geschwind is still acknowledged by most modern aphasiologists, it should be emphasized that it is only a very simplified model of the anatomical and psychological organization of language use. Recent studies using modern neuroimaging techniques have shown that cerebral lesions that cause aphasia are not always in (the vicinity of) the classical language areas of Broca and Wernicke. These studies have shown that damage to subcortical areas such as the thalamus or the basal ganglia can also result in aphasia (e.g. Cappa and Vignolo 1979; D'Esposito and Alexander 1995). Also, lesions to Broca's or Wernicke's area do not necessarily lead to Broca's and Wernicke's aphasia, respectively (e.g. Basso *et al.* 1985). However, most importantly, the classical localization doctrine cannot explain some very prominent symptoms that are characteristic for some aphasia syndromes, such as telegraphic speech and grammatical comprehension deficits in Broca's aphasia. This is not surprising because the classical localization doctrine only relates to word level. Research into sentence comprehension in aphasia only started in the 1970s (Parisi and Pizzamiglio 1970; Caramazza and Zurif 1976). This was the first time that sentence comprehension deficits in Broca's aphasia were investigated.

The above discussion shows that the classical localization doctrine cannot explain all aphasia symptoms. This lack of explanatory force is not surprising, however, since language functions such as speaking and understanding spoken language are, even when restricted to the word level, too complex from a psycholinguistic point of view to assume that they can be stored in a few isolated brain areas ('language centres'). They must be the result of collective functioning of several, probably overlapping networks of brain areas. As yet, little is known about the structure and functions of these cerebral networks, but it can be expected that in due course the classical localization doctrine can be refined and extended with the help of modern neurotechnology.

13.6   Recent developments

For the purposes of this section, the turn of the century is taken to represent the start of some recent developments in aphasia research. The word-production model that was described above only referred to nouns. However, we speak in sentences and sentences are built around verbs. Although the production of verbs and the comprehension of sentences have received considerable attention since the 1990s, no adequate anatomical model of these processes has so far been developed (see, however, Grodzinsky and Friederici 2006). Some theories of sentence comprehension and the production of verbs and sentences will be examined in this section. Also, an intensively debated issue in aphasiology will be addressed. This issue concerns whether linguistic knowledge is affected by brain damage in aphasia, or whether this knowledge is intact but not accessible to a normal extent. Finally, clinical researchers are increasingly examining aphasia across languages. It will be shown that studying language behaviour in bilingual aphasic speakers can reveal how language is represented in the (intact and damaged) brain.

13.6.1   Verbs and sentences in aphasia

It was in the late 1990s and early twenty-first century that retrieval of verbs began to receive the attention of investigators. Early studies focused on differences in performance on tests of object naming by nouns and action naming by verbs (e.g. Williams and Canter 1987; Miceli *et al.* 1988; Zingeser and Berndt 1990). They showed that both word classes may be selectively impaired in individual cases (e.g. Zingeser and Berndt 1988). However, group studies showed that the large majority of aphasic individuals (>95 per cent), regardless of aphasia type, have more problems with verb than noun production (Kohn *et al.* 1989; Jonkers 1998).

More recent studies of verb production do not focus on comparisons with nouns, but on differences within the class of verbs (Kemmerer and Tranel 2000a, 2000b; Luzzatti *et al.* 2002; Jonkers and Bastiaanse 2007) and on the inflection of verbs in the context of sentences (Berndt *et al.* 1997; Bastiaanse and Van Zonneveld 1998). Studies of different languages have shown that the argument structure of verbs plays an important role in verb production (English: Thompson 2004; German: De Bleser and Kauschke 2003; Hungarian: Kiss 2000; Italian: Luzzatti *et al.* 2002; Russian: Dragoy and Bastiaanse 2010). For example, 'to walk' is a verb that needs only one argument (the walker), whereas 'to give' needs three arguments (the person who gives, the person who receives and the gift). In agrammatic aphasia, the complexity of argument structure plays a role in verb retrieval (Thompson 2004). Other factors that play a role are instrumentality, which facilitates naming in agrammatic aphasia ('to cut' is an instrumental verb and is easier to retrieve than 'to push' for which no instrument is needed). Verbs with a name relation to a noun (e.g. 'to saw') are better retrieved than verbs without such a name relation (e.g. 'to cut') by individuals with anomic aphasia (Jonkers and Bastiaanse 2007).

At sentence level, most studies concern the comprehension of semantically reversible sentences, such as 'the woman is rescuing the man' compared to 'the man is rescued by the woman'. The latter sentence type, which is a passive construction, is harder to understand than the first one for individuals with Broca's aphasia. Sentences in which the agent (the one who performs the action, in the sentence above 'the woman') and the theme (the one who undergoes the action, here 'the man') are not in the preferred order are difficult to comprehend for individuals with a grammatical disorder as in Broca's aphasia. Many hypotheses have been proposed for why this should be the case. For comprehensive discussion of these hypotheses, the reader is referred to debates led by Grodzinsky (2000) and Drai and Grodzinsky (2006). Several studies have shown that these sentence comprehension problems are not restricted to Broca's aphasia and that similar performance has also been observed in Wernicke's aphasia (e.g. Bastiaanse and Edwards 2004).

Relatively few studies of sentence production have been conducted. Some researchers assume that it is only the beginning of sentences that is impaired, for example question words, and conjunctions such as 'because' and 'although' (Hagiwara 1995). However, several studies demonstrate problems further downstream in the sentence. These problems are found in sentences in which the word order is not the canonical one. Every language has its own canonical order, for example, subject-verb-object for English and subject-object-verb for Turkish. Usually, individuals with Broca's aphasia are able to produce these structures. However, when word order changes, sentence production and comprehension becomes harder for people with Broca's aphasia (Bastiaanse and Van Zonneveld 2006). This explains why sentences such as 'it is the man who the woman rescues' are hard for people with Broca's aphasia to understand. It also explains why yes/no questions in English (e.g. 'is the boy eating an apple?') are difficult for agrammatic speakers to produce: the auxiliary verb 'is' is not in its canonical position (Bastiaanse and Thompson 2003). In other languages, such as Hebrew, the word order remains the same in yes/no questions and only the intonation changes. In those languages, agrammatic speakers have no difficulty producing these questions (Friedmann 2002).

13.6.2   Representational versus processing deficit

In order to understand the nature of aphasia, to do experimental research and to treat aphasic individuals, it is important to know the possible effects of brain damage on linguistic knowledge. Is this knowledge or 'linguistic competence' still available to the aphasic speaker, that is, does the aphasic individual still know the rules of his or her language? All aphasiologists agree that at least some of this knowledge is retained, because aphasic speakers obey the rules of their language. For example, if the verb always precedes the object, as in English, an aphasic speaker will not produce sentences with an object preceding a verb. Also, phonological rules are followed. In Dutch and German, for example, obstruents that are pronounced with vibrating vocal cords, the so-called 'voiced obstruents' such as /d,b,z,v/, are devoiced at the end of a syllable to /t,p,s,f/. A Dutch or German aphasic speaker will obey this rule and will never produce words ending with voiced obstruents. Grammar and phonology may be simplified, but not basically altered. The question is whether knowledge of complex linguistic structures is erased by the lesion or is only less accessible.

Some aphasiologists assume that linguistic knowledge is lost. Grodzinsky (2000) and Friedmann (2000), for example, assume that critical grammatical knowledge is lost when Broca's area is damaged, with the result that grammatically complex sentences are no longer understood or produced. This assumption has serious consequences, because it implies that an aphasic individual can never produce grammatical structures, the representations of which are gone. According to Friedmann (2000), individuals with Broca's aphasia can no longer produce subordinate clauses, because they lack the grammatical rules to do so. If this were true, no such individual would ever be able to produce a subordinate clause, which is obviously incorrect.

Although it is true that individuals with Broca's aphasia produce subordinate clauses to a lesser extent than non-brain-damaged speakers, such clauses are produced every now and then. Therefore, most researchers agree that the aphasic individual still has linguistic knowledge available, but has insufficient resources to process more complex linguistic structures. The interesting question then is what determines the complexity of the structures. This can be answered by theoretical linguistics. At sentence level, for example, it has to do with the order of the constituents; at phoneme level with phonological markedness. At word level, complexity effects can be seen in the different performance on action and object naming tasks: verbs are more complex than nouns and, therefore, harder to retrieve.

13.6.3   Aphasia as an integration deficit

In the previous section, it was concluded that aphasia should be viewed as a processing disorder: in the large majority of the aphasic population, linguistic knowledge is still available, but is not always accessible. (In very severe cases of global aphasia, when lesions are large, linguistic knowledge may be lost, although this is hard to prove.) This is shown, for example, when a test for naming objects is assessed twice in a week. On both occasions the aphasic individual may name only 50 per cent of items correctly, but the correct and failed items will not be the same in each assessment. Also, on sentence production tests, a simple sentence type is usually easier for the aphasic individual to produce than a complex sentence type. But even a number of complex sentences will be produced correctly, showing that the aphasic individual is able to form a complex sentence, but cannot do so all the time.

In a study of the spontaneous speech of a woman with Broca's aphasia, Bastiaanse (1995) showed that she was able to form complex sentences, including embedded sentences, but at the cost of verb and noun retrieval: she produced semantic paraphasias and was hard to follow. In a later part of the same interview, her sentences became very simple, verbs were not inflected any more, articles and prepositions were omitted, but she gave much more information by producing correct verbs and nouns instead of paraphasias. On the basis of these data and data from other agrammatic speakers it was concluded that it is hard for agrammatic speakers to integrate semantic information in correct syntactic structures, leading to either ungrammatical sentences with correct lexical-semantic information or more complex structure that lacks lexical-semantic content. Therefore, agrammatic aphasia can be seen as a deficit in integrating lexical-semantic and grammatical information, a view that is shared by other researchers (e.g. Yarbay Duman *et al.* (2011) who formulated the integration deficit hypothesis).

Interestingly, this problem with integrating information of two linguistic levels has been observed in the spontaneous speech of fluent anomic speakers as well. Bastiaanse (2011) found that the retrieval of lexical verbs in these speakers decreased when more grammatical information in the form of inflection needed to be computed. This also points to an integration deficit: these fluent aphasic speakers are able to retrieve verbs in spontaneous speech, but when these verbs have to be inflected, retrievability diminishes due to an integration deficit. Of course, it is not true that all aphasic symptoms are due to integration problems. However, in general, most symptoms become more prominent in more demanding linguistic environments. Such a phenomenon can only be explained within the framework of a processing deficit.

13.6.4 Aphasia across languages

In the twentieth century, the majority of experimental studies of aphasia were conducted on English-speaking subjects. Nowadays, aphasia has been studied in many languages, including languages with a far more complex grammatical structure than English. As a result, we have gained deeper insight into the disorders underlying aphasia. In 1990, a notable book on this topic by Menn and Obler was published. They recruited fellow researchers from many different languages to collect samples of spontaneous speech from individuals with Broca's (agrammatic) aphasia, as well as data from several tests, such as sentence construction.

Cross-linguistically, investigations at phoneme and word level are less interesting than those at sentence level, because across languages there are far more differences in grammatical than in phonological structure. However, one interesting aspect at the phonological level, which involves lexical tones, should be reported here. Several languages (e.g. Norwegian, Mandarin, Cantonese) use 'lexical tone' as a distinctive feature. This means that the same phonemic string can have different meanings depending on whether it has a flat, rising, falling or rising-falling tone. A famous example is the word 'ma' in Mandarin. When this is spoken with a flat tone it means 'mother', when spoken with a rising tone it means 'hemp', with a falling tone it means 'scold' and with a rising tone followed by falling tone it means 'horse'. It turns out that Chinese individuals with Broca's aphasia are no longer sensitive to these distinctions. In fact, they respond to tone differences in a similar way to non-native speakers of Chinese who do not have a tone language as their mother tongue: they are insensitive to different tones (Liang 2006).

Particularly interesting with respect to aphasia across languages are investigations of bilingual aphasia. This field of study is rapidly growing. Studying the patterns of language deficits in the two or more languages bilingual individuals used before acquiring aphasia may reveal insights into the representations of more than one language in the brain. Although most descriptions are rather anecdotal, several interesting patterns have been observed. In a so-called early balanced bilingual person (someone who acquired both languages during early childhood and is equally proficient in both languages), one language may be more severely affected than the other. Different patterns may be seen in late 'balanced' bilingual persons (individuals who learned their second language after childhood but who are more or less equally proficient in both languages). In some bilingual aphasic speakers their native language is better preserved. In others, their second language is better preserved, especially when they used that language most often later in life. In both early and late 'non-balanced' bilingual aphasic speakers, either language may be worse.

These patterns have been seen in single case studies. There are only a few group studies. Kambanaros and Van Steenbrugge (2006) studied the production of verbs and nouns in Greek-English late bilingual aphasic immigrants in Australia. They found no difference between the use of verbs and nouns between the two languages, although verb production was more impaired than noun production in both languages. Abuom and Bastiaanse (2012) also reported qualitatively similar behaviour in a group study of Swahili-English bilingual agrammatic speakers: the nature and severity of the deficit were the same in both languages, which are very different from a grammatical point of view. This seems to be the general pattern: the aphasia manifests itself similarly in both languages, but exceptional cases have been reported (for examples, see Fabbro 1999). A few studies have been conducted on recovery of the different languages spoken by bilingual aphasic speakers (Gil and Goral 2004; Goral *et al.* 2010; for an overview, see Paradis 2001). They show that in some bilingual aphasic speakers only one language may improve (either the first or second language), whereas both languages may improve to the same extent in other speakers.

13.7   Summary

Aphasia is a language disorder caused by brain damage, usually in the left hemisphere. The symptoms are dependent on the site and the size of the lesion. Co-occurring symptoms have been classified as aphasia syndromes, but these syndromes do not often appear in pure form. The selective deficits in aphasia at the phoneme, word and sentence level contribute to our knowledge of how language is represented in and processed by the brain. Experimental aphasiology started in the second half of the twentieth century and is still blooming. In the twentieth century, the emphasis was on comprehension and production of words (mainly nouns) and sentences and on spontaneous speech production. Nowadays, aphasia is studied in a wide variety of languages, making cross-linguistic aphasiology an interesting topic. Much attention is also given to the contribution to language of the right hemisphere, bilingual aphasia and language disorders at the discourse level.

14

Right hemisphere damage and communication

Yves Joanette, Perrine Ferré and Maximiliano A. Wilson

14.1 Introduction

The contribution of the brain's right hemisphere to verbal communication has been established through clinical and theoretical reports since the mid-twentieth century and is well acknowledged nowadays. Many adults with acquired right brain lesions can exhibit impairment in one or more communication components. The presence of prosodic, discourse, pragmatic and/or lexico-semantic disorders can seriously alter communicative and social interactions. The goal of this chapter is to present, in a theoretically based and clinically driven manner, the different communication impairments that are present in individuals after right hemisphere damage (RHD). This description begins with a brief historical background and discussion of the role of the right hemisphere in language processing. The chapter then focuses on the estimated prevalence and clinical subtypes of communication impairments in RHD. The various impairment profiles are presented for each component of communication – prosody, lexico-semantics, discourse, pragmatics, reading and writing. Suggested relationships between communication deficits and cognitive impairments are described. Finally, assessment methods and intervention strategies will be addressed.

One important limitation on RHD research is the lack of proper terminology. Clinicians have witnessed a plethora of terms to describe individuals with language and communication impairments following RHD. Early terms used to describe the communication difficulties of this group of clients included 'alterations of the superordinate aspects of language' (Eisenson 1959) and 'latent sensory aphasia' (Boller and Vignolo 1966). In more recent times, the term 'aphasia' has been advocated by Joanette and Ansaldo (1999). This is because all components of communication that can be affected by RHD are now considered part of the language framework. However, this position has been challenged by some researchers

(Myers 2001). The use of the expression 'cognitive-communication disorder' reminds us that all communication impairments, including left hemisphere aphasia, are the expression of numerous underlying cognitive processes, some of them specific to language and communication. Additionally, 'cognitive-communication disorder' has been used to describe communication impairments in several other clinical populations in which there are significant cognitive deficits. These populations include individuals with traumatic brain injuries (TBI) and neurodegenerative diseases.

14.2   Some background

The pioneer writings of Broca and Wernicke in the late nineteenth century established the left hemisphere's dominance for language. In the twentieth century, Gazzaniga (1962), who studied split-brain patients, was one of the first researchers to ascribe certain language abilities to the right hemisphere. At about the same time, a few clinicians – demonstrating very good judgement considering that neither a theoretical framework nor accurate assessment tools were available at the time – noted that right-handed individuals suffering from RHD did not show total preservation of language and speech (for instance, Critchley 1962). These individuals displayed inappropriate communication behaviours, mostly of a pragmatic nature, in their interactions with others. At the time, pragmatics was only beginning to emerge as a distinct linguistic discipline, and its influence on the study of language disorders was still minimal. However, since the mid-twentieth century, an increasing number of studies have explored right hemisphere communication skills (for instance, Myers 1979; Joanette et al. 1990; Tompkins and Lehman 1998; Lehman Blake 2003). The contribution of pragmatics to impairment of these skills has also been extensively investigated (see Cummings (2009) for a review of studies).

There is now general agreement that both hemispheres of the brain are needed for accurate and appropriate communication skills. This view implies that all parts of the brain constantly interact to accomplish any task, regardless of its linguistic contents (Belin et al. 2008). The right hemisphere and left hemisphere do present some neuroanatomical differences, however; neurons in the right hemisphere have longer dendrites and synapses are more remote from the cell body than in the left hemisphere. The cellular columns leading to the right hemisphere are closer than in the left, with more overlap (Belin et al. 2008). Some authors have linked these neuroanatomical features to cognitive processes that are specific to the right hemisphere (Jung-Beeman 2005).

Recent findings suggest that the right hemisphere shows selectivity for long-term integration of information. The left hemisphere seems to be less selective (Hickok and Poeppel 2007) and is predisposed to process fast temporal acoustic information, semantic or otherwise (Schönwiesner *et al.* 2005) in a more categorical manner (Liebenthal *et al.* 2005). These findings provide some support for the view that the right hemisphere is especially involved in the comprehension of suprasegmental information (occurring over longer time intervals), such as stress, acoustic cues, lexical-tonal information and broader unspecified semantic information. According to Jodzio *et al.* (2005), damage in cortical or subcortical structures of the right hemisphere, except for the occipital lobe, is likely to lead to communication disorders. However, there is still no clear relationship between lesion site and impairment of a given component of communication.

In the future, new insights on the role of the right hemisphere in communication and communication disorders may come from techniques such as transcranial magnetic stimulation (TMS). This technique may offer new information on language specialization in the hemispheres. For example, Devlin and Watkins (2007) described how TMS was used to show that the right inferior frontal gyrus is essential to word production in patients who exhibit the strongest rightward asymmetries.

14.3   Communication deficits in adults with RHD

Following a right hemisphere stroke, it is estimated that some form of communication disorder occurs in 50 per cent (Benton and Bryan 1996) to 90 per cent of patients (Blake *et al.* 2002; Côté *et al.* 2007). Recent studies of a large population suggest that 75 per cent of right hemisphere stroke patients in rehabilitation facilities present with communication impairments (Ferré *et al.* 2009a, 2009b). Until recently, the incidence of communication impairment had been underestimated due to poor detection and referral (Foerch *et al.* 2005). No longitudinal study has yet been undertaken of the course of communication deficits in RHD adults over time. However, a recent cross-cultural study suggests that time post-onset has only a small impact on the severity of impairments when all communication components are considered and when no language-specific treatment has been offered (Ferré *et al.* 2012). This suggests that many individuals who sustain a right hemisphere stroke will have to live with long-term effects of their stroke on their communication abilities.

RHD individuals form a very heterogeneous population. Integrity of the right hemisphere can be challenged as a result of a cerebrovascular accident (or stroke), a TBI, a tumour or any neurodegenerative disease, especially Parkinson's disease and Alzheimer's disease. This chapter will focus on RHD communication disorders following stroke, as other populations often show diffuse brain lesions and consequently have mixed deficits (Blake 2007). The range of clinical manifestations is large even among right hemisphere stroke patients, in part depending on the size of the lesion, the type of stroke (ischaemic versus haemorrhagic) or the lesion site (cortical or subcortical) (Jodzio *et al.* 2005; Lajoie *et al.* 2010). For instance, haemorrhagic stroke can affect a vast brain territory. It may thus impair cognitive aspects other than communication and increase the severity of communication impairments.

Since the adult RHD population is so heterogeneous, the existence of profiles of impairment has been investigated. Myers (1979) pioneered this line of work in the first formal clinical study of communication deficits in RHD. However, she was initially unable to identify distinctive profiles in her eight RHD participants. For many years now, Yves Joanette and his research team have explored clinical profiles within the RHD population (Joanette *et al.* 1990; Côté *et al.* 2007; Ferré *et al.* 2009a, 2012). Recently, four different clinical profiles have been identified (Ferré *et al.* 2012) when 112 adult RHD subjects from three countries (Argentina, Brazil and Canada) were assessed for communication and executive abilities.

The first subgroup of RHD patients is mainly characterized by prosodic impairment. The second subgroup displays only conversational discourse disorders. The third subgroup presents with low to moderate impairment in narrative but not in conversational discourse, semantics or emotional prosody. Interestingly, the fourth subgroup shows extensive and more severe impairments in all the above-mentioned components. In all clusters but one, RHD adults are impaired in their conversational discourse. Variables such as age, education, time post-onset, type and site of the lesion do not seem to play a significant role in determining the subgroups' communicative profiles (Ferré *et al.* 2009b). Although these results need to be replicated with a different population and using different assessment tools, they suggest the existence of a series of clinical RHD communication profiles. These results also highlight the fact that different components of communication can be selectively impaired after RHD. These communication components will be discussed in detail below.

14.3.1 Prosody

The right hemisphere appears to be involved in the simultaneous processing of facial and prosodic information (Belin *et al.* 2008). The processing of emotional prosody relies on a complex cognitive mechanism which is supported at many different levels in the brain. There is evidence that subcortical networks, especially the basal ganglia and thalamus, might be involved specifically in a motor type of prosodic deficit (Blonder *et al.* 1995; Radanovic and Scaff 2003). Studies suggest that the right inferior frontal cortex specializes in the recognition of emotional prosody. For instance, a meta-analysis of 38 lesion studies indicates bihemispheric control of prosody comprehension with relative specialization of the right hemisphere for emotional prosody (Witteman *et al.* 2011).

Right hemisphere stroke can therefore affect both the reception and production of prosody. On the receptive side, RHD adults might show difficulties using prosody to identify emotions such as happiness, anger and sadness (Pell 2006) and, to a lesser extent, the intent of utterances (e.g. question, command) (Blonder *et al.* 1995). Difficulties are more pronounced for RHD adults when the semantic content is not congruent with the prosody used (Walker *et al.* 2002). Apart from anosognosia and difficulty recognizing emotional faces, especially in the case of anterior lesions (Harciarek and Heilman 2009), mood and mood perception of RHD individuals is generally normal. Because attitudes and emotions in personal relationships are expressed by the tone of voice and not by the explicit content of the verbal message, people living with RHD individuals sometimes complain that these patients do not pay enough attention to their feelings. Such observations constitute valuable hints in the assessment phase and should be addressed during therapy.

RHD individuals can also demonstrate a lack of facial expression. Associated with monotonous speech and an atypical or slowed rate, their expressions may evoke a depressed mood or seem neutral, irrespective of their communicative intent. This dissociation between the feeling experienced and its expression might represent a burden for family members, who have difficulties understanding this apparent lack of emotion. Pell (2006) notes that RHD subjects may use fewer prosodic cues than normal individuals to communicate emphasis in their utterances. Production of linguistic content is better preserved, especially at the lexical level. However, RHD adults may have difficulties producing prosodic boundaries to denote syntactic constituents, as in 'The father said, listen to the choirboy' versus 'The father said, listen to the choir, boy' (Walker *et al.* 2004).

14.3.2 Semantics

A right hemisphere lesion can affect semantic processing at the word and sentence level. Regarding the semantic processing of words, its anatomical bases in normal individuals are very complex and are still not well understood. However, lexico-semantic abilities are frequently linked with activations in the inferior frontal and temporal lobes bilaterally. The right hemisphere demonstrates an advantage for activation of distantly related concepts (Jung-Beeman 2005) with longer activation times (Kandhadai and Federmeier 2008), but some studies indicate low involvement of the right hemisphere when complexity is controlled (Lee and Dapretto 2006). Regarding metaphorical words and expressions, there are conflicting results. Brain stimulation with TMS has shown the right hemisphere to be involved in the processing of novel metaphorical expressions (Pobric *et al.* 2008). However, it has also been suggested that, beyond the single word level, metaphoric understanding of sentences relies on left hemisphere structures rather than on the right hemisphere (Mashal *et al.* 2009).

In general, RHD adults find words that are more abstract, less frequent or less imageable more difficult to process. RHD adults' ability to process secondary meanings of words and indirect speech acts depends on the complexity of the task and the capacity to integrate all the information provided. More specifically, it is thought that the right hemisphere is crucial when attentional or voluntary access to semantic processing is needed (Kahlaoui *et al.* 2008). For example, during a dual-modality (visuo-verbal versus visual) task, RHD patients' performance is poorer than that of non-brain-damaged individuals even after controlling for visuospatial difficulties (Rinaldi *et al.* 2004).

In terms of expressive semantics, studies have demonstrated that RHD adults can show impaired retrieval of words. Word-finding difficulties remain inconspicuous in conversation as well as in picture naming. Lexical fluency tasks are characterized by a smaller number of words produced, especially when a longer period of time is allowed and the criteria used are very productive, such as large semantic categories or unconstrained naming (Beausoleil *et al.* 2003). Qualitatively, RHD adults may show a tendency during these tasks to lack a clear strategy and to activate words that are more remote and less prototypical (Beausoleil *et al.* 2003).

14.3.3 Discourse

RHD individuals typically show deficits affecting linguistic units larger than single words, such as sentences and, to a greater extent, discourse. The majority of discourse studies in RHD have focused on narrative discourse, defined as a succession of verbal propositions that require inference revisions in order to create coherence and logical structure. Conversational discourse has been more thoroughly investigated in recent years, but research is still exploratory, given that most studies offer non-ecological or artificial contexts of communication. It is important to note that conversational discourse is inseparable from pragmatic abilities, since it requires constant adjustments by both speakers.

Neuroimaging studies in healthy individuals have shown that the left hemisphere alone is not sufficient to maintain adequate discourse comprehension (Jung-Beeman 2005). More interestingly, there is a direct link between task difficulty and right hemisphere activation (St. George *et al.* 1999). Recent findings in functional imaging have shed new light on the discourse level. Stephens *et al.* (2010) reported that speakers' and listeners' brain activity revealed spatiotemporal coupling between two patterns of activation when communication was efficient. Moreover, the extent of coupling was predictive of good comprehension. The activation pattern included Wernicke's and Broca's areas. A subset of brain regions in which the activity in the listener's brain precedes the activity in the speaker's brain has also been identified. In particular, bilateral activation of the pre-cuneus, dorsolateral prefrontal cortex, orbitofrontal cortex, striatum and medial prefrontal cortex was found in higher-order language processing such as semantics and social aspects of stories. In every case, only slightly greater left hemisphere than right hemisphere activation was observed. It may be the case that RHD compromises the quality of the coupling needed to achieve adequate discourse comprehension.

Indeed, some researchers have described discrepancies between RHD individuals' performance in experimental settings and as a conver-sational partner. Their performance is generally better in natural set-tings (Vanhalle *et al.* 2000; Barnes and Armstrong 2010). On the recep-tive side, RHD individuals are described as having trouble following a conversation. Difficulty retelling a narrative story as a whole has also been observed after RHD, especially under difficult conditions (rapid speech rate, presence of inferences) and even when memory is globally preserved (Titone *et al.* 2001; Tompkins *et al.* 2001). This is because infer-ence resolution while listening to a story is compromised. In terms of expressive discourse, RHD adults produce less informative narratives than other subjects. The content of narratives may be incoherent and self-oriented (Lehman Blake 2006). The structure of the discourse can be affected, especially when subjects are asked to order picture sequences and retell a story (Chantraine *et al.* 1998; Marini *et al.* 2005). Conversation behaviours have been claimed to be affected in up to 40 per cent of indi-viduals with RHD, most often associated with damage to frontal cortical or subcortical structures, or with very mild generalized damage (Jodzio *et al.* 2005; Ferré *et al.* 2012). Turn-taking and topic maintenance can be affected (Cocks *et al.* 2007).

Single-case studies, clinical observation and family members' comments generally mention discourse problems in the RHD population. However, scientific reports demonstrating significant differences between RHD and control groups are scarce. In particular, studies set in a naturalistic con-text reinforce the heterogeneity of the RHD population. For example, in a study including semi-structured conversation, procedural and picture description, the results showed no evidence of differences between the RHD and non-brain-damaged groups in topic use (Brady *et al.* 2003, 2005), with no difference over time (Brady *et al.* 2006). However, according to Hird and Kirsner (2003), RHD individuals were less likely than controls to sig-nal topic changes and were more reliant on their conversational partners for topic initiation and maintenance. In an analysis of spontaneous con-versation during a first encounter, turn-taking and topic management in RHD adults were similar to the non-brain-damaged population (Kennedy *et al.* 1994a). Yet, in the same study, RHD individuals made fewer requests, produced fewer words per speech turn and took more speech turns than non-brain-damaged controls. Further research is needed to appropriately incorporate pragmatic as well as non-verbal aspects in discourse analysis.

In this respect, conversation analysis is of special interest (Barnes and Armstrong 2010; Weed 2011).

14.3.4 Pragmatics

As described in section 14.2, pragmatics is an area of significant impairment in RHD adults. Among the pragmatic anomalies reported in the RHD population are deficits in the processing of implicatures and speech acts, and the understanding of humour and idioms. The ability to understand indirect speech acts or idioms is generally preserved in a natural context (Vanhalle *et al.* 2000; Tompkins *et al.* 2001). However, comprehension can be affected in some individuals, when less conventional stimuli are presented (Champagne-Lavau and Joanette 2009) and more generally when task demands are high (Tompkins and Lehman 1998). When asked to explain idioms or indirect speech acts, which constitutes a further step in extralinguistic processing, RHD individuals seem less able to give clear definitions. When offered a choice, some individuals favour a literal meaning over the correct, non-literal one (Tompkins *et al.* 1992; Papagno *et al.* 2006).

Both left and right cerebral damage leads to deficits in the processing of basic speech acts and implicatures relative to non-brain-damaged controls. However, the two hemispheres seem to rely on different mechanisms. For instance, the right hemisphere depends on a distributed network of specific verbal and non-verbal processors for pragmatics, with no strong correlation with the size of the lesion (Soroker *et al.* 2005). The left hemisphere has a more general representation of pragmatics, with no regard for verbal or non-verbal modality. Considering the wide range of communication behaviours encompassed by pragmatic abilities, no particular locus in the brain has been pinpointed. However, disruption of the right temporoparietal junction is presumed to reduce participants' reliance on the interlocutor's mental state (Young *et al.* 2010). In relation to mental states, it is noteworthy that pragmatic difficulties in RHD adults have been linked to problems with theory of mind (ToM). The reader is referred to Chapter 30 in this volume for discussion of the role of ToM deficits in the pragmatic impairments of these clients.

In real settings, RHD individuals may take little account of their communicative partner and therefore exhibit deficits in governing verbal exchanges. Chantraine *et al.* (1998) used a naturalistic task in which the patient sat in front of a screen with a series of unfamiliar visual figures. The participant then had to explain to a person sitting on the other side of the screen how to order the figures so as to reproduce the same series. Although there was great heterogeneity among RHD patients, the results nonetheless showed that some individuals displayed poor eye contact, produced incoherent or inappropriate comments, committed breaches in turn-taking and insufficiently considered shared knowledge. Finally, some individuals with RHD, especially affecting the frontal cortex, also have difficulties understanding humour and reacting physically to emotions by laughing or smiling (Shammi 1999). Comorbid deficits, such as depression, reduced auditory comprehension or perceptual deficits, can exacerbate humour appreciation problems in the RHD population (Lehman Blake 2003).

14.3.5 Reading

Although little systematic research has been conducted on this topic, it is clear that reading can be significantly affected after a right hemisphere stroke. The right hemisphere is involved in processing the visual shapes of letters and words, and also in the semantic processing of words (Beeman and Chiarello 1998). RHD can lead to various types of alexia, mostly belonging to the peripheral alexia subtypes (see Leff and Behrmann (2008) for a review). Hemianopic alexia, the most common type of peripheral alexia, results from a defect affecting the ipsilateral visual field. Because information located to the right of the fixation point typically allows planning of further eye movements, RHD and hemianopia of the right visual field prevent normal reading. This can lead to inappropriate returns to the next line or to partial reading of words that are long or are composed of two semantic entities (e.g. 'counterpart', 'vice-president').

Neglect or attentional alexia refers to difficulty reading the contralesional part of the word (e.g. 'house' read as *mouse*). This disorder usually appears after right parietal damage (Costello and Warrington 1987). Patients might complain of letter crowding and consequently perform better when words are presented in isolation (Warrington *et al.* 1993). Neglect alexia is influenced by lexicality (Riddoch 1990), frequency (Riddoch 1990) and length effects (Warrington 1991). Here again, compound words can be difficult for RHD individuals (Caramazza and Hillis 1990a).

Pure alexia is defined by preserved letter-by-letter reading but trouble reading words as a whole. This visuoperceptual encoding deficit is still poorly explained, but seems to be more specific to letters than to other material, such as numbers (Ingles and Eskes 2008). Transcranial magnetic stimulation (TMS) research suggests that pure alexia can occur after RHD. Coslett and Monsul (1994) asked a patient with pure alexia to name words while they applied TMS over the posterior temporal lobe. The patient's performance improved with high-frequency and high-imageability stimuli. When TMS was applied to the left hemisphere, no impact on performance was noticed.

Text comprehension disorders without perceptual deficits can also be encountered after RHD. Functional MRI studies with non-brain-damaged adults indicate the recruitment of right middle temporal regions for integrative processes needed to achieve global coherence during discourse reading, especially when the story has no title (St. George *et al.* 1999). Xu *et al.* (2005) also demonstrated that the right hemisphere's activity is at its maximum after actual reading, during resolution of the story. There is a significant effect of context, complexity and presentation – in columns or landscape format – on performance. In an experiment including RHD subjects and left-hemisphere-damaged and non-brain-damaged participants (Marini *et al.* 2005), only the RHD group showed significantly lower levels of informativeness when asked to produce short narratives on the basis of four stories arranged in a cartoon-like fashion. Thematic selection and number of thematic and lexical units were more impaired in the RHD group than in the other two groups. When asked to arrange the pictures by themselves, RHD individuals could not organize the propositions coherently, indicating difficulty generating a mental model.

14.3.6   Writing

Spatial agraphias are frequently observed after RHD, subsequent to perceptual and executive impairment affecting writing. Visuospatial agraphia, associated with hemineglect, commonly leads to topographic disorders in which writing may be squeezed to the right of the page, with difficulty maintaining a horizontal line. Also, some important features might be omitted, such as the dot on the 'i' or the horizontal line of the 't'. Afferent agraphia is defined as a disorder affecting the voluntary programming of motor gestures. This step is subsequent to the mental representation of letters and words. Symptoms include production of an incorrect number of strokes for a given letter, or identical letters for a given word, duplications and omissions. The errors arise mainly during the writing of duplicated letter sequences (e.g. 'tt' 'll') or letters with repeated strokes ('m', 'n'). This disorder might be experienced in some cases without the presence of hemineglect or spatial dysgraphia (Cubelli *et al.* 2000).

   Like impaired oral communication, written language disorders can damage interpersonal and professional communication skills. Speech-language assessment should encompass all of the above aspects to fully address the acquired communication disorders exhibited by RHD adults. Like other communication disorders in RHD, reading and writing can be impaired in isolation or in combination with perceptual and/or cognitive deficits. In the next section, the cognitive mechanisms underlying communication disorders in RHD will be examined.

14.4   Cognitive mechanisms in RHD communication disorders

Whether RHD communication disorders exist independently of other cognitive deficits or constitute specific impairments of language components has been a matter of debate for the past 20 years. So far, only a few explanatory models have been developed to account for communication deficits following RHD. These models include (1) the coarse coding hypothesis, (2) the suppression deficit hypothesis, (3) the theory of mind deficit hypothesis, (4) the use of context hypothesis and (5) the cognitive resources hypothesis. Each hypothesis will be examined in turn.

14.4.1   Coarse coding hypothesis

Burgess and Simpson (1988) first introduced the idea that the right hemisphere has a role in word processing with the coarse coding hypothesis. According to this view, automatic lexical processing occurs in both hemispheres, but while the right hemisphere hosts a wide, unspecified semantic network necessary to resolve ambiguity, only the left hemisphere engages in controlled processing. This line of research has been pursued and extended by Beeman (see Jung-Beeman 2005), who postulates that, when processing semantic material in context, the right hemisphere is weakly activated and sustains a diffuse network of semantic associates or distant concepts (e.g. *river* is more remote from *bank* than *money* is). The left hemisphere focuses on more dominant, often concrete meanings. In this view, both hemispheres work simultaneously and complementarily, with the role of the left hemisphere being exclusively to select the appropriate meaning and deactivate the inappropriate one within a short time (Faust and Chiarello 1998). RHD would then prevent activation of the distant semantic relationships necessary, for example, to understand secondary meanings such as metaphors, indirect requests and more abstract or polysemous words (Jung-Beeman 2005; Tompkins 2008), to compute inferences at the discourse level, or to solve problems (Kounios *et al.* 2006).

Other studies that used a wider variety of stimulus types, tasks and measures have failed to find evidence consistent with the coarse coding hypothesis (see, for instance, Kandhadai and Federmeier 2008). Only one recent study partially confirmed the coarse coding deficit hypothesis (Tompkins *et al.* 2008a, 2008b). In this study, discourse inference comprehension and lexical decisions on distantly related meanings of concrete nouns (e.g. *rotten* for *apple*) at two different presentation times were assessed in a group of individuals with RHD and a normal control group. The results showed that poor discourse comprehenders with RHD were less accurate than better comprehenders with RHD at making lexical decisions on semantically distant features 1,000 ms after they heard the target nouns, but not after 175 ms. This suggests that, for all RHD individuals, activation of distantly related features is preserved in an automatic condition, whereas maintenance of peripheral semantic features of nouns over longer intervals is impaired in some individuals, thus affecting discourse inference comprehension.

14.4.2 Suppression deficit hypothesis

The suppression deficit hypothesis was put forward by Tompkins and colleagues (2000, 2001, 2008b) to explain RHD individuals' problems understanding ambiguity in narratives. Contrary to the coarse coding explanation, this hypothesis suggests that adults with RHD can generate and select revised interpretations but are slow to reject unrelated meanings. The rationale underlying the hypothesis is that suppression is a secondary, more controlled processing step, and thus is seen at longer time intervals. Tompkins and colleagues asserted that some RHD individuals show longer response times than controls when asked to choose between two competing meanings in a given context. For example, after the probe word 'concert', participants had to choose between the experimental stimulus 'they installed more fans' and the comparison stimulus 'they installed more windows'. It appears that individuals with suppression deficits were also poor narrative comprehenders, even after controlling for working memory, vocabulary and age.

Recent studies have questioned the validity of the suppression deficit explanation. For instance, Lehman Blake (2009) tested the initial hypothesis with a similar design to that used by Tompkins *et al.* (2001). The results did not replicate a deficit in maintenance of inferences in most participants. Tompkins *et al.* (2008b) eventually reconciled the suppression and coarse coding deficit hypotheses by stating that the two mechanisms are complementary and hence can appear in the same individual but operate at different stages of the comprehension process. Tompkins also suggests that a coarse coding deficit may be evident only for particularly remote semantic relations, whereas a suppression deficit can be detected with closer semantic relations.

14.4.3 Theory of mind deficit hypothesis

Theory of mind (ToM) describes the ability to attribute mental states such as beliefs and knowledge to one's own mind and to the minds of others. Based on the assumption that the right hemisphere hosts a network dedicated to the computation of mental states (Caramazza and Mahon 2006), it is to be expected that RHD adults will exhibit ToM deficits. Moreover, difficulties with ToM have been suspected to cause pragmatic production (Sabbagh 1999) and perception deficits in RHD (Winner *et al.* 1998; Champagne-Lavau and Joanette 2009). ToM is also integral to social cognition, which is a complex hierarchical organization involving different parts of the right frontal cortex, among other cerebral systems. The question of whether ToM is domain-specific and thus independent from communication skills (Siegal and Varley 2002, 2006) is still a matter of debate.

As underscored by Martin and McDonald (2003), new approaches are needed to investigate the causes of pragmatic disorders. The complexity of the task has to be considered a critical factor, since it has been suggested that, when a task is well controlled, a ToM deficit does not seem to influence comprehension (Tompkins 2008). It has also been suggested that executive disorders, when combined with ToM deficits, might be better predictors of pragmatic deficits than ToM deficits alone (Champagne-Lavau and Joanette 2009). In fact, Siegal and Varley (2002, 2006) suggested that ToM deficits might be explained by executive dysfunction. For further discussion of the role of ToM in pragmatics in RHD, the reader is referred to Cummings (2014a).

14.4.4   Use of context hypothesis

There is growing evidence that the key to understanding impaired verbal behaviours in RHD might be found in the use of context rather than in basic semantic processes. This view recalls the weak central coherence hypothesis, which has been much discussed in studies of autism (see Chapter 9, this volume). People who display weak central coherence have problems forming an integrated whole out of individual pieces of information. This type of processing is similar to RHD individuals' functioning (Martin and McDonald 2003) and might be suspected to underlie pragmatic deficits in discourse comprehension such as elaborative inferences. However, no study has so far explored the plausibility of such a link.

Contextual information is indeed needed to determine appropriate interpretations or integrate multiple cues (Lehman Blake 2010). For example, Grindrod (2003) obtained similar results to those of Tompkins' team (i.e. difficulty resolving ambiguous words), but she attributes the RHD individuals' deficit to an acquired inability to access context, resulting in an over-reliance on frequency in the activation of ambiguous word meanings. In other words, the most frequent meaning is activated by default. This is claimed to be the case in sentence (Grindrod 2003) and discourse contexts (Grindrod *et al.* 2004). Since RHD individuals were able to generate multiple predictive inferencing in some studies (Blake and Lesniewicz 2005), a difficulty resolving inferences might be related to problems integrating multiple cues (Tompkins and Lehman 1998), such as different sources of information, simultaneous modalities or conflicting pieces of information. Such deficits have been proposed mainly in studies manipulating the relationship between characters in stories, suggesting a link with the ability to interpret intention and shared knowledge of the world (Winner *et al.* 1998).

Difficulties resolving inferences could also arise from other deficits, such as perceptual deficits (visual interpretation), prosodic impairment, or facial and emotional decoding (Lehman Blake 2010). But this line of research faces important challenges since context is a multifaceted concept that communication theories still need to clarify and little is known about the influence of contextual variables on language processing.

14.4.5   Cognitive resources hypothesis

In recent years, it has been suggested that so-called 'underlying deficits' could at least partially explain communication deficits in RHD adults. This explanation is based on the observation that adults with RHD perform well on tasks requiring few or no metalinguistic or metacognitive processes (Tompkins *et al.* 2002). A number of theoretical approaches have been suggested in the literature on cognitive resources (for instance, Friedman *et al.* 1982; Schneider and Detweiler 1988). Although these approaches differ in their view of the exact relationship between language and allocation of resources, or of the cerebral localization of the attentional pool, all models agree that cognitive resources constitute a limited-capacity system. Based on this assumption, Monetta *et al.* (2006) explored the hypothesis that normal adults could show a similar pattern of deficits in processing of metaphorical words to RHD adults when asked to perform a dual-task paradigm. Their results show quite conclusively that right hemisphere integrity is necessary to perform the most demanding word-processing tasks. Nonetheless, the authors emphasize that they do not rule out the possibility that other more specific theories of language deficits in RHD individuals may complement their explanation.

Attention deficits have often been reported in the RHD literature. At first, the striking perceptual neglect frequently exhibited by adults with RHD was suspected to be a possible mechanism underlying pragmatic and discourse disorders. But as noted by Myers (2001), it is not surprising that neglect often co-occurs with more severe communication impairments in RHD patients, even though a causal link cannot be presumed from that simple logical connection. Also, sustained attention could be involved during inference and story comprehension (Saldert and Ahlsén 2007; Tompkins 2008; Tompkins *et al.* 2009).

Executive functions describe an array of cognitive skills including organization, inhibition, planning, sequencing and working memory. Executive function deficits have frequently been posited to be responsible for communication disorders in RHD individuals. Limited mental flexibility has been linked to deficits in inferences (Brownell 1986), understanding of metaphors (Monetta *et al.* 2006) and indirect speech acts (Champagne-Lavau and Joanette 2009). Difficulties interpreting texts have been reported when attentional demands are high (Blake *et al.* 2002) or when working memory resources are limited (Tompkins *et al.* 1994; Lehman and Tompkins 1998). Pragmatic abilities may be affected when cognitive dysfunction is extensive (McDonald 2000a) or when inhibition is low (Champagne-Lavau and Joanette 2009). Although these studies are suggestive of a relationship between executive dysfunction and communication deficits in RHD, a link has yet to be definitively established.

In a retrospective study, Blake *et al.* (2002) reported that no relationship could be identified between cognitive impairments and communication disorders in 123 adults with RHD, even though all but eight adults exhibited at least one cognitive or communicative impairment. Marini *et al.* (2005) demonstrated that a group of 11 RHD individuals with no cognitive disorders showed discourse deficits. Other findings confirm that, although RHD individuals with the most extensive communicative disorders also showed various executive disorders, discrepancies were observed at the individual level and no linear relationship could be defined: some individuals exhibit communication impairments without executive disorders and vice versa (Côté *et al.* 2007; Fonseca *et al.* 2010; Ferré *et al.* 2012). McDonald (2000a) also places great emphasis on interindividual variability and suggests that only severe executive disorders disrupt pragmatic communication skills.

In conclusion, the cognitive resources hypothesis has found convincing support in recent years and is the first general-domain account of comprehension disorders. The caveat is that the hypothesis lacks specificity: no account so far has demonstrated that it is exclusively able to elucidate all communication deficits exhibited by RHD adults. This seems to be true also for the two main semantic processing theories formulated by Tompkins and Beeman.

14.5   Assessment of RHD communication disorders

Contextual aspects of communication have not been successfully assessed by traditional language batteries. Nowadays, it is commonly accepted that highly complex or highly structured tasks will intensify the deficits as well as the heterogeneity observed in the performance of RHD adults with communication disorders (Marini *et al.* 2005). For this reason, clinicians should favour an assessment that combines tasks with both structured and natural settings (Lehman Blake 2010; Ferré *et al.* 2011). Such assessment tools are available in several languages. In English, three batteries have been published: the Burns Brief Inventory of Communication and Cognition (Burns 1997); the Mini Inventory of Right Brain Injury – Revised (Pimental and Knight 2000); and the Rehabilitation Institute of Chicago Evaluation of Communication Problems in Right Hemisphere Dysfunction – Revised (Halper *et al.* 1996). Likewise, the Protocole Montréal d'Évaluation de la Communication (MEC) (Joanette *et al.* 2004), originally published in French, Spanish and Portuguese, is currently being standardized in English. Most of these instruments were published over 10 years ago and have psychometric and theoretical limitations.

More assessment tasks with ecological validity should be used to examine RHD communication disorders. These tasks assess the performance of clients in natural language settings. Conversational analysis (Barnes and Armstrong 2010) and communication grids constitute appropriate tools to address functional outcome measures. Assessment tools designed for general populations exhibiting pragmatic disorders are also available. They include the ASHA Functional Communication Measure (American Speech-Language-Hearing Association 1998) and the Functional Assessment of Communication in Adults (Frattali 1998).

As Côté et al. (2004) remind us, comparison with former communication habits and skills is also strongly advised through early discussions with RHD clients and their families. Questionnaires can be administered to the patient that will provide, after comparison with family members' and therapists' opinions, an overview of the client's awareness of deficits, and an assessment of his or her request for an intervention. The Burden of Stroke Scale (Doyle et al. 2003), the Communicative Effectiveness Index (Lomas et al. 1989), the Communicative Activity Log (Pulvermüller et al. 2001) and the MEC (Joanette et al. 2004) provide such questionnaires. They are known to be more sensitive to improvements in everyday communication than standardized tests in some cases (Lomas et al. 1989). A thorough assessment will provide a good foundation upon which to determine the goals of intervention and the methods to be used.

14.6   Rehabilitation strategies

Communication intervention in the RHD population has been a focus of research for the last decade. However, evidence-based treatments are only beginning to emerge. Therapy with RHD adults may be less rewarding for therapists: anosognosia and other cognitive disorders (irritability, lack of flexibility, impulsivity) make it more difficult to interact with these patients. For that reason, defining relevant intervention goals with the patient and his or her family is a key component of a successful intervention. As Tompkins (2012) states, for the RHD population in particular, intervention aims should be decided based on daily-life needs. Thus, therapeutic experiential exercises might be advocated to help the patient become aware of the acquired deficits and to allow agreement on specific subgoals of the intervention.

Two main approaches to intervention are advanced by expert clinicians. Process-oriented treatment targets core cognitive processing (e.g. auditory attention, memory) and its impact on various communication abilities (see Tompkins (2012) for a review). Task-specific treatment aims to improve a specific function of the person's everyday life using facilitatory and compensatory techniques (Myers 1999; Blake 2007). The most obvious limitation of the former approach is the lack of agreement on the theoretical basis of communicative deficits. Intervention can only be based on a precise description of the pattern of impairment, with no consideration of its aetiology or its cognitive profile. In the case of the RHD population, a combination of the two approaches seems to be the most reasonable option. Clinicians can use treatments that have an evidence base in other populations, such as TBI. TBI patients are often associated with RHD individuals because of the similarity of their deficits, especially during discourse (Coelho *et al.* 2003). Such a choice should be made with caution, however, as we do not have conclusive evidence that those two populations are comparable.

Ferré *et al.* (2011) propose three intervention guidelines for use with RHD clients. Firstly, it is important to raise the client's awareness of his or her communication deficits post-stroke. Awareness-raising can be achieved through the use of videos in which communication deficits are interpreted by others. This is important in overcoming anosognosia in the client and in addressing maladapted behaviours in real-life communication situations. Analogies can be used to demonstrate conversational and discourse difficulties, e.g. a highway illustrating the main theme and exit roads suggesting diverging commentaries. Pictographic symbols are also valuable in providing active feedback during conversation. Secondly, it is vital to organize activities and stimuli into a hierarchy of increasing difficulty. Within this hierarchy, activities can be varied according to the type and modality of the task, the answer modality, time constraints, perceptibility and characteristics of stimuli and type of context. Thirdly, clinicians must take the client's cognitive impairments into account. For the hemineglect patient, for example, it may be necessary to control the presentation of stimuli in the visual space. On the basis of these guidelines, therapists can take advantage of the numerous strengths of the RHD population such as their formal verbal aptitudes (Tompkins 2012).

Intervention may also target specific components of communication in RHD adults. Prosodic, lexico-semantic, pragmatic and discourse treatments are described in four recent reviews (Blake 2007; Lehman Blake 2010; Ferré *et al.* 2011; Tompkins 2012). Recently, two types of prosodic treatment were explored in one study involving 14 RHD patients (León and Rodriguez 2008). The first treatment is based on a motor-deficit hypothesis of aprosodia. It requires imitation of increasingly complex motor exercises. The second treatment aims to restore knowledge of emotional and prosodic curves. Both treatments were found to be effective. Other single-case studies report on the positive impact of therapy, and the possible generalization to daily life (for a complete review, see Ferré *et al.* 2011).

Lexico-semantics can be remediated using context. For instance, Blake (2007) suggests the use of lists of multiple-meaning words (e.g. 'ball') and different contextual sentences. The words can be paired with related words or inserted into contextual sentences (e.g. 'The prince danced at the ball'; 'The prince threw the ball to his dog'). Ambiguous sentences can also be presented, followed by a disambiguating sentence (e.g. 'The prince threw a ball. He invited the entire kingdom to celebrate his engagement'). Complexity can also be managed by varying the number of cues or the relationships between speakers. For example, scenarios can be created and role-played with changing contexts and characters, possibly in group sessions. Moreover, Lundgren *et al.* (2011) have explored metaphor processing through semantic association with encouraging preliminary results.

Treatment of discourse processing has been addressed by a few researchers. Mackenzie and Brady (2008) recommend the use of several types of stimuli (e.g. a picture, a verbally related story or a video watched by both the patient and the clinician) to encourage more relevant discourse production. Verbal production can also be recorded and then discussed. To improve comprehension, the main information should be repeated and inferences resolved with the help of the therapist. Complexity can be managed at the discourse level by manipulating the length of discourse, the number of cues and distractors, and the distance between the cues. The goals in conversational discourse production may include maintaining the theme, sharing knowledge and appropriate use of turn-taking. No formal study of this aspect of treatment has been undertaken so far (Ferré *et al.* 2011).

Pragmatics has only been touched on in exploratory intervention studies (Ferré *et al.* 2011). Pragmatic aspects can be practised with barrier or procedure tasks (how to make or do something) as well as role-playing in daily situations, with the goal of continuously adapting the information given to the interlocutor. Indirect speech acts can be included in a natural activity, such as reading the newspaper, with indirect commentaries inserted (e.g. 'I can't hear you well', 'We could read another one'). Preliminary studies have also addressed the remediation of ToM through the use of thought bubbles. The patient is asked to determine the thoughts of characters and to predict their behaviours in various situations (Lundgren *et al.* 2007).

14.7   Summary

In this chapter, profiles of communication impairment in individuals with RHD have been examined. Adults with RHD often show impairment in one or more components of communication. These components include, most notably, prosody, lexico-semantics, discourse, pragmatics, reading and writing. It has been emphasized that RHD patients present with a heterogeneous profile of communication impairments, making theoretical explanation of these impairments difficult. Moreover, there is no clear consensus on the role of cognitive impairments in executive functions and ToM in communication deficits after RHD. A range of assessments for use with RHD adults was described. It was argued that there is a need for assessment tasks and batteries to display greater ecological validity. Also, as our understanding of the interaction between ageing, communication and cognitive domains such as executive functions increases, this should lead to the development of more sensitive assessment tools. Finally, a number of general principles that guide rehabilitation in the RHD population were examined, along with treatments that target specific components of communication.

15

Dementia and communication

Jamie Reilly and Jinyi Hung

15.1   Introduction

Human longevity is rapidly increasing across much of the industrialized world, and this changing mosaic of ageing has created unprecedented challenges for healthcare systems. We are now in the midst of a public health crisis with respect to the management of Alzheimer's disease and associated forms of dementia. Moreover, all demographic indicators predict an exponential growth of dementia over the next three decades as a large proportion of the world's population approaches late middle age (Hebert *et al.* 2001, 2004; Alzheimer's Association 2010). In recognition of this looming epidemic, legislators have recently implemented a number of initiatives targeting dementia prevention and management. Much of this effort has focused on promoting advances in protein structure, genetics and molecular biomarkers. Recent advances in each of these domains hold great promise for identifying new drug targets and/or vaccines. Nonetheless, the state of cognitive rehabilitation for this rapidly growing segment of our society remains fundamentally limited. This is especially true with respect to disorders of speech, language and human communication.

It is now clear that we must find ways to promote functional independence and forgo institutionalized care (e.g. skilled nursing) for the many millions of adults who will soon be directly impacted by dementia. Communicative disorders are among the most functionally debilitating symptoms incurred in many different forms of dementia. Thus, the development of effective speech-language interventions is of paramount

This work was funded in part by a grant from the US Public Health Service, National Institute on Deafness and Other Communicative Disorders (K23 DC010197). We thank the following members of the University of Florida Cognition and Language Laboratory for their assistance with this work: Jamie Fisher, Kali Woodruff Carr, Sachit Mishra, Rachel Rosalsky, John Peterson, Jeri Parker, Patricia Hessen, Natalie O'Steen and Justine Allen.

importance. It is paradoxical that formal training in dementia is not yet mandated within the graduate clinical curricula of many national speech-language therapy organizations (American Speech-Language-Hearing Association 2008). Moreover, many speech-language clinicians continue to espouse outmoded ideas about the potential for learning in the dementias (e.g. 'What's the use when they are getting worse anyway?'). A number of recent studies have questioned this deeply ingrained view by showing that certain techniques can indeed promote functional communication for patients with various forms of dementia, especially when paired with common drug adjuvants (Grandmaison and Simard 2003; Boyle 2004; Fridriksson *et al.* 2005; Gonzalez-Rothi *et al.* 2009).

We have learned a number of important lessons from studies of language learning in the dementias to date. Perhaps most importantly, treatment effectiveness is moderated by disease aetiology. Techniques that 'work' for promoting communication in one dementia variant (e.g. Alzheimer's disease) are likely to have very limited effectiveness for other dementia variants (e.g. frontal variant frontotemporal dementia). Therefore, variability across the dementia subtypes demands an aetiology-specific treatment approach. The dominant rate-limiting factor undermining treatment development is a lack of understanding about the unique cognitive profiles of the dementia subtypes and their relation to anatomical distributions of cortical atrophy. Here we address this issue by providing an overview of the cognitive communication profiles of several of the most common forms of dementia. These forms are Alzheimer's disease, frontotemporal dementia, Lewy body spectrum disease and vascular dementia. We issue a caveat that this review is necessarily highly selective with respect to both its breadth and depth. Space restrictions preclude coverage of all forms of dementia (e.g. HIV-AIDS dementia complex, Wernicke–Korsakoff dementia, dementia pugilistica) and all cognitive domains within the populations we do address. Thus, we focus specifically on speech, language and the essential cognitive processes that support human communication.

15.2   What is dementia?

Ageing refers to a constellation of physical, psychological and social changes in a person over time. Structurally, the ageing brain decreases in volume significantly across the lifespan (Drag and Bieliauskas 2010). However, these changes in structure are often compensated for by functional reorganization (Cabeza 2002). Healthy cognitive ageing is associated with preserved social and occupational functioning (Rowe and Kahn 1997), but for many people this trajectory is compromised. The transitional state between healthy normal ageing and frank dementia is known as mild cognitive impairment (MCI). Accordingly, a person with MCI is often subjectively classified as not normal but not demented.

MCI can persist in a chronic, relatively stable form for many years. However, a proportion of MCI cases show evidence for progressive deterioration. These patients experience a shift from MCI to dementia. Current diagnostic criteria for MCI include (1) objective or subjective concern regarding a change in cognition, (2) impairment in one or more cognitive domains, (3) preservation of independence in functional abilities and (4) no evidence of dementia. The incorporation of biomarkers is also suggested, especially in the diagnosis of MCI due to Alzheimer's disease (Albert *et al.* 2011). Clinical diagnostic criteria delineate three distinct subtypes of MCI (i.e. amnestic, multiple cognitive domains and single non-memory domain) based on the dominant presenting cognitive impairment. Amnestic MCI presents as a dominant impairment of episodic memory (Petersen *et al.* 2001). Postmortem histological studies have shown that this particular MCI subtype has the highest likelihood of evolving to Alzheimer's disease (Jicha *et al.* 2006). MCI can also manifest as a more heterogeneous condition involving the compromise of other cognitive functions such as attention, language and visuospatial functioning (Petersen 2004; Winblad *et al.* 2004; Petersen and Negash 2008). Language may appear to be relatively unaffected in the amnestic variant of MCI. However, subtle impairments are often detectable when the complexity of the linguistic demands is increased (Fleming and Harris 2008).

MCI will often gradually evolve to a frank form of dementia over time. From a probabilistic standpoint, MCI is most likely to evolve to Alzheimer's disease. However, probabilistic reasoning and a chronic lack of specificity has led to the common misconception that dementia and Alzheimer's disease (AD) are synonymous. AD is indeed the most common form of dementia, accounting for approximately 60 per cent of all new cases (Alzheimer's Association 2010). However, there exist a number of non-Alzheimer's dementia variants. These variants are classified by means of their dominant protein aggregations (e.g. Lewy body dementia involves synucleinopathy, while frontotemporal dementia involves tauopathy), or metabolic and systemic causes (e.g. vascular dementia, Wernicke–Korsakoff dementia, HIV-AIDS dementia complex). Each of these dementia subtypes manifests in a unique cognitive profile. However, there are also many overlapping phenotypic similarities that complicate differential diagnosis. Thus, 'dementia' is a non-specific umbrella term describing a set of broad features which the many disparate subtypes share in common.

Two dominant systems of criteria exist for establishing a diagnosis of dementia: the International Classification of Diseases (ICD-10; World Health Organization 1993) and the Diagnostic and Statistical Manual of Mental Disorders (DSM-IV-TR; American Psychiatric Association 2000). According to the ICD-10, a diagnosis of dementia is appropriate in the context of two or more cognitive declines (e.g. memory, judgement, thinking, learning, orientation, language, comprehension or calculation) that compromise one's daily functioning significantly. The DSM-IV-TR suggests dementia is a gradual and progressive memory disturbance with one or more of the following: aphasia, apraxia, agnosia and dysexecutive disorder without the occurrence of other reversible causes. As the reader may surmise, these criteria are necessarily broad. There is no single objective measure, either psychometric or physiological, that can definitively confirm the presence of dementia. Instead, diagnosis is a probabilistic process whereby clinicians must weigh evidence from a variety of sources, including behavioural testing, neuroimaging, family history and other biomarkers (e.g. cerebrospinal fluid proteins) (Dubois *et al.* 2007; Ewers *et al.* 2011; Holtzman *et al.* 2011).

Speech and language characteristics provide powerful diagnostic markers that can aid in detecting the presence of dementia (i.e. sensitivity). Consideration of unique speech and language impairments can also aid in the more challenging task of discriminating between dementia subtypes (i.e. specificity). We now turn to discussion of the profiles of communicative impairment associated with a range of dementia subtypes.

15.3   Alzheimer's disease

Our most common association of AD is that of a disorder of impaired episodic memory (i.e. recall of specific events). Episodic memory impairment is one of the dominant cognitive symptoms during the mild to moderate stages of AD prior to the onset of personality changes and a constellation of other perceptual and linguistic problems. AD has historically been classified as an amyloidopathy in that its phenotype has been linked to depositions of the protein beta-amyloid. Although recent work has implicated a range of other proteins in AD (e.g. tau), much of our understanding about the nosology and progression of the disease has been informed by studies that track the progression of amyloid plaque and tangle pathology.

AD tends to follow a canonical progression with respect to the distribution and sequence of brain regions commonly impacted (McKhann *et al.* 1984, 2011). This progression is reflected in the Braak staging system (Braak and Braak 1997; Braak *et al.* 2006). This system posits the presence of a series of discrete stages of AD characterized by a period of clinically silent degradation in structural connectivity between the medial temporal lobe and the cortex proper (i.e. transentorhinal stage), followed by degradation of the hippocampal formation and later by diffuse plaque and tangle pathology in many other cortical and subcortical regions (Holtzman *et al.* 2011).

The preclinical or prodromal stage of AD may extend for many years prior to the onset of frank dementia symptoms (Morris 2005; Sperling *et al.* 2011). One of the challenges for medical management of AD is to establish precise differential diagnosis and begin treatment (both pharmacological and cognitive) prior to the onset of debilitating cognitive impairments (Parasuraman and Haxby 1993; Perry and Hodges 1999; Belleville *et al.* 2007). The most recent clinical criteria for AD diagnosis reflect a range of signs and symptoms, and further redefine the classification of the disease (i.e. probable AD dementia, possible AD dementia, and probable or possible AD dementia with evidence of the AD pathophysiological process). They also emphasize the incorporation of fluid or imaging biomarkers of the underlying disease state (McKhann *et al.* 2011).

Cognitive and linguistic impairments in AD are linked to a combination of diffuse synaptic loss and deposition of neuritic plaques within specific regions of the cortex (e.g. hippocampus, visual association cortex). In addition to gross structural grey and white matter loss, AD is also associated with a depletion of acetylcholine, a neurotransmitter that is essential for learning and memory encoding (Holtzman *et al.* 2011). Impairment in recent episodic memory, linked primarily to disconnection and atrophy of the medial temporal lobe, is one of the most common symptoms of AD. As hippocampal damage worsens, patients experience worsening anterograde amnesia, a condition characterized by a failure to effectively encode new memories (Nestor *et al.* 2006). During the early stages of AD patients tend to show a temporal gradient in forgetting that is characterized by worse recall for recent, relative to remote, episodic memories. For example, a patient might better recall details of her wedding day 50 years ago than the physician she met 15 minutes ago. Patients during later-stage AD typically show deficits in other forms of memory, including working memory and semantic memory. In addition to these associated amnestic impairments, AD also compromises a range of other cognitive domains related to language perception, executive function, attention, working memory and visuospatial abilities (Lambon Ralph *et al.* 2003; Nestor *et al.* 2004; Stopford *et al.* 2007). One useful diagnostic shortcut for detecting the presence of AD is that clinicians should look for the three As: Aphasia, Agnosia and Apraxia (but see Kramer and Duffy 1996).

Anomia (i.e. impaired naming) is a core feature of AD. Patients tend to show deficits in naming proper nouns and have also shown category-specific naming impairments for biological natural kinds relative to manufactured artefacts (Garrard *et al.* 1998; Capitani *et al.* 2003). In addition, patients tend to show a pattern of graceful degradation that is apparent in errors such as the overuse of superordinate category labels (e.g. animal, thing) in place of more descriptive basic or subordinate terms (e.g. dog, spaniel) (Martin and Fedio 1983; Hodges *et al.* 1992a).

The aetiology of the naming impairment in AD remains controversial. Some have attributed it to bottom-up degradation of a hierarchically organized semantic memory system (e.g. spaniels → dogs → mammals → animals → things). This claim receives converging support from impairments on other semantic tasks in AD, such as word-picture matching, priming and semantic fluency naming (Hodges *et al.* 1992a;

Rosser and Hodges 1994; Cerhan *et al.* 2002; Henry and Crawford 2004; Henry *et al.* 2004; Rogers and Friedman 2008). Another strong source of evidence in support of a semantic degradation account of anomia in AD is that patients tend to show strong correlations between 'naming and knowing' (Hodges *et al.* 1996). In a classic study, Hodges *et al.* (1996) demonstrated that the quality of concept definitions was worse for items patients could not name relative to successfully named targets. As counterpoint, others have argued that anomia in AD has a basis in impaired linguistic and/or perceptual access to semantic knowledge (Nebes *et al.* 1984, 1989). There exist complex and compelling arguments for both points of view. However, it is undeniable that deficits in visual perception (e.g. agnosia) and lexical retrieval moderate naming ability in AD and that these factors must be considered when planning treatments (Harnish *et al.* 2010).

As a general heuristic, output phonology, morphology and syntactic processing tend to remain intact relative to the massive loss of semantic memory and naming ability in AD. There are, however, noteworthy exceptions. Croot *et al.* (2000) reported non-fluent, agrammatic production in a series of AD patients with atypical perisylvian atrophy (see also Biassou *et al.* 1995). Barring exceptions such as these, people with AD tend to produce narrative discourse that is morphosyntactically well-formed but impoverished in terms of semantic content (for a review, see Almor *et al.* 1999). Patients tend to revert to over-learned phrases and idioms (e.g. 'You know, it's that thing') as ineffective means of circumlocution. Reductions in mean length of utterance (MLU) syntactic complexity and idea density are also common macro-scale features of discourse in AD (Almor *et al.* 1999). In summary, narrative discourse in AD is in many ways consistent with the lyric of the Talking Heads song *Psycho Killer*, 'You're talking a lot, but you're not saying anything' (Byrne *et al.* 1977).

Sentence comprehension is often compromised in AD, and there is much debate as to the cause(s) of this impairment. Causes include impairments in processing the meaning of single words and in comprehending the syntactic rules that govern word order. Patients with AD do show worse impairment as syntactic complexity increases. However, this relationship is non-linear and open to alternative explanations (Kempler *et al.* 1998). Sentence comprehension difficulties in AD may also be attributable to limitations in working memory. Although this issue remains controversial, the evidence to date seems to favour the hypothesis that sentence comprehension problems are related to impaired working memory rather than to a domain-specific syntactic impairment.

In addition to a range of frank impairments in single word, sentence and narrative comprehension, AD also compromises many higher-level linguistic processes linked to figurative language. Patients with AD commonly experience impairments in comprehension of non-literal language such as metaphor, idiomatic expressions, proverbs, irony, humour and sarcasm (see Rapp and Wild (2011) for a review). These difficulties manifest as overly concrete and rigid interpretation of word meaning and consequent failure to grasp nuanced messages (see also Cummings 2007a). However, further investigation is still needed to expand current findings.

15.4   Frontotemporal dementia

Frontotemporal dementia (FTD) is a non-Alzheimer's dementia with an onset approximately a decade earlier than that of AD. The onset of FTD follows a roughly normal distribution with a mean early in the sixth decade of life and tapering incidence in older age. This Gaussian/normal distribution of onset distinguishes FTD from other forms of dementia such as AD that show a linear increase in risk as a function of advancing age (Ratnavalli *et al.* 2002). Neurodegeneration in FTD has been linked to proteins such as tau, ubiquitin and TDP-43 (Bian and Grossman 2007; Seelaar *et al.* 2008). Tau abnormalities, in particular, have been linked to neuronal microtubule collapse and subsequent cell death (but see Avila *et al.* 2002). Accordingly, FTD has been classified within a family of dementias known as tauopathies which also include motor neuron disease, cortical basal degeneration and progressive supranuclear palsy (Kertesz *et al.* 2000; McKhann *et al.* 2001; Boxer and Miller 2005).

FTD is a histological designation that subsumes a variety of behavioural subtypes (i.e. phenotypes). These behavioural presentations are linked to the primary distribution of atrophy incurred during the disease course. For unknown reasons, cortical atrophy remains relatively circumscribed within specific regions of the cortex during early stages of FTD. Patients commonly show hemispheric asymmetry in disease progression as well as unique patterns of lobar degeneration within each hemisphere. For example, one variant of FTD (i.e. semantic dementia) tends to produce atrophy most evident in the left lateral inferior temporal lobe (Snowden *et al.* 1989). We focus our discussion to follow on three of the most commonly recognized FTD syndromes: progressive non-fluent aphasia, semantic dementia and frontal variant FTD (Gorno-Tempini *et al.* 2011). A fourth syndrome, logopenic progressive aphasia, has also been identified. However, the most recent postmortem clinicopathological correlation studies have shown that this subtype may in fact more commonly represent an atypical form of AD (Mesulam *et al.* 2008).

15.4.1   Progressive non-fluent aphasia

Progressive non-fluent aphasia (PNFA) profoundly compromises a person's ability to produce fluent and grammatically well-formed speech (Gorno-Tempini *et al.* 2004). The most recent core diagnosis of PNFA includes agrammatism and effortful speech. Patients with PNFA invariably show slowed speech output and articulatory struggles along with the presence of restarts, repeated syllables and phonemic paraphasias (Ash *et al.* 2004, 2010). Additional supportive features include difficulty comprehending syntactically complex sentences, spared single word comprehension and spared object knowledge (Gorno-Tempini *et al.* 2011). PNFA often evolves to complete mutism (Gorno-Tempini *et al.* 2004; Gunawardena *et al.* 2010; Rabinovici and Miller 2010).

The aetiology of the output impairment associated with PNFA remains controversial. Some have noted the presence of apraxia of speech in PNFA, which compromises motor aspects of production (Gorno-Tempini *et al.* 2004; Ogar *et al.* 2007). Others have argued that many of the deficits in production in PNFA share higher-level linguistic bases such as deficient phonological encoding, agrammatism and gross executive function limitations (Libon *et al.* 2007; Knibb *et al.* 2009; Ash *et al.* 2010; Gunawardena *et al.* 2010). Supporting this latter view, there is a tendency for patients with PNFA to produce reduced frequency of grammatically complex sentences (Ash *et al.* 2010; Gunawardena *et al.* 2010).

In our own work we have found that patients with PNFA tend to experience severe anomia, and these effects may be worse for manufactured artefacts than for animals or other biologically natural kinds (Reilly *et al.* 2011a). Others have reported that the naming impairment in PNFA is worse for verbs relative to nouns (Hillis *et al.* 2004b). In addition to category effects in naming, we also found evidence of verbal and non-verbal semantic impairment in PNFA, suggesting that difficulties incurred by these patients transcend modality-specific impairments of language (but see Kempler and Goral 2008).

Patients with PNFA typically have difficulties in comprehending syntactically complex sentences in the context of relatively intact single word recognition (Rabinovici and Miller 2010). A definitive basis for this impairment is elusive. Some have argued the comprehension impairment is indeed related to a grammatical/syntactic deficit (Ash *et al.* 2010; Gunawardena *et al.* 2010). Others have argued that sentence comprehension deficits are more likely attributable to impaired working memory (Grossman and Moore 2005; Peelle *et al.* 2008).

15.4.2 Semantic dementia

Semantic dementia (SD) is a variant of FTD associated with progressive bilateral degeneration of the temporal lobes (Hodges 2001; Grossman *et al.* 2002; Rabinovici and Miller 2010). During the early stages of SD, cortical atrophy is often asymmetric (left hemisphere damage is greater than right) and most prominent in anterolateral aspects of the temporal lobe (Peelle and Grossman 2008; Rabinovici and Miller 2010). SD is distinct from AD in that the pathology typically spares medial temporal

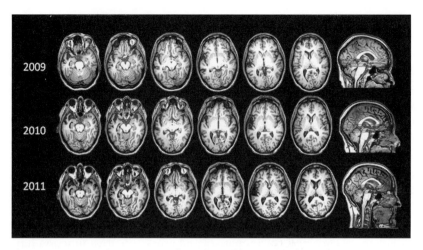

Figure 15.1 Successive MRI scans of a patient with semantic dementia.

structures that support episodic memory encoding and new anterograde learning. Figure 15.1 represents the distribution of atrophy in a patient with SD scanned successively over a 3-year period.

The most pronounced feature of SD is its associated degradation of semantic knowledge. Patients often display a homogeneous loss of semantic knowledge that transcends representational modality (e.g. written or spoken text, pictures, environmental sounds) and mode of input or output (e.g. comprehension versus expression) (Bozeat *et al.* 2000). During the progression of the disease, patients with SD show relative preservation of anterograde memory for recent day-to-day events as well as preserved sensory processing (these traits are commonly disturbed in AD). It is not uncommon for patients to successfully discriminate pictures or sounds (same/different) or complete other perceptual matching tasks with relative ease. Output phonology, syntax and speech articulation are also relatively preserved during much of the course of SD (Jefferies *et al.* 2006). Preserved single word repetition and fluent speech are core features of the disease (Neary *et al.* 1998). This range of apparently preserved abilities is in stark contrast to the profound loss of conceptual knowledge that underlies word and object meaning.

Warrington (1975) famously described the selective impairment of semantic memory we now regard as semantic dementia (Snowden *et al.* 1989). In the decades following Warrington's seminal article, SD has provided a powerful, yet highly controversial, lesion model for parsing the organization of human conceptual knowledge. SD has also informed cognitive science about the interplay between disturbed semantic knowledge and its effect on other cognitive processes (e.g. word recognition, colour perception) (Reilly *et al.* 2007a, 2007b, 2011b; Reilly and Peelle 2008).

Patients with SD usually produce fluent but empty speech with frequent semantic paraphasias (Grossman and Ash 2004; Kempler and Goral
2008; Kertesz *et al.* 2010). Spontaneous speech is often characterized by
profound anomia with better performance on typical, familiar and high-
frequency words (Patterson 2007; Meteyard and Patterson 2009). Patients
also commonly revert to deictic phrases, idioms and non-specific names
(e.g. things, stuff) (Grossman and Ash 2004). Importantly, there appears
to be a strong correlation in SD between 'naming and knowing' with
patients unable to produce words for which their conceptual knowledge
is disrupted. Patients tend to show minimal benefits from overt semantic cueing and demonstrate minimal priming effects (Reilly *et al.* 2005).
The naming impairment in SD is one manifestation of a more pervasive
loss of object knowledge that is also evident in non-verbal domains (e.g.
demonstrating object function and use, categorizing pictures of objects)
(Bozeat *et al.* 2000; Adlam *et al.* 2006).

SD is associated with severe impairments in single word comprehension, paralleling the impairment in naming (Reilly *et al.* 2007a; Gorno-
Tempini *et al.* 2011). Comprehension deficits are moderated by factors
such as disease severity, concept familiarity, word frequency and item
typicality (Adlam *et al.* 2006). Sentence processing impairments are also
common in SD, and these deficits are most often attributed to a semantic
locus relative to other cognitive processes (e.g. agrammatism or working
memory deficiencies) (Gorno-Tempini *et al.* 2004; Peelle *et al.* 2008).

One of the most ubiquitous and striking symptoms of SD is its associated pattern of reading impairment, known as surface dyslexia (Woollams
et al. 2007). Surface dyslexia is remarkable for the preserved ability to read
aloud words with transparent orthography in the context of impaired
reading of orthographically irregular words (e.g. sew, yacht). A similar
error pattern of orthographic regularization known as surface dysgraphia
is also evident in written production (Grossman and Ash 2004; Wilson
et al. 2009; Kertesz *et al.* 2010).

Dual route models of reading provide a compelling account of surface
dyslexia in SD. That is, patients revert to preserved phonological knowledge to rigidly convert graphemes to phonemes. Healthy adults supplement this phonological process using word meaning and whole-word
recognition. This putative semantic route is, however, unavailable in the
context of SD (Woollams *et al.* 2007). Further evidence for this pattern was
derived from Japanese patients with SD who were asked to read aloud
words in the two orthographic systems of Japanese, i.e. Kana and Kanji.
Kana is transparent in the relationship between orthography and phonology whereas the pronunciation of Kanji characters is context driven.
Japanese patients with SD consistently performed well when reading
Kana. However, they were selectively impaired in reading Kanji with atypical correspondences (Fushimi *et al.* 2009).

15.4.3   Frontal variant FTD/behavioural variant FTD

The frontal/behavioural variant of frontotemporal dementia (fvFTD) is not typically associated with the profound communicative impairments that are evident in SD and PNFA. The anterior cingulate, insular and orbit-ofrontal cortex are most affected in fvFTD (Rosen *et al.* 2002; Seeley *et al.* 2008). fvFTD is also sometimes referred to as social dysexecutive disorder due to its range of progressive deficits in executive functioning, inhibitory control and emotional regulation. A recent proposal by the International Behavioral Variant FTD Criteria Consortium (Rascovsky *et al.* 2011) introduces a hierarchy of diagnostic certainty including possible, probable and definite fvFTD. The diagnosis of possible fvFTD requires three random presentations of six behavioural/cognitive symptoms: disinhibition, apathy/inertia, loss of sympathy/empathy, perseverative/compulsive behaviour hyperorality/dietary changes and dysexecutive neuropsychological profile. The diagnosis of probable fvFTD further includes evidence of daily functional decline and pathological support from imaging results. fvFTD with definite pathology is only to be applied to those patients who show clinical syndromes with clear histopathological evidence or a known pathogenic mutation.

Unlike previous consensus criteria, this revised proposal emphasizes the distinctive behaviours of early stages of fvFTD and attempts to increase the sensitivity of diagnosis. Its reliability and specificity await further investigation (Rascovsky *et al.* 2007, 2011). Previous diagnostic criteria also list speech and language as supportive features of fvFTD including altered speech output, stereotypy of speech, echolalia, perseveration and mutism (Neary *et al.* 1998). These impairments are often apparent at the level of discourse and connected speech (Libon *et al.* 2007).

Patients with fvFTD are commonly impaired in measures of semantic and phonemic verbal fluency (e.g. 'Tell me as many animals as you can in one minute') (Libon *et al.* 2009). Many of these limitations have been attributed to deficits in switching and task vigilance that are classically subsumed under the domain of executive functions (Libon *et al.* 2009). Patients with fvFTD do not commonly experience the severity of anomia that is present at the single word level in PNFA or SD. However, deficits in expressive language are indeed present at the discourse level. Ash *et al.* (2006) examined aspects of discourse such as narrative coherence and maintenance of theme as patients with fvFTD narrated the story depicted in the wordless children's book *Frog, where are you?* (Mayer 1969). These authors found that fvFTD patients were able to find words to describe a picture, but that their narratives lacked connections to bind information into a coherent story, reflecting difficulty organizing their narratives (Ash *et al.* 2006).

Patients with fvFTD display relatively preserved comprehension of single words but show deficits for tasks that load on executive and working memory demands. This includes manipulations of syntactic and narrative complexity (Peelle and Grossman 2008). Patients have also been reported to have difficulties in understanding non-literal language critical for the appreciation of humour, irony and metaphor (Kosmidis *et al.* 2008; Kipps *et al.* 2009). As a result, fvFTD language comprehension often assumes a degree of rigid literality.

15.5   Vascular dementia

Vascular dementia (VaD) is a common form of dementia caused by a variety of cerebrovascular pathologies, including multiple strokes and small vessel ischaemic disease. The phenotype of VaD is moderated by a number of factors including nature of the arterial disease (i.e. small or large), type of stroke (i.e. ischaemic or haemorrhagic), site of lesion (e.g. cortical or subcortical), number of infarcts and other comorbid health factors (Román *et al.* 1993; Jellinger 2008). There exist no less than four distinct sets of diagnostic criteria for VaD in active use today. These include the State of California Alzheimer's Disease Diagnostic and Treatment Centers (Chui *et al.* 1992), the National Institute of Neurological Disorders and Stroke-Association Internationale pour la Recherche et l'Enseignement en Neurosciences (Román *et al.* 1993), the Diagnostic and Statistical Manual of Mental Disorders (American Psychiatric Association 1994) and the International Classification of Diseases (World Health Organization 1993). The variability of these diagnostic criteria reflects the heterogeneous nature of the disease.

Diagnostic specificity for VaD is complicated by high comorbidity with other neurological disorders such as Alzheimer's disease and traumatic brain injury (O'Brien *et al.* 2003; Nagata *et al.* 2007; Benisty *et al.* 2008). A number of studies have recently contrasted language and amnestic impairment in VaD and AD (Lafosse *et al.* 1997; Almkvist *et al.* 1999; Graham *et al.* 2004). Although some of these studies reveal differences between VaD and AD, there is not universal agreement as to the discriminative neuropsychological features of these disorders. The differential diagnosis of VaD is further complicated by the fact that there is no definitive threshold for dementia in the presence of multiple strokes. These challenges in diagnostic specificity are illustrated by a simple hypothetical example of two patients with chronic vascular disease. Patient A has sustained multiple ischaemic injuries to the left inferior frontal cortex resulting in non-fluent aphasia. Patient B has sustained diffuse white matter damage resulting from small vessel ischaemic disease. Patients A and B both satisfy many criteria for VaD, and yet they are likely to present with two very different behavioural profiles.

Despite inherent variability introduced by the diffuse nature of the human cerebral vasculature, there are some common features of VaD. Vascular damage tends to prominently affect the white matter, resulting in a condition known as leukoaraiosis (van Gijn 1998). White matter damage (as incurred in HIV-AIDS dementia) is associated with a specific range of cognitive deficits including slowed information processing, impaired working memory, poor sequencing, lack of inhibitory control, and a number of related impairments in executive functioning and attention (Starkstein *et al.* 1996; Mendez *et al.* 1997; Yuspeh *et al.* 2002; McGuinness *et al.* 2010). These deficits are commonly seen in VaD and many have been hypothesized to provide a substrate for associated impairments in language comprehension and expression.

One common finding regarding expressive language in VaD is that patients tend to show reduced verbal fluency relative to other dementia control groups (Starkstein *et al.* 1996; Lafosse *et al.* 1997). It is suggested that executive dysfunction, especially mental processing speed, contributes to decrements in fluency in VaD (Lafosse *et al.* 1997; Jones *et al.* 2006). For non-aphasic patients with VaD, naming is not typically as impaired as that of AD (Lukatela *et al.* 1998; Graham *et al.* 2004). Very few studies have investigated the integrity of receptive language in VaD (Desmond *et al.* 1999; Vuorinen *et al.* 2000; Desmond 2004). While comprehension impairments have indeed been reported, the basis of these deficits remains unclear and potentially multifactorial.

15.6   Synucleinopathy spectrum disorders

Parkinson's disease dementia (PDD) and Lewy body dementia (LBD) represent a spectrum of dementias known as synucleinopathies. In both conditions, large aggregations of destructive alpha-synucleinated proteins known as Lewy bodies accumulate in specific brain regions. When Lewy bodies destroy more than about 80 per cent of the dopaminergic cells within the substantia nigra, patients tend to show the overt motor symptoms of classical Parkinson's disease (Louis and Frucht 2007). In contrast, Lewy body deposition in the cortex produces a different syndrome known as LBD. In reality, these spectrum disorders are not always easily disentangled due to the fact that Lewy body damage tends to affect both the substantia nigra and the cortex in both conditions. For this reason, neurologists commonly employ what is known as the 'one year rule' when establishing a differential diagnosis of PDD or LBD. A diagnosis of PDD is appropriate when cognitive symptoms emerge within the context of a movement disorder lasting more than one year. By contrast, a diagnosis of LBD applies when movement disorders emerge in the context of a pre-existing dementia. When we describe the nature of language and communication in PDD and LBD below, we operate under an assumption that these syndromes have similar histopathological courses and many shared traits (McKeith 2000). It should be noted, however, that the lumping of PDD and LBD as spectrum disorders is not a universally accepted practice (Revuelta and Lippa 2009). We will describe these clinical populations as unique entities while also acknowledging a similarity bias.

15.6.1 Parkinson's disease dementia

Parkinson's disease (PD) is a chronic neurodegenerative condition that has historically been regarded as a movement disorder. Patients with PD commonly present with cardinal motor symptoms such as bradykinesia, tremor, rigidity and postural instability (Román *et al.* 2004; Bartels and Leenders 2009). However, a growing body of research implicates a range of cognitive impairments that are associated with non-demented PD, suggesting that PD cannot be classified exclusively as a movement disorder (Lewis *et al.* 2005; Williams-Gray *et al.* 2007; Mamikonyan *et al.* 2009; Aarsland *et al.* 2010; Kehagia *et al.* 2010). For example, one pooled analysis showed that 26 per cent of 1,346 patients with PD satisfied diagnostic criteria for mild cognitive impairment (MCI) due to impairments in a variety of domains, including delayed recall, attention/executive functioning, language and visuospatial functioning (Aarsland *et al.* 2010). The incidence of MCI in the larger population of patients with PD remains unclear.

Another factor that remains unclear is the rate/risk of evolution to dementia in PD. Some studies have reported that up to 80 per cent of patients satisfy criteria for dementia one decade after motor symptom onset. Others have reported more conservative estimates of 48 per cent (Emre *et al.* 2007). In either case, when dementia emerges within the context of a patient with non-demented PD, that patient may be classified as having PDD. In addition to a prior diagnosis of PD, diagnostic criteria for PDD require the gradual decline in more than one cognitive domain (i.e. attention, executive functions, visuospatial functions, memory or language) and the presence of at least one behavioural symptom (i.e. apathy, personality/mood changes, hallucinations, delusions or excessive daytime sleepiness) (Emre *et al.* 2007).

The communicative profiles of AD and FTD have been investigated extensively to date. However, the same cannot be said of PDD. A few studies have contrasted PDD with AD. The most common finding is that patients with PDD tend to fare slightly better in terms of the severity of their expressive language impairments (Emre 2003; Emre *et al.* 2007). Most studies link impairments in expressive language in PDD to processing limitations, some of which are compounded by concurrent motor impairments (e.g. working memory compounded by slowed speech output). Impaired verbal fluency is common in PDD and is often worse than that of AD (Henry and Crawford 2004). PDD is also associated with naming impairment, with some studies reporting worse performance for verbs and actions relative to nouns and objects (Cotelli *et al.* 2007; Murray 2008; Rodriguez-Ferreiro *et al.* 2009).

PDD presents a unique set of challenges in terms of comprehension impairment. Sentence comprehension deficits are common in PDD, especially for utterances with non-canonical syntactic structures (Grossman *et al.* 1991; Goetz *et al.* 2008). The nature of this impairment is controversial and follows similar lines to that seen in aphasia and also AD (i.e. 'Is the problem grammatical or attributable to a more general processing impairment?'). Some have argued for the presence of a grammatical impairment based on selective deficits in understanding specific syntactic structures (Lieberman *et al.* 1992). However, the bulk of recent behavioural and neuroimaging evidence appears to favour a processing account that may affect syntax along with a variety of other supportive cognitive functions (Grossman *et al.* 2002). There has been relatively little work examining the integrity of semantic memory in PDD, and much remains unclear about the effects of extensive subcortical damage on semantic processing (Crosson 1992). In late stage PDD, patients may experience visual hallucinations and fluctuating periods of consciousness that compromise comprehension (Ibarretxe-Bilbao *et al.* 2010).

It is becoming increasingly apparent that non-demented PD compromises cognition and communication. Hypokinetic dysarthria is an associated motor speech disorder that tends to compromise speech intelligibility in PD, and micrographia (i.e. illegibly tiny writing) is also commonly seen in PD (Jankovic 2008). Patients with PD do not typically manifest the profound deficits in naming and language comprehension that characterize FTD or AD. Non-demented PD patients do, however, experience high-level language impairments, including comprehension and production of complex narrative. Many have argued that the primary basis for high-level language impairment in PD lies at the level of processing limitations. Executive dysfunction and working memory impairments are prominent in PD (with or without dementia), resulting in deficits in planning, inhibition, set-switching, goal-directed behaviour, strategy formation and working memory (Henry and Crawford 2004; Emre *et al.* 2007; Murray 2008).

Patients with PD commonly show diminished pitch and amplitude contours in their vocal output consistent with dysprosodia. These prosodic deficits are also accompanied by diminished variability of facial expressions, a phenomenon known as masked facies (Pell 1996; Pell and Leonard 2003; Pell *et al.* 2006). These characteristics often lead to the impression that a communicative partner with PD has undergone emotional blunting and loss of empathy. Indeed, PD is thought to compromise aspects of emotional communication both receptively and expressively (Pell and Leonard 2005).

Many of the deficits that are apparent in prosodic speech output in PD manifest as analogous impairments in comprehension. Patients with PD often experience insensitivity to two dissociable forms of prosody (i.e. affective and linguistic prosody) (Heilman *et al.* 1984; Hillier *et al.* 2007).

Deficits in affective prosody compromise a patient's ability to detect emotional content conveyed by fluctuations in pitch and amplitude of a speaker's voice. Such cues are essential for conveying many non-literal aspects of language and communication such as irony and humour, domains that can become difficult for patients with PD to appreciate. PD also compromises perception of linguistic prosody that is critical for disambiguating word meaning or grammatical class based on unique stress patterns. For example, 'content' can mean two different things depending on its syllabic stress. In the absence of additional contextual linguistic detail, PD patients often experience difficulties detecting such subtle acoustic cues (Kotz *et al.* 2009).

15.6.2　Lewy body dementia

Although prevalence estimates vary, it is believed that Lewy body dementia (LBD) is often under-diagnosed and may in fact represent the second most common dementia behind AD (Zaccai *et al.* 2005). Core clinical features of LBD include fluctuating attention, repeated visual hallucinations and spontaneous parkinsonism (McKeith *et al.* 1996). Suggestive features include rapid eye movement (REM) sleep behaviour disorder, profound neuroleptic sensitivity and low dopamine transporter uptake in the basal ganglia on functional neuroimaging. Patients with LBD commonly experience frequent falls and syncope, transient loss of consciousness, severe autonomic dysfunction, multimodal hallucinations, delusions, depression and paranoia (McKeith 2006; Weisman and McKeith 2007).

Cognitive dysfunction emerges early during the course of LBD. Executive dysfunction, inattention and visuospatial/visuoperceptual dysfunction are the most consistently reported complaints (Ferman and Boeve 2007). Working memory, episodic memory and semantic memory are also compromised in LBD, but the underlying mechanism and the impaired aspect of memory processing (e.g. encoding, retrieval or consolidation) remains unclear (Metzler-Baddeley 2007). The phenotype of LBD is often conceptualized as a multifactorial blend of visuospatial, amnestic and dysexecutive impairments (Doubleday *et al.* 2002). Although LBD is prominently associated with visual disturbance, primary language impairment is a less common presentation. Prominent language impairments include confabulatory speech production, incoherent conversation, irrelevant responses, anomia and reduced verbal fluency (Lambon Ralph *et al.* 2001; McShane *et al.* 2001; Doubleday *et al.* 2002; Ash *et al.* 2012).

The receptive language impairment associated with LBD has been linked to decrements in verbal working memory and executive functioning. That is, impairments often emerge beyond the single word level within the domain of narrative discourse. Patients with LBD experience difficulties in online processing of syntactically ambiguous sentences (Grossman *et al.* 2012) and complex sentence structures (e.g. strategically padded sentences with additional prepositional phrases) (Gross *et al.* 2012).

15.7   Dementia and primary progressive aphasia

In a groundbreaking and highly cited series of works, neurologist Marcel Mesulam outlined formal criteria for the condition known as primary progressive aphasia (PPA) (Mesulam 1982, 2001, 2003, 2007). PPA manifests as a relatively focal impairment in the production and/or comprehension of language in the absence of frank dementia symptoms. PPA was accordingly described as 'slowly progressive aphasia without generalized dementia' (Mesulam 1982: 592). The most recent clinical diagnostic criteria for PPA delineate three distinct subtypes: non-fluent/agrammatic, logopenic and semantic PPA (Gorno-Tempini *et al.* 2011).

Unlike stroke aphasia, which tends to present as either stable or improving, PPA is by nature progressive. As speech and language impairments worsen across time, patients also tend to experience more of the classical symptoms of dementia, a stage recently termed PPA+ (Mesulam *et al.* 2003, 2009). Importantly, the progression from isolated speech-language impairment in PPA to more generalized dementia in PPA+ is continuous rather than punctuated. That is, no definitive threshold exists for when a person with PPA has crossed into the realm of dementia. For this reason, PPA has engendered great controversy (Snowden *et al.* 1989; Adlam *et al.* 2006).

PPA is the physical manifestation (i.e. phenotype) of one or more neurodegenerative processes. For example, one form of PPA (i.e. logopenic progressive aphasia) has been linked to primary AD pathology (Mesulam *et al.* 2008). PPA has been reported in autopsy-confirmed cases of FTD, LBD and VaD. However, the majority of PPA cases have been linked to the family of tauopathies that includes FTD (Grossman 2010). As such, some have argued that fluent variants of PPA do in fact represent early stage FTD.

Our discussion of PPA and dementia underscores a larger theoretical debate about the nature of aphasia in dementia. For over a century, aphasiology and neurology have been united in the belief that dementia does not fit easily within a classical cortical aphasia taxonomy (Wernicke 1874). One particularly influential dichotomy that has guided both assessment and treatment of aphasia in dementia is the distinction between disorders of access versus storage (Warrington and McCarthy 1983). Many speech-language pathologists, for example, operate under the assumption that dementia represents a core deficit of degraded storage whereas deficits in stroke aphasia are better characterized by impaired access to knowledge. This storage–access heuristic offers an intuitive and utilitarian framework for conceptualizing aphasia in dementia. However, this distinction is not without controversy, especially as it pertains to guiding one's treatment rationale (Rapp and Caramazza 1993; Reilly *et al.* 2011b).

15.8 Concluding remarks

In this chapter, we have presented an overview of communication in the dementias. The focus of the chapter has been on speech and language functioning in a small subset of dementia variants. Of course, this is problematic because human communication involves much more than speech and language. A comprehensive understanding of communicative impairment must also consider non-verbal expression and the ways that communication partners adapt to dementia. These aspects of communication in the dementias are still largely empirically uncharted. It is becoming increasingly evident that these gaps must be filled if we are to develop viable communicative interventions for the many millions of people living with dementia.

16

Traumatic brain injury and communication

Leanne Togher

16.1 Traumatic brain injury: causes and outcomes

According to the World Health Organization, traumatic brain injury (TBI) will overtake many diseases as the major cause of death and disability by the year 2020 (Hyder *et al.* 2007). Each year over 10 million people are affected by TBI resulting in significant pressure on healthcare resources. TBI most often affects young adults who sustain devastating life-long disabilities. However, there is also a higher incidence in early childhood and the elderly (Bruns and Hauser 2003). The most common cause of TBI for young adults is road traffic accidents, while children and the elderly typically sustain injuries as a result of falls. There has also been an increase in the number of injuries resulting from violence and war, particularly in low- and middle-income countries (Hyder *et al.* 2007).

The term 'traumatic brain injury' refers to brain injury caused by trauma rather than by disease, vascular accidents or alcohol abuse. Traumatic brain injury is a consequence of a head injury of sufficient severity to cause damage to the brain beneath the skull and can be either penetrating or blunt in nature. With the exception of war wounds, penetrating or open head injuries are an uncommon cause of traumatic brain injury. They occur when a missile, such as a bullet, pierces the skull and traverses the brain tissue. High velocity missile wounds cause catastrophic focal and diffuse damage and are usually fatal while low velocity missiles or missile fragments produce focal lesions restricted to the area of direct damage (Grafman and Salazar 1987). The more common mechanism of injury is an acceleration–deceleration movement. This movement impacts on the brain in a number of ways, causing both localized damage at the site of impact and at distant points due to the ricocheting movement of the brain. This type of trauma causes a series of catastrophic sequelae at the cellular level including diffuse axonal injury, where the nerve fibres are twisted and stretched by the force of the injury. Secondary injuries can exacerbate the initial insult and include oedema or swelling, hypoxic damage due to lack of oxygen after the injury, metabolic disturbances, hypothermia and hypotension (McHugh *et al.* 2007).

Communication problems may be a consequence of disabilities within both physical and social domains and represent a unique challenge for clinicians and researchers alike. With considerable advances in the fields of discourse analysis, pragmatics, social cognition and quality of life assessment, there has been an evolution of the descriptions of disordered language following TBI. These will be outlined in this chapter.

16.2   Cognitive-communication disorders

Communication problems following a TBI are distinctly different from those that result from a focal lesion such as occurs in a cerebrovascular accident. As such, they necessitate different approaches to assessment and remediation. Due to the multifocal nature of TBI, there is a complex interplay of cognitive, linguistic, physical, behavioural, organic and psychosocial factors which may contribute to the communication difficulties experienced by clients. Traditional communication impairments can result from TBI. These include aphasia, which has been reported to occur in up to 30 per cent of cases, and dysarthria, which typically affects about one-third of cases (Sarno *et al.* 1986). However, it is the social communication disabilities that predominate in TBI.

Traumatic brain injury typically affects the ventrolateral surfaces of the frontal and temporal lobes, and involves shearing of the white matter (Gentry *et al.* 1988; Bigler 2001). This results in slowed information processing, impaired working memory and attention and executive dysfunction, leading to problems such as inertia, rigidity, poor conceptualization and planning or, alternatively, poor regulation and control of cognition and behaviour (Tate *et al.* 1991). Communication disturbances reflect these different kinds of cognitive problems. Thus, adults with severe TBI have been described as being overtalkative (Hagen 1984; Milton and Wertz 1986), inefficient (Hartley and Jensen 1991), tangential (Prigatano *et al.* 1986) or as drifting from topic to topic (Snow *et al.* 1997). Alternatively, those with language deficiencies may have a paucity of language (Hartley and Jensen 1991; Chapman *et al.* 1992), in which their speech is characterized by slow, incomplete responses, numerous pauses and a reliance on set expressions (Thomsen 1975). People with TBI may also demonstrate confused, inaccurate and confabulatory verbal behaviour with frequent interruptions, disinhibited inappropriate responses, swearing, tangential topic changes or perseveration on topics, or some other combination of these basic features (Hartley and Jensen 1992). Likewise, in adolescents with TBI, there is reduced conversational fluency and inability to juggle multiple demands of conversation (Douglas 2010).

It became clear to researchers in the late 1980s and early 1990s that traditional language tests such as the Western Aphasia Battery (now in a revised edition; Kertesz 2006) were not suitable for detecting these 'higher-level' language deficits (Holland 1982a). The unique constellation of cognitive and linguistic deficits following TBI has led to the development of new theories of social communication and new methods of standardized and non-standardized assessment (Coelho *et al.* 2005a; Turkstra *et al.* 2005). As a result of these developments, a new era of research commenced in the late 1980s where investigations focused on connected speech samples, also known as discourse (e.g. Milton *et al.* 1984; Mentis and Prutting 1987; Penn and Cleary 1988).

16.3   Discourse analysis

Discourse is a unit of language which conveys a message (Ulatowska *et al.* 1981). There are different types of discourse, which have been referred to as discourse genres. A genre is a particular text type, which has its own structure and sequence. Types of discourse genres include narrative discourse (or recounting a story), procedural discourse (conveying a set of instructions for doing something), expository discourse (giving an opinion or discussing a topic in detail) and conversation. As discourse is the primary level of communication breakdown for people with TBI, clinicians commonly focus on a range of discourse genres during treatment. Narrative and conversation are the most commonly reported genres used in treatment, as these text types are commonly used during everyday contexts (Larkins *et al.* 1999). Treatment can focus on the person with TBI's ability to engage in conversation with family and friends by teaching them skills such as introducing new topics and maintaining conversations (Togher *et al.* 2009, 2013).

Narratives have also been the focus of treatment, whereby the person with TBI is taught to produce complete episodes within their story productions (Cannizzaro and Coelho 2002). In this single case study of an individual who was 12 years post TBI, treatment emphasized metalinguistic comprehension of story grammar structure and identification and generation of episode components within stories. Treatment consisted of twenty 60-minute sessions over a period of seven weeks. While there was a marked increase in the number of complete episodes generated by the participant during treatment, there was poor generalization of treatment effects. This poor outcome was attributed to factors such as the limited duration and intensity of the treatment programme, presence of chronic, moderately severe cognitive deficits and the acontextual nature of the treatment. This suggests that discourse treatment may be facilitated by focusing on contexts relevant to the individual's daily life.

Discourse analyses have been classified into microlinguistic, micro-structural, macrostructural and superstructural levels (Coelho 2007). Microlinguistic analyses or within-sentence analyses include productivity measures (e.g. words per T-unit), grammatical complexity (e.g. subordinate clauses per T-unit) or tallies of propositions and content units (such as the utterance with new information (UNI) and correct information unit (CIU)). Microstructural analyses or across-sentence analyses involve measures of cohesion and cohesive adequacy (Halliday and Hasan 1976) which examine the degree to which the speaker uses lexical items across a text to create a cohesive story (Armstrong 1987; Davis and Coelho 2004). Macrostructural analyses measure local and global coherence, which are indicators of the thematic unity of a narrative. Local coherence examines the relationship of the meaning or content of an utterance to that of a preceding utterance, while global coherence refers to the relationship of the meaning or content of an utterance to the general topic of the story.

Another macrostructural analysis is exchange structure analysis. This measures the amount of information giving, information requesting and receiving, and the amount of negotiation that is used to convey messages during interaction (Togher *et al.* 1997a). Coelho *et al.* (2002) proposed a discourse analysis procedure in which the middle 6 minutes of a 15-minute conversation are transcribed and analysed according to whether the person is a speaker-initiator or speaker-responder. A speaker-initiator's utterances are evaluated according to their 'summoning power', where those that clearly summon or demand a response are designated obliges, while those that do not are comments. The utterances of the speaker-responder are evaluated according to their appropriateness or adequacy within the interaction: adequate plus, adequate or inadequate (Coelho *et al.* 2002). Finally, superstructural analyses encompass the overall organization of content or information and include the analysis of story grammar, topic maintenance (Coelho 2007) and the essential and optional macrostructural elements within a text (Hasan 1985; Togher *et al.* 1997b).

Another way to classify discourse analysis is to examine the theoretical underpinnings of the measurement approach. Broadly, analysts have used either psycholinguistic approaches or sociolinguistic perspectives. Psycholinguistic approaches to evaluating language arise from an intra-psychological framework where the breakdown is seen as a disruption to the linguistic rule system within the individual or as a blockage of access to particular modules within that individual (Nickels 2002). Psycholinguistic analyses include measures of syntax (Liles *et al.* 1989; Glosser and Deser 1990; Chapman *et al.* 1992; Ewing-Cobbs *et al.* 1998; Ellis and Peach 2009), productivity (Mentis and Prutting 1987; Hartley and Jensen 1991; Jorgensen and Togher 2009) and content (Hartley and Jensen 1991) including propositional analysis (Coelho *et al.* 2005b).

Syntactic aspects of discourse have been investigated using measures such as the percentage of T-units containing dependent clauses (Chapman *et al.* 1992), embeddedness of subordinate clauses (Glosser and Deser 1990) and subordinate clauses per T-unit (Liles *et al.* 1989), with no differences being found between TBI and control participants. Glosser and Deser (1990) found that their TBI participants made significantly more grammatical errors than control participants (such as omissions of the subject, main verb and other grammatical morphemes), even though they demonstrated an adequate range of grammatical constructions in their spontaneous speech. While useful in explaining the reduced complexity of TBI discourse, psycholinguistic analyses at word level failed to delineate discourse problems and, therefore, researchers trialled analyses examining sentence-level processing (Ellis and Peach 2009) and the connectedness of TBI participants' discourse.

Sociolinguistic perspectives differ from psycholinguistic approaches to discourse analysis because, rather than focusing on the forms of language, there is an emphasis on language in use (Halliday 1994). Language is seen as a semantic, rather than a grammatical unit, which must be examined in the context in which it occurs. Context encompasses the situation in which the language has occurred, the purpose of the language use and the people involved in the situation. Context is interdependent with the text that occurs, so that, for example, the purpose of a text (which might be telling a story) realizes or leads to the use of particular words, phrases, sentences and genres. From this viewpoint, language analysis is always interpreted with the underlying context in mind.

Sociolinguistic analyses used to examine TBI discourse have included cohesion analysis (Mentis and Prutting 1987; Coelho *et al.* 1991; Hartley and Jensen 1991; McDonald 1993; Coelho 2002; Davis and Coelho 2004), analysis of coherence (Chapman *et al.* 1992; McDonald 1993), story grammar (Cannizzaro and Coelho 2002), analysis of topic (Mentis and Prutting 1991) and compensatory strategies (Penn and Cleary 1988).

Cohesion analysis has provided mixed results in the delineation of discourse deficits of individuals with TBI. The analysis of cohesion (Halliday and Hasan 1976) examines the components of the linguistic system that enable a text to function as a single, meaningful whole. The semantic relations that function to achieve cohesion are expressed partly through the vocabulary such as when the same person, place or event is referred to more than once but in different ways. This can be done by repetition of the same word, or by use of a synonym, superordinate or a more general word, e.g. 'The surfer strode along the beach at *sunrise*. He thought the best waves of the day occur just after *dawn*.' The other type of cohesion is grammatical cohesion, which can be achieved through reference, substitution and ellipsis. Referential cohesion, for example, relies on devices such as pronouns, e.g. 'There was outrage at the announcement of *the train strike.* While passengers complained about the inconvenience, they acknowledged there was little to be done about *it.*'

In a seminal study, Mentis and Prutting (1987) compared three TBI participants with three uninjured speakers using an analysis of cohesion during conversational and narrative samples with a familiar partner. While syntax was relatively well preserved in all three TBI participants, qualitative and quantitative differences in the TBI participants' cohesion abilities were reported, including the use of fewer cohesive ties in the narrative tasks.

Davis and Coelho (2004) recorded eight participants with TBI and compared them to eight control participants on a sample of six stories with tasks of cartoon-elicited story-telling and auditory-oral retelling. Deficits were found in the clinical group with respect to referential cohesion, logical coherence and accuracy of narration. Interestingly, the occurrence of deficits depended on the condition of narrative production and, to some extent, on the particular story used. Impairment of referential cohesion and accuracy was found with picture elicitation, whereas impairment of logical coherence occurred during retelling. This suggested that both the discourse feature being studied and the processing demands of the task should be considered when studying TBI discourse. The importance of the elicitation task was confirmed by Jorgensen and Togher (2009) who found that their 10 participants with TBI had fewer cohesive ties in a monologue picture narrative task compared to a matched control group, but no significant differences in a jointly produced narrative task.

16.4   Pragmatics

One of the challenges in measuring communication in people with TBI has been finding assessment tools sensitive to the unique communication deficits in this population. Early attempts at measuring everyday communication were based in pragmatics (Levinson 1983) and employed Grice's cooperative principle and four maxims of conversation: quality, quantity, relation and manner (Grice 1975). Penn and Cleary (1988) were among the first investigators to publish a profile of communicative appropriateness that took the following pragmatic parameters into account: non-verbal communication, sociolinguistic sensitivity, fluency, cohesion, control of semantic content and responsiveness to the interlocutor.

Prutting and Kirchner (1987) published a seminal work in which they used a Pragmatic Protocol. This was based on the tenets of Levinson's (1983) treatise that the range of pragmatic aspects of interaction exists on a continuum and includes context-dependent aspects of language structure (e.g. cohesion) in addition to aspects relying on principles of language use, such as physical proximity of communication partners and use of eye gaze (Prutting and Kirchner 1987). These authors

recommended that individuals be observed during a 15-minute spontaneous, unstructured conversation with a communicative partner. A rater
would then complete the protocol with ratings of appropriateness. The
Pragmatic Protocol was used widely subsequently in clinical contexts
and as a research tool (Penn and Cleary 1988), and fostered continued
interest in studying language use of people with TBI (rather than language performance) (Turkstra *et al.* 1996).

Pragmatic theory underpins two distinct approaches to the assessment
of communication after TBI (Body *et al.* 1999). One approach has led to
a proliferation of checklists or profiles of communication (Milton *et al.*
1984; Linscott *et al.* 1996; Snow *et al.* 1998). Based on Grice's theories,
the Profile of Functional Impairment in Communication (PFIC; Linscott
et al. 1996) includes feature summary scales that assess communication
skills on a 6-point scale from normative (0) to very severely impaired
(5), with lower scores indicating better performance. These summary
scales include logical content, general participation, quantity, quality,
internal relation, external relation, clarity of expression, social style,
subject matter and aesthetics. There are 84 specific behaviour items,
which assess the frequency of communication impairments from 'not
at all' to 'almost always/always'. Dahlberg and colleagues (2007) used
this scale as their primary outcome measure in a randomized controlled
trial of social skills treatment, finding that their treated group of 26 participants with chronic TBI improved on seven of the 10 summary scales
after 12 weeks of treatment, with no significant changes in a deferred
treatment group. The authors concluded that the PFIC was an appropriate outcome measure to evaluate the social communication of people
with TBI (Dahlberg *et al.* 2007).

At about the same time that Prutting and Kirchner were publishing the Pragmatic Protocol, Damico (1985) published Clinical Discourse
Analysis. This observational communication measure was also based on
Grice's maxims and eventually influenced the development of the La
Trobe Communication Questionnaire (Douglas *et al.* 2007). The La Trobe
Communication Questionnaire represents a significant advance in the
assessment of communication in a person with TBI. Rather than relying
on a standardized test of communication, it investigates the perception of
communication skills from the perspective of the person with TBI and also
their significant other. It is designed to assess social communication skills
by asking the person with TBI and a significant other a total of 30 questions, 22 of which are based on Damico's Clinical Discourse Analysis and
eight of which are based on commonly reported communication problems after TBI such as tangentiality and disinhibition. The person is asked
a question such as 'When talking to others do you go over and over the
same ground in conversation?' and then given a Likert scale which ranges
from 1 (never or rarely) to 4 (usually or always). While the use of self-report
can be limited if the person with TBI has impairments in insight, the use

of an 'other report' enables the clinician to determine whether communicative competence has been compromised by the brain injury and also
gain an insight into the level of awareness of the person with TBI.

Another approach that has evolved out of pragmatics is a focus on
specific aspects of interpersonal communication including the ability to
make inferences. This approach is exemplified by the body of work by
McDonald and colleagues (McDonald 1992, 1993; McDonald and Pearce
1996; Turkstra *et al.* 1996). This research has shown that a proportion
of TBI adults misinterpret conversational inferences generated by discrete speech acts. Given that linguistic performance is relatively normal
in these people, it is thought that they have difficulty utilizing the contextual information necessary to generate these inferences. However,
the nature of the contextual cues involved and whether any particular
sources of contextual cues are more poorly processed than others is not
well understood (McDonald 2000b).

Examining how contextual information is detected by conversational
speakers has led to advances in the study of sarcasm (McDonald and
Pearce 1996) and the use of hints (McDonald and van Sommers 1993). It is
thought that the ability to detect sarcasm is impaired because the frontal
lobes, which are commonly damaged in TBI, control executive processes.
These processes enable us to respond adaptively to novel stimuli by over-
riding routine, habit-driven responses. Damage to executive processes
may lead to automatic responses, which are either stimulus bound or
habit driven. This results in reduced appreciation of inferential meanings
in language because people with TBI are not able to suppress their tendency to respond to the most concrete aspects of the information given.
They are, therefore, unable to appreciate alternative meanings or associations (McDonald and Pearce 1996).

More recently, the role of theory of mind (ToM) in the pragmatic skills
of people with TBI has been examined (Bibby and McDonald 2005; Martin
and McDonald 2005). ToM is defined as the ability to generate inferences
about others' mental states and to use those inferences to understand
and predict behaviour. ToM has been described as the core cognitive
skill in pragmatic functioning (Cummings 2009, 2014a). It is also viewed
as an aspect of social cognition which is now recognized as a domain
that is frequently impaired for people with TBI (Stronach and Turkstra
2008). Deficits have been linked to an insensitivity to social cues, indif-
ference to others' opinions, poor foresight, egocentrism, lack of restraint
and inappropriate affect (Rowe *et al.* 2001). Martin and McDonald (2005)
considered both ToM and executive dysfunction in their discussion of
explanatory models of pragmatic disorders.

Another promising avenue of research in the field of social cognition
after TBI is the investigation of the role of emotion in cognition. The
ability to recognize emotion in others is obviously critical to our ability
to respond appropriately to communication partners in conversational

interactions. People with TBI can present with difficulties in emotional control, with poor frustration tolerance, temper outbursts, disinhibition and irritability. Clearly, this is likely to penalize the person in their every-day interactions. This difficulty was first described in the early 1980s in a study where people with TBI were shown a series of pictures depicting happy, sad, fearful and angry faces. They were asked to identify verbally the facial emotion and later freely recall the affect when shown some of the faces having neutral expressions (Prigatano and Pribram 1982). People with unilateral and bilateral lesions were reported to have difficulty, particularly with the memory component of this task.

These early observations have been confirmed across a range of visual and auditory media including photographs, videoed portrayals of emotion and audio tapes of emotionally charged voices (Spell and Frank 2000; Hopkins *et al.* 2002; Milders *et al.* 2003; Green *et al.* 2004). It is now well established that people with TBI have difficulty with this task, as emotion processing is mediated in the frontal lobes, which are frequently impaired after injury. Specifically, animal, neuroimaging and human lesion studies have consistently attributed impaired emotion recognition to dysfunction within a frontolimbic circuit that involves the striatum and anterior cingulate gyrus, ventromedial prefrontal cortex and dorsomedial nucleus of the thalamus. Of particular importance to the identification of emotional stimuli are the amygdala and anterior insula (Phillips 2003).

The task in the future is to develop treatments to remediate emotion recognition. While this area of research is in its infancy there has been a promising first study, which aimed to teach people with TBI to attend to salient features of various emotions (Bornhofen and McDonald 2008). This investigation employed a randomized controlled trial to evaluate the treatment of a group of 12 individuals with TBI using a programme specifically designed to address the perception of static and dynamic emotion cues. They found that the TBI participants who received the treatment showed improved accuracy when judging dynamic cues related to basic emotions (happiness, surprise, disgust, sadness, anger and anxiety) and that participants improved on distinguishing these emotions from a neutral emotional presentation. The treatment group also improved in their ability to draw inferences on the basis of emotional cues in order to judge whether a speaker was being sarcastic, sincere or deceptive. The authors suggested that participants who received the treatment may have been better able to monitor multiple, simultaneously occurring, dynamic cues such as eye contact, facial expression, voice tone and body language and to integrate these carefully to make higher-order judgements about a speaker's attitude, intentions and opinions. Clearly, much more needs to be done in this area, and ideally, emotion perception training could be combined with conversational skills treatment programmes to facilitate social interactions.

16.5   Quality of life and psychosocial outcomes

Many people with severe TBI have difficulty in everyday social situations, making participation in activities such as shopping, conversation with family and friends, and engaging with colleagues in a work interaction awkward and, in some cases, impossible. Social communication disability can result in difficulty for the person with a TBI in making and maintaining relationships with consequent social isolation and loss of leisure activities. This is particularly apparent when the long-term outcomes of individuals with TBI are examined. While the majority of people with TBI achieve independence in areas of activities of daily living (Tate *et al.* 1989), they experience poor outcomes in their psychosocial functioning. For example, almost 50 per cent of people with a severe TBI have been found to have no social contacts and few leisure interests one year or more after injury (Tate *et al.* 1989), with a greater reliance on family for emotional support following injury (Olver *et al.* 1996). A TBI can deleteriously affect vocational outcomes, and the ability to form new relationships (Olver *et al.* 1996). Impairments of communication underlie each of these adverse outcomes.

The combination of cognitive-communication deficits and problems of memory, fatigue and irritability in TBI commonly leads to interpersonal interactions which can be challenging, distressing or unsatisfactory for all concerned (O'Flaherty and Douglas 1997). Overall, loss of communicative competence presents a major obstacle to reintegration into the community because it makes the person with TBI more taxing and less rewarding to interact with socially (Bond and Godfrey 1997). Friends, carers and family members begin avoiding the individual with TBI and this generally limits his or her ability to maintain pre-injury relationships (Elsass and Kinsella 1987; Shorland and Douglas 2010). This can lead to marital and family breakdown (Tate *et al.* 1989) and disastrous vocational outcomes (Athanasou 2003), with estimates of only 7–10 per cent of people with severe TBI returning to their previous employment position. In addition, people with severe TBI often misjudge social situations, appearing to be overly familiar with potential acquaintances. This affects adversely their ability to establish new relationships.

As a result of diminished communication skills, people with TBI become socially isolated and may even require caregivers to help them with everyday tasks such as shopping or pursuing leisure options (Olver *et al.* 1996). But even among caregivers, the poor communication skills of people with TBI are problematic. Caring for people with TBI is stressful, with high levels of caregiver burden and depression (Knight *et al.* 1998). The main sources of this stress have been identified as problems communicating with the person with TBI (Motor Accidents Authority 1998), behavioural disturbance (Knight *et al.* 1998; Marsh *et al.* 1998) and the level of cognitive processing difficulties of the person with TBI (Wallace *et al.* 1998).

Social integration has been rated as the most important aspect of community integration by people with TBI (McColl *et al.* 1998). Struchen and colleagues showed that social communication scores added statistically significant predictive value to measures of social integration and occupational functioning (Struchen *et al.* 2008). Facial affect perception was a significant predictor of occupational outcomes and self-rating of communication skills was a significant predictor of social integration. Evaluation and treatment of social communication skills is therefore critical for the successful rehabilitation of these individuals as they work towards reintegration into community life.

16.6   Treatment approaches

Two approaches have been shown to improve the communication of those with TBI. Training in social skills is helpful, as is training partners to deal with difficult communication behaviours. Both these approaches will be addressed in turn, with a focus on those studies addressing the social communication skills of people with TBI.

16.6.1   Conversational and social skills treatments

Traditionally, communication training has focused on improving the social skills and interpersonal abilities of the person with TBI. Since the 1980s, there have been only a handful of empirical studies that have evaluated social skills remediation with TBI individuals. These studies have been aimed at overall social interaction deficits, or specific elements of such deficits (e.g. excessive talkativeness or inappropriate remarks) (Helffenstein and Wechsler 1982; Gajar *et al.* 1984; Schloss *et al.* 1985; Braunling-McMorrow *et al.* 1986; Johnson and Newton 1987; Brotherton *et al.* 1988; Flanagan *et al.* 1995; Dahlberg *et al.* 2007; McDonald *et al.* 2008). Communication training programmes have been in the form of games (Braunling-McMorrow *et al.* 1986), individual programmes (Gajar *et al.* 1984; Schloss *et al.* 1985) or small group activities (Flanagan *et al.* 1995). In general the gains are few, if any, despite the amount of resources required. Although this may suggest that such interventions are unsupportable, it needs to be emphasized that even a small improvement in problem behaviour can sometimes make a large difference in the social opportunities that are available to individuals with TBI (Lewis *et al.* 1988). Nevertheless, an inherent limitation to social skills and communication training with people with TBI is that these individuals usually experience a range of severe and disabling cognitive deficits which limit the extent to which they are able to compensate for their impairments or learn and apply new knowledge and skills.

As an indication, a systematic review of cognitive rehabilitation following TBI found very few interventions in this group to have demonstrable effectiveness (Carney *et al.* 1999). Nonetheless, in a recent randomized controlled trial of 39 participants, those receiving a 12-week programme of social skills intervention improved on one measure of social behaviour, the partner-directed behaviour scale of the Behaviourally Referenced Rating System of Intermediary Social Skills-Revised (Farrell *et al.* 1985; Wallander *et al.* 1985). The scale focuses on the ability to adapt to the social requirements of others. The self-centred behaviour and partner involvement behaviour subscales, in particular, showed improvement, indicating that participants with social skills training were less inclined to talk about themselves and more inclined to encourage their conversational partner to contribute to the conversation. Improving these interpersonal skills has clear implications for those situations where the person is meeting a new person at a social gathering or in a work context. It is encouraging that poor social skills which are related to impaired executive function appeared amenable to treatment (McDonald *et al.* 2008).

16.6.2   Training families and community agencies

In a similar vein to work done in aphasia, training programmes are now beginning to emerge to help families and other caregivers deal with the ongoing problems that can follow TBI (Ylvisaker *et al.* 1993; Carnevale 1996; Holland and Shigaki 1998). Ylvisaker *et al.* (1993) described the importance of providing a positive communication culture within the rehabilitation context. They suggest that role-playing and modelling combined with ongoing coaching and support are appropriate methods to facilitate communication training for communication partners of people with TBI. Further work is needed, however, to develop such training programmes to address individual communication profiles in collaboration with the family and peer network of the person with TBI. Importantly, there are few communication training programmes for community groups who interact with people with TBI. Thus, although community reintegration is frequently suggested as the primary objective of TBI rehabilitation (Ylvisaker *et al.* 2005), there are few documented cases where community agencies have been assisted to encourage more appropriate participation for these clients. This is despite the fact that there are now a number of studies that have clearly documented the nature of social interaction difficulties that commonly occur when people with TBI communicate in everyday settings.

In any conversation, the person with communication difficulties represents only one side of the interaction. The behaviour of the conversational partner is important as it can facilitate or diminish opportunities for the individual with brain injury to continue the conversation in a successful manner. Indeed, it has been found that TBI individuals are often disadvantaged in interactions because of the way their communication partners interact with them. For example, in a study of telephone conversations where TBI participants requested information from a range of communication partners, they were asked for and were given less information than matched control participants (Togher *et al.* 1996, 1997a, 1997b). Therapists and mothers never asked people with TBI questions to which they did not already know the answer. Additionally, TBI participants were more frequently questioned regarding the accuracy of their contributions and contributions were followed up less often than matched control participants. Communication partners used patronizing comments, flat voice tone and slowed speech production when talking to people with TBI. This was in contrast to the control interactions, where participants were asked for unknown information, encouraged to elaborate, did not have their contributions checked frequently, and had their contributions followed up.

Importantly, it has also been found that communication can be improved by manipulating the speaking situation for the person with TBI. For example, when people with TBI were placed in a powerful information-giving role, e.g. as a guest speaker talking about the experience of having a serious injury, their communication approximated matched control participants (who had a spinal injury) (Togher and Hand 1999). Thus, when provided with a facilitative context, such as an equal communicative opportunity, TBI participants are able to match the performance of control participants. One very important aspect of the context is *who* is involved in the interaction. This raises the question as to whether changing the communication partners' behaviours will impact on the way a person with TBI communicates.

To examine this question, our research team developed and evaluated a communication-training programme for police officers, as members of a service industry who are likely to encounter people with TBI. We trained the police officers to manage specific service encounters with people with TBI whom they had not previously met. This was evaluated in a randomized controlled trial (Togher *et al.* 2004). The TBI speakers rang the police to ask their advice both before and after the police had been trained. Training resulted in more efficient, focused interactions. In other words, this study confirmed that training communication partners improved the competence of people with TBI. What is unknown is whether this approach is better than, or equal to, the efficacy of direct remediation work with the person with TBI or whether a combined approach is more effective still.

One of the key ramifications of training police officers is that a well-trained communication partner can improve the communication of people with TBI. This study raises the possibility that training family members could lead to improved communication for the person with TBI. In a non-randomized clinical trial, 44 people with chronic, severe TBI and their chosen communication partners were allocated to one of the three groups: a TBI only group, where only the person with TBI was trained;

a joint group, where both the communication partner and person with TBI were trained together; and a delayed treatment control condition. Tests, questionnaires and ratings of video conversations were used to evaluate outcomes for communication, as well as measures of social skills, carer burden and self-esteem (Togher *et al.* 2009, 2013).

The communication partner-training programme was divided into seven modules which ran over 10 weeks. Each person with TBI and their communication partner attended a 2.5 hour group session with three to four other pairs as well as a one-hour individual session. This session focused on the pair's specific needs and also reviewed the week's home practice tasks that were recorded onto supplied tape recorders. The training programme consisted of an introductory session where the aims of training, group guidelines and home practice expectations were established. Session 2 contained an educational component on TBI and communication. Sessions 3 and 4 explored communication roles and rules in society as well as some general communication strategies. Collaborative conversation techniques were the focus of session 5. The aim of this module was to help conversations to be a collaborative process where both the 'feel' and information exchange are more equal, shared and organized.

In session 6, participants learned about the concept of 'keeping conversations going' (elaboration) with techniques that help to organize and link simple and more complex topics, with the use of both questions and comments. Session 7 explored the use of questions with particular attention on how to use helpful questions. It also provided methods to avoid using negative or 'testing' questions where communication partners asked for information when they already knew the answer. Sessions 8 to 10 then revised the information and practised each technique learnt in previous sessions with more intensive conversational practice. Every group session contained session handouts, a mix of role-plays, information content and conversational practice. Additionally, each pair was encouraged to play recorded home practice tapes to enable peer problem solving of conversational difficulties as well as peer support for good use of techniques or successful conversations. The programme taught communication partners how to help the person with TBI actively engage in conversations in everyday life and so the strategies were immediately applicable in everyday situations.

The finding was that the communication partner training led to greater improvements in the communication of the person with brain injury compared to the other two conditions. In addition to quantitative data analysis, data were collected from participants about their experiences of the training (Togher *et al.* 2012, 2013). This comment from one pair illustrates their experience with the training programme:

Participant with TBI: My communication after the programme is very good with my three kids, I communicate better with them, especially my kids, they're older now and I just communicate a lot better, a lot better.

Participant's communication partner: And they actually want to socialise with us whereas before they just walked away. Now we'll never get rid of them [laughs]. They want to sit and have a conversation with him but they used to only talk to me.

The training programme for communication partners consisted of a series of key components (listed below) that have been central to successful interactions between partners and their relative or friend with TBI. The communication partner and the person with TBI were encouraged to approach their interactions with an improved awareness of how *both* participants were contributing to the topic. In many cases, communication partners, who were frequently mothers or wives, were not consciously aware of how they were communicating. Once this awareness had been raised, they were able to change some communication behaviours that had interfered with a successful interaction.

Approach conversations with the goal of collaborating with each other in order to reach a common understanding or decision: Conversations need a balance of asking questions, listening and understanding, and sharing information about your own ideas and experiences. One participant said: 'I realized I just asked questions all the time like "Did you enjoy the holiday, and what did we do?". Now I use comments and give her time to spark her own memory from what I say rather than from nothing at all. I say, "It was a great holiday, my favourite day was the zoo and the white tiger, he was amazing". When I give her a little bit of information she can build on it.'

Use conversations as a way of introducing new and more complex information and ideas (elaboration): People with traumatic brain injury may have a limited range of topics they can talk about. By talking about new topics in daily conversations, people with TBI can expand their knowledge of the world and have more interesting things to talk about with other people. One of the participants found that by introducing her son to other topics and exploring those topics, he was able to provide many opinions she thought he wasn't capable of expressing. He also reduced the amount of time he spent on the same topic and, consequently, the frustration his family experienced with his repetition.

Use thinking supports as part of daily conversations: For example, make reference to a diary when planning for the future, look back at photos when talking about past events, use a written organizer with headings (e.g. who, what, where, when) when talking about planning for an event. One participant remarked that over the previous eight years, she had organized all her son's events, but in using this technique she realized with 'back-up support' he could do most of it himself.

Avoid asking questions to which you already know the answer: Instead, try to use real questions, which explore ideas, feelings and opinions. This creates a more natural, adult conversation and gives more confidence to the person with TBI in front of others. One participant said: 'He went to the movies and I knew what he saw. Before the course I would have asked him, did he remember what it was called and who went with him. How boring! I was like a teacher correcting him. Now I ask him, what was the best bit of the movie, or did he prefer the other *Die Hard* movies or this one, how were they different? It's amazing what he remembers then. It's not perfect but wouldn't you rather talk about that ... I would!'

Feedback: When you have a successful conversation with the person with TBI, or when you notice the person having a successful conversation with someone else, give specific, positive feedback.

Instructional materials included teaching the communication partner how to ask questions in a positive, non-demanding manner, encouraging discussion of opinions in conversations, and working through difficult communication situations collaboratively. For further information, the reader is referred to Togher *et al.* (2011).

16.7 Future directions

The social communication difficulties that typically follow severe TBI are complex and multilayered and are therefore difficult to describe and treat. This chapter has outlined some of the approaches that have investigated this area. Given the vastly different approaches that have been taken, ranging from discourse analysis to pragmatics and theory of mind, it is impossible to reconcile them neatly into a composite. This possibly reflects the heterogeneous nature of communication breakdown after TBI, which mirrors the complex interplay between cognitive and language processes interacting with the fast moving everyday environments in which communication occurs. It is heartening, however, that theoretical advances have been made and that these are now being translated into novel treatment approaches. It is reasonable to say that no single treatment is the panacea to communication difficulties and that a combination of approaches is needed to assist people with TBI and their families re-engage with their lives and society after the chaos that traumatic brain injury can bring. Nonetheless, there are some exciting new directions on the horizon which can only lead to improved integration into everyday life and enhanced quality of life for people with TBI.

17

Psychiatric disorders and communication

Karen Bryan

17.1 The epidemiology and aetiology of mental illness

The aetiology of mental illness is complex and not fully understood. Conditions such as schizophrenia are widely accepted as disorders of the brain but a comprehensive neurobiological account of such conditions remains elusive (Meyer and Feldon 2010). A complex interplay of genetic factors, perinatal exposure to environmental insults, early developmental problems and/or early adversity such as abuse, and lifestyle factors are thought to be involved. Many psychiatric disorders have their origin in adolescence. This is a time of brain development particularly involving the prefrontal cortex (Blakemore 2008). It is also a period of life when individuals may take risks which expose them to jeopardizing that cognitive development, such as smoking cannabis which is thought to contribute to gene expression in some individuals with an underlying genetic susceptibility towards schizophrenia (Barkus and Murray 2010). The aetiology of each of the disorders considered in this chapter will be addressed in more detail within the relevant sections.

Mental health disorders make a substantial contribution to the global burden of disease, with 14 per cent of this burden attributed to neuropsychiatric diseases (Prince *et al.* 2007). These conditions include depression, alcohol and substance use disorders, and psychoses. The full classification of mental and behavioural disorders by the World Health Organization (WHO) is given in the International Statistical Classification of Diseases and Related Health Problems (WHO 1992–1994). Apart from in sub-Saharan Africa, non-communicable diseases are rapidly becoming the dominant causes of ill health. Mathers and Loncar (2006) used the disability-adjusted life-year measure, which is the sum of the years lived with disability and years of life lost, to show that neuropsychiatric disorders accounted for up to a third of those attributed to non-communicable diseases, with 32 per cent in high income countries such as the UK and the USA. The five major contributors to this figure were unipolar depression (11.8%), alcohol-use disorder (3.3%), schizophrenia (2.8%), bipolar depression (2.4%) and dementia (1.6%).

However, the disease burden of mental health disorders is likely to be underestimated given that mental health disorders increase the risk for communicable and non-communicable diseases and contribute to intentional and unintentional injury (Prince *et al.* 2007). In addition, many health conditions increase the risk for mental health disorders, and comorbidity complicates help-seeking, diagnosis, prognosis and treatment. For example, disability is a significant risk factor for depression in older people (Cole and Dendukuri 2003). Mental health disorders also contribute to mortality, with WHO reporting 40,000 deaths per year due to mental health problems (Mathers and Loncar 2006). However, this is almost certainly an underestimate, as deaths from suicide are classed as intentional injury (Prince *et al.* 2007). Every year about 800,000 people commit suicide worldwide, and in the western world suicide is the leading cause of death in young men (Office for National Statistics 2011).

There is evidence for comorbidity between mental health disorders and physical health disorders. Possible mechanisms for this may be that mental health disorders affect the rate of other health conditions, e.g. mental health problems are associated with risk factors for chronic diseases such as smoking and obesity (de Leon *et al.* 2002), and conditions such as depression affect serotonin metabolism and inflammatory processes which are associated with cardiovascular disease and cancer (Zorrilla *et al.* 2001). Alternatively, some chronic health conditions create a psychological burden which increases the risk of mental health problems. In addition, some comorbid mental health problems affect treatment and outcomes for other health conditions (Robson and Gray 2007).

People with mental health problems are also at higher risk of criminal victimization than the general population (Maniglio 2009). Walsh *et al.* (2003) showed that 16 per cent of psychotic patients in a UK study reported violent victimization over one year, which was 2.3 times higher than the UK population at the time of the study. Violent victimization was significantly associated with illegal drug usage, homelessness, committing a violent crime in the previous two years, comorbid personality disorder and greater current symptomatology.

The World Health Organization's proposition that there can be 'no health without mental health' (World Health Organization 2005) has been widely endorsed by organizations including the EU Council of Ministers, the World Federation of Mental Health and the Royal College of Psychiatrists in the UK. There are universal calls for mental health awareness to be integrated into public health programmes, all aspects of health and social care policy (Saxena *et al.* 2007), health-system planning (Epping-Jordan *et al.* 2004) and delivery of healthcare (Patel *et al.* 2006).

Speech, language and communication difficulties are common in psychiatric conditions. They may be an intrinsic part of the disorder (as in schizophrenia), a side effect of treatment (as in drug-induced dysarthria) or a pre-existing disorder such as a stammer or social language difficulties associated with autism spectrum disorder. Treatments may be disease modifying, e.g. pharmacological intervention to address the underlying physiological processes, or symptomatic and supportive therapies designed to help maximize function and coping. In this chapter, the communication difficulties in three psychiatric disorders are examined. These disorders are schizophrenia, personality disorder and depression. Neuropsychiatric disorders, which involve neurological and psychiatric considerations, will also be discussed.

17.2   Schizophrenia

17.2.1   Symptoms and purported causes

Schizophrenia affects about 1 per cent of the population worldwide (Ross *et al.* 2006). The fourth edition of the *Diagnostic and Statistical Manual of Mental Disorders* (DSM-IV; American Psychiatric Association 1994) defines schizophrenia as a physiological disorder which typically has its onset between adolescence and early adulthood for males and a few years later for females, and is usually as a result of a stressful period (such as beginning college or starting a first full-time job). Initial symptoms may include delusions and hallucinations, disorganized behaviour and/or speech. As the disorder progresses, symptoms such as flattening or inappropriate affect may develop. There is no cure for this disorder so prognosis is poor. However, medication has been shown to be effective to some extent against the psychotic symptoms, and therapy can help the individual cope with the illness better and improve social functioning. Absence of what is termed the negative symptoms (flattened affect, avolition and poor social interaction) improves the prognosis significantly.

People diagnosed with schizophrenia usually experience a combination of positive, negative and cognitive symptoms. Positive symptoms are features that are not normally present (i.e. hallucinations, delusions, racing thoughts). Negative symptoms describe behaviours that are normally present but which are reduced or absent due to the disease (i.e. apathy, lack of emotion, poor or non-existent social functioning). Cognitive symptoms involve disturbances of executive functions, working memory and attention which give rise to difficulties such as disorganized thoughts, difficulty concentrating and following instructions, difficulty completing tasks and memory problems. Psychosis can occur in a number of psychiatric disorders and its diagnosis is not without controversy (Van Os 2011). However, the term 'schizophrenia' is applied to a syndrome that is characterized by longer duration, bizarre delusions, negative symptoms and few affective symptoms (Van Os 2010).

Currently, most professionals believe that schizophrenia is a physiological condition that is triggered by a life stressor. Theoretical models of the disorder include neurocognitive models. Hallucinations are a hallmark symptom of schizophrenia and neuroimaging studies suggest that during hallucinations patients experience activity in the secondary sensory cortices, prefrontal premotor, cingulate, subcortical and cerebellar regions of the brain (Allen *et al.* 2008). Based on these findings, a neurocognitive model of hallucinations is proposed where both top-down and bottom-up processes interact to produce the hallucinations.

According to the neurodevelopmental hypothesis of schizophrenia, an interaction between early neurodevelopmental disturbances and periadolescent brain maturation is necessary to trigger the onset of schizophrenia (Meyer and Feldon 2010). In the fetal brain, there is defective neuronal migration particularly in the second trimester of pregnancy which results in an increase in the size of the lateral and third ventricles (Mata *et al.* 2009), and agenesis of the corpus callosum (Walterfang *et al.* 2008), both of which are more prevalent in people with schizophrenia than in non-schizophrenic subjects. This perinatal damage is thought to be due to abnormalities in a number of genes that are important for early neurodevelopment. These genes are triggered by perinatal exposure to environmental insults (which may be infections, nutritional deficits or stress) that predispose the developing child to long-term changes in subsequent behaviour development (Meyer and Feldon 2010).

Animal models suggest that the effects of the perinatal environmental insults often only emerge after puberty. Pantelis *et al.* (2003) have shown that the transition from the non-psychotic phase to the psychotic phase is associated with significant bilateral reduction in the cingulate gyri, and the left parahippocampal and orbitofrontal regions. This is associated with a marked reduction in grey matter that may be an exaggeration of the grey matter reduction that normally occurs in adolescence (Wood *et al.* 2008). The exact relationship between genetic factors and environmental insults is not understood, but schizophrenia is widely accepted as a genetic disorder. However, recent studies suggest that there is a synergistic interaction between factors which is referred to as the stress-vulnerability model. For example, Clarke *et al.* (2009) suggest that prenatal exposure to infection and a positive family history of psychotic disorder interact synergistically to increase the risk of later developing schizophrenia. Nicodemus *et al.* (2008) suggest that some schizophrenia susceptibility genes, which are regulated by hypoxia, interact with obstetric complications.

Social behaviour (e.g. mentalization or 'theory of mind') is guided by social cognition which involves concepts such as attribution, intention, agency and emotion. Van Os *et al.* (2010) suggest that social cognition is particularly vulnerable to environmental disruption. Such disruption might be hearing impairment (Stefanis *et al.* 2006), exposure to deprivation or cruelty during critical developmental phases (Colvert *et al.* 2008) or head injury (Malaspina *et al.* 2001). Disruption to mentalization affects social interaction and suggests a link between the environment, social cognition and psychotic disorder. Early neglect and life course environmental insults that disinhibit stress signalling pathways can lead to impaired neuronal responsiveness and symptoms of profound prefrontal cortical dysfunction, providing a direct link between the environment and the cognitive impairments observed in schizophrenia (Arnsten 2009).

17.2.2   Social communication

Individuals with schizophrenia have social communication difficulties. Corcoran and Frith (1996) described the pragmatic difficulties that people with schizophrenia may show and how these problems affect conversation by making it difficult to convey a message or an intention. Social communication draws on several aspects of social competence which is often disordered in people with schizophrenia (Couture *et al.* 2006). This includes inaccurate social perceptions (Addington *et al.* 2006), difficulty in interpreting emotional facial expressions (J. Edwards *et al.* 2002; Schneider *et al.* 2006), difficulty in gaining emotional information from eyes (Bora *et al.* 2006), difficulty in gaining emotional information from prosody (Kucharska-Pietura *et al.* 2005) and a tendency to interpret averted gaze as directed at self (Hooker and Park 2005).

Also, Bucci *et al.* (2008) showed that people with schizophrenia had more difficulty than controls in interpreting communicative gestures. In particular, people with schizophrenia interpreted incidental movements as gestures and were more likely to misinterpret these as insulting, e.g. a hand held up to indicate 'stop' interpreted as 'you smell bad'. This is consistent with Frith's (2004) notion of over-mentalization associated with paranoia. Pinkham and Penn (2006) also showed that problems with social cognition (specifically measured via tests of emotion perception, social knowledge, theory of mind and interpersonal skill) rather than general neurocognition predicted social functioning in schizophrenia even when the level of education was controlled. Therefore, patients with schizophrenia who present with social communication difficulties are at risk of not achieving positive functional outcomes. It is important that their social communication difficulties are identified so that other people can compensate for these impairments and so that intervention can be offered. Studies by Horan *et al.* (2008, 2009) and Roberts and Penn (2009) suggest that social cognition training can be successful in people with schizophrenia.

17.2.3   Speech and language

Speech and language abnormalities have been documented in adults with schizophrenia and are described as one of the most important clinical diagnostic features of the disorder (Thomas 1995; McKenna and Tomasina 2005). The abnormalities can include poverty of speech, perseveration, echolalia, blocking and empty speech (Andreasen 1979). However, some of these descriptions relate to unmedicated schizophrenia which is now rarely encountered within rehabilitation settings.

Linguistic models have been applied to the study of speech and language disorders in schizophrenia with evidence to support disordered syntactic and semantic processing (Morice and Ingram 1983; Sanders *et al.* 1995; Newby 1998). Abnormalities in verbal production and comprehension, reduced sentence complexity and semantic processing deficits have been reported (Li *et al.* 2009). Disordered speech has been attributed to degradation of the semantic system (Goldberg and Weinberger 2000). Done *et al.* (1998) used narratives written by children at age 11, who later developed schizophrenia, to show that they did not differ from normal controls in syntactic production, grammatical errors or spelling. This suggests that syntactic difficulties seen in people with schizophrenia are a consequence of the psychosis rather than a premorbid deficit.

Action word retrieval (via reading an object name and producing a verb that describes what the object does) suggests that people with schizophrenia have noun and verb retrieval difficulties (Marvel *et al.* 2004; Woods *et al.* 2007). Kambanaros *et al.* (2010) used confrontation naming to investigate noun and verb retrieval. They confirmed that people with schizophrenia have significantly lower levels of word retrieval than controls, and that they have significantly greater difficulty retrieving verbs than nouns. The authors suggest that this may be due to action word generation placing greater demands on the prefrontal cortex (Kubota *et al.* 2005).

Pragmatic approaches have also been widely applied to the language difficulties in schizophrenia based on the premise that language processing is intact, but that the individual is unable to use this to communicate meaningfully with others (Frith and Allen 1988). Lack of cohesion (Harvey 1983) and difficulties in pragmatic comprehension (Langdon *et al.* 2002) have been reported as primary pragmatic impairments. Other behaviours include difficulties understanding non-literal language (Drury *et al.* 1998), ironic speech (Mitchley *et al.* 1998), indirect information (Corcoran *et al.* 1995), and conversational cues (Corcoran and Frith 1996).

Individuals with schizophrenia may show reading impairments such as difficulties with reading rate, functional reading and comprehension of single words, sentences, paragraphs and stories (Hayes and O'Grady 2003; Revheim *et al.* 2006). These reading impairments are thought to exist before the onset of schizophrenia (Done *et al.* 1998; Fuller *et al.* 2002) and may be related to structural abnormalities of related neuroanatomical regions primarily in the left temporoparietal region (Leonard *et al.* 2001). Jamadar *et al.* (2011) suggest that reading difficulties in people with schizophrenia may be related to structural grey matter abnormality in the cortical language networks, which may arise from impaired embryonic neuronal migration.

More recent imaging studies emphasize a range of brain dysfunction related to language disorder in people with schizophrenia. Li *et al.* (2009) reviewed imaging studies of people with schizophrenia and showed that schizophrenia is associated with structural and functional abnormalities in brain regions that are involved with language perception and processing. Individuals at high genetic risk of schizophrenia also have structural and functional deficits in brain pathways for language processing. The review also suggests that there is consistent evidence of disruption to the normal pattern of left hemisphere dominance for language processing. Further evidence for dysfunction in the language processing areas of the brain comes from studies of hallucinations. Strik *et al.* (2008) suggest that auditory hallucinations and formal thought disorder involve the regions of the brain that generate inner speech, as well as the primary acoustical cortex and the intrahemispheric fibres that connect the left frontal lobe with the temporal lobe. The authors suggest that a dynamic imbalance of the language system triggered by subtle structural changes is the neurobiological basis of hallucinations and thought disorder.

However, it may be unrealistic to search for unitary explanations of language symptoms in schizophrenia given the variation in language presentation. Langdon *et al.* (2002) showed that theory of mind deficits were associated with difficulty in understanding irony and were related to positive aspects of thought disorder, while negative features of thought disorder and poor understanding of metaphor were associated with abnormal semantic processing. Other studies have cited right hemisphere dysfunction (Mitchell and Crow 2005) and difficulty in context processing associated with inflexibility (Champagne-Lavau *et al.* 2006).

Patients in mental health settings may have a history of recreational drug usage. Illegal drug usage is associated with language and cognitive difficulties. Murphy *et al.* (2009) reviewed the literature and concluded that ecstasy (3,4-methylenedioxymethamphetamine, MDMA) causes working memory deficits that can impact on word finding and verbal fluency even in users who are now abstinent. The performance deficit was particularly evident in the updating of both verbal and visuospatial material and was associated with increased activity in the left prefrontal cortex for verbal material (Collette *et al.* 2006). In addition, studies have reported impaired cognitive functioning in ecstasy users in everyday life (Heffernan *et al.* 2001; Parrott *et al.* 2002). Clinicians working with patients with schizophrenia who have a history of drug usage or who appear to have memory difficulties should be alert to possible contributory factors and the need for accurate assessment.

Motor speech dysfunction may be found in people with schizophrenia as a side effect of antipsychotic medication. Krämer *et al.* (2010) suggest that 15 per cent of patients treated with clozapine (a drug used in treatment-resistant patients) present with dysarthria. Hypersalivation also occurs in these patients and this can affect communication directly and indirectly where the patient is reluctant to open his or her mouth. Extrapyramidal symptoms may also compromise speech production. These are frequently found in people with schizophrenia and are attributed to drug side effects although comorbidity with idiopathic Parkinson's disease should be excluded (Lan *et al.* 2011). Tardive dyskinesia (a movement disorder characterized by involuntary choreoathetoid movements in the orofacial region, limbs, trunk and respiratory system) may also develop in patients treated with antipsychotic medication, although it remains unclear as to whether this is a side effect of medication or a manifestation of dopamine dysfunction (Tenback *et al.* 2009). Antipsychotic medication, mood stabilizers and antidepressants may cause xerostomia (reduction in salivary flow). This changes the oral environment and can lead to periodontal disease (Friedlander and Marder 2002). In addition, poor dental health may be related to diet, smoking and poor dental hygiene (McCreadie *et al.* 2004). Where people with schizophrenia have drug-induced dysarthria, tooth loss following dental disease may compromise articulation further, resulting in increasingly reduced intelligibility.

Individuals with schizophrenia who are experiencing speech, language or communication difficulties should be referred to speech and language therapy. They require full language assessment to identify strengths and weaknesses and any particular difficulties. It is advisable to assess all areas of language and it is important to establish whether particular skills are (a) present for the individual and (b) used by the individual. It is common for people with schizophrenia who do not communicate as expected to have the language skills but not to use them. In other patients the expected skills are not present.

Speech and language therapy (SLT) has demonstrable value for people with schizophrenia who experience communication difficulties. Kramer *et al.* (2001) showed that discourse problems could be identified using a theoretically driven, multi-level linguistic framework analysis (Frederiksen *et al.* 1990) in two patients with very different language presentations. Five sessions of individually targeted discourse therapy resulted in measurable gains for both patients. Walsh (2008) demonstrated the value of conversation analysis in enabling a patient with schizophrenia to understand the impact of his voices on communication. Clegg *et al.* (2007) used a case study approach to address communication difficulties in a 53-year-old man presenting with severe poverty of speech. Two phases of therapy were used, one to desensitize the patient to verbal communication, and one to develop the patient's language productivity and to increase his awareness of social communication skills. The patient's verbal communication increased and he developed more appropriate social communication skills. However, his attitude to communication continued to be negative. The authors suggest that speech and language therapy should be considered as part of the treatment for schizophrenia and should be more widely available. Boucard and Laffy-Beaufils (2008) suggest that SLT assessment in patients with schizophrenia assists the clinical team in characterizing communication deficits, and that language remediation should proceed in the same way as for language impairments arising from neurological damage in conditions such as stroke and brain injury. They demonstrated that functional language improvement arises from SLT intervention when appropriate interventions are selected which capitalize on spared abilities to compensate for impaired abilities.

17.2.4 Dysphagia

Dysphagia or swallowing difficulty can also be caused by antipsychotic medication with possible consequences of choking and aspiration pneumonia. However, there may be other causes of eating difficulties. Dziewas *et al.* (2007) reviewed the literature and found five types of difficulty: (1) paralytic dysphagia involving weakness of the tongue, palate or pharynx attributed to another disease such as a stroke; (2) medical dysphagia which is caused by other conditions that affect swallowing such as obstructive pulmonary disease or gastro-oesophageal reflux; (3) fast-eating syndrome which is behavioural in nature rather than a swallowing disturbance (Bazemore *et al.* 1991); (4) bradykinetic dysphagia caused by extrapyramidal symptoms and resembling dysphagia in Parkinson's disease (Bushmann *et al.* 1989); and (5) dyskinetic dysphagia which is possibly a result of tardive dyskinesia involving involuntary lip, jaw and tongue movements that affect swallowing (Gregory *et al.* 1992). The latter two forms are the most common, occurring in 20–50% of patients depending on the sample (McCreadie *et al.* 1992; Muscettola *et al.* 1999).

Regan *et al.* (2006) examined the prevalence of dysphagia in acute and community mental health settings. They found a prevalence rate of 35% in an inpatient unit and 27% in those attending the day hospital, which compares to 6% in the general population (Groher and Bukatman 1986). There is also evidence for an elevated rate of death due to asphyxia in psychiatric inpatients (Corcoran and Walsh 2003). This is thought to be due to the effects of medication, neurological disorder and institutionalization (Bazemore *et al.* 1991). Fioritti *et al.* (1997) suggest that clinical staff should enquire regularly about swallowing difficulties and that all inpatients should be screened on admission to hospital, with patients who have polypharmacy and those over 60 years of age being recognized as particularly at risk.

Although some studies suggest that extrapyramidal symptoms including dysphagia are less common with newer atypical antipsychotics such as risperidone and clozapine, there are reports of dysphagia arising from these drugs (McCarthy and Terkelsen 1994; Varanese *et al.* 2011) with oesophageal dysfunction thought to be the cause. Dysphagia can

be treated by medication adjustment where possible, dietary modification using the Dysphagia Diet Food Texture Descriptors (National Patient
Safety Agency 2011) and swallowing training (Tang and Hsieh 2010).
Dysphagia assessment such as that described by Logemann (1997), and
management adhering to relevant clinical guidelines such as those from
the American Speech-Language-Hearing Association (2001) and the Royal
College of Speech and Language Therapists (2005), should be available to
patients with mental health conditions who are experiencing eating and
swallowing difficulties.

17.3   Personality disorder

Personality disorder or psychopathy is characterized by a callous, shallow and manipulative affective-interpersonal style combined with antisocial and reckless behaviour (Hare 1991). Personality disorders are not
particularly associated with overt communication problems. However,
where patients have a disrupted social and/or educational history, language and literacy skills may be limited. These limitations may contribute to difficulties in expressing needs and opinions and may contribute
to over-reliance on behaviours such as hitting out when explanation
is not within the person's language capability. Pervasive developmental disorders such as a stammer or articulatory difficulties may also be
evident. Iverach *et al.* (2009a) suggest that personality disorder is over-
represented in people with a stammer. However, other authors have
suggested that this may be due to both groups having increased anxiety
(Manning and Beck 2011).

   Research suggests that individuals with psychopathy may have more
subtle problems with emotional and interpersonal aspects of language.
They understand and apply the meanings of emotional words but do not
experience the affective value attached to them (Hare *et al.* 1998). Louth
et al. (1998) showed that adults with psychopathy were insensitive to the
emotional connotations of language and that their vocal characteristics
were designed to manipulate and control interpersonal interactions. Blair
et al. (2006) demonstrated that adults with psychopathy showed reduced
affective priming and suggested that the semantic representation of emotional words is dysfunctional in individuals with psychopathy. Gawda
(2010) examined the written emotional narratives of adults with and
without psychopathy and found that those with psychopathy contained
more repetitions, pauses and negations. Gawda suggests that analysis of
syntax can contribute to the assessment of affective characteristics in
antisocial individuals.

   A number of authors suggest that young people who go on to develop
psychopathy show verbal deficits (Vermeiren *et al.* 2002; Leech *et al.* 2003).
This appears to be at least partially independent of ethnicity and socioeconomic status. Moffit and Henry (1991) suggest that deficient verbal

abilities could relate to impaired executive functioning, which is critical for behaviour regulation. This suggestion is not surprising given that at least 40 per cent of adults with personality disorder or psychopathy present with conduct disorder as a child (Lahey *et al.* 2002).

Kiehl (2006) suggests that paralimbic system deficits underlie the language processing difficulties evident in individuals with psychopathy, particularly the right anterior superior temporal gyrus, amygdala, and anterior and posterior cingulate. Other authors suggest that subtle and complex difficulties in interhemispheric integration may underlie the abstract and emotional language processing difficulties found in individuals with psychopathy (Hiatt and Newman 2007; Lopez *et al.* 2007).

However, aspects of personality disorder may rely on relatively intact verbal abilities which can be used to manipulate and influence others (Salekin *et al.* 2004). In other words, it may be an advantage to a psychopath to have intact verbal abilities. Klaver *et al.* (2007) showed that adult psychopaths spoke more words, talked for longer and talked faster, which is consistent with the finding that psychopathic individuals can dominate interpersonal situations (Ekman 1999). High verbal ability (and higher intelligence) are both associated with lower likelihood of delinquency (Cornell and Wilson 1992; Lahey *et al.* 2002). Some authors suggest that intact verbal ability in young people with psychopathy is not a predictor of violence on its own, but when intact verbal ability is combined with other risk factors for aggression such as impulsivity and callous-unemotional states it may predict aggression (Frick and Dickens 2006). Muñoz *et al.* (2008) suggest that high verbal ability is only associated with reduced risk of violent offending in boys who do not show the callous and unemotional traits. These studies suggest that there are different causal mechanisms leading to violent behaviour and there may be identifiable subgroups of young people with antisocial behaviour problems (Loney *et al.* 2003) who need specific and appropriate intervention. Frick and Marsee (2006) suggest that adolescents with low verbal ability need interventions focused on their verbal deficits in order to avoid the problems that these may lead to, such as school difficulties. In contrast, young people with callous-unemotional traits may need intervention to increase their emotional awareness (Dadds *et al.* 2006).

La Vigne and Van Rybroek (2011) provide a detailed review of language impairments in adolescents and adults who are in contact with the criminal justice system written from the perspective of legal service provision. They outline the effects of language difficulty on the administration of justice, rehabilitation and public safety. Snow (2009) also outlines the accumulating risk factors that arise from early attachment difficulties, language problems and in turn educational difficulties, all of which may adversely impact on mental health. These language difficulties then affect the ability to give evidence (Snow and Powell 2004) and to take part in rehabilitation approaches (Snow and Sanger 2011).

Some studies have demonstrated differences in non-verbal communication in people with personality disorder. Rimé *et al.* (1978) showed that adolescents with psychopathy in a minimum security institution leaned towards the interviewer more, thus reducing the distance between them and the interviewer, used more gesture, smiled less and had longer periods of eye contact than adolescents without psychopathy. Blair (2003) suggests that psychopaths respond less to fearful and sad facial expressions and this interferes with socialization, resulting in an individual who fails to learn to avoid actions that result in harm to others.

17.4   Depression

Uher and McGuffin (2008) conclude that as with schizophrenia, depression arises through a gene–environment interaction. Depression varies in severity from brief episodes, for example after bereavement or other adverse life events, to lifelong difficulties that usually emerge during the period from puberty to mid-twenties (Kessler *et al.* 2005). Attempts have been made to distinguish mental illness from transitory and normative changes in emotions and behaviours, but how symptoms are acquired, intensify and coalesce into syndromes has not been widely considered (Eaton *et al.* 1995). McGorry *et al.* (2010) suggest a clinical staging method of diagnosis where earlier and milder clinical phenomena are distinguished from those that accompany illness extension, progression and chronicity. It also encourages treatment of early stage difficulties to try to avoid treatments delivered later in the course of the illness. Treatment approaches such as psychoeducation, self-help and e-health, exercise therapy and related behavioural approaches have been shown to be effective in the earlier stages of depression (Hetrick *et al.* 2008). A small number of studies suggest that the risk of major depression can be reduced in adolescents with subthreshold depression, particularly those with a family history (Stice *et al.* 2008; Garber *et al.* 2009). However, further research is needed to test whether such interventions prevent people from progressing to later stages of depressive disorders more generally.

Depressed patients are often reluctant to talk and avoid social contact where possible. Eye contact, facial expression and intonation may be reduced and response latencies may be increased. Responses tend to be short, but patients with depression may perform better on structured tasks such as picture description (Maxim 1991). It is important that depression is differentiated from dementia and there is some evidence that language assessment can be useful (Stevens *et al.* 1996).

Alexithymia is the inability to describe emotions with words (Bagby *et al.* 1994). Alexithymia has clinical implications because it creates interpersonal problems but also limits the responsiveness to psychotherapy (Kim *et al.* 2008). Research has indicated that there is a strong association between depression and alexithymia in both depressive populations (Honkalampi *et al.* 2001) and general populations (Honkalampi *et al.* 2000). Kim *et al.* (2008) suggest that the severity of the alexithymia is positively associated with the severity of the depression. Speech and language therapy may be able to assist in differentiating alexithymia from word-finding difficulty, and may also be able to work with patients to improve their ability to describe emotions with appropriate vocabulary.

Depression in mothers is recognized to place the young child at risk for cognitive and language difficulties. Sustained depression during pregnancy may increase the risk of language and cognitive delays by impacting on fetal growth rates (Walker *et al.* 1999) and fetal development of biological systems related to attention (Quas *et al.* 2004; Blair *et al.* 2005). Postnatal depression in mothers may affect the infant's electrical brain activity as measured using an electroencephalogram (EEG). Infants of depressed mothers show less left frontal activity than children of non-depressed mothers (Dawson *et al.* 2003). Newborn infants of depressed mothers show lower cardiac vagal tone. In addition to maintaining slowed heart rate, the vagus nerve activates facial expressions and vocalization. Six-month-olds with lower vagal tone have been shown to be less facially and vocally expressive (Field 2002). The vagal tone and electrical activity differences together result in a reduced ability to learn from the environment (Sohr-Preston and Scaramella 2006).

Adverse childbirth experiences, health complications for mother or baby, single parent status, poor social support and accompanying marital, social, financial or health problems have been shown to increase the risk for lifetime depression (Bernazzani and Bifulco 2003). Children of chronically depressed mothers may be more vulnerable to learning difficulties at least in part because they are less exposed to the facilitative components of infant-directed speech (Kaplan *et al.* 2002). Also, there is evidence that depressed mothers interact less and play less with their children, which may also impact on language and cognitive development (Sohr-Preston and Scaramella 2006) with a particular vulnerability for boys (Sharp *et al.* 1995). However, these effects can be reduced by close involvement of other adults with the child and interventions to increase maternal talk. It is vitally important that staff working in early years services appreciate the potential adverse effects of maternal depression on the child's speech so that early referral to speech and language therapy can take place in order to minimize the risk to the child's emerging language skills. Further research is needed to understand the benefits of early preventative intervention and to demonstrate the economic case for such intervention.

Depression may also be associated with chronic health conditions. Mudge *et al.* (2011) screened continuous hospital admissions for one year and showed that in older people with chronic disease comorbidities, weight loss associated with poor nutritional status and depression were the key risks for readmission to hospital. Depression may be encountered within speech and language therapy services more often when it arises in conjunction with other conditions. Code and Herrmann (2003) showed that depression is a common reaction to acquired communication impairment. Whilst there may be an interaction between depression and communication difficulty, the link is not inevitable and the interaction may be bidirectional (Miller *et al.* 2008). Further research is needed to understand the nature of this interaction. Wilkinson *et al.* (1997) showed that 36 per cent of stroke patients followed up in the community presented with depression. Emotional, social and psychological difficulties arising in people with aphasia are well recognized (Cruice *et al.* 2011).

17.5   Neuropsychiatric disorders

The term 'neuropsychiatric disorder' is often used to denote disorders where a combination of organic and functional disorder occurs. In many of these disorders both neurological and psychiatric problems can affect communication. Examples of such disorders are Parkinson's disease, multiple sclerosis and Huntington's disease, which are considered briefly below.

Miller *et al.* (2008) showed that almost without exception, Parkinson's disease has a negatively perceived influence on communication irrespective of age and gender. Individuals report a loss of control in communication, less confidence, and difficulty in conveying information which leads to feelings of inadequacy and loss of independence. These feelings may in turn lead to withdrawal from communication, and passing the burden of communication on to carers (Miller *et al.* 2006). Miller *et al.* (2008) suggest that early perceived changes in communication, even where there is no apparent decline in intelligibility, should trigger early referral to speech and language therapy.

Patients in the later stages of Parkinson's disease are also vulnerable to psychiatric sequelae including hallucinations, psychosis and depression (Varanese *et al.* 2011). This may arise partly due to the underlying damage caused by the disease and the psychological consequences for the person, for example, finding it difficult to communicate, walk and socialize. Speech and language therapy has a key role to play in the later stages of Parkinson's disease (Varenese *et al.* 2011). Heisters (2011) suggests that speech and language therapy can improve volume of speech and ability to participate in conversations which in turn enables people with Parkinson's disease to maintain a sense of independence and improve quality of life. Gage and Storey (2004) showed that interventions can have positive effects on patients' lives in many different ways, but continuous follow-up may be needed to maintain improvements (Wade *et al.* 2003).

Multiple sclerosis is a degenerative disease in which lesions caused by demyelination occur throughout the brain and spinal cord (Joy and Johnston 2001). The disease has a remitting and relapsing course. There are a number of patterns to the presentation so that patients present with varying types of difficulties. Up to 40 per cent of people with multiple sclerosis present with dysarthria and more severe speech symptoms are associated with disease progression and other symptoms such as mobility difficulties, visual changes, fatigue and depression (Yorkston *et al.* 2003a). Cognitive impairment is also common including problems with memory, attention, speed and information processing and executive functions (Shevil and Finlayson 2006). The interaction between any communication impairments and physical and cognitive impairments may be important in determining the impact on the person. Baylor *et al.* (2010) reported that the most significant associations with communicative participation in a large sample of people with multiple sclerosis were, in order of importance, strength, fatigue, slurred speech, depression, problems thinking, employment and perceived social support. This suggests that variables that influence communication difficulties should be addressed in communication interventions. However, further research is needed to address directionality of associations. For example, it is not established whether treating depression improves communication and vice versa.

Another example of a disease with a significant neuropsychiatric element is Huntington's disease. This is an inherited disease that typically begins in the third or fourth decade of life. It has a disease duration of 15 to 20 years and a steadily progressive course. Difficulties that affect communication are motor problems initially affecting facial expression and gesture, and involuntary movements that affect posture, balance, movement, speech and swallowing. Progressive cognitive problems are also evident with decline of intellect, memory and conceptual thought (Brandt 1991) and depression in the earlier stages of the disease. Dysarthria with slurred speech is a common symptom with weight loss arising from dysphagia in later stages of the disease (Kagel and Leopold 1992). Zinzi *et al.* (2007) showed that an individually tailored, coordinated, multidisciplinary programme including speech and language therapy with input at respiratory, speech motor and language levels improved physical, motor and functional measures with initial indications of longer-term maintenance of baseline functioning, although further follow-up studies would be needed to verify this.

Common to rehabilitation interventions for these complex diseases is that heterogeneity of therapy methods and of outcome measures makes it difficult to provide conclusive evidence for any particular form of intervention, or indeed to determine the exact effects of one element of multidisciplinary provision. However, lack of evidence should not constitute a proof of lack of effect (Deane *et al.* 2002). Delaying progression of functional impairment may be valuable in preserving quality of life, but also in delaying the onset of institutional care, which is expensive as well as limiting for the individual (Wheelock *et al.* 2003).

The biopsychosocial framework for exploring health conditions outlines how interactions among impairments, activity performance, participation and environmental factors may shape individual experiences with health conditions. The World Health Organization's International Classification of Functioning, Disability and Health (ICF; World Health Organization 2001) provides such a framework. Biopsychosocial frameworks specifically for communication disorders have been proposed to emphasize the interrelationships between participation, the severity of the communication disorder, the communication environment and each individual's personal identity and attitudes (Kagan *et al.* 2008).

17.6   Managing communication disorders in people with mental illness

Speech, language and communication assessment in psychiatry may have a number of functions. Assessment may assist psychiatric diagnosis, may contribute to differential diagnosis (e.g. dementia and dysphasia; dementia and depression; schizophrenia and dysphasia; paranoia and hearing impairment; language disorder and intellectual impairment), and may highlight specific communication problems. Assessment may also provide a diagnosis of any speech and language difficulties that may be part of the psychiatric disorder, may be pre-existing (e.g. a stammer), may arise due to treatment side effects (e.g. dysarthria) or may arise due to another medical condition such as a stroke.

Information about speech, language and communication difficulties may be important to assist the multidisciplinary team in understanding the patient's communication difficulties, and any frustration that these may cause. It will also enable the patient's care plan to be adapted to ensure that other interventions utilize an appropriate level of expressive and receptive language. In some cases, verbally mediated interventions such as psychotherapy, anger management or any individual or group based talking therapy might have to be adjusted to require a lower level of language. These intervention approaches may even be contraindicated if the patient does not currently have sufficient communication skills. This is important not only to ensure that treatment resources are not wasted, but also to ensure that judgements about why a patient may be deemed to be failing to progress are accurate. This is vital where psychological progress may be a condition for progress within care systems. For example, a patient detained under the Mental Health Act (2007) may be deemed to require better insight into their illness before they can be released. Patients may also benefit from understanding their speech, language and communication difficulties and how these affect other people during interpersonal communication.

There appears to be a higher incidence of hearing problems within the mentally ill population (Department of Health 2005), although there are a number of methodological difficulties associated with the studies in this field (see Denmark (1995) for a detailed review of this subject). Observation of a patient may indicate that he or she is relying heavily on lip-reading. A lack of attention may suggest a hearing problem or sometimes patients tend to turn slightly towards the speaker to use their 'better' ear. Patients may report continuous or buzzing noises that are suggestive of tinnitus. In other cases, patients may be adept at hiding a problem, particularly if they are concerned about the stigma of deafness. Freefield testing and screening audiometry may be useful in identifying patients who require more detailed investigation. Where a hearing problem is suspected or apparent, patients should undergo aural examination in order to eliminate build-up of wax secretions as a cause of hearing problems.

Assessments should include a full case history including early development, language history, educational progress, interpersonal communication and any difficulties with communication. For example, a depressed patient may on enquiry have reading difficulties from childhood or a poor memory as a result of an earlier head injury. There are few tests specifically designed to assess speech and language in people with mental illness. Typically, developmental tests or tests primarily devised for the assessment of acquired aphasia are applied to this population. There are no standardized speech, language and communication tests for the mental health population, and norms from other tests must be interpreted cautiously as people with mental illness may have other associated difficulties. These may range from drug side effects to subtle brain damage, pervasive learning difficulties, lack of opportunities for social interaction, institutionalization and a whole host of other potential difficulties. These problems may affect a person's response to assessment and may mask or exacerbate any speech, language and communication problems that they have.

The application of existing norms for language tests may also be questionable. The language and pictorial material used in tests may be of little relevance or may even be inappropriate for people who may have led impoverished, street or institutionalized lifestyles. For example, material referring to family events may be irrelevant or upsetting for some patients. Fluctuation in performance is a feature of many mental health disorders, raising issues of when to test and the need to monitor performance over time. Medication side effects may increase fluctuation and any change in drug regimens may alter the client's speech and language profile (although language levels may be a useful indicator of the positive effects of drug treatment).

Intervention for speech, language and communication should be tailored to the needs of the individual patient. A hypothesis testing approach, with outcomes clearly demonstrated, is advocated. Therapy should include evidence-based approaches relevant to the presenting disorder or combination of disorders that the patient presents with. These interventions may need to be modified to accommodate other problems such as memory difficulties or difficulties with abstract thinking. However, this would be no different from working practices with other patient groups such as those with stroke or head injury. There is a need for greater access to speech and language therapy services for people with mental health problems who experience communication difficulties, and for more research into the efficacy of speech and language therapy intervention.

Part III

Voice, fluency and hearing disorders

18

Functional and organic voice disorders

Nadine P. Connor and Diane M. Bless

18.1 Introduction

Voice production disorders result in deviations in vocal quality that can impair communicative function and quality of life (Benninger *et al.* 1998; Krischke *et al.* 2005; Cohen *et al.* 2006). These disorders are found in approximately 7.5 million Americans, have multiple aetiologies, and occur throughout the lifespan (National Institute on Deafness and Other Communication Disorders 2007). Lifetime prevalence of voice disorders has been reported at up to 47 per cent (Roy *et al.* 2007; Cohen 2010; Merrill *et al.* 2011). One estimate suggests that approximately 28 million workers in the United States have problems with their voices every day and that these voice problems have an impact on occupational function and quality of life (Verdolini and Ramig 2001). Definitions of what constitutes a voice disorder vary across the literature. In this chapter, we will define voice disorders as manifestations of abnormal vocal quality, or a voice that does not meet the needs of an individual. This may result from poor respiratory support, vocal fatigue, abnormal vocal fold closure or resonance imbalance, whether due to the presence of a lesion, irregular vocal fold margins, abnormally long or short vocal fold closure durations, irregular vibration or other abnormal biomechanical pattern.

Voice disorders may arise from a number of aetiologies (Verdolini *et al.* 2006). To provide clinically meaningful care, it follows that aetiologies of voice quality disruptions must be carefully defined and that treatment strategies must be geared directly to these identified causes. Unfortunately, identifying the causes and making a clear differential diagnosis are often not straightforward. Thus, a complete voice evaluation involves a multi-pronged approach consisting of at least the following: a complete history and examinations of auditory-perceptual and acoustic parameters, laryngeal imaging, aerodynamic measurements, quality of life assessments and determination of patient self-efficacy and readiness for behavioural change (van Leer *et al.* 2008; van Leer and Connor 2010). Data from all these assessments are combined to assist the identification of causation, diagnosis and treatment planning.

The most widely used classification scheme for voice disorder aetiology is the dichotomy of 'functional' versus 'organic', although some classifications differentiate 'organic' and 'neurogenic' (Boone *et al.* 2010). In this chapter, we will discuss the merits and flaws in classifying voice disorders as 'functional' versus 'organic', and will conclude that the functional-organic dichotomy is artificial and no longer useful, despite its widespread use for over 100 years (see Brodnitz (1969) for presentation of the 1889 German monograph by Schnitzler). As noted by Greene (1964: 88): 'Functional dysphonia can be a symptom of a great variety of aetiologically different organic and psychological states. In the majority of cases it is virtually impossible to separate one from the other since they overlap, and combine '.

18.2   'Functional' versus 'organic' voice disorders

It is disruptions in vocal quality that lead individuals to seek care (Carding *et al.* 2009), and therefore it is important to be able to describe vocal disruption. In his 1964 book, Murphy reviewed the existing literature and found the following descriptors of voice quality: 'mellow, rich, clear, bright, ringing, sharp, hollow, hooty, smooth, harmonious, pleasing, velvety, heady, clangy, chesty, throaty, covered, open, breathy, blanched, coarse, crude, heavy, golden, warm, brilliant, cool, flat, round, dull, pointed, pingy, pectoral, shallow, deep, buzzy, reedy, whiney, orotund, light, toothy, white, dark, metallic, dead, cutting, constricted, strident, shrill, blatant, poor, faulty, whispery, thin, whining, sharp, piercing, hollow, raspy, guttural, pinched, tight, twangy, hard' (Murphy 1964: 26). Some of these terms are still used to characterize voice quality disorders. In addition, other auditory-perceptual terminology is widely used in perceptual rating scales, including terms like breathiness, strain and roughness. The term 'hoarseness' has been used to denote a combination of roughness and breathiness (Verdolini *et al.* 2006: 41).

Thus, there is no shortage of descriptive terminology for vocal quality. The quest to accurately describe what we hear when listening to voices has been active for many decades and continues to be elusive, with often limited reliability even among experienced clinicians using standardized rating scales and methods (Zraick *et al.* 2011). Classification of voice disorders into categories has been thought to provide guidance regarding aetiology. However, the perceptual descriptors listed above do not assist with differentiating between 'functional' and 'organic' voice disorders because of the great variability within and across classifications and aetiologies. That is, vocal function can be influenced by the presence of a lesion, its size and location, and often the maladaptive efforts used to compensate for the lesion. Alternatively, the primary vocal disruption may not be related to a lesion at all, but to maladaptive vocal techniques that may serve as precursors to the development of a lesion. Thus, it is often the case that what we hear in the voice is a combination of multiple factors and is not grounded within 'functional' or 'organic' domains. They are not separable entities.

As noted, deviations in vocal quality have traditionally been classified according to various schemes and theoretical principles. The goal is to establish a diagnosis based on aetiology and to guide treatment. It is with these goals of classification and diagnosis that the 'functional' versus 'organic' dichotomy has traditionally been applied to voice disorders. Generally, a voice disorder is thought to have an 'organic' aetiology if it associated with an abnormal structural finding within the larynx or a systemic medical or neurological condition, and is classified as 'functional' if it does not (Murphy 1964; Aronson 1980; Bridger and Epstein 1983; Roy 2003). Use of the term 'functional' as applied to a voice disorder is an application of medical terminology where 'functional' is applied to symptoms lacking a clear medical explanation (Deary and Miller 2011). The obvious benefit, or merit, of this classification scheme is its simplicity. The obvious flaw is that it is not that simple.

Whether a 'functional' or 'organic' classification is associated with voice disorder severity or the effect on perception of voice-related quality of life (VR-QOL) is not known. While one study reported no statistically significant difference in health-related quality of life between patients classified with 'organic' versus 'functional' voice disorders, or between women and men (Krischke *et al.* 2005), other reports have suggested an increased impact of neurologically based voice disorders on VR-QOL versus other 'organic' aetiologies (Cohen *et al.* 2006).

The definitions and diagnostic descriptions of 'functional' versus 'organic' voice disorders have been associated with a great deal of confusion in the fields of laryngology and speech-language pathology (Greene 1964). In a paper by Aronson *et al.* (1964), a list of criteria for what constitutes a 'functional' voice order was assembled, based on a survey study of professionals working in the field (it was published in French by Perello 1962). This list of criteria was quoted as follows:

A functional voice disorder exists when: (1) there is no apparent alteration in structure detected by laryngoscopic examination; (2) the laryngoscopic examination is negative, but the stroboscopic examination is positive; (3) the dysphonia is disproportionately severe in contrast to existing anatomic lesions or inflammation; (4) the disorder is of nervous origin, has variable symptoms, and is conducive to the formation of organic lesions; (5) the disorder is reversible (an organic one is irreversible); (6) function is altered (the disorder disappears when the organ is used correctly); (7) motor utilization is incorrect (therefore, it is a dysfunction); or (8) there is a desire to mask ignorance of the exact cause. (Aronson *et al.* 1964: 367)

While (1) is the classic definition of a 'functional' voice disorder, further interpretation is offered in (2), where a 'functional' aetiology can be defined by abnormal vocal fold movement or closure patterns during stroboscopy without abnormal findings observable with laryngoscopy. For a voice disorder to be considered 'functional', it is also clear that the vocal folds do not need to be completely free of 'organic' pathology, as noted in (3) and (4), and that behavioural therapy could be effective (5), in contrast to presumed therapeutic ineffectiveness for 'organic' cases. The variability in symptoms is addressed by (4). Number (4) also appears to include neurological aetiologies unless 'nervous origin' refers to psychogenic aetiology. Numbers (6) and (7) speak to maladaptive vocal behaviours, or motor function, while (8) may further refer to psychogenesis or malingering. Thus, it is clear that 50 years ago there was thinking that 'functional' voice disorders could present in many ways, perhaps contributing to the many different views and definitions used by practitioners today.

Murphy (1964: 1) discouraged the idea of 'functional' and 'organic' voice disorders being conceptualized as a 'two-valued system' and suggested that a continuum exists. The notion that misuse of the vocal apparatus (i.e. a 'functional' disorder) can lead to 'organic or structural changes' was communicated as early as 1913 (Mills 1913). However, where one draws the line between a 'functional' and an 'organic' voice disorder is not clear and has never been adequately defined. Murphy (1964: 3) described the artificial nature of the 'functional' and 'organic' distinction in the following way:

> Although the terms 'functional' and 'organic' represent an untenable dichotomy, most voice clinicians, for the sake of convenience alone, have continued to use the terms despite their imprecision. They recognize that in many functional cases subtle organic factors exist, and that in most, if not all, organic cases functional factors can be found.

Although Murphy spoke of these terms as convenient, given the lack of clarity in meaning of 'functional' and 'organic', it is surprising that these diagnostic and aetiological categories are still used today.

18.3   Voice disorders typically described as functional

Functional voice disorders are found at least twice as frequently in women as in men (Bridger and Epstein 1983). Recently, these disorders were reported to be the most common reason for visiting a speech-language pathologist in the United Kingdom with up to 40,000 new cases per year

(Deary and Miller 2011). In the field of speech-language pathology, there is a long history of use of the term 'functional' to describe disorders of psychogenic origin or those relating to 'personality variables' (Bloch and Goodstein 1971). As such, historically, functional voice disorders were thought to be somewhat synonymous with psychogenic voice disorders. In this vein, Aronson (1980) put forth a list of proposed aetiologies for functional voice disorders with the view that functional and psychogenic voice disorders could share a set of common aetiologies. Under this assumption, functional voice disorders were thought to be caused by 'psychoneuroses, personality disorders, or faulty habits of voice usage' (Aronson 1980: 11) in an environment of normal laryngeal anatomy and physiology. Specific aetiologies included stress, musculoskeletal tension and conflict associated with sex identification.

Modern definitions of 'functional' voice disorders are careful to apply this term to a deviation in how the vocal apparatus is *used* – that is, how it *functions* – versus the more psychological or psychiatric associations, which are now typically labelled as 'psychogenic voice disorders'. However, the confusion caused by this terminology remains. The major subtypes of functional voice disorders generally fall into the following rough categories: psychogenic voice disorders, voice disorders resulting from phonotrauma, and muscle tension dysphonia. More description of these entities is provided below.

Psychogenic voice disorders are characterized by a vocal disruption attributed to a psychological or psychiatric problem and referral to a professional trained in those areas is indicated (Boone *et al.* 2010). Cases of mutational falsetto and functional aphonia are placed in this category (Boone *et al.* 2010). Mutational falsetto is seen in post-pubescent males with abnormally high-pitched voices and vocal quality, and normal appearing larynges. When there is no underlying laryngeal pathology, individuals with mutational falsetto respond within 1–5 sessions of laryngeal reposturing and other techniques of behavioural management (Peppard 1996; Lim *et al.* 2007). It is important to recognize that the abnormal pitch and quality can be compensatory for an underlying problem such as paralysis or laryngeal web (Lundy and Casiano 1995), in which case any psychogenic component would be secondary to having a voice that calls attention to itself. Functional aphonia is a voice disorder that also occurs in the presence of a normal appearing larynx (Freidl *et al.* 1993). It occurs most commonly in females who score higher on introversion than their normal voiced counterparts (Roy *et al.* 2000a, 2000b).

It has been suggested that personality plays a role in determining how a person copes vocally with his or her environment (van Mersbergen 2011). Having a voice that does not meet one's occupational or social needs may be a form of unconscious coping that allows one to avoid stressful or unpleasant environments for a while, but eventually becomes too cumbersome to allow it to persist. Used long enough, the maladapted laryngeal behaviour becomes habituated and the individual is unable to return the voice to normal without professional help. The voice disorder may range from being a completely aphonic whisper to being a nearly aphonic, high-pitched, strained, strangled voice. Like mutational falsetto, the symptoms of functional aphonia respond readily to behavioural management techniques. Because the voice problems are only symptoms, it is necessary that the individual sees professionals who can assist in finding successful means of handling his or her environment.

Functional voice disorders can be associated with phonotrauma, such as yelling, excessive talking at high intensities, strain, singing in styles requiring screaming or hard glottal attack, and non-communicative vocal behaviours such coughing or throat clearing. Phonotrauma is not to be confused with exogenous laryngeal trauma injuries such as those resulting from intubation trauma, automobile accidents, or surgery. Phonotraumatic vocal behaviours are often associated with the appearance of vocal fold lesions, such as nodules or polyps, and oedema and hyperaemia. Nodules occur most commonly in young boys and young women (Hunter *et al.* 2011), and are thought to result from a constellation of factors such as length of the vocal fold, impact stress related to vocal intensity (Jiang *et al.* 1998; Gunter 2004), frequency and duration of vocal fold vibration, lifestyle behaviour, laryngeal oesophageal reflux (Arruda *et al.* 2011), personality traits (Roy and Bless 2000) and, in the case of adults, occupation. Histologically, the nodules are an accumulation of fluid in Reinke's space at the mid-membranous section of the vocal folds where impact stress is greatest. For the same level of vocal intensity the shorter the vocal fold the greater the impact stress, suggesting that individuals with shorter vocal folds may be at greater risk for developing phonotrauma disorders.

Phonotraumatic vocal behaviours may be chronic patterns of misuse or abuse, such as loud, high-frequency voicing that does not cause problems until the speaker reaches a threshold of tolerance that may be influenced by tissue irritation from laryngopharyngeal reflux, an upper respiratory infection or increased duration of speaking. The typical patient with vocal nodules is a young female who works as a teacher, singer or waiter, and who may be an extravert who uses her voice extensively to meet her occupational and vocational needs. Her voice is often characterized by a variable hoarse quality that is worse in the evening than in the morning and is accompanied by vocal fatigue and increased effort to produce voice. The choice of treatment is, nearly always, behavioural management which is directed at educating the patient about the causes of phonotrauma and changing vocal behaviours to create a better balance between vocal aerodynamic forces and laryngeal closure patterns, in order to minimize impact stress (Holmberg *et al.* 2001; Roy *et al.* 2002; Verdolini-Abbot 2008; Boone *et al.* 2010; Valadez *et al.* 2012). Most patients demonstrate a change in vocal quality within 1–2 weeks and near resolution of symptoms within

6–12 weeks (Murry and Woodson 1992; Ramig and Verdolini 1998). Even when symptoms seem to have resolved as judged by improved vocal quality and vocal fold appearance, and reduction in vocal effort, it is likely that changes to the delicate histoarchitecture of the vocal fold basement membrane zone are permanent and may render the individual more vulnerable to developing voice problems in the future under similar vocal circumstances. When a patient is not responsive to behavioural management, it may be that he or she has not adhered to treatment recommendations, that the treatment administered is inappropriate or that the diagnosis of nodules was incorrect. In patients recalcitrant to behavioural modification, other treatments such as medical management or surgery need to be considered.

Muscle tension dysphonia (MTD) is often observed along with the appearance of excessive tension within the neck area, associated laryngeal hyperfunction and vocal fatigue (Altman *et al.* 2005). MTD can be manifested as a primary functional voice disorder or as compensatory for an underlying organic pathology (Belafsky *et al.* 2002). MTD can be confused with neurological disorders and can mask underlying disorders for which the compensatory movements have been adapted. One of the most commonly occurring MTD diagnostic challenges is differentiating it from adductor spasmodic dysphonia (ADSD). In a recent review article, Roy (2010) reported using a task-specific protocol controlling for phonetic environments to help influence the severity of sign expression in ADSD and assist in differential diagnoses. He suggested that while the two problems may sound and appear similar, intra-word phonatory breaks should raise suspicions of ADSD. However, he concludes that no single test reliably differentiates the two disorders.

MTD may also mask underlying pathology such as vocal fold bowing (Belafsky *et al.* 2002). Thus, the multifactorial nature of MTD requires an interdisciplinary approach to both diagnosis and treatment (Altman *et al.* 2005). The functional voice pattern of hyperfunction, excessive muscle force, is relatively easy to identify from stroboscopic examination, and from perceptual quality (Van Houtte *et al.* 2011). Typically, stroboscopic examinations reveal long closed phase, bulging or approximation of the ventricular folds and anterior-posterior vocal fold compression to varying degrees. In extreme cases, hyperfunction can be associated with use of ventricular phonation and can be confused with ADSD. Perceptually, MTD is characterized by a strained strangled voice quality similar to that of ADSD, making differential diagnosis challenging. It is particularly problematic not only because they can exhibit similar auditory and visual voice patterns but also because MTD may be a secondary problem in response to ADSD.

Adductor and abductor spasmodic dysphonia, previously called spastic dysphonia, were also included in the list of psychogenic or functional voice disorders advanced by Aronson (1980). One might ask, why? While it is clear that the manner of physical 'function', as exemplified by the vibratory pattern, differs for the speaker with spasmodic dysphonia, the definition of 'function' 30 years ago focused on psychogenesis. What may or may not constitute a functional voice disorder has undergone some change over the past few decades, because spasmodic dysphonia is now considered to have a neurogenic or organic aetiology. As previously stated, the vocal signs and symptoms of spasmodic dysphonia are difficult to distinguish clinically from those of patients manifesting muscle tension dysphonia, either in acoustic characteristics or upon laryngeal examination (Roy 2003). Thus, as well stated by Roy, categorization of functional versus organic voice disorders and their sub-classifications may have limited clinical utility. He wrote that '[w]hen applied clinically, these various diagnostic labels often reflect clinician supposition, bias or perception' (Roy 2003: 144). Roy noted that distinguishing between functional and organic aetiologies is not reliable because there are very few clear differences between these entities. Given the overlapping nature of these classifications, the presumed multifactorial aetiologies and their complex interactions, it appears overly optimistic and ill-advised to continue describing voice disorders as either functional or organic.

As the case of spasmodic dysphonia and MTD demonstrates, distinguishing among voice disorder categories of functional and organic may be unreliable. But, clearly, it should be possible to differentiate characteristics of a functional voice disorder from normal phonation. However, this has not been shown to be the case when laryngeal video segments were examined in an attempt to differentiate normal from disordered vocal fold movement. Using functional dysphonia features described by different workers in the field, as well as global ratings of 'normal' or 'abnormal', two masked investigators who specialized in voice disorders rated laryngoscopic video samples (with no sound) from voice patients with a functional dysphonia and another group described as non-dysphonic controls (Sama et al. 2001). Results demonstrated a clear inability to differentiate patients with functional dysphonia from non-dysphonic controls based on laryngological video findings. Even when potential study limitations noted by the authors are considered, it is revealing that long-held beliefs regarding the laryngeal movement hallmarks of functional dysphonia were not substantiated when put to the test.

Recent research has suggested, as previously indicated, that some voice disorders may be associated with particular personality characteristics or traits (Roy and Bless 2000; Roy et al. 2000a, 2000b; van Mersbergen et al. 2008; O'Hara et al. 2011; Dietrich et al. 2012). Specifically, introversion, extraversion, stress reaction, neuroticism, anxiety and perfectionism may be associated with maladaptive laryngeal responses, such as excess tension often observed in muscle tension dysphonia patients (introversion) or vocal fold vocal nodules (extroversion) (Roy et al. 2000b; O'Hara *et al.* 2011). Specific personality traits have not been identified in people with organic voice disorders, such as spasmodic dysphonia and unilateral vocal fold paralysis (Roy *et al.* 2000a, 2000b).

18.4   Voice disorders typically described as organic

Aronson (1980) also listed several causes of organic voice disorders in his textbook. This list included congenital disorders, such as cri du chat syndrome and laryngomalacia; cysts; inflammation; tumours; endocrine disorders; and a variety of neurological diseases. Boone *et al.* (2010) group organic voice disorders into subcategories including cancer; congenital abnormalities (laryngomalacia, subglottal stenosis, tracheo-oesophageal fistulas and oesophageal atresia); contact ulcers and granulomas; cysts; endocrine changes; haemangioma; hyperkeratosis; infectious laryngitis; laryngectomy; leukoplakia; papilloma; pubertal changes; laryngopharyngeal reflux; sulcus vocalis; and webbing. Nodules and polyps were not on Boone *et al.*'s list because these lesions were classified as aetiologies of functional voice disorders.

Anomalies of the larynx alter the physical plant or structure of the vocal apparatus. Vocal symptoms can be present at birth or can develop at a later time. The reader is referred to a comprehensive chapter on this topic by Tewfik *et al.* (2006), which includes a detailed table that notes multiple syndromes or conditions, inheritance and manifestations. As indicated in this chapter, laryngomalacia is the most common congenital anomaly of the larynx, has no known cause, and is a significant concern related to respiratory function. Vocal fold paralysis is the second most common congenital anomaly, according to Cotton and Prescott (1988). Bilateral vocal fold paralysis is a significant concern related to respiratory function. For unilateral vocal fold paralysis, Tewfik *et al.* (2006: 353) note signs of hoarseness, breathy cry and possibly feeding difficulties. Recurrent respiratory papillomatosis (RRP) is a disease that affects the larynx and can occur congenitally, appearing at birth or in early childhood (Aronson 1980: 10). RRP is a benign, viral disease related to human papillomavirus (HPV, types 6 and 11) that leads to substantial concerns regarding airway patency in the first instance with secondary concerns for voice (Derkay *et al.* 1998). This disease is often noted as the most commonly occurring, benign neoplasm found in the larynx (Derkay *et al.* 1998). Care for RRP is palliative, inasmuch as neoplastic disease is removed repeatedly, as needed, via laser or other surgical technique. Children and adults with RRP can have hundreds of surgeries, with associated potential for vocal fold scarring and other sequelae contributing to voice problems. The use of antiviral drugs, such as cidofovir, has been attempted via injection into the tumour base with varying levels of success (Snoeck *et al.* 1998; Pransky *et al.* 1999, 2000; Chhetri *et al.* 2002; McMurray *et al.* 2008).

Benign and malignant tumours also alter the physical plant or structure of the larynx and affect voice due to mass loading of vocal fold tissues, glottal obstruction or other cause. Correction of the problem may require surgical, medical or behavioural interventions or a combination of these treatments. The extent to which a tumour affects voice depends largely on its size and location within the vocal apparatus and on how the neoplasm may alter vocal fold mechanics (Jiang *et al.* 1998). The range of voice changes resulting from vocal fold masses is nearly infinite. They can range from a mild disturbance in quality to a severely dysphonic voice to little change in quality but increased vocal effort. Normal vocal fold vibration requires a soft, pliable, layered structure with smooth edges that approximate during phonation with adequate pulmonary pressure. The presence of a mass alters the normal relationship between the respiratory driving forces and the vocal folds. For example, in the presence of added stiffness, opening the vocal fold requires more pulmonary power, which may be perceived by the patient as more effort. In the most extreme cases of vocal stiffness, as might be associated with papillomas or laryngeal cancer, the vocal folds cannot vibrate and the speaker is aphonic. If a mass is irregular in appearance, creating a rough edge to the vocal fold margins, the vocal folds will be unable to close completely. This causes turbulent airflow at the irregular edges, which adds noise to the voice signal. It is because of the wide range of mass size and shape, which can cause variable interference with the vibratory pattern, that the acoustic consequences are not always predictable. The consequences are further complicated by a person's ability to compensate for the presence of a tumour.

The influence of endocrine systems on voice has long been suspected. Because hormones regulate many critical body functions, it is not surprising that alterations in endocrine status can affect vocal function. Endocrine aetiologies are systemic in nature and thus are often classified as organically based voice disorders (Aronson 1980). In the *Classification Manual for Voice Disorders-I* (Verdolini *et al.* 2006: 105–11), endocrine diseases or disorders affecting voice are sub-classified under the headings of hypothyroidism, hyperthyroidism, sexual hormone imbalance and growth hormone abnormalities (hyperpituitarism). In the most general terms, the voice may be low in pitch and hoarse in hypothyroidism (Aronson and Bless 2009b: 31), while hyperthyroidism may be characterized by an unstable, breathy, quiet voice (Aronson and Bless 2009b: 32). Hyperpituitarism (acromegaly) may be accompanied by low pitch and hoarseness (Aronson and Bless 2009b: 32). Alterations in sex hormones can result in virilization or feminization of the voice relative to expected or baseline conditions. The normal menstrual cycle can also influence vocal characteristics presumably due to tissue oedema within the vocal apparatus (J. Abitbol *et al.* 1999). A historical account of sex hormones and the female voice, along with a study of hormonal influence on the voices of 197 women, is found in J. Abitbol *et al.* (1999).

Thyroid cancer is most often treated with thyroidectomy. This surgical procedure can affect voice due to thyroid hormone depletion and/or dysregulation, and also due to iatrogenic injury of the recurrent and/or superior laryngeal nerves, often resulting in vocal fold paralysis or paresis (Hundahl *et al.* 2000; Cheah *et al.* 2002; Sippel and Chen 2009). Insufficient thyroid hormone or dysregulation negatively affects quality of life (McMillan *et al.* 2008). Even without overt laryngeal nerve injury, voice can be negatively affected (Akyildiz *et al.* 2008), but the mechanisms remain unclear. Voice symptoms and aberrant vocal function measures have been reported soon after thyroid surgery in 30–87 per cent of patients, with 14 per cent reporting difficulty with voice at three months post-surgery (Stojadinovic *et al.* 2002; Sinagra *et al.* 2004; de Pedro Netto *et al.* 2006). Using the Dysphonia Severity Index (DSI), negative voice outcomes have been reported, with decreased early post-thyroidectomy DSIs predictive of later voice dysfunction (Henry *et al.* 2010). Acoustic analysis of the voices of 54 patients (45 female) before and after thyroidectomy revealed significant reductions in speaking fundamental frequency and fundamental frequency range (Hong and Kim 1997).

Neurological diseases have been classified based on point of lesion, whether in lower or upper motor neurons, basal ganglia, cerebellum, brainstem or cortex. Because the nervous system controls multiple key components of vocal function, such as the muscles of the larynx and respiratory system, it is easy to imagine how neurological diseases or disorders in neuromuscular function can have an effect on voice (Smith and Ramig 2006). Tables of neurological voice disorders, their classifications and potential points of lesion can be found in multiple textbooks (Aronson 1980; Smith and Ramig 2006). As classically defined (Darley *et al.* 1969a), each different point of lesion may have a distinct effect on voice and speech, albeit distinctiveness using auditory perceptual analysis may be more difficult to determine in practice than in theory. Vocal fold paralysis is an example of a neuromuscular disorder that affects voice, generally resulting is breathiness, weakness and vocal fatigue. Electromyography may assist with diagnosis of this condition (Lovelace *et al.* 1992; Ludlow *et al.* 1994). Other examples of neurological causes for voice disorders may include Parkinson's disease, spasmodic dysphonia, myasthenia gravis, stroke, cerebral palsy and amyotrophic lateral sclerosis.

Exogenous laryngeal trauma injuries such as that resulting from intubation trauma, automobile accidents or surgery may result in damage to any part of the larynx, causing both voice and airway problems. Injuries may include dislocated or fractured cartilages, muscle damage and vocal fold scarring. These injuries occur less frequently nowadays than they did in the past because of increased safety measures. Smaller intubation tubes are used and anaesthesiologists are better informed about how to avoid damage to the vocal apparatus. The use of safety belts in automobiles has reduced injuries, and changes in surgical practices have reduced iatrogenic vocal fold injuries. Nevertheless, exogenous laryngeal traumas do occur and often are the most difficult to correct because of resultant changes in biomechanics. The most common consequence of injury is scarring which changes the tissue composition and viscoelasticity of the vocal folds, resulting in stiffness and an abnormal sound generator. Currently, there is no reliable treatment for vocal fold scarring. Consequently, the goal of treatment is often to get the best voice possible from the damaged vocal instrument rather than attempting to achieve normal voice.

The role of laryngopharyngeal reflux (LPR), defined as the intermittent, retrograde movement of gastric contents into the hypopharynx, in development of laryngeal inflammation and voice disorders is now relatively well accepted (Koufman *et al.* 2002). It has been estimated that LPR is associated with up to two-thirds of all cases of laryngeal pathology and hoarseness presenting to an otolaryngology specialty clinic (Koufman 1991; Koufman *et al.* 2000). The characteristics of dysphonia associated with LPR may not differ substantially from those observed with other causes of dysphonia and the differential diagnosis is complex (Ross *et al.* 1998). Perception of health-related quality of life (HR-QOL) can be influenced by the presence of LPR (Carrau *et al.* 2004). A survey study from our institution involving a large sample of adult participants (who were not voice or laryngology patients) found that 26 per cent reported symptoms suggestive of LPR (Connor *et al.* 2007). Of those with LPR symptoms, 38 per cent reported a voice disorder and significant reductions in perception of HR-QOL.

18.5   Revised classification schemes

Because the 'functional' versus 'organic' classification scheme often provides limited information concerning the aetiology and presentation of a particular patient's voice, other classification systems have been proposed or the existing dichotomy has been expanded. For example, 30 years ago the functional voice disorder category was expanded into four subtypes based on a review of medical records (Koufman and Blalock 1982). This scheme included: Type 1, hysterical aphonia/dysphonia of sudden onset; Type 2, habituated hoarseness; Type 3, falsetto; and Type 4, vocal abuse. Criteria for laryngeal and voice findings for each of the types were provided.

Morrison and Rammage (1993) suggested the term 'muscle misuse voice disorders' for cases in which a normal appearing larynx co-occurs with muscle tension or other behavioural process affecting voice. They proposed several types of muscle misuse dysphonias. Type 1 includes the muscle tension dysphonias labelled by others as 'non-organic' (Bos-Clark and Carding 2011), which Morrison and Rammage refer to as the laryngeal isometric. The authors indicated that this disorder is observed most frequently in occupational and professional voice users. The other classifications included: Type 2, lateral contraction of hyperadduction; Type 3, anteroposterior contraction of the supraglottic larynx; Type 4, conversion aphonia; Type 5, psychogenic dysphonia with bowed vocal cords; and Type 6, adolescent transitional dysphonia.

Often, the use of alternative terminology has resulted in a larger number of categories. For example, the following five categories were recently used in a textbook to classify voice disorders: structural, neurogenic, systemic (organic) disease, functional and idiopathic (Sapienza and Hoffman-Ruddy 2009). Another recent textbook increased the number of classifications (Stemple *et al.* 2010). These authors divided voice disorder aetiologies into the following classifications: structural pathologies of the vocal fold, congenital and maturational changes affecting voice, inflammatory conditions of the larynx, trauma or injury of the larynx, systemic conditions, non-laryngeal aerodigestive disorders affecting voice, psychiatric and psychological disorders affecting voice, movement disorders affecting voice, central neurological disorders affecting voice, and other disorders of voice use. The *Classification Manual for Voice Disorders-I* used eight similar categories to organize voice disorder aetiologies (Verdolini *et al.* 2006). Thus, recent attempts to organize voice disorder aetiologies have resulted in a larger number of categories, have alleviated some of the confusion regarding terminology, but have resulted in greater complexity.

Voice disorder clusters represent another conceptualization of grouping perceptual voice characteristics to shed light on potential biomechanical factors underlying what we are hearing (Aronson and Bless 2009b). While the aetiology for each cluster may be different for each patient, this conceptualization was presented as a starting place for diagnostic probing. The clusters presented were: (1) husky breathy whispered–continuous group, with incomplete glottal closure as the unifying biomechanical factor; (2) strained hoarse-continuous group; (3) strained hoarse voice arrest–intermittent arrhythmic group; (4) strained hoarse voice arrest–intermittent rhythmic group; (5) voice tremor group; (6) breathy whispered–intermittent group; (7) low-pitched hoarse group; and (8) high-pitched group. Aronson and Bless provided detailed discussion of further probing that may be done in the complete voice evaluation for each cluster. For instance, using 'husky breathy whispered–continuous' as an example, with presumed glottal insufficiency as the underlying cause, the clinician should investigate a series of avenues including potential lesions, glottal margin discontinuity, vocal fold vibratory dysfunction, potential neurological involvement and potential psychogenic components. The cluster concept, therefore, presented a framework based on perceptual voice characteristics to direct further diagnostic work and treatment planning.

18.6   Variables influencing voice disorders

Multiple variables influence vocal function including integrity of the central and peripheral nervous systems, respiratory system, vascular system, as well as the laryngeal and resonance mechanisms. Other variables that may affect voice disorders include comorbid medical conditions, behavioural variables, occupation and compensatory strategies employed by the specific individual with the voice disorder. As such, the presence of a lesion on the vocal folds, either as a primary aetiology or as secondary aetiology based on misuse or compensation, is compounded on multiple levels. In addition, due to mind–body connections, stress, emotional, psychosocial, psychiatric and personality variables are likely to be important in any list of variables related to a voice disorder. Teasing out the variables operating in the care of the individual patient with a voice disorder is the duty of the treating clinicians when performing a complete voice evaluation (Welham 2009).

Morrison (1997: 109) discussed the tendency for clinicians to engage in classification, arguing that attempting to perform such classifications may be 'artificial and restrictive when one considers the complex clinical pattern present in any one patient'. Instead of classifying, Morrison suggested that the individual patient should be studied with the goal of uncovering patterns of potentially causative factors. In Morrison's schema, the major overlapping/interacting categories of causative factors for muscle misuse dysphonia are: (1) posture, muscle use and technical skill (including the larynx, shoulders, tongue, jaw and neck); (2) behaviour ('smoker', 'yeller', 'vocaholic'); (3) emotion (depression, anger, anxiety); and (4) reflux (dysmotility, inflammation). The clinician is, therefore, charged with determining the extent to which each of these major contributors is influencing the vocal manifestations of a particular patient. Certainly, these four components interact, overlap and load onto the voice outcome with different weightings or strengths. Morrison illustrated this concept with four partially overlapping ovals of different sizes, demonstrating the strength of contribution of particular factors in different patients.

In Figure 18.1, we have attempted to summarize our view of major factors that may influence the development of a voice disorder with or without the presence of vocal fold lesions, thus bypassing any attempt at classification. Individual characteristics that may be associated with voice disorder vulnerability are found in box A. These characteristics may interact with each other. For instance, future development of a voice disorder may be more likely in individuals with small vocal folds with thin covers (tissue characteristics), and/or people who are extraverts (personality traits), who may have compromised neurological systems (neurological sensorimotor integrity), and/or compromised physical or psychological health, such as an upper respiratory infection with vocal fold oedema. While these premorbid factors are operating throughout the lifespan,

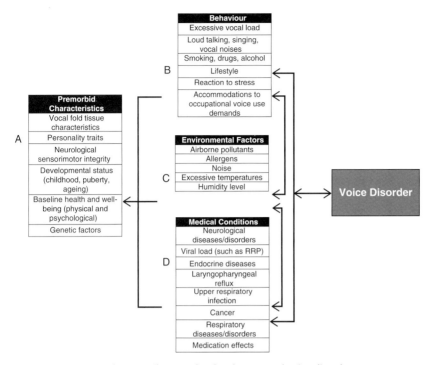

Figure 18.1 Factors that contribute to the development of voice disorders.

their relative influence and interaction with other factors differ at different stages of life. However, with the exception of congenital disorders, if internal and external factors noted in boxes B, C and D are not activated, a voice disorder may not develop. These factors also interact within and among boxes. In this view, the voice disorder found upon presentation to the clinic is the amalgamation of premorbid factors that long preceded that clinic visit, in addition to influence from multiple, interrelated contingencies that load into a disruption in vocal quality with differing and ever-changing weights or strengths. This schema demonstrates why voice disorders cannot be easily classified into the traditional functional and organic categories.

18.7   Research gained over the last two decades

In the last 10 to 20 years, there has been an explosion of research in areas related to voice. Here, we provide a short overview and references to review articles that provide state-of-the-art information as we know it today. Our brief review will focus on highlights of what we have learned regarding the complexity of the vocal mechanism, implications for assessment and treatment decisions, and how evidence-based studies and translational research might fill current gaps in our knowledge in the future.

Often discussions about voice therapy lead to the inevitable question of 'Is it art or science?' This same question was addressed by Tate (2006) in her John Stanley Coulter Memorial Lecture on the state of rehabilitation research. She makes the point that qualitative approaches make an 'artful' complement to quantitative methods, and that the information can be used as research tools to aid investigators in seeking knowledge about complexities associated with treatment. According to Tate, there are four major principles of scientific complexity: (1) interconnectivity among diverse components; (2) iteration of activity patterns; (3) emergence of order discovered by operating iterative cycles; and (4) holism resulting from interaction between the component elements of the system. Understanding this complexity requires studying the elements in isolation, in different combinations, and as a whole (Tate 2006). Although Tate was discussing physical rehabilitation, the same relationship with complex processes applies to our understanding of voice. It is because of these complex processes that we cannot easily classify a voice disorder as functional or organic. Furthermore, we must recognize the importance of clinicians having access to information beyond the traditional study of anatomy and physiology. For effective treatments, it is crucial to understand mechanisms on the microscopic level with clear pathways to translation evidenced at each stage of the research process on which the treatment is based.

For the most part, information on the microscopic level comes from bench-to-bedside translational research. This research is expensive and has a long life cycle. According to an analysis performed by Contopoulos-Ioannidis *et al.* (2008), of 101 research findings with highly promising clinical potential between 1979 and 1983, only five resulted in clinical interventions by 2003, only one had extensive clinical use, and median translational lag was 24 years. Nevertheless, translational research findings have the potential to transform treatment in this century. Our increased understanding of molecular and cellular events opens new horizons for prevention and treatment of voice disorders (Bartlett *et al.* 2012). Our current and future goal is to prevent voice disorders, not simply to treat already existing vocal manifestations, by understanding pre-clinical events and by detecting patients at risk. This can only be achieved by employing new knowledge of cellular and molecular events as they relate to other variables.

Methods in molecular biology provide a sensitive means to examine the relationships and interrelationships between biology and behaviour. The environment and behaviour influence the expression of genes (Titze *et al.* 2004; Wang and Thampatty 2006), which in turn induces changes in brain function and behaviour. In this vein, vocal fold vibration and subsequent forces may alter vocal fold extracellular matrix properties and cell biology. This knowledge has led to an exciting new area of research with bioreactors that permit simulation of phonatory activities to determine cellular changes caused by mechanical forces, such as heavy vocal loads used by professional voice users (Titze *et al.* 2004; Gaston *et al.* 2012). This illustrates the importance of clinicians having a holistic approach to assessment and treatment of dysphonia. It is necessary to recognize that change may occur at levels other than overt behaviour.

Using a modern lens to look at the vocal apparatus, we have learned a considerable amount about the delicate histoarchitecture of the vocal folds that is so critical to vocal fold vibration. As an example, recent research has shown that the vocal fold epithelium is not a passive cover. It is dynamic, exhibits specific permeability characteristics and may have effects on underlying tissues, as evidenced in several studies (Morrison *et al.* 1999; Fisher *et al.* 2001; Sivasankar *et al.* 2010; Rousseau *et al.* 2011). These studies show that vocal intensity, surface fluid and smoking alter epithelial barrier function by increasing its permeability. These findings suggest that pharmacological treatments aimed at restoring hydration level and chemical composition of vocal fold surface fluid might be a fruitful avenue of future treatment.

Similarly, from a microscopic perspective, understanding wound healing is an important factor in treating voice disorders. Inflammatory processes have a key role in initiating and coordinating various wound healing mechanisms after injury (Branski *et al.* 2006; Ling *et al.* 2010). Tissue engineering focuses on the function of cells and on the role of biomaterials in actively stimulating tissue healing and regeneration (Duflo *et al.* 2006). Factors influencing wound healing have been the central focus of interdisciplinary studies in tissue engineering. These studies have the potential to modify injured vocal folds.

Not all of the research advances have been in biology. Most notable have been advances in laryngeal imaging, because they have changed the way we assess and treat dysphonic patients. Through recent laryngeal imaging techniques, we can detect micro-level changes in vocal fold tissue and vibration (Svec *et al.* 2007; Burns 2012). This knowledge has been used to develop imaging assessment protocols to improve diagnostics and to use as outcome measures to document changes resulting from treatment (Kaszuba and Garrett 2009; Svec *et al.* 2007; Bonilha *et al.* 2012; Mehta *et al.* 2012). Similarly, recognition of the problems associated with auditory perceptual judgements has led to the development of instruments such as the Consensus Auditory-Perceptual Evaluation of Voice (CAPE-V) (Kempster *et al.* 2009). Such instruments assist the standardization of perceptual judgements, which allows comparisons to be made between patient visits and among different clinics (Kempster *et al.* 2009). Recognition of the need for patient input has resulted in tools to measure quality of life and impact of the voice disorder. Additionally, acknowledgement of the need for a holistic approach to assessment has given rise to multidimensional assessment protocols (Yumoto 2004; Lim *et al.* 2007).

With improved diagnostic- techniques and knowledge of the vocal system one might anticipate major improvements in treatment outcomes. Despite a large body of work (Carding and Horsley 1992; Carding *et al.* 1999; Mackenzie *et al.* 2001; McCrory 2001; Roy *et al.* 2002, 2003; Speyer 2006; Hapner *et al.* 2009; Smith *et al.* 2010), it is difficult to make comparisons among studies because of differences in populations, type and intensity of treatment and outcome measures used. Considering participant characteristics is critical in interpreting treatment outcomes, because genetic studies suggest that Reinke's oedema, polyps and nodules can be similar in appearance, but genetically different (Duflo *et al.* 2006). This leads us to suspect that treatment should also differ. Interpretations of treatment success are further complicated because infections, allergies, LPR and environmental irritants known to impact the larynx must be considered when interpreting findings (Pedersen *et al.* 2004).

A number of direct voice therapy techniques (Kotby *et al.* 1991; Stemple *et al.* 1994; Sabol *et al.* 1995; Verdolini-Marston *et al.* 1995; Roy *et al.* 1997; Verdolini *et al.* 1998a; Chen *et al.* 2007) often paired with vocal education or vocal hygiene have been reported as successfully treating dysphonias from a variety of aetiologies. Information on which of these techniques is best for any specific individual is lacking. There may be a host of reasons for treatment failure. The treatment administered may be inappropriate for the problem, the treatment may not be sufficiently intense, the patient may not be following treatment recommendations, and/or the patient may not be ready for change. During the past decade, several of these potential obstacles have been addressed (Behrman 2006; van Leer *et al.* 2008; Patel *et al.* 2011; van Leer and Connor 2012) and further work in this area is warranted.

In summary, the information presented here presents a few highlights of research accomplished in the last two decades. Evidence-based research on treatment of voice problems is sparse, whether behavioural management or surgery. This is due, at least in part, to the individual variations from patient to patient, from clinician to clinician, and to the resultant difficulty in conducting systematic studies in this population. Thus, much of the information speech-language pathologists and laryngologists must rely on for direction in treating patients with voice disorders comes from animal studies, cellular studies, research on successfully preventing or treating problems elsewhere in the body, and studies done on small populations. These works provide valuable information upon which we can build current treatment and research strategies, but more work must be done in translating these data to the clinic and in optimizing clinical treatment protocols for any individual patient. It is likely that advances in other fields such as technology, tissue engineering and muscle physiology will have an increasingly important role in treatment of voice disorders, including better behavioural therapies. Furthermore, information gained from cell responses to bioreactors and animal models may provide speech-language pathologists with prescriptive information about types, timing and dosages of treatment. Thus, although we have much to learn about the treatment of voice disorders, the future promises to have an interdisciplinary treatment that is likely to be reliable, durable and tailor-made for each individual patient.

18.8 Summary

Voice production disorders result in deviations in vocal quality that can impair not only communicative function but also the quality of life. At any given point in time across the lifespan, anywhere from 3 to 9 per cent of the population has some type of voice dysfunction (Berry *et al.* 2001). Although voice problems traditionally have been classified into disorders of functional and organic origin, division between the two cannot be easily distinguished. Definitions in the literature have been confusing and often do not take variables influencing disorders, or responses to treatment, into consideration.

What can be identified as contributing to the voice disorder in the individual patient depends on the tools and training of the clinician and on the current state of knowledge, which is always rapidly changing. The ultimate clinical goal is to provide the best treatment possible for each individual patient. This can only be achieved by using results from a multi-pronged vocal assessment approach that examines the whole person and how variables such as pre-existing conditions, medical conditions, occupation and vocal load requirements impact on the voice problem. Without this approach, we may not be able to uncover variables interfering with compliance and success of treatment. Moreover, we are unlikely to design research studies that will contribute to advancing our knowledge rather than obscuring it with conflicting results. Thus, it appears that the dichotomy of functional versus organic is too simple, and does not take sufficient account of the 'impact variables' (summarized in Figure 18.1) or the interactions among variables, tissue changes and voice production. It is only when one looks at the whole person, regardless of whether or not there are visible tissue changes, that successful treatment can be reliably administered.

Despite the gains we have made in holistic assessment of the individual voice patient, much more needs to be known before we can accurately diagnose and choose the most reliable and efficient treatment. For instance, we do not know the effects of muscle training on muscle fibres, nerve–muscle connections and mucosa, nor do we know how the amount, intensity and distribution of voice use and/or voice therapy affect the outcomes of treatment. Animal studies and bioreactors are likely to provide necessary insight to begin clinical trials. Unfortunately, this type of translational research often takes years before it can be routinely applied in the clinic. Occupations hazardous to voice have been identified, as have both internal and external environmental factors, but we know little about the interaction of factors. Research in this arena is expensive and difficult to accomplish, because placebo, double-blind treatment is difficult or nearly impossible to achieve in voice therapy.

Vocal hygiene is routinely administered to voice patients, but there is limited evidence that it makes a significant difference in resolution of symptoms. Similarly, many treatment plans include vocal warm-ups and cool-downs but evidence supporting their efficacy is weak. Directly related to the discussion here about functional versus organic disorders is research done elsewhere in the body in the field of psychoneuroimmunology. That research has demonstrated that thoughts and emotions affect our bodies at the cellular level, in the same way as genes, lifestyle and things we ingest (Bradley-Hagerty 2009). Psychological stress has been linked to nearly every disease of the body including suppressed immune systems and heart attacks. Why wouldn't these same types of stressors affect the laryngeal respiratory system similarly? And if so, how does one separate functional from organic? In this chapter, we argue that it cannot be reliably accomplished.

19

Stuttering and cluttering

Kathleen Scaler Scott

19.1   Stuttering

Stuttering is defined as a fluency disorder whereby a speaker's forward flow of speech is impeded. In stuttering, the speaker knows what he or she wishes to say, has the message formulated, but has difficulty getting the speech sounds out to produce the message in a fluent manner. The speech sounds are repeated, prolonged and/or blocked so that that speaker has difficulty moving forward to the next sound. Although stuttering is often considered a low incidence disorder, it carries with it potential negative social, academic and/or vocational consequences.

19.1.1   Speech features of stuttering

Given that all speakers are disfluent at one time or another, and that the presence of disfluency does not necessarily result in a diagnosis of stuttering, disfluent speech is typically broken down into two types (Yairi and Ambrose 1992a; Ambrose and Yairi 1999). The first type of disfluency is known as stuttering-like disfluencies (SLDs), those most typically produced by individuals diagnosed with stuttering. These disfluencies include blocks (i.e. the speaker becomes 'stuck' on a sound in a word and cannot move to the next sound; attempts at producing the sound may or may not be audible), prolongations of sounds, part-word repetitions and single-syllable whole-word repetitions with tension. Non-stuttering-like disfluencies (NSLDs) are produced by all speakers, and are related more to thought formulation than to the sound production problems observed in stuttering. These include repetitions of single-syllable or multisyllabic words without tension, repetitions of phrases, and interjections and/or filler words. One component involved in diagnosing a speaker with stuttering includes the frequency with which SLDs occur in their speech. Part

Table 19.1 *Definitions of disfluency by type*

Name	Acronym	Example
Stuttering-like disfluencies	SLDs	
Repetitions of:		
Single-syllable whole words (with tension)	SSWWR	'I-I-I'
Sounds or syllables (part-word repetition)	PWR	'd-d-uck' 'Spi-spiderman'
Prolongations	PR	'sssometimes'
Blocks/Tense pauses	TP	'st – uck'[a]
Non-stuttering-like disfluencies	NSLDs	
Repetitions of:		
Multisyllable whole words	MSWWR	'open-open'
Phrases	PHR	'I want – I want'
Revisions	REV	'I like unicorns, no, I mean dragons'
Interjections/Fillers	INT	'um, uh, er, well, like, so'[b]

[a] Defined as a break in phonation accompanied by audible or inaudible tension.
[b] Words such as 'well', 'like' and 'so' not counted as interjections when used to add to sentence meaning (e.g. 'I got water from the *well*', 'She looks *like* her mother', 'I'm going to sleep *so* I can get up early tomorrow').

of the criteria for diagnosis of stuttering in a child includes the presence of SLDs in their speech 3 per cent or more of the time (Conture 2001). Table 19.1 outlines examples of the various types of SLDs and NSLDs.

19.1.2 Non-speech features of stuttering

The non-speech features of stuttering include secondary behaviours. Such behaviours involve visible tension or struggle in the face, articulators or other parts of the body, and other mannerisms such as eye blinks, facial grimaces, pounding fists, etc. during the moment of struggle. These behaviours are thought to occur first as stutterers attempt to work through a moment of stuttering, and then to be conditioned as the stutterer's automatic response to their speech struggles (Brutten and Shoemaker 1967).

Other non-speech features of stuttering include what has come to be known as the affective and cognitive components of stuttering. Historically, these components of stuttering were not recognized as a part of the disorder, which was evaluated and diagnosed based only on its overt symptoms (i.e. SLDs and secondary behaviours). More recently, the World Health Organization (WHO) has taken the view that a disorder can have an impact on the whole person. Yaruss (1998a, 1998b, 2001) and Yaruss and Quesal (2004a, 2004b) adapted the WHO's original International Classification of Functioning, Disability and Health to stuttering. As part of this adaptation, emphasis was placed not only on the observable behavioural characteristics of stuttering, but also on the affective and cognitive components of stuttering.

Affective components are defined as the feelings one has about one's stuttering, and may include (but are not restricted to) such feelings as guilt, shame, frustration, sadness and embarrassment (Yaruss and Quesal 2006). Cognitive components are defined as a person's interpretations of his or her stuttering. These interpretations shape how a person views his or her stuttering and ultimately how he or she reacts to it (Yaruss and Quesal 2006). For example, an interpretation of a moment of stuttering by a preschooler may be 'I can't talk'. This preschooler may then shut down after experiencing a moment of stuttering. An interpretation of stuttering by a school-age child may be 'I can't say my name'. Accordingly, the child may 'change' his or her name to something else, such as taking on a middle name as the first name, or using a completely different name. An adolescent may interpret his or her stuttering to mean that a career which involves speaking cannot be pursued. This may result in the adolescent taking high school and/or college coursework outside of his or her interest area. An adult may interpret his or her stuttering in a similar fashion, and consequently be held back from achieving a true career potential. These affective and cognitive components of stuttering can have significant negative consequences for the person who stutters (PWS), regardless of level of frequency of outward disfluencies (Yaruss and Quesal 2004b).

19.1.3   Relationship between speech and non-speech features of stuttering

The main advantage to understanding both the speech and non-speech features of stuttering is that this understanding can help one to further make sense of the interaction between the two. Feelings of shame or embarrassment (i.e. affective components) may cause the PWS to try to push through a moment of stuttering quickly rather than give themselves time to access a speech strategy to help them move through the word. In trying to push through a moment of stuttering, the PWS may exhibit secondary struggle behaviours such as eye blinks, and tension in the face or other parts of the body. Thus, there is often a relationship between the physical behaviours of stuttering one sees and the feelings underlying these behaviours. This should not be mistaken as feelings causing the physical behaviours, but rather as feelings in response to a moment of stuttering contributing to how the physical behaviours manifest themselves.

A person's cognitive perception of their stuttering may directly affect how a PWS communicates a message. For example, if a PWS feels that they cannot say their name or hometown, they may 'talk around' this word, inserting lots of filler words and/or substitutions, thereby possibly appearing to have intellectual difficulties or other limitations. The speech may appear as 'My name is uh, uh, uh, well, my name is uh, my name is Jim', or 'I live in that city next to Toronto. The one where …'. A PWS may come to feel their opinion has less value, and therefore show a decrease in class participation or participation in work meetings. Each PWS experiences the affective, behavioural and cognitive components of stuttering in different proportions relative to their own life experience with the disorder.

19.1.4 Epidemiology of stuttering

The prevalence rate is highest among preschool children, when stuttering most frequently begins (Andrews and Harris 1964). In a study of 3,164 African American and European American preschool children, Proctor *et al.* (2008) found a prevalence rate of 2.52%, with more boys than girls stuttering. Recovery from stuttering has been found to occur in preschoolers without intervention at a rate of 65% within the first two years of stuttering onset (Yairi and Ambrose 1999) and up to 85% (with some intervention reported; Månsson 2000) five to six years after onset.

Studies to determine the prevalence of stuttering among school-age children have been conducted from the nineteenth century to the present day. Averages from these studies indicate a prevalence of approximately 1% occurrence of stuttering among school-age children in the United States and Europe. Although there have been criticisms of certain study designs (see Craig *et al.* 2002), such as collecting data from non-random samples, the average prevalence rate in developed countries tends to hover around 1% (Bloodstein and Bernstein Ratner 2008). However, the most recent studies have suggested that the prevalence in children beyond preschool years may be slightly lower than 1% (Yairi and Ambrose 2013).

Regarding incidence of stuttering, Andrews and Harris (1964) studied 1,000 children over a 16-year period. The investigators found an incidence rate of 4.9% between birth and 16 years. Andrews and Harris also found that the risk factor for developing stuttering slowly declined after preschool years, and was significantly decreased after puberty. Updated studies beginning in the year 2000 indicated that incidence rates might be as high as 8% (Yairi and Ambrose 2013).

19.1.5 Aetiology of stuttering

While there are cases of stuttering following neurological insults, the majority of cases of stuttering occur during normal development of speech and are not related to insult, injury or disease. Developmental stuttering has many proposed aetiologies. Theories have been developed, refined and/or expanded over time. The current thinking reflects the view that no one factor seems to result in stuttering, and that various components may combine in different individuals to produce stuttering. Three of the main potential components studied are genetic, neurological and linguistic factors. This section will also consider factors that are believed to play a role in the maintenance of stuttering once it is established.

Genetic findings in stuttering: Twin studies, adoption studies, family studies and population studies have shown a genetic contribution in some but not all cases of non-syndromic stuttering. The first studies that examined the relationships between stuttering in families arose when families seeking services for their children who stutter (CWS) identified relatives who also stutter. Twin studies have shown that stuttering has a moderate to high heritability factor (Drayna 2011). As the field of genetics has advanced, studies have found genetic variants for stuttering linked to specific chromosomes. New methods in biological genetics including linkage analysis, candidate gene analysis, genome-wide association study, and functional genome-wide association have provided a start to confirming that multiple genes are involved in stuttering and interact in a complex manner (see Yairi and Ambrose 2013 for a review). Identifying specific genotypes and their contribution to stuttering requires replication and analysis.

Neurological findings in stuttering: Studies have identified anatomical differences in the brains of those who stutter in terms of lateralization, size of structures, and/or amounts of white and grey matter. The field of stuttering has a long history of considering differences in brain lateralization among those who stutter (Travis 1928; Orton and Travis 1929). Early twenty-first-century evidence supporting these differences was related to changes in lateralization/dominance following stuttering treatment (De Nil *et al.* 2003). Because the studies were conducted on adults, it has been unclear whether differences in lateralization/dominance are related to causal factors in stuttering, or secondary to compensatory mechanisms used in response to stuttering. Recent research involving comparison of children aged 9 to 12 years with persistent stuttering, those who recovered from stuttering and those who never stuttered failed to confirm differences in lateralization that were previously found with adults (Chang *et al.* 2008). These findings offered the first possible confirmation that the lateralization differences found in adults were related to the consequence of living with stuttering rather than a causal agent in stuttering.

Chang *et al.*'s study of 9- to 12-year-olds did reveal reduced grey matter volume connected to both groups of children at risk for stuttering (i.e. the groups with recovered and persistent stuttering). Decreased left white matter integrity was found for the group of children with persistent stuttering. This study included seven to eight children in each group and needs to be replicated with larger samples. However, it provides preliminary information regarding the role of anatomical differences in those at risk for stuttering.

A later study using near infrared spectroscopy and comparing pre-schoolers, school-age children and adults who stutter to controls showed that there was no pattern of functional brain lateralization for speech processing among those who stutter, including preschoolers (Sato *et al.* 2011). This pattern of functional brain lateralization was identified in control participants, however, suggesting that the idea that differences in lateralization are a consequence of dealing with stuttering may not in fact be the case. Replication of such studies is needed with larger samples of participants. The increasing sophistication and safety of imaging technology hold promise for further study of structural and functional differences in children who stutter.

Psycholinguistic findings in stuttering: Some of the psycholinguistic theories of the aetiology of stuttering are related to the role of disordered encoding of language. Specifically, theories have proposed difficulties in encoding speech at phonological (Wingate 1988), lexical (Karniol 1995), syntactical (Bernstein 1981; Bernstein Ratner 1997a; Bloodstein 2002, 2006), or suprasegmental (Perkins *et al.* 1991; Packman *et al.* 1996) levels. Some of these models have suggested problems in more than one area of encoding (Karniol 1995), or a dyssynchrony between linguistic planning and motor execution (the Execution and Planning (EXPLAN) Model; Dworzynski *et al.* 2003). A psycholinguistic model frequently cited as a potential source for stuttering has been the Covert Repair hypothesis (Postma and Kolk 1993; Kolk and Postma 1997). In this model, it is proposed that a PWS over-monitors speech for errors in the planning stages. During this monitoring, true errors are caught and resolved before they become overt errors, but errors that are caught and are not true errors result in various forms of stuttering. Specific sources of encoding errors (i.e. phonemic, syntactic, semantic, lexical) result in specific types of disfluency. Components of all proposed psycholinguistic theories have undergone testing, but further work is needed to draw final conclusions regarding any of the psycholinguistic models.

Stuttering as a learned behaviour: No current theories hold that the development of stuttering is *rooted* in learned behaviour. However, some theories propose that although stuttering may begin from some multifactorial origin, the behaviour is often maintained by the PWS's reaction to it (see Bloodstein and Bernstein Ratner (2008) for a review). For example, the struggle against one's stuttering may be maintained by pairing of the struggle with successful attempts to get through a moment of stuttering, that is, by operant conditioning (Brutten and Shoemaker 1967). Some of the current treatment methodology works to address specific learned behaviours in response to the moment of stuttering. For example, stuttering modification therapy involves use of the strategy cancellation, which involves a 'time out' from the moment of stuttering to cancel automatic reactions of struggle and to begin again with a control strategy (Van Riper 1938). The Lidcombe Program (Onslow and Packman 1999), a stuttering intervention programme used with preschoolers, is based on operant principles. Thus, although stuttering is not known to be caused by learned behaviours, some treatments reflect the fact that learned behaviours can follow from an individual's experience with stuttering.

Stuttering and self-regulation: Once established, there is some evidence that self-regulation problems may play a role in the maintenance of stuttering. Anderson *et al.* (2003) found significant differences in self-regulatory skills of a group of 31 preschool CWS versus controls. The authors speculated that such differences, although not changeable learned behaviours, may be a factor regarding those who persist in stuttering versus those who recover. Responses to parent questionnaires regarding temperament revealed CWS as a group to be less adaptable to change and less distracted by environmental stimuli, and to exhibit less predictable biological functions than children who do not stutter (CWNS). The investigators proposed relationships between each of these temperamental characteristics and stuttering. For example, the authors postulated that CWS may be less adaptable to change because of their stuttering and its unpredictability in novel situations. Alternatively, the authors proposed that it may be possible that general temperamental differences, such as decreased adaptability to change, may result in a decreased comfort among CWS in entering new speaking situations.

Investigators suggested a third possibility for the relationship between decreased adaptability to change and stuttering. This third possibility reflects some combination of the prior two explanations. That is, a child who is less adaptable to change may be more likely to avoid new situations, and may also be more likely to stutter in these situations. In terms of less distractibility and its relationship to stuttering, the authors proposed that perhaps CWS are more focused upon mistakes in their speech and therefore are more likely to react with tension and struggle against these mistakes, which can exacerbate stuttering. Finally, the investigators proposed that unpredictable biological functions may lead to increased stress and anxiety, which may indirectly contribute to the maintenance of stuttering. Differences in temperament have been confirmed in a more recent sample of 116 CWS and matched controls (Eggers *et al.* 2010). Further study is needed to confirm any of these potential connections between temperament and stuttering. The study of self-regulation in CWS and its relationship to the larger picture of stuttering is still in its infancy.

19.1.6 Stuttering and language

Within the stuttering literature, investigators have been building a case of potential subtle linguistic differences in CWS (Bernstein Ratner and Sih 1987; Silverman and Bernstein Ratner 2002; Zackheim and Conture 2003; Hartfield and Conture 2006; Wagovich and Bernstein Ratner 2007).

Bernstein Ratner and Sih reported a 'growing clinical impression of subtle language differences in CWS' (1987: 278), but were unable to support
this finding for a sentence repetition task in preschoolers who stutter.
Over the years, researchers have suggested that perhaps the reason such
differences were suspected rather than identified was related to the sensitivity and validity of the measures being used to test for language differences. Watkins and Yairi (1997) examined the language of preschoolers who stutter via language sampling rather than through standardized
test measures. The investigators measured the mean length of utterance (MLU), number of different words and number of total words in
32 preschoolers separated into three different groups: persistent stutterers, late recovered stutterers and early recovered stutterers. Results
indicated that the majority of CWS in all groups exhibited language
that was at or above average in comparison to established developmental norms. Although there were no significant differences in language
between persistent stutterers and early and late recovered CWS, children in the persistent group were noted to exhibit more variation in
their performance in comparison to the other two groups of children
for all language variables measured (i.e. MLU, number of different words
and number of total words).

Similarly, Watkins *et al.* (1999) completed a longitudinal study of 84
children who stuttered between the ages of 2 and 5 years. Spontaneous
language samples were taken from each child at the time of entrance
to the study. Participants were followed for a minimum of four years,
at the end of which time 62 were classified as recovered from stuttering
and 22 were classified as persistent stutterers. Language skills at the time
of entry into the study were compared to a normative sample. Results
revealed that regardless of their eventual grouping, all children scored at
least within the average range of performance on the language variables
of MLU, number of different words, number of total words and syntactic
and morphological analyses. Children who entered the study at earlier
ages tended to score one year above their peers entering the study at later
ages. Dissociations were suggested when it was noted that no such precocious findings were identified for these children in the area of phono-
logical/articulation development. Thus, although this subgroup of children exhibited precocious expressive language skills, these skills were
dissociated from their phonological development. Children who persisted
in stuttering exhibited phonological development that progressed in the
same sequence as their recovered peers and used the same substitution
patterns as their peers. However, the persistent group tended to score
lower than their recovered peers on all formal testing measures of phonological development. The investigators concluded that CWS who exhibit
delays in phonological development are at increased risk for persistent
stuttering (Paden *et al.* 1999). Given delays in phonological development
and at least average expressive language skills, dissociations between

different areas of speech and language are suggested early on in the development of persistent stuttering.

Anderson and Conture (2000) were the first to identify dissociations in standardized testing between CWS and CWNS. The researchers found that among a sample of preschoolers who did and did not stutter, both groups scored within the average range of performance on measures of receptive vocabulary and measures of receptive/expressive language. However, the sample of CWS exhibited a larger difference between the two measures than did the CWNS. Although these differences did not correlate with increased measures of stuttering, the investigators speculated that semantic development may be somewhat slower than syntactic development in CWS, and that such a mismatch may be related to disruptions in fluency of speech. In a study of the language abilities of 45 preschoolers who stuttered and 45 preschoolers who did not stutter, Anderson *et al.* (2005) found that the CWS exhibited three times the amount of dissociations between the speech and language domains (measured via standardized testing) as CWNS. Findings remained significant even when groups were matched for overall oral language abilities. Results of this study revealed variability in the patterns of dissociation. The consistent pattern observed was not a specific type of dissociation. However, it is important to note that dissociations *did* occur among CWS.

Investigators have identified specific trends of linguistic differences among children who stutter in the area of lexical abilities. Silverman and Bernstein Ratner (2002) examined vocabulary diversity in a sample of 15 CWS (diagnosed with stuttering within four months of study participation) and 15 CWNS. The researchers found no indications of language disorder among the CWS as compared to the CWNS on either standardized measures of vocabulary or use of a measure of vocabulary diversity (i.e. vocd; Malvern and Richards 1997). However, although both groups exhibited average scores, the CWS did exhibit significantly lower average scores than the CWNS on the Expressive One-Word Picture Vocabulary Test-Revised (Gardner 1990) and measures of vocd and lexical rarity (Bernstein Ratner and Silverman 2000; Miles and Ratner 2001), suggesting possible subtle language differences among the CWS. In a sample of 26 preschoolers, half of whom did and half of whom did not stutter, Hartfield and Conture (2006) found no significant differences in error production in picture-naming tasks between CWS and CWNS, but slower speech reaction times for naming among CWS, even when words were said without stuttering. CWS exhibited slower reaction times than matched peers under four different categories of priming (i.e. tone, word physically related to target word, word functionally related to target word, and word categorically related to target word). Thus, there is an emerging trend of potential delays in word retrieval among CWS.

From an early age, investigators are finding that some children with language impairments present with specific disfluency types that distinguish them from children with normal development. N.E. Hall *et al.* (1993) found increased patterns of NSLDs and SLDs in a subgroup of 3- to 5-year-olds with developmental language disorders. This difference has also been demonstrated in children with only a *history* of language disorders. Boscolo *et al.* (2002) studied children with a history of specific expressive language impairment (HSLI-E) as compared to age-, gender- and socioeconomic-status-matched typically developing (TD) children. Participants were recruited from a previous study in which they participated at 2 years of age (Rescorla 1989). Participants were re-examined at 9 years of age for the Boscolo *et al.* study. By age 9, standardized testing no longer revealed the language impairments originally seen among the group of HSLI-E children. Yet, subtle differences in language skills, including average but significantly lower scores than those of the TD group on tests of standardized language, were present for the HSLI-E group.

Participants' narratives produced in response to a wordless picture book were analysed for patterns of disfluency. Boscolo *et al.* broke analysis of disfluency down into 'normal disfluency' (defined as whole-word repetitions, phrase repetitions, revisions and interjections) and SLDs (defined as part-word repetitions, prolongations, broken words, and blocks/tense pauses). Results of this study revealed that the children with HSLI-E exhibited a significantly greater amount of total disfluencies in their speech than did the TD children. When analyses were broken down by type of disfluency, differences between the groups reached significance for the proportion of SLDs in the samples but not for the proportion of NSLDs in the samples. Although the authors reported that there were few occurrences of SLDs among all participants, in terms of frequency of occurrence of SLDs, the HSLI-E group exhibited significantly more SLDs than did the TD group. In addition, a greater percentage (78%) of the HSLI-E children exhibited SLDs than did those within the TD group (52%). No statistically significant differences were found between groups in terms of types of SLDs.

A description of the SLDs revealed that the HSLI-E group produced seven times more blocks and three times more part-word repetitions than their matched peers. Broken words were found to occur the least frequently of all SLDs among both groups. Part-word repetitions and prolongations were reported to have occurred most frequently among the HSLI-E group. The investigators found that the HSLI-E group tended to produce more SLDs on function rather than content words, which is reflective of earlier developmental stuttering patterns (Brown 1945; Tetnowski 1998). By contrast, the TD group tended to produce SLDs on content rather than function words, which has been found to be a pattern among older children and adults who stutter (Howell *et al.* 1999). The authors proposed that such consistency in SLD patterns among the HSLI-E group suggests a relationship to difficulties in sentence planning, as might be observed in developmental stuttering.

Boscolo *et al.* further support possible linguistic relationships to the disfluencies among the HSLI-E group by noting that a hallmark seeming to distinguish the SLDs of the children with HSLI-E from children diagnosed with stuttering was a lack of any struggle or avoidance behaviours in the HSLI-E group. Given definitional issues regarding specific language impairment (SLI) as a diagnostic category, and the contention that those with SLI do not catch up (Muma and Cloud 2008) as these participants seem to have, it seems probable that the participants in this study merely had delayed language rather than SLI. Nonetheless, even when achieving average performance on standardized measures at school age, the children exhibited significantly lower patterns of performance than their peers. This pattern is consistent with identified performance of CWS in comparison to non-stuttering peers (Westby 1974; Yairi *et al.* 1996; Bernstein Ratner 1997a; Anderson and Conture 2000; Anderson *et al.* 2005). Taken together, findings of relationships between language impairments and/or delays and patterns of disfluency demonstrate that disfluency may suggest information about language development.

19.2 Cluttering

Cluttering is a fluency disorder that affects a person's ability to convey messages to others in a clear and/or concise manner (Scaler Scott *et al.* 2007). People with cluttering tend to state that their listeners have difficulty understanding them. The difficulties in listener comprehension may be related to the speaker's rate of speech, the clarity of their speech and/or the organization or relevance of their message. Some who clutter have said they have often received such feedback as 'Slow down!', 'Don't mumble' or 'Where did that comment come from?' (Scaler Scott *et al.* 2007). Because cluttering is misunderstood by the public and professionals alike, those who clutter may be misdiagnosed as stutterers or as 'anxious speakers' (Scaler Scott *et al.* 2007). Often, listeners give advice to the person who clutters (PWC) to improve their communication, but cannot articulate exactly what needs to be improved upon. Cluttering often coexists with stuttering.

Cluttering has been documented in Europe since 1717. The first textbook detailing this communication disorder was produced by Deso Weiss (1964). Although cluttering has always been recognized and researched in Europe, there was a time in the United States when the validity of cluttering as a true communication disorder was questioned (see St. Louis *et al.* (2007) for a review). Much of this questioning appeared to be related to controversy and disagreement regarding the characteristics which constitute the true features of cluttering. For example, cluttering was described by Weiss (1964) as a 'central language imbalance'. The description of features which Weiss offered went beyond those of speech characteristics and included language, gross motor skills, fine motor skills, grapho-motor skills, pragmatic language and personality traits. Those with the central language imbalance were described as having handwriting that deteriorates over time, similar to their speech. They were also described as clumsy in gross motor movements and discoordinated in fine motor tasks. People with cluttering were described as frequently interrupting others in conversation, changing the topic and being rude or inconsiderate when speaking with others.

Some of the components Weiss outlined have undergone empirical investigation in small groups of PWC. For example, one study of cluttering confirmed the presence of possible pragmatic language issues in a small group of adolescents with cluttering (Teigland 1996). Other characteristic traits such as difficulties in auditory processing were reported in three children with cluttering and coexisting disorders (Molt 1996). After mixed findings in many of the areas, a call was put out for a specific definition of cluttering in future studies (Bakker 1996), and for use of definitions that only focus upon speech characteristics (Preus 1996). This fundamental flaw of definition in existing research studies resulted in many non-believers in the existence of cluttering in the United States (St. Louis *et al.* 2007).

The definition of cluttering cyclically broadened and narrowed over a 30-year period (see St. Louis and Schulte (2011) for a review). In 1987, the American Psychiatric Association included cluttering among the diagnoses in the Diagnostic and Statistical Manual of Mental Disorders (DSM; American Psychiatric Association 1987). Part of the diagnostic criteria for cluttering was lack of awareness of the disorder, as it was felt that those with cluttering were unaware of how their speech was unclear to others. This particular criterion became a means of differentially diagnosing cluttering from stuttering in the minds of many clinicians. Simply put, those with stuttering were aware of their communication difficulties, while those with cluttering were not. Due to the more recent involvement of adults with cluttering in online support groups, discussions and face-to-face meetings, the idea that those with cluttering are unaware of their difficulties has been questioned as a consistent trait. Although some may be unaware of their difficulties altogether, others are aware in general of difficulties communicating but are unaware of either the exact nature of their communication difficulties, or their exact moments of cluttered speech as they occur. In 1994, cluttering was removed from the DSM as its own diagnostic category, and has since been grouped with stuttering.

In 1999, the World Health Organization included reference to rate, phrasing and disfluency in its definition of cluttering, similar to the more recent 'lowest common denominator' definition (see below; St. Louis and Schulte 2011). In the same year, the definition of cluttering was once again broadened in the United States when a Special Interest Committee of the American Speech-Language-Hearing Association was established to develop a more *specific* definition (American Speech-Language-Hearing Association 1999). The resulting definition included some of the original broad characteristics defined by Weiss including phonological, language and attention-related symptoms. Rather than narrowing the definition of cluttering, the committee brought together both broad and narrow viewpoints on the definition of cluttering, resulting in a compromise between broad and narrow definitions.

In 1996, a special edition of the *Journal of Fluency Disorders* was published featuring current work on cluttering. The most recent works in cluttering throughout the world were featured and the current status of cluttering research was analysed. The call for a consistent definition was reiterated (Bakker 1996; Preus 1996). In the 10 years following this publication, new research in cluttering began to emerge. Among this research, it is perhaps the work of Kenneth O. St. Louis that has most consistently addressed the issue of a definition of cluttering. St. Louis had been working towards a 'lowest common denominator' definition of cluttering (St. Louis 1992). He acknowledged that beyond speech issues, other features such as attention, processing, memory, handwriting and pragmatic language might be present in some people with cluttering. However, St. Louis contended that there was currently no research to confirm that any of these characteristics were consistent features of all people who clutter.

St. Louis and colleagues examined what features were considered to be consistent across cluttering (St. Louis *et al.* 2003, 2007). These features formed the basis of what speech-language professionals would agree upon as cluttering symptoms. Agreed-upon characteristics related to rate, fluency and speech clarity. As St. Louis called for making these features a part of the 'lowest common denominator' definition of cluttering, he and Katrin Schulte of Germany collaborated in obtaining multiple data sources on a variety of clients with cluttering. Schulte examined areas such as receptive and expressive language, handwriting and auditory memory. As in previous studies, no pattern of difficulties emerged consistently among those with cluttering. What emerged consistently were features related to rate of speech, clarity of speech and fluency of speech. Thus, St. Louis and Schulte developed the 'lowest common denominator' definition of cluttering which includes the mandatory criteria of perceived rapid and/or irregular rate of speech accompanied by the presence of at least one of the following symptoms: (1) excessive NSLDs; (2) excessive collapsing or deletion of syllables; (3) abnormal pauses, syllable stress or speech rhythm (St. Louis and Schulte 2011).

Around the same time that St. Louis and Schulte were developing this definition, a resurgence of worldwide interest in cluttering resulted in the First World Congress on Cluttering in Katerino, Bulgaria in May 2007. This was a momentous turning point in the field of cluttering. It was the first time that people with cluttering, clinicians and researchers came together in an organized fashion to discuss the latest research and current needs in the area of cluttering. From this congress, the International Cluttering Association was established. This is a global organization that fosters collaborations among consumers (people who clutter), researchers and clinicians. Out of this collaboration came increased partnerships among researchers worldwide, among researchers and clinicians, and among researchers and consumers. As a result, current research is showing significant improvements over former studies. Participants are becoming better defined in studies of cluttering. It appears that as research progresses, cluttering is also gaining increased respect and validity in contexts where it was previously overlooked or afforded little significance.

19.2.1   Speech features of cluttering

Although the focus in defining cluttering has not always been upon speech characteristics, the current working definition has been scaled down to its 'lowest common denominator', or core features of speech. Those features include first as a mandatory criterion a rate of speech that is perceived to be rapid and/or irregular in presentation. The rate does not have to exceed normal limits, but often will be perceived as doing so by the listener. Once this mandatory criterion is met, the speaker would also have to present with at least one of the following three speech characteristics to be diagnosed with cluttering: (1) excessive NSLDs; (2) excessive collapsing or deletion of syllables; (3) abnormal pauses, syllable stress or speech rhythm. As with stuttering, these features of cluttering do not need to occur the majority of the time in a person's speech for a diagnosis of cluttering to be made. Instead, clear examples of cluttering in naturalistic conversation 'are sufficient for a diagnosis' to be made (St. Louis and Schulte 2011).

19.2.2   Non-speech features of cluttering

Although the current focus on definition of cluttering targets speech-related aspects of the disorder, PWC are like PWS in that they may experience a negative impact of their communication disorder. In the past, lack of awareness was presented as a key feature of cluttering. Given this lack of awareness, the assumption was that PWC do not experience the negative thoughts and feelings that are a feature of stuttering. However, qualitative interviews with adults who clutter have indicated that some individuals do in fact experience, and are acutely aware of, the negative reactions of others to their communication disorder (Scaler Scott and St. Louis 2011).

What some adults report is that the awareness is not of the specific name for the communication disorder, but a more general awareness that others do not understand their attempts at communication. PWC report that listeners express advice to them to improve their communication skills. However, because there is a lack of understanding among the public about what cluttering is, the listeners giving such advice do not have a term to label the communication impairment. Although stuttering is often poorly understood by the public, in general many laypeople can identify stuttering when they hear it. This is not so with cluttering, a disorder that is often confused by the layperson with hoarding and/or disorganization of space and/or materials. Consequently, many adults who clutter, when reflecting back upon their experience of having cluttering pointed out to them, indicate vague feedback from others about overall communication. Advice-givers are unable to suggest a course of action (Dewey 2005). As a result, many with cluttering may be aware that there is a problem with their communication, but not always aware of where their communication breaks down and/or what to do about it.

Even without the speaker or listener being aware of exactly what is going on, adults who clutter have reported negative reactions from others such as 'Slow down!', 'Are you drunk?', and/or 'Are you stupid?' (Kissagizlis 2010; Scaler Scott and St. Louis 2011). Individuals with cluttering have been unfairly judged in these ways as the listener reacted to the symptoms and did not have a known diagnosis to put to the symptoms. This has resulted in negative attitudes toward speaking, avoidance of speaking, and/or difficulties in advancing one's career (Exum *et al.* 2010). These negative reactions have shaped the feelings of those with cluttering toward communication. We do not yet have enough data from those who clutter to measure the full impact of the disorder upon a clutterer's perception of their speech (i.e. cognitive components), resulting in reactions such as communication avoidance. As with stuttering, all those who clutter do not experience negative feelings and attitudes towards communication. The most important idea to convey is that cluttering has the potential to elicit these negative reactions in those who experience the disorder.

19.2.3   Relationship between speech and non-speech features of cluttering

As in stuttering, the feelings and attitudes of a person who clutters about his or her communication skills may negatively impact on overall patterns of speech. For example, some clients have reported becoming quieter and less clear at the ends of sentences as a result of years of others not acknowledging their opinion, simply because their opinion was not clear enough to be understood. The person who clutters may avoid communication. When a person stutters in addition to cluttering, a complex pattern of communication avoidance may emerge. For example, a PWS may increase their rate of speech to get out as much information as possible while fluent. If this is a person who stutters and clutters, that increase in rate will trigger cluttering symptoms, such as unintelligible speech. This complex pattern is difficult to unravel as it is uncertain whether the person is cluttering due to rapid speech alone or due to rapid speech secondary to stuttering avoidance. These symptoms must be carefully analysed in the therapeutic process to ensure the use of relevant strategies at appropriate times.

19.2.4 Epidemiology of cluttering

There has been little systematic investigation of the epidemiology of cluttering. Among those studies which have been undertaken, it appears that the disorder is more common in males than in females. Estimates of the male to female ratio for cluttering have been reported to range from 3:1 to 6:1 (Arnold 1960; St. Louis and Hinzman 1986; St. Louis and Rustin 1996). Cluttering has been noted to be among the presenting symptoms of some children on the autism spectrum (see Scaler Scott (2011) for review), children with Down's syndrome (see Van Borsel (2011) for review) and children with learning disabilities (Wiig and Semel 1984). It is important to note that no studies have indicated that cluttering occurs in all participants with these disorders. Furthermore, some studies used a broader definition of cluttering than others, focusing not only on the speech characteristics but also on other accompanying symptoms. Further research is needed to rule out the presence of cluttered speech in co-occurring language, learning and neurobehavioural disorders. Experts in the field of cluttering have consistently estimated that approximately one-third of people who stutter also present with at least some components of cluttering (Preus 1981; Daly 1986; Ward 2006). It is important to note that there are more clinical anecdotes to support this statement than data, and that further research in this area is needed.

19.2.5 Aetiology of cluttering

There has also been little systematic investigation of the aetiology of cluttering. However, a number of factors have been proposed to play a causal role in this disorder. These factors will be briefly reviewed in this section. As with stuttering, it is likely that suspected and otherwise unidentified components combine in some multifactorial way to contribute to the development and/or maintenance of cluttering. Further research will be required to establish these components and to reveal the complex interrelationships which exist between them.

Rate exceeds speech production capability: It has been proposed that cluttering arises when the rate of speech exceeds a level that is not always higher than that of the average speaker, but which is nonetheless greater than a speaker's articulatory system can handle (Bakker *et al.* 2011). A recent study conducted by Bakker *et al.* compared the rate of speech of eight PWC, eight exceptionally rapid speakers (ERS) and eight controls. Participants were asked to perform several speaking tasks at a slow rate, a comfortable rate, the fastest rate possible, and even faster than the 'fastest rate'. The speaking tasks the participants were asked to perform included diadochokinetic tasks, reading, reciting nursery rhymes and repeating sentences modelled by an investigator at a typical speaking rate. Results revealed no statistically significant differences in rate during diadochokinetic tasks. Those in the ERS and PWC groups exhibited significantly higher rates of speech than controls during reading and sentence repetition tasks only under the 'comfortable' condition. Because in this study ERS and the PWC only demonstrated higher rates of speaking when the speech rate was chosen by themselves (rather than directed by the examiner), the researchers hypothesized that these two groups may feel 'driven' to speak at a faster speech rate, even when this rate is not needed.

A synergistic view of cluttering: Myers (1992) has consistently called for a synergistic view of cluttering, contending that it may be more the interaction of the speech components of cluttering rather than any one component in isolation that results in the perception of cluttered speech. Under a conversation condition in the study by Bakker *et al.* (2011), there were also no significant differences between eight PWC, eight ERS and eight controls in terms of amount of disfluency. When a qualitative analysis of the types of disfluencies was undertaken, it was hypothesized that perhaps the type of disfluency rather than the amount would make a person's speech sound more 'cluttered'. The authors further investigated this in a study of disfluency 'clusters', that is, when different types of NSLDs were seen together. The researchers compared 18 PWC to 20 people without cluttering under the same speaking conditions (Myers *et al.* 2012). Results of this study revealed that the two groups did not differ in terms of frequency or type of disfluency, with the exception of revisions and word repetitions, which were significantly more frequent in the PWC group than in the group without cluttering. These revisions and word repetitions tended to occur together in clusters in the PWC. The researchers called for further investigation of the frequency and types of disfluency in understanding cluttering.

Neurological underpinnings of cluttering: Like stuttering, there have been reported cases of cluttering following neurological insult. However, the majority of instances are not related to specific trauma, illness or injury. Alm (2011) summarized new hypotheses regarding the potential neurological underpinnings of cluttering. On the basis of a review of existing literature related to pharmacological treatments of cluttering, brain imaging studies and studies of those with brain lesions, Alm concluded that dysregulation of the anterior cingulate cortex (ACC) and the supplementary motor area (SMA) might play a role in the development of cluttering. Specifically, dysregulation in these areas relates to potential dysregulation of initiation of movement, inhibition of impulses, planning, sequencing, word selection, timing and self-monitoring. Alm proposed that all of these areas controlled by the ACC/SMA fit with areas of breakdown in the communication disorder of cluttering. These hypotheses, Alm suggested, require further testing.

Potential linguistic differences: Van Zaalen *et al.* (2011) proposed that there are two types of cluttering, namely, syntactic and phonological cluttering. According to these authors, phonological cluttering is related to motoric difficulties, while syntactic cluttering is related to linguistic difficulties. In a recent examination of a small group of adults with cluttering, Bretherton-Furness and Ward (2012) found that the adults with cluttering showed an increase in response time for lexical tasks and increased linguistic maze behaviours for some tasks but not for others. The authors concluded that there may be subgroups within the diagnosis of cluttering that present with language differences, but cautioned that further research is needed to establish this in larger samples.

The role of disinhibition: Another possibility regarding the origin of cluttering is the role of disinhibition in people who clutter. Studies of individuals with attention deficit hyperactivity disorder have found disinhibition in verbal responses, that is, linguistic messages which emerge before the linguistic plan is ready. The idea of thoughts emerging before they are ready has been noted across qualitative interviews with those who clutter (Scaler Scott and St. Louis 2011). Pilot studies have generated some potentially valuable ideas regarding the role of disinhibition in cluttering (Scaler Scott and Barone 2010). Further exploration of this concept is warranted.

19.3   Conclusion

Many advances have been made in the field of fluency disorders. These have helped us to understand components that contribute to the development and/or maintenance of stuttering and cluttering. Significant advances have also been made in our understanding of how both disorders affect the consumer. This has strengthened the speech-language clinician's ability to provide comprehensive services. With future expansion in areas such as genetics, neuroimaging and consumer involvement, the next generation of knowledge in fluency disorders holds exciting promise.

20

Hearing disorders

R. Steven Ackley

20.1 Introduction

Disorders of hearing and balance are fundamental to an understanding
of communication disorders. This chapter will examine the causes, diagnosis and treatment of hearing disorders. Audiologists and otolaryngologists are involved in the diagnosis of these disorders in the clinic, and
also in developing a treatment plan. Rehabilitative treatment is generally
provided by audiologists, while medical and surgical remediation is the
responsibility of otolaryngologists. Medical and surgical intervention is
often successful at restoring lost hearing when the condition is located
in the external or middle ear. Inner ear disorders are more often treated
rehabilitatively. Disorders of the auditory central nervous system (CNS),
such as neuroma, may require surgical intervention when the condition
is life-threatening, whereas CNS conditions such as 'auditory processing
disorder' require therapeutic intervention. The causes of hearing and balance disorders are also discussed.

20.2 External ear pathology and treatment

20.2.1 Anatomy and physiology

The external ear consists of the pinna or auricle (see Figure 20.1), ear canal
and epidermal layer of the tympanic membrane. It is that part of the auditory mechanism which can be seen without surgically invading the body.
The pinna is evident without instrument for visual inspection, but the ear
canal (external auditory meatus) and eardrum (tympanic membrane) are
not. An otoscope serves the purpose of viewing these two components of
the outer ear, but direct inspection of the normal middle ear is impossible
without surgical exploration. On rare occasions, the eardrum may be thin

(monomeric) allowing for limited view of middle ear structures, or the eardrum may be eroded away (necrosed) from infection which may allow limited inspection.

The pinna serves slightly more than an ornamental purpose. The concha resonates sounds in a narrow frequency spectrum (~5 kHz), and the other pinna structures help in a limited way to direct high-frequency sounds into the concha. However, the full contribution of the pinna to the loudness dimension of hearing is only a few decibels (dB). The ear canal length measured from the tragus base to the tympanic membrane is 2.35 cm. The ear canal amplifies sound an average of 10–15 dB in the 2,500–4,000 Hz frequency range because of the physical dimensions of the canal. This frequency range is important for the understanding of human speech, and the additional contribution of the concha resonance also aids speech intelligibility.

20.2.2   Pathology and clinical management

Disorders of the pinna and external ear canal are usually visible and do not normally threaten hearing acuity. These pathologies are frequently painful, or at least appear to be so to the observer. Disorders of the pinna may occur because of trauma, infection, cancer, gene mutation or congenital event. Genetic pinna defect may signal an internal condition such as middle ear deformity or propensity to recurrent ear infections. Traumatic pinna pathologies include chondrodermatitis nodularis, a precursor to cauliflower ear, and keloids. The former condition is common among boxers, wrestlers and such athletes who fail to wear protective headgear. It can be corrected with cosmetic surgery, and it does not result in hearing loss. Keloids are benign growths on the lobule which may follow long-term ear piercing.

The two cancers of the external ear are squamous cell carcinoma and basal cell carcinoma. Basal cell carcinoma is the most common skin cancer with an incidence of about 25 females per 100,000 population and 20 males per 100,000 (Christenson *et al.* 2005). Skin cancers may be a result of solar radiation and as such the helix of the pinna is a potential damage site from repeated sunburn. Treatment for either cancer is excision of the area, often including the pinna. Radiation and chemotherapy are generally effective, particularly in treating squamous cell carcinoma. Basal cell carcinoma is quite tenacious and ugly, and is referred to as 'rodent ulcer'. Infections of the pinna are not common or disabling. Conditions affecting branchial arch development (e.g. Treacher Collins syndrome, oculo-auriculo-vertebral spectrum or OAVS) may manifest as pre-auricular tags or pits, and pre-auricular appendages (see left panel in Figure 20.2). A branchial arch defect may result in no ear canal development, which produces complete conductive hearing loss (see right panel in Figure 20.2).

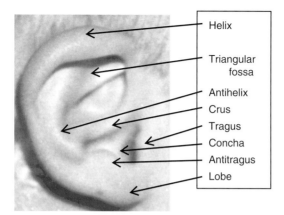

Helix

Triangular
    fossa

Antihelix

Crus

Tragus

Concha

Antitragus

Lobe

Figure 20.1 Pinna of person with Down's syndrome showing slight deformity (thick, overlapping helix) with parts of the pinna labelled (photo taken by the author).

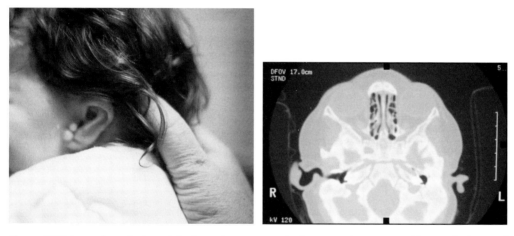

Figure 20.2 In oculo-auriculo-vertebral spectrum, pre-auricular appendages are evidence of abnormal branchial arch development. The CT scan in the right panel shows failure of the left ear canal to develop (photo taken by the author).

Any pinna malformation, however subtle, may suggest pathology. Consider the pinna of the child with Down's syndrome (see Figure 20.1). A thick, overlapping helix is characteristic of Down's syndrome along with a stenotic ear canal (Mazzoni *et al.* 1994). In this case, the deformity is indicative of branchial arch/branchial groove maldevelopment. The vast majority of children with Down's syndrome have recurrent ear infections related to poor Eustachian tube function (branchial groove maldevelopment). A more extreme example is Treacher Collins syndrome, which frequently produces complete atresia and associated ear canal and middle ear deformity. Malformed pinna and middle ear pathology coexist not coincidentally, but rather because of shared embryological development.

Both parts of the ear emerge from the same branchial arches and the genetic condition or traumatic event which produced the maldeveloped pinna is also likely to have damaged unseen middle ear structures.

Other disorders of the external ear canal may be somewhat more obscure and difficult to identify than those of the pinna and canal atresia. This is because this category of pathology requires use of the otoscope and knowledge of normal structure. Furthermore, the ear canal may be obstructed with cerumen (wax), or the canal may be stenotic preventing a clear view. Unlike problems with the pinna, the highest incidence of ear canal pathology is usually the result of infection and may be diagnosed as external otitis. It includes swimmer's ear and bullous myringitis. Swimmer's ear is a fungus infection which grows because of inadequate drying of the ear canal. It is prevented by using boric acid following swimming. Rare cases of hearing loss may occur when oedema causes blockage of the ear canal resulting in temporary conductive hearing impairment.

Bullous myringitis is identified as blisters on the eardrum. It often self-limits, and it rarely causes hearing loss. The disorder is frequently accompanied by intense pain, and attempts to perform hearing testing may be unsuccessful because the pain prevents the patient from cooperating with the test procedure. All types of external otitis are treated in the physician's office quite effectively using antibiotic and anaesthetic topical treatments. Painless and non-infectious ear canal disorders include osteomas and exostoses, which are benign growths of the ear canal. They are removed surgically only when they lead to cerumenous accumulation and subsequent canal occlusion.

20.2.3 Hearing loss

Hearing loss is not common in most cases of external ear pathology. Cerumenous impaction is an exception to this rule, but build-up of ear wax is a questionable 'pathology' in the true sense of disorders of hearing. In most cases, cerumen is designed to move laterally toward the ear canal opening. By so doing, the ear canal is cleansed of debris. Unusual ear canal shapes may prevent this normal process from occurring. Also, growths in the ear canal, such as osteomas and exostoses, may present a barrier to effective cerumen evacuation. Cerumenous impaction causes a mild-moderate hearing loss and the remedy is the removal of the impaction. This may be aided with commercially available products designed to liquefy the wax and allow it to drain out. Physicians and audiologists can perform cerumen removal using a curette and suction.

Hearing loss may occur in rare cases of ear canal oedema where swelling of tissue underlying the epidermis is so extreme that the swollen canal occludes sound transmission to the tympanic membrane. This might also cause a mild-moderate hearing loss. Treatment of the oedema is accomplished using a cotton 'wick' saturated with topical anaesthetic and antibacterial medication. Treatment outcome is realized within 24 hours in most cases.

Hearing loss in congenital external ear pathologies is more common than in acquired conditions. All cases of congenital pinna deformity raise suspicion of potential inadequate ear canal development. Stenotic canal as seen commonly in patients with Down's syndrome does not produce hearing loss, but becomes a location where cerumen collects and prevents sound transmission. Atresia of the ear canal shows up on CT scan (Figure 20.2, right panel) as no airway to the tympanic membrane and results in maximum conductive hearing loss of 40–50 dB.

20.3   Middle ear pathology and treatment

20.3.1   Anatomy and physiology

The middle ear is an air-filled space ventilated to ambient atmospheric pressure via the Eustachian tube (see Figure 20.3). The cavity volume is less than 5 cubic centimetres in the adult and may be substantially less when some volume is occupied by a mass, such as a cholesteatoma. The tympanic membrane serves as the lateral boundary of the middle ear with the manubrium of the malleus bone attached to the medial surface of this membrane. Only the manubrium is visible during otoscopic examination of the ear canal. The greater mass of the malleus is located superiorly in the attic or epitympanic recess of the middle ear space and is not visible otoscopically.

The malleus is surrounded by the same mucosal tissue that is the inside layer of the drum membrane. Functionally, it is situated such that when the eardrum moves in response to sound-disturbed air, the malleus moves. The head of the malleus is attached to the head of the incus which is also in the attic. The malleus and incus are of similar mass, each weighing about 25 mg. Because of their mass and off-centre point of balance, they offer leverage for increasing sound intensity. This is known as the 'ossicular lever action'. The stapes is the third ossicle and is the smallest bone in the human body. It weighs 2.5 mg, or one-tenth the weight of either the incus or malleus. It compensates architecturally for its small weight. It is arch shaped, a design that has been known for centuries to be capable of holding up tall buildings at doorways. It is attached to the lenticular process of the incus. The lenticular process is delicate and the connection between incus and stapes (incudostapedial joint) may be a vulnerable site for disarticulation following physical trauma. Still, the stapes bone itself is quite resistant to fracture despite the enormous physical pressure (an order of 10^{14} sound intensity magnitude above threshold) focused at its apex when sound becomes painfully loud.

The ossicles develop embryologically from the first and second branchial arches which also give rise to the pinna. They develop during the

Malleus   Incus   Stapes   Oval window

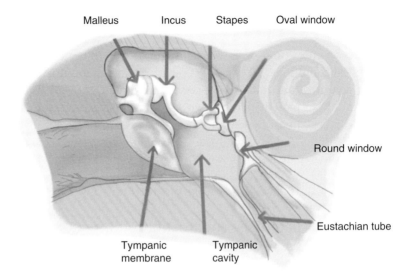

Round window

Eustachian tube

Tympanic
membrane

Tympanic
cavity

Figure 20.3 Middle ear anatomy (original artwork by Rachel Walters, PhD student, Gallaudet University).

first eight weeks of embryonic life. Certain structures continue to develop after birth. The stapes, for example, is not truly adult-like until early childhood. The Eustachian tube links the middle ear (tympanic) cavity to the outside world by interconnecting this space to the nasopharynx. Although this tube is normally closed in the nasopharynx, it opens when we swallow, yawn or move our mandible to extremes. The tensor veli palatini and levator veli palatini muscles provide the majority of muscle contraction necessary to effect the air passage link. The Eustachian tube has been implicated in chronic/recurrent otitis media with effusion (OME) in children. It is not the angle of the tube that is the culprit – all infants have the same Eustachian tube angle – but a small percentage have chronic Eustachian tube dysfunction leading to OME.

Two muscles, the tensor tympani and stapedius, are contained in the tympanic cavity. The tensor tympani is roughly six times the diameter of the stapedius. It is attached to the head of the malleus after wrapping around the cochleariform process to get a better angle of pull. The stapedius is attached to the posterior neck of the stapes, exiting around the cone opening of the pyramidal eminence to get a better angle of pull. These two muscles function antagonistically to each other in order to produce a synergistic effect. That is, the tensor tympani muscle pulls the malleus, and therefore the eardrum, medially, and the stapedius moves the stapes, and therefore the eardrum, somewhat laterally. When they both contract, they serve to lock the ossicles eliminating distortion when vocalizing and when external noise is loud.

Other structures of note in the middle ear are the eight ligaments which help suspend the ossicles in the tympanic space, the epitympanic recess, where cholesteatomas may hide, and the chorda tympani nerve, which passes between the malleus and incus and innervates the anterior two-thirds of the tongue. The promontory is a bony bulge in the medial wall of the middle ear space that corresponds to the basal turn (4,000 Hz region) of the cochlea. It is a physical landmark that is found between the round window and the stapes. The promontory may become blood engorged during an active stage of otosclerosis, and may appear as a positive Schwartze's sign through the eardrum when viewed otoscopically. The round window is located inferiorly to the promontory and is the release valve for sound pressure waves travelling through the fluid-filled cochlea. This event occurs in response to a plunger-like action of the stapes footplate moving in and out of the oval window in response to eardrum sound pressure activity.

It is important to note that the facial nerve and carotid artery meander within a few millimetres of the middle ear space. This leaves the facial nerve susceptible to Bell's palsy if erosive otitis media invades the nerve. The carotid artery may produce a pulsatile tinnitus because of its close proximity to the cochlea and in patients with high blood pressure. The jugular vein is in close proximity to the floor of the tympanic cavity, and may enlarge into the cavity creating a glomus jugulare tumour. Finally, there is the infrequently referred to Prussak's space located just medial to the pars flaccida. It is the site of the attic retraction pocket, which occurs on occasion during otitis media and is seen during otoscopy as an intrusion of the superior eardrum into the tympanic cavity. It may lead to cholesteatoma if the retraction pocket persists.

20.3.2 Pathology and clinical management

Otitis media: Disorders of the middle ear commonly involve fluid. Indeed, the most common chronic or recurrent disease in childhood is otitis media, or middle ear infection. This condition occurs after blockage of the Eustachian tube because of allergy or upper respiratory infection. The mucosal lining of the middle ear space absorbs the available oxygen supply forcing the eardrum into retraction. Fluid secretion from the mucosal cells then accumulates in the middle ear, resulting in otitis media with effusion. The effusion is either serous (a simple serum exudate from the cells without infection) or it may be purulent or infected. Either condition may produce the same degree and category of hearing loss, which is a mild to moderate conductive loss.

Diagnosis of otitis media is uncomplicated. Physicians determine this after reviewing audiometric records, patient symptoms and physical examination of the eardrum. Aiding in this diagnosis is immittance testing, which determines ear canal volume, eardrum mobility, acoustic reflex ability, Eustachian tube function and a few other peripheral and lower brainstem auditory processes. Treatment for each type of otitis media might be quite different. Serous otitis media will not be affected by antibiotic treatment, because there is no infection. However, medications which dry out the middle ear or medications which reduce swelling around the opening of the Eustachian tube at the nasopharynx (torus tubarius) may be effective. Medications which perform these functions fall into the categories of antihistamines, decongestants and steroids.

In cases of purulent otitis media, antibiotics are prescribed in addition to the medications that are used to treat serous otitis media. The problem with medication prescription is that the fluid content is frequently not known, because to sample the fluid requires invading the middle ear space. Therefore, antibiotics are often prescribed in case infection is present. As a last resort, treatment for otitis media with effusion involves surgery. The surgery of choice is tympanostomy with tubal insertion. This procedure involves myringotomy incision in the eardrum, suctioning out fluid in the middle ear as necessary, and inserting a pressure equalizing tube into the incision site. The tubes stay in place for six months to one year in most children, and after that time they are expelled by the eardrum epithelium. As long as the tube is in place and patent, middle ear infection is virtually cured.

Cholesteatoma: This is a benign accumulation of epithelium in the middle ear which tends to grow superiorly in the attic of the tympanic cavity (see Figure 20.4). Cholesteatoma may be congenital or is occasionally a complication of the perforation of the tympanic membrane. The perforation may go unnoticed and is often asymptomatic. Congenital, or primary, cholesteatoma is present at birth and probably develops embryologically from adjacent ectoderm of the neural crest. The meninges of the brain, for example, are in proximity to the primary cholesteatoma growth site in the attic, and derive from ectoderm. The cholesteatoma itself is painless, but it continues to grow and may become erosive. It may erode away the ossicles. This might go undetected, because as it destroys the ossicles, it can form a sound conducting link between the eardrum and stapes. Eventually, it will become symptomatic causing muffled hearing, damage to the eardrum, tinnitus or pressure. In extreme cases, it will erode through the tegmen tympani, or thin bone barrier which separates the epitympanic recess (middle ear attic) from the brain, and cause meningitis.

Treatment of cholesteatoma involves surgical removal and middle ear reconstruction, as needed. Surgical removal of cholesteatoma and ossicular reconstruction are frequently performed in stages. First, the mass is removed and the ear is allowed to heal. Next, an ossicular reconstruction prosthesis, made of bone, Teflon or stainless steel, is anchored between the eardrum and stapes footplate. The prosthesis is either a total or a partial ossicular reconstruction prosthesis. If the former is used, then a single new ossicle connects the medial surface of the drum membrane to the stapes footplate. If the latter is adopted, then usually the malleus and incus are intact and a prosthesis replacing the stapes crura is inserted.

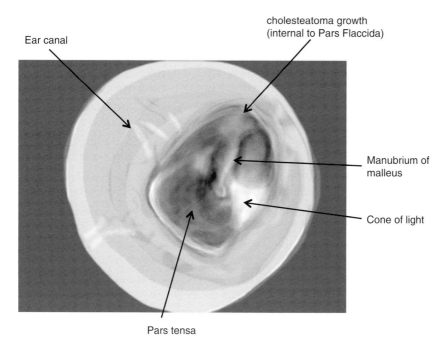

Figure 20.4 Tympanic membrane showing location of cholesteatoma (original artwork by Rachel Walters, PhD student, Gallaudet University).

Otosclerosis: Of the various middle ear disorders, none is more intriguing to the audiologist than otosclerosis. This disease is caused by new bone growth on the anterior stapes footplate. Initially, and in its active stage, the growth is 'otospongiosis' and not yet thoroughly ossified. In its quiescent stage, the growth hardens and impedes or completely immobilizes stapes motion. The result can be conductive hearing loss of up to 50 dB, with an 'artificial' bone conduction hearing loss at 2,000 Hz. The latter loss occurs because of lost ossicular resonance and is therefore 'artificial' because it is not a true sensorineural loss.

The cause of the disease is as yet undetermined. The prevalence in white people is 0.3–0.4 per cent (Ealy and Smith 2011). Because the growth originates just anterior to the stapes footplate, the fissula ante fenestram has been implicated. This is a plugged conduit linking the perilymphatic space of the inner ear to the middle ear. It is no doubt open at some time during embryology, but seals with connective tissue before birth. Pathological discharge of fluid from the perilymphatic space may leave calcium deposits and otosclerotic growth.

Physical examination of the eardrum is usually unremarkable, with the rare exception of a positive 'Schwartze's sign' seen during the active stage of the disease. This is a reddening of the promontory of the medial wall of the middle ear space as seen through the eardrum. If the eardrum is less than transparent or if the disease is quiescent, which is usually the case when the patient becomes symptomatic, this sign is not evident.

Diagnosis of otosclerosis is made with the aid of a characteristic audiogram showing conductive hearing loss, and 'Carhart notch' at 2,000 Hz on bone conduction testing which restores to normal after the ossicular chain is re-mobilized. (Carhart notch is a 2 kHz loss of hearing by bone conduction. This audiometric pattern in the presence of conductive hearing loss indicates stapes fixation, which is usually otosclerosis.) Also, immittance audiometry is useful in showing normal middle ear air pressure, and slightly reduced eardrum mobility (type A shallow tympanogram). Acoustic reflex test, a measurement of stapedius muscle contraction using immittance equipment, fails to record a muscle contraction. The stapedius muscle is unaffected by the disease process, but its pull on the stapes is insufficient to overcome the bony growth anchoring the stapes bone to the oval window.

Treatment of choice for otosclerosis is stapedectomy surgery. The technique involves removing the crura of the stapes and then connecting the lenticular process of the incus to the oval window with a piston, wire or bone. Most surgeons who perform stapedectomy surgery report improvement in hearing in the majority of cases (Kisilevsky *et al.* 2010). On account of the nature of the procedure, which involves entering the perilymphatic space of the inner ear, a possible complication can be perilymphatic fistula. Another complication of the procedure may be endolymphatic hydrops, a condition of over-supply of endolymph that is thought to be the pathophysiological mechanism for the symptoms of Ménière's disease.

Glomus jugulare tumour: Like cholesteatoma, glomus jugulare tumour is a benign growth in the middle ear. Unlike cholesteatoma, it grows from the floor of the middle ear rather than the attic, and it is blood engorged. It grows as an appendage from the jugular bulb, which is inferior to the middle ear floor. It is asymptomatic with the exception of pulsatile tinnitus. Other conditions, including hypertension, give this tinnitus symptom, but glomus tumour may be visible on otoscopic examination as a blue smear through the inferior tympanic membrane. Tympanometry may trace a pulsation pattern timed with heart rate which is transmitted from the glomus to the drum membrane. As the tympanogram is traced, a pulsating line will appear superimposed on this record rather than the typically smooth trace. This line is precisely in synchrony with the patient's heartbeat. This tracing is not to be confused with undulations of the tympanometric record occurring in accord with breathing. A tympanogram which shows rhythmic pattern corresponding to the patient's breathing is indicative of an abnormally open Eustachian tube.

Treatment for glomus tumour is radiation therapy to reduce the mass, followed by surgical excision. Complications can be heavy bleeding, temporal bone invasion and facial nerve damage. If the tumour is detected later, the ossicles may be eroded and the tumour may break through the tympanic membrane and appear to be a polyp in the ear canal. They are rarely malignant, and also on rare occasions may occur bilaterally.

Squamous cell carcinoma: Middle ear squamous cell carcinoma is more serious than that arising in the ear canal. The disease is the most common malignancy of the ear, and it easily escapes detection when growing in the middle ear. Early symptoms may be obscured by ear discharge (otorrhoea), which can be mistaken for otitis media, and the discharge is typically treated as a chronic condition for several months before final diagnosis. The disease has an equal incidence among young (<40 years old) male and female patients with a rate of about 4 per 100,000 population (Christenson *et al.* 2005). Growth of squamous cell carcinoma in the middle ear seems unusual in a place where there are no naturally occurring squamous cells. However, migration of these cells into the middle ear cavity must first occur, or the growth originates elsewhere and grows internally.

A variety of sequelae may emerge from whatever disease process invades the middle ear cavity. When otitis media is chronic or in cases of tuberculous middle ear, erosion of tissue and bone may develop. This is necrotizing otitis media, and it is often characterized by a kidney-bean-shaped perforation dominating the tympanic membrane. Treatment is surgical reconstruction after the erosive process is controlled. Catarrhal otitis, a serous otitis media variant, is often associated with 'glue ear'. The fluid is non-purulent, but frequently more tenacious and of higher viscosity than simple serum. It may occur naturally as untreated otitis media, or it may be an iatrogenic by-product of unsuccessful medication therapy to treat middle ear infection. Its cure is myringotomy and suctioning of the fluid. Meningitis is a rare complication of middle ear disease, because antibiotic treatment usually destroys the infection before it invades the meninges of the brain. Before penicillin, however, otitis media was the leading cause of meningitis.

20.3.3 Hearing loss

Hearing loss in cholesteatoma, otitis media and other middle ear disorders never exceeds 50–55 dB. Logically, it would be concluded erroneously that conductive hearing loss could not exceed 30 dB. After all, sound travelling from air into any seawater-like medium (cochlear fluid) loses 99.9 per cent of its energy which, on the logarithmic decibel scale, is 30. The reason the hearing loss is greater than 30 dB has to do with the bone and tissue barriers standing between the sound in air and the fluid-filled inner ear. These barriers account for the additional 20–25 dB. Therefore, as sound reaches the non-functional middle ear, it may need to vibrate the skull in order to be transmitted to the cochlea. The bones of the skull begin to respond to airborne sound at 50–55 dB. Once this intensity is reached, the skull is an effective sound conductor. The purpose of the external and middle ear is to recover the otherwise lost 30 dB.

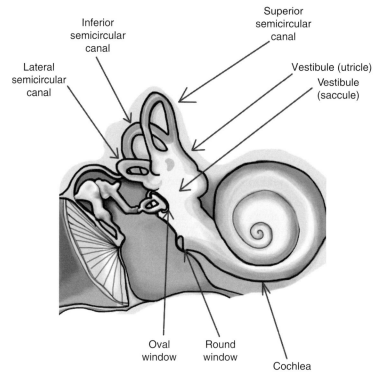

Figure 20.5 Structures of the inner ear (original artwork by Rachel Walters, PhD student, Gallaudet University).

20.4   Cochlear damage and treatment

20.4.1   Anatomy and physiology

The lateral boundary of the inner ear is the medial wall of the tympanic cavity. Internal to this medial wall are found the cochlea, vestibule and semicircular canals (see Figure 20.5). Divisions within the cochlea include scala tympani, scala vestibuli, both containing perilymph, and scala media containing endolymph. The boundaries of the scala media are the basilar membrane and Reissner's membrane. Located on the basilar membrane are inner and outer hair cells held in place by various supporting cells (Deiter's, Claudius, Boetcher, Held). Stereocilia bundles project from the tops of each hair cell body and move with wave action in the cochlear fluids or with mechanical action of the tectorial membrane. As stereocilia are deflected during wave action of cochlear fluids, potassium flows from endolymph into the cell body, initiating a nerve response.

20.4.2   Cochlear pathology and hearing loss

Disorders of the inner ear affect the cochlea, vestibule, semicircular canals or any combination of these organs. Symptoms may include tinnitus, hearing loss, aural pressure, vertigo and imbalance, which may lead to nausea, headache and emotional distress. The most common causes of hearing loss in adulthood are presbycusis and noise-induced hearing loss, both of which involve damage to the inner ear.

Presbycusis: Deterioration of the cochlea and auditory nerve occurs as a consequence of the natural ageing process. Hearing loss because of age-ing becomes evident audiometrically during the end of the fifth decade and into the sixth decade of life and is known medically as presbycusis, or presbyacusis. There are at least four levels of presbycusis. The most basic level and perhaps the first evident involves simple deterioration of hair cells. Outer hair cells are least resistant to insult and are dam-aged before inner hair cells. Stereocilia fracture, disintegrate, swell or in some way become non-functional as a prelude to cell body atrophy. The basal hair cells are first to disappear, and once gone they fail to regen-erate in humans. With high-frequency hearing situated at the cochlear base, frequencies above 4,000 Hz are lost initially. Eventually, hair cell deterioration progresses usually not beyond the cochlear midpoint, or the 2,000 Hz cell region. Therefore, although hearing loss can be rather complete in high frequencies as a result of presbycusis, it seldom involves low-frequency hearing.

Other levels or stages of presbycusis are metabolic, cochlear conductive and neural in nature. In metabolic presbycusis, the balance of cochlear fluid chemistry is disturbed. Endolymph, which is manufactured in the stria vascularis, is high in potassium and low in sodium. It also contains amino acids and chloride. As blood flow to the richly vascular stria vas-cularis becomes restricted in elderly people, the endolymph manufactur-ing process is affected. Without proper endolymphatic chemical compos-ition, adequate flow of potassium ions into the hair cell body is altered. This affects the function of the cell body.

Cochlear conductive presbycusis is not to be confused with conductive hearing loss. There is no middle ear involvement in cochlear conduct-ive presbycusis. In this instance, the ageing process affects the elasticity and flexibility of cochlear tissue. The basilar membrane, which is 'tuned' from base to apex and undergoes a several-fold increase in flexibility and fibre mass along its course, is particularly affected. Adequate flexibility in the cochlear partition is essential if the travelling wave through the coch-lea is to have full effect on stereocilia displacement.

Neural presbycusis involves deterioration of the auditory nerve and brainstem nervous system. This condition is perhaps the most devastat-ing of all forms of the disease, because it impairs speech understanding. The condition was first described by John Gaeth in his doctoral disser-tation at Northwestern University in the late 1940s. He noted that in many elderly people, pure tone hearing sensitivity suggests mild hear-ing loss, whereas speech understanding ability is very poor. He gave the term 'phonemic regression' to describe this condition where word recognition ability is worse than would be predicted from the pure tone audiogram.

A common symptom of presbycusis is recruitment, which is intolerance to loud sound. It seems odd that people with cochlear hearing loss should have a lower tolerance to amplified sound than those with normal hearing. However, this is precisely what occurs, and it is more than a psychological phenomenon. Loss of outer hair cells associated with presbycusis may decouple the inner and outer hair cell interconnections and leave the remaining cell units less tolerant to sound exceeding 90 dB. This is because the dynamic range of inner hair cells, when functioning without their outer hair cell counterparts, is 50–90 dB. When sound reaches 90+ dB, it becomes intolerable. Another common symptom of those with presbycusis is tinnitus, or 'ringing in the ears'. This symptom comes in many versions, but the type suffered by elderly people is the standard high-pitched variety. It is constant, although it might only be noticed in quiet settings. It is usually not debilitating, and it is rarely of sufficient intensity to interfere with sleep.

Inability to understand conversation in the presence of background noise is another common complaint associated with high-frequency hearing loss, and is common among elderly people. With lost hearing sensitivity in high frequencies, and with predominantly low-frequency background noise interference (most background noise is below 1,000 Hz, because of the inability of higher frequencies to move around objects), there is nothing left to interpret speech. Directional hearing is also impaired, but this is more of an embarrassment than a disability. Those with high-frequency hearing loss have a damaged sound field localization centre – the input to the lateral superior olive. Therefore, only lower-frequency information can be detected directionally, which is handled by the medial superior olive. Consequently, only lower-frequency information can be effectively localized, and higher-frequency consonant information is not localized. Often, individuals with presbycusis complain of looking in the wrong direction when their name is called out.

Noise-induced hearing loss: Hearing loss because of noise exposure or acoustic trauma is a leading cause of auditory complaint in adults. Indeed, this may be the reason for presbycusis. The oft-quoted study by Rosen and colleagues in the 1960s showed that the Mabaans, a tribe in Sudan, had normal hearing at age 70 (Rosen *et al.* 1962). This suggests that only industrialized societies, with concomitant noise, impose the insidious growth of hair cell loss on its members. This was termed 'socioacusis' by Aram Glorig, who attributed inner ear damage to society rather than to nature (Glorig and Nixon 1962).

Noise-induced hearing loss (NIHL) damages the cochlear base at first, and then widens its focus. Initially, the loss is typified by 4,000 Hz notch configuration as evidenced on the pure tone audiogram. That is, frequencies from 125 to 8,000 Hz will show hearing within a normal range with the single exception of the 4,000 Hz frequency. This is convenient for diagnosis of the disorder, because cochlear damage from other causes rarely results in this pattern. Why the damage is limited to this site is still debated. It may have to do with ear canal resonance, which is suspiciously close to 4,000 Hz. It may have to do with the travelling wave in the cochlea, which snaps the basilar membrane like a whip at the 4,000 Hz region when sound is dangerously loud. Or it may have to do with inadequate blood supply in this region of the cochlea.

Complaints of those with NIHL are much like the auditory symptoms of presbycusis. Tinnitus, again of a high register, is typical and in rare cases may be somewhat debilitating. It is occasionally reported as more intense than background highway noise when travelling in a car with the window down. This is of sufficient amplitude to impair sleep and disturb mental health. Recruitment, impaired directional hearing and poor speech understanding in the presence of background noise are common in NIHL. (Recruitment is an abnormal growth in loudness function that manifests as hypersensitivity to loud sounds.) The mechanisms for these symptoms are likely to be the same as in presbycusis.

The site of lesion of NIHL is 8–10 mm from the base of the basilar membrane. Hair cells responsible for 4,000 Hz signals are located in this region. When noise exposure is tolerated, stereocilia may swell and stretch tip links and full recovery is expected. This condition is known as 'temporary threshold shift' (TTS), which usually recovers completely within a day. When the noise is not tolerated, stereocilia fracture. As noise continues, stereocilia are expelled and cell body atrophy follows (see Figure 20.6). Recovery is impossible after this level of damage, and the TTS becomes a 'permanent threshold shift' (PTS). TTS has long been thought to predict ultimate PTS but such a relationship has not been proven to date.

Ototoxicity: More than 200 prescription and over-the-counter medications are known to be ototoxic, affecting either hearing or balance, or both (Cone *et al.* 2012). Chemical damage to hair cells is well documented (Wake *et al.* 1993; Campbell 2007). Excessive aspirin (acetylsalicylic acid) ingestion causes a temporary loss in hearing, which may be caused by a chemical imbalance in endolymph. Tinnitus accompanies the complaint and both conditions improve after aspirin intake declines. Another reversible ototoxic agent is quinine, which is used to treat malaria and eliminate heroin addiction. Certain diuretics, such as furosemide (Lasix), may produce reversible auditory symptoms when given in high doses and usually intravenously.

A class of medications which causes permanent hearing loss, vestibular damage and tinnitus are the aminoglycoside antibiotics. The most ototoxic agent available is neomycin, which is a powerful antibiotic used in life-threatening situations. Its ototoxic effects can be seen in the

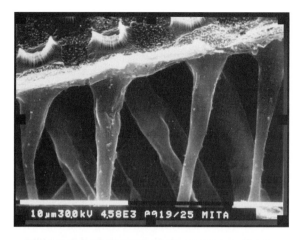

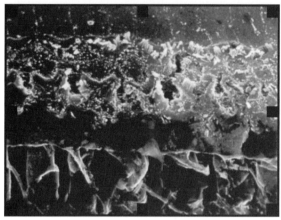

Figure 20.6 Normal cochlear hair cells (top panel) and hair cell damage following noise exposure (bottom panel) (photomicrographs taken by the author).

destruction of hair cells. Streptomycin, another medication in this category, is more frequently vestibulotoxic than ototoxic. This medication has been used extensively to treat tuberculosis. Other drugs under this heading are dihydrostreptomycin (another anti-tuberculin), kanamycin, gentamicin, tobramycin and framycetin. Between 2 and 5 per cent of patients who are treated with aminoglycosides have irreparable hearing loss (Waguespack and Ricci 2005). Hearing loss is usually high frequency and bilaterally symmetrical, although exceptions to this pattern are not rare. The loss may be immediate or, in the case of neomycin ototoxicity, it can be delayed by up to six months after ingestion. Monitoring of hearing is frequently done at bedside in the hospital, but it may continue for months after discharge. A 15 dB or greater drop in hearing at any frequency is significant, and alerts the physician to modify the regimen, if possible.

20.5   Vestibular damage and treatment

20.5.1   Anatomy and physiology

The inner ear contains balance organs in addition to the cochlea which serves hearing. The gravitationally sensitive organs, saccule and utricle, are located in the vestibule of the inner ear which is interior to the stapes footplate. Within the saccule and utricle are the maculae which contain otoconia. The otoconia are calcium carbonate crystals which respond to gravitation pull and send a message to the cerebellum which locates where the head is with respect to the centre of the Earth. The organs which respond to angular acceleration are at the base of each of three semicircular canals and are contained within an ampulla. Inside each ampulla is a cupula, which responds to wave action and stimulates stereocilia of type I and type II hair cells. (Type I and type II hair cells are the functional correlates of cochlear inner and outer hair cells.)

20.5.2   Pathology

This section will examine the following conditions: Ménière's disease, vestibular schwannoma and benign paroxysmal positional vertigo (BPPV).

Ménière's disease: A disease involving the symptom triad of tinnitus, vertigo and deafness was first identified as an inner ear disorder, and not as a neurological disease as previously thought, by Prosper Ménière in France in 1861. Too much endolymph, or endolymphatic hydrops, is thought to be the pathophysiological mechanism for the symptom triad (see Figure 20.7). However, there is still controversy about the inner ear mechanism of Ménière's disease. Without access to the inner ear for diagnosis, the disease remains diagnosed solely on the basis of symptoms. It is apparent from patient history that the disease process is quite slow in many cases and is affected by body metabolism, viral infection and stress. There is some evidence that cells in the stria vascularis can provide a temporary compensatory mechanism and withdraw endolymph from the cochlear duct in cases of hydrops, perhaps when the endolymphatic duct is non-functional. However, changes in body metabolism or blood flow changes associated with stress may reduce the absorbent capacity of this compensatory mechanism.

In Ménière's disease, the tinnitus must be a low-pitched 'roaring' or 'buzzing' sensation. Sensorineural hearing loss is low frequency and fluctuates. Vertigo must be true 'hallucination of motion' such that either the patient spins or the room spins around the patient. In addition, the symptom of aural pressure was added to the triad in the 1950s. Hearing loss is always sensorineural in nature and fluctuates in the low frequencies in early stages of the disease. Serial audiograms may document the fluctuation, or it can be documented by having the patient ingest a dehydration medication such as glycerol which allegedly dehydrates the cochlea

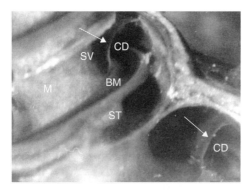

Figure 20.7 Arrows pointing to distended Reissner's membrane at second and third turns of a guinea pig cochlea showing endolymphatic hydrops. 'M' is modiolus; 'SV' is scala vestibule; 'BM' is basilar membrane; 'ST' is scala tympani; 'CD' is cochlear duct (photo taken by the author).

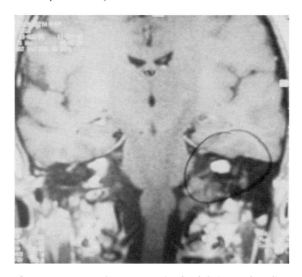

Figure 20.8 Acoustic neuroma in the left internal auditory canal (photo taken by the author).

and eliminates endolymphatic hydrops temporarily. Hearing level may improve from mild-moderate low-frequency loss to normal levels during this procedure. In advanced stages of Ménière's disease the hearing loss extends across the frequency range tested audiometrically and reaches a severe level of hearing loss.

Vestibular schwannoma: The acoustic neuroma, or vestibular schwannoma, is the most commonly occurring tumour in the head and neck with an annual incidence of newly diagnosed tumours of about 1 in 100,000 (Hain 2008). This mass appears on CT scan and MRI when it is of sufficient size to be scanned (see Figure 20.8), but may be evident on an auditory brainstem response test before then. The most common symptom is hearing loss. In patients with asymmetrical hearing loss the incidence of vestibular schwannoma is 1 in 1,000 (Hain 2008). Other symptoms may include tinnitus, imbalance and difficulty using the telephone with the affected ear.

Benign paroxysmal positional vertigo: BPPV is a common vestibular complaint which is described by the patient as 'dizziness which is triggered by head movement'. When tested using a head positioning procedure (Dix–Hallpike procedure), the sensation decreases with repetition of the positioning process. This defines a condition where imbalance 'fatigues'. The treatment (Epley manoeuvre) is to move the patient into a series of positions beginning with the patient seated upright, then moving to supine position and rolling to one side and moving again to the original seated position. The purpose of this chiropractic-like manoeuvre is to migrate dislocated cell debris away from a semicircular canal and into the endolymphatic duct where it will not trigger imbalance.

20.6　Disorders of the auditory central nervous system

In 1996, the American Speech-Language-Hearing Association's Task Force on Central Auditory Processing defined six behaviours that constitute central auditory processing, or CAP (Keith 1999). These behaviours include sound localization and lateralization, auditory discrimination, auditory pattern recognition, temporal aspects of audition (resolution, masking, integration and ordering), and auditory performance with acoustic signals that are degraded and signals that are present with competing signals. All listed behaviours hold true for both speech and non-speech acoustic stimuli. Any problem in one or more of these behaviours and an individual is considered to have difficulty with central auditory processing.

A working definition of auditory processing disorder (APD) is an auditory perceptual disorder that cannot be explained on the basis of peripheral hearing loss. It has a high occurrence in children who have a learning disability, reading disorder and/or speech and language disorders. It is also important to note that APD typically does not become apparent until the child attends school. It is at this point that a child becomes reliant on hearing and understanding spoken language in the presence of background noise. Therefore, an early sign or symptom of APD is poor hearing in the presence of background noise. An audiometric procedure to test for this condition is presentation of word recognition lists with competing background noise. If this test is positive, various behavioural tests can be administered to determine the extent of the difficulty. Also, evoked potential procedures such as middle latency response (see section 20.7) are useful at giving objective assessment of the auditory nervous system in APD.

As a brainstem dysfunction, APD may involve defective reticular formation function, which may fail to screen out unnecessary sensory input thereby overloading the auditory nervous system. This may result in hyperactivity which is often controlled with medication that stimulates the auditory brainstem. As a subtle brainstem problem, auditory localization and auditory comprehension in the presence of background noise may be impaired. In more involved brainstem or cortical CAP disability, the patient may require medication to achieve minimal functional capability in the classroom. The disorder dominates the sufferer's life in such cases, and leaves them an exhausted asocial loner at the end of each day. They seek approving, easily manipulated or predictable relationships with others, usually caring adults or younger children. They daydream incessantly. They fail to attend to tasks, and are capable of completing only the most facile of school assignments. However, the child may experience islands of skill in the school curriculum with some teachers, those few for whom the child produces unselfishly, serving as advocates while others are adversarial.

Diagnosis and treatment of APD is the responsibility of the audiologist. Tests mainly use speech or phonemic stimuli presented with the signals in some way degraded (e.g. filtered) or presented simultaneously to each ear. Certain tests are focal to brainstem pathology, while other tests target the auditory cortex. Once identified, treatment involves intensive, one-on-one remediation of the faulty incoming auditory signal. The behaviours need not be treated, although if the child is misdiagnosed as 'emotionally disturbed' and only the behaviours treated, the problem will intensify. In other words, effective treatment requires retraining of the auditory nervous system and then the aberrant behaviours normalize.

20.7   Audiometric tests

Audiologists have a range of audiometric tests available to them to assist in the assessment and diagnosis of hearing disorders. These tests include pure tone audiometry, speech audiometry, immittance audiometry and auditory brainstem response. Each test will be examined in turn in this section.

Pure tone audiometry: The most commonly performed hearing test is the pure tone air conduction procedure which is graphed on the audiogram. It gives a record of hearing level by frequency (125–8 kHz) when sound is delivered to the ear canal via either headphones or ear inserts. A less frequently performed procedure is bone conduction pure tone assessment, which requires signal delivery via a bone oscillator in contact with the patient's skull and delivers a 250–6 kHz frequency range. If bone conduction and air conduction symbols are at the same hearing loss level, a sensorineural hearing loss is identified. When bone conduction hearing is better than air conduction hearing, the difference between the two symbols on the audiogram identifies a conductive hearing loss. A mixed hearing loss is a combination of conductive and sensorineural loss.

Speech audiometry: Typically performed with the pure tone procedure, a speech threshold and word recognition score are documented on the audiogram. The speech threshold is a hearing level (in dB) which identifies where each ear responded to a series of bisyllabic familiar words. The word recognition score is a percentage of 50 monosyllabic words identified correctly. The speech threshold is used to verify the pure tone audiogram, and suggests non-organic hearing loss when agreement is not found between pure tone sensitivity and speech threshold. The word recognition score is sensitive to cochlear damage and retro-cochlear (central nervous system) pathology. When the word recognition score is poorer than that predicted by the pure tone audiogram (a somewhat complicated process), 'phonemic regression' is identified and the patient has CNS damage. A variation on the standard word recognition procedure is to introduce competing noise while presenting the monosyllabic word lists. This is called 'speech in noise' test and may help to diagnose auditory processing disorder.

Immittance audiometry: Measurement of eardrum mobility is commonly performed in hospitals and clinics. When eardrum movement is measured as a function of air pressure changes introduced into a sealed ear canal, the procedure produces a 'tympanogram'. This procedure can be used to diagnose a blocked Eustachian tube, eardrum perforation and stages of otitis media. When the measurement of eardrum mobility is done by introducing a loud sound and identifying a muscle reflex, the procedure is known as the 'acoustic reflex' test. This test is sensitive to cochlear damage and acoustic nerve tumour. An 'acoustic reflex decay' version of the test sustains a pure tone for 10 seconds and increases tumour detection sensitivity when the muscle does not stay contracted for the prescribed duration.

Auditory brainstem response (ABR): ABR is an evoked potentials measurement of the auditory nervous system. Signals are delivered usually to each ear independently with electrodes taped to the skull. These electrodes detect microvolt sensory responses from the auditory nerve and brainstem. The responses are delivered to an amplifier and fed to a signal averaging computer which extracts the response from a background of electrical noise. The result is a highly predictable waveform consisting of a series of waves representing the auditory nerve response (waves I and II), lower pons (wave III) and upper pons (waves IV and V). Travel time from wave I to wave V is 4.00 milliseconds in normal subjects. When time of travel is delayed by 0.5 milliseconds or more there is suspicion of tumour. The test is also useful in identifying hearing level (loss) in newborns.

Middle latency response: Slight changes in the ABR protocol will yield an evoked response that occurs between the brainstem and auditory cortex. This is known as the 'middle latency response' or MLR. Instead of amplifying the waves in the first 10 milliseconds following signal delivery as seen with the ABR, responses occurring in 100 milliseconds after the stimulus are collected. The MLR gives objective electrophysiological data that corresponds to midbrain and cortical centres.

20.8   Concluding remarks

The audiologist plays a key role in the diagnosis and management of most auditory and vestibular disorders. Technological advances in biomedical instrumentation have brought sophistication to the field of audiology that would not have been predicted in the early days of pure tone audiometry. However, the case history and basic audiometric work-up provide the fundamental components to identifying additional audiometric test procedures that might need to be performed. These basic elements along with advanced biomedical procedures assist the physician in making an accurate diagnosis of auditory pathologies and in instituting appropriate treatment plans.

Part IV

Management of communication disorders

21

Developmental motor speech disorders

Kirrie J. Ballard and Patricia McCabe

21.1   Introduction

Motor speech disorders in children can take several forms. These include apraxia, dysarthria or co-occurring apraxia and dysarthria. The origin of the disorder, whether developmental or acquired, and the course of the disorder (improving, chronic/static or degenerating) has important implications for assessment and for treatment. (The focus of this chapter is improving and chronic/static conditions.) Although there are some similarities in assessment and treatment of motor speech disorders in children, relative to adults, there are also some critically important differences.

Children with motor speech disorders face a special set of challenges during the process of speech development (Maassen 2002). First, like all children, they face the challenge of development itself and the associated gradual emergence of speech. Second, they face the impact of a neuromotor disorder. Third, they must contend with the poorly understood, but likely pervasive, interactions between development and a superimposed neuromotor disorder. In particular, the impact of neuromotor speech disorders on the development of an intact or impaired cognitive or linguistic system complicates both differential diagnosis and treatment planning processes.

In this chapter, a framework is presented for the assessment and treatment of children with motor speech disorders. Naturally, the framework borrows heavily from prominent textbooks and researchers in the field and is aligned with the World Health Organization's International Classification of Functioning, Disability, and Health (ICF) and the ICF-Children/Youth (ICF-CY) (World Health Organization 2001; McLeod and McCormack 2007). While the ICF draws attention to five domains, we will focus here on the levels of Body Structure and Function (i.e. the impairment), and Activity and Participation. The Body Structure and Function level considers the presence of craniofacial or neuromuscular anomalies across the subsystems of respiration, phonation, resonance and articulation. The Activity level considers ability in communication activities and focuses on measures and ratings of speech intelligibility and perceptions of communication success. The Participation level considers the degree and quality of the child's involvement in a range of social communication contexts.

21.2   Frameworks for assessment of children with motor speech disorders

21.2.1   Background

Assessment of children with motor speech disorders occurs in a dynamic environment where the child is developing cognitively, linguistically and neurologically at the same time as acquiring speech motor skills. This means, of course, that a surface approach to assessment will result in inaccurate diagnosis. There are a number of assessment frameworks which have been proposed for differential diagnosis of speech sound disorders in children. These frameworks operate predominantly at the Body Structure and Function level of the ICF/ICF-CY with limited examination of either Activity or Participation. Each takes a specific theoretical framework and uses that structure systematically to evaluate the child's speech system. Some frameworks focus on motor control (e.g. the approach developed at the Mayo Clinic in Rochester, Minnesota, in the USA, and updated by Duffy 2005), some emphasize aetiology (e.g. Shriberg *et al.* 2010b), while others treat speech output as one component of a larger speech and language system (e.g. Stackhouse and Wells 1997). The reader is referred to Waring and Knight (2013) for a thorough critique of the main paediatric speech sound disorder classification systems.

Generally, clinicians report being ill-equipped to examine, diagnose and treat paediatric motor speech disorders (e.g. Forrest 2003). Additionally, within the child motor speech literature, each medical diagnosis is examined separately, with causal factors as the major grouping rather than type of dysarthria or accuracy of speech output. For example, there are Cochrane reviews examining treatment of children with dysarthria associated with cerebral palsy (Pennington *et al.* 2004) and acquired brain injury (Morgan and Vogel 2009). While it is true that aetiology leads to variable outcomes, it could be argued that children with early-acquired spastic dysarthria, regardless of aetiology, would be more similar to each other than children with ataxic dysarthria of similar aetiology. The justification for a disorders-based approach, rather than an aetiology-based one, is found in the well-established adult motor speech disorders classification schema of the Mayo Clinic mentioned earlier.

The Mayo Clinic classification schema has two main components: (a) a structural and functional non-speech evaluation of the respiratory, phonatory, articulatory and resonatory subsystems and (b) perceptual judgements of the isolated and combined performance of these subsystems in speech and speech-like tasks. These tasks range from sustained phonation of vowels and voiced and voiceless consonants through production of syllables and polysyllabic words, sentences and connected speech. While the Mayo system has a 50-year history and has been refined to accommodate thousands of patient cases, it has some limitations. It is perceptually based and so is vulnerable to all the biases and challenges of perceptual analysis such as clinician experience and perceptual drift (see Kent (1996) for an excellent review of some of these challenges). Furthermore, it was designed primarily to classify neuromotor speech disorders in adults. It is, however, routinely applied to differential diagnosis of paediatric motor speech disorders (e.g. Yorkston *et al.* 2010), with the knowledge that the neuromotor system of a child has the same basic organization as that of an adult, albeit it is immature.

Another predominant approach to diagnosis of paediatric speech sound disorders is that of Stackhouse and Wells (1997), which has been widely used in the United Kingdom. Their Speech Processing Profile is based on a psycholinguistic approach to speech production and provides 12 possible sources of speech error including input and output errors. Use of the Speech Processing Profile provides a systematic approach to child speech assessment. Various steps in the model are designed to differentiate motor speech disorders from linguistically-based speech disorders. Case study reports in book chapters and in the research literature suggest that differential diagnosis of childhood apraxia of speech (CAS) from phonological disorder is possible using this approach (e.g. Corrin 2001). However, the model is limited as the only component that relates to motor control alone, without linguistic overlay, is the component 'K: Does the child have adequate sound production capacity'.

It has been suggested that the field needs a well-grounded classification system specific to paediatric dysarthria that is sensitive to behavioural, neurological and genetic profiles and sensitive to the interaction with an immature linguistic and cognitive system (van Mourik *et al.* 1998; Morgan and Liegeois 2010). However, Cahill *et al.* (2002) reported concordance between the natural groupings of dysarthria type in their sample of 24 children with traumatic brain injury and the dysarthria types of the Mayo Clinic schema. Additionally, the main types of dysarthria associated with cerebral palsy (spastic and athetoid) align with the Mayo schema, consistent with the neural sites and networks affected (Yorkston *et al.* 2010).

As suggested by the study of Cahill *et al.* (2002), the Mayo system may be most appropriate for children with motor speech disorders acquired after foundational speech and language skills have developed. Furthermore, Cahill *et al.* (2003) state that, when lesion–behaviour relationships do not match expectation in children, this may be due to the different types of injury typically seen in the two populations as well as differences in how the neuroanatomical systems respond to and compensate for injury. Naturally, the diagnosis of children (and adults) with impairment across multiple domains and with potentially mixed motor speech disorders will always be more challenging. Perhaps it is less important to develop a new paediatric dysarthria classification system than to ensure that clinicians are well prepared to skilfully integrate knowledge about the presenting speech, language and cognitive impairments, the ICF/ICF-CY framework and current evidence-based principles of neuroplasticity and motor learning of new skills when designing treatments.

For the present, we focus on the speech motor system but stress the importance of understanding concomitant, or related, delays in other developmental areas for the design of appropriate, functional and motivating therapeutic activities. Below, we propose an assessment framework focused on motor speech that is guided by the ICF and ICF-CY. It utilizes the Mayo Clinic diagnostic classification system along with the well-known staging system of Yorkston and colleagues (Yorkston *et al.* 2010) that identifies a child's functional ability and relative reliance on speech versus augmentative and alternative communication (AAC) for communication and learning.

21.2.2   Proposed assessment framework

In all clinical decision-making, a certain statement holds true: the most common diagnoses are common and treat what you see. This can be overlooked when a clinician feels inexperienced and ill-prepared. The logical approach is to follow a systematic and comprehensive procedure that will lead naturally to the outcome of assigning a diagnosis and a level of functional ability. This will guide in turn the balance of impairment, activity and participation based components in treatment.

In this section, we present a schematic representation of the assessment process in Figure 21.1, and suggestions for published tests and protocols to support the diagnostic process in Table 21.1. Figure 21.1 outlines the procedure from the first stages of analysing responses to assessment tasks, to deciding whether motor speech disorder, language and/or cognitive delays are evident, to establishing the stage of functioning and degree of need for AAC tools and techniques, and finally to designing therapy to stimulate development of communicative functions, activities and participation. Table 21.1 contains primarily oral and speech motor assessment tasks, but also some basic language and cognitive assessment tasks. Several published protocols are available for assessing oral and speech motor control and for identification of concomitant language and cognitive impairment. Regardless of whether one subscribes to the Mayo Clinic

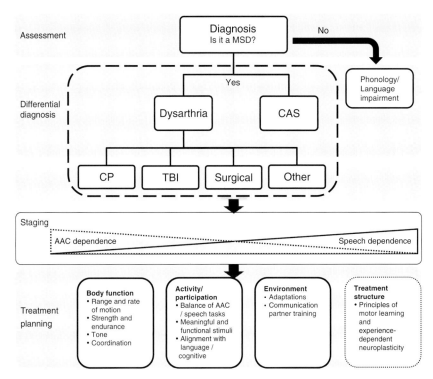

Figure 21.1 Assessment process for developmental motor speech disorders. AAC, augmentative and alternative communication; CAS, childhood apraxia of speech; CP, cerebral palsy; MSD, motor speech disorder; TBI, traumatic brain injury.

approach (Duffy 2005; see also Yorkston *et al.* 2010 and Freed 2011), it provides a clear, structured assessment protocol to identify any contributing structural abnormalities, and gather information on a broad range of non-speech and speech functions that can guide differential diagnosis.

Given the focus of this chapter on motor speech disorders, the language and cognitive assessment tasks are intended (a) to aid in the design of therapy tasks of appropriate difficulty that might also stimulate development across systems, and (b) to provide information on the potential for therapy response to be influenced by complicating factors. Concomitant language and cognitive impairments will alter the structure and complexity of an intervention programme directed at speech motor learning. While we acknowledge that underperformance on language assessment may reflect either a concomitant language system impairment and/or the impact of the motor speech disorder on the developing language system, in-depth discussion of this issue is beyond the scope of this chapter. We suggest that, in either case, carefully crafted therapy can serve to stimulate development in both areas.

The next stage in diagnosis, prior to building therapeutic stimuli and tasks, is to determine at which stage the child is functioning. Stages range

Table 21.1 *Suggested areas for assessment in differential diagnosis of paediatric motor speech disorders with examples of published tests and protocols to support each task*

ICF-CY level	Domain	Task	Example
Body Systems	Oral and auditory mechanisms*	Oral structure exam Cranial nerve exam Assessment of respiration, phonation and resonance for speech and swallow	Comprehensive Oral Motor Evaluation (e.g. Robbins and Klee 1987; Yorkston *et al.* 2010; Freed 2011)
		Hearing test	(American Speech-Language-Hearing Association 1997)
		Case history: family history, development, feeding, gross and fine motor skills	(Yorkston *et al.* 2010)
Body Functions	Speech-like oro-motor function*	Assessment of diadochokinesis (DDK)	Time by Count (Fletcher 1972)
	Speech accuracy*	Single word sample – accuracy (articulation) and phonology – at least 50 words and examination of spontaneous vs. imitated production	Diagnostic Evaluation of Articulation and Phonology (DEAP; Dodd *et al.* 2006)
		Polysyllabic words especially in older children	Test of Polysyllables (Gozzard *et al.* 2008)
		Non-word repetition test	Children's Nonword Repetition Test (Gathercole *et al.* 1994)
		Connected speech sample – 100 utterances	(McLeod 1997)
		Consistency and variability	DEAP Consistency Subtest (Dodd *et al.* 2006)
		Stimulability	Dynamic Evaluation of Motor Speech Skills (Miccio 2002; Strand *et al.* 2013)
	Prosody*	Assessment of prosody	Profiling Elements of Prosody in Speech-Communication (Peppé and McCann 2003) Pairwise Variability Indices (Ballard *et al.* 2012)
	Receptive and expressive language*	Language/cognitive skills	Language battery of choice
	Phonological awareness		Preschool and Primary Inventory of Phonological Awareness (Dodd *et al.* 2000)
	Related cognitive skills	Speech perception testing Verbal working memory	Test of Auditory Processing Skills (Martin and Brownell 2000)

ICF-CY level	Domain	Task	Example
Activity		Intelligibility score	Percent Consonants Correct (Shriberg *et al.* 1997d) Intelligibility measures in words, sentences, and in context (Flipsen 2006; Hodge and Daniels 2007; McLeod *et al.* 2012). Computerized Assessment of Intelligibility of Dysarthric Speech (Yorkston *et al.* 1984a) may be suitable for older children (Flipsen 2012)
		Comprehensibility evaluation	Parent ratings on a 7-point equal-appearing interval scale (Hustad *et al.* 2012) See Yorkston *et al.* (2010)
		Evaluation of compensatory strategies	See Yorkston *et al.* (2010)
Participation			Speech Participation and Activity Assessment – Children (SPAA-C) version 2 (McLeod 2004*)*
			Quality of life questionnaire with parent and child
			Observation in classroom and at home

Note: It is beyond the scope of this chapter to provide more than a basic framework for such an assessment protocol. To aid clinicians in building their own protocol, we provide references with useful tools for each component of the protocol.

* Indicates essential component; other assessment tasks will inform treatment planning for individuals.

from no functional speech through to no detectable disorder (Yorkston *et al.* 2010). In the case of disorders that are improving (i.e. are non-degenerative), children assigned to Stage 1 will rely on augmentative/alternative communication (AAC) for participating in communicative interactions, with impairment-based treatment possibly focused on precursors to speech production, such as differentiated tongue and jaw movement, or developing basic articulatory gestures and syllable structures. Children in Stage 2 will be able to express basic daily needs with familiar listeners through vocalization or speech but rely on AAC for more complex communication needs. Children in Stage 3 will use speech for most interactions but will utilize AAC to resolve communication breakdowns or scaffold new language skills. Those in Stage 4 rely on speech production, with no/minimal AAC supplementation. Those in Stage 5 rely entirely on speech with no noticeable disorder. While most children in Stages 1 to

4 are likely to benefit from treatment targeted at both impairment and activity/participation levels, those in Stage 4 are thought to be most suitable for an intervention that is primarily impairment-based.

It must be noted, however, that such classification will be accurate only at the time of the assessment. Due to the interactive, concurrent development of speech, language and cognition, the goal is naturally to shift children along the continuum toward Stage 5. Also, while such classification may be highly appropriate for children with dysarthria, it may lead to most children with apraxia being classed in Stages 3 and 4 and being incorrectly perceived as less impaired. Finally, while this classification may guide us in deciding the involvement of AAC in intervention, it does not inform the selection of processes, levels or stimulus categories for impairment- or activity-based intervention programmes (see sections 21.4 and 21.5).

A comprehensive assessment may take several hours, and many will argue that there is not time in a stretched clinical service to execute such comprehensive protocols. Clearly, some children will come with a clear diagnosis and others will present with relatively simple profiles that require a more streamlined assessment process. However, the trade-off with a brief assessment for our more complex or challenging clients is a less accurate picture, increased risk of misdiagnosis (see section 21.3) and perhaps an explanation for our history of slow and painfully incremental progress for many of our intervention approaches. As the cost of healthcare increases, more time getting it right in the beginning will almost guarantee a more time- and cost-efficient outcome and better outcomes for our clients. It should be noted, however, that dynamic assessment can and should be used where possible, as described below.

Dynamic assessment is a philosophy which captures both the changing nature of developmental disorders and the learning potential of the child being assessed (Hasson and Joffe 2007). Dynamic assessment allows the clinician systematically to evaluate how children respond to the prompts, cues and stimuli of treatment. The information gathered may prove to be more useful for differential diagnosis of motor versus linguistic/cognitive impairment than many of our traditional diagnostic tests (Hasson and Joffe 2007). To date, one dynamic assessment tool has been developed for children with developmental motor speech disorders, the Dynamic Evaluation of Motor Speech Skills (Strand *et al.* 2013). This tool is designed for use with severe and complex speech sound disorders in young children and provides a structured approach to evaluating speech potential.

With application of the proposed framework, clinicians have the tools they need to provide a more accurate picture of the individual, where they need to move next, and what factors will potentially influence the response of clients to intervention. Assessment will ideally be structured within the ICF framework. It will include stand-alone assessments of subsystems in isolation and in coordinated non-speech and speech movements, as well as dynamic assessment to confirm diagnosis and better understand how the child's system is responding to tasks, cues and stressors.

21.3   Differential diagnosis: dysarthria versus apraxia versus phonological disorders

> Differentiation between movement planning versus movement execution can be conceptually and practically difficult and is often at the heart of differential diagnosis of severe speech impairment. (Strand and McCauley 2008)

Developing linguistic, cognitive and neurological systems complicate the differential diagnosis of motor speech disorders in children. Speech-language pathologists are known to find complex differential diagnosis difficult (e.g. Forrest 2003; Shriberg *et al.* 2011). This was clearly demonstrated by Murray *et al.* (2012a), who found that 19 of 47 children presenting with a community diagnosis of CAS were incorrectly diagnosed. Among these 19 children, two were found to have a dysarthria, three had an undiagnosed submucous cleft palate, eight had a phonological disorder rather than CAS and two had combinations of phonological disorder and stuttering. Additionally, four children who had been thought to have CAS alone were reclassified as CAS plus dysarthria. Based on these findings, the authors recommended that a minimum assessment inventory for motor speech disorder must include a formal oral structure and function evaluation including intra-oral examination, speech diadochokinesis (DDK) tasks (e.g. repetition of 'papapa' and 'pataka' sequences) and a speech sample of 50 or more polysyllabic words (three or more syllables). While additional, larger-scale studies are required, Murray *et al.* (2012a) were able to reliably separate CAS, dysarthria and phonologically-based speech sound disorders on the basis of this assessment inventory. With the data generated from a comprehensive assessment protocol, such as in Table 21.1, a clinician is well situated for the task of differential diagnosis.

It should be noted that some features that are associated with dysarthria and CAS can also be symptomatic of other diagnoses. For example, resonance problems may be indicative of muscular weakness (dysarthria) or an error of timing (CAS) or they may be structural in nature such as in cleft palate. The revisions and repetitions thought to be part of CAS could be stuttering either in isolation or in combination with, for example, a phonological disorder (Murray *et al.* 2012a). Vowel distortions could be diagnostic of dysarthria or CAS (Duffy 2005). It is also worth keeping in mind that the power of many proposed diagnostic markers (e.g. dysprosody) to differentiate CAS from the other dysarthria types

Table 21.2 *Primary symptoms which may differentiate childhood apraxia of speech, dysarthria and phonological disorders*

Childhood apraxia of speech	Dysarthria	Phonological disorder
• Initiation, sequencing and prosody distortions • Difficulty moving from syllable to syllable (e.g. robotic, staccato or very slow speech) • Influenced by word length: increasing breakdown with increasing complexity • Inconsistent errors • No paralysis or paresis – normal muscle tone • Normal resonance, respiration and phonation	• Known brain injury, other neurological signs • Sound distortions • Not generally influenced by word length • Usually consistent (except spasticity) • Paralysis, paresis, asymmetry • Abnormal resonance, respiration or phonation	• Normal prosody • Consistent, rule governed, even if not developmentally typical • Influenced by word position not length • Rarely any oral signs • Responsive to phonological feedback

(e.g. ataxic dysarthria) has not been rigorously tested. Some older definitions of CAS are based on these markers, leading to false diagnostic criteria and misleading results (McCabe *et al.* 1998). Finally, dysarthria and CAS can co-occur along with sensory, language and cognitive disorders. Table 21.2 shows how these three main diagnostic categories might be differentiated.

In general, it is recommended that three simple steps are followed in diagnosis: (1) form a diagnostic hypothesis based on the initial available information; (2) consider other information as it becomes available, such as case history, medical information and test results; and (3) further test the diagnostic hypothesis by observing how the child responds to the challenges of stimulability tasks and initial treatment activities, as some diagnostic features may not manifest clearly until the speech system is challenged. Other questions that may aid in diagnostic decision-making include the following:

(1) *Is the child consistent? Is there an observable pattern, even if not developmentally expected?* If the answer to both of these questions is 'yes', then consider a diagnosis of phonological impairment, articulation disorder or dysarthria. If the answer is 'no', consider a diagnosis of CAS or ataxic dysarthria.
(2) *Does the child have speech distortions, oral, feeding and/or gross motor impairments?* If the answer is 'yes', then consider a diagnosis of dysarthria (or resonance difficulties, if no gross motor problems are apparent).
(3) *Are there deviant speech errors?* If the answer is 'yes', then consider dysarthria, the speaker's accent, or cleft palate.
(4) *Does the child have any other recognized condition that could explain your results, e.g. hearing impairment?*

21.4 A framework for treatment of children with motor speech disorders

21.4.1 Impairment-based or activity/participation-based treatment?

Interventions for paediatric motor speech disorders have been classified using the ICF framework as either impairment-based or activity/participation-based. However, this distinction is not as clear-cut at it seems. Treatment focused on improving respiratory, phonatory, articulatory and resonatory performance for speech production (i.e. multiple muscular contractions that are coordinated and precise in space and time) is considered impairment-based. Ultimately, the outcome of an impairment-based intervention is to improve speech production accuracy, speech rate and prosodic contours, and hence speech intelligibility and naturalness and the ability to participate in communicative interactions. All of these outcome measures are considered to tap the activity and participation levels within the ICF framework (Yorkston *et al.* 2010).

Treatment focused on developing compensatory strategies to obtain rapid or immediate improvements in speech intelligibility and communicative success would be considered activity/participation-based (Hustad and Weismer 2007; Hustad 2012). While compensations can include AAC tools and techniques such as hand gestures and alphabet and/or topic cues through a word/picture display, other compensations include slowing speech rate, using clear or 'over-articulated' speech, inserting strategic pauses or breaths, and emphasizing key words through manipulations of speech segment duration, pitch and loudness (see Hustad and Weismer (2007) and Yorkston *et al.* (2010) for detailed descriptions of these methods). If the child can implement the strategy, the speech should immediately be more intelligible. Note that, as with any new skill, habituating independent use of the strategy may require considerable practice (not a trivial exercise in children or adults). Just like impairment-based therapy activities, motivation and compliance with practice are facilitated by therapy activities that are functional and meaningful. However, as many of these strategies require use of an impaired system (e.g. over-articulation requires weak articulators to use a greater range of movement and force), the impairment may be reduced over time with practice of these strategies during speaking. So, again, this intervention approach spans the three ICF levels.

Perhaps a more useful way to consider these two different therapy approaches is by the timeframe over which they aim to operate. Compensatory strategies can be applied to improve immediately activity and participation in daily communication contexts. Impairment-based treatment can be applied to work on a longer timescale, with the aim of increasing muscle strength, range of motion, and coordinated, multi-articulator movements for further improvements in speech intelligibility and naturalness. While changes in intelligibility and naturalness of speech are attainable with impairment-based interventions (e.g. Morgan *et al.* 2007), it is unlikely that widespread changes in more complex, functional, daily, connected speech will be seen in the typical 2- to 6-week timeframe of most impairment-based treatment studies. As Hustad (2012) suggests, it is reasonable to propose that the most effective approach for children at Stages 2 to 4 of Yorkston *et al.*'s scheme will target the impairment as well as compensatory strategies, with careful selection of speech stimuli and tasks that are specific to the communication goals of the child and designed to maximize potential generalization to related but untreated speech behaviours and contexts. Furthermore, practice and feedback should be thoughtfully structured according to evidence-based principles of experience-dependent neuroplasticity and motor learning, in order to maximize long-term maintenance and generalization of newly acquired skills.

21.4.2   Principles of motor learning

The human and animal motor learning literature provides a wealth of evidence for structuring more effective speech interventions (Clark 2004; Schmidt and Lee 2005; Kleim and Jones 2008; Maas *et al.* 2008b). The principles of motor learning (PML) approach of Schmidt and colleagues (e.g. Schmidt and Lee 2005) is probably the most prescriptive intervention and has now been applied to a range of developmental and acquired motor speech disorders across several studies (see Maas *et al.* (2008b) for a review). To date, very few studies with children have trialled speech interventions that comply with the PML approach. Those that have include interventions in children with CAS (Strand and Debertine 2000; Strand *et al.* 2006; Ballard *et al.* 2010; Murray *et al.* 2011, 2012b), children with cerebral palsy and spastic dysarthria (Fox and Boliek 2012) and typically developing children (Van Rees *et al.* 2012). A brief description of the PML approach and its main principles follows.

The PML approach guides the level of stimuli selected and the structure of practice within a treatment session as well as the nature, frequency and timing of feedback provided (Schmidt and Lee 2005). The focus is not on performance within the session but rather on long-term learning. This is indexed by maintenance of skill from session to session and after a speech behaviour is removed from treatment, as well as generalization of skill to related behaviours and to other speaking contexts or tasks. Each session is usually divided into pre-practice and practice. Pre-practice serves (a) to orient the child to the tasks and stimuli that will be practised, (b) to define what is considered a correct production of the speech behaviour, (c) to provide supported attempts at production and experience with producing an accurate response and (d) to motivate the child to engage in the therapeutic activities. Once some successful responses have been produced, the child is moved into practice. This aims to maximize the amount of supervised practice the child has in producing accurate responses with minimal assistance from the clinician. Early in treatment the child may need to remain in pre-practice for several sessions until he or she can produce some correct productions of the targeted speech behaviours. But, ideally, practice occupies about three-quarters of the session time.

There are several key principles of practice, which have been shown to facilitate long-term maintenance of treated behaviours and promote generalization of skills to untreated behaviours and untreated speaking tasks. These have been reviewed extensively elsewhere (e.g. Schmidt and Lee 2005; Maas *et al.* 2008b; Bislick *et al.* 2012). The principles are presented as dichotomous but are, in reality, ends of a continuum. As an example, it has been demonstrated frequently that random practice of motor skills facilitates more robust learning while blocked practice facilitates performance in the moment but actually inhibits long-term learning. If the goal is to improve production of CVC words beginning with /p/ or /t/, blocked practice would involve practising all /p/ words together, then switching to /t/ words, while random practice would involve switching randomly back and forth between /p/ and /t/ words within a session. Random practice is much harder than blocked practice and, at least initially, elicits more errors of production. However, the maintenance and generalization of the treated speech skills will be more robust. But for some children, jumping into random practice may be too difficult at first. The art is in finding the point on the continuum – the optimal challenge point – that is hard enough to ensure robust learning but is not so hard that the child cannot succeed or loses motivation (Guadagnoli and Lee 2004). These children may benefit from shifting along the continuum and practising a series of randomized blocks: producing 5–10 trials of each word type, with order of trial-blocks randomized.

Other facilitative principles of practice include (a) variable versus constant practice, such as practising two or three different speech rates or loudness levels rather than one to improve control of these parameters, (b) high versus low intensity practice, with over 100 practice trials per session and 3–5 sessions per week, and (c) using stimuli of high versus low complexity, such as words or multisyllabic sequences rather than single sounds, syllables or non-speech behaviours.

Three main principles of feedback guide the type and structure of feedback provided by the clinician. Motor learning studies concur with a long history from behavioural psychology in recommending intermittent provision of feedback on accuracy for only 50–60 per cent of production attempts (i.e. low-frequency feedback), rather than 100 per cent (Schmidt and Lee 2005). While detailed feedback on the nature or shortfalls of a child's response during pre-practice helps to shape production and helps the child understand what is correct or incorrect, simple, low-frequency feedback on accuracy alone (i.e. knowledge of results) is usually sufficient during practice to promote learning. Finally, pausing for 3–5 seconds before providing the feedback (i.e. delayed feedback) is more effective than delivering it immediately following a response.

These principles of feedback type and structure, like the practice principles, usually make the learning process harder and engage the child in more active learning processes. This ensures that the child takes responsibility for problem solving to independently modify speech and gradually reduce errors. Specifically, intermittent and delayed feedback encourage the child to actively self-evaluate their production attempts, hypothesize what was wrong and how they can change their production next time, and compare their evaluation with the clinician's evaluation when available. This inherent training of self-evaluation and analysis supports generalization of new skills to contexts outside the therapy session and to similar, untrained speech behaviours. It also increases the likelihood that any home practice will be of high quality, as close to the quality of the clinical session as possible. The conceptualization of the principles as a series of continua rather than as dichotomies also allows flexible application for children whose impairments are more severe, or who have more cognitive involvement that limits self-evaluation or support from explicit memory of trial-and-error practice experiences.

21.5   Evaluating the treatment evidence base

High-level evidence for treatment of children with motor speech disorders is sparse. Cochrane systematic reviews in both CAS (Morgan and Vogel 2008) and dysarthria (Pennington *et al.* 2004, 2009a; Morgan and Vogel 2009) show no randomized control trials have been published to date. However, children with dysarthria or apraxia still need intervention to develop the most effective communication.

Murray and colleagues' recent narrative review of the CAS literature shows that more than 40 controlled treatment studies (with data) have been reported, although most are case description and experimental, single-case designs (Murray *et al.* 2012c). This pool of evidence is significantly larger than the potential, data-based speech interventions available for children with dysarthria. Leaving aside interventions that are primarily focused on language development including AAC, few treatments are supported by systematic programmes of research that demonstrate treatment efficacy, efficiency or sustainability.

Figure 21.2 shows treatments that have any well-controlled, peer-reviewed research evidence to support their efficacy. These are most frequently experimental, single-case design studies. Interventions are included based on reporting speech-related outcomes. To date, there has

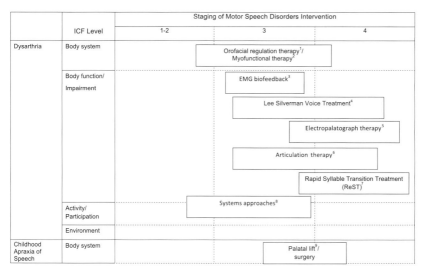

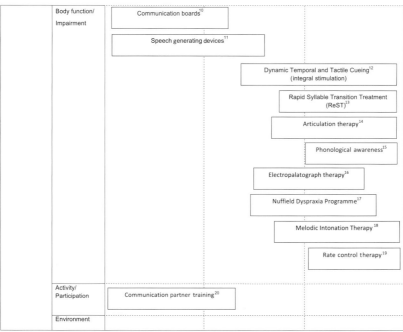

Figure 21.2 Interventions for paediatric motor speech disorders based on reported speech-related outcomes and treated participants. *Key: Research evidence for dysarthria interventions:* 1, Orofacial regulation therapy (Fischer-Brandies *et al.* 1987); 2, Myofunctional (Ray 2001); 3, EMG (Gallegos *et al.* 1992); 4, Lee Silverman Voice Treatment (Fox *et al.* 2005, 2008); 5, Electropalatograph therapy (Thompson-Ward *et al.* 1997); 6, Articulation therapy (Wu and Jeng 2004; Marchant *et al.* 2008); 7. Rapid Syllable Transition Treatment (Murray *et al.* 2011); 8, Systems approaches and multiple mixed methods (Hartley *et al.* 2003; Puyuelo and Rondal 2005; Pennington *et al.* 2006, 2008, 2010; Robson *et al.* 2009). *Research evidence for apraxia interventions:* 9, Palatal lift (Hall *et al.* 1990); 10, Communication boards (Binger and Light 2007; Binger *et al.* 2008); 11, Speech generating devices, alone or in combination (Cumley and Swanson 1999; Bornman *et al.* 2001; Binger *et al.* 2011); 12, Dynamic Temporal and Tactile Cueing (and integral stimulation)

been a range of treatment approaches covering all or most of the ICF/ICF-CY and all stages of habilitation in children with motor speech disorders. Treatment of children outside this range would be experimental and should be undertaken cautiously. We do not present a full-scale, systematic review here and, therefore, the list of interventions is not exhaustive. Some commonly used treatments have been omitted as studies of their efficacy are not well controlled or they have only been reported in combination with a number of other interventions.

The development of effective treatments for paediatric motor speech disorders is an emerging field. In recent years, there has been a significant increase in the number and quality of studies examining CAS treatments. Much of this work has followed the seminal reviews of the late 2000s (American Speech-Language-Hearing Association 1997; Morgan and Vogel 2008) in which a clear call for treatment research was articulated. At least three of the treatments in Figure 21.2 are based in whole or in part on the PML approach discussed above (i.e. Dynamic Temporal and Tactile Cueing; Nuffield Dyspraxia Programme-3; Rapid Syllable Transition Treatment), and the efficacy of two of these has been demonstrated in a recent randomized controlled trial (Murray et al. 2012b). Other treatments for CAS with an emerging evidence base include Integrated Phonological Awareness (McNeill et al. 2009a, 2009c), which uses a combination of phonological interventions with articulation cueing as required by the child, and various AAC interventions using communication boards alone or in combination with voice generating devices to focus on language development (e.g. Binger and Light 2007; Binger et al. 2008, 2011).

By contrast, there is a critical shortfall in high-quality, research evidence to guide speech treatments for paediatric dysarthria. Dysarthria is considerably more common than CAS and, consistent with Yorkston et al.'s (2010) stages of functioning, the majority of these children stand to benefit from well-designed interventions to improve their speech production skills and their speech intelligibility and naturalness. Given the stigma and other negative social, academic and emotional outcomes that speech disorders impose on children and adolescents (Ruben 2000; Pennington et al. 2010), a concerted effort needs to be made to develop theoretically driven, proven interventions for this population. In the absence of such research evidence, clinicians are encouraged to use expert clinical

Caption for Figure 21.2 (cont.)

(Rosenbek *et al.* 1974; Strand and Debertine 2000; Strand *et al.* 2006; Baas *et al.* 2008; Edeal and Gildersleeve-Neumann 2011; Maas and Farinella 2012); 13, Rapid Syllable Transition Treatment (Ballard *et al.* 2010; Murray *et al.* 2012b); 14, Articulation therapy (Stokes and Griffiths 2010); 15, Phonological awareness (Tempest and Parkinson 1993; Gillon and Moriarty 2007; McNeill *et al.* 2009a, 2009c, 2010; Zaretsky *et al.* 2010); 16, Electropalatograph therapy (Carter and Edwards 2004; Lundeborg and McAllister 2007); 17, Nuffield Dyspraxia Programme (Murray *et al.* 2012b); 18, Melodic intonation therapy (Krauss and Galloway 1982; Helfrich-Miller 1994; LaGasse 2012); 19, Rate control therapy (Rosenthal 1994); 20, Communication partner training (Culp 1989).

judgement, evidence from other populations including adults and children with dysarthria and CAS, and a strong, single-case methodology in designing treatment programmes for their clients. The information in this chapter is intended to provide a guide for such efforts.

21.6 Conclusions

As our knowledge expands in the coming years, it is possible that frameworks for assessment and treatment of motor speech disorders in children will merge, and the dynamic assessment approaches of researchers like Strand and colleagues will become more developed and mainstream (Strand *et al.* 2013). It is likely that the diagnosis of motor speech disorders will rest not only on the presenting symptoms, but on the specific approaches and changes that a child demonstrates in response to therapeutic exercises. Here, we argue for the importance of a comprehensive assessment protocol that allows a consensus diagnosis over different domains and sources of information. As noted by Hustad (2012), it is likely that the treatments which will have the greatest impact on both short-term needs and long-term outlook will be those that combine impairment-based and activity/participation-based interventions and outcome measures, based on sound theories of experience-dependent neuroplasticity. One can envisage treatments that will (a) target gradual improvement in articulation and prosody within multi-phoneme and multisyllable sequences, (b) train compensatory strategies to maximize intelligibility, success and motivation as quickly as possible and (c) place all therapy activities within meaningful and motivating contexts.

22

Acquired motor speech disorders

Anja Lowit

22.1   Introduction

This chapter examines current assessment and intervention techniques in the management of acquired motor speech disorders (MSDs). Publications on MSD management can be found from early in the twentieth century. However, focused research on these disorders largely started with the publication of seminal papers by Darley *et al.* on the classification of different types of MSDs (Darley *et al.* 1969a, 1969b), and their subsequent volume on the management of these disorders (Darley *et al.* 1975). Current clinical practice is still heavily based on some of these early techniques, although a number of new areas have since been developed. It is outside the scope of this chapter to go into any of these methods in depth. Instead reference is made to research studies and systematic reviews that discuss the appropriateness of assessment tools and the available evidence on effectiveness of treatment techniques to allow the reader to gain further details on the issues addressed here.

22.2   Assessment of acquired motor speech disorders

22.2.1   General principles of assessment

Following Darley *et al.*'s influential publication on the characteristics of different types of motor speech disorders (Darley *et al.* 1969a, 1969b), clinical assessment of dysarthria and apraxia of speech (AOS) focused largely on physiological function and intelligibility, i.e. on 'body' and 'activity' in terms used in the International Classification of Functioning, Disability and Health (ICF; World Health Organization 2001). At the body level, the functioning of the various speech subsystems, i.e. respiratory, laryngeal and velopharyngeal function, and oral musculature are investigated. In terms of the activity level, a variety of data elicitation methods are available to assess intelligibility, ranging from evaluations of single words and phrases to reading passages and spontaneous speech. Following the publication of Darley *et al.*'s (1975) protocol, a number of assessments for dysarthria were developed including the Frenchay Dysarthria Assessment (now in its revised version, FDA-2, Enderby and Palmer 2008), the Robertson Dysarthria Profile (Robertson 1982) and the Dysarthria Examination Battery (Drummond 1993).

All of these assessments follow the medical model of initially investigating the physiological level, then moving on to evaluations of intelligibility, based on the premise that problems affecting activity have a direct link to those at the body level. This idea is not only reflected in published assessment protocols but is mirrored in common treatment practice where, for example, the use of diadochokinetic (DDK) exercises is still widespread as a technique to improve articulatory clarity (Mackenzie *et al.* 2010).

Research evidence suggests that links between physiology and speech intelligibility are not as clear cut as is often assumed. Assessment of physiological performance through maximum performance tasks is not always reliable. Patient performance can be variable due to practice effects (Kent *et al.* 1987) and some tasks, particularly those looking at movement force, are prone to poor reliability of scoring unless instrumental techniques are available. More importantly, research has shown that there is often little correspondence between performance on non-speech tasks and actual speech (Ziegler 2003). Finally, one could argue that the most important issues to consider in patient management are not the effects of the disorder on body and activity, but how the combination of these impact on the patient's participation in daily activities, i.e. the third level of the ICF framework. It is at this level that other factors such as awareness, attitude, confidence, mood, fatigue, etc. affect speech performance, often irrespective of what a physiological assessment has highlighted.

Published assessment batteries for dysarthria are largely consistent in their approach to what is being assessed, but vary in the types of tasks designed for this purpose. In particular, the assessment follows a specific order, starting with non-speech, physiological investigations, generally followed by evaluations of intelligibility and naturalness. One might want to argue that order of assessment is inconsequential as long as all levels are assessed appropriately. However, there is a danger that the clinical decision-making path might follow along the same lines, i.e. clinicians might be biased in basing their choice of management more on the severity of impairment at physiological and intelligibility levels instead of first considering which factors have the greatest impact on the communication participation of the client.

It is suggested, therefore, that in order to arrive at a holistic assessment of patients with MSDs, the clinician should first of all identify the person's current level of functioning and why this might be affected. This will inform whether or not the patient should be offered treatment and whether the speech and language therapist is the most appropriate person to deliver it. In most, but not all cases, the prominent underlying reason will be a reduction in intelligibility and naturalness. In this situation, a comprehensive assessment of how well the person can be understood should be performed in different contexts and speaking tasks, with a focus on segmental as well as prosodic aspects of speech production. Finally, one should assess the patient with maximum performance tests to discover any particular impairments in motor function and control that might cause the intelligibility deficits previously identified.

In line with this suggested order, the chapter will now proceed to discuss available assessment options for each of the levels of functioning, starting with impact and participation, followed by intelligibility, prosody and finally underlying physiology.

22.2.2   Assessment of impact and participation

It has long been good practice to look beyond a person's speech or language impairment and find out about personal circumstances which can inform clinical decision-making. However, clinicians have not always had access to formalized assessments which provide a reliable, holistic account of medical, environmental and personal factors and which can be used as an outcome measure of treatment. Researchers have tried to rectify this since the late 1990s and a number of different tools have been published. Although not all of these are specifically designed for people with MSDs, clinicians now have access to a good range of resources and more are being validated at present. Walshe (2011) provides a comprehensive overview of the framework for assessments of impact and of a range of published tools currently available in this area (see also Yorkston and Baylor 2011).

Essentially, impact assessment is concerned with how a communication disorder affects a person's quality of life (QOL) and participation in communicative activities. QOL is a multifaceted concept which encompasses personal as well as external factors. Byng *et al.* (2000) describe a psychosocial model which tries to take account of these various factors in the context of aphasia. Psychological factors describe the direct impact of the communication disorder on the person, i.e. changes in identity and self-esteem, as well as in the person's role and their relationship with others. Depression is also a significant factor in this category. Qualitative research on people's perceptions following acquired MSDs has been undertaken by several authors and reveals fear of communication, anger and frustration about how speech has changed, and feelings of isolation and loneliness, depression and a negative self-image as consequences of MSDs (Miller *et al.* 2006; Dickson *et al.* 2008; Hartelius *et al.* 2008; Bloch *et al.* 2011; Brady *et al.* 2011; N. Miller *et al.* 2011; Walshe and Miller 2011).

The effects of such feelings include partial or complete withdrawal from communication. Avoidance of the telephone, shortening of communication exchanges, as well as reductions in social use of language, are also often noted.

From a social point of view, the communication disorder can impact on lifestyle, employment, social networks, as well as leisure activities. The importance of each of these to the speaker will depend on their age, as well as on the degree to which they are engaged in social activities. Although most research on social aspects has been done on aphasia, one can assume some parallels with dysarthria and AOS. One must not forget the family and carers who will also be affected by at least some of these issues, in particular changes in family relationships and employment status. It is as important to explore perceptions of carers as it is to consider those of the client, both from a duty of care point of view and because a supportive communication environment can significantly facilitate participation for the client, thus indirectly improving their QOL.

Walshe (2011) lists a number of impact assessments that address the areas mentioned above. She refers to Thomas (2010) for an overview of screening tools for anxiety and depression. Such screening tests are quick to administer and will assist the clinician in deciding if onward referral to other relevant health professionals is necessary. Table 22.1 lists available tools for other areas such as self-esteem, QOL and social factors. It should be noted that many of these have been developed for patients with aphasia or voice problems, but they are also appropriate for those with MSDs. The most recent development has focused on measures of actual communicative participation. An example is the communicative participation item bank by Yorkston and co-workers (Yorkston *et al.* 2006; Baylor *et al.* 2009, 2011) that can be used to quantify the activities a speaker engages in. An overview of its development can be found in Yorkston and Baylor (2011). The tool has been validated for a number of disorders already, with more studies currently underway to extend its applicability.

22.2.3 Intelligibility

Intelligibility is one of the most important concepts to assess in a person with MSD. It refers to how accurately the acoustic signal is understood by the listener. Intelligibility represents the most global reflection of type and severity of the speech disorder and is a measure of the effects of any impairment at the physiological level on speech. In addition, intelligibility impairments are the most common reason for a reduction in participation. Intelligibility thus plays a pivotal role in identifying a speaker's problem, deciding on the best management pathway, and functioning as an outcome measure of such management.

Alongside intelligibility, it is important to consider the comprehensibility of speech. Comprehensibility takes into account any non-verbal

Table 22.1 *Selection of published scales to assess psychosocial effects of acquired communication disorders*

Assessment	Author
Visual Analog Mood Scales	Stern (1997)
Stroke and Quality of Life Scale – 39 (SAQOL-39)	Hilari *et al.* (2003)
Quality of Communication Life Scale (QCL)	Paul *et al.* (2004)
Stroke Impact Scale	Duncan *et al.* (1999)
Psychosocial Well-being Index	Lyon *et al.* (1997)
Dysarthria Impact Profile	Walshe *et al.* (2009)
Living with Dysarthria Questionnaire	Hartelius *et al.* (2008)
Communication Effectiveness Survey (CETI)	Ball *et al.* (2004)
Communicative Effectiveness Survey (CES)	Donovan *et al.* (2008)
Social Activities Checklist (SOCACT)	Cruice *et al.* (2006)
Voice Handicap Index (VHI)	Jacobson *et al.* (1997)
Voice-Related Quality of Life scale (V-RQOL)	Hogikyan and Sethuraman (1999)
Voice Activity and Participation Profile (VAPP)	Ma and Yiu (2001)
Voice Symptoms Scale (VoiSS)	Deary *et al.* (2003)

messages that might accompany speech, as well as cues provided by the context, e.g. topic choice and grammatical structure of the utterance. Although many clinicians and researchers refer to evaluating intelligibility, they might in fact be looking at comprehensibility. Any face-to-face assessment of speech beyond single word level is by its nature one of comprehensibility. Another common descriptor is communication effectiveness, which again implies more than intelligibility. 'Decipherability' is the term used by the Frenchay Dysarthria Assessment in its intelligibility section. It is employed for both single word and connected speech assessments and it is therefore unclear whether it relates to intelligibility or comprehensibility. There is no right or wrong choice of terminology to describe how well patients get their messages across. What is important is for the clinician to realize that this depends on more factors than just the accuracy of speech production and to consider any facilitating or limiting factors in the evaluation of assessment.

The usual task hierarchy moving from structured to unstructured speech material is frequently applied to intelligibility assessments. Published batteries include tasks ranging from single words at one end of the continuum to reading sentences and passages, and producing monologues or conversational speech at the other. Within this larger framework, assessments differ in relation to how data are elicited and what listeners have to pay attention to or evaluate. Early single word tests (those included in the Robertson Dysarthria Profile (Robertson 1982), for example, tended to consist of lists of monosyllabic words that were phonetically balanced in order to assess the client across a range of speech sounds. Researchers soon came to realize that clinician familiarity with the test items could significantly skew their evaluation of the speaker's intelligibility and larger word pools were constructed from which test items could be randomly selected (e.g. ASSISD single word intelligibility section (Yorkston *et al.* 1984b), FDA-2 (Enderby and Palmer 2008)). However, a criticism of that methodology was that despite yielding a more valid reflection of the person's intelligibility level, the outcomes of the assessment did not necessarily provide any systematic guidance on why the person was unintelligible. As a result, the multi-word intelligibility test (Kent *et al.* 1989) was developed, which provides a pool of words that not only sound similar, but actually form a minimal pair with the test item for all relevant phonetic contrasts. The results still yield a percentage intelligibility score but in addition provide information on which phonetic contrasts could not be achieved by the patient. This information can then be put into the context of the physiological assessment to see what strategies might help the speaker achieve adequate production of the phoneme type in question.

There is general agreement that single word assessment is not sufficient to gain a comprehensive picture of a speaker's functional level. This is reflected in most assessment batteries which also evaluate connected speech samples. There is a wide range of material at hand to look at larger speech units. The next step up from single words is sentence reading. Validated tests for this task include the sentence section of the Assessment of Intelligibility of Dysarthric Speech (ASSIDS; Yorkston *et al.* 1984b) or the FDA-2 (Enderby and Palmer 2008), which provide clinicians with a pool of sentences. In the ASSIDS, the clinician is also provided with a choice of sentence lengths in order to assess whether this has any impact on intelligibility. Unpredictability of material has been taken a step further by McHenry and Parle (2006), who provide a pool of sentences that do not make sense lexically. The listener is thus not guided by the lexical content of the utterance, and results more clearly reflect intelligibility rather than comprehensibility.

Elicitation tasks for longer stretches of speech tend to centre around reading passages, monologues and conversational assessments of the client. The most commonly applied reading passages are the grandfather passage (Darley *et al.* 1975) or the rainbow passage (Fairbanks 1960). Others have been developed over the years in an attempt to include more prosodic variation into the text and can thus form the basis for a wider range of analysis than purely intelligibility (Brown and Docherty 1995; Lowit *et al.* 2006; Patel *et al.* 2013).

If spontaneous speech is assessed, the clinician needs to ensure that samples are comparable over time. Rate and pausing behaviour in particular are affected by the cognitive load of the task, and they in turn can have a significant impact on the intelligibility of the speaker. A number of monologue topics have been applied in research studies, involving story retelling, procedural descriptions (e.g. how to make a cup of tea) or descriptions of events such as a holiday. Any of these topics can be easily extended into conversational tasks by the clinician asking questions about the information provided in the monologue. An alternative dialogue task that retains greater control over speech output comes in the form of a map task, where both the client and the clinician have to provide instructions to each other on how to reach a particular point on a map (Anderson *et al.* 1991). There is also the more recently designed Diapix (Bradlow *et al.* 2007), where interlocutors discuss differences on two versions of the same picture.

Researchers have identified some discrepancy between intelligibility inside and outside the clinical environment. A number of variations of the above listed tasks have been proposed by research studies in order to make task performance and listening conditions more similar to normal communication situations. Dromey and Benson (2003) and Dromey and Bates (2005), for example, noticed differences in speech performance in healthy speakers when they were asked to perform concurrent cognitive, manual or syntactic tasks. Another possibility is to ask listeners to evaluate the patient's speech under noisy conditions (Adams *et al.* 2008).

A range of evaluation or scoring methods is available for any of these elicitation tasks. The most global judgement method is interval scaling, where the patient's performance is judged on a 5-point scale, for example, with a score of 1 indicating no impairment and 5 indicating severe impairment. These scales are common in assessment batteries such as the Robertson Dysarthria Profile (Robertson 1982) or the FDA-2 (Enderby and Palmer 2008). The main problem associated with this scoring method is that the intervals on these scales tend not to be equidistant and vary considerably across listeners. Although good agreement is generally reached at the extreme ends of the scale, the middle parts are associated with greater variability. An advantage of scaling methods is that a descriptor can be attached to each scale. This allows the use of more refined scales that consider not just how much the listener understands, but also the effort involved in understanding (e.g. FDA-2).

Another popular method is percentage scoring. Here one needs to distinguish between global estimates of how much the listener thinks they understood and actual measures of how many words in a sample were identified or transcribed correctly. The latter technique can only be applied if the target utterances are known to the clinician, and thus cannot be used with spontaneous speech tasks. To quantify intelligibility in those samples, a more global measure such as percentage estimates needs to be applied. Kent and Kim (2011) favour visual analogue scales in such cases, where the listener places a mark on a line to show how much they thought they understood. This can then be turned back into a percentage mark for quantification purposes. A further technique that is predominantly used in research is direct magnitude estimation where a speech sample is compared to a standard (Weismer and Laures 2002; Whitehill *et al.* 2002). The standard could be a sample from a moderately impaired speaker against which the patient in question can be judged in terms of how much better or worse their intelligibility is. Alternatively, samples of the same speaker can be compared with each other if collected pre- and post-treatment, with one acting as the standard. In this case, it is important that the listener is unaware of which time point they are listening to.

Whatever evaluation method one chooses to adopt, assessment of intelligibility needs to go beyond simple estimates of severity level. Whilst these are important as outcome measures, the assessment should also serve a diagnostic purpose, i.e. it should allow the clinician to identify the reasons for the intelligibility deficit. This will require more detailed analysis of segmental and suprasegmental issues that are contributing to reduced clarity of speech. In addition, it is important to take account of the listener as well. There are a number of environmental changes or behavioural strategies that can improve comprehensibility without direct work on the patient's articulatory system.

22.2.4 Prosody

The term 'prosody' refers to those aspects of speech that are applied to structures larger than segments. At the phonetic level, these aspects consist of pitch, loudness, duration, silence and voice quality. At the phonological level, these features can then be used to express linguistic meaning through the manipulation of tempo, pause, intonation, stress and rhythm. Underlying the phonetic level are the same physiological functions as those used in segmental speech production, i.e. the respiratory and laryngeal system, as well as the oral musculature. Thus, they do not require separate assessment and can be examined using the same tasks as described in section 22.2.5.

As is the case for assessment in general, all levels of prosodic production need to be assessed. The speaker should be required to signal contrasts in linguistic or emotive meaning through the use of prosody. This could be in the form of contrastive stress tasks at lexical level (**ob**ject vs. ob**ject**) or sentence level (**Tom** drinks coffee vs. Tom drinks **coffee**), signalling different illocutionary acts via intonation ('He is going home' expressed as a statement, command or question), producing utterances with different emotive meanings (neutral, sad, angry, etc.), using pause to disambiguate different syntactic structures ('Jane said ¦ the boss was very competent.' vs. 'Jane ¦ said the boss ¦ was very competent.') or by judging the frequency and appropriateness of pause placement in a longer stretch of speech. It is important to note that these linguistic functions of prosody can only be assessed perceptually via judgements of appropriateness. As there are many different prosodic patterns that can be applied to particular utterances, none of which are necessarily correct or incorrect if viewed out of context, it is best to use highly structured exercises as exemplified above to establish whether a client is capable of using prosody to signal linguistic meaning.

Rhythm and tempo must also be considered. Rhythm is generally judged for its appropriateness in longer stretches of speech. If a problem is suspected, the clinician can assess the patient across different tasks to identify more clearly what the problem is and what type of rhythm is most problematic for the patient. Tasks can elicit regular rhythms in syllable repetitions (/pa, pa, pa/), a more natural speech rhythm in reading or spontaneous discourse, or highly rhythmic speech in poems and limericks.

Speech tempo is important in the management of intelligibility problems and is probably the most widely assessed aspect of prosody. Perception of tempo largely depends on the speed of articulatory movement as well as the amount, length and location of pauses. Tempo can be judged as appropriate or too fast or slow, and clinicians can perform quantitative measures of speech or articulation rate for more objective results via instrumental analysis (see section 22.3.4). In addition to judgements of natural rate, patients should be asked to slow down their rate. This will inform the clinician about the patient's ability to manipulate rate, their natural strategy for rate reduction (insertion of pauses and/or segment prolongation), as well as whether and to what degree slowed rate contributes to improvements in intelligibility. Should the patient be unable to reduce rate by themselves, the latter needs to be investigated with the help of the clinician pacing their speech.

If a problem is detected at a functional level, further investigation is necessary to identify the origin of the poor performance. It is important to remember that the correct functional use of prosody depends not only on adequate articulation, but also on higher-order processing, such as being able to select the appropriate intonation contour to express a particular syntactic or pragmatic meaning, or deciding which word needs to be stressed in an utterance. It can be difficult to tease these two levels apart purely on the basis of a few sentences, and the patient's performance needs to be evaluated holistically across a range of tasks to identify whether a cognitive or language problem impacts most on speech production.

Phonetic prosodic components can be assessed via speech and non-speech tasks. Non-speech tasks come in the form of maximum performance tests. Care should be taken in the interpretation of these tests, as there is often no direct relationship between, for example, maximum phonation time and management of breath support during speech, or pitch range in a glide and the degree of monopitch in connected speech. It is thus better to continue to look at functional speech tasks, but with the aim of identifying what prosodic aspect is not being manipulated appropriately. For example, does the client fail to highlight a particular word in the utterance because they cannot increase the pitch on the item, or because the pitch peak is produced in the wrong place? Such detailed analysis is extremely difficult to perform reliably without instrumental support, and in addition, can be time-consuming. It is thus not surprising that clinicians rarely go down the route of such investigations and rely on maximum performance tests instead.

A number of prosodic assessments have been published over the years, such as the Prosody-Voice-Screening Profile (Shriberg *et al.* 1990) and the Profile of Prosody (Crystal 1992). There have been some more recent developments in the paediatric field (Peppé and McCann 2003) which could potentially also be used with adults. Otherwise, research papers outlining assessments of particular prosodic functions can be consulted for further indications of suitable tasks and normative data (see Patel (2011) for a more detailed review of procedures).

22.2.5 Physiological level

One area where physiological assessment can be helpful is in the differential diagnosis of MSDs. Despite the problems associated with maximum performance tests alluded to above, research has shown that they can highlight differences in underlying motor pathology (Kent *et al.* 1998; Kent and Kent 2000; Kent and Kim 2003). Clinicians cannot rely on generically applicable treatment programmes for specific types of dysarthria and should always base their management plan firmly on the symptom complex of each individual patient. This is because techniques that are suitable for flaccid muscle tone, for example, can be counterproductive in someone with problems of spasticity. The physiological examination should thus also take careful note of any aspects that inform of the appropriateness of disorder-specific treatment techniques.

A full investigation of motor speech physiology will require the use of instrumental measures to quantify the patient's performance (see Murdoch (1998, 2011) for a comprehensive review of available systems). However, not many of these are readily available to clinicians. The most frequently seen assessment tools are for respiratory function and voice quality, and are generally used within the context of a joint voice clinic with an ENT consultant (see Chapter 25). Most practitioners largely rely on maximum performance tasks to assess the functioning of each speech subsystem in their patients with MSDs.

Standard dysarthria assessment protocols such as the FDA-2 (Enderby and Palmer 2008) or the Robertson Dysarthria Profile (Robertson 1982) provide a template for a comprehensive assessment of the speech subsystems. Typical tasks for the respiratory and laryngeal systems include maximum phonation time (prolonged /a/, /s/ and /z/, counting to 20 on one breath, etc.), and pitch and loudness manipulations (producing maxima and minima on /a/, while counting to 5, singing up and down a scale). To assess velopharyngeal function, the patient can be required to repeat a series of /a/ sounds while movement of the velum is observed, and may be asked to produce word pairs such as 'may–bay'. Oral movements are assessed through observation of articulator range (e.g. moving tongue from side to side), strength (e.g. maintaining lip closure to blow up the cheeks), as well as speed and coordination (e.g. sequential and alternate motion rates in DDK tasks). As already discussed, clinicians need to take care when interpreting the results of DDK tasks. However, they can highlight which subsystems are more severely affected and need to be addressed specifically and which subsystems could be explored as compensatory tools.

22.2.6   Apraxia of speech

Apraxia of speech does not benefit from the same number of assessment tools as dysarthria. One of the major problems is that there is still no consensus on which criteria differentiate AOS from other disorders. In addition, AOS frequently co-occurs with aphasia, which complicates the execution of some of the linguistically more demanding tasks such as reading. The most disputed aspects of differential diagnosis are in fact whether the observed speech difficulties are more based on articulatory difficulties (AOS) or lexical retrieval issues (aphasia). This is discussed in Chapter 12 (this volume). The distinction between AOS and dysarthria is more clear cut, although again patients can present with both types of difficulty at the same time, and certain symptoms can overlap. Physiological assessment will be most useful here, as AOS is not associated with neuromuscular weakness. Performance in speech tasks might see more of an overlap between the two disorders, i.e. prosodic disturbances have been reported for both AOS and dysarthria. It will be difficult to base the differential diagnosis on just a few tasks, and it is therefore important that clinicians look holistically at the patient's speech performance to make their decision.

One of the few assessments specifically designed for AOS is the Apraxia Battery for Adults (Dabul 2000). Originally developed in 1979, this test was revised in 2000 to account for new research evidence about specific areas of difficulty for speakers with AOS, resulting in several additions to the task pool. The test consists of six sections, which focus on DDK rate, production of words with increasing length, tasks to identify symptoms of limb and oral apraxia, response latency and speech rate for polysyllabic words, articulatory variability across repetitions of polysyllabic words and an evaluation of the nature of speech errors on the basis of automatic speech, reading and spontaneous output.

22.3   Intervention in acquired motor speech disorders

Although a number of intervention techniques have been developed over the years for various components of speech production, very few of them are supported by sufficiently high levels of evidence to demonstrate their effectiveness. A range of reports is now available that summarize information on treatment efficacy. Several have been commissioned by the Academy of Neurological Communication Disorders and Sciences (ANCDS), resulting in reviews of treatment studies for spasmodic dysphonia, velopharyngeal and respiratory deficiency, as well as the use of speech supplementation (Yorkston *et al.* 2001, 2003b, 2007; Duffy and Yorkston 2003). In addition, the American Speech-Language-Hearing Association has published a series of papers on the evidence base for speaking rate management (Hammen 2004), as well as the involvement of augmentative and alternative communication (AAC) (Mathy 2004) and non-speech exercises in treatment (Hodge 2004). Three Cochrane reviews, two on Parkinson's disease and one on non-progressive dysarthria as a consequence of stroke (Deane *et al.* 2001a, 2001b; Sellars *et al.* 2001), have considered the evidence that is available from randomized controlled trials in these areas. Furthermore, the Royal College of Speech and Language Therapists has produced a resource manual that pulls together information of the ANCDS and Cochrane reviews to provide some guidelines for the evidence-based treatment of dysarthria (RCSLT 2009). A further Cochrane review has been conducted for AOS (Hesketh *et al.* 2007b).

The gold standard for assessing treatment effectiveness is a randomized controlled trial. Such trials are seen as difficult to execute in speech and language therapy due to the wide variability in presenting symptoms and the need for individualized treatment approaches. Only very few treatment techniques have thus been evaluated via this paradigm. The most prolific of these is the Lee Silverman Voice Treatment (LSVT). However, caution is required in judging the strength of the evidence, as early studies did not include a particularly large number of participants. Moreover, they only compared LSVT to respiratory treatment, which is not representative of much wider-ranging techniques commonly used to treat people with Parkinson's disease.

Given that there is little evidence that any particular treatment technique is more effective than any other, clinicians will need to exercise their own judgement as to which method is most appropriate for a client's profile and needs, and monitor changes during therapy carefully in order to evaluate whether this choice was appropriate. The following sections will provide a brief overview of treatment approaches that have been suggested for the various speech subsystems. It is outside the scope of this chapter to go into any of these in detail, and the reader is therefore referred to the original sources for more specific guidance. Initial information will relate to dysarthria treatment, followed by a discussion of AOS management.

22.3.1 General principles of intervention

One overarching factor that needs to be considered in the choice of management approach for MSDs is whether the patient presents with a stable or progressive pathology. Although the intervention technique for particular speech subsystems might not differ much between these two clinical pictures, treatment goals and follow-up procedures will. For example, a person in the early stages of motor neuron disease (MND) might present with similar intelligibility problems as someone who has recently suffered a stroke. However, whilst it is realistic to tackle the various components that contribute to the intelligibility problem in the stroke patient in an attempt to improve speech, the degenerative nature of MND precludes any significant chances of improvement in the long term. Instead, it would be more appropriate to prepare the patient for use of alternative means of communication in addition to maximizing their communicative effectiveness at the time.

Another issue that is independent of particular techniques is frequency of treatment. There appears to be some consensus in the clinical community that higher frequency is advantageous compared to the traditional schedule of one session a week. Probably the most intensive treatment is LSVT, which is administered in four sessions a week over a period of four weeks. Although the importance of this schedule is stressed for proper retention of the skills, a study looking into reducing this intensity by half, i.e. providing two sessions a week over eight weeks, found no significant differences in speech outcomes (Spielman *et al.* 2007). However, there is a lack of well-controlled studies on the effects of treatment frequency and little guidance is thus available on the best schedule.

Finally, many treatment techniques described in the literature involve practice of non-speech tasks. As discussed in section 22.2.1, it is doubtful to what degree these movements are representative of the problems that occur in speech, and treatment via these methods might also not be appropriate. Real speech tasks should therefore form the foundation of all rehabilitation whenever possible.

22.3.2   Treatment of speech subsystems

Respiratory and phonatory systems: Respiration is fundamental to speech production. It is one of the areas that needs to be addressed in treatment if it is identified to be deficient. As with most speech subsystems, there are two aspects of respiration that require consideration: the speed, range and force of muscular movement, and the control of this movement coordination with other articulatory systems during speech.

One of the first things clinicians will look at is whether the patient's posture might have an impact on their respiratory support. A slumped posture will make it more difficult to expand the diaphragm during inspiration, thus reducing the amount of air that can be inhaled. Postural adjustments that go beyond facilitating normal breathing activity are those that address specific inspiratory versus expiratory problems. For example, it has been suggested that patients with expiratory difficulties can be aided by being placed in a supine position, and those with inspiratory difficulties in an upright position, in order for gravity to help the respiratory movements. Besides the obvious psychosocial implications of having to speak in a supine position, there is little research evidence for the effectiveness of such techniques (Yorkston *et al.* 2003b; Spencer and Yorkston 2004). Breathing against resistance is a popular treatment technique that can be implemented by asking the patient to exhale through a water manometer (Netsell and Daniel 1979; Hixon *et al.* 1982). In addition, breath support can be addressed during speech tasks by focusing on appropriate breathing patterns for speech, and practising to maintain appropriate breath support during speech. Biofeedback is helpful in enhancing patient performance and can be used in speech and non-speech tasks. This largely takes the form of acoustic measures or pressure transducers.

Disturbances of respiratory support are frequently accompanied by reduced phonatory function. Whilst a range of MSDs can have similar effects on breath support, phonatory dysfunction depends more on the underlying physiology. Thus, the high muscle tone characteristic of spastic or hyperkinetic dysarthria leads to hyper-adduction of the vocal folds, whereas flaccid or hypokinetic dysarthrias are more associated with hypo-adduction. Management of the two problems differs and an accurate diagnosis is thus essential. Behavioural techniques to improve hypo-adduction focus on increasing effort during voice production. The Lee Silverman Voice Treatment (LSVT) broadly falls under this category. Physical aids such as clasping hands during phonation can be used, although they do have some limitations as discussed by Solomon and Charron (1998). Postural adjustments as well as manipulations of the thyroid cartilage have been suggested in the literature (Spencer and Yorkston 2004). Surgical intervention to reposition the vocal folds is also an option, although it is rarely used (Dworkin and Meleca 1997).

Techniques for hyper-adduction focus on reducing instead of increasing tension. There is limited evidence for effectiveness of non-speech tasks, where whole body relaxation and the use of biofeedback to monitor vocal fold tension have been advocated. A small number of studies have demonstrated improvements in speech with effort-reducing strategies for speech tasks, such as easy onset of phonation, yawning, etc. (Dworkin and Johns 1980; Murry and Woodson 1995). Biofeedback has also been suggested as beneficial during speech, however, this again lacks evidence (Spencer and Yorkston 2004).

Resonance: Velopharyngeal dysfunction results in hypo- or hypernasality, with the latter the more common scenario. Hypernasality affects a greater number of sounds than hyponasality and thus has a more significant impact on intelligibility. Whilst hypernasality would not be the only cause for unintelligible speech, it can contribute to unintelligibility when other articulatory features are impaired.

The management of velopharyngeal dysfunction is rarely a major focus of treatment and will thus not be covered in detail. A review of techniques has been published by Yorkston *et al.* (2001). Available techniques range from behavioural to prosthetic and surgical methods. Yorkston *et al.* (2001) conclude that there is little evidence for the effectiveness of surgical procedures. More success is reported for prosthetic devices, which come mainly in the form of palatal lifts. These can reduce hypernasality but are not tolerated by some speakers. Additional desensitization therapy might have to be offered. Other prostheses include nasal obturators in various forms to block nasal airflow. Behavioural techniques summarized by Yorkston *et al.* (2001) include reducing speech rate and asking the speaker to over-articulate. Resistance training against air pressure exerted from above the velopharyngeal port during speech (Kuehn and Wachtel 1994; Cahill *et al.* 2004) has been reported as successful in a small number of patients, but Yorkston *et al.* (2001) conclude that there is no evidence for the effectiveness of strength or other training in non-speech tasks. In all of the above techniques, speakers might benefit from biofeedback to monitor the amount of nasal airflow.

Articulation: Although intelligibility is influenced by a multitude of physiological, prosodic and segmental factors, articulatory precision is often regarded as the most direct correlate of how well a speaker can be understood. It thus receives considerable focus in the treatment of MSDs. The literature describes direct and indirect methods of treating articulatory difficulties. Direct methods address the articulatory system, while indirect methods aim to facilitate more accurate sound production by modulating other variables.

Direct treatment of articulation has traditionally involved attempts to improve the strength, range and speed of articulator movements through oro-motor exercises. A recent review conducted by Mackenzie *et al.* (2010) shows that such techniques are still widely used by clinicians. However, the research literature has now established that there is no clear evidence for any functional benefit of such exercises (see Hodge (2004) for a review) and clinicians thus need to consider carefully the aim of such exercises and whether they are an effective use of their and the patient's time. Another form of direct treatment is to work on the articulation of speech sounds. Such techniques are still popular in the treatment of AOS but could also be appropriate for some speakers with dysarthria, particularly those who are severely impaired. In this context, it is important to approach exercises at the syllable rather than individual segment level in order to avoid similar problems as have been raised with oro-motor exercises.

For less severely impaired speakers where work on individual phonemes is not appropriate, the concept of clear speech can be helpful. The speaker is essentially asked to over-articulate speech sounds, thus resulting in greater clarity and precision of gestures. A number of studies have demonstrated that intelligibility is increased compared to normal conversational speech with the use of this technique (Kennedy *et al.*

1994b; Beukelman *et al.* 2002). Recently, Lam and Tjaden (2011) investigated the effects of instructions to patients to speak more loudly versus more clearly or as if talking to someone with a hearing impairment. They noticed that speech intelligibility increased progressively with these instructions, suggesting that the latter would be an appropriate concept to use with patients.

The over-articulation suggested above will not just affect articulatory gestures, but also enhances pitch variation and reduces speaking rate. Reduced speaking rate is a frequently applied indirect technique to improve intelligibility. It provides the speaker with more time to perform articulatory gestures, thus compensating for reductions in movement speed. At the same time, it aids the listener as word boundaries will often be more clearly delineated and listeners have more time to process the distorted speech signal. Following early reports on improvements in intelligibility as a result of rate reduction (e.g. Yorkston *et al.* 1990), this strategy is nowadays widely applied in treatment. However, clinicians should be aware that success is not guaranteed for each client. Turner *et al.* (1995) found inconsistent improvements in their participants with amyotrophic lateral sclerosis, and more recently, Van Nuffelen *et al.* (2009, 2010) observed similar results across a wide range of dysarthria types and rate reduction techniques. Rate reduction strategies include rigid techniques such as pacing boards, metronomes or ABC boards, and methods which retain the rhythmicity of the speech signal and result in more natural speech (Yorkston *et al.* 1999; Hammen 2004; Blanchet and Snyder 2010).

In addition to addressing rate reduction directly, there is also evidence that carry-over to speaking rate can occur from other targeted areas. For example, a number of studies have observed changes in the velocity and displacement of articulatory movements (Dromey 2000), as well as greater movement stability, when speaking with a louder voice in Parkinson's disease as well as in healthy speakers (Kleinow *et al.* 2001). This is consistent with the rate reductions observed as a result of LSVT (Ramig *et al.* 1995). In addition, Simmons (1983) observed that exercises to improve loudness and pitch variation resulted in reduced rate, because more time was needed in which to execute the required prosodic modulations.

Prosody: With the exception of modifications of speaking rate, prosodic aspects of speech have been relatively neglected in treatment studies. The most researched aspect is loudness, which has been investigated as part of the many evaluations of LSVT that have been published (see Yorkston *et al.* (2007) for a review). Most of these studies relate to speakers with Parkinson's disease, but some investigations have been conducted with other populations, such as traumatic brain injury, multiple sclerosis and stroke. Any treatment of loudness needs to go hand in hand with establishing adequate respiratory support and must monitor adverse effects on voice quality. Treatment of pitch modulation is generally achieved through tasks which are similar to those used for assessment, i.e. pitch glides or producing particular intonation patterns on short phrases.

Emphatic stress or focus tasks are another widely used technique. These tasks allow the client to practise coordinated control of pitch, loudness and duration. There are no reports of tasks designed to specifically address speech rhythm. English speech rhythm is strongly related to lexical stress patterns, and any significant disturbance in this area could therefore initially be addressed via stress tasks, as well as reading of rhythmical materials such as limericks. Yorkston *et al.* (2007) reviewed the available literature and concluded that with the exception of loudness in speakers with Parkinson's disease, evidence is currently inconclusive as to the effectiveness of prosodic treatment and which technique to apply to particular clients.

22.3.3 Apraxia of speech

Compared to dysarthria, AOS has received relatively little attention in relation to treatment evaluations. A review by Wambaugh *et al.* (2006b) identified that only 58 papers have been published in this area since 1950. One of the most important issues to be considered by clinicians is the fact that AOS is generally confounded with aphasia. In particular, some of the overt speech symptoms can be very similar despite different underlying disturbances of the motor and language systems (see Chapter 12, this volume). The clinician therefore needs to (1) decide at what point the speech difficulties should be addressed in relation to language disturbances, and (2) put in place procedures to be able to review the efficacy of treatment, i.e. to evaluate whether the correct underlying structure is being targeted.

Wambaugh *et al.* (2006a) categorize existing AOS treatment techniques into four main categories: articulatory/kinematic; rate/rhythm; AAC; and inter-systemic facilitation or reorganization. Probably the best known articulatory approach is Rosenbek's eight-step continuum (Rosenbek *et al.* 1973), which sets out the basic treatment hierarchy of modelling, followed by joint production and then individual attempts by the patient. In addition to the visual and auditory cues provided by modelling, kinematic stimulation, such as described in the PROMPT approach (Bose *et al.* 2001), can further aid the patient in their speech production. Wambaugh *et al.* (2006a) highlight the importance of implementing principles of motor learning into the treatment regimen. In addition, and in contrast to some early descriptions of AOS treatment, it is now acknowledged that treatment targets should at least start at the syllable instead of single phoneme level due to differences in motor control (see Ziegler *et al.* (2010) for a review of the evidence). One of the most recent treatment programmes developed with the above principles in mind, is a computerized system that promotes errorless learning of whole words (Varley and Whiteside 2008).

There are other types of AOS treatment which have been less frequently reported in the literature (Wambaugh *et al.* 2006a). Rate and
rhythm approaches tend to consist of reductions of speaking rate with
similar means as used for speakers with dysarthria. Pacing can be regular with, for example, the use of a metronome (Dworkin *et al.* 1988), or
maintain the natural rhythmic pattern of a word or utterance (Brendel
et al. 2000; Brendel and Ziegler 2008). Insufficient evidence is currently
available to evaluate which technique is effective and for what client
type. Inter-systemic techniques aim to exploit abilities in less impaired
or unimpaired areas of functioning to aid speech production. This type of
treatment generally refers to the use of gesture or other vocal behaviour
in therapy, such as melodic intonation therapy (Sparks 1981). Due to the
paucity of evaluative studies for the above approaches, the level of evidence is not strong for any particular method (Wambaugh *et al.* 2006b).
The final category of AOS treatment is the use of AAC aids. A range of symbolic systems have been successfully used with patients, and total communication approaches similar to those used with patients with aphasia
are also described in the literature (Wambaugh *et al.* 2006a).

22.3.4   Instrumentation and AAC devices

Technology can be used to provide biofeedback in the treatment of
MSDs or as an augmentative and alternative means of communication.
Biofeedback systems are designed to provide visual or tactile feedback to
clients about an aspect of their speech behaviour. Many of these are based
on instrumental analysis techniques and can present information on
phonation, nasality, pitch, loudness and durational aspects of speech (e.g.
the Kay Pentax Voice Games, Nasometers, or the lingWAVES TheraVox
from Wevosys). Further feedback can be provided for air pressure and
airflow, as well as muscle force (e.g. the Iowa Performance Instrument
(Robin *et al.* 1992)). For example, recent work by Johansson *et al.* (2012)
has shown that expiratory muscle training using a positive expiratory
pressure threshold trainer improved the speech of people with multiple
sclerosis. Devices that have been developed for training as well as for
daily use by people with Parkinson's disease to increase their speaking
volume include the Voxlog™ (Schalling *et al.* 2012) which provides feedback on loudness while a person is speaking. If voluntary volume control cannot be achieved consistently, the SpeechVive™ (Huber *et al.* 2012)
induces an automatic increase in the Lombard effect (i.e. the fact that
we speak louder in the presence of background noise) by playing babble
noise through headphones when the speaker phonates. There is generally good evidence that biofeedback can enhance a client's progression
through therapy (e.g. Austermann Hula *et al.* 2008). However, the clinician
needs to consider how the principles of motor learning theory affect the
timing, type and frequency of biofeedback, as over-reliance on externally

provided feedback can lead to poorer internalization of the new behaviour, and thus less carry-over into natural speech behaviour.

In terms of AAC, a wide variety of low- and high-tech aids have been used with people with MSDs. Mathy (2004) and Hanson *et al.* (2004) provide a comprehensive review of the various issues that have to be considered when deciding on which aid is appropriate for which client and at what stage, as well as the range of aids available to the patient. The choice of AAC aid will depend not only on the severity and type of speech problem the client experiences, but also on their cognitive and language skills, and visual and fine motor abilities. Acceptability to the patient and their communication partners is also a highly important factor to be considered.

AAC aids divide into three main categories: speech supplementation techniques, and high- and low-tech aids that replace speech. A common speech supplementation system used in MSDs is the alphabet board. Speakers can use this board either to spell out complete words or to indicate the first letter of a word to aid listener comprehension. A number of authors have reported on the success of this technique (Hustad and Garcia 2005; Hanson and Beukelman 2006; Hanson *et al.* 2010). Speech replacement systems can be as low tech as pen and paper, or in the form of aids that speak for the patient. It is important to assess each client individually to determine what form of AAC is most suitable, taking into account the client's communication needs as well as attitudes towards the use of the aid and support required from carers. More detailed information on choosing the right AAC for clients with MSDs can be found in texts such as Beukelman *et al.* (2007).

22.4   Conclusion

The term 'motor speech disorder' encompasses a wide range of symptom complexes, with the clinical picture being further complicated by differences in how each patient is affected by their speech impairment. This means that the clinician is required to develop individual treatment plans that are tailored to their clients' specific needs, rather than being able to follow recipes for particular speech parameters and subsystems. Although studies are increasingly being published to widen the evidence base for intervention approaches, the field still has a long way to go in order to accumulate sufficient information on the effectiveness of the various treatments that have been proposed.

23

Developmental language disorders

Laurence B. Leonard

23.1   Introduction

This chapter deals with the assessment and treatment of children with developmental language disorders (DLD). This label is an over-arching term used to refer to children with a significant deficit in spoken language ability that is apparent from the outset. Central to this clinical category are those children who exhibit specific language impairment (SLI) (see Chapter 5, this volume). However, the term DLD can also be applied to language impaired children whose non-verbal cognitive abilities are more than one standard deviation below the mean for their age, but well above levels reflecting intellectual disability. The category of DLD includes as well children whose language impairments are accompanied by subtle deficits in motor skill.

Much of the published research on children with DLD has been aimed at evaluating alternative theories of the nature and causes of these children's difficulties (see Chapter 5). However, there is also a growing literature concerned with the accurate assessment of language in these children. These two literatures are mutually supportive. A satisfactory theory of DLD cannot be developed unless there is confidence that the children whose difficulty is to be explained have been accurately identified. In turn, the development of assessment instruments can be informed by research findings indicating potentially vulnerable areas in DLD.

A third literature, which is also rapidly expanding, focuses on language treatment methods for children with DLD. As is true for theory development, the development of appropriate treatment methods should depend on the accurate identification of children with DLD. If children are not accurately identified at the beginning, mixed results regarding the success of treatment may be difficult to interpret, as some of the children receiving treatment may have been misplaced. Treatment will also benefit from theory. For example, some theories may posit that a skill which serves as a prerequisite for language is lacking in these children. Such a skill may therefore form a focus of treatment prior to attending to language itself. The theory–treatment relationship can also operate in the opposite direction. As will be seen later, treatment studies can offer a rather rigorous test of theoretical proposals concerning the relationships among different components of language. Given the advances in the literatures on language assessment and treatment, we review here many of these developments. We will take these two areas of study in turn.

23.2   Assessment

23.2.1   Some preliminaries

Along with the principal need to document and describe a child's language deficit, assessment should include an evaluation of other areas of the child's functioning. Hearing is one such area. Typically, a hearing screening is performed, using a recognized standard such as 20 dB in each ear at the frequencies of 500, 1,000, 2,000, and 4,000 Hz. It is also important to rule out abnormalities in oral structure that might impede language production.

There is evidence that some children with SLI and related DLDs exhibit atypical neuroanatomical configurations or show reduced responses to certain stimuli in electrophysiological studies. These characteristics appear to represent part of the DLD profile. However, it is important to rule out frank neurological impairment in the form of focal brain lesions, seizure disorders, cerebral palsy or traumatic brain injury, as such conditions will result in a different type of diagnosis.

Non-verbal intelligence is regularly assessed in the evaluation of children with DLD. Traditionally, a non-verbal IQ score within one standard deviation of the mean for a child's age (85 or above) has been required. However, somewhat lower IQ scores are now acceptable (Tager-Flusberg and Cooper 1999), given that the available evidence does not reveal differences between these children and those with IQs of at least 85 in either their linguistic profile or in their response to language treatment. In the past, these children were in a state of clinical limbo, as their level of non-verbal functioning placed them outside of both the intellectual disability category (their non-verbal scores were too high), and the category of SLI (their non-verbal scores were too low).

Finally, it is important to determine if children show symptoms of impaired reciprocal social interaction or restriction of activities that characterize children on the autism spectrum. Evidence of such symptoms would place a child outside of the traditional boundaries of SLI. However, there are children with pragmatic language impairments whose difficulties include problems with social interaction. Bishop and Norbury (2002) have suggested that such children might represent an intermediate point between SLI and autism spectrum disorder. It is also the case that some children with autism spectrum disorders also show a profile of language impairment that closely resembles that seen in SLI (Kjelgaard and Tager-Flusberg 2001). However, these children are more likely to be regarded as a subtype of children with autism spectrum disorder rather than as a subtype of SLI.

23.2.2 The language deficit

Diagnostic accuracy: In years past, low scores on standardized tests of spoken language ability formed the basis for documenting a language impairment. However, such documentation now requires a somewhat higher standard. Tests must exhibit acceptable levels of both sensitivity and specificity. The former refers to the percentage of truly language impaired children that the test correctly identifies as exhibiting a language impairment; the latter refers to the percentage of truly typically developing children that the test accurately identifies as showing no language impairment. Here, 'truly' is defined according to a recognized gold standard, which is often another well-studied test in combination with clinical judgement by experienced practitioners. Values of at least 80 per cent for both sensitivity and specificity are expected for tests used for identification purposes (Plante and Vance 1994). Tests in English that report acceptable levels of diagnostic accuracy include the *Rice/Wexler Test of Early Grammatical Impairment* (Rice and Wexler 2001), *Clinical Evaluation of Language Fundamentals – 4* (CELF-4; Semel *et al.* 2003), and the *Structured Photographic Expressive Language Test – Preschool 2* (Dawson *et al.* 2005), among others.

Recently, positive and negative likelihood ratios have also been used to convey the same general types of diagnostic accuracy (Dollaghan 2007). Positive likelihood ratios, computed as sensitivity/(1 – specificity), should be greater than 10, whereas negative likelihood ratios, computed as (1 – sensitivity)/specificity should be less than 0.10. The positive and negative likelihood ratios are interpreted as the odds that a score above or below a particular level, respectively, has come from a child with a true language impairment.

It is important to note that acceptable levels of diagnostic accuracy (sensitivity and specificity and/or likelihood ratios) need not conform to traditional points on a normal distribution (e.g. a standard score of 70, placing the child 2 standard deviations below the mean). Cut-off scores above and below traditional levels have been found for several standardized tests (e.g. Plante and Vance 1994). When faced with an apparent discrepancy between using the cut-off score that yields the best sensitivity and specificity and a score that conforms more closely to a conventional cut-off point, the former is preferred over the latter. For example, if a score of 90 yields ideal sensitivity and specificity, the use of, say, 80 will result in a failure to identify many children at risk for language impairment (and hence lower sensitivity).

Thus far, we have discussed diagnostic accuracy without singling out the particular language weaknesses that seem most closely associated with DLD. Based on their use of a twin study design, Bishop *et al.* (2006) have identified two such weaknesses. One of these is phonological short-term memory, often revealed through poor performance on non-word repetition tasks. The other is grammatical computation, revealed through inconsistent use of tense/agreement morphology (e.g. inconsistent use of past tense *–ed* and auxiliary *is* among others) and poor syntactic comprehension. These weaknesses had already been noted in the literature prior to the Bishop *et al.* investigation. However, Bishop *et al.* made the important discovery that these types of problems seem to be genetic in origin. Interestingly, they are also separable. That is, although many children have weaknesses in both phonological short-term memory and grammatical computation, some children have a problem in only one of these two areas. Measures of both types have revealed good sensitivity and specificity (Bedore and Leonard 1998; Graf Estes *et al.* 2007).

The type of language being acquired plays an important role in shaping the details of language that are most diagnostically useful in distinguishing children with SLI from their typically developing peers. For example, Italian has a rich system of inflectional morphology, and Italian-speaking children with SLI have much less difficulty with this area of grammar than do their Germanic language-speaking counterparts (Leonard 2009b). For Italian, the omission and/or substitution of clitic pronouns serves as a measure with good sensitivity and specificity (Bortolini *et al.* 2006). A growing literature in Spanish (Bedore and Leonard 2001) and French (Paradis *et al.* 2003) suggests that clitic use may prove to be a promising diagnostic feature in other Romance languages as well.

Non-word repetition also seems to have good diagnostic accuracy beyond English, judging from work done on Italian (Bortolini *et al.* 2006). It may also have potential based on findings from Swedish (Sahlén *et al.* 1999) and Spanish (Girbau and Schwartz 2007). However, for certain languages, such as Cantonese, this type of measure seems less successful (Stokes *et al.* 2006). It is possible that non-word repetition performance differences between children with SLI and typically developing peers in languages such as Cantonese are less differentiated because of the phonological properties of these languages. For example, in Cantonese all syllables carry a tone and the consonant inventory is smaller than in many other languages.

Points on a continuum or a discrete disorder? It may seem paradoxical but our ability to distinguish children with a language impairment from those with no such disorder does not rule out the possibility that the two groups populate different points on a single continuum of language ability. A qualitative difference between the two groups does not have to be assumed. To be classified as exhibiting a language impairment, it might be sufficient for children to simply cross some threshold in their difficulty with certain features of language – especially those deemed important according to the gold standard. This seems all the more plausible considering the apparently multifactorial nature of the aetiology of SLI. No mutation or disruption of any single gene seems to be responsible for this condition. Instead, intricate combinations of genetic factors, possibly in interaction with environmental factors, seem to be necessary in order to create this type of language impairment. Importantly, many of these same factors, in fewer or slightly different combinations, might lead to below-average language abilities that are not sufficiently severe to cross the clinical threshold.

Assessment for linguistic description and clinical planning: Language assessment is not limited to the goal of determining if a child is at risk for language impairment. Another goal is to provide a comprehensive description of a child's linguistic profile with an eye toward identifying additional areas of special weakness. Such areas may serve as the focus of treatment. The tests used to identify additional areas of weakness may not even exhibit good sensitivity and specificity. For example, children with SLI can show a considerable range of ability in receptive vocabulary. Although some children with SLI score low in this area, the average or even above-average receptive vocabulary abilities of other children with SLI could render sensitivity rather poor. However, because some children have weaknesses in receptive vocabulary, it would be important to identify those cases in which special assistance might be needed in this area.

One distinction that is traditionally made is that between language comprehension and language production. Some comprehensive language tests (e.g. the CELF-4) include tasks of both comprehension and production, and allow for the computation of separate comprehension and production composite scores. Many children with SLI earn higher scores in comprehension than in production. The implicit assumption is that children whose problems centre on production rather than comprehension might benefit from treatment that emphasizes production practice, as they already have an understanding of the material that they are not producing well. However, this assumption relies on a close correspondence between the details of language included in the comprehension test and those included in the production test. Often these details do not correspond closely, rendering the comprehension–production gap somewhat artificial in these cases (Leonard 2009a).

Another distinction often made during assessment is the distinction between lexical and morphosyntactic skills. Although many children with SLI are slow in their initial lexical development, by preschool age morphosyntax is often the most conspicuous area of difficulty for them (Leonard 1998). As noted earlier, measures of receptive vocabulary can vary from very weak to age-appropriate. Pragmatic skills are not assessed as systematically as should be the case (see Chapter 30, this volume). This state of affairs may change when psychometrically appropriate measures of pragmatic ability begin to appear. Phonology is routinely assessed for two important reasons. First, of course, children may have phonological deficits that are comorbid with problems in other areas of language and such deficits, too, can be targets for intervention. Second, phonological difficulties can affect grammatical morphology. In English, for example, noun plural –s, third person singular –s, and past tense –ed require an ability to produce word-final consonants. Similarly, articles and other unstressed monosyllabic function words often appear in sentence- or phrase-initial positions – positions that are more vulnerable to deletion (McGregor and Leonard 1994). It is important to determine if observed weaknesses in grammatical morphology are caused or exacerbated by weaknesses in the requisite phonology.

Language assessment tasks: Many different tasks are employed to assess a child's command of language. To assess comprehension ability, many tests employ a simple picture pointing or identification task, in which the child points to a drawing in a booklet or on a computer screen that corresponds to the word or sentence spoken by the examiner. Other tasks require the child to act out a sentence produced by the examiner, using toys or other relevant objects. The truth value judgement task has also proven to be useful. Here, the examiner tells a story, perhaps with visual aids, and the child has to judge whether a sentence produced by the examiner (e.g. *The dog was chased by the cat*) described the events that took place. Grammaticality judgement tasks are also employed. In this case, children hear a sentence that is grammatical or ungrammatical and must judge its acceptability. To render the task more suitable for children, two characters (e.g. a teacher and an alien) might be introduced. The examiner tells the children that some of the sentences will be spoken by someone (the alien, in this case) who doesn't know how to speak properly yet, and the children must decide which sentences these are.

For infants and toddlers at risk for language impairment, methods borrowed from the infant speech perception literature are beginning to be applied. These include the preferential looking paradigm and the head-turn procedure. In these tasks, comprehension is inferred when infants or toddlers look longer at a picture that corresponds to the word presented auditorily (as opposed to a picture that constitutes a mismatch), or turn towards the loudspeaker that is the source of a recognizable passage as opposed to the loudspeaker through which an unrecognizable passage is played. Applications of electrophysiological measures such as event-related potentials (ERPs) are also beginning to appear. For example, it appears that typically developing 19-month-olds show distinct electrophysiological responses to mismatches between a picture and a spoken word, whereas 19-month-olds at risk for language impairment fail to show this type of response (Friedrich and Friederici 2006). Although evidence is emerging that the performance of infants and toddlers on early speech perception and processing tasks is related to later language test scores (e.g. Benasich *et al.* 2005), the methodology does not yet show a sufficient level of reliability at the individual child level to be employed as a standard clinical assessment procedure. With refinements in these methods, the goal of using these procedures to identify infants at risk for language impairment may well be realized.

There are several different tasks that have been employed to assess children's language production abilities. Elicited imitation tasks are common. Sentence imitation tasks are the most common and are usually designed to assess children's grammatical skills. The assumption is that children filter the sentence through their own linguistic system and respond in a manner that matches or approximates the way they would produce the sentence spontaneously. Sentence completion tasks are also employed, in which the examiner describes one picture and begins a sentence that would describe a second picture. The child has to complete the sentence (e.g. *Here is one car, but here are two* ____ [*books*]). Paraphrase tasks are also used. Typically, the examiner reads a story that can be understood by the child but is too long for the child to recall verbatim. The script of the story contains numerous examples of the grammatical forms or vocabulary of interest. The child is then asked to retell the story (perhaps to another listener). Even if the child only provides the gist of the story, the heavy concentration of target forms in the story ensures that the child will attempt some of these forms. As a result, the examiner will be in a position to assess the child's proficiency with the target forms in a multi-sentence context.

Finally, samples of children's spontaneous speech frequently serve as a basis for assessing language production. The advantage of this method, of course, is that the language form and content of the samples are likely to be representative of the children's language skills, given that the children, themselves, generated these utterances without prompting. The disadvantage is that less frequently occurring forms in the language may not appear in the sample. The analysis of children's language samples has been greatly facilitated by the appearance of computer-assisted methods of analysis such as Systematic Analysis of Language Transcripts (SALT; J. Miller *et al.* 2011). First employed with samples from English-speaking children, these methods are now applied to languages such as Spanish, Swedish and Turkish (e.g. Miller and Iglesias 2006). Even with the advent of computer-assisted language sample analysis programs, transcription of the audio-recordings of children's language samples has remained a challenge, given the labour- (and time-) intensive nature of this activity. However, the Language Environment Analysis System, referred to as LENA (LENA Research Foundation 2011) – a portable system of recording and (approximately) categorizing 16 hours of a child's language (and that of the child's interlocutors) – may have the potential of significantly aiding the transcription process. At present, the system is best suited for extracting and counting vocalizations of infants, presumed words of children and adults, and conversational turns. However, with further development, the system might be capable of extracting and quantifying much finer linguistic detail. It is likely that examiners will still need to check for LENA's accuracy and perform additional analyses. However, with further refinement, this system is likely to significantly change the language sample and analysis process.

23.3   Treatment

Available treatment methods cover a wide range of territory. They differ in the type of linguistic detail they are designed to help teach, the amount of structure they place on the child, whether they involve leading the child or following the child's lead, and whether they emphasize production or comprehension. They also differ in how much empirical support they receive in the scientific literature.

23.3.1   Standards of evidence

In recent years, a premium has been placed on treatment studies that meet the highest standards of evidence. The design that meets the highest standard is the randomized controlled trial. The term highlights one important feature of the design – assigning children randomly to a treatment group and a comparison group. The comparison group might be a no-treatment group, for example a group on a waiting list that will receive treatment when the first group has completed its treatment. It could also be a group that receives a more traditional form of treatment. Through random assignment to groups, there is reduced risk that the groups will differ significantly in pre-treatment characteristics that might differentially affect their relative success in treatment. Even with random assignment, if the groups are small in size there may be unintended pre-treatment differences between the groups. In this case, propensity score analysis can also be applied. This form of analysis involves statistically controlling for factors (e.g. mean length of utterance, scores on a temperament measure) that might give one group a greater likelihood of treatment gains than the other group.

Randomized controlled trials also have other important features. The judges who assess the children's progress are blind to whether the children being assessed were in the treatment or comparison group. Of course, the ideal would be a double-blind study. Unfortunately, this design feature is usually not practical (and in most cases is not even possible) in language treatment studies. Unlike, say, a study of a particular drug, in which the persons administering the drug are not aware if they are administering the drug of interest or a placebo, in any language treatment study involving an experimenter interacting with the child, the experimenter can't help but know if treatment, and which treatment, is being provided. In theory, for interventions that are entirely computer-based, a double-blind design might be possible. However, strict provisions that made it impossible for the researchers to know which computer program a child was engaged in would have to be put in place. High-quality interventions should also document low attrition, and for the children who leave the study, investigators should ensure that there was not a systematic pattern (e.g. children with the most severe impairment dropping out) which could bias the findings.

A review by Law *et al.* (2004) revealed that only a minority of published language intervention studies possessed these characteristics. Of these studies, the evidence for real gains in expressive vocabulary skills was stronger than the evidence for demonstrable gains in expressive syntax. Within each of these areas, the studies varied greatly in the method used, their specific language targets and the ages of the participants. Since the Law *et al.* review, several additional randomized controlled trials have appeared in the literature, though the numbers are still relatively small.

One example of this type of study was the investigation by Fey *et al.* (1993). Children received treatment immediately or were placed on a waiting list for later enrolment in treatment. The treatment was provided by either the clinician or the parent. The treatment procedure employed both focused stimulation and recasting. Focused stimulation is a procedure in which the clinician provides multiple examples of the target form for the child, usually in a naturalistic context such as in play or in a story read to the child. Recasting is a procedure in which the clinician replies to a child's utterance in a manner that is conversationally appropriate and contains an example of the target form. The children in both clinician-administered and parent-administered treatment made gains that exceeded those seen in the waiting-list group. The two types of administration (clinician or parent) yielded comparable results. Other studies that have employed recasting and random assignment of children to treatment conditions include Nelson *et al.* (1996) and Fey and Loeb (2002).

Randomized controlled trials have also been conducted on procedures designed to facilitate skills assumed to underlie many language impairments. One well-known procedure is Fast ForWord (Tallal *et al.* 1996). A major assumption behind this approach is that many children with language impairments have significant difficulty processing speech that is rapidly presented and/or brief in duration, and that by altering the input to accommodate this type of deficit, gains can be made in both perception and language itself. However, randomized controlled trials have reported either no gains or gains with Fast ForWord that were comparable in degree to that seen in groups assigned to other types of treatment (Pokorni *et al.* 2004; Cohen *et al.* 2005; Gillam *et al.* 2008).

Although randomized controlled trials are invaluable, they must be implemented in conjunction with a sound rationale for a method of treatment and a choice of targets that are consistent with that rationale. In the extreme, one can imagine an immaculately designed study aimed at teaching children an overly specialized vocabulary. If gains are assessed by means of, say, the number of different words used in a 100-utterance spontaneous speech sample obtained in an everyday situation, the results might prove to be quite disappointing. Such an outcome should probably not be interpreted as meaning that the vocabulary treatment is scientifically without merit. Rather, the outcome derived from a mismatch between the vocabulary actually taught and the vocabulary that usually occurs in spontaneous speech and that most often distinguishes children with DLD from their typically developing peers in everyday life.

There are treatment studies in the literature that have employed designs with some, but not all of the features of a randomized controlled trial. A series of studies conducted by Leonard and his colleagues serves as a good example (L. Leonard *et al.* 2004, 2006, 2008). In these studies, a premium was placed on keeping the clinicians blind to the fact that several grammatical details were being monitored in addition to those serving as targets. For this reason, children seen at one site received treatment on one particular target (third person singular –*s*) and children seen at another site received treatment on another target (auxiliary *is/are/was* forms). After a change in clinical personnel, the two sites reversed the grammatical forms serving as new targets as new children entered the treatment study. This was not random assignment because, for example, a child entering treatment in the beginning of the project at site A would automatically be assigned to receive the target that was the focus at that site at the time. However, in all other respects (e.g. blinding of the examiners who evaluated progress, ensuring low attrition), the studies possessed the rigour seen in randomized controlled trials. A combination of focused stimulation and recasting was employed. The children receiving treatment on third person singular –*s* and those receiving treatment on auxiliary *is/are/was* showed greater gains on their respective targets than a group of children receiving general language stimulation with no special focus on any particular grammatical detail.

Although focused stimulation and recasting have been widely used in the intervention literature, there are also several other treatment approaches that have produced encouraging results and might well be incorporated into future randomized controlled trials. Some are imitation-based approaches; the clinician produces the exact sentence, phrase or word required of the child and the child is asked to repeat it. As accuracy increases, the imitative prompt is gradually faded. Some variations of this approach have been employed. For example, Warren and Kaiser (1986) taught children to use two- to five-word utterances in a programme that included pointing to pictures, describing pictures and performing requested actions along with imitating the target sentence.

Modelling is another approach that has been implemented in many treatment studies. In this approach, the child observes someone (the model) produce examples of the target form. Typically, the child is instructed that the model will be talking in a special way. After several or more productions of the target form by the model, the child is asked to take turns with the model producing new examples of the target form. In one variation of modelling, the child continues to observe without taking a turn at producing the target form. A wide variety of targets have been employed in modelling. Although most have involved morphosyntax (e.g. Leonard 1975; Ellis Weismer and Murray-Branch 1989), semantic and pragmatic goals have also been pursued within this approach (e.g. Bedrosian and Willis 1987).

Milieu teaching and a modified version termed enhanced milieu teaching are also approaches that have been applied. Although much of milieu teaching has focused on children with global developmental deficits, children with SLI have also been included in select studies (Warren *et al.* 1984). As the names of these approaches suggest, the emphasis is on teaching language within a naturalistic context. A common component in this type of approach is that the clinician arranges the physical and communicative setting to increase the likelihood that the child will make some attempt at communication. When the child indicates interest in an activity, the clinician shows attention and, as necessary, provides increasingly specific cues to increase the likelihood that the child will produce the target.

23.3.2 Maintenance, generalization and the efficacy–effectiveness distinction

Thus far, we have discussed treatment studies in terms of gains observed immediately after treatment. Often studies also include assessments one to six months following treatment, to determine if the gains are maintained. Evidence of maintenance serves as important documentation that the gains reflect more than transient response strategies developed through continuous practice. For example, in the Leonard *et al.* (2008) investigation, the children's use of third person singular –*s* and auxiliary *is/are/was* was assessed one month after treatment ended. The gains were maintained.

A distinction is made between efficacy of treatment and effectiveness of treatment. Efficacy refers to treatment effects observed under tightly controlled conditions, with clinicians who administer the treatment following carefully prescribed procedures, pre- and post-treatment measures that are carefully targeted, and other controls. The step of establishing that a treatment is efficacious is crucial, because if a treatment cannot be shown to be successful when careful controls are in place, it will be difficult to argue that the treatment should be applied more generally. The majority of well-designed treatment studies in the literature would be considered to be studies of efficacy.

In contrast, effectiveness of treatment refers to the treatment as it is likely to be applied under real-world circumstances. This means that the children participating may not be as narrowly selected in terms of age, purity of developmental profile, and other factors. Furthermore, those administering the treatment may be less prone to follow to the letter every detail of the prescribed procedure, but may instead have to adapt the procedure slightly to fit the everyday circumstance. The measures, too, can be somewhat less precise than in efficacy studies, provided, of course, that they have general validity. The Fey *et al.* (1993) study described earlier has many properties that are seen in effectiveness studies. Of particular note is the fact that their outcome measure was a more general measure of grammatical use in spontaneous speech. This measure is important for two reasons. First, spontaneous speech seems to be a more ecologically valid way of assessing children's progress than, say, responses to sentence completion items. Second, the score on this spontaneous speech measure reflected the children's use of a wide variety of grammatical details, not just one or two specific grammatical forms. Fey *et al.* found that the children in both the clinician-administered and the parent-administered treatment groups demonstrated the broad gains reflected by this measure.

Generalization is crucial to the success of language treatment. One often hears how speakers of a language are capable of generating utterances they have never heard before. If language treatment were confined to teaching children only how to produce or comprehend the sentences used as exemplars, the treatment would be a failure. Most studies designed to facilitate children's use of sentence structure will include post-treatment probes that assess the children's ability to use the sentence structure with new combinations of words. For example, in a study by Wilcox and Leonard (1978), children were taught to ask questions such as *What does the boy push?* Subsequently, the children showed evidence of producing similar questions that were not included in treatment, such as *What does the baby want?*

Fewer studies have examined whether treatment on one grammatical form results in gains in different but presumably related grammatical forms. Hegde (1980) found that treatment gains in the use of copula *is* forms result in gains in the use of auxiliary *is* forms, and vice versa. Leonard *et al.* (2004) found that gains in the use of third person singular –*s* lead to gains as well in the use of auxiliary *is*. This generalization was attributed to the fact that both forms reflect the features of present tense, third person and singular. Leonard *et al.* also found, as predicted, that generalization did not extend to past tense –*ed*, a form that differs from the target form third person –*s* on several features.

23.3.3   Factors influencing treatment gains

As noted earlier, in some instances, the groups to be compared are not well matched on some potentially important variable (e.g. receptive vocabulary ability, mean length of utterance), even after random assignment, and, in these instances, propensity analysis might be necessary. In other instances, investigators might wish to conduct analyses to determine why the outcomes varied even within a particular group. For example, after observing that children in the Leonard *et al.* (2004) study varied in their degree of gains during treatment of third person singular –s, Pawłowska *et al.* (2008) asked whether the children's degree of pre-treatment use of other types of grammatical details might have served as a type of prerequisite skill. In particular, they hypothesized that two details – the use of noun plural –s and the use of subject–verb combinations – might be predictive. They reasoned that third person singular –s required awareness of the singular–plural distinction (hence the use of noun plural –s as a predictor), and that the subject–verb agreement that dictates use of third person singular –s might be more readily learned by children if they already tended to produce verbs with preceding subjects. In fact, these investigators found that higher frequencies of these two measures prior to treatment were significant predictors of greater gains on the target form.

Whereas some predictors may constitute pre-treatment characteristics of the child, others may be factors that occur during treatment itself. 'Dosage' seems to be one such factor. In the recast literature, dosage refers to the density of recasts provided during the treatment sessions (Proctor-Williams *et al.* 2001; Proctor-Williams and Fey 2007). Warren *et al.* (2007) divide the notion of dosage into subtypes. The term 'dose' itself is reserved for the number of recasts provided during a single session. 'Dose frequency' is the number of times a recast is provided in a given period, such as a week. 'Total intervention duration' is the time period over which treatment was provided (e.g. six months), and 'cumulative intervention intensity' is the product of dose × dose frequency × total intervention duration. For example, in the L. Leonard *et al.* (2008) study, children received 12 recasts per session. Sessions were held three times per week for 32 weeks. Thus, the cumulative intervention intensity was $12 \times 3 \times 32 = 1{,}152$ recasts. Proctor-Williams *et al.* (2001) provided evidence that, for children with SLI, recast density must exceed the frequency expected in typical interactions with a child. Another important factor is attendance (Justice *et al.* 2008). Children may vary in their attendance, which, in turn, will affect the dosage.

In some treatment procedures, certain clinician or child behaviours are free to vary, provided that the components viewed as essential are properly carried out. For example, in the L. Leonard *et al.* (2006, 2008) studies, the number of recasts provided per session and the target forms themselves were fixed elements in the procedure, but the clinician was free to select the particular child utterances to recast and even, when necessary, to elicit an utterance by the child that could then receive a recast. Hassink and Leonard (2010) examined the types of child utterances that were recast and found that high frequencies of non-corrective recasts were associated with greater gains in the use of the target third person singular –s. Non-corrective recasts were instances in which the recast (e.g. *She runs*) followed either a grammatical (e.g. *She's running*) or ungrammatical (e.g. *She running*) utterance by the child that did not contain an obligatory context for third person singular –s. In contrast, a corrective recast followed a child utterance that contained an obligatory context for the target form (e.g. *She run*). Hassink and Leonard hypothesized that at an early stage of grammatical learning, the children were more likely to treat a similar form – that is, a corrective recast – as an acknowledgement of their previous utterance rather than as a correction. On the other hand, the larger difference between the children's utterances and a non-corrective recast might have drawn the children's attention to the grammatical details of the recast. Hassink and Leonard proposed that this relationship probably changes as children reach a later stage of grammatical development. At that point, the subtle difference between child utterances and corrective recasts might be more easily discernible and therefore have a facilitative effect on their use of the grammatical target.

23.3.4   What can intervention teach us about developmental language disorders?

Although the identification of appropriate treatment approaches must continue given that higher standards of evidence are now the norm, we have already learned a great deal from the many intervention studies that have been conducted. Much of the information we have learned is about the nature of DLD. Since the early 1990s, we have known that most children with DLD receive a language input that, ordinarily, would be adequate for normal language acquisition (see Leonard 1998). Obviously for children with DLD, such an input is not sufficient to acquire language at a normal pace. Most of the treatment approaches used in intervention studies seem to be designed to make the language input ideal for the language learner. The manipulations of input involve increasing the frequency with which children hear the forms to be learned (e.g. focused stimulation), showing how the forms to be learned relate to the children's own (preceding) utterance (e.g. recasting), and showing the functional value of the forms to be learned (e.g. milieu teaching). Children with DLD seem to benefit from these manipulations. The significance of this observation is that clinicians have not had to rely on teaching compensatory strategies, or changing input modalities (e.g. sign language) to assist these children in the acquisition of language. These children certainly require assistance, but this assistance can probably take the form of ensuring that the input is provided frequently, in unambiguous contexts. The apparent success of using ideal input, in turn, suggests that whatever are the causes of DLD, these children's language learning systems are less 'broken' than they are inefficient or immature. When these children acquire the use of target forms during treatment, these forms are usually maintained in their speech. Generalization to untrained forms also occurs, certainly to the point where it can be said that the children have acquired more than a finite set of rote sentence-like responses. Although effectiveness studies are not as common as efficacy studies, it appears that gains made in treatment are reflected in the children's language use in more naturalistic contexts, as seen in improvements on relatively broad measures obtained from spontaneous speech.

23.3.5   Additional goals of treatment: contributions to theory

Treatment designs offer a benefit that goes beyond assisting children in the acquisition of language skills. These designs also permit an examination of the relationships among features of language – features that may be assumed to be related according to some theory. For example, to test the assumption that grammatical detail A is closely related to grammatical detail B, children lacking detail A, detail B and a third, theoretically unrelated grammatical detail (detail C) might be recruited. Treatment and subsequent gains on detail A might be expected and, if the theory is on the mark, corresponding gains on detail B should also be observed. In contrast, grammatical detail C should continue to lag behind. The monitoring of detail C is crucial to ensure that gains in detail B along with A can be attributed to treatment and not to a maturational spurt.

The study by Leonard *et al.* (2004) was conducted in part to test the theoretical relationship between two grammatical morpheme types associated with the functional category Agreement (AGR). As noted earlier, children received treatment in the use of third person singular –*s* or auxiliary *is/are/was*, and their use of third person singular –*s*, auxiliary *is/are/was* and past tense –*ed* was monitored before, during and after treatment. For children assigned to treatment on third person singular –*s*, this morpheme served as grammatical detail A and auxiliary *is/are/was* constituted grammatical detail B. The reverse was true for children assigned to treatment on auxiliary *is/are/was*. It was assumed that the use of both third person singular –*s* and auxiliary *is/are/was* requires that AGR be projected; otherwise, the sentence will be produced without these morphemes. If treatment was successful in increasing the children's facility with the target morpheme (detail A), gains in the other morpheme (detail B) were expected, given their joint reliance on AGR. Because past tense –*ed* is associated with a different functional category, Tense (T), it was assumed that it was sufficiently independent to serve as grammatical detail C. Indeed, the results were consistent with these predictions. Gains in both detail A and detail B were significantly greater than those seen for grammatical detail C. On the other hand, grammatical detail A also outpaced detail B, suggesting that children were learning details about the specific target morpheme over and beyond the fact that AGR is obligatory.

Clahsen and Hansen (1993) also employed a treatment study to test a theoretical account of the relationship between grammatical details. Because the study did not have some of the controls expected in treatment studies, the study is in need of replication. However, the question posed by these investigators serves as a good illustration. Children with SLI in German have difficulties with both agreement inflections and the verb-second rule. The latter is a rule that requires the finite verb to appear as the second constituent of the sentence, even if the sentence begins with something other than the subject. In these instances, the finite verb precedes rather than follows the subject. In the theoretical framework adopted by Clahsen and Hansen, the verb-second rule depends on a finite verb located in AGR that is then moved to the functional category, Complementizer (C). They hypothesized that greater consistency of subject–verb agreement inflection use (e.g. use of present third person singular, as in *tanzt* 'dances') through treatment would increase the likelihood of projecting AGR which, in turn, would allow for a finite verb in AGR to move to C. Put more simply, increases in the children's use of subject–verb agreement inflections through treatment were expected to lead to increases in the children's ability to produce sentences reflecting the verb-second rule even though the latter was not the focus of intervention. Clahsen and Hansen reported data that were consistent with their prediction.

23.4   Conclusions

Children with DLD have a language impairment that appears to be primary, though subtle deficits in other areas of functioning are seen. Children with SLI are the most widely known group that falls within DLD, though the category of DLD is sufficiently broad to include children with related deficits who do not meet the criteria for categories such as autism spectrum disorder or intellectual disability.

The assessment of language impairments in children with DLD has become increasingly sophisticated across time. This progression began with the increasing precision with which we have been able to describe the details of children's language profiles. Although this precision has been extremely useful for selecting targets for treatment, instruments for accurately identifying children with language impairments in the first place were surprisingly slow to arrive on the scene. However, in recent years, such instruments have begun to appear. Most of these instruments evaluate children's morphosyntactic abilities. Whether weaknesses in this area of language are the most accurate way of identifying children with DLD, or whether this fact is simply due to more intense test development in this area of language, is not yet clear.

Language treatment has also undergone a revolution of sorts. Early treatment studies reported success with a variety of approaches and language targets. However, these earlier efforts often lacked the scientific rigour needed to be confident that the approach could produce reliably positive outcomes. In recent years, randomized controlled trials have emerged in the literature. The design properties of such studies are invaluable. However, they must be implemented in conjunction with a sound rationale for a method of treatment and the choice of targets that are consistent with that rationale. Future studies of language treatment are likely to include many of the safeguards seen in randomized controlled trials, including the random assignment of children to treatment and comparison groups and the blinding of examiners who assess the children's progress. In addition, these studies are likely to have provisions for testing children's maintenance of target forms, their ability to use these forms under more naturalistic circumstances, and their ability to take the information gleaned from the learning of target forms and generalize it to related but untaught forms. This last detail is of importance not only because language facility requires the ability to create wholly new, never-before-heard utterances, but also because such generalization can shed light on theoretically important relationships between components of language that are difficult to discern with other types of methods.

24

Acquired aphasia

Anne Whitworth, Janet Webster and Julie Morris

24.1   Introduction

Drawing from a range of disciplines that stretch from neuroscience to sociology, our understanding of aphasia, both as a neuropsychological and linguistic entity and from the perspective of the person with aphasia, has seen major advances over the past few decades. This has led to a burgeoning of different approaches to assessment and intervention. This chapter provides an overview of aphasia assessment and therapy. It sets out the different assessment and therapeutic approaches that reflect current practice in the management of aphasia. In doing so, no attempt is made to provide an exhaustive list of the approaches and techniques currently, or previously, reported in the field. Rather, the objective is to provide an insight into why approaches have developed and how they aim to achieve change in aphasia, to consider briefly the evidence base of these approaches and to highlight the often complementary nature of seemingly different perspectives on aphasia. It is also not the aim of this chapter to closely examine the effectiveness of these approaches. The reader is directed to review papers (e.g. Robey 1998; Bhogal *et al.* 2003; Moss and Nicholas 2006; Cherney *et al.* 2008) and the Cochrane library (Greener *et al.* 1999; Kelly *et al.* 2010; Brady *et al.* 2012) to obtain more detailed coverage and closer scrutiny of therapy impact within certain research paradigms, e.g. randomized controlled trials (RCTs).

The broadening of approaches to aphasia management in recent years can be attributed to a number of influences, including the widespread international adoption of a more comprehensive definition of physical and mental health, a heightened interest in issues related to therapy effectiveness and measurement of real-life outcomes, and the influences of the healthcare context and user engagement in driving the health agenda in many countries. This chapter will provide an overview of the main approaches to aphasia management using the World Health Organization's International Classification of Functioning, Disability and Health (ICF) (World Health Organization 2001) as a framework to consider the multifaceted and integrated nature of these approaches.

The approaches themselves, however, only form a part of any discussion of therapy with people with aphasia, with the complex therapeutic process providing the broader context in which change in communicative ability is sought. The distinction between therapy approaches to aphasia and the therapeutic process is an important one. Given the complexity of the processes involved in therapy (e.g. therapy medium, task hierarchy, feedback) and the interaction between a host of individual characteristics (e.g. motivation, severity, family support, home environment) and contextual factors (e.g. timing, dosage, change agent), considerable attention has been directed towards the development of a theory of therapy and how such a theory would guide and shape the delivery and outcome of therapy (Byng and Black 1995; Wertz 1999; Basso 2003; Nickels *et al.* 2010). While this interplay is undeniably influential in determining therapy impact, with these outcomes often feeding back into the theoretical views held of aphasia, detailed examination of this aspect will not be the focus of this chapter and as such will be addressed only when it is integral to other discussion. This chapter will, however, consider intervention in the widest sense, exploring the range of theoretical influences, the different assessment approaches and the therapy approaches that ensue.

24.2 Approaches to assessment and treatment of aphasia and the ICF framework

The ICF framework (World Health Organization 2001) has provided an opportunity to structure our thinking around the diversity within aphasia management. Whilst interconnected and overlapping, the domains set out in the ICF provide a framework to describe and understand the needs of people with aphasia and to consider the approaches to assessment and treatment that address these needs. The transparent mapping of the ICF to the management of aphasia has been highlighted by Kagan and colleagues in an aphasia-specific framework called 'Living with Aphasia: Framework for Outcome Measurement (A-FROM)' (Kagan *et al.* 2008). The A-FROM domains include (1) the linguistic and cognitive deficits observed as part of the impairment in aphasia; (2) the impact of the aphasia on a wide range of activities and participation in life situations; (3) the communication and language environment, considering the factors influencing effective interaction and understanding barriers and facilitators; and (4) the impact of the aphasia (and its wider implications) on personal factors such as identity, self-esteem and quality of life.

The A-FROM framework places the person with aphasia at the centre of the intervention process. It will be used here to loosely organize the description of approaches in relation to the overall aims and theoretical underpinnings of each domain. These four domains are by no means mutually exclusive. The particular needs of individual people with aphasia may require a specific focus on one of these areas or, more commonly, in order to maximize functional gains, the rehabilitation team will draw on a combination of approaches from different domains. The interaction between domains is often complex. Intervention may focus on one domain while the aim of therapy, or the desired outcome, may be within another domain. For example, the aim of therapy may be to facilitate telephone use and promote participation while the focus of therapy may be on improving word retrieval and the ability to read out a set of everyday phrases. Similarly, when evaluating the effect of intervention, there is a need to consider impact across domains. As domains overlap, therapies too fall across domains, despite being presented here within one domain for ease of readership.

24.3   Approaches targeting linguistic and/or cognitive impairment

24.3.1   Theoretical perspectives

Linguistic and/or cognitive approaches to aphasia intervention focus on aphasia as a multimodality language disorder which can impact spoken and/or written comprehension and spoken and/or written production at single word or sentence level. There are a number of theoretical approaches, historical and current, that have contributed to our understanding of the language difficulties in aphasia and influenced approaches to assessment and treatment within this domain (see Howard and Hatfield (1987) for an historical overview). Classical and neo-classical approaches to aphasia are syndrome based, defining people with aphasia by the location of their brain lesion and the cluster of language features that frequently co-occur as a consequence of damage in that region. Cognitive neuropsychological approaches to aphasia emerged from the need to recognize and explain individual differences in performance. These approaches investigate language difficulties in relation to models of normal language processing, initially at single word level (e.g. Patterson and Shewell 1987) and then in relation to models of sentence production (e.g. Garrett 1982).

The single word model – described in depth in Ellis and Young (1988) and Whitworth *et al.* (2013) – provides a detailed, although underspecified, description of the processes involved in the spoken and written comprehension and production of single words. Within this approach, the language deficits reflect specific damage to one or more of the component processes or the mappings between them. At a sentence level, models of production are even less well specified but distinguish pre-verbal conceptual processing, semantic processing of verb argument structure, syntactic processing of phrasal structure and word order and phonological processing (Garrett 1982; Thompson and Faroqi-Shah 2002). Schwartz (1987) elaborates the processes involved in the production of semantic and syntactic structure, emphasizing the central importance of the verb for sentence production. At the sentence level, there has also been the emergence of linguistic and neurolinguistic approaches (e.g. Thompson and Shapiro 1994; Bastiaanse *et al.* 2009; Bastiaanse and Jonkers 2012). These are grounded in linguistic theory, with specific predictions about the co-occurrence of deficits for particular structures, cross-linguistic differences and the rationale for therapy emerging from an understanding of the linguistic processes and transformations involved in the comprehension and production of specific structures.

While aphasia is primarily a language disorder, there is increasing evidence that aphasia can occur with subtle cognitive deficits affecting visual recognition memory, attention, executive problem solving, monitoring and learning (Helm-Estabrooks 2002; Fillingham *et al.* 2006; Conroy *et al.* 2009b). These cognitive deficits may interact with and exacerbate the linguistic deficits, influencing the person's ability to engage in the therapy process, and requiring therapy methods and materials to be selected that consider both the language and cognitive abilities of an individual (Lambon Ralph *et al.* 2010). There is some evidence that treating co-occurring cognitive deficits can result in gains on primarily linguistic activities (e.g. Coelho 2005; Salis 2012). Performance on cognitive tasks has also been shown to be one predictor (alongside language) of therapy gains following anomia therapy (Lambon Ralph *et al.* 2010).

24.3.2   Aims of assessment and intervention

The primary aim of assessment within this domain is to gain an in-depth understanding of the language abilities of the person with aphasia, characterizing the individual's relative strengths and weaknesses across modalities and levels of processing. By examining the convergence of performance across tasks, each assessment contributes to hypotheses as to the underlying nature of breakdown. The assessment process is often underpinned by formal assessment of specific linguistic skills, comparing performance to participants without brain damage and monitoring performance over time. Therapy approaches then aim to promote change in linguistic ability. This is achieved by stimulation or reactivation of the impaired function, relearning of specific knowledge or procedures, or a relay strategy that promotes the language function via an alternative route through the processing system, often drawing on more intact processes (Whitworth *et al.* 2013). Facilitating compensatory strategies, which aim to maximize communication without focusing on the impairment, equally requires an in-depth understanding of the person's strengths.

24.3.3   Assessment approaches

Assessments emerging from the classical approach assess a range of language skills in order to classify an individual within an aphasia type, e.g. global, conduction, Wernicke's or Broca's aphasia. These assessments often have an overall measure of aphasia severity. A number of examples exist, including the widely used Boston Diagnostic Aphasia Examination (BDAE) (Goodglass *et al.* 2001) and Western Aphasia Battery-Revised (WAB-R) (Kertesz 2006).

Within a cognitive neuropsychological framework, the process of assessment involves identifying impaired and retained processes by examining the relationship between performance on different tasks, the pattern of errors and the effect of a range of psycholinguistic variables, e.g. imageability, length, word frequency (see Whitworth *et al.* (2013) for a detailed discussion). A number of assessment batteries are available, for example the Psycholinguistic Assessments of Language Processing in Aphasia (PALPA) (Kay *et al.* 1992) and the Psycholinguistic Assessment of Language (PAL) (Caplan and Bub 1990), each with carefully controlled subtests. The Comprehensive Aphasia Test (CAT) (Swinburn *et al.* 2004) emerged more recently as a screening test. While grounded in a cognitive neuropsychological framework, the CAT is complemented by a cognitive section and a questionnaire investigating activity, participation and personal factors.

Assessment at the sentence level is driven by the same principles, with particular consideration of the relationship between sentence comprehension and production, the relationship between verb retrieval and sentence production, and the influence of sentential variables, e.g. reversibility, word order, verb argument structure and grammatical complexity. Further detail about the assessment of sentence processing can be found in Webster and Howard (2012) and Marshall (2013), highlighting the range of verb and sentence assessments drawn on by clinicians (e.g. Whitworth 1996; Marshall *et al.* 1999; Druks and Masterson 2000; Webster and Bird 2000; Bishop 2003c).

24.3.4   Therapy approaches

With their emphasis on syndromes, classical approaches have focused on identifying therapy techniques likely to be applicable for groups of participants all displaying similar surface symptoms. Therapy approaches are, therefore, often symptom focused (Lesser and Milroy 1993). Melodic intonation therapy (Albert *et al.* 1973), for example, concentrates on the non-fluent speech production in people with Broca's aphasia, with minimal focus on the syntactic, morphological and/or phonological difficulties that may underpin this symptom pattern. Other approaches in this para-digm include Visual Action Therapy (Helm-Estabrooks *et al.* 1982) and therapy aimed at gaining voluntary control of involuntary utterances (Helm-Estabrooks and Baressi 1980).

In contrast, cognitive neuropsychological and neurolinguistic approaches are processing focused (Lesser and Milroy 1993) and empha-size the need to consider the skills and processes underpinning the lan-guage abilities within treatment. There is an extensive literature regarding therapy approaches underpinned by a cognitive neuropsychological per-spective despite there being no straightforward relationship between the identification of an impaired process and the type of therapy (Caramazza 1989; Nickels *et al.* 2010). Whitworth *et al.* (2013) provide a comprehensive overview of therapy for single word comprehension and production. This section will provide a brief overview of these approaches, drawing out key issues, and will direct readers to relevant review articles and book chapters where these are described in greater depth.

Single word-level therapies: By far the majority of the therapy litera-ture has focused on spoken word retrieval and therapy for anomia (see Nickels and Best 1996a; Nickels 2002; Whitworth *et al.* 2013). Therapy has included reactivation of links between word meaning and word form via a variety of semantic and phonological tasks (e.g. Nettleton and Lesser 1991; Nickels and Best 1996b; Hickin *et al.* 2002; Boyle 2010) or cognitive relay strategies, using written naming or access to initial letters to pro-mote spoken naming (e.g. Nickels 1992; Best *et al.* 1997). The relationship between the nature of the therapy tasks and the level of the impairment, however, is not transparent. Semantic tasks are used with people with lexical impairments and phonological tasks have been used with people with semantic impairments, lexical deficits and post-lexical deficits in phonological assembly.

A number of reasons underlie this. Therapy tasks often rely on a combin-ation of semantic and phonological processing, such that all approaches, regardless of their intent, focus on the link between semantic represen-tations and the word form (Howard 2000). Further, people often present with a combination of difficulties which are being targeted simultan-eously. While this may argue against the need to consider the potential origin of the naming difficulty, it has been shown that the presence of a semantic impairment may restrict therapy gains (C. Leonard *et al.* 2008), and an understanding of both the nature of the impairment and the type of therapy may be important in predicting the nature of the gains post-therapy.

Lexical therapy targeting access to spoken word forms, whether via phonological cues, orthographic cues or word repetition, has been found to result in item-specific improvement. If gains are specific to the words that are treated, this emphasizes the need to select personally relevant words for therapy (McKelvey *et al.* 2010) to ensure functional gains. There is some evidence that semantic therapy tasks, when they focus explicitly on differences between items and are used with people with semantic deficits, result in generalization to the naming of untreated words (Nickels and Best 1996b; Kiran and Thompson 2003). Generalized therapy gains may be dependent on the task and feedback given (Nickels and Best 1996b). Kiran and Thompson (2003) found generalization to untreated items was greatest when therapy focused on atypical items within a semantic category. Gains in untreated items may, however, reflect repeated probing during therapy (Coelho *et al.* 2000) and are often short-lived (Nickels and Best 1996a). Phonological tasks for people with difficulties in post-lexical phonological processing (phonological assembly) have been shown to result in generalized gains across phonemes and modalities (Franklin *et al.* 2002), but co-occurring lexical or motor speech difficulties may restrict these gains (Waldron *et al.* 2011a, 2011b).

When considering the introduction of cognitive relay strategies, a clear understanding of the relationship between spoken naming, written naming and reading aloud is required if therapy is to be successful (Nickels 1992). When a strategy is introduced, gains are predicted for both treated and untreated stimuli. However, improvement may be restricted by the extent of difficulties in written naming, the success of initial phoneme cues and/or the ability to blend phonemes and read written words aloud.

Over recent years, there have been an increasing number of studies investigating the impact of therapy for verb retrieval (see Conroy *et al.* 2006; Webster and Whitworth 2012). These studies have shown that, despite the differences between nouns and verbs (Druks 2002; Black and Chiat 2003; Vigliocco *et al.* 2011), verbs can be treated in similar ways to nouns using semantic and phonological tasks. Lexical therapies again result in item-specific improvements. Some therapy approaches have acknowledged the role that verbs play in sentence production and have either treated verbs in a sentence context (e.g. Links *et al.* 2010) or have combined work on verb retrieval and argument structure production (e.g. Webster *et al.* 2005). These approaches have resulted in wider gains in sentence production, with more verbs, a greater proportion of sentences and/or a greater proportion of grammatically correct sentences in connected speech. These gains can be explained by models of sentence production where the processes involved in argument structure production and grammatical specification are not lexically driven.

As with spoken production, written word retrieval has been targeted using similar tasks, relatively independently of the underlying impairment. These tasks have included repeated picture naming with various cues, anagram sorting and copying, and repeated copy and recall treatment (see Beeson *et al.* 2003). Therapy has resulted in significant gains in the writing of treated words, although the number of words treated and the extent of the gains are often limited. For individuals with more peripheral impairments in the graphemic output buffer, some generalization to untreated words has been reported (Rapp and Kane 2002), with therapy improving the efficiency of the buffering process.

Therapy for single word spoken comprehension (described in Morris *et al.* 2009; Morris and Franklin 2013; Whitworth *et al.* 2013) has attracted less attention. It involves specific tasks and strategies targeting, predominantly, phonological analysis, spoken word recognition and access to meaning via spoken forms. Tasks are specifically targeted at the level of impairment. Similar principles underpin therapy for written word comprehension, with tasks and strategies targeting orthographic analysis and written word recognition. Significant gains have been found post-therapy. Treatments targeting peripheral processes (e.g. Morris *et al.* 1996) have resulted in gains in both treated and untreated words, whilst lexical-based treatments (e.g. Francis *et al.* 2001) have resulted in item-specific gains. There are a small number of studies that have aimed to improve access to category knowledge and word meaning with the aim of improving comprehension. These studies show that gains extend across modality, but that they may be specific to a particular category or type of meaning (e.g. Behrmann and Lieberthal 1989). The effects of therapy may also be dependent on the exact profile of performance, with different therapy effects seen in clients with broadly similar profiles of language ability (e.g. Morris and Franklin 2013).

Sentence-level therapies: Therapies targeting sentence production and comprehension have primarily focused on the relationship between sentence meaning (semantic structure) and sentence form (syntactic structure). Verb-centred mapping therapies (reviewed in Marshall 1995) increase awareness of the verb and its arguments and of how the arguments map onto syntactic structure in simple canonical sentences. Following therapy, people show improved comprehension of treated structures but with minimal generalization to different sentence structures. General structural gains are, however, seen in production with individuals producing more verbs and more sentences in connected speech.

Linguistic-specific therapy that treats underlying forms (Thompson and Shapiro 1994; Thompson 2001) extended this type of therapy to more complex structures, e.g. *wh* questions, passives, object clefts, subject raising sentences. Within this cognitive neurolinguistic approach, Thompson and colleagues have trained specific linguistic operations, examining patterns of generalization between sentences involving similar or different types of linguistic movement/trace-antecedent relations. Therapy has been shown to result in improved comprehension and production of targeted structures with generalization to structures that are linguistically similar. More recently, Thompson and colleagues have shown that optimal generalization is seen when treatment is applied to the most complex structure first (Thompson *et al.* 2003). The Complexity Account of Treatment Effects (CATE) has now been extended across a number of linguistic domains within aphasia and in other client groups (see Clinical Forum introduced by Thompson 2007). More detailed descriptions of therapy approaches for sentence processing difficulties in aphasia can be found in Faroqi-Shah and Thompson (2012), Marshall (2013) and Webster *et al.* (2009).

A number of therapies focusing on single word and sentence production fall under the rubric of Constraint Induced Language Therapy (CILT) (Pulvermüller and Berthier 2008; see Cherney *et al.* (2008) and Meinzer *et al.* (2012) for reviews). CILT uses barriers to encourage the person with aphasia to use spoken output to communicate and constrain the use of other modalities. The approach is based on a number of principles including behaviourally relevant treatment setting, non-use hypothesis from motor learning theory, intensive and massed practice and shaping of behaviours, with studies demonstrating changes in communicative behaviours (e.g. Maher *et al.* 2006).

24.4   Approaches targeting participation in life situations

24.4.1   Theoretical perspectives

Maximizing participation in usual life activities has long been a characteristic of aphasia therapy (e.g. Holland 1977, 1982b; Green 1984). While this is either implicit or explicit in many of the approaches discussed within the other A-FROM domains, a broad alliance of approaches focus specifically on participation through facilitation of compensatory behaviours and/or strategies and an emphasis on the everyday event. Having their antecedents in the 1980s, a wave of approaches emerged predominantly as a reaction to symptom-based approaches to aphasia therapy. These shifted the focus to communication and enabling the person with aphasia to participate in functional, everyday activities (e.g. Green 1982). They initially drew on developments in the pragmatic dimension of language (see Holland (1991) for an overview) and many now embrace a social model of disability (Oliver 1983). Simmons-Mackie (2008: 290) states the goal of a social approach to aphasia is 'to promote membership in a communicating society and participation in personally relevant activities'.

Given the nature of everyday activities and a focus on the use of language, early approaches were labelled 'functional' and were contrasted with approaches that focused on the linguistic and/or cognitive impairment. While this term is still applied, the goals of participation or social interaction assume a greater focus over the functionality of the aim or task. Quality of life is a key construct in a social model of participation (see World Health Organization (1999) and Cruice *et al.* (2000) for discussion). A host of factors including attitudes towards and personal beliefs about aphasia, feelings of control and independence, family and social relationships and environment all converge to influence the quality of each individual's life. Quality of life, therefore, relates to all domains and is elaborated in this section in relation to a person's unique participation needs and individual situations in which communication takes place.

24.4.2   Aims of assessment and intervention

The primary aim of assessment within the participation domain is to capture a holistic view of the person in their usual life, their habits, their roles and the activities they engage in on a day-to-day basis (Simmons-Mackie 2008). A detailed analysis of the person's linguistic and cognitive strengths and weaknesses may or may not be undertaken, despite the intervention approaches often incorporating aspects of the language profile and often drawing on other linguistic paradigms to capture changes in linguistic competence, e.g. analysis of discourse (Yorkston and Beukelman 1980; Helm-Estabrooks and Albert 1991; Nicholas and Brookshire 1993; and see Armstrong (2000) for an overview). Given the situational contexts of communication, examination of the barriers and facilitators to effective communication are often addressed, e.g. in the workplace or within social groups or settings. Intervention aims to facilitate participation in naturally occurring activities/situations that may take place in the home or in broader society. It frequently focuses explicitly on the communicative skills of the person with aphasia but also aims to reduce the barriers and enhance the facilitators to communication within person-specific situations.

24.4.3   Assessment approaches

Assessment of participation frequently focuses on communication ability within particular situations, drawing on a range of assessment protocols used within the clinical setting, the home, in the workplace or in social settings. Early examples of assessments to emerge within this paradigm included the Functional Communication Profile (Sarno 1969), Communicative Activities of Daily Living (Holland 1980), subsequently revised (Holland *et al.* 1999), and the Amsterdam-Nijmegen Everyday Language Test (ANELT) (Blomert *et al.* 1994). These involve simulated activities of daily living and ask the person with aphasia to respond as they might in a particular situation. With the focus on communicative effectiveness, assessments of participation frequently look across different modalities, e.g. assessment of writing or gestural abilities, as well as at how successfully the message has been communicated, via whichever modality and irrespective of the semantic, phonological or grammatical accuracy of the spoken output.

Spoken output may instead be analysed according to number of content units (Yorkston and Beukelman 1980) or number of correct information units (Nicholas and Brookshire 1993) to capture the degree of information conveyed. The impact of compensatory strategies, taught or novel, on communication success may be gauged through rating of communication by significant others such as carers (e.g. Communicative Effectiveness Index, Lomas *et al.* 1989). While necessarily individualized, other formalized tools are available to assess participation, primarily through self-report, logs and contextual inventories, and often drawing on models of social networking (e.g. Simmons-Mackie and Damico 1996, 2001; Code 2003; Davidson *et al.* 2008; Kagan *et al.* 2010; and see Dalemanns *et al.* (2008) for a systematic review of measures for rating social participation). Assessments of participation may also assess the component skills required for person-specific situations, such as employment, often involving a component analysis of tasks as well as assessment of communication, for example, in the workplace itself. Information from assessments is considered in the light of relevance for the individual to ensure the resulting therapy approach is meaningful to the individual (Davidson *et al.* 2003).

24.4.4 Therapy approaches

Approaches to increasing participation follow a number of themes (see Chapey *et al.* (2008) and Simmons-Mackie (2008) for a comprehensive discussion of some of these approaches). Early approaches arose from developments in pragmatics and the knowledge that pragmatic skills are relatively well preserved and may be utilized in facilitating effective communication. Promoting Aphasic Communicative Effectiveness (PACE) (Davis and Wilcox 1985) was an early example of this approach where communication is encouraged through creating meaningful contexts and the person with aphasia can communicate their message in any way. Total communication approaches (e.g. Pound *et al.* 2000; Lawson and Fawcus 2001) constitute a further set of approaches that are aimed at maximizing participation through any modality, or combination of modalities, which are available and effective for the person with aphasia. The use of gesture, functional writing abilities, drawing, a prosthetic device or a communication aid are examples of therapy approaches within this domain, each aiming to develop or facilitate compensatory strategies to maximize communication in everyday activities.

Total communication approaches have frequently been reported in relation to severe aphasia (Simmons-Mackie 2009). These approaches target specific modalities and enhance communication through whichever means available in order to achieve participation of the individual with aphasia. The use of gesture, in particular (see Rose (2006) for a review), has been explored as an alternative method of communication and also for its ability to enhance verbal communication. Beginning with the adoption by Skelly and colleagues of Amer-Ind (Skelly *et al.* 1974), a gesture code developed by North American Indians, studies have shown that people with aphasia can learn gestures for communication. However, similar to the therapies aimed at improving lexical retrieval, improvement tends to be item specific and does not generalize across modalities (Marshall *et al.* 2012), although more evidence is present for improvement of non-treated items (Daumuller and Goldenberg 2010). Gesture therapies have also been shown to facilitate lexical retrieval (Rose and Sussmilch 2008; Boo and Rose 2011). It is, however, difficult to communicate all ideas via gesture and the effectiveness of such approaches is influenced by the comorbidity of motor impairments such as limb apraxia (Raymer 2007).

Therapy targeting strategies for the individual will often involve communication partners. Drawing approaches, for example, have been used within a conversational context (Lyon 1995; Sacchett *et al.* 1999), along with graphic topic setters to construct conversations (Garrett and Huh 2002). These approaches focus on strategies that facilitate conversational interaction and maximize participation in communication with others. Delivering aphasia therapy in groups has also attracted considerable attention as a method of promoting participation, practising communication within a meaningful communication environment and providing emotional and psychosocial support (e.g. Fawcus 1989, 1991; Holland and Beeson 1999; Marshall 1999; and see Elman (2007) for a review).

24.5 Approaches targeting the communication and language environment

24.5.1 Theoretical perspectives

The influence of the social model of disability in aphasia therapy is particularly pronounced in those interventions that have taken an environmental perspective and sought to embed interventions for people with aphasia within a social context, be it the individual's own context or society more generally (see Pound *et al.* 2000). With the World Health Organization (1999: 3) defining quality of life as being affected by 'social relationships, personal beliefs and their relationship to salient features of their environment', these areas have assumed a key focus in aphasia therapy over the past two decades. Lubinski's early work on communication-impaired environments in relation to both aphasia (Lubinski 1981a) and dementia (Lubinski 1981b) has been built on in the closer examination of communication-friendly environments by Howe *et al.* (2007). A broader environmental perspective is seen in those who have sought to remove environmental barriers more generally through promoting self-advocacy and empowerment (e.g. Pound *et al.* 2000) and social action (e.g. Byng and Duchan 2005). The interaction with quality of life is particularly apparent here with the focus on families, communication partners and broader society.

Theoretical developments in how conversation and interaction take place have heavily influenced aphasia intervention. The application of Conversation Analysis (CA) (Sacks *et al.* 1974) has had considerable impact on aphasia therapy within this domain, giving rise to systematic training of conversational partners within the person's immediate environment. A related perspective is the view that aphasia impedes communicative access and results in reduced participation in social communication more generally. This view has directed attention to training people who interact with people with aphasia in the general principles of conversation. By training conversation partners, communication is enhanced within larger contexts such as nursing homes or rehabilitation centres.

24.5.2   Aims of assessment and intervention

Assessment within this domain aims to identify both the barriers to communication, often involving communication partners, and the factors that may facilitate communication within the environment of the person with aphasia. Environmental therapies then aim to promote effective interaction by removing or reducing barriers in the environment, including the broader community, and increasing the awareness and skills of the person with aphasia and/or communication partners. Therapies focused on everyday conversations between people with aphasia and significant others (e.g. family, carers) in their environment generally aim to modify the conversational behaviour of the partner, emphasizing the collaborative nature of conversations and the partner's potential to provide a more facilitative conversational environment (see Turner and Whitworth (2006a) and Simmons-Mackie *et al.* (2010) for reviews).

24.5.3   Assessment approaches

Assessment may take a variety of forms. They include structured or semi-structured interviews with carers and/or the person with aphasia, personal narratives and self-report rating scales. Within a CA approach, conversation sampling is usually undertaken in conjunction with an interview of the person with aphasia and/or partner in order to identify any problematic issues in the conversations between two partners. Examples of this approach include the Conversation Analysis Profile for People with Aphasia (CAPPA) (Whitworth *et al.* 1997) and Supporting Partners of People with Aphasia in Relationships and Conversation (SPPARC) (Lock *et al.* 2001). Social network approaches further facilitate analysis of the communication environment (e.g. Simmons-Mackie and Damico 1996). Aphasia-specific interview tools such as the Assessment of Living with Aphasia (ALA) (Kagan *et al.* 2010), the Communication Disability Profile (CDP) (Swinburn and Byng 2006) and the Communication Outcome after Stroke (COAST) scale (Long *et al.* 2008) provide structured protocols for gathering information on the communication and language environment among other areas.

24.5.4 Therapy approaches

Those therapies targeting conversation partners often revolve around the structural organization of conversations and facilitate turn taking, management of topics, and repair strategies for when lexical retrieval and other difficulties arise (e.g. Lesser and Algar 1995; Perkins 1995; Wilkinson and Wierlaert 2012). They are intended to assist the conversational partner, and sometimes also the person with aphasia, in structuring and maintaining effective conversation. Notions of appropriateness and accuracy do not motivate these therapies. Instead, therapy is motivated by supporting people with aphasia to communicate effectively through enabling the person's competence to emerge rather than achieving linguistic accuracy (Perkins 1995; Kagan *et al.* 2001). The approach is predicated on the belief that conversation partners can be trained to enable the conversational and interactional skills of the person with aphasia. This, in turn, results in increased communicative access for the person with aphasia and ultimately reduces the negative psychosocial consequences of aphasia (Wilkinson and Wierlaert 2012). The training process itself is designed to change the expectations and perceptions of both partners and expand the opportunities for communication (Simmons-Mackie 2008).

Studies applying CA to conversation between the person with aphasia and his or her partner have produced a steady stream of results, each demonstrating the effectiveness of this approach (e.g. Lesser and Algar 1995; Booth and Swabey 1999; Turner and Whitworth 2006b; Wilkinson *et al.* 2010). Two examples of published therapy approaches used here are interaction therapy (Wilkinson 1995) and SPPARC (Lock *et al.* 2001). The latter involves an additional support component for the conversation partner. These aim to reduce the impact of aphasia on the interaction between the conversation partners, enhancing the psychosocial aspects of the relationship.

A related approach is Supported Conversation for Adults with Aphasia (SCA) (Kagan 1998), which focuses on the training of conversation partners to provide communication opportunities for people with aphasia. While based on many similar principles, SCA places a key emphasis on revealing the competence of people with aphasia by recognizing conversation as key to participation and facilitating access through a set of procedures and supportive pictorial resources. Communication Partners (Lyon *et al.* 1997) combines elements from both of the above approaches. It trains volunteers to interact with specific people with aphasia and increase their life participation, often focusing on activities unrelated to communication. This has been built on in the Life-Participation Approach to Aphasia (LPAA) (Chapey *et al.* 2008). This approach has broadened the concept of participation to re-engagement with life and the point at which the person no longer perceives that therapy or support is required.

24.6   Approaches targeting personal identity, attitudes and self-esteem

24.6.1   Theoretical perspectives

It is uncontentious that aphasia represents more than a disturbance of language and can have profound effects in many domains. Barrow (2008: 43) states that 'acquiring aphasia changes one's life', with the effects extending beyond communication to impact on personal identity, attitudes and self-esteem. This impact is frequently related to altered roles in relationships, and within the family and community (Code and Herrmann 2003). However, the domination of a medical model in the literature with the focus on fix or cure has potentially influenced people with aphasia's own narrative, resulting in a narrow focus on restitution and a more limited focus on personal aspects of aphasia (Barrow 2008). Barrow argues that alternative models, such as the social model of disability, may help people consider a different perspective on their individual situation and facilitate living with aphasia.

The effect of aphasia on identity and the subsequent process of renegotiation of identity has also been addressed (Shadden 2005), with Code and Herrmann (2003) discussing the notion of 'loss of self'. Identity and communication are seen as strongly linked. The same processes through which communication is used to express who we are and shape our identity then influence the altered communicative experiences caused by the aphasia. Brown *et al.* (2012) consider recent work on 'living successfully with aphasia', moving from a focus on improving the aphasia (or minimizing its effects) to a focus on personal qualities and positive factors, e.g. determination, sense of humour, which can be used within therapy to help people in living with their aphasia.

24.6.2   Aims of assessment and intervention

The aims of assessment within this domain are to explore, with the individual, what the relevant personal factors are from the person's perspective, the interaction between these and the other domains, and the impact on the person with aphasia. This domain is closely related to the person's perception of their quality of life. Intervention aims include assisting the person to live successfully with their aphasia, for example by exploring motivation or confidence, or utilizing therapy techniques which aim to improve confidence in communication skills. Hilari and Cruice (2013) suggest that using a quality of life approach to assessment and intervention across the domains would facilitate this, commencing with determining the person's perspective and basing any further stages (of assessment or intervention) on this. Having quality of life at the forefront is then mutually compatible with a variety of therapy approaches.

24.6.3　Assessment approaches

Assessment in this area is less developed than in the other domains, with semi-structured interviews being used frequently to explore the person's perspective and personal factors. There is clearly a challenge in probing complex factors with people with aphasia. This has led to the development of assessment tools that are aphasia-friendly. Examples include the CDP (Swinburn and Byng 2006) and the ALA (Kagan *et al.* 2010). The CDP aims to allow 'the administrator and person with aphasia to explore and rate the impact of acquiring and living with aphasia' (Swinburn and Byng 2006: 5) and considers activities, participation and external influences on this process. The ALA gathers both qualitative and quantitative information and perspectives that map directly onto the A-FROM framework.

Assessment of the perception of quality of life is relevant here, as these measures aim to develop further understanding of the person with aphasia's perspective in decision-making, goal setting and rehabilitation more generally. While a variety of measures are available to examine these factors in the general population and to some extent in the stroke population, there are few assessment approaches that are tailored to people with aphasia. Measures such as the Stroke and Aphasia Quality of Life-39 (SAQOL) (Hilari *et al.* 2009) have been used widely and consider the person's perception of functioning across communication, energy, physical and psychosocial domains. Measures of emotional distress are available with the Visual Analogue Mood Scale (Stern *et al.* 1997) designed specifically for aphasia. Many of these assessments use a visual analogue scale to allow for easier, more reliable responses from people with aphasia, e.g. Visual Analogue Self-Esteem Scale (VASES) (Brumfit and Sheeran 1999). Some authors have aimed to assess aspects of social networks (e.g. Cruice *et al.* 2006) to inform therapy in relation to goals and communication partners. These assessment approaches are often intended as a starting point, highlighting areas for further investigation through their relevance for the individual.

24.6.4　Therapy approaches

Person-centred therapy is essential to this domain. Negotiated and joint goal setting arise from diverse and holistic assessment of the client, including attempts to understand the concerns of the individual and the unique impact of the aphasia. Byng and Duchan (2005) set out social practice principles which underpin a philosophy of aphasia therapy rather than an approach per se. These principles include an equal and collaborative therapeutic relationship between the person with aphasia and the therapy provider, authentic decision-making, meaningful and engaging therapies, control resting or shared with the person with aphasia and accountability by the provider of therapy at all levels of the process, including to the person with aphasia (see Simmons-Mackie (2008) for an overview). Therapy approaches include counselling and support, confidence building, and approaches focused on living (well/successfully) with aphasia (e.g. Brumfitt 1993; Cunningham 1998).

Group therapy and group support/self-help models are often drawn on to achieve the goals in this domain. Groups provide opportunities for increased participation through conversational opportunities, but also reinforce the importance of being with peers which, in turn, contributes to the renegotiation of identity (Shadden 2005). Simmons-Mackie and Elman (2011: 314) suggest that therapy 'must focus on both improved communication and enhanced identity in order to maximize outcomes', cautioning that focusing only on communication may give rise to issues for development/renegotiation of a positive or healthy identity. They propose that group therapy is one possible vehicle where goals can be combined, identifying, through analysis of group interaction, several important aspects that might contribute to the process of achieving positive identity, e.g. the person with aphasia being heard and being assumed to be competent. Simmons-Mackie and Elman (2011) further discuss the clinician's role as facilitator or mediator in this process, ensuring messages are understood, reinforced and valued.

Life coaching is also frequently used within aphasia therapy to provide an increased focus on personal factors. Holland (2007) and Worrall *et al.* (2010) consider coaching to be a form of counselling and suggest that it may take different forms at different times, from providing information and support through to enabling individuals to develop their own goals and problem-solving ability. Worrall *et al.* (2010) state that coaching is underpinned by certain assumptions including the importance of time being required to live successfully with aphasia, that aphasia is beyond the individual (it is a family problem) and that aphasia is chronic with people learning to live with it within their lives.

24.7   Integrating approaches to aphasia assessment and management

While the ICF framework provides a useful way of grouping the evidence base and therapy approaches for discussion, the framework suggested by Kagan and colleagues (2008) reinforces the overlapping nature of the domains and appropriately places the person at the centre of them. At any one time, and driven by the individual needs of the person with aphasia, different aspects of the aphasia may be focused on. Such an integrated approach to assessment and intervention is reliant on a collaborative, negotiated, goal-setting process (e.g. Hersh *et al.* 2012) which is under-pinned by a belief that the person with aphasia is a key stakeholder in the therapy process. This process involves the person with aphasia (with their knowledge of their needs, their experience of aphasia, their preferences), the aphasia clinician (with their knowledge of aphasia, of the strengths and weaknesses within the communication profile, the evidence base for therapeutic interventions) and often significant others. While the different theoretical perspectives and therapy approaches are available to the clinician, the person's individual needs and abilities, and subsequently negotiated goals, will drive the therapy process.

The combination of different approaches is further facilitated through the ongoing nature of goal setting (as opposed to a static, one-off process), with evaluation and revision of goals as part of a cycle (Hersh *et al.* 2012). Several tools are available to guide this process, examples of which include the CDP (Swinburn and Byng 2006), the Functional Communication Therapy Planner (Worrall 1999), the ALA (Kagan *et al.* 2010), Talking Mats (Murphy 1997) and Goal Attainment Scaling (Turner-Stokes 2009). Each considers the individual's needs at a particular point in time. Goals will interact with the selection of an approach, either explicitly or through analysis of the component parts of the goal, the necessary skills involved and how these relate to the person's communicative strengths and weaknesses. Different aspects may be targeted simultaneously using a variety of therapeutic approaches, with the clinician drawing on an extensive, evidence-based 'toolkit' of therapy approaches. This complexity is rarely represented in the literature.

Equally influential in the integration of approaches is the ubiquitous goal of improving real-life communication for the person with aphasia. Even where the focus is, for example, on eliciting highly non-contextualized linguistic or cognitive behaviours, therapy is predicated on an implicit belief that gains from therapy will ultimately contribute to more effective communication and, where possible, generalize to the skills required by the individual in daily communication (see Carragher *et al.* (2012) for a review). Within the literature on word retrieval, Herbert *et al.* (2008) demonstrated that performance on constrained-naming tasks was related to lexical retrieval in conversation, suggesting that if gains were seen on naming tasks, improvements should be seen in connected speech. Anomia therapy has been shown to result in gains on lexical measures in conversation (Best *et al.* 2011) as well as improved participation in everyday activities and interaction (Best *et al.* 2008). Verb- and sentence-based therapies have also demonstrated gains in connected speech, showing that the impact of therapy extends beyond constrained tasks.

While many approaches seek to monitor this generalization with a view to understanding the interaction between therapy tasks and discourse (viewed as being closer to real-life communication), other studies have sought to combine approaches. For example, Clausen and Beeson

(2003) aimed to improve the use of writing as a communicative strategy in people with severe aphasia, combining Copy and Recall Treatment, or CART, delivered in individual sessions, with group sessions where the use of the practised words was facilitated via structured conversations. While therapy effects were largely restricted to the items involved in treatment, the items for treatment were carefully chosen and of direct functional relevance to maximize their usefulness within conversation. Therapy outcomes were assessed in a standard elicitation task and within group sessions, but also via interaction with a new person, aiming to capture impact on conversational communication.

Panton and Marshall (2008) also reported a study where therapy, aimed at a real-life goal of note taking in the workplace, used a combined therapy approach to focus both on the underlying impairment and on the development of strategies. Panton and Marshall argued that both elements contributed to progress. Robson *et al.* (1998) also exemplified this in a single case study where therapy involved improving access to written word forms. Although improvement was seen, it did not generalize to a communicative context. However, when therapy subsequently focused on making explicit how the person with aphasia could use these learnt items in a functional way, improvement took place. In this study, the initial (impairment-based) work was 'necessary but not sufficient'; therapy focusing on 'generalization' or communicative contexts was also needed. Herbert *et al.* (2003) combined approaches within their study, with lexical therapy which targeted a specific set of items, combined with communicative use of those items. They describe this as a combination of 'a lexical approach with an interactional approach' (2003: 1178). Therapy tasks included picture naming, naming from definition, exchange of information task, list task, and topic based conversations, all using the same set of words. Herbert *et al.* also attempted to measure outcome both at the single word level and in a more communicative context.

24.8　Efficacy of therapy approaches

To date, the efficacy of specific therapy approaches in aphasia has been evaluated primarily via single case studies and case series. These studies involve detailed pre-therapy language assessment, a period of therapy, monitoring of performance during therapy and/or post-therapy assessment evaluating the effect of treatment. Different experimental designs have been used (described in Howard 1986; Willmes 1990; Franklin 1995; Thompson 2006) to ensure gains are due to specific therapy effects, and are not non-specific gains as a consequence of spontaneous recovery or the 'charm effect'. Some studies use statistical evaluation of pre- and post-therapy or look at effect size to consider the significance of change. These designs are particularly conducive to evaluating linguistic and cognitive therapies where the aim is to effect change in language behaviour. Change in communicative behaviour within the other domains may also be measured within a pre-/post-therapy design. However, these domains are also likely to employ more ecologically valid protocols, such as interviews with carers, perceptual ratings of change or observation of change in real-life situations, all of which provide rigour to the process and confidence in the outcomes. Evaluating the efficacy of multifaceted, individualized therapy approaches, however, remains a challenge for researchers. While feasible at the single case level, it is more challenging beyond this.

Case series studies and small group studies replicate a specific therapy across a number of different individuals, using standard assessment and therapy procedures. Performance may be considered across the group, for individuals and between individuals. There have been a range of case series studies looking at particular therapy techniques targeting linguistic behaviours, with some contrasting different therapy approaches, e.g. errorless and errorful therapy for word retrieval (Fillingham *et al.* 2006; Conroy *et al.* 2009b), the use of increasing and decreasing cues for word retrieval (Conroy *et al.* 2009a), the use of phonological and orthographic cues for word retrieval (Hickin *et al.* 2002), phonological components analysis for anomia (C. Leonard *et al.* 2008) and the use of copy and recall treatment to target written production (Beeson *et al.* 2003). These studies have provided strong evidence that therapy can be effective and have contributed to an understanding of the factors that underpin individual variability, e.g. the severity of the initial impairment (Conroy *et al.* 2009a, 2009b), the origin of the naming deficit (Hickin *et al.* 2002; C. Leonard *et al.* 2008), client preference (Fillingham *et al.* 2006; Conroy *et al.* 2009b) and communicative need and motivation (Beeson *et al.* 2003). They have also contributed to a wider understanding of factors that influence the therapy process, e.g. the number of naming attempts (Fillingham *et al.* 2005) and active engagement in therapy either by the selection of cues (Best *et al.* 2008) or by pitching tasks at an appropriate level of difficulty for the individual (Conroy *et al.* 2009a).

24.9   Conclusion

Our understanding of aphasia and the interplay between the acquired language difficulty, the person and the environment has grown exponentially over the past few decades in relation to intervention. The application of increasingly rigorous and controlled experimental designs, within both research and clinical settings, has partly paved the way. However, the receptiveness of the field to the social dimensions of assessing and managing aphasia has also been a significant development. The result of this process has been more holistic, client-centred intervention that is driven by the needs of the person with aphasia and is underpinned by an understanding of the likely impact of intervention.

In parallel, attention has focused on the therapy process itself. The nature and style of the client–clinician relationship, the timeliness and dosage of therapy and the medium through which therapy is delivered are some of the factors that interact with the therapy process (see Whitworth *et al.* (2013) for an overview). These factors set the agenda for continued research into aphasia therapy, both for the benefit of the individuals and their families and for the organization of services. As always, there remain as many new questions as those answered and the complex impact of specific approaches and combinations of approaches across domains needs to be considered and demonstrated more rigorously. The quest to understand the nature of aphasia, the impact on the individual and how this intersects with therapy and its outcome should continue to be at the heart of this agenda and progress our understanding of why, how and for whom aphasia therapy is effective.

25

Disorders of voice

Linda Rammage

25.1 Integrative management of individuals with voice dysfunction

Voice production for communication is among the most intricate physiological functions that characterize humans as a unique species. In the twenty-first century, healthcare practitioners ascribe to the concept of complex mind–body interactions that are represented in all human disorders, and that validate the concept of 'dysfunction' as a physiological entity. This understanding is as essential for effective management of individuals suffering voice dysfunction as it is for other complex health issues.

One of the greatest assets of the voice clinic is a multi-professional team of individuals dedicated to sharing their discipline-specific expertise, while working together in a cross-disciplinary model to analyse and synthesize clinical problems in a comprehensive manner. This allows for integrative management, and it is this approach that has allowed us to understand voice dysfunction at multiple physiological levels, as has been described in Chapter 18.

25.2 Evaluating the problem

25.2.1 The management team

At the core of the management team is the client. Client-centred care was introduced by psychologist Carl Rogers (1959). A commonly adopted interpretation of this care for occupational rehabilitation defines client-centred therapy as 'an approach … which embraces a philosophy of respect for and partnership with people receiving services. It recognizes the autonomy of individuals, the need for client choice in making decisions about … needs, the strength clients bring to … an encounter and the benefits of client–therapist partnership and the need to ensure that services are accessible and fit the context in which the client lives' (Law *et al.* 1995: 251).

The speech-language pathologist is a key member of the voice care team, and traditionally works in concert with the otolaryngologist throughout the comprehensive evaluation and treatment planning process. Medical specialists in psychiatry, respiratory medicine, endocrinology, neurology and internal medicine are often collaborators, as are audiologists, physical therapists, osteopaths, vocal pedagogues and psychologists.

25.2.2 The tools

Self-report inventories: Many voice clinics employ intake forms to gather information from clients/caregivers before meeting them. This can help clients recognize the breadth of factors that may contribute to symptoms, and also provides triage information for the voice clinic team. Typically, these forms enquire about clients' current and previous occupations, presenting symptoms, medications, allergies, illnesses, surgeries and hospitalizations. There are also questions about smoking, the amount and type of fluid intake, hearing status, family history of speech and hearing problems, and changes in and use of voice.

A number of self-report tools have been developed based on quality of life concepts or on World Health Organization (WHO) constructs for defining the impact of voice dysfunction on individuals. Quality of life inventories are employed in healthcare disciplines worldwide. To be client-centred, these measures need to be socio-culturally relevant, and derived from clients' perspectives (Carr and Higginson 2001). Yiu *et al.* (2011) reported differences in self-report profiles using the same tool for individuals from two distinct cultures. WHO constructs have evolved to include self-report of participation in activities such as communication. Eadie *et al.* (2006) used the International Classification of Functioning, Disability and Health framework (ICF; World Health Organization 2001) to examine and compare self-report inventories, concluding that none of the commonly used tools measure communicative participation exclusively.

Self-report tools may enhance client-centred approaches to management and are used to determine treatment outcomes. Client-report data may not have strong statistical relationships with other assessment measurements (Ma and Yiu 2001; Hsuing *et al.* 2002; Murry *et al.* 2004; da Costa de Ceballos *et al.* 2010; de Alarcon *et al.* 2009). These findings emphasize the unique nature of this clinical information. Examples of self-report inventories include the Voice Handicap Index-10 (Rosen *et al.* 2004) and Voice-Related Quality of Life (Hogikyan and Sethuraman 1999).

Instruments of the modern voice clinic: The voice clinic of the twenty-first century typically includes an array of sophisticated equipment that allows clinicians to gather objective data on acoustics, aerodynamics and dynamics of the laryngopharyngeal mechanisms. Medical diagnostic procedures that are also frequently used to evaluate voice dysfunction include pulmonary function testing, electromyography (EMG), oesophageal manometry and pH testing, and radiographic imaging procedures such as magnetic resonance imaging (MRI) and computerized tomography (CT).

Data obtained during instrumental measures can be compared to normative data when they are available. To be socially valid the normative data referenced must reflect those of the client's cultural-linguistic milieu. Objective measures are often used to track and document changes with treatment. Instrumental assessment will be discussed in detail in section 25.2.4.

25.2.3   The assessment process

History interview: In keeping with client-centred principles, the history interview provides an opportunity to establish the critical relationship of mutual respect and trust between client and voice care professional(s), while facilitating information-sharing in a non-directive approach. The client's role as 'expert' in his/her experiences of the problem is established at the outset, and the clinician demonstrates 'unconditional positive regard' by listening to and acknowledging the client's perspective without making judgement (Rogers 1959).

Using open-ended questions, clinicians encourage the client's 'expert' role while reducing clinician reductive biases that are reinforced by 'yes/ no' questions. Examples of appropriate open-ended phrases include 'Tell us about your concerns'; 'Tell us about any patterns that you have noticed in these symptoms'; 'Tell us how this is affecting your life'. Client responses and any previously submitted history information will naturally invoke clinician requests for clarification on specific issues.

One interview model 'alerts' clinicians to probe four common areas (components) of factors that may contribute to voice dysfunction: **l**ifestyle, **e**motion, **r**eflux and **t**echnique (Rammage *et al.* 2001). Since **a**natomical changes to the vocal system related to developmental or ageing processes, injuries, lesions or disease may also be relevant, the model has been expanded to include five general areas of inquiry, and is represented by the ALERT acronym (see Figure 25.1). Anatomical factors may be primary or secondary and may interact with other components. For each client, a profile can be developed delineating specific aetiological factors for each component, the degree to which each area contributes to the symptoms, and interactions.

During the history discussion, some topics may evoke emotional responses from the client, whereas others will be emotionally neutral. This provides the clinician with an opportunity to observe changes in

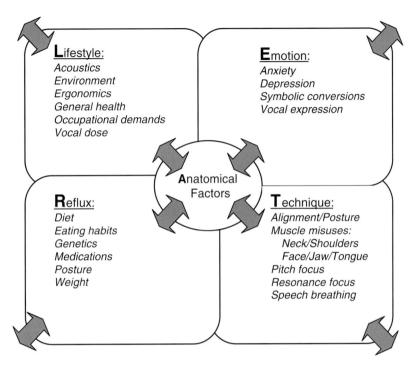

Figure 25.1 The ALERT model for management of voice disorders.

clients' speech and voice, posture, facial expression and pragmatics associated with the contrasting emotions elicited.

Perceptual evaluations: Clinicians rely on their own acoustic, visual, tactile and other perceptual processes to obtain information that only humans can interpret. This clinical activity, invaluable as it is, may nevertheless introduce biases to the assessment process. Perceptual biases may be influenced by a number of factors including listener knowledge, experience or training (Gelfer 1988; Chan and Yiu 2002, 2006; Eadie and Baylor 2006; Eadie and Kapsner-Smith 2011); number of perceptual channels accessing information (Martens *et al.* 2007); terminology/operational definitions (Kreiman *et al.* 2007); type of rating scale (Eadie and Doyle 2002; Yiu and Ng 2004; Kreiman *et al.* 2007); and use of reference anchors (Chan and Yiu 2002, 2006; Kreiman *et al.* 2007; Eadie and Kapsner-Smith 2011). To some extent, person biases can be minimized and meaningful communication about perceptual features maximized by ensuring common protocols are employed by all judges, and that these tools meet appropriate levels of validity and reliability.

Auditory perceptual assessment: Auditory perceptual assessment is the single most commonly used tool by speech-language pathologists during voice assessment (Oates 2009). A number of models have been used to develop protocols and scales to rate psychoacoustic features of voice such as loudness, pitch and quality, prosodic characteristics such as phrasing, speech rate and phonation duration and psycholinguistic interpretations such as degree of perceived pleasantness, politeness or bizarreness. Auditory perceptual assessment is a complex task challenged by numerous factors related to stimulus materials, terminology, rating scales, interdependence of perceptual features and listener knowledge, skills and perceptual biases (Kent 1996). None of the tools developed to date meet all criteria for an ideal and all-encompassing tool, but many protocols in current use are associated with acceptable validity and reliability. Theoretical influences on the various tools range from semantic differential coding (Gelfer 1988, 1993) to perceptual correlates of laryngeal function and spectral acoustics (Hiroto 1967; Takahashi and Koike 1976; Yoshida 1979) to phonetic analysis of the entire vocal tract output (Laver 1980, 2000; Laver and Mackenzie Beck 1991). Examples of auditory perceptual protocols include GRBAS (Hirano 1981), the Consensus Auditory-Perceptual Evaluation of Voice (American Speech-Language-Hearing Association 2002) and the Prosody-Voice Screening Profile (Shriberg *et al.* 1990, 1992).

Visual perceptual assessment: Clinicians routinely use visual observation to evaluate structural and body-use features that may contribute to voice dysfunction. Visual perceptual judgements of vocal fold activity observed during laryngostroboscopy are a core activity in voice function assessment and will be discussed in section 25.2.4. Visual perception information may be supplemented by manual palpation techniques which can be used to assess the larynx and laryngeal suspension system (Lieberman 2011).

General body posture/alignment: During the assessment, common patterns of body misalignment that have a deleterious effect on breathing, phonation, resonance and/or articulation are documented. Ergonomics of daily activities often plays a major role in the development and reinforcement of postural misuses and these should be captured in the client's history. Examples include poor seating arrangement at the computer station, long-term use of telephone handsets, or inappropriate/use of corrective eye-wear.

Orofacial postures and laryngeal suspensory system: The larynx is suspended from the lower cranial and facial structures by various muscle groups and other soft tissue. Many of these structures, such as the muscles governing temporomandibular movements and the suprahyoid muscle group, have primary vegetative functions related to deglutition but are sometimes inappropriately active during inspiration and phonation. Since dysfunction in orofacial muscles that impact on resonance or articulatory functions will also affect the final vocal output, it is critical to document these during the comprehensive evaluation. Facial muscles are known to play a critical, innate and perhaps even universal role in conveying emotions (Ekman 1973, 1982). Interpretation of facial muscle misuse patterns can be complex as they may represent psychological defence mechanisms such as repression (Eriksen 1965; Rammage 2011). Often, the expertise of a mental health professional is required.

Speech breathing: The speech breathing literature makes it clear that there is no single profile for normal speech breathing and documents many examples of 'adaptive control' and motor equivalence for adults during vocal activities (Hixon 1987). Since the primary function of the respiratory system during speech is to provide sufficient airflow to support build-up and maintenance of appropriate subglottal pressure, it is important to identify anatomical factors and postural/muscle misuses that impact on speech breathing. In some instances, unorthodox use of the speech breathing mechanism to maintain adequate subglottal pressure may reflect adaptive control, but more often it reflects interactions between structures of speech breathing and phonation due to misuse in one system or the other. For example, chronic contraction of abdominal muscles may result in exaggerated inspiratory movements in the rib cage and accessory muscles in the laryngeal suspensory system. This pattern has been associated with excessive lung volumes at the onset of phonation and an abductory biomechanical effect on the vocal folds (Sundberg *et al.* 1991). Maladaptive patterns such as laryngeal hyperadduction may subsequently be adopted in an attempt to overcome excessive flow rates.

25.2.4   Instrumental assessment

Speech breathing measures: Hixon and Hoit (2005) provide detailed protocols for instrumental evaluation of speech breathing in three areas of investigation: measurements of volume, pressures and shapes; acoustics; and physical status. Assessment of speech breathing kinematics (movements) involves use of electromagnetic devices known as magnetometers or dedicated respiratory inductance plethysmographs to measure changes in positions for the upper torso (the rib cage) and the lower torso (the diaphragm–abdomen). These non-invasive measures can be used to describe clients' speech breathing patterns and the relationships between lung volumes and specific movement patterns. Several commonly used measures of lung volume, air pressures and flow rates can be made during phonation and are discussed under aerodynamic measures.

Aerodynamic measures: Clinical measures of phonatory flow rates, volumes and subglottal pressure and resistance allow the clinician to obtain information about voice function in a non-invasive manner. This can be achieved through the use of air-rate meters (pneumotachometers) that quantify output through a face mask at the oral and/or nasal cavities (see Figure 25.2). Airflow/pressure from the oral and/or nasal cavities is directed towards flow/pressure transducers which convert the aerodynamic signals to electrical signals. These signals are measured and may be analysed further and displayed through software programs. Pneumotachometers are recommended for aerodynamic speech breathing measurements as they are most responsive to the rapid changes of flow rate associated with

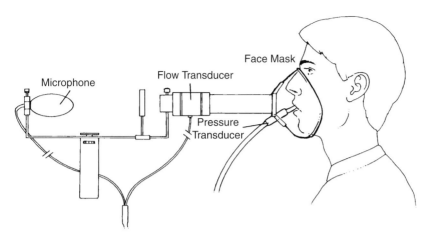

Figure 25.2 Aerodynamic voice assessment using an air-rate meter. (From Rammage/ Morrison. *Management of the Voice and Its Disorders*, 2E. © 2001 Delmar Learning, a part of Cengage Learning, Inc. Reproduced by permission. www.cengage.com/permissions.)

speech (Hixon and Hoit 2005). Holmberg *et al.* (2003) demonstrated the superiority of aerodynamic over acoustic measures as indicators of various vocal fold pathologies.

Acoustic assessment: A comprehensive acoustic evaluation provides objective data that complements aerodynamic, endoscopic, perceptual and self-report information. Dedicated software is often used with acoustic microphones to make physical measures of fundamental frequency (f_0), vocal intensity, acoustic spectra and timing. However, impedance microphones typically used to drive the stroboscope light, or electroglottography, can also be used to derive f_0 measures, and vocal intensity can be measured from sound level meters.

A vocal range profile can be derived by plotting f_0 and dynamic ranges on a phonetogram. This type of visual display is helpful for both clinicians and clients to identify changes in the physiological ranges and their relationships over time (Speyer *et al.* 2003). Dedicated software is available to guide the process of gathering the many vocal productions required to complete phonetograms. In Figure 25.3, f_0 (axis labelled Hertz) is plotted against vocal intensity (axis labelled dB). The pre-treatment profile is depicted in the light area, and post-treatment profiles are represented by dark shading, indicating gains in both f_0 and intensity with treatment.

Vocal efficiency is a measure that reflects how well the larynx converts aerodynamic to acoustic energy. It is determined by dividing the radiated acoustic intensity (I_R) by subglottal pressure (P_s) times mean flow rate (MFR): $I_R/P_s \times$ MFR. Vocal efficiency may help clinicians estimate the effects of glottal 'leakiness'. However, the values co-vary with production factors such as f_0 and intensity, thus careful control is necessary to ensure meaningful data comparisons (Titze 2000).

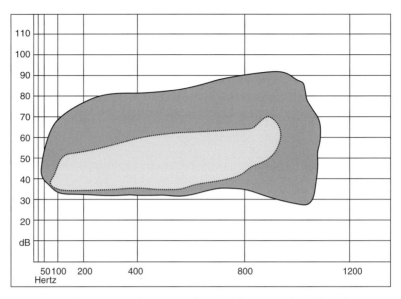

Figure 25.3 Phonetogram showing fundamental frequency (f_0) and vocal intensity. (From Rammage/Morrison. *Management of the Voice and Its Disorders*, 2E. © 2001 Delmar Learning, a part of Cengage Learning, Inc. Reproduced by permission. www.cengage.com/permissions.)

Spectral-acoustic analysis of voice: Numerous software programs are available for measuring spectral acoustic features of the voice, including those that use inverse-filtering techniques to subtract the effect of the vocal tract resonance features. Measures of cycle-to-cycle stability of f_0 (jitter) and amplitude (shimmer) reflect short-term irregularities in the vocal fold vibratory pattern (see Figure 25.4). Relative intensity of vocal harmonics to aperiodic noise can be measured to determine harmonics to noise ratios (HNR) or signal to noise ratios (SNR). Since these measures assume some degree of regularity or periodicity in the voice signal, they are not always a good choice for measuring very aperiodic ('noisy') voices. Further, these parameters vary with vocal production factors such as f_0, intensity, and effort level, so meaningful comparisons across trials demand careful control.

The importance of observing consistent recording and stimulus material for acoustic analysis cannot be overstated. Furthermore, algorithms used in one software program may vary in fundamental ways from those in other programs. For example, measures may be based on either time or frequency domains. Some programs are better suited to certain clinical measures than others, and it may not be meaningful to compare one with another despite similarities in terminology (Pinto and Titze 1990). Normative data referenced for comparison with clinical data should be based on the same hardware, software and stimuli as those used for the clinical assessment.

Although one-to-one correspondence between single acoustic measures and perceptual acoustic terms has not been demonstrated, some

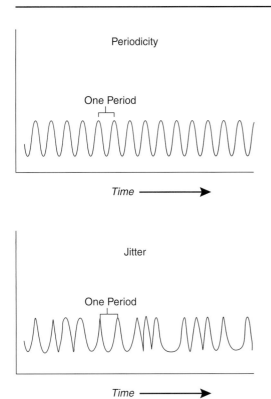

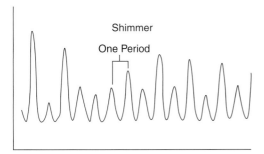

Figure 25.4 Perturbations (jitter and shimmer) in the glottal source waveform. (From Rammage/Morrison. *Management of the Voice and Its Disorders*, 2E. © 2001 Delmar Learning, a part of Cengage Learning, Inc. Reproduced by permission. www.cengage.com/permissions.)

correlations have been made. Thus, acoustic analysis may serve to validate perceptual scales and train listeners (Sodersten *et al.* 1991; Shoji *et al.* 1992; Martens *et al.* 2007).

Measures of rate and duration: Typically, abnormal speaking rates are readily perceived. In instances where an abnormally slow or fast speaking rate is affecting phrasing, coordination of respiration and phonation, intelligibility or vocal tract tension, it is useful to document this using syllable or word counts from contextual speech to compare with normative data and treatment outcome measures.

Maximum phonation time (MPT), typically measured during sustained vowels, has been heralded as a cost-effective and reliable measure of the efficiency of the respiratory mechanism during phonation (Speyer *et al.* 2010). However, performance on MPT tasks is subject to a variety of performance variables such as practice effects and clinician modelling. Further, MPT represents a dynamic interaction between glottal closure and speech breathing patterns, thus the measure is difficult to interpret accurately in isolation (Kent *et al.* 1987). One study demonstrated that MPT is not related to vital capacity (Solomon *et al.* 2000). Clinicians should not assume that longer MPTs necessarily represent more appropriate phonation patterns. Wide ranges for MPT normative values are cited in the literature: 13.1 to 16.2 seconds for children; 16.7 to 25.7 seconds for women; and 22 to 34.6 seconds for men (Hirano 1981).

A variant of the MPT involves comparison of minimal pair voiced and voiceless fricative productions to produce an s/z ratio. Boone (1971) proposed this measure as a way of differentiating respiratory from phonatory contributions to compromised MPT, suggesting that children with benign vocal fold pathology performed worse on the voiced phoneme. Normative values have been presented for children, adults and elderly people and they suggest that age and gender affect s/z ratios (Kent *et al.* 1987).

Measures of phonatory fluency and rhythm may be included in the acoustic protocol. Data on phonation breaks/voice onset times or intensity/f_0 variations can be used to characterize vocal tremors, spasmodic dysphonias or other motor speech disorders.

Assessment of vocal tract postures and vocal fold vibratory features: A variety of instrumental measures can be used to evaluate movements and postures in the vocal tract. Most clinicians agree that video-endoscopic techniques with both continuous and stroboscopic light provide invaluable information about structures and function of the voice mechanism.

Clinicians may use trans-nasal flexible fibreoptic endoscopes to observe the entire upper vocal tract during connected speech and other phonation activities. This technique may be used exclusively with continuous and stroboscopic light for individuals who have recalcitrant gag reflexes and for young children. It can be helpful to illustrate to clinicians and clients any changes in pharyngo-laryngeal postures that occur with probe therapy techniques.

Most clinicians still prefer to use a rigid trans-oral laryngoscope in conjunction with stroboscopic light sources to assess detailed parameters of vocal fold vibratory patterns, owing to the optical clarity and magnification achieved through this technique. This typically involves tongue protrusion and is evaluated during production of /i/ to facilitate anterior tongue displacement, making the larynx more visually accessible. Neck extension and tongue protrusion may affect laryngeal closure patterns, so this must be considered during data interpretation (Sodersten and Lindestad 1992).

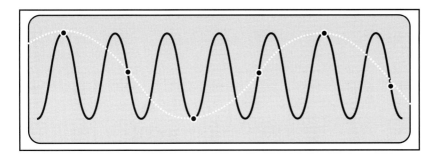

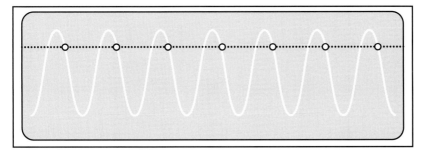

Figure 25.5 Sampling of the phonatory cycle in stroboscopy. (From Rammage/Morrison. *Management of the Voice and Its Disorders*, 2E. © 2001 Delmar Learning, a part of Cengage Learning, Inc. Reproduced by permission. www.cengage.com/permissions.)

During direct and indirect examination of the larynx, a continuous light source is generally used to examine gross structural, postural and movement characteristics. In stroboscopy, a flashing light source creates an apparent slow-motion image by flashing just below or just above the f_0, averaged over many cycles of phonation. An impedance or acoustic microphone detects the f_0 and drives the stroboscope light so that it samples progressive parts of the phonatory cycle (top frame, Figure 25.5) to create an apparent slow motion image, or the same portion of the vocal fold cycle each time (bottom frame, Figure 25.5) to allow for assessment of regularity. One limitation of the stroboscopic technique is its reliance on quasi-periodic vocal fold vibration to detect f_0 that drives the strobe light.

The Stroboscopy Evaluation Rating Form (SERF) is used in many voice clinics to guide the assessment (see Figure 25.6). It provides verbal instructions and diagrams to enhance consistency of visual perceptual ratings by clinicians (Poburka 1999). We discussed above the importance of recognizing and mitigating potential biasing factors in such ratings. For example, one study demonstrated the potential biasing influence that knowledge of clients' history could have on laryngo-stroboscopic judgements (Teitler 1992). Detailed descriptions of the principles, instrumentation, protocols and interpretation of stroboscopic evaluation of the voice is provided by Hirano and Bless (1993).

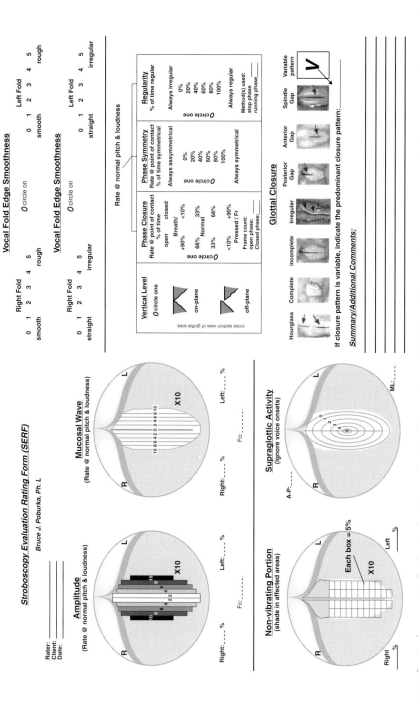

Figure 25.6 The Stroboscopy Evaluation Rating Form. (Reprinted from *Journal of Voice*, volume 13, issue 3, Bruce J. Poburka, A new stroboscopy rating form, 403–13, 1999, with permission from Elsevier.)

Other methods for evaluating vibratory patterns: Electroglottography (EGG) measures changes in electrical impedance of the glottis, as high-frequency electric currents pass between the vocal folds. Two or more electrodes are held on the surface of the neck, one over each thyroid lamina. Measures of the relative vocal fold contact area can be illustrated on a cycle-to-cycle basis. No direct relationships have been established between the amplitude of the EEG signal and acoustic amplitude or intensity. However, the rate of repetition of signals recorded with EGG provides an accurate and reliable representation of vocal f_0 unless a vocal signal is very aperiodic (Baken 1992). Because of inherent difficulties encountered in interpreting EGG, it is often combined with other measures of vocal fold vibratory patterns.

Flow glottography uses a special face mask that effectively subtracts the effect of the vocal tract filter on the flow output during phonation (Rothenberg 1973). The resulting flow glottograms provide aerodynamic characteristics of vocal fold vibratory patterns such as peak glottal flow, direct current (DC) flow offset ('leakiness' factor), open, closed and closing speed quotients. Hertegard *et al.* (1992) demonstrated an inverse relationship between EGG recordings and flow glottograms in depicting vocal fold vibratory patterns.

Videokymography is a laryngeal imaging technique that uses a high-speed mode of nearly 8000 images per second, from one cross-sectional line of the glottis displayed on the X axis of the monitor, while the Y axis represents the time dimension. This provides a detailed image of very short timeframes in phonation, allowing the clinician to identify small vocal fold asymmetries, open quotient differences along the glottis, movements of the upper vocal fold margins and lateral propagation of mucosal waves. Kymography overcomes the problems encountered with the stroboscope when assessing very aperiodic and/or unstable vocal fold vibration, and can thus provide a sensitive assessment of the effects of various pathologies. This is not currently a practical technique for measuring changes in phonatory patterns over extended time. Kymography can be combined with videostroboscopy to take advantage of the strengths of the two procedures. This is achieved by rearranging one active horizontal line from successive frames of pre-recorded stroboscopic images and displaying it from top to bottom along the time axis for a static image of vibration at a specific part of the vocal folds over time (Sung *et al.* 1999).

Probing facilitative techniques: Recommendations regarding voice therapy are based on both the clinicians' knowledge of relevant and effective techniques and results of probe therapy. Probe therapy can demonstrate conditions impacting on variability in voice function and techniques that improve the condition, and is used when considering prognosis for improvement in a voice therapy programme. By demonstrating variability in function under controlled conditions, the diagnostic therapy process can be used to modify or eliminate the apparent significance of some organic disease processes. For example, dysphonic clients with bilateral vocal fold nodules often also exhibit a large posterior glottal gap which is reduced during semi-occluded vocal tract exercises such as humming, resulting in clearer voice quality. Probe therapy confirms that vocal technique changes rather than surgical reduction of vocal nodules should be the primary management goal. Selection of probes depends on the primary clinical features of vocal dysfunction. For example, when the vocal folds are hyper-adducting, facilitation techniques will target less forceful closure. Therapy probes are derived from direct therapy techniques which are discussed in section 25.3.5.

Describing, classifying and diagnosing the problem: Once all the relevant evaluation information and instrumental measures have been obtained, they can be used to form a profile for the client, and should inform the course of treatment. In some instances, comparison of a client's vocal function profile with documented classification schemes, such as is provided in the American Speech-Language-Hearing Association *Classification Manual for Voice Disorders* (CMVD-I), will lead the voice clinic team to a diagnosis that also informs treatment course (Verdolini *et al.* 2006). In many cases, however, the complex interactions between contributing factors make assignment of an exclusive diagnosis impossible. In that instance, a detailed description of symptoms, ALERT components and interactions as well as the impact of voice dysfunction on a client's life provide the foundation for the clinical description and intervention goal-setting. Aronson and Bless (2009a) proposed eight categories of symptom clusters based on auditory perceptual features of voice dysfunction (see Chapter 18). The auditory perceptual classification is intended to provide a starting point for differential diagnosis, by narrowing possible aetiologies and guiding the clinical team in selection of assessment protocols.

25.3   Planning effective intervention

25.3.1 Therapy approaches

The speech-language pathologist works with the client to set realistic outcome priorities, then plan and direct the most effective and efficient voice therapy programme. A voice therapy programme can consist of direct strategies, indirect strategies or both. Direct strategies involve training clients to acquire specific physical-technical skills. Indirect strategies involve education about conditions and behaviours that are required to improve vocal function and support in achieving the goals. When the cause of voice dysfunction is multifactorial, there may be advantages to combining direct and indirect therapy approaches. For example, vocal load and environmental and psychological stress have all been implicated in the development of occupational voice problems (Dejonckere 2001).

Outcome studies show little agreement on the effectiveness of direct versus indirect approaches. Roy *et al.* (2001) compared two approaches for teachers with voice dysfunction in a prospective randomized trial and concluded that a direct therapy approach was more effective than an indirect approach consisting of vocal hygiene guidelines. However, in two subsequent studies, indirect therapy involving use of portable voice amplifiers by dysphonic teachers resulted in better outcomes than either vocal hygiene instruction alone or direct voice therapy approaches (Roy *et al.* 2002, 2003). Chan (1994) found that a two-month vocal hygiene programme resulted in improved vocal health in a group of preschool teachers. Sodersten *et al.* (2002) recognized the advantage of voice rest throughout the teaching day in preschool teachers.

25.3.2 Factors influencing selection and success of therapy programmes

In order to participate in direct therapy approaches, the client must be able to access feedback channels to assist in motor learning. These may include the auditory, visual and tactile–kinaesthetic processing systems. Some therapy approaches may be more adaptable than others to accommodate individuals with sensory deficits. Since both indirect therapy and technique change involve cognitive processes, participation requires adequate attention skills to process instructions, adequate memory for retrieval of information critical to effective practice and behaviour changes, and psychological motivation that is unimpeded by psychological conflict or apathy. The choice of therapy approaches is often influenced by a number of socioeconomic factors affecting programme or client funding. It is incumbent on the speech-language pathologist to determine the most efficient approach to meet each client's treatment goals.

Clients often develop maladaptive patterns in response to anatomical changes. These patterns can effect neuroplastic changes when reinforced by use over time (Rosenbek 2009) and influence not only motor activity, but also an individual's ability to perceive the changes. Koufman and Blalock (1982) referred to a state of habituated hoarseness. In the case of long-standing lesions, such as a fibrotic nodules, or neuromuscular processes such as benign essential tremor, maladaptive behaviours may have become habituated. The same may hold true for individuals with psychogenic dysphonia, where the conflict is since resolved, but the habituated muscle misuse is reinforced by use over time. In such cases voice therapy may require longer and more comprehensive intervention than in those with more recent onset of voice dysfunction.

Regardless of the approach taken, voice therapy requires commitment from both clinician and client. Compliance requirements may extend to communication partners, spouses, caretakers, teachers and others involved in daily routines for the therapy programme to have a positive impact on the client's life. The most commonly reported compliance breaches for voice clients include missed appointments and failure to follow through with assignments (Behrman 2006; Portone *et al.* 2008; Hapner *et al.* 2009). Factors that may contribute to non-compliance include advanced age, lower socioeconomic status, general health problems and more severe voice problems (Smith *et al.* 2010). Van Leer and Connor (2010) highlighted the importance of client-perceived clinician support. This involves collaboration between client and clinician in identifying barriers to participation, and specific clinician behaviours such as provision of a variety of analogies for the desired behaviours, individualized exercises, feedback regarding productions and specific suggestions for carry-over of voice skills to speech. Verdolini-Marston *et al.* (1995) identified client compliance as the best predictor of positive outcomes for two common treatments in individuals with vocal fold nodules.

25.3.3   Role of technology

Instrumental advances that facilitate assessment in the modern voice clinic also provide choices for the client and clinician during treatment. Endoscopy and dedicated acoustic software technology may provide salient feedback during practice, and may enhance information from other feedback channels. In cases where clients are unable to use information from certain sensory channels, as may be the case for hard-of-hearing individuals or those who are initially unable to perceive discrete voice changes, programs that display acoustic features of voice in real-time can be invaluable in providing the necessary models and feedback about target vocal productions. Fortunately, dedicated programs that appeal to both children and adults are widely accessible to provide information on aspects of vocal intensity, f_0, spectral features, timing and fluency.

Portable feedback devices, 'dosimeters', provide clients with vocal dose information such as cumulative daily voice use time, f_0 and intensity (Cheyne *et al.* 2003). Van Leer and Connor have used MP4 players with video recordings of the client and clinician performing voice therapy to improve client practice compliance. In a randomized controlled trial of 40 clients, those clients who had been provided with MP4 home-practice support achieved significantly better motivation and generalization of vocal skills than those who were provided with written practice instructions only (van Leer and Connor 2010, 2012; van Leer 2010). The Lee Silverman Voice Treatment (LSVT) Companion™ provides a computer-based program to guide training and practice sessions in the LSVT®Loud therapy programme. The clinician programs the goals for each activity in both the clinician edition used during therapy sessions, and the home edition used by the client for home practice. LSVT®Loud therapy has also been conducted through tele-practice methods, which makes it more accessible to clients.

25.3.4 Indirect therapy

Indirect therapy may address lifestyle, emotion and reflux components of the ALERT model. Lifestyle factors are mitigated in a variety of ways. For example, the speech-language pathologist mentors the client on strategies for reducing vocally traumatizing behaviours and improving vocal health, and advocates for the client to improve environmental factors such as poor acoustics, vocal demands and ergonomics that are contributing to voice dysfunction.

The role of hydration in vocal health programmes has been highlighted by a number of studies. Increased hydration has been associated with lower phonation threshold pressures (Verdolini-Marston *et al.* 1990). Improved voice function with increased hydration has been demonstrated in studies of amateur singers (Yiu and Chan 2003), kindergarten teachers with vocal fatigue (Chan 1994) and individuals with benign vocal fold lesions (Verdolini-Marston *et al.* 1994).

Vocal rest and voice conservation measures are sometimes prescribed to treat voice dysfunction. Absolute voice rest is most frequently prescribed following acute vocal fold trauma, such as vocal fold haemorrhage, or following phonosurgery, such as ablation of vocal fold lesions or laryngeal web resection. In these situations, absolute voice rest may promote healing and minimize post-surgical scarring (Ishikawa and Thibeault 2010). A survey of otolaryngologists revealed that approximately 50 per cent recommend absolute voice rest following phonosurgery, whereas approximately 15 per cent do not prescribe any type of voice rest (Behrman and Sulica 2003). Prescribing absolute voice rest may not be advisable in individuals who are susceptible to psychogenic voice disorders (Aronson and Bless 2009a). Individuals who are predisposed to anxiety and hypochondriasis may be particularly susceptible to warnings about hazards of voice use, as may those for whom the voice is involved in repressing emotional expression, such as in conversion dysphonias. Koufman and Blalock (1989) concluded that conservative voice use provided adequate protection against postoperative dysphonia post-surgically in a study of patients with benign and invasive vocal fold lesions. Conservative voice use is frequently incorporated in vocal hygiene programmes. A Voice Use Reduction Program has been reported to improve laryngeal and voice symptoms (Van der Merwe 2004).

Indirect therapy with occupational voice users and vocal performers may include use of voice dosimetry to monitor voice use, optimizing room acoustics and providing appropriate sound field amplification. Guidelines for optimizing room acoustics have been provided by Howard and Angus (2001). The benefit that teachers derive from voice amplification was demonstrated in studies by Sapienza *et al.* (1999) and Roy *et al.* (2002, 2003). Guidelines for selection and use of voice amplification systems in occupational voice use settings are provided by McGlashan and Howard (2001). Voice amplification has also been recommended for individuals with reduced vocal intensity due to unilateral vocal fold paralysis (Baylor *et al.* 2006; Woo and Carroll 2009).

Emotional factors contributing to voice dysfunction may require an interdisciplinary approach. In collaboration with mental health professionals, the speech-language pathologist assists the client in understanding how emotional factors contribute to muscle misuses affecting voice function. Special considerations for management of psychogenic voice disorders are discussed in section 25.3.9. Indirect therapy may also involve reflux management. As a professional trained in facilitating behavioural changes, the speech-language pathologist may assist clients in planning and monitoring compliance with regimens prescribed by physicians to reduce reflux and other laryngeal irritants.

25.3.5   Direct therapy

In contrast to indirect intervention strategies, direct therapy involves training clients in the acquisition of physical skills involved in vocal production. Direct therapy thus addresses the technique factors in the ALERT model.

Principles underlying technique change: Programmes designed to facilitate vocal technique adjustments are based on the same principles of motor learning and neuroplasticity that underlie all intervention programmes targeting changes in neuromotor and neuropsychological patterns. The principles of motor learning are well established and are based on the concept of neuroplasticity – the brain's propensity for anatomical and physiological change when the necessary physical and motor learning conditions are met. Activity specificity, saliency, complexity, intensity, repetition, feedback and timing are key to neuroplasticity (Kleim and Jones 2008). Therapy activities that facilitate motor learning may include establishing clients' understanding of the purpose and expected sensory result of an appropriate movement pattern, modelling the desired movement pattern, repeated practice of the movement pattern at the appropriate intensity, frequency and complexity, and use of sensory feedback to correct inappropriate responses and confirm appropriate responses (Adams 1986; Schmidt 1988; Schneider *et al.* 1997).

Theoretical assumptions for voice therapy techniques: Most direct therapy approaches published to date are holistic and are based on an assumption that improved coordination among speech breathing, vocal fold vibration and upper vocal tract resonance systems can be achieved with a targeted strategy. Strategies include improving speech breathing during phonation, optimizing resonance effects, relaxing the laryngeal suspension system, changing laryngeal postures or exercising the laryngeal apparatus. Most methods are not disorder-specific, and are used to manage a wide variety of voice dysfunction profiles. Although outcome research has been published supporting some methods, it may be difficult to interpret which aspect(s) of a particular therapy approach contributed to positive outcome measures. Examples of direct voice therapy techniques include LSVT®Loud (Ramig *et al.* 1994) and Confidential Voice (Colton *et al.* 2006).

Role of relaxation and posture training: Some protocols include techniques for general muscle relaxation and/or posture-alignment. However, clients who exhibit muscle and postural misuses that have a negative impact on speech breathing, phonation, resonance and/or articulation may need more extensive work in these areas to benefit fully from more focused voice therapy techniques. This is particularly the case if emotional factors are present and/or there has been long-term maladaptive muscle misuse. These techniques may be introduced in conjunction with psychotherapy. Mental health practitioners and speech-language pathologists often train clients in progressive relaxation (Jacobson 1938). Physical, massage or osteopathic therapy, and Alexander (Barlow 1973) or Feldenkrais (1949) techniques may also be beneficial. Manual therapy may be used in combination with certain focused techniques to reduce specific muscle misuses (Harris 1998). Speech-language pathologists need to undertake training and to understand their limitations in order to ensure they perform manual therapy safely and effectively (Harris 1998; Lieberman 1998).

Speech breathing exercises: When clients exhibit muscle tension or weakness affecting speech breathing, therapy exercises may be introduced to improve awareness and efficiency of speech breathing muscles. Cooper and Cooper (1977) suggested training relaxed abdominal rest breathing, initially in supine position with the client's hands monitoring movement on the rib cage and abdomen. Supine position may provide a gravitational advantage for clients who have a poor awareness of respiratory movements, since it forces them to resist gravity during inspiration and may enhance the experience of the abdominal muscle activity during phonation. Individuals whose breathing patterns are disrupted by neuromuscular weakness or incoordination may benefit from exercises that strengthen respiratory muscles, or prosthetic devices that increase intra-abdominal pressure during speech (Hixon and Hoit 2005).

25.3.6 Role of voice therapy in individuals with anatomically based voice dysfunction

The ALERT model directs the clinician to consider anatomical contributions to voice dysfunction related to ageing/development, injuries, lesions and diseases. The role of voice therapy may depend on whether anatomical factors are primary or secondary to voice dysfunction. For example, individuals with lesions such as papilloma on the vocal folds or a long-standing paretic vocal fold that is fixed in an abducted position will probably require primary phonosurgery. Voice therapy may be instituted preoperatively, postoperatively or both. Individuals who present with vocal fold lesions that are secondary to lifestyle, emotional, reflux or technical factors, such as those with bilateral vocal fold nodules, will typically undergo voice therapy as a primary treatment, with surgical intervention reserved for cases where therapy outcomes are not satisfactory and efficacy of surgery has been demonstrated.

Therapy and phonosurgery: In instances where phonosurgery is the primary treatment for individuals with anatomically based voice dysfunction, preoperative therapy typically focuses on vocal hygiene, reflux and elimination of maladaptive behaviours. Postoperatively, therapy activities include voice conservation during recovery and direct techniques that maximize surgical outcomes and minimize post-surgical scarring. Patients may benefit from therapy in conjunction with a number of medical-surgical procedures including surgical removal of benign or neoplastic lesions, surgical augmentation of vocal folds (by injection of inert substances or by thyroplasty), botulinum toxin injections, thyroplasty procedures to modify pitch in gender dysphoria, nerve anastomosis or other micro-nerve surgery, radiation treatment for cancers, and partial or total laryngectomy. The speech-language pathologist will need to understand basic goals and procedures of the various phonosurgical techniques in order to select the most appropriate direct therapy techniques.

Stiff/scarred vocal folds: Although phonosurgical techniques for ablation of vocal fold lesions have evolved to minimize long-term scarring, some degree of post-surgical stiffness is common. Scarring can also result from intubation during medical-surgical interventions, injuries, burns and congenital anomalies such as sulcus vocalis. Voice therapy is considered the first treatment choice for vocal fold scar (Rosen *et al.* 2000). Techniques are based on principles of stretching and massage used by physical therapists to manage body scars. Vocal function exercises (Stemple *et al.* 1994) and pitch glissandos during lip and tongue trills have been advocated based on the assumption that vocal fold lengthening during pitch ascension effectively stretches vocal fold tissue (Casper 1999; Hapner and Klein 2009). Lip bubbling/tongue trilling or nasalizing activities of resonant voice therapy (Verdolini 1998: 28–9) provide the semi-occluded vocal tract condition advocated by Titze (2006) to minimize phonation threshold pressure and relax supra-glottal structures, while ensuring wide vocal fold excursions that may effectively massage the vocal fold layer structure.

Flaccid vocal fold paralysis: Voice therapy may play a role for the patient with unilateral vocal fold paralysis during the 9- to 12-month spontaneous recovery period, or thereafter as a primary treatment approach or as an adjunct to phonosurgery. In addition to direct therapy protocols, techniques may be used to facilitate vocal fold adduction. These include forced adduction techniques (phonating while pushing, pulling, lifting); breath-holding/swallowing gestures; lateral pressure on the thyroid lamina and turning the head to one side (McFarlane *et al.* 1991, 1998; Stemple *et al.* 1996). Since forced adduction exercises are typically associated with supra-glottal as well as glottal compression, they are not always the best option during the spontaneous recovery period as they may encourage maladaptive behaviours. Some clinicians reserve forced adduction activities for situations where individuals need to recruit any and all vibrating structures in the larynx. Pitch lowering may be an appropriate alternative in the spontaneous recovery period. In the lower modal register the vocal fold margins are thick, increasing the chance of vocal fold closure particularly in the membranous portions. Since low f_0 is also associated with low phonation threshold pressure, this approach may increase vocal efficiency and optimize communication, particularly when reinforced by vocal amplification.

Hypokinetic dysarthrias: Vocalization therapies are most often used for hypophonia related to hypokinetic dysarthrias. The LSVT®Loud approach is one of the few voice therapy programmes currently supported by Class I research evidence (based on randomized controlled trials), including evidence of post-treatment neuroplastic changes demonstrated by positron emission tomography (Liotti *et al.* 2003). Problems related to programme access and physical limitations of clients have led to modified protocols using the LSVT®Loud principles and tasks. Spielman *et al.* (2007) reported positive outcomes in a programme extended over eight weeks with two, rather than four, sessions per week. Tele-practice holds promise for making LSVT®Loud therapy accessible to clients who have difficulty accessing service in person (Tindall *et al.* 2008; Howell *et al.* 2009; Little *et al.* 2009; Constantinescu *et al.* 2010).

A recent clinical study explored the effectiveness of a vocalization therapy approach which blended techniques from the LSVT®Loud protocol with singing activities in small groups of individuals with idiopathic Parkinson's disease. Singing pedagogy exercises were used to improve vocal stamina, flexibility and strength. Singing was used to maximize self-expression and peer support while capitalizing on the Lombard effect and the choral effect. The Lombard effect contributes to increased vocal intensity in the presence of competing noise, whereas choral singing facilitates recall of memorized text and fluency. Positive outcomes were reported for both acoustic measures and self-rating scales (Tanner 2012).

Hyperkinetic dysarthrias: Essential voice tremor (EVT) is characterized by f_0 and intensity modulations of 4–8 Hz (Barkmeier-Kraemer *et al.* 2011). The degree to which other structures are involved, or co-occurrence with neurogenic spasmodic dysphonia may influence treatment focus. Indirect voice therapy may minimize mild tremor symptoms when it includes reducing psychological stressors and tremor-inducing chemicals such as caffeine, and taking small amounts of alcohol (Chen and Swope 2007).

Direct voice therapy approaches may be helpful in increasing laryngeal stability, minimizing maladaptive techniques, or both. Voice therapy may also be adjunctive to pharmaceutical treatment using β-adrenergic blockers, anticonvulsants or botulinum toxin injections. Since EVT symptoms are most evident during loud phonation at low f_0, therapy tactics typically target increasing pitch and reducing intensity or laryngeal effort. Dworkin and Meleca (1999) advocate f_0 increase of approximately 50 Hz. They also advocate chanting and stabilizing the larynx manually or with an elastic neckband. Barkmeier-Kraemer *et al.* (2011) described a therapy programme that included training in relaxation/breathing, increasing speaking rate to reduce voiced segment durations, increasing f_0 and upward phrase-end inflections, using breathiness to reduce vocal intensity and vocal fold adduction and anterior facial resonance with 'open' throat. Results of the single-subject study revealed subject satisfaction and improved auditory perceptual ratings by naïve listeners.

(Neurogenic) spasmodic dysphonias: Speech-voice therapy for patients experiencing spasmodic dysphonias (SD) may be primary or secondary. Primary therapy programmes target reduction of the dominant symptoms. Secondary speech therapy is used as an adjunct to other surgical, medical or psychological treatment programmes to enhance the primary treatment. Botulinum toxin injections, first introduced by Blitzer *et al.* (1988), compromise the primary management approach for most clients with neurogenic spasmodic dysphonia symptoms, but other surgical procedures such as recurrent laryngeal nerve section/resection or vocal fold lateralization are also offered in some centres (Dedo 1976; Berke *et al.* 1999; Isshiki *et al.* 2000, 2001). Adjunctive therapy may be undertaken to optimize communication in the presence of post-treatment symptoms such as vocal fold weakness or asymmetry (Izdebski *et al.* 1999).

Primary voice therapy is generally intensive and long term. It may encompass any of a number of facilitative techniques that reduce primary symptoms of laryngeal hypervalving (adductor SD) or hypovalving (abductor SD). Voice therapy may also address secondary symptoms that exacerbate communication attempts, such as respiratory overloading and incoordination, head retraction, facial tension and grimacing, jaw and tongue splinting and pitch lowering. Therapy techniques that have been advocated for adductor SD include the Accent Method (Kotby *et al.* 1991), pitch register therapy (Barkmeier and Verdolini-Marston 1992), inhalation phonation (Shulman 1989) and voice onset tactics associated with automatic speech and low lung volumes (Cooper 1973; Rammage *et al.* 2001).

Transgender voice: The immediate voice problem for most individuals who have undergone gender reassignment relates to inappropriate pitch due to the significant discrepancy between the adult male and female larynx (Spencer 1988). Since increased vocal fold mass is an expected result of male hormone treatment, inappropriate vocal pitch is not typically a significant problem among individuals undergoing female to male transition (FTM individuals represent a minority of the transgender population). Those undergoing male to female transition represent the majority of patients consulting the voice clinic, because administration of female hormones has no demonstrated effect of raising f_0.

Phonosurgery, such as crico-thyroid approximation (Isshiki 1989) or induction of anterior laryngeal webbing (Rammage *et al.* 2001), may be the primary intervention for raising f_0, but this goal may also be targeted in primary or secondary therapy. Since other physical and behavioural discrepancies affecting communication also contribute to gender perception, voice therapy typically targets multiple factors (Spencer 1988). Therapy goals may include elevating speaking f_0 to fall between 180 Hz and 200 Hz, raising formant frequencies, altering intonation patterns, reducing speaking intensity, increasing breathiness and adopting feminine syntax, vocabulary, articulation and communicative gestures (Gelfer 1999; Soderpalm *et al.* 2004; Mayer and Gelfer 2008). Individuals with gender dysphoria experience ongoing physical, emotional and lifestyle stressors that increase their susceptibility to muscle misuse, and therapy must address these stressors to ensure best outcomes. Voice therapy should be timed appropriately by taking other life-altering priorities into account.

25.3.7 Paediatric population: special considerations

Therapy for children may need to address factors related to any or all of the ALERT components. Special consideration needs to be given to the developmental stage of each child, as the laryngeal mechanism is not fully mature until mid to late adolescence in males and the third decade in females (Kahane 1983). The immature vocal fold layer structure and relative small size of the larynx may make it more susceptible to injury during sustained loud phonation or other vocal behaviours that may put undue stress on the larynx. Psychosocial and speech-language development may also be considerations when planning therapy with children.

Phonotrauma: Since vocal behaviours in children may reflect both internal and external influences, intervention may involve the child's family, educators and peers. Indirect therapy may need to address psychosocial factors that contribute to inappropriate vocal behaviours. Verdolini Abbott (2011) advocates therapy targeting improved technique for producing loud voice, rather than taking the prohibitive approach associated with many vocal hygiene programmes. There may be benefits to integrating therapy into group activities involving peers to provide social support and vocal training for all participants.

Adolescent transitional voice disorder: Some adolescent boys do not adjust their vocal function in modal register in response to larynx maturation. Rather, they adopt falsetto register for speech. Typically, they require direct voice therapy but indirect intervention by a psychologist or psychiatrist may also be required in cases where emotional factors play a role in the persistent use of falsetto phonation. The primary goal of direct therapy is to establish and generalize modal register phonation in the f_0 range appropriate to the mature larynx. Since the larynx is usually held high, manual therapy or postural adjustments are often used to lower the larynx. Modal register is typically identified during vegetative vocalizations such as coughing and throat-clearing and when vocal intensity is increased during glottal fry phonation. Kinaesthetic feedback can be enhanced by having the client monitor vibrations over the thyroid cartilage. Visual feedback devices may be useful in instances where an individual's auditory pitch perception is biased by habituated misuse or psychological influences.

25.3.8   Geriatric population: special considerations

Anatomical processes associated with ageing contribute to predictable voice changes. These can be compounded by additional physiological or disease factors affecting laryngeal function that arise most commonly in geriatric years. Since decline in other motor speech, respiratory and cognitive functions is also associated with ageing, therapy goals will necessarily need to be tailored to accommodate these changes.

   Direct therapy targets reduction of muscle misuses that reflect attempts to maintain the acoustic signal the individual is accustomed to hearing, and/or techniques to optimize vocal fold adduction. Surgical techniques such as injecting substances to augment vocal fold mass may be offered to geriatric individuals with age-related atrophy. Indirect therapy may be focused on reducing the environmental and psychosocial barriers to communication and may involve communication partners and caregivers. Goals include helping clients understand and accept expected ageing changes. These changes include elevated f_0, breathiness and reduced intensity range associated with vocal fold atrophy in elderly men, and lower f_0 related to mucosal thickening in post-menopausal women. Vocal amplification may allow an elderly person to communicate more effectively, especially with hard-of-hearing communication partners.

25.3.9   Psychogenic voice dysfunction

Voice disorders can be caused by a variety of psychogenic and personality-based factors, primarily through misuse of the voluntary nervous system (Rammage *et al.* 1987; Rammage 2011; Roy 2011; van Mersbergen 2011). Anxiety reactions, depression, repression and conversion are among the psychological mechanisms that may be represented through muscle misuses resulting in dysphonia. Management often requires an inter-professional approach, as direct therapy may not be relevant or effective in the face of unresolved psychological conflict or personality disorders that perpetuate vocally traumatizing behaviours and muscle misuse. Medical intervention such as reflux management may also be required to reduce symptoms such as globus pharyngeus that reinforce anxiety. Most clients want to be reassured unconditionally about the absence of cancer.

Reviewing recorded images of the larynx with the client can allay their fear about disease processes.

Once the speech-language pathologist is reassured that psychological mechanisms are not interfering with client motivation, therapy is introduced to alter vocal behaviours and extinguish muscle misuses contributing to abnormal voice features. Components of the programme may include education about vocal misuse and normal voice function, exploration of direct techniques that allow the client to access more appropriate voice, carry-over to speech activities in a variety of situations and follow-up. Involving family or friends may provide socio-emotional support and the opportunity to generalize appropriate vocal skills to conversation.

Specific techniques used to normalize voice use depend on the primary features contributing to dysphonia. For example, in the case of aphonia due to vocal fold hyper-abduction, vegetative gestures such as coughing, throat-clearing, effort closure, or phonation in non-modal modes such as laughter or glottal fry are probed to effect vocal fold adduction. Conversely, when dysphonia is caused by vocal fold/supra-glottal hyper-adduction, techniques such as yawn–sigh may be used to reduce vocal tract constriction.

If, in the course of therapy for psychogenic voice dysfunction, the clinician detects resistance or unexpected responses, referral to a mental health professional is advisable. Indicators of psychological interference include reduced motivation, inappropriate response to a demonstrated voice improvement, recurrence of dysphonia following normal voice recovery, persistent signs of anxiety, depression or psychological conflict, and request by a client for a mental health referral (Rammage *et al.* 2001).

25.3.10   Irritable larynx syndrome

Irritable larynx syndrome (ILS) is a condition that is thought to be related to central sensitivity syndromes (CSS) such as irritable bowel, irritable bladder, chronic fatigue syndrome and fibromyalgia (Morrison and Rammage 2010). Muscle tension symptoms in the larynx may result in laryngospasm during inspiration, chronic cough, globus pharyngeus and/or voice dysfunction. Contributing factors often arise from all components of the ALERT model. Thus, management of ILS requires an inter-professional approach.

Comprehensive management of ILS involves several levels of intervention to minimize symptom triggers, both internal (e.g. reflux) and external (e.g. odours), reprogram laryngeal muscle responses through desensitizing activities and direct therapy approaches, and reprogram central nervous system responses with pharmaceutical intervention such as antidepressants, antiepileptic and anti-spasmolytic medications (Morrison and Rammage 2010). Botox injections in the larynx are also sometimes used to reduce laryngospasm and/or chronic cough. Direct strategies for laryngospasm and chronic cough may include gestures such as 'pursed-lips breathing' and/or sniffing that capitalize on the vocal fold abductory response to breathing through an upper vocal tract restriction (Blager 2005). Indirect therapy involves counselling clients about the nature of the neuromuscular reactions and lifestyle changes required to reduce internal and external triggers.

25.4   Measuring treatment outcomes

We have discussed the application of a variety of client-report, perceptual and instrumental tools that help describe, classify and/or diagnose voice disorders and are used to document and measure treatment outcomes. Public and private funding for voice management is increasingly contingent on evidence-based practice. It is incumbent on clinicians to ensure that reliable and valid measures are made to document voice function changes at regular intervals, and that the most relevant tools are used to define therapy outcomes.

Client-centred approaches highlight the importance of the client's perspective in determining when treatment is complete and success-ful. Clinical outcome studies rely increasingly on self-report inventories as socially valid measures. However, we have seen that relationships between self-report tools and other clinical measures are weak at best. Some funding programmes require objective instrumental measures as evidence of intervention success.

25.5   Challenges and needs

Modern evaluative techniques such as video-laryngeal stroboscopy and radiographic imaging techniques have rendered identification of structural anomalies a relatively easy clinical endeavour. In fact, our ready access to elaborate technology for identifying structural anomalies affecting voice function may tempt us to focus on this type of evidence to the exclusion of less technologically sophisticated assessment activities. For successful, long-term management outcomes clinicians should assume that multiple factors are interacting to affect function in the larynx, and not all these factors can be captured by instrumental measures.

As quickly as we begin to understand how the mind–body complex generates voice dysfunction, and the role of biological features such as sensorimotor learning and neuroplasticity in rehabilitation processes, new evidence reveals even more astounding complexities in the systems involved. Making the management process even more complex are continual advances in diagnostic and treatment technologies that present clinicians with the responsibility and challenges of staying abreast of current technology, not to mention accessing fiscal resources to ensure access to the most effective tools.

Research supporting specific voice treatment approaches is still in its infancy. Speech-language pathologists often have no choice but to offer therapy approaches without the benefit of evidence-based research. The majority of voice therapy techniques in common use have been affirmed, at best, by studies of small-group or single-subject design and few Class I (randomized controlled trials) exist (Verdolini *et al.* 1998b; Carding 2000). The paucity of outcome research supporting voice therapy can negatively influence client motivation, programme funding and clinician confidence. Given the significant cost that medical and speech-language pathology services impose on individual consumers and society, there is also a need for clinical research to include efficiency as a critical parameter defining successful management.

26

Disorders of fluency

J. Scott Yaruss

26.1 Overview

Stuttering is a complex communication disorder that can have far-reaching effects on a person's life. The primary observable symptoms of stuttering involve disruptions in the flow of speech, commonly termed 'speech disfluencies' (Bloodstein and Bernstein Ratner 2008). Speech disfluencies can take a variety of forms. Some are considered to be 'non-stuttered', presumably because they represent a normal interruption in language planning or speech production. Common examples include interjections ('um', 'uh'), phrase repetitions ('I want- I want that'), and revisions ('I want- I need that'). All speakers produce these types of disfluencies, though they are more likely to be seen in individuals who do not stutter (Conture 2001). Other disfluencies are considered to be 'stuttered' or 'stutter-like' (Yairi 1996), presumably because they represent an atypical interruption in language planning or speech production. Common examples include repetitions of parts of words ('li-li-like this'), prolongations ('lllllike this') and blocks (moments when the speaker is unable to produce any sound at all, 'l - -ike this'). These disfluencies are most likely to be seen in individuals who stutter (Conture 2001). Speech disfluencies may be accompanied by physical tension or struggle behaviours as the speaker attempts to force words out. For example, speakers may blink their eyes, tense the muscles in their jaw or lips, or exhibit movements of the head or arms as they attempt to speak.

Although observable disfluencies are among the most identifiable aspects of the stuttering disorder, stuttering can involve far more than just the surface behaviours that may be perceived by a listener. In fact, the experience of stuttering can affect nearly every aspect of daily life, and many authors have described the broad-based experience of individuals who stutter (Starkweather and Givens-Ackerman 1997; Yaruss 1998a; Yaruss and Quesal 2004a, 2006; Bennett 2006; Gabel *et al.* 2008;

Craig *et al.* 2009; Manning 2010; Yaruss 2010; Shapiro 2011). For example, people who stutter may experience emotional reactions, such as embarrassment or shame. They may develop negative communication attitudes, including reduced self-confidence, or low self-esteem. They may have difficulty performing common daily tasks such as introducing themselves to others, engaging in conversations, talking on the telephone or giving presentations at work or in school. And people in their environment may react negatively, leading to problems such as discrimination and bullying. In essence, any task that involves speaking can be affected by stuttering, and together, these aspects of the experience of stuttering can lead to a significant negative effect on a speaker's overall quality of life.

Stuttering has been studied for millennia, but no cure has yet been identified (Bloodstein 1993). Many approaches to assessment and treatment have been presented and debated over the years. Interestingly, recommended treatment approaches differ depending upon the age of the client (Bloodstein and Bernstein Ratner 2008). Of course, this is partly due to differences in linguistic, motor and cognitive abilities of individuals in different age groups. The chances of recovery from stuttering also diminish significantly as a person ages (Andrews and Harris 1964; Yairi and Ambrose 1999). In young children close to the onset of stuttering, the chances of a complete recovery, even without treatment, are quite good, so treatment for younger children is typically focused on eliminating stuttering entirely. For older children, adolescents or adults, the chances of a complete recovery diminish dramatically, so most treatments for these age groups focus on modifying speech to reduce the amount of stuttering and minimizing the impact of stuttering on the speaker's life as a whole (e.g. Starkweather and Givens-Ackerman 1997; Guitar 2006; Manning 2010; Shapiro 2011).

Regardless of the age of the client, differences of opinion regarding appropriate assessment and treatment procedures abound. At times, strident disagreements have developed between groups of practitioners favouring one approach or another (Gregory 1979; Bloodstein 1993). Because of the wide range of opinions and positions about stuttering treatment that have been offered over the years, no single chapter can provide a complete review. Instead, an attempt will be made in this chapter to address certain key trends in stuttering treatment across age groups.

Finally, stuttering is not the only disorder that can affect speech fluency. The fluency disorder addressed throughout the majority of this chapter is often called 'developmental stuttering' (or, more recently, 'persistent developmental stuttering') to differentiate it from other, less common fluency disorders that are also associated with disruptions in the forward flow of speech. These other conditions, specifically cluttering, 'neurogenic' stuttering and 'psychogenic' stuttering, will be briefly reviewed at the end of this chapter.

26.2   Assessment and intervention for very young children who stutter

Stuttering tends to arise between the ages of 2.5 and 4 years, though later onset is sometimes reported (Yairi *et al.* 1993). This age represents a period of rapid expansion in children's language development, as they learn to express more complicated concepts in more complicated ways using more complicated vocabulary. This is also a period of rapid growth in children's motor skills, as they develop better coordination of the fine movements necessary for producing speech. One apparent consequence of the rapid expansion of these abilities is the fact that many young children exhibit an increased frequency of disfluencies in their speech as they are learning to integrate their newly developing speech and language skills (Yairi and Ambrose 1992a, 1992b; Ambrose and Yairi 1999). This complicates the assessment process for speech-language pathologists, for one of the first tasks a clinician must perform when presented with a young child who may be stuttering is determining whether the child is exhibiting disfluencies that may be indicative of a developing stuttering disorder (Yaruss *et al.* 1998).

A sizeable literature has developed on the procedures that can be used for evaluating observable speech disfluencies (see review in Yaruss 1997b). Such measures have not been without controversy, some of which is related to concerns about the reliability of disfluency frequency counts (e.g. Cordes 1994), and some of which is related to differences of opinion about what should be measured (e.g. Cordes and Ingham 1995; Einarsdottir and Ingham 2005). Still, speech-language pathologists routinely complete measures of children's speech fluency in order to make a determination of whether a child is stuttering and, if so, how much. Clinicians typically accomplish this goal by observing a child's speech and tallying the number of words or syllables the child produces fluently and disfluently, and assessing whether disfluencies appear to be 'normal' or 'stuttered' (Yaruss 1997b, 1998c; Conture 2001). The more a child is exhibiting stuttered types of disfluencies, the more confident the clinician can be in the diagnosis that the child is indeed stuttering. Other measures, such as the duration of disfluencies (e.g. Zebrowski 1991) and the presence of secondary characteristics, can also help to support this determination. Because of the variability of stuttering, such measures should be made across a variety of different speaking situations, both within the clinical setting and in real-world settings (Costello and Ingham 1984; Yaruss 1997a). Resulting disfluency counts can be used as part of a broader severity measure, such as the Stuttering Severity Instrument (Riley 2009). Clinicians can also use a measure such as the Test of Childhood Stuttering (Gillam *et al.* 2009), to provide an indication of how a child's stuttering behaviours compare with those of other children.

The assessment of young children who stutter is complicated by the fact that the majority of young children who start to stutter also recover (Yairi and Ambrose 1999). Although the exact recovery figure is not entirely clear, it has been estimated that at least 75 per cent of children who begin to stutter ultimately make a complete recovery (Yairi and Ambrose 1999; Reilly *et al.* 2009). Thus, even after a clinician has made the determination that a child is stuttering, an additional determination then needs to be made of whether the child is likely to continue to stutter. Unfortunately, there is no single factor that differentiates which children are at greatest risk for continuing to stutter, though there has been a concerted research effort to identify factors that contribute to the likelihood that a child will continue to stutter (e.g. Paden and Yairi 1996; Yairi *et al.* 1996; Ambrose *et al.* 1997; Watkins and Yairi 1997; Yaruss *et al.* 1998; Watkins *et al.* 1999; Reilly *et al.* 2009). This research provides important guidance for clinicians seeking to determine whether a young child is at risk for continuing to stutter.

For example, research has documented the fact that stuttering runs in families and that there is a strong genetic basis for stuttering (see review in Kraft and Yairi (2012) and Chapter 19, this volume). Determining whether a child has a family history of stuttering thus forms an important component of the evaluation process. Likewise, the longer a child stutters, the more likely he or she is to continue stuttering (Yairi and Ambrose 1999). Thus, clinicians should ascertain the time since onset of the child's stuttering. This is typically done through a parent interview, which also gives clinicians the opportunity to learn more about the child's speech behaviours at home and in other settings outside of the clinic. Also, because males are more likely to stutter than females (see review in Bloodstein and Bernstein Ratner (2008) and Chapter 19, this volume) and because females are more likely to recover in early childhood (Ambrose *et al.* 1997), the child's sex figures strongly within a determination of a child's risk for persistent stuttering.

Research has also uncovered certain aspects of a child's development that appear to be associated with the development of stuttering. Prominent examples in the literature include language development (e.g. Watkins and Yairi 1997; Watkins *et al.* 1999), motor development (e.g. Olander *et al.* 2010) and temperament (Anderson *et al.* 2003; Karrass *et al.* 2006; K.N. Johnson *et al.* 2010). These areas are also relevant because research has shown that many preschool children exhibit concomitant disorders of language formulation or speech production (see review in Yaruss *et al.* 1998). Thus, the evaluation should consider the child's development in these areas as well. Finally, although not directly linked through research to the risk for continued stuttering, there has also been research on the child's awareness or concern about his or her speaking difficulties that may factor into a clinician's recommendations for treatment (Ezrati-Vinacour *et al.* 2001; Vanryckeghem and Brutten 2007; Langevin *et al.* 2010). Taken together, results of this research suggest that the evaluation of a young child who stutters should examine the child's stuttering history and overall development so clinicians will have the greatest chance of determining the risk for continued stuttering and need for treatment.

Once all data from an evaluation have been collected, clinicians need to make a recommendation about whether a child should receive treatment. Those children who appear to be at greater risk for chronic stuttering should receive treatment. Still, there has been a significant debate in the field about whether to recommend treatment for young children who may still recover from stuttering (e.g. Bernstein Ratner 1997b; Curlee and Yairi 1997; Zebrowski 1997). Some clinicians recommend early treatment, with the goal of minimizing the likelihood of continued stuttering while diminishing the child's (and family's) concerns about speaking. Citing high natural recovery rates, other clinicians suggest that it is better to wait some fixed period of time to see if a child recovers before initiating treatment. There is no best answer to the question of when to recommend therapy for young children who stutter. In practice, many clinicians seek to combine their assessment of a child's risk for continued stuttering with their understanding of the child's and family's concerns about stuttering in making their recommendations (Yaruss *et al.* 1998; Hill 2003; Millard *et al.* 2008; Gottwald 2010; Langevin *et al.* 2010).

Whenever treatment is recommended, the first step in the process is to consider the ultimate goals of that treatment. For very young children who stutter, there is general agreement across practitioners about what those goals should be. Specifically, treatment for preschool children who stutter is typically aimed at eliminating the stuttering behaviours, preventing the development of persistent stuttering, and helping the child develop normal speech fluency (Guitar and McCauley 2010). Research on various treatment approaches suggests very high success rates for achieving these goals (Jones *et al.* 2005; Yaruss *et al.* 2006; Millard *et al.* 2008). However, as with many topics in the field of fluency disorders, there is disagreement between practitioners about the best way to achieve these goals (Onslow and Yaruss 2007; Onslow and Millard 2012). In general, there appear to be three methods for working with young children who stutter that have been evaluated through varying degrees of empirical research. These can be described as indirect treatments, direct treatments and operant treatments (Guitar and McCauley 2010).

Indirect treatments are aimed at minimizing communication stressors in the environment that may contribute to a child's difficulty maintaining fluent speech (Starkweather *et al.* 1990; Melnick and Conture 1999; Hill 2003; Yaruss *et al.* 2006; Richards and Conture 2007; Millard *et al.* 2008; Botterill and Kelman 2010; Gottwald 2010). For many years, indirect treatment was the most commonly recommended form of treatment for young children who stutter (Starkweather *et al.* 1990; Conture 2001). The reasons for this can presumably be traced to some clinicians' reluctance to talk openly with young children about their speaking difficulties for fear that drawing attention to stuttering might cause the child to feel self-conscious about speaking. Pure indirect treatments involve no specific recommendations or suggestions for children to make any changes in their speech. The primary mechanism for achieving improved fluency is modelling of a modified speaking style by the clinician, parents and others in the environment. One common modification is slowed speech, sometimes called 'turtle speech', though a variety of other strategies for reducing the overall pace of conversation have also been employed (Starkweather *et al.* 1990; Meyers and Woodford 1992; Conture 2001). Such treatment helps to reduce time pressures that may make it harder for children to speak fluently, while providing a model that children can utilize in their own speech to enhance fluency. Indirect treatment may also incorporate changes in the parents' language model (e.g. Richels and Conture 2010) and focus on parents' ability to manage demands in the environment that may contribute to the child's speaking difficulties (e.g. Yaruss *et al.* 2006; Botterill and Kelman 2010; Gottwald 2010; Richels and Conture 2010).

Some clinicians supplement these indirect treatments with more direct strategies aimed at helping children develop the ability to modify their own speech to enhance fluency (Walton and Wallace 1998; Hill 2003; Yaruss *et al.* 2006; Gottwald 2010). Such strategies, which are more commonly used with older clients, build upon the models provided through indirect treatment by specifically encouraging children to implement reductions in their own speaking rates, linguistic complexity or physical tension that may be exacerbating their stuttering. Direct treatment can also include other speech and stuttering modification strategies, such as increased pausing, easier stuttering, and desensitization exercises. The fact that even very young children may react negatively to stuttering (Ezrati-Vinacour *et al.* 2001; Langevin *et al.* 2010) suggests that there is value in helping children accept their stuttering in the context of a broader therapy approach aimed at helping them develop normal fluency. Therefore, some practitioners work specifically with young children to encourage the development of appropriate communication attitudes by talking openly about speaking and stuttering (Williams 1985; Logan and Yaruss 1999; Yaruss *et al.* 2006). The goal of these components of treatment is to provide a model of acceptance, so children will be less likely to develop the negative communication attitudes that are often found in school-age children, adolescents and adults who stutter.

The third primary approach follows the principles of operant conditioning to help parents learn to selectively reinforce a child's production of fluent speech while reducing production of speech disfluencies through encouragement and reminders. The most prominent example of an operant approach is the Lidcombe programme (Onslow *et al.* 1997, 2003; Harris *et al.* 2002; Harrison and Onslow 2010). The Lidcombe programme involves two stages. First, parents meet regularly with clinicians for train-ing about how to provide appropriate reinforcements and corrections, and they frequently provide these contingencies for their children at home and in other settings. This continues until the child is exhibiting stuttering levels below a set criterion, at which time treatment shifts so that parents continue to check in with clinicians and provide feedback to their children on a less frequent basis. Throughout treatment, parents provide regular ratings of their child's level of fluency, and measures of stuttering frequency are completed in the clinical setting. The Lidcombe programme is supported by a sizeable literature which demonstrates clearly that many children who stutter improve their speech fluency dra-matically through treatment and maintain these gains over time (Jones *et al.* 2005, 2008). In contrast, other treatments (including the indirect and direct treatments described above) have not been subjected to nearly the same level of empirical research (Bothe *et al.* 2006a).

Interestingly, although there have been notable disagreements between practitioners about the best way to treat young children who stutter, there also appear to be some similarities between approaches (Guitar and McCauley 2010). For example, all treatment approaches mentioned above rely heavily on the support of parents throughout the treatment process and, as noted above, all seek the same goals. Moreover, it appears that the outcomes of these various treatment approaches are quite positive and generally comparable (Franken *et al.* 2005), though more research on traditional indirect and direct treatments is clearly needed. For the present, it appears that clinicians have a number of seemingly effective options for helping preschool and young school-age children overcome early stuttering.

26.3   Assessment and intervention for older individuals who stutter

As speakers grow older, assessment and treatment procedures change. This is due, in part, to the reduction in the likelihood of recovery that occurs as stuttering continues, combined with a growing acceptance of the idea that some individuals may not be able to recover completely from stuttering, even with treatment (Cooper 1987). As a result, many clinicians broaden their goals of assessment and treatment to encompass the speaker's entire experience of the stuttering disorder. That said, there are a number of practitioners who assert that the development and main-tenance of normal speech fluency is possible, even in older children and adults, so 'normal' fluency should be the primary (or sole) focus of inter-vention (Webster 1980; Ryan and Ryan 1996). Thus, clinicians are again faced with controversy about what constitutes appropriate treatment for individuals who stutter.

Regardless of the specific goals that might ultimately be selected for treatment, the first step in the process is still assessment, and one of the key components of any comprehensive assessment of stuttering involves an evaluation of the speaker's observable speech disfluencies. Previously, this task was described in terms of determining whether a preschool child is exhibiting disfluencies indicative of stuttering. With older clients, there is generally little question that a speaker who reports a history of stuttering is indeed stuttering, particularly if the behaviour started in early childhood. Thus, the assessment of speech fluency for these age groups is not typically aimed at differential diagnosis, except as it might relate to differentiating stuttering from other types of fluency disorders.

Measurement of stuttering frequency, duration and severity is aimed at developing a greater understanding of the characteristics of the person's speech both with a view to planning treatment and establishing a baseline for later evaluation of treatment outcomes. As before, this can be done through observation and tallying of fluent and stuttered speech, as well as through various tests of speech fluency. And, as before, assessment should be conducted in a variety of speaking situations because of the inherent variability of the stuttering behaviour. That said, the task of determining the severity of observable stuttering in these age groups can be complicated by the fact that speakers are increasingly aware of, and often quite concerned about, their stuttering. It is not uncommon for speakers to learn that one way of minimizing the negative consequences associated with overt stuttering is to try to avoid moments of stuttering. Thus, some speakers may attempt to change words and select only words they think they can say fluently. Other speakers may engage in circumlocution to 'talk around' the perceived moment of stuttering. Some speakers avoid sounds or particular words, while others may avoid entire situations, like speaking in front of a group or on the telephone. Some individuals who stutter may get so adept at hiding their stuttering that the casual listener (or even a certified clinician) may not detect overt signs of stuttering in the person's speech. Such 'covert' stuttering can come at a very high cost to the speaker, for such extensive avoidance can dramatically limit what the person is able to say (Murphy *et al.* 2007a).

In order to describe adequately the experiences of school-age children, adolescents and adults, clinicians must consider more than just observable speech behaviours. Numerous measurement tools have been developed for assessing how stuttering can affect a person's life (Woolf 1967; Erickson 1969; Andrews and Cutler 1974; Brutten and Shoemaker 1974; Ornstein and Manning 1985; Wright and Ayre 2000; Riley *et al.* 2004; Brutten and Vanryckeghem 2006; Yaruss and Quesal 2006). These instruments can help clinicians understand factors such as how the speaker reacts to stuttering, including affective and cognitive reactions such as embarrassment, shame, anxiety or frustration (Murphy 1999); how stuttering varies across speaking situations (Brutten and Shoemaker 1974);

how much stuttering hinders the speaker's functional communication abilities (Yaruss and Quesal 2010); and how stuttering affects the speaker's quality of life (Craig *et al.* 2009). A complete assessment of stuttering takes these issues into account, not only because they provide a more complete description of what affects the individual who stutters on a day-to-day basis, but also because they help the clinician and client work together to establish specific, individualized goals for treatment.

Inherent in the statement that assessment should examine more than just the speaker's observable speech fluency is the assumption that treatment, too, will address more than just speech fluency. This assumption is not universally accepted, however, for there has been disagreement about how to help school-age children, adolescents and adults who stutter (Nippold 2011; Yaruss *et al.* 2012). Of course, there is general agreement that one of the key goals of therapy is to reduce the frequency or severity of the observable stuttering behaviours, and several approaches for accomplishing this goal have been proposed. These include changes in the person's speech production strategies and changes in the moments of stuttering themselves (see Bloodstein (1993), Guitar (2006), Bloodstein and Bernstein Ratner (2008) and Blomgren (2010) for reviews).

Strategies for enhancing speech fluency, often called 'fluency shaping' or 'speech modification' therapies, involve helping speakers make a variety of changes to their speech production method in order to reduce the likelihood that stuttering events will occur (e.g. Webster 1980; Howie *et al.* 1981; Ingham *et al.* 2001, 2012; O'Brian *et al.* 2010). Examples include reduced speaking rate (e.g. slow speech, prolonged speech, phrased speech, easy starts), reductions in physical tension (e.g. gentle voice onsets, light contact) and other techniques in which the speaker changes the typical method of speech production (e.g. modified phonation intervals). Sometimes, these treatments begin with exaggerated speech modifications which are then 'shaped' towards more natural-sounding speech patterns. Fluency can also be enhanced through operant procedures that involve praise for fluent speech as utterances of increasing length and complexity are produced (Ryan and Van Kirk Ryan 1995; Riley and Ingham 2000).

Strategies aimed at changing the moment of stuttering, often called 'stuttering modification' therapies, involve helping speakers learn to reduce the physical tension and struggle inherent in the act of stuttering itself (Sheehan 1970; Van Riper 1973; Breitenfeld and Lorenz 1989). The most common strategies include Van Riper's (1973) classic trio of preparatory set (to reduce physical tension prior to an anticipated moment of stuttering), pull-out (to reduce tension during a moment of stuttering) and cancellation (to reduce tension after a moment of stuttering has already occurred). Other strategies include helping speakers learn to stutter more easily, for example by allowing stuttering to occur and 'bouncing' through the disfluency or by using pseudostuttering (fake stuttering) to manage and reduce physical tension (e.g. Johnson 1956; Sheehan 1970). Participants in stuttering modification treatment also learn to confront their fears about stuttering directly through desensitization exercises which are aimed at minimizing their negative reactions to stuttering (Sheehan 1970; Breitenfeld and Lorenz 1989; Murphy *et al.* 2007b).

Although these two basic approaches have often been presented as being in opposition to one another, there has been a growing consensus among many clinicians that treatment must involve more that 'just' increasing speech fluency or 'just' changing moments of stuttering. Indeed, the majority of modern treatments for school-age children, adolescents and adults who stutter involve an integration of these historically competing approaches (e.g. Boberg and Kully 1984; Healey *et al.* 1995; Bennett 2006; Guitar 2006; Montgomery 2006; Kully *et al.* 2007; Blomgren 2010; Kroll and Scott-Sulsky 2010; Manning 2010; Yaruss *et al.* 2010; Shapiro 2011). The ultimate goal of treatment in these approaches is to ensure that speakers are able to communicate effectively and say what they want to say without being hindered by stuttering.

Research has clearly demonstrated the value of treatments for helping people improve their speech fluency (e.g. Andrews *et al.* 1980; Thomas and Howell 2001; Bothe *et al.* 2006b) and, to a lesser extent, modify moments of stuttering (Blomgren *et al.* 2005; Reitzes and Snyder 2006; Prins and Ingham 2009). However, challenges still remain. For example, any treatment that requires speakers to make changes in their speaking method must contend with the reduction in speech naturalness that typically accompanies the fluency-enhancing speech modification (e.g. Ingham and Onslow 1985; Martin and Haroldson 1992). Such reductions in naturalness can be minimized, however, and a sizeable literature has developed surrounding the issue of helping speakers maintain naturalness while producing more fluent speech. Another challenge is the high rates of relapse following treatment (e.g. Craig and Andrews 1985; Craig 2002). Again, many researchers and clinicians have considered ways to minimize the likelihood of relapse following successful stuttering treatment. In the end, it is clear that people who stutter can enhance their speech fluency by making modifications to their speaking style, and such modifications form the core of many approaches to therapy.

In addition to changing speech production, many treatments also incorporate methods which help speakers change their reactions to stuttering. This includes desensitization to moments of stuttering in stuttering modification approaches (Sheehan 1970; Van Riper 1973; Murphy *et al.* 2007b) and psychologically based treatments such as cognitive-behavioural therapy, acceptance and commitment therapy and mindfulness approaches (e.g. Menzies *et al.* 2009; Boyle 2011; Beilby and Byrnes 2012). Historically, psychological approaches have been used with people who stutter, generally with limited success (Bloodstein 1993; Bloodstein and Bernstein Ratner 2008). What appears to be different about more recent work in this area is a greater focus on helping people learn to manage the effects of stuttering (e.g. Plexico *et al.* 2009a, 2009b) and the integration of these approaches with more traditional treatments aimed at enhancing fluency or modifying moments of stuttering. Moreover, many proponents of these broader treatment paradigms do not necessarily suggest that people who stutter have a psychological problem, although some do (Iverach *et al.* 2009a, 2009b, 2010), and a lively debate has developed around this topic (Iverach *et al.* 2011; Manning and Beck 2011). Results from these combination therapies appear to be quite promising, although additional research is needed (Menzies *et al.* 2008; Beilby *et al.* 2012).

Alongside these traditional forms of therapy, other approaches are available, including medications, fluency enhancing devices, and self-help and support groups. Numerous medications have been examined (Brady 1991; Bothe *et al.* 2006a), with results indicating a reduction in frequency and severity of stuttering for some individuals but not for others (e.g. Maguire *et al.* 2004, 2010). None of the medications studied thus far have eliminated stuttering entirely, and there is presently no approved pharmacological treatment that can be prescribed to treat stuttering. Similarly, there have been many attempts to develop effective delayed auditory feedback and frequency altered feedback devices over the years (Andrews *et al.* 1982; Stuart *et al.* 2006, 2008; Antipova *et al.* 2008). Results indicate that many people who stutter do experience improvements in speech fluency with these devices. However, their long-term effectiveness is still being studied and there is also some controversy regarding their use (Ingham *et al.* 1997; Van Borsel *et al.* 2003a; Finn *et al.* 2005; Kalinowski *et al.* 2007; Lincoln and Walker 2007; Pollard *et al.* 2009; Lincoln *et al.* 2010; Saltuklaroglu *et al.* 2010). Finally, there has recently been increased consideration of the role that self-help and support groups may play in the lives of people who stutter, and it has become clear that many people find help through these organizations, either as an adjunct to or in lieu of traditional speech therapy (Yaruss *et al.* 2007). Again, more research is needed, but preliminary results suggest that self-help groups can help people improve their communication and their overall ability to cope with stuttering (Yaruss *et al.* 2002; Trichon and Tetnowski 2011).

26.4   Other fluency disorders

Although this chapter has focused on stuttering (or 'developmental' stuttering), there are other types of fluency disorders that can affect communication. Some of these disorders are also called stuttering, though they differ in terms of their cause, their manifestation and their treatment. Specifically, 'neurogenic' stuttering is associated with a known neurological trauma that at least partially explains its aetiology and onset. 'Psychogenic' stuttering is also associated with a known onset, though in this case the aetiology is psychological trauma. Cluttering is a disorder for which the key feature may not be speech disfluencies, but which still involves a disruption in the fluency and flow of speech (see Chapter 19, this volume).

Neurogenic stuttering (also called acquired stuttering, stuttering associated with acquired neurological disorders, and other labels indicating a neurological aetiology) is generally considered to be a rare condition. Still, case studies and clinical reviews have appeared in the literature for many years and surveys indicate that a significant proportion of clinicians in medical settings have seen neurogenic stuttering in their patients (De Nil *et al.* 2007; Theys *et al.* 2011). Onset typically follows a cerebrovascular accident or head injury, though there is no single locus that is consistently associated with the occurrence of stuttering behaviours (Market *et al.* 1990). Onset may also be associated with extrapyramidal disease, drug usage and other neurological events, and there may be subtypes of neurogenic stuttering (Van Borsel *et al.* 2003b). Neurogenic stuttering differs from developmental stuttering in its sudden onset, but other characteristics (e.g. disfluency types) may be similar or different depending upon the specific aetiology and the individual's reactions to the speaking difficulties.

Psychogenic stuttering also has a known time of onset, but it differs from neurogenic stuttering, in that there is no known organic cause. Like neurogenic stuttering, psychogenic stuttering is believed to be rare, although there have been numerous case reports in the literature (e.g. Deal 1982; Roth *et al.* 1989; Mahr and Leith 1992; Baumgartner 1999). Individuals with psychogenic stuttering have generally experienced some type of significant psychological event or trauma preceding the onset of disfluent speech, though there is no single type of event that has been consistently related to the development of stuttering-like behaviours.

Differential diagnosis between psychogenic stuttering, neurogenic stuttering and developmental stuttering can be complicated by the fact that the disorders can co-occur and by the fact that the surface behaviours may appear to be quite similar. Several authors have proposed factors that may differentiate these conditions (e.g. Canter 1971; Roth *et al.* 1989; Helm-Estabrooks 1993; Baumgartner 1999; Van Borsel and Taillieu 2001; Seery 2005; De Nil *et al.* 2007), and the distinctions may be subtle. Therefore, assessment must involve several components including a detailed case history that attempts to ascertain a speaker's premorbid abilities and potential events (neurological or psychological) that may have been associated with onset; careful testing of language, speech and cognitive abilities; and a thorough evaluation of the surface speech characteristics. Even if a differential diagnosis can be made, there is relatively little research to guide treatment planning. It appears that many approaches have been tried including treatment strategies typically used with developmental stuttering, as well as altered auditory feedback, medications and psychological counselling. Outcomes seem to be highly individual-ized, with success probably tied to the nature and extent of the trauma and the degree of recovery experienced in the underlying disorder. Given the relatively rarity of these disorders, more research is needed to provide clinicians with meaningful guidance about treatment strategies that may help people with acquired stuttering improve their communication.

Finally, cluttering is a communication disorder that has its onset in childhood like developmental stuttering. However, the characteristics of cluttering differ from developmental stuttering (Weiss 1964; Daly and Burnett 1999; St. Louis *et al.* 2004, 2007; Ward and Scaler Scott 2011). Some of the primary symptoms of cluttering include a speaking rate that is perceived to be faster than normal or irregular in its rhythm, atypical prosody, excessive coarticulation between sounds, poor organization of thought, frequent revisions or maze behaviour, and possible difficulties with pragmatic language and social skills. Disfluencies may occur, but they are not necessarily the primary symptom, and they are not necessar-ily of the 'stuttered' types described at the beginning of this chapter. The result is speech that may be unintelligible and hard for listeners to follow. Individuals who clutter may be unaware of their communication difficul-ties, and their self-monitoring abilities may be minimal.

Cluttering can also co-occur with stuttering, and this can complicate differential diagnosis. Therefore, assessment must involve a careful con-sideration of the characteristics of the client's speech output and com-munication as a whole. Clinicians cannot make a diagnosis of cluttering simply on the basis of 'fast speaking rate'. Moreover, many researchers view cluttering as an outward manifestation of an underlying language processing or planning disorder (e.g. Weiss 1964; Daly and Burnett 1999), so it is important to consider a client's language development in addition to speech production characteristics. Treatment of cluttering typically involves rate management strategies, although the focus cannot be solely placed on speaking rate. Increasing self-awareness and self-monitoring, supporting language development, enhancing social skills and improving prosody can also be helpful strategies for improving the overall fluency of speech and flow of communication. There are very few studies of treat-ment outcomes in cluttering. More research on appropriate assessment and treatment strategies is needed.

26.5   Conclusion

There is a wide range of options aimed at helping people who stutter to enhance their speech fluency and minimize the impact of their commu-nication difficulty on their lives. A large and growing literature points to very high success rates for young children close to the onset of stuttering. For those who continue to stutter into school-age years and beyond, there are still many options for treatment, and success is closely tied to the specific goals that are selected for treatment. Indeed, different people appear to benefit from different approaches, and many people benefit from a combination of approaches. In fact, recent research in fluency disorders has started to examine not just differences between approaches, but also similarities across treatments (Plexico *et al.* 2010). Such research, which is based on the 'common factors' model prevalent in psychology (Wampold 2001), indicates that the specific strategies used in treatment may not be as important for determining overall outcomes as factors such as the therapeutic alliance that develops between the client and clinician. This finding helps to explain the wide range of seemingly successful options described in the literature and offers hope for individuals who stutter. Indeed, as research findings continue to accumulate, there is reason for optimism that future efforts will continue to uncover new ways to help people who stutter overcome the burden of their disorder so they can improve their communication and their lives as a whole.

Part V

Theoretical developments in communication disorders

27

Motor speech disorders and models of speech production

Karen Croot

27.1 Introduction

Fluent speech production by neurologically intact adult speakers is a highly skilled motor ability in the service of human communication. Thus, 'in one breath, most people are able to realise a sequence of 20 syllables or 40 phoneme targets … an extraordinary rapid fire sequence of action' compared to limb movements (Grimme *et al.* 2011: 14). Yet, despite the speed of speech movements, the spatial precision of articulatory placement is within one millimetre and the temporal precision in coordinating two articulators is within 10 milliseconds (Kent and Moll 1975; Gay *et al.* 1981). A range of models and theories are available that structure current knowledge about normal speech motor control, provide a basis for practical application of that knowledge, and guide further research in the field (Schmidt 2003).

Models of speech motor control can also help us understand, research, assess and deliver interventions for the various types of motor speech disorder that impair the planning and execution of movements of the lungs, larynx and supralaryngeal vocal tract (velum, tongue, lips, jaw) during speech communication. A number of motor speech disorders will be considered in this chapter. Apraxia of speech is a disorder of motor planning in which the speaker's ability to translate phonological representations into an articulatory plan is disrupted (McNeil *et al.* 2009). Dysarthria impairs neuromuscular control over the respiratory, laryngeal and supralaryngeal movements of speech (Duffy 2005; Ackermann *et al.* 2010; Miller 2012). Stuttering is characterized by repeated, prolonged or delayed speech movements (Max 2004). Chapters elsewhere in this volume describe the presentation and management of these disorders. This chapter instead discusses a selection of models of speech motor control that have emerged from the study of normal speech production and/or motor speech disorders. These models have contributed to our understanding of motor speech disorders or have the potential to do so.

A scientific model is a representation (a diagram, a verbal description, a computer program, etc.) of an empirical phenomenon that captures the fundamental characteristics of that phenomenon. Building and testing models is a means of developing our understanding of the phenomenon. A model simplifies and substitutes for the phenomenon (Pease and Bull 1992). Developing a model thus involves selecting the aspects of the phenomenon that are important, specifying the relationships between them and representing these aspects and their interrelationships as clearly as possible. Evaluating a model involves testing whether the model is a good fit to the real world – whether the empirical data (information collected from observations and experiments) support the structure and organization of the phenomenon as proposed by the model. In general, scientific theories are broader than models, but they too are analytical tools: they organize knowledge and make predictions, and their predictions can be tested against data. Past models and theories that are no longer supported are also useful in showing which aspects of a phenomenon have previously been considered important and how these have or have not been supported by data (Kuhn 1996).

The models and theories of speech production discussed here capture diverse aspects of speech motor control, modelling speech motor control at cognitive, neuroanatomical, physiological and mathematical levels of description. The chapter will describe the ongoing influence of the clinico-anatomical model of motor speech disorders developed by Darley and colleagues at the Mayo Clinic, the dynamic systems and psycholinguistic approaches to speech motor control, and the growing importance of approaches that rely on adaptive internal models. It will discuss the production of prosody and the basis of motor learning theory and its application to motor speech disorders. The models presented here are intended to provide an illustrative rather than an exhaustive survey, but the references provided will allow readers to gain a deeper understanding of topics of interest.

27.2   The Mayo Clinic view

Darley, Aronson and Brown (1969a, 1969b, 1975) proposed a clinico-anatomical account of dysarthria, according to which perceptually distinct subtypes of dysarthria (defined by clusters of auditory-perceptual features) were linked to different lesions of the brain and cranial nerves. The subtypes (with hypothesized lesion site) they proposed were flaccid dysarthria (associated with damage to the lower motor neurons, i.e. one or more of the cranial nerves), spastic dysarthria (upper motor neurons), spastic-flaccid dysarthria (upper and lower motor neurons), ataxic dysarthria (cerebellum or its efferent pathways), hypokinetic dysarthria (basal ganglia, especially substantia nigra) and hyperkinetic dysarthria (basal ganglia especially putamen or caudate) (Kent *et al.* 2000). Dysarthria was defined as a disorder of 'muscular control over the speech mechanism due to damage to the central or peripheral nervous system' (Darley *et al.* 1969a: 246) with the language aspects of speech production unimpaired. Later clinical subtypes were added to those proposed by Darley and colleagues, including dysarthria associated with spasmodic dystonia, tremor and unilateral upper motor neuron lesion (Duffy 2005; Miller 2012).

Around the time that the clinical work developing these dysarthria subtypes was in progress, Darley (1967), cited in McNeil *et al.* (2009), also reported a motor speech disorder that was qualitatively different to the dysarthrias. Muscular innervation did not appear to be deficient, thus it was not a dysarthria, but language processing was also preserved, thus it was not an aphasia. Darley named this new disorder 'apraxia of speech' in analogy to the limb apraxias, disorders of purposeful movement reported by Liepmann and others in the late nineteenth century (Goldenberg 2003). In this new speech disorder, it was the planning of voluntary speech movements that was assumed to be impaired, not the linguistic formulation of utterances, nor the execution of articulatory movements per se.

Although Weismer (2006: 317) suggests that there is only 'a rough sense of theory … implied by the link between classical signs of neurological disease and the speech production problems in dysarthria', the Mayo Clinic view of the dysarthrias and apraxia of speech is a model in the sense that it provides guidelines on what to assess, what to diagnose and, to a lesser extent, how to intervene (Duffy and Kent 2001; Duffy 2005). This view still dominates research and clinical practice in dysarthria (Duffy 2005; Weismer 2006; Ackermann *et al.* 2010; Lowit Chapter 22, this volume). There is controversy, however, as to whether the perceptual clusters *can* be reliably distinguished in clinical practice, thus whether the subtypes can be reliably diagnosed (Miller 2012). There are also questions about whether the perceptually identified subtypes are in fact associated with the lesion sites predicted by Darley *et al.* (Duffy and Kent 2001; Weismer 2006). The relationship between the clusters of auditory-perceptual disruptions and their anatomical substrates has proven to be more complex than initially proposed (Netsell 1986), and the neuroanatomical basis for speech motor planning and execution (and, thus, for apraxic and dysarthric disorders, respectively) has been revised and elaborated (e.g. see section 27.6 below). Duffy and Kent (2001) provide further reflection on the substantial contributions of Darley and his colleagues to speech science, and to clinical practice in speech-language pathology.

27.3 Early cognitive models and cognitive neuropsychology

In effect, Darley, Aronson and Brown, and the colleagues they trained at the Mayo Clinic, gave us not one, but two influential models of speech motor control. The first was the clinico-anatomical account described

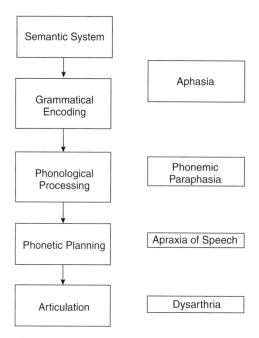

Figure 27.1 Box-and-arrow diagram of the language production system (left), showing the disorders corresponding to impairment in the various processing components (right). (Reprinted from Code (1998) in *Clinical Linguistics & Phonetics* by Taylor & Francis Ltd. Reproduced with permission of Taylor & Francis Ltd.)

above. The second was a broad tripartite division of the cognitive processes relevant to spoken language production, with each division associated with a specific type of disorder. Breakdown in linguistic processing was classed as aphasia, breakdown in planning of speech movements as apraxia of speech, and breakdown in movement execution due to neuromuscular impairment as dysarthria (see Figure 27.1). These divisions are alive and well today in psycholinguistic approaches to language production, and in all clinical approaches to disorders of speech production that distinguish aphasia, apraxia of speech and dysarthria as different classes of disorders (e.g. Jordan and Hillis 2006).

Aphasia is an acquired disorder of language processing, and phonemic paraphasias involve hypothesized disruption to the retrieval or assembly of the phonological representation of the word. A useful distinction between the planning and execution of articulatory movements is that planning comprises 'all processes of movement preparation that take place before a movement is initiated' (Grimme *et al.* 2011: 6). The term 'programming' (or 'motor programming') is used to describe the same stage of processing by many authors (e.g. Schmidt 2003), and further terms for processes corresponding to articulatory planning include 'phonetic planning' (e.g. Figure 27.1) and 'phonetic encoding' (section 27.5 below). Articulation (or motor execution, articulatory implementation) refers to the final stage when the speech movements have been initiated and the articulatory plan or programme is being executed.

The model in Figure 27.1 is an example of an information-processing or representational model, typical of the information-processing framework that arose with the development of cognitive science from the late 1950s. In cognitive science, the mind is conceived as a symbol-processing system in analogy to the computer. It is capable of representing things in the world and of acquiring, storing and manipulating information (information-processing) (Green 1996; Pinker 1999). Cognitive theories specify the nature of the representations (forms in which information is processed), and the processes (operations or algorithms) carried out on the representations to transform inputs, retrieve relevant symbolic knowledge and generate outputs (Marr 1982). Theories and models have often been written down in a format known as a 'box-and-arrow diagram', showing the types of representations being manipulated and/or the sequence of processes that manipulate representations. The series of boxes and arrows on the left in Figure 27.1 is a box-and-arrow diagram of speech production, in which the boxes show a sequence of cognitive processes (grammatical encoding, phonological processing, phonetic planning and articulation) hypothesized to occur after the semantic system generates a meaning or message to be communicated. The boxes standing alone on the right are not part of the box-and-arrow model, but show the clinical syndromes presumed to arise from impairments in the corresponding cognitive processing components of the model.

One sub-discipline of cognitive science that is particularly well suited to the parallel consideration of normal cognitive processing and its disorders, as exemplified in Figure 27.1, is cognitive neuropsychology. Cognitive neuropsychology has two complementary aims: to consider how data from people with acquired brain damage can inform theories of normal cognitive processing, and to use theories of normal cognitive processing to characterize patterns of cognitive impairment. In the early days of cognitive neuropsychology in the 1970s and 1980s, theory development involved the making of box-and-arrow diagrams that were built up incrementally by observing patterns of double dissociations between two or more people with highly selective cognitive impairments. A double dissociation is demonstrated when one person (or more) shows an impairment on task X and unimpaired performance on task Y, while another person (or more) shows the reverse pattern (impairment on Y with preserved performance on X). A double dissociation implies that the cognitive processes involved in tasks X and Y are not identical, and that there must be a processing component in X but not Y that is impaired in the first case, and a separate processing component in Y but not X that is impaired in the second case (Coltheart 2001). Although Darley *et al.* did not set out to analyse the symptoms of apraxia of speech and dysarthria in this way, the distinction between apraxic and dysarthric speech disorders – impaired planning and intact muscle innervation versus intact planning and impaired muscle innervation, respectively – implies that there are separate processing components of articulatory planning and articulation proper (motor execution) in the speech production architecture. This is shown by the representation of these processes in separate boxes in Figure 27.1.

Early cognitive neuropsychology and other information-processing models assumed transparency between impairment or disruption of a function and the mechanism or processing component responsible for it. For example, Fromkin (1973) claimed that if a particular type of unit can be involved in a speech error, then that unit must be one of the types of representation processed during speech production. In this way, because unimpaired speakers and people with aphasia make errors that can be analysed in terms of disruption to a sequence of phonemes (e.g. saying 'real feely bad' instead of the intended 'feel really bad' exchanges the word-initial phonemes /f/ and /r/), phonemes were assumed to be important units of processing in spoken word production. Incorporating phonemes as units of production raised the problem, however, of how these discrete, invariant units of linguistic processing were transformed to produce the continuous, variable acoustic speech signal (Saltzman and Munhall 1989). Dynamical systems theory provided a way forward in regard to this problem.

27.4   Dynamical systems theory

While information-processing accounts of cognitive processes focus on the manipulation of symbolic information, an alternative framework called dynamical systems theory eschews symbolic processing (Neilson and Neilson 2005). In dynamical systems theory, human movement control has its basis in the self-organizing properties of perception-action networks proposed within ecological psychology and direct realism, as pioneered by Gibson (1986) and applied to speech by Fowler and others (e.g. Fowler 1986). Movement control is seen as emerging spontaneously in response to the environment without the need for the stored movement plans and motor commands posited by representational models (Van Lieshout 2004). The state of a dynamic system at a particular time depends on previous states of the system, allowing complex behaviours such as radical changes between stable states (attractors) to be captured by what Rosenbaum (2010: 400) describes as 'deceptively simple' equations.

An important construct in these models is the task-dependent synergy or coordinative structure, in which an ensemble of muscles and joints functions together as a single unit to achieve a task-specific goal (Van Lieshout 2004). This reduces the degrees of freedom problem, that is, that there are approximately 700 functional muscles involved in speech production, yet people do not have the cognitive resources to control each one separately (Neilson and Neilson 2005). In synergies, groups of muscles related to task-specific goals are controlled together. Other key concepts are the control parameters which transition the system from one stable state to another, the order parameters (also called 'collective variables') which both capture and limit key behaviours of the system at particular values of one or more of the control parameters, and the self-organizing coupling dynamics of the system which govern the coordination between articulators under functional constraints (for further discussion, see Van Lieshout 2004).

An influential model to emerge from the dynamical systems theory approach was the task dynamic model of Saltzman and Munhall (1989). In this model, the invariant linguistic units that are the inputs to the model are gestural (action-based) units, rather than phonemes. These units are arranged in a gestural score that specifies the onset and offset of each gesture produced by each of the speech articulators over time (see (a) in Figure 27.2), analogous to a musical score that indicates on different staves which notes a number of different instruments should play and when. The gestural scores are mapped to a three-layer dynamical system comprising intergestural and interarticulator levels (see (b) in Figure 27.2). At the intergestural level, activation coordinates determine the degree to which individual gestures shape the vocal tract over time. At the two interarticulator levels, tract variable coordinates specify context-independent location and degree of constriction for a set of articulators (glottis, velum, tongue dorsum, tongue tip, lips), and model articulator coordinates specify the context-dependent activity of the articulators in an articulatory synthesizer. Critically, 'the spatiotemporal patterns of speech emerge as behaviours implicit in a dynamical system' (Saltzman and Munhall 1989: 335).

Dynamical systems theory has been applied less to speech production than have other theoretical frameworks (Van Lieshout 2004). However, gestural scores and articulatory coupling mechanisms of the type described in the task dynamic model have generated some theoretical and empirical interest in relation to motor speech disorders (Kent 1997). For example, Pouplier and Hardcastle (2005) noted that kinematic studies of people with dysarthria, apraxia of speech and aphasia have shown that people with these disorders produce intrusion errors (additional gestures) consistent with an erroneous entrainment of two articulators in a dynamically stable 1:1 in-phase coupling mode. Kent and Rosen (2004) review evidence that tremor in a range of motor speech disorders can be used to entrain phasic voluntary movement. Ziegler (2011) found evidence for strong synchronization between gestures even in speakers with apraxia of speech, as would be predicted if the gestures were produced as a task-dependent synergy. Tjaden (1999) demonstrated that scanning speech in some individuals with apraxia of speech or dysarthria could be attributed to reduced temporal overlap of gestures.

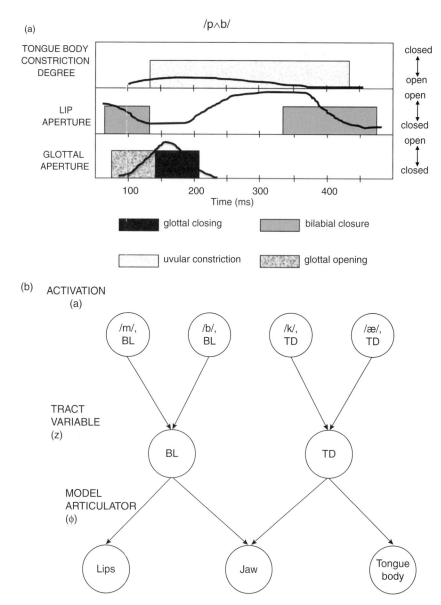

Figure 27.2 (a) Gestural score used to synthesize the syllable 'pub', showing gestures for the tongue body, lips and glottis over time. Filled boxes indicate intervals of gestural activation, box heights show either 0 (no activation where there is no box) or 1 (full activation where there is a box). The waveform lines show tract-variable trajectories generated during the simulation. (b) An example of a connectivity pattern between coordinates at the three levels of the model (BL, bilabial constriction; TD, tongue dorsum constriction). (Reprinted from Saltzman and Munhall (1989) in *Ecological Psychology* by Taylor & Francis Ltd. Reproduced with permission of Taylor & Francis Ltd.)

27.5 Psycholinguistic models of articulatory planning

At the same time as direct realist and dynamical systems theory accounts of speech motor control were being developed, there was extensive investigation of processes occurring earlier in speech production within the disciplines of psycholinguistics and cognitive psychology (Dell 1986; Levelt 1999; Rapp and Goldrick 2006). Among these processes, lexical retrieval is the activation of representations of words in the mental lexicon, and phonological encoding is the retrieval of the sounds of words from memory and their assembly for production. For a long period, however, models of the earlier processes did not consider in any detail how phonological encoding was connected to the generation of neuromuscular activity producing the acoustic speech signal (Miller 2002; Ziegler 2003; Smith 2006). Conversely, models of speech motor control had almost nothing to say about prior lexical and phonological encoding processes, or they simply assumed an adequately specified phonological representation as the input to the model (e.g. Guenther *et al.* 2006). Miller (2002) therefore described 'a major divide over what counts as a speech production model. Some deal with supposed processes in lexical and phonological retrieval but leave motor speech control to happen in some *terra incognita* off the bottom of the page. Others tackle motor control but can be equally non-specific about what and how input arrives into their scheme from off the top of the page' (Miller 2002: 224).

This state of affairs was particularly problematic for the diagnosis, investigation and rehabilitation of apraxia of speech, which affects speech production at precisely the phonological-articulatory interface (Ziegler 2002). It was also becoming necessary to explain the reciprocal effects seen when precise details of speech articulation are influenced by linguistic variables (Fougeron and Keating 1997) and the characteristics of the motor system influence linguistic processing (Smith 2006).

Levelt and colleagues (most significantly Levelt 1989 and Levelt *et al.* 1999) proposed an influential model of speech production that incorporated gestural scores retrieved subsequent to phonological encoding (see Figure 27.3). Empirical support for this move came from speech errors (Crompton 1982), and the fact that the syllable is the primary domain of coarticulation, or overlap, between the movements of the different speech articulators (larynx, velum, tongue and lips) (Lindblom 1983). According to Levelt *et al.* (1999), during the process of phonological encoding, a speaker retrieves the phonological representations of words represented in the mental lexicon (word form retrieval in Figure 27.3), and assigns the phonological segments to locations in a metrical frame for phonological words (segment-to-frame association) that specifies number of syllables, and which syllables receive lexical stress. Next, in a process corresponding to phonetic planning in Figure 27.1, speakers retrieve gestural scores from a syllabary, a library of stored gestural scores for syllables. Levelt and

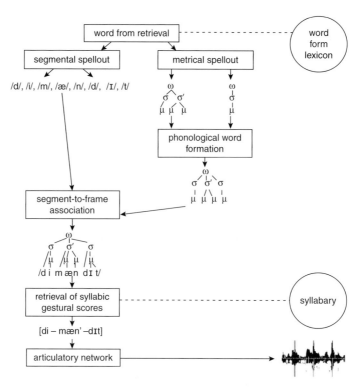

Figure 27.3 Model of phonological encoding and articulatory planning showing the retrieval of gestural syllabic scores from the syllabary. (Reprinted from *Cognition*, 50, Levelt, W.J.M. & Wheeldon, L., 'Do speakers have access to a mental syllabary?', 239–69, Copyright (1994), with permission from Elsevier.)

colleagues suggested that because speakers of languages such as English and Dutch do 80 per cent of their talking with approximately 6 per cent of their language's syllables (Levelt *et al.* 1999), it would be of computational advantage to store only high-frequency syllable plans in the syllabary, computing the others online as required.

Varley and Whiteside (2001) described this as a 'dual route' model of speech planning, because speakers may either retrieve gestural scores from the syllabary (high-frequency syllables), or compile them online when preparing to speak (low-frequency syllables). They proposed that in apraxia of speech, speakers have lost access to the syllabary, and thus to gestural scores for high-frequency syllables, and must compile all required gestural scores online. Varley and Whiteside suggested that this account can explain the key features of apraxic speech. The slow speech rate in apraxia of speech is attributed to the fact that syllable assembly in real-time results in longer syllable durations, and the reduced coarticulation to the fact that people with apraxia of speech lose the benefit of storing plans for highly practised units as pre-compiled wholes. Further, there is some indication that people with apraxia of speech show no difference in response times to high- versus low-frequency syllables, whereas high-frequency syllables are produced faster by unimpaired speakers (Cholin 2008).

The hypothesized dissolution of the pre-assembled gestural scores also allowed a unitary account of the range, and the within- and between-speaker variability, of apraxic speech symptoms (see Robin and Flagmeier Chapter 12, this volume), since the noisy, online compilations could differ from the pre-compiled syllables in a variety of ways. This hypothesis was also consistent with the non-linear dynamics of speech as proposed by the task dynamic model, rather than requiring different mechanisms to account for different impairments (e.g. a timing disruption to account for prolongations, impaired combination of segmental movement plans to explain reduced coarticulation, etc.). However, although the proposal generated considerable discussion, and highlighted the value of considering apraxia of speech within a framework proposed for normal speech production, the empirical evidence in support of it (Whiteside and Varley 1998) was weak. Further, while there is positive evidence for syllable-sized, stored phonetic plans in normal speakers in a number of languages (Cholin 2008), evidence that these are important for unimpaired English speakers is somewhat equivocal (Croot and Rastle 2004; Cholin 2008).

A logical alternative to the hypothesis that articulatory planning involves syllable-sized units only is that it embraces syllable-sized units together with units both larger and smaller than the syllable (Croot and Rastle 2004; Varley *et al.* 2006; Cholin 2008). Investigations of apraxia of speech especially by Ziegler, Aichert, Staiger and colleagues suggest a role for sub-syllabic, syllabic *and* supra-syllabic units in phonetic encoding, as all of these units influence speech production accuracy and therapy efficacy in apraxia of speech (Aichert and Ziegler 2004, 2008; Brendel and Ziegler 2008; Staiger and Ziegler 2008). A mathematical model based on a number of the hierarchically organized linguistic units that comprise words (including foot structure, word stress, syllable composition, types of segment, and articulatory gestures) provided a better fit to error data from 20+ people with apraxia of speech than did models fitting syllables or segments alone (Ziegler 2005, 2009).

Smith and Goffman (2004) similarly proposed that 'the signals that drive muscle activity in speech are integrated over multiple levels of units simultaneously' and that 'adults may have stored speech motor commands for phrases, words, and syllables' (Smith 2006: 338). A range of experimental results from the Laboratory Phonology community also supports a role for probabilistic relationships between phonological and phonetic representations at different grain sizes (Croot 2010; Cohn *et al.* 2011). Thus, closer examination of articulatory planning suggests there is likely to be a many-to-many mapping between linguistic and motor control units. The models discussed here pertain to speech production in English or in Indo-European languages (especially German and Dutch), however, and the nuances of mapping from linguistic to motor control units in other languages are less well understood (O'Seaghdha *et al.* 2010).

27.6   Adaptive internal models

The class of theories of speech motor control that are currently most influential (Kent 2000; Weismer 2006; Grimme *et al.* 2011) utilize cognitive structures called adaptive internal models. Such theories are derived from the neuroscience of motor control (Max *et al.* 2004). They are implemented in part or in whole by using computational neural networks to simulate the multiple inputs and outputs in movement control and the non-linear dynamic relationships between them. The key assumption in these theories is that the central nervous system continuously monitors the efferent (outgoing) motor commands and their afferent (proprioceptive and sensory) consequences, and contains the computational apparatus required to model (or map) the inverse relationship between them (Neilson and Neilson 1987). People are able to 'compute from the desired sensory consequences the … commands necessary to achieve those consequences' (Max *et al.* 2004: 111). These learned internal models are stored in memory and adaptively maintained; in other words, they are updated as necessary when the efferent–afferent relationships change (Neilson and Neilson 1987).

One important factor contributing to the adoption of internal models in theories of movement control was 'the idea that sensory feedback could potentially establish an adaptive inverse model as the basis of a feedforward controller of movement' (Neilson and Neilson 2005: S279), seen, for example, in adaptation effects to changes in sensory input (Neilson and Neilson 1987). Another was the discovery that the cerebellum contained the requisite computational apparatus to develop adaptive models (Neilson and Neilson 2005). A third factor was the recognition that feedback control based on a forward model can occur much earlier than feedback can be provided by perception of afferent signals during the actual movement (Schmidt 2003; Grimme *et al.* 2011).

A major contribution of this theoretical approach is the integration of feedback and feedforward control (Max *et al.* 2004), and the resulting emphasis on movement control as *sensori*motor control. In feedforward (sometimes referred to as open loop) control, motor commands are prepared before the movement and executed without modification. In feedback (closed loop) control, motor commands may be continuously modified depending on feedback from an ongoing comparison of the intended and actual movement. Max *et al.* (2004) described a generic adaptive model of motor control (see Figure 27.4), the fundamental components of which can be found in the other adaptive models of speech sensorimotor control discussed below (Neilson and Neilson 2005; Guenther *et al.* 2006; Kroeger *et al.* 2011). This generic model will be briefly described below,

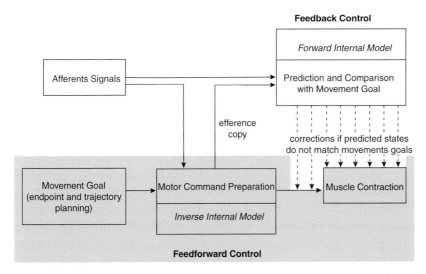

Figure 27.4 Schematic representation of a generic adaptive model of speech motor control. The model integrates a feedforward controller and a feedback controller that use inverse and forward internal models, respectively. (Republished with permission of American Speech-Language-Hearing Association, from Max, L., Guenther, F.H., Gracco, V.L., Ghosh, S.S. and Wallace, M.E. 'Unstable or insufficiently activated internal models and feedback-biased motor control as sources of dysfluency: a theoretical model of stuttering', *Contemporary Issues in Communication Science and Disorders* 31, 2004, permission conveyed through Copyright Clearance Center, Inc.)

but for a more detailed introduction to these types of models, the reader is referred to Max *et al.* (2004).

In the feedforward movement controller within this model (shaded grey in Figure 27.4), the movement goal determines the motor commands required to reach that goal on the basis of an inverse internal model of the movement. The inverse internal model works back (inversely) from the movement goal to compute the motor commands that would achieve the goal given the current state of the system. Thus, for example, an inverse kinematic transformation may be used to compute the required joint angles given a particular target position for a given movement effector (arm, leg, jaw, etc.), or an inverse dynamic transformation may be used to compute the required muscular forces (in the context of other forces acting on the effector) to compute the motor commands required to generate those forces (Max *et al.* 2004). The current state of the system is determined from the afferent signals received from proprioceptive and sensory mechanisms (e.g. joints, muscles, skin, visual and auditory systems). Thus, the inverse internal model allows the feedforward controller to prepare motor commands that can be sent via the motor neurons to the appropriate muscles.

In the feedback movement controller within Max *et al.*'s (2004) generic adaptive model (occupying the top half of Figure 27.4), a forward internal model specifies the relationships between motor commands and their sensory consequences, and allows a comparison between the anticipated consequences of a prepared motor command and the desired consequences. Thus, when the feedforward system has prepared a motor command, a copy of that command (called an efference copy or a corollary discharge) is sent to the feedback system, which uses the forward internal model component to predict the sensory consequences of the command, compares the predicted consequences with the goal, and adjusts the muscle contractions for the movement if there is a mismatch.

Although the basic principles of inverse and forward models as described above are relatively straightforward, the number of subsystems potentially involved in human motor control is large, and adaptive models rapidly become complex when they begin to include the multiple motor and sensory structures known to be involved in human movement. To give an example of this complexity, in Neilson and Neilson's (2005) adaptive model theory, the adaptive feedforward/feedback control system models forward and inverse relationships between various types of afferent feedback from a muscle control subsystem, a biomechanical subsystem and a subsystem consisting of the respiratory system, larynx and vocal tract. It also models the elemental movements and their co-contractions that are produced by the three aforementioned subsystems working in concert. The model proposes roles for Golgi tendon organs, muscle spindle endings, mechanoreceptors and other sensory organs (visual, auditory, labyrinthine, etc.) in mapping the consequences of motor commands, as well as in forming two types of synergies. One type of synergy specifies the particular efferent pathway to be used given the redundancy of the musculoskeletal system (the fact that there are an infinite number of muscle activations that could produce a particular movement). The other type is the task-dependent type of synergy that reduces the degrees of freedom of movement to be controlled.

Adaptive model theory was developed under the impetus to explain disordered limb movement control in cerebral palsy and disordered speech motor control in stuttering (Neilson and Neilson 2005). Neilson and Neilson (1987) suggested that stuttering could be explained by a reduced ability to form inverse auditory-motor models (computing the motor commands required to achieve auditory targets). The hypothesis was that people who stutter are more fluent during white noise masking because masking removes the need to monitor and update auditory-motor relationships. They are also hypothesized to be more fluent when they use slower and 'smoother' speech (involving rate control, gentle voicing onset and offset, soft articulatory contacts, appropriate and natural prosody – see Neilson (1999) for further details), because these characteristics of speech reduce the demands on the speech motor system as a whole.

Adaptive model theory, as described above, takes as the plant – the body part being controlled – 'the entire musculoskeletal system in interaction with its environment' (Neilson and Neilson 2005: S280). It thus has the important advantage of generality in proposing mechanisms that apply to all human movements. An additional consideration for theories specific to *speech* motor control, however, is that speech movement is also different from other types of human movement. For example, speech movements are intermediate in speed between limb and oculomotor movement (Netsell 1986), speech muscles fibres are different from limb and other muscle fibres in their contraction properties and fatigue resistance (Kent 2004), the same muscles of the articulatory tract contract differently in speech versus non-speech tasks (Smith 2006), and speech movements are subserved by dedicated neural structures that develop with exceptionally high levels of practice over a lifetime (Ziegler 2003). Questions about the extent to which certain principles are specific to speech motor control or overlap with those of other motor control systems have been controversial, especially with regard to selecting the appropriate materials and tasks to be used in the clinical management of motor speech disorders (Ziegler 2003; Weismer 2006). Grimme *et al.*'s (2011: 24) thoughtful integration of issues in limb versus speech motor control concludes that 'the best strategy has been to avoid simple ... dichotomies and instead uncover the underlying processes' in both domains.

An adaptive model specific to speech planning and execution that is gaining ascendancy as an account of unimpaired speech production is the DIVA (Directions Into Velocities of Articulators) neural network developed by Guenther and colleagues over the past two decades (Guenther *et al.* 2006; Tourville and Guenther 2011). This model specifies processing components involved in feedforward and feedback control of speech, and associates these with brain regions hypothesized to provide the neuroanatomical substrates of these components (see Figure 27.5). Further, the model is instantiated as a neural network that takes as input a string of speech sounds and produces as output a series of articulatory positions that control the movements of an articulatory synthesizer to produce an acoustic speech signal. Because the model is mathematically explicit, simulations of the model provide quantitative predictions about the performance of various components of the model under specific conditions. Model outputs (formant frequencies, articulatory positions, learning rates, predicted activity levels in various brain structures) can be compared with human data (Tourville and Guenther 2011).

The DIVA model is powerful and broad in application because it models speech sensorimotor control at three levels of description, and it indicates how these levels are related. First, the neural maps and their interrelationships as depicted in Figure 27.5 constitute an information-processing model of processing components and their connections, described in detail below. Second, brain regions associated with the neural maps (also indicated in Figure 27.5) provide a neuroanatomical model. Third, the algorithms instantiated in the neural network provide a mathematical model of the operations within and between components. For

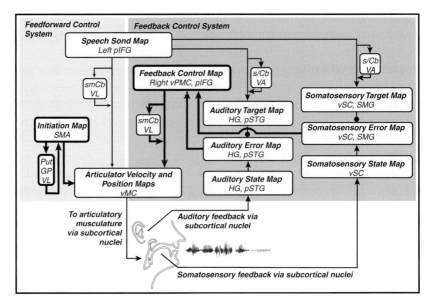

Figure 27.5 The DIVA model of speech acquisition and production. Model components are associated with hypothesized neuroanatomical substrates. GP, globus pallidus; HG, Heschl's gyrus; pIFg, posterior inferior frontal gyrus; pSTg, posterior superior temporal gyrus; Put, putamen; slCB, superior lateral cerebellum; smCB, superior medial cerebellum; SMA, supplementary motor area; SMG, supramarginal gyrus; VA, ventral anterior nucleus of the thalamus; VL, ventral lateral nucleus of the thalamus; vMC, ventral motor cortex; vPMC, ventral premotor cortex; vSC, ventral somatosensory cortex. (Reprinted from Tourville and Guenther 2011 in *Language and Cognitive Processes* by Taylor & Francis Ltd. Reproduced with permission of Taylor & Francis Ltd.)

more information about the neuroanatomy and algorithms for DIVA, see Tourville and Guenther (2011) and Guenther *et al.* (2006).

The processing components of the DIVA model will be described briefly here (for further information see Tourville and Guenther 2011). The large boxes in Figure 27.5 correspond to neural representations (maps), and the arrows correspond to transformations from one type of representation to another that are specified by weights in the network analogous to synapses between sets of neurons. The model initially learns to control the movements of the vocal tract (that is, to develop the articulator velocity and position maps for lips, jaw, tongue and larynx that determine the positions of the articulators in the articulatory synthesizer) during a simulated early babbling phase and an imitation learning phase. In the early babbling phase, the associations between motor commands producing random articulatory states and their auditory and somatosensory (proprioceptive and tactile) consequences (represented as the auditory state map and the somatosensory state map) are used to tune the weights between the auditory and somatosensory error maps and the feedback control map so that it issues corrective motor commands. These mappings, therefore, constitute inverse internal models.

During the imitation learning phase, the model receives speech sounds as input and forms a cell for each sound in the speech sound map. With repeated presentations of sounds, each cell becomes associated with a target region for the first three formants of the sound in the auditory target map and a multidimensional vector specifying the predicted proprioceptive and tactile feedback in the somatosensory target map. Once the auditory targets have been learned, initial attempts to produce those targets are imprecise. This generates large error signals, and places heavy demand on the feedback from the auditory and somatosensory error maps to the articulator velocity and position map that produces corrective motor commands. With practice, however, the model learns to reduce the error and comes to rely more on the feedforward system than the feedback system.

Feedforward control thus begins with the activation of a cell in the speech sound map, where cells represent motor programmes for frequently used phonemes, syllables, words and short phrases (somewhat similar to the representations in the syllabary proposed by Levelt and colleagues and discussed in section 27.5), although the units are of various sizes. Cells in the speech sound map activate cells in the articulator velocity and position maps that represent the feedforward motor commands to produce that sound, coding for the articulatory velocities of the lips, jaw, tongue and larynx that determine the positions of the articulators in the synthesizer. Each cell in the speech sound map is also associated with a cell in one final component of the model, the initiation map, that regulates the release of motor commands from the articulator velocity and position maps to the model's articulatory tract (synthesizer). This final step is under the control of processes described in the GODIVA (Gradient Order DIVA) model of phonological and phonetic encoding (Bohland *et al.* 2010), with further description beyond the scope of the current chapter.

Feedback control in the DIVA model involves two forward internal models that predict the sensory consequences of movements in the mappings between the speech sound map and the auditory target map, and the speech sound map and somatosensory target map. The auditory and somatosensory target maps inhibit the regions within their respective error maps (auditory and somatosensory error maps) corresponding to the expected feedback for the sound being produced (analogous to the receipt of an efference copy of the movement commands). Each of the two error maps receives excitatory input from their corresponding state maps (auditory state map and somatosensory state map), which estimate the current auditory or somatosensory state, respectively. The error maps, therefore, compute the difference between the expected and actual sensory states for the sound being produced, and send an error signal to the feedback control map if the predicted consequences are off-target.

DIVA has not yet been widely applied to the understanding of motor speech disorders, but some work is beginning in this area, and there is rich potential given the advantages of the model already discussed. Max *et al.* (2004) hypothesized that stuttering may arise when the internal models are insufficiently activated or when there is too much reliance on feedback control, and tested these hypotheses with simulations of the DIVA model. The articulatory synthesizer produced sound repetitions consistent with stuttering behaviour under these conditions. The DIVA model has also been used to generate hypotheses about the mechanisms in apraxia of speech (Tourville and Guenther 2011). A similar computational model of speech production, which also drives an articulatory-acoustic synthesizer, has been used to model apraxia of speech (Kroeger *et al.* 2011). Kroeger *et al.*'s model has been trained to simulate three possible types of apraxia of speech and produces the trial-and-error articulatory groping behaviour and segmental distortion errors characteristic of apraxia of speech.

27.7   Prosodic encoding and speech motor control

The prosody of spoken language refers to the sound-related features of speech such as the melody and rhythm that occur over stretches of speech longer than an individual segment (Keating and Shattuck-Hufnagel 2002). Prosody is the *way* something is said, rather than what is said (McCann and Peppé 2003). In the phenomenon of articulatory strengthening, the articulators become stronger, and in the case of consonants, form a more extreme constriction, on prominent syllables and on the initial segments of prosodic constituents such as phonological words or prosodic phrases (Beckman *et al.* 1992; Fougeron and Keating 1997). Articulatory strengthening indicates that the prosodic form of an utterance influences the force, duration and distance of the articulatory movements during speech.

Most current models of speech production have little to say, however, about how the production of prosodic information is integrated with phonological encoding, articulatory planning and motor execution. Levelt (1989: 365) proposed a 'rough sketch of a possible architecture' underlying the prosodic formulation of connected speech (Figure 27.6). The key component of this architecture is the prosody generator, which combines surface structure, number of syllables and lexical stress information to build a prosodic structure that details a pattern of accented versus unaccented syllables and larger and smaller prosodic phrases. Next, the speaker's intonational meanings (not captured in the grammar) are consulted to determine which phrase accents and boundary tones will apply to each phrase, and which syllables will receive prominence. Finally, the prosody generator computes how the segments associated with individual words will be combined into phonological words and structured into syllables.

The outputs from the prosody generator are a prosodic frame for the whole utterance that details durations, loudness, fundamental frequency

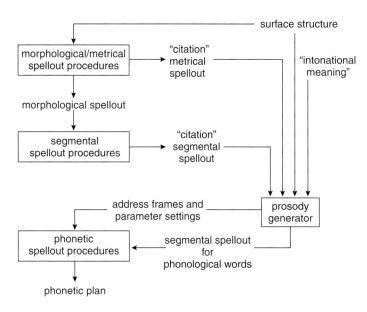

Figure 27.6 Model of phonological encoding, articulatory planning and prosody generation in connected speech. (Levelt, Willem J. M., *Speaking: From Intention to Articulation*, Fig. 10.1, p. 366, © 1989 Massachusetts Institute of Technology, by permission of The MIT Press.)

(f_0) and pausing (the address frames and parameter settings in Figure 27.6), and a string of segments tagged with their syllable position ready to be allocated to phonological words (Levelt 1989; Keating and Shattuck-Hufnagel 2002). The gestural scores are then generated (phonetic spellout procedures in Figure 27.6), and these are specified for utterance-level and phrase-level prosody, a development from the gestural scores described in section 27.5 above. Although Levelt *et al.* (1999) later suggested that the prosodic form could not be specified until after the allocation of segments to frames during phonological encoding, a number of observations about normal prosodic structure and the influence of prosodic factors on segmental error rates (Keating and Shattuck-Hufnagel 2002; Croot *et al.* 2010) suggest that prosodic structure must be available before the specification of phonological words, as in Levelt's (1989) original proposal.

Van Lancker Sidtis *et al.* (2006) reviewed a number of perspectives on the relationship between normal prosodic functions (e.g. communicating affective, attitudinal, pragmatic, linguistic and indexical/personal information), presentations of dysprosodic speech in people with acquired brain injury, and brain regions associated with processing prosody and the physical correlates of prosody in the speech signal. These authors suggested that available models of prosodic processing are immature for a number of reasons, including the need for a codification of 'normal' prosody, the need for more sophisticated cognitive theories, the difficulty of hearing the components of prosody independently and training clinicians to do so reliably, and the non-trivial individual differences and context effects in speech prosody. Progress towards building models of prosodic production can be seen in the availability of a general annotation framework for annotating prosody in several languages (the ToBI framework; Ohio State University Department of Linguistics 1999) and moves to train speech pathologists to assess prosody in the speech pathology clinic (Kuschmann *et al.* 2011; Patel 2011; White *et al.* 2011). Nevertheless, the absence of a model of the clinical presentations of dysprosodic speech and their neural bases, and the underspecification of prosodic processing in psycholinguistic models, currently hamper our understanding and management of prosodic impairments associated with motor speech disorders.

27.8   Motor schema theory and principles of motor learning

The schema theory for discrete motor skill learning (Schmidt 1976) has predominantly been applied to limb motor control. However, it has recently received considerable attention in the literature on treatment for motor speech disorders because it makes predictions about the effects of practice and feedback schedules on the learning of motor skills. According to motor schema theory, a discrete action such as a golf swing (by contrast with an action such as driving or juggling that is ongoing over time) is controlled by sets of motor commands called motor programmes. These programmes are prepared in advance and specify information about the action such as the relative timing required for the elements of the action. Programmes are generalized in the sense that they allow for the redundancy in the motor system by which the programme can be executed in multiple ways to achieve the same outcome (Schmidt 2003). Generalized motor programmes, therefore, do not contain the specific parameters required to achieve the movement in a given context on a given occasion, such as the absolute timing, force or amplitude of the movement, or the specific effectors or muscles to be used (Maas *et al.* 2008b). Instead, people acquire motor schemas that allow them to parameterize generalized motor programmes to produce movements in specific contexts. A series of generalized motor programmes, which are used in a particular order (e.g. generalized motor programmes for syllables in a word), may be chunked into a larger generalized motor programme (for the whole word) as a result of practice.

Motor schemas are memory representations of the 'relationship between the outcomes achieved on past attempts at running a program and the parameters chosen on those attempts' (Schmidt 2003: 367). Schmidt proposed two types of motor schemas: recall schemas and recognition schemas (see Schmidt 2003; Schmidt and Lee 2005 and Maas *et al.* 2008b for further details). A recall schema for a particular generalized motor programme represents the relationship between the initial conditions, the movement parameters and the outcome of the movement. Given the movement goal and information about the current conditions, the recall schema calculates the required parameters (Schmidt 2003; Maas *et al.* 2008b). A recognition schema for a particular generalized motor programme represents the relationship between the initial conditions, the sensory consequences of a movement and the outcome of the movement. If there is a mismatch between the intended sensory consequences and the actual sensory consequences, the resulting error signal is used to update the recall schema. Information on movement outcome provides feedback about whether the sensory consequences were on target. Recall and recognition schemas, therefore, encode somewhat similar information to inverse and forward internal models, respectively (compare Figure 27.4). The aim of motor learning is to acquire motor schemas that can generate appropriate parameterizations for generalized motor programmes, even in novel contexts (Maas *et al.* 2008b).

Schmidt (2003: 372) reflected that he was 'amazed by the number of statements that could be made about how to teach [motor skills] that are possible from the empirical data surrounding schema theory and from the theory itself'. Such statements apply especially to practice conditions (amount, distribution, scheduling and variability of practice) and feedback conditions (type, frequency and timing of feedback), and are summarized as principles of motor learning. Table 27.1, which is reproduced from Bislick *et al.* (2012), summarizes the practice and feedback variables discussed by Schmidt and Lee (2005), with the most effective manipulations shown in bold.

Maas *et al.* (2008b) summarized how apraxia of speech, hypokinetic dysarthria and ataxic dysarthria can be conceptualized in terms of impaired activation or parameterizing of generalized motor programmes. They further noted that other acquired dysarthrias will alter the premorbid relations between motor commands, sensory consequences and movement outcomes, necessitating the updating of schemas acquired prior to the onset of the disorder. Recently, attention has turned to the question of whether the principles that facilitate non-speech motor learning also predict success in learning and relearning speech motor control in the context of motor speech disorders (e.g. Wambaugh *et al.* 2006a; Mass *et al.* 2008b; McNeil *et al.* 2009; Bislick *et al.* 2012). Bislick *et al.* (2012) evaluated three randomized controlled trials and four single-participant designs in which principles of motor learning were investigated in people with apraxia of speech (four studies), hypokinetic dysarthria (one study) and healthy adults (two studies). They concluded that the evidence for effectiveness is promising. Further empirical testing of the various principles of motor learning with different populations at different levels of severity

Table 27.1 *Summary of the primary principles of limb motor learning. Bolded principles are those proven effective for long-term retention of trained limb movements by Schmidt and Lee 2005. (Reprinted from Bislick et al. 2012 in Aphasiology by Taylor & Francis Ltd. Reproduced with permission of Taylor & Francis Ltd.)*

STRUCTURE OF PRACTICE
Massed practice (practise a given number of trials/sessions in a small period of time) versus
Distributed practice (practise a given number of trials/sessions over a longer period of time)
Blocked practice (different targets practised in separate, successive blocks, e.g., aaaa, bbbb) versus
Random practice (different targets are randomly intermixed, e.g., acbbcadabc)
Constant practice (practise targets in same context) versus
Varied practice (practise targets in different contexts)
Low number of trials (i.e., <50/target) versus
High number of trials (i.e., >50/target)

STRUCTURE OF FEEDBACK
Knowledge of Performance (feedback related to specific aspects of performance) versus
Knowledge of Results (feedback only related to correctness of response)
High-frequency feedback (feedback after every trial) versus
Low-frequency feedback (feedback only after some attempts)
Immediate feedback (feedback immediately following attempt) versus
Delayed feedback (feedback provided with a delay, e.g., 5 seconds)

is required, however, and there is substantial theoretical work still to be done. Schmidt (2003) proposed that motor schema theory needs to be updated. Or, perhaps, the principles of motor learning need to be recast instead within the framework of other well-specified models such as DIVA, which is notably also a model that can learn, that can generate quantitative predictions and that can be applied to motor speech disorders.

27.9   Concluding remarks

The survey of models of speech production presented above yields a number of themes. One theme is that models are available at different levels of description and serve different purposes. The clinico-anatomical model of Darley, Aronson and Brown links clusters of clinical symptoms with hypothesized neuroanatomical structures. It has been widely used in the clinical management of motor speech disorders (Duffy 2005) and the diagnosis of neurological disease and lesion site. Although newer imaging and neuropathological analyses are superseding the use of dysarthria subtypes in the diagnosis of neurological disease (Weismer 2006), interventions are still targeted at perceptually prominent symptoms

(Ackermann *et al.* 2010; Miller 2012). Identifying these symptoms thus remains clinically invaluable.

The empirical testing of information-processing models over time has demonstrated the heuristic value of models that can explain unimpaired as well as impaired speech motor control, and the potential for data from both unimpaired and impaired speakers to constrain theory development about speech production. It has also raised a critical question about how to model the interface between discrete linguistic representations and dynamical continuous movements. Other models discussed above have highlighted the role of the environment in movement control. These have shown how complex behaviours could emerge from a relatively small number of parameters in a non-linear, self-organizing, dynamical system, and demonstrated the utility of internal models of the current and predicted states of the speech system in explaining aspects of speech motor control. A number of approaches emphasized the power of computational models that can generate quantitative predictions, explain factors associated with learning, and model speech motor control at multiple levels.

Extending our current understanding of the mechanisms involved in speech motor control and motor speech disorders requires well-designed, theory-driven experiments in research settings (Max 2004). Research is also possible in the speech pathology clinic when the speech-language pathologist works within a scientist-practitioner model, is informed by current theory and research, and evaluates his or her own therapy on a client-by-client basis. The reader is referred to Wilson (1987, 1997) for suggestions about how to design interventions that control for the effects of extraneous factors and allow clinicians to determine whether a treatment was effective. The models discussed in the current chapter model speech motor control at the level of body structures and functions in the International Classification of Functioning, Disability and Health (ICF) framework (World Health Organization 2001), and thus contribute to thinking in the clinic about impairment-directed interventions. It is, however, also essential not to lose sight of the functioning of the person with a motor speech disorder at the activity and participation levels of the ICF framework, and to promote intelligibility and opportunities to participate in communication according to the personal goals of the individual (Miller 2012; Lowit Chapter 22, this volume).

28

Adult neurological disorders and semantic models

Tobias Bormann

28.1 Case vignette

A 62-year-old man in good general health (no hypertension, no history of substance abuse) introduced himself to the outpatient unit of a neurology department accompanied by his wife. He was seen by a neurologist, a psychologist and a speech therapist. Asked about his problems, he and his wife reported that his 'memory' had deteriorated and that he had difficulty finding the correct words. Questioned in more detail, his wife noted that his difficulty with 'memory' affected mainly words and names but that, in general, his knowledge of events in the recent past appeared preserved. His wife recalled that the initial complaint, which was also noted by their children, concerned problems finding the correct words, using descriptions, occasionally using a related, but wrong, word and occasional confusion over the meaning of words. There had been several occasions in which she had asked him to get her some fruit and he had picked the wrong fruit at the shop. The family had the impression that their father's condition was worsening, although he continued to use his car without ever getting lost or putting anyone in danger.

The family lived in an area in which a new shopping mall was being built. On being asked about that project, the patient reported, albeit with several hesitations, word-finding difficulties and circumlocutions, that the mall was to host more than forty different shops and would also include three restaurants and a movie theatre. He said that there had been a recent delay of the opening date and that there had been concerns about local businesses losing customers. He also reported that he had attended the foundation stone ceremony two months earlier and that the mayor and the state's governor had been there.

He was then shown a picture of a frog and was asked to name it. He said that this thing might live in the water or in the desert but that he couldn't get the name. He was asked whether the animal was a 'lizard'.

His response was: 'A lizard? What's a lizard? It could be a lizard though I am not quite sure.' When shown pictures of 12 twelve different animals and asked to pick the lizard, after a considerable delay he picked the picture of a snake.

A formal neuropsychological assessment revealed severely impaired object naming, impaired comprehension of words and objects but well preserved visual-spatial skills, including perfect production of a clock. This latter test is known as the Shulman clock drawing test (Shulman 2000). During object naming, semantic errors, word-finding difficulties and circumlocutions were observed. His anomia interfered with tests of verbal memory but he exhibited good learning and retention of pictures of faces, buildings and nonsense drawings. His recognition of the pictures after a delay of 30 minutes was in the normal range. His performance on the Trail Making Test A, in which the numbers 1 to 25 have to be connected with a pencil as quickly as possible (Reitan 1955), was in the normal range. Cognitive slowing was not observed, and the client had preserved digit spans as measures of verbal short-term memory.

An MRI scan of the patient's brain revealed selective atrophy of anterior temporal areas which was more pronounced in the left hemisphere. Other regions of the brain, including frontal and parietal areas, were normal for his age. The hippocampi, which are regions associated with encoding, consolidation and retrieval of episodic memory, appeared to be spared from atrophy. A PET scan, which provides information on oxygen and glucose metabolism in the brain, revealed reduced perfusion in anterior temporal areas.

An experienced clinician can draw several inferences from this case description (Garrard 2008). As the onset of his condition was insidious and it appears to be progressive, a stroke is rather unlikely to be the cause while some variant of a degenerative disease is likely. As the patient was otherwise in good health, other causes of progressive worsening of his cognitive skills, such as long-standing type II diabetes or cerebrovascular disease, can also be ruled out.

It is quite common for patients and their families to report some 'memory impairment'. However, this report should be taken to indicate an impairment of any cognitive skill, including language, attention, way-finding and planning. Forgetfulness is a more salient impairment and is easier to recognize than, say, attentional problems. Therefore, when mentioned by a patient and his family, memory problems should be considered an umbrella term for different cognitive deficits (Garrard 2008).

'Memory' is not a unitary system but is a collective term for different contents. Long-term memory is to be distinguished from short-term and working memory. Long-term memory can, in turn, be episodic or semantic in nature. Episodic memory refers to individually experienced episodes of memory or autobiographical memory, whereas 'semantic memory' is a term for culturally shared knowledge about objects, words and facts. One could think of this distinction in terms of what a person did during the last elections versus knowledge of what an election is in that person's country.

In the present case, episodic memory appears to be intact while semantic memory is impaired. This is an important observation from a clinical point of view as an impairment of episodic memory is the most significant symptom of the typical variant of Alzheimer's type dementia. The client's orientation for time and place as well as his detailed account of the progress of the shopping mall project in his neighbourhood further suggest preserved episodic memory, making a diagnosis of Alzheimer's disease less likely. Preserved episodic memory would be rather atypical for Alzheimer's disease as is the onset of the disease in someone who is only 62 years old. This short case description is a fictitious, yet typical, example of a condition named 'semantic dementia' which consists of a progressive worsening of semantic knowledge or semantic memory. It has been studied extensively in the last few years by both clinicians and cognitive scientists.

The term 'semantic memory' refers to knowledge of objects, concepts, words and people irrespective of the personal context in which this knowledge was acquired (Warrington 1975). This knowledge also includes the semantic category of the object, visual information about the object's shape along with other sensory information (e.g. the sound an animal makes; the smell of fruits), the relationship to other concepts and the possible contexts in which these objects are encountered. It can also be thought of as a multimodal dictionary that can be accessed in different ways (Humphreys and Forde 2001: 455). Semantic memory can be distinguished from episodic memory, which refers to personally experienced episodes or autobiographical memory (Tulving 1972). Semantic memory is culturally shared, does not contain the specific contexts in which knowledge is acquired, and is established for the most part early in life.

There are several neurological conditions that may lead to impaired semantic memory. This chapter will review four of these conditions: semantic impairment in the context of aphasia resulting from stroke, semantic impairment due to herpes simplex encephalitis (HSE), semantic dementia and Alzheimer's disease. The chapter will also use the results from the study of neurological populations to infer something about the organization of semantic knowledge both in the mind and in the brain.

28.2 Neurological disorders associated with semantic impairment

28.2.1 Aphasia

Aphasia is an acquired impairment of language processing following brain damage. The impairment may affect any aspect of language production and comprehension including phonological, lexical, semantic or syntactic processing as well as reading and writing. Aphasia usually results from infarction or a stroke in the middle cerebral artery. This artery has two major branches and supplies the region around the sylvian fissure, usually in the left hemisphere. However, aphasia can also be caused by traumatic brain injury and brain tumours.

Traditionally, two cortical regions have been considered particularly important for language. These regions are the posterior parts of the left inferior frontal gyrus, often referred to as 'Broca's area' (area 44/45 in Brodmann's cytoarchitectonic map), as well as the posterior part of the left superior temporal gyrus (area 22). Lesions in these areas frequently result in distinct aphasic syndromes known as 'Broca's aphasia' and 'Wernicke's aphasia'. There are other aphasic syndromes including global aphasia, anomic aphasia, conduction aphasia and variants of transcortical aphasias (sensory, motor, mixed). (The reader is referred to Dronkers and Larsen (2001) and Stemmer and Whitaker (2008) for a review of aphasic syndromes and their associated symptoms.) Infarctions in the anterior branch of the left middle cerebral artery result in non-fluent aphasia in which 'agrammatic' speech and impaired comprehension of syntactically complex sentences are dominant symptoms. By contrast, superior temporal lesions yield fluent aphasia with patients exhibiting paragrammatic errors, semantic and/or phonemic errors as well as impaired comprehension of words and sentences. The aphasic syndromes associated most reliably with impaired word comprehension and semantic deficits are Wernicke's aphasia, transcortical sensory aphasia and global aphasia.

While infarction of the left middle cerebral artery is reliably associated with aphasia, a recent case series study by Capitani *et al.* (2009) documented category-specific semantic impairments in patients with infarcts in the posterior cerebral artery. More frequently, ischaemia in the posterior cerebral artery may also lead to mild impairments of word finding and may lead to a severe reading impairment (pure alexia or 'letter by letter reading'). Ischaemia in the anterior cerebral artery can occasionally lead to transcortical motor aphasia. It may also impair executive functions which are supported by prefrontal cortical regions.

Aphasia has been a major focus of clinical and cognitive studies. Some studies have focused on category-specific deficits in aphasia (Warrington and McCarthy 1983). Other studies have discussed the implications of aphasia for modelling the role of the semantic system in a general framework of word processing (Hillis *et al.* 1990) or have investigated access to semantic information (Jefferies and Lambon Ralph 2006). Virtually all aphasic individuals exhibit word-finding difficulties ('anomia'). Within a cognitive model of word production, however, anomia can result from different impairments. Besides a semantic impairment, a lexical access deficit may be the cause of anomia. In this case, one may also observe failures to provide a response, circumlocutions or semantic errors (Caramazza and Hillis 1990b). That means that a semantic error in picture naming, for example saying 'lion' in response to the picture of a tiger, is not necessarily a sign of a semantic impairment. Distinguishing between the different underlying causes of anomia requires additional testing (Nickels 1997). In the case of lexical or phonological anomia the subject may benefit from phonological cues (e.g. the word's onset) and may not exhibit a comparable degree of comprehension problems.

28.2.2 Herpes simplex encephalitis

Herpes simplex encephalitis (HSE) is a viral encephalitis that accounts for about 5–10 per cent of all cases of viral or bacterial encephalitis (Malessa and Tyler 1996; Adams *et al.* 1997). About 90 per cent of those affected have HSE-1 virus infection which can also cause cold sores, but both complaints occur independently. After a prodrome of some days which may include symptoms of a viral infection (i.e. fever, headache and meningism), patients frequently develop psychiatric symptoms with acute psychosis, language impairment, changes in behaviour and personality, confusion and altered states of consciousness. They may also have epileptic seizures and fall into coma or stupor. The virus can be detected in the patient's cerebrospinal fluid after a lumbar puncture but this takes several days and treatment for suspected HSE should begin immediately. When untreated, HSE has a mortality rate of 30–70 per cent (Adams *et al.* 1997). When treated with aciclovir, mortality rate is much lower (25 per cent), although there remain severe neurological deficits (McGrath *et al.* 1997). The typical imaging finding is focal necrosis in the temporal and frontal lobes.

The neuropsychological sequelae of HSE consist of severe episodic memory impairments (anterograde amnesia), anomic aphasia and, in cases with extensive temporal lobe damage affecting lateral and medial regions, impairments of semantic knowledge. The semantic impairment is less pronounced than in other conditions, such as semantic dementia (see section 28.2.4). By contrast, there is a higher rate of category-specific semantic deficits in HSE in that living or non-living things are affected (Lambon Ralph *et al.* 2007; Noppeney *et al.* 2007; Patterson *et al.* 2007). The majority of studies on HSE have reported a pronounced impairment for living things (Capitani *et al.* 2003; Lambon Ralph *et al.* 2007). Warrington and Shallice (1984) reported on four patients who displayed a greater deficit for living things, animals and plants, in comparison to non-living things. This affected object naming but also more general access to knowledge about objects. Knowledge about musical instruments and some other categories was impaired while knowledge about body parts was spared. These observations led to the development of a prominent cognitive model of semantic knowledge, the sensory-functional model, which will be discussed in section 28.3.1.

28.2.3 Alzheimer's disease

Alzheimer's disease is the most common cause of dementia. Onset is usually insidious and progression is slow, but it may appear faster when a person moves to a new environment (e.g. a nursing home) or during a stay in hospital. Patients (about 5 per cent) in whom the disease starts before the age of 65 years are cases of early-onset dementia, while patients with an onset after the age of 65 are late-onset dementia cases. There appear to be no pathological differences between early- and late-onset dementia, although recently differences in the topography of grey matter atrophy have been reported (e.g. Frisoni *et al.* 2007). The majority of late-onset cases are sporadic in that there is no positive family history. In the familial variant of the disease, onset may be between the thirties and sixties.

The hallmark feature of Alzheimer's disease is a severe impairment of episodic memory. The memory impairment becomes obvious when patients repeatedly ask the same questions or tell the same stories, forget appointments, lose things like keys and their glasses, have difficulty with names and problems coping with complex everyday activities such as taking care of finances. Patients usually have problems finding their way around in new environments, learning new routines (e.g. how to use a new mobile phone) and may give incorrect responses when asked about the date and name of the clinic. The memory impairment shows a temporal gradient with a more severe deficit for recently learned contents. Besides progressive episodic memory deficits, Alzheimer's patients develop visual-spatial impairments and many develop semantic deficits with anomia and comprehension impairments (Larner 2008).

Dementia due to Alzheimer's disease is preceded by a phase of variable length in which there is evidence of a cognitive impairment that is not severe enough to impair daily functioning (Albert *et al.* 2011). This phase of mild cognitive impairment is due to the progressive accumulation of Alzheimer's pathology in the brain. It is difficult to validate by a clinician but performance on standardized neuropsychological tests will be below the typical level for a given age and education. Although a definite diagnosis of Alzheimer's disease is only possible postmortem after autopsy, a diagnosis of 'probable' Alzheimer's dementia or 'possible' Alzheimer's dementia can be made fairly accurately. Clinical diagnosis proceeds by means of criteria that are set out in the fourth edition of the Diagnostic and Statistical Manual of Mental Disorders (American Psychiatric Association 2000), the tenth edition of the International Classification of Diseases (World Health Organization 1993), and by the National Institute of Neurological and Communicative Disorders and Stroke – Alzheimer's Disease and Related Disorders Association (NINCDS-ADRDA) (McKhann *et al.* 1984). The NINCDS-ADRDA criteria have recently been revised (McKhann *et al.* 2011).

The semantic impairment of Alzheimer's patients was investigated by Chertkow and Bub (1990). Subjects had impaired object naming when compared to a group of age-matched control participants. There was a certain correspondence between the ability to name objects and to answer questions about these objects. This was taken to indicate the presence of damaged representations of these concepts in semantic memory and was distinguished from the more variable deficits which are observed in aphasia. As a group, Alzheimer patients were more impaired on natural objects (animals, fruits, vegetables) with the exception of body parts. A comparable relationship between semantic knowledge about objects and the ability to name these objects was reported by Hodges *et al.* (1996).

Hodges and Patterson (1995) studied Alzheimer's patients at different stages of illness. They observed that even the minimally affected group (Mini-Mental State score >23) was impaired in object naming and naming to verbal description, a semantic fluency task ('Please tell me as many animals as you can think of in one minute') and a test of semantic knowledge based on associatively related pictures. The group also performed poorly on questions about semantic features. With more advanced cognitive decline, patients had additional difficulties in sorting pictures according to semantic categories and matching a word to one of several pictures. While the study revealed semantic impairments early in the course of the disease, a considerable variation was observed, with some subjects in the mild or moderate stage of the illness still performing in the normal range on some tests. By contrast, all subjects were impaired in tests of episodic memory, e.g. recognition of unknown faces which had been presented in a study phase some time earlier.

28.2.4   Semantic dementia

Semantic dementia is a progressive neurological disorder from the spectrum of frontotemporal lobar degeneration (FTLD) or frontotemporal dementia (FTD). FTD comprises language and behavioural variants (Neary *et al.* 1998). At present, a variety of pathologies at the cell level are known to underlie the clinical deficits in FTD, e.g. ubiquitin-positive, tau-negative inclusions comparable to the changes typically found in motor neuron disease, tau-positive Pick bodies, as well as Alzheimer's pathology (Davies *et al.* 2005). The different variants of FTD are associated with different atrophy patterns in the brain. Bilateral frontal atrophy is associated with behavioural variant FTD. Symptoms include early changes in behaviour and personality, reduced insight and concern, as well as disinhibited and socially inappropriate behaviour (Rascovsky *et al.* 2011). This variant is the most common form of FTD. Another variant, progressive non-fluent aphasia, is associated with atrophy predominantly in the left perisylvian area including the left inferior frontal gyrus (Mesulam 1982). Individuals with the logopenic variant show atrophy in posterior superior temporal and inferior parietal areas of the left hemisphere. Onset before the age of 65 years, a positive family history in first-degree relatives as well as bulbar palsy, muscular weakness and fasciculations are supportive for any disorder from the spectrum of FTLD.

Criteria for three different language variants of FTD, i.e. non-fluent/ agrammatic primary progressive aphasia (PPA), semantic PPA and logo-penic PPA, were recently defined by Gorno-Tempini *et al.* (2011). For semantic PPA, also referred to as semantic dementia, two core symptoms need to be present: impaired confrontation naming and impaired single word comprehension. In addition, three of the following diagnostic features must be present: impaired object knowledge, surface dyslexia or dysgraphia, spared repetition and spared speech production with preserved grammar and articulation. According to Neary *et al.* (1998), core diagnostic features of semantic dementia include insidious onset and gradual progression, language disorder characterized by fluent spontaneous speech with a lack of content words, loss of meaning of words which affects comprehension and production, semantic errors in production, a perceptual disorder comparable to associative agnosia, preserved perceptual matching and drawing, preserved single word repetition and preserved reading and writing of orthographically regular words. Supportive features include press of speech, idiosyncratic word usage, absence of phonemic paraphasias, surface dyslexia and dysgraphia, preserved calculation, and behavioural changes (loss of empathy; narrowed preoccupations; parsimony). On neurological examination, patients do not exhibit primitive reflexes, but may exhibit Parkinson-like symptoms (akinesia, rigidity and tremor) while the EEG is normal (Neary *et al.* 1998: 1549). The case vignette from the beginning of this chapter was the description of an individual with semantic dementia.

In modern times, semantic dementia was first described by Warrington (1975), who reported on patients with selective impairments of semantic memory. At the same time, these subjects exhibited preserved episodic and working memory and preserved general cognitive skills. It was only later that some of these individuals were identified as cases of semantic dementia. A short time later, Mesulam (1982) reported cases of what he called primary progressive aphasia. Initially primarily anomic, his subjects exhibited a decrease in their language skills with their language becoming progressively non-fluent over the course of 5 to 11 years. They developed language deficits similar to Broca's aphasia. The term 'primary progressive aphasia' was later applied to another group of patients who developed fluent aphasia (Poeck and Luzzatti 1988) with relative sparing of other cognitive skills. Snowden *et al.* (1989) introduced the term 'semantic dementia' for the group of progressive fluent aphasic patients.

A first set of neuropsychological symptoms of semantic dementia as well as their association with temporal lobe atrophy was reported by Hodges *et al.* (1992b). The pathological mechanism is a degeneration of anterior temporal and frontal cortical areas. The anterior temporal lobes are affected, usually bilaterally although asymmetric atrophy is common.

Cognitive symptoms include a selective impairment of semantic memory leading to anomia, word comprehension problems and reduced semantic fluency (Snowden *et al.* 1989; Patterson *et al.* 2007). When sensitive tests are employed, impaired processing of non-verbal semantic information can be demonstrated (Bozeat *et al.* 2000). Other aspects of language such as syntax and phonology are reported to be spared, as are basic perceptual and problem-solving skills as well as episodic and autobiographical memory. However, it has been argued that processing of irregular stimuli critically rests upon contributions from semantic memory (Patterson *et al.* 2006). This may also apply to the processing of irregular past-tense morphology of verbs and the drawing of atypical animals (e.g. an ostrich). Furthermore, phonemic errors have been observed frequently in the repetition of word lists (Patterson *et al.* 1994). Therefore, at least one cognitive model of language processing assigns semantic knowledge a central role in supposedly non-semantic tasks (Patterson *et al.* 2006).

Reading and writing in semantic dementia are characterized by a so-called surface dyslexic and surface dysgraphic pattern. Surface dyslexia and dysgraphia are acquired impairments of reading and spelling, respectively, which affect low-frequency irregular words for which the correct pronunciation and spelling has to be retrieved from a long-term store. Patients exhibit so-called 'phonologically plausible errors' in reading and spelling. For example, the written word 'pint' may be pronounced incorrectly and analogously to 'mint'. An irregular word like 'campaign' may be spelled 'campain'. By contrast, regular words may be written just by their sound without retrieval of the correct spelling from the orthographic lexicon. Languages which do not have a transparent orthography (e.g. English, French) offer numerous opportunities to violate the correct spelling or pronunciation of words, while languages with transparent orthographies (e.g. Russian, Italian, Finnish, Spanish, German) have more regular correspondence between sounds and letters.

28.3   Cognitive models of semantic memory

In the 1970s, a research programme was revived which made use of data from neurological patients to develop models of complex cognitive skills (Shallice 1988; Rapp 2001). A major focus has always been language processing, most notably single word reading, word writing, lexical access in speaking as well as sentence processing. An important paper by Marshall and Newcombe (1973) discussed errors of patients with dyslexia in relation to a model of normal, unimpaired reading. After this paper, neurologists, psychologists, and speech and language therapists reported in detail upon individuals in their clinics who presented with selective, often unexpected impairments.

While many aspects of human language processing, such as word reading, sentence processing, lexical access in oral naming as well as in auditory perception, have also been investigated in unimpaired subjects, representation of semantic knowledge has been a field in which data from neurological populations have been of particular importance. Psycholinguistic studies have been less suited to addressing issues of how semantic information is represented and accessed.

Research has focused on impairments of specific semantic categories, most notably the distinction between living and non-living things. The category of living things usually comprises animals, plants, fruits and vegetables while non-living things include mainly artefacts and tools. Food items as well as body parts have been subsumed under the label of either 'living' or 'non-living'. Neurological subjects were reported who appeared to have lost their knowledge about concepts of specific categories, which suggested that different semantic categories are organized independently of each other in semantic memory (Caramazza 1999; Capitani *et al.* 2003). Therefore, research has often been limited to categories of concrete concepts (e.g. animals, plants, tools, furniture). Few studies have focused on the representation of abstract concepts, although a recent study suggests that concrete and abstract concepts are organized in a qualitatively different way in semantic memory (Crutch and Warrington 2005).

A standard observation in work with language impaired people is that concreteness affects performance. Most aphasic individuals have more difficulties processing abstract words (e.g. 'agenda', 'schedule') in comparison to concrete words (Crutch and Warrington 2005). Empirical studies of semantic memory have identified a number of other variables known to affect processing. These variables can be used to infer an aphasic subject's functional impairment. At the same time, these variables need to be controlled in empirical studies. For example, a comparison of naming performance for items of different semantic categories (e.g. living versus non-living) requires that the two sets of target words are matched for word frequency, familiarity, visual complexity and other variables.

The familiarity of objects is an important variable, as is the frequency of occurrence of words. Many animals are less familiar than, for example, body parts, pieces of furniture, or tools. Processing of words in either perception or production is influenced by the word's frequency in everyday conversation, TV shows and newspapers. In addition, word processing is affected by the age at which the word was learned (age of acquisition). Early acquired words (e.g. 'dog') are represented more robustly than late acquired words (e.g. 'ocelot'). Concepts that are typical of their category are represented more robustly and are, thus, easier to process than rather atypical members of a semantic category. Frequently discussed examples are birds such as 'robins' and 'penguins' which are a typical and an atypical member of that category, respectively. For visual materials, visual complexity plays a role especially in studies employing line drawings of objects. This makes recognition of animals and fruits more difficult as colour is important for these categories whereas overall shape is rather similar (cf. four-legged animals).

The initial clinical study of Warrington (1975) reported on subjects with impaired semantic memory in the face of spared episodic memory. Together with the opposite dissociation in anterograde amnesia – preserved semantic knowledge but impaired episodic memory – this strongly suggests that the two compartments of explicit long-term memory, semantic and episodic memory, could doubly dissociate. It can, thus, be concluded that they are represented independently of each other.

Most cognitive models of semantic memory share the basic assumption that concepts are composed of semantic features. Animals live, they breathe, they move, they eat and drink. They may be carnivores (predators, scavengers), herbivores or omnivores. Subordinate concepts inherit features from superordinate concepts. A poodle is a dog and inherits features which apply to all dogs. In turn, dogs are mammals which are part of the category of animals. A poodle, thus, inherits features like 'breathes', 'moves', 'eats', etc. from the 'animals' category, but also has specific features that do not necessarily apply to other breeds of dogs. This leads to typical exemplars sharing more features. A penguin and an ostrich are considered atypical birds as they cannot fly. Yet, like all birds they lay eggs.

28.3.1   Sensory-functional model

A seminal study by Warrington and Shallice (1984) sparked research on category-specific semantic impairments. The authors described four individuals with HSE who had pronounced difficulties with living things. The term 'living things' referred to the categories of animals and plants, which were compared to inanimate things. The four individuals were impaired on naming pictures of animals and plants as well as producing semantic information when hearing the name. As frequently cited examples, one of the subjects ('JBR') described a compass as 'tools for telling the direction you are going' and a tent as a 'temporary outhouse, living home', while describing a snail as 'an insect animal' and an ostrich as 'unusual' (Warrington and Shallice 1984: 838). Comparably clear dissociations were also observed for object naming. These observations provided clear examples of significant difficulties with objects from specific semantic categories. The dissociation was independent of word frequency, which was controlled for by the authors.

However, JBR also exhibited impaired knowledge of food, musical instruments, flowers and precious stones while knowledge about furniture and body parts was spared. This latter observation, namely that JBR's impairment did not strictly obey the distinction of living versus non-living objects, led the authors to suggest that the representation of living things and some artefacts was based more heavily on sensory features while many non-living things were represented predominantly through their functional features. The clustering of animals, plants, food, musical instruments and precious stones seems to support this conclusion. It can be argued that items of these categories are represented mainly through their sensory features. Man-made objects or artefacts are represented through their functional features. After all, a hammer is *for hammering* but can take many different shapes and forms. Likewise, things like a jug or a vase are defined through their use and less so through their appearance. By contrast, different animals are identified through their shape and colour while 'functional features' are less salient.

Yet, the authors reported a second important observation, namely, a rather consistent pattern of performance for individual items across repeated sessions. Consistency, however, was observed only when the same modality was used but was less evident when the same item was assessed in tasks employing different modalities. From this and previous observations in the literature, Warrington and Shallice argued for separate verbal and visual semantic stores. In the literature, these two hypotheses about the representation of semantic categories and different semantic stores have been discussed as the 'sensory-functional account' of category-specific deficits and the 'multiple semantics' hypothesis. Of particular relevance for the latter hypothesis were reports of a condition named 'optic aphasia'. In this condition, subjects can apparently identify objects from vision yet they are unable to name the item. This deficit is, however, only confined to confrontation naming while subjects may be able to name objects placed in their hand or name according to definitions (Beauvois 1982).

Both sensory-functional and multiple semantics proposals have been challenged on theoretical and empirical grounds. The sensory-functional account predicts that subjects with impaired knowledge of living things should exhibit impaired knowledge of sensory features while individuals with selective impairment of non-living categories should have impaired knowledge of functional features. This association, however, has not been observed reliably (Capitani *et al.* 2003). The commentaries to Humphreys and Forde (2001) summarize in detail different arguments for and against the account. The verbal–visual distinction is challenged by item-specific impairments across different tasks (e.g. Hillis *et al.* 1990).

28.3.2   Intercorrelation accounts

As mentioned above, semantic features tend to cluster. Birds have feathers, wings, and beaks, they lay eggs, most of them fly but, obviously, there are exceptions. It has been argued that intercorrelation of features is stronger in living things while artefacts are made up from distinctive properties that have lower intercorrelations. This is at the heart of various theoretical accounts which all assume a unitary semantic system where category-specific deficits may not arise because of damage to discrete semantic categories but because of unspecific damage to semantic representations (e.g. Caramazza *et al.* 1990). The conceptual structure account is one example (e.g. Tyler *et al.* 2000; Moss *et al.* 2002).

Proponents of this model hold that semantic knowledge is represented in a single, highly distributed network in which concepts consist of features. Conceptual processing means that nodes of the network receive activation which they pass along to related nodes. The organization of concepts differs between different semantic categories yet these categories are not hard-wired or built-in a priori but result from intercorrelation of features (e.g. animals that have fur are likely to have claws). Living things share features with other living things while non-living things share fewer features with other non-living things. Correlated features are more resistant to damage than are highly distinctive properties. More specifically, proponents of this model hold that in the realm of non-living things, idiosyncratic features are tightly linked to their specific function. A hammer has been designed to fulfil a specific purpose while a screwdriver serves a completely different purpose. By contrast in the area of living things, shared sensory features are related to a specific function (e.g. eyes to see, nose to smell, the fangs of big cats to prey). Shared features (e.g. animals breathe, animals move and drink) point to vital functions common to many species. By contrast, individual features of specific exemplars are less relevant because other species can do without them.

From these assumptions, the prediction can be derived that an impairment should affect all categories but to a different degree. A mild impairment should affect non-living things more because these are composed of distinctive features which are shared less with other items from this category. Distinctive, idiosyncratic features are less resistant to damage than are widely shared features. The latter prediction has been confirmed repeatedly and in different contexts. Patterson *et al.* (2006) reported that semantic dementia patients lost knowledge about idiosyncratic and irregular features while exhibiting better preserved knowledge of regular, widely shared features. As discussed above, this pattern of impairment affects processing of irregular stimuli, e.g. reading and writing irregular or ambiguous words and producing the correct irregular past tense for verbs (such as 'go, went, gone'). Subjects with semantic dementia also tend to omit idiosyncratic features when drawing animals, even after they have seen a drawing which they have to reproduce after a certain delay. For example, they may fail to reproduce an elephant's large ears or trunk. These observations, however, would be compatible with other theoretical positions.

The study of Gonnerman *et al.* (1997) assessed specifically the prediction that mild and more severe semantic deficits should differentially affect different categories of knowledge. The authors studied the effect of the degree of semantic impairment in Alzheimer's patients and also implemented a computational model to which they applied artificial lesions. (Computational modelling has become a common method in cognitive neuroscience. It usually involves an artificial computer model which is 'lesioned' by adding noise to the processes or damaging representations. The lesioned model then produces 'symptoms', i.e. output patterns, which can be compared to empirical data from neurological populations.) With mild semantic impairments, the patients as a group were more impaired on non-living things, reflecting the resistance of shared features to damage. With more severe damage, patients as well as the model exhibited greater impairment for living things.

28.3.3 The domain-specific account

This account is based on a single case study by Caramazza and Shelton (1998). Their subject, EW, exhibited a selective impairment for animals with spared knowledge of fruits, vegetables and non-living artefacts. For example, she named about 30 per cent of animal pictures correctly while achieving scores of 100 per cent on fruits and vegetables and above 90 per cent on body parts. She also performed poorly on recognizing animals and answering questions about animals, thus attesting to a modality-independent semantic impairment. Knowledge of sensory versus functional features was impaired to a comparable degree.

The opposite dissociation of impaired knowledge of fruit and vegetables but preserved knowledge of animals has also been reported (cf. Caramazza 1999). Caramazza and Shelton argued that dissociations within the broader category of living things were difficult to explain on the basis of impairment to sensory or functional features. Instead, they claimed that evolutionary pressure has led to independent representation of different domains, including animals, plant life (fruits, vegetables) and artefacts. Rapid recognition of animals was vital because animals are both prey as well as predators. Specialization for fruits and vegetables was essential as these are an important source of food.

28.3.4 A neurocognitive model: the hub-and-spoke model

Drawing on extensive research with semantic dementia patients, Patterson *et al.* (2007) proposed a revised model of semantic knowledge. The anterior temporal lobes, which are affected in semantic dementia and herpes simplex encephalitis, play a central role in binding knowledge from different domains. It has been argued that these lobes act as a 'semantic hub' binding modality-specific knowledge from association cortices. The model accords with other accounts in that semantic knowledge is represented in a distributed fashion. Information relating to the perception and action of objects is represented close to or even overlapping with cortical areas responsible for perception. In addition to these modality-specific attributes there are amodal hubs which serve to bind the different representations into a unified conceptual representation.

Patterson *et al.* argue that their 'distributed-plus-hub' view predicts a modality-independent semantic impairment. As the 'hub' is located in anterior temporal regions, selective lesions to these sites should produce amodal semantic impairment, a prediction confirmed by studies with semantic dementia patients. Recall that the impairment in semantic dementia is, indeed, independent of modality of input or output and affects all verbal and non-verbal semantic tasks. The model can also accommodate category-specific semantic deficits or deficits of certain types of knowledge because it assumes modality-specific information to be represented in different cortical areas close to visual, auditory or other areas. The 'hub', however, allows for generalization and differentiation between concepts independently of the sensory features. If the 'hub' was missing, conceptual similarities between perceptually distinct objects, for example different drinking vessels or fruits, may be missed. This account has been supported by extensive computational modelling studies as well as clinical studies with large groups of subjects (Rogers *et al.* 2004; Patterson *et al.* 2006, 2007; Lambon Ralph *et al.* 2007, 2011). Not all aspects of this model have, however, been universally accepted, and it remains to be seen whether the model can accommodate observations of contradictory cases (e.g. Coltheart *et al.* 2010).

28.4   Accessing semantic knowledge

A frequent observation in work with language impaired individuals is the considerable variation in their performance. Performance on the same items is inconsistent and processing of an item may be successful on one occasion and unsuccessful on another occasion. This suggests that mental representations of specific concepts may not be permanently lost but that access to these concepts may be affected. The distinction between impaired access to concepts or lexical representations on the one hand and damage to stored representations on the other hand – often referred to as 'access versus storage deficits' – has received quite a bit of attention in cognitive neuropsychology.

Warrington and Shallice (1979) proposed a set of criteria to distinguish storage from access disorders. A storage deficit was more likely if the following could be observed: A subject would exhibit impairment on the same items repeatedly and across different tasks; frequency or familiarity of the concept would affect performance while presentation rate would not; superordinate information would be preserved. Consistent performance across tasks would suggest that the item is 'lost' from semantic memory while inconsistent performance would prove that on some occasions, the item is available. An effect of frequency or familiarity would indicate a storage deficit since the frequency of usage would, according to the argument, affect the representations. A higher frequency of usage could, for example, influence the activation states of these representations, with more frequently used representations having higher states of activation. Alternatively, these items could be easier to activate by having, for example, a lower activation threshold.

Effects of presentation rate would suggest a specific type of access deficit in which access to a representation would render this representation 'refractory' for a period of time. With longer intervals, the representation would become accessible again. Finally, an access deficit should equally affect superordinate as well as subordinate information. A similar distinction has recently been revived by Jefferies and Lambon Ralph (2006). These authors introduced the notion of impaired control over semantic processing as exhibited by patients with stroke aphasia. Impaired semantic control would affect the ability to direct activation to subserve specific tasks. Obviously, a deficit of semantic control rather than semantic knowledge per se would have considerable implications for therapy.

The above criteria have, however, been criticized (e.g. Rapp and Caramazza 1993). The observation of frequency effects, for example, is equally compatible with access disorders. If frequency affected an item's activation threshold, it should be easier to access because less activation is required to exceed its threshold. Also, items in semantic memory may be permanently inaccessible but still be represented. Finally, patients who have been argued to suffer from impaired access or degraded storage often presented with less clear-cut or rather mixed symptoms. It remains to be seen how the more recent proposal of Jefferies and Lambon Ralph (2006) will fare.

28.5   Semantic disorders in clinical practice

Deficits of semantic knowledge may affect object use and impair awareness of appropriate precautionary measures which are vital for a person's safety. Formal investigations are therefore needed if a semantic impairment is suspected. From the discussion in this chapter, guidelines for assessment and treatment of semantic impairments can be derived. Formal tests of semantic knowledge require that confounding variables are controlled for.

Object naming is a sensitive formal test. Incorrect responses may consist of semantic errors (category coordinates, associated words, superordinate names), omissions and circumlocutions. Comprehension may be assessed by asking a subject to point to a picture from a set of related pictures in response to a word (word–picture matching). Distractors from the same semantic category make the task more challenging than distractors from different categories. A person may be asked about semantic features (e.g. 'Does an elephant have tusks?') or to judge synonyms (e.g. 'Is a stool the same as a chair?') but any impairment of speech processing clearly interferes with this task. Non-verbal semantic tests have been published and can be used in different countries. The Pyramids and Palm Trees Test (Howard and Patterson 1992) as well as subtests of the Birmingham Object Recognition Battery (Riddoch and Humphreys 1993) assess knowledge about associations between concepts. Sorting pictures into different semantic categories would be another test but visual similarity needs to be controlled for. When unpublished tests are used, adequate norms from a larger sample of unimpaired subjects are required for comparison.

It has sometimes been reported that a semantic therapy leads to longer-lasting effects and generalization across items while remediation of lexical access is item-specific and has short-term effects (Howard *et al.* 1985; Hillis 1989). However, this has not been observed in other studies (Doesborgh *et al.* 2004). Doesborgh *et al.* (2004) compared semantic therapy to phonological therapy in a large group of aphasic subjects. Therapy effects were training-specific. The semantic group exhibited improved performance on semantic measures whereas the phonological group improved selectively on measures of phonological processing. Both groups exhibited comparable improvement on a measure of everyday communication. A review of therapies for aphasic impairments can be found in Nickels (2002) and Horton and Byng (2002).

28.6   Conclusions

The present chapter has reviewed neurological disorders leading to semantic impairments. Data from these neurological patients have been used to inform cognitive models of semantic memory. Category-specific deficits are among the most fascinating impairments in cognitive neuroscience and cognitive neuropsychology, and the relevance of semantic deficits is obvious. Although much has been learned in the past 30 years, more work has to be done in order to arrive at a complete theory of semantic processing, semantic representations in the brain and effective remediation strategies.

29

Language in genetic syndromes and cognitive modularity

Vesna Stojanovik

29.1   Introduction

In recent years, research into the impact of genetic abnormalities on cognitive development, including language, has become recognized for its potential to make valuable contributions to our understanding of the brain–behaviour relationships underlying language acquisition as well as to understanding the cognitive architecture of the human mind. The publication of Fodor's (1983) book *The Modularity of Mind* has had a profound impact on the study of language and the cognitive architecture of the human mind. Its central claim is that many of the processes involved in comprehension are undertaken by special brain systems termed 'modules'. This domain specificity of language or *modularity* has become a fundamental feature that differentiates competing theories and accounts of language acquisition (Fodor 1983, 1985; Levy 1994; Karmiloff-Smith 1998).

However, although the fact that the adult brain is modularized is hardly disputed, there are different views of how brain regions become specialized for specific functions. A question of some interest to theorists is whether the human brain is modularized from the outset (nativist view) or whether these distinct brain regions develop as a result of biological maturation and environmental input (neuroconstructivist view). One source of insight into these issues has been the study of developmental disorders, and in particular genetic syndromes, such as Williams syndrome (WS) and Down's syndrome (DS). Because of their uneven profiles characterized by dissociations of different cognitive skills, these syndromes can help us address theoretically significant questions. Investigations into the linguistic and cognitive profiles of individuals with these genetic abnormalities have been used as evidence to advance theoretical views about innate modularity and the cognitive architecture of the human mind.

The present chapter will be organized as follows. To begin, two different theoretical proposals in the modularity debate will be presented. Then studies of linguistic abilities in WS and in DS will be reviewed. Here, the emphasis will be mainly on WS due to the fact that theoretical debates have focused primarily on WS, there is a larger body of literature on WS, and DS subjects have typically been used for the purposes of comparison. Finally, the modularity debate will be revisited in light of the literature review of both WS and DS. Conclusions will be drawn regarding the contribution of these two genetic syndromes to the issue of cognitive modularity, and in particular innate modularity.

29.2   Nativist approach to language acquisition and cognitive architecture

The first half of the twentieth century was dominated by a behaviourist view of language acquisition. According to this view, linguistic abilities are acquired in childhood as a result of training provided by the members of the child's immediate linguistic environment. Skinner (1957), the main proponent of behaviourism, proposed that language is just another behaviour which can be acquired through explicit teaching and reinforcement.

In an attempt to reject behaviourist explanations of language acquisition, Noam Chomsky launched in the late 1950s what has become known as a 'nativist' revolution. The adherents of the nativist tradition oppose the behaviourist's simplistic and rather mechanical way of explaining language acquisition. They propose instead that a generative grammar is to be taken as a starting point for explaining language acquisition. A generative grammar is a set of rules or procedures which allow one to generate all and only the grammatical sentences in a language, characterize all the sentences which already exist in the language corpus and predict the existence and properties of new sentences (Chomsky 1965).

Another crucial aspect of nativist theories with regard to the organization of human cognitive architecture is the assumption that the human mind is modular and that language is a separate, independent module. This idea has been clearly articulated by Jerry Fodor. Fodor (1983) argued that many of the processes involved in the comprehension of language are undertaken by specialized brain systems termed 'modules'. This domain specificity of language or modularity has become a fundamental feature that differentiates competing linguistic theories and accounts of language acquisition (Fodor 1983, 1985; Bates *et al.* 1988, 1995). Fodor argues for a distinction between a central system responsible for rational thought and the fixation of belief, and a number of modular input systems which deliver input into the central system. The theory posits that while cognitive processes, such as long-term memory and problem solving, are carried out by non-modular, relatively slow, central processes, input systems such as those involved in perception are modular in nature. The language faculty is viewed as an input system on a par with the senses, such as vision.

Fodor's main examples of modules are language comprehension and visual perception. Fodor (1983: 98) points out that 'the key to modularity is informational encapsulation'. Informational encapsulation describes the feature of modules whereby they only have access to information of a certain type. A visual perception module, for example, only has access to visual perceptual data. Other characteristics of modules, such as domain specificity, shallow output and neural localization, may be present, but they are not crucial. Given that modules are informationally encapsulated, one would expect there to be minimal interference in the event of breakdown. So, for example, difficulties in the visuospatial domain should not affect comprehension of syntactic structures. In order to test this hypothesis, one inevitably needs to refer to atypical populations which present with breakdowns of different cognitive functions resulting in cognitive dissociations.

As mentioned above, a commonly assumed approach to language acquisition within the nativist view is represented by generative grammar. According to proponents of generative grammar, children's knowledge of morphosyntax and possibly phonology consists of knowledge of formal rules or operations (Ambridge and Lieven 2011). A large body of literature on language acquisition has emerged within the nativist and generativist frameworks (for a review of studies, see Ambridge and Lieven 2011). Discussion of this literature on typical language acquisition is beyond the scope of this chapter. However, it is worth pointing out that dissociations between language and other cognitive skills, such as is often found in atypical populations, have been used by nativist theorists as evidence in support of an innate language (or more often, 'syntax') module. Evidence of this type will be presented in a discussion of Williams syndrome in section 29.4.1, with subsequent consideration of its theoretical implications in section 29.5.

In addition, there have been some theoretical developments within the nativist view since the publication of Fodor's landmark book in 1983. Evolutionary psychologists have proposed what is known as the massive modularity hypothesis (Machery 2011). According to this hypothesis, human cognitive architecture is built from a number of different systems and most of these systems are believed to be adaptations selected for specific purposes (Machery 2011). Unlike Fodorian modularity, this hypothesis does not propose informational encapsulation of the different systems. Importantly, it does not say anything about whether the different systems are specified from birth and it proposes that development involves an interaction between the genome and the environment.

Evidence in support of the massive modularity hypothesis should come from developmental disorders. This is because developmental disorders often show dissociations between different cognitive skills, dissociations which are assumed to provide support for distinct components in human cognitive architecture (Machery 2011). The massive modularity hypothesis also proposes that the component parts of the human cognitive system are adaptations. The question of how the massive modularity hypothesis can provide evidence that these components are adaptations is still to be answered. However, the answer is to be sought in developmental disorders. This is because dissociations found in developmental disorders will need to show how specific systems fulfil specific functions and *only these functions*. For the time being, the evidence is not very strong (see discussion of Clahsen and Almazan's (1998) work on WS in section 29.4.1).

29.3   Neuroconstructivist approach

In the 1970s, a second stream of thought regarding language acquisition was derived largely from the work of Jean Piaget. Even though it seemed that this stream would be some kind of continuation of the empiricist thinking of the seventeenth and eighteenth centuries, this was not quite the case, as Piaget (1980: 23–4) explicitly acknowledged:

> The critique of empiricism is not tantamount to negating the role of experimentation, but the 'empirical' study of the genesis of knowledge shows from the onset the insufficiency of an 'empiricist' interpretation of experience. In fact, no knowledge is based on perceptions alone, for these are always directed, and accompanied by schemes of action. Knowledge, therefore, proceeds from action, and all action that is repeated or generalised through application to new objects engenders by this very fact a 'scheme', that is, a kind of practical concept.

This quotation from the Piaget–Chomsky debate suggests that although Piaget does not fully discard the role of experience in knowledge acquisition, he emphasizes the necessity of the human subject having an important role in structuring activity. Thus, knowledge is supposed to proceed from action, or what Piaget terms 'assimilation' of objects to the schemes of the subject. What is the relevance of such a proposal to language acquisition?

According to Piaget, language is facilitated by the development of sensory-motor schemas that represent the joint outcomes of perception and action. Sensory-motor schemas undergo orderly changes which are nourished, but not shaped by, continuing experience in acting on the world. This means that the child will be able to separate thought from action in her schemas in due course, and her concepts of objects and events in the world will become independent of the actions to be performed on them. Thus, in order for the infant who is acquiring language to be able to make linguistic distinctions such as Object and Action (i.e. NP and VP), she needs to acquire the concept that Object is independent of Action.

For Piaget, language is a manifestation of intelligence and is, hence, not dissociable from it. It is also argued that certain cognitive prerequisites are necessary for the acquisition of language. The idea is that normal development of language is parasitic on the prior mental development of such abilities as 'seriation' and 'conservation'. In order to acquire linguistic structures such as correct word order or the passive, children are supposed to have reached a level of cognitive development at which they could carry out tasks such as putting items in ascending order of size (seriation), or judging that the amount of liquid poured from a tall thin glass into a short one remained the same (conservation).

Thinking has moved on from the time when Piaget first proposed his view of language acquisition. Although some of Piaget's fundamental principles are still very much present, there have been a number of theoretical developments. For example, there is a large body of literature which addresses the issue of cognitive precursors to language acquisition. The very concept of cognitive precursors or prerequisites suggests that it is taken for granted that language acquisition is dependent upon the development of other cognitive skills. These skills include speech segmentation (Newman *et al.* 2006) and joint attention (Morales *et al.* 1998, 2000; Markus *et al.* 2000), amongst others.

Pertinent to the current chapter are challenges to the innateness of modularity, and the proposal that modularity is a product of development (Karmiloff-Smith 1994, 1998). This viewpoint recognizes the existence of innate biological constraints on language acquisition but it considers these constraints to be not so detailed and less domain-specific as far as higher-level cognitive functions such as language are concerned. Development is seen as playing a crucial role in shaping phenotypical outcomes and the protracted period of postnatal growth is seen as essential in influencing the resulting domain specificity of the developing neocortex (Karmiloff-Smith 1998). As with the nativist view, it is difficult to test the idea that language acquisition is an inseparable part of general cognitive development, because in typically developing children different cognitive abilities develop in synchrony with each other. Assuming this theoretical approach, a child with a developmental disorder would be expected to show language acquisition in line with their general cognitive abilities.

29.4 Genetic syndromes

Over the past four decades, language breakdown and atypical linguistic and cognitive development have played a very important role in the ongoing debate on modularity. In particular, genetic syndromes have played a major role in this debate. A 'syndrome' is defined as the presence of multiple anomalies in the same individual with all of those anomalies having a single cause. So far, over 300 different genetic syndromes have been identified (Shprintzen 1997). Populations affected by genetic syndromes have been studied for different reasons. One strong motivation is to gain knowledge about the behavioural manifestations of a specific genetic abnormality, with a view to having a better understanding of the condition and informing diagnosis and remediation. Another reason for studying genetic syndromes is the potential contribution that they can make to theoretical debates on the role of general cognitive mechanisms for language acquisition. Developmental disorders provide a naturalistic way of testing the relation between the biological (and psychological) basis of language and the biological (and psychological) basis of other cognitive or neural systems (Marcus and Rabagliati 2006).

Two syndromes which have attracted more interest than others are Williams syndrome (WS) and Down's syndrome (DS). There are a number of reasons for this. The foremost reason is the fact that affected individuals present with uneven, and qualitatively different, profiles of cognitive abilities within the context of similar IQ levels (~40 to 60; Udwin and Yule 1991; Roizen 2002). In DS, relatively good visuospatial abilities contrast with poor expressive language skills (Fowler *et al.* 1994; Rondal and Comblain 1996; Chapman *et al.* 1998; Klein and Mervis 1999; Jarrold *et al.* 2002; Laws 2002). Individuals with WS display relatively good expressive language abilities and poor visuospatial abilities (Bellugi *et al.* 1994; Grant *et al.* 1997; Howlin *et al.* 1998). Within the context of language abilities, the two populations also show uneven profiles. Syntactic abilities are a relative weakness in DS but a relative strength in WS (Bellugi *et al.* 2000). Expressive prosodic skills, which are a relative weakness in DS (Pettinato and Verhoeven 2009; Stojanovik 2011), are relatively unimpaired in WS as they are in line with level of language comprehension (Stojanovik *et al.* 2007). Finally, pragmatic aspects of language are impaired in the context of WS (Laws and Bishop 2004; Stojanovik 2006), but are a relative strength for those with DS (Laws and Bishop 2004). Each of these syndromes will be reviewed separately below.

29.4.1   Williams syndrome

Williams syndrome is a relatively rare genetic condition which was first identified in 1961 by Williams and his colleagues in New Zealand (Williams *et al.* 1961). They labelled the syndrome following a clinical study of four patients with mental retardation and a peculiar facial appearance. WS occurs in one of 15,000–20,000 live births, although a study in Norway suggested an incidence rate of 1 in 7,500 (Strømme *et al.* 2002). WS results from a micro-deletion of one copy of about 20 contiguous genes in chromosome 7, affecting one of the alleles of the elastin gene (Frangistakis *et al.* 1996; Korenberg *et al.* 2000). Molecular genetic testing by means of fluorescence in situ hybridization (or FISH) can now be used to confirm the deletion of one copy of the elastin gene and other surrounding genes in a small region of chromosome 7 at 7q11.23. WS is characterized by a range of moderate to severe physical abnormalities, including elevated blood calcium levels, high blood pressure, failure to thrive in infancy and abnormal sensitivity to certain classes of sounds (hyperacusis).

On the level of brain organization, WS typically presents with no evidence of focal lesions. Given that approximately 22 out of the 28 genes within the WS critical region are thought to be expressed in the brain, it is very likely that brain development in WS differs from typical development (Karmiloff-Smith 2011). There have been few studies of the WS brain during development (i.e. childhood) and most of what we know about brain structure in WS comes from adult studies. Brain volume in WS reaches about 80 per cent of normal brain volume (Chiang *et al.* 2007) and there is increased cortical thickness (Thompson *et al.* 2005). The frontal lobes, superior temporal gyrus, amygdala, fusiform gyrus and cerebellum in WS adult brains are relatively preserved whereas the parietal and occipital lobes, the thalamus, the basal ganglia and the midbrain are smaller in volume (Karmiloff-Smith 2011). An interesting finding is that the amygdala and the cerebellum are larger than the rest of the WS brain and a large cerebellum has been shown to be present in young children with WS (Jones *et al.* 2002).

Although WS was first identified in the 1960s, it was not until about two decades later that it started attracting increasing interest from researchers. The most striking phenomenon linked to the syndrome was the reported uneven cognitive-linguistic profile. This profile includes moderate to severe learning difficulties, impairments in planning, problem solving and spatial cognition alongside relative strengths in social cognition, linguistic abilities, face processing and auditory rote memory (Mervis and Klein-Tasman 2000). Despite the fact that performance IQ is around 50 on average for people with WS, the general view is that linguistic abilities are a relative strength. However, this view has been seriously challenged in recent years.

Early studies on Williams syndrome (1970s and 1980s)

Early studies of WS were typically multidimensional investigations which incorporated behavioural, medical, physiological, cognitive and linguistic aspects of the WS profile. These studies provided a rather broad picture of the WS phenotype. However, they suggested the existence of possible dissociations in the WS profile. For example, Von Arnim and Engel (1964) described the profiles of four individuals with WS who were aged 5 to 15 years. The IQs of these children ranged from 43 to 56. They had physical growth problems, poor motor coordination, outgoing personalities, recurrent signs of unreasonable anxiety, and an unusual command of language. Von Arnim and Engel (1964: 375) stated that '[t]heir loquacity combined with friendliness and a great ability to make interpersonal contacts makes them appear brighter and more intelligent than in fact they are'. A decade later, Jones and Smith (1975) presented evaluation data on 14 children and adults with WS between the ages of 3 months and 23 years. The children were reported to have full IQ scores which ranged between 41 and 80 and a mean IQ of 56. This study also makes special mention of linguistic abilities in WS, but with not much elaboration. The personality of individuals with WS was described as 'friendly, loquacious, and cocktail party manner' (Jones and Smith 1975: 719).

It was not until 1978 that the first attempt was made to systematically quantify data on individuals with WS. Bennett et al. (1978) studied seven children with WS who were 4;6–8;5 years of age. The children had mild to moderate learning difficulties as revealed by scores (range 30–81, mean IQ 53.9) on the McCarthy Scales of Children's Abilities (McCarthy 1972). All seven children performed better on measures of verbal ability than on fine motor and gross motor measures. Bennett et al. concluded that verbal abilities in WS were superior in the face of impaired motor skills and cognitive deficits. Thus, a debate was begun which remains unresolved as yet.

A number of studies investigating linguistic abilities in WS followed throughout the 1980s. As the research base started to grow, so too did the controversy regarding 'superior' language skills in WS. Kataria et al. (1984) did not find evidence of superior verbal skills over motor abilities. Nor did they find evidence of an 'unusual command of language' (previously considered to be a marker of the syndrome). Arnold et al. (1985) found no difference in the performance of children with WS on the verbal and non-verbal subtests of the Wechsler Intelligence Scale for Children (WISC; Wechsler 1976). Furthermore, on the Reynell Developmental Language Scale (Reynell 1977), the language skills of only three children exceeded the 7-year ceiling of the test, while those of the remainder ranged from 3 to 7 years. Most children, though, were able to produce and respond to simple sentences.

Pagon et al. (1987) also administered the WISC to a group of individuals with WS. Seven of the group scored above the floor of the verbal scale, and had verbal IQs of between 47 and 85. Five of these individuals also scored above the floor on the performance scale and their performance IQs were between 45 and 69. These differences were non-significant. Only one individual with a high verbal IQ score showed a verbal advantage. Similarly, Crisco et al. (1988) found no significant verbal advantage on the Illinois Test of Psycholinguistic Abilities (Kirk et al. 1968) for a group of children with WS when matched on mental age with another group of children with non-specific developmental disabilities. However, they did observe significantly poorer performance for the WS group in comparison to the control group on visual reception, visual closure and visual memory. No verbal advantage on the WISC was reported by Dall'Oglio and Milani (1995) and Greer *et al.* (1997) on the Stanford-Binet Intelligence Scale.

Unlike the studies mentioned above, significant differences between verbal and performance IQ were reported in a series of papers by Udwin and colleagues (Udwin *et al.* 1986, 1987; Udwin and Yule 1990, 1991). These four papers give details from a single, large group of 44 individuals with infantile hypercalcaemia (former label for WS) aged between 6;0 and 15;9 years who were administered the WISC. A number of participants scored below floor on the verbal and performance scales. But verbal IQs for the remaining participants ranged between 45 and 109 (mean = 62.4), while performance IQs ranged between 45 and 73 (mean = 55.9). This suggests a verbal advantage for the majority of the participants albeit a fairly marginal one.

In summary, the majority of studies which have used IQ measures with the WS population have found no significant differences between their verbal and non-verbal profiles. The exceptions are Udwin and Yule (1990, 1991) and Udwin *et al.* (1986, 1987), who reported a marginal verbal advantage. The problem with using IQ measures for the purposes of investigating verbal and non-verbal skills is that the verbal part of both the WISC and the Stanford-Binet scales requires the use of metalinguistic skills and knowledge of social situations. Both scales examine knowledge of vocabulary by asking the participant to provide a definition (a metalinguistic skill) as opposed to, for example, only asking the participant to name a picture. Also, both scales have a comprehension sub-part which requires practical problem solving and social information. It has been widely documented across studies that individuals with WS have difficulties with problem-solving tasks (Bellugi *et al.* 1988, 1989, 1994).

More recent studies on Williams syndrome (from 1990s to present day)

From the 1990s onwards, research into WS became more systematic. Researchers started investigating various levels of language including phonology, morphosyntax, lexical semantics and pragmatics. Each of these levels will be reviewed in this section. Some studies argued that each of these areas of linguistic functioning is somewhat 'spared' or is a relative strength in WS. A series of studies from the Bellugi group mainly involving older children and young adults with WS suggested that individuals with WS have 'spared' or 'preserved' syntactic abilities (Bellugi *et al.* 1988, 1994, 1999). The evidence came from individuals with WS whose comprehension of complex syntactic structures such as reversible passives, negative clauses and conditionals was better than that of age- and IQ-matched individuals with DS. Also, individuals with WS were reported to be better than age- and IQ-matched individuals with DS at detecting syntactic anomalies and correcting ungrammatical sentences.

A study by Clahsen and Almazan (1998) also reported that individuals with WS are able to comprehend reversible passives, regular past-tense morphology and reflexive anaphors. A recent study by Musolino *et al.* (2010) argued that individuals with WS are able to understand core syntactic and semantic relations. These authors claimed that 'knowledge of core, abstract principles of grammar is present and engaged in WS' (Musolino *et al.* 2010: 155). Performance on regular as opposed to irregular morphology has been shown to be a relative strength for individuals with WS in different languages (Pleh *et al.* 2003; Clahsen *et al.* 2004). However, individuals with WS have never been shown to outperform mental age controls.

The study by Clahsen and Almazan (1998) has been referred to as an example of how a genetic disorder such as WS can support the massive modularity hypothesis. This is because the study revealed a dissociation between regular and irregular morphology, suggesting the existence of two systems: a computational system which involves the application of syntactic rules (such as 'add –ed to regular verbs'), and a lexical system responsible for lexical knowledge. Importantly, however, when Thomas *et al.* (2001) employed a developmental trajectory approach and controlled for mental age when analysing data from the performance on regular versus irregular morphology, they did not find an effect of regularity on performance in the WS group. This throws into question the original claim that children with WS are better at regular than irregular inflectional morphology. This, in turn, raises doubts about the existence of two separate computational and lexical systems.

There is no evidence in the research corpus so far to show that individuals with WS perform better than expected for their level of non-verbal ability on morphosyntactic tasks. In fact, some studies have even shown that children with WS perform below levels expected for their non-verbal mental age. For example, Joffe and Varlocosta (2007) reported that participants with WS performed significantly worse than mental-age-matched controls on a task requiring them to repeat wh- questions and also on a standardized test of grammar, the Test of the Reception of Grammar (Bishop 2003c).

With regard to lexical abilities in WS, one striking finding that has emerged from the existent literature is the relative strength in receptive vocabulary. Receptive vocabulary is one language domain in which individuals with WS tend to score better than might be predicted by their mental age (Bellugi *et al.* 1988; Rossen *et al.* 1996; Clahsen *et al.* 2004). This relative strength seems to hold for concrete rather than conceptual/relational vocabulary (Mervis and John 2008). There has been debate as to whether individuals with WS have atypical semantic organization. Some studies have shown that naming, when accurate, is faster in individuals with WS than mental age controls (Temple *et al.* 2002). Ypsilanti *et al.* (2005) reported atypical responses by individuals with WS on a word definition task. However, Tyler *et al.* (1997) did not find any different priming effects of category structure and functional relations in an online task in individuals with WS compared to controls, suggesting that semantic organization was not atypical.

Studies have also shown that individuals with WS may show delayed semantic development. For example, individuals with WS showed frequency and semantic category effects in a speeded picture-naming task which were in line with their receptive language skills (Thomas *et al.* 2006). Although some early research pointed out that individuals with WS may sometimes use rare and low-frequency vocabulary (Bellugi *et al.* 1992), which was taken as evidence that lexical semantics may be independent of general cognitive abilities (Bellugi *et al.* 2000), such findings have not been replicated. For example, Jarrold *et al.* (2000b) reported that individuals with WS did not produce more novel items in a semantic fluency task than a control group of individuals with learning difficulties matched on receptive vocabulary. More recently, Stojanovik and van Ewijk (2008) showed that, when the conversational context was controlled for, children with WS did not produce more low-frequency words than controls matched for language age, non-verbal mental age and chronological age.

Phonological abilities in WS have perhaps attracted least attention. This is possibly due to the fact that individuals with WS, unlike those with DS, have intelligible speech by and large. Suprasegmental features have attracted more interest. A seminal study by Reilly *et al.* (1990), which included only four participants with WS, reported that individuals with WS have expressive prosody which is over-rich in affect intonation. Abnormally high pitch range, which results in individuals with WS being perceived as twice as emotionally involved as children of a similar language and chronological age, was confirmed in a larger study by Setter *et al.* (2007).

Research involving a developmental trajectory approach to data analysis showed that children and teenagers with Williams syndrome show a delayed onset (relative to chronological age) in the development of some prosodic skills, such as the ability to use prosody to signal which is the most important word in a phrase (Stojanovik 2010). This same study demonstrated a delayed rate of development in the ability to use prosody to achieve the disambiguation of potentially ambiguous phrases and to produce questioning versus declarative intonation (Stojanovik 2010). In addition, children with WS have different prosodic profiles from children with DS despite having similar levels of receptive language and non-verbal abilities. In particular, children with WS were significantly better than children with DS at perceiving and producing affect and questioning versus declarative intonation (Stojanovik 2010). This cross-syndrome difference is interesting as it suggests some syndrome-specific characteristic and has implications for how we evaluate the evidence that genetic syndromes provide for innate modularity. This issue will be discussed in more detail in the conclusions of the chapter.

Last but not least, we need to mention pragmatic abilities in WS. Early studies of WS reported relative strengths in the domain of communication skills in WS. For example, Reilly *et al.* (1990) characterized individuals with WS as being 'highly social' and as 'having remarkable social understanding'. A series of studies by Jones *et al.* (2000) reported that individuals with WS used a greater number of descriptions of affective states and evaluative comments during an interview task. They also included more inferences about the affective state and motivation of story characters than children with DS or typically developing children.

However, other studies have shown that individuals with WS use more stereotyped conversation than children with DS or specific language impairment (Laws and Bishop 2004) and have difficulties with establishing social relationships and making friends (Davies *et al.* 1998). Social interaction deficits, and specifically difficulties with exchange structure, responding appropriately to interlocutor's requests for information and clarification, interpreting meaning and providing enough information for the conversational partner were reported by Stojanovik (2006). Individuals with WS also have difficulties with the understanding of idiomatic expressions (Mervis *et al.* 2003) and figurative language, in particular lexicalized metaphor comprehension, which was reported to be lower than expected for receptive language abilities (Annaz *et al.* 2009).

29.4.2 Down's syndrome

DS is the most common genetic cause of developmental delay (Martin *et al.* 2009). It results from extra genetic material on chromosome 21 (Rondal and Edwards 1997). The majority of cases (about 95%) are caused by complete duplication of chromosome 21. The remainder of cases are caused either by translocation of material from chromosome 21 to another chromosome, typically 13 or 18 (4%), or mosaicism (i.e. a mixture of trisomy and unaffected cells) (1%) (Baum *et al.* 2008). A person of any race, socioeconomic status or geographic location can have a child with DS, and the only aetiological factor definitely linked to DS is increasing maternal age (Hassold and Sherman 2002). DS has an incidence of 1 in 1,000 (Down's Syndrome Association 2012). The syndrome is characterized by a range of physiological and anatomical anomalies. Individuals with DS often have characteristic facial features due to midfacial hypoplasia. These include a flat broad face, flat nasal bridge and a flat facial profile (Baum *et al.* 2008). Physical features such as short stature, hypotonia and hyperflexibility of the joints are also present (Baum *et al.* 2008).

At the level of brain organization, some anomalies have been reported. For example, individuals with DS seem to present a right cerebral hemisphere lateralization for receptive language and a left cerebral hemisphere lateralization for production of simple and complex movements (Heath *et al.* 2007). A study by Shoji *et al.* (2009) has also reported atypical linguistic lateralization in a dichotic listening task in which individuals with DS showed a left ear advantage when presented with words with two consonant–vowel syllables. This is a different pattern to that seen in the neuro-typical brain, where language processing typically occurs in the left hemisphere. This has been supported by hand-preference studies (which are believed to be a marker of functional hemispheric specialization). For instance, children with DS were found to show weaker hand preference than typically developing children (Groen *et al.* 2008).

The linguistic and cognitive profile of individuals with DS is often characterized as 'uneven'. There are weaknesses in auditory short-term memory relative to visual short-term memory and other aspects of cognition (Chapman 2003), and strengths in social functioning abilities (Kasari and Bauminger 1998). Children with DS are slow to acquire language. General language performance in individuals with DS tends to be lower than expected from their level of cognitive development (Fowler *et al.* 1994; Chapman and Hesketh 2000; Vicari *et al.* 2000; Perovic 2001, 2002). Exceptionally, language abilities may in some cases be higher than other cognitive abilities (Rondal 1994), but such cases are rare.

Vocabulary knowledge seems to be stronger than grammatical abilities (Chapman *et al.* 1991; Miller 1996). Many children with DS do not acquire their first words before the age of 2 years (Rondal 2001). However, early lexical development generally shows a positive linear relationship with mental age (Rondal and Edwards 1997). Receptive vocabulary has also been reported to be in line with mental age (Laws and Bishop 2003). Although vocabulary is a relative strength in the language profile of the DS population, there is individual variation. In a study of 43 children with DS, Miller (1999) reported that 65 per cent scored below their mental age on vocabulary and 35 per cent had vocabulary scores consistent with their mental age on the MacArthur Communicative Development Inventories (Fenson *et al.* 1993). Jarrold *et al.* (2002) also reported that children and adults with DS often have receptive vocabulary deficits compared to typically developing individuals matched for mental age.

Morphosyntactic abilities in children with DS are a relative weakness. Eadie *et al.* (2002) compared the accuracy of marking finiteness in spontaneous speech in children with DS to that of children with specific language impairment. The study found that the profiles of the two groups of children were similar, suggesting that grammatical abilities in children with DS are comparable to those of children with known language impairments. A study by Ring and Clahsen (2005) reported that adolescents with DS have marked difficulties with tense marking, plural marking and the marking of comparative and superlative on adjectives. Interestingly, the participants with DS had equal difficulties with tense and non-tense related morphemes, suggesting that the grammatical morpheme difficulties in DS extend beyond the finiteness cluster of morphemes.

Phonological abilities in DS have been investigated more frequently than those of individuals with WS, due to the fact that individuals with DS have difficulties with producing intelligible speech. A study by Cleland *et al.* (2010) reported that two-thirds of a cohort of 15 individuals with DS (mean age 14;3 years) had severe speech disorders to the extent that they failed to meet the basal age-equivalent of 3;0 years in the Diagnostic Evaluation of Articulation and Phonology (Dodd *et al.* 2002). The most common phonological process evidenced was consonant cluster reduction followed by final consonant deletion and initial consonant deletion. Prosodic abilities are mainly in line with non-verbal mental age apart from production of affective intonation and pre-final narrow focus which seem lower than expected for non-verbal mental age (Stojanovik 2011). In addition, and similar to morphosyntactic and lexical skills, prosodic abilities seem better with regard to comprehension as opposed to production.

With regard to pragmatic and social communication skills, it has been shown that people with DS are very keen to engage in conversation and to keep the conversation going but often lack the appropriate language skills to do so (Rondal 2001). Two studies described in Abbeduto and Murphy (2004) report relative strengths and weaknesses in the DS communication profile. For example, in a barrier task, individuals with DS were less likely than typically developing individuals matched for mental age and individuals with fragile X syndrome to provide listeners with referential frames which help the listener's comprehension. Also, individuals with DS were less likely than mental-age-matched controls to signal non-comprehension. This suggests that they may be unable to monitor their own comprehension, which can seriously disrupt the flow of conversations. However, individuals with DS were found to appreciate shared knowledge in conversational exchanges. They were also able to make appropriate shifts from indefinite descriptions such as 'a house' to definite descriptions such as 'the house'.

29.5 Critical evaluation of the modularity debate

As already mentioned in the introduction (section 29.1), comparing linguistic abilities in children with WS and those with DS is relevant for addressing theoretical questions about the architecture of human cognition. This is because both genetic disorders present with similar levels of non-verbal IQ, but different linguistic profiles. The literature on linguistic abilities in WS is richer than the literature on DS, and aspects of linguistic abilities in WS, such as morphosyntactic, lexical and pragmatic abilities, have been studied more systematically and in greater detail in WS than in DS. Although it is obvious that there are areas of strengths and weaknesses in both genetic disorders, what is also striking is the fact that linguistic abilities in WS rarely, if ever, exceed non-verbal abilities. The literature review on WS in section 29.4.1 suggests that individuals with WS present with language deficits relative to chronological age, but in line with non-verbal mental age (e.g. Thomas *et al.* 2001; Stojanovik *et al.* 2004, 2007). Interestingly, language abilities in some studies have been shown to be even lower than non-verbal mental age (Joffe and Varlocosta 2007). This suggests that it is very unlikely that linguistic and non-verbal abilities are dissociable. It seems that linguistic abilities (with the exception of, perhaps, receptive vocabulary) develop in synchrony with non-verbal skills.

The innate modularity view and, in particular, the massive modularity hypothesis are based on the premise that typical cognitive architecture consists of a number of different systems. If this view is correct, it is expected that these systems will dissociate in developmental disorders. The lack of dissociations found in WS means that one cannot accept the nativist view and must accept the alternative neuroconstructivist view. This latter view posits that it is impossible for language abilities to exceed an individual's level of cognitive functioning as these abilities are not dissociable from general cognition. Studies which argue that language abilities in WS are superior to non-verbal abilities – a claim which supports the nativist view – do not have convincing evidence that this is really the case. Given that most individuals with WS reach a non-verbal mental age of between 5 and 7 years, it is not surprising that they are able to comprehend core syntactic and semantic relations (Musolino *et al.* 2010). These relations are expected to have been acquired by typically developing children by 5 years of age. Hence, there is no compelling evidence for clear dissociations between general cognitive abilities and language.

Although not as rich, evidence from DS is still very informative. This evidence leads to a different conclusion in the theoretical debate between innate modularity and neuroconstructivism. So far, research has shown that linguistic abilities in DS often lag behind non-verbal abilities. In particular, morphosyntactic skills and, in some individuals, vocabulary knowledge seem to be poorer than expected given non-verbal mental age. Such findings suggest that linguistic abilities may not be fully dependent upon non-verbal functioning, otherwise one would not expect to find language skills that are below a person's general level of cognitive functioning. It seems that in individuals with DS (although there are a few exceptions), non-verbal cognitive ability does not necessarily interact with language in the same way as it appears to in individuals with WS. This leads to the conclusion that perhaps language skills (or at least some language skills) do develop independently of other cognitive abilities, as the innate modularity hypothesis would suggest.

Interestingly, it has been research into WS rather than DS that has been referred to as the prototypical example of a dissociation between linguistic and non-verbal abilities in theoretical debates on innate modularity. However, the literature review above suggests that there may also be a dissociation between linguistic and non-verbal skills in DS. Unfortunately, linguistic abilities in DS have not received the detailed investigation, scrutiny and analyses needed in order to assess the magnitude of possible associations or dissociations between linguistic and non-verbal functioning. In addition, there have not been many studies that have adopted a developmental trajectory approach in order to explain the delay in language and other cognitive abilities often reported in individuals with DS. If it turns out that the developmental trajectory of language and other cognitive abilities is atypical in DS and that there are no clear dissociations between language and non-verbal cognitive abilities, one could argue that DS provides evidence for the neuroconstructivist view.

Despite the fact that research into developmental disorders over the past few decades has not resolved the theoretical debate between nativism and constructivism, the fields of language acquisition, developmental psychology and cognitive neuroscience have gained much from this research. For example, we now have a much more comprehensive understanding of the complexities of developmental disorders, in particular Williams syndrome and, to some extent, Down's syndrome. The evidence from these two disorders (at least what we have so far) does not exclusively support one or the other theoretical viewpoint. It would be fair to say that research into WS and DS has been driving the development of new thinking about how the theoretical frameworks we are currently working with may need to be modified. For example, based on a detailed overview of the language acquisition literature on inflectional morphology and with reference to the two competing theories (nativism and constructivism), Ambridge and Lieven (2011: 190) conclude that if nativist-generativist accounts of language acquisition could explain early errors reported in child language, and if constructivist accounts could explain how the adult state of language knowledge is reached, 'the field would be able to move closer to a complete understanding of the domain of inflectional morphology'.

In a similar manner, given that developmental disorders such as WS and DS provide evidence for both theoretical viewpoints, it seems that a more unified account is needed. This would bring the two views together so that instead of opposing each other, they would complement each other. For example, it is true that a number of cognitive skills in WS develop atypically and that there are no strong language and non-verbal dissociations in children with WS. Yet, there are dissociations found in the adult state. It seems that the neuroconstructivist view is focusing exclusively on development whereas the nativist view is focusing on the end state. However, both these viewpoints are crucial for the ultimate understanding of human cognitive architecture, and they need to be viewed in synergy with each other in order to have the optimum explanatory power.

In this respect, research into developmental disorders may lead the way to a more unified theoretical framework. Such a framework will have the power to explain developmental and end-state cognitive patterns reported not only for WS and DS but for developmental disorders in general.

29.6 Directions for future research

What is particularly lacking in our present knowledge base are investigations of early linguistic and non-verbal skills in WS and DS. There have been only a small number of studies of infants with WS and DS. Mundy *et al.* (1995) identified non-verbal requesting as a possible predictor of expressive language in DS. However, although this study was longitudinal in nature, it did not go beyond the age of 36 months. This is the age at which many children with DS would still be in the holophrastic stage of language acquisition. Hence, it is impossible to know how language development proceeds beyond this age. Laing *et al.* (2002) investigated early language development in infants with WS, also in the context of how well early social communication skills predict language outcomes. The study does not provide a longitudinal examination of language skills per se, so we do not know how linguistic skills unfold over time in the first few years of life.

However, an interesting finding emerged from Laing *et al.*'s study. These investigators found that pointing may not necessarily precede the onset of first words in WS as it does in typically developing children. The question arises as to whether an atypical trajectory of development, as evidenced from behavioural studies, means by default that modules are not specified for certain cognitive functions from birth. Unless behavioural studies are complemented by neurophysiological investigations, it will be very difficult to move the innate modularity debate forward. Our current state of knowledge would also benefit from carefully constructed, longitudinal studies including both behavioural and neurophysiological measures. These studies should examine in detail the acquisition of linguistic abilities as well as non-verbal skills in children with DS and WS from the onset of the two-word stage until about 10 years of age.

It goes without saying that the linguistic and general cognitive profiles of individuals with WS and DS are the result of brain development which occurs under certain genetic constraints. Given technological advances in cognitive neuroscience, and in particular the availability of a range of neurophysiological measures such as magnetic resonance imaging and electroencephalography, future research has the potential to explain the neurophysiological bases of resulting phenotypes. Possible neural localization and impenetrability of different 'modules' from infancy would directly address the issue of innate modularity. Studies using event related potentials (ERPs) have shown that individuals with WS do not develop the hemispheric asymmetries associated with the processing of closed versus open class words by individuals in the general population (Neville *et al.* 1994). This suggests that the neural organization of some aspects of language in WS may be different from that of the general population. However, we still do not know exactly what this means in terms of whether modules are innately specified or are a product of development. ERP studies of infants with WS would help address this issue.

30

Pragmatic disorders and theory of mind

Louise Cummings

30.1   Introduction

For approximately 40 years, clinical investigators have actively pursued research into pragmatic disorders in children and adults (Cummings 2010). During that time, there has been considerably less concern on the part of researchers to *explain* pragmatic disorders than there has been on the attempt to *characterize* these disorders. The result has been a large and somewhat disjointed body of research findings, not all of which relate in a meaningful way to pragmatic disorders (Cummings 2005, 2007a, 2007b, 2008, 2009, 2011, 2012a, 2014a, 2014b).

While many investigators have appeared content with the task of characterizing pragmatic disorders, other investigators have pursued a deeper form of analysis by striving for cognitive explanations of these disorders. These investigators have appealed to cognitive factors and frameworks such as inferential load (Bara 2010), relevance processing (Leinonen and Kerbel 1999) and weak central coherence (Norbury and Bishop 2002) to account for the pragmatic deficits that are seen to compromise communication in child and adult clients. However, one type of cognitive explanation has had more prominence than all others. This is the attempt to explain pragmatic deficits in terms of an impairment of the cognitive capacity to attribute mental states to the minds of others. This capacity, known as *theory of mind*, has had a powerful and transformative effect on research into pragmatic disorders in recent years. This chapter seeks to examine that effect and assess what gains, if any, it has delivered in terms of our understanding of pragmatic disorders.

It is apt to begin a discussion of theory of mind (ToM) by considering a definition of this cognitive capacity by Simon Baron-Cohen. Baron-Cohen's investigations of ToM deficits in autism (see section 30.3) set the scene for subsequent work in the application of ToM to the study of a range of

clinical populations. With its inclusion of *intentions*, Baron-Cohen's definition demonstrates the relevance of ToM to pragmatics, the linguistic discipline that studies utterance interpretation in terms of the attribution of
communicative intentions to the minds of speakers and hearers:

> By theory of mind we mean being able to infer the full range of men-
> tal states (beliefs, desires, intentions, imagination, emotions, etc.) that
> cause action. In brief, to be able to reflect on the contents of one's own
> and other's minds. (Baron-Cohen 2000: 3)

Mental state attribution, and specifically the attribution of communicative intentions, is such a fundamental part of the cognitive processes by
means of which pragmatic interpretation proceeds that it is impossible
to consider pragmatic notions such as implicature, deixis and presupposition without reference to these states. In this way, when Sally utters 'My
parents are visiting' in response to a question posed by her friend Bill,
'Do you want to join me for dinner this evening?', Sally may be taken
to implicate that she does not wish to accept Bill's invitation to dinner.
This implicature can only be realized if Bill is able to recover the communicative intention that has motivated Sally's utterance, the intention to
decline his (Bill's) invitation to dinner.

In arriving at this communicative intention, Bill has drawn upon his
knowledge of Sally's mental states. Amongst other things, he has used his
knowledge that Sally will want to accommodate her parents to derive the
implicature of Sally's utterance. For her part, Sally is able to issue such an
implicature because she knows certain things about Bill's mental states.
Sally knows, for example, that Bill knows that family commitments often
take priority over social engagements and that someone who is receiving
visitors cannot simultaneously have dinner with a friend. Sally's (albeit
indirect) communication of her intention to Bill is only possible to the
extent that Sally and Bill are both able to entertain thoughts about the
mental states of their interlocutor. (In fact, Sally's choice of an implicature as an indirect means of conveying her communicative intention to
Bill is also motivated by her understanding of Bill as an agent that entertains mental states, in this case, feelings which could be hurt by an out-
right rejection of his dinner invitation.) Utterance interpretation, as this
example demonstrates, is none other than an exercise in mental state
attribution. It is thus a ToM-based activity through and through.

That some type of ToM capacity is integral to utterance interpretation
is beyond doubt. The question which will concern us in this chapter is
whether deficits in this capacity can account, either in whole or in part,
for the multitude of ways in which pragmatics has been shown to be
disordered in children and adults. We will see in sections 30.3 and 30.4
that an answer to this question is not nearly as well developed as other
aspects of ToM research. One such aspect concerns the development of
ToM in young children (see Cummings 2014a). Much is now known about

the developmental stages through which children pass on their way to acquiring a theory of mind. Normally developing 4-year-olds can pass false belief tasks (a standard test of ToM), a skill that is not present in normally developing 3-year-olds. Also, certain mental states (e.g. desires, emotions) are more easily acquired by children than other mental states (e.g. beliefs, knowledge) and are first to emerge in children's use of language.

Studies of ToM in normally developing children provide theorists and clinicians with normative data against which to judge ToM achievements in neurodevelopmental disorders such as autism. It is now widely established, for example, that children with autism are on average 10 years of age before they are able to complete the same false belief tests that are passed at 4 years of age by their normally developing counterparts. Deficits in the acquisition of ToM skills by children with neurodevelopmental disorders are likely to differ in significant ways from ToM deficits in neurodevelopmentally healthy adults who sustain a brain injury, for example. ToM deficits in a range of adult clinical populations must, therefore, be examined separately. However, before we can engage with developmental and acquired ToM deficits, something more must be said about the role of ToM in pragmatic interpretation. It is to this issue that we now turn.

30.2   Pragmatic interpretation and theory of mind

In section 30.1, Sally's use of an implicature to decline Bill's invitation to dinner, and Bill's recovery of this implicature, were shown to be an exercise in mental state attribution. Both interlocutors in this exchange attributed a rich array of beliefs, desires and knowledge to each other's minds in an effort to recover the particular communicative intention that had motivated Sally's utterance to Bill. This was at all possible because Sally and Bill had a fully developed theory of each other's minds, or at least as developed as it needed to be in order to engage in utterance interpretation. Yet, implicature is not a unique pragmatic concept in respect of the role played by ToM in its recovery. All pragmatic interpretation draws to a greater or lesser extent on the same processes of mental state attribution that were evident in this example. Consider the utterances in (1) to (5) below:

(1) It was the teenager who vandalized the shop.
(2) What a delightful child! (uttered in the presence of a boisterous 5-year-old)
(3) Can you tell me the time? (uttered by a woman to a passer-by)
(4) I would love to live here.
(5) The girls looked after the children all day. They were exhausted.

The utterance in (1) contains a presupposition to the effect that someone vandalized the shop. The speaker who utters (1) is able to presuppose such a thing because he knows that the hearer knows that someone vandalized the shop. Presupposition is a means of leaving unstated in communication that which can be assumed between the speaker and hearer. Yet, this is only possible to the extent that the speaker is able to establish the beliefs and knowledge that a hearer is likely to possess. The speaker in (2) is clearly producing this utterance with considerable ironic intent. The speaker's irony is only detectable by a hearer who is able to witness the boisterous child and who knows that the speaker is also witnessing this child. The hearer can then go on to infer not just that the speaker believes that the child is boisterous but also that the speaker believes that the hearer believes that the child is boisterous. It is only with the attribution of this latter belief to the mind of the speaker that the hearer can be said to understand anything of the ironic intent with which this utterance is produced. The passer-by in (3) is able to use his knowledge of the mental state of the woman who addresses him to establish that she wants to be given the time. Moreover, the woman is only able to use this indirect speech act as a means of requesting the time because she knows that the passer-by knows that a complete stranger is unlikely to make an enquiry about one's time-telling ability.

Imagine that the utterance in (4) is produced by a passenger in a car that is being driven through a picturesque village. The other passengers in the car have little difficulty in establishing the speaker's intended referent of 'here' – it is the village the speaker would love to live in rather than the car itself or the road on which the car is travelling. This example of spatial deixis demonstrates that mental state attribution also plays an important role in the assignment of referents to linguistic expressions. The car passengers who hear the utterance in (4) know certain things about the speaker's mental states. They know, for example, that the speaker wants to live in a house rather than in a car or on a road. They also know that the speaker entertains certain beliefs such as the belief that the area is attractive to live in. It is through their knowledge of the speaker's desires and beliefs that the passengers are able to establish the intended referent of 'here'. Mental state attribution is also integral to the assignment of a referent to the pronoun 'they' in example (5). A hearer has little difficulty in establishing that a speaker intends to refer to the girls by the use of 'they' and not to the children. The question of interest is how this is possible given that either of the preceding plural noun phrases ('girls' and 'children') could be referents of this pronoun. Once again, the answer lies in mental state attribution. The hearer of the utterances in (5) knows, and knows that the speaker knows, that looking after children is a tiring activity which can lead to exhaustion.

Whether we are dealing with presuppositions, ironic utterances, speech acts, deictic expressions or reference assignment, the lesson to emerge is the same. The interpretation of pragmatic phenomena is only possible to the extent that speakers and hearers are able to attribute a range of mental states to their respective interlocutors during verbal communication. Closer examination of these mental states is necessary. In first-order mental state attribution, one person infers that another person has a certain belief about the world. In inferring that the speaker of the utterance in (2) above believes that the child is boisterous, the hearer of this utterance has engaged in first-order ToM reasoning. However, the hearer of this utterance must engage in second-order mental state attribution if he or she is to recover the ironic communicative intention that motivates the production of this utterance. Specifically, the hearer must infer not just that the speaker believes that the child is boisterous (first-order ToM reasoning), but also that the speaker believes that the hearer believes that the child is boisterous. To the extent that this latter inference does not concern what the speaker believes about the world but rather concerns what the speaker believes about the hearer's beliefs, it is a form of second-order ToM reasoning. It is this latter type of mental state attribution that is integral to pragmatic interpretation and to social interaction in general, as these comments by Sullivan and Tager-Flusberg (1999) indicate:

> Being able to represent what one person thinks about what a second person thinks allows us to understand not only another's belief about the world (a first-order belief) but also to understand that person's concern about yet another person's belief about the world (a second-order belief). This sort of reasoning is necessary for any sophisticated understanding of the subtleties inherent in social interactions. (1999: 524)

To the extent that pragmatic interpretation requires second-order mental state attribution, an important observation can be made based on what is known about ToM development in normal children. We can expect, for example, that young children will experience difficulty with many aspects of pragmatic interpretation until such time as they have the ToM skills that make pragmatic interpretation possible. It was described in section 30.1 that most normally developing 4-year-olds can pass tests of false belief. However, these tests usually examine first-order ToM reasoning (i.e. a child's understanding of an actor's beliefs about the world), a form of reasoning which we have seen does not suffice for pragmatic interpretation. Based on what we know about normal ToM development, it should not be surprising to learn that children who are 4 years of age cannot appreciate ironic utterances at a point in their language development when many structural language skills are already acquired.

The ToM reasoning that makes the interpretation of irony possible is a later developmental achievement. Although findings vary with method of assessment, we now know that children first begin to experience success on second-order ToM tasks at around 5 or 6 years of age (Miller 2009). And, as one might expect, there is considerable evidence that recognition of irony in normally developing children also begins around

6 years of age. For example, Glenwright and Pexman (2010) presented ironic utterances to 71 5 to 6-year-olds and 71 9 to 10-year-olds. These investigators found that children can determine the non-literal meanings of ironic utterances by 6 years of age, although they were not able to distinguish between sarcasm and other ironic remarks until later in middle childhood.

To date, most ToM research has focused on the developmental transition that allows normally developing children to pass false belief tests for the first time at around 4 years of age. This ToM milestone has also featured extensively in the study of neurodevelopmental disorders such as autism spectrum disorders, where investigators have been concerned to ask why children with autism take until 10 years of age to attain the ToM skills of the normally developing 4-year-old. But if the observation discussed above is correct, it would seem that most ToM research is not addressing the ToM developmental period that is likely to be of most relevance to the acquisition of pragmatics. (For other criticisms of ToM research in pragmatics, see Chapter 7 in Cummings (2009).)

Certainly, there is evidence which indicates that if investigators wish to understand the type of ToM developments which make pragmatic interpretation possible, they must extend considerably the rather limited developmental period that has been the focus of studies thus far. Levorato and Cacciari (2002) have demonstrated, for example, that the ability to use figurative language requires 'a long developmental time span'. These investigators examined the development of figurative language across four age groups: children aged 9;6 and 11;3 years, adolescents aged 18;5 years and adults. Although the ability to produce certain conventional figurative expressions is achieved by 15 years of age, the metalinguistic ability that is needed to make innovative figurative expressions communicatively appropriate and conceptually sensible continues to evolve up to adulthood. The extended developmental achievements, which make the use of figurative language possible, demand that investigators chart ToM skills into adulthood. There is some evidence that this is beginning to happen (e.g. Dumontheil *et al.* 2010).

30.3   Theory of mind deficits in developmental pragmatic disorders

It has already been stated that normally developing 4-year-olds pass tests of false belief, a developmental achievement which indicates that they are in possession of first-order ToM skills. False belief tests have been at the centre of developmental and clinical studies of ToM. For this reason, the standard format of these tests will now be described. The type of scenario typically presented in these tests is characterized in an early study by Baron-Cohen *et al.* (1985) as follows:

There were two doll protagonists, Sally and Anne. First, we checked that the children knew which doll was which (Naming Question). Sally first placed a marble into her basket. Then she left the scene, and the marble was transferred by Anne and hidden in her box. Then, when Sally returned, the experimenter asked the critical Belief Question: 'Where will Sally look for her marble?'. If the children point to the previous location of the marble, then they pass the Belief Question by appreciating the doll's now false belief. If however, they point to the marble's current location, then they fail the question by not taking into account the doll's belief. These conclusions are warranted if two control questions are answered correctly: 'Where is the marble really?' (Reality Question); 'Where was the marble in the beginning?' (Memory Question). (1985: 41)

Baron-Cohen *et al.* presented this scenario, which is an adaptation of Wimmer and Perner's (1983) puppet play paradigm, to three groups of children: 27 normally developing children (mean chronological age 4;5 years), 20 children with autism (mean chronological age 11;11 years) and 14 children with Down's syndrome (mean chronological age 10;11 years). Naming, Reality and Memory Questions were passed by all three groups of children. However, while 85 per cent of normal children and 86 per cent of children with Down's syndrome passed the Belief Question, 80 per cent of children with autism failed this question, a finding that was highly significant. The four children with autism who passed the Belief Question had chronological ages from 10;11 to 15;10 years. Clearly, the children with autism had a severe deficit in first-order mental state attribution which could not be accounted for by their reduced verbal and non-verbal mental ages (the verbal and non-verbal mental ages of the subjects with autism were higher than those of the subjects with Down's syndrome in the study).

Baron-Cohen *et al.*'s study demonstrates that while the acquisition of a theory of mind is an unproblematic achievement for normally developing children, for children with a neurodevelopmental disorder such as autism, ToM skills are acquired much later, if at all. The same neurodevelopmental disorders that compromise ToM development can also cause problems with the acquisition of language, and specifically the acquisition of pragmatic language skills. The co-occurrence of ToM deficits and pragmatic disorders in children has led investigators to ask if the former might not somehow be causally related to the latter.

It was argued in section 30.2 that there were plausible grounds for believing that ToM plays a central role in pragmatic interpretation – to the extent that utterance interpretation requires speakers and hearers to engage in mental state attribution, a ToM capacity would appear to be a fundamental part of the cognitive apparatus by means of which such interpretation is achieved. On conceptual grounds, arguments in support of a role for a ToM capacity in pragmatic interpretation appear indisputable. Ultimately, however, this is an issue that can only be properly addressed in an empirical way. In this section, we examine studies that have assessed theory of mind in four clinical populations with developmental pragmatic disorders: autism spectrum disorders, developmental language disorders, emotional and behavioural disorders and intellectual disability. We consider what these studies reveal about ToM deficits in developmental pragmatic disorders before pursuing a critical evaluation of this research in section 30.5.

By far the most widely examined clinical population with regard to ToM is the autism spectrum disorders (ASDs) (see Chapter 9, this volume). Beyond the well-established finding that children with autism experience a significant delay in their ability to engage in first-order ToM reasoning (such children are typically 10 years of age before they can pass false belief tasks), there is clear evidence of a range of mentalizing impairments in children and adults with autism spectrum disorders. Individuals with ASD display diminished awareness of their own and others' intentions (Williams and Happé 2010), impaired understanding of the perception–knowledge relationship (Lind and Bowler 2010), impaired visual perspective-taking (i.e. knowledge that different people may see the same thing differently at the same time) (Hamilton *et al.* 2009) and difficulty recognizing emotions and other mental states from faces and voices (Kleinman *et al.* 2001; Rutherford *et al.* 2002; Golan *et al.* 2006).

A parallel development has been the proliferation of studies that have examined different aspects of pragmatics in autism spectrum disorders. Investigators have found that subjects with ASDs use a limited range of assertive speech acts, particularly those involving mental states (Ziatas *et al.* 2003), display difficulty interpreting irony and detecting violations of Grice's maxims (Surian *et al.* 1996; Martin and McDonald 2004), are unable to use features of context in the interpretation of utterances (Loukusa *et al.* 2007) and produce narratives which lack coherence and referential expressions (Diehl *et al.* 2006; Colle *et al.* 2008) (see Barnes and Baron-Cohen (2010) for a discussion of narrative comprehension and production in ASD). Conversational difficulties have also been reported in children and adults with ASDs, including problems in dealing with communication breakdown by responding appropriately to requests for clarification (Volden 2004).

The presence of ToM deficits and pragmatic impairments in children and adults with ASDs is thus supported by a substantial evidential base. However, to date only a small part of that base has examined if ToM deficits are directly contributing to those impairments. While Ziatas *et al.* (2003) explain the reduced use of mental assertions that refer to thoughts and beliefs in terms of ToM impairments in the children with autism in their study, other investigators have established correlations between ToM deficits and pragmatic impairments in children and adults with ASDs. In this way, Martin and McDonald (2004) found that second-order ToM reasoning was significantly associated with the ability of subjects with Asperger's syndrome in their study to interpret non-literal utterances (ironic jokes). Surian *et al.* (1996) reported that the performance of children with autism on a task requiring the detection of utterances that violate Grice's maxims was related to their ability to attribute false beliefs.

Hale and Tager-Flusberg (2005b) examined discourse skills – specifically, the use of topic-related contingent utterances – and theory of mind in 57 children with autism. Over one year, these children made significant gains in the ability to maintain a topic of discourse. Theory of mind contributed unique variance in the contingent discourse skills of these children beyond the significant contribution made by language skills. Capps *et al.* (2000) found that the narrative abilities of 13 children with autism were linked to performance on measures of ToM and to an index of conversational competence. The limited number of studies in this area, and the fact that some investigations have failed to relate pragmatic disorders in ASD to ToM abilities (e.g. Losh and Capps 2003), suggests that more research must be undertaken before any firm conclusions can be drawn about the role of ToM deficits in pragmatic impairments in ASD.

Pragmatic impairments have been reported in children with developmental language disorder (Cummings 2014c, 2014d). This clinical population includes children with specific language impairment (SLI) in whom there is a primary impairment of structural language skills (see Chapter 5, this volume). It also includes children who have a primary impairment of pragmatics in a disorder called pragmatic language impairment (PLI). Laws and Bishop (2004) and Botting (2004) found that 41 per cent and 15 per cent of children with SLI, respectively, attained a score indicative of pragmatic impairment on the pragmatic composite of the Children's Communication Checklist (CCC; Bishop 1998). In Botting's study, 37 per cent of children with PLI scored on or below the 132 cut-off point for pragmatic impairment on this composite. Such pragmatic impairments as have been reported in children with SLI and PLI include the use of inappropriate conversational responses (Bishop *et al.* 2000b), problems in using context to understand implied meanings (Rinaldi 2000) and difficulty in performing a range of inferences that are essential to pragmatic interpretation (Botting and Adams 2005; Spanoudis *et al.* 2007; Ryder *et al.* 2008; Adams *et al.* 2009).

To date, the relationship between ToM skills in children with SLI and pragmatic deficits has not been directly examined. However, this is not to overlook the substantial number of studies that have investigated ToM in SLI. Typically, these studies have examined the relationship between structural language skills and performance on ToM tasks (e.g. Farrar *et al.* 2009). One aspect of language in particular, the syntax of complement structures, has received considerable attention on account of its role in false belief tasks. In order to entertain the thought *Sally thinks that the marble is in the basket*, subjects in a false belief task must appreciate the embedded nature of the clause *the marble is in the basket*. Miller (2004) found that performance on sentence complement structures predicted false belief performance in children with SLI.

Recently, researchers have started to investigate pragmatic impairments in children with emotional and behavioural disorders (see Chapter 8, this volume). Bishop and Baird (2001) found that 73 per cent of children in their study with attention deficit hyperactivity disorder (ADHD) scored below the 132 cut-off point indicative of pragmatic impairment on the CCC. Particularly poor scores were obtained on the scale measuring inappropriate initiation of conversation. Children with ADHD have also been reported to have difficulty drawing inferences when listening to spoken expository passages and comprehending figurative language (McInnes *et al.* 2003; Bignell and Cain 2007). Gilmour *et al.* (2004) found pragmatic language impairments and other behavioural features similar to those found in autism in two-thirds of the children with conduct disorder in their study.

There is now substantial evidence to support claims of ToM deficits in children with emotional and behavioural disorders. Buitelaar *et al.* (1999) found that children with ADHD performed significantly worse than normal children and similarly to children with autism on second-order ToM tasks. Donno *et al.* (2010) reported poorer mentalizing abilities in 26 persistently disruptive children than in comparison subjects. These children also possessed poorer pragmatic language skills than comparisons. Hughes *et al.* (1998) found that hard-to-manage preschoolers showed poor prediction or recall of a false belief. Few of these studies have attempted to relate ToM deficits to pragmatic skills. One study which has done so is that by Adachi *et al.* (2004). Using a metaphor and sarcasm scenario test, these investigators found that children with ADHD and children with high-functioning pervasive developmental disorder (HFPDD) could not understand metaphor, while only children with HFPDD could not understand a sarcastic situation. There was a high correlation between comprehension of sarcasm and success in a ToM task, which was not replicated in the case of metaphor.

The population of individuals with learning disability or intellectual disability is clinically heterogeneous, thus making it difficult to advance general statements about the pragmatic skills of this group. This heterogeneity has led to investigators characterizing pragmatic impairments in relation to the individual genetic syndromes that constitute at least part of this population (see Chapters 7 and 29, this volume). Studies have reported that subjects with Williams syndrome have difficulty with the interpretation of irony (Sullivan *et al.* 2003), that subjects with fragile X syndrome produce tangential language during conversation and engage in topic repetition (Sudhalter and Belser 2001; Murphy and Abbeduto 2007) and that individuals with Down's syndrome display impairments of referential communication and have difficulty with the comprehension of metaphors and idioms (Papagno and Vallar 2001; Abbeduto *et al.* 2006).

Individuals with these same genetic syndromes have also been found to have ToM deficits, notwithstanding Baron-Cohen *et al.*'s (1985) finding of intact ToM skills in subjects with Down's syndrome (Yirmiya *et al.* 1996; Garner *et al.* 1999; Sullivan and Tager-Flusberg 1999; Abbeduto *et al.* 2001; Cornish *et al.* 2005). Few studies have examined the relationship between ToM and pragmatics in subjects with intellectual disability. An exception is Abbeduto *et al.* (2004), who found that limited narrative language skills in subjects with intellectual disability contributed substantially to the failure of these subjects on a false belief task. This study is significant in that it suggests a different direction in the ToM–pragmatics relationship. Where poor ToM skills have thus far been credited with causing pragmatic impairments, Abbeduto *et al.*'s study raises the possibility that these impairments may be a contributory factor in poor ToM performance.

30.4 Theory of mind deficits in acquired pragmatic disorders

Many diseases and injuries that cause pragmatic disorders have their onset in adulthood or at least in the period when most language and pragmatic development is believed to be complete. Adults can sustain a cerebrovascular accident or stroke which may cause a lesion in the right hemisphere of the brain. Right hemisphere damage can have significant (and often overlooked) implications for communication, particularly within the area of pragmatics. Where damage to the brain is multifocal in nature, such as occurs in traumatic brain injury, the patient may experience subtle pragmatic and discourse deficits which are not readily identified on formal assessment, but which nevertheless act as a significant barrier to communication.

The onset of mental illness in adulthood can lead to a marked pragmatic disturbance in conditions such as schizophrenia. A growing number of neurodegenerative disorders, including most notably the dementias, but also conditions such as Parkinson's disease and Huntington's disease, are associated with pragmatic disorders in adults. Alongside the expansion in our knowledge of pragmatic disorders in adults, there has been increasing interest on the part of researchers in the role of ToM deficits in these various clinical populations. Whilst many ToM studies of adults have been conducted in isolation from pragmatic concerns, a smaller number have undertaken to examine the relationship of ToM deficits to pragmatic disorders. This section will examine adult-onset pragmatic disorders and will discuss the role of ToM deficits within them.

Right hemisphere damage (RHD) has been linked to significant pragmatic and discourse deficits (see Chapter 14, this volume). These deficits were first formally characterized by Penelope Myers in 1979. Myers described how her stroke patients with dysarthria and RHD were communicating inadequately, notwithstanding their intact language skills (see Cummings (2009: 97) for discussion). Since this early investigation, the pragmatic impairments of the RHD population have been extensively examined. Subjects with RHD display problems with the comprehension of non-literal language such as occurs in idioms, proverbs and humour (Brundage 1996; Cheang and Pell 2006; Papagno *et al.* 2006). Discourse skills are noticeably deviant. These skills have been described as tangential and egocentric with speakers with RHD displaying extreme verbosity or paucity of speech (Blake 2006). Narratives produced by these patients are noteworthy for their poor information content and lack of cohesion and coherence (Marini *et al.* 2005). Subjects with RHD fail to respond to violations of Gricean maxims, do not assume equal responsibility for the development of an intentional structure in conversation and experience problems with inferencing (Rehak *et al.* 1992; Hird and Kirsner 2003; Saldert and Ahlsén 2007).

Cognitive features of the RHD population, including ToM, have been the focus of numerous studies. These studies have revealed problems with a range of mentalizing skills (Griffin *et al.* 2006; Weed *et al.* 2010). However, few of these studies have attempted to examine the relationship between ToM and pragmatics in patients with RHD. One study which does is that by Winner *et al.* (1998). These investigators found that patients with RHD performed significantly worse than controls on measures of second-order belief attribution and that the ability to distinguish lies from ironic jokes correlated strongly with these measures.

Subjects with traumatic brain injury (TBI) display marked pragmatic and discourse impairments (see Chapter 16, this volume). Many of these impairments are related to the significant cognitive deficits that are found in this clinical population (see Cummings (2009: 107) for discussion). These impairments have been captured in studies that have investigated the performance of subjects with TBI in conversation and in narrative and procedural discourse. Performance in these domains was used by MacLennan *et al.* (2002) to study pragmatic impairments in 144 patients with TBI. A pragmatic rating scale revealed pragmatic impairments in 86 per cent of these patients, with the highest frequency of impairment in cohesion, repair, elaboration, initiation and relevance. Subjects with TBI examined by Angeleri *et al.* (2008) performed worse than controls on all scales of a communication battery that was used to examine pragmatic features of communicative exchanges. These subjects also showed a trend of increasing difficulty in understanding and producing pragmatic phenomena, with standard communication acts easier than deceits which were in turn easier than ironies. Other pragmatic impairments include difficulty with topic management and the use of politeness markers in conversation (Togher and Hand 1998; Coelho *et al.* 2002).

ToM deficits have been extensively reported in adolescents and adults with TBI (Turkstra *et al.* 2004; Henry *et al.* 2006; Milders *et al.* 2006; Muller *et al.* 2010). The relationship of these deficits to pragmatic impairments is, however, still uncertain. McDonald and Flanagan (2004) reported that the second-order ToM judgements of the adults with TBI in their study were related to the ability to understand conversational inference. However, other investigators believe that ToM deficits in TBI are probably distinct from the pragmatic communication skills of these clients (e.g. Muller *et al.* 2010).

Schizophrenia is a relatively common mental illness which has adverse implications for language in general and pragmatic skills in particular (see Chapter 17, this volume). Pragmatic impairments in this population include difficulty recognizing the communicative intentions behind violations of Gricean maxims, problems with topic management and referential communication and difficulty processing aspects of linguistic context (Bazin *et al.* 2000; Sitnikova *et al.* 2002; Tényi *et al.* 2002; Docherty *et al.* 2003; Meilijson *et al.* 2004) (see Cummings (2012b) for a discussion of context in clinical pragmatics). Increasingly, investigators are characterizing pragmatic impairments in relation to the different symptom profiles of patients with schizophrenia (see Cummings (2012c) for a discussion of the diagnostic value of pragmatic deficits in schizophrenia). For example, Corcoran and Frith (1996) examined politeness and appreciation of the Gricean maxims of quantity, quality and relation in patients with schizophrenia who have positive symptoms (paranoid delusions) and patients with negative symptoms.

Some pragmatic impairments have been examined in the context of ToM deficits in schizophrenia. Brüne and Bodenstein (2005) investigated the relation of proverb understanding to ToM in 31 patients with schizophrenia. These investigators found that approximately 39 per cent of the variance of proverb comprehension in these patients was predicted by ToM performance. Champagne-Lavau *et al.* (2009) used a referential communication task to examine ToM in a study of 31 patients with schizophrenia. As well as having difficulty attributing mental states in a classic ToM task, these patients were unable to mark new and old information and use information they shared with the experimenter in a referential communication task. Investigators have also attempted to characterize ToM impairments in relation to different symptom profiles in individuals with schizophrenia. Montag *et al.* (2011) found that negative symptoms in schizophrenia are associated with a lack of a mental state concept, while positive symptoms like delusions are associated with 'overmentalizing'.

The population of adults with neurodegenerative diseases is large, and includes individuals with a range of dementias and conditions such as Huntington's disease and Parkinson's disease (see Chapter 15, this volume). The pragmatic features of Alzheimer's disease (AD), the most common cause of dementia, are by now well documented. Subjects with AD have problems with discourse coherence and produce irrelevant, redundant and incorrect utterances during discourse production tasks (Cherney and Canter 1992; Chapman *et al.* 1995). Referential communication, conversational repair and topic management are also problematic areas of pragmatic functioning (Mentis *et al.* 1995; Orange *et al.* 1996; Carlomagno *et al.* 2005). The comprehension of figurative language is impaired, although this is not an early symptom of AD (Papagno 2001).

More recently, researchers have started to investigate the pragmatic skills of patients with other types of dementia (e.g. Rousseaux *et al.* 2010). Kertesz *et al.* (2010) examined the language and pragmatic skills of subjects with four different types of dementia: semantic dementia, progressive non-fluent aphasia, Alzheimer's disease and a behavioural variant of frontotemporal dementia (FTD). Significant pragmatic disturbance was identified in patients with semantic dementia with 75.7 per cent exhibiting problems in this area. Pragmatic impairments have also been reported in patients with Parkinson's disease. Such impairments include problems with the comprehension of speech acts, metaphor and irony as well as difficulty with conversational appropriateness and turn-taking (McNamara and Durso 2003; Monetta and Pell 2007; Monetta *et al.* 2009; Holtgraves and McNamara 2010). Studies of pragmatic skills in the non-Alzheimer's dementias and Parkinson's disease are to be welcomed for expanding this area of work beyond its traditional focus on pragmatic impairments in Alzheimer's disease.

Much is now known about the ToM skills of adults with neurodegenerative disorders. Modinos *et al.* (2009) studied ToM in several patients with early-stage dementias. The subject with AD in their study did not display a specific ToM deficit. A clear ToM deficit was reported in a patient with frontal or behavioural variant FTD. This patient misattributed beliefs, assumed intentionality in comments that could hurt somebody else's feelings and attributed wrong emotions to eye expressions. A patient with Lewy body dementia and a patient with vascular dementia also displayed ToM deficits, although these were not as severe as those recorded in the patient with FTD. The finding of poor ToM skills in frontal or behavioural variant FTD has been replicated in other studies, some of which have also reported impairments in second-order false belief tasks in patients with AD (Gregory *et al.* 2002; Fernandez-Duque *et al.* 2009). Increasingly, ToM impairments are being reported in patients with Parkinson's disease (Saltzman *et al.* 2000). These impairments include deficits in both affective and cognitive subcomponents of ToM (Bodden *et al.* 2010).

Few studies of ToM skills in patients with neurodegenerative disorders have examined the relationship between ToM performance and pragmatic impairments. Two exceptions are noteworthy. Cuerva *et al.* (2001) studied 34 patients with probable Alzheimer's disease. These investigators reported a significant association between performance on a test of second-order false belief and pragmatic deficits in the interpretation of indirect requests and conversational implications. Monetta *et al.* (2009) examined irony comprehension and ToM in 11 non-demented patients with Parkinson's disease. A significant correlation was reported in these patients between the ability to interpret an utterance as a lie or an ironic remark and second-order belief questions.

30.5 Critical evaluation of theory of mind research in pragmatic disorders

The literature on ToM is now particularly well developed. Investigations of ToM have moved substantially beyond the developmental period to examine how these skills mature and change in adolescent, adult and ageing subjects (see Cummings 2014a). Among clinical studies, the traditionally dominant focus on ToM skills in the autism spectrum disorders has been superseded by investigations of mentalizing in neuropsychiatric, neurodegenerative and neurocognitive populations. Tests of ToM have also proliferated and include, in addition to first- and second-order false belief tasks, tests of faux pas detection, deception and reading mental states from eye gaze and facial expressions (although the extent to which these different ToM tests may be said to measure skills of mental state attribution has been challenged, e.g. Saltzman *et al.* 2000).

In short, there is much within ToM research to be commended. Yet, there is also a clear sense in which some of this research has failed to throw an explanatory light on mentalizing skills as these skills relate to pragmatic disorders. The issue of concern goes beyond the limited number of empirical studies that have attempted to examine the relationship between ToM and pragmatics, a point that was raised on several occasions in sections 30.3 and 30.4. Rather, the issue goes to the very heart of what constitutes a ToM capacity, or at least a ToM capacity that is able to subserve pragmatic interpretation. When we consider the type of ToM capacity that is required for utterance interpretation, we find that ToM studies often fall short of capturing that capacity in significant ways. It is to an examination of this issue that we now turn.

In a review of ToM research in autism, Baron-Cohen (2000: 4) lists no less than 20 different tests which have been used to examine mentalizing skills in children and adults with this disorder. Of these tests, the following three relate directly to pragmatics: (1) tests of understanding metaphor, sarcasm and irony, (2) tests of pragmatics in speech, (3) tests of recognition of violations of pragmatic rules. Among the tests of pragmatics in speech in (2), Baron-Cohen mentions studies which examine the recognition of faux pas. These three categories of ToM test are worth examining further for the problems they reveal about ToM research in relation to pragmatics. In demonstration of the tests subsumed by (1), consider the following investigation by Mo *et al.* (2008) of metaphor and irony comprehension in patients with schizophrenia. These patients, who were all in remission at the time of the study, also completed first- and second-order

ToM tasks. Metaphor and irony comprehension was assessed by means of narrated stories. These stories were followed by questions which were intended to test patients' understanding of the metaphorical and ironical content of the narrated passages. One of the passages used in this study is shown below, along with the questions which were intended to probe the patients' understanding of metaphor and irony:

> Xiao Zhang could never make up his mind about anything. One day when Li Qi and Wang Li asked him if he would like to go to the cinema, Xiao Zhang could not decide. It took him so long to make up his mind that by the time he did, they had already missed the first half of the film …

> On the metaphorical presentation, the story continued … Li Qi said: 'Xiao Zhang, you are a ship without a captain!'

> **Metaphor** question: What does Li Qi mean? Does he mean Xiao Zhang is good or not good at making decisions?

> On the ironical presentation, the story continued … Wang Li said to Xiao Zhang: 'You really are so good at making decisions!'

> **Irony** question: What does Wang Li mean? Does he mean Xiao Zhang is good or not good at making up his mind?

This passage and its accompanying probe questions are typical of those used by investigators who examine the relation of ToM to pragmatics in clinical subjects. Yet, neither the metaphor nor the irony question is successfully tapping the particular pragmatic phenomenon it purports to examine. In the metaphorical presentation of the passage, regardless of how the respondent answers the metaphor question, he or she becomes committed to a presupposition of that question, a presupposition to the effect that the utterance 'You are a ship without a captain!' is stating something about Xiao Zhang's ability to make decisions. In not allowing the respondent the opportunity to deny a metaphorical interpretation of the passage, the probe question is itself not felicitous.

This somewhat ironical pragmatic error on the part of these investigators is accompanied by an even greater problem in the irony version of the same passage. The irony question 'What does Wang Li mean?' invites the response 'Wang Li thinks that Xiao Zhang is good/not good at making up his mind'. This question and its response involve a first-order belief, Wang Li's belief about Xiao Zhang's decision-making ability. Yet, this is quite different from the second-order ToM reasoning which, it was argued in section 30.2, is the basis of the interpretation of irony in language. In order for *this* interpretation to be adequately tested, Mo *et al.* needed to pose a quite different question, a question to the effect 'What does Wang Li think that Xiao Zhang believes the utterance *You really are so good at making decisions* means?' The response to this question – Wang Li thinks that Xiao Zhang believes the utterance means *x* – is the belief that the respondent must attribute to Wang Li's mind in order to be said to have appreciated the ironic intent of Wang Li's utterance. It is only by asking this latter question that Mo *et al.* can expect to assess the second-order ToM reasoning and irony comprehension of the subjects with schizophrenia in their study.

Within his category of tests of pragmatics of speech, Baron-Cohen (2000) includes tasks which assess the recognition of faux pas. In Baron-Cohen *et al.* (1999), the format of these tasks is described in detail. In this study, Baron-Cohen and his colleagues investigated the recognition of faux pas by children with Asperger's syndrome (AS) or high-functioning autism (HFA). Twelve children with AS or HFA, and 16 normal controls were presented with 10 short stories on audio cassette. In one of these stories, a girl called Kim is helping her Mum make an apple pie for her Uncle Tom who is visiting. Kim carried the pie out of the kitchen and, upon seeing her uncle, said 'I made it just for you'. Uncle Tom replied 'Mmm, that looks lovely. I love pies, except for apple, of course!' Subjects were then asked a series of questions. One of these questions assessed if subjects had detected the faux pas in the story ('In the story did someone say something that they should not have said?'). A further question required subjects to identify the faux pas ('What did they say that they should not have said?'). A third question tested subjects' understanding of the language used in the story ('What kind of pie had Kim made?'). A fourth question aimed to assess if subjects were aware that the faux pas was a consequence of a false belief on the part of the speaker in the story ('Did Uncle Tom know that the pie was an apple pie?').

Scenarios of the kind just described create a substantial difficulty for ToM researchers. Tests of faux pas recognition, according to Baron-Cohen (2000), relate to 'pragmatics in speech'. Yet, when they recognize or fail to recognize faux pas, the children in this study are not engaging in the type of mental state attribution that is integral to pragmatic interpretation. In recognizing or failing to recognize Uncle Tom's mistaken belief in the above scenario, the children are merely attributing a first-order belief to Tom, a belief that the pie made by Kim is not apple. However, this is something quite different from the attribution of communicative intentions that is the basis of all pragmatic interpretation.

We have already seen how communicative intentions take the form of second-order mental representations, in which interlocutors are attributing beliefs about a hearer's beliefs to the minds of speakers. This second-order ToM reasoning is not even beginning to be assessed through the type of faux pas recognition study conducted by Baron-Cohen *et al.* (1999). To the extent that the recognition of faux pas is none other than the recognition of false belief, it is not surprising that only 18 per cent of children with AS or HFA passed this faux pas test (75 per cent of normal children passed this test, a difference that was highly significant). For we have described from the outset of this chapter that performance on tests of false belief is impaired in subjects with ASDs over and above any impairment that might be contributed by factors such as reduced intellectual functioning, for example. It emerges that Baron-Cohen *et al.*'s faux pas study tells us little about ToM skills used in pragmatic interpretation and serves only to repeat the well-established finding of impaired false belief performance in subjects with ASDs.

ToM researchers have also examined the ability of children with autism to recognize violations of Gricean rules (one of Baron-Cohen's 'tests of recognition of violations of pragmatic rules'). The rationale for these studies is articulated by Surian *et al.* (1996: 58) in a study of high-functioning children with autism: 'if children with autism have deficits in ascribing mental states, and particularly ascribing intentions, then they should fail to recognize when such Gricean maxims are being violated'. The following violation of the quality maxim is one of the examples used in Surian *et al.*'s study:

A: Where do you live?

B: I live on the moon.

In this exchange, B has produced a response which is evidently false and thus violates the Gricean maxim of quality. However, in so recognizing this maxim violation, the child with autism cannot be said to have engaged in any form of pragmatic interpretation. The pragmatic significance of Grice's maxims resides, not in their mere recognition by interlocutors within an exchange, but in their use in a process of reasoning which terminates in an implicature intended by the speaker of an utterance.

In relation to the above exchange, A assumes that B is attempting to be cooperative within the exchange, notwithstanding B's use of an utterance that is clearly false. A uses this assumption of cooperation to derive an implicature of B's utterance. B may be attempting to implicate that he does not wish to tell A where he lives or that he believes A has posed a somewhat intrusive question. Simply recognizing that a maxim has been violated is not in any way a test of an individual's ToM skills. These skills only truly come into action (and are only properly tested) when the recognition that a maxim has been violated becomes the first step in a process of reasoning that issues forth in an implicature. Surian *et al.* found that while most children with autism performed at chance on this maxim task, all children with specific language impairment and all normal controls performed above chance. Yet, this finding lacks any real implications for our knowledge of ToM skills and pragmatics in autism, given the failure of this maxim task to assess adequately the processes at work in both these domains.

An examination of each of the categories of ToM test relating to pragmatics identified by Baron-Cohen (2000) has revealed certain problems in how ToM skills, pragmatic phenomena, or both are conceptualized. Tests of the understanding of irony (category 1) were shown to use questions that probed first-order beliefs when an appreciation of irony requires that hearers attribute second-order beliefs to the minds of speakers. Tests of faux pas recognition (category 2) were shown to be little more than first-order false belief tasks which failed to represent the ToM skills that are necessary for pragmatic interpretation (notwithstanding their categorization as 'tests of the pragmatics of speech'). Tests of the recognition of the violation of Gricean maxims (category 3) failed to assess how speakers and hearers use their knowledge of maxim violation to generate implicatures. Merely identifying that a maxim is violated by a speaker involves no mental state attribution whatsoever if the hearer does not then use that maxim violation to attribute certain communicative intentions to the speaker.

The upshot of each of these scenarios is that ToM investigators still have some way to go if they are to succeed in capturing the processes of mental state attribution that subserve pragmatic interpretation. The only way to make progress on this task, I have contended, is to consider in conceptual terms what constitutes pragmatic interpretation (see Chapter 7 in Cummings 2009). It is not until investigators are clear on this issue that they can develop a ToM framework capable of capturing the mentalizing skills that speakers and hearers use during utterance interpretation. Such a pragmatic reorientation of ToM research promises to make a substantial contribution to our understanding of the role of ToM in pragmatic disorders.

30.6 Concluding remarks

Increasingly, clinical pragmatic research is moving beyond merely characterizing pragmatic disorders in children and adults to providing a cognitive explanation of these disorders. A cognitive account that is of growing significance is to be found in the construct of a theory of mind. In this way, it is argued that individuals with pragmatic disorders fail to interpret and produce utterances in context because of a reduced capacity to attribute mental states both to their own minds and to the minds of others. This chapter examined evidence in support of this claim by considering the findings of studies which have investigated ToM deficits in a range of developmental and acquired pragmatic disorders. While clinical studies in this area are still small in number, their findings suggest that the relationship between ToM and pragmatics is a potentially productive line of enquiry in terms of achieving a better understanding of pragmatic disorders. The chapter considered some of the ways in which ToM researchers have examined mentalizing and pragmatic language skills to date. It was concluded that ToM research requires some pragmatic reorientation if it is to properly capture the mentalizing skills that are involved in utterance interpretation.

References

Aarsland, D., Bronnick, K., Williams-Gray, C., Weintraub, D., Marder, K., Kulisevsky, J., Burn, D., Barone, P., Pagonabarraga, J., Allcock, L., Santangelo, G., Foltynie, T., Janvin, C., Larsen, J.P., Barker, R.A. and Emre, M. 2010. 'Mild cognitive impairment in Parkinson disease: a multicenter pooled analysis', *Neurology* 75:12, 1062–9.

Abbeduto, L. (ed.) 2003. *International review of research in mental retardation (volume 27). Language and communication in mental retardation*, San Diego, CA: Academic Press.

Abbeduto, L. and Chapman, R. 2005. 'Language and communication skills in children with Down syndrome and fragile X', in P. Fletcher and J. Miller (eds.), *Trends in language acquisition research: developmental theory and language disorders*, Amsterdam: John Benjamins, 53–72.

Abbeduto, L. and Hagerman, R.J. 1997. 'Language and communication in fragile X syndrome', *Mental Retardation and Developmental Disabilities* 3:4, 313–22.

Abbeduto, L. and Hesketh, L.J. 1997. 'Pragmatic development in individuals with mental retardation: learning to use language in social interactions', *Mental Retardation and Developmental Disabilities Research Reviews* 3:4, 323–33.

Abbeduto, L. and Murphy, M.M. 2004. 'Language, social cognition, maladaptive behaviour, and communication in Down syndrome and fragile X syndrome', in M.L. Rice and S.F. Warren (eds.), *Developmental language disorders: from phenotype to aetiologies*, Mahwah, NJ: Erlbaum, 77–97.

Abbeduto, L., Brady, N. and Kover, S.T. 2007b. 'Language development and fragile X syndrome: profiles, syndrome-specificity, and within-syndrome differences', *Mental Retardation and Developmental Disabilities Research Reviews* 13:1, 36–46.

Abbeduto, L., Davies, B., Solesby, S. and Furman, L. 1991. 'Identifying the referents of spoken messages: the use of context and clarification requests by children with and without mental retardation', *American Journal on Mental Retardation* 95:5, 551–62.

Abbeduto, L., Murphy, M.M., Cawthon, S.W., Richmond, E.K., Weissman, M.D., Karadottir, S. and O'Brien, A. 2003. 'Receptive language skills of adolescents and young adults with Down syndrome or fragile x syndrome', *American Journal on Mental Retardation* 108:3, 149–60.

Abbeduto, L., Murphy, M.M., Richmond, E.K., Amman, A., Beth, P., Weissman, M.D., Kim, J., Cawthon, S.W. and Karadottir, S. 2006. 'Collaboration in referential communication: comparison of youth with Down syndrome or fragile X syndrome', *American Journal on Mental Retardation* 111:3, 170–83.

Abbeduto, L., Pavetto, M., Kesin, E., Weissman, M.D., Karadottir, S., O'Brien, A. and Cawthon, S. 2001. 'The linguistic and cognitive profile of Down syndrome: evidence from a comparison with fragile X syndrome', *Down Syndrome Research and Practice* 7:1, 9–15.

Abbeduto, L., Short-Meyerson, K., Benson, G. and Dolish, J. 2004. 'Relationship between theory of mind and language ability in children and adolescents with intellectual disability', *Journal of Intellectual Disability Research* 48:2, 150–9.

Abbeduto, L., Short-Meyerson, K., Benson, G., Dolish, J. and Weissman, M. 1998. 'Understanding referential expressions in context: use of common ground by children and adolescents with mental retardation', *Journal of Speech, Language, and Hearing Research* 41:6, 1348–62.

Abbeduto, L., Warren, S.F. and Conners, F.A. 2007a. 'Language development in Down syndrome: from the prelinguistic period to the acquisition of literacy', *Mental Retardation and Developmental Disabilities Research Reviews* 13:3, 247–61.

Abitbol, A., Friedland, J.D., Lewin, A.A., Rodrigues, M.-A. and Mishra, V. 1999. 'Radiation therapy in oncologic management with special emphasis on head and neck carcinoma', in P.A. Sullivan and A.M. Guilford (eds.), *Swallowing intervention in oncology*, San Diego, CA: Singular, 47–63.

Abitbol, J., Abitbol, P. and Abitbol, B. 1999. 'Sex hormones and the female voice', *Journal of Voice* 13:3, 424–46.

Abuom, T.O. and Bastiaanse, R. 2012. 'Characteristics of Swahili-English bilingual agrammatic spontaneous speech and the consequences for understanding agrammatic aphasia', *Journal of Neurolinguistics* 25:4, 276–93.

Achenbach, T.M. 2001. *Manual for the child behavior checklist/4–18 and 2001 profile*, Burlington: University of Vermont, Department of Psychiatry.

Ackerman, P., Dykman, R. and Gardner, M. 1990. 'Counting rate, naming rate, phonological sensitivity and memory span: major factors in dyslexia', *Journal of Learning Disabilities* 23:5, 325–7.

Ackermann, H., Hertrich, I. and Ziegler, W. 2010. 'Dysarthria', in J. Damico, N. Müller and M. Ball (eds.), *The handbook of language and speech disorders*, Chichester, West Sussex: Wiley-Blackwell, 362–90.

Adachi, T., Koeda, T., Hirabayashi, S., Maeoka, Y., Shiota, M., Wright, E.C. and Wada, A. 2004. 'The metaphor and sarcasm scenario test: a new instrument to help differentiate high functioning pervasive developmental disorder from attention deficit/hyperactivity disorder', *Brain & Development* 26:5, 301–6.

Adams, C. 2005. 'Social communication intervention for school-age children: rationale and description', *Seminars in Speech and Language* 26:3, 181–8.

Adams, C., Clarke, E. and Haynes, R. 2009. 'Inference and sentence comprehension in children with specific or pragmatic language impairments', *International Journal of Language & Communication Disorders* 44:3, 301–18.

Adams, C., Green, J., Gilchrist, A. and Cox, A. 2002. 'Conversational behaviour of children with Asperger syndrome and conduct disorder', *Journal of Child Psychology and Psychiatry* 43:5, 679–90.

Adams, J.A. 1986. 'Use of the model's knowledge of results to increase observer's performance', *Journal of Human Movement Studies* 12, 89–98.

Adams, L., Fletcher, S. and McCutcheon, M. 1989. 'Cleft palate speech assessment through oral-nasal acoustic measures', in K. Bzoch (ed.), *Communicative disorders related to cleft lip and palate*, Boston, MA: College Hill Press, 246–57.

Adams, M.J. 1990. *Beginning to read: thinking and learning about print*, Cambridge, MA: MIT Press.

Adams, R.D., Victor, M. and Ropper, A.H. 1997. *Principles of neurology*, sixth edition, New York: McGraw-Hill.

Adams, S.G., Dykstra, A.D., Jenkins, M. and Jog, M. 2008. 'Speech-to-noise levels and conversational intelligibility in hypophonia and Parkinson's disease', *Journal of Medical Speech-Language Pathology* 16, 165–72.

Addington, J., Saeedi, H. and Addington, D. 2006. 'Influence of social perception and social knowledge on cognitive and social functioning in early psychosis', *British Journal of Psychiatry* 189:4, 373–8.

Adlam, A.L., Patterson, K., Rogers, T.T., Nestor, P.J., Salmond, C.H., Acosta-Cabronero, J. and Hodges, J.R. 2006. 'Semantic dementia and fluent primary progressive aphasia: two sides of the same coin?', *Brain* 129:11, 3066–80.

Aichert, I. and Ziegler, W. 2004. 'Syllable frequency and syllable structure in apraxia of speech', *Brain and Language* 88:1, 148–59.

Aichert, I. and Ziegler, W. 2008. 'Learning a syllable from its parts: cross-syllabic generalisation effects in patients with apraxia of speech', *Aphasiology* 22:11, 1216–29.

Akyildiz, S., Ogut, F., Akyildiz, M. and Engin, E.Z. 2008. 'A multivariate analysis of objective voice changes after thyroidectomy without laryngeal nerve injury', *Archives of Otolaryngology – Head and Neck Surgery* 134:6, 596–602.

Al Otaiba, S. and Fuchs, D. 2002. 'Characteristics of children who are unresponsive to early literacy intervention', *Remedial and Special Education* 23:5, 300–16.

Albert, G.W., Menezes, A.H., Hansen, D.R., Greenlee, J.D.W. and Weinstein, S.L. 2010. 'Chiari malformation type I in children younger than age 6 years: presentation and surgical outcome', *Journal of Neurosurgery: Pediatrics* 5:6, 554–61.

Albert, M., Sparks, R. and Helm, N.A. 1973. 'Melodic intonation therapy for aphasia', *Archives of Neurology* 29:2, 130–1.

Albert, M.S., DeKosky, S.T., Dickson, D., Dubois, B., Feldman, H.H., Fox, N.C., Gamst, A., Holtzman, D.M., Jagust, W.J., Petersen, R.C., Snyder, P.J., Carrillo, M.C., Thies, B. and Phelps, C.H. 2011. 'The diagnosis of mild cognitive impairment due to Alzheimer's disease: recommendations from the National Institute on Aging-Alzheimer's Association workgroups on diagnostic guidelines for Alzheimer's disease', *Alzheimer's & Dementia* 7:3, 270–9.

Allen, M.M. 2009. 'The impact of treatment intensity on a phonological intervention', American Speech, Language and Hearing Association Conference: New Orleans, Louisiana, 18–21 November 2009.

Allen, P., Larøi, F., McGuire, P.K. and Aleman, A. 2008. 'The hallucinating brain: a review of structural and functional neuroimaging studies of hallucinations', *Neuroscience and Biobehavioral Reviews* 32:1, 175–91.

Alm, P.A. 2011. 'Cluttering: a neurological perspective', in D. Ward and K. Scaler Scott (eds.), *Cluttering: research, intervention and education*, East Sussex: Psychology Press, 3–28.

Almkvist, O., Fratiglioni, L., Aguero-Torres, H., Viitanen, M. and Backman, L. 1999. 'Cognitive support at episodic encoding and retrieval: similar patterns of utilization in community-based samples of Alzheimer's disease and vascular dementia patients', *Journal of Clinical Experimental Neuropsychology* 21:6, 816–30.

Almor, A., Kempler, D., MacDonald, M.C., Andersen, E.S. and Tyler, L.K. 1999. 'Why do Alzheimer patients have difficulty with pronouns? Working memory, semantics, and reference in comprehension and production in Alzheimer's disease', *Brain and Language* 67:3, 202–27.

Almost, D. and Rosenbaum, P. 1998. 'Effectiveness of speech intervention for phonological disorders: a randomized controlled trial', *Developmental Medicine and Child Neurology* 40:5, 319–25.

Alt, M. and Plante, E. 2006. 'Factors that influence lexical and semantic fast mapping of young children with specific language impairment', *Journal of Speech, Language, and Hearing Research* 49:5, 941–54.

Altman, K.W., Atkinson, C. and Aazrus, C. 2005. 'Current and emerging concepts in muscle tension dysphonia: a 30-month review', *Journal of Voice* 19:2, 261–7.

Alzheimer's Association. 2010. '2010 Alzheimer's disease facts and figures', *Alzheimer's & Dementia* 6:2, 158–94.

Ambridge, B. and Lieven, E. 2011. *Child language acquisition: contrasting theoretical approaches*, Cambridge University Press.

Ambrose, N.G. and Yairi, E. 1999. 'Normative disfluency data for early childhood stuttering', *Journal of Speech, Language, and Hearing Research* 42:4, 895–909.

Ambrose, N.G., Cox, N.J. and Yairi, E. 1997. 'The genetic basis of persistence and recovery in stuttering', *Journal of Speech, Language, and Hearing Research* 40:3, 567–80.

American Academy of Child and Adolescent Psychiatry. 1999. 'Summary of the practice parameters for the assessment and treatment of children, adolescents, and adults with mental retardation and comorbid mental disorders', *Journal of the American Academy of Child & Adolescent Psychiatry* 38:12, 1606–10.

American Academy of Pediatrics, Council on Children with Disabilities, American Academy of Ophthalmology, American Association for Pediatric Ophthalmology and Strabismus, and American Association of Certified Orthoptists. 2009. 'Learning disabilities, dyslexia and vision', *Pediatrics*, 124:2, 837–44.

American Cancer Society. 2007. *Global cancer facts and figures 2007*, Atlanta, GA: American Cancer Society.

American Cleft Palate-Craniofacial Association. 2009. *Parameters for evaluation and treatment of patients with cleft lip/palate or other craniofacial anomalies*, Chapel Hill, NC: American Cleft Palate-Craniofacial Association.

American Psychiatric Association 1987. *Diagnostic and statistical manual of mental disorders*, Washington, DC: American Psychiatric Association.

American Psychiatric Association 1994. *Diagnostic and statistical manual of mental disorders*, fourth edition, Washington, DC: American Psychiatric Association.

American Psychiatric Association 2000. *Diagnostic and statistical manual of mental disorders, text revision*, Washington, DC: American Psychiatric Association.

American Psychiatric Association 2013. *Diagnostic and statistical manual of mental disorders*, fifth edition, Washington, DC: American Psychiatric Association.

American Speech-Language-Hearing Association. 1997. *Guidelines for audiologic screening* (online, available at: www.asha.org/policy/GL1997-00199.htm; last accessed 12 June 2013).

American Speech-Language-Hearing Association. 1998. *ASHA's functional communication measure*, Rockville, MD: American Speech-Language-Hearing Association.

American Speech-Language-Hearing Association. 1999. *Terminology pertaining to fluency and fluency disorders: guidelines*, ASHA Special Interest Division 4: Fluency and Fluency Disorders (online, available at: www.asha.org/docs/html/GL1999-00063.html; last accessed 12 June 2013).

American Speech-Language-Hearing Association. 2001. *Roles of speech-language pathologists in swallowing and feeding disorders: technical report*, Rockville, MD: American Speech-Language-Hearing Association.

American Speech-Language-Hearing Association. 2002. *Consensus auditory–perceptual evaluation of voice (CAPE-V)*, Rockville, MD: American Speech-Language-Hearing Association.

American Speech-Language-Hearing Association. 2007. *Childhood apraxia of speech*, Technical Report (online, available at: www.asha.org/policy/TR2007-00278.htm; last accessed 12 June 2013).

American Speech-Language-Hearing Association. 2008. *Standards for accreditation of graduate education programs in audiology and speech-language pathology* (online, available at: www.asha.org/academic/accreditation/accredmanual/section3; last accessed 12 June 2013).

Anastasiou, D. and Polychronopoulou, S. 2009. 'Identification and overidentification of specific learning disabilities (dyslexia) in Greece', *Learning Disability Quarterly* 3:2, 55–69.

Anderson, A.H., Bader, M., Bard, E.G., Boyle, E., Doherty, G., Garrod, S., Isard, S., Kowtko, J., McAllister, J., Miller, J., Sotillo, C., Thompson, H.S. and Weinert, R. 1991. 'The HCRC map task corpus', *Language and Speech* 34:4, 351–66.

Anderson, J.A., Kutash, K. and Duchnowski, A.J. 2001. 'A comparison of the academic progress of students with EBD and students with LD', *Journal of Emotional and Behavioral Disorders* 9:2, 106–15.

Anderson, J.D. and Conture, E.G. 2000. 'Language abilities of children who stutter: a preliminary study', *Journal of Fluency Disorders* 25:4, 283–304.

Anderson, J.D., Pellowski, M.W. and Conture, E.G. 2005. 'Childhood stuttering and dissociations across linguistic domains', *Journal of Fluency Disorders* 34:4, 219–53.

Anderson, J.D., Pellowski, M.W., Conture, E.G. and Kelly, E.M. 2003. 'Temperamental characteristics of young children who stutter', *Journal of Speech, Language, and Hearing Research* 46:5, 1221–33.

Anderson, R.T. 1996. 'Nasometric values for normal Spanish-speaking females: a preliminary report', *Cleft Palate-Craniofacial Journal* 33:4, 333–6.

Andreasen, N.C. 1979. 'Thought, language and communication disorders', *Archives of General Psychiatry* 36:12, 1315–21.

Andrews, G. and Cutler, J. 1974. 'Stuttering therapy: the relation between changes in symptom level and attitudes', *Journal of Speech and Hearing Disorders* 39:3, 312–19.

Andrews, G. and Harris, M. 1964. *The syndrome of stuttering*, Clinics in Developmental Medicine, No. 17. London: Spastics Society Medical Education and Information Unit in association with W. Heinemann Medical Books.

Andrews, G., Guitar, B. and Howie, P. 1980. 'Meta-analysis of the effects of stuttering treatment', *Journal of Speech and Hearing Research* 45:3, 287–307.

Andrews, G., Howie, P.M., Dozsa, M. and Guitar, B.E. 1982. 'Stuttering: speech pattern characteristics under fluency-inducing conditions', *Journal of Speech and Hearing Research* 25:2, 208–16.

Angeleri, R., Bosco, F.M., Zettin, M., Sacco, K., Colle, L. and Bara, B.G. 2008. 'Communicative impairment in traumatic brain injury: a complete pragmatic assessment', *Brain and Language* 107:3, 229–45.

Annaz, D., Van Herwegen, J., Thomas, M., Fishman, R., Karmiloff-Smith, A. and Rundblad, G. 2009. 'Comprehension of metaphor and metonymy in children with Williams syndrome', *International Journal of Language & Communication Disorders* 44:6, 962–78.

Anthony, J.L., Aghara, R., Dunkelberger, M., Anthony, T.I., Williams, J.M. and Zhang, Z. 2011. 'What factors place children with speech sound disorders at risk for reading problems?', *American Journal of Speech-Language Pathology* 20:2, 146–60.

Antipova, E.A., Purdy, S.C., Blakeley, M. and Williams, S. 2008. 'Effects of altered auditory feedback (AAF) on stuttering frequency during monologue speech production', *Journal of Fluency Disorders* 33:4, 274–90.

Appleton, J. and Marchin, J. 1995. *Working with oral cancer*, Bicester: Winslow.

Archibald, L. and Gathercole, S. 2007. 'Nonword repetition in specific language impairment: more than a phonological short-term memory deficit', *Psychonomic Bulletin & Review* 14:5, 919–24.

Armstrong, E. 1987. 'Cohesive harmony in aphasic discourse and its significance to listener perception of coherence', in R.H. Brookshire (ed.), *Clinical aphasiology conference proceedings*, Minneapolis: BRK Publishers, 210–15.

Armstrong, E. 2000. 'Aphasic discourse analysis: the story so far', *Aphasiology* 14:9, 875–92.

Arnold, G. 1960. 'Studies in tachyphemia: III. Signs and symptoms', *Logos* 3, 82–95.

Arnold, R., Yule, W. and Martin, N. 1985. 'The psychological characteristics of infantile hypercalcaemia: a preliminary investigation', *Developmental Medicine and Child Neurology* 27:1, 49–59.

Arnsten, A.F. 2009. 'Stress signalling pathways that impair prefrontal cortex structure and function', *Nature Reviews. Neuroscience* 10:6, 410–22.

Aronson, A. 1980. *Clinical voice disorders: an interdisciplinary approach*, New York: Thieme-Stratton.

Aronson, A.E. and Bless, D.M. 2009a. 'Studies in clinical diagnosis', in A.E. Aronson and D.M. Bless (eds.), *Clinical voice disorders*, fourth edition, New York: Thieme, 204–30.

Aronson, A.E. and Bless, D.M. 2009b. 'Voice disorders of structural origin', in A.E. Aronson and D.M. Bless (eds.), *Clinical voice disorders*, fourth edition, New York: Thieme, 24–38.

Aronson, A.E., Peterson, H.W. and Litin, E.M. 1964. 'Voice symptomatology in functional dysphonia and aphonia', *Journal of Speech and Hearing Disorders* 29, 367–80.

Arruda, H., Martins, R.H. and Lerco, L.L. 2011. 'Gastroesophageal reflux disease and vocal disturbances', *Journal of Voice* 25:2, 202–7.

Ash, S., McMillan, C., Gross, R.G., Cook, P., Gunawardena, D., Morgan, B., Boller, A., Siderowf, A. and Grossman, M. 2012. 'Impairments of speech fluency in Lewy body spectrum disorder', *Brain and Language* 120:3, 290–302.

Ash, S., McMillan, C., Gunawardena, D., Avants, B., Morgan, B., Khan, A., Moore, P., Gee, J. and Grossman, M. 2010. 'Speech errors in progressive non-fluent aphasia', *Brain and Language* 113:1, 13–20.

Ash, S., Moore, P., Antani, S., McCawley, G., Work, M. and Grossman, M. 2006. 'Trying to tell a tale: discourse impairments in progressive aphasia and frontotemporal dementia', *Neurology* 66:9, 1405–13.

Ash, S., Moore, P., Hauck, R., Antani, S., Katz, J. and Grossman, M. 2004. 'Quantitative analysis of paraphasic errors in frontotemporal dementia', *Neurology* 62A: 166–83.

Athanasou, J.A. 2003. 'Acquired brain injury and return to work in Australia and New Zealand', *Australian Journal of Career Development* 12:1, 58–65.

Austermann Hula, S.N., Robin, D.A., Maas, E., Ballard, K.J. and Schmidt, R.A. 2008. 'Effects of feedback frequency and timing on acquisition, retention, and transfer of speech skills in acquired apraxia of speech', *Journal of Speech, Language, and Hearing Research* 51:5, 1088–113.

Austin, J.L. 1962. *How to do things with words*, Oxford: Clarendon Press.

Avery, C.M., Crank, S.T., Neal, C.P., Hayter, J.P. and Elton, C. 2010. 'The use of the pectoralis major flap for advanced and recurrent head and neck malignancy in the medically compromised patient', *Oral Oncology* 46:11, 829–33.

Avila, J., Lim, F., Moreno, F., Belmonte, C. and Cuello, A.C. 2002. 'Tau function and dysfunction in neurons: its role in neurodegenerative disorders', *Molocular Neurobiology* 25:3, 213–31.

Baas, B.S., Strand, E.A., Leanne, M. and Barbaresi, W.J. 2008. 'Treatment of severe childhood apraxia of speech in a 12-year-old male with CHARGE association', *Journal of Medical Speech-Language Pathology* 16:4, 180–90.

Baddeley, A.D. 1996. 'Exploring the central executive', *Quarterly Journal of Experimental Psychology* 49:1, 5–28.

Badecker, W. and Caramazza, A. 1985. 'On considerations of method and theory governing the use of clinical categories in neurolinguistics and cognitive neuropsychology: the case against agrammatism', *Cognition* 20:2, 97–125.

Badian, N.A. 1994. 'Preschool prediction: orthographic and phonological skills, and reading', *Annals of Dyslexia*, 44:1, 1–25.

Bae, Y., Kuehn, D., Charles, A., Conway, C. and Sutton, B.P. 2011. 'Real-time magnetic resonance imaging of velopharyngeal activities with simultaneous speech recordings', *Cleft Palate-Craniofacial Journal* 48:6, 695–707.

Bagby, R.M., Parker, J.D. and Taylor, G.J. 1994. 'The twenty-item Toronto Alexithymia Scale-1. Item selection and cross-validation of the factor structure', *Journal of Psychosomatic Research* 38:1, 23–32.

Baken, R.J. 1992. 'Electroglottography', *Journal of Voice* 6:2, 98–110.

Baker, L. and Cantwell, D.P. 1982. 'Developmental, social and behavioral characteristics of speech and language disordered children', *Child Psychiatry and Human Development* 12:4, 195–206.

Baker, L. and Cantwell, D.P. 1987a. 'A prospective psychiatric follow-up of children with speech/language disorders', *Journal of the American Academy of Child and Adolescent Psychiatry* 26:4, 546–53.

Baker, L. and Cantwell, D.P. 1987b. 'Factors associated with the development of psychiatric illness in children with early speech/language problems', *Journal of Autism and Developmental Disorders* 17:4, 499–510.

Bakker, K. 1996. 'Cluttering: current scientific status and emerging research and clinical issues', *Journal of Fluency Disorders* 21:3, 359–65.

Bakker, K., Myers, F.L., Raphael, L.J. and St. Louis, K.O. 2011. 'A preliminary comparison of speech rate, self-evaluation, and disfluency of people who speak exceptionally fast, clutter, or speak normally', in D. Ward and K. Scaler Scott (eds.), *Cluttering: research, intervention and education*, East Sussex: Psychology Press, 45–66.

Baldwin, D.A. 1991. 'Infants' contribution to the achievement of joint reference', *Child Development* 62:5, 875–90.

Baldwin, D.A. 1993. 'Infants' ability to consult the speaker for clues to word reference', *Journal of Child Language* 20:2, 395–418.

Ball, L.J., Beukelman, D. and Pattee, G.L. 2004. 'Communication effectiveness of individuals with amyotrophic lateral sclerosis', *Journal of Communication Disorders* 37:3, 197–215.

Ballard, K.J. and Robin, D.A. 2007. 'Influence of continual biofeedback on jaw pursuit-tracking in healthy adults and in adults with apraxia plus aphasia', *Journal of Motor Behavior* 39:1, 19–28.

Ballard, K.J., Djaja, D., Arciuli, J., James, D.G. and van Doorn, J. 2012. 'Developmental trajectory for production of prosody: lexical stress contrastivity in children 3 to 7 years and adults', *Journal of Speech, Language, and Hearing Research* 55:6, 1822–35.

Ballard, K.J., Granier, J., Robin, D.A. 2000. 'Understanding the nature of apraxia of speech: theory, analysis, and treatment', *Aphasiology* 14:10, 969–95.

Ballard, K.J., Robin, D.A., McCabe, P. and McDonald, J. 2010. 'Treating dysprosody in childhood apraxia of speech', *Journal of Speech, Language, and Hearing Research* 53:5, 1227–45.

Balm, A.J.M. 2007. 'Laryngeal and hypopharyngeal cancer: intervention approaches', in E.C. Ward and C.J. van As-Brooks (eds.), *Head and neck cancer:*

treatment, rehabilitation, and outcomes, San Diego, CA: Plural Publishing, Inc., 122–43.

Bara, B.G. 2010. *Cognitive pragmatics: the mental processes of communication*, Cambridge, MA and London: The MIT Press.

Barañano, C.F., Rosenthal, E.L., Morgan, B.A., McColloch, N.L. and Magnuson, J.S. 2011. 'Dynasplint for the management of trismus after treatment of upper aerodigestive tract cancer: a retrospective study', *Ear, Nose, and Throat Journal* 90:12, 584–90.

Barkmeier, J. and Verdolini-Marston, K. 1992. 'Behavioral treatment for adductory spasmodic dysphonia', Second Biennial Phonosurgery Symposium: Madison WI, July 1992.

Barkmeier-Kraemer, J.M., Lato, A. and Wiley, K. 2011. 'Development of a speech treatment program for a client with essential tremor', *Seminars in Speech and Language* 32:1, 43–57.

Barkus, E. and Murray, R.M. 2010. 'Substance use in adolescence and psychosis: clarifying the relationship', *Annual Review of Clinical Psychology* 6, 365–89.

Barlow, J.A. and Gierut, J.A. 2002. 'Minimal pair approaches to phonological remediation', *Seminars in Speech and Language* 23:1, 57–67.

Barlow, W. 1973. *The Alexander technique*, New York: Warner Books, Inc.

Barnes, J. and Baron-Cohen, S. 2010. 'Language in autism: pragmatics and theory of mind', in J. Guendouzi, F. Loncke and M.J. Williams (eds.), *The handbook of psycholinguistic and cognitive processes: perspectives in communication disorders*, London: Psychology Press, 731–45.

Barnes, M.A. and Dennis, M. 1998. 'Discourse after early-onset hydrocephalus: core deficits in children of average intelligence', *Brain and Language* 61:3, 309–34.

Barnes, S. and Armstrong, E. 2010. 'Conversation after right hemisphere brain damage: motivations for applying conversation analysis', *Clinical Linguistics & Phonetics* 24:1, 55–69.

Barnett, D.W., Carey, K.T. and Hall, J.D. 1993. 'Naturalistic intervention design for young children: foundations, rationales, and strategies', *Topics in Early Childhood Special Education* 13:4, 430–44.

Baron-Cohen, S. 2000. 'Theory of mind and autism: a fifteen year review', in S. Baron-Cohen, H. Tager-Flusberg and D.J. Cohen (eds.), *Understanding other minds: perspectives from developmental cognitive neuroscience*, New York: Oxford University Press, 3–20.

Baron-Cohen, S., Leslie, A.M. and Frith, U. 1985. 'Does the autistic child have a "theory of mind"?', *Cognition* 21:1, 37–46.

Baron-Cohen, S., O'Riordan, M., Stone, V., Jones, R. and Plaisted, K. 1999. 'Recognition of faux pas by normally developing children and children with Asperger syndrome or high-functioning autism', *Journal of Autism and Developmental Disorders* 29:5, 407–18.

Barratt, J., Littlejohns, P. and Thompson, J. 1992. 'Trial of intensive compared with weekly speech therapy in preschool children', *Archives of Disease in Childhood* 67:1, 106–8.

Barriga, A.Q., Doran, J.W., Newell, S.B., Morrison, E.M., Barbetti, V. and Robbins, B.D. 2002. 'Relationships between problem behaviors and academic achievement in adolescents: the unique role of attention problems', *Journal of Emotional and Behavioral Disorders* 10:4, 233–40.

Barrow, R. 2008. 'Listening to the voice of living life with aphasia: Anne's story', *International Journal of Language & Communication Disorders* 43:Suppl 1, 30–46.

Bartels, A.L. and Leenders, K.L. 2009. 'Parkinson's disease: the syndrome, the pathogenesis and pathophysiology', *Cortex* 45:8, 915–21.

Bartlett, R.S., Jette, M.E., King, S.N., Schaser, A. and Thibeault, S.L. 2012. 'Fundamental approaches in molecular biology for communication sciences and disorders', *Journal of Speech, Language, and Hearing Research* 55:4, 1220–31.

Barty, E. and Caynes, K. 2009. 'Development of a functional communication classification scale', International Cerebral Palsy Conference: Sydney, Australia, 18–21 February 2009.

Basso, A. 2003. *Aphasia and its therapy*, Oxford University Press.

Basso, A., Lecours, A.R., Moraschini, S. and Vanier, M. 1985. 'Anatomoclinical correlations of the aphasias as defined through computerized tomography: exceptions', *Brain and Language* 26:2, 201–29.

Bastiaanse, R. 1995. 'Broca's aphasia: a syntactic and/or morphological disorder? A case study', *Brain and Language* 48:1, 1–32.

Bastiaanse, R. 2010. *Afasie*, Houten, Netherlands: Bohn Stafleu Van Loghum.

Bastiaanse, R. 2011. 'The retrieval and inflection of verbs in the spontaneous speech of fluent aphasic speakers', *Journal of Neurolinguistics* 24:2, 163–72.

Bastiaanse, R. and Edwards, S. 2004. 'Word order and finiteness in Dutch and English Broca's and Wernicke's aphasia', *Brain and Language* 89:1, 91–107.

Bastiaanse, R. and Jonkers, R. 2012. 'Linguistic accounts of agrammatic aphasia', in R. Bastiaanse and C.K. Thompson (eds.), *Perspectives on agrammatism*, Hove, East Sussex: Psychology Press, 17–33.

Bastiaanse, R. and Thompson, C.K. 2003. 'Verb and auxiliary movement in agrammatic Broca's aphasia', *Brain and Language* 84:2, 286–305.

Bastiaanse, R. and Van Zonneveld, R. 1998. 'On the relation between verb inflection and verb position in Dutch agrammatic aphasics', *Brain and Language* 64:2, 165–81.

Bastiaanse, R. and Van Zonneveld, R. 2006. 'Comprehension of passives in Broca's aphasia', *Brain and Language* 96:2, 135–42.

Bastiaanse, R., Bouma, G. and Post, W. 2009. 'Linguistic complexity and frequency in agrammatic speech production', *Brain and Language* 109:1, 18–28.

Bates, E., Bretherton, I. and Snyder, L. 1988. *From first words to grammar: individual differences and dissociable mechanisms*, Cambridge University Press.

Bates, E., Dale, P.S. and Thal, D. 1995. 'Individual differences and their implications for theories of language development', in P. Fletcher and B. MacWhinney (eds.), *Handbook of child language*, Oxford: Basil Blackwell, 96–151.

Baum, R.A., Nash, P.L., Foster, J.E.A., Spader, M., Ratliff-Schaub, K. and Coury, D.L. 2008. 'Primary care of children and adolescents with Down syndrome: an update', *Current Problems in Paediatric and Adolescent Health Care* 38:8, 241–61.

Bauman-Waengler, J. 2008. *Articulatory and phonological impairments: a clinical focus*, Boston, MA: Pearson Education, Inc.

Baumgartner, J.M. 1999. 'Acquired psychogenic stuttering', in R.F. Curlee (ed.), *Stuttering and related disorders of fluency*, second edition, New York: Thieme Medical Publishers, 269–88.

Bax, M., Tydeman, C. and Flodmark, O. 2006. 'Clinical and MRI correlates of cerebral palsy: the European cerebral palsy study', *Journal of the American Medical Association* 296:13, 1601–8.

Baylor, C., Burns, M., Eadie, T., Britton, D. and Yorkston, K. 2011. 'A qualitative study of interference with communicative participation across communication disorders in adults', *American Journal of Speech-Language Pathology* 20:4, 269–87.

Baylor, C., Yorkston, K., Bamer, A., Britton, D. and Amtmann, D. 2010. 'Variables associated with communicative participation in people with multiple sclerosis: a regression analysis', *American Journal of Speech-Language Pathology* 19:2, 143–53.

Baylor, C.R., Yorkston, K.M., Eadie, T.L., Miller, R.M. and Amtmann, D. 2009. 'Developing the communicative participation item bank: Rasch analysis results from a spasmodic dysphonia sample', *Journal of Speech, Language, and Hearing Research* 52:5, 1302–20.

Baylor, C.R., Yorkston, K.M., Eadie, T.L., Strand, E.A. and Duffy, J. 2006. 'A systematic review of outcome measurement in unilateral vocal fold paralysis', *Journal of Medical Speech-Language Pathology* 14:1, xxvii–lvii.

Bazemore, P.H., Tonkonogy, J. and Ananth, R. 1991. 'Dysphagia in psychiatric patients: clinical and videofluoroscopic study', *Dysphagia* 6:1, 2–5.

Bazin, N., Perruchet, P., Hardy-Bayle, M.C. and Feline, A. 2000. 'Context-dependent information processing in patients with schizophrenia', *Schizophrenia Research* 45:1-2, 93–101.

Beausoleil, N., Fortin, R., Le Blanc, B. and Joanette, Y. 2003. 'Unconstrained oral naming performance in right- and left-hemisphere-damaged individuals: when education overrides the lesion', *Aphasiology* 17:2, 143–58.

Beauvois, M.-F. 1982. 'Optic aphasia: a process of interaction between vision and language', *Philosophical Transactions of the Royal Society London B* 298:1089, 35–47.

Beck, J.M., Wrench, A., Jackson, M., Soutar, D., Robertson, A.G. and Laver, J. 1998. 'Surgical mapping and phonetic analysis in intra-oral cancer', in W. Ziegler and K. Deger (eds.), *Clinical phonetics and linguistics*, London: Whurr, 481–92.

Beckman, M.E. and Edwards, J. 2000. 'The ontogeny of phonological categories and the primacy of lexical learning in linguistic development', *Child Development* 71:1, 240–9.

Beckman, M.E., Edwards, J. and Fletcher, J. 1992. 'Prosodic structure and tempo in a sonority model of articulatory dynamics', in G.J. Docherty and D.R. Ladd (eds.), *Papers in laboratory phonology II: gesture, segment, prosody*, Cambridge University Press, 68–86.

Bedore, L. and Leonard, L. 1998. 'Specific language impairment and grammatical morphology: a discriminant function analysis', *Journal of Speech, Language, and Hearing Research* 41:5, 1185–92.

Bedore, L. and Leonard, L. 2001. 'Grammatical morphology deficits in Spanish-speaking children with specific language impairment', *Journal of Speech, Language, and Hearing Research* 44:4, 905–24.

Bedrosian, J. and Willis, T. 1987. 'Effects of treatment on the topic performance of a school-age child', *Language, Speech, and Hearing Services in Schools* 18:2, 158–67.

Beeghly, M., Weiss-Perry, B. and Cicchetti, D. 1990. 'Beyond sensorimotor functioning: early communicative and play development of children with Down syndrome', in D. Cicchetti and M. Beeghly (eds.), *Children with Down syndrome: a developmental perspective*, New York: Cambridge University Press, 329–68.

Beeman, M. and Chiarello, C. 1998. *Right hemisphere language comprehension: perspectives from cognitive neuroscience*, Mahwah, NJ: Lawrence Erlbaum Associates.

Beeson, P., Rising, K. and Volk, J. 2003. 'Writing treatment for severe aphasia: who benefits?', *Journal of Speech, Language, and Hearing Research* 46:5, 1038–60.

Behrman, A. 2006. 'Facilitating behavioural change in voice therapy: the relevance of motivational interviewing', *American Journal of Speech-Language Pathology* 15:3, 215–25.

Behrman, A. and Sulica, L. 2003. 'Voice rest after microlaryngoscopy: current opinion and practice', *The Laryngoscope* 113:12, 2182–86.

Behrmann, M. and Lieberthal, T. 1989. 'Category-specific treatment of a lexical-semantic deficit: a single case study of global aphasia', *British Journal of Disorders of Communication* 24:3, 281–99.

Beilby, J.M. and Byrnes, M.L. 2012. 'Acceptance and commitment therapy for people who stutter', *Perspectives on Fluency and Fluency Disorders* 22:1, 34–46.

Beilby, J.M., Byrnes, M.L. and Yaruss, J.S. 2012. 'Acceptance and commitment therapy for adults who stutter: psychosocial adjustment and speech fluency', *Journal of Fluency Disorders* 37:4, 289–99.

Beitchman, J.H., Brownlie, E.B., Inglis, A., Wild, J., Ferguson, B., Schachter, D., Lancee, W., Wilson, B. and Mathews, R. 1996. 'Seven-year follow-up of speech/language impaired and control children: psychiatric outcome', *Journal of Child Psychology and Psychiatry* 37:8, 961–70.

Beitchman, J.H., Nair, R., Clegg, M., Patel, P.G., Ferguson, B., Pressman, E. and Smith, A. 1986. 'Prevalence of speech and language disorders in 5-year-old kindergarten children in the Ottawa-Carleton region', *Journal of Speech and Hearing Disorders* 51:2, 98–110.

Beitchman, J.H., Wilson, B., Johnson, C.J., Atkinson, L., Young, A.R., Adlaf, E., Escobar, M. and Douglas, L. 2001. 'Fourteen-year follow-up of speech/language-impaired and control children: psychiatric outcome', *Journal of the American Academy of Child and Adolescent Psychiatry* 40:1, 75–82.

Belafsky, P.C., Postma, G.N., Reulbach, T.R., Holland, B.W. and Koufman, J.A. 2002. 'Muscle tension dysphonia as a sign of underlying glottal insufficiency', *Otolaryngology – Head and Neck Surgery* 127:5, 448–51.

Belin, C., Faure, S. and Mayer, E. 2008. 'Spécialisation hémisphérique versus coopération inter-hémisphérique [Hemispheric specialisation versus inter-hemispheric cooperation]', *Revue Neurologique* 164:3, 148–53.

Belleville, S., Chertkow, H. and Gauthier, S. 2007. 'Working memory and control of attention in persons with Alzheimer's disease and mild cognitive impairment', *Neuropsychology* 21:4, 458–69.

Bellugi, U., Bihrle, A., Neville, H., Jernigan, T. and Doherty, S. 1992. 'Language, cognition, and brain organization in a neurodevelopmental disorder', in M. Gunnar and C. Nelson (eds.), *Developmental behavioral neuroscience*, Hillsdale, NJ: Lawrence Erlbaum, 201–32.

Bellugi, U., Lai, Z. and Wang, P. 1997. 'Language, communication, and neural systems in Williams syndrome', *Mental Retardation and Developmental Disabilities Research Review* 3:4, 334–42.

Bellugi, U., Lichtenberger, L., Jones, W., Lai, Z. and St. George, M. 2000. 'The neurocognitive profile of Williams syndrome: a complex pattern of strengths and weaknesses', *Journal of Cognitive Neuroscience*, 12:S1, 7–29.

Bellugi, U., Lichtenberger, L., Mills, D., Galaburda, A. and Korenberg, J.R. 1999. 'Bridging cognition, the brain and modular genetics: evidence from Williams syndrome', *Trends in Neurosciences* 22:5, 197–207.

Bellugi, U., Marks, S., Bihrle, A. and Sabo, H. 1988. 'Dissociations between language and cognitive functions in Williams Syndrome', in D. Bishop and K. Mogford (eds.), *Language development in exceptional circumstances*, Edinburgh: Churchill Livingstone, 177–89.

Bellugi, U., Poizner, H. and Klima, E. 1989. 'Language modality and the brain', *Trends in Neurosciences* 12:10, 380–8.

Bellugi, U., Wong, P. and Jernigan, T.L. 1994. 'Williams syndrome: an unusual neuropsychological profile', in S.H. Broman and J. Grafman (eds.), *Atypical cognitive deficits in developmental disorders: implications for brain function*, Hillsdale, NJ: Lawrence Erlbaum Associates, 23–56.

Benasich, A. and Tallal, P. 2002. 'Infant discrimination of rapid auditory cues predicts later language impairment', *Behavioural Brain Research*, 136:1, 31–49.

Benasich, A., Choudhury, N., Friedman, J., Realpe-Bonilla, T., Chojnowska, C. and Gou, Z. 2005. 'The infant as a prelinguistic model for language learning impairment: predicting from event-related potentials to behavior', *Neuropsychologia* 44:3, 396–411.

Benisty, S., Hernandez, K., Viswanathan, A., Reyes, S., Kurtz, A., O'Sullivan, M., Bousser, M.G., Dichgans, M. and Chabriat, H. 2008. 'Diagnostic criteria of vascular dementia in CADASIL', *Stroke* 39:3, 838–44.

Benner, G.J., Mattison, R.E., Nelson, J.R. and Ralston, N.C. 2009. 'Types of language disorders in students classified ED: prevalence and association with learning disabilities and psychopathology', *Education and Treatment of Children* 32:4, 631–53.

Benner, G.J., Nelson, J.R., Allor, J.H., Mooney, P. and Dai, T. 2008. 'Academic processing speed mediates the influence of both externalizing behavior and language skills on the academic skills of students with emotional disturbance', *Journal of Behavioral Education* 17:1, 63–78.

Benner, G.J., Nelson, J.R. and Epstein, M.H. 2002. 'The language skills of children with emotional and behavioral disorders: a review of the literature', *Journal of Emotional and Behavioral Disorders* 10:1, 43–59.

Benner, G.J., Nelson, J.R., Ralston, N.C. and Mooney, P. 2010. 'A meta-analysis of the effects of reading instruction on the reading skills of students with or at-risk of behavioral disorders', *Behavioral Disorders* 35:2, 86–102.

Bennett, E.M. 2006. *Working with people who stutter: a lifespan approach*, Upper Saddle River, NJ: Pearson Merrill/Prentice Hall.

Bennett, F., La Veck, B. and Sells, C. 1978. 'The Williams elfin faces syndrome: the psychological profile as an aid in syndrome identification', *Paediatrics* 61:2, 303–6.

Bennett, K.E. and Haggard, M.P. 1999. 'Behavior and cognitive outcomes from middle ear disease', *Archives of Disease in Childhood* 80:1, 28–35.

Bennetto, L. and Pennington, B. 2002. 'The neuropsychology of fragile X syndrome', in R.J. Hagerman and A.C. Cronister (eds.), *Fragile X syndrome: diagnosis, treatment, and research*, second edition, Baltimore, MD: Johns Hopkins University Press, 210–48.

Benninger, M.S., Ahuja, A.S., Gardner, G. and Grywalski, C. 1998. 'Assessing outcomes for dysphonic patients', *Journal of Voice* 12:4, 540–50.

Benton, E. and Bryan, K. 1996. 'Right cerebral hemisphere damage: incidence of language problems', *International Journal of Rehabilitation Research* 19:1, 47–54.

Berglund, E., Eriksson, M. and Johansson, I. 2001. 'Parental reports of spoken language skills in children with Down syndrome', *Journal of Speech and Hearing Research* 44:1, 179–91.

Berke, G.S., Blackwell, K.E., Gerratt, B.R., Verneil, A., Jackson, K.S. and Sercarz, J.A. 1999. 'Selective laryngeal adductor denervation-reinnervation: a new surgical treatment for adductor spasmodic dysphonia', *Annals of Otology, Rhinology and Laryngology* 108:3, 227–31.

Bernazzani, O. and Bifulco, A. 2003. 'Motherhood as a vulnerability factor in major depression: the role of negative pregnancy experiences', *Social Science and Medicine* 56:6, 1249–60.

Berndt, R., Haendiges, A., Mitchum, C.C. and Sandson, J. 1997. 'Verb retrieval in aphasia. 2. Relationship to sentence processing', *Brain and Language* 56:1, 107–37.

Bernhardt, B. and Major, E.M. 2005. 'Speech, language and literacy skills three years later: a follow-up study of early phonological and metaphonological intervention', *International Journal of Language & Communication Disorders* 40:1, 1–27.

Bernhardt, B. and Stemberger, J.P. 1998. *Handbook of phonological development from the perspective of constraint-based phonology*, San Diego, CA: Academic Press.

Berninger, V.W. 2006. 'Converging evidence for triple word form theory in children with dyslexia', *Developmental Neuropsychology* 30:1, 547–89.

Berninger, V.W. 2007. *Process assessment of the learner: diagnostics for reading and writing*, second edition, San Antonio, TX: Pearson.

Berninger, V.W. 2011. 'Evidence based differential diagnosis and treatment of reading disabilities with and without comorbidities in oral language, writing and math: prevention, problem-solving consultation and specialized instruction', in D. Flanagan and V. Alfonso (eds.), *Essentials of specific learning disabilities identification*, Hoboken, NJ: John Wiley, 203–32.

Berninger, V.W. and O'Malley-May, M. 2011. 'Evidence-based diagnosis and treatment for specific learning disabilities involving impairments in written and/or oral language', *Journal of Learning Disabilities* 44:2, 167–83.

Berninger, V.W. and Richards, T.L. 2002. *Brain literacy for educators and psychologists*, New York: Academic Press.

Berninger, V.W. and Wolf, B.J. 2009. *Teaching students with dyslexia and dysgraphia: lessons from teaching and science*, Baltimore, MD: Paul H. Brookes.

Berninger, V.W., Abbott, R.D. and Thompson, S. 2006. 'Modeling phonological core deficits within a working memory architecture in children and adults with developmental dyslexia', *Scientific Studies of Reading* 10:2, 165–98.

Berninger, V.W., Raskind, W., Richards, T., Abbott, R. and Stock, P. 2008. 'A multidisciplinary approach to understanding developmental dyslexia within working-memory architecture: genotypes, phenotypes, brain, and instruction', *Developmental Neuropsychology* 33:6, 707–44.

Bernstein, N.E. 1981. 'Are there constraints on childhood disfluency?', *Journal of Fluency Disorders* 6:4, 341–50.

Bernstein Ratner, N. 1997a. 'Stuttering: a psycholinguistic perspective', in R. Curlee and G. Siegel (eds.), *Nature and treatment of stuttering: new directions*, second edition, Needham, MA: Allyn & Bacon, 99–127.

Bernstein Ratner, N. 1997b. 'Leaving Las Vegas: clinical odds and individual outcomes', *American Journal of Speech-Language Pathology* 6:2, 29–33.

Bernstein Ratner, N. and Sih, C. 1987. 'Effects of gradual increases in sentence length and complexity on children's dysfluency', *Journal of Speech and Hearing Disorders* 52:3, 278–87.

Bernstein Ratner, N. and Silverman, S. 2000. 'Parental perceptions of children's communicative development at stuttering onset', *Journal of Speech, Language, and Hearing Research* 43:5, 1252–63.

Berry, D.A., Verdolini, K., Montequin, D.W., Hess, M.M., Chan, R.W. and Titze, I. 2001. 'A quantitative output-cost ratio in voice production', *Journal of Speech, Language, and Hearing Research* 44:1, 29–37.

Best, W., Grassly, J., Greenwood, A., Herbert, R., Hickin, J. and Howard, D. 2011. 'A controlled study of changes in conversation following aphasia therapy for anomia', *Disability and Rehabilitation* 33:3, 229–42.

Best, W., Greenwood, A., Grassly, J. and Hickin, J. 2008. 'Bridging the gap: can impairment based therapy for anomia have an impact at the psychosocial level?', *International Journal of Language & Communication Disorders* 43:4, 390–407.

Best, W., Howard, D., Bruce, C. and Gatehouse, C. 1997. 'Cueing the words: a single case study of treatments for anomia', *Neuropsychological Rehabilitation* 7:2, 105–41

Beukelman, D., Fager, S., Ullman, C., Hanson, E.K. and Logemann, J.A. 2002. 'The impact of speech supplementation on the intelligibility of persons with traumatic brain injury', *Journal of Medical Speech-Language Pathology* 10, 237–42.

Beukelman, D., Garrett, K.L. and Yorkston, K.M. 2007. *Augmentative communication strategies for adults with acute or chronic medical conditions*, Baltimore, MD: Paul H. Brookes Pub. Co.

Beukelman, D.R. and Mirenda, P. 2005. *Augmentative and alternative communication*, third edition, New York: Cambridge University Press.

Beukelman, D.R., Kraft, G.H. and Freal, J. 1985. 'Expressive communication disorders in persons with multiple sclerosis: a survey', *Archives of Physical Medicine and Rehabilitation* 66:10, 675–7.

Bhogal, S.K., Teasell, R. and Speechley, M. 2003. 'Intensity of aphasia therapy, impact on recovery', *Stroke* 34:4, 987–93.

Bian, H. and Grossman, M. 2007. 'Frontotemporal lobar degeneration: recent progress in antemortem diagnosis', *Acta Neuropathologica* 114:1, 23–9.

Biassou, N., Grossman, M., Onishi, K., Mickanin, J., Hughes, E., Robinson, K.M. and D'Esposito, M. 1995. 'Phonologic processing deficits in Alzheimer's disease', *Neurology* 45:12, 2165–9.

Bibby, H. and McDonald, S. 2005. 'Theory of mind after traumatic brain injury', *Neuropsychologia* 43:1, 99–114.

Bigler, E.D. 2001. 'The lesion(s) in traumatic brain injury: implications for clinical neuropsychology', *Archives of Clinical Neuropsychology* 16:2, 95–131.

Bignell, S. and Cain, K. 2007. 'Pragmatic aspects of communication and language comprehension in groups of children differentiated by teacher ratings of inattention and hyperactivity', *British Journal of Developmental Psychology* 25:4, 499–512.

Binger, C. and Light, J. 2007. 'The effect of aided AAC modeling on the expression of multi-symbol messages by preschoolers who use AAC', *AAC: Augmentative and Alternative Communication* 23:1, 30–43.

Binger, C., Kent-Walsh, J., Berens, J., Del Campo, S. and Rivera, D. 2008. 'Teaching Latino parents to support the multi-symbol message productions of their children who require AAC', *AAC: Augmentative and Alternative Communication* 24:4, 323–38.

Binger, C., Maguire-Marshall, M. and Kent-Walsh, J. 2011. 'Using aided AAC models, recasts, and contrastive targets to teach grammatical morphemes to children who use AAC', *Journal of Speech, Language, and Hearing Research* 54:1, 160–76.

Bird, J., Bishop, D.V.M. and Freeman, N.H. 1995. 'Phonological awareness and literacy development in children with expressive phonological impairments', *Journal of Speech and Hearing Research* 38:2, 446–62.

Bishop, D.V.M. 1997. *Uncommon understanding*, Hove, East Sussex: Psychology Press.

Bishop, D.V.M. 1998. 'Development of the children's communication checklist (CCC): a method for assessing qualitative aspects of communicative impairment in children', *Journal of Child Psychology and Psychiatry* 39:6, 879–91.

Bishop, D.V.M. 2000. 'Pragmatic language impairment: a correlate of SLI, a distinct subgroup, or part of the autistic spectrum?', in D.V.M. Bishop and L.B. Leonard (eds.), *Speech and language impairments in children*, Hove, East Sussex: Psychology Press, 99–113.

Bishop, D.V.M. 2003a. 'Autism and specific language impairment: categorical distinction or continuum?', in G. Bock and J. Goode (eds.), *Autism: neural basis and treatment possibilities*, Novartis Foundation Symposium 251, Chichester, West Sussex: Wiley, 213–26.

Bishop, D.V.M. 2003b. *Children's communication checklist, version 2 (CCC-2)*, San Antonio, TX: Pearson.

Bishop, D.V.M. 2003c. *Test for the reception of grammar*, London: Harcourt Assessment.

Bishop, D.V.M. 2006a. 'What causes specific language impairment in children?', *Current Directions in Psychological Science* 15:5, 217–21.

Bishop, D.V.M. 2006b. 'Developmental cognitive genetics: how psychology can inform genetics and vice versa', *Quarterly Journal of Experimental Psychology (Colchester)* 59:7, 1153–68.

Bishop, D.V.M. 2008. 'Specific language impairment, dyslexia and autism: using genetics to unravel their relationship', in C.F. Norbury, J.B. Tomblin and D.V.M. Bishop (eds.), *Understanding developmental language disorders: from theory to practice*, New York: Psychology Press, 67–78.

Bishop, D.V.M. 2009. 'Genes, cognition, and communication: insights from neurodevelopmental disorders', *Annals of the New York Academy of Sciences* 1156:1, 1–18.

Bishop, D.V.M. 2010a. 'Specific language impairment', in C.L. Cooper, U. Goswami, B.J. Sahakian, J. Field and R. Jenkins (eds.), *Mental capital and wellbeing*, Chichester, West Sussex: Wiley-Blackwell, 767–73.

Bishop, D.V.M. 2010b. 'Overlaps between autism and language impairment: phenomimicry or shared etiology?', *Behavior Genetics* 40:5, 618–29.

Bishop, D.V.M. and Adams, C. 1990. 'A prospective study of the relationship between specific language impairment, phonological disorders and reading retardation', *Journal of Child Psychology and Psychiatry* 31:7, 1027–50.

Bishop, D.V.M. and Adams, C. 1992. 'Comprehension problems in children with specific language impairment: literal and inferential meaning', *Journal of Speech and Hearing Research* 35:1, 119–29.

Bishop, D.V.M. and Baird, G. 2001. 'Parent and teacher report of pragmatic aspects of communication: use of the Children's Communication Checklist in a clinical setting' *Developmental Medicine and Child Neurology* 43:12, 809–18.

Bishop, D.V.M. and Edmundson, A. 1987. 'Language-impaired 4-year-olds: distinguishing transient from persistent impairment', *Journal of Speech and Hearing Disorders* 52:2, 156–73.

Bishop, D.V.M. and Hayiou-Thomas, M.E. 2008. 'Heritability of specific language impairment depends on diagnostic criteria', *Genes, Brain and Behavior* 7:3, 365–72.

Bishop, D.V.M. and Norbury, C.F. 2002. 'Exploring the borderlands of autistic disorder and specific language impairment: a study using standardized diagnostic instruments', *Journal of Child Psychology and Psychiatry* 43:7, 916–29.

Bishop, D.V.M. and Snowling, M.J. 2004. 'Developmental dyslexia and specific language impairment: same or different?', *Psychological Bulletin* 130:6, 858–86.

Bishop, D.V.M., Adams, C. and Norbury, C.F. 2006. 'Distinct genetic influences on grammar and phonological short-term memory deficits: evidence from 6-year-old twins', *Genes, Brain and Behavior* 5:2, 158–69.

Bishop, D.V.M., Bright, P., James, C., Bishop, S.J. and van der Lely, H.K. 2000a. 'Grammatical SLI: a distinct subtype of developmental language impairment?', *Applied Psycholinguistics* 21:2, 159–81.

Bishop, D.V.M., Chan, J., Adams, C., Hartley, J. and Weir, F. 2000b. 'Conversational responsiveness in specific language impairment: evidence of disproportionate pragmatic difficulty in a subset of children', *Development and Psychopathology* 12:2, 177–99.

Bishop, D.V.M., Holt, G., Line, E., McDonald, D., McDonald, S. and Watt, H. 2012. 'Parental phonological memory contributes to prediction of outcome of late talkers from 20 months to 4 years: a longitudinal study of precursors of specific language impairment', *Journal of Neurodevelopmental Disorders* 4:1, 3–13.

Bishop, D.V.M., Maybery, M., Wong, D., Maley, A., Hill, W. and Hallmayer, J. 2004. 'Are phonological processing deficits part of the broad autism phenotype?', *American Journal of Medical Genetics Part B: Neuropsychiatric Genetics* 128B:1, 54–60.

Bishop, D.V.M., North, T. and Donlan, C. 1995. 'Genetic basis of specific language impairment: evidence from a twin study', *Developmental Medicine and Child Neurology* 37:1, 56–71.

Bishop, D.V.M., North, T. and Donlan, C. 1996. 'Nonword repetition as a behavioural marker for inherited language impairment: evidence from a twin study', *Journal of Child Psychology and Psychiatry* 36:1, 1–13.

Bislick, L.P., Weir, P.C., Spencer, K., Kendall, D. and Yorkston, K.M. 2012. 'Do principles of motor learning enhance retention and transfer of speech skills? A systematic review', *Aphasiology* 26:5, 709–28.

Bister, D., Set, P., Cash, C., Coleman, N. and Fanshawe, T. 2011. 'Incidence of facial clefts in Cambridge, United Kingdom', *European Journal of Orthodontics* 33:4, 372–6.

Black, M. and Chiat, S. 2003. 'Noun-verb dissociations: a multi-faceted phenomenon', *Journal of Neurolinguistics* 16:2–3, 231–50.

Blager, F.B. 2005. *'Breathing exercises for cough. Pursed lips breath'*, Denver, CO: National Jewish Medical and Research Center.

Blair, C., Granger, D. and Razza, R.P. 2005. 'Cortisol reactivity is positively related to executive functioning in preschool children attending head start', *Child Development* 76:3, 554–67.

Blair, K.S., Richell, R.A., Mitchell, D.G.V., Leonard, A., Morton, J. and Blair, R.J.R. 2006. 'They know the words, but not the music: affective and semantic priming in individuals with psychopathy', *Biological Psychology* 73:2, 114–23.

Blair, R.J.R. 2003. 'Facial expressions, their communicatory functions and neuro-cognitive substrates', *Philosophical Transactions of the Royal Society B: Biological Sciences* 358:1431, 561–72.

Blake, M.L. 2006. 'Clinical relevance of discourse characteristics after right hemisphere brain damage', *American Journal of Speech-Language Pathology* 15:3, 255–67.

Blake, M.L. 2007. 'Perspectives on treatment for communication deficits associated with right hemisphere brain damage', *American Journal of Speech-Language Pathology* 16:4, 331–42.

Blake, M.L. and Lesniewicz, K. 2005. 'Contextual bias and predictive inferencing in adults with and without right hemisphere brain damage', *Aphasiology* 19:3–5, 423–34.

Blake, M.L., Duffy, J., Myers, P. and Tompkins, C. 2002. 'Prevalence and patterns of right hemisphere cognitive/communicative deficits: retrospective data from an inpatient rehabilitation unit', *Aphasiology* 16:4–6, 537–47.

Blakeley, R.W. 1972. *The practice of speech pathology: a clinical diary*, Springfield, IL: Charles C. Thomas.

Blakemore, S. 2008. 'The social brain in adolescence', *Nature Reviews. Neuroscience* 9:4, 267–77.

Blanchet, P.G. and Snyder, G.J. 2010. 'Speech rate treatments for individuals with dysarthria: a tutorial', *Perceptual and Motor Skills* 110:3 Pt 1, 965–82.

Blitzer, A., Brin, M.F., Fahn, S. and Lovelace, R.E. 1988. 'Localized injections of botulinum toxin for the treatment of focal laryngeal dystonia (spastic dysphonia)', *Laryngoscope* 98:2, 193–7.

Bloch, E.L. and Goodstein, L.D. 1971. 'Functional speech disorders and personality: a decade of research', *Journal of Speech and Hearing Disorders* 36:3, 295–314.

Bloch, S., Beeke, S. and Miller, N. 2011. 'Acquired communication disorders: looking beyond impairment', *Disability and Rehabilitation* 33:3, 175–7.

Blom, E.D. 2000. 'Tracheoesophageal voice restoration: origin-evolution-state-of-the-art', *Folia Phoniatrica et Logopaedica* 52:1–3, 14–23.

Blomert, L., Kean, M.L., Koster, C. and Schokker, J. 1994. 'Amsterdam-Nijmegen Everyday Language Test: construction, reliability and validity', *Aphasiology* 8:4, 381–407.

Blomgren, M. 2010. 'Stuttering treatment for adults: an update on contemporary approaches', *Seminars in Speech and Language* 31:4, 272–82.

Blomgren, M., Roy, N., Callister, T. and Merrill, R.M. 2005. 'Intensive stuttering modification therapy: a multidimensional assessment of treatment outcomes', *Journal of Speech, Language, and Hearing Research* 48:3, 509–23.

Blonder, L.X., Pickering, J.E., Heath, R.L., Smith, C.D. and Butler, S.M. 1995. 'Prosodic characteristics of speech pre- and post- right hemisphere stroke', *Brain and Language* 51:2, 318–35.

Bloodstein, O. 1993. *Stuttering: the search for a cause and cure*, Boston, MA: Allyn & Bacon.

Bloodstein, O. 2002. 'Early stuttering as a type of language difficulty', *Journal of Fluency Disorders* 27:2, 163–6.

Bloodstein, O. 2006. 'Some empirical observations about early stuttering: a possible link to language development', *Journal of Communication Disorders* 39:3, 185–91.

Bloodstein, O. and Bernstein Ratner, N. 2008. *A handbook on stuttering*, sixth edition, Clifton Park, NY: Thomson/ Delmar Learning.

Bloomberg, K. and Johnson, H. 1990. 'A statewide demographic survey of people with severe communication impairments', *AAC: Augmentative and Alternative Communication* 6:1, 50–60.

Blumstein, S. 1981. *Acquired aphasia*, New York: Academic Press.

Boberg, E. and Kully, D. 1984. *Comprehensive stuttering program: client manual*, San Diego, CA: College Hill Press.

Bodden, M.E., Mollenhauer, B., Trenkwalder, C., Cabanel, N., Eggert, K.M., Unger, M.M., Oertel, W.H., Kessler, J., Dodel, R. and Kalbe, E. 2010. 'Affective and cognitive theory of mind in patients with Parkinson's disease', *Parkinsonism & Related Disorders* 16:7, 466–70.

Body, R., Perkins, M. and McDonald, S. 1999. 'Pragmatics, cognition, and communication in traumatic brain injury', in S. McDonald, L. Togher and C. Code (eds.), *Communication disorders following traumatic brain injury*, Hove, East Sussex: Psychology Press, 81–112.

Boes, A.D., Murko, V., Wood, J.L., Langbehn, D.R., Canady, J., Richman, L. and Nopoulos P. 2007. 'Social function in boys with cleft lip and palate: relationship to ventral frontal cortex morphology', *Behavioral Brain Research* 181:2, 224–31.

Bogart, K. and Matsumoto, D. 2010. 'Living with Moebius syndrome: adjustment, social competence, and satisfaction with life', *Cleft Palate-Craniofacial Journal* 47:2, 134–42.

Bohland, J.W., Bullock, D. and Guenther, F.H. 2010. 'Neural representations and mechanisms for the performance of simple speech sequences', *Journal of Cognitive Neuroscience* 22:7, 1504–29.

Boller, F. and Vignolo, L. 1966. 'Latent sensory aphasia in hemisphere-damaged patients: an experimental study with the token test', *Brain* 89:4, 815–30.

Bond, F. and Godfrey, H.P.D. 1997. 'Conversation with traumatically brain-injured individuals: a controlled study of behavioural changes and their impact', *Brain Injury* 11:5, 319–29.

Bonilha, H.S., Deliyski, D.D., Whiteside, J.P. and Gerlach, T.T. 2012. 'Vocal fold phase asymmetries in patients with voice disorders: a study across visualization techniques', *American Journal of Speech-Language Pathology* 21:1, 3–15.

Bonneh, Y.S., Levanon, Y., Dean-Pardo, O., Lossos, L. and Adini, Y. 2011. 'Abnormal speech spectrum and increased pitch variability in young autistic children', *Frontiers in Human Neuroscience* 4, 237.

Boo, M. and Rose, M.L. 2011. 'The efficacy of repetition, semantic and gesture treatments for verb retrieval and use in Broca's aphasia', *Aphasiology* 25:2, 154–75.

Boone, D.R. 1971. *The voice and voice therapy*, Englewood Cliffs, NJ: Prentice-Hall.

Boone, D.R., McFarlane, S.C., Von Berg, S.L. and Zraick, R.I. 2010. *The voice and voice therapy*, eighth edition, Boston, MA: Allyn & Bacon.

Booth, S. and Swabey, D. 1999. 'Group training in communication skills for carers of adults with aphasia', *International Journal of Language & Communication Disorders* 34:3, 291–309.

Bora, E., Eryavuz, A., Kayahan, B., Sungu, G. and Veznedaroglu, B. 2006. 'Social functioning, theory of mind and neurocognition in outpatients with schizophrenia: mental state decoding may be a better predictor of social functioning than mental state reasoning', *Psychiatry Research* 145:2–3, 95–103.

Bornhofen, C. and McDonald, S. 2008. 'Treating deficits in emotion perception following traumatic brain injury', *Neuropsychological Rehabilitation* 18:1, 22–44.

Bornman, J., Alant, E. and Meiring, E. 2001. 'The use of a digital voice output device to facilitate language development in a child with developmental apraxia of speech: a case study', *Disability and Rehabilitation* 23:14, 623–34.

Bortolini, U., Arfé, B., Caselli, M.C., Degasperi, L., Deevy, P. and Leonard, L. 2006. 'Clinical markers for specific language impairment in Italian: the contribution of clitics and nonword repetition', *International Journal of Language & Communication Disorders* 41:6, 695–712.

Bos-Clark, M. and Carding, P. 2011. 'Effectiveness of voice therapy in functional dysphonia: where are we now?', *Current Opinion in Otolaryngology & Head and Neck Surgery* 19:3, 160–4.

Boscolo, B., Bernstein Ratner, N. and Rescorla, L. 2002. 'Fluency of school-aged children with a history of specific expressive language impairment: an exploratory study', *American Journal of Speech-Language Pathology* 11:1, 41–9.

Bose, A., Square, P.A., Schlosser, R. and Van Lieshout, P. 2001. 'Effects of PROMPT therapy on speech motor function in a person with aphasia and apraxia of speech', *Aphasiology* 15:8, 767–85.

Bothe, A.K., Davidow, J.H., Bramlett, R.E., Franic, D.M. and Ingham, R.J. 2006a. 'Stuttering treatment research 1970–2005: II. systematic review incorporating trial quality assessment of pharmacological approaches', *American Journal of Speech-Language Pathology* 15:4, 342–52.

Bothe, A.K., Davidow, J.H., Bramlett, R.E. and Ingham, R.J. 2006b. 'Stuttering treatment research 1970–2005: I. systematic review incorporating trial quality assessment of behavioral, cognitive, and related approaches', *American Journal of Speech-Language Pathology* 15:4, 321–41.

Botterill, W. and Kelman, E. 2010. 'Palin parent-child interaction', in B. Guitar and R.J. McCauley (eds.), *Treatment of stuttering: established and emerging interventions*, Baltimore, MD: Lippincott Williams & Wilkins, 63–90.

Botting, N. 2004. 'Children's communication checklist (CCC) scores in 11-year-old children with communication impairments', *International Journal of Language & Communication Disorders* 39:2, 215–27.

Botting, N. and Adams, C. 2005. 'Semantic and inferencing abilities in children with communication disorders',

International Journal of Language & Communication Disorders 40:1, 49–66.

Botting, N. and Conti-Ramsden, G. 1999. 'Pragmatic language impairment without autism', *Autism* 3:4, 371–96.

Botting, N. and Conti-Ramsden, G. 2003. 'Autism, primary pragmatic difficulties, and specific language impairment: can we distinguish them using psycholinguistic markers?', *Developmental Medicine and Child Neurology* 45:8, 515–24.

Botting, N., Simkin, Z. and Conti-Ramsden, G. 2006. 'Associated reading skills in children with a history of specific language impairment (SLI)', *Reading and Writing* 19:1, 77–98.

Boucard, C. and Laffy-Beaufils, B. 2008. 'Qualifying language disorders of schizophrenia through the speech therapists' assessment', *Encephale* 34:3, 226–32.

Boudreau, D. and Chapman, R.S. 2000. 'The relationship between event representation and linguistic skill in narratives of children and adolescents with Down syndrome', *Journal of Speech, Language, and Hearing Research* 43:5, 1146–59.

Bowers, P. 1996. 'The effects of single and double deficits in phonemic awareness and naming speed on new tests of orthographic knowledge', Annual Meeting of the Society for the Scientific Study of Reading: New York, 12–13 April 1996.

Bowers, P. 2001. 'Exploration of the basis for rapid naming's relationship to reading', in M. Wolf (ed.), *Dyslexia, fluency and the brain*, Timonium, MD: York Press, 41–64.

Bowers, P. and Wolf, M. 1993. 'Theoretical links among naming speed, precise timing mechanisms, and orthographic skill in dyslexia', *Reading and Writing: An Interdisciplinary Journal* 5:1, 69–85.

Bowers, P., Sunseth, K. and Golden, J. 1999. 'The route between rapid naming and reading progress', *Scientific Studies of Reading* 3:1, 31–54.

Boxer, A.L. and Miller, B.L. 2005. 'Clinical features of frontotemporal dementia', *Alzheimer Disease and Associated Disorders* 19:Suppl 1, S3–S6.

Boyle, M. 2004. 'Semantic feature analysis treatment for anomia in two fluent aphasia syndromes', *American Journal of Speech-Language Pathology* 13:3, 236–49.

Boyle, M. 2010. 'Semantic feature analysis treatment for aphasic word retrieval impairments: what's in a name?', *Topics in Stroke Rehabilitation* 17:6, 411–22.

Boyle, M. 2011. 'Mindfulness training in stuttering therapy: a tutorial for speech-language pathologists', *Journal of Fluency Disorders* 36:2, 122–9.

Bozeat, S., Lambon Ralph, M.A., Patterson, K., Garrard, P. and Hodges, J. 2000. 'Non-verbal semantic impairment in semantic dementia', *Neuropsychologia* 38:9, 1207–15.

Braak, H. and Braak, E. 1997. 'Staging of Alzheimer-related cortical destruction', *International Psychogeriatrics* 9:1, 257–61.

Braak, H., Alafuzoff, I., Arzberger, T., Kretzschmar, H. and Del Tredici, K. 2006. 'Staging of Alzheimer disease-associated neurofibrillary pathology using paraffin sections and immunocytochemistry', *Acta Neuropathologica* 112:4, 389–404.

Bracken, B.A. and McCallum, R.S. 1998. *Universal nonverbal intelligence test (UNIT)*, Itasca, IL: Riverside.

Bradley, R., Doolittle, J. and Bartolotta, R. 2008. 'Building on the data and adding to the discussion: the experiences and outcomes of students with emotional disturbance', *Journal of Behavioral Education* 17:1, 4–23.

Bradley-Hagerty, B. 2009. *Fingerprints of God: the search for the science of spirituality*, New York: Riverhead Books.

Bradlow, A.R., Bakes, R.E., Choi, A., Kim, M. and van Engen, K.J. 2007. 'The Wildcat corpus of native- and foreign-accented English', *Journal of the Acoustical Society of America* 121:5 Pt 2, 3072.

Brady, J.P. 1991. 'The pharmacology of stuttering: a critical review', *American Journal of Psychiatry* 148:10, 1309–16.

Brady, M., Armstrong, L. and Mackenzie, C. 2005. 'Further evidence on topic use following right hemisphere brain damage: procedural and descriptive discourse', *Aphasiology* 19:8, 731–47.

Brady, M., Armstrong, L. and Mackenzie, C. 2006. 'An examination over time of language and discourse production abilities following right hemisphere brain damage', *Journal of Neurolinguistics* 19:4, 291–310.

Brady, M., Mackenzie, C. and Armstrong, L. 2003. 'Topic use following right brain damage during three semi-structured conversational discourse samples', *Aphasiology* 17:9, 881–904.

Brady, M.C., Clark, A.M., Dickson, S., Paton, G. and Barbour, R.S. 2011. 'The impact of stroke-related dysarthria on social participation and implications for rehabilitation', *Disability and Rehabilitation* 33:3, 178–86.

Brady, M.C., Kelly, H., Godwin, J. and Enderby, P. 2012. 'Speech and language therapy for aphasia following stroke', *Cochrane Database of Systematic Reviews*, Issue 5, CD000425.

Brady, N.C. 2000. 'Improved comprehension of object names following voice output communication aid use: two case studies', *AAC: Augmentative and Alternative Communication* 16:3, 197–204.

Brandt, J. 1991. 'Cognitive impairments in Huntington's disease: insights into the neuropsychology of the striatum', in F. Boller and J. Grafman (eds.), *Handbook of neuropsychology*, Amsterdam: Elsevier Science, 261–4.

Branski, R.C., Verdolini, K., Sandulache, V., Rosen, C.A. and Hebda, P.A. 2006. 'Vocal fold wound healing: a review for clinicians', *Journal of Voice* 20:3, 432–42.

Braunling-McMorrow, D., Lloyd, K. and Fralish, K. 1986. 'Teaching social skills to head injured adults', *Journal of Rehabilitation* 52:1, 39–44.

Breitenfeld, D. and Lorenz, D.R. 1989. *Successful stuttering management program (SSMP) for adolescent and adult stutterers*, Cheney, WA: Eastern Washington University School of Health Sciences.

Brendel, B. and Ziegler, W. 2008. 'Effectiveness of metrical pacing in the treatment of apraxia of speech', *Aphasiology* 22:1, 77–102.

Brendel, B., Ziegler, W. and Deger, K. 2000. 'The synchronization paradigm in the treatment of apraxia of speech', *Journal of Neurolinguistics* 13:4, 254–7.

Bressmann, T., Ackloo, E., Heng, C.L. and Irish, J.C. 2007. 'Quantitative three-dimensional ultrasound imaging of partially resected tongues', *Otolaryngology – Head and Neck Surgery* 136:5, 799–805.

Bressmann, T., Jacobs, H., Quintero, J. and Irish, J.C. 2009. 'Speech outcomes for partial glossectomy surgery: measures of speech articulation and listener perception', *Canadian Journal of Speech-Language Pathology and Audiology* 33:4, 204–10.

Bressmann, T., Thind, P., Uy, C., Bollig, C., Gilbert, R.W. and Irish, J.C. 2005b. 'Quantitative three-dimensional ultrasound analysis of tongue protrusion, grooving and symmetry: data from 12 normal speakers and a partial glossectomee', *Clinical Linguistics & Phonetics* 19:6–7, 573–88.

Bressmann, T., Uy, C. and Irish, J.C. 2005a. 'Analysing normal and partial glossectomee tongues using ultrasound', *Clinical Linguistics & Phonetics* 19:1, 35–52.

Bretherton-Furness, J. and Ward, D. 2012. 'Lexical access, story re-telling, and sequencing skills in adults who clutter and those who do not', *Journal of Fluency Disorders* 37:4, 214–24.

Bridger, M.W. and Epstein, R. 1983. 'Functional voice disorders: a review of 109 patients', *Journal of Laryngology and Otology* 97:12, 1145–8.

Brier, N. 1995. 'Predicting antisocial behavior in youngsters displaying poor academic achievement: a review of risk factors', *Developmental and Behavioral Pediatrics* 16:4, 271–6.

Brinton, B., Fujiki, M. and Higbee, L.M. 1998. 'Participation in cooperative learning activities by children with specific language impairment', *Journal of Speech, Language, and Hearing Research* 41:5, 1193–206.

Brinton, B., Fujiki, M. and Powell, J. 1997. 'The ability of children with language impairment to manipulate topic in a structured task', *Language, Speech, and Hearing Services in Schools* 28:1, 3–11.

Broca, P. [1861]1977. 'Remarks on the seat of the faculty of articulate speech, followed by the report of a case of aphemia (loss of speech)', in D.A. Rottenberg and F.H. Hochburg (eds.), *Neurological classics in modern translation*, New York: Hafner Press, 136–49.

Broca, P. 1861. 'Remarques sur le siège de la faculté du langage articulé, suivies d'une observation d'aphémie (perte de la parole)', *Bulletin de la Société d'Anatomie* 6: 330–57.

Broca, P. 1865. 'Sur le siège de la faculté du langage articulé', *Bulletin de la Société d'Anthropologie* 6: 337–93.

Brock, J., Norbury, C., Einav, S. and Nation, K. 2008. 'Do individuals with autism process words in context? Evidence from language-mediated eye-movements', *Cognition* 108:3, 896–904.

Broder, H.L., Richman, L.C. and Matheson, P.B. 1998. 'Learning disability, school achievement, and grade retention among children with cleft: a two-center study', *Cleft Palate-Craniofacial Journal* 35:2, 127–31.

Brodnitz, F.S. 1969. 'Functional aphonia', *Annals of Otology, Rhinology and Laryngology* 78:6, 1244–53.

Broomfield, J. and Dodd, B. 2004. 'The nature of referred subtypes of primary speech disability', *Child Language Teaching and Therapy* 20:2, 135–51.

Brosky, M.E. 2007. 'The role of saliva in oral health: strategies for prevention and management of xerostomia', *Journal of Supportive Oncology* 5:5, 215–25.

Brotherton, F.A., Thomas, L.L., Wisotzek, I.E. and Milan, M.A. 1988. 'Social skills training in the rehabilitation of patients with traumatic closed head injury', *Archives of Physical Medicine and Rehabilitation* 69:10, 827–32.

Brouha, X., Tromp, D., Hordijk, G.J., Winnubst, J. and De Leeuw, R. 2005. 'Role of alcohol and smoking in diagnostic delay of head and neck cancer patients', *Acta Oto-Laryngologica* 125:5, 552–6.

Brown, A. and Docherty, G.J. 1995. 'Phonetic variation in dysarthric speech as a function of sampling task', *European Journal of Disorders of Communication* 30:1, 17–35.

Brown, J.R., Darley, F.L. and Aronson, A.E. 1970. 'Ataxic dysarthria', *International Journal of Neurology* 7, 302–18.

Brown, K., Worrall, L.E., Davidson, B. and Howe, T. 2012. 'Living successfully with aphasia: a qualitative meta-analysis of the perspectives of individuals with aphasia, family members, and speech-language pathologists', *International Journal of Speech-Language Pathology* 14:2, 141–55.

Brown, S.F. 1945. 'The loci of stutterings in the speech sequence', *Journal of Speech Disorders* 10:3, 181–92.

Brownell, H. 1986. 'Inference deficits in right brain-damaged patients', *Brain and Language* 27:2, 310–21.

Brownell, M.D. and Whiteley, J.H. 1992. 'Development and training of referential communication in children with mental retardation', *American Journal on Mental Retardation* 97:2, 161–71.

Brownlee, E.B., Beitchman, J.H., Escobar, M., Young, A.R., Atkinson, L., Johnson, C., Wilson, B. and Douglas, L. 2004. 'Early language impairment and young adult delinquency and aggressive behavior', *Journal of Abnormal Child Psychology* 32:4, 453–67.

Brown-Schmidt, S. 2009. 'The role of executive function in perspective taking during online language comprehension', *Psychonomic Bulletin & Review* 16:5, 893–900.

Brumfitt, S. 1993. 'Losing your sense of self: what aphasia can do', *Aphasiology* 7:6, 569–75.

Brumfitt, S.M. and Sheeran, P. 1999. 'The development and validation of the Visual Analogue Self-Esteem Scale (VASES)', *British Journal of Child Psychology* 38:4, 387–400.

Brundage, S. 1996. 'Comparison of proverb interpretations provided by right-hemisphere-damaged adults and adults with probable dementia of the Alzheimer type', *Clinical Aphasiology* 24, 215–31.

Brüne, M. and Bodenstein, L. 2005. 'Proverb comprehension reconsidered – "theory of mind" and the pragmatic use of language in schizophrenia', *Schizophrenia Research* 75:2–3, 233–9.

Bruni, O., Novelli, L., Mallucci, A., Corte, M.D., Romeo, A. and Ferri, R. 2012. 'Benign rolandic and occipital epilepsies of childhood', *Sleep Medicine Clinics* 7:1, 135–45.

Bruns, J.J. and Hauser, W. 2003. 'The epidemiology of traumatic brain injury: a review', *Epilepsia* 44 (Suppl 10), 2–10.

Brutten, E.J. and Shoemaker, D.J. 1967. *The modification of stuttering*, Englewood Cliffs, NJ: Prentice-Hall.

Brutten, E.J. and Vanryckeghem, M. 2006. *The behavior assessment battery for school-age children who stutter*, San Diego, CA: Plural Publishers.

Brutten, G. and Shoemaker, D. 1974. *Speech situation checklist*, Carbondale, IL: Southern Illinois University.

Bucci, S., Startup, M., Wynn, P., Baker, A. and Lewin, T.J. 2008. 'Referential delusions of communication and interpretations of gestures', *Psychiatry Research* 158:1, 27–34.

Buitelaar, J.K., van der Wees, M., Swaab-Barneveld, H. and van der Gaag, R.J. 1999. 'Theory of mind and emotion-recognition functioning in autistic spectrum disorders and in psychiatric control and normal children', *Development and Psychopathology* 11:1, 39–58.

Burgess, C. and Simpson, G.B. 1988. 'Cerebral hemispheric mechanisms in the retrieval of ambiguous word meanings', *Brain and Language* 33:1, 86–103.

Burns, J.A. 2012. 'Optical coherence tomography: imaging the larynx', *Current Opinion in Otolaryngology & Head and Neck Surgery*, 20:6, 477–81.

Burns, M.S. 1997. *Burns brief inventory of communication and cognition*, San Antonio, TX: Psychological Corporation.

Burns, M.S. 2011. 'Apraxia of speech in children and adolescents: applications of neuroscience to differential diagnosis and intervention', *Perspectives on Neurophysiology and Neurogenic Speech and Language Disorders* 21:1, 33–42.

Bushmann, M., Dobmeyer, S.M., Leeker, L. and Perlmutter, J.S. 1989. 'Swallowing abnormalities and their responses to treatment in Parkinson's disease', *Neurology* 39:10 1309–14.

Byng, S. and Black, M. 1995. 'What makes a therapy? Some parameters of therapeutic intervention in aphasia', *International Journal of Language & Communication Disorders* 30:3, 303–16.

Byng, S. and Duchan, J. 2005. 'Social model philosophies and principles: their applications to therapies for aphasia', *Aphasiology* 19:10–11, 906–22.

Byng, S., Pound, C. and Parr, S. 2000. 'Living with aphasia: a framework for therapy interventions', in I. Papathanasiou (ed.), *Acquired neurogenic communication disorders: a clinical perspective*, London: Whurr, 49–75.

Byrne, D., Frantz, C. and Weymouth, T. 1977. 'Psycho killer' on Talking Heads: 77, Sire Records.

Cabeza, R. 2002. 'Hemispheric asymmetry reduction in older adults: the HAROLD model', *Psychology and Aging* 17:1, 85–100.

Cahill, L.M., Murdoch, B.E. and Theodoros, D.G. 2002. 'Perceptual analysis of speech following traumatic brain injury in childhood', *Brain Injury* 16:5, 415–46.

Cahill, L.M., Murdoch, B.E. and Theodoros, D.G. 2003. 'Perceptual and instrumental analysis of laryngeal function after traumatic brain injury in childhood', *Journal of Head Trauma and Rehabilitation* 18:3, 268–83.

Cahill, L.M., Turner, A.B., Stabler, P.A., Addis, P.E., Theodoros, D.G. and Murdoch, B.E. 2004. 'An evaluation of continuous positive airway pressure (CPAP) therapy in the treatment of hypernasality following traumatic brain injury: a report of 3 cases', *Journal of Head Trauma Rehabilitation* 19:3, 241–53.

Cain, K., Oakhill, J. and Lemmon, K. 2005. 'The relation between children's reading comprehension level and their comprehension of idioms', *Journal of Experimental Child Psychology* 90:1, 65–87.

Calandrella, A.M. and Wilcox, M.J. 2000. 'Predicting language outcomes for young prelinguistic children with developmental delay', *Journal of Speech, Language, and Hearing Research* 43:5, 1061–71.

Calnan, J.S. 1971. 'Permanent nasal escape after adenoidectomy', *British Journal of Plastic Surgery* 24:2, 197–204.

Campbell, K.C.M. 2007. 'Ototoxicity', in R.S. Ackley, T.N. Decker and C. Limb, C. (eds.), *An essential guide to hearing and balance disorders*, Mahwah, NJ: Lawrence Erlbaum Publishers, 117–37.

Campbell, T.F., Dollaghan, C.A., Rockette, H.E., Paradise, J.L., Feldman, H.M., Shriberg, L.D., Sabo, D.L. and Kurs-Lasky, M. 2003. 'Risk factors for speech delay of unknown origin in 3-year-old children', *Child Development* 74:2, 346–57.

Canadian Cancer Society. 2011. *Canadian cancer statistics 2011*, Mississauga, ON: Canadian Cancer Society.

Cannizzaro, M.S. and Coelho, C.A. 2002. 'Treatment of story grammar following traumatic brain injury: a pilot study', *Brain Injury* 16:12, 1065–73.

Canter, G.J. 1971. 'Observations on neurogenic stuttering: a contribution to differential diagnosis', *British Journal of Disorders of Communication* 6:2, 139–43.

Cao, F., Bitan, T., Chou, T.-L., Burman, D.D. and Booth, J.R. 2006. 'Deficient orthographic and phonological representations in children with dyslexia revealed by brain activation patterns', *Journal of Child Psychology and Psychiatry* 47:10, 1041–50.

Capitani, E., Laiacona, M., Mahon, B. and Caramazza, A. 2003. 'What are the facts of semantic category-specific deficits? A critical review of the clinical evidence', *Cognitive Neuropsychology* 20:3, 213–61.

Capitani, E., Laiacona, M., Pagain, R., Capasso, R., Zampetti, P. and Miceli, G. 2009. 'Posterior cerebral artery infarcts and semantic category dissociations: a study of 28 patients', *Brain* 132:4, 965–81.

Caplan, D. and Bub, D.N. 1990. 'Psycholinguistic assessment of aphasia', American Speech and Hearing Association Conference: Seattle, WA, 1990.

Cappa, S. and Vignolo, L. 1979. '"Transcortical" features of aphasia following left thalamic hemorrhage', *Cortex* 15:1, 121–30.

Capps, L., Losh, M. and Thurber, C. 2000. '"The frog ate the bug and made his mouth sad": narrative competence in children with autism', *Journal of Abnormal Child Psychology* 28:2, 193–204.

Caramazza, A. 1989. 'Cognitive neuropsychology and rehabilitation: an unfulfilled promise?', in X. Seron and G. Deloche (eds.), *Cognitive approaches in neuropsychological rehabilitation*, Hillsdale, NJ: Lawrence Erlbaum Associates, 383–98.

Caramazza, A. 1999. 'The organization of conceptual knowledge in the brain', in M.S. Gazzaniga (ed.), *The new cognitive neurosciences*, second edition, Cambridge, MA: MIT Press, 1037–46.

Caramazza, A. and Hillis, A.E. 1990a. 'Spatial representation of words in the brain implied by studies of a unilateral neglect patient', *Nature* 346, 267–9.

Caramazza, A. and Hillis, A.E. 1990b. 'Where do semantic errors come from?', *Cortex* 26:1, 95–122.

Caramazza, A. and Mahon, B.Z. 2006. 'The organisation of conceptual knowledge in the brain: the future's past and some future directions', *Cognitive Neuropsychology* 23:1, 13–38.

Caramazza, A. and McCloskey, M. 1988. 'The case for single-patient study', *Cognitive Neuropsychology* 5:5, 517–28.

Caramazza, A. and Shelton, J.R. 1998. 'Domain-specific knowledge systems in the brain: the animate-inanimate distinction', *Journal of Cognitive Neuroscience* 10:1, 1–34.

Caramazza, A. and Zurif, E.B. 1976. 'Dissociation of algorithmic and heuristic processes in sentence comprehension: evidence from aphasia', *Brain and Language* 3:4, 572–82.

Caramazza, A., Hillis, A.E., Rapp, B.C. and Romani, C. 1990. 'The multiple semantics hypothesis: multiple confusions?', *Cognitive Neuropsychology* 7:3, 161–89.

Caravolas, M., Volín, J. and Hulme, C. 2005. 'Phoneme awareness is a key component of alphabetic literacy skills in consistent and inconsistent orthographies: evidence from Czech and English children', *Journal of Experimental Child Psychology* 92:2, 107–39.

Carding, P. 2000. *Evaluating voice therapy: measuring the effectiveness of treatment*, New York: Wiley.

Carding, P.N. and Horsley, I.A. 1992. 'An evaluation study of voice therapy in non-organic dysphonia', *European Journal of Disorders of Communication* 27:2, 137–58.

Carding, P.N., Horsley, I.A. and Docherty, G.J. 1999. 'The effectiveness of voice therapy in the treatment of 45 patients with nonorganic dysphonia', *Journal of Voice* 13:1, 72–104.

Carding, P.N., Wilson, J.A., MacKenzie, K. and Deary, I.J. 2009. 'Measuring voice outcomes: state of the science review', *Journal of Laryngology and Otology* 123:8, 823–9.

Cardoso-Martins, C. and Pennington, B.F. 2004. 'The relationship between phoneme awareness and rapid serial naming skills and literacy acquisition: the role of developmental period and reading ability', *Scientific Studies of Reading* 8:1, 27–52.

Carlomagno, S., Santoro, A., Menditti, A., Pandolfi, M. and Marini, A. 2005. 'Referential communication in Alzheimer's type dementia', *Cortex* 41:4, 520–34.

Carmichael, C.T. 2006. 'Cellular and molecular mechanisms of neural repair after stroke: making waves', *Annals of Neurology* 59:5, 735–42.

Carnevale, G. 1996. 'Natural-setting behavior management for individuals with traumatic brain injury: results of a three-year caregiver training program', *Journal of Head Trauma Rehabilitation* 11:1, 27–38.

Carney, N., Chesnut, R., Maynard, H., Mann, N., Patterson, P. and Helfand, M. 1999. 'Effect of cognitive rehabilitation on outcomes for persons with traumatic brain injury: a systematic review', *Journal of Head Trauma Rehabilitation* 14:3, 277–307.

Carothers, A.D., Hecht, C.A. and Hook, E.B. 1999. 'International variation in reported live birth prevalence rates of Down syndrome, adjusted for maternal age', *Journal of Medical Genetics* 36:5, 386–93.

Carr, A.J. and Higginson, I.J. 2001. 'Are quality of life measures patient centred?', *British Medical Journal* 322:7298, 1357–60.

Carragher, M., Conroy, P., Sage, K. and Wilkinson, R. 2012. 'Can impairment-focused therapy change the everyday conversations of people with aphasia? A review of the literature and future directions', *Aphasiology* 26:7, 895–916.

Carrau, R.L., Khidr, A., Crawley, J.A., Hillson, E.M., Davis, J.K. and Pashos, C.L. 2004. 'The impact of laryngopharyngeal reflux on patient-reported quality of life', *Laryngoscope* 114:4, 670–4.

Carter, P. and Edwards, S. 2004. 'EPG therapy for children with long-standing speech disorders: predictions and outcomes', *Clinical Linguistics & Phonetics* 18:6–8, 359–72.

Casper, J. 1999. 'Voice therapy in the treatment of vocal fold stiffness and scar: a roundtable', *Phonoscope* 2:3, 139–44.

Castles, A. and Coltheart, M. 2004. 'Is there a causal link from phonological awareness to success in learning to read?', *Cognition* 91:1, 77–111.

Catts, H.W. and Hogan, T.P. 2003. 'Language basis of reading disabilities and implications for early identification and remediation', *Reading Psychology* 24:3–4, 223–46.

Catts, H.W. and Kamhi, A.G. 1986. 'The linguistic basis of reading disorders: implications for the speech-language pathologist', *Language, Speech, and Hearing Services in Schools* 17:4, 329–41.

Catts, H., Adlof, S. and Ellis Weismer, S. 2006. 'Language deficits in poor comprehenders: a case for the simple view of reading', *Journal of Speech, Language, and Hearing Research* 49:2, 278–93.

Catts, H., Adlof, S., Hogan, T. and Ellis Weismer, S. 2005. 'Are specific language impairment and dyslexia distinct disorders?', *Journal of Speech, Language, and Hearing Research* 48:6, 1378–96.

Catts, H.W., Bridges, M.S., Little, T.D. and Tomblin, J.B. 2008. 'Reading achievement growth in children with language impairments', *Journal of Speech, Language, and Hearing Research* 51:6, 1569–79.

Catts, H.W., Compton, D., Tomblin, J.B. and Bridges, M.S. 2012. 'Prevalence and nature of late-emerging poor readers', *Journal of Educational Psychology* 104:1, 166–81.

Catts, H.W., Fey, M.E., Tomblin, J.B. and Zhang, X. 2002. 'A longitudinal investigation of reading outcomes in children with language impairments', *Journal of Speech, Language, and Hearing Research* 45:6, 1142–57.

Catts, H.W., Fey, M.E., Xuyang, Z. and Tomblin, J.B. 1999. Language basis of reading and reading disabilities: evidence from a longitudinal investigation', *Scientific Studies of Reading* 3:4, 331–62.

Catts, H.W., Fey, M.E., Zhang, X. and Tomblin, J.B. 2001. 'Estimating the risk of future reading difficulties in kindergarten children: a research-based model and its clinical implementation', *Language, Speech, and Hearing Services in Schools* 32:1, 38–50.

Centers for Disease Control and Prevention. 2006. 'Improved national prevalence estimates for 18 selected major birth defects – United States, 1999–2001', *Morbidity and Mortality Weekly Report* 54:51 & 52, 1301–5.

Cerhan, J.H., Ivnik, R.J., Smith, G.E., Tangalos, E.C., Petersen, R.C. and Boeve, B.F. 2002. 'Diagnostic utility of letter fluency, category fluency, and fluency difference scores in Alzheimer's disease', *The Clinical Neuropsychologist* 16:1, 35–42.

Chalstrey, S.E., Bleach, N.R., Cheung, D. and van Hasselt, V.A. 1994. 'A pneumatic artificial larynx popularized in Hong Kong', *Journal of Laryngology and Otology* 108:10, 852–4.

Champagne-Lavau, M. and Joanette, Y. 2009. 'Pragmatics, theory of mind and executive functions after a right-hemisphere lesion: different patterns of deficits', *Journal of Neurolinguistics* 22:5, 413–26.

Champagne-Lavau, M., Fossard, M., Martel, G., Chapdelaine, C., Blouin, G., Rodriguez, J.P. and Stip, E. 2009. 'Do patients with schizophrenia attribute mental states in a referential communication task?', *Cognitive Neuropsychiatry* 14:3, 217–39.

Champagne-Lavau, M., Stip, E. and Joanette, Y. 2006. 'Social cognition deficit in schizophrenia: accounting for pragmatic deficits in communication abilities?', *Current Psychiatry Reviews* 2:3, 309–15.

Chan, K.M.K. and Yiu, E.M.-L. 2002. 'The effect of anchors and training on the reliability of perceptual voice evaluation', *Journal of Speech, Language, and Hearing Research* 45:1, 111–26.

Chan, K.M.K. and Yiu, E.M.-L. 2006. 'A comparison of two perceptual voice evaluation training programs for naive listeners', *Journal of Voice* 20:2, 229–41.

Chan, R.W. 1994. 'Does the voice improve with vocal hygiene education? A study of some instrumental voice measures in a group of kindergarten teachers', *Journal of Voice* 8:3, 279–91.

Chandu, A., Smith, A.C. and Rogers, S.N. 2006. 'Health-related quality of life in oral cancer: a review', *Journal of Oral and Maxillofacial Surgery* 64:3, 495–502.

Chang, S.-E., Erickson, K.I., Ambrose, N.G., Hasegawa-Johnson, M.A. and Ludlow, C.L. 2008. 'Brain anatomy differences in childhood stuttering', *Neuroimage* 39:3, 1333–44.

Chantraine, Y., Joanette, Y. and Ska, B. 1998. 'Conversational abilities in patients with right hemisphere damage', *Journal of Neurolinguistics* 11:1–2, 21–32.

Chapey, R., Duchan, J.F., Elman, R.J., Garcia, L.J., Kagan, A., Lyon, J. and Simmons Mackie, N. 2008. 'Life-participation approach to aphasia: a statement of values for the future', in R. Chapey (ed.), *Language intervention strategies in aphasia and related neurogenic communication disorders*, fifth edition, Philadelphia, PA: Lippincott Williams & Wilkins, 279–89.

Chapman, R. 1997. 'Language development in children and adolescents with Down syndrome', *Mental Retardation and Developmental Disabilities Research Reviews* 3:4, 307–12.

Chapman, R.S. 2003. 'Language and communication in individuals with Down syndrome', in L. Abbeduto (ed.), *International review of research in mental retardation (volume 27). Language and communication in mental retardation*, San Diego, CA: Academic Press, 1–34.

Chapman, R.S. and Hesketh, L.J. 2000. 'Behavioural phenotype of individuals with Down syndrome', *Mental Retardation and Developmental Disabilities Research Reviews* 6:2, 84–95.

Chapman, R., Hesketh, L. and Kistler, D. 2002. 'Predicting longitudinal change in language production and comprehension in individuals with Down syndrome: hierarchical linear modelling', *Journal of Speech, Language, and Hearing Research* 45:5, 902–15.

Chapman, R.S., Schwartz, S.E. and Kay-Raining Bird, E. 1991. 'Language skills of children and adolescents with Down syndrome: I. Comprehension', *Journal of Speech, Language, and Hearing Research* 34:5, 1106–20.

Chapman, R.S., Seung, H.-K., Schwartz, S.E. and Kay-Raining Bird, E. 1998. 'Language skills of children and adolescents with Down syndrome: II. Production deficits', *Journal of Speech, Language, and Hearing Research* 41:4, 861–73.

Chapman, S., Ulatowska, H., King, K., Johnson, J. and McIntire, D. 1995. 'Discourse in early Alzheimer's disease versus normal advanced aging', *American Journal of Speech-Language Pathology* 4:4, 124–9.

Chapman, S.B., Culhane, K.A., Levin, H.S., Harward, H., Mendelsohn, D., Ewing-Cobbs, L., Fletcher, J.M. and Bruce, D. 1992. 'Narrative discourse after closed head injury in children and adolescents', *Brain and Language* 43:1, 42–65.

Charcot, J.M. 1877. *Lectures on diseases of the nervous system*, London: New Sydenham Society.

Charman, T., Baron-Cohen, S., Swettenham, J., Baird, G., Drew, A. and Cox, A. 2003. 'Predicting language outcome in infants with autism and pervasive developmental disorder', *International Journal of Language & Communication Disorders* 38:3, 265–85.

Cheah, W.K., Arici, C., Ituarte, P.H., Siperstein, A.E., Duh, Q.Y. and Clark, O.H. 2002. 'Complications of neck dissection for thyroid cancer', *World Journal of Surgery* 26:8, 1013–6.

Cheang, H. and Pell, M. 2006. 'A study of humour and communicative intention following right hemisphere stroke', *Clinical Linguistics & Phonetics* 20:6, 447–62.

Chen, A.Y., Fedewa, S. and Zhu, J. 2011. 'Temporal trends in the treatment of early and advanced-stage laryngeal cancer in the United States, 1985–2007', *Archives of Otolaryngology – Head and Neck Surgery* 137:10, 1017–24.

Chen, J.J. and Swope, D.M. 2007. 'Essential tremor', *Journal of Pharmacology Practice* 20:6, 258–68.

Chen, S.H., Hsiao, T.-Y., Hsiao, L.-C., Chung, Y.-M. and Chiang, S.-C. 2007. 'Outcome of resonant voice therapy for female teachers with voice disorders: perceptual,

physiological, acoustic, aerodynamic, and functional measurements', *Journal of Voice* 21:4, 415–25.

Chenery, H.J., Murdoch, B.E. and Ingram, J.C.L. 1988. 'Studies in Parkinson's disease 1: perceptual speech analysis', *Australian Journal of Human Communication Disorders* 16:2, 17–29.

Cherney, L. and Canter, G. 1992. 'Informational content in the discourse of patients with probable Alzheimer's disease and patients with right brain damage', *Clinical Aphasiology* 21, 123–34.

Cherney, L.R., Patterson, J.P., Raymer, A., Frymark, T. and Schooling, T. 2008. 'Evidence-based systematic review: effects of intensity of treatment and constraint-induced language therapy for individuals with stroke-induced aphasia', *Journal of Speech, Language, and Hearing Research* 51:5, 1282–99.

Chertkow, H. and Bub, D. 1990. 'Semantic memory loss in Alzheimer-type dementia', in M.F. Schwartz (ed.), *Modular deficits in Alzheimer's disease*, Cambridge, MA: MIT Press, 207–44.

Cheyne, H.A., Hanson, H.M., Genereux, R.P., Stevens, K.N. and Hillman, R.E. 2003. 'Development and testing of a portable vocal accumulator', *Journal of Speech, Language, and Hearing Research* 46:6, 1457–67.

Chhetri, D.K., Blumin, J.H., Shapiro, N.L. and Berke, G.S. 2002. 'Office-based treatment of laryngeal papillomatosis with percutaneous injection of cidofovir', *Otolaryngology – Head and Neck Surgery* 126:6, 642–8.

Chiang, M.-C., Reiss, A.L., Lee, A.D., Bellugi, U., Galaburda, A.M., Korenberg, J.R., Mills, D.L., Toga, A.W. and Thompson, P.M. 2007. '3D pattern of brain abnormalities in Williams syndrome visualised using tensor-based morphometry', *NeuroImage* 36:4, 1096–109.

Chiat, S. 1982. 'If I were you and you were me: the analysis of pronouns in a pronoun-reversing child', *Journal of Child Language* 9:2, 359–79.

Cho, S.J. 2008. 'Current practices and future directions of special education in the republic of Korea', *Intellectual and Developmental Disabilities* 46:2, 150–3.

Cholin, J. 2008. 'The mental syllabary in speech production: an integration of different approaches and domains', *Aphasiology* 22:11, 1127–41.

Chomsky, N. 1965. *Aspects of the theory of syntax*, Cambridge, MA: MIT Press.

Christensen, C.A. 2000. 'Preschool phonological awareness and success in reading', in N.A. Badian (ed.), *Prediction and prevention of reading failure*, Baltimore, MD: York Press, 153–78.

Christenson, L.J., Borrowman, T.A., Vachon, C.M., Tollefson, M.M., Otley, C.C., Weaver, A.L. and Roenig, R.K. 2005. 'Incidence of basal cell and squamous cell carcinomas in a population younger than 40 years', *Journal of the American Medical Association* 294:6, 681–90.

Christo, C. 1995. *'Contributions of orthographic representations, phonological processing and rapid naming to reading and spelling'*, American Educational Research Association Annual Meeting: San Francisco, CA, 18–22 April 1995.

Christo, C. 2005. 'Critical characteristics of a three tiered model applied to reading interventions', *The California School Psychologist* 10, 33–44.

Christo, C. and Davis, J. 2008. 'Rapid naming and phonological processing as predictors of reading and spelling', *The California School Psychologist* 13, 7–18.

Christo, C., Davis, J. and Brock, S.E. 2009. *Identifying, assessing, and treating dyslexia at school*, New York: Springer Science and Business Media.

Chui, H.C., Victoroff, J.I., Margolin, D., Jagust, W., Shankle, R. and Katzman, R. 1992. 'Criteria for the diagnosis of ischemic vascular dementia proposed by the State of California Alzheimer's Disease Diagnostic and Treatment Centers', *Neurology* 42:3:Pt 1, 473–80.

Clahsen, H. and Almazan, M. 1998. 'Syntax and morphology in Williams syndrome', *Cognition* 68:3, 197–8.

Clahsen, H. and Hansen, D. 1993. 'The missing agreement account of specific language impairment: evidence from therapy experiments', *Essex Research Reports in Linguistics* 2, 1–36.

Clahsen, H., Ring, M. and Temple, C. 2004. 'Lexical and morphological skills in English-speaking children with Williams syndrome', in S. Bartke and J. Siegmüller (eds.), *Williams syndrome across languages*, Amsterdam: Benjamins, 221–44.

Clark, H.M. 2004. 'Neuromuscular treatments for speech and swallowing: a tutorial', *American Journal of Speech-Language Pathology* 12:4, 400–15.

Clark, H.M. and Robin, D.A. 1998. 'Generalized motor programme and parameterization accuracy in apraxia of speech and conduction aphasia', *Aphasiology* 12:7–8, 699–713.

Clark, M. and Neville, B. 2008. 'Familial and genetic associations in Worster-Drought syndrome and perisylvian disorders', *American Journal of Medical Genetics* 146A:1, 35–42.

Clark, M., Carr, L., Reilly, S. and Neville, B. 2000. 'Worster-Drought syndrome, a mild tetraplegic perisylvian cerebral palsy: review of 47 cases', *Brain* 123:10, 2160–70.

Clark, M., Harris, R., Jolleff, N., Price, K. and Neville, B. 2010. 'Worster-Drought syndrome: poorly recognized despite severe and persisting difficulties with feeding and speech', *Developmental Medicine and Child Neurology* 52:1, 27–32.

Clarke, M.C., Tanskanen, A., Huttunen, M., Whittaker, J.C. and Cannon, M. 2009. 'Evidence for an interaction between familial liability and prenatal exposure to infection in the causation of schizophrenia', *American Journal of Psychiatry* 166:9, 1025–30.

Clausen, N.S. and Beeson, P.M. 2003. 'Conversational use of writing in severe aphasia: a group treatment approach', *Aphasiology* 17:6–7, 625–44.

Cleft Palate Foundation. 2012. *Feeding your baby* (online, available at: www.cleftline.org/parents-individuals/feeding-your-baby; last accessed 12 June 2013).

Clegg, J., Brumfitt, S., Parks, R.W. and Woodruff, P.W.R. 2007. 'Speech and language therapy intervention in schizophrenia: a case study', *International Journal of Language & Communication Disorders* 42:S1, 81–101.

Clegg, J., Hollis, C., Mawhood, L. and Rutter, M. 2005. 'Developmental language disorders – a follow-up in later adult life. Cognitive, language, and psychosocial outcomes', *Journal of Child Psychology and Psychiatry* 46:2, 128–49.

Cleland, J., Wood, S., Hardcastle, W., Wishart, J. and Timmins, C. 2010. 'The relationship between speech, oromotor, language and cognitive abilities in children with Down's syndrome', *International Journal of Language & Communication Disorders* 45:1, 83–95.

Clements, K.S., Rassekh, C.H., Seikaly, H., Hokanson, J.A. and Calhoun, K.H. 1997. 'Communication after laryngectomy: an assessment of patient satisfaction', *Archives of Otolaryngology – Head and Neck Surgery* 123:5, 493–6.

Cocks, N., Hird, K. and Kirsner, K. 2007. 'The relationship between right hemisphere damage and gesture in spontaneous discourse', *Aphasiology* 21:3–4, 299–319.

Code, C. 1998. 'Models, theories and heuristics in apraxia of speech', *Clinical Linguistics & Phonetics* 12:1, 47–65.

Code, C. 2003. 'The quantity of life for people with chronic aphasia', *Neuropsychological Rehabilitation* 13:3, 379–90.

Code, C. 2010. 'Aphasia', in J.S. Damico, N. Müller and M. Ball (eds.), *The handbook of language and speech disorders*, Oxford: Wiley-Blackwell, 317–36.

Code, C. and Herrmann, M. 2003. 'The relevance of emotional and psychosocial factors in aphasia to rehabilitation', *Neuropsychological Rehabilitation* 13:1–2, 109–32.

Coelho, C.A. 2002. 'Story narratives of adults with closed head injury and non-brain-injured adults: influence of socioeconomic status, elicitation task, and executive functioning', *Journal of Speech, Language, and Hearing Research* 45:6, 1232–48.

Coelho, C.A. 2005. 'Direct attention training as a treatment of reading impairment in aphasia', *Aphasiology* 19:3–5, 275–83.

Coelho, C.A. 2007. 'Management of discourse deficits following traumatic brain injury: progress, caveats, and needs', *Seminars in Speech and Language* 28:2, 122–35.

Coelho, C., Grela, B., Corso, M., Gamble, A. and Feinn, R. 2005b. 'Microlinguistic deficits in the narrative discourse of adults with traumatic brain injury', *Brain Injury* 19:13, 1139–45.

Coelho, C.A., Liles, B.Z. and Duffy, R.J. 1991. 'Discourse analysis with closed head injured adults: evidence for differing patterns of deficits', *Archives of Physical Medicine and Rehabilitation* 72:7, 465–8.

Coelho, C.A., McHugh, R.E. and Boyle, M. 2000. 'Semantic feature analysis as a treatment for aphasic dysnomia', *Aphasiology* 14:2, 133–42.

Coelho, C., Ylvisaker, M. and Turkstra, L.S. 2005a. 'Nonstandardized assessment approaches for individuals with traumatic brain injuries', *Seminars in Speech and Language* 26:4, 223–41.

Coelho, C., Youse, K. and Le, K. 2002. 'Conversational discourse in closed-head-injured and non-brain-injured adults', *Aphasiology* 16:4–6, 659–72.

Coelho, C., Youse, K., Le, K. and Feinn, R. 2003. 'Narrative and conversational discourse of adults with closed head injuries and non-brain-injured adults: a discriminant analysis', *Aphasiology* 17:5, 499–510.

Coggins, T., Carpenter, R. and Owings, N. 1983. 'Examining early intentional communication in Down syndrome and nonretarded children', *British Journal of Disorders of Communication* 18:2, 99–107.

Cohen, N.J. 2001. *Language impairment and psychopathology in infants, children, and adolescents*, Thousand Oaks, CA: Sage.

Cohen, N.J., Barwick, M.A., Horodezky, N.B., Vallance, D.D. and Im, N. 1998. 'Language, achievement, and cognitive processing in psychiatrically disturbed children with previously identified and unsuspected language impairments', *Journal of Child Psychology and Psychiatry* 39:6, 865–77.

Cohen, N.J., Davine, M., Horodezsky, N., Lipsett, L. and Isaacson, L. 1993. 'Unsuspected language impairment in psychiatrically disturbed children: prevalence and language and behavioral characteristics', *Journal of the American Academy of Child and Adolescent Psychiatry* 32:3, 595–603.

Cohen, S.M. 2010. 'Self-reported impact of dysphonia in a primary care population: an epidemiological study', *Laryngoscope* 120:10, 2022–32.

Cohen, S.M., Dupont, W.D. and Courey, M.S. 2006. 'Quality-of-life impact of non-neoplastic voice disorders: a meta-analysis', *Annals of Otology, Rhinology and Laryngology* 115:2, 128–34.

Cohen, W., Hodson, A., O'Hare, A., Boyle, J., Durrani, T., McCartney, E., Mattey, M., Naftalin, L. and Watson, J. 2005. 'Effects of computer-based intervention through acoustically modified speech (Fast ForWord) in severe mixed receptive-expressive language impairment: outcomes from a randomized controlled trial', *Journal of Speech, Language, and Hearing Research* 48:3, 715–29.

Cohn, A.C., Fougeron, C. and Huffman, M.K. 2011. 'Introduction', in A.C. Cohn, C. Fougeron and M.K. Huffman (eds.), *The Oxford handbook of laboratory phonology*, New York: Oxford University Press, 3–9.

Cole, K.N., Dale, P.S. and Mills, P.E. 1990. 'Defining language delay in young children by cognitive referencing: are we saying more than we know?', *Applied Psycholinguistics* 11:3, 291–302.

Cole, K., Mills, P. and Kelly, D. 1994. 'Agreement of assessment profiles used in cognitive referencing', *Language, Speech, and Hearing Services in Schools* 25:1, 25–31.

Cole, M.G. and Dendukuri, N. 2003. 'Risk factors for depression among elderly community subjects: a systematic review and meta-analysis', *American Journal of Psychiatry* 160:6, 1147–56.

Colle, L., Baron-Cohen, S., Wheelwright, S. and van der Lely, H.K. 2008. 'Narrative discourse in adults with high-functioning autism or Asperger syndrome', *Journal of Autism and Developmental Disorders* 38:1, 28–40.

Collette, F., Hogge, M., Salmon, E. and van der Linden, M. 2006. 'Exploration of the neural substrates of executive functioning by functional neuroimaging', *Neuroscience* 139:1, 209–21.

Collins, M.J., Rosenbek, J.C. and Wertz, R.T. 1983. 'Spectrographic analysis of vowel and word duration in apraxia of speech, *Journal of Speech and Hearing Research* 26:2, 224–30.

Coltheart, M. 2001. 'Assumptions and methods in cognitive neuropsychology', in B. Rapp (ed.), *The handbook of cognitive neuroscience: what deficits reveal about the human mind*, Philadelphia, PA: Psychology Press, 3–21.

Coltheart, M., Tree, J.J. and Saunders, S.J. 2010. 'Computational modeling of reading in semantic dementia: comments on Woollams, Lambon Ralph, Plaut, and Patterson (2007)', *Psychological Review* 117:1, 256–72.

Colton, R.H. and Casper, J.K. 1996. *Understanding voice problems: a physiological perspective for diagnosis and treatment*, second edition, Baltimore, MD: Williams & Wilkins.

Colton, R.H., Casper, J.K. and Leonard, R. 2006. *Understanding voice problems: a physiological perspective for diagnosis and treatment*, third edition, Baltimore, MD: Williams & Wilkins.

Colver, A. 2010. *SPARCLE: A study of participation and quality of life of children with cerebral palsy living in Europe*, Executive Summary (online, available at: http://research.ncl.ac.uk/sparcle/Publications_files/Executive%20Summary%20SPARCLE1%20.pdf; last accessed 12 June 2013).

Colvert, E., Rutter, M., Kreppner, J., Beckett, C., Castle, J., Groothues, C., Hawkins, A., Stevens, S. and Sonuga-Barke, E.J. 2008. 'Do theory of mind and executive function deficits underlie the adverse outcomes associated with profound early deprivation?: findings from the English and Romanian adoptees study', *Journal of Abnormal Child Psychology* 36:7, 1057–68.

Cone, B., Dorn, P., Konrad-Martin, P., Lister, J., Ortiz, C. and Shairer, J. 2012. *Ototoxic medications (medication effects)*, American Speech-Language-Hearing Association (online, available at: www.asha.org/public/hearing/Ototoxic-Medications; last accessed 12 June 2013).

Connor, N.P., Palazzi-Churas, K.L., Cohen, S.B., Leverson, G.E. and Bless, D.M. 2007. 'Symptoms of extraesophageal reflux in a community-dwelling sample', *Journal of Voice* 21:2, 189–202.

Conrad, A.L., Canady, J., Richman, L. and Nopoulos, P. 2008. 'Incidence of neurological soft signs in children with isolated cleft of the lip or palate', *Perceptual and Motor Skills* 106:1, 197–206.

Conrad, A.L., Dailey, S., Richman, L., Canady, J., Karnell, M.P., Axelson, E. and Nopoulos, P. 2010. 'Cerebellum structure differences and relationship to speech in boys and girls with nonsyndromic cleft of the lip and/or palate ', *Craniofacial Journal* 47:5, 469–75.

Conroy, P., Sage, K. and Lambon-Ralph, M.A. 2009a. 'The effects of decreasing and increasing cue therapy on improving naming speed and accuracy for verbs and nouns in aphasia', *Aphasiology* 23:6, 707–30.

Conroy, P., Sage, K. and Lambon-Ralph, M.A. 2009b. 'Errorless and errorful therapy for verb and noun naming in aphasia', *Aphasiology* 23:11, 1311–37.

Conroy, P., Sage, K. and Ralph, M.A.L. 2006. 'Towards theory-driven therapies for aphasic verb impairments: a review of current theory and practice', *Aphasiology* 20:12, 1159–85.

Constantinescu, G.A., Theordoros, D.G., Russell, T.G., Ward, E.C., Wilson, S.J. and Wootton, R. 2010. 'Home-based speech treatment for Parkinson's disease delivered remotely: a case report', *Journal of Telemedicine and Telecare* 16:2, 100–4.

Conti-Ramsden, G. and Botting, N. 1999. 'Characteristics of children attending language units in England: a national study of 7-year-olds', *International Journal of Language & Communication Disorders* 34:4, 359–66.

Conti-Ramsden, G. and Botting, N. 2004. 'Social difficulties and victimization in children with SLI at 11 years of age', *Journal of Speech, Language, and Hearing Research* 47:1, 145–61.

Conti-Ramsden, G. and Botting, N. 2008. 'Emotional health in adolescents with and without a history of specific language impairment (SLI)', *Journal of Child Psychology and Psychiatry* 49:5, 516–25.

Conti-Ramsden, G. and Durkin, K. 2008. 'Language and independence in adolescents with and without a history of specific language impairment (SLI)', *Journal of Speech, Language, and Hearing Research* 51:1, 70–83.

Conti-Ramsden, G., Durkin, K., Simkin, Z. and Knox, E. 2009. 'Specific language impairment and school outcomes I: identifying and explaining variability at the end of compulsory education', *International Journal of Language & Communication Disorders* 44:1, 15–35.

Contopoulos-Ioannidis, D.G., Alexiou, G.A., Gouvias, T.C. and Ioannidis, J.P.A. 2008. 'Life cycle of translational research for medical interventions', *Science* 321:5894, 1298–9.

Conture, E.G. 2001. *Stuttering: its nature, diagnosis, and treatment*, Boston, MA: Allyn and Bacon.

Cooley Hidecker, M.J., Paneth, N., Rosenbaum, P.L., Kent, R.D., Lillie, J., Eulenberg, J.B., Chester, K., Johnson, B., Michalsen, L., Evatt, M. and Taylor, K. 2011. 'Developing and validating the Communication Function Classification System for individuals with cerebral palsy', *Developmental Medicine and Child Neurology* 53:8, 704–10.

Cooper, E.B. 1987. 'The chronic perseverative stuttering syndrome: incurable stuttering', *Journal of Fluency Disorders* 12:6, 381–8.

Cooper, M. 1973. *Modern techniques of vocal rehabilitation*, Springfield, IL: Charles C. Thomas.

Cooper, M. and Cooper, M.H. 1977. 'Direct vocal rehabilitation', in M. Cooper and M.H. Cooper (eds.), *Approaches to vocal rehabilitation*, Springfield, IL: Charles C. Thomas, 22–41.

Cooper, M.E., Ratay, J.S. and Marazita, M.L. 2006. 'Asian oral-facial cleft birth prevalence', *Cleft Palate-Craniofacial Journal* 43:5, 580–9.

Coplan, J. and Gleason, J.R. 1988. 'Unclear speech: recognition and significance of unintelligible speech in preschool children', *Pediatrics* 82:3, 447–52.

Corcoran, E. and Walsh, D. 2003. 'Obstructive asphyxia: a cause of excess mortality in psychiatric patients', *Irish Journal of Psychological Medicine* 20:3, 88–90.

Corcoran, R. and Frith, C.D. 1996. 'Conversational conduct and the symptoms of schizophrenia', *Cognitive Neuropsychiatry* 1:4, 305–18.

Corcoran, R., Mercer, G. and Frith, C.D. 1995. 'Schizophrenia, symptomatology and social inference: investigating "theory of mind" in people with schizophrenia', *Schizophrenia Research* 17:1, 5–13.

Cordes, A.K. 1994. 'The reliability of observational data: I. theories and methods for speech-language pathology', *Journal of Speech and Hearing Research* 37:2, 264–78.

Cordes, A.K. and Ingham, R.J. 1995. 'Stuttering includes both within-word and between-word disfluencies', *Journal of Speech and Hearing Research* 38:2, 382–6.

Cornell, D.G. and Wilson, L.A. 1992. 'The PIQ > VIQ discrepancy in violent and nonviolent delinquents', *Journal of Clinical Psychology* 48:2, 256–61.

Cornish, K., Burack, J.A., Rahman, A., Munir, F., Russo, N. and Grant, C. 2005. 'Theory of mind deficits in children with fragile X syndrome', *Journal of Intellectual Disability Research* 49:5, 372–8.

Correa, A., Gilboa, S.M., Besser, L.M., Botto, L.D., Moore, C.A., Hobbs, C.A., Cleves, M.A., Riehle-Colarusso, T.J., Waller, D.K. and Reece, E.A. 2008. 'Diabetes mellitus and birth defects', *American Journal of Obstetrics & Gynecology* 199:3, 237.

Corrin, J. 2001. 'From profile to programme: steps 1–2', in J. Stackhouse and B. Wells (eds.) *Children's speech and literacy difficulties: identification and intervention*, Book 2, London: Whurr Publishers, 96–132.

Coslett, H.B. and Monsul, N. 1994. 'Reading with the right hemisphere: evidence from transcranial magnetic stimulation', *Brain and Language* 46:2, 198–211.

Costello, A.D. and Warrington, E.K. 1987. 'The dissociation of visuospatial neglect and neglect dyslexia', *Journal of Neurology, Neurosurgery and Psychiatry* 50:9, 1110–6.

Costello, J.M. and Ingham, R.J. 1984. 'Assessment strategies for stuttering', in R.F. Curlee and W.H. Perkins (eds.), *Nature and treatment of stuttering: new directions*, San Diego, CA: College Hill Press, 303–33.

Côté, H., Moix, V. and Giroux, F. 2004. 'Évaluation des troubles de la communication des cérébrolésés droits [Assessment of communication problems in right-brain-damaged subjects]', *Rééducation Orthophonique* 219, 107–33.

Côté, H., Payer, M., Giroux, F. and Joanette, Y. 2007. 'Towards a description of clinical communication impairment profiles following right-hemisphere damage', *Aphasiology* 21, 739–49.

Cotelli, M., Borroni, B., Manenti, R., Zanetti, M., Arévalo, A., Cappa, S.F. and Padovani, A. 2007. 'Action and object naming in Parkinson's disease without dementia', *European Journal of Neurology* 14:6, 632–7.

Coté-Reschny, K.J. and Hodge, M.M. 2010. 'Listener effort and response time when transcribing words spoken by children with dysarthria', *Journal of Medical Speech-Language Pathology* 18:4, 24–34.

Cotton, R.T. and Prescott, A.J. 1988. 'Congenital anomalies of the larynx', in R.T. Cotton and C.M. Myers III (eds.), *A practical approach to pediatric otolaryngology*, Philadelphia, PA: Lippincott, 497–513.

Couture, S.M., Penn, D.L. and Roberts, D.L. 2006. 'The functional significance of social cognition in schizophrenia: a review', *Schizophrenia Bulletin* 32:S1, S44–S63.

Coyne, M.D. and Harn, B.A. 2006. 'Promoting beginning reading success through meaningful assessment of early literacy skills', *Psychology in the Schools* 43:1, 33–43.

Coyne, M.D., Kame'enui, E.J. and Simmons, D.C. 2001. 'Prevention and intervention in beginning reading: two complex systems', *Learning Disabilities Research & Practice* 16:2, 62–73.

Craig, A.R. 2002. 'Fluency outcomes following treatment for those who stutter', *Perceptual and Motor Skills* 94:3 Pt 1, 772–4.

Craig, A. and Andrews, G. 1985. 'The prediction and prevention of relapse in stuttering. The value of self-control techniques and locus of control measures', *Behavior Modification* 9:4, 427–42.

Craig, A., Blumgart, E. and Tran, Y. 2009. 'The impact of stuttering on the quality of life in adults who stutter', *Journal of Fluency Disorders* 34:2, 61–71.

Craig, A., Hancock, K., Tran, Y., Craig, M. and Peters, K. 2002. 'Epidemiology of stuttering in the community across the entire lifespan', *Journal of Speech, Language, and Hearing Research* 45:6, 1097–1105.

Craig, H.K. and Washington, J.A. 1993. 'Access behaviors of children with specific language impairment', *Journal of Speech and Hearing Research* 36:2, 322–37.

Crawford, D.C., Acuna, J.M. and Sherman, S.L. 2001. 'FMR1 and the fragile X syndrome: human genome epidemiology review', *Genetics in Medicine* 3:5, 359–71.

Cress, C. and Marvin, C. 2003. 'Common questions about AAC services in early intervention', *AAC: Augmentative and Alternative Communication* 19:4, 254–72.

Crevier-Buchman, L., Laccourreye, O. and Weinstein, G.S. 1995. 'Evolution of speech and voice following supracricoid partial laryngectomy', *Journal of Laryngology and Otology*, 109:5, 410–13.

Crisco, J.J., Dobbs, J.M. and Mulhern, R.K. 1988. 'Cognitive processing of children with Williams syndrome', *Developmental Medicine and Child Neurology* 30:5, 650–6.

Critchley, M. 1962. 'Speech and speech-loss in relation to duality of the brain', in V.B. Mountcastle (ed.), *Interhemispheric relations and cerebral dominance*, Baltimore, MD: Johns Hopkins Press, 208–13.

Crockett, D.M., Bumstead, R.M. and Van Demark, D.R. 1988. 'Experience with surgical management of velopharyngeal incompetence', *Otolaryngology – Head and Neck Surgery* 99:1, 1–9.

Croen, L.A., Shaw, G.M., Wasserman, C.R. and Tolarová, M.M. 1998. 'Racial and ethnic variations in the prevalence of orofacial clefts in California, 1983–1992', *American Journal of Medical Genetics* 79:1, 42–7.

Cromer, R.F. 1991. *Language and thought in normal and handicapped children*, Cambridge: Blackwell.

Crompton, A. 1982. 'Syllables and segments in speech production', in A. Cutler (ed.), *Slips of the tongue and language production*, Berlin: Mouton, 109–62.

Croot, K. 2010. 'The emergent paradigm in Laboratory Phonology: phonological categories and statistical generalisation in Cutler, Beckman and Edwards, Frisch and Brea-Spahn, Kapasinski, and Walter', *Journal of Laboratory Phonology* 1:2, 415–24.

Croot, K. and Rastle, K. 2004. 'Is there a syllabary containing stored articulatory plans for speech production in English?', The 10th Australian International Conference on Speech Science and Technology: Macquarie University, Sydney, 8–10 December 2004.

Croot, K., Au, C. and Harper, A. 2010. 'Prosodic structure and tongue twister errors', in C. Fougeron, B. Kuehnert, M. D'Imperio and N. Vallee (eds.), *Laboratory phonology 10*, Berlin: de Gruyter, 433–59.

Croot, K., Hodges, J.R., Xuereb, J. and Patterson, K. 2000. 'Phonological and articulatory impairment in Alzheimer's disease: a case series', *Brain and Language* 75:2, 277–309.

Crosbie, S., Holm, A. and Dodd, B. 2005. 'Intervention for children with severe speech disorder: a comparison of two approaches', *International Journal of Language & Communication Disorders* 40:4, 467–91.

Crosson, B. 1992. *Subcortical functions in language and memory*, New York: Guilford Press.

Cruice, M., Worrall, L. and Hickson, L. 2000. 'Quality of life measurement in speech pathology and audiology', *Asia Pacific Journal of Speech, Language and Hearing* 5:1, 1–20.

Cruice, M., Worrall, L. and Hickson, L. 2006. 'Quantifying aphasic people's social lives in the context of their non-aphasic peers', *Aphasiology* 20:12, 1210–25.

Cruice, M., Worrall, L. and Hickson, L. 2011. 'Reporting on psychological well-being of older adults with chronic aphasia in the context of unaffected peers', *Disability and Rehabilitation* 33:3, 219–28.

Crutch, S.J. and Warrington, E.K. 2005. 'Abstract and concrete concepts have structurally different representational frameworks', *Brain* 128:3, 615–27.

Crystal, D. 1992. *Profiling linguistic disability*, second edition, London: Whurr.

Cubelli, R., Guiducci, A. and Consolmagno, P. 2000. 'Afferent dysgraphia after right cerebral stroke: an autonomous syndrome?', *Brain and Cognition* 44:3, 629–44.

Cuerva, A.G., Sake, L., Kuzis, G., Tiberti, C., Dorrego, F. and Starkstein, S.E. 2001. 'Theory of mind and pragmatic abilities in dementia', *Neuropsychiatry, Neuropsychology, and Behavioral Neurology* 14:3, 153–8.

Culp, D.M. 1989. 'Developmental apraxia and augmentative or alternative communication: a case example', *AAC: Augmentative and Alternative Communication* 5:1, 27–34.

Cumley, G.D. and Swanson, S. 1999. 'Augmentative and alternative communication options for children with developmental apraxia of speech: three case studies', *AAC: Augmentative and Alternative Communication* 15:2, 110–25.

Cummings, C.W., Haughey, B.H., Thomas, J.R., Harker, L.A., Robbin, K.T., Schuller, D.E., Flint, P.W. and Richardson, M.A. 2004. *Otolaryngology: head and neck surgery*, fourth edition, St Louis, MO: Mosby.

Cummings, L. 2005. *Pragmatics: a multidisciplinary perspective*, Edinburgh University Press.

Cummings, L. 2007a. 'Pragmatics and adult language disorders: past achievements and future directions', *Seminars in Speech and Language* 28:2, 98–112.

Cummings, L. 2007b. 'Clinical pragmatics: a field in search of phenomena?', *Language and Communication* 27:4, 396–432.

Cummings, L. 2008. *Clinical linguistics*, Edinburgh University Press.

Cummings, L. 2009. *Clinical pragmatics*, Cambridge University Press.

Cummings, L. 2010. 'Clinical pragmatics', in L. Cummings (ed.), *The Routledge pragmatics encyclopedia*, London and New York: Routledge, pp. 40–3.

Cummings, L. 2011. 'Pragmatic disorders and their social impact', *Pragmatics and Society* 2:1, 17–36.

Cummings, L. 2012a. 'Pragmatic disorders', in H.-J. Schmid (ed.), *Cognitive pragmatics*, Handbooks of Pragmatics 4, Berlin and Boston, MA: Mouton de Gruyter, pp. 291–315.

Cummings, L. 2012b. 'Theorising context: the case of clinical pragmatics', in R. Finkbeiner, J. Meibauer and P. Schumacher (eds.), *What is a context? Theoretical and empirical approaches*, Amsterdam: John Benjamins, pp. 55–80.

Cummings, L. 2012c. 'Establishing diagnostic criteria: the role of clinical pragmatics', *Lodz Papers in Pragmatics* 8:1, 61–84.

Cummings, L. 2013. 'Clinical pragmatics and theory of mind', in A. Capone, F. Lo Piparo and M. Carapezza (eds.), *Perspectives on pragmatics and philosophy*, Dordrecht: Springer.

Cummings, L. 2014a. 'Clinical pragmatics and theory of mind,' in A. Capone, F. Lo Piparo and M. Carapezza (eds.), *Perspectives on Linguistic Pragmatics, Perspectives in Pragmatics, Philosophy & Psychology*, Vol. 2, Dordrecht, Heidelberg, London and New York: Springer.

Cummings, L. 2014b. 'Clinical pragmatics', in Y. Huang (ed.), *Oxford handbook of pragmatics*, Oxford University Press.

Cummings, L. 2014c. *Communication disorders*, Houndmills, Basingstoke: Palgrave Macmillan.

Cummings, L. 2014d. *Pragmatic disorders*, Dordrecht: Springer .

Cummings, L. In press. 'Clinical pragmatics', in Y. Huang (ed.), *Oxford handbook of pragmatics*, Oxford University Press.

Cunningham, A.E. and Stanovich, K.E. 1997. 'Early reading acquisition and its relation to reading experience and ability 10 years later', *Developmental Psychology* 33:6, 934–45.

Cunningham, R. 1998. 'Counselling someone with severe aphasia: an explorative case study', *Disability and Rehabilitation* 20:9, 346–54.

Curlee, R.F. and Yairi, E. 1997. 'Early intervention with early childhood stuttering: a critical examination of the data', *American Journal of Speech-Language Pathology* 6:2, 8–18.

da Costa de Ceballos, A.G., Carvalho, F.M., de Araujo, T.M. and Borges dos Reis, E.J.F. 2010. 'Diagnostic validity of voice handicap index-10 (VHI-10) compared with perceptive-auditory and acoustic speech pathology evaluations of the voice', *Journal of Voice* 24:6, 715–18.

Dabul, B. 2000. *Apraxia battery for adults*, Austin, TX: Pro-Ed.

Dadds, M.R., Perry, Y., Hawes, D.J., Merz, S., Riddell, A.C., Haines, D.J., Solak, E. and Abeygunawardane, A.I. 2006. 'Attention to the eyes and fear-recognition deficits in child psychopathy', *British Journal of Psychiatry* 189:3, 280–1.

Dahlberg, C.A., Cusick, C.P., Hawley, L.A., Newman, J.K., Morey, C.E., Harrison-Felix, C.L. and Whiteneck, G.G. 2007. 'Treatment efficacy of social communication skills training after traumatic brain injury: a randomized treatment and deferred treatment controlled trial', *Archives of Physical Medicine and Rehabilitation* 88:12, 1561–73.

Dale, P.S., Price, T.S., Bishop, D.V.M. and Plomin, R. 2003. 'Outcomes of early language delay: I. Predicting persistent and transient language difficulties at 3 and 4 years', *Journal of Speech, Language, and Hearing Research* 46:3, 544–60.

Dalemanns, R., de Witte, L.P., Lemmens, J. and van der Heuvel, W.J.A. 2008. 'Measures for rating social participation in people with aphasia: a systematic review', *Clinical Rehabilitation* 22:6, 542–55.

Dall'Oglio, A.M. and Milani, L. 1995. 'Analysis of the cognitive development in Italian children with Williams syndrome', *Genetic Counselling* 6, 175–6.

Dalston, R.M. and Stuteville, O.H. 1975. 'A clinical investigation of the efficacy of primary nasopalatal pharyngoplasty', *Cleft Palate Journal* 12, 177–92.

Dalston, R.M. and Warren, D.W. 1986. 'Comparison of tonar II, pressure flow, and listener judgments of hypernasality in the assessment of velopharyngeal function', *Cleft Palate Journal* 23:2, 108–15.

Dalston, R.M., Marsh, J.L., Vig, K.W., Witzel, M.A. and Burnsted, R.M. 1988. 'Minimal standards for reporting the results of surgery on patients with cleft lip, cleft palate, or both: a proposal', *Cleft Palate Journal* 25:1, 3–7.

Dalston, R.M., Warren, D.W. and Dalston, E.T. 1991a. 'Use of nasometry as a diagnostic tool for identifying patients with velopharyngeal impairment', *Cleft Palate Journal* 28:2, 184–8.

Dalston, R.M., Warren, D.W. and Dalston, E.T. 1991b. 'A preliminary investigation concerning the use of nasometry in identifying patients with hyponasality and/or nasal airway impairment', *Journal of Speech and Hearing Research* 34:1, 11–8.

Daly, D.A. 1986. 'The clutterer', in K.O. St. Louis (ed.), *The atypical stutterer: principles and practices of rehabilitation*, New York: Academic Press, 155–92.

Daly, D.A. and Burnett, M.L. 1999. 'Cluttering: traditional views and perspectives', in R.F. Curlee (ed.), *Stuttering and related disorders of fluency*, second edition, New York: Thieme Medical Publishers, 222–54.

Damasio, H. and Damasio, A.R. 1989. *Lesion analysis in neuropsychology*, New York: Oxford University Press.

Damico, J.S. 1985. 'Clinical discourse analysis: a functional approach to language assessment', in C.S. Simon (ed.), *Communication skills and classroom success*, London: Taylor and Francis, 165–203.

Darley, F.L. 1968. *'Apraxia of speech: 107 years of terminological confusion'*, American Speech and Hearing Association Convention: Denver, CO.

Darley, F.L. 1969. *'Aphasia: input and output disturbances in speech and language processing'*, American Speech and Hearing Association Convention: Chicago, November 1969.

Darley, F.L., Aronson, A.E. and Brown, J.R. 1969a. 'Differential diagnostic patterns of dysarthria', *Journal of Speech and Hearing Research* 12:2, 246–69.

Darley, F.L., Aronson, A.E. and Brown, J.R. 1969b. 'Clusters of deviant speech dimensions in the dysarthrias', *Journal of Speech and Hearing Research* 12:3, 462–96.

Darley, F.L., Aronson, A.E. and Brown, J.R. 1975. *Motor speech disorders*, Philadelphia, PA: W.B. Saunders.

Darley, F.L., Brown, J.R. and Goldstein, N.P. 1972. 'Dysarthria in multiple sclerosis', *Journal of Speech and Hearing Research* 15:2, 229–45.

Daumuller, M. and Goldenberg, G. 2010. 'Therapy to improve gestural expression in aphasia: a controlled clinical trial', *Clinical Rehabilitation* 24:1, 55–65.

Davidson, B., Howe, T., Worrall, L. and Hickson, L. 2008. 'Social participation for older people with aphasia: the impact of communication disability on friendships', *Topics in Stroke Rehabilitation* 15:4, 325–40.

Davidson, B., Worrall, L. and Hickson, L. 2003. 'Identifying the communication activities of older people with aphasia: evidence from naturalistic observation', *Aphasiology* 17:3, 243–64.

Davies, M., Udwin, O. and Howlin, P. 1998. 'Adults with Williams syndrome: preliminary study of social, emotional and behavioural difficulties', *British Journal of Psychiatry* 172:3, 273–6.

Davies, R.R., Hodges, J.R., Kril, J.J., Patterson, K., Halliday, G.M. and Xuereb, J.H. 2005. 'The pathological basis of semantic dementia', *Brain* 128:9, 1984–95.

Davis, G.A. and Coelho, C.A. 2004. 'Referential cohesion and logical coherence of narration after closed head injury', *Brain and Language* 89:3, 508–23.

Davis, G.A. and Wilcox, J. 1985. *Adult aphasia rehabilitation: applied pragmatics*, San Diego, CA: College Hill Press.

Davis, G.N., Lindo, E.J. and Compton, D.L. 2007. 'Children at risk for reading failure', *Teaching Exceptional Children* 39:5, 32–9.

Dawson, G., Ashman, S.B., Panagiotides, H., Hessl, D., Self, J., Yamada, E. and Embry, L. 2003. 'Preschool outcomes of children of depressed mothers: role of maternal behaviour, contextual risk, and children's brain activity', *Child Development* 74:4, 1158–75.

Dawson, J., Stout, C., Eyer, J., Tattersall, P., Fonkalsrud, J. and Croley, K. 2005. *Structured photographic expressive language test – preschool 2*, DeKalb, IL: Janelle Publications.

De Alarcon, A., Brehm, S.B., Kelchner, L.N., Meinzen-Derr, J., Middendorf, J. and Weinrich, B. 2009. 'Comparison of pediatric voice handicap index scores with perceptual voice analysis in patients following airway reconstruction', *Annals of Otology, Rhinology and Laryngology* 118:8, 581–6.

De Bleser, R. and Kauschke, C. 2003. 'Acquisition and loss of nouns and verbs: parallel or divergent patterns?', *Journal of Neurolinguistics* 16:2–3, 213–29.

De Carvalho-Teles, V., Sennes, L.U. and Gielow, I. 2008. 'Speech evaluation after palatal augmentation in patients undergoing glossectomy', *Archives of Otolaryngology – Head and Neck Surgery* 134:10, 1066–70.

De Fossé, L., Hodge, S.M., Makris, N., Kennedy, D.N., Caviness Jr, V.S., McGrath, L., Steele, S., Ziegler, D.A., Herbert, M.R., Frazier, J.A., Tager-Flusberg, H. and Harris, G.J. 2004. 'Language-association cortex asymmetry in autism and specific language impairment', *Annals of Neurology* 56:6, 757–66.

De Giacomo, A. and Fombonne, E. 1998. 'Parental recognition of developmental abnormalities in autism', *European Child & Adolescent Psychiatry* 7:3, 131–6.

De Leon, J., Becona, E., Gurpegui, M., Gonzalez-Pinto, A. and Diaz, F.J. 2002. 'The association between high nicotine dependence and severe mental illness may be consistent across countries', *Journal of Clinical Psychiatry* 63:9, 812–16.

De Nil, L.F., Kroll, R.M., Lafaille, S.J. and Houle, S. 2003. 'A positron emission tomography study of short- and long-term treatment effects on functional brain activation in adults who stutter', *Journal of Fluency Disorders* 28:4, 357–80.

De Nil, L.F., Jokel, R. and Rochon, E.A. 2007. 'Etiology, symptomatology, and treatment of neurogenic stuttering', in E.G. Conture and R.F. Curlee (eds.), *Stuttering and related disorders of fluency*, third edition, New York: Thieme Publishers, 323–42.

de Pedro Netto, I., Fae, A., Vartanian, J.G., Barros, A.P., Correia, L.M., Toledo, R.N., Testa, J.R., Nishimoto, I.N., Kowalski, L.P. and Carrara-de Angelis, E. 2006. 'Voice and vocal self-assessment after thyroidectomy', *Head & Neck* 28:12, 1106–14.

De Smet, H.J., Catsman-Berrevoets, C., Aarsen, F., Verhoeven, J., Mariën, P. and Paquier, P.F. 2012. 'Auditory-perceptual speech analysis in children with cerebellar tumours: a long-term follow-up study', *European Journal of Paediatric Neurology* 16:5, 434–42.

Deal, J.L. 1982. 'Sudden onset of stuttering: a case report', *Journal of Speech and Hearing Disorders* 47:3, 301–4.

Deal, J.L. and Darley, F.L. 1972. 'The influence of linguistic and situational variables on phonemic accuracy in apraxia of speech', *Journal of Speech and Hearing Research* 15:3, 639–53.

Dean, E. and Howell, J. 1986. 'Developing linguistic awareness: a theoretically based approach to phonological disorders', *British Journal of Disorders of Communication* 21:2, 223–38.

Deane, K.H., Ellis-Hill, C., Jones, D., Whurr, R., Ben-Shlomo, Y., Playford, E.D. and Clarke, C.E. 2002. 'Systematic review of paramedical therapies for Parkinson's disease', *Movement Disorders* 17:5, 984–91.

Deane, K.H., Whurr, R., Playford, E.D., Ben-Shlomo, Y. and Clarke, C.E. 2001a. 'Speech and language therapy for dysarthria in Parkinson's disease' *Cochrane Database of Systematic Reviews*, Issue 2, CD002812.

Deane, K.H., Whurr, R., Playford, E.D., Ben-Shlomo, Y. and Clarke, C.E. 2001b. 'A comparison of speech and language therapy techniques for dysarthria in Parkinson's disease' *Cochrane Database of Systematic Reviews*, Issue 2, CD002814.

Deary, I.J., Wilson, J.A., Carding, P.N. and MacKenzie, K. 2003. 'VoiSS: a patient-derived voice symptom scale', *Journal of Psychosomatic Research* 54:5, 483–9.

Deary, V. and Miller, T. 2011. 'Reconsidering the role of psychosocial factors in functional dysphonia', *Current Opinion in Otolaryngology & Head and Neck Surgery* 19:3, 150–4.

Dedo, H.H. 1976. 'Recurrent laryngeal nerve section for spastic dysphonia', *Annals of Otology, Rhinology and Laryngology* 85:4 Pt 1, 451–59.

Deger, K. and Ziegler, W. 2002. 'Speech motor programming in apraxia of speech', *Journal of Phonetics* 30:3, 321–35.

Dehaene, S. 2009. *Reading in the brain*, New York: Viking.

Dejonckere, P.H. 2001. 'The concept of occupational voice disorders', in P.H. Dejonckere (ed.), *Occupational voice: care and cure*, The Hague, The Netherlands: Kugler, vii–xii.

Delaney, A.L. and Kent, R.D. 2004. *'Developmental profiles of children diagnosed with apraxia of speech'*, Annual Convention of the American-Speech-Language-Hearing Association: Philadelphia, USA, 20–22 November 2004.

Dell, G.S. 1986. 'A spreading-activation theory of retrieval in sentence production', *Psychological Review* 93:3, 283–321.

Denckla, M.B. and Rudel, R.G. 1976a. 'Naming of object-drawings by dyslexic and other learning disabled children', *Brain and Language* 3:1, 1–15.

Denckla, M.B. and Rudel, R.G. 1976b. 'Rapid "automatized" naming (R.A.N.): dyslexia differentiated from other learning disabilities', *Neuropsychologia* 14:4, 471–9.

Deng, J., Ridner, S.H. and Murphy, B.A. 2011. 'Lymphedema in patients with head and neck cancer', *Oncology Nursing Forum* 38:1, E1–E10.

Denmark, J.C. 1995. *Deafness and mental health*, London: Jessica Kingsley.

Dennis, M. and Barnes, M.A. 2001. 'Comparison of literal, inferential, and intentional text comprehension in children with mild or severe closed head injury', *Journal of Head Trauma Rehabilitation* 16:5, 456–68.

Department of Health. 2005. *Mental health and deafness*, London: Department of Health.

Derkay, C.S., Malis, D.J., Zalzal, G., Wiatrak, B.J., Kashima, H.K. and Coltrera, M.D. 1998. 'A staging system for assessing severity of disease and response to therapy in recurrent respiratory papillomatosis', *Laryngoscope* 108:6, 935–7.

Deroost, N., Zeischka, P., Coomans, D., Bouazza, S., Depessemier, P. and Soetens, E. 2010. 'Intact first- and second-order implicit sequence learning in secondary-school-aged children with developmental dyslexia', *Journal of Clinical and Experimental Neuropsychology* 32:6, 561–72.

Desmond, D.W. 2004. 'Vascular dementia', *Clinical Neuroscience Research* 3:6, 437–48.

Desmond, D.W., Erkinjuntti, T., Sano, M., Cummings, J.L., Bowler, J.V., Pasquier, F., Moroney, J.T., Ferris, S.H., Stern, Y., Sachdev, P.S. and Hachinski, V.C. 1999. 'The cognitive syndrome of vascular dementia: implications for clinical trials', *Alzheimer Disease and Associated Disorders* 13:Suppl 3, S21–S29.

D'Esposito, M. and Alexander, M.P. 1995. 'Subcortical aphasia: distinct profiles following left putaminal hemorrhage', *Neurology* 45:1, 38–41.

Devlin, J.T. and Watkins, K.E. 2007. 'Stimulating language: insights from TMS', *Brain* 130:3, 610–22.

Dewey, D., Roy, E., Square-Storer, P. and Hayden, D. 1998. 'Limb and oral praxic abilities in children with verbal sequencing deficits', *Developmental Medicine and Child Neurology* 30:6, 743–51.

Dewey, J. 2005. My experiences with cluttering, Eighth Annual International Stuttering Awareness Day (ISAD) On-line Conference (online, available at: www.mnsu.edu/comdis/isad8/papers/dewey8.html; last accessed 12 June 2013).

Dickinson, D.K. and Tabors, P.O. (eds.) 2001. *Building literacy with language: young children learning at home and school*, Baltimore, MD: Brookes.

Dickson, S., Barbour, R.S., Brady, M., Clark, A.M. and Paton, G. 2008. 'Patients' experiences of disruptions associated with post-stroke dysarthria', *International Journal of Language & Communication Disorders* 43:2, 135–53.

Diehl, J.J., Bennetto, L. and Young, E.C. 2006. 'Story recall and narrative coherence of high-functioning children with autism spectrum disorders', *Journal of Abnormal Child Psychology* 34:1, 87–102.

Dietrich, M., Andreatta, R.D., Jiang, Y., Joshi, A. and Stemple, J.C. 2012. 'Preliminary findings on the relation between the personality trait of stress reaction and the central neural control of human vocalization', *International Journal of Speech-Language Pathology* 14:4, 377–89.

Docherty, N.M., Cohen, A.S., Nienow, T.M., Dinzeo, T.J. and Dangelmaier, R.E. 2003. 'Stability of formal thought disorder and referential communication disturbances in schizophrenia', *Journal of Abnormal Psychology* 112:3, 469–75.

Dockrell, J., Messer, D., George, R. and Wilson, G. 1998. 'Children with word-finding difficulties – prevalence, presentation and naming problems', *International Journal of Language & Communication Disorders* 33:4, 445–54.

Dockrell, J.E., Messer, D., George, R. and Ralli, A. 2003. 'Beyond naming patterns in children with WFDs – definitions for nouns and verbs', *Journal of Neurolinguistics* 16:2–3, 191–211.

Dodd, B. 2005. *Differential diagnosis and treatment of children with speech disorder*, London: Whurr.

Dodd, B. and McIntosh, B. 2008. 'The input processing, cognitive linguistic and oro-motor skills of children with speech difficulty', *International Journal of Speech-Language Pathology* 10:3, 169–78.

Dodd, B., Crosbie, S., McIntosh, B., Teitzel, T. and Ozanne, A. 2000. *The primary and preschool inventory of phonological awareness*, London: Psychological Corporation.

Dodd, B., Holm, A., Hua, Z. and Crosbie, S. 2003. 'Phonological development: a normative study of British English-speaking children', *Clinical Linguistics & Phonetics* 17:8, 617–43.

Dodd, B., Hua, Z., Crosbie, S., Holm, A. and Ozanne, A. 2002. *Diagnostic evaluation of articulation and phonology*, London: Psychological Corporation.

Dodd, B., Hua, Z., Crosbie, S., Holm, A. and Ozanne, A. 2006. *Diagnostic evaluation of articulation and phonology*, London: Psychological Corporation.

Dodd, B., McCormack, P. and Woodyatt, G. 1994. 'Evaluation of an intervention program: relation between children's phonology and parents' communicative behavior', *American Journal on Mental Retardation* 98:5, 632–45.

Doesborgh, S.J., van de Sandt-Koenderman, M.W.E., Dippel, D.W.J., van Harskamp, F., Koudstaal, P.J. and Visch-Brink, E.G. 2004. 'Effects of semantic treatment on verbal communication and linguistic processing in aphasia after stroke. A randomized controlled trial', *Stroke* 35:1, 141–6.

Dolan, T.R. 1997. 'Overview: communication processes and developmental disabilities', *Mental Retardation and Developmental Disabilities Research Reviews* 3:4, 279–81.

Dollaghan, C. 1987. 'Fast mapping in normal and language impaired children', *Journal of Speech and Hearing Disorders* 52:3, 218–22.

Dollaghan, C. 2007. *The handbook for evidence-based practice in communication disorders*, Baltimore, MD: Paul H. Brookes.

Dollaghan, C. and Campbell, T. 1998. 'Nonword repetition and child language impairment', *Journal of Speech, Language, and Hearing Research* 41:5, 1136–46.

Done, D.J., Leinoneen, E., Crow, T.J. and Sacker, A. 1998. 'Linguistic performance in children who develop schizophrenia in adult life. Evidence for normal syntactic ability', *British Journal of Psychiatry* 172:2, 130–5.

Donno, R., Parker, G., Gilmour, J. and Skuse, D.H. 2010. 'Social communication deficits in disruptive primary-school children', *British Journal of Psychiatry* 196, 282–9.

Donovan, N.J., Kendall, D.L., Young, M.E. and Rosenbek, J.C. 2008. 'The communicative effectiveness survey: preliminary evidence of construct validity', *American Journal of Speech-Language Pathology* 17:4, 335–47.

Dorf, D.S. and Curtin, J.W. 1982. 'Early cleft palate repair and speech outcome', *Plastic and Reconstructive Surgery* 70:1, 74–81.

Doubleday, E.K., Snowden, J.S., Varma, A.R. and Neary, D. 2002. 'Qualitative performance characteristics differentiate dementia with Lewy bodies and Alzheimer's disease', *Journal of Neurology, Neurosurgery and Psychiatry* 72:5, 602–7.

Douglas, J.M. 2010. 'Using the La Trobe Communication Questionnaire to measure perceived social communication ability in adolescents with traumatic brain injury', *Brain Impairment* 11:2, 171–82.

Douglas, J.M., Bracy, C.A. and Snow, P.C. 2007. 'Measuring perceived communicative ability after traumatic brain injury: reliability and validity of the La Trobe Communication Questionnaire', *Journal of Head Trauma Rehabilitation* 22:1, 31–8.

Douklias, S.D., Masterson, J. and Hanley, J.R. 2009. 'Surface and phonological developmental dyslexia in Greek', *Cognitive Neuropsychology* 26:8, 705–23.

Down's Syndrome Association. 2012. What is the incidence of Down's syndrome? (online, available at: www.downs-syndrome.org.uk/component/content/article/35-general/159-3-what-is-the-incidence-of-downs-syndrome.html; last accessed 12 June 2013).

Doyle, P.C. 1994. *Foundation of voice and speech rehabilitation following laryngeal cancer*, San Diego, CA: Singular.

Doyle, P., McNeil, M., Hula, W. and Mikolic, J. 2003. 'The Burden of Stroke Scale (BOSS): validating patient-reported communication difficulty and associated psychological distress in stroke survivors', *Aphasiology* 17:3, 291–304.

Drag, L.L. and Bieliauskas, L.A. 2010. 'Contemporary review 2009: cognitive aging', *Journal of Geriatric Psychiatry and Neurology* 23:2, 75–93.

Dragoy, O. and Bastiaanse, R. 2010. 'Verb production and word order in Russian agrammatic speakers', *Aphasiology* 24:1, 28–55.

Drai, D. and Grodzinsky, Y. 2006. 'A new empirical angle on the variability debate: quantitative neurosyntactic analyses of a large data set from Broca's aphasia', *Brain and Language* 96:2, 117–28.

Drayna, D. 2011. 'Possible genetic factors in cluttering', in D. Ward and K. Scaler Scott (eds.), *Cluttering: research, intervention and education*, Hove, East Sussex: Psychology Press, 29–33.

Dromey, C. 2000. 'Articulatory kinematics in patients with Parkinson disease using different speech treatment approaches', *Journal of Medical Speech-Language Pathology* 8:8, 155–61.

Dromey, C. and Bates, E. 2005. 'Speech interactions with linguistic, cognitive, and visuomotor tasks', *Journal of Speech, Language, and Hearing Research* 48:2, 295–305.

Dromey, C. and Benson, A. 2003. 'Effects of concurrent motor, linguistic, or cognitive tasks on speech motor performance', *Journal of Speech, Language, and Hearing Research* 46:5, 1234–46.

Dronkers, N.F. 1996. 'A new brain region for coordinating speech articulation', *Nature* 384:6605, 159–61.

Dronkers, N.F. and Larsen, J. 2001. 'Neuroanatomy of the classical syndromes of aphasia', in R.S. Berndt (ed.), *Handbook of neuropsychology, Vol. 3: Language and aphasia*, second edition, Amsterdam: Elsevier, 19–30.

Druks, J. 2002. 'Verbs and nouns – a review of the literature', *Journal of Neurolinguistics* 15:3–5, 289–315.

Druks, J. and Masterson, J. 2000. *An object and action naming battery*, London: Taylor & Francis.

Drummond, S.S. 1993. *Dysarthria examination battery*, Tucson, AZ: Communication Skill Builders.

Drury, V.M., Robinson, E.J. and Birchwood, M. 1998. '"Theory of mind" skills during an acute episode of psychosis and following recovery', *Psychological Medicine* 28:5, 1101–12.

Dubois, B., Feldman, H.H., Jacova, C., Dekosky, S.T., Barberger-Gateau, P., Cummings, J., Delacourte, A., Galasko, D., Gauthier, S., Jicha, G., Meguro, K., O'Brien, J., Pasquier, F., Robert, P., Rossor, M., Salloway, S., Stern, Y., Visser, P.J. and Scheltens, P. 2007. 'Research criteria for the diagnosis of Alzheimer's disease: revising the NINCDS-ADRDA criteria', *Lancet Neurology* 6:8, 734–46.

Duffy, J.R. 1995. *Motor speech disorders: substrates, diagnosis and management*, St Louis, MO: Mosby.

Duffy, J.R. 2005. *Motor speech disorders: substrates, differential diagnosis, and management*, second edition, St Louis, MO: Elsevier Mosby.

Duffy, J.R. 2012. *Motor speech disorders: substrates, differential diagnosis, management*, third edition, St Louis, MO: Elsevier Mosby.

Duffy, J.R. and Kent, R.D. 2001. 'Darley's contributions to the understanding, differential diagnosis, and scientific study of the dysarthrias', *Aphasiology* 15:3, 275–89.

Duffy, J.R. and Yorkston, K.M. 2003. 'Medical interventions for spasmodic dysphonia and some related conditions: a systematic review', *Journal of Medical Speech-Language Pathology* 11:4, ix–lviii.

Duflo, S., Thibeault, S.L., Li, W., Shu, X.A. and Xiao, Z.S. 2006. 'Vocal fold tissue repair in vivo using a synthetic extracellular matrix', *Tissue Engineering* 12:8, 2171–80.

Dumontheil, I., Apperly, I.A. and Blakemore, S.J. 2010. 'Online usage of theory of mind continues to develop in late adolescence', *Developmental Science* 13:2, 331–8.

Duncan, P.W., Wallace, D., Lai, S.M., Johnson, D., Embretson, S. and Laster, L.J. 1999. 'The stroke impact scale version 2.0: evaluation of reliability, validity, and sensitivity to change', *Stroke* 30:10, 2131–40.

Dunn, L.M., Dunn, L.M., Whetton, C. and Burley, J. 1997. *British picture vocabulary scale*, second edition, Windsor: NFER-Nelson.

Dunst, C.J., Bruder, M.B., Trivette, C.M., Hamby, D., Raab, M. and McLean, M. 2001a. 'Characteristics and consequences of everyday natural learning opportunities', *Topics in Early Childhood Special Education* 21:2, 68–92.

Dunst, C.J., Trivette, C.M., Humphries, T., Raab, M. and Roper, N. 2001b. 'Contrasting approaches to natural learning environment interventions', *Infants and Young Children* 14:2, 48–63.

Durgunoglu, A.Y. 2006. 'Learning to read in Turkish', *Developmental Science* 9:5, 437–9.

Durkin, K. and Conti-Ramsden, G. 2007. 'Language, social behavior, and the quality of friendships in adolescents with and without a history of specific language impairment', *Child Development* 78:5, 1441–57.

Durkin, K., Simkin, Z., Knox, E. and Conti-Ramsden, G. 2009. 'Specific language impairment and school outcomes II: educational context, student satisfaction, and post-compulsory progress', *International Journal of Language & Communication Disorders* 44:1, 36–55.

Dworkin, J.P. 1980. 'Characteristics of frontal lispers clustered according to severity', *Journal of Speech and Hearing Disorders* 45:1, 37–44.

Dworkin, J.P. and Culatta, R.A. 1980. 'Tongue strength: its relationship to tongue thrusting, open-bite, and articulatory proficiency', *Journal of Speech and Hearing Disorders* 45:2, 277–82.

Dworkin, J.P. and Johns, D.F. 1980. 'Management of velopharyngeal incompetence in dysarthria: a historical review', *Clinical Otolaryngology and Allied Sciences* 5:1, 61–74.

Dworkin, J.P. and Meleca, R.J. 1997. *Vocal pathologies: diagnosis, treatment, and case studies*, San Diego, CA: Singular.

Dworkin, J.P. and Meleca, R.J. 1999. 'Behavioral therapy for organic voice tremor', *Phonoscope* 2:2, 113–19.

Dworkin, J.P., Abkarian, G.G. and Johns, D.F. 1988. 'Apraxia of speech: the effectiveness of a treatment regimen', *Journal of Speech and Hearing Disorders* 53:3, 280–94.

Dworzynski, K., Howell, P. and Natke, U. 2003. 'Predicting stuttering from linguistic factors for German speakers in two age groups', *Journal of Fluency Disorders* 28:2, 95–114.

Dykens, E.M., Hodapp, R.M. and Evans, E.W. 1994. 'Profiles and development of adaptive behavior in children with Down syndrome', *American Journal on Mental Retardation* 98:5, 580–7.

Dykens, E.M., Hodapp, R.M. and Evans, E.W. 2006. 'Profiles and development of adaptive behavior in children with Down syndrome', *Down Syndrome: Research and Practice* 9:3, 45–50.

Dziewas, R., Warnecke, T., Schnabel, M., Ritter, M., Nabavi, D.G., Schilling, M., Ringelstein, E.B. and Reker, T. 2007. 'Neuroleptic-induced dysphagia: case report and literature review', *Dysphagia* 22:1, 63–7.

Eadie, P., Fey, M., Douglas, J. and Parsons, C. 2002. 'Profiles of grammatical morphology and sentence imitation in children with specific language impairment and Down syndrome', *Journal of Speech, Language, and Hearing Research* 45:4, 720–32.

Eadie, T.L. and Baylor, C.R. 2006. 'The effect of perceptual training on inexperienced listeners' judgments of dysphonic voice', *Journal of Voice* 20:4, 527–44.

Eadie, T.L. and Doyle, P.C. 2002. 'Direct magnitude estimation and interval scaling of pleasantness and severity in dysphonic and normal speakers', *Journal of the Acoustical Society of America* 112:6, 3014–21.

Eadie, T.L. and Kapsner-Smith, M. 2011. 'The effect of listener experience and anchors on judgments of dysphonia', *Journal of Speech, Language, and Hearing Research* 54:2, 430–47.

Eadie, T.L., Yorkston, K.M., Klasner, E.R., Dudgeon, B.J., Deitz, J.C., Baylor, C.R., Miller, R.M. and Amtmann, D. 2006. 'Measuring communication participation: a review of self-report instruments in speech-language pathology', *American Journal of Speech-Language Pathology* 15:4, 307–20.

Ealy, M. and Smith, R.J. 2011. 'Otosclerosis', *Advances in Oto-Rhino-Laryngology* 70, 122–9.

Eaton, W.W., Badawi, M. and Melton, B. 1995. 'Prodromes and precursors: epidemiologic data for primary prevention of disorders with slow onset', *American Journal of Psychiatry* 152:7, 967–72.

Edeal, D.M. and Gildersleeve-Neumann, C. 2011. 'The importance of production frequency in therapy for childhood apraxia of speech', *American Journal of Speech-Language Pathology* 20:2, 95–110.

Eden, G., Van Meter, J., Rumsey, J., Maisog, J., Woods, R. and Zeffiro, T. 1996. 'Abnormal processing of visual motion in dyslexia revealed by functional brain imaging', *Nature* 382:6586, 66–9.

Edwards, J. and Lahey, M. 1998. 'Nonword repetitions of children with specific language impairment: exploration of some explanations for their inaccuracies', *Applied Psycholinguistics* 19:2, 279–309.

Edwards, J., Jackson, H.J. and Pattison, P.E. 2002. 'Emotion recognition via facial expression and affective prosody in schizophrenia: a methodological review', *Clinical Psychology Review* 22:6, 789–832.

Edwards, J., Fox, R.A. and Rogers, C.L. 2002. 'Final consonant discrimination in children: effects of phonological disorder, vocabulary size, and articulatory accuracy', *Journal of Speech, Language, and Hearing Research* 45:2, 231–42.

Eggers, K., De Nil, L.F. and Van den Bergh, B.R.H. 2010. 'Temperament dimensions in stuttering and typically developing children', *Journal of Fluency Disorders* 35:4, 355–72.

Ehri, L.C. 2005. 'Learning to read words: theory, findings, and issues', *Scientific Studies of Reading* 9:2, 167–88.

Eigsti, I.M., Bennetto, L. and Dadlani, M.B. 2007. 'Beyond pragmatics: morphosyntactic development in autism', *Journal of Autism and Developmental Disorders* 37:6, 1007–23.

Einarsdottir, J. and Ingham, R.J. 2005. 'Have disfluency-type measures contributed to the understanding and treatment of developmental stuttering?', *American Journal of Speech-Language Pathology* 14:4, 260–73.

Eisenson, J. 1959. 'Language dysfunctions associated with right brain damage', *American Speech and Hearing Association* 1, 107.

Eiserman, W.D., Weber, C. and McCoun, M. 1992. 'Two alternative program models for serving speech-disordered preschoolers: a second year follow-up', *Journal of Communication Disorders* 25:2–3, 77–106.

Eiserman, W.D., Weber, C. and McCoun, M. 1995. 'Parent and professional roles in early intervention: a longitudinal comparison of the effects of two intervention configurations', *Journal of Special Education* 29:1, 20–44.

Ekelman, B.L. and Aram, D. 1983. 'Syntactic findings in developmental verbal apraxia', *Journal of Communication Disorders* 16:4, 237–50.

Ekman, P. 1973. *Darwin and facial expression: a century of research in review*, New York: Academic Press.

Ekman, P. 1982. *Emotion in the human face*, second edition, Cambridge University Press.

Ekman, P. 1999. 'Emotional and conversational nonverbal signals', in L.S. Messing and R. Campbell (eds.), *Gesture, speech and sign*, New York: Oxford University Press, 45–56.

Elin Thordardottir, E. and Ellis Weismer, S. 2002. 'Verb argument structure weakness in specific language impairment in relation to age and utterance length', *Clinical Linguistics & Phonetics* 16:4, 233–350.

Ellis Weismer, S. 2007. 'Typical talkers, late talkers, and children with specific language impairment: a language endowment spectrum?', in R. Paul (ed.), *The influence of developmental perspectives on research and practice in communication disorders: a festschrift for Robin S. Chapman*, Mahwah, NJ: Erlbaum, 83–102.

Ellis Weismer, S. and Edwards, J. 2006. 'The role of phonological storage deficits in specific language impairment: a reconsideration', *Applied Psycholinguistics* 27:4, 556–62.

Ellis Weismer, S. and Elin Thordardottir, E. 2002. 'Cognition and language', in P. Accardo, B. Rogers and A. Capute (eds.), *Disorders of language development*, Timonium, MD: York Press, 21–37.

Ellis Weismer, S. and Hesketh, L.J. 1996. 'Lexical learning by children with specific language impairment: effects of linguistic input presented at varying speaking rates', *Journal of Speech and Hearing Research* 39:1, 177–88.

Ellis Weismer, S. and Murray-Branch, J. 1989. 'Modeling versus modeling plus evoked production training: a comparison of two language intervention methods', *Journal of Speech and Hearing Disorders* 54:2, 269–81.

Ellis Weismer, S., Evans, J. and Hesketh, L.J. 1999. 'An examination of verbal working memory capacity in children with specific language impairment', *Journal of Speech, Language, and Hearing Research* 42:5, 1249–60.

Ellis Weismer, S., Tomblin, B., Zhang, X., Buckwalter, P., Chyoweth, J. and Jones, M. 2000. 'Nonword repetition performance in school-age children with and without language impairment', *Journal of Speech, Language, and Hearing Research* 43:4, 865–78.

Ellis, A.W. and Young, A.W. 1988. *Human cognitive neuropsychology*, Hove, East Sussex: Lawrence Erlbaum Associates.

Ellis, C. and Peach, R. 2009. 'Sentence planning following traumatic brain injury', *NeuroRehabilitation* 24:3, 255–66.

Elman, R.J. 2007. 'The importance of aphasia group treatment for rebuilding community and health', *Topics in Language Disorders* 27:4, 300–8.

Elsass, L. and Kinsella, G. 1987. 'Social interaction after severe closed head injury', *Psychological Medicine* 17:1, 67–78.

Emre, M. 2003. 'Dementia associated with Parkinson's disease', *Lancet Neurology* 2:4, 229–37.

Emre, M., Aarsland, D., Brown, R., Burn, D.J., Duyckaerts, C., Mizuno, Y., Broe, G.A., Cummings, J., Dickson, D.W., Gauthier, S., Goldman, J., Goetz, C., Korczyn, A., Lees, A., Levy, R., Litvan, I., McKeith, I., Olanow, W., Poewe, W., Quinn, N., Sampaio, C., Tolosa, E. and Dubois, B. 2007. 'Clinical diagnostic criteria for dementia associated with Parkinson's disease' *Movement Disorders* 22:12, 1689–1707.

Enderby, P. 1986. 'Relationships between dysarthric groups', *British Journal of Disorders of Communication* 21:2, 187–97.

Enderby, P. and Palmer, R. 2008. *Frenchay dysarthria assessment*, second edition, Austin, TX: Pro-Ed.

Engelmann, S. and Bruner, E.C. 1983. Reading Mastery I and II: DISTAR Reading, Chicago, IL: Science Research Associates.

Epping-Jordan, J.E., Pruitt, S.D., Bengoa, R. and Wagner, E.H. 2004. 'Improving the quality of health care for chronic conditions', *Quality and Safety in Health Care* 13:4, 299–305.

Erickson, K.A. and Koppenhaver, D.A. 1995. 'Developing a literacy program for children with severe disabilities', *Reading Teacher* 48:8, 676–84.

Erickson, R.L. 1969. 'Assessing communication attitudes among stutterers', *Journal of Speech and Hearing Research* 12:4, 711–24.

Eriksen, C.W. 1965. 'Perceptual defense', *Proceedings of the 53rd Annual Meeting of the American Psychopathological Association, Psychopathology of Perception*, New York: Grune and Stratton.

Evans, J., Saffran, J. and Robe-Torres, K. 2009. 'Statistical learning in children with specific language impairment', *Journal of Speech, Language, and Hearing Research* 52:2, 321–35.

Eveson, J.W. 2008. 'Xerostomia', *Periodontology 2000* 48:1, 85–91.

Eveson, J.W. 2011. 'Salivary tumours', *Periodontology 2000* 57:1, 150–9.

Ewers, M., Sperling, R.A., Klunk, W.E., Weiner, M.W. and Hampel, H. 2011. 'Neuroimaging markers for the prediction and early diagnosis of Alzheimer's disease dementia', *Trends in Neurosciences* 34:8, 430–42.

Ewing-Cobbs, L., Brookshire, B., Scott, M. and Fletcher, J. 1998. 'Children's narratives following traumatic brain injury: linguistic structure, cohesion and thematic recall', *Brain and Language* 61:3, 395–419.

Exum, T., Abasalon, C., Smith, B. and Reichel, I. 2010. People with cluttering and stuttering have room for success, International Cluttering On-Line Conference (online, available at: www.mnsu.edu/comdis/ica1/papers/exumc.html; last accessed 12 June 2013).

Ezrati-Vinacour, R., Platzky, R. and Yairi, E. 2001. 'The young child's awareness of stuttering-like disfluency', *Journal of Speech, Language, and Hearing Research* 44:2, 368–80.

Fabbro, F. 1999. *The neurolinguistics of bilingualism*, Hove, East Sussex: Psychology Press.

Facon, B., Facon-Bollengier, T. and Grubar, J. 2002. 'Chronological age, receptive vocabulary and syntax comprehension in children and adolescents with mental retardation', *American Journal on Mental Retardation* 107:2, 91–8.

Fairbanks, G. 1960. *Voice and articulation drillbook*, second edition, New York: Harper & Row.

Fairbanks, G. and Bebout, B. 1950. 'A study of minor organic deviations in "functional" disorders of articulation: 3. The tongue', *Journal of Speech and Hearing Disorders* 15:4, 348–52.

Falcaro, M., Pickles, A., Newbury, D.F., Addis, L., Banfield, E., Fisher, S.E., Monaco, A.P., Simkin, Z., Conti-Ramsden, G. and SLI Consortium. 2008. 'Genetic and phenotypic effects of phonological short-term memory and grammatical morphology in specific language impairment', *Genes, Brain and Behavior* 7:4, 393–402.

Farmer, M. 2000. 'Language and social cognition in children with specific language impairment', *Journal of Child Psychology and Psychiatry* 41:5, 627–36.

Faroqi-Shah, Y. and Thompson, C.K. 2012. 'Approaches to treatment of agrammatism', in R. Bastiaanse and C.K. Thompson (eds.), *Perspectives on agrammatism*, Hove, East Sussex: Psychology Press, 158–91.

Farrar, M.J., Johnson, B., Tompkins, V., Easters, M., Zilisi-Medus, A. and Benigno, J.P. 2009. 'Language and theory of mind in preschool children with specific language impairment', *Journal of Communication Disorders* 42:6, 428–41.

Farrell, A.D., Rabinowitz, J.A., Wallander, J.L. and Curran, J.P. 1985. 'An evaluation of two formats for the intermediate-level assessment of social skills', *Behavioural Assessment* 7:2, 155–71.

Farrell, J. 2011. *AAC apps – speaking APPropriately* (online, available at: www.spectronicsinoz.com/blog/tools-and-resources/aac-apps-speaking-appropriately/; last accessed 12 June 2013).

Faust, M. and Chiarello, C. 1998. 'Sentence context and lexical ambiguity resolution by the two hemispheres', *Neuropsychologia* 36:9, 827–35.

Fawcett, A.J. and Nicolson, R.I. 2000. 'Systemic screening and intervention for reading difficulty', in N.A. Badian (ed.), *Prediction and prevention of reading failure*, Baltimore, MD: York Press, 57–86.

Fawcett, A.J., Nicolson, R. and Lee, R. 2004. *Ready to learn*, San Antonio, TX: Harcourt Assessment.

Fawcus, M. 1989. 'Group therapy: a learning situation', in C. Code and D.J. Muller (eds.), *Aphasia therapy*, second edition, London: Cole and Whurr, 113–19.

Fawcus, M. 1991. 'Managing group therapy: further considerations', *Aphasiology* 5:6, 555–7.

Feifer, S. 2011. 'How SLD manifests in reading', in D. Flanagan and V. Alfonso (eds.), *Essentials of learning disability identification*, Hoboken, NJ: John Wiley and Sons, 21–42.

Feldenkrais, M. 1949. *Body and mature behavior*, New York: International University.

Felsenfeld, S., Broen, P.A. and McGue, M. 1994. 'A 28-year follow-up of adults with a history of moderate phonological disorder: educational and occupational results', *Journal of Speech and Hearing Research* 37:6, 1341–53.

Felton, R.H. and Brown, I.S. 1990. 'Phonological processes as predictors of specific reading skills in children at risk for reading failure', *Reading and Writing* 2:1, 39–59.

Felton, R., Wood, F., Brown, I., Campbell, S. and Harter, M. 1987. 'Separate verbal memory and naming deficits in attention deficit disorder and reading disability', *Brain and Language* 31:1, 171–84.

Fenson, L., Dale, P.S., Reznick, J.S., Bates, E., Pethick, S.J., Hartung, J. and Reilly, J. 1993. *MacArthur communicative development inventories*, San Diego, CA: Singular Publishing.

Ferguson, C. and Farwell, C.B. 1975. 'Words and sounds in early acquisition', *Language* 51:2, 419–39.

Ferman, T.J. and Boeve, B.F. 2007. 'Dementia with Lewy bodies', *Neurologic Clinics* 25:3, 741–60.

Fernald, D.D. 1995. 'When in London…: differences in disability language preferences among English-speaking countries', *Mental Retardation* 33:2, 9–103.

Fernandez-Duque, D., Baird, J.A. and Black, S.E. 2009. 'False-belief understanding in frontotemporal dementia and Alzheimer's disease', *Journal of Clinical and Experimental Neuropsychology* 31:4, 489–97.

Ferré, P., Clermont, M., Lajoie, C., Côté, H. Ska, B. and Joanette, Y. 2009a. '*Clinical profiles of communication impairments after a right-hemisphere stroke*', Annual Meeting of the Academy of Aphasia: Boston, MA, 9 October 2009.

Ferré, P., Clermont, M.F., Lajoie, C., Côté, H., Abusamra, V., Ska, B. and Fonseca, R.P. 2009b. 'Identification de profils communicationnels parmi les individus cérébrolésés droits: profils transculturels [Identification of communicative profiles among right-brain-damaged individuals: cross-cultural profiles]', *Neuropsicologia Latinoamericana* 1:1, 32–40.

Ferré, P., Fonseca, R.P., Ska, B. and Joanette, Y. 2012. 'Communicative clusters after a right-hemisphere stroke: are there universal clinical profiles?', *Folia Phoniatrica et Logopaedica* 64:6, 199–207.

Ferré, P., Ska, B., Lajoie, C. and Joanette, Y. 2011. 'Clinical focus on prosodic, discursive and pragmatic treatment for right hemisphere damaged adults: what's right?', *Rehabilitation Research and Practice* (online, available at: www.hindawi.com/journals/rerp/2011/131820/cta/; last accessed 12 June 2013).

Fey, M. and Loeb, D. 2002. 'An evaluation of the facilitative effects of inverted yes-no questions on the acquisition of auxiliary verbs', *Journal of Speech, Language, and Hearing Research* 45:1, 160–74.

Fey, M., Cleave, P., Long, S. and Hughes, D. 1993. 'Two approaches to the facilitation of grammar in children with language impairment: an experimental evaluation', *Journal of Speech and Hearing Research* 36:1, 141–57.

Fey, M.E., Long, S.H. and Finestack, L.H. 2003. 'Ten principles of grammar facilitation for children with specific language impairments', *American Journal of Speech-Language Pathology* 12:1, 3–15.

Fidler, D.J., Hepburn, S. and Rogers, S. 2006. 'Early learning and adaptive behaviour in toddlers with Down syndrome: evidence for an emerging behavioural phenotype?', *Down Syndrome: Research and Practice* 9:3, 37–44.

Fidler, D.J., Philofsky, A. and Hepburn, S.L. 2007. 'Language phenotypes and intervention planning: bridging research and practice', *Mental Retardation and Developmental Disabilities Research Review* 13:1, 47–57.

Field, T. 2002. 'Prenatal effects of maternal depression', in S.H. Goodman and I.H. Gotlib (eds.), *Children of depressed parents: mechanisms of risk and implications for treatment*, Washington, DC: American Psychological Association, 59–88.

Fillingham, J.K., Sage, K. and Lambon Ralph, M.A. 2005. 'Further explorations and an overview of errorless and errorful therapy for aphasic word-finding difficulties: the number of naming attempts during therapy affects outcome', *Aphasiology* 19:7, 597–614.

Fillingham, J.K., Sage, K. and Lambon Ralph, M.A. 2006. 'The treatment of anomia using errorless learning', *Neuropsychological Rehabilitation* 16:2, 129–54.

Finestack, L.H. and Abbeduto, L. 2010. 'Expressive language profiles of verbally expressive adolescents and young adults with Down syndrome or fragile X', *Journal of Speech, Language, and Hearing Research* 53:5, 1334–48.

Finn, J.D., Stott, M.W.R. and Zarichny, K.T. 1988. 'School performance and adolescents in juvenile court', *Urban Education* 23:2, 150–61.

Finn, P., Bothe, A.K. and Bramlett, R.E. 2005. 'Science and pseudoscience in communication disorders: criteria and applications', *American Journal of Speech-Language Pathology* 14:3, 172–86.

Fioritti, A., Giaccotto, L. and Melega, V. 1997. 'Choking incidents among psychiatric patients: retrospective analysis of thirty-one cases from the west Bologna psychiatric wards', *Canadian Journal of Psychiatry* 42:5, 515–20.

Fischer-Brandies, H., Avalle, C. and Limbrock, G.J. 1987. 'Therapy of orofacial dysfunctions in cerebral palsy according to Castillo-Morales: first results of a new treatment concept', *European Journal of Orthodontics* 9:2, 139–43.

Fisher, K.V., Telser, A., Phillips, J.E. and Yeates, D.B. 2001. 'Regulation of vocal fold transepithelial water fluxes', *Journal of Applied Physiology* 91:3, 1401–11.

Fisher, M. and Meyer, L.H. 2002. 'Development and social competence after two years for students enrolled in inclusive and self-contained educational programs', *Research and Practice for Persons with Severe Disabilities* 27:3, 165–74.

Fisher, S.E., Vargha-Khadem, F., Watkins, K.E., Monaco, A.P. and Pembrey, M.E. 1998. 'Localisation of a gene implicated in a severe speech and language disorder', *Nature Genetics* 18:3, 168–70.

Flamand-Rouvière, C., Guettard, E., Moreau, C., Bahi-Buisson, N., Valayannopoulos, V., Grabli, D., Motte, J., Rodriguez, D., Roubertie, A., Maintigneux, L., Kemlin, I., Ceballos-Picot, I., Adams, D., Vidailhet, M. and Roze, E. 2010. 'Speech disturbances in patients with dystonia or chorea due to neurometabolic disorders', *Movement Disorders* 25:11, 1605–11.

Flanagan, D. and Alfonso, V. 2011. *Essentials of learning disability identification*, Hoboken, NJ: John Wiley and Sons.

Flanagan, S., McDonald, S. and Togher, L. 1995. 'Evaluating social skills following traumatic brain injury: the BRISS as a clinical tool', *Brain Injury* 9:4, 321–38.

Fleming, V. and Harris, J. 2008. 'Complex discourse production in mild cognitive impairment: detecting subtle changes', *Aphasiology* 22:7–8, 729–40.

Fletcher, J.M., Lyon, G.R., Fuchs, L.S. and Barnes, M.A. 2007. *Learning disabilities: from identification to intervention*, New York: Guilford Press.

Fletcher, S.G. 1972. 'Time-by-count measurement of diadochokinetic syllable rate', *Journal of Speech and Hearing Research* 15:4, 763–70.

Flipsen, P. 2006. 'Measuring the intelligibility of conversational speech in children', *Clinical Linguistics & Phonetics* 20:4, 303–12.

Flipsen, P. 2012. '*Intelligibility measures in children with speech sound disorders*', Illinois Speech-Language-Hearing Association Annual Convention: Rosemont, IL, 10–11 February 2012.

Fodor, J.A. 1983. *The modularity of mind*, Cambridge, MA: MIT Press.

Fodor, J.A. 1985. 'Précis of the Modularity of Mind', *Behavioral and Brain Sciences* 8:1, 1–5.

Foerch, C., Misselwitz, B., Sitzer, M., Berger, K., Steinmetz, H. and Neumann-Haefelin, T. 2005. 'Difference in recognition of right and left hemispheric stroke', *Lancet* 366:9483, 392–3.

Folstein, S.E. and Mankoski, R.E. 2000. 'Chromosome 7q: where autism meets language disorder?', *American Journal of Human Genetics* 67:2, 278–81.

Fonseca, R.P., Ferré, P., Wilson, M.A., Ska, B. and Joanette, Y. 2010. '*Communication profiles and their relationship with executive dysfunction*', Academy of Aphasia: Athens, Greece, 24–26 October 2010.

Foorman, B.R. 2003. *Preventing and remediating reading difficulties: bringing science to scale*, Baltimore, MD: York Press.

Foreman, P., Arthur-Kelly, M., Pascoe, S. and King, B.S. 2004. 'Evaluating the educational experiences of children with profound and multiple disabilities in inclusive and segregated classroom setting: an Australian perspective', *Research and Practice for Persons with Severe Disabilities* 29:3, 183–93.

Forrest, K. 2002. 'Are oral motor exercises useful in the treatment of phonological/articulatory disorders?', *Seminars in Speech and Language* 23:1, 15–25.

Forrest, K. 2003. 'Diagnostic criteria of developmental apraxia of speech used by clinical speech-language pathologists', *American Journal of Speech-Language Pathology* 12:3, 376–80.

Forrest, K., Adams, S., McNeil, M.R. and Southwood, H. 1991. *Dysarthria and apraxia of speech: perspectives on management*, Baltimore, MD: Paul H. Brookes Publishing Co.

Forrest, K., Elbert, M. and Dinnsen, D.A. 2000. 'The effect of substitution patterns on phonological treatment outcomes', *Clinical Linguistics & Phonetics* 14:7, 519–31.

Fougeron, C. and Keating, P.A. 1997. 'Articulatory strengthening at the edges of prosodic domains', *Journal of the Acoustical Society of America* 101:6, 3728–40.

Fowler, A., Gelman, R. and Gleitman, L. 1994. 'The course of language learning in children with Down syndrome', in H. Tager-Flusberg (ed.), *Constraints on language acquisition: studies of atypical children*, Hillsdale, NJ: Lawrence Erlbaum Associates, 91–140.

Fowler, C.A. 1986. 'An event approach to the study of speech perception from a direct-realist perspective', *Journal of Phonetics* 14:1, 3–28.

Fox, A.V. and Dodd, B. 2001. 'Phonologically disordered German-speaking children', *American Journal of Speech-Language Pathology* 10:3, 291–307.

Fox, A.V., Dodd, B. and Howard, D. 2002. 'Risk factors for speech disorders in children', *International Journal of Language & Communication Disorders* 37:2, 117–31.

Fox, C.M. and Boliek, C.A. 2012. 'Intensive voice treatment (LSVT Loud) for children with spastic cerebral palsy and dysarthria', *Journal of Speech, Language, and Hearing Research* 55:3, 930–45.

Fox, C., Boliek, C., Namdaran, N., Nickerson, C., Gardner, B., Piccott, C., Hilstad, J. and Archibald, E. 2008. 'Intensive voice treatment (LSVTR LOUD) for children with spastic cerebral palsy', *Movement Disorders* 23:S1, S378.

Fox, C.M., Boliek, C.A. and Ramig, L.O. 2005. 'The impact of intensive voice treatment (LSVT) on speech intelligibility in children with spastic cerebral palsy', *Movement Disorders* 20:S10, S149.

Francis, D.R., Riddoch, M.J. and Humphreys, G.W. 2001. 'Cognitive rehabilitation of word meaning deafness', *Aphasiology* 15:8, 749–66.

Francomano, C.A. 2010. 'Stickler syndrome', in S.B. Cassidy and J.E. Allanson (eds.), *Management of genetic syndromes*, third edition, Hoboken, NJ: John Wiley & Sons, 787–96.

Frangistakis, J.M., Ewart, A.K., Moris, C.A., Mervis, C.B., Bertrand, J., Robinson, B.F., Klein, B.P., Ensing, G.J., Everett, L.A., Green, E.D., Pröschel, C., Gutowski, N.J., Noble, M., Atkinson, D.L., Odelberg, S.J. and Keating, M.T. 1996. 'LIM-kinase 1 hemizygosity implicated in impaired visuospatial constructive cognition', *Cell* 86:1, 59–69.

Franken, M.C., Kielstra-Van der Schalk, C.J. and Boelens, H. 2005. 'Experimental treatment of early stuttering: a preliminary study', *Journal of Fluency Disorders* 30:3, 189–99.

Franklin, S. 1995. 'Designing single case treatment studies for aphasic patients', *Neuropsychological Rehabilitation* 7:4, 401–18.

Franklin, S., Buerk, F. and Howard, D. 2002. 'Generalised improvement in speech production for a subject with reproduction conduction aphasia', *Aphasiology* 16:10–11, 1087–1114.

Frattali, C.M. 1998. 'Assessing functional outcomes: an overview', *Seminars in Speech and Language* 19:3, 209–20.

Frederiksen, C.H., Bracewell, R.J., Breuleux, A. and Renaud, A. 1990. 'The cognitive representation and processing of discourse function and dysfunction', in

Y. Joanette and H.H. Brownell (eds.), *Discourse ability and brain damage: theoretical and empirical perspectives*, New York: Springer-Verlag, 69–112.

Freed, D.B. 2011. *Motor speech disorders: diagnosis and treatment*, Independence, KY: Delmar Cengage Learning.

Freidl, W., Friedrich, G., Egger, J. and Fitzek, T. 1993. 'Psychogenic aspects of functional dysphonia', *Folia Phoniatrica* 45:1, 10–2.

Freund, L.S., Reiss, A.L. and Abrams, M. 1993. 'Psychiatric disorders associated with fragile X in the young female', *Pediatrics* 91:2, 321–9.

Frick, P.J. and Dickens, C. 2006. 'Current perspectives on conduct disorder', *Current Psychiatry Reports* 8:1, 59–72.

Frick, P.J. and Marsee, M.A. 2006. 'Psychopathy and developmental pathways to antisocial behaviour in youth', in C.J. Patrick (ed.), *Handbook of psychology*, New York: Guilford, 355–74.

Fridriksson, J., Holland, A.L., Beeson, P. and Morrow, L. 2005. 'Spaced retrieval treatment of anomia', *Aphasiology* 19:2, 99–109.

Frieden, L. 2004. *Improving outcomes for students with disabilities*, Washington, DC: National Council on Disabilities.

Friedlander, A.H. and Marder, S.R. 2002. 'The psychopathology, medical management and dental implications of schizophrenia', *Journal of American Dental Association* 133:5, 603–10.

Friedman, A., Polson, M.C., Dafoe, C.G. and Gaskill, S.J. 1982 'Dividing attention within and between hemispheres: testing a multiple resources approach to limited-capacity information processing', *Journal of Experimental Psychology. Human Perception and Performance* 8:5, 625–50.

Friedman, J., Roze, E., Abdenur, J.E., Chang, R., Gasperini, S., Saletti, V., Wali, G.M., Eiroa, H., Neville, B., Felice, A., Parascandalo, R., Zafeiriou, D.I., Arrabal-Fernandez, L., Dill, P., Eichler, F.S., Echenne, B., Gutierrez-Solana, L.G., Hoffmann, G.F., Hyland, K., Kusmierska, K., Tijssen, M.A., Lutz, T., Mazzuca, M., Penzien, J., Poll-The, B.T., Sykut-Cegielska, J., Szymanska, K., Thöny, B. and Blau, N. 2012. 'Sepiapterin reductase deficiency: a treatable mimic of cerebral palsy', *Annals of Neurology* 71:4, 520–30.

Friedman, M.A., Miletta, N., Roe, C., Wang, D., Morrow, B.E., Kates, W.R., Higgins, A.M. and Shprintzen, R.J. 2011. 'Cleft palate, retrognathia and congenital heart disease in velo-cardio-facial syndrome: a phenotype correlation study', *International Journal of Pediatric Otorhinolaryngology* 75:9, 1167–72.

Friedmann, N. 2000. 'Moving verbs in agrammatic production', in R. Bastiaanse and Y. Grodzinsky (eds.), *Grammatical disorders in aphasia: a neurolinguistic perspective*, London: Whurr, 152–70.

Friedmann, N. 2002. 'Question production in agrammatism: the tree pruning hypothesis,' *Brain and Language* 80:2, 160–87.

Friedrich, M. and Friederici, A. 2006. 'Early N400 development and later language acquisition', *Psychophysiology* 43:1, 1–12.

Frisoni, G.B., Pievani, M., Testa, C., Sabattoli, F., Bresciani, L., Bonetti, M., Beltramello, A., Hayashi, K.M., Toga, A.W. and Thompson, P.M. 2007. 'The topography of grey matter involvement in early and late onset Alzheimer's disease', *Brain* 130:3, 720–30.

Frith, C.D. 2004. 'Schizophrenia and theory of mind', *Psychological Medicine* 34:3, 385–9.

Frith, C.D. and Allen, H.A. 1988. 'Language disorders in schizophrenia and their implications for neuropsychology', in P. Bebbington and P. McGuffin (eds.), *Schizophrenia: the major issues*, Oxford: Heinemann, 172–86.

Frith, U. 2003. *Autism: explaining the enigma*, Oxford: Blackwell Publishing.

Fromkin, V.A. 1973. *Speech errors as linguistic evidence*, The Hague: Mouton.

Fromm, D. 1981. *Investigation of movement/EMG parameters in apraxia of speech*, unpublished dissertation, University of Wisconsin-Madison.

Fromm, D., Abbs, J.H., McNeil, M.R. and Rosenbek, J.C. 1982. 'Simultaneous perceptual-physiological method for studying apraxia of speech', *Clinical Aphasiology* 10, 155–71.

Frost, R. 2006. 'Becoming literate in Hebrew: the grain size hypothesis and Semitic orthographic systems', *Developmental Science* 9:5, 439–40.

Fry, A.F. and Hale, S. 1996. 'Processing speed, working memory, and fluid intelligence: evidence for a developmental cascade', *Psychological Science* 7:4, 237–41.

Fucci, D. 1972. 'Oral vibrotactile sensation: an evaluation of normal and defective speakers', *Journal of Speech and Hearing Research* 15:1, 179–84.

Fuchs, D., Mock, D., Morgan, P.L. and Young, C.L. 2003. 'Responsiveness-to-intervention: definitions, evidence, and implications for the learning disabilities construct', *Learning Disabilities Research & Practice* 18:3, 157–71.

Fuijkschot, J., Maassen, B., Gorter, J.W., Gerven, M.V. and Willemsen, M. 2009. 'Speech-language performance in Sjogren-Larsson syndrome', *Developmental Neurorehabilitation* 12:2, 106–12.

Fujiki, M. and Brinton, B. 2009. 'Pragmatics and social communication in child language disorders', in R.G. Schwartz (ed.), *Handbook of child language disorders*, New York: Psychology Press, 406–23.

Fujiki, M., Brinton, B. and Clarke, D. 2002. 'Emotion regulation in children with specific language impairment', *Language, Speech, and Hearing Services in Schools* 33:2, 102–11.

Fujiki, M., Brinton, B., Morgan, M. and Hart, C.H. 1999. 'Withdrawn and sociable behavior of children with language impairment', *Language, Speech, and Hearing Services in the Schools* 30:2, 183–95.

Fukushiro, A.P. and Trindade, I.E. 2011. 'Nasometric and aerodynamic outcome analysis of pharyngeal flap surgery for the management of velopharyngeal insufficiency', *Journal of Craniofacial Surgery* 22:5, 1647–51.

Fuller, R., Nopoulos, P., Arndt, S., O'Leary, D., Ho, B.C. and Andreasen, N.C. 2002. 'Longitudinal assessment of premorbid cognitive functioning in patients with schizophrenia through examination of standardized scholastic test performance', *American Journal of Psychiatry* 159:7, 1183–9.

Furia, C.L.D., Kowalski, L.P., Latorre, M.R.D.O., Angelis, E.C., Martins, N.M.S., Barros, A.P.B. and Ribeiro, K.C.B. 2001. 'Speech intelligibility after glossectomy and speech rehabilitation', *Archives of Otolaryngology – Head and Neck Surgery*, 127:7, 877–83.

Furlow, L.T. 1986. 'Cleft palate repair by double opposing Z-plasty', *Plastic and Reconstructive Surgery* 78:6, 724–38.

Fushimi, T., Komori, K., Ikeda, M., Lambon Ralph, M.A. and Patterson, K. 2009. 'The association between semantic dementia and surface dyslexia in Japanese', *Neuropsychologia* 47:4, 1061–8.

Gaab, N., Gabrielli, J.D., Deutsch, G.K., Tallal, P. and Temple, E. 2007. 'Neural correlates of rapid auditory processing are disrupted in children with developmental dyslexia and ameliorated with training: an fMRI study', *Restorative Neurology and Neuroscience* 25:3–4, 295–310.

Gabel, R.M., Hughes, S. and Daniels, D. 2008. 'Effects of stuttering severity and therapy involvement on role entrapment of people who stutter', *Journal of Communication Disorders* 41:2, 146–58.

Gage, H. and Storey, L. 2004. 'Rehabilitation for Parkinson's disease: a systematic review of available evidence', *Clinical Rehabilitation* 18:5, 463–82.

Gajar, A. 1979. 'Educable mentally retarded, learning disabled, emotionally disturbed: similarities and differences', *Exceptional Children* 45:6, 470–2.

Gajar, A., Schloss, P., Schloss, C. and Thompson, C. 1984. 'Effects of feedback and self-monitoring on head trauma youth's conversation skills', *Journal of Applied Behavior Analysis* 17:3, 353–8.

Gallagher, T.M. 1999. 'Interrelationships among children's language, behavior, and emotional problems', *Topics in Language Disorders* 19:2, 1–15.

Gallegos, X., Medina, R., Espinoza, E. and Bustamante, A. 1992. 'Electromyographic feedback in the treatment of bilateral facial paralysis: a case study', *Journal of Behavioral Medicine* 15:5, 533–9.

Gallon, N., Harris, J. and van der Lely, H. 2007. 'Non-word repetition: an investigation of phonological complexity in children with grammatical SLI', *Clinical Linguistics & Phonetics* 21:6, 435–55.

Garber, J., Clarke, G.N., Weersing, V.R., Beardslee, W.R., Brent, D.A., Gladstone, T.R., Debar, L.L., Lynch, F.L., D'Angelo, E., Hollon, S.D., Shamseddeen, W. and Iyengar, S. 2009. 'Prevention of depression in at-risk adolescents: a randomised controlled trial', *Journal of the American Medical Association* 302:21, 2215–24.

Gardner, M.F. 1990. *Expressive one-word picture vocabulary test – revised*, Novato, CA: Academic Therapy Publications.

Garner, C., Callias, M. and Turk, J. 1999. 'Executive function and theory of mind performance of boys with fragile-X syndrome', *Journal of Intellectual Disability Research* 43:6, 466–74.

Garrard, P. 2008. 'Differential diagnosis in dementia', in S.F. Cappa, J. Abutalebi, J.-F. Démonet, P.C. Fletcher and P. Garrard (eds.), *Cognitive neurology: a clinical textbook*, Oxford University Press, 185–98.

Garrard, P., Patterson, K., Watson, P.C. and Hodges, J.R. 1998. 'Category specific semantic loss in dementia of Alzheimer's type. Functional-anatomical correlations from cross-sectional analyses', *Brain* 121:4, 633–46.

Garrett, K.L. and Huh, C. 2002. 'The impact of graphic contextual information and instruction on the conversational behaviours of a person with severe aphasia', *Aphasiology* 16:4–6, 523–36.

Garrett, M.F. 1982. 'Production of speech: observation from normal and pathological language use', in A.W. Ellis (ed.), *Normality and pathology in cognitive functions*, London: Academic Press, 19–76.

Gaston, J., Quinchia Rios, B., Bartlett, R., Berchtold, C. and Thibeault, S.L. 2012. 'The response of vocal fold fibroblasts and mesenchymal stromal cells to vibration', *PLoS ONE* 7:2, e30965.

Gathercole, S.E. 2006. 'Nonword repetition and word learning: the nature of the relationship', *Applied Psycholinguistics* 27:4, 513–43.

Gathercole, S.E. and Baddeley, A.D. 1990. 'Phonological memory deficits in language disordered children:

is there a causal connection?', *Journal of Memory and Language* 29:3, 336–60.

Gathercole, S.E., Willis, C.S. and Baddeley, A.D. 1994. 'The children's test of nonword repetition: a test of phonological working memory', *Memory* 2:2, 103–27.

Gawda, B. 2010. 'Syntax of emotional narratives of persons diagnosed with antisocial personality', *Journal of Psycholinguistic Research* 39:4, 273–83.

Gay, T., Lindblom, B. and Lubker, J. 1981. 'Production of bite-block vowels: acoustic equivalence by selective compensation', *Journal of the Acoustical Society of America* 69:3, 802–10.

Gazzaniga, M.S., Bogen, J.E. and Sperry, R.W. 1962. 'Some functional effects of sectioning the cerebral commissures in man', *Proceedings of the National Academy of Sciences of the United States of America*, 48:10, 1765–9.

Gelfer, M.P. 1988. 'Perceptual attributes of voice: development and use of rating scales', *Journal of Voice* 2:4, 320–6.

Gelfer, M.P. 1993. 'A multidimensional scaling study of voice quality in females', *Phonetica* 50:1, 15–27.

Gelfer, M.P. 1999. 'Voice treatment for the male-to-female transgendered client', *American Journal of Speech-Language Pathology* 8:3, 201–8.

Gentry, L.R., Godersky, J.C. and Thompson, B. 1988. 'MR imaging of head trauma: review of the distribution and radiopathologic features of traumatic lesions', *American Journal of Roentgenology* 150:3, 663–72.

Georgiou, G.K. 2006. 'The effect of orthography on literacy development: evidence from studies in different languages. A review of 'Handbook of Orthography and Literacy' by Joshi, M. and Aaron, P.G.', *Journal of Research in Reading* 29:4, 457–8.

Gerber, S. and Kraat, A. 1992. 'Use of a developmental model of language acquisition: applications to children using AAC systems', *AAC: Augmentative and Alternative Communication* 8:1, 19–32.

German, D.J. 2000. *Test of word finding*, second edition (TWF-2), Austin, TX: Pro Ed.

Gernsbacher, M.A. and Pripas-Kapit, S.R. 2012. 'Who's missing the point? A commentary on claims that autistic persons have a specific deficit in figurative language comprehension', *Metaphor and Symbol* 27:1, 93–105.

Geschwind, N. 1972. 'Language and the brain', *Scientific American* 226:4, 76–83.

Geschwind, N. 1974. *Selected papers on language and the brain*, Dordrecht and Boston, MA: D. Reidel Publishing Company.

Geurts, H. and Embrechts, M. 2008. 'Language profiles in ASD, SLI, and ADHD', *Journal of Autism and Developmental Disorders* 38:10, 1931–43.

Giancola, P. 2000. 'Neuropsychological functioning and antisocial behavior: implications for etiology and prevention', in D.H. Fishbein (ed.), *The science, treatment, and prevention of antisocial behaviors: application to the criminal justice system*, Kingston, NJ: Civic Research Institute, 11-1 to 11-16.

Gibbon, F.E. 1999. 'Undifferentiated lingual gestures in children with articulation/phonological disorders', *Journal of Speech, Language, and Hearing Research* 42:2, 382–97.

Gibbon, F.E. and Wood, S.E. 2002. 'Articulatory drift in the speech of children with articulation and phonological disorders', *Perceptual and Motor Skills* 95:1, 295–307.

Gibbon, F., Lee, A., Yuen, I. and Crampin, L. 2008. 'Clicks produced as compensatory articulations in two adolescents with velocardiofacial syndrome', *Cleft Palate-Craniofacial Journal* 45:4, 381–92.

Gibson, J.J. 1986. *The ecological approach to visual perception*, Hillsdale, NJ: Lawrence Erlbaum.

Gierut, J.A. 1998. 'Treatment efficacy: functional phonological disorders in children', *Journal of Speech, Language, and Hearing Research* 41:1, S85–S100.

Gijsel, M.A., Bosman, A.M.T. and Verhoeven, L. 2006. 'Kindergarten risk factors, cognitive factors, and teacher judgments as predictors of early reading in Dutch', *Journal of Learning Disabilities* 39:6, 558–71.

Gil, M. and Goral, M. 2004. 'Nonparallel recovery in bilingual aphasia: effects of language choice, language proficiency and treatment', *International Journal of Bilingualism* 8:2, 191–219.

Gillam, R., Loeb, D.F., Hoffman, L., Bohman, T., Champlin, C., Thibodeau, L., Widen, J., Brandel, J. and Friel-Patti, S. 2008. 'The efficacy of Fast ForWord language intervention in school-age children with language impairment: a randomized controlled trial', *Journal of Speech, Language, and Hearing Research* 51:1, 97–119.

Gillam, R., Logan, K.J. and Pearson, N. 2009. *Test of childhood stuttering (TOCS)*, Austin, TX: Pro-Ed.

Gillingham, A. and Stillman, B. 1960. *Remedial training for children with specific disability in reading*, Cambridge, MA: Educators Publishing Service.

Gillon, G.T. and Moriarty, B.C. 2007. 'Childhood apraxia of speech: children at risk for persistent reading and spelling disorder', *Seminars in Speech and Language* 28:1, 48–57.

Gilmour, J., Hill, B., Place, M. and Skuse, D.H. 2004. 'Social communication deficits in conduct disorder: a clinical and community survey', *Journal of Child Psychology and Psychiatry* 45:5, 967–78.

Girbau, D. and Schwartz, R. 2007. 'Nonword repetition in Spanish-speaking children with specific language impairment', *International Journal of Language & Communication Disorders* 42:1, 59–75.

Glennen, S. 2000. 'AAC assessment myths and realities', ASHA SID 12 Leadership Conference on Augmentative and Alternative Communication: Sea Island, GA, 8–11 January 2000.

Glenwright, M. and Pexman, P.M. 2010. 'Development of children's ability to distinguish sarcasm and verbal irony', *Journal of Child Language* 37:2, 429–51.

Glorig, A. and Nixon, J. 1962. 'Hearing loss as a function of age', *Laryngoscope* 72:11, 1596–610.

Glosser, G. and Deser, T. 1990. 'Patterns of discourse production among neurological patients with fluent language disorders', *Brain and Language* 40:1, 67–88.

Goetz, C.G., Emre, M. and Dubois, B. 2008. 'Parkinson's disease dementia: definitions, guidelines, and research perspectives in diagnosis', *Annals of Neurology* 64:Suppl 2, S81–S92.

Goffman, L., Gerken, L. and Lucchesi, J. 2007. 'Relations between segmental and motor variability in prosodically complex nonword sequences', *Journal of Speech, Language, and Hearing Research* 50:2, 444–58.

Golalipour, M.J., Mirfazeli, A. and Behnampour, N. 2007. 'Birth prevalence of oral clefting in northern Iran', *Cleft Palate-Craniofacial Journal* 44:4, 378–80.

Golan, O., Baron-Cohen, S. and Hill, J. 2006. 'The Cambridge Mindreading (CAM) Face-Voice Battery: testing complex emotion recognition in adults with and without Asperger syndrome', *Journal of Autism and Developmental Disorders* 36:2, 169–83.

Goldberg, T.E. and Weinberger, D.R. 2000. 'Thought disorder in schizophrenia: a reappraisal of older formulations and an overview of some recent studies', *Cognitive Neuropsychiatry* 5:1, 1–19.

Goldenberg, G. 2003. 'Apraxia and beyond: life and work of Hugo Liepmann', *Cortex* 39:3, 509–24.

Goldstein, H. 2006. 'Language intervention considerations for children with retardation and developmental disabilities', *Perspectives on Language, Learning and Education* 13:3, 21–6.

Goldstein, H. and Cisar, C.L. 1992. 'Promoting interaction during sociodramatic play: teaching scripts to typical preschoolers and classmates with disabilities', *Journal of Applied Behavior Analysis* 25:2, 265–80.

Goldstein, H. and Kaczmarek, L. 1992. 'Promoting communicative interaction among children in integrated intervention settings', in S. Warren and J. Reichle (eds.), *Causes and effects in communication and language intervention*, Baltimore, MD: Paul H. Brookes, 81–111.

Goldstein, H., English, K., Shafer, K. and Kaczmarek, L. 1997. 'Interaction among preschoolers with and without disabilities: effects of across-the-day peer interaction', *Journal of Speech, Language, and Hearing Research* 40:1, 33–48.

Gonnerman, L.M., Andersen, E.S., Devlin, J.T., Kempler, D. and Seidenberg, M.S. 1997. 'Double dissociation of semantic categories in Alzheimer's disease', *Brain and Language* 57:2, 254–79.

González, B.S., López, M.L., Rico, M.A. and Garduño, F. 2008. 'Oral clefts: a retrospective study of prevalence and predisposal factors in the State of Mexico', *Journal of Oral Science* 50:2, 123–9.

Gonzalez-Rothi, L.J., Fuller, R., Leon, S.A., Kendall, D.L., Moore, A., Wu, S.S., Crosson, B., Heilman, K.M. and Nadeau, S.E. 2009. 'Errorless practice as a possible adjuvant to donepazil in Alzheimer's disease', *Journal of the International Neuropsychological Society* 15:2, 311–22.

Good, R.H. and Kaminski, R.A. (eds.) 2002. *Dynamic indicators of basic early literacy skills*, sixth edition, Eugene, OR: Institute for the Development of Education Achievement.

Good, R.H., Kaminski, R.A., Moats, L.C., Laimon, D., Smith, S. and Dill, S. 2003. *DIBELS: dynamic indicators of basic early literacy skills*, sixth edition, Longmont, CO: Sopris West.

Good, R.H., Simmons, D.C. and Kame'enui, E.J. 2001. 'The importance and decision-making utility of a continuum of fluency-based indicators of foundational reading skills for third-grade high-stakes outcomes', *Scientific Studies of Reading* 5:3, 257–88.

Goodglass, H. and Kaplan, E. 1972. *Boston diagnostic aphasia examination*, Philadelphia, PA: Lea & Febiger.

Goodglass, H. and Kaplan, E. 1983. *The assessment of aphasia and related disorders*, Philadelphia, PA: Lea & Febiger.

Goodglass, H., Kaplan, E. and Barresi, B. 2001. *Boston diagnostic aphasia examination*, third edition, Philadelphia, PA: Lippincott Williams & Wilkins.

Goozée, J.V., Murdoch, B., Ozanne, A., Cheng, Y., Hill, A. and Gibbon, F. 2007. 'Lingual kinematics and coordination in speech-disordered children exhibiting differentiated versus undifferentiated lingual gestures', *International Journal of Language & Communication Disorders* 42:6, 703–24.

Gopnik, M. 1990. 'Feature-blind grammar and dysphasia', *Nature* 344:7, 715.

Gopnik, M. and Crago, M.B. 1991. 'Familial aggregation of a developmental language disorder', *Cognition* 39:1, 1–50.

Goral, M., Levy, E.S. and Kastl, R. 2010. 'Cross-language treatment generalisation: a case of trilingual aphasia', *Aphasiology* 24:2, 170–87.

Goran, L.G. and Gage, N.A. 2011. 'A comparative analysis of language, suspension, and academic performance of students with emotional disturbance and students with learning disabilities', *Education and Treatment of Children* 34:4, 469–88.

Gorno-Tempini, M.L., Dronkers, N.F., Rankin, K.P., Ogar, J.M., Phengrasamy, L., Rosen, H.J., Johnson, J.K., Weiner, M.W. and Miller, B.L. 2004. 'Cognition and anatomy in three variants of primary progressive aphasia', *Annals of Neurology* 55:3, 335–46.

Gorno-Tempini, M.L., Hillis, A.E., Weintraub, S., Kertesz, A., Mendez, M., Cappa, S.F., Ogar, J.M., Rohrer, J.D., Black, S., Boeve, B.F., Manes, F., Dronkers, N.F., Vandenberghe, R., Rascovsky, K., Patterson, K., Miller, B.L., Knopman, D.S., Hodges, J.R., Mesulam, M.M. and Grossman, M. 2011. 'Classification of primary progressive aphasia and its variants', *Neurology* 76:11, 1006–14.

Goswami, U. 2000. 'Phonological representations, reading development and dyslexia: towards a cross-linguistic theoretical framework', *Dyslexia* 6:2, 133–51.

Goswami, U. 2001. 'Early phonological development and the acquisition of literacy', in S. Neumann and D.K. Dickinson (eds.), *Handbook of early literacy research*, New York: Guilford Press, 111–25.

Gottwald, S.R. 2010. 'Stuttering prevention and early intervention: a multidimensional approach', in B. Guitar and R.J. McCauley (eds.), *Treatment of stuttering: established and emerging interventions*, Baltimore, MD: Lippincott Williams & Wilkins, 91–117.

Gough, P.B. and Tunmer, W.E. 1986. 'Decoding, reading and reading disability', *Remedial and Special Education* 7:1, 6–10.

Gozzard, H., Baker, E. and McCabe, P. 2008. 'Requests for clarification and children's speech responses: changing "pasghetti" to "spaghetti"', *Child Language Teaching and Therapy* 24:3, 249–63.

Graetz, P., De Bleser, R. and Willmes, C. 1992. *Akense Afasietest*, Amsterdam: Hogrefe.

Graf Estes, K., Evans, J. and Else-Quest, N. 2007. 'Differences in nonword repetition performance of children with and without specific language impairment: a meta-analysis', *Journal of Speech, Language, and Hearing Research* 50:1, 177–95.

Grafman, J. and Salazar, A. 1987. 'Methodological considerations relevant to the comparison of recovery from penetrating and closed head injuries', in H.S. Levin, J. Grafman and H.M. Eisenberg (eds.), *Neurobehavioral recovery from head injury*, New York: Oxford University Press, 44–54.

Graham, M.S. 1997. *The clinician's guide to alaryngeal speech therapy*, Boston, MA: Butterworth-Heinemann.

Graham, M.S. 2005. 'Taking it to the limits: achieving proficient esophageal speech', in P.C. Doyle and R.L. Keith (eds.), *Contemporary considerations in the treatment and rehabilitation of head and neck cancer*, Austin: Pro-Ed, 379–430.

Graham, N.L., Emery, T. and Hodges, J.R. 2004. 'Distinctive cognitive profiles in Alzheimer's disease and subcortical vascular dementia', *Journal of Neurology, Neurosurgery and Psychiatry* 75:1, 61–71.

Grandmaison, E. and Simard, M. 2003. 'A critical review of memory stimulation programs in Alzheimer's disease', *Journal of Neuropsychiatry and Clinical Neurosciences* 15:2, 130–44.

Grant, J., Karmiloff-Smith, A., Gathercole, S., Patterson, S., Howlin, P., Davies, M. and Udwin, O. 1997. 'Verbal short-term memory and its relation to language acquisition in Williams syndrome', *Cognitive Neuropsychology* 2:2, 81–99.

Gray, S. 2003. 'Word learning by preschoolers with specific language impairment: what predicts success?', *Journal of Speech, Language, and Hearing Research* 46:1, 56–67.

Gray, S. 2005. 'Word learning by preschoolers with specific language impairment: effect of phonological or semantic cues', *Journal of Speech, Language, and Hearing Research* 48:6, 1452–67.

Gray, S. 2006. 'The relationship between phonological memory, receptive vocabulary, and fast mapping in young children with specific language impairment', *Journal of Speech, Language, and Hearing Research* 49:5, 955–69.

Gray, S., Plante, E., Vance, R. and Henrichsen, M. 1999. 'The diagnostic accuracy of four vocabulary tests administered to preschool-age children', *Language, Speech, and Hearing Services in Schools* 30:2, 196–206.

Gray, S., Reiser, M. and Brinkley, S. 2012. 'Effect of onset and rhyme primes in preschoolers with typical development and specific language impairment', *Journal of Speech, Language, and Hearing Research* 55:1, 32–44.

Great Ormond Street Hospital for Children NHS Foundation Trust. 2007. Integrated care pathways (online, available at: www.gosh.nhs.uk/health-professionals/integrated-care-pathways/; last accessed 12 June 2013).

Green, D. 1996. 'Introduction', in D.W. Green (ed.), *Cognitive science: an introduction*, Oxford: Blackwell, 1–22.

Green, G. 1982. 'Assessment and treatment of the adult with severe aphasia: aiming for functional generalisation', *Australian Journal of Human Communication Disorders* 10, 11–23.

Green, G. 1984. 'Communication in aphasia therapy: some of the procedures and issues involved', *British Journal of Disorders of Communication* 19:1, 35–46.

Green, R.E.A., Turner, G.R. and Thompson, W.F. 2004. 'Deficits in facial emotion perception in adults with recent traumatic brain injury', *Neuropsychologia* 42:2, 133–41.

Greenbaum, P.E., Dedrick, R.F., Friedman, R.M., Kutash, K., Brown, E.C., Lardieri, S.P. and Pugh, A.M. 1996. 'National Adolescent and Child Treatment Study (NACTS): outcomes for children with serious emotional and behavioral disturbance', *Journal of Emotional and Behavioral Disorders* 4:3, 130–46.

Greene, C.L. 1964. *The voice and its disorders*, second edition, Philadelphia, PA: J.B. Lippincott.

Greener, J., Enderby, P. and Whurr, R. 1999. 'Speech and language therapy for aphasia following stroke', *Cochrane Database of Systematic Reviews*, Issue 4, CD000425.

Greer, M.K., Brown, F.R., Shashidhar, G., Choudry, S.H. and Klein, A.J. 1997. 'Cognitive, adaptive, and behavioural characteristics of Williams syndrome', *American Journal of Medical Genetics (Neuropsychiatric Genetics)* 74:5, 521–5.

Gregg, T.A., Leonard, A.G., Hayden, C., Howard, K.E. and Coyle, C.F. 2008. 'Birth prevalence of cleft lip and palate in Northern Ireland (1981 to 2000)', *Cleft Palate-Craniofacial Journal* 45:2, 141–7.

Gregory, C., Lough, S., Stone, V., Erzinclioglu, S., Martin, L., Baron-Cohen, S. and Hodges, J.R. 2002. 'Theory of mind in patients with frontal variant frontotemporal dementia and Alzheimer's disease: theoretical and practical implications', *Brain* 125:4, 752–64.

Gregory, H.H. 1979. *Controversies about stuttering therapy*, Baltimore, MD: University Park Press.

Gregory, R.P., Smith, P.T. and Rudge, P. 1992. 'Tardive dyskinesia presenting as severe dysphagia', *Journal of Neurology, Neurosurgery and Psychiatry* 55:12, 1203–4.

Grela, G. 2003. 'The omission of subject arguments in children with specific language impairment', *Clinical Linguistics & Phonetics* 17:2, 153–69.

Gresham, F.M., MacMillan, D.L. and Bocian, K. 1996. 'Behavioral earthquakes: low frequency, salient behavior events that differentiate students at-risk for behavioral disorders', *Behavioral Disorders* 21:4, 277–92.

Grice, H.P. 1975. 'Logic and conversation', in P. Cole and J.L. Morgan (eds.), *Syntax and semantics, Vol. 3, Speech acts*, New York: Academic Press, 41–58.

Griffin, R., Friedman, O., Ween, J., Winner, E., Happe, F. and Brownell, H. 2006. 'Theory of mind and the right cerebral hemisphere: refining the scope of impairment', *Laterality* 11:3, 195–225.

Grigorencko, E.L., Wood, F.B., Meyer, M.S., Hart, L.A., Speed, W.C., Shuster, A. and Pauls, D. 1997. 'Susceptibility loci for distinct components of developmental dyslexia on chromosome 6 and 15', *American Journal of Human Genetics* 60:1, 27–39.

Grimme, B., Fuchs, S., Perrier, P. and Schoener, G. 2011. 'Limb versus speech motor control: a conceptual review', *Motor Control* 15:1, 5–33.

Grindrod, C. 2003. 'Sensitivity to local sentence context information in lexical ambiguity resolution: evidence from left- and right-hemisphere-damaged individuals', *Brain and Language* 85:3, 503–23.

Grindrod, C.M., Blumstein, S.E., Myers, E.B. and Bilenko, N.Y. 2004. 'An event-related fMRI study of competition in selecting among semantically ambiguous word meanings' (online, available at: www.cog.brown.edu/~seb/posters/Grindrod%20et%20al.%20CNS%202006.pdf; last accessed 12 June 2013).

Grodzinsky, Y. 1990. *Theoretical perspectives on language deficits*, Cambridge and London: MIT Press.

Grodzinsky, Y. 2000. 'The neurology of syntax: language use without Broca's area', *Behavioral and Brain Sciences* 23:1, 1–21.

Grodzinsky, Y. and Friederici, A.D. 2006. 'Neuroimaging of syntax and syntactic processing', *Current Opinions in Neurobiology* 16:2, 240–6.

Groen, M.A., Yasin, I., Laws, G., Barry, J.G. and Bishop, D.V.M. 2008. 'Weak hand preference in children with Down syndrome is associated with language deficits', *Developmental Psychobiology* 50:3, 242–50.

Groher, M.E. and Bukatman, R. 1986. 'Prevalence of swallowing disorders in two teaching hospitals', *Dysphagia* 1:1, 3–6.

Gross, R.G., McMillan, C.T., Chandrasekaran, K., Dreyfuss, M., Ash, S., Avants, B., Cook, P., Moore, P., Libon, D.J., Siderowf, A. and Grossman, M. 2012. 'Sentence processing in Lewy body spectrum disorder: the role of working memory', *Brain and Cognition* 78:2, 85–93.

Grossman, M. 2010. 'Primary progressive aphasia: clinico-pathological correlations', *Nature Reviews Neurology* 6:2, 88–97.

Grossman, M. and Ash, S. 2004. 'Primary progressive aphasia: a review', *Neurocase* 10:1, 3–18.

Grossman, M. and Moore, P. 2005. 'A longitudinal study of sentence comprehension difficulty in primary progressive aphasia', *Journal of Neurology, Neurosurgery and Psychiatry* 76:5, 644–9.

Grossman, M., Carvell, S., Gollomp, S., Stern, M.B., Vernon, G. and Hurtig, H.I. 1991. 'Sentence comprehension and praxis deficits in Parkinson's disease', *Neurology* 41:10, 1620–6.

Grossman, M., Gross, R.G., Moore, P., Dreyfuss, M., McMillan, C.T., Cook, P.A., Ash, S. and Siderowf, A. 2012. 'Difficulty processing temporary syntactic ambiguities in Lewy body spectrum disorder', *Brain and Language* 120:1, 52–60.

Grossman, M., Zurif, E., Lee, C., Prather, P., Kalmanson, J., Stern, M.B. and Hurtig, H.I. 2002. 'Information processing speed and sentence comprehension in Parkinson's disease', *Neuropsychology* 16:2, 174–81.

Guadagnoli, M. and Lee, T. 2004. 'Challenge point: a framework for conceptualizing the effects of various practice conditions in motor learning', *Journal of Motor Behavior* 36:2, 212–24.

Guenther, F. 2008. 'ASHA 2007 Zemlin memorial award lecture: the neural control of speech', *Perspectives on Speech Science and Orofacial Disorders* 18:1, 7–14.

Guenther, F.H., Ghosh, S.S. and Tourville, J.A. 2006. 'Neural modeling and imaging of the cortical interactions underlying syllable production', *Brain and Language* 96:3, 280–301.

Guitar, B. 2006. *Stuttering: an integrated approach to its nature and treatment*, third edition, Baltimore, MD: Lippincott Williams & Wilkins.

Guitar, B. and McCauley, R.J. 2010. 'An overview of treatments for preschool stuttering', in B. Guitar and R.J. McCauley (eds.), *Treatment of stuttering: established and emerging interventions*, Baltimore, MD: Lippincott Williams & Wilkins, 56–62.

Gunawardena, D., Ash, S., McMillan, C., Avants, B., Gee, J. and Grossman, M. 2010. 'Why are patients with progressive nonfluent aphasia nonfluent?', *Neurology* 75:7, 588–94.

Gunter, H.E. 2004. 'Modeling mechanical stresses as a factor in the etiology of benign vocal fold lesions', *Journal of Biomechanics* 37:7, 1119–24.

Gunter, E., Wisser, J.R., Cohen, M.A. and Brown, A.S. 1998. 'Palatoplasty: Furlow's double reversing Z-plasty versus intravelar veloplasty', *Cleft Palate-Craniofacial Journal* 35:6, 546–9.

Guralnick, M.J. 2001. 'Social competence with peers and early childhood inclusion: need for alternative approaches', in M.J. Guralnick (ed.), *Early childhood inclusion: focus on change*, Baltimore, MD: Paul H. Brookes, 481–502.

Guralnick, M.J. and Neville, B. 1997. 'Designing early intervention programs to promote children's social competence', in M.J. Guralnick (ed.), *The effectiveness of early intervention*, Baltimore, MD: Paul H. Brookes, 579–610.

Guralnick, M.J. and Paul-Brown, D. 1989. 'Peer-related communicative competence of preschool children; developmental and adaptive characteristics', *Journal of Speech and Hearing Research* 32:4, 930–43.

Hageman, C.F., Robin, D.A., Moon, J.B. and Folkins, J.W. 1994. 'Visuomotor tracking in normal and apraxic speakers', *Clinical Aphasiology* 22, 219–29.

Hagen, C. 1984. 'Language disorders in head trauma' in A. Holland (ed.), *Language disorders in adults*, San Diego, CA: College Hill Press, 245–81.

Hagerman, R. and Hagerman, P.J. 2002. 'Fragile X syndrome', in P. Howlin and O. Udwin (eds.), *Outcomes in neurodevelopmental and genetic disorders*, New York: Cambridge University Press, 198–219.

Hagiwara, H. 1995. 'The breakdown of functional categories and the economy of derivation', *Brain and Language* 50:1, 92–116.

Hain, T.C. 2008. *Acoustic neuroma*, American Hearing Research Foundation (online, available at: http://american-hearing.org/disorders/acoustic-neuroma/; last accessed 12 June 2013).

Hale, C.M. and Tager-Flusberg, H. 2005a. 'Brief report: the relationship between discourse deficits and autism symptomatology', *Journal of Autism and Developmental Disorders* 35:4, 519–24.

Hale, C.M. and Tager-Flusberg, H. 2005b. 'Social communication in children with autism: the relationship between theory of mind and discourse development', *Autism* 9:2, 157–78.

Hale, J.B. and Fiorello, C.A. 2004. *School neuropsychology: a practitioner's handbook*, New York: Guilford Press.

Hall, C.D., Golding-Kushner, K.J., Argamaso, R.V. and Strauch, B. 1991. 'Pharyngeal flap surgery in adults', *Cleft Palate Journal* 28:2, 179–82.

Hall, N.E., Yamashita, T.S. and Aram, D.M. 1993. 'Relationship between language and fluency in children with language disorders', *Journal of Speech and Hearing Research* 36:3, 568–79.

Hall, P.K., Hardy, J.C. and LaVelle, W.E. 1990. 'A child with signs of developmental apraxia of speech with whom a palatal lift prosthesis was used to manage palatal dysfunction', *Journal of Speech and Hearing Disorders* 55:3, 454–60.

Hall, P.K., Jordan, L.S. and Robin, D.A. 1993. *Developmental apraxia of speech: theory and clinical practice*, Austin, TX: Pro-Ed.

Halle, J. and Holt, B. 1991. 'Assessing stimulus control in natural settings: an analysis of stimuli that acquire control during training', *Journal of Applied Behavior Analysis* 24:3, 579–89.

Halliday, M.A.K. 1994. *An introduction to functional grammar*, second edition, London: Edward Arnold.

Halliday, M.A.K. and Hasan, R. 1976. *Cohesion in English*, London: Longman.

Halper, A.S., Cherney, L.R. and Burns, M.S. 1996. *RICE-R. Clinical management of right hemisphere dysfunction*, second edition, Gaithersburg, MD: Aspen Publishers.

Hamaker, R.C., Singer, M.I., Blom, E.D. and Daniels, H.A. 1985. 'Primary voice restoration at laryngectomy', *Archives of Otolaryngology – Head and Neck Surgery*, 111:3, 182–6.

Hamilton, A.F., Brindley, R. and Frith, U. 2009. 'Visual perspective taking impairment in children with autistic spectrum disorder', *Cognition* 113:1, 37–44.

Hammen, V.L. 2004. 'Managing speaking rate in dysarthria', in E. Strand (ed.), *Treatment of dysarthria: evidence-based practice*, Rockville, MD: American Speech-Language-Hearing Association, 19–24.

Hannus, S., Kauppila, T. and Launonen, K. 2009. 'Increasing prevalence of specific language impairment (SLI) in primary healthcare of a Finnish town, 1989–1999', *International Journal of Language & Communication Disorders* 44:1, 79–97.

Hanson, E.K. and Beukelman, D.R. 2006. 'Effect of omitted cues on alphabet supplemented speech intelligibility', *Journal of Medical Speech-Language Pathology* 14:3, 185–96.

Hanson, E.K., Beukelman, D.R., Heidemann, J.K. and Shutts-Johnson, E. 2010. 'The impact of alphabet supplementation and word prediction on sentence intelligibility of electronically distorted speech', *Journal of Speech Communication* 52:2, 99–105.

Hanson, E.K., Yorkston, K.M. and Beukelman, D.R. 2004. 'Speech supplementation techniques for dysarthria: a systematic review', *Journal of Medical Speech-Language Pathology* 12:2, ix–xxix.

Hapner, E. and Klein, A. 2009. 'A synopsis of the management of vocal fold scar', *Perspectives on Voice and Voice Disorders* 19:1, 15–23.

Hapner, E., Portone-Maira, C. and Johns III, M.M. 2009. 'A study of voice therapy dropout', *Journal of Voice* 23:3, 337–40.

Happé, F.G.E. 1993. 'Communicative competence and theory of mind in autism: a test of relevance theory', *Cognition* 48:2, 101–19.

Happé, F.G.E. 1997. 'Central coherence and theory of mind in autism: reading homographs in context', *British Journal of Developmental Psychology* 15:1, 1–12.

Happé, F.G.E. 1999. 'Autism: cognitive deficit or cognitive style?', *Trends in Cognitive Science* 3:6, 216–22.

Happé, F. and Frith, U. 2006. 'The weak coherence account: detail-focused cognitive style in autism spectrum disorders', *Journal of Autism and Developmental Disorders* 36:1, 5–25.

Harciarek, M. and Heilman, K.M. 2009. 'The contribution of anterior and posterior regions of the right hemisphere to the recognition of emotional faces', *Journal of Clinical and Experimental Neuropsychology* 31:3, 322–30.

Hardcastle, W.J. 1987. *Phonetic approaches to speech production in aphasia and related disorders*, Boston, MA: College Hill Press.

Hardin, M.A., Van Demark, D.R., Morris, H.L. and Payne, M.M. 1992. 'Correspondence between nasalance scores and listener judgments of hypernasality and hyponasality', *Cleft Palate Journal* 29:4, 346–51.

Hare, R.D. 1991. *The Hare psychopathy checklist – revised*, Toronto: Multi-Health Systems.

Hare, R.D., Williamson, S.E. and Harpur, T.J. 1998. 'Psychopathy and language', in T.E. Moffitt and A.M. Sarnoff (eds.), *Biological contributions to crime causation*, NATO Advanced Science Series D: Behavior and Social Sciences, Dordrecht, The Netherlands: Martinus Nijhoff Publishing, 68–92.

Harnish, S.M., Neils-Strunjas, J., Eliassen, J., Reilly, J., Meinzer, M., Clark, J.G. and Joseph, J. 2010. 'Visual discrimination predicts naming and semantic association accuracy in Alzheimer disease', *Cognitive Behavioral Neurology* 23:4, 231–9.

Harris, L., Doyle, E.S. and Haaf, R. 1996. 'Language treatment approach for users of AAC: experimental single-subject investigation', *AAC: Augmentative and Alternative Communication* 12:4, 230–43.

Harris, S. 1998. 'Speech therapy for dysphonia', in T. Harris, S. Harris, J.S. Rubin and D.M. Howard (eds.), *The voice clinic handbook*, London: Whurr, 139–206.

Harris, V., Onslow, M., Packman, A., Harrison, E. and Menzies, R. 2002. 'An experimental investigation of the impact of the Lidcombe program on early stuttering', *Journal of Fluency Disorders* 27:3, 203–13.

Harrison, E. and Onslow, M. 2010. 'The Lidcombe program for preschool children who stutter', in B. Guitar and R.J. McCauley (eds.), *Treatment of stuttering: established and emerging interventions*, Baltimore, MD: Lippincott Williams & Wilkins, 118–66.

Harry, B. 1994. *The disproportionate representation of minority students in special education: theories and recommendations*, Alexandria, VA: Project FORUM, National Association of State Directors of Special Education.

Hart, K.I., Fujiki, M., Brinton, B. and Hart, C.H. 2004. 'The relationship between social behavior and severity of language impairment', *Journal of Speech, Language, and Hearing Research* 47:3, 647–62.

Hartelius, L. and Svensson, P. 1994. 'Speech and swallowing symptoms associated with Parkinson's disease and multiple sclerosis: a survey', *Folia Phoniatrica et Logopaedica* 46:1, 9–17.

Hartelius, L., Elmberg, M., Holm, R., Lövberg, A.-S. and Nikolaidis, S. 2008. 'Living with dysarthria: evaluation of a self-report questionnaire', *Folia Phoniatrica et Logopaedica* 60:1, 11–19.

Hartelius, L., Svensson, P. and Bubach, A. 1993. 'Clinical assessment of dysarthria: performance on a dysarthria test by normal adult subjects and by individuals with Parkinson's disease or with multiple sclerosis', *Scandinavian Journal of Logopedics and Phoniatrics* 18:4, 131–41.

Hartfield, K.N. and Conture, E.G. 2006. 'Effects of perceptual and conceptual similarity in lexical priming of young children who stutter: preliminary findings', *Journal of Fluency Disorders* 31:4, 303–24.

Hartley, C.L., Grove, N., Lindsey, J. and Pring, T. 2003. 'Treatment effects on speech production and speech intelligibility of dysarthric speech in children with cerebral palsy', Fifth European CPLOL Congress: Edinburgh, UK, 5–7 September 2003.

Hartley, L. and Jensen, P. 1991. 'Narrative and procedural discourse after closed head injury', *Brain Injury* 5:3, 267–85.

Hartley, L. and Jensen, P. 1992. 'Three discourse profiles of closed-head-injury speakers: theoretical and clinical implications', *Brain Injury* 6:3, 271–82.

Harvey, P.D. 1983. 'Speech competence in manic and schizophrenic psychosis: the association between clinically rated thought disorder and cohesion and reference performance', *Journal of Abnormal Psychology* 92:3, 368–77.

Hasan, R. 1985. *Language, context, and text: aspects of language in a social-semiotic perspective*, Geelong, Victoria: Deakin University Press.

Haskill, A.M. and Tyler, A.A. 2007. 'A comparison of linguistic profiles in subgroups of children with specific language impairment', *American Journal of Speech-Language Pathology* 16:3, 209–21.

Hassink, J. and Leonard, L. 2010. 'Within-treatment factors as predictors of outcomes following conversational recasting', *American Journal of Speech-Language-Pathology* 19:3, 213–24.

Hassold, T. and Sherman, S. 2002. 'The origin and etiology of trisomy 21', in W.I. Cohen, L. Nadel and M.E. Madnick (eds.), *Down syndrome: visions for the 21st century*, New York: Wiley-Liss, 295–301.

Hasson, N. and Joffe, V. 2007. 'The case for dynamic assessment in speech and language therapy', *Child Language Teaching and Therapy* 23:1, 9–25.

Hauner, K.K.Y., Shriberg, L.D., Kwiatkowski, J. and Allen, C.T. 2005. 'A subtype of speech delay associated with developmental psychosocial involvement', *Journal of Speech, Language, and Hearing Research* 48:3, 635–50.

Hayden, D. and Square, P. 1999. *Verbal motor production assessment for children*, Toronto, ON: The Psychological Corporation.

Hayes, R.L. and O'Grady, B.M. 2003. 'Do people with schizophrenia comprehend what they read?', *Schizophrenia Bulletin* 29:3, 499–507.

Hayiou-Thomas, M., Bishop, D. and Plunkett, K. 2004. 'Simulating SLI: general cognitive processing stressors can produce a specific linguistic profile', *Journal of Speech, Language, and Hearing Research* 47:6, 1347–62.

Hayiou-Thomas, M., Oliver, B. and Plomin, R. 2005. 'Genetic influences on specific versus nonspecific language impairment in 4-year-old twins', *Journal of Learning Disabilities* 38:3, 222–32.

Healey, E.C., Scott, L.A. and Ellis, G. 1995. 'Decision making in the treatment of school-age children who stutter', *Journal of Communication Disorders* 28:2, 107–24.

Heath, M., Grierson, L., Binsted, G. and Elliott, D. 2007. 'Interhemispheric transmission time in persons with Down syndrome', *Journal of Intellectual Disability Research* 51:12, 972–81.

Hebert, L.E., Beckett, L.A., Scherr, P.A. and Evans, D.A. 2001. 'Annual incidence of Alzheimer's disease in the United States projected to the years 2000 through 2050', *Alzheimer's Disease and Associated Disorders* 15:4, 169–73.

Hebert, L.E., Scherr, P.A., Bienias, J.L., Bennett, D.A. and Evans, D.A. 2004. 'State-specific projections through 2025 of Alzheimer disease prevalence', *Neurology* 62:9, 1645.

Heffernan, T.M., Jarvis, H., Rodgers, J., Scholey, A.B. and Ling, J. 2001. 'Prospective memory, everyday cognitive failure and central executive functioning in recreational users of ecstasy', *Human Psychopharmacology* 16:8, 607–12.

Hegde, M. 1980. 'An experimental-clinical analysis of grammatical and behavioral distinctions between verbal auxiliary and copula', *Journal of Speech and Hearing Research* 23:4, 864–77.

Heilman, K.M., Bowers, D., Speedie, L. and Coslett, H.B. 1984. 'Comprehension of affective and nonaffective prosody', *Neurology* 34:7, 917–21.

Heisters, D. 2011. 'Parkinson's: symptoms, treatments and research', *British Journal of Nursing* 20:9, 548–54.

Helffenstein, D.A. and Wechsler, F.S. 1982. 'The use of Interpersonal Process Recall (IPR) in the remediation of interpersonal and communication skill deficits in the newly brain-injured', *Clinical Neuropsychology* 4, 139–43.

Helfrich-Miller, K.R. 1994. 'A clinical perspective: melodic intonation therapy for developmental apraxia', *Clinical Communication Disorders* 4:3, 175–82.

Helm-Estabrooks, N. 1993. 'Stuttering associated with acquired neurological disorders', in R.F. Curlee (ed.), *Stuttering and related disorders of fluency*, New York: Thieme Medical Publishers, 205–18.

Helm-Estabrooks, N. 2002. 'Cognition and aphasia: a discussion and a study', *Journal of Communication Disorders* 35:2, 171–86.

Helm-Estabrooks, N. and Albert, M.L. 1991. *Manual of aphasia therapy*, Austin, TX: Pro-Ed.

Helm-Estabrooks, N. and Baressi, B.A. 1980. *Voluntary control of involuntary utterances: a treatment approach for severe aphasia*, Clinical Aphasiology Conference: Minneapolis, 1980.

Helm-Estabrooks, N., Fitzpatrick, P.M.R. and Baresi, B. 1982. 'Visual action therapy for global aphasia', *Journal of Speech and Hearing Disorders* 47:4, 385–9.

Henrichs, J., Rescorla, L., Schenk, J.J., Schmidt, H.G., Jaddoe, V.W.V., Hofman, A., Raat, H., Verhulst, F.C. and Tiemeier, H. 2011. 'Examining continuity of early expressive vocabulary development: the generation R study', *Journal of Speech, Language, and Hearing Research* 54:3, 854–69.

Henry, J.D. and Crawford, J.R. 2004. 'Verbal fluency deficits in Parkinson's disease: a meta-analysis', *Journal of the International Neuropsychological Society* 10:4, 608–22.

Henry, J.D., Crawford, J.R. and Phillips, L.H. 2004. 'Verbal fluency performance in dementia of the Alzheimer's type: a meta-analysis', *Neuropsychologia* 42:9, 1212–22.

Henry, J.D., Phillips, L.H., Crawford, J.R., Ietswaart, M. and Summers, F. 2006. 'Theory of mind following traumatic brain injury: the role of emotion recognition and executive dysfunction', *Neuropsychologia* 44:10, 1623–8.

Henry, L.A. 2001 'How does the severity of a learning disability affect working memory performance?', *Memory* 9:4–6, 233–47.

Henry, L.A. and MacLean, M. 2002. 'Working memory performance in children with and without intellectual disabilities', *American Journal on Mental Retardation* 107:6, 421–32.

Henry, L.R., Helou, L.B., Solomon, N.P., Howard, R.S., Gurevich-Uvena, J., Coppit, G. and Stojadinovic, A. 2010. 'Functional voice outcomes after thyroidectomy: an assessment of the Dysphonia Severity Index (DSI) after thyroidectomy', *Surgery* 147:6, 861–70.

Herbert, M.R., Ziegler, D.A., Makris, N., Filipek, P.A., Kemper, T.L., Normandin, J.J., Sanders, H.A., Kennedy, D.N. and Caviness, V.S. 2004. 'Localization of white matter volume increase in autism and developmental language disorder', *Annals of Neurology* 55:4, 530–40.

Herbert, R., Best, W., Hickin, J., Howard, D. and Osborne, F. 2003. 'Combining lexical and interactional approaches to therapy for word finding deficits in aphasia', *Aphasiology* 17:2, 1163–86.

Herbert, R., Hickin, J., Howard, D., Osbourne, F. and Best, W. 2008. 'Do picture-naming tests provide a valid assessment of lexical retrieval in conversation in aphasia?', *Aphasiology* 22:2, 184–203.

Hersh, D., Worrall, L., Howe, T., Sherratt, S. and Davidson, B. 2012. 'SMARTER goal setting in aphasia rehabilitation', *Aphasiology* 26:2, 220–33.

Hertegard, S., Gauffin, J. and Karlsson, I. 1992. 'Physiological correlates of the inverse filtered flow waveform', *Journal of Voice* 6:3, 224–34.

Hesketh, A., Dima, E. and Nelson, V. 2007a. 'Teaching phoneme awareness to pre-literate children with speech disorder: a randomized controlled trial', *International Journal of Language & Communication Disorders* 42:3, 251–71.

Hesketh, A., Mumby, K. and Bowen, A. 2007b. 'Apraxia of speech: how reliable are speech and language therapists' diagnoses?', *Clinical Rehabilitation* 21:8, 760–7.

Hetrick, R.D. and Sommers, R.K. 1988. 'Unisensory and bisensory processing skills of children having misarticulations and normally speaking peers', *Journal of Speech and Hearing Research* 31:4, 575–81.

Hetrick, S.E., Parker, A.G., Hickie, I.B., Purcell, R., Yung, A.R. and McGorry, P.D. 2008. 'Early identification and intervention in depressive disorders: towards a clinical staging model', *Psychotherapy and Psychosomatics* 77:5, 263–70.

Hiatt, K.D. and Newman, J.P. 2007. 'Behavioural evidence of prolonged interhemispheric transfer time among psychopathic offenders', *Neuropsychology* 21:3, 313–18.

Hickin, J., Best, W., Herbert, R., Howard, D. and Osbourne, F. 2002. 'Phonological therapy for word-finding difficulties: a re-evaluation', *Aphasiology* 16:10–11, 981–99.

Hickok, G. and Poeppel, D. 2007. 'The cortical organization of speech processing', *Nature Reviews. Neuroscience* 8:5, 393–402.

Hilari, K. and Cruice, M. 2013. 'Quality-of-life approach to aphasia', in I. Papathanasiou, P. Coppens and C. Potagas (eds.), *Aphasia and related neurogenic communication disorders*, Burlington, MA: Jones and Bartlett Learning, 233–54.

Hilari, K., Byng, S., Lamping, D.L. and Smith, S.C. 2003. 'Stroke and aphasia quality of life scale-39', *Stroke* 34:8, 1944–50.

Hilari, K., Lamping, D.L., Smith, S.C., Northcott, S., Lamb, A. and Marshall, J. 2009. 'Psychometric properties of the Stroke and Aphasia Quality of Life scale (SAQOL-39) in a generic stroke population', *Clinical Rehabilitation* 23:6, 544–57.

Hilgers, F.J., Aaronson, N.K., Ackerstaff, A.H., Schouwenburg, P.F. and van Zandwikj, N. 1991. 'The influence of a heat and moisture exchanger (HME) on the respiratory symptoms after total laryngectomy', *Clinical Otolaryngology and Allied Sciences* 16:2, 152–6.

Hill, D. 2003. 'Differential treatment of stuttering in the early stages of development', in H. Gregory (ed.), *Stuttering therapy: rationale and procedures*, Needham Heights, MA: Allyn & Bacon, 142–85.

Hill, E.L. 2004. 'Executive dysfunction in autism', *Trends in Cognitive Science* 8:1, 26–32.

Hillier, A., Beversdorf, D.Q., Raymer, A.M., Williamson, D.J. and Heilman, K.M. 2007. 'Abnormal emotional word ratings in Parkinson's disease', *Neurocase* 13:2, 81–5.

Hillis, A.E. 1989. 'Efficacy and generalisation of treatment for aphasic naming errors', *Archives of Physical Medicine and Rehabilitation* 70:8, 632–6.

Hillis, A.E., Oh, S. and Ken, L. 2004b. 'Deterioration of naming nouns versus verbs in primary progressive aphasia', *Annals of Neurology* 55:2, 268–75.

Hillis, A.E., Rapp, B., Romani, C. and Caramazza, A. 1990. 'Selective impairment of semantics in lexical processing', *Cognitive Neuropsychology* 7:3, 191–243.

Hillis, A.E., Work, M., Barker, P.B., Jacobs, M.A., Breese, E.L. and Maurer, K. 2004a. 'Re-examining the brain regions crucial for orchestrating speech articulation', *Brain* 127:7, 1479–87.

Hinshaw, S.P. 1992. 'Externalizing behavior problems and academic underachievement in childhood and adolescence: causal relationships and underlying mechanisms', *Psychological Bulletin* 111:1, 127–55.

Hinshelwood, J. 1917. *Congenital word blindness*, London: H.K. Lewis.

Hinton, V., De Viva, D., Nereo, N., Goldstein, E. and Stern, Y. 2000. 'Poor verbal working memory across intellectual levels in boys with Duchenne dystrophy', *Neurology* 54:13, 2127–32.

Hirano, M. 1981. *Clinical examination of the voice*, New York: Springer-Verlag.

Hirano, M. and Bless, D.M. 1993. *Videostroboscopic examination of the larynx*, San Diego, CA: Singular.

Hird, K. and Kirsner, K. 2003. 'The effect of right cerebral hemisphere damage on collaborative planning in conversation: an analysis of intentional structure', *Clinical Linguistics & Phonetics* 17:4–5, 309–15.

Hiroto, I. 1967. 'Hoarseness. Viewpoints of voice physiology', *Japanese Journal of Logopedics and Phoniatrics* 8:1, 9–15.

Hixon, T.J. 1987. *Respiratory function in speech and song*, Baltimore, MD: Williams & Wilkins.

Hixon, T.J. and Hoit, J.D. 2005. *Evaluation and management of speech breathing disorders: principles and methods*, Tucson, AZ: Redington Brown.

Hixon, T.J., Hawley, M.S. and Wilson, J.M. 1982. 'An around-the-house device for the clinical determination of respiratory driving pressure', *Journal of Speech and Hearing Disorders* 47:4, 413–15.

Hodge, M. 1999. 'Relationship between F2/F1 vowel quadrilateral area and speech intelligibility in a child with progressive dysarthria', *Canadian Acoustics* 27:3, 84–5.

Hodge, M. 2004. 'Nonspeech oral motor treatment approaches for dysarthria: perspectives on a controversial clinical practice', in E. Strand (ed.), *Treatment of dysarthria: evidence-based practice*, Rockville, MD: American Speech-Language-Hearing Association, 25–32.

Hodge, M. 2010. 'Intervention for developmental dysarthria', in R. McCauley and S. McLeod (eds.), *Treatment of speech sound disorders in children*, Baltimore, MD: Brookes Publishing, 557–78.

Hodge, M. and Daniels, J. 2007. *Test of Children's Speech Plus (TOCS+)*, Edmonton, AB: University of Alberta.

Hodge, M. and Gotzke, C.L. 2010. 'Stability of intelligibility measures for children with dysarthria and cerebral palsy', *Journal of Medical Speech-Language Pathology* 18:4, 61–5.

Hodge, M. and Gotzke, C.L. 2011. 'Minimal pair distinctions and intelligibility in preschool children with and without speech sound disorders', *Clinical Linguistics & Phonetics* 25:10, 853–63.

Hodge, M. and Wellman, L. 1999. 'Management of children with dysarthria', in A. Caruso and E. Strand (eds.), *Clinical management of motor speech disorders in children*, New York: Thieme, 209–80.

Hodge, M. and Whitehill, T. 2010. 'Intelligibility impairments', in J.S. Damico, M.J. Ball and N. Müller (eds.), *Handbook of language and speech disorders*, Oxford: Wiley-Blackwell, 99–114.

Hodge, M., Brown, C. and Kuzyk, T. 2012. 'Predicting intelligibility scores of children with dysarthria and cerebral palsy from phonetic measures of speech accuracy', *Journal of Medical Speech-Language Pathology* 20:4, 41–6.

Hodge, S.M., Makris, N., Kennedy, D.N., Caviness, V.S., Howard, J., McGrath, L., Steele, S., Frazier, J.A., Tager-Flusberg, H. and Harris, G.J. 2010. 'Cerebellum, language, and cognition in autism and specific language impairment', *Journal of Autism and Developmental Disorders* 40:3, 300–16.

Hodges, J.R. 2001. 'Frontotemporal dementia (Pick's disease): clinical features and assessment', *Neurology* 56:Suppl 4, S6–S10.

Hodges, J.R. and Patterson, K. 1995. 'Is semantic memory consistently impaired early in the course of Alzheimer's disease? Neuroanatomical and diagnostic implications', *Neuropsychologia* 33:4, 441–59.

Hodges, J.R., Patterson, K., Graham, N. and Dawson, K. 1996. 'Naming and knowing in dementia of Alzheimer's type', *Brain and Language* 54:2, 302–25.

Hodges, J.R., Patterson, K., Oxbury, S. and Funnell, E. 1992b. 'Semantic dementia. Progressive fluent aphasia with temporal lobe atrophy', *Brain* 115:6, 1783–1806.

Hodges, J.R., Salmon, D.P. and Butters, N. 1992a. 'Semantic memory impairment in Alzheimer's disease: failure of access or degraded knowledge?', *Neuropsychologia* 30:4, 301–14.

Hodson, B.W. 2007. *Evaluating and enhancing children's phonological systems: research and theory to practice*, Wichita, KS: Phonocomp Publishers.

Hodson, B.W. and Paden, E.P. 1983. *Targeting intelligible speech: a phonological approach to remediation*, Boston, MA: College Hill.

Hoeft, F., Hernandez, A., McMillon, G., Taylor-Hill, H., Martindale, J.L., Meyler, A., Keller, T.A., Ting Siok, W., Deutsch, G.K., Just, M.A., Whitfield-Gabrieli, S. and Gabrieli, J.D.E. 2006. 'Neural basis of dyslexia: a comparison between dyslexic and nondyslexic children equated for reading ability', *Journal of Neuroscience* 26:42, 10700–8.

Hogan, V.M. 1973. 'A clarification of the surgical goals in cleft palate speech and the introduction of the lateral port control (LPC) pharyngeal flap', *Cleft Palate Journal* 10, 331–45.

Hogikyan, N.D. and Sethuraman, G. 1999. 'Validation of an instrument to measure voice-related quality of life (V-RQOL)', *Journal of Voice* 13:4, 557–69.

Holland, A.L. 1977. 'Some practical considerations in aphasia rehabilitation', in M. Sullivan and M. Kommers (eds.), *Rationale for adult aphasia therapy*, Omaha: University of Nebraska Medical Center, 167–80.

Holland, A.L. 1980. *Communication activities of daily living*, Austin, TX: Pro-Ed.

Holland, A.L. 1982a. 'When is aphasia aphasia? The problem of closed head injury', in R.H. Brookshire (ed.), *Clinical aphasiology conference proceedings*, Minneapolis: BRK Publishers, 345–9.

Holland, A.L. 1982b. 'Observing functional communication of aphasic adults', *Journal of Speech and Hearing Disorders* 47:1, 50–6.

Holland, A.L. 1991. 'Pragmatic aspects of intervention in aphasia', *Journal of Neurolinguistics* 6:2, 197–211.

Holland, A.L. 1998. 'Why can't clinicians talk to aphasic adults? Comments on supported conversation for adults with aphasia: methods and resources for training conversation partners', *Aphasiology* 12:9, 844–7.

Holland, A.L. 2007. 'Counselling/coaching in chronic aphasia: getting on with life', *Topics in Language Disorders* 27:4, 339–50.

Holland, A.L. and Beeson, P. 1999. 'Aphasia groups: the Arizona experience', in R. Elman (ed.), *Group treatment of neurogenic communication disorders: the expert clinician's approach*, Woburn, MA: Butterworth-Heinemann, 77–84.

Holland, A.L., Frattali, C. and Fromm, D. 1999. *Communication activities of daily living*, second edition, Austin, TX: Pro-Ed.

Holland, D. and Shigaki, C. 1998. 'Educating families and caretakers of traumatically brain injured patients in the new health care environment: a three phase model and bibliography', *Brain Injury* 12:12, 993–1009.

Hollich, G., Hirsh-Pasek, K. and Golinkoff, R. 2000. 'Breaking the language barrier: an emergentist coalition model of word learning', *Monographs of the Society for Research in Child Development* 65:3, 1–135.

Holmberg, E.B., Doyle, P., Perkell, J.S., Hammarberg, B. and Hillman, R.E. 2003. 'Aerodynamic and acoustic voice measurements of patients with vocal nodules: variation in baseline and changes across voice therapy', *Journal of Voice* 17:2, 269–82.

Holmberg, E.B., Hillman, R.E., Hammarberg, B., Sodersten, M. and Doyle, P. 2001. 'Efficacy of a behaviorally based voice therapy protocol for vocal nodules', *Journal of Voice* 15:3, 395–412.

Holtgraves, T. and McNamara, P. 2010. 'Pragmatic comprehension deficit in Parkinson's disease', *Journal of Clinical and Experimental Neuropsychology* 32:4, 388–97.

Holtzman, D.M., Morris, J.C. and Goate, A.M. 2011. 'Alzheimer's disease: the challenge of the second century', *Science Translational Medicine* 3:77, 77sr1.

Honein, M.A., Rasmussen, S.A., Reefhuis, J., Romitti, P., Lammer, E.J., Sun, L. and Correa, A. 2007. 'Maternal smoking, environmental tobacco smoke, and the risk of oral clefts', *Epidemiology* 18:2, 226–33.

Hong, C.H.L., Napeñas, J.J., Hodgson, B.D., Stokman, M.A., Mathers-Stauffer, V., Elting, L.S., Spijkervet, F.K.L. and Brennan, M.T. 2010. 'A systematic review of dental disease in patients undergoing cancer therapy', *Supportive Care in Cancer*, 18:8, 1007–21.

Hong, K.H. and Kim, Y.K. 1997. 'Phonatory characteristics of patients undergoing thyroidectomy without laryngeal nerve injury', *Otolaryngology – Head and Neck Surgery* 117:4, 399–404.

Honkalampi, K., Hintikka, J., Laukkanen, E., Lehtonen, J. and Viinamäki, H. 2001. 'Alexithymia and depression: a prospective study of patients with major depressive disorder', *Psychosomatics* 42:3, 229–34.

Honkalampi, K., Hintikka, J., Tanskanen, A., Lehtonen, J. and Viinamäki, H. 2000. 'Depression is strongly associated with alexithymia in the general population', *Journal of Psychosomatic Research* 48:1, 99–104.

Hooker, C. and Park, S. 2005. 'You must be looking at me: the nature of gaze perception in schizophrenia patients', *Cognitive Neuropsychiatry* 10:5, 327–45.

Hooper, S.R. and Tramontana, M.G. 1997. 'Advances in the neuropsychological bases of child and adolescent psychopathology: proposed models, findings, and ongoing issues', in T.H. Ollendick and R.J. Prinz (eds.), *Advances in clinical child psychology*, New York: Plenum, 133–75.

Hooper, S.R., Roberts, J.E., Zeisel, S.A. and Poe, M. 2003. 'Core language predictors of behavioral functioning in early elementary school children: concurrent and longitudinal findings', *Behavior Disorders* 29:1, 10–24.

Hoover, W. and Gough, P. 1990. 'The simple view of reading', *Reading and Writing* 2:2, 127–60.

Hopkins, M.J., Dywan, J. and Segalowitz, S.J. 2002. 'Altered electrodermal response to facial expression after closed head injury', *Brain Injury* 16:3, 245–57.

Horan, W.P., Kern, R.S., Green, M.F. and Penn, D.L. 2008. 'Social cognition training for individuals with schizophrenia: emerging evidence', *American Journal of Psychiatric Rehabilitation* 11:3, 205–52.

Horan, W.P., Kern, R.S., Shokat-Fadai, K., Sergi, M.J., Wynn, J.K. and Green, M.F. 2009. 'Social cognitive skills training in schizophrenia: an initial efficacy study of stabilized outpatients', *Schizophrenia Research* 107:1, 47–54.

Horowitz, S.M., Bility, K.M., Plichta, S.B., Leaf, P.J. and Haynes, N. 1998. 'Teacher assessment of children's behavioral disorders: demographic correlates', *American Journal of Orthopsychiatry* 68:1, 117–25.

Horton, S. and Byng, S. 2002. '"Semantic therapy" in day-to-day clinical practice: perspectives on diagnosis and therapy related to semantic impairments in aphasia', in A.E. Hillis (ed.), *The handbook of adult language disor-*

ders: integrating cognitive neuropsychology, neurology, and rehabilitation, New York: Psychology Press, 229–49.

Hough, M.S. and Klich, R.J. 1987. 'Effects of word length on lip EMG activity in apraxia of speech', *Clinical Aphasiology* 15, 271–6.

Howard, D. 1986. 'Beyond randomised controlled trials: the case for effective case studies of the effects of treatment in aphasia', *British Journal of Communication Disorders* 21:1, 89–102.

Howard, D. 2000. 'Cognitive neuropsychology and aphasia therapy: the case of word retrieval', in I. Papathanasiou (ed.), *Acquired neurogenic communication disorders*, London: Whurr Publishers, 76–99.

Howard, D. and Angus, J. 2001. 'Room acoustics: how they affect vocal production and perception', in P.H. Dejonckere (ed.), *Occupational voice: care and cure*, The Hague, The Netherlands: Kugler, 29–46.

Howard, D. and Hatfield, F.M. 1987. *Aphasia therapy: historical and contemporary issues*, London: Lawrence Erlbaum Associates.

Howard, D. and Patterson, K. 1992. *The pyramids and palm trees test*, Bury St Edmunds: Thames Valley.

Howard, D., Patterson, K.E., Franklin, S., Orchard-Lisle, V. and Morton, J. 1985. 'The facilitation of picture naming in aphasia', *Cognitive Neuropsychology* 2:1, 49–80.

Howe, T., Worrall, L. and Hickson, L. 2007. 'Interviews with people with aphasia: environmental factors that influence their community participation', *Aphasiology* 22:10, 1–26.

Howell, P., Au-Yeung, J. and Sackin, S. 1999. 'Exchange of stuttering from function words to content words with age', *Journal of Speech, Language, and Hearing Research* 42:2, 345–54.

Howell, S., Tripoliti, E. and Pring, T. 2009. 'Delivering the Lee Silverman Voice Treatment (LSVT) by web camera: a feasibility study', *International Journal of Language & Communication Disorders* 44:3, 287–300.

Howie, P.M., Tanner, S. and Andrews, G. 1981. 'Short- and long-term outcome in an intensive treatment program for adult stutterers', *Journal of Speech and Hearing Research* 46:1, 104–9.

Howlin, P. 1984. 'The acquisition of grammatical morphemes in autistic children: a critique and replication of the findings of Bartolucci, Pierce, and Streiner, 1980', *Journal of Autism and Developmental Disorders* 14:2, 127–36.

Howlin, P. 2003. 'Outcome in high-functioning adults with autism with and without early language delays: implications for the differentiation between autism and Asperger syndrome', *Journal of Autism and Developmental Disorders* 33:1, 3–13.

Howlin, P., Davies, M. and Udwin, O. 1998. 'Syndrome specific characteristics in Williams syndrome: to what extent do early behavioural patterns persist into adult life', *Journal of Applied Research in Intellectual Disabilities* 11:3, 207–26.

Howlin, P., Goode, S., Hutton, J. and Rutter, M. 2004. 'Adult outcome for children with autism', *Journal of Child Psychology and Psychiatry* 45:2, 212–29.

Howlin, P., Mawhood, L. and Rutter, M. 2000. 'Autism and developmental receptive language disorder – a follow-up comparison in early adult life. II: Social, behavioural, and psychiatric outcomes', *Journal of Child Psychology and Psychiatry* 41:5, 561–78.

Hsuing, M.W., Pai, L. and Wang, H.W. 2002. 'Correlation between voice handicap index and voice laboratory measurements in dysphonic patients', *European Archives of Otorhinolaryngology* 259:2, 169–74.

Huber, J., Bradley, K., Spiegler, B. and Dennis, M. 2007. 'Long-term neuromotor speech deficits in survivors of childhood posterior fossa tumours: effects of tumor type, radiation, age at diagnosis, and survival years', *Journal of Child Neurology* 22:7, 848–54.

Huber, J., Stathopoulos, E., Sussman, H., Darling, M., Snyder, S. and Richardson, K. 2012. *'Changes to physiology as a result of a new treatment, SpeechVive for individuals with Parkinson's disease'*, Conference on Motor Speech: Santa Rosa, CA, 29 February – 4 March 2012.

Hughes, C., Dunn, J. and White, A. 1998. 'Trick or treat?: uneven understanding of mind and emotion and executive dysfunction in "hard-to-manage" preschoolers', *Journal of Child Psychology and Psychiatry* 39:7, 981–94.

Hultman, C.S., Riski, J.E., Cohen, S.R., Burstein, F.D., Boydston, W.R., Hudgins, R.J., Grattan-Smith, D., Uhas, K. and Simms, C. 2000. 'Chiari malformation, cervical spine anomalies, and neurologic deficits in velocardiofacial syndrome', *Plastic and Reconstructive Surgery* 106:1, 16–24.

Humphreys, G.W. and Forde, E.M.E. 2001. 'Hierarchies, similarity, and interactivity in object-recognition: "Category-specific" neuropsychological deficits', *Behavioral and Brain Sciences* 24:3, 453–76.

Hundahl, S.A., Cady, B., Cunningham, M.P., Mazzaferri, E., McKee, R.F., Rosai, J., Shah, J.P., Fremgen, A.M., Stewart, A.K. and Hölzer, S. 2000. 'Initial results from a prospective cohort study of 5583 cases of thyroid carcinoma treated in the United States during 1996. U.S. and German Thyroid Cancer Study Group. An American College of Surgeons Commission on Cancer Patient Care Evaluation study', *Cancer* 89:1, 202–17.

Hunter, E.J., Tanner, K. and Smith, M.E. 2011. 'Gender differences affecting vocal health of women in vocally demanding careers', *Logopedics, Phoniatrics, Vocology* 36:3, 128–36.

Hurst, J.A., Baraitser, M., Auger, E., Graham, S. and Norell, S. 1990. 'An extended family with a dominantly inherited speech disorder', *Developmental Medicine and Child Neurology* 32:4, 352–5.

Hus, V., Pickles, A., Cook, E.H., Risi, S. and Lord, C. 2007. 'Using the autism diagnostic interview – revised to increase phenotypic homogeneity in genetic studies of autism', *Biological Psychiatry* 61:4, 438–48.

Huskie, C.F. and Jackson, I.T. 1977. 'The sphincter pharyngoplasty: a new approach to the speech problem of velopharyngeal incompetence', *British Journal of Disorders of Communication* 12:1, 31–5.

Hustad, K.C. 2012. 'Speech intelligibility in children with speech disorders', *Perspectives on Language Learning and Education* 19:1, 7–11.

Hustad, K.C. and Garcia, J.M. 2005. 'Aided and unaided speech supplementation strategies: effect of alphabet cues and iconic hand gestures on dysarthric speech', *Journal of Speech, Language, and Hearing Research* 48:5, 996–1012.

Hustad, K.C. and Weismer, G. 2007. 'Interventions to improve intelligibility and communicative success for speakers with dysarthria', in G. Weismer (ed.), *Motor speech disorders*, San Diego, CA: Plural Publishing, 261–303.

Hustad, K.C., Gorton, K. and Lee, J. 2010. 'Classification of speech and language profiles in 4-year-old children with cerebral palsy: a prospective preliminary study', *Journal of Speech, Language, and Hearing Research* 53:6, 1496–513.

Hustad, K.C., Schueler, B., Schulz, L. and DuHadway, C. 2012. 'Intelligibility of 4-year-old children with and without cerebral palsy', *Journal of Speech, Language, and Hearing Research* 55:4, 1177–89.

Hyder, A.A., Wunderlich, C.A., Puvanachandra, P., Gururaj, G. and Kobusingye, O.C. 2007. 'The impact of traumatic brain injuries: a global perspective', *NeuroRehabilitation* 22:5, 341–53.

Hynes, W. 1951. 'Pharyngoplasty by muscle transposition', *British Journal of Plastic Surgery* 3, 128–35.

Hynes, W. 1953. 'The results of pharyngoplasty by muscle transplantation in "failed cleft palate" cases, with special reference to the influence of the pharynx on voice production', *Annals of the Royal College of Surgeons of England* 13:1, 17–35.

Iacono, T.A. and Duncum, J.E. 1995. 'Comparison of sign alone and in combination with an electronic communication device in early language intervention: case study', *AAC: Augmentative and Alternative Communication* 11:4, 249–59.

Ibarretxe-Bilbao, N., Ramirez-Ruiz, B., Junque, C., Marti, M.J., Valldeoriola, F., Bargallo, N., Juanes, S. and Tolosa, E. 2010. 'Differential progression of brain atrophy in Parkinson's disease with and without visual hallucinations', *Journal of Neurology, Neurosurgery and Psychiatry* 81:6, 650–7.

Iles, J., Walsh, V. and Richardson, A. 2000. 'Visual search performance in dyslexia', *Dyslexia* 6:3, 163–77.

Imai, S. and Michi, K. 1992. 'Articulatory function after resection of the tongue and floor of the mouth: palatometric and perceptual evaluation', *Journal of Speech and Hearing Research* 35:1, 68–78.

Im-Bolter, N., Johnson, J. and Pascual-Leone, J. 2006. 'Processing limitations in children with specific language impairment: the role of executive function', *Child Development* 77:6, 1822–41.

Individuals with Disabilities Education Improvement Act. 2004. 20 U.S.C. 1400 et seq. (2004) (reauthorization of Individuals with Disabilities Education Act 1990).

Ingham, R.J. and Onslow, M. 1985. 'Measurement and modification of speech naturalness during stuttering therapy', *Journal of Speech and Hearing Research* 50:3, 261–81.

Ingham, R.J., Bothe, A.K., Wang, Y., Purkhiser, K. and New, A. 2012. 'Phonation interval modification and speech performance quality during fluency-inducing conditions by adults who stutter', *Journal of Communication Disorders* 45:3, 198–211.

Ingham, R.J., Kilgo, M., Ingham, J.C., Moglia, R., Belknap, H. and Sanchez, T. 2001. 'Evaluation of a stuttering treatment based on reduction of short phonation intervals', *Journal of Speech, Language, and Hearing Research* 44:6, 1229–44.

Ingham, R.J., Moglia, R.A., Frank, P., Ingham, J.C. and Cordes, A.K. 1997. 'Experimental investigation of the effects of frequency-altered auditory feedback on the speech of adults who stutter', *Journal of Speech, Language, and Hearing Research* 40:2, 361–72.

Ingles, J.L. and Eskes, G.A. 2008. 'A comparison of letter and digit processing in letter-by-letter reading', *Journal of the International Neuropsychological Society* 14:1, 164–73.

Ingram, D. 2012. 'Prologue: cross-linguistic and multilingual aspects of speech sound disorders in children', in

S. McLeod and B.A. Goldstein (eds.), *Multilingual aspects of speech sound disorders in children*, Bristol, UK: Multilingual Matters, 3–12.

International Dyslexia Association. 2007. *Framework for informed reading and language instruction: matrix of multisensory structured language programs* (online, available at: www.interdys.org/ewebeditpro5/upload/MSL2007finalR1.pdf; last accessed 12 June 2013).

International Dyslexia Association 2009. *IDA position statement: dyslexia treatment programs* (online, available at: www.interdys.org/ewebeditpro5/upload/IDA_Position_Statement_Dyslexia_Treatment_Programs_template(1).pdf; last accessed 12 June 2013).

Irwin, O. 1968. 'Correct status of vowels and consonants in the speech of children with cerebral palsy as measured by an integrated test', *Cerebral Palsy Journal* 29:1, 9–15.

Ishikawa, K. and Thibeault, S. 2010. 'Voice rest versus exercise: a review of the literature', *Journal of Voice* 24:4, 379–87.

Isshiki, N. 1989. *Phonosurgery: theory and practice*, Tokyo: Springer-Verlag.

Isshiki, N., Haji, R., Yamamoto, Y. and Mathieu, H.F. 2001. 'Thyroplasty for adductor spasmodic dysphonia: further experiences', *Laryngoscope* 111:4, 615–21.

Isshiki, N., Tsuji, D.H., Yamamoto, Y. and Izuka, Y. 2000. 'Midline lateralization thyroplasty for adductor spasmodic dysphonia', *Annals of Otolaryngology, Rhinology and Laryngology* 109:2, 187–93.

Itoh, M., Sasanuma, S., Hirose, H., Yoshioka, H. and Ushijima, T. 1980. 'Abnormal articulatory dynamics in a patient with apraxia of speech: X-ray microbeam observation', *Brain and Language* 11:1, 66–75.

Iverach, L., Jones, M., Menzies, R., O'Brian, S., Packman, A. and Onslow, M. 2011. 'Response to Walter Manning and J. Gayle Beck: comments concerning Iverach, Jones et al. (2009a)', *Journal of Fluency Disorders* 36:1, 66–71.

Iverach, L., Jones, M., O'Brian, S., Block, S., Lincoln, M., Harrison, E., Hewat, S., Menzies, R.G., Packman, A. and Onslow, M. 2009a. 'Screening for personality disorders among adults seeking speech treatment for stuttering', *Journal of Fluency Disorders* 34:3, 173–86.

Iverach, L., Jones, M., O'Brian, S., Block, S., Lincoln, M., Harrison, E., Hewat, S., Cream, A., Menzies, R.G., Packman, A. and Onslow, M. 2009b. 'The relationship between mental health disorders and treatment outcomes among adults who stutter', *Journal of Fluency Disorders* 34:1, 29–43.

Iverach, L., O'Brian, S., Jones, M., Block, S., Lincoln, M., Harrison, E., Hewat, S., Menzies, R.G., Packman, A. and Onslow, M. 2010. 'The five factor model of personality applied to adults who stutter', *Journal of Communication Disorders* 43:2, 120–32.

Izdebski, K., Reed, C.G., Ross, J.C. and Hilsinger, R.L. 1994. 'Problems with tracheoesophageal fistula voice restoration in totally laryngectomized patients: a review of 95 cases', *Archives of Otolaryngology – Head and Neck Surgery* 120:8, 840–5.

Izdebski, K., Ward, R.R. and Dedo, H.H. 1999. 'Voice therapy following surgical (or chemical) treatment for adductor spasmodic dysphonia', *Phonoscope* 2:3, 149–58.

Jackson, H. [1893]1915. 'Words and other symbols in mentation', *Brain* 38:1–2, 175–86.

Jackson, I.T. and Silverton, J.S. 1977. 'The sphincter pharyngoplasty as a secondary procedure in cleft palates', *Plastic and Reconstructive Surgery* 59:4, 518–24.

Jacobson, B.H., Johnson, A., Grywalski, C., Silbergleit, A., Jacobson, G., Benninger, M.S. and Newman, C.W. 1997. 'The voice handicap index (VHI): development and validation', *American Journal of Speech-Language Pathology* 6:3, 66–70.

Jacobson, E. 1938. *Progressive relaxation*, second edition, Chicago: University of Chicago.

Jacobson, M.C., Franssen, E., Fliss, D.M., Birt, B.D. and Gilbert, R.W. 1995. 'Free forearm flap in oral reconstruction: functional outcome', *Archives of Otolaryngology – Head and Neck Surgery* 121:9, 959–64.

Jacoby, G.P., Levin, L., Lee, L., Creaghead, N.A. and Kummer, A.W. 2002. 'The number of individual treatment units necessary to facilitate functional communication improvements in the speech and language of young children', *American Journal of Speech-Language Pathology* 11:4, 370–80.

Jacques, S. and Zelazo, P.D. 2005. 'Language and the development of cognitive flexibility: implications for theory of mind', in J.W. Astington and J.A. Baird (eds.), *Why language matters for theory of mind*, New York: Oxford University Press, 144–62.

Jamadar, S., Powers, N.R., Meda, S.A., Gelernter, J., Gruen, J.R. and Pearlson, G.D. 2011. 'Genetic influences of cortical gray matter in language-related regions in healthy controls and schizophrenia', *Schizophrenia Research* 129:2–3, 141–8.

Jankovic, J. 2008. 'Parkinson's disease: clinical features and diagnosis', *Journal of Neurology, Neurosurgery and Psychiatry* 79:4, 368–76.

Jarrold, C. and Baddeley, A.D. 1997. 'Short-term memory for verbal and visuospatial information in Down's syndrome', *Cognitive Neuropsychiatry* 2:2, 101–22.

Jarrold, C., Baddeley, A.D. and Hewes, A.K. 2000a. 'Verbal short-term memory deficits in Down syndrome: a consequence of problems in rehearsal?', *Journal of Child Psychology and Psychiatry* 41:2, 233–44.

Jarrold, C., Baddeley, A.D. and Phillips, C.E. 2002. 'Verbal short-term memory deficits in Down syndrome: a problem of memory, audition or speech?', *Journal of Speech, Language, and Hearing Research* 45:3, 531–44.

Jarrold, C., Hartley, S.J., Phillips, C. and Baddeley, A.D. 2000b. 'Word fluency in Williams syndrome: evidence for unusual semantic organisation?', *Cognitive Neuropsychology* 5:4, 293–319.

Järvinen-Pasley, A., Peppé, S., King-Smith, G. and Heaton, P. 2008. 'The relationship between form and function level receptive prosodic abilities in autism', *Journal of Autism and Developmental Disorders* 38:7, 1328–40.

Jeanner, P.-Y., Marcoz, P., Kuntzer, T. and Roulet-Perez, E. 2008. 'Isolated facial and bulbar paresis: a persistent manifestation of neonatal myasthenia gravis', *Neurology* 70:3, 237–8.

Jefferies, E. and Lambon Ralph, M.A. 2006. 'Semantic impairment in stroke aphasia versus semantic dementia: a case-series comparison', *Brain* 129:8, 2132–47.

Jefferies, E., Patterson, K. and Lambon Ralph, M.A. 2006. 'The natural history of late-stage "pure" semantic dementia', *Neurocase* 12:1, 1–14.

Jellinger, K.A. 2008. 'Morphologic diagnosis of "vascular dementia" – a critical update', *Journal of the Neurological Sciences* 270:1–2, 1–12.

Jiang, J.J., Diaz, C.E. and Hanson, D.B. 1998. 'Fine element modeling of vocal fold vibration in normal phonation and hyperfunctional dysphonia: implications for the pathogenesis of vocal nodules', *Annals of Otology, Rhinology and Laryngology* 107:7, 603–10.

Jicha, G.A., Parisi, J.E., Dickson, D.W., Johnson, K., Cha, R., Ivnik, R.J., Tangalos, E.G., Boeve, B.F., Knopman, D.S., Braak, H. and Petersen, R.C. 2006. 'Neuropathologic outcome of mild cognitive impairment following progression to clinical dementia', *Archives of Neurology* 63:5, 674–81.

Jissendi-Tchofo, P., Pandit, F., Vallée, L., Vinchon, M., Pruvo, J.P., Baleriaux, D. and Soto Ares, G. 2012. 'Brain regional glucose uptake changes in isolated cerebellar cortical dysplasia: qualitative assessment using coregistrated FDG-PET/MRI', *Cerebellum* 11:1, 280–8.

Joanette, Y. and Ansaldo, A.I. 1999. 'Clinical note: acquired pragmatic impairments and aphasia', *Brain and Language* 68:3, 529–34.

Joanette, Y., Goulet, P. and Daoust, H. 1990. 'Incidence et profils des troubles de la communication verbale chez les cérébrolésés droits' (online, available at: rnp.resodys.org/IMG/pdf/Incidence_et_profils_des_.pdf; last accessed 12 June 2013).

Joanette, Y., Keller, E. and Lecours, A.R. 1980. 'Sequences of phonemic approximations in aphasia', *Brain and Language* 11:1, 30–44.

Joanette, Y., Ska, B. and Côté, H. 2004. *Protocole Montréal d'évaluation de la communication*, Isbergues, France: Ortho Edition.

Jodzio, K., Lojek, E. and Bryan, K. 2005. 'Functional and neuroanatomical analysis of extralinguistic disorders in right hemisphere-damaged patients', *Psychology of Language and Communication* 9:1, 55–73.

Joffe, B. and Reilly, S. 2004. 'The evidence base of the evaluation and management of motor speech disorders in children', in S. Reilly, J. Douglas and J. Oates (eds.), *Evidence-based practice in speech pathology*, London: Whurr, 219–57.

Joffe, V. and Varlocosta, S. 2007. 'Patterns of syntactic development in children with Williams syndrome and Down's syndrome: evidence from passives and wh-questions', *Clinical Linguistics & Phonetics* 21:9, 705–27.

Johansson, K., Fredrikson, S., Hartelius, L. and Schalling, E. 2012. 'Effects of EMST (expiratory muscle strength training) on speech and respiration in individuals with multiple sclerosis', Conference on Motor Speech: Santa Rosa, CA, 29 February – 4 March 2012.

John, A.E., Rowe, M.L. and Mervis, C.B. 2009. 'Referential communication skills of children with Williams syndrome: understanding when messages are not adequate', *American Journal on Intellectual and Developmental Disabilities* 114:2, 85–99.

Johnson, C.J., Beitchman, J.H. and Brownlie, E.B. 2010. 'Twenty-year follow-up of children with and without speech-language impairments: family, educational, occupational, and quality of life outcomes', *American Journal of Speech-Language Pathology* 19:1, 51–65.

Johnson, D. and Newton, A. 1987. 'Social adjustment and interaction after severe head injury: II. Rationale and bases for intervention', *British Journal of Clinical Psychology* 26:4, 289–98.

Johnson, E.P., Pennington, B.F., Lee, N.R. and Boada, R. 2009. 'Directional effects between rapid auditory processing and phonological awareness in children', *Journal of Child Psychology and Psychiatry* 50:8, 902–10.

Johnson, K.N., Walden, T.A., Conture, E.G. and Karrass, J. 2010. 'Spontaneous regulation of emotions in preschool children who stutter: preliminary findings', *Journal of Speech, Language, and Hearing Research* 53:6, 1478–95.

Johnson, N. 2001. 'Tobacco use and oral cancer: a global perspective', *Journal of Dental Education* 65:4, 328–39.

Johnson, W. 1956. 'Stuttering', in W. Johnson, S.J. Brown, J.J. Curtis, C.W. Edney and J. Keaster (eds.), *Speech handicapped school children*, New York: Harper & Bros, 202–300.

Johnston, J., Miller, J. and Tallal, P. 2001. 'Use of cognitive state predicates by language-impaired children', *International Journal of Language & Communication Disorders* 36:3, 349–70.

Jolliffe, T. and Baron-Cohen, S. 2000. 'Linguistic processing in high-functioning adults with autism or Asperger's syndrome. Is global coherence impaired', *Psychological Medicine* 30:5, 1169–87.

Jones, G., Tamburelli, M., Watson, S.E., Gobet, R. and Pine, J.M. 2010. 'Lexicality and frequency in specific language impairment: accuracy and error data from two nonword repetition tests', *Journal of Speech, Language, and Hearing Research* 53:6, 1642–55.

Jones, K.L. and Smith, D.W. 1975. 'The Williams elfin facies syndrome: a new perspective', *Journal of Paediatrics* 86:5, 718–23.

Jones, M., Onslow, M., Packman, A., O'Brian, S., Hearne, A., Williams, S., Ormond, T. and Schwarz, I. 2008. 'Extended follow-up of a randomized controlled trial of the Lidcombe program of early stuttering intervention', *International Journal of Language & Communication Disorders* 43:6, 649–61.

Jones, M., Onslow, M., Packman, A., Williams, S., Ormond, T., Schwarz, I. and Gebski, V. 2005. 'Randomised controlled trial of the Lidcombe programme of early stuttering intervention', *British Medical Journal* 331:7518, 659.

Jones, S., Laukka, E.J. and Backman, L. 2006. 'Differential verbal fluency deficits in the preclinical stages of Alzheimer's disease and vascular dementia', *Cortex* 42:3, 347–55.

Jones, W., Bellugi, U., Lai, Z., Chiles, M., Reilly, J., Lincoln, A. and Adolphs, R. 2000. 'Hypersociability in Williams syndrome', *Journal of Cognitive Neuroscience* 12:S1, 30–46.

Jones, W., Hesselink, J.R., Courchesne, E., Duncan, T., Matsuda, K. and Bellugi, U. 2002. 'Cerebellar abnormalities in infants and toddlers with Williams syndrome', *Developmental Medicine and Child Neurology* 44:10, 688–94.

Jonkers, R. 1998. *Comprehension and production of verbs in aphasic speakers*, University of Groningen: Groningen Dissertations in Linguistics (GRODIL).

Jonkers, R. and Bastiaanse, R. 2007. 'Action naming in anomic speakers: effects of instrumentality and name relation', *Brain and Language* 102:3, 262–72.

Jordan, L.C. and Hillis, A.E. 2006. 'Disorders of speech and language: aphasia, apraxia and dysarthria', *Current Opinion in Neurology* 19:6, 580.

Jorgensen, M. and Togher, L. 2009. 'Narrative after traumatic brain injury: a comparison of monologic and jointly-produced discourse', *Brain Injury* 23:9, 727–40.

Joseph, R.M., Tager-Flusberg, H. and Lord, C. 2002. 'Cognitive profiles and social-communicative functioning in children with autism spectrum disorder', *Journal of Child Psychology and Psychiatry* 43:6, 807–21.

Josephs, K.A., Duffy, J.R., Fossett, T.R., Strand, E.A., Claassen, D.O. and Whitwell, J.L. 2010. 'Fluorodeoxyglucose F18 positron emission tomography in progressive apraxia of speech and primary progressive aphasia variants', *Archives of Neurology* 67:5, 596–605.

Josephs, K.A., Duffy, J.R., Strand, E.A., Machulda, M.M., Senjem, M.L., Master, A.V., Lowe, V.J., Jack Jr, C.R. and Whitwell, J.L. 2012. 'Characterizing a neurodegenerative syndrome: primary progressive apraxia of speech', *Brain* 135:5, 1522–36.

Josephs, K.A., Duffy, J.R., Strand, E.A., Whitwell, J.L., Layton, K.F., Parisi, J.E., Hauser, M.F., Witte, M.F., Boeve, B.F., Knopman, D.S., Dickson, D.W., Jack, C.R. and Petersen, R.C. 2006. 'Clinicopathological and imaging correlates of progressive aphasia and apraxia of speech', *Brain* 129:6, 1385–98.

Joy, J.E. and Johnston, R.B. 2001. *Multiple sclerosis: current status and strategies for the future*, Washington, DC: National Academy Press.

Jung-Beeman, M. 2005. 'Bilateral brain processes for comprehending natural language', *Trends in Cognitive Sciences* 9:11, 512–18.

Justice, L., Mashburn, A., Pence, K. and Wiggins, A. 2008. 'Experimental evaluation of preschool language curriculum: influence on children's expressive language skills', *Journal of Speech, Language, and Hearing Research* 51:4, 983–1001.

Kagan, A. 1998. 'Supported conversation for adults with aphasia: methods and resources for training conversation partners', *Aphasiology* 12:9, 816–30.

Kagan, A., Black, S., Duchan, J., Simmons-Mackie, N. and Square, P. 2001. 'Training volunteers as conversation partners using "supported conversation for adults with aphasia" (SCA): a controlled trial', *Journal of Speech, Language, and Hearing Research*, 44:3, 624–38.

Kagan, A., Simmons-Mackie, N., Rowland, A., Huijbregts, M., Shumway, E., McEwen, S., Threats, T. and Sharp, S. 2008. 'Counting what counts: a framework for capturing real-life outcomes of aphasia intervention', *Aphasiology* 22:3, 258–80.

Kagan, A., Simmons-Mackie, N., Victor, J.C., Carling-Rowland, A., Hoch, J., Huijbregts, M., Streiner, D. and Mok, A. 2010. *Assessment for living with aphasia (ALA)*, Toronto, Canada: The Aphasia Institute.

Kagel, M.C. and Leopold, N.A. 1992. 'Dysphagia in Huntington's disease: a 16 year retrospective', *Dysphagia* 7:2, 106–14.

Kahane, J.C. 1983. 'Postnatal development and aging of the human larynx', *Seminars in Speech and Language* 4:3, 189–203.

Kahlaoui, K., Scherer, L.C. and Joanette, Y. 2008. 'The right hemisphere's contribution to the processing of semantic relationships between words', *Language and Linguistics Compass* 2:4, 550–68.

Kail, R. and Salthouse, T. 1994. 'Processing speed as a mental capacity', *Acta Psychologica* 86:2–3, 199–225.

Kaiser, A.P. and Hester, P.P. 1996. 'How everyday environments support children's communication', in L. Koegel, R.L. Dunlap and L.G. Koegel (eds.), *Positive behavioral support: including people with difficult behavior in the community*, Baltimore, MD: Paul H Brookes Publishing, 145–62.

Kaiser, A.P., Hester, P.P. and McDuffie, A.S. 2001. 'Supporting communication in young children with developmental disabilities', *Mental Retardation and Developmental Disabilities Research Reviews* 7:2, 143–50.

Kalinowski, J., Saltuklaroglu, T., Stuart, A. and Guntupalli, V.K. 2007. 'On the importance of scientific rhetoric in stuttering: a reply to Finn, Bothe, and Bramlett (2005)', *American Journal of Speech-Language Pathology* 16:1, 69–76.

Kambanaros, M. and van Steenbrugge, W. 2006. 'Noun and verb processing in Greek-English bilingual individuals with anomic aphasia and the effect of instrumentality and verb-noun name relation', *Brain and Language* 97:2, 162–77.

Kambanaros, M., Messinis, L., Georgiou, V. and Papathanassopoulos, P. 2010. 'Action and object naming in schizophrenia', *Journal of Clinical and Experimental Neuropsychology* 32:10, 1083–94.

Kamio, Y. and Toichi, M. 2000. 'Dual access to semantics in autism: is pictorial access superior to verbal access?', *Journal of Child Psychology and Psychiatry* 41:7, 859–67.

Kamio, Y., Robins, D., Kelley, E., Swainson, B. and Fein, D. 2007. 'Atypical lexical/semantic processing in high-functioning autism spectrum disorders without early language delay', *Journal of Autism and Developmental Disorders* 37:6, 1116–22.

Kandhadai, P. and Federmeier, K.D. 2008. 'Summing it up: semantic activation processes in the two hemispheres as revealed by event-related potentials', *Brain Research* 1233, 146–59.

Kanner, L. 1943. 'Autistic disturbances of affective contact', *Nervous Child* 2, 217–50.

Kaplan, P.S., Bachorowski, J., Smoski, M.J. and Hudenko, W.J. 2002. 'Infants of depressed mothers, although competent learners, fail to learn in response to their own mothers' infant-directed speech', *Psychological Sciences* 13:3, 268–71.

Karasinski, C. and Ellis Weismer, S. 2010. 'Comprehension of inferences in discourse processing by adolescents with and without language impairment', *Journal of Speech, Language, and Hearing Research* 53:5, 1268–79.

Karmiloff-Smith, A. 1994. *Beyond modularity: a developmental perspective on cognitive science*, Cambridge, MA: MIT Press.

Karmiloff-Smith, A. 1998. 'Development itself is the key to understanding developmental disorders', *Trends in Cognitive Neurosciences* 2:10, 389–98.

Karmiloff-Smith, A. 2011. 'Brain: the neuroconstructivist approach', in E.K. Farran and A. Karmiloff-Smith (eds.), *Neurodevelopmental disorders across the lifespan: a neuroconstructivist approach*, Oxford University Press, 37–58.

Karnell, M.P. and Van Demark, D.R. 1986. 'Longitudinal speech performance in patients with cleft palate: comparisons based on secondary management', *Cleft Palate Journal* 23:4, 278–88.

Karniol, R. 1995. 'Stuttering, language, and cognition: a review and a model of stuttering as suprasegmental sentence plan alignment (SPA)', *Psychological Bulletin* 117:1, 104–24.

Karrass, J., Walden, T.A., Conture, E.G., Graham, C.G., Arnold, H.S., Hartfield, K.N. and Schwenk, K.A. 2006. 'Relation of emotional reactivity and regulation to childhood stuttering', *Journal of Communication Disorders* 39:6, 402–23.

Kasari, C. and Bauminger, N. 1998. 'Social and emotional development in children with mental retardation', in J.A. Burack, R.M. Hodapp and E. Ziegler (eds.), *Handbook of mental retardation and development*, New York: Cambridge University Press, 411–33.

Kaszuba, S.M. and Garrett, C.G. 2009. 'Strobovideolaryngoscopy and laboratory voice evaluation', *Otolaryngologic Clinics of North America* 40:5, 991–1001.

Kataria, S., Goldstein, D.J. and Kushnik, T. 1984. 'Developmental delays in Williams ("elfin facies") syndrome', *Applied Research in Mental Retardation* 5:4, 419–23.

Katz, W., Machetanz, J., Orth, U. and Schonle, P. 1990. 'A kinematic analysis of anticipatory coarticulation in the speech of anterior aphasic subjects using electromagnetic articulography', *Brain and Language* 38:4, 555–75.

Kauffman, J.M. and Landrum, T.J. 2013. *Characteristics of emotional and behavioral disorders of children and youth*, 10th edition, Upper Saddle River, NJ: Merrill.

Kaufman, A.S. and Kaufman, N. 2004. *Kaufman test of educational achievement*-second edition, comprehensive form, Bloomington, MN: Pearson.

Kay, J., Lesser, R. and Coltheart, M. 1992. *PALPA: psycholinguistic assessments of language processing in aphasia*, Hove, East Sussex: Lawrence Erlbaum Associates.

Kay-Raining Bird, E., Chapman, R.S. and Schwartz, S. 2004. 'Fast mapping of words and story recall by children with Down syndrome', *Journal of Speech, Language, and Hearing Research* 47:6, 1286–1300.

Kazdin, A.E. 1993. 'Treatment of conduct disorders: progress and directions in psychotherapy', *Development and Psychopathology* 5:1–2, 277–310.

Keating, P. and Shattuck-Hufnagel, S. 2002. 'A prosodic view of word form encoding for speech production', *UCLA Working Papers in Phonetics* 101, 112–56.

Kehagia, A.A., Barker, R.A. and Robbins, T.W. 2010. 'Neuropsychological and clinical heterogeneity of cognitive impairment and dementia in patients with Parkinson's disease', *Lancet Neurology* 9:12, 1200–13.

Keith, R. 1999. 'Clinical issues in central auditory processing disorders', *Language, Speech, and Hearing Services in Schools* 30:4, 339–44.

Keith, R.L., Shanks, J.C. and Doyle, P.C. 2005. 'Historical highlights: laryngectomy rehabilitation', in P.C. Doyle and R.L. Keith (eds.), *Contemporary considerations in the treatment and rehabilitation of head and neck cancer*, Austin: Pro-Ed, 17–57.

Kelley, E., Paul, J.J., Fein, D. and Naigles, L.R. 2006. 'Residual language deficits in optimal outcome children with a history of autism' *Journal of Autism and Developmental Disorders* 36:6, 807–28.

Kelly, H., Brady, M.C. and Enderby, P. 2010. 'Speech and language therapy for aphasia following stroke', *Cochrane Database of Systematic Reviews*, Issue 5, CD000425.

Kelly, L.E. 2007. 'Radiation and chemotherapy', in E.C. Ward and C.J. van As-Brooks (eds.), *Head and neck cancer: treatment, rehabilitation, and outcomes*, San Diego, CA: Plural Publishing, Inc., 57–86.

Kemmerer, D. and Tranel, D. 2000a. 'Verb retrieval in brain-damaged subjects: 1. Analysis of stimulus, lexical, and conceptual factors', *Brain and Language* 73:3, 347–92.

Kemmerer, D. and Tranel, D. 2000b. 'Verb retrieval in brain-damaged subjects: 2. Analysis of errors', *Brain and Language* 73:3, 393–420.

Kempler, D. and Goral, M. 2008. 'Language and dementia: neuropsychological aspects', *Annual Review of Applied Linguistics* 28, 73–90.

Kempler, D., Almor, A., Tyler, L.K., Andersen, E.S. and MacDonald, M.C. 1998. 'Sentence comprehension deficits in Alzheimer's disease: a comparison of off-line vs. on-line sentence processing', *Brain and Language* 64:3, 297–316.

Kempster, G.B., Gerratt, B.R., Verdolini Abbott, K., Barkmeier-Kramer, J. and Hillman, R.E. 2009. 'Consensus auditory-perceptual evaluation of voice: development of a standardized clinical protocol', *American Journal of Speech-Language Pathology* 18:2, 124–32.

Kendeou, P., Savage, R. and van den Broek, P. 2009. 'Revisiting the simple view of reading', *British Journal of Educational Psychology* 79:2, 353–70.

Kennedy, M.R.T., Strand, E., Burton, W. and Peterson, C. 1994a. 'Analysis of first-encounter conversations of right-hemisphere-damaged adults', *Clinical Aphasiology* 22, 67–80.

Kennedy, M.R.T., Strand, E.A. and Yorkston, K.M. 1994b. 'Selected acoustic changes in the verbal repairs of dysarthric speakers', *Journal of Medical Speech-Language Pathology* 2:4, 263–80.

Kent, R.D. 1996. 'Hearing and believing: some limits to the auditory-perceptual assessment of speech and voice disorders', *American Journal of Speech-Language Pathology* 5:3, 7–23.

Kent, R.D. 1997. 'Gestural phonology: basic concepts and applications in speech-language pathology', in M.J. Ball and R.D. Kent (eds.), *The new phonologies: developments in clinical linguistics*, San Diego, CA: Singular, 247–68.

Kent, R.D. 2000. 'Research on speech motor control and its disorders: a review and prospective', *Journal of Communication Disorders* 33:5, 391–428.

Kent, R.D. 2004. 'The uniqueness of speech among motor systems', *Clinical Linguistics & Phonetics* 18:6–8, 495–505.

Kent, R.D. and Kent, J.F. 2000. 'Task-based profiles of the dysarthrias', *Folia Phoniatrica et Logopaedica* 52:1–3, 48–53.

Kent, R.D. and Kim, Y.J. 2003. 'Toward an acoustic typology of motor speech disorders', *Clinical Linguistics & Phonetics* 17:6, 427–45.

Kent, R.D. and Kim, Y.J. 2011. 'The assessment of intelligibility in motor speech disorders', in A. Lowit and R.D. Kent (eds.), *Assessment of motor speech disorders*, San Diego, CA: Plural Publishing, 21–38.

Kent, R.D. and Moll, K.L. 1975. 'Articulatory timing in selected consonant sequences', *Brain and Language* 2, 304–23.

Kent, R.D. and Rosen, K. 2004. 'Motor control perspectives on motor speech disorders', in B. Maassen, R. Kent, H. Peters, P.V. Lieshout and W. Hulstijn (eds.), *Speech motor control in normal and disordered speech*, New York: Oxford University Press, 285–311.

Kent, R.D. and Rosenbek, J.C. 1983. 'Acoustic patterns of apraxia of speech', *Journal of Speech and Hearing Research* 26:2, 231–49.

Kent, R.D., Kent, J.F. and Rosenbek, J.C. 1987. 'Maximum performance tests of speech production', *Journal of Speech and Hearing Disorders* 52:4, 367–87.

Kent, R.D., Kent, J.F., Duffy, J. and Weismer, G. 1998. 'The dysarthrias: speech-voice profiles, related dysfunctions, and neuropathology', *Journal of Medical Speech-Language Pathology* 6, 165–211.

Kent, R.D., Kent, J.F., Weismer, G. and Duffy, J.R. 2000. 'What dysarthrias can tell us about the neural control of speech', *Journal of Phonetics* 28:3, 273–302.

Kent, R.D., Weismer, G., Kent, J.F. and Rosenbek, J.C. 1989. 'Toward phonetic intelligibility testing in dysarthria', *Journal of Speech and Hearing Disorders* 54:4, 482–99.

Kertesz, A. 1981. 'Evolution of aphasic syndromes', *Topics in Language Disorders* 1:4, 15–27.

Kertesz, A. 1984. *Subcortical lesions and verbal apraxia*, San Diego, CA: College Hill Press.

Kertesz, A. 2006. *Western aphasia battery – revised*, San Antonio, TX: Pearson.

Kertesz, A. and Sheppard, B. 1981. 'The epidemiology of aphasic and cognitive impairment in stroke – age, sex, aphasia type and laterality differences', *Brain* 104:1, 117–28.

Kertesz, A., Jesso, S., Harciarek, M., Blair, M. and McMonagle, P. 2010. 'What is semantic dementia?: a cohort study of diagnostic features and clinical boundaries', *Archives of Neurology* 67:4, 483–9.

Kertesz, A., Martinez-Lage, P., Davidson, W. and Munoz, D.G. 2000. 'The corticobasal degeneration syndrome overlaps progressive aphasia and frontotemporal dementia', *Neurology* 55:9, 1368–75.

Kessler, R.C., Berglund, P., Demler, O., Jin, R., Merikangas, K.R. and Waters, E.E. 2005. 'Lifetime prevalence and age-of-onset distributions of DSM-IV disorders in the National Comorbidity Survey Replication', *Archives of General Psychiatry* 62:6, 593–602.

Kiehl, K.A. 2006. 'A cognitive neuroscience perspective on psychopathy: evidence for paralimbic system dysfunction', *Psychiatry Research* 142:2–3, 107–28.

Kier, W.M. and Smith, K.E. 1985. 'Tongues, tentacles and trunks: the biomechanics of movement in muscular hydrostats', *Zoological Journal of the Linnean Society* 83:4, 307–24.

Kim, J.H., Lee, S.J., Rim, H.D., Kim, H.W., Bae, G.Y. and Chang, S.M. 2008. 'The relationship between alexithymia and general symptoms of patients with depressive disorders', *Psychiatry Investigation* 5:3, 179–85.

Kim, Y.T. and Lombardino, L.J. 1991. 'The efficacy of script contexts in language comprehension intervention with children who have mental retardation', *Journal of Speech and Hearing Research* 34:4, 845–57.

Kimata, Y., Sakuraba, M., Hishinuma, S., Ebihara, S., Hayashi, R., Asakage, T., Nakatsuka, T. and Harii, K. 2003. 'Analysis of the relations between the shape of the reconstructed tongue and postoperative functions after subtotal or total glossectomy', *Laryngoscope* 113:5, 905–9.

King, B., Wood, C. and Faulkner, D. 2008. 'Sensitivity to visual and auditory stimuli in children with developmental dyslexia', *Dyslexia* 14:2, 116–41.

Kipps, C.M., Nestor, P.J., Acosta-Cabronero, J., Arnold, R. and Hodges, J.R. 2009. 'Understanding social dysfunction in the behavioural variant of frontotemporal dementia: the role of emotion and sarcasm processing', *Brain* 132:3, 592–603.

Kiran, S. and Thompson, C.K. 2003. 'The role of semantic complexity in treatment of naming deficits: training semantic categories in fluent aphasia by controlling exemplar typicality', *Journal of Speech, Language, and Hearing Research* 46:4, 773–87.

Kirby, J.R. and Savage, R.S. 2008. 'Can the simple view deal with the complexities of reading?', *Literacy* 42:2, 75–82.

Kirk, S.A., James, M. and Kirk, W.D. 1968. *Illinois test of psycholinguistic abilities*, Urbana, IL: Illinois University Press.

Kisilevsky, V.E., Bailie, N.A. and Halik, J.J. 2010. 'Results of stapedectomy in otosclerosis with severe and profound hearing loss', *Journal of Otolaryngology – Head and Neck Surgery* 39:3, 244–52.

Kiss, K. 2000. 'Effects of verb complexity on agrammatic aphasics' sentence production', in R. Bastiaanse and Y. Grodzinsky (eds.), *Grammatical disorders in aphasia*, London: Whurr Publishers, 123–51.

Kissagizlis, P. 2010. An interview with Peter Kissagizlis: cluttering and me, International Cluttering On-line Conference (online, available at: www.mnsu.edu/comdis/ica1/papers/kissagizlisc.html; last accessed 12 June 2013).

Kitsiou-Tzeli, S., Kolialexi, A., Fryssira, H., Galla-Voumvouraki, A., Salavoura, K., Kanariou, M., Tsangaris, G.Th., Kanavakis, E. and Mavrou, A. 2004. 'Detection of 22q11.2 deletion among 139 patients with DiGeorge/velocardiofacial syndrome features', *In Vivo* 18:5, 603–8.

Kitz, W.R. and Tarver, S.G. 1989. 'Comparison of dyslexic and nondyslexic adults on decoding and phonemic awareness tasks', *Annals of Dyslexia* 39:1, 196–205.

Kjelgaard, M.M. and Tager-Flusberg, H. 2001. 'An investigation of language impairment in autism: implications for genetic subgroups', *Language and Cognitive Processes* 16:2-3, 287–308.

Klapp, S.T. 1995. 'Motor response programming during simple and choice reaction time: the role of practice', *Journal of Experimental Psychology: Human Perception and Performance* 21:5, 1015–27.

Klaver, J.R., Lee, Z. and Hart, S.D. 2007. 'Psychopathy and nonverbal indicators of deception in offenders', *Law and Human Behaviour* 31:4, 337–51.

Kleim, J.A. and Jones, T.A. 2008. 'Principles of experience-dependent neural plasticity', *Journal of Speech, Language, and Hearing Research* 51:1, S225–39.

Klein, B.P. and Mervis, C.B. 1999. 'Cognitive strengths and weaknesses of 9- and 10-year-olds with Williams syndrome or Down syndrome', *Developmental Neuropsychology* 16:2, 177–96.

Klein, E.S. 1996. 'Phonological/traditional approaches to articulation therapy: a retrospective group comparison', *Language, Speech, and Hearing Services in Schools* 27:4, 314–23.

Kleinman, J., Marciano, P.L. and Ault, R.L. 2001. 'Advanced theory of mind in high-functioning adults with autism', *Journal of Autism and Developmental Disorders* 31:1, 29–36.

Kleinow, J., Smith, A. and Ramig, L.O. 2001. 'Speech stability in idiopathic Parkinson disease: effects of rate and loudness manipulations', *Journal of Speech, Language, and Hearing Research* 44:5, 1041–51.

Kleinsmith, L.J. 2006. *Principles of cancer biology*, San Francisco, CA: Pearson Benjamin Cummings.

Klin, A., Jones, W., Schultz, R. and Volkmar, F. 2003. 'The enactive mind, or from actions to cognition: lessons from autism' *Philosophical Transactions of the Royal Society London B Biological Sciences* 358:1430, 345–60.

Klin, A., Jones, W., Schultz, R., Volkmar, F. and Cohen, D. 2002. 'Visual fixation patterns during viewing of naturalistic social situations as predictors of social competence in individuals with autism', *Archives of General Psychiatry* 59:9, 809–16.

Knibb, J.A., Woollams, A.M., Hodges, J.R. and Patterson, K. 2009. 'Making sense of progressive non-fluent aphasia: an analysis of conversational speech', *Brain* 132:10, 2734–46.

Knight, R., Devereux, R. and Godfrey, H. 1998. 'Caring for a family member with traumatic brain injury', *Brain Injury* 12:6, 467–81.

Knitzer, J. and Olson, L. 1982. Unclaimed children: The failure of public responsibility to children and adolescents in need of mental health services, Washington, DC: Children's Defense Fund.

Knorr, S.G. and Zwitman, D.H. 1977. 'The design of a wireless-controlled intra-oral electrolarynx', *Journal of Bioengineering* 1:3, 165–71.

Koegel, L.K., Koegel, R.L. and Ingham, J.C. 1986. 'Programming rapid generalization of correct articulation through self-monitoring procedures', *Journal of Speech and Hearing Disorders* 51:1, 24–32.

Kohn, S.E. 1984. 'The nature of the phonological disorder in conduction aphasia', *Brain and Language* 23:1, 97–115.

Kohn, S.E., Lorch, M.P. and Pearson, D.M. 1989. 'Verb finding in aphasia', *Cortex* 25:1, 57–69.

Kolb, D.A. 1984. *Experiential learning: experience as the source of learning and development*, Englewood Cliffs, NJ: Prentice-Hall.

Kolk, H. and Postma, A. 1997. 'Stuttering as a covert repair phenomenon', in R. Curlee and G. Siegel (eds.), *Nature and treatment of stuttering: new directions*, second edition, Boston, MA: Allyn & Bacon, 182–203.

Komatsu, Y., Genba, R. and Kohama, G. 1982. 'Morphological studies of the velopharyngeal orifice in cleft palate', *Cleft Palate Journal* 19:4, 275–80.

Konstantinovic, V.S. and Dimic, N.D. 1998. 'Articulatory function and tongue mobility after surgery followed by radiotherapy for tongue and floor of the mouth cancer patients', *British Journal of Plastic Surgery* 51:8, 589–93.

Koppenhaver, D.A. and Erickson, K.A. 2003. 'Natural emergent literacy supports for preschoolers with autism and severe communication impairments', *Topics in Language Disorders* 23:4, 283–92.

Korenberg, J., Chen, X.-N., Hirota, H., Lai, Z., Bellugi, U., Burian, D., Roe, B. and Matsuoka, R. 2000. 'Genome structure and cognitive map of Williams syndrome', *Journal of Cognitive Neurosciences* 12:1, 89–107.

Korpijaakko-Huuhka, A.M., Söderholm, A.L. and Lehtihalmes, M. 1999. 'Long-lasting speech and oral-motor deficiencies following oral cancer surgery: a retrospective study', *Logopaedics, Phoniatrics and Vocology* 24:3, 97–106.

Kosmidis, M.H., Aretouli, E., Bozikas, V.P., Giannakou, M. and Ioannidis, P. 2008. 'Studying social cognition in patients with schizophrenia and patients with fronto-temporal dementia: theory of mind and the perception of sarcasm', *Behavioural Neurology* 19:1-2, 65–9.

Kotby, M.N., El-Sady, S.R., Basiouny, S.D., Abou-Rass, Y.A. and Hegazi, M.A. 1991. 'Efficacy of the accent method of voice therapy', *Journal of Voice* 5:4, 316–20.

Kotz, S.A., Schwartze, M. and Schmidt-Kassow, M. 2009. 'Non-motor basal ganglia functions: a review and proposal for a model of sensory predictability in auditory language perception', *Cortex* 45:8, 982–90.

Koufman, J.A. 1991. 'The otolaryngologic manifestations of gastroesophageal reflux disease (GERD): a clinical investigation of 225 patients using ambulatory 24-hour pH monitoring and an experimental investigation of the role of acid and pepsin in the development of laryngeal injury', *Laryngoscope* 101:4 Pt 2 Suppl 53, 1–78.

Koufman, J.A. and Blalock, P.D. 1982. 'Classification and approach to patients with functional voice disorders', *Annals of Otology, Rhinology and Laryngology* 91:4 Pt 1, 372–77.

Koufman, J.A. and Blalock, P.D. 1989. 'Is voice rest never indicated?', *Journal of Voice* 3:1, 87–91.

Koufman, J.A., Amin, M.R. and Panetti, M. 2000. 'Prevalence of reflux in 113 consecutive patients with laryngeal and voice disorders', *Otolaryngology – Head and Neck Surgery* 123:4, 385–8.

Koufman, J.A., Aviv, J.E., Casiano, R.R. and Shaw, G.Y. 2002. 'Laryngopharyngeal reflux: position statement of the Committee on Speech, Voice, and Swallowing Disorders of the American Academy of Otolaryngology-Head and Neck Surgery', *Otolaryngology – Head and Neck Surgery* 127:1, 32–5.

Kounios, J., Frymiare, J.L., Bowden, E.M., Fleck, J.I., Subramaniam, K., Parrish, T.B. and Jung-Beeman, M. 2006. 'The prepared mind: neural activity prior to problem presentation predicts subsequent solution by sudden insight', *Psychological Science* 17:10, 882–90.

Kraft, S.J. and Yairi, E. 2012. 'Genetic bases of stuttering: the state of the art, 2011', *Folia Phoniatrica et Logopaedica* 64:1, 34–47.

Krämer, I., Rauber-Lüthy, C., Kupferschmidt, H., Krähenbühl, S. and Ceschi, A. 2010. 'Minimal dose for severe poisoning and influencing factors in acute human clozapine intoxication: a 13-year retrospective study', *Clinical Neuropharmacology* 33:5, 230–4.

Kramer, J.H. and Duffy, J.M. 1996. 'Aphasia, apraxia, and agnosia in the diagnosis of dementia', *Dementia* 7:1, 23–6.

Kramer, S., Bryan, K. and Frith, C.D. 2001. 'Mental illness and communication', *International Journal of Language & Communication Disorders* 36:S1, 132–7.

Krauss, T. and Galloway, H. 1982. 'Melodic intonation therapy with language delayed apraxic children', *Journal of Music Therapy* 19:2, 102–13.

Kreiman, J., Gerratt, B.R. and Ito, M. 2007. 'When and why listeners disagree in voice quality assessment tasks', *Journal of the Acoustical Society of America* 122:4, 2354–64.

Kreimer, A., Clifford, G., Boyle, P. and Franceschi, S. 2005. 'Human papillomavirus types in head and neck squamous cell carcinomas worldwide: a systematic review', *Cancer Epidemiology, Biomarkers and Prevention* 14:2, 467–75.

Krischke, S., Weigelt, S., Hoppe, U., Köllner, V., Klotz, M., Eysholdt, U. and Rosanowski, F. 2005. 'Quality of life in dysphonic patients', *Journal of Voice* 19:1, 132–7.

Kroeger, B.J., Miller, N., Lowit, A. and Neuschaefer-Rube, C. 2011. 'Defective neural motor speech mappings as a source for apraxia of speech', in A. Lowit and R. Kent (eds.), *Assessment of motor speech disorders*, Abingdon, Oxfordshire: Plural Publishing, 325–46.

Kroll, R.M. and Scott-Sulsky, L. 2010. 'The fluency plus program: an integration of fluency shaping and cognitive restructuring procedures for adolescents and adults who stutter', in B. Guitar and R.J. McCauley (eds.), *Treatment of stuttering: established and emerging interventions*, Baltimore, MD: Lippincott Williams & Wilkins, 277–312.

Kubert, H.L., Stepp, C.E., Zeitels, S.M., Gooey, J.E., Walsh, M.J., Prakash, S.R., Hillman, R.E. and Heaton, J.T. 2009. 'Electromyographic control of a hands-free electrolarynx using neck strap muscles', *Journal of Communication Disorders* 42:3, 211–25.

Kubota, Y., Toichi, M., Shimizu, M., Mason, R.A., Coconcea, C.M., Findling, R.L., Yamamoto, K. and Calabrese, J.R. 2005. 'Prefrontal activation during verbal fluency tests in schizophrenia – a near infra-red spectroscopy (NIRS) study', *Schizophrenia Research* 77:1, 65–73.

Kucharska-Pietura, K., David, A.S., Masiak, M. and Phillips, M.L. 2005. 'Perception of facial and vocal affect by people with schizophrenia in early and late stages of illness', *British Journal of Psychiatry* 187:6, 523–8.

Kuehn, D.P. 1991. 'New therapy for treating hypernasal speech using continuous positive airway pressure (CPAP)', *Plastic and Reconstructive Surgery* 88:6, 959–66.

Kuehn, D.P. and Wachtel, J.M. 1994. 'CPAP therapy for treating hypernasality following closed head injury', in J.A. Till, K.M. Yorkston and D. Beukelman (eds.), *Motor speech disorders: advances in assessment and treatment*, Baltimore, MD: Paul H. Brooks, 207–12.

Kugler, S.L., Bali, B., Lieberman, P., Strug, L., Gagnon, B., Murphy, P.L., Clarke, T., Greenberg, D.A. and Pal, D.K. 2008. 'An autosomal dominant genetically heterogeneous variant of rolandic epilepsy and speech disorder', *Epilepsia* 49:6, 1086–90.

Kuhl, P.K., Coffey-Corina, S., Padden, D. and Dawson, G. 2005. 'Links between social and linguistic processing of speech in preschool children with autism: behavioral and electrophysiological measures', *Developmental Science* 8:1, F1–F12.

Kuhl, P.K., Conboy, B.T., Coffey-Corina, S., Padden, D., Rivera-Gaxiola, M. and Nelson, T. 2008. 'Phonetic learning as a pathway to language: new data and native language magnet theory expanded (NLEM-e)', *Philosophical Transactions of the Royal Society Bulletin* 363:1493, 979–1000.

Kuhn, T.S. 1996. *The structure of scientific revolutions*, third edition, Chicago: University of Chicago Press.

Kully, D., Langevin, M. and Lomheim, H. 2007. 'Intensive treatment of stuttering in adolescents and adults', in E. Conture and R.F. Curlee (eds.), *Stuttering and related disorders of fluency*, third edition, New York: Thieme Medical Publishers, 213–32.

Kumin, L. 2006. 'Speech intelligibility and childhood verbal apraxia in children with Down syndrome', *Down Syndrome Research and Practice* 10:1, 10–22.

Kunnari, S., Savinainen-Makkonen, T., Leonard, L., Mäkinen, L., Tolonen, A.-K., Luotonen, M. and Leinonen, E. 2011. 'Children with specific language impairment in Finnish: the use of tense and agreement inflections', *Journal of Child Language* 38:5, 999–1027.

Kuschmann, A., Miller, N., Lowit, A. and Mennen, I. 2011. 'Assessment of intonation', in A. Lowit and R. Kent (eds.), *Assessment of motor speech disorders*, Oxfordshire, UK: Plural Publishing, 253–68.

Kushner, K.G. 2000. *Therapy techniques for cleft palate speech and related disorders*, San Diego, CA: Singular.

Laccourreye, H., Laccourreye, O. and Weinstein, G.S. 1990. 'Supracricoid laryngectomy with cricohyoidoepiglottopexy: a partial laryngeal procedure for glottic carcinoma', *Annals of Otology, Rhinology and Laryngology* 99, 421–6.

Lafosse, J.M., Reed, B.R., Mungas, D., Sterling, S.B., Wahbeh, H. and Jagust, W.J. 1997. 'Fluency and memory differences between ischemic vascular dementia and Alzheimer's disease', *Neuropsychology* 11:4, 514–22.

LaGasse, B. 2012. 'Evaluation of melodic intonation therapy for developmental apraxia of speech', *Music Therapy Perspectives* 30:1, 49.

Lahey, B.B., Loeber, R., Burke, J. and Rathouz, P.J. 2002. 'Adolescent outcomes of childhood conduct disorder among clinic-referred boys: predictors of improvement', *Journal of Abnormal Child Psychology* 30:4, 333–48.

Lai, C.S., Fisher, S.E., Hurst, J.A., Vargha-Khadem, F. and Monaco, A.P. 2001. 'A novel forkhead-domain gene is mutated in a severe speech and language disorder', *Nature* 413:6855, 519–23.

Laing, E., Butterworth, G., Ansari, D., Gsödl, M., Longhi, E., Panagiotaki, G., Paterson, S. and Karmiloff-Smith, A. 2002. 'Atypical development of language and social communication in toddlers with Williams syndrome', *Developmental Science* 5:2, 233–46.

Lajoie, C., Ferré, P. and Ska, B. 2010. 'L'impact de la nature des lesions sur les troubles de la communication consécutifs à une lesion cérébrale droite [The impact of the nature of lesions on communication problems further to a right brain lesion]', *Neuropsicologia Latinoamericana* 2:3, 12–20.

Lam, J. and Tjaden, K. 2011. 'Intelligibility of clear speech: effect of instruction', 6th International Conference on Speech Motor Control: Groningen, The Netherlands, 8–11 June 2011.

Lambert, N., Nihira, K. and Leland, H. 1993. *AAMR adaptive behavioral scale-school*, second edition, Austin, TX: Pro-Ed.

Lambon Ralph, M.A., Lowe, C. and Rogers, T.T. 2007. 'Neural basis of category-specific semantic deficits for living things: evidence from semantic dementia, HSVE and a neural network model', *Brain* 130:4, 1127–37.

Lambon Ralph, M.A., Patterson, K., Graham, N., Dawson, K. and Hodges, J.R. 2003. 'Homogeneity and heterogeneity in mild cognitive impairment and Alzheimer's disease: a cross-sectional and longitudinal study of 55 cases', *Brain* 126:11, 2350–62.

Lambon Ralph, M.A., Powell, J., Howard, D., Whitworth, A.B., Garrard, P. and Hodges, J.R. 2001. 'Semantic memory is impaired in both dementia with Lewy bodies and dementia of Alzheimer's type: a comparative neuropsychological study and literature review', *Journal of Neurology, Neurosurgery and Psychiatry* 70:2, 149–56.

Lambon Ralph, M.A., Sage, K., Jones, R.W. and Mayberry, E.J. 2011. 'Coherent concepts are computed in the anterior temporal lobes', *Proceedings of the National Academy of Sciences of the United States of America* 107:6, 2717–22.

Lambon Ralph, M.A., Snell, C., Fillingham, J.K., Conroy, P. and Sage, K. 2010. 'Predicting the outcome of anomia therapy for people with aphasia post CVA: both language and cognitive status are key predictors', *Neuropsychological Rehabilitation* 20:2, 289–305.

Lan, C.C., Su, T.P., Chen, Y.S. and Bai, Y.M. 2011. 'Treatment dilemma in comorbidity of schizophrenia and idiopathic Parkinson's disease', *General Hospital Psychiatry* 33:4, 411.e3–411.e5.

Landa, R.J. and Goldberg, M.C. 2005. 'Language, social, and executive functions in high functioning autism: a continuum of performance', *Journal of Autism and Developmental Disorders* 35:5, 557–73.

Lane, K.L. 1999. 'Young students at risk for antisocial behavior: the utility of academic and social skills interventions', *Journal of Emotional and Behavioral Disorders* 7:4, 211–24.

Lane, K.L., Fletcher, T., Carter, E.W., Dejud, C. and DeLorenzo, J. 2007. 'Paraprofessional-led phonological awareness training with youngsters at risk for reading and behavior problems', *Remedial and Special Education* 28:5, 266–76.

Lane, K.L., O'Shaughnessy, T.E., Lambros, K.M., Gresham, F.M. and Beebe-Frankenberger, M.E. 2001. 'The efficacy of phonological awareness training with first-grade students who have behavior problems and reading difficulties', *Journal of Emotional and Behavioral Disorders* 9:4, 219–31.

Langdon, R., Coltheart, M., Ward, P.B. and Catts, S.V. 2002. 'Disturbed communication in schizophrenia: the role of poor pragmatics and poor mind-reading', *Psychological Medicine* 32:7, 1273–84.

Langevin, M., Packman, A. and Onslow, M. 2010. 'Parent perceptions of the impact of stuttering on their preschoolers and themselves', *Journal of Communication Disorders* 43:5, 407–23.

Larkins, B., Worrall, L. and Hickson, L. 1999. 'Everyday communication activities of individuals with traumatic brain injury living in New Zealand', *Asia Pacific Journal of Speech, Language and Hearing* 4:3, 183–91.

Larner, A.J. 2008. 'Alzheimer's disease', in S.F. Cappa, J. Abutalebi, J.-F. Démonet, P.C. Fletcher and P. Garrard (eds.), *Cognitive neurology: a clinical textbook*, Oxford University Press, 199–228.

Larrivee, L.S. and Catts, H.W. 1999. 'Early reading achievement in children with expressive phonological disorders', *American Journal of Speech-Language Pathology* 8:2, 118–28.

Lauridsen, H., Hansen, B.F., Reintoft, I., Keeling, J.W. and Kjær, I. 2001. 'Histological investigation of the palatine bone in prenatal trisomy 21', *Cleft Palate-Craniofacial Journal* 38:5, 492–7.

Laver, J. 1980. *The phonetic description of voice quality*, Cambridge University Press.

Laver, J. 2000. 'Phonetic evaluation of voice quality', in R.D. Kent and M.J. Ball (eds.), *The handbook of voice quality measurement*, San Diego, CA: Singular, 37–48.

Laver, J. and Mackenzie Beck, J. 1991. *Vocal profiles analysis*. Edinburgh: Queen Margaret College and University of Edinburgh Centre for Speech Technology Research.

LaVigne, M. and van Rybroek, G.J. 2011. 'Breakdown in the language zone: the prevalence of language impairments among juvenile and adult offenders and why it matters', *US Davis Journal of Juvenile Law and Policy* 15:1, 37.

Law, J., Boyle, J., Harris, F., Harkness, A. and Nye, C. 2000. 'Prevalence and natural history of primary speech and language delay: findings from a systematic review of the literature', *International Journal of Language & Communication Disorders* 35:2, 165–88.

Law, J., Garrett, Z. and Nye, C. 2003. 'Speech and language therapy interventions for children with primary speech and language delay or disorder', *Cochrane Database of Systematic Reviews*, Issue 3, CD004110.

Law, J., Garrett, Z. and Nye, C. 2004. 'The efficacy of treatment for children with developmental speech and language delay/disorder: a meta-analysis', *Journal of Speech, Language, and Hearing Research* 47:4, 924–43.

Law, M., Baptiste, S. and Mills, J. 1995. 'Client-centred practice: what does it mean and does it make a difference?', *Canadian Journal of Occupational Therapy* 62:5, 250–7.

Laws, G. 2002. 'Working memory in children and adolescents with Down syndrome: evidence from a colour memory experiment', *Journal of Child Psychology and Psychiatry and Allied Disciplines* 43:3, 353–64.

Laws, G. and Bishop, D. 2003. 'A comparison of language abilities in adolescents with Down syndrome and children with specific language impairment', *Journal of Speech, Language, and Hearing Research* 46:6, 1324–39.

Laws, G. and Bishop, D. 2004. 'Pragmatic language impairment and social deficits in Williams syndrome: a comparison with Down's syndrome and specific language impairment', *International Journal of Language & Communication Disorders* 39:1, 45–64.

Lawson, R. and Fawcus, M. 2001. 'Increasing effective communication using a total communication approach: early stages in treating a person with non-fluent aphasia', in S. Byng and K. Swinburn (eds.), *The aphasia therapy file*, Hove, East Sussex: Psychology Press, 61–74.

Lazarus, C.L., Ward, E.C. and Yiu, E.M. 2007. 'Speech and swallowing following oral, oropharyngeal, and nasopharyngeal cancers', in E.C. Ward and C.J. van As-Brooks (eds.), *Head and neck cancer: treatment, rehabilitation, and outcomes*, San Diego, CA: Plural Publishing, Inc., 103–22.

Leafstedt, J.M., Richards, C.R. and Gerber, M.M. 2004. 'Effectiveness of explicit phonological-awareness instruction for at-risk English learners', *Learning Disabilities Research & Practice* 19:4, 252–61.

Leanderson, R., Korlof, B., Nylen, B. and Eriksson, G. 1974. 'The age factor and reduction of open nasality following superiorly-based velopharyngeal flap operation in 124 cases', *Scandinavian Journal of Plastic and Reconstructive Surgery* 8:1–2, 156–60.

Lebrun, Y., Buyssens, E. and Henneaux, J. 1973. 'Phonetic aspects of anarthria', *Cortex* 9:1, 126–35.

Lee, S.S. and Dapretto, M. 2006. 'Metaphorical versus literal word meanings: fMRI evidence against a selective role of the right hemisphere', *NeuroImage* 29:2, 536–44.

Lee, T.D. and Magill, R.A. 1983. 'The locus of contextual interference in motor-skill acquisition', *Journal of Experimental Psychology: Learning, Memory, and Cognition* 9:4, 730–46.

Leech, S.L., Day, N.L., Richardson, G.A. and Goldschmidt, L. 2003. 'Predictors of self-reported delinquent behaviour in a sample of young adolescents', *Journal of Early Adolescence* 23:1, 78–106.

Leeper, H.A., Gratton, D.G., Lapointe, H.J. and Armstrong, J.E.A. 2005. 'Maxillofacial rehabilitation for oral cancer: surgical, prosthodontic and communication aspects of management', in P.C. Doyle and R.L. Keith (eds.), *Contemporary considerations in the treatment and rehabilitation of head and neck cancer*, Austin: Pro-Ed, 261–314.

Leff, A.P. and Behrmann, M. 2008. 'Treatment of reading impairment after stroke', *Current Opinion in Neurology* 21:6, 644–8.

Lehman Blake, M. 2003. 'Affective language and humor appreciation after right hemisphere brain damage', *Seminars in Speech and Language* 24:2, 107–19.

Lehman Blake, M. 2006. 'Clinical relevance of discourse characteristics after right hemisphere brain damage', *American Journal of Speech-Language Pathology* 15:3, 255–67.

Lehman Blake, M. 2009. 'Inferencing processes after right hemisphere brain damage: maintenance of inferences', *Journal of Speech, Language, and Hearing Research* 52:2, 359–72.

Lehman Blake, M. 2010. 'Communication deficits associated with right hemisphere brain damage', in J.S. Damico, N. Müller and M.J. Ball (eds.), *Handbook of language and speech disorders*, Oxford: Wiley-Blackwell, 556–76.

Lehman, M.T. and Tompkins, C.A. 1998. 'Reliability and validity of an auditory working memory measure: data from elderly and right-hemisphere damaged adults', *Aphasiology* 12:7–8, 771–85.

Leinonen, E. and Kerbel, D. 1999. 'Relevance theory and pragmatic impairment', *International Journal of Language & Communication Disorders* 34:4, 367–90.

LENA Research Foundation. 2011. *Language Environment Analysis System (LENA)*, Boulder, CO: LENA Research Foundation.

Leon, S.A. and Rodriguez, A.D. 2008. 'Aprosodia and its treatment', *Perspectives on Neurophysiology and Neurogenic Speech and Language Disorders* 18:2, 66–72.

Leonard, C., Rochon, E. and Laird, L. 2008. 'Treating naming impairments in aphasia: findings from a phonological components analysis treatment', *Aphasiology* 22:9, 923–47.

Leonard, C.M., Eckert, M.A., Lombardino, L.J., Oakland, T., Kranzler, J., Mohr, C.M., King, W.M. and Freeman, A. 2001. 'Anatomical risk factors for phonological dyslexia', *Cerebral Cortex* 11:2, 148–57.

Leonard, L. 1975. 'Developmental considerations in the management of language disabled children', *Journal of Learning Disabilities* 8:4, 232–37.

Leonard, L. 1998. *Children with specific language impairment*, Cambridge, MA: MIT Press.

Leonard, L. 2009a. 'Is expressive language disorder an accurate diagnostic category?', *American Journal of Speech-Language Pathology* 18:2, 115–23.

Leonard, L. 2009b. 'Cross-linguistic studies of child language disorders', in R. Schwartz (ed.), *Handbook of child language disorders*, Hove, East Sussex: Psychology Press, 308–24.

Leonard, L., Camarata, S., Brown, B. and Camarata, M. 2004. 'Tense and agreement in the speech of children with specific language impairment: patterns of generalization through intervention', *Journal of Speech, Language, and Hearing Research* 47:6, 1363–79.

Leonard, L., Camarata, S., Pawłowska, M., Brown, B. and Camarata, M. 2006. 'Tense and agreement morphemes in the speech of children with specific language impairment during intervention: phase II', *Journal of Speech, Language, and Hearing Research* 49:4, 749–70.

Leonard, L., Camarata, S., Pawłowska, M., Brown, B. and Camarata, M. 2008. 'The acquisition of tense and agreement morphemes by children with specific language impairment during intervention: phase 3', *Journal of Speech, Language, and Hearing Research* 51:1, 120–5.

Leonard, L.B., Ellis Weismer, S., Miller, C., Francis, D., Tomblin, J.B. and Kail, R. 2007. 'Speed of processing, working memory, and language impairment in children', *Journal of Speech, Language, and Hearing Research* 50:2, 408–28.

Leonard, L.B., Miller, C.A. and Finneran, D. 2009. 'Grammaticality judgments in adolescents with and without language impairment', *International Journal of Language & Communication Disorders* 43:3, 346–57.

Leonard, R.J. 1994. 'Characteristics of speech in speakers with glossectomy and other oral/oropharyngeal ablation', in J.E. Bernthal and N.W. Bankson (eds.), *Child phonology: characteristics, assessment, and intervention with special populations*, New York: Thieme, 54–78.

Leonard, R.J. and Gillis, R. 1990. 'Differential effects of speech prostheses in glossectomized patients', *Journal of Prosthetic Dentistry* 64:6, 701–8.

Lesniak-Karpiak, K., Massocco, M. and Ross, J. 2003. 'Behavioral assessment of social anxiety in females with Turner or fragile X syndrome', *Journal of Autism and Developmental Disorders* 33:1, 55–67.

Lesser, R. and Algar, L. 1995. 'Towards combining the cognitive neuropsychological and the pragmatic in aphasia therapy', *Neuropsychological Rehabilitation* 5:1–2, 67–92.

Lesser, R. and Milroy, L. 1993. *Linguistics and aphasia: psycholinguistic and pragmatic aspects of intervention*, London: Longman.

Levelt, W.J.M. 1989. *Speaking: from intention to articulation*, Cambridge, MA: MIT Press.

Levelt, W.J.M. 1999. 'Models of word production', *Trends in Cognitive Sciences* 3:6, 223–32.

Levelt, W.J.M. and Wheeldon, L. 1994. 'Do speakers have access to a mental syllabary?', *Cognition* 50:1–3, 239–69.

Levelt, W.J.M., Roelofs, A. and Meyer, A.S. 1999. 'A theory of lexical access in speech production', *Behavioural and Brain Sciences* 22:1, 1–75.

Levinson, S.C. 1983. *Pragmatics*, Cambridge University Press.

Levorato, M.C. and Cacciari, C. 2002. 'The creation of new figurative expressions: psycholinguistic evidence in Italian children, adolescents and adults', *Journal of Child Language* 29:1, 127–50.

Levy, B.A. and Bourassa, D.C. 1999. 'Fast and slow namers: benefits of segmentation and whole word training', *Journal of Experimental Child Psychology* 73:2, 115–38.

Levy, Y. 1994. *Other languages, other children: issues in the theory of language acquisition*, Hillsdale, NJ: Lawrence Erlbaum Associates.

Lewis, B.A. and Thompson, L.A. 1992. 'A study of developmental speech and language disorders in twins', *Journal of Speech and Hearing Research* 35:5, 1086–94.

Lewis, B.A., Chen, X., Freebairn, L., Holland, S. and Tkach, J. 2010. *'Neural correlates of speech production in speech sound disorders'*, American Speech, Language and Hearing Association Conference: Philadelphia, PA, 17–20 November 2010.

Lewis, B.A., Freebairn, L., Hansen, A., Iyengar, S. and Taylor, H. 2004b. 'School-age follow-up of children with childhood apraxia of speech', *Language, Speech, and Hearing Services in Schools* 35:2, 122–40.

Lewis, B.A., Freebairn, L.A. and Taylor, H.G. 2000. 'Follow-up of children with early expressive phonology disorders', *Journal of Learning Disabilities* 33:5, 433–44.

Lewis, B.A., Freebairn, L.A., Hansen, A.J., Taylor, H.G., Iyengar, S.K. and Shriberg, L.D. 2004a. 'Family pedigrees of children with suspected childhood apraxia of speech', *Journal of Communication Disorders* 37:2, 157–75.

Lewis, B.A., Shriberg, L.D., Freebairn, L.A., Hansen, A.J., Stein, C.M., Taylor, H.G. and Iyengar, S.K. 2006. 'The genetic bases of speech sound disorders: evidence from spoken and written language', *Journal of Speech, Language, and Hearing Research* 49:6, 1294–1312.

Lewis, F., Nelson, J., Nelson, C. and Reusink, P. 1988. 'Effect of three feedback contingencies on the socially inappropriate talk of a brain-injured adult', *Behavior Therapy* 19:2, 203–11.

Lewis, S.J., Foltynie, T., Blackwell, A.D., Robbins, T.W., Owen, A.M. and Barker, R.A. 2005. 'Heterogeneity of Parkinson's disease in the early clinical stages using a data driven approach', *Journal of Neurology, Neurosurgery and Psychiatry* 76:3, 343–8.

Lewit, E.M., Terman, D.L. and Behrman, R.E. 1997. 'Children and poverty: analysis and recommendations', *The Future of Children* 7:2, 4–24.

Leyfer, O.T., Tager-Flusberg, H., Dowd, M., Tomblin, J.B. and Folstein, S.E. 2008. 'Overlap between autism and specific language impairment: comparison of Autism Diagnostic Interview and Autism Diagnostic Observation Schedule scores', *Autism Research* 1:5, 284–96.

Lhermitte, F. and Gauthier, J.-C. 1969. 'Aphasia', in P.J. Vinken and G.W. Bruyn (eds.), *Handbook of clinical neurology: Vol. 4: Disorders of speech, perception and symbolic behaviour*, Amsterdam: North-Holland Publishing Co., 84–104.

Li, X., Branch, C.A. and DeLisi, L.E. 2009. 'Language pathway abnormalities in schizophrenia: a review of fMRI and other imaging studies', *Current Opinion in Psychiatry* 22:2, 131–9.

Li, Y. and Wright, D.L. 2000. 'An assessment of the attention demands during random-and blocked-practice schedules', *Quarterly Journal of Experimental Psychology* 53:2, 591–606.

Liang, J. 2006. *Experiments on the modular nature of word and sentence phonology in Chinese Broca patients*, PhD thesis University of Leiden, Leiden: LOT.

Liberman, A.M. 1999. 'The reading researcher and the reading teacher need the right theory of speech', *Scientific Studies of Reading* 3:2, 95–111.

Liberman, I.Y. and Shankweiler, D. 1985. 'Phonology and problems of learning to read and write', *Remedial and Special Education* 6:6, 8–17.

Liberman, I.Y., Shankweiler, D. and Liberman, A.M. 1989. 'The alphabetic principle and learning to read', in A.M. Liberman and D. Shankweiler (eds.), *Phonology and reading disabiity: solving the reading puzzle*, Ann Arbor: University of Michigan Press, 1–34.

Libon, D.J., McMillan, C., Gunawardena, D., Powers, C., Massimo, L., Khan, A., Morgan, B., Farag, C., Richmond, L., Weinstein, J., Moore, P., Coslett, H.B., Chatterjee, A., Aguirre, G. and Grossman, M. 2009. 'Neurocognitive contributions to verbal fluency deficits in frontotemporal lobar degeneration', *Neurology* 73:7, 535–42.

Libon, D.J., Xie, S.X., Moore, P., Farmer, J., Antani, S., McCawley, G., Cross, K. and Grossman, M. 2007. 'Patterns of neuropsychological impairment in frontotemporal dementia', *Neurology* 68:5, 369–75.

Lichtheim, L. 1885. 'Über aphasie', *Deutsches Archiv für Klinische Medizin*, 36, 204–68.

Liebenthal, E., Binder, J.R., Spitzer, S.M., Possing, E.T. and Medler, D.A. 2005. 'Neural substrates of phonemic perception', *Cerebral Cortex* 15:10, 1621–31.

Lieberman, J. 1998. 'Principles and techniques of manual therapy: applications in the management of dysphonia', in T. Harris, S. Harris, J.S. Rubin and D.M. Howard (eds.), *The voice clinic handbook*, London: Whurr, 103–15.

Lieberman, J. 2011. 'Lieberman manual assessment of the larynx and laryngeal suspension system', personal communication.

Lieberman, P., Kako, E., Friedman, J., Tajchman, G., Feldman, L.S. and Jiminez, E.B. 1992. 'Speech production, syntax comprehension, and cognitive deficits in Parkinson's disease', *Brain and Language* 43:2, 169–89.

Liederman, J., Kantrowitz, L. and Flannery, K. 2005. 'Male vulnerability to reading disability is not likely to be a myth: a call for new data', *Journal of Learning Disabilities* 38:2, 109–29.

Liégeois, F.J. and Morgan, A.T. 2012. 'Neural bases of childhood speech disorders: lateralization and plasticity for speech functions during development', *Neuroscience and Biobehavioral Reviews* 36:1, 439–58.

Liepmann, H. 1913. 'Motor aphasia, anarthria and apraxia', *Transactions of the 17th International Congress of Medicine*, Section XI, Part II, 97–106.

Light, J., Collier, B. and Parnes, P. 1985a. 'Communicative interaction between young nonspeaking physically disabled children and their primary caregivers: part 1-discourse patterns', *AAC: Augmentative and Alternative Communication* 1:2, 74–83.

Light, J., Collier, B. and Parnes, P. 1985b. 'Communicative interaction between young nonspeaking physically disabled children and their primary caregivers: part 2-communicative function', *AAC: Augmentative and Alternative Communication* 1:3, 98–107.

Liles, B.Z., Coelho, C.A., Duffy, R.J. and Zalagens, M.R. 1989. 'Effects of elicitation procedures on the narratives of normal and closed head-injured adults', *Journal of Speech and Hearing Disorders* 54:3, 356–66.

Lim, J.L., Lim, S.E., Choi, S.H., Kim, J.H., Kim, K.M. and Choi, H.S. 2007. 'Clinical characteristics and voice analysis of patients with mutational dysphonia: clinical significance of diplophonia and closed quotients', *Journal of Voice* 21:1, 12–19.

Lincoln, M. and Walker, C. 2007. 'A survey of Australian adult users of altered auditory feedback devices for stuttering: use patterns, perceived effectiveness and satisfaction', *Disability and Rehabilitation* 29:19, 1510–7.

Lincoln, M., Packman, A., Onslow, M. and Jones, M. 2010. 'An experimental investigation of the effect of altered auditory feedback on the conversational speech of adults who stutter', *Journal of Speech, Language, and Hearing Research* 53:5, 1122–31.

Lind, S.E. and Bowler, D.M. 2010. 'Impaired performance on see-know tasks amongst children with autism: evidence of specific difficulties with theory of mind or domain-general task factors?', *Journal of Autism and Developmental Disorders* 40:4, 479–84.

Lindblom, B. 1983. 'Economy of speech gestures', in P.F. MacNeilage (ed.), *The production of speech*, New York: Springer-Verlag, 217–45.

Lindgren, K.A., Folstein, S.E., Tomblin, J.B. and Tager-Flusberg, H. 2009. 'Language and reading abilities of children with autism spectrum disorders and specific language impairment and their first-degree relatives', *Autism Research* 2:1, 22–38.

Ling, C., Yamashita, M., Zhang, J., Bless, D.M. and Welham, N.V. 2010. 'Reactive response of fibrocytes to vocal fold mucosal injury in rat', *Wound Repair Regeneration* 18:5, 514–23.

Links, P., Hurkmans, J. and Bastiaanse, R. 2010. 'Training verb and sentence production in agrammatic Broca's aphasia', *Aphasiology* 24:11, 1303–25.

Linscott, R.J., Knight, R.G. and Godfrey, H.P.D. 1996. 'The Profile of Functional Impairment of Communication (PFIC): a measure of communication impairment for clinical use', *Brain Injury* 10:6, 397–412.

Liotti, M., Ramig, L., Vogel, D., New, P., Cook, C.I., Ingham, R.J., Ingham, J.C. and Fox, P.T. 2003. 'Hypophonia in Parkinson's disease, neural correlates of voice treatment revealed by PET', *Neurology* 60:1, 432–40.

Little, J., Cardy, A. and Munger, R.G. 2004. 'Tobacco smoking and oral clefts: a meta-analysis', *Bulletin of the World Health Organization* 82:3, 213–18.

Little, M.A., McSharry, P.E., Hunter, E.J., Spielman, J. and Ramig, L.O. 2009. 'Suitability of dysphonia measurements for telemonitoring of Parkinson's disease', *IEEE Transactions of Biomedical Engineering* 56:4, 1015–22.

Lock, S., Wilkinson, R. and Bryan, K. 2001. *Supporting partners of people with aphasia in relationships and conversation: a resource pack*, Bicester: Speechmark.

Lof, G. 2003. 'Oral motor exercises and treatment outcomes', *Perspectives on Language Learning and Education* 10:1, 7–11.

Logan, K.J. and Yaruss, J.S. 1999. 'Helping parents address attitudinal and emotional factors with young children who stutter', *Contemporary Issues in Communication Science and Disorders* 26:1, 69–81.

Logemann, J.A. 1994. 'Rehabilitation of the head and neck cancer patient', *Seminars in Oncology* 21:3, 359–65.

Logemann, J.A. 1997. *Evaluation and treatment of swallowing disorders*, Nerang East, Australia: Pro-Ed.

Lomas, J., Pickard, L., Bester, S., Elbard, H., Finlayson, A. and Zoghaib, C. 1989. 'The communicative effectiveness index: development and psychometric evaluation of a functional communication measure for adult aphasia', *Journal of Speech and Hearing Disorders* 54:1, 113–24.

Lonegan, D.S. 1974. 'Vibrotactile thresholds and oral stereognosis in children', *Perceptual and Motor Skills* 38:1, 11–14.

Loney, B.R., Frick, P.J., Clements, C.B., Ellis, M.L. and Kerlin, K. 2003. 'Callous-unemotional traits, impulsivity, and emotional processing in adolescents with antisocial behaviour problems', *Journal of Clinical Child and Adolescent Psychology* 32:1, 66–80.

Long, A.F., Hesketh, A., Paszek, G., Booth, M. and Bowen, A. 2008. 'Development of a reliable self-report outcome measure for pragmatic trials of communication therapy following stroke: the communication outcome after stroke (COAST) scale', *Clinical Rehabilitation* 22:12, 1083–94.

Lopez, A.D., Mathers, C.D., Ezzati, M., Jamison, D.T. and Murray, C.J.L. 2006. 'Global and regional burden of disease and risk factors, 2001: systematic analysis of population health data', *Lancet* 367:9524, 1747–57.

Lopez, M., Kosson, D.S., Weissman, D.H. and Banich, M.T. 2007. 'Interhemispheric integration in psychopathic offenders', *Neuropsychology* 21:1, 82–93.

Losh, M. and Capps, L. 2003. 'Narrative ability in high-functioning children with autism or Asperger's syndrome', *Journal of Autism and Developmental Disorders* 33:3, 239–51.

Losh, M., Reilly, J. and Bellugi, U. 1997. 'Linguistically encoded affect is abnormally high in Williams Syndrome children', *International Behavioral Neuroscience Society Abstracts* 6, 2–53.

Losken, A., Williams, J.K., Burstein, F.D., Malick, D.N. and Riski, J.E. 2003. 'An outcome evaluation of sphincter pharyngoplasty for the management of velopharyngeal insufficiency', *Plastic and Reconstructive Surgery* 112:7, 1755–61.

Losken, A., Williams, J.K., Burstein, F.D., Malick, D.N. and Riski, J.E. 2006. 'Surgical correction of velopharyngeal insufficiency in children with velocardiofacial syndrome', *Plastic and Reconstructive Surgery* 117:5, 1493–8.

Loucas, T., Charman, T., Pickles, A., Simonoff, E., Chandler, S., Meldrum, D. and Baird, G. 2008. 'Autistic symptomatology and language ability in autism spectrum disorder and specific language impairment', *Journal of Child Psychology and Psychiatry* 49:11, 1184–92.

Loucas, T., Riches, N.G., Charman, T., Pickles, A., Simonoff, E., Chandler, S. and Baird, G. 2010. 'Speech perception and phonological short-term memory capacity in language impairment: preliminary evidence from adolescents with specific language impairment (SLI) and autism spectrum disorders (ASD)', *International Journal of Language & Communication Disorders* 45:3, 275–86.

Louhiala, P. 2004. *Preventing Intellectual Disability: Ethical and Clinical Issues*. New York: Cambridge University Press.

Louis, E.D. and Frucht, S.J. 2007. 'Prevalence of essential tremor in patients with Parkinson's disease vs. Parkinson-plus syndromes', *Movement Disorders* 22:10, 1402–7.

Loukusa, S., Leinonen, E., Kuusikko, S., Jussila, K., Mattila, M.L., Ryder, N., Ebeling, H. and Moilanen, I. 2007. 'Use of context in pragmatic language comprehension by children with Asperger syndrome or high-functioning autism', *Journal of Autism and Developmental Disorders* 37:6, 1049–59.

Louth, S.M., Williamson, S., Alpert, M., Pouget, E.R. and Hare, R.D. 1998. 'Acoustic distinctions in the speech of male psychopaths', *Journal of Psycholinguistic Research* 27:3, 375–84.

Love, R.J. 1999. *Childhood motor speech disability*, second edition, Toronto: Maxwell Macmillan Canada.

Lovegrove, W.J. 1994. 'Visual deficits in dyslexia: evidence and implications', in A.J. Fawcett and R.I Nicolson (eds.), *Dyslexia in children: multidisciplinary perspectives*, New York: Harvester Press, 113–35.

Lovelace, R.E., Blitzer, A. and Ludlow, C.L. 1992. 'Clinical laryngeal electromyography', in A. Blitzer, M.F. Brin, C.T. Sasaki, S. Fahn and K.S. Harris (eds.), *Neurologic disorders of the larynx*, New York: Thieme Medical Publishers, Inc., 66–81.

Lovett, M., Steinback, K. and Fritjers, J. 2000. 'Remediating the core deficits of developmental reading disability: a double deficit perspective', *Journal of Learning Disabilities* 33:4, 334–59.

Lowit, A., Brendel, B., Dobinson, C. and Howell, P. 2006. 'An investigation into the influences of age pathology and cognition on speech production', *Journal of Medical Speech-Language Pathology* 14:4, 253–62.

Lubinski, R. 1981a. 'Environmental language intervention', in R. Chapey (ed.), *Language intervention strategies in adult aphasia*, Baltimore, MD: Williams & Wilkins, 223–45.

Lubinski, R. 1981b. 'Language and aging: an environmental approach to intervention', *Topics in Language Disorders* 1:4, 89–97.

Luckasson, R., Borthwick-Duffy, S., Buntinx, W.H.E., Coulter, D.L., Craig, E.M., Reeve, A., Shalock, R.L., Snell, M.E., Spitalnik, D.M., Spreat, S. and Tasse, M.J. 2002. *Mental retardation: definition, classification, and systems of supports*, tenth edition, Washington, DC: American Association on Mental Retardation.

Ludlow, C.L., Yeh, J., Cohen, L.G., Van Pelt, F., Rhew, K. and Hallett, M. 1994. 'Limitations of electromyography and magnetic stimulation for assessing laryngeal muscle control', *Annals of Otology, Rhinology and Laryngology* 103:1, 16–27.

Lukatela, K., Malloy, P., Jenkins, M. and Cohen, R. 1998. 'The naming deficit in early Alzheimer's and vascular dementia', *Neuropsychology* 12:4, 565–72.

Lum, J., Gelgic, C. and Conti-Ramsden, G. 2010. 'Research report: procedural and declarative memory in children with and without specific language impairment', *International Journal of Language & Communication Disorders* 45:1, 96–107.

Lundeborg, I. and McAllister, A. 2007. 'Treatment with a combination of intra-oral sensory stimulation and electropalatography in a child with severe developmental dyspraxia', *Logopedics Phoniatrics Vocology* 32:2, 71–9.

Lundgren, K., Brownell, H., Cayer-Meade, C., Milione, J. and Kearns, K. 2011. 'Treating metaphor interpretation deficits subsequent to right hemisphere brain damage: preliminary results', *Aphasiology* 25:4, 456–74.

Lundgren, K., Brownell, H., Cayer-Meade, C. and Spitzer, J. 2007. 'Training theory of mind following right hemisphere damage: a pilot study', *Brain and Language* 103:1–2, 209–10.

Lundy, D.S. and Casiano, R.R. 1995. 'Compensatory falsetto: effects on vocal quality', *Journal of Voice* 9:4, 439–42.

Luria, A.R. 1970. *Traumatic aphasia: its syndromes, psychology and treatment*, The Hague: Mouton.

Luyster, R. and Lord, C. 2009. 'Word learning in children with autism spectrum disorders', *Developmental Psychology* 45:6, 1774–86.

Luzzatti, C., Raggi, R., Zonca, G., Pistarini, C., Contardi, A. and Pinna, G.D. 2002. 'Verb-noun double dissociation in aphasic lexical impairments: the role of word frequency and imageability', *Brain and Language* 81:1–3, 432–44.

Lynam, D. and Henry, B. 2001. 'The role of neuropsychological deficits in conduct disorders', in J. Hill and B. Maughan (eds.), *Conduct problems in childhood and adolescence*, Mahwah, NJ: Erlbaum, 235–63.

Lyon, G.R., Shaywitz, S.E. and Shaywitz, B.A. 2003. 'Defining dyslexia, comorbidity, teachers' knowledge of language and reading: a definition of dyslexia', *Annals of Dyslexia* 53:1, 1–14.

Lyon, J.G. 1995. 'Drawing: its value as a communication aid for adults with aphasia', *Aphasiology* 9:1, 33–94.

Lyon, J.G., Cariski, D., Keisler, L., Rosenbek, J., Levine, R., Kumpula, J., Ryff, C., Coyne, S. and Blanc, M. 1997. 'Communication partners: enhancing participation in life and communication for adults with aphasia in natural settings', *Aphasiology* 11:7, 693–708.

Ma, E.P.-M. and Yiu, E.M.-L. 2001. 'Voice activity and participation profile: assessing the impact of voice disorders on daily activities', *Journal of Speech, Language, and Hearing Research* 44:3, 511–24.

Maas, E. and Farinella, K.A. 2012. 'Random versus blocked practice in treatment for childhood apraxia of speech', *Journal of Speech, Language, and Hearing Research* 55:2, 561–78.

Maas, E., Robin, D.A., Austermann Hula, S.N., Freedman, S.E., Wulf, G., Ballard, K.J. and Schmidt, R.A. 2008b. 'Principles of motor learning in treatment of motor speech disorders', *American Journal of Speech-Language Pathology* 17:3, 277–98.

Maas, E., Robin, D.A., Steinhauer, V., Ballard, K.J., Magnuson, C. and Wright, D. 2006. 'Motor programming in apraxia of speech: a reaction time approach', 5th International Conference on Speech Motor Control: Nijmegen, 7–10 June 2006.

Maas, E., Robin, D.A., Wright, D.L. and Ballard, K.J. 2008a. 'Motor programming in apraxia of speech', *Brain and Language* 106:2, 107–18.

Maassen, B. 2002. 'Issues contrasting adult acquired versus developmental apraxia of speech', *Seminars in Speech and Language* 23:4, 257–66.

Maassen, B., Nijland, L. and Terband, H. 2010. 'Developmental models of childhood apraxia of speech', in B. Maassen and P. van Lieshout (eds.), *Speech motor control: new developments in basic and applied research*, New York: Oxford University Press, 243–58.

Machery, E. 2011. 'Developmental disorders and cognitive architecture', in A. De Block and P. Adriaens (eds.), *Darwin and psychiatry: philosophical perspectives*, Oxford University Press, 89–114.

Machin, J. and Shaw, C. 1998. 'A multidisciplinary approach to head and neck cancer', *European Journal of Cancer Care* 7:2, 93–6.

Mackenzie, C. and Brady, M. 2008. 'Communication difficulties following right-hemisphere stroke: applying evidence to clinical management', *Evidence-Based Communication Assessment and Intervention* 2:4, 235–47.

Mackenzie, C., Muir, M. and Allen, C. 2010. 'Non-speech oro-motor exercise use in acquired dysarthria management: regimes and rationales', *International Journal of Language & Communication Disorders* 45:6, 617–29.

Mackenzie, K., Millar, A., Wilson, J.A., Sellars, C. and Deary, I.J. 2001. 'Is voice therapy an effective treatment for dysphonia? A randomized controlled trial', *British Medical Journal* 323:7314, 658–61.

MacLennan, D.L., Cornis-Pop, M., Picon-Nieto, L. and Sigford, B. 2002. 'The prevalence of pragmatic communication impairments in traumatic brain injury', *Premier Outlook* 3:4, 38–45.

Madison, L.S., George, C. and Moeschler, J.B. 1986. 'Cognitive functioning in the fragile X syndrome: a study of intellectual, memory, and communication skills', *Journal of Mental Deficiency Research* 30:2, 129–48.

Magnuson, C.E., Robin, D.A. and Wright, D.L. 2008. 'Motor programming when sequencing multiple elements of the same duration', *Journal of Motor Behavior* 40:6, 532–44.

Maguire, G., Franklin, D., Vatakis, N.G., Morgenshtern, E., Denko, T., Yaruss, J.S., Spotts, C., Davis, L., Davis, A., Fox, P., Soni, P., Blomgren, M., Silverman, A. and Riley, G. 2010. 'Exploratory randomized clinical study of pagoclone in persistent developmental stuttering: the EXamining Pagoclone for peRsistent dEvelopmental Stuttering Study', *Journal of Clinical Psychopharmacology* 30:1, 48–56.

Maguire, G.A., Riley, G.D., Franklin, D.L., Maguire, M.E., Nguyen, C.T. and Brojeni, P.H. 2004. 'Olanzapine in the treatment of developmental stuttering: a double-blind, placebo-controlled trial', *Annals of Clinical Psychiatry* 16:2, 63–7.

Maher, L., Kendall, D., Swearengin, J., Rodriguez, A., Leon, S., Pingel, K., Holland, A. and Rothi, L. 2006. 'A pilot study of use-dependent learning in the context of constraint induced language therapy', *Journal of the International Neuropsychological Society* 12:1, 843–52.

Mahoney, G. and Wheeden, C.A. 1999. 'The effect of teacher style on interactive engagement of preschool-aged children with special learning needs', *Early Childhood Research Quarterly* 14:1, 51–68.

Mahr, G. and Leith, W. 1992. 'Psychogenic stuttering of adult onset', *Journal of Speech and Hearing Research* 35:2, 283–6.

Malaspina, D., Goetz, R.R., Friedman, J.H., Kaufmann, C.A., Faraone, S.V., Tsuang, M., Cloninger, C.R., Numberger, J.I. and Blehar, M.C. 2001. 'Traumatic brain injury and schizophrenia in members of schizophrenia and bipolar disorder pedigrees', *American Journal of Psychiatry* 158:3, 440–6.

Malessa, R. and Tyler, K.L. 1996. 'Viral infections of the central nervous system', in T. Brandt, L.R. Caplan, J. Dichgans, H.C. Diener and C. Kennard (eds.), *Neurological disorders: course and treatment*, San Diego, CA: Academic Press, 443–54.

Malvern, D.D. and Richards, B.J. 1997. 'A new measure of lexical diversity', in A. Ryan and A. Wray (eds.), *Evolving models of language*, Clevedon: Multilingual Matters, 58–71.

Mamikonyan, E., Moberg, P.J., Siderowf, A., Duda, J.E., Have, T.T., Hurtig, H.I., Stern, M.B. and Weintraub, D. 2009. 'Mild cognitive impairment is common in Parkinson's disease patients with normal Mini-Mental State Examination (MMSE) scores', *Parkinsonism & Related Disorders* 15:3, 226–31.

Maniglio, R. 2009. 'Severe mental illness and criminal victimization: a systematic review', *Acta Psychiatrica Scandinavica* 119:3, 180–91.

Manis, F.R. and Freedman, L. 2001. 'The relationship of naming speed to multiple reading measures in disabled and normal readers', in M. Wolf (ed.), *Dyslexia, fluency and the brain*, Timonium, MD: York Press, 65–92.

Manis, F.R., Seidenberg, M.S. and Doi, L.M. 1999. 'See Dick RAN: rapid naming and the longitudinal prediction of reading subskills in first and second grade', *Scientific Studies of Reading* 3:2, 129–57.

Manning, W.H. 2010. *Clinical decision making in fluency disorders*, third edition, Clifton Park, NY: Cengage Learning.

Manning, W. and Beck, J.G. 2011. 'Comments concerning Iverach, *et al.*, Screening for personality disorders among adults seeking speech treatment for stuttering [J. Fluency Disorders 34 (2009) 173–186]', *Journal of Fluency Disorders* 36:1, 61–5.

Månsson, H. 2000. 'Childhood stuttering: incidence and development', *Journal of Fluency Disorders* 25:1, 47–57.

Marchant, J., McAuliffe, M.J. and Huckabee, M. 2008. 'Treatment of articulatory impairment in a child with spastic dysarthria associated with cerebral palsy', *Developmental Neurorehabilitation* 11:1, 81–90.

Marcus, G. and Rabagliati, H. 2006. 'What developmental disorders can tell us about the nature and origins of language', *Nature Neuroscience* 9:10, 1226–9.

Marfo, K. 1991. 'The maternal directiveness theme in mother-child interaction research: implications for early intervention', in K. Marfo (ed.), *Early intervention in transition: current perspectives on programs for handicapped children*, New York: Praeger Publishers, 177–203.

Marini, A., Carlomagno, S., Caltagirone, C. and Nocentini, U. 2005. 'The role played by the right hemisphere in the organization of complex textual structures', *Brain and Language* 93:1, 46–54.

Marinis, T. and van der Lely, H.K. 2007. 'On-line processing of wh-questions in children with G-SLI and typically developing children', *International Journal of Language & Communication Disorders* 42:5, 557–82.

Market, K.E., Montague, J.C., Buffalo, M.D. and Drummond, S.S. 1990. 'Acquired stuttering: descriptive data and treatment outcome', *Journal of Fluency Disorders* 15:1, 21–33.

Markus, J., Mundy, P., Morales, M., Delgado, C.E.F. and Yale, M. 2000. 'Individual differences in infant skill as predictors of child-caregiver joint attention and language', *Social Development* 9:3, 302–15.

Marquardt, T. and Sussman, H. 1984. 'The elusive lesion-apraxia of speech link in Broca's aphasia', in J.C. Rosenbek, M.R. McNeil and A.E. Aronson (eds.), *Apraxia of speech: physiology, acoustics, linguistics, management*, San Diego, CA: College Hill Press, 91–112.

Marquardt, T.P., Jacks, A. and Davis, B.L. 2004. 'Token-to-token variability in developmental apraxia of speech: three longitudinal case studies', *Clinical Linguistics & Phonetics* 18:2, 127–44.

Marquardt, T.P., Sussman, H.M., Snow, T. and Jacks, A. 2002. 'The integrity of the syllable in developmental apraxia of speech', *Journal of Communication Disorders* 35:1, 31–49.

Marr, D. 1982. *Vision: a computational investigation into the human representation and processing of visual information*, San Francisco, CA: W.H. Freeman.

Marsh, N., Kersel, D., Havill, J. and Sleigh, J. 1998. 'Caregiver burden at 1 year following severe traumatic brain injury', *Brain Injury* 12:12, 1045–59.

Marshall, C. and van der Lely, H. 2007. 'The impact of phonological complexity on past tense inflection in children with grammatical-SLI', *Advances in Speech-Language Pathology* 9:3, 191–203.

Marshall, D., Christo, C. and Davis, J. 2013. 'Performance of school age reading disabled students on the phonological awareness subtests of the comprehensive test of phonological processing (CTOPP)', *Contemporary School Psychologist*, 17:1, 93–102.

Marshall, J. 1995. 'The mapping hypothesis and aphasia therapy', *Aphasiology* 9:6, 517–39.

Marshall, J. 2013. 'Disorders of sentence processing in aphasia', in I. Papathanasiou, P. Coppens and C. Potagas (eds.), *Aphasia and related neurogenic communication disorders*, Burlington, MA: Jones and Bartlett Learning, 197–216.

Marshall, J., Best, W., Cocks, N., Cruice, M., Pring, T., Bulcock, G., Creek, G., Eales, N., Mummery, A.L., Matthews, N. and Caute, A. 2012. 'Gesture and naming therapy for people with aphasia: a group study', *Journal of Speech, Language, and Hearing Research* 55:3, 726–38.

Marshall, J., Black, M., Byng, S., Chiat, S. and Pring, T. 1999. *The sentence processing resource pack*, London: Winslow Press.

Marshall, J.C. and Newcombe, F. 1973. 'Patterns of paralexia: a psycholinguistic approach', *Journal of Psycholinguistic Research* 2:3, 175–99.

Marshall, R.C. 1999. *Introduction to group treatment for aphasia: design and management*, Woburn, MA: Butterworth Heinemann.

Martens, J.W.M.A.F., Versnel, H. and Dejonckere, P.H. 2007. 'The effect of visible speech in the perceptual rating of pathological voices', *Archives of Otolaryngology – Head and Neck Surgery* 133:2, 178–85.

Martens, M.A., Wilson, S.J. and Reutens, D.C. 2008. 'Research review: Williams syndrome: a critical review of the cognitive, behavioural, and neuroanatomical phenotype', *Journal of Child Psychology and Psychiatry* 49:6, 576–608.

Martin, A. and Fedio, P. 1983. 'Word production and comprehension in Alzheimer's disease: the breakdown of semantic knowledge', *Brain and Language* 19:1, 124–41.

Martin, A.D. 1974. 'Some objections to the term apraxia of speech', *Journal of Speech and Hearing Disorders* 39:1, 53–64.

Martin, G.E., Klusek, J., Estigarribia, B. and Roberts, J.E. 2009. 'Language characteristics of individuals with Down syndrome', *Topics in Language Disorders* 29:2, 112–32.

Martin, I. and McDonald, S. 2003. 'Weak coherence, no theory of mind, or executive dysfunction? Solving the puzzle of pragmatic language disorders', *Brain and Language* 85:3, 451–66.

Martin, I. and McDonald, S. 2004. 'An exploration of causes of non-literal language problems in individuals with Asperger syndrome', *Journal of Autism and Developmental Disorders* 34:3, 311–28.

Martin, I. and McDonald, S. 2005. 'Evaluating the causes of impaired irony comprehension following traumatic brain injury', *Aphasiology* 19:8, 712–30.

Martin, N.A. and Brownell, R. 2000. *Test of auditory processing skills*, third edition, Academic Therapy Publications.

Martin, R.R. and Haroldson, S.K. 1992. 'Stuttering and speech naturalness: audio and audiovisual judgments', *Journal of Speech and Hearing Research* 35:3, 521–8.

Marton, K. 2008. 'Visuo-spatial processing and executive functions in children with specific language impairment', *International Journal of Language & Communication Disorders* 43:2, 181–200.

Marunick, M. and Tselios, N. 2004. 'The efficacy of palatal augmentation prostheses for speech and swallowing in patients undergoing glossectomy: a review of the literature', *Journal of Prosthetic Dentistry* 91:1, 67–74.

Marvel, C.L., Schwartz, B.L. and Isaacs, K.L. 2004. 'Word production deficits in schizophrenia', *Brain and Language* 89:1, 182–91.

Mashal, N., Faust, M., Hendler, T. and Jung-Beeman, M. 2009. 'An fMRI study of processing novel metaphoric sentences', *Laterality* 14:1, 30–54.

Mason, R.M. and Warren, D.W. 1980. 'Adenoid involution and developing hypernasality in cleft palate', *Journal of Speech and Hearing Disorders* 45:4, 469–80.

Mata, I., Perez-Iglesias, R., Roiz-Santiañez, R., Tordesillas-Gutierrez, D., Gonzalez-Mandly, A., Vazquez-Barquero, J.L. and Crespo-Facorro, B. 2009. 'A neuregulin 1 variant is associated with increased lateral ventricle volume in patients with first-episode schizophrenia', *Biological Psychiatry* 65:6, 535–40.

Mather, N., Roberts, R., Hammill, D.D. and Allen, E.A. 2008. *Test of orthographic competence*, Austin, TX: Pro-Ed.

Mathers, C.D. and Loncar, D. 2006. 'Projections of global mortality and burden of disease from 2002 to 2030', *Public Library of Science Medicine* 3:11 e442, 2011–29.

Mathes, P.G., Denton, C.A., Fletcher, J.M., Anthony, J.L., Francis, D.J. and Schatschneider, C. 2005. 'The effects of theoretically different instruction and student characteristics on the skills of struggling readers', *Reading Research Quarterly* 40:2, 148–82.

Mathy, P. 2004. 'Augmentative and alternative communication intervention in neurogenic disorders with acquired dysarthria', in E. Strand (ed.), *Treatment of dysarthria: evidence-based practice*, Rockville, MD: American Speech-Language-Hearing Association, 33–41.

Matthews, T.W. and Lampe, H.B. 2005. 'Treatment options in oral cancer', in P.C. Doyle and R.L. Keith (eds.), *Contemporary considerations in the treatment and rehabilitation of head and neck cancer*, Austin: Pro-Ed, 153–70.

Mattison, R.E., Hooper, S.R. and Carlson, G.A. 2006. 'Neuropsychological characteristics of special education students with serious emotional/behavioral disorders', *Behavioral Disorders* 31:2, 176–88.

Mattison, R.E., Spitznagel, E.L. and Felix, B.C. 1998. 'Enrollment predictors of the special education outcome for students with SED', *Behavioral Disorders* 23:4, 243–56.

Maulik, P.K. and Harbour, C.K. 2011. 'Epidemiology of intellectual disability', in J.H. Stone and M. Blouin (eds.), *International encyclopedia of rehabilitation* (online, available at: http://cirrie.buffalo.edu/encyclopedia/en/article/144/; last accessed 12 June 2013).

Max, L. 2004. 'Stuttering and internal models for sensorimotor control: a theoretical perspective to generate testable hypotheses', in B. Maassen, R. Kent, H. Peters, P.V. Lieshout and W. Hulstijn (eds.), *Speech motor control in normal and disordered speech*, New York: Oxford University Press, 357–87.

Max, L., Guenther, F.H., Gracco, V.L., Ghosh, S.S. and Wallace, M.E. 2004. 'Unstable or insufficiently activated internal models and feedback-biased motor control as sources of dysfluency: a theoretical model of stuttering', *Contemporary Issues in Communication Science and Disorders* 31, 105–22.

Maxim, J. 1991. 'Can elicited language be used to diagnose dementia? A comparison of demented, depressed, aphasic and normal elderly subjects', *NHCSS Work in Progress* 1, 13–21.

Mayer, M. 1969. *Frog, where are you?*, New York: Penguin Books.

Mayer, R.M. and Gelfer, M.P. 2008. 'Outcomes of voice therapy for male-to-female transgendered individuals', ASHA Convention: Chicago, IL, November 2008.

Mazzocco, M.M., Kates, W.R., Baumgardner, T.L., Freund, L.S. and Reiss, A.L. 1997. 'Autistic behaviors among girls with fragile X syndrome', *Journal of Autism and Developmental Disorders* 27:4, 415–35.

Mazzoni, D.S., Ackley, R.S. and Nash, D.J. 1994. 'Abnormal pinna type and hearing loss correlations in Down syndrome', *Journal of Intellectual Disability Research* 38:11, 481–7.

McBride-Chang, C., Lam, F., Lam, C., Doo, S., Wong, S.W.L. and Chow, Y.Y.Y. 2008. 'Word recognition and cognitive profiles of Chinese pre-school children at risk for dyslexia through language delay or familial history of dyslexia', *Journal of Child Psychology and Psychiatry* 49:2, 211–18.

McCabe, P., Rosenthal, J. and McLeod, S. 1998. 'Features of developmental dyspraxia in the general speech-impaired population?', *Clinical Linguistics & Phonetics* 12:2, 105–26.

McCann, J. and Peppé, S. 2003. 'Prosody in autism spectrum disorders: a review', *International Journal of Language & Communication Disorders* 38:4, 325–50.

McCarthy, D. 1972. *McCarthy scales of children's abilities*, San Antonio, TX: Psychological Corporation.

McCarthy, R.H. and Terkelsen, K.G. 1994. 'Esophageal dysfunction in two patients after clozapine treatment', *Journal of Clinical Psychopharmacology* 14:4, 281–3.

McCartney, K. 1984. 'Effect of quality of day care environment on children's language development', *Developmental Psychology* 20:2, 244–60.

McCathren, R.B., Yoder, P.J. and Warren, S.F. 1999. 'The relationship between prelinguistic vocalization and later expressive vocabulary in young children with developmental delay', *Journal of Speech, Language, and Hearing Research* 42:4, 915–24.

McColl, M.A., Carlson, P., Johnston, J., Minnes, P., Shue, K., Davies, D. and Karlovits, T. 1998. 'The definition of community integration: perspectives of people with brain injuries', *Brain Injury* 12:1, 15–30.

McConaughy, S.H. and Skiba, R.J. 1994. 'Comorbidity of externalizing and internalizing problems', *School Psychology Review* 22:3, 421–36.

McCormack, J., McLeod, S., Harrison, L.J. and McAllister, L. 2010. 'The impact of speech impairment in early childhood: investigating parents' and speech-language pathologists' perspectives using the ICF-CY', *Journal of Communication Disorders* 43:5, 378–96.

McCormack, J., McLeod, S., McAllister, L. and Harrison, L.J. 2009. 'A systematic review of the association between childhood speech impairment and participation across the lifespan', *International Journal of Speech-Language Pathology* 11:2, 155–70.

McCreadie, R., Stevens, H., Henderson, J., Hall, D., McCaul, R., Filik, R., Young, G., Sutch, G., Kanagaratnam, G., Perrington, S., McKendrick, J., Stephenson, D. and Burns, T. 2004. 'The dental health of people with schizophrenia', *Acta Psychiatrica Scandinavica* 110:4, 306–10.

McCreadie, R.G., Robertson, L.J. and Wiles, D.H. 1992. 'The Nithsdale schizophrenia surveys. IX: akathisia, parkinsonism, tardive dyskinesia and plasma neuroleptic level', *British Journal of Psychiatry* 160:6, 793–9.

McCrory, E. 2001. 'Voice therapy outcomes in vocal fold nodules: a retrospective audit', *International Journal of Language & Communication Disorders* 36:suppl, 19–24.

McCune, L. and Vihman, M.M. 2001. 'Early phonetic and lexical development: a productivity approach', *Journal of Speech, Language, and Hearing Research* 44:3, 670–84.

McDonald, S. 1992. 'Communication disorders following closed head injury: new approaches to assessment and rehabilitation', *Brain Injury* 6:3, 283–92.

McDonald, S. 1993. 'Pragmatic skills after closed head injury: ability to meet the informational needs of the listener', *Brain and Language* 44:1, 28–46.

McDonald, S. 2000a. 'Exploring the cognitive basis of right-hemisphere pragmatic language disorders', *Brain and Language* 75:1, 82–107.

McDonald, S. 2000b. 'Neuropsychological studies of sarcasm', *Metaphor and Symbol* 15:1–2, 85–98.

McDonald, S. and Flanagan, S. 2004. 'Social perception deficits after traumatic brain injury: interaction between emotion recognition, mentalizing ability, and social communication', *Neuropsychology* 18:3, 572–9.

McDonald, S. and Pearce, S. 1996. 'Clinical insights into pragmatic theory: frontal lobe deficits and sarcasm', *Brain and Language* 53:1, 81–104.

McDonald, S. and van Sommers, P. 1993. 'Differential pragmatic language loss following closed head injury: ability to negotiate requests', *Cognitive Neuropsychology* 10:4, 297–315.

McDonald, S., Tate, R., Togher, L., Bornhofen, C., Long, E., Gertler, P. and Bowen, R. 2008. 'Social skills treatment for people with severe, chronic acquired brain injuries: a multicenter trial', *Archives of Physical Medicine and Rehabilitation* 89:9, 1648–59.

McFarlane, S.C., Holt-Romeo, T.L., Lavorato, A.S. and Warner, L. 1991. 'Unilateral vocal fold paralysis: perceived vocal quality following three methods of treatment', *American Journal of Speech-Language Pathology* 1:1, 45–8.

McFarlane, S.C., Watterson, T.L., Lewis, K. and Boone, D.R. 1998. 'Effect of voice therapy facilitation techniques on airflow in unilateral paralysis patients', *Phonoscope* 1:3, 187–91.

McGlashan, J.A. and Howard, D.M. 2001. 'Theoretical and practical considerations in the occupational use of voice amplification devices', in P.H. Dejonckere (ed.), *Occupational voice: care and cure*, The Hague, The Netherlands: Kugler, 165–86.

McGorry, P.D., Nelson, B., Goldstone, S. and Yung, A.R. 2010. 'Clinical staging: a heuristic and practical strategy for new research and better health and social outcomes for psychotic and related mood disorders', *Canadian Journal of Psychiatry* 55:8, 486–97.

McGrath, L.M., Pennington, B.F., Willcutt, E.G., Boada, R., Shriberg, L.D. and Smith, S.D. 2007. 'Gene × environment interactions in speech sound disorder predict language and preliteracy outcomes', *Development and Psychopathology* 19:4, 1047–72.

McGrath, N., Anderson, N.E., Croxson, M.C. and Powell, K.F. 1997. 'Herpes simplex encephalitis treated with acyclovir: diagnosis and long term outcome', *Journal of Neurology, Neurosurgery and Psychiatry* 63:3, 321–6.

McGregor, K. and Appel, A. 2002. 'On the relationship between mental representation and naming in a child with specific language impairment', *Clinical Linguistics & Phonetics* 16:1, 1–20.

McGregor, K. and Leonard, L. 1994. 'Subject pronoun and article omissions in the speech of children with specific language impairment: a phonological interpretation', *Journal of Speech and Hearing Research* 37:1, 171–81.

McGregor, K.K., Berns, A.J., Owen, A.J., Michels, S.A., Duff, D., Bahnsen, A.J. and Lloyd, M. 2012. 'Associations between syntax and the lexicon among children with or without ASD and language impairment', *Journal of Autism and Developmental Disorders* 42:1, 35–47.

McGrew, K.S. and Wendling, B.J. 2010. 'Cattell–Horn–Carroll cognitive-achievement relations: what we have learned from the past 20 years of research', *Psychology in the Schools* 47:7, 651–75.

McGuinness, B., Barrett, S.L., Craig, D., Lawson, J. and Passmore, A.P. 2010. 'Attention deficits in Alzheimer's disease and vascular dementia', *Journal of Neurology, Neurosurgery and Psychiatry* 81:2, 157–9.

McHenry, M.A. and Parle, A.M. 2006. 'Construction of a set of unpredictable sentences for intelligibility testing', *Journal of Medical Speech-Language Pathology* 14:4, 269–72.

McHugh, G., Doortje, C., Butcher, I., Steyerberg, E., Lu, J., Mushkudiani, N., Hernández, A.V., Marmarou, A., Maas, A.I. and Murray, G.D. 2007. 'Prognostic value of secondary insults in traumatic brain injury: results from the IMPACT study', *Journal of Neurotrauma* 24:2, 287–93.

McInnes, A., Humphries, T., Hogg-Johnson, S. and Tannock, R. 2003. 'Listening comprehension and working memory are impaired in attention-deficit hyperactivity disorder irrespective of language impairment', *Journal of Abnormal Child Psychology* 31:4, 427–43.

McKeith, I.G. 2000. 'Spectrum of Parkinson's disease, Parkinson's dementia, and Lewy body dementia', *Neurologic Clinics* 18:4, 865–902.

McKeith, I.G. 2006. 'Consensus guidelines for the clinical and pathologic diagnosis of dementia with Lewy bodies (DLB): report of the Consortium on DLB international workshop', *Journal of Alzheimer's Disease* 9:3 Suppl, 417–23.

McKeith, I.G., Galasko, D., Kosaka, K., Perry, E.K., Dickson, D.W., Hansen, L.A., Salmon, D.P., Lowe, J., Mirra, S.S., Byrne, E.J., Lennox, G., Quinn, N.P., Edwardson, J.A., Ince, P.G., Bergeron, C., Burns, A., Miller, B.L., Lovestone, S., Collerton, D., Jansen, E.N., Ballard, C., de Vos, R.A., Wilcock, G.K., Jellinger, K.A. and Perry, R.H. 1996. 'Consensus guidelines for the clinical and pathologic diagnosis of dementia with Lewy bodies (DLB): report of the consortium on DLB international workshop', *Neurology* 47:5, 1113–24.

McKelvey, M.L., Hux, K., Dietz, A. and Beukelman, D.R. 2010. 'Impact of personal relevance and contextualization on word-picture matching by people with aphasia', *American Journal of Speech-Language Pathology* 19:1, 22–33.

McKenna, P. and Tomasina, O.H. 2005. *Schizophrenic speech*, Cambridge University Press.

McKhann, G., Albert, M.S., Grossman, M., Miller, B., Dickson, D. and Trojanowski, J.Q. 2001. 'Clinical and pathological diagnosis of frontotemporal dementia: report of the Work Group on Frontotemporal Dementia and Pick's Disease', *Archives of Neurology* 58:11, 1803–9.

McKhann, G.M., Drachman, D., Folstein, M., Katzman, R., Price, D. and Stadlan, E.M. 1984. 'Clinical diagnosis of Alzheimer's disease: report of the NINCDS-ADRAA work group under the auspices of Department of Health and Human Services task force on Alzheimer's disease', *Neurology* 34:7, 939–44.

McKhann, G.M., Knopman, D.S., Chertkow, H., Hyman, B.T., Jack, C.R., Kawas, C.H., Klunk, W.E., Koroshetz, W.J., Manly, J.J., Mayeux, R., Mohs, R.C., Morris, J.C., Rossor, M.N., Scheltens, P., Carrillo, M.C., Thies, B., Weintraub, S. and Phelps, C.H. 2011. The diagnosis of dementia due to Alzheimer's disease: recommendations from the National Institute on Aging and Alzheimer's Association workgroups on diagnostic guidelines for Alzheimer's disease', *Alzheimer's & Dementia* 7:3, 263–9.

McLean, J.E. and Snyder-McLean, L. 1988. 'Application of pragmatics to severely mentally retarded children and youth', in R.L. Schiefelbusch and L. Lloyd (eds.), *Language perspectives: acquisition, retardation, and intervention*, Austin, TX: Pro-Ed., 255–90.

McLeod, S. 1997. 'Sampling consonant clusters: four procedures designed for Australian children', *Australian Communication Quarterly*, Autumn, 9–12.

McLeod, S. 2004. 'Speech pathologists' application of the ICF to children with speech impairment', *Advances in Speech-Language Pathology* 6:1, 75–81.

McLeod, S. and Harrison, L.J. 2009. 'Epidemiology of speech and language impairment in a nationally representative sample of 4- to 5-year-old children', *Journal of Speech, Language, and Hearing Research* 52:5, 1213–29.

McLeod, S. and McCormack, J. 2007. 'Application of the ICF and ICF-children and youth in children with speech impairment', *Seminars in Speech and Language* 28:4, 254–64.

McLeod, S. and Threats, T. 2008. 'The ICF-CY and children with communication disabilities', *International Journal of Speech-Language Pathology* 10:1–2, 92–109.

McLeod, S., Harrison, L.J. and McCormack, J. 2012. 'The intelligibility in context scale: validity and reliability of a subjective rating measure', *Journal of Speech, Language, and Hearing Research* 55:2, 648–56.

McMaster, K.L., Fuchs, D., Fuchs, L.S. and Compton, D.L. 2005. 'Responding to nonresponders: an experimental field trial of identification and intervention methods', *Exceptional Children* 71:4, 445–63.

McMillan, C., Bradley, C., Razvi, S. and Weaver, J. 2008. 'Evaluation of new measures of the impact of hypothyroidism on quality of life and symptoms: the ThyDQoL and ThySRQ', *Value in Health* 11:2, 285–94.

McMurray, J.S., Connor, N. and Ford, C.N. 2008. 'Cidofovir efficacy in recurrent respiratory papillomatosis: a randomized, double-blind, placebo-controlled study', *Annals of Otology, Rhinology and Laryngology* 117:7, 477–83.

McNamara, P. and Durso, R. 2003. 'Pragmatic communication skills in patients with Parkinson's disease', *Brain and Language* 84:3, 414–23.

McNeil, M.R. and Adams, S. 1991. 'A comparison of speech kinematics among apraxic, conduction aphasic, ataxic dysarthric and normal geriatric speakers', *Clinical Aphasiology* 18, 279–94.

McNeil, M.R. and Kent, R.D. 1990. *Cerebral control of speech and limb movements*, North-Holland: Elsevier Science Publishers.

McNeil, M.R., Caligiuri, M. and Rosenbek, J.C. 1989. 'A comparison of labiomandibular kinematic durations, displacements, velocities, and dysmetrias in apraxic and normal adults', in *Clinical aphasiology conference*, Cape Cod, MA: College Hill Press, 173–93.

McNeil, M.R., Fossett, T.R.D., Katz, W.F., Garst, D., Carter, G., Szuminsky, N. and Doyle, P.J. 2007. 'Effects of on-line kinematic feedback treatment for apraxia of speech', *Brain and Language*, 103:1–2, 223–5.

McNeil, M.R., Robin, D.A. and Schmidt, R.A. 1997. 'Apraxia of speech: definition, differentiation, and treatment', in M.R. McNeil (ed.), *Clinical management of sensorimotor speech disorders*, New York: Thieme Medical Publishers, 311–44.

McNeil, M.R., Robin, D.A. and Schmidt, R.A. 2009. 'Apraxia of speech: definition and differential diagnosis', in M.R. McNeil (ed.), *Clinical management of sensorimotor speech disorders*, second edition, New York: Thieme, 249–68.

McNeill, B.C. and Gillon, G.T. 2011. 'Prospective evaluation of features of childhood apraxia of speech', American Speech-Language-Hearing Association (ASHA) Convention: San Diego, CA, 17–19 November 2011.

McNeill, B.C., Gillon, G.T. and Dodd, B. 2009a. 'Effectiveness of an integrated phonological awareness approach for children with childhood apraxia of speech (CAS)', *Child Language Teaching and Therapy* 25:3, 341–66.

McNeill, B.C., Gillon, G.T. and Dodd, B. 2009b. 'Phonological awareness and early reading development in childhood apraxia of speech', *International Journal of Language & Communication Disorders* 44:2, 175–92.

McNeill, B.C., Gillon, G.T. and Dodd, B. 2009c. 'A longitudinal case study of the effects of an integrated phonological awareness program for identical twin boys with childhood apraxia of speech (CAS)', *International Journal of Speech-Language Pathology* 11:6, 482–95.

McNeill, B.C., Gillon, G.T. and Dodd, B. 2010. 'The longer term effects of an integrated phonological awareness intervention for children with childhood apraxia of speech', *Asia Pacific Journal of Speech, Language and Hearing* 13:3, 145–61.

McNutt, J.C. 1977. 'Oral sensory and motor behaviors of children with /s/ or /r/ misarticulations', *Journal of Speech and Hearing Research* 20:4, 694–704.

McShane, R.H., Nagy, Z., Esiri, M.M., King, E., Joachim, C., Sullivan, N. and Smith, A. 2001. 'Anosmia in dementia is associated with Lewy bodies rather than Alzheimer's pathology', *Journal of Neurology, Neurosurgery and Psychiatry* 70:6, 739–43.

McWilliam, R.A. 1992. *Family-centered intervention planning: a routines-based approach*, Tucson, AZ: Communication Skill Builders.

McWilliam, R.A. 2000. 'It's only natural … to have early intervention in the environments where it is needed', in S. Sandall and M. Ostrosky (eds.), *Natural environments and inclusion – young exceptional children monograph no. 2*, Longmont, CO: Sopris West, 17–26.

Meaburn, E., Dale, P.S., Craig, I.W. and Plomin, R. 2002. 'Language-impaired children: no sign of the FOXP2 mutation', *Neuro Report* 13:8, 1075–7.

Meadows, N.B., Neel, R.S., Scott, C.M. and Parker, G. 1994. 'Academic performance, social competence, and mainstream accommodations: a look at mainstreamed and non-mainstreamed students with serious behavioral disorders', *Behavioral Disorders* 19:3, 170–80.

Mehta, D.D., Zeitels, S.M., Burns, J.A., Friedman, A.D., Deliyski, D.D. and Hillman, R.E. 2012. 'High-speed videoendoscopic analysis of relationships between cepstral-based acoustic measures and voice production mechanisms in patients undergoing phonomicrosurgery', *Annals of Otology, Rhinology and Laryngology* 121:5, 341–7.

Mei, C. and Morgan, A.T. 2011. 'Incidence of mutism, dysarthria and dysphagia associated with childhood posterior fossa tumour', *Child's Nervous System* 27:7, 1129–36.

Meilijson, S.R., Kasher, A. and Elizur, A. 2004. 'Language performance in chronic schizophrenia: a pragmatic approach', *Journal of Speech, Language, and Hearing Research* 47:3, 695–713.

Meinzer, M., Rodriguez, A.D. and Gonzalez Rothi, L.J. 2012. 'First decade of research on constrained-induced treatment approaches for aphasia rehabilitation', *Archives of Physical Medicine and Rehabilitation* 93:1, S35–45.

Mellard, D. and Woods, S. 2007. 'Adult life with dyslexia', *Perspectives* 33:4, 15–18.

Melnick, K. and Conture, E.G. 1999. 'Parent-child group approach to stuttering in preschool and school-age children', in M. Onslow and A. Packman (eds.), *Early stuttering: a handbook of intervention strategies*, San Diego, CA: Singular Publishing, 17–51.

Meltzner, G.S. and Hillman, R.E. 2005. 'Impact of aberrant acoustic properties on the perception of sound quality in electrolarynx speech', *Journal of Speech, Language, and Hearing Research* 48:4, 766–79.

Mendez, M.F., Cherrier, M.M. and Perryman, K.M. 1997. 'Differences between Alzheimer's disease and vascular dementia on information processing measures', *Brain and Cognition* 34:2, 301–10.

Menn, L. and Obler, L. 1990. *Agrammatic aphasia*, Amsterdam: Benjamins.

Menn, L., Schmidt, E. and Nicholas, B. 2009. 'Conspiracy and sabotage in the acquisition of phonology: dense data undermine existing theories, provide scaffolding for a new one', *Language Sciences* 31:2–3, 285–304.

Mentis, M. and Prutting, C.A. 1987. 'Cohesion in the discourse of normal and head-injured adults', *Journal of Speech and Hearing Research* 30:1, 88–98.

Mentis, M. and Prutting, C.A. 1991. 'Analysis of topic as illustrated in a head-injured and a normal adult', *Journal of Speech and Hearing Research* 34:3, 583–95.

Mentis, M., Briggs-Whittaker, J. and Gramigna, G.D. 1995. 'Discourse topic management in senile dementia of the Alzheimer's type', *Journal of Speech and Hearing Research* 38:5, 1054–66.

Menzies, R.G., O'Brian, S., Onslow, M., Packman, A., St Clare, T. and Block, S. 2008. 'An experimental clinical trial of a cognitive-behavior therapy package for chronic stuttering', *Journal of Speech, Language, and Hearing Research* 51:6, 1451–64.

Menzies, R.G., Onslow, M., Packman, A. and O'Brian, S. 2009. 'Cognitive behavior therapy for adults who stutter: a tutorial for speech-language pathologists', *Journal of Fluency Disorders* 34:3, 187–200.

Merrill, R.M., Anderson, A.E. and Sloan, A. 2011. 'Quality of life indicators according to voice disorders and voice-related conditions', *Laryngoscope* 121:9, 2004–10.

Mervis, C.B. and John, A.E. 2008. 'Vocabulary abilities of children with Williams syndrome: strengths, weaknesses and relation to visuospatial construction ability', *Journal of Speech, Language, and Hearing Research* 51:4, 967–82.

Mervis, C.B. and Klein-Tasman, B.P. 2000. 'Williams syndrome: cognition, personality, and adaptive behaviour', *Mental Retardation and Developmental Disabilities Research Reviews* 6:2, 148–58.

Mervis, C.B., Morris, J., Bertrand, J. and Robinson, B.F. 1999. 'Williams syndrome: findings from an integrated program of research', in H. Tager-Flusberg (ed.), *Neurodevelopmental disorders*, Cambridge, MA: MIT Press, 65–110.

Mervis, C.B., Robinson, B.F., Rowe, M.L., Becerra, A.M. and Klein-Tasman, B.P. 2003. 'Language abilities of individuals with Williams syndrome', in L. Abbeduto (ed.), *International review of research in mental retardation (volume 27). Language and communication in mental retardation*, San Diego, CA: Academic Press, 35–81.

Messer, D. and Dockrell, J.E. 2006. 'What constitutes a word-finding problem?', *Journal of Speech, Language, and Hearing Research* 49:2, 309–32.

Mesulam, M.M. 1982. 'Slowly progressive aphasia without generalized dementia', *Annals of Neurology* 11:6, 592–8.

Mesulam, M.M. 2001. 'Primary progressive aphasia', *Annals of Neurology* 49:4, 425–32.

Mesulam, M.M. 2003. 'Primary progressive aphasia – a language-based dementia', *New England Journal of Medicine* 349:16, 1535–42.

Mesulam, M.M. 2007. 'Primary progressive aphasia: a 25-year retrospective', *Alzheimer Disease and Associated Disorders* 21:4, S8-S11.

Mesulam, M.M., Grossman, M., Hillis, A.E., Kertesz, A. and Weintraub, S. 2003. 'The core and halo of primary progressive aphasia and semantic dementia', *Annals of Neurology* 54:Suppl 5, S11–S14.

Mesulam, M.M., Rogalski, E., Wieneke, C., Cobia, D., Rademaker, A., Thompson, C. and Weintraub, S. 2009. 'Neurology of anomia in the semantic variant of primary progressive aphasia', *Brain* 132:9, 2553–65.

Mesulam, M.M., Wicklund, A., Johnson, N., Rogalski, E., Leger, G.C., Rademaker, A., Weintraub, S. and Bigio, E.H. 2008. 'Alzheimer and frontotemporal pathology in subsets of primary progressive aphasia', *Annals of Neurology* 63:6, 709–19.

Meteyard, L. and Patterson, K. 2009. 'The relation between content and structure in language production: an analysis of speech errors in semantic dementia', *Brain and Language* 110:3, 121–34.

Metsala, J.L. and Walley, A.C. 1998. 'Spoken vocabulary growth and the segmental restructuring of lexical representations: precursors to phonemic awareness and early reading ability', in J.L. Metsala and L.C. Ehri (eds.), *Word recognition in beginning literacy*, Mahwah, NJ: Lawrence Erlbaum Associates, 89–120.

Metter, E.J. and Hanson, W.R. 1986. 'Clinical and acoustical variability in hypokinetic dysarthria', *Journal of Communication Disorders* 19:5, 347–66.

Metzler-Baddeley, C. 2007. 'A review of cognitive impairments in dementia with Lewy bodies relative to Alzheimer's disease and Parkinson's disease with dementia', *Cortex* 43:5, 583–600.

Meyer, M.S., Wood, F.B., Hart, L.A. and Felton, R.H. 1998. 'Longitudinal course of rapid naming in disabled and nondisabled readers', *Annals of Dyslexia* 48:1, 89–114.

Meyer, U. and Feldon, J. 2010. 'Epidemiology-driven neurodevelopmental animal models of schizophrenia', *Progress in Neurobiology* 90:3, 285–326.

Meyers, S.C. and Woodford, L.L. 1992. *The fluency development system for young children (ages 2–9)*, Buffalo, NY: United Educational Services.

Miccio, A.W. 2002. 'Clinical problem solving: assessment of phonological disorders', *American Journal of Speech-Language Pathology* 11:3, 221–9.

Miceli, G., Silveri, M.C., Nocentini, U. and Caramazza, A. 1988. 'Patterns of dissociation in comprehension and production of nouns and verbs', *Aphasiology* 2:3–4, 251–8.

Miceli, G., Silveri, M.C., Romani, C. and Caramazza, A. 1989. 'Variations in the pattern of omissions and substitutions of grammatical morphemes in the spontaneous speech of so-called agrammatic patients', *Brain and Language* 36:3, 447–92.

Middleton, S., Barnett, J. and Reeves, D. 2001. *What is an integrated care pathway?* www.evidence-based-medicine.co.uk, volume 3, issue 3 (online, available at: www.medicine.ox.ac.uk/bandolier/painres/download/whatis/What_is_an_ICP.pdf; last accessed 12 June 2013).

Milders, M., Fuchs, S. and Crawford, J.R. 2003. 'Neuropsychological impairments and changes in emotional and social behaviour following severe traumatic brain injury', *Journal of Clinical and Experimental Neuropsychology* 25:2, 157–72.

Milders, M., Ietswaart, M. and Crawford, J.R. 2006. 'Impairments in theory of mind shortly after traumatic brain injury and at 1-year follow-up', *Neuropsychology* 20:4, 400–8.

Miles, S. and Chapman, R. 2002. 'Narrative content as described by individuals with Down syndrome and typically-developing children', *Journal of Speech, Language, and Hearing Research* 45:1, 175–89.

Miles, S. and Ratner, N. 2001. 'Parental language input to children at stuttering onset', *Journal of Speech, Language, and Hearing Research* 44:5, 1116–30.

Millard, S.K., Nicholas, A. and Cook, F.M. 2008. 'Is parent-child interaction therapy effective in reducing stuttering?', *Journal of Speech, Language, and Hearing Research* 51:3, 636–50.

Miller, C. 2004. 'False belief and sentence complement performance in children with specific language impairment', *International Journal of Language & Communication Disorders* 39:2, 191–213.

Miller, E.H. and Quinn, A.I. 2006. 'Dental considerations in the management of head and neck cancer patients', *Otolaryngological Clinics of North America* 39:2, 319–29.

Miller, J. 1996. 'The search for the phenotype of disordered language performance', in M.L. Rice (ed.), *Towards a genetics of language*, Mahwah, NJ: Lawrence Erlbaum Associates, 297–314.

Miller, J. 1999. 'Profiles of language development in children with Down syndrome', in J.F. Miller, M. Leddy and L.A. Leavitt (eds.), *Improving the communication of people with Down syndrome*, Baltimore, MD: Paul H. Brookes, 11–39.

Miller, J. and Iglesias, A. 2006. *Systematic Analysis of Language Transcripts (SALT), English and Spanish, Version 9*, Madison, WI: Language Analysis Laboratory, University of Wisconsin, Madison.

Miller, J., Andriacchi, K. and Nockerts, A. 2011. *Assessing language production using SALT software: a clinician's guide to language sample analysis*, Madison, WI: Language Analysis Laboratory, University of Wisconsin, Madison.

Miller, J., Leddy, J., Miolo, G. and Sedey, A. 1995. 'The development of early language skills in children with Down syndrome', in L. Nade and D. Rosenthal (eds.), *Down syndrome: living and learning in the community*, New York: Wiley-Liss, 115–20.

Miller, N. 2002. 'The neurological bases of apraxia of speech', *Seminars in Speech and Language* 23:4, 223–30.

Miller, N. 2012. 'Dysarthria', in J.H. Stone and M. Blouin (eds.), *International encyclopedia of rehabilitation* (online, available at: http://cirrie.buffalo.edu/encyclopedia/en/article/242/; last accessed 12 June 2013.

Miller, N., Andrew, S., Noble, E. and Walshe, M. 2011. 'Changing perceptions of self as a communicator in Parkinson's disease: a longitudinal follow-up study', *Disability and Rehabilitation* 33:3, 204–10.

Miller, N., Noble, E., Jones, D., Allcock, L. and Burn, D.J. 2008. 'How do I sound to me? Perceived changes in communication in Parkinson's disease', *Clinical Rehabilitation* 22:1, 14–22.

Miller, N., Noble, E., Jones, D. and Burn, D. 2006. 'Life with communication changes in Parkinson's disease', *Age and Ageing* 35:3, 235–9.

Miller, S.A. 2009. 'Children's understanding of second-order mental states', *Psychological Bulletin* 135:5, 749–73.

Mills, W. 1913. *Voice production in singing and speaking, based on scientific principles*, fourth edition, Philadelphia, PA: Lippincott.

Milton, S. and Wertz, R. 1986. 'Management of persisting communication deficits in patients with traumatic brain injury', in B.P. Uzzell and Y. Gross (eds.), *Clinical neuropsychology of intervention*, Boston, MA: Martinus Nijhoff, 223–82.

Milton, S.B., Prutting, C.A. and Binder, G.M. 1984. 'Appraisal of communicative competence in head injured adults', in R.H. Brookshire (ed.), *Clinical aphasiology conference proceedings*, Minneapolis, MN: BRK Publishers, 114–23.

Mitchell, R.L.C. and Crow, T.J. 2005. 'Right hemisphere language functions and schizophrenia: the forgotten hemisphere?', *Brain* 128:5, 963–78.

Mitchley, N.J., Barber, J., Gray, J.M., Brooks, N. and Livingston, M.G. 1998. 'Comprehension of irony in schizophrenia', *Cognitive Neuropsychiatry* 3:2, 127–38.

Mo, S., Su, Y., Chan, R.C.K. and Liu, J. 2008. 'Comprehension of metaphor and irony in schizophrenia during remission: the role of theory of mind and IQ', *Psychiatry Research* 157:1–3, 21–29.

Modinos, G., Obiols, J.E., Pousa, E. and Vicens, J. 2009. 'Theory of mind in different dementia profiles', *Journal of Neuropsychiatry and Clinical Neurosciences* 21:1, 100–1.

Mody, M. and Studdert-Kennedy, M. 1997. 'Speech perception deficits in poor readers: auditory processing or phonological coding?', *Journal of Experimental Child Psychology* 64:2, 199–231.

Moffitt, T.E. and Henry, B. 1991. 'Neuropsychological studies of juvenile delinquency and juvenile violence', in J.S. Milner (ed.), *Neuropsychology of aggression*, Boston, MA: Kluwer Academic Publishers, 67–91.

Moll, K.R., Huffman, W.C., Lierle, D.M. and Smith, J.K. 1963. 'Factors related to the success of pharyngeal flap procedures', *Plastic and Reconstructive Surgery* 32:6, 581–8.

Molt, L.F. 1996. 'An examination of various aspects of auditory processing in clutterers', *Journal of Fluency Disorders* 21:3–4, 215–25.

Monetta, L. and Pell, M.D. 2007. 'Effects of verbal working memory deficits on metaphor comprehension in patients with Parkinson's disease', *Brain and Language* 101:1, 80–9.

Monetta, L., Grindrod, C.M. and Pell, M.D. 2009. 'Irony comprehension and theory of mind deficits in patients with Parkinson's disease', *Cortex* 45:8, 972–81.

Monetta, L., Ouellet-Plamondon, C. and Joanette, Y. 2006. 'Simulating the pattern of right-hemisphere-damaged patients for the processing of the alternative metaphorical meanings of words: evidence in favor of a cognitive resources hypothesis', *Brain and Language* 96:2, 171–7.

Montag, C., Dziobek, I., Richter, I.S., Neuhaus, K., Lehmann, A., Sylla, R., Heekeren, H.R., Heinz, A. and Gallinat, J. 2011. 'Different aspects of theory of mind in paranoid schizophrenia: evidence from a video-based assessment', *Psychiatry Research* 186:2–3, 203–9.

Montgomery, C.S. 2006. 'The treatment of stuttering: from the hub to the spoke', in N. Bernstein Ratner and J.A. Tetnowski (eds.), *Current issues in stuttering research and practice*, Mahwah, NJ: Lawrence Erlbaum, 159–204.

Montgomery, J. 1995. 'Sentence comprehension in children with specific language impairment: the role of phonological working memory', *Journal of Speech and Hearing Research* 38:1, 187–99.

Montgomery, J. 2000. 'Verbal working memory and sentence comprehension in children with specific language impairment', *Journal of Speech, Language, and Hearing Research* 43:2, 293–308.

Montgomery, J. 2004. 'Sentence comprehension in children with specific language impairment: effects of input rate and phonological working memory', *International Journal of Language & Communication Disorders* 39:1, 115–34.

Montgomery, J. and Evans, J. 2009. 'Complex sentence comprehension and working memory in children with specific language impairment', *Journal of Speech, Language, and Hearing Research* 52:2, 269–88.

Montgomery, J., Magimairaj, B.M. and Finney, M.C. 2010. 'Working memory and specific language impairment: an update on the relation and perspectives on assessment and treatment', *American Journal of Speech-Language Pathology* 19:1, 78–94.

Montgomery, J.K. and Bonderman, I.R. 1989. 'Serving preschool children with severe phonological disorders', *Language, Speech, and Hearing Services in Schools* 20:1, 76–84.

Morales, M., Mundy, P. and Rojas, J. 1998. 'Following the direction of gaze and language development in 6-month-olds', *Infant Behavior and Development* 21:2, 373–7.

Morales, M., Mundy, P., Delgado, C., Yale, M., Messinger, D., Neal, R. and Schwartz, H.K. 2000. 'Responding to joint attention across the 6- through 24-month age period and early language acquisition', *Journal of Applied Developmental Psychology* 21:3, 283–98.

Morgan, A.T. and Liegeois, F. 2010. 'Re-thinking diagnostic classification of the dysarthrias: a developmental perspective', *Folia Phoniatrica et Logopaedica* 62:3, 120–6.

Morgan, A.T. and Vogel, A.P. 2008. 'Intervention for childhood apraxia of speech', *Cochrane Database of Systematic Reviews*, Issue 3, CD006278.

Morgan, A.T. and Vogel, A.P. 2009. 'A Cochrane review of treatment for dysarthria associated with acquired brain injury in children and adolescents', *European Journal of Physical & Rehabilitation Medicine* 45:2, 197–204.

Morgan, A.T., Liegeois, F. and Occomore, L. 2007. 'Electropalatography treatment for articulation impairment in children with dysarthria post-traumatic brain injury', *Brain Injury* 21:11, 1183–93.

Morgan, A.T., Mageandran, S.D. and Mei, C. 2010. 'Incidence and clinical presentation of dysarthria and dysphagia in the acute setting following paediatric traumatic brain injury', *Child: Care, Health and Development* 36:1, 44–53.

Moriarty, B.C. and Gillon, G.T. 2006. 'Phonological awareness intervention for children with childhood apraxia of speech', *International Journal of Language & Communication Disorders* 41:6, 713–34.

Morice, R.D. and Ingram, J.C. 1983. 'Language complexity and age of onset of schizophrenia', *Psychiatry Research* 9:3, 233–42.

Morley, M.E., Court, D. and Miller, H. 1954. 'Developmental dysarthria', *British Medical Journal* 1:4852, 8–10.

Morr, K.E., Warren, D.W., Dalston, R.M., Smith, L.R., Seaton, D. and Hairfield, W.M. 1988. 'Intraoral speech pressures after experimental loss of velar resistance', *Folia Phoniatrica* 40:6, 284–9.

Morris, J. and Franklin, S. 2013. 'Disorders of auditory comprehension', in I. Papathanasiou, P. Coppens and C. Potagas (eds.), *Aphasia and related neurogenic communication disorders*, Burlington, MA: Jones and Bartlett Learning, 113–30.

Morris, J., Franklin, S., Ellis, A.W., Turner, J.E. and Bailey, P.J. 1996. 'Remediating a speech perception deficit in an aphasic patient', *Aphasiology* 10:2, 137–58.

Morris, J., Webster, J., Whitworth, A. and Howard, D. 2009. *Newcastle university aphasia therapy resources: auditory processing*, Newcastle upon Tyne, UK: Newcastle University.

Morris, J.C. 2005. 'Early-stage and preclinical Alzheimer disease', *Alzheimer Disease and Associated Disorders* 19:3, 163–5.

Morris, R.D. and Shaywitz, S.E. 1998. 'Subtypes of reading disability: variability around a phonological core', *Journal of Educational Psychology* 90:3, 347–73.

Morris, R.D., Lovett, M.W., Wolf, M., Sevcik, R.A., Steinbach, K.A., Frijters, J.C. and Shapiro, M.B. 2012. 'Multiple-component remediation for developmental reading disabilities: IQ, socioeconomic status, and race as factors in remedial outcome', *Journal of Learning Disabilities*, 45:2, 99–127.

Morrison, D., Rahman, I., Lannan, S. and MacNee, W. 1999. 'Epithelial permeability, inflammation, and oxidant stress in the air spaces of smokers', *Respiratory and Critical Care Medicine* 159:2, 473–9.

Morrison, M. 1997. 'Pattern recognition in muscle misuse voice disorders: how I do it', *Journal of Voice* 11:1, 108–14.

Morrison, M.D. and Rammage, L.A. 1993. 'Muscle misuse voice disorders: description and classification', *Acta Oto-Laryngologica* 113:3, 428–34.

Morrison, M.D. and Rammage, L.A. 2010. 'The irritable larynx syndrome as a central sensitivity syndrome', *Canadian Journal of Speech-Language Pathology and Audiology* 34:4, 282–9.

Mortimer, J. and Rvachew, S. 2010. 'A longitudinal investigation of morpho-syntax in children with speech sound disorders', *Journal of Communication Disorders* 43:1, 61–76.

Moss, A. and Nicholas, M. 2006. 'Language rehabilitation in chronic aphasia and time postonset: a review of single-subject data', *Stroke* 37:12, 3043–51.

Moss, A.L., Pigott, R.W. and Albery, E.H. 1987. 'Hynes pharyngoplasty revisited', *Plastic and Reconstructive Surgery* 79:3, 354–5.

Moss, H.E., Tyler, L.K. and Devlin, J.P. 2002. 'The emergence of category-specific deficits in a distributed semantic system', in E.M.E. Forde and G.W. Humphreys (eds.), *Category specificity in mind and brain*, Hove, East Sussex: Psychology Press, 115–45.

Motor Accidents Authority. 1998. *Training needs of attendant carers*, Sydney: Motor Accidents Authority.

Mottron, L. 2004. 'Matching strategies in cognitive research with individuals with high-functioning autism: current practices, instrument biases, and recommendations', *Journal of Autism and Developmental Disorders* 34:1, 19–27.

Mowrer, D.E. 1971. 'Transfer of training in articulation therapy', *Journal of Speech and Hearing Disorders* 36:4, 427–46.

Moyle, M.J., Karasinski, C., Ellis Weismer, S. and Gorman, B. 2011. 'Grammatical morphology in school-age children with and without language impairment: a discriminant function analysis', *Language, Speech, and Hearing Services in Schools* 42:4, 550–60.

Msall, M. and Park, J. 2009. 'The changing panorama of preschool disability: biomedical and social risks', in M. Shevell (ed.), *Neurodevelopmental disabilities: clinical and scientific foundations*, London: Mac Keith Press, 27–42.

Mudge, A.M., Kasper, K., Clair, A., Redfern, H., Bell, J.J., Barras, M.A., Dip, G. and Pachana, N.A. 2011. 'Recurrent readmissions in medical patients: a prospective study', *Journal of Hospital Medicine* 6:2, 61–7.

Muller, F., Simion, A., Reviriego, E., Galera, C., Mazaux, J.M., Barat, M. and Joseph, P.A. 2010. 'Exploring theory of mind after severe traumatic brain injury', *Cortex* 46:9, 1088–99.

Müller, U., Zelazo, P.D., Hood, S., Leone, T. and Rohrer, L. 2004. 'Interference control in a new rule use task: age-related changes, labeling, and attention', *Child Development* 75:5, 1594–609.

Muma, J. and Cloud, S. 2008. *Advancing communication disorders: 60 basic issues*, Hattiesburg, MS: Natural Child Publisher.

Mundy, P., Kasari, C., Sigman, M. and Ruskin, E. 1995. 'Non-verbal communication and early language acquisition in children with Down's syndrome and in normally developing children', *Journal of Speech, Language, and Hearing Research* 38:1, 157–67.

Muñoz, L.C., Frick, P.J., Kimonis, E.R. and Aucoin, K.J. 2008. 'Verbal ability and delinquency: testing the moderating role of psychopathic traits', *Journal of Child Psychology and Psychiatry* 49:4, 414–21.

Munson, B., Edwards, J. and Beckman, M.E. 2005a. 'Phonological knowledge in typical and atypical speech-sound development', *Topics in Language Disorders* 25:3, 190–206.

Munson, B., Edwards, J. and Beckman, M.E. 2005b. 'Relationships between nonword repetition accuracy and other measures of linguistic development in children with phonological disorders', *Journal of Speech, Language, and Hearing Research* 48:1, 61–78.

Murdoch, B. 2011. 'Physiological assessment', in A. Lowit and R.D. Kent (eds.), *Assessment of motor speech disorders*, San Diego, CA: Plural Publishing, 39–74.

Murdoch, B.E. (ed.) 1998. *Dysarthria: a physiological approach to assessment and treatment*, Cheltenham: Stanley Thornes Ltd.

Murdoch, B.E. and Hudson-Tennent, L. 1994. 'Speech disorders in children treated for posterior fossa tumours: ataxic and developmental features', *European Journal of Disorders of Communication* 29:4, 379–97.

Murdoch, B.E., Attarch, M.D., Ozanne, A. and Stokes, P.D. 1995. 'Impaired tongue strength and endurance in developmental verbal dyspraxia: a physiological analysis', *European Journal of Disorders of Communication* 30:1, 51–64.

Murdoch, B.E., Ozanne, A.E. and Cross, J.A. 1990. 'Acquired childhood speech disorders: dysarthria and dyspraxia', in B.E. Murdoch (ed.), *Acquired neurological speech/language disorders in childhood*, London: Taylor & Francis, 308–41.

Murdoch, B.E., Ward, E.C. and Theodoros, D.G. 2008. 'Spastic dysarthria', in M. McNeil (ed.), *Clinical management of sensorimotor speech disorders*, second edition, New York: Thieme Medical Publishers, 187–203.

Murphy, A.T. 1964. *Functional voice disorders*, Englewood Cliffs, NJ: Prentice-Hall.

Murphy, J. 1997. *Talking mats*, Stirling: AAC Research Team, Dept of Psychology, University of Stirling.

Murphy, M.M. and Abbeduto, L. 2007. 'Gender differences in repetitive language in fragile X syndrome', *Journal of Intellectual Disability Research* 51:5, 387–400.

Murphy, P.N., Wareing, M., Fisk, J.E. and Montgomery, C. 2009. 'Executive working memory deficits in abstinent ecstasy/MDMA users: a critical review', *Neuropsychobiology* 60:3–4, 159–75.

Murphy, W.P. 1999. 'A preliminary look at shame, guilt, and stuttering', in N. Bernstein Ratner and E.C. Healey (eds.), *Stuttering research and practice: bridging the gap*, Mahwah, NJ: Lawrence Erlbaum Associates, Inc., 131–43.

Murphy, W.P., Quesal, R.W. and Gulker, H. 2007a. 'Covert stuttering', *Perspectives on Fluency and Fluency Disorders* 17:2, 4–9.

Murphy, W.P., Yaruss, J.S. and Quesal, R.W. 2007b. 'Enhancing treatment for school-age children who stutter: I. reducing negative reactions through desensitization and cognitive restructuring', *Journal of Fluency Disorders* 32:2, 121–38.

Murray, E., McCabe, P. and Ballard, K. 2011. 'Using ReST intervention for paediatric cerebellar ataxia: a pilot study', *Stem-, Spraal-en Taalpathologie* 17, S55.

Murray, E., McCabe, P. and Ballard, K. 2012b. 'The first randomised control trial for childhood apraxia of speech (ReST vs Nuffield dyspraxia program-3)', Speech Pathology Australia National Conference: Hobart, 24–27 June 2012.

Murray, E., McCabe, P. and Ballard, K.J. 2012c. 'The first randomised control trial for childhood apraxia of speech (ReST vs Nuffield Dyspraxia Program, 3rd edition). Speech Pathology Australia Annual Conference, Hobart, 25 June 2012.

Murray, E., McCabe, P. and Ballard, K. 2013. 'A review of treatment outcomes for children with childhood apraxia of speech', submitted.

Murray, E., McCabe, P., Heard, R. and Ballard, K. 2012a. *'Differential diagnosis of 56 children with suspected childhood apraxia of speech'*, Motor Speech Conference: Santa Rosa, CA, 29 February–4 March 2012.

Murray, L. 2008. 'Language and Parkinson's disease', *Annual Review of Applied Linguistics* 28, 113–27.

Murry, T. and Woodson, G. 1992. 'Comparison of three methods for the management of vocal fold nodules', *Journal of Voice* 6:3, 271–6.

Murry, T. and Woodson, G. 1995. 'Combined-modality treatment of adductor spasmodic dysphonia with botulinum toxin and voice therapy', *Journal of Voice* 9:4, 460–5.

Murry, T., Medraldo, R., Hogikyan, N. and Aviv, J.E. 2004. 'The relationship between ratings of voice quality and quality of life measures', *Journal of Voice* 18:2, 183–92.

Muscettola, G., Barbato, G., Pampallona, S., Casiello, M. and Bollini, P. 1999. 'Extrapyramidal syndromes in neuroleptic-treated patients: prevalence, risk factors, and association with tardive dyskinesia', *Journal of Clinical Psychopharmacology* 19:3, 203–8.

Musolino, J., Chunyo, G. and Landau, B. 2010. 'Uncovering knowledge of core syntactic and semantic principles in individuals with Williams syndrome', *Language Learning and Development* 6:2, 126–61.

Muter, V. 2000. 'Screening for early reading failure', in N.A. Badian (ed.), *Prediction and prevention of reading failure*, Timonium, MD: York Press, 1–30.

Muter, V., Hulme, C. and Snowling, M. 1997. *Phonological abilities test*, Minneapolis, MN: Pearson Assessment.

Myers, C. 2005. 'Quality of life in head and neck cancer', in P.C. Doyle and R.L. Keith (eds.), *Contemporary considerations in the treatment and rehabilitation of head and neck cancer*, Austin, TX: Pro-Ed, 697–736.

Myers, F.L. 1992. 'Cluttering: a synergistic framework', in F.L. Myers and K.O. St. Louis (eds.), *Cluttering: a clinical perspective*, Kibworth, Great Britain: Far Communications, 71–84.

Myers, F.L., Bakker, K., St. Louis, K.O. and Raphael, L. 2012. 'Disfluencies in cluttered speech', *Journal of Fluency Disorders* 37:1, 9–19.

Myers, P.S. 1979. 'Profiles of communication deficits in patients with right cerebral hemisphere damage: implications for diagnosis and treatment', in R.H. Brookshire (ed.), *Clinical aphasiology conference proceedings*, Minneapolis, MN: BRK Publishers, 38–46.

Myers, P.S. 1999. 'Process-oriented treatment of right hemisphere communication disorders', *Seminars in Speech and Language* 20:4, 319–32.

Myers, P.S. 2001. 'Toward a definition of RHD syndrome', *Aphasiology* 15:10–11, 913–18.

Nadig, A., Lee, I., Singh, L., Bosshart, K. and Ozonoff, S. 2010. 'How does the topic of conversation affect verbal exchange and eye gaze? A comparison between typical development and high-functioning autism', *Neuropsychologia* 48:9, 2730–9.

Nadig, A., Vivanti, G. and Ozonoff, S. 2009. 'Adaptation of object descriptions to a partner under increasing communicative demands: a comparison of children with and without autism', *Autism Research* 2:6, 334–47.

Nagata, K., Saito, H., Ueno, T., Sato, M., Nakase, T., Maeda, T., Satoh, Y., Komatsu, H., Suzuki, M. and Kondoh, Y. 2007. 'Clinical diagnosis of vascular dementia', *Journal of the Neurological Sciences* 257:1–2, 44–8.

Naglieri, J.A. 1996. *Naglieri nonverbal ability test*, San Antonio, TX: The Psychological Corporation.

Nash, M. and Donaldson, M. 2005. 'Word learning in children with vocabulary deficits', *Journal of Speech, Language, and Hearing Research* 48:2, 439–58.

Nathan, L., Stackhouse, J., Goulandris, N. and Snowling, M.J. 2004. 'The development of early literacy skills among children with speech difficulties: a test of the "critical age hypothesis"', *Journal of Speech, Language, and Hearing Research* 47:2, 377–91.

Nathan, P.W. 1947. 'Facial apraxia and apraxic dysarthria', *Brain* 70:4, 449–78.

National Cancer Institute. 2004. *Childhood cancers* (online, available at: www.cancer.gov/cancertopics/factsheet/Sites-Types/childhood#r2; last accessed 12 June 2013).

National Center on Response to Intervention. 2010. *Essential components of RTI – a closer look at response to intervention*, Washington, DC: US Department of Education.

National Institute of Child Health & Human Development. 2010. *Learning disabilities* (online, available at: http://www.nichd.nih.gov/health/topics/learning/Pages/default.aspx; last accessed 12 June 2013).

National Institute of Neurological Disorders and Stroke. 2011. *NINDS dyslexia information page* (online, available at: www.ninds.nih.gov/disorders/dyslexia/dyslexia.htm; last accessed 12 June 2013).

National Institute on Deafness and Other Communication Disorders. 2007. Quick statistics (online, available at: www.nidcd.nih.gov/health/statistics/vsl/Pages/stats.aspx); last accessed 12 June 2013).

National Patient Safety Agency. 2011. *Dysphagia diet food texture descriptors*, London: National Patient Safety Agency.

National Reading Panel. 2000. *Report of the national reading panel. Teaching children to read: an evidence-based assessment of the scientific research literature and its implications for reading instruction*, Publication No. 00-4754, Rockville, MD: NICHD Clearinghouse (online, available at: www.nichd.nih.gov/publications/pubs/nrp/Pages/smallbook.aspx; last accessed 12 June 2013).

Neary, D., Snowden, J.S., Gustafson, L., Passant, U., Stuss, D., Black, S., Freedman, M., Kertesz, A., Robert, P.H., Albert, M., Boone, K., Miller, B.L., Cummings, J. and Benson, D.F. 1998. 'Frontotemporal lobar degeneration: a consensus on clinical diagnostic criteria', *Neurology* 51:6, 1546–54.

Nebes, R.D., Brady, C.B. and Huff, F.J. 1989. 'Automatic and attentional mechanisms of semantic priming in Alzheimer's disease', *Journal of Clinical and Experimental Neuropsychology* 11:2, 219–30.

Nebes, R.D., Martin, D.C. and Horn, L.C. 1984. 'Sparing of semantic memory in Alzheimer's disease', *Journal of Abnormal Psychology* 93:3, 321–30.

Neilson, M.D. 1999. 'Cognitive-behavioral treatment of adults who stutter: the process and the art', in R. Curlee (ed.), *Stuttering and related disorders of fluency*, second edition, New York: Thieme, 188–91.

Neilson, M.D. and Neilson, P.D. 1987. 'Speech motor control and stuttering: a computational model of adaptive sensory-motor processing', *Speech Communication* 6:4, 325–33.

Neilson, P.D. and Neilson, M.D. 2005. 'An overview of adaptive model theory: solving the problems of redundancy, resources, and nonlinear interactions in human movement control', *Journal of Neural Engineering* 2:3, S279–S312.

Nelson, I.W., Parkin, J.L. and Potter, J.F. 1975. 'The modified Tokyo larynx: an improved pneumatic speech aid', *Archives of Otolaryngology* 101:2, 107–8.

Nelson, J.R., Benner, G.H. and Cheney, D.A. 2005a. 'An investigation of the language skills of students with emotional disturbance served in public school settings', *Journal of Special Education* 39:2, 97–105.

Nelson, J.R., Benner, G.J. and Gonzalez, J. 2003. 'Learner characteristics that influence the treatment effectiveness of early literacy interventions: a meta analytic review', *Learning Disabilities Research & Practice* 18:4, 255–67.

Nelson, J.R., Benner, G.J., Lane, K. and Smith, B. 2004. 'Academic skills of K-12 students with emotional and behavioral disorders', *Exceptional Children* 71:1, 59–74.

Nelson, J.R., Benner, G.J., Neill, S. and Stage, S. 2006. 'The interrelationships among language skills, externalizing behavior, and academic fluency and their impact on the academic skills of students with emotional disturbance', *Journal of Emotional and Behavioral Disorders* 14:4, 209–16.

Nelson, J.R., Stage, S.A., Epstein, M.H. and Pierce, C.D. 2005b. 'Effects of a prereading intervention on the literacy and social skills of children', *Exceptional Children* 72:1, 29–45.

Nelson, K.E., Camarata, S., Welsh, J., Butovsky, L. and Camarata, M. 1996. 'Effects of imitative and conversational recasting treatment on the acquisition of grammar in children with specific language impairment and younger normal children', *Journal of Speech, Language, and Hearing Research* 39:4, 850–9.

Nestor, P.J., Fryer, T.D. and Hodges, J.R. 2006. 'Declarative memory impairments in Alzheimer's disease and semantic dementia', *Neuroimage* 30:3, 1010–20.

Nestor, P.J., Scheltens, P. and Hodges, J.R. 2004. 'Advances in the early detection of Alzheimer's disease', *Nature Medicine* 5, S34–S41.

Netsell, R. 1986. *A neurobiologic view of speech production and the dysarthrias*, San Diego, CA: College Hill.

Netsell, R. 1990. 'Commentary on maintaining speech pressures in the presence of velopharyngeal impairment regulation', *Cleft Palate Journal* 27:1, 58–60.

Netsell, R. and Daniel, B. 1979. 'Dysarthria in adults: physiologic approach to rehabilitation', *Archives of Physical Medicine and Rehabilitation* 60:11, 502–8.

Nettleton, J. and Lesser, R. 1991. 'Therapy for naming difficulties in aphasia: application of a cognitive neuropsychological model', *Journal of Neurolinguistics* 6:2, 139–57.

Neville, H.J., Mills, D.L. and Bellugi, U. 1994. 'Effects of altered auditory sensitivity and age of language acquisition on the development of language-relevant neural systems: preliminary studies of Williams syndrome', in S. Borman and J. Grafman (eds.), *Atypical cognitive deficits in developmental disorders: implications of brain function*, Hillsdale, NJ: Erlbaum, 67–83.

Newbury, D.F., Fisher, S.E. and Monaco, A.P. 2010. 'Recent advances in the genetics of language impairment', *Genome Medicine* 2:1, 6.

Newby, D. 1998. '"Cloze" procedure refined and modified: "modified cloze", "reverse cloze" and the use of predictability as a measure of communication problems in psychosis', *British Journal of Psychiatry* 172:2, 136–41.

Newman, R., Ratner, N.B., Jusczyk, A.M., Jusczyk, P.W. and Dow, K.A. 2006. 'Infants' early ability to segment the conversational speech signal predicts later language development: a retrospective analysis', *Developmental Psychology* 42:4, 643–55.

NICHD Early Child Care Research Network. 2005. 'Pathways to reading: the role of oral language in the transition to reading', *Developmental Psychology* 41:2, 428–42.

Nicholas, L.E. and Brookshire, R.H. 1993. 'A system for quantifying the informativeness and efficiency of the connected speech of adults with aphasia', *Journal of Speech and Hearing Research* 36:2, 338–50.

Nickels, L. 1992. 'The autocue? Self-generated phonemic cues in the treatment of a disorder of reading and naming', *Cognitive Neuropsychology* 9:2, 155–82.

Nickels, L. 1997. *Spoken word production and its breakdown in aphasia*, Hove, East Sussex: Psychology Press.

Nickels, L. 2002. 'Therapy for naming disorders: revisiting, revising, and reviewing', *Aphasiology* 16:10–11, 935–79.

Nickels, L. and Best, W. 1996a. 'Therapy for naming disorders (part I): principles, puzzles and progress', *Aphasiology* 10:1, 21–47.

Nickels, L. and Best, W. 1996b. 'Therapy for naming disorders (part II): specifics, surprises and suggestions', *Aphasiology* 10:2, 109–36.

Nickels, L., Kohnen, S. and Biedermann, B. 2010. 'An untapped resource: treatment as a tool for revealing the nature of cognitive processes', *Cognitive Neuropsychology* 27:7, 539–62.

Nicodemus, K.K., Marenco, S., Batten, A.J., Vakkalanka, R., Egan, M.F., Straub, R.E. and Weinberger, D.R. 2008. 'Serious obstetric complications interact with hypoxia-regulated/vascular-expression genes to influence schizophrenia risk', *Molecular Psychiatry* 13:9, 873–7.

Nicoletti, G., Soutar, D.S., Jackson, M.S., Wrench, A.A., Robertson, G. and Robertson, C. 2004. 'Objective assessment of speech after surgical treatment for oral cancer: experience from 196 selected cases', *Plastic and Reconstructive Surgery* 113:1, 114–25.

Nicolson, R. and Fawcett, A. 2008. *Dyslexia, learning and the brain.* Cambridge: MIT Press

Nippold, M.A. 2011. 'Stuttering in school-age children: a call for treatment research', *Language, Speech, and Hearing Services in Schools* 42:2, 99–101.

Noonan, M. and McCormick, L. 1993. *Early intervention in natural environments: methods and procedures*, Pacific Grove: Brooks/Cole Publishing.

Nopoulos, P., Boes, A.D., Jabines, A., Conrad, A.L., Canady, J., Richman, L. and Dawson, J.D. 2010. 'Hyperactivity, impulsivity, and inattention in boys with cleft lip and palate: relationship to ventromedial prefrontal cortex morphology', *Journal of Neurodevelopmental Disorders* 2:4, 235–42.

Nopoulos, P., Langbehn, D.R., Canady, J., Magnotta, V. and Richman, L. 2007. 'Abnormal brain structure in children with isolated clefts of the lip or palate', *Archives of Pediatrics and Adolescent Medicine* 161:8, 753–8.

Noppeney, U., Patterson, K., Tyler, L.K., Moss, H., Stamatakis, E.A., Bright, P., Mummery, C. and Price, C.J. 2007. 'Temporal lobe lesions and semantic impairment: a comparison of herpes simplex virus encephalitis and semantic dementia', *Brain* 130:4, 1138–47.

Norbury, C.F. 2004. 'Factors supporting idiom comprehension in children with communication disorders', *Journal of Speech, Language, and Hearing Research* 47:5, 1179–93.

Norbury, C.F. 2005a. 'Barking up the wrong tree? Lexical ambiguity resolution in children with language impairments and autistic spectrum disorders', *Journal of Experimental Child Psychology* 90:2, 142–71.

Norbury, C.F. 2005b. 'The relationship between theory of mind and metaphor: evidence from children with language impairment and autistic spectrum disorder', *British Journal of Developmental Psychology* 23:3, 383–99.

Norbury, C.F. and Bishop, D.V. 2002. 'Inferential processing and story recall in children with communication problems: a comparison of specific language impairment, pragmatic language impairment and high-functioning autism', *International Journal of Language & Communication Disorders* 37:3, 227–51.

Norbury, C.F. and Bishop, D.V. 2003. 'Narrative skills of children with communication impairments', *International Journal of Language & Communication Disorders* 38:3, 287–313.

Norbury, C.F. and Nation, K. 2011. 'Understanding variability in reading comprehension in adolescents with autism spectrum disorders: interactions with language status and decoding skill', *Scientific Studies of Reading* 15:3, 191–210.

Norbury, C.F., Bishop, D.V.M. and Briscoe, J. 2002. 'Does impaired grammatical comprehension provide evidence for an innate grammar module?', *Applied Psycholinguistics* 23:2, 247–68.

Norbury, C.F., Brock, J., Cragg, L., Einav, S., Griffiths, H. and Nation, K. 2009. 'Eye-movement patterns are associated with communicative competence in autistic spectrum disorders', *Journal of Child Psychology and Psychiatry* 50:7, 834–42.

Norbury, C.F., Gemmell, T. and Paul, R. 2013. 'Pragmatic abilities in narrative production: a cross-disorder comparison', *Journal of Child Language*, published online 30 April 2013 (DOI: http://dx.doi.org/10.1017/S030500091300007X).

Norbury, C.F., Griffiths, H. and Nation, K. 2010. 'Sound before meaning: word learning in autistic disorders', *Neuropsychologia* 48:14, 4012–19.

Numminen, H., Service, E., Ahonen, T. and Ruoppila, I. 2001. 'Working memory and everyday cognition in adults with Down syndrome', *Journal of Intellectual Disability Research* 45:2, 157–68.

Numminen, H., Service, E. and Ruoppila, I. 2002. 'Working memory, intelligence and knowledge base in adult persons with intellectual disability', *Research in Developmental Disabilities* 23:2, 105–18.

Oates, J. 2009. 'Auditory-perceptual evaluation of disordered voice quality. Pros, cons and future directions', *Folia Phoniatrica* 61:1, 49–56.

Obler, L.K., Albert, M.L., Goodglass, H. and Benson, D.F. 1978. 'Aphasia type and aging', *Brain and Language* 6:3, 318–22.

O'Brian, S., Packman, A. and Onslow, M. 2010. 'The Camperdown program', in B. Guitar and R.J. McCauley (eds.), *Treatment of stuttering: established and emerging interventions*, Baltimore, MD: Lippincott Williams, & Wilkins, 256–76.

O'Brien, E., Zhang, X., Nishimura, C., Tomblin, J.B. and Murray, J.C. 2003. 'Association of specific language impairment (SLI) to the region of 7q31', *American Journal of Human Genetics* 72:6, 1536–43.

O'Brien, N., Langhinrichsen-Rohling, J. and Shelley-Tremblay, J. 2007. 'Reading problems, attentional deficits, and current mental health status in adjudicated adolescent males', *Journal of Correctional Education* 58:3, 293–315.

O'Connor, M., Arnott, W., McIntosh, B. and Dodd, B. 2009. 'Phonological awareness and language intervention in preschoolers from low socio-economic backgrounds: a longitudinal investigation', *British Journal of Developmental Psychology* 27:4, 767–82.

Odell, K. and Shriberg, L.D. 2001. 'Prosody-voice characteristics of children and adults with apraxia of speech', *Clinical Linguistics & Phonetics* 15:4, 275–307.

Odell, K., McNeil, M.R., Rosenbek, J.C. and Hunter, L. 1990. 'Perceptual characteristics of consonant production by apraxic speakers', *Journal of Speech and Hearing Disorders* 55:2, 345–59.

Odell, K., McNeil, M.R., Rosenbek, J.C. and Hunter, L. 1991. 'Perceptual characteristics of vowel and prosody production in apraxic, aphasic, and dysarthric speaker', *Journal of Speech and Hearing Research* 34:1, 67–80.

O'Dell, K. and Sinha, U. 2011. 'Osteoradionecrosis', *Oral and Maxillofacial Surgery Clinics of North America* 23:3, 455–64.

Odom, S.L., Favazza, P.C., Brown, W.H. and Horn, E.M. 2000. 'Approaches to understanding the ecology of early childhood environments for children with disabilities', in T. Thompson, D. Felce and F.J. Symons (eds.), *Behavioral observation: technology and applications in developmental disabilities*, Baltimore, MD: Paul H. Brookes Publishing, 193–214.

Office for National Statistics. 2011. *Leading causes of death in England and Wales, 2009*, London: Office for National Statistics.

Office of Special Education and Rehabilitative Services. 2003. *IDEA '97 The Law* (online, available at: www2.ed.gov/offices/OSERS/Policy/IDEA/the_law.html; last accessed 12 June 2013).

O'Flaherty, C.A. and Douglas, J.M. 1997. 'Living with cognitive-communicative difficulties following traumatic brain injury: using a model of interpersonal communication to characterize the subjective experience', *Aphasiology* 11:9, 889–911.

Ogar, J.M., Dronkers, N.F., Brambati, S.M., Miller, B.L. and Gorno-Tempini, M.L. 2007. 'Progressive nonfluent aphasia and its characteristic motor speech deficits', *Alzheimer Disease and Associated Disorders* 21:4, S23-S30.

O'Gara, M.M. and Logemann, J.A. 1988. 'Phonetic analyses of the speech development of babies with cleft palate', *Cleft Palate Journal* 25:2, 122–34.

Ogletree, B.T., Bruce, S.M., Finch, A., Fahey, R. and McLean, L. 2011. 'Recommended communication-based interventions for individuals with severe intellectual disabilities', *Communication Disorders Quarterly* 32:3, 164–75.

O'Hara, J., Miller, T., Carding, P., Wilson, J. and Deary, V. 2011. 'Relationship between fatigue, perfectionism, and functional dysphonia', *Otolaryngology – Head and Neck Surgery* 144:6, 921–6.

Ohio State University Department of Linguistics. 1999. *ToBI* (online, available at: www.ling.ohio-state.edu/~tobi/; last accessed 12 June 2013).

Olander, L., Smith, A. and Zelaznik, H.N. 2010. 'Evidence that a motor timing deficit is a factor in the development of stuttering', *Journal of Speech, Language, and Hearing Research* 53:4, 876–86.

Oliver, M. 1983. *Social work with disabled people*, Basingstoke: Macmillan.

Olver, J.H., Ponsford, J.L. and Curran, C.A. 1996. 'Outcome following traumatic brain injury: a comparison between 2 and 5 years after injury', *Brain Injury* 10:11, 841–8.

O'Neill, R., Horner, R., Albin, R., Sprager, J., Storey, K. and Newton, S. 1997. *Functional assessment and program development for problem behavior: a practical handbook*, second edition, Pacific Grove: Brooks/Cole.

Onslow, M. and Millard, S. 2012. 'Palin parent child interaction and the Lidcombe program: clarifying some issues', *Journal of Fluency Disorders* 37:1, 1–8.

Onslow, M. and Packman, A. 1999. 'The Lidcombe program of early stuttering intervention', in N. Bernstein Ratner and E.C. Healey (eds.), *Stuttering research and practice: bridging the gap*, Mahwah, NJ: Lawrence Erlbaum Associates, 193–210.

Onslow, M. and Yaruss, J.S. 2007. 'Differing perspectives on what to do with a stuttering preschooler and why', *American Journal of Speech-Language Pathology* 16:1, 65–8.

Onslow, M., O'Brian, S. and Harrison, E. 1997. 'The Lidcombe programme of early stuttering intervention: methods and issues', *European Journal of Disorders of Communication* 32:2, 231–50.

Onslow, M., Packman, A. and Harrison, E. 2003. *Lidcombe program of early stuttering intervention: a clinician's guide*, Austin, TX: Pro-Ed.

Orange, J.B., Lubinski, R.B. and Higginbotham, D.J. 1996. 'Conversational repair by individuals with dementia of the Alzheimer's type', *Journal of Speech and Hearing Research* 39:4, 881–95.

Ornstein, A.F. and Manning, W.H. 1985. 'Self-efficacy scaling by adult stutterers', *Journal of Communication Disorders* 18:4, 313–20.

Orticochea, M. 1968. 'Construction of a dynamic muscle sphincter in cleft palates', *Plastic and Reconstructive Surgery* 41:4, 323–7.

Orticochea, M. 1970. 'Results of the dynamic muscle sphincter operation in cleft palates', *British Journal of Plastic Surgery* 23:2, 108–14.

Orticochea, M. 1983. 'A review of 236 cleft palate patients treated with dynamic muscle sphincter', *Plastic and Reconstructive Surgery* 71:2, 180–8.

Orton, S. 1928. 'Specific reading disability – strephosymbolia', *Journal of the American Medical Association* 90:20, 1649–50.

Orton, S. and Travis, L.E. 1929. 'Studies in stuttering: IV. Studies of action currents in stutterers', *Archives of Neurology and Psychiatry* 21:1, 61–8.

O'Seaghdha, P.G., Chen, J.Y. and Chen, T.M. 2010. 'Proximate units in word production: phonological encoding begins with syllables in Mandarin Chinese but with segments in English', *Cognition* 115:2, 282–302.

Otapowicz, D., Sobaniec, W., Kułak, W. and Sendrowski, K. 2007. 'Severity of dysarthric speech in children with infantile cerebral palsy in correlation with the brain CT and MRI', *Advances in Medical Sciences* 52:Suppl 1, 188–90.

Owen, A. 2010. 'Factors affecting accuracy of past tense production in children with specific language impairment and their typically developing peers: the influence of verb transitivity, clause location, and sentence type', *Journal of Speech, Language, and Hearing Research* 53:4, 993–1014.

Owen, A. and Leonard, L. 2006. 'The production of finite and nonfinite complement clauses by children with specific language impairment and their typically developing peers', *Journal of Speech, Language, and Hearing Research* 49:3, 548–71.

Owens, R. 2008. *Language development: an introduction*, Boston, MA: Allyn & Bacon.

Ozanne, A. 2005. 'Childhood apraxia of speech', in B. Dodd (ed.), *Differential diagnosis and treatment of children with speech disorder*, London: Whurr, 71–82.

Packman, A., Onslow, M., Richard, E. and van Doorn, J. 1996. 'Syllabic stress and variability: a model of stuttering', *Clinical Linguistics & Phonetics* 10:3, 235–63.

Paden, E.P. and Yairi, E. 1996. 'Phonological characteristics of children whose stuttering persisted or recovered', *Journal of Speech and Hearing Research* 39:5, 981–90.

Paden, E.P., Yairi, E. and Ambrose, N.G. 1999. 'Early childhood stuttering II: initial status of phonological abilities', *Journal of Speech, Language, and Hearing Research* 42:5, 1113–24.

Pagon, R., Bennet, F., La Veck, B., Stewart, K. and Johnson, J. 1987. 'Williams syndrome: features in late childhood and adolescence', *Paediatrics* 80:1, 85–91.

Palisano, R., Rosenbaum, P., Bartlett, D. and Livingston, M. 2007. *Gross motor function classification system expanded and revised*, Hamilton, ON: CanChild Centre for Childhood Disability Research, McMaster University.

Pamplona, M.C., Ysunza, A. and Espinoza, J. 1999. 'A comparative trial of two modalities of speech intervention for compensatory articulation in cleft palate children: phonological approach versus articulatory approach', *International Journal of Pediatric Otorhinolaryngology* 49:1, 21–6.

Pamplona, M.C., Ysunza, A., González, M., Ramírez, E. and Patiño, C. 2000. 'Linguistic development in cleft palate patients with and without compensatory articulation disorder', *International Journal of Pediatric Otorhinolaryngology* 54:2–3, 81–91.

Pannbacker, M. 1988. 'Management strategies for developmental apraxia of speech: a review of the literature', *Journal of Communication Disorders* 21:5, 363–71.

Pantelis, C., Velakoulis, D., McGorry, P.D., Wood, S.J., Suckling, J., Yung, A.R., Bullmore, E.T., Brewer, W., Soulsby, B., Desmond, P. and McQuire, P.K. 2003. 'Neuroanatomical abnormalities before and after onset of psychosis: a cross-sectional and longitudinal MRI comparison', *Lancet* 361:9354, 281–8.

Panton, A. and Marshall, J. 2008. 'Improving spelling and everyday writing after a CVA: single case therapy study', *Aphasiology* 22:2, 164–83.

Pany, D. and McCoy, K.M. 1988. 'Effects of corrective feedback on word accuracy and reading comprehension of readers with learning disabilities', *Journal of Learning Disabilities* 21:9, 546–50.

Papagno, C. 2001. 'Comprehension of metaphors and idioms in patients with Alzheimer's disease: a longitudinal study', *Brain* 124:7, 1450–60.

Papagno, C. and Vallar, G. 2001. 'Understanding metaphors and idioms: a single-case neuropsychological study in a person with Down syndrome', *Journal of the International Neuropsychological Society* 7:4, 516–28.

Papagno, C., Curti, R., Rizzo, S., Crippa, F. and Colombo, M. 2006. 'Is the right hemisphere involved in idiom comprehension? A neuropsychological study', *Neuropsychology* 20:5, 598–606.

Papanicolaou, A.C., Simos, P.G., Breier, J.I., Fletcher, J.M., Foorman, B.R., Francis, D., Castillo, E. and David, R. 2003. 'Brain mechanisms for reading in children with and without dyslexia: a review of studies of normal development and plasticity', *Developmental Neuropsychology* 24:2–3, 593–612.

Paradis, J., Crago, M. and Genesee, F. 2003. 'Object clitics as a clinical marker of SLI in French: evidence from French-English bilingual children', in B. Beachley, A. Brown and F. Conlin (eds.), *Proceedings of the 27th annual Boston university conference on language development*, Somerville, MA: Cascadilla Press, 638–49.

Paradis, M. 2001. 'Bilingual and polyglot aphasia', in R.S. Berndt (ed.), *Language and aphasia*, Amsterdam: Elsevier Science, 69–91.

Parasuraman, R. and Haxby, J. 1993. 'Attention and brain function in Alzheimer's disease: a review', *Neuropsychology* 7:3, 242–72.

Parish-Morris, J., Hennon, E.A., Hirsh-Pasek, K., Golinkoff, R.M. and Tager-Flusberg, H. 2007. 'Children with autism illuminate the role of social intention in word learning', *Child Development* 78:4, 1265–87.

Parisi, D. and Pizzamiglio, L. 1970. 'Syntactic comprehension in aphasia', *Cortex* 6, 204–15.

Park, J.H., Shea, C.H. and Wright, D.L. 2000. 'Reduced-frequency concurrent and terminal feedback: a test of the guidance hypothesis', *Journal of Motor Behavior* 32:3, 287–96.

Parker, S.E., Mai, C.T., Canfield, M.A., Rickard, R., Wang, Y., Meyer, R.E., Anderson, P., Mason, C.A., Collins, J.S., Kirby, R.S. and Correa, A. 2010. 'Updated national birth prevalence estimates for selected birth defects in the United States, 2004–2006', *Birth Defects Research. Part A, Clinical and Molecular Teratology* 88:12, 1008–16.

Parladé, M.V. and Iverson, J.M. 2011. 'The interplay between language, gesture, and affect during communicative transition: a dynamic systems approach', *Developmental Psychology* 47:3, 820–33.

Parmenter, B. 2010. 'Taking mental illness beyond the DSM-IV-TR and into a new frontier', *The Clinical Neuropsychologist* 24:6, 1081–3.

Parrott, A.C., Buchanan, T., Scholey, A.B., Heffernan, T., Ling, J. and Rodgers, J. 2002. 'Ecstasy/MDMA-attributed problems reported by novice, moderate, and heavy recreational users', *Human Psychopharmacology* 17:6, 309–12.

Patel, R. 2011. 'Assessment of prosody', in A. Lowit and R.D. Kent (eds.), *Assessment of motor speech disorders*, San Diego, CA: Plural Publishing, 75–96.

Patel, R., Connaghan, K., Franco, D., Edsall, E., Forgit, D., Olsen, L., Ramage, L., Tyler, E. and Russell, S. 2013. '"The Caterpillar": a novel reading passage for assessment of motor speech disorders', *American Journal of Speech-Language Pathology* 22:1, 1–9.

Patel, R.R., Bless, D.M. and Thibeault, S.L. 2011. 'Boot camp: a novel intensive approach to voice therapy', *Journal of Voice* 25:5, 562–9.

Patel, V., Saraceno, B. and Kleinman, A. 2006. 'Beyond evidence: the moral case for international mental health', *American Journal of Psychiatry* 163:8, 1312–15.

Paterson, S., Brown, J.H., Gsödl, M., Johnson, M.H. and Karmiloff-Smith, A. 1999. 'Cognitive modularity and genetic disorders', *Science* 286:5448, 1355–8.

Patterson, K. 2007. 'The reign of typicality in semantic memory', *Philosophical Transactions of the Royal Society of London. Series B, Biological Sciences* 362:1481, 813–21.

Patterson, K. and Shewell, C. 1987. 'Speak and spell: dissociations and word-class effects', in M. Coltheart, R. Job and G. Sartori (eds.), *The cognitive neuropsychology of language*, Hillsdale, NJ: Lawrence Erlbaum, 273–94.

Patterson, K., Graham, N. and Hodges, J.R. 1994. 'The impact of semantic memory loss on phonological representations', *Journal of Cognitive Neuroscience* 6:1, 57–69.

Patterson, K., Lambon Ralph, M., Jefferies, E., Woollams, A., Jones, R., Hodges, J.R. and Rogers, T.T. 2006. '"Presemantic" cognition in semantic dementia: six deficits in search of an explanation', *Journal of Cognitive Neuroscience* 18:2, 169–83.

Patterson, K., Nestor, P.J. and Rogers, T.T. 2007. 'Where do you know what you know? The representation of semantic knowledge in the human brain', *Nature Reviews Neuroscience* 8:12, 976–87.

Patzko, A. and Shy, M.E. 2012. 'Charcot-Marie-Tooth disease and related genetic neuropathies', *CONTINUUM Lifelong Learning in Neurology* 18:1, 39–59.

Paul, D.R., Frattali, C., Holland, A.L., Thompson, C.K., Caperton, C.J. and Slater, S.C. 2004. *Quality of communication life scale*, Rockville, MD: American Speech-Language-Hearing Association.

Paul, R. 2007. *Language disorders from infancy through adolescence*, third edition, St Louis, MO: Elsevier Science.

Paul, R. and Shriberg, L.D. 1982. 'Associations between phonology and syntax in speech-delayed children', *Journal of Speech and Hearing Research* 25:4, 536–47.

Paul, R., Chawarska, K., Fowler, C., Cicchetti, D. and Volkmar, F. 2007. '"Listen my children and you shall hear": auditory preferences in toddlers with autism spectrum disorders', *Journal of Speech, Language, and Hearing Research* 50:5, 1350–64.

Paul-Brown, D. and Caperton, C. 2001. 'Inclusive practices for preschool children with specific language impairment', in M.J. Guralnick (ed.), *Early childhood inclusion: focus on change*, Baltimore, MD: Paul H. Brookes, 433–63.

Paulesu, E., DeMonet, J.F., Fazio, F., McCrory, E., Chanoine, V., Brunswick, N., Cossu, G., Habib, M., Frith, C.D. and Frith, U. 2001. 'Dyslexia: cultural diversity and biological unity', *Science* 291:5511, 2165–7.

Paulooski, B.R., Logemann, J.A., Colangelo, L.A., Rademaker, A.W., McConnel, F.M., Heiser, M.A., Cardinale, S., Shedd, D., Stein, D., Beery, Q., Myers, E., Lewin, J., Haxer, M. and Esclamado, R. 1998. 'Surgical variables affecting speech in treated patients with oral and oropharyngeal cancer', *Laryngoscope* 108:6, 908–16.

Pawłowska, M., Leonard, L., Camarata, S., Brown, B. and Camarata, M. 2008. 'Factors accounting for the ability of children with SLI to learn agreement morphemes in intervention', *Journal of Child Language* 35:1, 25–53.

Pearce, W., James, D. and McCormack, P. 2010. 'A comparison of oral narratives in children with specific language and non-specific language impairment', *Clinical Linguistics & Phonetics* 24:8, 622–45.

Pearson Publishing. 2010. *Aimsweb* (online, available at: www.aimsweb.com; last accessed 12 June 2013).

Pease, C.M. and Bull, J.J. 1992. 'Is science logical?', *Bioscience* 42:4, 293–8.

Pedersen, M., Beranova, A. and Moller, S. 2004. 'Dysphonia: medical treatment and a medical voice hygiene advice approach. A prospective randomized pilot study', *European Archive of Otorhinolaryngology* 261:6, 312–15.

Peelle, J.E. and Grossman, M. 2008. 'Language processing in frontotemporal dementia: a brief review', *Language and Linguistics Compass* 2:1, 18–35.

Peelle, J.E., Troiani, V., Gee, J., Moore, P., McMillan, C., Vesely, L. and Grossman, M. 2008. 'Sentence comprehension and voxel-based morphometry in progressive nonfluent aphasia, semantic dementia, and nonaphasic frontotemporal dementia', *Journal of Neurolinguistics* 21:5, 418–32.

Peetsma, T., Vergeer, M., Roeleveld, J. and Karsten, S. 2001. 'Inclusion in education: comparing pupils' development in special and regular education', *Educational Review* 53:2, 125–35.

Pell, M.D. 1996. 'On the receptive prosodic loss in Parkinson's disease', *Cortex* 32:4, 693–704.

Pell, M.D. 2006. 'Cerebral mechanisms for understanding emotional prosody in speech', *Brain and Language* 96:2, 221–34.

Pell, M.D. and Leonard, C.L. 2003. 'Processing emotional tone from speech in Parkinson's disease: a role for the basal ganglia', *Cognitive, Affective & Behavioral Neuroscience* 3:4, 275–88.

Pell, M.D. and Leonard, C.L. 2005. 'Facial expression decoding in early Parkinson's disease', *Cognitive Brain Research* 23:2, 327–40.

Pell, M.D., Cheang, H.S. and Leonard, C.L. 2006. 'The impact of Parkinson's disease on vocal-prosodic communication from the perspective of listeners', *Brain and Language* 97:2, 123–34.

Pellicano, E. 2010. 'Individual differences in executive function and central coherence predict developmental changes in theory of mind in autism', *Developmental Psychology* 46:2, 530–44.

Penn, C. and Cleary, J. 1988. 'Compensatory strategies in the language of closed head injured patients', *Brain Injury* 2:1, 3–17.

Pennington, B.F. 2006. 'From single to multiple deficit models of developmental disorders', *Cognition* 101:2, 385–413.

Pennington, B.F. and Bishop, D.V.M. 2009. 'Relations among speech, language, and reading disorders', *Annual Review of Psychology* 60, 283–306.

Pennington, B.F. and Olson, R.K. 2005. 'Genetics of dyslexia', in M.J. Snowling and C. Hulme (eds.), *The science of reading: a handbook*, Malden, MA: Blackwell Publishing, 453–72.

Pennington, L. 2008. 'Cerebral palsy and communication', *Paediatrics and Child Health* 18:9, 405–9.

Pennington, L. and Noble, E. 2010. 'Acceptability and usefulness of the group interaction training program it takes two to talk to parents of preschool children with motor disorders', *Child Care, Health and Development* 36:2, 285–96.

Pennington, L., Goldbart, J. and Marshall, J. 2004. 'Speech and language therapy to improve the communication skills of children with cerebral palsy', *Cochrane Database of Systematic Reviews*, Issue 2, CD003466.

Pennington, L., Miller, N. and Robson, S. 2009a. 'Speech therapy for children with dysarthria acquired before three years of age', *Cochrane Database of Systematic Reviews*, Issue 4, CD006937.

Pennington, L., Miller, N., Robson, S. and Steen, N. 2010. 'Intensive speech and language therapy for older children with cerebral palsy: a systems approach', *Developmental Medicine and Child Neurology* 52:4, 337–44.

Pennington, L., Robson, S., Miller, N. and Steen, N. 2008. 'Improving the intelligibility of children with dysarthria: results from a pilot study', Developmental Medicine and Child Neurology: 20th Annual Meeting of the EACD: Zagreb, Croatia, 5–7 June 2008.

Pennington, L., Smallman, C.E. and Farrier, F. 2006. 'Intensive dysarthria therapy for older children with cerebral palsy: findings from six cases', *Child Language Teaching & Therapy* 22:3, 255–73.

Pennington, L., Thomson, K., James, P., Martin, L. and McNally, R. 2009b. 'Effects of it takes two to talk – the Hanen program for parents of preschool children with cerebral palsy: findings from an exploratory study', *Journal of Speech, Language, and Hearing Research* 52:5, 1121–38.

Peppard, R.C. 1996. 'Management of functional voice disorders in adolescents', *Language, Speech, and Hearing Services in Schools* 27:3, 257–70.

Peppé, S. and McCann, J. 2003. 'Assessing intonation and prosody in children with atypical language development: the PEPS-C test and the revised version', *Clinical Linguistics & Phonetics* 17:4–5, 345–54.

Peppé, S., McCann, J., Gibbon, F., O'Hare, A. and Rutherford, M. 2007. 'Receptive and expressive prosodic ability in children with high-functioning autism', *Journal of Speech, Language, and Hearing Research* 50:4, 1015–28.

Perello, J. 1962. 'Functional dysphonias. Phonoponosis and phononeurosis', *Folia Phoniatrica* 14, 150–205.

Perkins, L. 1995. 'Applying conversation analysis to aphasia: clinical implications and analytic issues', *International Journal of Language & Communication Disorders* 30:3, 372–83.

Perkins, W.H., Kent, R.D. and Curlee, R.F. 1991. 'A theory of neuropsycholinguistic function in stuttering', *Journal of Speech and Hearing Research* 34:4, 734–52.

Perovic, A. 2001. 'Binding principles in Down syndrome', *UCL Working Papers in Linguistics* 13, 425–45.

Perovic, A. 2002. 'Language in Down syndrome: delay of principle A effect?', *Durham Working Papers in Linguistics* 8, 97–110.

Perovic, A., Modyanova, N. and Wexler, K. 2013. 'Comprehension of reflexive and personal pronouns in children with autism: a syntactic or pragmatic deficit?', *Applied Psycholinguistics*, 34:4, 813–835.

Perry, R.J. and Hodges, J.R. 1999. 'Attention and executive deficits in Alzheimer's disease. A critical review', *Brain* 122:3, 383–404.

Petersen, R.C. 2004. 'Mild cognitive impairment as a diagnostic entity', *Journal of Internal Medicine* 256:3, 183–94.

Petersen, R.C. and Negash, S. 2008. 'Mild cognitive impairment: an overview', *CNS Spectrums* 13:1, 45–53.

Petersen, R.C., Stevens, J.C., Ganguli, M., Tangalos, E.G., Cummings, J.L. and DeKosky, S.T. 2001. 'Practice parameter: early detection of dementia: mild cognitive impairment (an evidence-based review). Report of the Quality Standards Subcommittee of the American Academy of Neurology', *Neurology* 56:9, 1133–42.

Peterson, R.L. and McGrath, L.M. 2009. 'Speech and language disorders', in B.F. Pennington (ed.), *Diagnosing learning disorders: a neuropsychological framework*, second edition, New York: Guilford, 83–107.

Peterson, R.L., Pennington, B.F., Shriberg, L.D. and Boada, R. 2009. 'What influences literacy outcome in children with speech sound disorder?', *Journal of Speech, Language, and Hearing Research* 52:5, 1175–88.

Peterson, S.J. 1975. 'Nasal emission as a component of the misarticulation of sibilants and affricates', *Journal of Speech and Hearing Disorders* 40:1, 106–14.

Peterson-Falzone, S.J., Hardin-Jones, M.A. and Karnell, M.P. 2010. *Cleft palate speech*, fourth edition, St Louis, MO: Mosby Elsevier.

Pettinato, M. and Verhoeven, J. 2009. 'Production and perception of word stress in children and adolescents with Down syndrome', *Down Syndrome Research and Practice* 13:1, 48–61.

Phillips, M.L. 2003. 'Understanding the neurobiology of emotion perception: implications for psychiatry', *British Journal of Psychiatry* 182:3, 190–2.

Philofsky, A., Fidler, D.J. and Hepburn, S. 2007. 'Pragmatic language profiles of school-age children with autism spectrum disorders and Williams syndrome', *American Journal of Speech-Language Pathology* 16:4, 368–80.

Piaget, J. 1980. 'The psychogenesis of knowledge and its epistemological significance', in M. Piattelli-Palmarini (ed.), *Language and learning: the debate between Jean Piaget and Noam Chomsky*, London: Routledge & Kegan Paul, 23–34.

Pierce, R.S. 1991. 'Apraxia of speech vs. phonemic paraphasia: theoretical, diagnostic, and treatment considerations', in D. Vogel and M.P. Cannito (eds.), *Treating disordered speech motor control: for clinicians by clinicians*, Austin, TX: Pro-Ed, 185–216.

Pierrehumbert, J. 2003. 'Phonetic diversity, statistical learning, and acquisition of phonology', *Language and Speech* 46:2–3, 115–54.

Pigott, R.W. 1993. 'The results of pharyngoplasty by muscle transplantation by Wilfred Hynes', *British Journal of Plastic Surgery* 46:5, 440–2.

Pijnacker, J., Hagoort, P., Buitelaar, J., Teunisse, J.P. and Geurts, B. 2009. 'Pragmatic inferences in high-functioning adults with autism and Asperger syndrome', *Journal of Autism and Developmental Disorders* 39:4, 607–18.

Pimental, P.A. and Knight, J.A. 2000. *Mini inventory of right brain injury – revised*, Nerang East, Australia: Pro-Ed.

Pinker, S. 1999. *How the mind works*, London: Penguin.

Pinkham, A.E. and Penn, D.L. 2006. 'Neurocognitive and social cognitive predictors of interpersonal skill in schizophrenia', *Psychiatry Research* 143:2–3, 167–78.

Pinto, N.B. and Titze, I.R. 1990. 'Unification of perturbation measures in speech signals', *Journal of the Acoustical Society of America* 87:3, 1278–89.

Plante, E. and Vance, R. 1994. 'Selection of preschool language tests: a data-based approach', *Language, Speech, and Hearing Services in Schools* 25:1, 15–24.

Pleh, C., Likacs, A. and Racsmany, M. 2003. 'Morphological patterns in Hungarian children with Williams syndrome and the rule debates', *Brain and Language* 86:3, 377–83.

Plexico, L.W., Manning, W.H. and DiLollo, A. 2010. 'Client perceptions of effective and ineffective therapeutic alliances during treatment for stuttering', *Journal of Fluency Disorders* 35:4, 333–54.

Plexico, L.W., Manning, W.H. and Levitt, H. 2009a. 'Coping responses by adults who stutter: part II. approaching the problem and achieving agency', *Journal of Fluency Disorders* 34:2, 108–26.

Plexico, L.W., Manning, W.H. and Levitt, H. 2009b. 'Coping responses by adults who stutter: part I. protecting the self and others', *Journal of Fluency Disorders* 34:2, 87–107.

Pobric, G., Mashal, N., Faust, M. and Lavidor, M. 2008. 'The role of the right cerebral hemisphere in processing novel metaphoric expressions: a transcranial magnetic stimulation study', *Journal of Cognitive Neuroscience* 20:1, 170–81.

Poburka, B.J. 1999. 'A new stroboscopy rating form', *Journal of Voice* 13:3, 403–13.

Poeck, K. and Luzzatti, C. 1988. 'Slowly progressive aphasia in three patients. The problem of accompanying deficit', *Brain* 111:1, 151–68.

Pokorni, J., Worthington, C. and Jamison, P. 2004. 'Phonological awareness intervention: comparison of Fast ForWord, Earobics, and LiPS', *Journal of Educational Research* 97:3, 147–57.

Pollard, R., Ellis, J.B., Finan, D. and Ramig, P.R. 2009. 'Effects of the SpeechEasy on objective and perceived aspects of stuttering: a 6-month, phase I clinical trial in naturalistic environments', *Journal of Speech, Language, and Hearing Research* 52:2, 516–33.

Poretti, A., Limperopoulos, C., Roulet-Perez, E., Wolf, N.I., Rauscher, C., Prayer, D., Müller, A., Weissert, M., Kotzaeridou, U., Du Plessis, A.J., Huisman, T.A. and Boltshauser, E. 2010. 'Outcome of severe unilateral cerebellar hypoplasia', *Developmental Medicine and Child Neurology* 52:8, 718–24.

Porter, J.H. and Hodson, B.W. 2001. 'Collaborating to obtain phonological acquisition data for local schools', *Language, Speech, and Hearing Services in Schools* 32:3, 165–71.

Portone, C., Johns III, M.M. and Hapner, E.R. 2008. 'A review of patient adherence to the recommendations for voice therapy', *Journal of Voice* 22:2, 192–6.

Postma, A. and Kolk, H. 1993. 'The covert repair hypothesis: prearticulatory repair processes in normal and stuttered disfluencies', *Journal of Speech and Hearing Research* 36:3, 472–87.

Potter, N.L. 2011. 'Voice disorders in children with classic galactosemia', *Journal of Inherited Metabolic Disease* 34:2, 377–85.

Pound, C., Parr, S., Lindsay, J. and Woolf, C. 2000. *Beyond aphasia: therapies for living with communication disability*, Bicester: Speechmark.

Pouplier, M. and Hardcastle, W.J. 2005. 'A re-evaluation of the nature of speech errors in normal and disordered speakers', *Phonetica* 62:2–4, 227–43.

Pransky, S.M., Brewster, D.F., Magit, A.E. and Kearns, D.B. 2000. 'Clinical update on 10 children treated with intralesional cidofovir injections for severe recurrent respiratory papillomatosis', *Archives of Otolaryngology – Head and Neck Surgery* 126:10, 1239–43.

Pransky, S.M., Magit, A.E., Kearns, D.B., Kang, D.R. and Duncan, N.O. 1999. 'Intralesional cidofovir for recurrent respiratory papillomatosis in children', *Archives of Otolaryngology – Head and Neck Surgery* 125:10, 1143–8.

Preisser, D.A., Hodson, B.W. and Paden, E.P. 1988. 'Developmental phonology: 18–29 months', *Journal of Speech and Hearing Disorders* 53:2, 125–30.

Preston, J.L. 2010. 'Speech and literacy: the connections and the relevance to clinical populations', in A.E. Harrison (ed.), *Speech disorders: causes, treatments and social effects*, Hauppauge, NY: Nova Science Publishers, Inc., 43–73.

Preston, J.L. and Edwards, M.L. 2010. 'Phonological awareness and types of sound errors in preschoolers with speech sound disorders', *Journal of Speech, Language, and Hearing Research* 53:1, 44–60.

Preston, J.L., Felsenfeld, S., Frost, S.J., Fulbright, R.K., Mencl, W., Goen, A. and Pugh, K.R. 2010. 'An fMRI investigation of childhood speech sound disorders', American Speech, Language and Hearing Association Conference, Philadelphia, PA, 17–20 November 2010.

Preus, A. 1981. *Identifying subgroups of stutterers*, Oslo: Universitetsforlaget.

Preus, A. 1996. 'Cluttering upgraded', *Journal of Fluency Disorders* 21:3, 349–57.

Price, J.R., Roberts, J.E., Hennon, E.A., Berni, M.C., Anderson, K.L. and Sideris, J. 2008. 'Syntactic complexity during conversation of boys with fragile X syndrome and Down syndrome', *Journal of Speech, Language, and Hearing Research* 51:1, 3–15.

Price, J.R., Roberts, J.E., Vandergrift, N. and Martin, G. 2007. 'Language comprehension in boys with fragile X syndrome and boys with Down syndrome', *Journal of Intellectual Disability Research* 51:4, 318–26.

Prigatano, G.P. and Pribram, K.H. 1982. 'Perception and memory of facial affect following brain injury', *Perceptual and Motor Skills* 54:3, 859–69.

Prigatano, G.P., Roueche, J.R. and Fordyce, D.J. 1986. *Neuropsychological rehabilitation after brain injury*, Baltimore, MD: Johns Hopkins University Press.

Prince, M., Patel, V., Saxena, S., Maj, M., Maselko, J., Phillips, M.R. and Rahman, A. 2007. 'No health without mental health', *Lancet* 370:9590, 859–77.

Prins, D. and Ingham, R.J. 2009. 'Evidence-based treatment and stuttering – historical perspective', *Journal of Speech, Language, and Hearing Research* 52:1, 254–63.

Prins, R.S., Snow, C.E. and Wagenaar, E. 1978. 'Recovery from aphasia: spontaneous speech versus language comprehension', *Brain and Language* 6:2, 192–211.

Prizant, B. and Duchan, J. 1981. 'The functions of immediate echolalia in autistic children', *Journal of Speech, Language, and Hearing Research* 46:3, 241–9.

Prizant, B.M. and Wetherby, A.M. 1988. 'Providing services to children with autism (0–2 years) and their families', *Topics in Language Disorders* 9:1, 1–23.

Proctor, A., Yairi, E., Duff, M.C. and Zhang, J. 2008. 'Prevalence of stuttering in African-American preschoolers', *Journal of Speech, Language, and Hearing Research* 51:6, 1465–79.

Proctor-Williams, K. and Fey, M. 2007. 'Recast density and acquisition of novel irregular past tense verbs', *Journal of Speech, Language, and Hearing Research* 50:4, 1029–47.

Proctor-Williams, K., Fey, M. and Loeb, D. 2001. 'Parental recasts and production of copulas and articles by children with specific language impairment and typical language', *American Journal of Speech-Language Pathology* 10:2, 155–68.

Prutting, C.A. and Kirchner, D.M. 1987. 'A clinical appraisal of the pragmatic aspects of language', *Journal of Speech and Hearing Disorders* 52:2, 105–19.

Pugh, K.R. 2006. 'A neurocognitive overview of reading acquisition and dyslexia across languages', *Developmental Science* 9:5, 448–50.

Pugh, K.R., Mencl, W.E., Jenner, A.R., Lee, J.R., Katz, L., Frost, S.J., Shaywitz, S. and Shaywitz, B. 2001. 'Neuroimaging studies of reading development and reading disability', *Learning Disabilities Research & Practice* 16:4, 240–9.

Pulvermüller, F. and Berthier, M.L. 2008. 'Aphasia therapy on a neuroscience basis', *Aphasiology* 22:6, 563–99.

Pulvermüller, F., Neininger, B., Elbert, T., Mohr, B., Rockstroh, B., Koebbel, P. and Taub, E. 2001. 'Constraint-induced therapy of chronic aphasia after stroke', *Stroke* 32:7, 1621–6.

Puolakanaho, A., Ahonen, T., Aro, M., Eklund, K., Leppanen, P.H.T., Poikkeus, A., Tolvanen, A., Torppa, M. and Lyytinen, H. 2007. 'Very early phonological and language skills: estimating individual risk of reading disability', *Journal of Child Psychology and Psychiatry* 48:9, 923–31.

Puyuelo, M. and Rondal, J.A. 2005. 'Speech rehabilitation in 10 Spanish-speaking children with severe cerebral palsy: a 4-year longitudinal study', *Pediatric Rehabilitation* 8:2, 113–16.

Quas, J.A., Bauer, A. and Boyce, W.T. 2004. 'Physiological reactivity, social support, and memory in early childhood', *Child Development* 75:3, 797–814.

Rabinovici, G.D. and Miller, B.L. 2010. 'Frontotemporal lobar degeneration: epidemiology, pathophysiology, diagnosis and management', *CNS Drugs* 24:5, 375–98.

Radanovic, M. and Scaff, M. 2003. 'Speech and language disturbances due to subcortical lesions', *Brain and Language* 84:3, 337–52.

Ramig, L. and Verdolini, K. 1998. 'Treatment efficacy: voice disorders', *Journal of Speech, Language, and Hearing Research* 41:1, S101–16.

Ramig, L., Bonitati, C., Lemke, J. and Horii, Y. 1994. 'Voice treatment for patients with Parkinson's disease: development of an approach and preliminary efficacy data', *Journal of Medical Speech-Language Pathology* 2, 191–209.

Ramig, L.O., Pawlas, A.A. and Countryman, S. 1995. *The Lee Silverman voice treatment: a practical guide to treating the voice and speech disorders in Parkinson's disease*, Iowa City: National Center for Voice and Speech.

Rammage, L. 2011. 'Emotional expression and voice dysfunction', *Perspectives on Voice and Voice Disorders* 21:1, 8–16.

Rammage, L., Morrison, M., Nichol, H., Pullan, B., Salkeld, L. and May, P. 2001. *Management of the voice and its disorders*, San Diego, CA: Singular Thomson Learning.

Rammage, L.A., Nichol, H. and Morrison, M.D. 1987. 'The psychopathology of voice disorders', *Human Communication Canada* 11:4, 21–5.

Ramus, F., Rosen, S., Dakin, S.C., Day, B.L., Castellotte, J.M. and White, S. 2003. 'Theories of developmental dyslexia: insights from a multiple case study of dyslexic adults', *Brain* 126:4, 841–65.

Randall, P. 1972. 'Cleft palate', in W.C. Grabb and J.W. Smith (eds.), *Plastic surgery: a concise guide to clinical practice*, Boston, MA: Little Brown, 179–210.

Rapp, A.M. and Wild, B. 2011. 'Nonliteral language in Alzheimer dementia: a review', *Journal of the International Neuropsychological Society* 17:2, 207–18.

Rapp, B. 2001. *Handbook of cognitive neuropsychology: what deficits reveal about the mind*, Hove, East Sussex: Psychology Press.

Rapp, B. and Caramazza, A. 1993. 'On the distinction between deficits of access and deficits of storage: a question of theory', *Cognitive Neuropsychology* 10:2, 113–41.

Rapp, B. and Goldrick, M. 2006. 'Speaking words: contributions of cognitive neuropsychological research', *Cognitive Neuropsychology* 23:1, 39–73.

Rapp, B. and Kane, A. 2002. 'Remediation of deficits affecting different components of the spelling process', *Aphasiology* 16:4-6, 439–54.

Rascovsky, K., Hodges, J.R., Kipps, C.M., Johnson, J.K., Seeley, W.W., Mendez, M.F., Knopman, D., Kertesz, A., Mesulam, M., Salmon, D.P., Galasko, D., Chow, T.W., Decarli, C., Hillis, A., Josephs, K., Kramer, J.H., Weintraub, S., Grossman, M., Gorno-Tempini, M.L. and Miller, B.M. 2007. 'Diagnostic criteria for the behavioral variant of frontotemporal dementia (bvFTD): current limitations and future directions', *Alzheimer Disease and Associated Disorders* 21:4, S14–S18.

Rascovsky, K., Hodges, J.R., Knopman, D., Mendez, M.F., Kramer, J.H., Neuhaus, J., van Swieten, J.C., Seelaar, H., Dopper, E.G.P., Onyike, C.U., Hillis, A.E., Josephs, K.A., Boeve, B.F., Kertesz, A., Seeley, W.W., Rankin, K.P., Johnson, J.K., Gorno-Tempini, M.-L., Rosen, H., Prioleau-Latham, C.E., Lee, A., Kipps, C.M., Lillo, P., Piguet, O., Rohrer, J.D., Rossor, M.N., Warren, J.D., Fox, N.C., Galasko, D., Salmon, D.P., Black, S.E., Mesulam, M., Weintraub, S., Dickerson, B.C., Diehl-Schmid, J., Pasquier, F., Deramecourt, V., Lebert, F., Pijnenburg, Y., Chow, T.W., Manes, F., Grafman, J., Cappa, S.F., Freedman, M., Grossman, M. and Miller, B.L. 2011. 'Sensitivity to revised diagnostic criteria for the behavioral variant of frontotemporal dementia', *Brain* 134:9, 2456–77.

Rasmussen, T. and Millner, B. 1977. 'The role of early left-brain injury in determining lateralization of cerebral speech functions', *Annals of the New York Academy of Sciences* 299, 355–69.

Rastadmehr, O., Bressmann, T., Smyth, R. and Irish, J.C. 2008. 'Increased midsagittal tongue velocity as indication of articulatory compensation in patients with lateral partial glossectomies', *Head and Neck* 30:6, 718–26.

Ratnavalli, E., Brayne, C., Dawson, K. and Hodges, J.R. 2002. 'The prevalence of frontotemporal dementia', *Neurology* 58:11, 1615–21.

Ray, J. 2001. 'Functional outcomes of orofacial myofunctional therapy in children with cerebral palsy', *International Journal of Orofacial Myology* 27, 5–17.

Raymer, A. 2007. 'Gestures and words: facilitating recovery in aphasia', *ASHA Leader* (online, available at: www.asha.org/Publications/leader/2007/070619/f070619a.htm; last accessed 12 June 2013).

Redmond, S. and Rice, M. 1998. 'The socioemotional behaviors of children with SLI: social adaptation or social deviance?', *Journal of Speech, Language, and Hearing Research* 41:3, 688–700.

Regan, J., Sowman, R. and Walsh, I. 2006. 'Prevalence of dysphagia in acute and community mental health settings', *Dysphagia* 21:2, 95–101.

Rehak, A., Kaplan, J. and Gardner, H. 1992. 'Sensitivity to conversational deviance in right-hemisphere-damaged patients', *Brain and Language* 42:2, 203–17.

Reid, D., Hresko, W. and Hammill, D.D. 2004. *Test of Early Reading Ability – 3*, Austin, TX: Pro-Ed.

Reilly, J. and Peelle, J.E. 2008. 'Effects of semantic impairment on language processing in semantic dementia', *Seminars in Speech and Language* 29:1, 32–43.

Reilly, J., Cross, K., Troiani, V. and Grossman, M. 2007a. 'Single word semantic judgments in semantic dementia: do phonology and grammatical class count?', *Aphasiology* 21:6-8, 558–69.

Reilly, J., Klima, E.S. and Bellugi, U. 1990. 'Once more with feeling: affect and language in atypical populations', *Development and Psychopathology* 2:4, 367–91.

Reilly, J., Martin, N. and Grossman, M. 2005. 'Verbal learning in semantic dementia: is repetition priming a useful strategy?', *Aphasiology* 19:3, 329–39.

Reilly, J., Peelle, J.E., Antonucci, S.M. and Grossman, M. 2011b. 'Anomia as a marker of distinct semantic memory impairments in Alzheimer's disease and semantic dementia', *Neuropsychology* 25:4, 413–26.

Reilly, J., Peelle, J.E. and Grossman, M. 2007b. 'A unitary semantics account of reverse concreteness effects in semantic dementia', *Brain and Language* 103:1-2, 86–7.

Reilly, J., Rodriguez, A., Peelle, J.E. and Grossman, M. 2011a. 'Frontal lobe damage impairs process and content in semantic memory: evidence from category specific effects in progressive nonfluent aphasia', *Cortex* 47:6, 645–58.

Reilly, S., Onslow, M., Packman, A., Wake, M., Bavin, E.L., Prior, M., Eadie, P., Cini, E., Bolzonello, C. and Ukoumunne, O.C. 2009. 'Predicting stuttering onset by the age of 3 years: a prospective, community cohort study', *Pediatrics* 123:1, 270–7.

Reitan, R.M. 1955. 'The relation of the trail making test to organic brain damage', *Journal of Consulting Psychology* 19:5, 393–4.

Reitzes, P. and Snyder, G. 2006. 'Response to "Intensive stuttering modification therapy: a multidimensional assessment of treatment outcomes" by Blomgren, Roy, Callister, and Merrill (2005)', *Journal of Speech, Language, and Hearing Research* 49:6, 1420–2.

Reschly, D.J. 2002. 'Minority overrepresentation: the silent contributor to learning disability prevalence and diagnostic confusion', in R. Bradley, L. Danielson and D.P. Hallahan (eds.), *Identification of learning disabilities: research to practice*, Mahwah, NJ: Lawrence Erlbaum, 361–8.

Rescorla, L. 1989. 'The language development survey: a screening tool for delayed language in toddlers', *Journal of Speech and Hearing Disorders* 54:4, 587–99.

Revheim, N., Butler, P.D., Schechter, I., Jalbrzikowski, M., Silipo, G. and Javitt, D.C. 2006. 'Reading impairment and visual processing deficits in schizophrenia', *Schizophrenia Research* 87:1–3, 238–45.

Revuelta, G.J. and Lippa, C.F. 2009. 'Dementia with Lewy bodies and Parkinson's disease dementia may best be viewed as two distinct entities', *International Psychogeriatrics* 21:2, 213–16.

Reynell, J.K. 1977. *Manual for the Reynell developmental language scales*, Windsor: NFER.

Rice, K., Moriuchi, J.M., Jones, W. and Klin, A. 2012. 'Parsing heterogeneity in autism spectrum disorders: visual scanning of dynamic social scenes in school-aged children', *Journal of the American Academy of Child and Adolescent Psychiatry* 51:3, 238–48.

Rice, M. and Smolik, F. 2007. 'Genetics of language disorders: clinical conditions, phenotypes, and genes', in M.G. Gaskell (ed.), *Oxford handbook of psycholinguistics*, Oxford University Press, 685–700.

Rice, M. and Wexler, K. 1996a. 'A phenotype of specific language impairment: extended optional infinitive', in M.L. Rice (ed.), *Toward a genetics of language*, Hillsdale, NJ: Lawrence Erlbaum Associates, 215–37.

Rice, M. and Wexler, K. 1996b. 'Toward tense as a clinical marker of specific language impairment in English-speaking children', *Journal of Speech and Hearing Research* 39:6, 1239–57.

Rice, M. and Wexler, K. 2001. *Rice/Wexler test of early grammatical impairment*, San Antonio, TX: Psychological Corporation.

Rice, M., Buhr, J. and Nemeth, M. 1990. 'Fast mapping word learning abilities of language-delayed preschoolers', *Journal of Speech and Hearing Disorders* 55:1, 33–42.

Rice, M., Hoffman, L. and Wexler, K. 2009a. 'Judgments of omitted BE and DO in questions as extended finiteness clinical markers of specific language impairment (SLI) to 15 years: a study of growth and asymptote', *Journal of Speech, Language, and Hearing Research* 52:6, 1417–33.

Rice, M., Oetting, J., Marquis, J., Bode, J. and Pae, S. 1994. 'Frequency of input on word comprehension of children with specific language impairment', *Journal of Speech and Hearing Research* 37:1, 106–22.

Rice, M., Smith, S. and Gayán, J. 2009b. 'Convergent genetic linkage and associations to language, speech and reading measures in families of probands with specific language impairment', *Journal of Neurodevelopmental Disorders* 1:4, 264–82.

Rice, M., Taylor, C. and Zubrick, S. 2008. 'Language outcomes of 7-year-old children with or without a history of late language emergence at 24 months', *Journal of Speech, Language, and Hearing Research* 51:2, 394–407.

Rice, M., Warren, S.F. and Betz, S. 2005. 'Language symptoms of developmental language disorders: an overview of autism, Down syndrome, fragile X, specific language impairment, and Williams syndrome', *Applied Psycholinguistics* 26:1, 7–27.

Rice, M., Wexler, K. and Hershberger, S. 1998. 'Tense over time: the longitudinal course of tense acquisition in children with specific language impairment', *Journal of Speech, Language, and Hearing Research* 41:6, 1412–31.

Richards, C. and Conture, E.G. 2007. 'An indirect treatment approach for early intervention for childhood stuttering', in E.G. Conture and R.F. Curlee (eds.), *Stuttering and related disorders of fluency*, third edition, New York: Thieme Publishers, 77–99.

Richards, T.L., Aylward, E.H., Field, K.M., Grimme, A.C., Raskind, W., Richards, A.L., Nagy, W., Ekert, M., Leonard, C., Abbot, D. and Berninger, V. 2006. 'Converging evidence for triple word form theory in children with dyslexia', *Developmental Neuropsychology* 30:1, 547–89.

Richels, C. and Conture, E.G. 2010. 'Indirect treatment of childhood stuttering: diagnostic predictors of treatment outcome', in B. Guitar and R.J. McCauley (eds.), *Treatment of stuttering: established and emerging interventions*, Baltimore, MD: Lippincott Williams & Wilkins, 18–55.

Riches, N.G., Loucas, T., Baird, G., Charman, T. and Simonoff, E. 2010. 'Sentence repetition in adolescents with specific language impairments and autism: an investigation of complex syntax', *International Journal of Language & Communication Disorders* 45:1, 47–60.

Richman, L.C. and Eliason, M. 1984. 'Type of reading disability related to cleft type and neuropsychological patterns', *Cleft Palate Journal* 21:1, 1–6.

Richman, L.C., Eliason, M.J. and Lindgren, S.D. 1988. 'Reading disability in children with clefts', *Cleft Palate Journal* 25:1, 21–5.

Riddoch, J. 1990. 'Neglect and the peripheral dyslexias', *Cognitive Neuropsychology* 7:5–6, 369–89.

Riddoch, M.J. and Humphreys, G.W. 1993. *Birmingham object recognition battery (BORB)*, Hove, East Sussex: Lawrence Erlbaum.

Rieger, J.M., Wolfaardt, J.F., Jha, N. and Seikaly, H. 2003. 'Maxillary obturators: the relationship between patient satisfaction and speech outcome', *Head and Neck* 25:11, 895–903.

Riley, G. 2009. *Stuttering severity instrument*, fourth edition, Austin, TX: Pro-Ed.

Riley, G.D. and Ingham, J.C. 2000. 'Acoustic duration changes associated with two types of treatment for children who stutter', *Journal of Speech, Language, and Hearing Research* 43:4, 965–78.

Riley, J., Riley, G. and Maguire, G. 2004. 'Subjective screening of stuttering severity, locus of control and avoidance: research edition', *Journal of Fluency Disorders* 29:1, 51–62.

Rimé, B., Bouvy, H., Leborgne, B. and Rouillon, F. 1978. 'Psychopathy and nonverbal behaviour in an interpersonal situation', *Journal of Abnormal Psychology*, 87:6, 636–43.

Rinaldi, M.C., Marangolo, P. and Baldassari, F. 2004. 'Metaphor comprehension in right brain-damaged patients with visuo-verbal and verbal material: a dissociation (re)considered', *Cortex* 40:3, 479–90.

Rinaldi, W. 2000. 'Pragmatic comprehension in secondary school-aged students with specific developmental language disorder', *International Journal of Language & Communication Disorders* 35:1, 1–29.

Ring, M. and Clahsen, H. 2005. 'Morpho-syntax in Down's syndrome: is the extended optional infinitive an option?', *Stem-, Spraak-en Taalpathologie* 13:1, 3–13.

Ringel, R.L., House, A.S., Burk, K.W., Dolinsky, J.P. and Scott, C.M. 1970. 'Some relations between orosensory discrimination and articulatory aspects of speech production', *Journal of Speech and Hearing Disorders* 35:1, 3–11.

Riski, J.E. 1979. 'Articulation skills and oral-nasal resonance in children with pharyngeal flaps', *Cleft Palate Journal* 16:4, 421–8.

Riski, J.E. 1984. 'Functional velopharyngeal incompetence: diagnoses and management,' in H. Winitz (ed.), *Treating articulation disorders: for clinicians by clinicians*, Baltimore, MD: University Park Press, 224–34.

Riski, J.E. 1995. 'Speech assessment of adolescents', *Cleft Palate Journal* 32:2, 109–13.

Riski, J.E. 2006. *'Educating parents of newborns with cleft lip/palate: are we meeting the challenge?'*, American Cleft Palate-Craniofacial Association: Vancouver, BC, Canada, 3–8 April 2006.

Riski, J.E. 2011. *'Hemifacial microsomia: feeding, resonance and articulation'*, American Cleft Palate-Craniofacial Association, San Juan, Puerto Rico, 3 April 2011.

Riski, J.E. and DeLong, E. 1984. 'Articulation development in children with cleft lip/palate', *Cleft Palate Journal* 21:2, 57–64.

Riski, J.E. and Mason, R.M. 1994. 'Adenoid involution as a cause of velopharyngeal incompetence in children with cleft palate', Annual Meeting of the American Cleft Palate-Craniofacial Association: Toronto, Canada, 16–21 May 1994.

Riski, J.E. and Millard, R.T. 1979. 'The process of speech evaluation and treatment', in H. Cooper, R. Harding, W. Krogman, M. Mazaheri and R.T. Millard (eds.), *Cleft palate and cleft lip: a team approach to clinical management and rehabilitation of the patient*, Philadelphia, PA: W.B. Saunders, 431–84.

Riski, J.E., Georgiade, N.G., Serafin, D., Barwick, W., Georgiade, G.S. and Riefkohl, R. 1987. 'The orticochea pharyngoplasty and primary palatoplasty: an evaluation', *Annals of Plastic Surgery* 18:4, 303–9.

Riski, J.E., Hoke, J.A. and Dolan, E.A. 1989. 'The role of pressure flow and endoscopic assessment in successful palatal obturator revision', *Cleft Palate Journal* 26:1, 56–62.

Riski, J.E., Ruff, G.L., Georgiade, G.S., Barwick, W.J. and Edwards, P.D. 1992. 'Evaluation of the sphincter pharyngoplasty', *Cleft Palate-Craniofacial Journal* 29:3, 254–61.

Riski, J.E., Serafin, D., Riefkohl, R., Georgiade, G.S. and Georgiade, N.G. 1984. 'A rationale for modifying the site of insertion of the orticochea pharyngoplasty', *Plastic and Reconstructive Surgery* 73:6, 892–4.

Rizos, M. and Spyropoulos, M.N. 2004. 'Van der Woude syndrome: a review. Cardinal signs, epidemiology, associated features, differential diagnosis, expressivity, genetic counselling and treatment. *European Journal of Orthodontics* 26:1, 17–24.

Robbins, J. and Klee, T. 1987. 'Clinical assessment of oropharyngeal motor development in young children', *Journal of Speech and Hearing Disorders* 52:3, 271–7.

Roberts, D.L. and Penn, D.L. 2009. 'Social cognition and interaction training (SCIT) for outpatients with schizophrenia: a preliminary study', *Psychiatry Research* 166:2–3, 141–7.

Roberts, J.A., Rice, M.L. and Tager-Flusberg, H. 2004. 'Tense marking in children with autism', *Applied Psycholinguistics* 25, 429–48.

Roberts, J.E., Burchinal, M.R. and Zeisel, S.A. 2002. 'Otitis media in early childhood in relation to children's school-age language and academic skills', *Pediatrics* 110:4, 696–706.

Roberts, J.E., Chapman, R.S., Martin, G.E. and Moskowitz, L. 2008. 'Language of preschool and school-age children with Down syndrome and fragile X syndrome', in J.E. Roberts, R.S. Chapman and S.F. Warren (eds.), *Speech and language development and intervention in Down syndrome and fragile X syndrome*, Baltimore, MD: Paul Brookes Publishing, 77–115.

Roberts, J.E., Price, J. and Malkin, C. 2007a. 'Language and communication development in Down syndrome', *Mental Retardation and Developmental Disabilities Research Review* 13:1, 26–35.

Roberts, J.E., Price, J., Barnes, E., Nelson, L., Burchinal, M., Hennon, E.A., Moskowitz, L., Edwards, A., Malkin, C., Anderson, K., Misenheimer, J. and Hooper, S.R. 2007b. 'Receptive vocabulary, expressive vocabulary, and speech production of boys with fragile X syndrome in comparison to boys with Down syndrome', *American Journal on Mental Retardation* 112:3, 177–93.

Roberts, J.E., Rosenfeld, R.M. and Zeisel, S.A. 2004. 'Otitis media and speech and language: a meta-analysis of prospective studies', *Pediatrics* 113:3, e238–48.

Roberts, T.F. and Brown, B.J. 1983. 'Evaluation of a modified sphincter pharyngoplasty in the treatment of speech problems due to palatal insufficiency', *Annals of Plastic Surgery* 10:3, 209–13.

Robertson, S.J. 1982. *Dysarthria profile*, Tucson, AZ: Communication Skill Builders.

Robey, R.R. 1998. 'A meta-analysis of clinical outcomes in the treatment of aphasia', *Journal of Speech, Language, and Hearing Research* 41:1, 172–87.

Robin, D.A., Bean, C. and Folkins, J.W. 1989. 'Lip movement in apraxia of speech', *Journal of Speech and Hearing Research* 32:3, 512–23.

Robin, D.A., Goel, A., Somodi, L.B. and Luschei, E.S. 1992. 'Tongue strength and endurance: relation to highly skilled movements', *Journal of Speech and Hearing Research* 35:6, 1239–45.

Robin, D.A., Jacks, A., Hageman, C., Clark, H.M. and Woodworth, G. 2008. 'Visuomotor tracking abilities of speakers with apraxia of speech or conduction aphasia', *Brain and Language* 106:2, 98–106.

Robin, D.A., Maas, E., Sandberg, Y. and Schmidt, R.A. 2007. 'Motor control and learning and childhood apraxia of speech', in P.K. Hall, L. Jordan and D.A. Robin, *Developmental apraxia of speech: theory and clinical practice*, second edition, Austin, TX: Pro-Ed, 67–86.

Robin, D.A., Somodi, C.B. and Luschei, E.S. 1991. 'Measurement of tongue strength and endurance in normal and articulation disordered subjects', in C.A. Moore, K.M. Yorkston and D.R. Beukelman (eds.), *Dysarthria and apraxia of speech: perspectives on management*, Baltimore, MD: Paul H. Brookes, 173–84.

Robson, D. and Gray, R. 2007. 'Serious mental illness and physical health problems: a discussion paper', *International Journal of Nursing Studies* 44:3, 457–66.

Robson, J., Pring, T., Marshall, J., Morrison, S. and Chiat, S. 1998. 'Written communication in undifferentiated jargon aphasia: a therapy study', *Journal of Language and Communication Disorders* 33:3, 305–28.

Robson, S., Eftychiou, E., Le Couteur, J., Pennington, L., Miller, N. and Steen, N. 2009. 'Associations between speech intelligibility of children with cerebral palsy and the loudness and clarity of their voice', Royal College of Speech and Language Therapists Scientific Conference, Partners in Progress: Spreading the Word: London, 17–18 March 2009.

Rodriguez-Ferreiro, J., Menendez, M., Ribacoba, R. and Cuetos, F. 2009. 'Action naming is impaired in Parkinson disease patients', *Neuropsychologia* 47:14, 3271–4.

Rogers, C. 1959. 'A theory of therapy, personality and interpersonal relationships, as developed in the client-centered framework', in S. Koch (ed.), *Psychology: a study of a science, Vol 3: Formulations of the person and the social context*, New York: McGraw Hill, 184–256.

Rogers, S.L. and Friedman, R.B. 2008. 'The underlying mechanisms of semantic memory loss in Alzheimer's disease and semantic dementia', *Neuropsychologia* 46:1, 12–21.

Rogers, T.T., Lambon Ralph, M.A., Garrard, P., Bozeat, S., McClelland, J.L., Hodges, J.R. and Patterson, K. 2004. 'Structure and deterioration of semantic memory: a neuropsychological and computational investigation', *Psychological Review* 111:1, 2005–35.

Rogers-Adkinson, D.L. 2003. 'Language processing in children with EBD', *Behavioral Disorders* 29:1, 43–7.

Roizen, N.J. 2002. 'Down syndrome', in M.L. Batshaw (ed.), *Children with disabilities*, Baltimore, MD: Brookes, 307–20.

Román, G.C., Sachdev, P., Royall, D.R., Bullock, R.A., Orgogozo, J.M., Lopez-Pousa, S., Arizaga, R. and Wallin, A. 2004. 'Vascular cognitive disorder: a new diagnostic category updating vascular cognitive impairment and vascular dementia', *Journal of the Neurological Sciences* 226:1–2, 81–7.

Román, G.C., Tatemichi, T.K., Erkinjuntti, T., Cummings, J.L., Masdeu, J.C., Garcia, J.H., Amaducci, L., Orgogozo, J.-M., Brun, A., Hofman, A., Moody, D.M., O'Brien, M.D., Yamaguchi, T., Grafman, J., Drayer, B.P., Bennett, D.A., Fisher, M., Ogata, J., Kokmen, E., Bermejo, F., Wolf, P.A., Gorelick, P.B., Bick, K.L., Pajeau, A.K., Bell, M.A., DeCarli, C., Culebras, A., Korczyn, A.D., Bogousslavsky, J., Hartmann, A. and Scheinberg, P. 1993. 'Vascular dementia: diagnostic criteria for research studies. Report of the NINDS-AIREN international workshop', *Neurology* 43:2, 250–60.

Romski, M. and Sevcik, R.A. 1996. *Breaking the speech barrier: language development through augmented means*, Baltimore, MD: Paul H. Brookes.

Romski, M. and Sevcik, R.A. 1997. 'Augmentative and alternative communication for children with developmental disabilities', *Mental Retardation and Developmental Disabilities Research Reviews* 3:4, 363–8.

Romski, M. and Sevcik, R.A. 2005. 'Early intervention and augmentative communication: myths and realities', *Infants and Young Children* 18:3, 174–85.

Romski, M., Sevcik, R.A. and Adamson, L.B. 1999. 'Communication patterns of youth with mental retardation with and without their speech-output communication devices', *American Journal on Mental Retardation* 104:3, 249–59.

Romski, M., Sevcik, R.A. and Fonseca, A.H. 2003. 'Augmentative and alternative communication for persons with mental retardation', in L. Abbeduto (ed.), *International review of research in mental retardation (volume 27). Language and communication in mental retardation*, San Diego, CA: Academic Press, 255–80.

Rondal, J. 1994. 'Exceptional language development in mental retardation: the relative autonomy of language as a cognitive system', in H. Tager-Flusberg (ed.), *Constraints on language acquisition: studies of atypical children*, Hillsdale, NJ: Lawrence Erlbaum Associates, 155–74.

Rondal, J. 2001. 'Language in mental retardation: individual and syndromic differences and neurogenetic variation', *Swiss Journal of Psychology* 60:3, 161–78.

Rondal, J. and Comblain, A. 1996. 'Language in adults with Down Syndrome', *Down Syndrome Research and Practice* 4:1, 3–14.

Rondal, J. and Edwards, S. 1997. *Language in mental retardation*, London: Whurr Publishers.

Roper, N. and Dunst, C.J. 2003. 'Communication intervention in natural learning environments: guidelines for practice', *Infants and Young Children* 16:3, 215–26.

Rose, M. 2006. 'The utility of arm and hand gestures in the treatment of aphasia', *Advances in Speech-Language Pathology* 8:2, 92–109.

Rose, M. and Sussmilch, G. 2008. 'The effects of semantic and gesture treatments on verb retrieval and verb use in aphasia', *Aphasiology* 22:7–8, 691–706.

Rosen, C.A., Murry, T., Zinn, A., Zullo, T. and Sonbolian, M. 2000. 'Voice handicap index change following treatment of voice disorders', *Journal of Voice* 14:4, 619–23.

Rosen, C.A., Osborne, J., Zullo, T. and Murry, T. 2004. 'Development and validation of the voice handicap index-10', *Laryngoscope* 114:9, 1549–56.

Rosen, H.J., Gorno-Tempini, M.L., Goldman, W.P., Perry, R.J., Schuff, N., Weiner, M., Feiwell, R., Kramer, J.H. and Miller, B.L. 2002. 'Patterns of brain atrophy in frontotemporal dementia and semantic dementia', *Neurology* 58:2, 198–208.

Rosen, S., Bergman, M., Plester, D., El-Mofty, A. and Satti, M.H. 1962. 'Presbycusis study of a relatively noise-free population in the Sudan', *Annals of Otology, Rhinology and Laryngology* 71, 727–43.

Rosenbaum, D.A. 2010. *Human motor control*, Burlington, MA: Elsevier.

Rosenbek, J. 2009. 'What do we mean when we say, "We know how to treat that problem?"', Annual Conference of British Columbia Association of Speech-Language Pathologists and Audiologists: Harrison Hot Springs, BC, Canada, 17 October 2009.

Rosenbek, J., Hansen, R., Baughman, C.H. and Lemme, M. 1974. 'Treatment of developmental apraxia of speech: a case study', *Language, Speech, and Hearing Services in Schools* 5:1, 13–22.

Rosenbek, J.C., Collins, M. and Wertz, R.T. 1976. 'Intersystemic reorganization for apraxia of speech', in R.H. Brookshire (ed.), *Clinical aphasiology conference proceedings*, Minneapolis: BRK Publishers, 255–60.

Rosenbek, J.C., Lemme, M.L., Ahern, M.B., Harris, E.H. and Wertz, R.T. 1973. 'A treatment for apraxia of speech in adults', *Journal of Speech and Hearing Disorders* 38:4, 462–72.

Rosenberg, S. and Abbeduto, L. 1993. *Language and communication in mental retardation: development, processes, and intervention*, Hillsdale, NJ: Lawrence Erlbaum Associates.

Rosenthal, J.B. 1994. 'Rate control therapy for developmental apraxia of speech', *Clinics in Communication Disorders* 4:3, 190–200.

Ross, C.A., Margolis, R.L., Reading, S.A., Pletnikov, M. and Coyle, J.T. 2006. 'Neurobiology of schizophrenia', *Neuron* 52:1, 139–53.

Ross, J.A., Noordzji, J.P. and Woo, P. 1998. 'Voice disorders in patients with suspected laryngo-pharyngeal reflux disease', *Journal of Voice* 12:1, 84–8.

Rossen, M., Klima, E.S., Bellugi, U., Bihrle, A. and Jones, W. 1996. 'Interaction between language and cognition: evidence from Williams syndrome', in J.H. Beitchman, N. Cohen, M. Konstantareas and R. Tannock (eds.), *Language, learning, and behavior disorders: developmental, biological, and clinical perspectives*, New York: Cambridge University Press, 367–92.

Rosser, A. and Hodges, J.R. 1994. 'Initial letter and semantic category fluency in Alzheimer's disease, Huntington's disease, and progressive supranuclear palsy', *Journal of Neurology, Neurosurgery and Psychiatry* 57:11, 1389–94.

Roth, C.R., Aronson, A.E. and Davis, L.J., Jr. 1989. 'Clinical studies in psychogenic stuttering of adult onset', *Journal of Speech and Hearing Disorders* 54:4, 634–46.

Rothenberg, M. 1973. 'A new inverse-filtering technique for deriving the glottic air flow waveform during voicing', *Journal of the Acoustical Society of America* 53:6, 1632–45.

Roulstone, S., Miller, L.L., Wren, Y. and Peters, T.J. 2009. 'The natural history of speech impairment of 8-year-old children in the Avon longitudinal study of parents and children: error rates at 2 and 5 years', *International Journal of Speech-Language Pathology* 11:5, 381–91.

Rousseau, B., Suehiro, A., Echemendia, N. and Sivasankar, M. 2011. 'Raised intensity phonation compromises vocal fold epithelial barrier integrity', *Laryngoscope* 121:2, 346–51.

Rousseaux, M., Sève, A., Vallet, M., Pasquier, F. and Mackowiak-Cordoliani, M.A. 2010. 'An analysis of communication in conversation in patients with dementia', *Neuropsychologia* 48:13, 3884–90.

Rowe, A.D., Bullock, P.R., Polkey, C.E. and Morris, R.G. 2001. '"Theory of mind" impairments and their relationship to executive functioning following frontal lobe excisions', *Brain* 124:3, 600–16.

Rowe, J.W. and Kahn, R.L. 1997. 'Successful aging', *Gerontologist* 37:4, 433–40.

Roy, N. 2003. 'Functional dysphonia', *Current Opinion in Otolaryngology & Head and Neck Surgery* 11:3, 144–8.

Roy, N. 2010. 'Differential diagnosis of muscle tension dysphonia and spasmodic dysphonia', *Current Opinion in Otolaryngology & Head and Neck Surgery*, 18:3, 165–70.

Roy, N. 2011. 'Personality and voice disorders', *Perspectives on Voice and Voice Disorders* 21:1, 18–23.

Roy, N. and Bless, D.M. 2000. 'Personality traits and psychological factors in voice pathology: a foundation for future research', *Journal of Speech, Language, and Hearing Research* 43:3, 737–48.

Roy, N., Bless, D.M. and Heisey, D. 2000a. 'Personality and voice disorders: a superfactor trait analysis', *Journal of Speech, Language, and Hearing Research* 43:3, 749–68.

Roy, N., Bless, D.M. and Heisey, D. 2000b. 'Personality and voice disorders: a multitrait-multidisorder analysis', *Journal of Voice* 14:4, 521–48.

Roy, N., Bless, D.M., Heisey, D. and Ford, C.N. 1997. 'Manual circumlaryngeal therapy for functional dysphonia: an evaluation of short- and long-term treatment outcomes', *Journal of Voice* 11:3, 321–31.

Roy, N., Gray, S.D., Simon, M., Dove, H., Corbin-Lewis, K. and Stemple, J.C. 2001. 'An evaluation of the effects of two treatment approaches for teachers with voice disorders: a prospective randomized clinical trial', *Journal of Speech, Language, and Hearing Research* 44:2, 286–96.

Roy, N., Stemple, J., Merrill, R.M. and Thomas, L. 2007. 'Epidemiology of voice disorders in the elderly: preliminary findings', *Laryngoscope* 117:4, 628–33.

Roy, N., Weinrich, B., Gray, S.D., Tanner, K., Stemple, J.C. and Sapienza, C.M. 2003. 'Three treatments for teachers with voice disorders: a randomized clinical trial', *Journal of Speech, Language, and Hearing Research* 46:3, 670–88.

Roy, N., Weinrich, B., Gray, S.D., Tanner, K., Walker Toledo, S., Dove, H., Corbin-Lewis, K. and Stemple, J.C. 2002. 'Voice amplification versus vocal hygiene instruction for teachers with voice disorders', *Journal of Speech, Language, and Hearing Research* 45:4, 625–38.

Royal College of Speech and Language Therapists. 2005. *Clinical guidelines*, London: Royal College of Speech and Language Therapists.

Royal College of Speech and Language Therapists 2009. *RCSLT resource manual for commissioning and planning services for SLCN: dysarthria*, London: Royal College of Speech and Language Therapists.

Ruben, R.J. 2000. 'Redefining the survival of the fittest: communication disorders in the 21st century', *Laryngoscope* 110:2 Pt 1, 241–5.

Ruhl, K.L., Hughes, C.A. and Camarata, S.M. 1992. 'Analysis of the expressive and receptive language characteristics of emotionally handicapped students served in public school settings', *Journal of Childhood Communication Disorders* 14:2, 165–76.

Ruscello, D.M. 2004. 'Considerations for behavioral management for velopharyngeal closure for speech', in K. Bzoch (ed.), *Communicative disorders related to cleft lip and palate*, Austin, TX: Pro Ed, 509–28.

Russell, J., Jarrold, C. and Henry, L. 1996. 'Working memory in children with autism and with moderate learning difficulties', *Journal of Child Psychology and Psychiatry* 37:6, 673–86.

Rutherford, M.D., Baron-Cohen, S. and Wheelwright, S. 2002. 'Reading the mind in the voice: a study with normal adults and adults with Asperger syndrome and high functioning autism', *Journal of Autism and Developmental Disorders* 32:3, 189–94.

Rutter, M. 1970. 'Autistic children: infancy to adulthood', *Seminars in Psychiatry* 2:4, 435–50.

Rutter, M., Bailey, A. and Lord, C. 2003. *The social communication questionnaire*, Los Angeles: Western Psychological Services.

Rvachew, S. 2007. 'Phonological processing and reading in children with speech sound disorders', *American Journal of Speech-Language Pathology* 16:3, 260–70.

Rvachew, S. and Brosseau-Lapré, F. 2012. *Developmental phonological disorders: foundations of clinical practice*, San Diego, CA: Plural Publishing.

Rvachew, S. and Grawburg, M. 2006. 'Correlates of phonological awareness in preschoolers with speech sound disorders', *Journal of Speech, Language, and Hearing Research* 49:1, 74–87.

Rvachew, S. and Grawburg, M. 2008. 'Reflections on phonological working memory, letter knowledge and phonological awareness: a reply to Hartmann (2008)', *Journal of Speech, Language, and Hearing Research* 51:5, 1219–26.

Rvachew, S. and Jamieson, D.G. 1995. 'Learning new speech contrasts: evidence from learning a second language and children with speech disorders', in W. Strange (ed.), *Speech perception and linguistic experience: theoretical and methodological issues in cross-language speech research*, Timonium, MD: York Press Inc., 411–32.

Rvachew, S., Chiang, P. and Evans, N. 2007. 'Characteristics of speech errors produced by children with and without delayed phonological awareness skills', *Language, Speech, and Hearing Services in Schools* 38:1, 60–71.

Rvachew, S., Gaines, B.R., Cloutier, G. and Blanchet, N. 2005. 'Productive morphology skills of children with speech delay', *Journal of Speech-Language Pathology and Audiology* 29:2, 83–9.

Rvachew, S., Nowak, M. and Cloutier, G. 2004. 'Effect of phonemic perception training on the speech production and phonological awareness skills of children with expressive phonological delay', *American Journal of Speech-Language Pathology* 13:3, 250–63.

Ryalls, J.H. 1984. 'Some acoustic aspects of fundamental frequency of CVC utterances in aphasia', *Phonetica* 41:2, 103–11.

Ryalls, J.H. 1986. 'An acoustic study of vowel production in aphasia', *Brain and Language* 29:1, 48–67.

Ryan, B.P. and Ryan, B.V. 1996. The rise and fall of operant programs for the treatment of stammering, *Folia Phoniatrica et Logopaedica* 48:6, 309–13.

Ryan, B.P. and Van Kirk Ryan, B. 1995. 'Programmed stuttering treatment for children: comparison of two establishment programs through transfer, maintenance, and follow-up', *Journal of Speech and Hearing Research* 38:1, 61–75.

Ryder, N., Leinonen, E. and Schulz, J. 2008. 'Cognitive approach to assessing pragmatic language comprehension in children with specific language impairment', *International Journal of Language & Communication Disorders* 43:4, 427–47.

Sabbagh, M.A. 1999. 'Communicative intentions and language: evidence from right-hemisphere damage and autism', *Brain and Language* 70:1, 29–69.

Sabol, J.W., Lee, L. and Stemple, J.C. 1995. 'The value of vocal function exercises in the practice regimen of singers', *Journal of Voice* 9:1, 27–36.

Sacchett, C., Byng, S., Marshall, J. and Pound, C. 1999. 'Drawing together: evaluation of a therapy programme for severe aphasia', *International Journal of Language & Communication Disorders* 34:3, 265–89.

Sacks, H., Schegloff, E.A. and Jefferson, G. 1974. 'A simplest systematics for the organization of turn-taking for conversation', *Language* 50:4, 696–735.

Sadagopan, N. and Smith, A. 2008. 'Developmental changes in the effects of utterance length and complexity on speech movement variability', *Journal of Speech, Language, and Hearing Research* 51:5, 1138–51.

Sahlén, B., Reuterskiold-Wagner, C., Nettelbladt, U. and Radeborg, K. 1999. 'Nonword repetition in children with language impairment – pitfalls and possibilities', *International Journal of Language & Communication Disorder* 34:3, 337–52.

Saldaña, D. and Frith, U. 2007. 'Do readers with autism make bridging inferences from world knowledge?', *Journal of Experimental Child Psychology* 96:4, 310–19.

Saldert, C. and Ahlsén, E. 2007. 'Inference in right hemisphere damaged individuals' comprehension: the role of sustained attention', *Clinical Linguistics & Phonetics* 21:8, 637–55.

Salekin, R.T., Neumann, C.S., Leistico, A.M. and Zalot, A.A. 2004. 'Psychopathy in youth and intelligence: an investigation of Cleckley's hypothesis', *Journal of Clinical Child and Adolescent Psychology* 33:4, 731–42.

Salis, C. 2012. 'Short-term memory treatment: patterns of learning and generalisation to sentence comprehension in a person with aphasia', *Neuropsychological Rehabilitation* 22:3, 428–48.

Saltuklaroglu, T., Kalinowski, J. and Stuart, A. 2010. 'Refutation of a therapeutic alternative? A reply to Pollard, Ellis, Finan, and Ramig (2009)', *Journal of Speech, Language, and Hearing Research* 53:4, 908–11.

Saltzman, E.L. and Munhall, K.G. 1989. 'A dynamical approach to gestural patterning in speech production', *Ecological Psychology* 1:4, 333–82.

Saltzman, J., Strauss, E., Hunter, M. and Archibald, S. 2000. 'Theory of mind and executive functions in normal human aging and Parkinson's disease', *Journal of the International Neuropsychological Society* 6:7, 781–8.

Salvador-Carulla, L., Reed, G.M., Vaez-Azizi, L.M., Cooper, S.A., Martinez-Leal, R., Bertelli, M., Adams, C., Cooray, S., Shoumitro, D., Akoury-Dirani, L., Girimaji, S.C., Katz, G., Kwok, H., Luckasson, R., Simeonson, R., Walsh, C., Munir, K. and Saxena, S. 2011. 'Intellectual developmental disorders: towards a new name, definition and framework for "mental retardation/intellectual disability" in ICD-11', *World Psychiatry* 10:3,175–80.

Sama, A., Carding, P.N., Price, S., Kelly, P. and Wilson, J.A. 2001. 'The clinical features of functional dysphonia', *Laryngoscope* 111:3, 458–63.

Sander, E.K. 1972. 'When are speech sounds learned?', *Journal of Speech and Hearing Disorders* 37:1, 55–63.

Sanders, L.M., Adams, J., Tager-Flusberg, H., Shenton, M.E. and Coleman, M. 1995. 'A comparison of clinical and linguistic indices of deviance in the verbal discourse of schizophrenia', *Applied Psycholinguistics* 16:3, 325–38.

Santos, R.M. and Lignugaris/Kraft, B. 1997. 'Integrating research on effective instruction with instruction in the natural environment for young children with disabilities', *Exceptionality* 7:2, 97–129.

Sapienza, C. and Hoffman-Ruddy, B. 2009. *Voice disorders*, San Diego, CA: Plural Publishing.

Sapienza, C.M., Crandell, C.C. and Curtis, B. 1999. 'Effects of sound-field frequency modulation amplification on reducing teachers' sound pressure level in the classroom', *Journal of Voice* 13:3, 375–81.

Sarno, M.T. 1969. *Functional communication profile*, Institute of Rehabilitation Medicine, New York University Medical Center.

Sarno, M.T., Buonagaro, A. and Levita, E. 1986. 'Characteristics of verbal impairment in closed head injured patients', *Archives of Physical Medicine and Rehabilitation* 67:6, 400–5.

Sasanuma, S. 1971. 'Speech characteristics of a patient with apraxia of speech – a preliminary case report', *Annual Bulletin: Research Institute of Logopedics and Phoniatrics* 5, 85–9.

Sato, Y., Mori, K., Koizumi, T., Minagawa-Kawai, Y., Tanaka, A., Ozawa, E. and Mazuka, R. 2011. 'Functional lateralization of speech processing in adults and children who stutter', *Frontiers in Psychology* 2, 70.

Saxena, S., Thornicroft, G., Knapp, M. and Whiteford, H. 2007. 'Resources for mental health: scarcity, inequity and inefficiency', *Lancet* 370:9590, 878–89.

Scaler Scott, K. 2011. 'Cluttering and autism spectrum disorders', in D. Ward and K. Scaler Scott (eds.), *Cluttering: research, intervention and education*, Hove, East Sussex: Psychology Press, 115–34.

Scaler Scott, K. and Barone, N. 2010. 'Disfluency, disinhibition, and cluttering: food for thought', Seminar presentation at the Annual ASHA Convention: Philadelphia, PA, 18–20 November 2010.

Scaler Scott, K. and St. Louis, K.O. 2011. 'Self-help and support groups for people with cluttering', in D. Ward and K. Scaler Scott (eds.), *Cluttering: research, intervention and education*, East Sussex: Psychology Press, 211–30.

Scaler Scott, K., Myers, F.L. and Kissagizlis, P. 2007. What is cluttering? (online, available at: http://associations.missouristate.edu/ica/; last accessed 12 June 2013).

Scarborough, H.S. 2005. 'Developmental relationships between language and reading: reconciling a beautiful hypothesis with some ugly facts', in H.W. Catts and A.G. Kamhi (eds.), *The connections between language and reading disabilities*, Mahwah, NJ: Lawrence Erlbaum, 3–24.

Scarborough, H., Rescorla, L., Tager-Flusberg, H., Fowler, A.E. and Sudhalter, V. 1991. 'Relation of utterance length to grammatical complexity in normal or language-disordered groups', *Applied Psycholinguistics* 12, 23–45.

Schalling, E., Bulukin-Wilen, F., Gustafson, J. and Södersten, M. 2012. 'Voice use and effects of biofeedback in Parkinson's disease, studied with a newly developed portable voice accumulator, VoxLog', Conference on Motor Speech: Santa Rosa, CA, 29 February – 4 March 2012.

Schalock, R.L., Borthwick-Duffy, S.A., Bradley, V.J., Buntinx, W.H.E., Coulter, D.L., Craig, E.M., Gomez, S.C., Lachapelle, Y., Luckasson, R., Reeve, A., Shogren, K.A., Snell, M.E., Spreat, S., Tassé, M.J., Thompson, J.R., Verdugo-Alonso, M.A., Wehmeyer, M.L. and Yeager, M.H. 2010. *Intellectual disability: definition, classification, and systems of supports*, Washington, DC: American Association on Intellectual and Developmental Disabilities.

Schatschneider, C. and Torgesen, J.K. 2004. 'Using our current understanding of dyslexia to support early identification and intervention', *Journal of Child Neurology* 19:10, 759–65.

Schatschneider, C., Carlson, C.D., Francis, D.J., Foorman, B.R. and Fletcher, J.M. 2002. 'Relationship of rapid automatized naming and phonological awareness in early reading development: implications for the double-deficit hypothesis', *Journal of Learning Disabilities* 35:3, 245–56.

Scheffer, I.E. 2000. 'Autosomal dominant rolandic epilepsy with speech dyspraxia', *Epileptic Disorders* 2:Suppl 1, S19–S22.

Schloss, P.J., Thompson, C.K., Gajar, A.H. and Schloss, C.N. 1985. 'Influence of self-monitoring on heterosexual conversational behaviours of head trauma youth', *Applied Research in Mental Retardation* 6:3, 269–82.

Schlosser, R.W., Wendt, O., Angermeier, K. and Shetty, M. 2005. 'Searching for evidence in augmentative and alternative communication: navigating a scattered literature', *AAC: Augmentative and Alternative Communication* 21:4, 233–55.

Schmidt, R.A. 1975. 'A schema theory of discrete motor learning', *Psychological Review* 82:4, 225–60.

Schmidt, R.A. 1976. 'The schema as a solution to some persistent problems in motor learning theory', in G.E. Stelmach (ed.), *Motor control: issues and trends*, New York: Academic Press, 41–65.

Schmidt, R.A. 1988. *Motor control and learning*, Champaign, IL: Human Kinetics.

Schmidt, R.A. 2003. 'Motor schema theory after 27 years: reflections and implications for a new theory', *Research Quarterly for Exercise and Sport* 74:4, 366–75.

Schmidt, R.A. and Lee, T.D. 1999. *Motor control and learning: a behavioral emphasis*, third edition, Champaign, IL: Human Kinetics.

Schmidt, R.A. and Lee, T.D. 2005. *Motor control and learning: a behavioral emphasis*, fourth edition, Champaign, IL: Human Kinetics.

Schmidt, R.A. and Young, D.E. 1991. 'Methodology for motor learning: a paradigm for kinematic feedback', *Journal of Motor Behavior* 23:1, 13–24.

Schneider, C.M., Dennehy, C.A. and Saxon, K.G. 1997. 'Exercise physiology principles applied to vocal performance: the improvement of postural alignment', *Journal of Voice* 11:3, 332–7.

Schneider, F., Gur, R.C., Koch, K., Backes, V., Amunts, K., Shah, N.J., Bilker, W., Gur, R.E. and Habel, U. 2006. 'Impairment in the specificity of emotion processing in schizophrenia', *American Journal of Psychiatry* 163:3, 442–7.

Schneider, W. and Detweiler, M. 1988. 'The role of practice in dual-task performance: toward workload modeling in a connectionist/control architecture', *Human Factors* 30:5, 539–66.

Schönwiesner, M., Rübsamen, R. and von Cramon, D.Y. 2005. 'Hemispheric asymmetry for spectral and temporal processing in the human antero-lateral auditory belt cortex', *European Journal of Neuroscience* 22:6, 1521–8.

Schooling, T.L. 2003. 'Lessons from the National Outcomes Measurement System (NOMS)', *Seminars in Speech and Language* 24:3, 245–56.

Schuchardt, K., Gebhardt, M. and Mähler, C. 2010. 'Working memory functions in children with different degrees of intellectual disability', *Journal of Intellectual Disability Research* 54:4, 346–53.

Schuele, C.M. and Dykes, J.C. 2005. 'Complex syntax acquisition: a longitudinal case study of a child with specific language impairment', *Clinical Linguistics & Phonetics* 19:4, 295–318.

Schwartz, M.F. 1987. 'Patterns of speech production deficit within and across aphasia syndromes: application of a psycholinguistic model', in M. Coltheart, G. Sartori and R. Job (eds.), *The cognitive neuropsychology of language*, London: Lawrence Erlbaum Associates, 163–99.

Scientific Learning Corporation. 1999. *Fast ForWord companion: a comprehensive guide to the training exercises*, Berkeley, CA: Scientific Learning Corporation.

Scrimger, R. 2011. 'Salivary gland sparing in the treatment of head and neck cancer', *Expert Review of Anticancer Therapy* 11:9, 1437–48.

Scruggs, T.E. and Mastropieri, M.A. 1986. 'Academic characteristics of behaviorally disordered and learning disabled students', *Behavioral Disorders* 11:3, 184–90.

Searle, J.R. 1969. *Speech acts: an essay in the philosophy of language*, Cambridge University Press.

Seddoh, S.A.K., Robin, D.A., Sim, H. and Hageman, C. 1996. 'Speech timing in apraxia of speech versus conduction aphasia', *Journal of Speech and Hearing Research* 39:3, 590–603.

Seelaar, H., Kamphorst, W., Rosso, S.M., Azmani, A., Masdjedi, R., de Koning, I., Maat-Kievit, J.A., Anar, B., Donker Kaat, L., Breedveld, G.J., Dooijes, D., Rozemuller, J.M., Bronner, I.F., Rizzu, P. and van Swieten, J.C. 2008. 'Distinct genetic forms of frontotemporal dementia', *Neurology* 71:16, 1220–6.

Seeley, W.W., Crawford, R., Rascovsky, K., Kramer, J.H., Weiner, M., Miller, B.L. and Gorno-Tempini, M.L. 2008. 'Frontal paralimbic network atrophy in very mild behavioral variant frontotemporal dementia', *Archives of Neurology* 65:2, 249–55.

Seery, C.H. 2005. 'Differential diagnosis of stuttering for forensic purposes', *American Journal of Speech-Language Pathology* 14:4, 284–97.

Seidenberg, M.S. and McClelland, J.L. 1989. 'A distributed, developmental model of word recognition and naming', *Psychological Review* 96:4, 523–68.

Seikaly, H., Jha, N., Harris, J.R., Barnaby, P., Liu, R., Williams, D., McGaw, T., Rieger, J., Wolfaardt, J.F. and Hanson, J. 2004. 'Long-term outcomes of submandibular gland transfer for prevention of postradiation xerostomia', *Archives of Otolaryngology – Head and Neck Surgery* 130:8, 956–61.

Sellars, C., Hughes, T. and Langhorne, P. 2001. 'Speech and language therapy for dysarthria due to non-progressive brain damage', *Cochrane Database of Systematic Reviews*, Issue 2, CD002088.

Semel, E., Wiig, E.H. and Secord, W.A. 1995. *Clinical evaluation of language fundamentals*, third edition, San Antonio, TX: The Psychological Corporation.

Semel, E., Wiig, E.H. and Secord, W.A. 2003. *Clinical evaluation of language fundamentals*, fourth edition, San Antonio, TX: Psychological Corporation.

Sennott, S. and Bowker, A. 2009. 'Autism, AAC and Proloquo2go', *Perspectives on Augmentative and Alternative Communication* 18:4, 137–45.

Sennott, S. and Niemeijr, D. 2009. *Proloquo2go*, Amsterdam: Assistiveware.

Setter, J., Stojanovik, V., van Ewijk, L. and Moreland, M. 2007. 'Affective prosody in children with Williams syndrome', *Clinical Linguistics & Phonetics* 21:9, 659–72.

Sevcik, R.A. and Romski, M.A. 1997. 'Comprehension and language acquisition: evidence from youth with severe cognitive disabilities', in L.B. Adamson and M.A. Romski (eds.), *Communication and language acquisition: discoveries from atypical development*, Baltimore, MD: Paul H. Brookes Publishing, 187–202.

Seyfer, A.E., Prohazka, D. and Leahy, E. 1988. 'The effectiveness of the superiorly based pharyngeal flap in relation to the type of palatal defect and timing of the operation', *Plastic and Reconstructive Surgery* 82:5, 760–4.

Shadden, B.B. 2005. 'Aphasia as identity theft: theory and practice', *Aphasiology* 19:3–5, 211–23.

Shah, A. and Frith, U. 1993. 'Why do autistic individuals show superior performance on the block design task?', *Journal of Child Psychology and Psychiatry* 34:8, 1351–64.

Shallice, T. 1988. *From neuropsychology to mental structure*, Cambridge University Press.

Shammi, P. 1999. 'Humour appreciation: a role of the right frontal lobe', *Brain* 122:4, 657–66.

Shankweiler, D., Harris, K.S. and Taylor, M.L. 1968. 'Electromyographic studies of articulation in aphasia', *Archives of Physical Medicine and Rehabilitation* 49:1, 1–8.

Shapiro, D.A. 2011. *Stuttering intervention: a collaborative journey to fluency freedom*, second edition, Austin, TX: Pro-Ed.

Sharp, D., Hay, D., Pawlby, S., Schmücker, G., Allen, H. and Kumar, R. 1995. 'The impact of postnatal depression on boys' intellectual development', *Journal of Child Psychology and Psychiatry* 36:8, 1315–36.

Shatil, E. and Share, D.L. 2003. 'Cognitive antecedents of early reading ability: a test of the modularity hypothesis', *Journal of Experimental Child Psychology* 86:1, 1–31.

Shaywitz, B.A., Shaywitz, S.E., Blachman, B.A., Pugh, K.R., Fulbright, R.K., Skudlarski, P., Mencl, W.E., Constable, R.T., Holahan, J.M., Marchione, K.E., Fletcher, J.M., Lyon, G.R. and Gore, J.C. 2004. 'Development of left occipito-temporal systems for skilled reading in children after a phonologically-based intervention', *Biological Psychiatry* 55:9, 926–33.

Shaywitz, S.E. 1996. 'Dyslexia', *Scientific American*, November 1996, 98–104.

Shaywitz, S.E. 2003. *Overcoming dyslexia*, New York: Random House.

Shaywitz, S.E., Escobar, M.D., Shaywitz, B.A., Fletcher, J.M. and Makuch, R. 1992. 'Evidence that dyslexia may represent the lower tail of a normal distribution of reading ability', *New England Journal of Medicine* 326:3, 145–50.

Sheehan, J.G. 1970. *Stuttering: research and therapy*, New York: Harper & Row.

Shelton, R.L., Johnson, A.F., Ruscello, D.M. and Arndt, W.B. 1978. 'Assessment of parent-administered listening training for preschool children with articulation deficits', *Journal of Speech and Hearing Disorders* 43:2, 242–54.

Sheng, L. and McGregor, K. 2010. 'Lexical-semantic organization in children with specific language impairment', *Journal of Speech, Language, and Hearing Research* 53:1, 146–59.

Shevell, M. 2009. 'Concepts and definitions in neurodevelopmental disability', in M. Shevell (ed.), *Neurodevelopmental disabilities: clinical and scientific foundations*, London: Mac Keith Press, 1–9.

Shevell, M., Majnemer, A. and Morin, I. 2003. 'Etiologic yield of cerebral palsy: a contemporary case series', *Pediatric Neurology* 28:5, 352–9.

Shevil, E. and Finlayson, M. 2006. 'Perceptions of persons with multiple sclerosis on cognitive changes and their impact on daily life', *Disability and Rehabilitation* 28:12, 779–88.

Shimodaira, K., Yoshida, H., Yusa, H. and Kanazawa, T. 1998. 'Palatal augmentation prosthesis with alternative palatal vaults for speech and swallowing: a clinical report', *Journal of Prosthetic Dentistry* 80:1, 1–3.

Shoji, H., Koizumi, N. and Ozaki, H. 2009. 'Linguistic lateralization in adolescents with Down syndrome revealed by a dichotic monitoring test', *Research in Developmental Disabilities* 30:2, 219–28.

Shoji, K., Regenbogen, E., Yu, J.D. and Blaugrund, S.M. 1992. 'High-frequency power ratio of breathy voice', *Laryngoscope* 102:3, 267–71.

Shorland, J. and Douglas, J.M. 2010. 'Understanding the role of communication in maintaining and forming friendships following traumatic brain injury', *Brain Injury* 24:4, 569–80.

Shprintzen, R.J. 1997. *Genetics, syndromes and communication disorders*, San Diego, CA: Singular.

Shprintzen, R.J., Lewin, M.L., Croft, C.B., Daniller, A.I., Argamaso, R.V., Ship, A.G. and Strauch, B. 1979. 'A comprehensive study of pharyngeal flap surgery: tailor-made flaps', *Cleft Palate Journal* 16:1, 46–55.

Shprintzen, R.J., McCall, G.N. and Skolnick, M.L. 1980. 'The effect of pharyngeal flap surgery on the movements of the lateral pharyngeal walls', *Plastic and Reconstructive Surgery* 66:4, 570–3.

Shriberg, L.D. 1994. 'Five subtypes of developmental phonological disorders', *Clinics in Communication Disorders* 4:1, 38–53.

Shriberg, L.D. 2003. 'Diagnostic markers for child speech-sound disorders: introductory comments', *Clinical Linguistics & Phonetics* 17:7, 501–5.

Shriberg, L.D. 2006. 'Research in idiopathic and symptomatic childhood apraxia of speech', 5th International Conference on Speech Motor Control: Nijmegen, 7–10 June 2006.

Shriberg, L.D. 2010. 'A neurodevelopmental framework for research in childhood apraxia of speech', in B. Maassen and P. van Lieshout (eds.), *Speech motor control: new developments in basic and applied research*, New York: Oxford University Press, 259–70.

Shriberg, L.D., Aram, D. and Kwiatkowski, J. 1997a. 'Developmental apraxia of speech I. Descriptive and theoretical perspectives', *Journal of Speech, Language, and Hearing Research* 40:2, 273–85.

Shriberg, L.D., Aram, D. and Kwiatkowski, J. 1997b. 'Developmental apraxia of speech II. Toward a diagnostic marker', *Journal of Speech, Language, and Hearing Research* 40:2, 286–312.

Shriberg, L.D., Austin, D., Lewis, B.A., McSweeny, J.L. and Wilson, D.L. 1997c. 'The Speech Disorders Classification System (SDCS): extensions and lifespan reference data', *Journal of Speech, Language, and Hearing Research* 40:4, 723–40.

Shriberg, L.D., Austin, D., Lewis, B.A., McSweeny, J.L. and Wilson, D.L. 1997d. 'The percentage of consonants correct (PCC) metric: extensions and reliability data', *Journal of Speech and Hearing Research* 40:4, 708–22.

Shriberg, L.D., Ballard, K.J., Tomblin, J.B., Duffy, J.R., Odell, K.H. and Williams, C.A. 2006. 'Speech, prosody, and voice characteristics of a mother and daughter with a 7;13 translocation affecting FOXP2', *Journal of Speech, Language, and Hearing Research* 49:3, 500–25.

Shriberg, L.D., Campbell, T.F., Karlsson, H., Brown, R., McSweeny, J. and Nadler, C. 2003. 'A diagnostic marker for childhood apraxia of speech: the lexical stress ratio', *Clinical Linguistics & Phonetics* 17:7, 549–74.

Shriberg, L.D., Fourakis, M., Hall, S.D., Karlsson, H.B., Lohmeier, H.L., McSweeny, J., Potter, N.L., Scheer-Cohen, A.R., Strand, E.A., Tilkens, C.M. and Wilson, D.L. 2010b. 'Extensions to the speech disorders classification system (SDCS)', *Clinical Linguistics & Phonetics* 24:10, 795–824.

Shriberg, L.D., Friel-Patti, S., Flipsen, P. and Brown, R.L. 2000. 'Otitis media, fluctuant hearing loss, and speech-language outcomes: a preliminary structural equation model', *Journal of Speech, Language, and Hearing Research* 43:1, 100–20.

Shriberg, L.D., Kwiatkowski, J. and Rasmussen, C. 1990. *The prosody-voice screening profile*, Tucson, AZ: Communication Skill Builder.

Shriberg, L.D., Kwiatkowski, J., Rasmussen, C., Lof, G.L. and Miller, J.F. 1992. 'The Prosody-Voice Screening Profile (PVSP): psychometric data and reference information for children', *Technical Report 1, Phonology Project*, Madison, WI: Waisman Centre on Mental Retardation and Human Development.

Shriberg, L.D., Lewis, B.A., Tomblin, J.B., McSweeny, J.L., Karlsson, H.B. and Scheer, A.R. 2005. 'Toward diagnostic and phenotypic markers for genetically transmitted speech delay', *Journal of Speech, Language, and Hearing Research* 48:4, 834–52.

Shriberg, L.D., Lohmeier, H.L., Campbell, T.F., Dollaghan, C.A., Green, J.R. and Moore, C.A. 2009. 'A nonword repetition task for speakers with misarticulations: the syllable repetition task', *Journal of Speech, Language, and Hearing Research* 52:5, 1189–212.

Shriberg, L.D., Lohmeier, H.L., Strand, E.A. and Jakielski, K.J. 2012. 'Encoding, memory, and transcoding deficits in childhood apraxia of speech', *Clinical Linguistics & Phonetics* 26:5, 445–82.

Shriberg, L.D., Paul, R., Black, L. and van Santen, J. 2010a. 'The hypothesis of apraxia of speech in children with autism spectrum disorder', *Journal of Autism and Developmental Disorders* 41:4, 405–26.

Shriberg, L.D., Paul, R., McSweeny, J.L., Klin, A.M., Cohen, D.J. and Volkmar, F.R. 2001. 'Speech and prosody characteristics of adolescents and adults with high-functioning autism and Asperger syndrome', *Journal of Speech, Language, and Hearing Research* 44:5, 1097–115.

Shriberg, L.D., Potter, N.L. and Strand, E. 2011. 'Prevalence and phenotype of childhood apraxia of speech in youth with galactosemia', *Journal of Speech, Language, and Hearing Research* 54:2, 487–519.

Shriberg, L.D., Tomblin, J.B. and McSweeny, J.L. 1999. 'Prevalence of speech delay in 6-year-old children and comorbidity with language impairment', *Journal of Speech, Language, and Hearing Research* 42:6, 1461–81.

Shriver, A.S., Canady, J., Richman, L., Andreasen, N.C. and Nopoulos, P.J. 2006. 'Structure and function of the superior temporal plane in adult males with cleft lip and palate: pathologic enlargement with no relationship to childhood hearing deficits', *Journal of Child Psychological Psychiatry* 47:10, 994–1002.

Shulman, K.I. 2000. 'Clock-drawing: is it the ideal cognitive screening test?', *International Journal of Geriatric Psychiatry* 15:6, 548–61.

Shulman, S. 1989. *Spasmodic dysphonia: techniques and approaches in successful voice therapy*, Rockville, MD: American Speech–Language–Hearing Association.

Siegal, M. and Varley, R. 2002. 'Neural systems involved in "theory of mind"', *Nature Reviews. Neuroscience* 3:6, 463–71.

Siegal, M. and Varley, R. 2006. 'Aphasia, language, and theory of mind', *Social Neuroscience* 1:3–4, 167–74.

Siegel, E. and Cress, C.J. 2002. 'Overview of the emergence of early AAC behaviors: progression from communicative to symbolic skills', in J. Reichle, D.R. Beukelman and J.C. Light (eds.), *Exemplary practices for beginning communicators: implications for AAC*, Baltimore, MD: Paul H. Brookes Publishing, 25–75.

Siegel, E. and Wetherby, A. 2000. 'Nonsymbolic communication', in M. Snell (ed.), *Instruction of students with severe disabilities*, Baltimore, MD: Paul H. Brookes Publishing.

Siegel, E.B., Maddox, L.L., Ogletree, B.T. and Westling, D.L. 2010. 'Communication-based services for persons with severe disabilities in schools: a survey of speech-language pathologists', *Journal of Communication Disorders* 43:2, 148–59.

Siegel, L. 2010. 'Early intervention: identification and appropriate treatment', World Dyslexia Forum: Paris, France, 3–5 February, 2010.

Siegel-Causey, E. and Bashinski, S. 1997. 'Enhancing initial communication and responsiveness of learners with multiple disabilities: a tri-focus framework for partners', *Focus on Autism and Other Developmental Disabilities* 12:2, 105–20.

Sigafoos, J., Arthur, M. and O'Reilly, M. 2003. *Challenging behavior and developmental disability*, Baltimore, MD: Paul H. Brookes Publishing.

Sigafoos, J., O'Reilly, M.F., Drasgow, E. and Reichle, J. 2002. 'Strategies to achieve socially acceptable escape and avoidance', in J. Reichle, D. Beukelman and J.C. Light (eds.), *Exemplary practice for beginning communicators: implications for AAC*, Baltimore, MD: Brookes, 157–86.

Sigman, M. and Rushkin, E. 1999. 'Continuity and change in the social competence of children with autism, Down syndrome, and developmental delays', *Monographs of the Society for Research in Child Development* 64:1, 1–130.

Sigurdardottir, S. and Vik, T. 2011. 'Speech, expressive language, and verbal cognition of preschool children with cerebral palsy in Iceland', *Developmental Medicine and Child Neurology* 53:1, 74–80.

Siller, M. and Sigman, M. 2008. 'Modeling longitudinal change in the language abilities of children with autism: parent behaviors and child characteristics as predictors of change', *Developmental Psychology* 44:6, 1691–704.

Silva, P.A., Justin, C., McGee, R. and Williams, S.M. 1984. 'Some developmental and behavioral characteristics of seven-year-old children with delayed speech development', *British Journal of Disorders of Communication* 19:2, 147–54.

Silverman, S. and Bernstein Ratner, N. 2002. 'Measuring lexical diversity in children who stutter: application of vocd', *Journal of Fluency Disorders* 27:4, 289–304.

Simkin, Z. and Conti-Ramsden, G. 2006. 'Evidence of reading difficulty in subgroups of children with specific language impairment', *Child Language Teaching and Therapy* 22:3, 315–31.

Simmons, N.N. 1983. 'Acoustic analysis of ataxic dysarthria: an approach to monitoring treatment', in W. Berry (ed.), *Clinical dysarthria*, Austin, TX: Pro-Ed, 283–94.

Simmons, N.N. 2008. 'Social approaches to aphasia intervention', in R. Chapey (ed.), *Language intervention strategies in aphasia and related neurogenic communication disorders*, Baltimore, MD: Lippincott Williams & Wilkins, 290–318.

Simmons, N.N. 2009. 'Thinking beyond language: intervention for severe aphasia', *Neurophysiology and Neurogenic Speech and Language Disorders* 19:1, 15–22.

Simmons-Mackie, N. and Damico, J.S. 1996. 'Accounting for handicaps in aphasia: communicative assessment from an authentic social perspective', *Disability and Rehabilitation* 18:11, 540–9.

Simmons-Mackie, N. and Damico, J.S. 2001. 'Intervention outcomes: a clinical application of qualitative methods' *Topics in Language Disorders* 22:1, 21–36.

Simmons-Mackie, N. and Elman, R.J. 2011. 'Negotiation of identity in group therapy for aphasia: the aphasia café', *International Journal of Language & Communication Disorders* 46:3, 312–23.

Simmons-Mackie, N., Raymer, A., Armstrong, E., Holland, A. and Cherney, L.R. 2010. 'Communication partner training in aphasia: a systematic review', *Archives of Physical Medicine and Rehabilitation* 91:12, 1814–37.

Simos, P.G., Fletcher, J.M., Bergman, E., Breier, J.I., Foorman, B.R., Castillo, E.M., Davis, N., Fitzgerald, M. and Papanicolaou, A.C. 2002. 'Dyslexia- specific brain activation profile becomes normal following successful remedial training', *Neurology* 58:8, 1203–13.

Simos, P.G., Fletcher, J.M., Denton, C., Sarkari, S., Billingsley-Marshall, R. and Papanicolaou, A.C. 2006. 'Magnetic source imaging studies of dyslexia interventions', *Developmental Neuropsychology* 30:1, 591–611.

Simos, P.G., Fletcher, J.M., Sarkari, S., Billingsley-Marshall, R., Denton, C.A. and Papanicolaou, A.C. 2007. 'Intensive instruction affects brain magnetic activity associated with oral word reading in children with persistent reading disabilities', *Journal of Learning Disabilities* 40:1, 37–48.

Sinagra, D.L., Montesinos, M.R., Tacchi, V.A., Moreno, J.C., Falco, J.E., Mezzadri, N.A., Debonis, D.L. and Curutchet, H.P. 2004. 'Voice changes after thyroidectomy without recurrent laryngeal nerve injury', *Journal of the American College of Surgeons* 199:4, 556–60.

Sippel, R.S. and Chen, H. 2009. 'Controversies in the surgical management of newly diagnosed and recurrent/ residual thyroid cancer', *Thyroid* 19:12, 1373–80.

Sitnikova, T., Salisbury, D.F., Kuperberg, G. and Holcomb, P.J. 2002. 'Electrophysiological insights into language processing in schizophrenia', *Psychophysiology* 39:6, 851–60.

Sivasankar, M., Erickson, E., Rosenblatt, M. and Branski, R.C. 2010. 'Hypertonic challenge to porcine vocal folds: effects on epithelial barrier function', *Otolaryngology – Head and Neck Surgery* 142:1, 79–84.

Skelly, M. 1973. *Glossectomee speech rehabilitation*, Springfield, IL: Thomas.

Skelly, M., Schinsky, L., Smith, R. and Fust, R. 1974. 'American Indian sign (Amer-Ind) as a facilitator of verbalisation for the oral verbal apraxic', *Journal of Speech and Hearing Disorders* 39:4, 445–56.

Skelly, M., Spector, D.J., Donaldson, R.C., Brodeur, A. and Paletta, F.X. 1971. 'Compensatory physiologic phonetics for the glossectomee', *Journal of Speech and Hearing Disorders* 36:1, 101–14.

Skinner, B.F. 1957. *Verbal behavior*, New York: Appleton Century Crofts.

Skolnick, M.L. 1970. 'Videofluoroscopic examination of the velopharyngeal portal during phonation in lateral and base projections – a new technique for studying the mechanics of closure', *Cleft Palate Journal* 7, 803–16.

Skolnick, M.L. 1975. 'Velopharyngeal function in cleft palate', *Journal of Clinical Plastic Surgery* 2:2, 285–97.

Skotko, B.G., Koppenhaver, D.A. and Erickson, K.A. 2004. 'Parent reading behaviors and communication outcomes in girls with Rett syndrome', *Exceptional Children* 70:2, 145–66.

Skottun, B.C. and Skoyles, J.R. 2006. 'Is coherent motion an appropriate test for magnocellular sensitivity?', *Brain and Cognition* 61:2, 172–80.

Skottun, B.C. and Skoyles, J.R. 2008. 'Dyslexia and rapid visual processing: a commentary', *Journal of Clinical and Experimental Neuropsychology* 30:6, 666–73.

Skuse, D. 2012. 'DSM-5's conceptualization of autistic disorders', *Journal of the American Association of Child and Adolescent Psychiatry* 51:4, 344–6.

Slavin, R.E., Madden, N.A., Karweit, N.L., Dolan, L. and Wasik, B.A. 1992. 'Success for All: a relentless approach to prevention and early intervention in elementary schools', Arlington, VA: Educational Research Service.

SLI Consortium. 2002. 'A genome-wide scan identifies two novel loci involved in specific language impairment (SLI)', *American Journal of Human Genetics* 70:2, 384–98.

SLI Consortium. 2004. 'Highly significant linkage to SLI1 locus in an expanded sample of individuals affected by specific language impairment (SLI)', *American Journal of Human Genetics* 94:6, 1225–38.

Smeele, L.E. 2007. 'Oral, oropharyngeal, and nasopharyngeal cancer: intervention approaches', in E.C. Ward and C.J. van As-Brooks (eds.), *Head and neck cancer: treatment, rehabilitation, and outcomes*, San Diego, CA: Plural Publishing, Inc., 87–102.

Smit, A.B., Hand, L., Freilinger, J.J., Bernthal, J.E. and Bird, A. 1990. 'The Iowa articulation norms project and its Nebraska replication', *Journal of Speech and Hearing Disorders* 55:4, 779–98.

Smith, A. 2006. 'Speech motor development: integrating muscles, movements, and linguistic units', *Journal of Communication Disorders* 39:5, 331–49.

Smith, A. and Goffman, L. 2004. 'Interaction of motor and language factors in the development of speech production', in B. Maassen, R. Kent, H. Peters, P.V. Lieshout and W. Hulstijn (eds.), *Speech motor control in normal and disordered speech*, New York: Oxford University Press, 225–52.

Smith, A. and Zelaznik, H.N. 2004. 'Development of functional synergies for speech motor coordination in childhood and adolescence', *Developmental Psychobiology* 45:1, 22–33.

Smith, B.E. and Kuehn, D.P. 2007. 'Speech evaluation of velopharyngeal dysfunction', *Journal of Craniofacial Surgery* 18:2, 251–61.

Smith, B.E., Kempster, G.B. and Sims, H.S. 2010. 'Patient factors related to voice therapy attendance and outcomes', *Journal of Voice* 24:6, 694–701.

Smith, M.E. and Ramig, L.O. 2006. 'Neurologic disorders and the voice', in J.S. Rubin, R.T. Sataloff and G.S. Korovin (eds.), *Diagnosis and treatment of voice disorders*, third edition, San Diego, CA: Plural Publishing, 349–69.

Smith, S.D., Pennington, B.F., Boada, R. and Shriberg, L.D. 2005. 'Linkage of speech sound disorder to reading disability loci', *Journal of Child Psychology and Psychiatry* 46:10, 1057–66.

Snell, M.E., Brady, N., McLean, L., Ogletree, B.T., Siegel, E., Sylvester, L., Mineo, B., Paul, D., Romski, M.A. and Sevcik, R. 2010. 'Twenty years of communication intervention research with individuals who have severe intellectual and developmental disabilities', *American Journal on Intellectual and Developmental Disabilities* 115:5, 364–80.

Snoeck, R., Wellens, W., Desloovere, C., Van Ranst, M., Naesens, L., De Clercq, E. and Feenstra, L. 1998. 'Treatment of severe laryngeal papillomatosis with intralesional injections of cidofovir [(S)-1-(3-hydroxy-2-phosphonylmethoxypropyl)cytosine]', *Journal of Medical Virology* 54:3, 219–25.

Snow, P.C. 2009. 'Oral language competence and equity of access to education and health', in K. Bryan (ed.), *Communication in healthcare*, Interdisciplinary Communication Studies Volume 1 (Series Editor: Colin B. Grant), Bern: Peter Lang European Academic Publishers, 101–34.

Snow, P.C. and Powell, M.B. 2004. 'Interviewing juvenile offenders: the importance of oral language competence', *Current Issues in Criminal Justice* 16:2, 220–5.

Snow, P.C. and Sanger, D.D. 2011. 'Restorative justice conferencing and the youth offender: exploring the role of oral language competence', *International Journal of Language & Communication Disorders* 46:3, 324–33.

Snow, P.C., Douglas, J.M. and Ponsford, J. 1997. 'Conversational assessment following traumatic brain injury: a comparison across two control groups', *Brain Injury* 11:6, 409–29.

Snow, P.C., Douglas, J.M. and Ponsford, J. 1998. 'Conversational discourse abilities following severe traumatic brain injury: a follow up study', *Brain Injury* 12:11, 911–35.

Snowden, J.S., Goulding, P.J. and Neary, D. 1989. 'Semantic dementia: a form of circumscribed cerebral atrophy', *Behavioural Neurology* 2:3, 167–82.

Snowling, M. and Frith, U. 1986. 'Comprehension in "hyperlexic" readers', *Journal of Experimental Child Psychology* 42:3, 392–415.

Snowling, M., Bishop, D.V.M. and Stothard, S.E. 2000. 'Is preschool language impairment a risk factor for dyslexia in adolescence?', *Journal of Child Psychology and Psychiatry* 41:5, 587–600.

Snowling, M.J. and Hayiou-Thomas, M. 2010. 'Specific language impairment', in K.O. Yeates, M.D. Ris, H.G. Taylor and B.F. Pennington (eds.), *Pediatric neuropsychology: research, theory, and practice*, second edition, New York: Guilford Press, 363–92.

Snowling, M.J., Gallagher, A. and Frith, U. 2003. 'Family risk of dyslexia is continuous: individual differences in the precursors of reading skill', *Child Development* 74:2, 358–73.

Snyder-McLean, L., Cripe, J. and McNay, V.J. 1988. *Using joint action routines in an early intervention program*, Parsons: Bureau of Child Research, University of Kansas Parsons Research Center.

So, L.K.H. and Dodd, B. 1994. 'Phonologically disordered Cantonese-speaking children', *Clinical Linguistics & Phonetics* 8:3, 235–55.

Social Security Administration. 2006. *Fast facts and figures about social security, 2006*, (online, available at: www.ssa.gov/policy/docs/chartbooks/fast_facts/2006/fast_facts06.pdf; last accessed 12 June 2013).

Soderpalm, E., Larsson, A.K and Almquist, S.A. 2004. 'Evaluation of a consecutive group of transsexual individuals referred for vocal intervention in the west of Sweden', *Logopedics, Phoniatrics, Vocology* 29:1, 18–30.

Sodersten, M. and Lindestad, P.-A. 1992. 'A comparison of vocal fold closure in rigid telescopic and flexible fiberoptic laryngostroboscopy', *Acta Otolaryngologica* 112:1, 144–50.

Sodersten, M., Grandqvist, S., Hammarberg, B. and Szabo, A. 2002. 'Vocal behaviour and vocal loading factors for preschool teachers at work studied with binaural DAT recordings', *Journal of Voice* 16:3, 356–71.

Sodersten, M., Lindestad, P.-A. and Hammarberg, B. 1991. 'Vocal fold closure, perceived breathiness, and acoustic characteristics in normal adult speakers', in J. Gauffin and B. Hammarberg (eds.), *Vocal fold physiology: acoustic, perceptual and physiological aspects of voice*, San Diego, CA: Singular, 217–24.

Sohr-Preston, S.L. and Scaramella, L.V. 2006. 'Implications of timing of maternal depressive symptoms for early cognitive and language development', *Clinical Child and Family Psychology Review* 9:1, 65–83.

Solomon, M., Olsen, E., Niendam, T., Ragland, J.D., Yoon, J., Minzenberg, M. and Carter, C.S. 2011. 'From lumping to splitting and back again: atypical social and language development in individuals with clinical-high-risk for psychosis, first episode schizophrenia, and autism spectrum disorders', *Schizophrenia Research* 131:1–3, 146–51.

Solomon, N.P. and Charron, S. 1998. 'Speech breathing in able-bodied children and children with cerebral palsy: a review of the literature and implications for clinical intervention', *American Journal of Speech-Language Pathology* 7:2, 61–78.

Solomon, N.P. and Robin, D.A. 2005. 'Perceptions of effort during handgrip and tongue elevation in Parkinson's disease', *Parkinsonism & Related Disorders* 11:6, 353–61.

Solomon, N.P., Milbrath, R.L. and Garlitz, S.J. 2000. 'Respiratory and laryngeal contributions to maximum phonation duration', *Journal of Voice* 14:3, 331–40.

Solomon, N.P., Robin, D.A. and Luschei, E.S. 1994. 'Strength, endurance and sense of effort: studies of the tongue and hand in people with Parkinson's disease and accompanying dysarthria', Speech Motor Control Conference: Sedona, AZ, March 1994.

Solomon, N.P., Robin, D.A., Mitchinson, S.I., VanDaele, D.J. and Luschei, E.S. 1996. 'Sense of effort and the effects of fatigue in the tongue and hand', *Journal of Speech and Hearing Research* 39:1, 114–25.

Sommers, R.K. 1962. 'Factors in the effectiveness of mothers trained to aid in speech correction', *Journal of Speech and Hearing Disorders* 27:2, 178–86.

Sommers, R.K., Cockerille, C.E., Paul, C.D., Bowser, D.C., Fichter, G.R., Fenton, A.K. and Copetas, F.G. 1961. 'Effects of speech therapy and speech improvement upon articulation and reading', *Journal of Speech and Hearing Disorders* 26:1, 27–38.

Sommers, R.K., Copetas, F.G., Bowser, D.C., Fichter, G.R., Furlong, A.K., Rhodes, F.E. and Saunders, Z.G. 1962. 'Effects of various durations of speech improvement upon articulation and reading', *Journal of Speech and Hearing Disorders* 27:1, 54–61.

Sommers, R.K., Cox, S. and West, C. 1972. 'Articulatory effectiveness, stimulability, and children's performances on perceptual and memory tasks', *Journal of Speech and Hearing Research* 15:3, 579–89.

Sommers, R.K., Furlong, A.K., Rhodes, F.E., Fichter, G.R., Bowser, D.C., Copetas, F.G. and Saunders, Z.G. 1964. 'Effects of maternal attitudes upon improvements in articulation when mothers are trained to assist in speech correction', *Journal of Speech and Hearing Disorders* 29:2, 126–32.

Sommers, R.K., Schaeffer, M.H., Leiss, R.H., Gerber, A., Bray, M.A., Fundrella, D., Olson, J.K. and Tomkins, E.R. 1966. 'The effectiveness of group and individual therapy', *Journal of Speech and Hearing Research* 9:2, 219–25.

Somodi, L.B., Robin, D.A. and Luschei, E.S. 1995. 'A model of "sense of effort" during maximal and submaximal contractions of the tongue', *Brain and Language* 51:3, 371–82.

Soroker, N., Kasher, A., Giora, R., Batori, G., Corn, C., Gil, M. and Zaidel, E. 2005. 'Processing of basic speech acts following localized brain damage: a new light on the neuroanatomy of language', *Brain and Cognition* 57:2, 214–17.

Spafford, C.A. and Grosser, G.S. 2005. *Dyslexia and reading difficulties: research and resource guide for working with all struggling readers*, second edition, Boston, MA: Pearson Education.

Spanoudis, G., Natsopoulos, D. and Panayiotou, G. 2007. 'Mental verbs and pragmatic language difficulties', *International Journal of Language & Communication Disorders* 42:4, 487–504.

Sparano, A., Ruiz, C. and Weinstein, G.S. 2004. 'Voice rehabilitation after external partial laryngeal surgery', *Otolaryngologic Clinics of North America* 37:3, 637–53.

Sparks, R.W. 1981. 'Melodic intonation therapy', in R. Chapey (ed.), *Language intervention strategies in adult aphasia*, Baltimore, MD: Williams & Wilkins, 320–32.

Speirs, R.L. and Dean, P.M. 1989. 'Toffee clearance and lingual sensory and motor activities in normal children and children with articulation problems of speech', *Archives of Oral Biology* 34:8, 637–44.

Spell, L.A. and Frank, E. 2000. 'Recognition of nonverbal communication of affect following traumatic brain injury', *Journal of Nonverbal Behavior* 24:4, 285–300.

Spence, S.J., Cantor, R.M., Chung, L., Kim, S., Geschwind, D.H. and Alarcón, M. 2006. 'Stratification based on language-related endophenotypes in autism: attempt to replicate reported linkage', *American Journal of Medical Genetics Part B Neuropsychiatric Genetics* 141B:6, 591–8.

Spencer, K.A. and Yorkston, K.M. 2004. 'Evidence for the treatment of respiratory/phonatory dysfunction from dysarthria', in E. Strand (ed.), *Treatment of dysarthria: evidence-based practice*, Rockville, MD: American Speech-Language-Hearing Association, 5–17.

Spencer, L.E. 1988. 'Speech characteristics of male-to-female transsexuals: a perceptual and acoustic study', *Folia Phoniatrica* 40, 31–42.

Sperling, R.A., Aisen, P.S., Beckett, L.A., Bennett, D.A., Craft, S., Fagan, A.M., Iwatsubo, T., Jack, C.R., Kaye, J., Montine, T.J., Park, D.C., Reiman, E.M., Rowe, C.C., Siemers, E., Stern, Y., Yaffe, K., Carrillo, M.C., Thies, B., Morrison-Bogorad, M., Wagster, M.V. and Phelps, C.H. 2011. 'Toward defining the preclinical stages of Alzheimer's disease: recommendations from the National Institute on Aging-Alzheimer's Association workgroups on diagnostic guidelines for Alzheimer's disease', *Alzheimer's & Dementia* 7:3, 280–92.

Speyer, R. 2006. 'Effects of voice therapy: a systematic review', *Journal of Voice* 22:5, 565–80.

Speyer, R., Bogaardt, H., Passos, V., Roodenburg, N., Zumach, A., Heijnen, M., Baijens, L., Fleskens, S. and Brunings, J. 2010. 'Maximum phonation time: variability and reliability', *Journal of Voice* 24:3, 281–4.

Speyer, R., Wieneke, G.H., van Wijck-Warnaar, I. and Dejonckere, P.H. 2003. 'Effects of voice therapy on the voice range profiles of dysphonic patients', *Journal of Voice* 17:4, 544–56.

Sphrintzen, R.J. 2000. 'Velo-cardio-facial syndrome: a distinctive behavioral phenotype', *Mental Retardation and Developmental Disabilities Research Reviews* 6:2, 142–7.

Spielman, J., Ramig, L.O., Mahler, L., Halpern, A. and Gavin, W.J. 2007. 'Effects of an extended version of the Lee Silverman Voice Treatment on voice and speech in Parkinson's disease', *American Journal of Speech-Language Pathology* 16:2, 95–107.

Spielmann, P.M., Majumdar, S. and Morton, R.P. 2010. 'Quality of life and functional outcomes in the management of early glottic carcinoma: a systematic review of studies comparing radiotherapy and transoral laser microsurgery', *Clinical Otolaryngology* 35:5, 373–82.

Spinelli, M., Rocha, A., Giacheti, C. and Richieri-Costa, A. 1995. 'Word-finding difficulties, verbal paraphasias, and verbal dyspraxia in ten individuals with fragile x syndrome', *American Journal of Medical Genetics* 60:1, 39–43.

Spring, C. and Davis, J.M. 1988. 'Relations of digit naming speed with three components of reading', *Applied Psycholinguistics* 9:4, 315–34.

St. George, M., Kutas, M., Martinez, A. and Sereno, M.I. 1999. 'Semantic integration in reading: engagement of the right hemisphere during discourse processing', *Brain* 122:7, 1317–25.

St. Louis, K.O. 1992. 'On defining cluttering', in F.L. Myers and K.O. St. Louis (eds.), *Cluttering: a clinical perspective*, Kibworth: Far Communications, 37–53.

St. Louis, K.O. and Hinzman, A.R. 1986. 'Studies of cluttering: perceptions of cluttering by speech-language pathologists and educators', *Journal of Fluency Disorders* 11:2, 131–49.

St. Louis, K.O. and Rustin, L. 1996. 'Professional awareness of cluttering', in F.L. Myers and K.O. St. Louis (eds.), *Cluttering: a clinical perspective*, San Diego, CA and London: Singular Publishing Group, 23–35.

St. Louis, K.O. and Schulte, K. 2011. 'Defining cluttering: the lowest common denominator', in D. Ward and K. Scaler Scott (eds.), *Cluttering: research, intervention and education*, Hove, East Sussex: Psychology Press, 233–53.

St. Louis, K.O., Myers, F.L., Bakker, K. and Raphael, L.J. 2007. 'Understanding and treating cluttering', in E.G. Conture and R.F. Curlee (eds.), *Stuttering and related disorders of fluency*, third edition, New York: Thieme, 297–325.

St. Louis, K.O., Myers, F.L., Faragasso, K., Townsend, P.S. and Gallaher, A.J. 2004. 'Perceptual aspects of cluttered speech', *Journal of Fluency Disorders* 29:3, 213–35.

St. Louis, K.O., Raphael, L.J., Myers, F.L. and Bakker, K. 2003. 'Cluttering updated', *ASHA Leader* 18:4–5, 20–1.

Stackhouse, J. 1992. 'Developmental verbal dyspraxia 1: a review and critique', *International Journal of Language & Communication Disorders* 27:1, 19–34.

Stackhouse, J. 2006. 'Speech and spelling difficulties: what to look for', in M.J. Snowling and J. Stackhouse (eds.), *Dyslexia, speech and language: a practitioner's handbook* second edition, Chichester, West Sussex: Whurr Publishers, 15–35.

Stackhouse, J. and Snowling, M. 1992. 'Barriers to literacy development in two cases of developmental verbal dyspraxia', *Cognitive Neuropsychology* 9:4, 273–99.

Stackhouse, J. and Wells, B. 1997. *Children's speech and literacy difficulties I: a psycholinguistic framework*, London: Whurr Publishers.

Staiger, A. and Ziegler, W. 2008. 'Syllable frequency and syllable structure in the spontaneous speech production of patients with apraxia of speech', *Aphasiology* 22:11, 1201–15.

Stanovich, K.E. 1991. 'Word recognition: changing perspectives', in D. Pearson, R. Barr, M. Kamil and M. Mosenthal (eds.), *Handbook of reading research*, New York: Longman, 418–52.

Stanovich, K.E. 2000. *Progress in understanding reading: scientific foundations and new frontiers*, New York: Guilford Press.

Starkstein, S.E., Sabe, L., Vazquez, S., Teson, A., Petracca, G., Chemerinski, E., Di Lorenzo, G. and Leiguarda, R. 1996. 'Neuropsychological, psychiatric, and cerebral blood flow findings in vascular dementia and Alzheimer's disease', *Stroke* 27:3, 408–14.

Starkweather, C.W. and Givens-Ackerman, J. 1997. *Stuttering*, Austin, TX: Pro-Ed.

Starkweather, C.W., Gottwald, S.R. and Halfond, M.M. 1990. *Stuttering prevention: a clinical method*, Englewood Cliffs, N.J.: Prentice Hall.

Steele, J.C., Richardson, J.C. and Olszewski, J. 1964. 'Progressive supra-nuclear palsy: a heterogeneous degeneration involving the brainstem, basal ganglia and cerebellum with vertical gaze and pseudobulbar palsy, nuchal dystonia and dementia', *Archives of Neurology* 10:4, 333–59.

Stefanis, N., Thewissen, V., Bakoula, C., van Os, J. and Myin-Germeys, I. 2006. 'Hearing impairment and psychosis: a replication in a cohort of young adults', *Schizophrenia Research* 85:1–3, 266–72.

Stein, C.M., Schick, J.H., Taylor, G., Shriberg, L.D., Millard, C., Kundtz-Kluge, A., Russo, K., Minich, N., Hansen, A., Freebairn, L.A., Elston, R.C., Lewis, B.A. and Iyengar, S. 2004. 'Pleiotropic effects of a chromosome 3 locus on speech-sound disorder and reading', *American Journal of Human Genetics* 74:2, 283–97.

Stein, J. 2001. 'The magnocellular theory of developmental dyslexia', *Dyslexia* 7:1, 12–36.

Stein, S. and Merrell, K.W. 1992. 'Differential perceptions of multidisciplinary team members: seriously emotionally disturbed vs. socially maladjusted', *Psychology in the Schools* 29:4, 320–30.

Steinthal, P. 1871. *Abris der Sprachwissenschaft*, Berlin: Karger.

Stemmer, B. and Whitaker, H.A. 2008. *Handbook of the neuroscience of language*, London: Academic Press.

Stemple, J.C. 2010. 'Principles of voice therapy', in J.C. Stemple and L.T. Fry (eds.), *Voice therapy: clinical case studies*, third edition, San Diego, CA: Plural Publishing, Inc., 1–11.

Stemple, J.C., Glaze, L.E. and Gerdeman, B.K. 1996. *Clinical voice pathology: theory and management*, San Diego, CA: Singular.

Stemple, J.C., Glaze, L.E. and Gerdeman-Klaben, B. 2000. *Clinical Voice Pathology: Theory and Management*, third edition, San Diego, CA: Singular.

Stemple, J.C., Glaze, L. and Klaben, B. 2010. *Clinical voice pathology: theory and management*, fourth edition, San Diego, CA: Plural Publishing, Inc.

Stemple, J.C., Lee, L., D'Amico, B. and Pickup, B. 1994. 'Efficacy of vocal function exercises as a method of improving voice production', *Journal of Voice* 8:3, 271–8.

Stephens, G.J., Silbert, L.J. and Hasson, U. 2010. 'Speaker-listener neural coupling underlies successful communication', *Proceedings of the National Academy of Sciences of the United States of America* 107:32, 14425–30.

Stern, R. 1997. *Visual analog mood scales manual*, Odessa, FL: Psychological Assessment Resources.

Stern, R.A., Arruda, J.E., Hooper, C.R. and Wolfner, G. 1997. 'Visual analogue mood scales to measure internal mood state in neurologically impaired patients: description and initial validity evidence', *Aphasiology* 11:1, 59–71.

Stevens, S.J., Harvey, R.J., Kelly, C.A., Nicholl, C.G. and Pitt, B.M.N. 1996. 'Characteristics of language performance in four groups of patients attending a memory clinic', *International Journal of Geriatric Psychiatry* 11:11, 973–82.

Stewart, F., Parkin, A.J. and Hunkin, N.M. 1992. 'Naming impairments following recovery from herpes simplex encephalitis: category-specific?', *Quarterly Journal of Experimental Psychology* 44:2, 261–84.

Stice, E., Rohde, P., Seeley, J.R. and Gau, J.M. 2008. 'Brief cognitive-behavioural depression prevention program for high-risk adolescents outperforms two alternative interventions: a randomised efficacy trial', *Journal of Consulting and Clinical Psychology* 76:4, 595–606.

Stojadinovic, A., Shaha, A.R., Orlikoff, R.F., Nissan, A., Kornak, M.F., Singh, B., Boyle, J.O., Shah, J.P., Brennan, M.F. and Kraus, D.H. 2002. 'Prospective functional voice assessment in patients undergoing thyroid surgery', *Annals of Surgery* 236:6, 823–32.

Stojanovik, V. 2006. 'Social interaction deficits and conversational inadequacy in Williams syndrome', *Journal of Neurolinguistics* 19:2, 157–73.

Stojanovik, V. 2010. 'Understanding and production of prosody in children with Williams syndrome: a developmental trajectory approach', *Journal of Neurolinguistics* 23:2, 112–26.

Stojanovik, V. 2011. 'Prosodic deficits in children with Down syndrome', *Journal of Neurolinguistics* 24:2, 145–55.

Stojanovik, V. and van Ewijk, L. 2008. 'Do children with Williams syndrome have unusual vocabularies?', *Journal of Neurolinguistics* 21:1, 18–34.

Stojanovik, V., Perkins, M. and Howard, S. 2004. 'Williams syndrome and specific language impairment do not support claims for developmental double dissociations and innate modularity', *Journal of Neurolinguistics* 17:6, 403–24.

Stojanovik, V., Perkins, M. and Howard, S. 2006. 'Linguistic heterogeneity in Williams syndrome', *Clinical Linguistics & Phonetics* 20:7–8, 547–52.

Stojanovik, V., Setter, J. and van Ewijk, L. 2007. 'Intonation abilities in children with Williams syndrome: a preliminary investigation', *Journal of Speech, Language, and Hearing Research* 50:6, 1610–17.

Stokes, S., Wong, A.M.-Y., Fletcher, P. and Leonard, L. 2006. 'Nonword repetition and sentence repetition as clinical markers of SLI: the case of Cantonese', *Journal of Speech, Language, and Hearing Research* 49:2, 219–36.

Stokes, S.F. and Griffiths, R. 2010. 'The use of facilitative vowel contexts in the treatment of post-alveolar fronting: a case study', *International Journal of Language & Communication Disorders* 45:3, 368–80.

Stokes, S.F. and Suredran, D. 2005. 'Articulatory complexity, ambient frequency, and functional load as predictors of consonant development in children', *Journal of Speech, Language, and Hearing Research* 48:3, 577–91.

Stopford, C.L., Snowden, J.S., Thompson, J.C. and Neary, D. 2007. 'Distinct memory profiles in Alzheimer's disease', *Cortex* 43:7, 846–57.

Stothard, S.E., Snowling, M.J., Bishop, D.V.M., Chipchase, B.B. and Kaplan, C.A. 1998. 'Language-impaired preschoolers: a follow-up into adolescence', *Journal of Speech, Language, and Hearing Research* 41:2, 407–18.

Stowe, L.A., Haverkort, M. and Zwarts, F. 2005. 'Re-thinking the neurological basis of language', *Lingua* 115:7, 997–1042.

Strain, P.S. 1983. 'Generalization of autistic children's social behavior change: effects of developmentally integrated and segregated settings', *Analysis and Intervention in Developmental Disabilities* 3:1, 23–34.

Strain, P.S. and Kohler, F.W. 1998. 'Peer-mediated social intervention for young children with autism', *Seminars in Speech and Language* 19:4, 391–405.

Strand, E.A. and Debertine, P. 2000. 'The efficacy of integral stimulation intervention with developmental apraxia of speech', *Journal of Medical Speech-Language Pathology* 8:4, 295–300.

Strand, E.A. and McCauley, R.J. 2008. 'Differential diagnosis of severe speech impairment in young children', *ASHA Leader* (online, available at: http://develop.asha.org/Publications/leader/2008/080812/f080812a.htm; last accessed 12 June 2013).

Strand, E.A., McCauley, R.J., Weigand, S.D., Stoeckel, R.E. and Baas, B.S. 2013. 'A motor speech assessment for children with severe speech disorders: reliability and validity evidence', *Journal of Speech, Language, and Hearing Research* 56:2, 505–20.

Strand, E.A., Stoeckel, R. and Baas, B. 2006. 'Treatment of severe childhood apraxia of speech: a treatment efficacy study', *Journal of Medical Speech-Language Pathology* 14:4, 297–307.

Stratoudakis, A.C. and Bambace, C. 1984. 'Sphincter pharyngoplasty for correction of velopharyngeal incompetence', *Annals of Plastic Surgery* 12:3, 243–8.

Strik, W., Dierks, T., Hubl, D. and Horn, H. 2008. 'Hallucinations, thought disorders, and the language domain in schizophrenia', *Clinical EEG and Neuroscience* 39:2, 91–4.

Strømme, P., Bjornstad, P.G. and Ramstad, K. 2002. 'Prevalence estimation of Williams syndrome', *Journal of Child Neurology* 17:4, 269–71.

Stronach, S.T. and Turkstra, L.S. 2008. 'Theory of mind and use of cognitive state terms by adolescents with traumatic brain injury', *Aphasiology* 22:10, 1054–70.

Strong, A.C., Wehby, J.H., Falk, K.B. and Lane, K.L. 2004. 'The impact of a structured reading curriculum and repeated reading on the performance of junior high students with emotional and behavioral disorders', *School Psychology Review* 33:4, 561–81.

Strong, G.K., Torgerson, C.J., Torgerson, D. and Hulm, C. 2011. 'A systematic meta-analytic review of evidence for the effectiveness of the "Fast ForWord" language intervention program', *Journal of Child Psychology and Psychiatry* 52:3, 224–35.

Struchen, M., Clark, A., Sander, A., Mills, M., Evans, G. and Kurtz, D. 2008. 'Relation of executive functioning and social communication measures to functional outcomes following traumatic brain injury', *NeuroRehabilitation* 23:2, 185–98.

Stuart, A., Frazier, C.L., Kalinowski, J. and Vos, P.W. 2008. 'The effect of frequency altered feedback on stuttering duration and type', *Journal of Speech, Language, and Hearing Research* 51:4, 889–97.

Stuart, A., Kalinowski, J., Saltuklaroglu, T. and Guntupalli, V.K. 2006. 'Investigations of the impact of altered auditory feedback in-the-ear devices on the speech of people who stutter: one-year follow-up', *Disability and Rehabilitation* 28:12, 757–65.

Stubblefield, M.D. 2011. 'Radiation fibrosis syndrome: neuromuscular and musculoskeletal complications in cancer survivors', *PM&R* 3:11, 1041–54.

Stuebing, K.K., Barth, A.E., Cirino, P.T., Francis, D.J. and Fletcher, J.M. 2008. 'A response to recent reanalyses of the National Reading Panel Report: effects of systematic phonics instruction are practically significant', *Journal of Educational Psychology* 100:1, 123–34.

Subtelny, J.D. 1957. 'A cephalometric study of the growth of the soft palate', *Plastic and Reconstructive Surgery* 19:1, 49–62.

Sudhalter, V. and Belser, R.C. 2001. 'Conversational characteristics of children with fragile X syndrome: tangential language', *American Journal on Mental Retardation* 106:5, 389–400.

Sullivan, K. and Tager-Flusberg, H. 1999. 'Second-order belief attribution in Williams syndrome: intact or impaired?', *American Journal on Mental Retardation* 104:6, 523–32.

Sullivan, K., Winner, E. and Tager-Flusberg, H. 2003. 'Can adolescents with Williams syndrome tell the difference between lies and jokes?', *Developmental Neuropsychology* 23:1–2, 85–103.

Sundberg, J., Leanderson, R., von Euler, C. and Knutsson, E. 1991. 'Influence of body posture and lung volume on subglottal pressure control during singing', *Journal of Voice* 5:4, 283–91.

Sung, M.W., Kim, K.H. and Koh, T.Y. 1999. 'Videostrobokymography: a new method for the quantitative analysis of vocal fold vibration', *Laryngoscope* 109:11, 1859–63.

Suresh, P. and Deepa, C. 2004. 'Congenital suprabulbar palsy: a distinct clinical syndrome of heterogeneous aetiology', *Developmental Medicine and Child Neurology* 46:9, 617–25.

Surian, L., Baron-Cohen, S. and Van der Lely, H. 1996. 'Are children with autism deaf to Gricean maxims?', *Cognitive Neuropsychiatry* 1:1, 55–72.

Svec, J.G., Sram, F. and Schutte H.K. 2007. 'Videokymography in voice disorders: what to look for?', *Annals of Otology, Rhinology and Laryngology* 116:3, 172–80.

Swanson, H.L. and Berninger, V.W. 1996. 'Individual differences in children's working memory and writing skill', *Journal of Experimental Child Psychology* 63:2, 358–85.

Swanson, H.L. and Siegel, L. 2001. 'Learning disabilities as a working memory deficit', *Issues in Education: Contributions of Educational Psychology* 7:1, 1–48.

Swanson, H.L., Howard, C.B. and Sáez, L. 2006. 'Do different components of working memory underlie different subgroups of reading disabilities?', *Journal of Learning Disabilities* 39:3, 252–69.

Swartz, S.L., Mosley, W.J. and Koenig-Jerz, G. 1987. *Diagnosing behavior disorders: an analysis of state definitions, eligibility criteria and recommended procedures*, Chicago, IL: Council for Exceptional Children.

Swinburn, K. and Byng, S. 2006. *The communication disability profile*, London: Connect.

Swinburn, K., Porter, G. and Howard, D. 2004. *The comprehensive aphasia test*, Hove, East Sussex: Psychology Press.

Swinnen, S., Schmidt, R.A., Nicholson, D.E. and Shapiro, D.C. 1990. 'Information feedback for skill acquisition: instantaneous knowledge of results degrades learning', *Journal of Experimental Psychology: Learning, Memory, and Cognition* 16:4, 706–16.

Szatmari, P., Bryson, S., Duku, E., Vaccarella, L., Zwaigenbaum, L., Bennett, T. and Boyle, M.H. 2009. 'Similar developmental trajectories in autism and Asperger syndrome: from early childhood to adolescence', *Journal of Child Psychology and Psychiatry* 50:12, 1459–67.

Tager-Flusberg, H. 1991. 'Semantic processing in the free recall of autistic children: further evidence for a cogni-

tive deficit', *British Journal of Developmental Psychology* 9:3, 417–30.

Tager-Flusberg, H. 2006. 'Defining language phenotypes in autism', *Clinical Neuroscience Research* 6:3–4, 219–24.

Tager-Flusberg, H. and Anderson, M. 1991. 'The development of contingent discourse ability in autistic children', *Journal of Child Psychology and Psychiatry* 32:7, 1123–34.

Tager-Flusberg, H. and Calkins, S. 1990. 'Does imitation facilitate the acquisition of grammar? Evidence from a study of autistic, Down's syndrome and normal children', *Journal of Child Language* 17:3, 591–606.

Tager-Flusberg, H. and Cooper, J. 1999. 'Present and future possibilities for defining a phenotype for specific language impairment', *Journal of Speech, Language, and Hearing Research* 42:5, 1275–8.

Tager-Flusberg, H. and Joseph, R.M. 2003. 'Identifying neurocognitive phenotypes in autism', *Philosophical Transactions of the Royal Society London B Biological Sciences* 358:1430, 303–14.

Tager-Flusberg, H., Paul, R. and Lord, C. 2005. 'Language and communication in autism', in F.R. Volkmar, R. Paul, A. Klin and D.J. Cohen (eds.), *Handbook of autism and pervasive developmental disorders*, New York: John Wiley and Sons, 335–64.

Takahashi, H. and Koike, Y. 1976. 'Some perceptual dimensions and acoustic correlates of pathological voices', *Acta Otolaryngologica* 338, 1–25.

Talcott, J.B., Hansen, P.C., Willis-Owen, C., McKinnell, I.W., Richardson, A.J. and Stein, J.F. 1998. 'Visual magnocellular impairment in adult developmental dyslexics', *Neuro-Ophthalmology* 20:4, 187–201.

Tallal, P. and Gaab, N. 2006. 'Dynamic auditory processing, musical experience and language development', *Trends in Neurosciences* 29:7, 382–90.

Tallal, P., Hirsch, L.S., Raelpe-Bonilla, T., Miller, S., Brzustowicz, L.M., Bartlett, C. and Flox, J.F. 2001. 'Familial aggregation in specific language impairment', *Journal of Speech, Language, and Hearing Research* 44:5, 1172–82.

Tallal, P., Miller, S., Bedi, G., Byma, G., Wang, X., Nagarajan, S., Schreiner, C., Jenkins, W. and Merzenich, M. 1996. 'Language comprehension in language learning impaired children improved with acoustically modified speech', *Science* 271:5245, 81–4.

Tallal, P., Miller, S.C. and Fitch, R. 1993. 'Neurobiological basis of speech: a case for the preeminence of temporal processing', *Annals of the New York Academy of Sciences* 682, 27–47.

Tang, K.T. and Hsieh, M.H. 2010. 'A case of schizophrenia with dysphagia successfully treated by a multidimensional approach', *General Hospital Psychiatry* 32:5, 599. e11–559.e13.

Tanner, M. 2012. *'Voice improvement for people with Parkinson's disease: vocal pedagogy and voice therapy combined'*, Doctoral Dissertation, Edmonton, Alberta: University of Alberta.

Tannock, R., Girolametto, L. and Siegel, L.S. 1992. 'Language intervention with children who have developmental delays: effects of an interactive approach', *American Journal on Mental Retardation* 97:2, 145–60.

Tartan, B.F., Sotereanos, G.C., Patterson, G.T. and Giuliani, M.J. 1991. 'Use of the pharyngeal flap with temporalis muscle for reconstruction of the unrepaired adult palatal cleft: report of two cases', *Journal of Oral and Maxillofacial Surgery* 49:4, 422–5.

Tate, D.G. 2006. 'The state of rehabilitation research: art or science?', *Archives of Physical Medicine and Rehabilitation* 87:2, 160–6.

Tate, R.L., Fenelon, B., Manning, M. and Hunter, M. 1991. 'Patterns of neuropsychological impairment after severe blunt head injury', *Journal of Nervous and Mental Disease* 179:3, 117–26.

Tate, R.L., Lulham, J.M., Broe, G.A., Strettles, B. and Pfaff, A. 1989. 'Psychosocial outcome for the survivors of severe blunt head injury: the results from a consecutive series of 100 patients', *Journal of Neurology, Neurosurgery and Psychiatry* 52:10, 1128–34.

Teigland, A. 1996. 'A study of pragmatic skills of clutterers and normal speakers', *Journal of Fluency Disorders* 21:3–4, 201–14.

Teitler, N. 1992. *'Examiner bias: influence of patient history on perceptual ratings of videostroboscopy'*, Master's Thesis, Madison, WI: University of Wisconsin.

Tempest, B. and Parkinson, E. 1993. 'A case study of a child with severe dyspraxia and reading difficulties', *Child Language Teaching and Therapy* 9:3, 242–50.

Temple, C.M., Almazan, M. and Sherwood, S. 2002. 'Lexical skills in Williams syndrome: a cognitive neuropsychological analysis', *Journal of Neurolinguistics* 15:6, 463–95.

Tenback, D.E., van Harten, P.N. and van Os, J. 2009. 'Non-therapeutic risk factors for onset of tardive dyskinesia in schizophrenia: a meta-analysis', *Movement Disorders* 24:16, 2309–15.

Tényi, T., Herold, R., Szili, I.M. and Trixler, M. 2002. 'Schizophrenics show a failure in the decoding of violations of conversational implicatures', *Psychopathology* 35:1, 25–7.

Tetnowski, J.A. 1998. 'Linguistic effects on disfluency', in R. Paul (ed.), *Exploring the speech-language connection*, Baltimore, MD: Paul Brookes Publishing Co., 227–47.

Teverovsky, E.G., Bickel, J.O. and Feldman, H.M. 2009. Functional characteristics of children diagnosed with childhood apraxia of speech, *Disability and Rehabilitation* 31:2, 94–102.

Tewfik, T.L., Sobol, S.E. and Al Macki, K. 2006. 'Congential anomalies of the larynx', in J.S. Rubin, R.T. Sataloff and G.S. Korovin (eds.), *Diagnosis and treatment of voice disorders*, third edition, San Diego, CA: Plural Publishing, 349–69.

Theys, C., van Wieringen, A., Sunaert, S., Thijs, V. and De Nil, L.F. 2011. 'A one year prospective study of neurogenic stuttering following stroke: incidence and co-occurring disorders', *Journal of Communication Disorders* 44:6, 678–87.

Thiemann, K. and Warren, S.F. 2010. 'Programs supporting young children's language development', *Encyclopedia of language and literacy development*, London: Canadian Language and Literacy Research Network, 1–8 (online, available at: http://literacyencyclopedia.ca/index.php? fa=items.show&topicId=10; last accessed 12 June 2013).

Thomas, C. and Howell, P. 2001. 'Assessing efficacy of stuttering treatments', *Journal of Fluency Disorders* 26:4, 311–33.

Thomas, M.S.C., Dockrell, J.E., Messer, D., Parmigiani, C., Ansari, D. and Karmiloff-Smith, A. 2006. 'Speeded naming, frequency and the development of the lexicon in Williams syndrome', *Language and Cognitive Processes* 21:6, 721–59.

Thomas, M.S.C., Grant, J., Barham, Z., Gsödl, M., Laing, E., Lakusta, L., Tyler, L.K., Grice, S., Paterson, S. and Karmiloff-Smith, A. 2001. 'Past tense formation in Williams syndrome', *Language and Cognitive Processes* 16:2, 143–76.

Thomas, P. 1995. 'Thought disorder or communication disorder: linguistic science provides a new approach', *British Journal of Psychiatry* 166:3, 287–90.

Thomas, S. 2010. 'Evaluation of anxiety and depression in people with acquired communication impairments', in S.M. Brumfitt (ed.), *Psychological well-being and acquired communication impairments*, Chichester, West Sussex: Wiley-Blackwell, 25–43.

Thompson, C.K. 2001. 'Treatment of underlying forms: a linguistic specific approach for sentence production deficits in agrammatic aphasia', in R. Chapey (ed.), *Language intervention strategies in aphasia and related neurogenic communication disorders*, fourth edition, Baltimore, MD: Lippincott Williams & Wilkins, 605–28.

Thompson, C.K. 2004. 'Unaccusative verb production in agrammatic aphasia: the argument structure complexity hypothesis', *Journal of Neurolinguistics* 16:2–3, 151–67.

Thompson, C.K. 2006. 'Single subject controlled experiments in aphasia: the science and the state of the science', *Journal of Communication Disorders* 39:4, 266–91.

Thompson, C.K. 2007. 'Clinical forum: complexity in language learning and treatment', *American Journal of Speech-Language Pathology* 16:1, 3–5.

Thompson, C.K. and Faroqi-Shah, Y. 2002. 'Models of sentence production', in A.E. Hillis (ed.), *The handbook of adult language disorders: integrating cognitive neuropsychology, neurology, and rehabilitation*, Hove, East Sussex: Psychology Press, 311–30.

Thompson, C.K. and Shapiro, L.P. 1994. 'A linguistic-specific approach to treatment of sentence production deficits in aphasia', in M.L. Lemme (ed.), *Clinical aphasiology*, Austin, TX: Pro-Ed, 307–23.

Thompson, C.K., Shapiro, L.P., Kiran, S. and Sobecks, J. 2003. 'The role of syntactic complexity in treatment of sentence deficits in agrammatic aphasia: the complexity account of treatment efficacy (CATE)', *Journal of Speech, Language, and Hearing Research* 46:3, 591–607.

Thompson, J.R., Bryant, B., Campbell, E.M., Craig, E.M., Hughes, C., Rotholz, D.A., Schalock, R., Silverman, W., Tassé, M. and Wehmeyer, M. 2004. *The supports intensity scale (SIS): users' manual*, Washington, DC: American Association on Mental Retardation.

Thompson, P.M., Lee, A.D., Dutton, R.A., Geaga, J.A., Hayashi, K.M., Eckert, M.A., Bellugi, U., Galaburda, A.M., Korenberg, J.R., Mills, D.L., Toga, A.W. and Reiss, A.L. 2005. 'Abnormal cortical complexity and thickness profiles mapped in Williams syndrome', *Journal of Neuroscience* 25:16, 4146–58.

Thompson-Ward, E.C., Murdoch, B.E. and Stokes, P.D. 1997. 'Biofeedback rehabilitation of speech breathing for an individual with dysarthria: a case study', *Journal of Medical Speech-Language Pathology* 5:4, 277–88.

Thomsen, I.V. 1975. 'Evaluation and outcome of aphasia in patients with severe closed head trauma', *Journal of Neurology, Neurosurgery and Psychiatry* 38:7, 713–18.

Thomson, M. 2009. *The psychology of dyslexia*, Chichester, West Sussex: Wiley-Blackwell.

Thoonen, G., Maassen, B., Gabreëls, F., Schreuder, R. and de Swart, B. 1997. 'Towards a standardized assessment procedure for developmental apraxia of speech', *European Journal of Disorders of Communication* 32:1, 37–60.

Thorndike, R.L., Hagen, E.P. and Sattler, J.M. 1986. *Stanford-Binet intelligence scale*, fourth edition, Chicago, IL: Riverside.

Tindall, L.R., Huebner, R.A., Stemple, J.C. and Klienert, H.L. 2008. 'Videophone-delivered voice therapy: a comparative analysis of outcomes to traditional delivery for adults with Parkinson's disease', *Telemedicine and eHealth* 14:10, 1070–7.

Titone, D., Wingfield, A., Caplan, D., Waters, G. and Prentice, K. 2001. 'Memory and encoding of spoken discourse following right hemisphere damage: evidence from the Auditory Moving Window (AMW) technique', *Brain and Language* 77:1, 10–24.

Titze, I.R. 2000. *Principles of voice production*, Denver, CO: National Center for Voice and Speech.

Titze, I.R. 2006. 'Voice training and therapy with a semi-occluded vocal tract: rationale and scientific underpinnings', *Journal of Speech, Language, and Hearing Research* 49:2, 448–59.

Titze, I.R., Hitchcock, R.W., Broadhead, K., Webb, K., Li, W., Gray, S.D. and Tresco, P.A. 2004. 'Design and validation of a bioreactor for engineering vocal fold tissues under combined tensile and vibrational stresses', *Journal of Biomechanics* 37:20, 1521–9.

Tjaden, K. 1999. 'Can a model of overlapping gestures account for scanning speech patterns?', *Journal of Speech, Language, and Hearing Research* 42:3, 604–17.

Togher, L. and Hand, L. 1998. 'Use of politeness markers with different communication partners: an investigation of five subjects with traumatic brain injury', *Aphasiology* 12:7–8, 755–70.

Togher, L. and Hand, L. 1999. 'The macrostructure of the interview: are traumatic brain injury interactions structured differently to control interactions?', *Aphasiology* 13:9–11, 709–23.

Togher, L., Hand, L. and Code, C. 1996. 'A new perspective on the relationship between communication impairment and disempowerment following head injury in information exchanges', *Disability and Rehabilitation* 18:11, 559–66.

Togher, L., Hand, L. and Code, C. 1997a. 'Analysing discourse in the traumatic brain injury population: telephone interactions with different communication partners', *Brain Injury* 11:3, 169–89.

Togher, L., Hand, L. and Code, C. 1997b. 'Measuring service encounters in the traumatic brain injury population', *Aphasiology* 11:4–5, 491–504.

Togher, L., McDonald, S., Code, C. and Grant, S. 2004. 'Training communication partners of people with traumatic brain injury: a randomised controlled trial', *Aphasiology* 18:4, 313–35.

Togher, L., McDonald, S., Tate, R., Power, E. and Rietdijk, R. 2009. 'Training communication partners of people with traumatic brain injury: reporting the protocol for a clinical trial', *Brain Impairment* 10:2, 188–204.

Togher, L., McDonald, S., Tate, R., Power, E. and Rietdijk, R. 2011. *TBI express partner training*, Disability and Community, The University of Sydney (online, available at: http://sydney.edu.au/health_sciences/disability_community/tbi_express/; last accessed 12 June 2013).

Togher, L., Power, E., Riedijk, R., McDonald, S. and Tate, R. 2012. 'An exploration of participant experience of a communication training program for people with trau-matic brain injury and their communication partners', *Disability and Rehabilitation* 34:18, 1562–74.

Togher, L., McDonald, S., Tate, R., Power, E. and Rietdijk, R. 2013. 'Training communication partners of people with severe traumatic brain injury improves everyday conversations: A multicenter single blind clinical trial', *Journal of Rehabilitation Medicine* 45:7, 637–45.

Tomblin, J.B. 1996. 'Genetic and environmental contributions to the risk for specific language impairment', in M. Rice (ed.), *Toward a genetics of language*, Mahwah, NJ: Lawrence Erlbaum, 191–210.

Tomblin, J.B. 2009. 'Genetics of child language disorders', in R.G. Schwartz (ed.), *Handbook of child language disorders*, New York: Psychology Press, 232–56.

Tomblin, J.B. 2011. 'Co-morbidity of autism and SLI: kinds, kin and complexity', *International Journal of Language & Communication Disorders* 46:2, 127–37.

Tomblin, J.B. and Buckwalter, P. 1998. 'Heritability of poor language achievement among twins', *Journal of Speech, Language, and Hearing Research* 41:1, 188–99.

Tomblin, J.B., Hafeman, L. and O'Brien, M. 2003. 'Autism and autism risk in siblings of children with specific language impairment', *International Journal of Language & Communication Disorders* 38:3, 235–50.

Tomblin, J.B., Mainela-Arnold, E. and Zhang, X. 2007. 'Procedural learning in adolescents with and without specific language impairment', *Language Learning and Development* 3:4, 269–93.

Tomblin, J.B., Records, N.L., Buckwalter, P., Zhang, X., Smith, E. and O'Brien, M. 1997. 'Prevalence of SLI in kindergarten children', *Journal of Speech, Language, and Hearing Research* 40:6, 1245–60.

Tompkins, C.A. 2008. 'Theoretical considerations for understanding "understanding" by adults with right hemisphere brain damage', *Perspectives on Neurophysiology and Neurogenic Speech and Language Disorders* 18:2, 45–54.

Tompkins, C.A. 2012. 'Rehabilitation for cognitive-communication disorders in right hemisphere brain damage', *Archives of Physical Medicine and Rehabilitation* 93:1 Suppl, S61–9.

Tompkins, C.A. and Lehman, M.T. 1998. 'Interpreting intended meanings after right hemisphere brain damage: an analysis of evidence, potential accounts, and clinical implications', *Brain* 5:1, 29–47.

Tompkins, C.A., Baumgaertner, A., Lehman, M.T. and Fassbinder, W. 2000. 'Mechanisms of discourse comprehension impairment after right hemisphere brain damage: suppression in lexical ambiguity resolution', *Journal of Speech, Language, and Hearing Research* 43:1, 62–78.

Tompkins, C.A., Bloise, C.G., Timko, M.L. and Baumgaertner, A. 1994. 'Working memory and inference revision in brain-damaged and normally aging adults', *Journal of Speech and Hearing Research* 37:4, 896–912.

Tompkins, C.A., Boada, R. and McGarry, K. 1992. 'The access and processing of familiar idioms by brain-damaged and normally aging adults', *Journal of Speech and Hearing Research* 35:3, 626–37.

Tompkins, C.A., Fassbinder, W., Lehman Blake, M. and Baumgaertner, A. 2002. 'The nature and implications of right hemisphere language disorders: issues in search of answers', in A.E. Hillis (ed.), *The handbook of adult language disorders: integrating cognitive neuropsychology, neurology, and rehabilitation*, New York: Psychology Press, 429–48.

Tompkins, C.A., Fassbinder, W., Scharp, V.L. and Meigh, K.M. 2008a. 'Activation and maintenance of peripheral semantic features of unambiguous words after right hemisphere brain damage in adults', *Aphasiology* 22:2, 119–38.

Tompkins, C.A., Lehman Blake, M.T., Baumgaertner, A. and Fassbinder, W. 2001. 'Mechanisms of discourse comprehension impairment after right hemisphere brain damage: suppression in inferential ambiguity resolution', *Journal of Speech, Language, and Hearing Research* 43:1, 62–78.

Tompkins, C.A., Meigh, K., Gibbs Scott, A. and Guttentag Lederer, L. 2009. 'Can high-level inferencing be predicted by discourse comprehension test performance in adults with right hemisphere brain damage?', *Brain, Behavior, and Immunity* 23:7, 1016–27.

Tompkins, C.A., Scharp, V.L., Meigh, K.M. and Fassbinder, W. 2008b. 'Coarse coding and discourse comprehension in adults with right hemisphere brain damage', *Aphasiology* 22:2, 204–23.

Torgesen, J.K. 1995. *Phonological awareness: a critical factor in dyslexia*, Baltimore, MD: International Dyslexia Association.

Torgesen, J.K. 2002. 'The prevention of reading difficulties', *Journal of School Psychology*, 40:1, 7–27.

Torgesen, J.K. 2004. 'Lessons learned from research on interventions for students who have difficulty learning to read', in V.P.C. McCardle (ed.), *The voice of evidence in reading research*, Baltimore, MD: Paul Brooks, 355–82.

Torgesen, J.K. and Bryant, P.E. 2004. *Test of phonological awareness – second edition: PLUS*, Austin, TX: Pro-Ed.

Torgesen, J.K., Alexander, A.W., Wagner, R.K., Rashotte, C.A., Voeller, K.S. and Conway, T. 2001. 'Intensive remedial instruction for children with severe reading disabilities: immediate and long-term outcomes from two instructional approaches', *Journal of Learning Disabilities* 34:1, 33–58.

Torgesen, J.K., Wagner, R.K., Rashotte, C.A., Burgess, S. and Hecht, S. 1997. 'Contributions of phonological awareness and rapid automatic naming ability to the growth of word-reading skills in second-to-fifth-grade children', *Scientific Studies of Reading* 1:2, 161–85.

Torgesen, J.K., Wagner, R.K., Rashotte, C.A., Herron, J. and Lindamood, P. 2010. 'Computer-assisted instruction to prevent early reading difficulties in students at risk for dyslexia: outcomes from two instructional approaches', *Annals of Dyslexia* 60:1, 40–56.

Torgesen, J.K., Wagner, R.K., Rashotte, C.A., Rose, E., Lindamood, P., Conway, T. and Garvan, C. 1999. 'Preventing reading failure in young children with phonological processing disabilities: group and individual responses to instruction', *Journal of Educational Psychology* 91:4, 579–93.

Tourville, J.A. and Guenther, F.H. 2011. 'The DIVA model: a neural theory of speech acquisition and production', *Language and Cognitive Processes* 26:7, 952–81.

Travis, L.E. 1928. 'A comparative study of the performances of stutterers and normal speakers in mirror tracing', *Psychology Monographs* 39:2, 45–50.

Trichon, M. and Tetnowski, J. 2011. 'Self-help conferences for people who stutter: a qualitative investigation', *Journal of Fluency Disorders* 36:4, 290–5.

Trost, J.E. 1981. 'Articulatory additions to the classical description of the speech of persons with cleft palate', *Cleft Palate Journal* 18:3, 193–203.

Trout, A., Nordness, P.D., Pierce, C.D. and Epstein, M.H. 2003. 'Research on the academic status of children and youth with emotional and behavioral disorders: a review of the literature from 1961–2000', *Journal of Emotional and Behavioral Disorders* 11:4, 198–210.

Tulving, E. 1972. 'Episodic and semantic memory', in E. Tulving and W. Donaldson (eds.), *Organization of memory*, New York: Academic Press, 381–403.

Turkstra, L.S., Coelho, C. and Ylvisaker, M. 2005. 'The use of standardized tests for individuals with cognitive-communication disorders', *Seminars in Speech and Language* 26:4, 215–22.

Turkstra, L.S., Dixon, T.M. and Baker, K.K. 2004. 'Theory of mind and social beliefs in adolescents with traumatic brain injury', *NeuroRehabilitation* 19:3, 245–5.

Turkstra, L.S., McDonald, S. and Kaufman, P.M. 1996. 'Assessment of pragmatic communication skills in adolescents after traumatic brain injury', *Brain Injury* 10:5, 329–45.

Turner, G.S., Tjaden, K. and Weismer, G. 1995. 'The influence of speaking rate on vowel space and speech intelligibility for individuals with amyotrophic lateral sclerosis', *Journal of Speech and Hearing Research* 38:5, 1001–13.

Turner, S. and Whitworth, A. 2006a. 'Clinicians' perceptions of candidacy for conversation partner training in aphasia: how do we select candidates for therapy and do we get it right?', *Aphasiology* 20:7, 616–43.

Turner, S. and Whitworth, A. 2006b. 'Conversational partner training programmes in aphasia: a review of key themes and participants' roles', *Aphasiology* 20:6, 483–510.

Turner-Stokes, L. 2009. 'Goal attainment scaling (GAS) in rehabilitation: a practical guide', *Clinical Rehabilitation* 23:4, 362–7.

Twistleton, E. 1873. *The tongue – not essential to speech*, London: John Murray.

Tyler, A.A., Lewis, K.E., Haskill, A. and Tolbert, L.C. 2003. 'Outcomes of different speech and language goal attack strategies', *Journal of Speech, Language, and Hearing Research* 46:5, 1077–94.

Tyler, L.K., Karmiloff-Smith, A., Voice, J.K., Stevens, T., Grant, J., Udwin, O., Davies, M. and Howlin, P. 1997. 'Do individuals with Williams syndrome have bizarre semantics? Evidence for lexical organization using an on-line task', *Cortex* 33:3, 515–27.

Tyler, L.K., Moss, H.E., Durrant-Peatfield, M. and Levy, J. 2000. 'Conceptual structure and the structure of concepts: a distributed account of category-specific deficits', *Brain and Language* 75:2, 195–231.

US Department of Education. 2002. *Twenty-fourth annual report to Congress on the implementation of the Education of the Handicapped Act*, Washington, DC: US Government Printing.

US Department of Health and Human Services. 1999. *A report of the Surgeon General*, Rockville, MD: US Public Health Service.

US Department of Health and Human Services. 2001. *Mental health: culture, race, and ethnicity. A supplement to mental health: a report of the Surgeon General*, Rockville, MD: US Public Health Service.

Udwin, O. and Yule, W. 1990. 'Expressive language of children with Williams syndrome' *American Journal of Medical Genetics* 37:S6, 108–14.

Udwin, O. and Yule, W. 1991. 'A cognitive and behavioural phenotype in Williams syndrome', *Journal of Clinical and Experimental Neuropsychology* 13:2, 232–44.

Udwin, O., Yule, W. and Martin, N. 1986. 'Age at diagnosis and abilities in idiopathic hypercalcaemia', *Archives of Disease in Childhood* 61:12, 1164–7.

Udwin, O., Yule, W. and Martin, N. 1987. 'Cognitive abilities and behavioural characteristics of children with idiopathic infantile hypercalcaemia', *Child Psychology and Psychiatry* 28:2, 297–308.

Uher, R. and McGuffin, P. 2008. 'The moderation by the serotonin transporter gene of environmental adversity in the aetiology of mental illness: review and methodological analysis', *Molecular Psychiatry* 13:2, 131–46.

Uhry, J.K. and Clark, D.B. 2004. *Dyslexia: theory and practice of instruction*, third edition, Austin, TX: Pro-Ed.

Ulatowska, H.K., North, A.J. and Macaluso-Haynes, S. 1981. 'Production of narrative and procedural discourse in aphasia', *Brain and Language* 13:2, 345–71.

Ullman, M. and Pierpont, E. 2005. 'Specific language impairment is not specific to language: the procedural deficit hypothesis', *Cortex* 41:3, 399–433.

Valadez, V., Ysunza, A., Ocharan-Hernandez, E., Garrido-Bustamante, N., Sanchez-Valerio, A. and Pamplona, M.C. 2012. 'Voice parameters and videonasolaryngoscopy in children with vocal nodules: a longitudinal study, before and after voice therapy', *International Journal of Pediatric Otorhinolaryngology* 76:9, 1361–5.

Valdois, S., Bosse, M.-L. and Tainturier, M.-J. 2004. 'The cognitive deficits responsible for developmental dyslexia: review of evidence for a selective visual attentional disorder', *Dyslexia* 10:4, 339–63.

Valls-Sole, J. 2007. 'Neurophysiology of motor control and movement disorders', in J. Jankovic and E. Tolosa (eds.), *Parkinson's disease and movement disorders*, Philadelphia, PA: Lippincott Williams & Wilkins, 7–22.

Van As-Brooks, C. and Fuller, D.P. 2007. 'Prosthetic tracheoesophageal voice restoration following total laryngectomy', in E.C. Ward and C.J. van As-Brooks (eds.), *Head and neck cancer: treatment, rehabilitation, and outcomes*, San Diego, CA: Plural Publishing, Inc., 229–66.

Van As-Brooks, C., Finizia, C.A. and Ward, E.C. 2007. 'Rehabilitation of olfaction and taste following total laryngectomy', in E.C. Ward and C.J. van As-Brooks (eds.), *Head and neck cancer: treatment, rehabilitation, and outcomes*, San Diego, CA: Plural Publishing, Inc., 325–46.

Van Borsel, J. 2011. 'Cluttering and Down syndrome', in D. Ward and K. Scaler Scott (eds.), *Cluttering: research, intervention and education*, Hove, East Sussex: Psychology Press, 90–9.

Van Borsel, J. and Taillieu, C. 2001. 'Neurogenic stuttering versus developmental stuttering: an observer judgement study', *Journal of Communication Disorders* 34:5, 385–95.

Van Borsel, J., Reunes, G. and Van den Bergh, N. 2003a. 'Delayed auditory feedback in the treatment of stuttering: clients as consumers', *International Journal of Language & Communication Disorders* 38:2, 119–29.

Van Borsel, J., van der Made, S. and Santens, P. 2003b. 'Thalamic stuttering: a distinct clinical entity?', *Brain and Language* 85:2, 185–9.

Van Demark, D.R. 1979. 'Predictability of velopharyngeal competency', *Cleft Palate Journal* 16:4, 429–35.

Van Demark, D.R. and Hammerquist, P.J. 1978. *'Longitudinal evaluation of articulation and velopharyngeal competency of patients with pharyngoplasties'*, American Cleft Palate Association: Atlanta, GA, 5–8 April 1978.

Van Demark, D.R. and Hardin, M.A. 1985. 'Longitudinal evaluation of articulation and velopharyngeal competence of patients with pharyngeal flaps', *Cleft Palate Journal* 22:3, 163–72.

Van Demark, D.R. and Morris, H.L. 1983. 'Stability of velopharyngeal competency', *Cleft Palate Journal* 20:1, 18–22.

Van Demark, D.R., Hardin, M.A. and Morris, H.L. 1988. 'Assessment of velopharyngeal competence: a long-term process', *Cleft Palate Journal* 25:4, 362–73.

van der Lely, H.K. 1998. 'SLI in children: movement, economy, and deficits in the computational-syntactic system', *Language Acquisition* 7:2–4, 161–92.

van der Lely, H.K. 2005. 'Domain-specific cognitive systems: insight from grammatical-SLI', *Trends in Cognitive Sciences* 9:2, 53–9.

van der Lely, H.K. and Marshall, C.R. 2011. 'Grammatical-specific language impairment: a window onto domain-specificity', in J. Guendouzi, F. Loncke and M.J. Williams (eds.), *The handbook of psycholinguistic and cognitive processes: perspectives in communication disorders*, London: Taylor & Francis, 401–18.

Van der Merwe, A. 1997. 'A theoretical framework for the characterization of pathological speech sensorimotor control', in M.R. McNeil (ed.), *Clinical management of sensorimotor speech disorders*, New York: Thieme Medical Publishers, 1–25.

Van der Merwe, A. 2004. 'The voice use reduction program', *American Journal of Speech-Language Pathology* 13:3, 208–18.

Van der Molen, M.J., Van Luit, J.E.H., Van der Molen, M.W., Klugkist, I. and Jongmans, M.J. 2010. 'Effectiveness of a computerized working memory training in adolescents with mild to borderline intellectual disabilities', *Journal of Intellectual Disability Research* 54:5, 433–47.

Van der Plas, E., Conrad, A., Canady, J., Richman, L. and Nopoulos, P. 2010. 'Effects of unilateral clefts on brain structure', *Archives of Pediatrics and Adolescent Medicine* 164:8, 763–8.

Van der Schuit, M., Segers, E., Van Balkom, H. and Verhoeven, L. 2011. 'How cognitive factors affect language development in children with intellectual disabilities', *Research in Developmental Disabilities* 32:5, 1884–94.

Van der Schuit, M., Segers, E., Van Balkom, H., Stoep, J. and Verhoeven, L. 2010. 'Immersive communication intervention for speaking and non-speaking children with intellectual disabilities', *AAC: Augmentative and Alternative Communication* 26:3, 203–20.

Van Doorne, J.M. 1994. 'Extra-oral prosthetics: past and present', *Journal of Investigative Surgery* 7:4, 267–74.

van Gijn, J. 1998. 'Leukoaraiosis and vascular dementia', *Neurology* 51:3 (Suppl 3), S3–S8.

Van Horne, A.J.O. and Lin, S. 2011. 'Cognitive state verbs and complement clauses in children with SLI and their typically developing peers', *Clinical Linguistics & Phonetics* 25:10, 881–98.

Van Houtte, E., Van Lierde, K. and Claeys, S. 2011. 'Pathophysiology and treatment of muscle tension dysphonia: a review of the current knowledge', *Journal of Voice* 25:2, 202–7.

Van Lancker Sidtis, D., Pachana, N., Cummings, J.L. and Sidtis, J.J. 2006. 'Dysprosodic speech following basal ganglia insult: toward a conceptual framework for the study of the cerebral representation of prosody', *Brain and Language* 97:2, 135–53.

van Leer, E. 2010. *'Role of social cognitive factors in voice therapy adherence and outcome'*, PhD Dissertation, Madison, WI: University of Wisconsin.

van Leer, E. and Connor, N.P. 2010. 'Patient perceptions of voice therapy adherence', *Journal of Voice* 24:4, 458–69.

van Leer, E. and Connor, N.P. 2012. 'Use of portable digital media players increases patient motivation and practice in voice therapy', *Journal of Voice* 26:4, 447–53.

van Leer, E., Hapner, E.R. and Connor, N.P. 2008. 'Transtheoretical model of health behavior change applied to voice therapy', *Journal of Voice* 22:6, 688–98.

Van Lieshout, P. 2004. 'Dynamical systems theory and its application in speech', in B. Maassen, R. Kent, H. Peters, P.V. Lieshout and W. Hulstijn (eds.), *Speech motor control in normal and disordered speech*, New York: Oxford University Press, 51–82.

van Mersbergen, M. 2011. 'Voice disorders and personality: understanding their interactions', *Perspectives on Voice and Voice Disorders* 21:1, 31–38.

van Mersbergen, M., Patrick, C. and Glaze, L. 2008. 'Functional dysphonia during mental imagery: testing the trait theory of voice disorders', *Journal of Speech, Language, and Hearing Research* 51:6, 1405–23.

van Mourik, M., Catsman-Berrevoets, C.E., Paquier, P.F., Yousef-Bak, E. and van Dongen, H.R. 1997. 'Acquired childhood dysarthria: review of its clinical presentation', *Pediatric Neurology* 17:4, 299–307.

van Mourik, M., Catsman-Berrevoets, C.E., Yousef-Bak, E., Paquier, P.F. and van Dongen, H.R. 1998. 'Dysarthria in children with cerebellar or brainstem tumors', *Pediatric Neurology* 18:5, 411–14.

Van Nuffelen, G., De Bodt, M., Vanderwegen, J., Van de Heyning, P. and Wuyts, F. 2010. 'Effect of rate control on speech production and intelligibility in dysarthria', *Folia Phoniatrica et Logopaedica* 62:3, 110–19.

Van Nuffelen, G., De Bodt, M., Wuyts, F. and Van de Heyning, P. 2009. 'The effect of rate control on speech rate and intelligibility of dysarthric speech', *Folia Phoniatrica et Logopaedica* 61:2, 69–75.

Van Os, J. 2010. 'Are psychiatric diagnoses of psychosis scientific and useful? The case of schizophrenia', *Journal of Mental Health* 19:4, 305–17.

Van Os, J. 2011. 'From schizophrenia metafacts to non-schizophrenia facts', *Schizophrenia Research* 127:1–3, 16–7.

Van Os, J., Kenis, G. and Rutten, B.P.F. 2010. 'The environment and schizophrenia', *Nature* 468:7321, 203–12.

Van Rees, L., Ballard, K.J., McCabe, P., McDonald-daSilva, A. and Arciuli, J. 2012. 'Training production of lexical stress in typically developing children with orthographically biased stimuli and principles of motor learning', *American Journal of Speech-Language Pathology* 21:3, 197–206.

Van Riper, C. 1938. 'A study of the stutterer's ability to interrupt stuttering spasms', *Journal of Speech Disorders* 3:2, 117–19.

Van Riper, C. 1973. *Treatment of stuttering*, Englewood Cliffs, NJ: Prentice-Hall.

Van Zaalen, Y., Wijnen, F. and Dejonckere, P. 2011. 'The assessment of cluttering: rationale, tasks, and interpretation', in D. Ward and K. Scaler Scott (eds.), *Cluttering: research, intervention and education*, Hove, East Sussex: Psychology Press, 137–51.

Vanhalle, C., Lemieux, S., Joubert, S., Goulet, P., Ska, B. and Joanette, Y. 2000. 'Processing of speech acts by right hemisphere brain-damaged patients: an ecological approach', *Aphasiology* 14:11, 1127–41.

Vanryckeghem, M. and Brutten, E.J. 2007. *KiddyCat: communication attitude test for preschool and kindergarten children who stutter*, San Diego, CA: Plural Publishers.

Varanese, S., Birnbaum, Z., Rossi, R. and Di Rocco, A. 2011. 'Treatment of advanced Parkinson's disease', *Parkinson's Disease* 2010, 480260.

Varley, R. and Whiteside, S. 2001. 'Forum: what is the underlying impairment in acquired apraxia of speech?', *Aphasiology* 15:1, 39–56.

Varley, R. and Whiteside, S. 2008. *SWORD*. Peebles: Propeller Multimedia Ltd.

Varley, R., Whiteside, S., Windsor, F. and Fisher, H. 2006. 'Moving up from the segment: a comment on Aichert and Ziegler's syllable frequency and syllable structure in apraxia of speech, Brain and Language, 88, 148–159, 2004', *Brain and Language* 96:2, 235–9.

Velleman, S.L. and Strand, E. 1994. 'Developmental verbal dyspraxia', in J.E. Bernthal and N.W. Bankson (eds.), *Child phonology: characteristics, assessment, and intervention with special populations*, New York: Thieme, 110–39.

Vellutino, F.R., Fletcher, J.M., Snowling, M. and Scanlon, D.M. 2004. 'Specific reading disability (dyslexia): what have we learned in the past four decades?', *Journal of Child Psychology and Psychiatry* 45:1, 2–40.

Vellutino, F.R., Scanlon, D.M., Small, S. and Fanuele, D.P. 2006. 'Response to intervention as a vehicle for distinguishing between children with and without reading disabilities: evidence for the role of kindergarten and first-grade interventions', *Journal of Learning Disabilities* 39:2, 157–69.

Verdolini Abbott, K. 2008. *Lessac-Madsen resonant voice therapy*, San Diego, CA: Plural Publishing.

Verdolini Abbott, K. 2011. 'Voice therapy with children: practical tips for a new generation', 2011 Fall Voice Conference at UCSF: San Francisco, CA, 5 November 2011.

Verdolini, K. 1998. *Guide to vocology*, Iowa City: National Center for Voice and Speech.

Verdolini, K. and Ramig, L. 2001. 'Occupational risks for voice problems', *Logopedics, Phoniatrics, Vocology* 26:1, 37–46.

Verdolini, K., Druker, D.G., Palmer, P.M. and Samawi, H. 1998a. 'Laryngeal adduction in resonant voice', *Journal of Voice* 12:3, 315–27.

Verdolini, K., Ramig, L. and Jacobson, B. 1998b. 'Outcome measurements in voice disorders', in C.M. Frattili (ed.), *Measuring outcomes in speech-language pathology*, New York: Thieme, 1354–86.

Verdolini, K., Rosen, C.A. and Branski, R.C. 2006. *Classification manual for voice disorders-I*, Mahwah, NJ: Lawrence Erlbaum.

Verdolini-Marston, K., Burke, M., Lesac, A., Glaze, L. and Caldwell, E. 1995. 'Preliminary study of two methods of treatment for laryngeal nodules', *Journal of Voice* 9:1, 74–85.

Verdolini-Marston, K., Sandage, M. and Titze, I.R. 1994. 'Effect of hydration treatments on laryngeal nodules and polyps and related voice measures', *Journal of Voice* 8:1, 30–47.

Verdolini-Marston, K., Titze, I.R. and Druker, D.G. 1990. 'Changes in phonation threshold pressure with induced conditions of hydration', *Journal of Voice* 4:2, 142–51.

Vermeiren, R., De Clippele, A., Schwab-Stone, M., Ruchkin, V. and Deboutte, D. 2002. 'Neuropsychological characteristics of three subgroups of Flemish delinquent adolescents', *Neuropsychology* 16:1, 49–55.

Vernes, S.C., Newbury, D.F., Abrahams, B.S., Winchester, L., Nicod, J., Groszer, M., Alarcón, M., Oliver, P.L., Davies, K.E., Geschwind, D.H., Monaco, A.P. and Fisher, S.E. 2008. 'A functional genetic link between distinct developmental language disorders', *New England Journal of Medicine* 359:22, 2337–45.

Vernon-Feagans, L. 1999. 'Impact of otitis media on speech, language, cognition and behavior', in R.M. Rosenfeld and C.D. Bluestone (eds), *Evidence-based otitis media*, Hamilton: BC Decker, 353–73.

Vicari, S., Caselli, M. and Tonucci, F. 2000. 'Asynchrony of lexical and morpho-syntactic development in children with Down syndrome', *Neuropsychologia* 38:5, 634–44.

Vigliocco, G., Vinson, D.P., Druks, J., Barber, H. and Cappa, S.F. 2011. 'Nouns and verbs in the brain: a review of behavioural, electrophysiological, neuropsychological and imaging studies', *Neuroscience and Biobehavioural Reviews* 35:3, 407–26.

Vihman, M.M. 2010. 'Phonological templates in early words: a cross-linguistic study', in C. Fougeron, B. Kühnert, M. d'Imperio and N. Vallé (eds), *Laboratory phonology 10: variation, phonetic detail and phonological representation*, New York: Mouton de Gruyter.

Vihman, M.M. and Croft, W. 2007. 'Phonological development: toward a "radical" templatic phonology', *Linguistics* 45:4, 683–725.

Volden, J. 2004. 'Conversational repair in speakers with autism spectrum disorder', *International Journal of Language & Communication Disorders* 39:2, 171–89.

Volden, J. and Lord, C. 1991. 'Neologisms and idiosyncratic language in autistic speakers', *Journal of Autism and Developmental Disorders* 21:2, 109–30.

Von Arnim, G. and Engel, P. 1964. 'Mental retardation related to hypercalcaemia', *Developmental Medicine and Child Neurology* 6:4, 366–77.

Vukovic, R.K. and Siegel, L.S. 2006. 'The double-deficit hypothesis: a comprehensive analysis of the evidence', *Journal of Learning Disabilities* 39:1, 25–47.

Vuorinen, E., Laine, M. and Rinne, J. 2000. 'Common pattern of language impairment in vascular dementia and in Alzheimer disease', *Alzheimer Disease and Associated Disorders* 14:2, 81–6.

Vygotsky, L.S. 1962. *Thought and language*, Cambridge, MA: MIT Press.

Waber, D.P., Forbes, P.W., Wolff, P.H. and Weiler, M.D. 2004. 'Neurodevelopmental characteristics of children with learning impairments classified according to the double-deficit hypothesis', *Journal of Learning Disabilities* 37:5, 451–61.

Wacker, D.P., Berg, W.K. and Harding, J.W. 2002. 'Replacing socially unacceptable behavior with acceptable communication responses', in J. Reichle, D.R. Beukelman and J.C. Light (eds), *Exemplary practices for beginning communicators: implications for AAC*, Baltimore, MD: Paul H. Brookes Publishing, 97–122.

Wade, D.T., Gage, H., Owen, C., Trend, P., Grossmith, C. and Kaye, J. 2003. 'Multidisciplinary rehabilitation for people with Parkinson's disease: a randomised controlled study', *Journal of Neurology, Neurosurgery and Psychiatry* 74:2, 158–62.

Wadman, R., Durkin, K. and Conti-Ramsden, G. 2008. 'Self-esteem, shyness, and sociability in adolescents with specific language impairment (SLI)', *Journal of Speech, Language, and Hearing Research* 51:4, 938–52.

Wagner, M. 1995. 'Outcomes for youths with serious emotional disturbance in secondary school and early adulthood', *The Future of Children: Critical Issues for Children and Youths* 5:2, 90–112.

Wagner, M., Friend, M., Bursuck, W.D., Kutash, K., Duchnowski, A.J., Sumi, W.C. and Epstein, M.H. 2006. 'Educating students with emotional disturbances: a national perspective on school programs and services', *Journal of Emotional and Behavioral Disorders* 14:1, 12–30.

Wagner, M., Kutash, K., Duchnowski, A.J., Epstein, M.H. and Sumi, C. 2005. 'The children and youth we serve: a national picture of the characteristics of students with emotional disturbances receiving special education', *Journal of Emotional and Behavioral Disorders* 13:2, 79–96.

Wagner, R.K., Torgesen, J.K., Laughon, P., Simmons, K. and Rashotte, C.A. 1993. 'Development of young readers' phonological processing abilities', *Journal of Educational Psychology* 85:1, 83–103.

Wagner, R.K., Torgesen, J.K. and Rashotte, C.A. 1994. 'Development of reading-related phonological processing abilities: new evidence of bidirectional causality from a latent variable longitudinal study', *Developmental Psychologist* 30:1, 73–87.

Wagner, R.K., Torgesen, J.K. and Rashotte, C.A. 1999. *Comprehensive test of phonological processing*, Austin, TX: Pro-Ed.

Wagner, R.K., Torgesen, J.K., Rashotte, C.A., Hecht, S.A., Barker, T.A., Burgess, S.R., Donahue, J. and Garon, T. 1997. 'Changing relations between phonological processing abilities and word-level reading as children develop from beginning to skilled readers: a 5-year longitudinal study', *Developmental Psychology* 33:3, 468–79.

Wagovich, S.A. and Bernstein Ratner, N. 2007. 'Frequency of verb use in young children who stutter', *Journal of Fluency Disorders* 32:2, 79–94.

Waguespack, J.R. and Ricci, A.J. 2005. 'Aminoglycoside ototoxicity: permeant drugs cause permanent hair cell loss', *Journal of Physiology* 567:2, 359–60.

Wake, M., Takeno, S., Ibrahim, D., Harrison, R. and Mount, R. 1993. 'Carboplatin ototoxicity: an animal model', *Journal of Laryngology and Otology* 107:7, 585–9.

Waldron, H., Whitworth, A. and Howard, D. 2011a. 'Comparing monitoring and production based approaches to the treatment of phonological assembly difficulties in aphasia', *Aphasiology* 25:10, 1153–73.

Waldron, H., Whitworth, A. and Howard, D. 2011b. 'Therapy for phonological assembly difficulties: a case series', *Aphasiology* 25:4, 434–55.

Walker, H. and Severson, H. 1990. *Systematic screening for behavior disorders (SSBD)*, Longmont, CO: Sopris West.

Walker, H. and Severson, H. 2002. 'Developmental prevention of at-risk outcomes for vulnerable antisocial children and youth', in K.L. Lane, F.M. Gresham and T.E. O'Shaughnessy (eds), *Interventions for children with or at risk for emotional and behavioral disorders*, Boston, MA: Allyn & Bacon, 177–94.

Walker, H.M., Schwarz, I.E., Nippold, M.A., Irvin, L.K. and Noell, J.W. 1994. 'Social skills in school-age children and youth: issues and best practices in assessment and intervention', *Topics in Language Disorders* 14:3, 70–82.

Walker, J.P., Daigle, T. and Buzzard, M. 2002. 'Hemispheric specialisation in processing prosodic structures: revisited', *Aphasiology* 16:12, 1155–72.

Walker, J.P., Pelletier, R. and Reif, L. 2004. 'The production of linguistic prosodic structures in subjects with right hemisphere damage', *Clinical Linguistics & Phonetics* 18:2, 85–106.

Walker, L.O., Cooney, A.T. and Riggs, M.W. 1999. 'Psychosocial and demographic factors related to health behaviours in the first trimester', *Journal of Obstetric, Gynecologic, and Neonatal Nursing* 28:6, 606–14.

Wallace, C., Bogner, J., Corrigan, J., Clinchot, D., Mysiw, W. and Fugate, L. 1998. 'Primary caregivers of persons with brain injury: life changes 1 year after injury', *Brain Injury* 12:6, 483–93.

Wallander, J.L., Conger, A.J. and Cohen Conger, J. 1985. 'Development and evaluation of a behaviourally referenced rating system for heterosocial skills', *Behavioural Assessment* 7:2, 137–53.

Walley, A. 1993. 'The role of vocabulary development in children's spoken word recognition and segmentation ability', *Developmental Review* 13:3, 286–350.

Walsh, E., Moran, P., Scott, C., McKenzie, K., Burns, T., Creed, F., Tyrer, P., Murray, R.M. and Fahy, T. 2003. 'Prevalence of violent victimisation in severe mental illness', *British Journal of Psychiatry* 183:3, 233–8.

Walsh, I.P. 2008. 'Whose voice is it anyway? Hushing and hearing "voices" in speech and language therapy interactions with people with chronic schizophrenia', *International Journal of Language & Communication Disorders* 43:S1, 81–95.

Walsh, R. 2009. 'Word games: the importance of defining phonemic awareness for professional discourse', *Australian Journal of Language and Literacy* 32:3, 211–25.

Walsh, S.F., Rous, B. and Lutzer, C. 2000. 'The federal IDEA natural environments provisions', in S. Sandall and M. Ostrosky (eds.), *Natural environments and inclusion – young exceptional children monograph no. 2*, Longmont, CO: Sopris West, 3–15.

Walshe, M. 2011. 'The psychological impact of acquired motor speech disorders', in A. Lowit and R.D. Kent (eds.), *Assessment of motor speech disorders*, San Diego, CA: Plural Publishing, 97–122.

Walshe, M. and Miller, N. 2011. 'Living with acquired dysarthria: the speaker's perspective', *Disability and Rehabilitation* 33:3, 195–203.

Walshe, M., Peach, R.K. and Miller, N. 2009. 'Dysarthria impact profile: development of a scale to measure psychosocial effects', *International Journal of Language & Communication Disorders* 44:5, 693–715.

Walterfang, M., Wood, A.G., Reutens, D.C., Wood, S.J., Chen, J., Velakoulis, D., McGorry, P.D. and Pantelis, C. 2008. 'Morphology of the corpus callosum at different stages of schizophrenia: cross-sectional study in first-episode and chronic illness', *British Journal of Psychiatry* 192:6, 429–34.

Walton, P. and Wallace, M. 1998. *Fun with fluency: direct therapy with the young child*, Bisbee, AZ: Imaginart.

Wambaugh, J., Duffy, J.R., McNeil, M.R., Robin, D.A. and Rogers, M.A. 2006a. 'Treatment guidelines for acquired apraxia of speech: treatment descriptions and recommendations', *Journal of Medical Speech-Language Pathology* 14:2, 35–67.

Wambaugh, J., Duffy, J.R., McNeil, M.R., Robin, D.A. and Rogers, M.A. 2006b. 'Treatment guidelines for acquired apraxia of speech: a synthesis and evaluation of the evidence', *Journal of Medical Speech-Language Pathology* 14:2, 15–34.

Wampold, B.E. 2001. *The great psychotherapy debate: models, methods, and findings*, Mahwah, NJ: Lawrence Erlbaum Associates.

Wang, J.H. and Thampatty, B.P. 2006. 'An introductory review of cell mechanobiology', *Biomechanics and Modeling in Mechanobiology* 5:1, 1–16.

Wang, X., Hu, C. and Eisbruch, A. 2011. 'Organ-sparing radiation therapy for head and neck cancer', *Nature Reviews Clinical Oncology* 26:8, 639–48.

Wang, Y., Ow, T.J. and Myers, J.N. 2012. 'Pathways for cervical metastasis in malignant neoplasms of the head and neck region', *Clinical Anatomy* 25:1, 54–71.

Warburton, P., Baird, G., Chen, W., Morris, K., Jacobs, B.W., Hodgson, S. and Docherty, Z. 2000. 'Support for linkage of autism and specific language impairment to 7q3 from two chromosome rearrangements involving band 7q31', *American Journal of Medical Genetics* 96:2, 228–34.

Ward, D. 2006. *Stuttering and cluttering: frameworks for understanding and treatment*, New York: Psychology Press.

Ward, D. and Scaler Scott, K. 2011. *Cluttering: a handbook of research, intervention, and education*, New York: Taylor and Francis Group.

Ward, E.C., Acton, L.M. and Morton, A.L. 2007a. 'Stoma care and appliances', in E.C. Ward and C.J. van As-Brooks (eds.), *Head and neck cancer: treatment, rehabilitation, and outcomes*, San Diego, CA: Plural Publishing, Inc., 289–311.

Ward, E.C., Kerle, S.M., Hancock, K.L. and Perkins, K. 2007b. 'Swallowing rehabilitation following total laryngectomy', in E.C. Ward and C.J. van As-Brooks (eds.), *Head and neck cancer: treatment, rehabilitation, and outcomes*, San Diego, CA: Plural Publishing, Inc., 267–88.

Wardill, W.E.M. 1928. 'Cleft palate', *British Journal of Surgery* 16:61, 127–48.

Wardill, W.E.M. 1933. 'Cleft palate', *British Journal of Surgery* 21:82, 347–69.

Waring, R. and Knight, R. 2013. 'How should children with speech sound disorders be classified? A review and critical evaluation of current classification systems', *International Journal of Language & Communication Disorders*, 48:1, 25–40.

Warren, S. and Kaiser, A. 1986. 'Generalization of treatment effects by young language-delayed children: a longitudinal analysis', *Journal of Speech and Hearing Disorders* 51:3, 239–51.

Warren, S. and Kaiser, A. 1988. 'Research in early language intervention', in S.I. Odom and M.A. Karnes (eds.), *Early intervention for infants and children with handicaps: an empirical base*, Baltimore, MD: Paul H. Brookes Publishing, 84–108.

Warren, S., Fey, M. and Yoder, P. 2007. 'Differential treatment intensity research: a missing link to creating optimally effective communication interventions', *Mental Retardation Reviews* 13:1, 70–7.

Warren, S., McQuarter, R. and Rogers-Warren, A. 1984. 'The effects of mands and models on the speech of unresponsive language-delayed preschool children', *Journal of Speech and Hearing Disorders* 49:1, 43–52.

Warren, S.F., Gazdag, G.E., Bambara, L.M. and Jones, H.A. 1994. 'Changes in the generativity and use of semantic relationships concurrent with milieu language intervention', *Journal of Speech and Hearing Research* 37:4, 924–34.

Warrington, E.K. 1975. 'The selective impairment of semantic memory', *Quarterly Journal of Experimental Psychology* 27:4, 635–57.

Warrington, E.K. 1991. 'Right neglect dyslexia: a single case study', *Cognitive Neuropsychology* 8:3–4, 193–212.

Warrington, E.K. and McCarthy, R.A. 1983. 'Category specific access dysphasia', *Brain* 106:4, 859–78.

Warrington, E.K. and Shallice, T. 1979. 'Semantic access dyslexia', *Brain* 102:1, 43–63.

Warrington, E.K. and Shallice, T. 1984. 'Category specific semantic impairments', *Brain* 107:3, 829–54.

Warrington, E.K., Cipolotti, L. and McNeil, J. 1993. 'Attentional dyslexia: a single case study', *Neuropsychologia* 31:9, 871–85.

Warr-Leeper, G., Wright, N.A. and Mack, A. 1994. 'Language disabilities of antisocial boys in residential treatment', *Behavior Disorders* 19:3, 159–69.

Watkins, K.E., Dronkers, N.F. and Vargha-Khadem, F. 2002. 'Behavioural analysis of an inherited speech and language disorder: comparison with acquired aphasia', *Brain* 125:3, 452–64.

Watkins, R.V. and Yairi, E. 1997 'Language production abilities of children whose stuttering persisted or recovered', *Journal of Speech, Language, and Hearing Research* 40:2, 385–99.

Watkins, R.V., Yairi, E. and Ambrose, N.G. 1999. 'Early childhood stuttering III: initial status of expressive language abilities', *Journal of Speech, Language, and Hearing Research* 42:5, 1125–35.

Webb, W. and Adler, R. 2008. *Neurology for the speech-language pathologist*, fifth edition, St Louis, MO: Mosby, Inc.

Webster, J. and Bird, H. 2000. *VAN: the verb and noun test*, Northumberland: STASS Publications.

Webster, J. and Howard, D. 2012. 'Assessment of agrammatic language', in R. Bastiaanse and C.K. Thompson (eds.), *Perspectives on agrammatism*, London: Psychology Press, 136–57.

Webster, J. and Whitworth, A. 2012. 'Treating verbs in aphasia: exploring the impact of therapy at the single word and sentence levels', *International Journal of Language & Communication Disorders* 47:6, 619–36.

Webster, J., Morris, J. and Franklin, S. 2005. 'Effects of therapy targeted at verb retrieval and the realisation of the predicate argument structure: a case study', *Aphasiology* 19:8, 748–64.

Webster, J., Morris, J., Whitworth, A. and Howard, D. 2009. *Newcastle University aphasia therapy resources: sentence processing*, Newcastle upon Tyne, UK: Newcastle University.

Webster, R.L. 1980. 'Evolution of a target-based behavioral therapy for stuttering', *Journal of Fluency Disorders* 5:3, 303–20.

Wechsler, D. 1976. *Wechsler intelligence scale for children-revised*, Windsor: NFER.

Wechsler, D. 2003. *Wechsler intelligence scale for children – fourth edition*, San Antonio, TX: The Psychological Corporation.

Weed, E. 2011. 'What's left to learn about right hemisphere damage and pragmatic impairment?', *Aphasiology* 25:8, 872–89.

Weed, E., McGregor, W., Feldbaek Nielsen, J., Roepstorff, A. and Frith, U. 2010. 'Theory of mind in adults with right hemisphere damage: what's the story?', *Brain and Language* 113:2, 65–72.

Wehby, J.H., Symons, F.J. and Hollo, A. 1997. 'Promote appropriate assessment', *Journal of Emotional and Behavioral Disorders* 5:1, 45–54.

Wehmeyer, M.L. and Obremski, S. 2011. 'Intellectual disabilities', in J.H. Stone and M. Blouin (eds.), *International encyclopedia of rehabilitation* (online, available at: http://cirrie.buffalo.edu/encyclopedia/en/article/15/; last accessed 12 June 2013).

Weinberg, S.M., Andreasen, N.C. and Nopoulos, P. 2009. 'Three-dimensional morphometric analysis of brain shape in nonsyndromic orofacial clefting', *Journal of Anatomy* 214:6, 926–36.

Weisman, D. and McKeith, I. 2007. 'Dementia with Lewy bodies', *Seminars in Neurology* 27:1, 42–7.

Weismer, G. 2006. 'Philosophy of research in motor speech disorders', *Clinical Linguistics & Phonetics* 20:5, 315–49.

Weismer, G. and Laures, J.S. 2002. 'Direct magnitude estimates of speech intelligibility in dysarthria: effects of a chosen standard', *Journal of Speech, Language, and Hearing Research* 45:3, 421–33.

Weiss, D.A. 1964. *Cluttering*, Englewood Cliffs, NJ: Prentice-Hall.

Welham, N.V. 2009. 'Clinical voice evaluation', in A.E. Aronson and D.M. Bless (eds.), *Clinical voice disorders*, fourth edition, New York: Thieme, 134–65.

Wernicke, C. 1874. *Der aphasische Symptomenkomplex: eine psychologische Studie auf anatomischer Basis*, Breslau: Cohn und Weigert.

Wertz, R.T. 1999. 'The role of theory in aphasia therapy: art or science?', in D.T. Stuss, G. Winocur and I.H. Robertson (eds.), *Cognitive neurorehabilitation*, Cambridge University Press, 265–78.

Wertz, R.T., Rosenbek, J.C. and Deal, J.L. 1970. 'A review of 228 cases of apraxia of speech: classification, etiology, and localization', American Speech and Hearing Association Convention: New York, November 1970.

Westby, C.E. 1974. 'Language performance of stuttering and nonstuttering children', *Journal of Communication Disorders* 12:2, 133–45.

Westerlund, M., Berglund, E. and Eriksson, M. 2006. 'Can severely language delayed 3-year-olds be identified at 18 months? Evaluation of a screening version of the Macarthur-Bates communicative development inventories', *Journal of Speech, Language, and Hearing Research* 49:2, 237–47.

Wetherby, A., Warren, S.F. and Reichle, J. (eds.) 1998. *Transitions in prelinguistic communication*, Baltimore, MD: Paul H. Brookes Publishing.

Wexler, K. 2003. 'Lenneberg's dream: learning, normal language development, and specific language impairment', in Y. Levy and J. Schaeffer (eds.), *Language competence across populations: toward a definition of specific language impairment*, Mahwah, NJ: Lawrence Erlbaum, 11–61.

Whaley, N.R., Fujioka, S. and Wszolek, Z.K. 2011. 'Autosomal dominant cerebellar ataxia type I: a review of the phenotypic and genotypic characteristics', *Orphanet Journal of Rare Diseases* 6:33.

Wharton, P. and Mowrer, D.E. 1992. 'Prevalence of cleft uvula among school children in kindergarten through grade five', *Cleft Palate-Craniofacial Journal* 29:1, 10–12.

What Works Clearinghouse. 2007. *Intervention: Fast ForWord ®* (online, available at: http://ies.ed.gov/ncee/wwc/interventionreport.aspx?sid=172; last accessed 12 June 2013).

What Works Clearinghouse. 2011. *Procedures and standards handbook* (online, available at: http://ies.ed.gov/ncee/wwc/pdf/reference_resources/wwc_procedures_v2_1_standards_handbook.pdf; last accessed 12 June 2013).

Wheelock, V.L., Tempkin, T., Marder, K., Nance, M., Myers, R.H., Zhao, H., Kayson, E., Orme, C. and Shoulson, I. 2003. 'Predictors of nursing home placement in Huntington disease', *Neurology* 60:6, 998–1001.

White, L., Liss, J.M. and Dellwo, V. 2011. 'Assessment of rhythm', in A. Lowit and R. Kent (eds.), *Assessment of motor speech disorders*, Abingdon, Oxfordshire: Plural Publishing, 231–51.

White, S., Milne, E., Rosen, S., Hansen, P., Swettenham, J., Frith, U. and Ramus, R. 2006. 'The role of sensorimotor impairments in dyslexia: a multiple case study of dyslexic children', *Developmental Science* 9:3, 237–55.

Whitehill, T.L., Lee, A.S. and Chun, J.C. 2002. 'Direct magnitude estimation and interval scaling of hypernasality', *Journal of Speech, Language, and Hearing Research* 45:1, 80–8.

Whitehouse, A.J., Barry, J.G. and Bishop, D.V.M. 2007. 'The broader language phenotype of autism: a comparison with specific language impairment', *Journal of Child Psychology and Psychiatry* 48:8, 822–30.

Whitehouse, A.J., Barry, J.G. and Bishop, D.V.M. 2008. 'Further defining the language impairment of autism: is there a specific language impairment subtype?', *Journal of Communication Disorders* 41:4, 319–36.

Whitehouse, A.J.O., Watt, H.J., Line, E.A. and Bishop, D.V.M. 2009. 'Adult psychosocial outcomes of children with specific language impairment, pragmatic language impairment and autism', *International Journal of Language & Communication Disorders* 44:4, 511–28.

Whitehurst, G.J. and Lonigan, C.J. 1998. 'Child development and emergent literacy', *Child Development* 69:3, 848–72.

Whiteside, S.P. and Varley, R.A. 1998. 'A reconceptualisation of apraxia of speech: a synthesis of evidence', *Cortex* 34:2, 221–31.

Whitworth, A. 1996. *Thematic roles in production (TRIP)*, London: Whurr Publishers.

Whitworth, A., Perkins, L. and Lesser, R. 1997. *Conversation analysis profile for people with aphasia*, London: Whurr Publishers.

Whitworth, A., Webster, J. and Howard, D. 2013. *A cognitive neuropsychological approach to assessment and intervention in aphasia: a clinician's guide*, second edition, London: Psychology Press.

Wiig, E.H. and Semel, E. 1984. *Language assessment and intervention for the learning disabled*, second edition, Columbus, OH: Charles E. Merrill.

Wilcox, M.J. and Leonard, L. 1978. 'Experimental acquisition of wh-questions in language-disordered children', *Journal of Speech and Hearing Research* 21:2, 220–39.

Wilkinson, K.M. and Hennig, S. 2007. 'The state of research and practice in augmentative and alternative communication for children with developmental/intellectual disabilities', *Mental Retardation and Developmental Disabilities Research Reviews* 13:1, 58–69.

Wilkinson, P.R., Wolfe, C.D., Warburton, F.G., Rudd, A.G., Howard, R.S., Ross-Russell, R.W. and Beech, R.R. 1997. 'A long term follow-up of stroke patients', *Stroke* 28:3, 507–12.

Wilkinson, R. 1995. 'Aphasia: conversation analysis of a non-fluent aphasic person', in M. Perkins and S. Howard (eds.), *Case studies in clinical linguistics*, London: Whurr Publishers, 271–92.

Wilkinson, R. and Wielaert, S.M. 2012. 'Rehabilitation for aphasic conversation: can we change the everyday talk of people with aphasia and their significant others?', *Archives of Physical Medicine and Rehabilitation* 93:Suppl 1, 70–6.

Wilkinson, R., Bryan, K., Lock, S. and Sage, K. 2010. 'Implementing and evaluating aphasia therapy targeted at couples' conversations: a single case study', *Aphasiology* 24:6–8, 869–86.

Willcutt, E.G., Pennington, B.F., Smith, S.D., Cardon, L.R., Gayan, J., Knopik, V.S., Olson, R.K. and DeFries, J.C. 2002. 'Quantitative trait locus for reading disability on chromosome 6p is pleiotropic for attention-deficit/hyperactivity disorder', *American Journal of Medical Genetics: Neuropsychiatric Genetics*, 114:3, 260–8.

Williams, D. and Happé, F. 2010. 'Representing intentions in self and other: studies of autism and typical development', *Developmental Science* 13:2, 307–19.

Williams, D., Botting, N. and Boucher, J. 2008. 'Language in autism and specific language impairment: where are the links?', *Psychological Bulletin* 134:6, 944–63.

Williams, D.E. 1985. 'Talking with children who stutter', in J.H. Fraser (ed.), *Counseling stutterers*, Memphis, TN: Stuttering Foundation of America, 35–45.

Williams, J.C.P., Barrat-Boyes, B.G. and Lowe, J.B. 1961. 'Supravalvular aortic stenosis', *Circulation* 24:6, 1311–18.

Williams, N. and Chiat, S. 1993. 'Processing deficits in children with phonological disorder and delay: a comparison of responses to a series of output tasks', *Clinical Linguistics & Phonetics* 7:2, 145–60.

Williams, S.E. and Canter, G.J. 1987. 'Action-naming performance in four syndromes of aphasia', *Brain and Language* 32:1, 124–36.

Williams, S.E. and Watson, J.B. 1987. 'Speaking proficiency variations according to method of alaryngeal voicing', *Laryngoscope* 97:6, 737–9.

Williams, W.N. and Eisenbach, O.R. 1981. 'Assessing VP function: the lateral still technique vs. cinefluorography', *Cleft Palate Journal* 18:1, 45–50.

Williams-Gray, C.H., Foltynie, T., Brayne, C.E., Robbins, T.W. and Barker, R.A. 2007. 'Evolution of cognitive dysfunction in an incident Parkinson's disease cohort', *Brain* 130:7, 1787–98.

Williamson, P., McLeaskey, J., Hoppey, D. and Rentz, T. 2006. 'Educating students with mental retardation in general education classrooms', *Exceptional Children* 72:3, 347–61.

Willmes, K. 1990. 'Statistical methods for a single case study approach to aphasia therapy research', *Aphasiology* 4:4, 415–36.

Wilson, B. 1987. 'Single-case experimental designs in neuropsychological rehabilitation', *Journal of Clinical and Experimental Neuropsychology* 9:5, 527–44.

Wilson, B. 1997. 'Research and evaluation in rehabilitation', in B. Wilson and D.L. McLellan (eds.), *Rehabilitation studies handbook*, Cambridge University Press, 161–87.

Wilson, L., Cone, T., Bradley, C. and Reese, J. 1986. 'The characteristics of learning disabled and other handicapped students referred for evaluation in the state of Iowa', *Journal of Learning Disabilities* 19:9, 553–7.

Wilson, S.A.K. 1908. 'A contribution to the study of apraxia with a review of the literature', *Brain* 31:1, 164–216.

Wilson, S.M., Brambati, S.M., Henry, R.G., Handwerker, D.A., Agosta, F., Miller, B.L., Wilkins, D.P., Ogar, J.M. and Gorno-Tempini, M.L. 2009. 'The neural basis of surface dyslexia in semantic dementia', *Brain* 132:1, 71–86.

Wimmer, H. 2006. 'Don't neglect reading fluency!', *Developmental Science* 9:5, 447–8.

Wimmer, H. and Mayringer, H. 2002. 'Dysfluent reading in the absence of spelling difficulties: a specific disability in regular orthographies', *Journal of Educational Psychology* 94:2, 272–7.

Wimmer, H. and Perner, J. 1983. 'Beliefs about beliefs: representation and constraining function of wrong beliefs in young children's understanding of deception', *Cognition* 13:1, 103–28.

Wimmer, H., Mayringer, H. and Raberger, T. 1999. 'Reading and dual-task balancing: evidence against the automatization deficit explanation of developmental dyslexia', *Journal of Learning Disabilities* 32:5, 473–8.

Winblad, B., Palmer, K., Kivipelto, M., Jelic, V., Fratiglioni, L., Wahlund, L.O., Nordberg, A., Bäckman, L., Albert, M., Almkvist, O., Arai, H., Basun, H., Blennow, K., de Leon, M., DeCarli, C., Erkinjuntti, T., Giacobini, E., Graff, C., Hardy, J., Jack, C., Jorm, A., Ritchie, K., van Duijn, C., Visser, P. and Petersen, R.C. 2004. 'Mild cognitive impairment – beyond controversies, towards a consensus: report of the International Working Group on Mild Cognitive Impairment', *Journal of Internal Medicine* 256:3, 240–6.

Wingate, M.E. 1988. *The structure of stuttering: a psycholinguistic analysis*, New York: Springer-Verlag.

Winitz, H. and Darley, F. 1980. 'Speech production', in F.M. Lassman, R.O. Fisch, D.K. Vetter and E.S. LaBenz (eds.), *Early correlates of speech, language and hearing*, Littleton, MA: PSG Publishing Co., 232–65.

Winner, E., Brownell, H., Happé, F., Blum, A. and Pincus, D. 1998. 'Distinguishing lies from jokes: theory of mind deficits and discourse interpretation in right hemisphere brain-damaged patients', *Brain and Language* 62:1, 89–106.

Winskel, H. 2006. 'The effects of an early history of otitis media on children's language and literacy skill development', *British Journal of Educational Psychology* 76:4, 727–44.

Winter, R. and Baraister, M. 1998. *London dysmorphology database*, Oxford University Press.

Witt, P.D., Marsh, J.L., Arlis, H., Grames, L.M., Ellis, R.A. and Pilgram, T.K. 1998. 'Quantification of dynamic velopharyngeal port excursion following sphincter pharyngoplasty', *Plastic and Reconstructive Surgery* 101:5, 1205–11.

Wittekind, C. and Sobin, L.H. 2002. *TNM classification of malignant tumours*, New York: Wiley-Liss.

Witteman, J., van IJzendoorn, M.H., van de Velde, D., van Heuven, V.J.J.P. and Schiller, N.O. 2011. 'The nature of hemispheric specialization for linguistic and emotional prosodic perception: a meta-analysis of the lesion literature', *Neuropsychologia* 49:13, 3722–38.

Wolf, M. 2001. 'Seven dimensions of time', in M. Wolfe (ed.), *Dyslexia, fluency and the brain*, Timonium, MD: York Press, ix–xix.

Wolf, M., and Bowers, P. 1999. 'The "double-deficit hypothesis" for the developmental dyslexias', *Journal of Educational Psychology* 91:3, 415–38.

Wolf, M., Bowers, P. and Biddle, K. 2000a. 'Naming-speed processes, timing, and reading: a conceptual review', *Journal of Learning Disabilities* 33:4, 387–407.

Wolf, M., Miller, L. and Donnelly, K. 2000b. 'Retrieval, automaticity, vocabulary elaboration, orthography (RAVE-O): a comprehensive, fluency-based reading intervention program', *Journal of Learning Disabilities* 33:4, 375–86.

Wolfe, V., Presley, C. and Mesaris, J. 2003. 'The importance of sound identification training in phonological intervention', *American Journal of Speech-Language Pathology* 12:3, 282–8.

Woo, P. and Carroll, L.M. 2009. 'Management of adult vocal fold nerve injury', *Perspectives on Voice and Voice Disorders* 19:1, 24–33.

Wood, S.J., Pantelis, C., Velakoulis, D., Yücel, M., Fornito, A. and McGorry, P.D. 2008. 'Progressive changes in the development toward schizophrenia: studies in subjects at increased symptomatic risk', *Schizophrenia Bulletin* 34:2, 322–9.

Woodcock, R.W., McGrew, K.S. and Mather, N. 2001. *Woodcock-Johnson III tests of achievement*, Itasca, IL: Riverside Publishing.

Woods, S.P., Weinborn, M., Posada, C. and O'Grady, J. 2007. 'Preliminary evidence for impaired rapid verb generation in schizophrenia', *Brain and Language* 102:1, 46–51.

Woolf, G. 1967. 'The assessment of stuttering as struggle, avoidance, and expectancy', *British Journal of Disorders of Communication* 2:2, 158–71.

Woollams, A.M., Ralph, M.A., Plaut, D.C. and Patterson, K. 2007. 'SD-squared: on the association between semantic dementia and surface dyslexia', *Psychological Review* 114:2, 316–39.

Workinger, M.S. 2005. *Cerebral palsy: resource guide for speech-language pathologists*, Clifton Park, NJ: Thomson-Delmar Learning.

World Health Organization. 1992–1994. *International statistical classification of diseases and related health problems*, 10th revision, Geneva: World Health Organization.

World Health Organization. 1993. *International classification of diseases*, Geneva: World Health Organization.

World Health Organization. 1999. *WHOQOL: measuring quality of life*, Geneva: World Health Organization.

World Health Organization. 2001. *International classification of functioning, disability and health*, Geneva: World Health Organization.

World Health Organization. 2005. *Mental health: facing the challenges, building solutions*, Report from the WHO European Ministerial conference. Copenhagen: WHO Regional Office for Europe.

World Health Organization. 2007a. *International classification of functioning, disability and health – children and youth version (ICF-CY)*, Geneva: WHO.

World Health Organization. 2007b. *Atlas: global resources for persons with intellectual disabilities*, Geneva: World Health Organization.

Worrall, L. 1999. *Functional communication therapy planner*, Bicester, Oxon.: Winslow Press.

Worrall, L., Brown, K., Cruice, M., Davidson, B., Hersh, D., Howe, T. and Sherratt, S. 2010. 'The evidence for a life-coaching approach to aphasia', *Aphasiology* 24:4, 497–514.

Wright, D.L., Black, C.B., Immink, M.A., Brueckner, S. and Magnuson, C. 2004. 'Long-term motor programming improvements occur via concatenation of movement sequences during random but not during blocked practice', *Journal of Motor Behavior* 36:1, 39–50.

Wright, D.L., Robin, D.A., Rhee, J., Vaculin, A., Jacks, A., Guenther, F.H. and Fox, P.T. 2009. 'Using the self-select paradigm to delineate the nature of speech motor programming', *Journal of Speech, Language, and Hearing Research* 52:3, 755–65.

Wright, L. and Ayre, A. 2000. *The Wright & Ayre stuttering self rating profile (WASSP)*, Bicester: Winslow Press.

Wu, P. and Jeng, J. 2004. 'Efficacy comparison between two articulatory intervention approaches for dysarthric cerebral palsy (CP) children', *Asia Pacific Journal of Speech, Language and Hearing* 9:1, 28–32.

Xiong, H., Bao, X.-H., Zhang, Y.-H., Xu, Y.-N., Qin, J., Shi, H.-P. and Wu, X.-R. 2012. 'Niemann-Pick disease type C: analysis of 7 patients', *World Journal of Pediatrics* 8:1, 61–6.

Xu, J., Kemeny, S., Park, G., Frattali, C. and Braun, A. 2005. 'Language in context: emergent features of word, sentence, and narrative comprehension', *NeuroImage* 25:3, 1002–15.

Yairi, E. 1996. 'Applications of disfluencies in measurements of stuttering', *Journal of Speech and Hearing Research* 39:2, 402–5.

Yairi, E. and Ambrose, N. 1992a. 'A longitudinal study of stuttering in children: a preliminary report', *Journal of Speech and Hearing Research* 35:4, 755–60.

Yairi, E. and Ambrose, N. 1992b. 'Onset of stuttering in preschool children: selected factors', *Journal of Speech and Hearing Research* 35:4, 782–8.

Yairi, E. and Ambrose, N. 1999. 'Early childhood stuttering. I. Persistency and recovery rates', *Journal of Speech, Language, and Hearing Research* 42:5, 1097–1112.

Yairi, E. and Ambrose, N. 2013. 'Epidemiology of stuttering: 21st century advances', *Journal of Fluency Disorders*, in press.

Yairi, E., Ambrose, N.G. and Niermann, R. 1993. 'The early months of stuttering: a developmental study', *Journal of Speech and Hearing Research* 36:3, 521–8.

Yairi, E., Ambrose, N.G., Paden, E. and Throneburg, R. 1996. 'Predictive factors of persistence and recovery: pathways of childhood stuttering', *Journal of Communication Disorders* 29:1, 51–77.

Yang, F.F., McPherson, B., Shu, H., Xie, N. and Xiang, K. 2012. 'Structural abnormalities of the central auditory pathway in infants with non-syndromic cleft lip and/or palate', *Cleft Palate-Craniofacial Journal* 49:2, 137–45.

Yarbay Duman, T., Ozgirgin, N., Altinok, N. and Bastiaanse, R. 2011. 'Comprehension in Turkish Broca's aphasia: an integration problem', *Aphasiology* 25:8, 908–26.

Yaruss, J.S. 1997a. 'Clinical implications of situational variability in preschool children who stutter', *Journal of Fluency Disorders* 22:3,187–203.

Yaruss, J.S. 1997b. 'Clinical measurement of stuttering behaviors', *Contemporary Issues in Communication Science and Disorders* 24, 33–44.

Yaruss, J.S. 1998a. 'Describing the consequences of disorders: stuttering and the International Classification of Impairments, Disabilities, and Handicaps', *Journal of Speech, Language, and Hearing Research* 41:2, 249–57.

Yaruss, J.S. 1998b. 'Treatment outcomes in stuttering: finding value in clinical data', in A. Cordes and R. Ingham (eds.), *Toward treatment efficacy in stuttering: a search for empirical bases*, Austin, TX: Pro-Ed, 213–42.

Yaruss, J.S. 1998c. 'Real-time analysis of speech fluency: procedures and reliability training', *American Journal of Speech-Language Pathology* 7:2, 25–37.

Yaruss, J.S. 2001. 'Evaluating treatment outcomes for adults who stutter', *Journal of Communication Disorders* 34:1–2, 163–82.

Yaruss, J.S. 2010. 'Assessing quality of life in stuttering treatment outcomes research', *Journal of Fluency Disorders* 35:3, 190–202.

Yaruss, J.S. and Quesal, R.W. 2004a. 'Stuttering and the International Classification of Functioning, Disability, and Health: an update', *Journal of Communication Disorders* 37:1, 35–52.

Yaruss, J.S. and Quesal, R.W. 2004b. 'Partnerships between clinicians, researchers, and people who stutter in the evaluation of stuttering treatment outcomes', *Stammering Research* 1:1, 1–15.

Yaruss, J.S. and Quesal, R.W. 2006. 'Overall assessment of the speaker's experience of stuttering (OASES): documenting multiple outcomes in stuttering treatment', *Journal of Fluency Disorders* 31:2, 90–115.

Yaruss, J.S. and Quesal, R.W. 2010. *Overall assessment of the speaker's experience of stuttering (OASES)*, Bloomington, MN: Pearson Assessments.

Yaruss, J.S., Coleman, C. and Hammer, D. 2006. 'Treating preschool children who stutter: description and preliminary evaluation of a family-focused treatment approach', *Language, Speech, and Hearing Services in Schools* 37:2, 118–36.

Yaruss, J.S., Coleman, C.E. and Quesal, R.W. 2012. 'Stuttering in school-age children: a comprehensive approach to treatment', *Language, Speech, and Hearing Services in Schools* 43:4, 536–48.

Yaruss, J.S., LaSalle, L.R. and Conture, E.G. 1998. 'Evaluating stuttering in young children: diagnostic data', *American Journal of Speech-Language Pathology* 7:4, 62–76.

Yaruss, J.S., Pelczarski, K.M. and Quesal, R.W. 2010. 'Comprehensive treatment for school-age children who stutter: treating the entire disorder', in B. Guitar and R.J. McCauley (eds.), *Treatment of stuttering: established and emerging interventions*, Baltimore, MD: Lippincott Williams & Wilkins, 215–44.

Yaruss, J.S., Quesal, R.W. and Reeves, P.L. 2007. 'Self-help and mutual aid groups as an adjunct to stuttering therapy', in E.G. Conture and R.F. Curlee (eds.), *Stuttering and related disorders of fluency*, third edition, New York: Thieme, 256–76.

Yaruss, J.S., Quesal, R.W., Reeves, L., Molt, L.F., Kluetz, B., Caruso, A.J., McClure, J.A. and Lewis, F. 2002. 'Speech treatment and support group experiences of people who participate in the National Stuttering Association', *Journal of Fluency Disorders* 27:2, 115–33.

Yeargin-Allsopp and Drews-Botsch, C. 2009. 'The epidemiology of selected neurodevelopmental disabilities: an overview', in M. Shevell (ed.), *Neurodevelopmental disabilities: clinical and scientific foundations*, London: Mac Keith Press, 10–26.

Yirmiya, N., Solomonica-Levi, D., Shulman, C. and Pilowsky, T. 1996. 'Theory of mind abilities in individuals with autism, Down syndrome, and mental retardation of unknown etiology: the role of age and intelligence', *Journal of Child Psychology and Psychiatry* 37:8, 1003–14.

Yiu, E.M. and Chan, R.M. 2003. 'Effect of hydration and vocal rest on vocal fatigue in amateur karaoke singers', *Journal of Voice* 17:2, 216–27.

Yiu, E.M., Ho, E.M., Ma, E.P., Verdolini Abbott, K., Branski, R., Richardson, K. and Li, N.Y. 2011. 'Possibility of cross-cultural differences in the perception and impact of voice disorders', *Journal of Voice* 25:3, 348–53.

Yiu, E.M.-L. and Ng, C.-Y. 2004. 'Equal-appearing interval and visual analog scaling of perceptual roughness and breathiness', *Clinical Linguistics & Phonetics* 18:3, 211–29.

Ylvisaker, M., Feeney, T.J. and Urbanczyk, B. 1993. 'Developing a positive communication culture for rehabilitation: communication training for staff and family members', in C.J. Durgin, N.D. Schmidt and L.J. Fryer (eds.), *Staff development and clinical intervention in brain injury rehabilitation*, Gaithersburg, MD: Aspen, 57–81.

Ylvisaker, M., Turkstra, L.S. and Coelho, C. 2005. 'Behavioral and social interventions for individuals with traumatic brain injury: a summary of the research with clinical implications', *Seminars in Speech and Language* 26:4, 256–67.

Yont, K.M., Snow, C.E. and Vernon-Feagans, L. 2003. 'Is chronic otitis media associated with differences in parental input at 12 months of age? An analysis of joint attention and directives', *Applied Psycholinguistics* 24:4, 581–602.

Yorkston, K.M. and Baylor, C.R. 2011. 'Measurement of communicative participation', in A. Lowit and R.D. Kent (eds.), *Assessment of motor speech disorders*, San Diego, CA: Plural Publishing, 123–40.

Yorkston, K.M. and Beukelman, D.R. 1980. 'An analysis of connected speech samples of aphasic and normal speakers', *Journal of Speech and Hearing Disorders* 45:1, 27–36.

Yorkston, K.M., Baylor, C.R., Klasner, E.R., Deitz, J., Dudgeon, B.J., Eadie, T., Miller, R.M. and Amtmann, D. 2006. 'Satisfaction with communicative participation as defined by adults with multiple sclerosis: a qualitative study', *Journal of Communication Disorders* 40:6, 433–51.

Yorkston, K.M., Beukelman, D.R., Strand, E.A. and Hakel, M. 2010. *Management of motor speech disorders in children and adults*, third edition, Austin, TX: Pro-Ed.

Yorkston, K.M., Beukelman, D. and Traynor, C.D. 1984a. *Computerised assessment of intelligibility of dysarthric speech*, Tigard: C.C. Publications.

Yorkston, K.M., Beukelman, D. and Traynor, C.D. 1984b. *Assessment of intelligibility of dysarthric speech*, Austin, TX: Pro-Ed.

Yorkston, K.M., Beukelman, D.R., Strand, E.A. and Bell, K.R. 1999. *Management of motor speech disorders in children and adults*, Austin, TX: Pro-Ed.

Yorkston, K.M., Hakel, M., Beukelman, D.R. and Fager, S. 2007. 'Evidence for effectiveness of treatment of loudness, rate, or prosody in dysarthria: a systematic review', *Journal of Medical Speech-Language Pathology* 15:2, xi–xxxvi.

Yorkston, K.M., Hammen, V.L., Beukelman, D.R. and Traynor, C.D. 1990. 'The effect of rate control on the intelligibility and naturalness of dysarthric speech', *Journal of Speech and Hearing Disorders* 55:3, 550–60.

Yorkston, K.M., Klasner, E.R., Bowen, J., Ehde, D.M., Gibbons, K. and Johnson, K. 2003a. 'Characteristics of multiple sclerosis as a function of the severity of speech disorders', *Journal of Medical Speech-Language Pathology* 11:2, 73–85.

Yorkston, K.M., Spencer, K.A. and Duffy, J.R. 2003b. 'Behavioral management of respiratory/phonatory dysfunction from dysarthria: a systematic review of the evidence', *Journal of Medical Speech-Language Pathology* 11:2, xiii–xxxviii.

Yorkston, K.M., Spencer, K.A., Duffy, J.R., Beukelman, D.R., Golper, L.A., Miller, R.M., Strand, E. and Sullivan, M. 2001. 'Evidence-based practice guidelines for dysarthria: management of velopharyngeal function', *Journal of Medical Speech-Language Pathology* 9:4, 257–73.

Yoshida, M. 1979. 'Study on perceptive and acoustical classification of pathological voices', *Practica Otolaryngologica* 72, 249–87.

Young, L., Camprodon, J.A., Hauser, M., Pascual-Leone, A. and Saxe, R. 2010. 'Disruption of the right temporoparietal junction with transcranial magnetic stimulation reduces the role of beliefs in moral judgments', *Proceedings of the National Academy of Sciences of the United States of America* 107:15, 6753–8.

Younger, R. and Dickson, R.I. 1985. 'Adult pharyngoplasty for velopharyngeal insufficiency', *Journal of Otolaryngology* 14:3, 158–62.

Ypsilanti, A., Grouios, G., Alevriadou, A. and Tsapkini, K. 2005. 'Expressive and receptive vocabulary in children with Williams and Down syndromes', *Journal of Intellectual Disability Research* 49:5, 353–64.

Ysunza, A., Pamplona, M.C., Molina, F., Chacon, E. and Collado, M. 1999. 'Velopharyngeal motion after sphincter pharyngoplasty: a videonasopharyngoscopic and electromyographic study', *Plastic and Reconstructive Surgery* 104:4, 905–10.

Yumoto, E. 2004. 'Aerodynamics, voice quality, and laryngeal image analysis of normal and pathologic voices', *Current Opinion in Otolaryngology & Head and Neck Surgery* 12:3, 166–73.

Yuspeh, R.L., Vanderploeg, R.D., Crowell, T.A. and Mullan, M. 2002. 'Differences in executive functioning between Alzheimer's disease and subcortical ischemic vascular dementia', *Journal of Clinical and Experimental Neuropsychology* 24:6, 745–54.

Zaccai, J., McCracken, C. and Brayne, C. 2005. 'A systematic review of prevalence and incidence studies of dementia with Lewy bodies', *Age and Ageing* 34:6, 561–6.

Zackheim, C.T. and Conture, E.G. 2003. 'Childhood stuttering and speech disfluencies in relation to children's mean length of utterance: a preliminary study', *Journal of Fluency Disorders* 28:2, 115–42.

Zadeh, Z.Y., Im-Bolter, N. and Cohen, N.J. 2007. 'Social cognition and externalizing psychopathology: an investigation of the mediating role of language', *Journal of Abnormal Child Psychology* 35:2, 141–52.

Zaretsky, E., Velleman, S.L. and Curro, K. 2010. 'Through the magnifying glass: underlying literacy deficits and remediation potential in childhood apraxia of speech', *International Journal of Speech-Language Pathology* 12:1, 58–68.

Zebrowski, P.M. 1991. 'Duration of the speech disfluencies of beginning stutterers', *Journal of Speech and Hearing Research* 34:3, 483–91.

Zebrowski, P.M. 1997. 'Assisting young children who stutter and their families: defining the role of the speech-language pathologist', *American Journal of Speech-Language Pathology* 6:2, 19–28.

Zeitels, S.M. 2005. 'Recent advances in the surgical treatment of laryngeal cancer', in P.C. Doyle and R.L. Keith (eds.), *Contemporary considerations in the treatment and rehabilitation of head and neck cancer*, Austin, TX: Pro-Ed, 171–94.

Zelazo, P.D. 2004. 'The development of conscious control in childhood', *Trends in Cognitive Science* 8:1, 12–17.

Zemlin, W.R. 1997. *Speech and hearing science: anatomy and physiology*, New York: Prentice Hall.

Ziatas, K., Durkin, K. and Pratt, C. 2003. 'Differences in assertive speech acts produced by children with autism, Asperger syndrome, specific language impairment, and normal development', *Development and Psychopathology* 15:1, 73–94.

Ziegler, J.C. and Goswami, U. 2005. 'Reading acquisition, developmental dyslexia, and skilled reading across languages: a psycholinguistic grain size theory', *Psychological Bulletin* 131:1, 3–29.

Ziegler, J.C. and Goswami, U. 2006. 'Becoming literate in different languages: similar problems, different solutions', *Developmental Science* 9:5, 429–36.

Ziegler, W. 2002. 'Psycholinguistic and motor theories of apraxia of speech', *Seminars in Speech and Language* 23:4, 231–44.

Ziegler, W. 2003. 'Speech motor control is task-specific: evidence from dysarthria and apraxia of speech', *Aphasiology* 17:1, 3–36.

Ziegler, W. 2005. 'A nonlinear model of word length effects in apraxia of speech', *Cognitive Neuropsychology* 22:5, 603–23.

Ziegler, W. 2009. 'Modelling the architecture of phonetic plans: evidence from apraxia of speech', *Language and Cognitive Processes* 24:5, 631–61.

Ziegler, W. 2011. 'Apraxic failure and the hierarchical structure of speech motor plans', in A. Lowit and R. Kent (eds.), *Assessment of motor speech disorders*, Abingdon, Oxfordshire: Plural Publishing, 305–24.

Ziegler, W., Aichert, I. and Staiger, A. 2010. 'Syllable- and rhythm-based approaches in the treatment of apraxia of speech', *Perspectives on Neurophysiology and Neurogenic Speech and Language Disorders* 20:3, 59–66.

Zingeser, L.B. and Berndt, R.S. 1988. 'Grammatical class and context effects in a case of pure anomia: implications for models of language processing', *Cognitive Neuropsychology* 5:4, 473–516.

Zingeser, L.B. and Berndt, R.S. 1990. 'Retrieval of nouns and verbs in agrammatism and anomia', *Brain and Language* 39:1, 14–32.

Zinzi, P., Salmaso, D., De Grandis, R., Graziani, G., Maceroni, S., Bentivoglio, A., Zappata, P., Frontali, M. and Jacopini, G. 2007. 'Effects of an intensive rehabilitation programme on patients with Huntington's disease: a pilot study', *Clinical Rehabilitation* 21:7, 603–13.

Zorrilla, E.P., Luborsky, L., McKay, J.R., Rosenthal, R., Houldin, A., Tax, A., McCorkle, R., Seligman, D.A. and Schmidt, K. 2001. 'The relationship of depression and stressors to immunological assays: a meta-analytic review', *Brain, Behavior and Immunity* 15:3, 199–226.

Zraick, R.I., Kempster, G.B., Connor, N.P., Thibeault, S., Klaben, B.K., Bursac, Z., Thrush, C.R. and Glaze, L.E. 2011. 'Establishing validity of the Consensus Auditory-Perceptual Evaluation of Voice (CAPE-V)', *American Journal of Speech-Language Pathology* 20:1, 14–22.

Index